COMMENTARIES AND CASES ON THE LAW
OF BUSINESS ORGANIZATION

ASPEN PUBLISHERS

COMMENTARIES AND CASES ON THE LAW OF BUSINESS ORGANIZATION

SECOND EDITION

William T. Allen
Jack Nusbaum Professor of Law and Business
New York University
Of Counsel, Wachtell, Lipton, Rosen & Katz

Reinier Kraakman
Ezra Ripley Thayer Professor of Law
Harvard Law School

Guhan Subramanian
Joseph Flom Professor of Law and Business
Harvard Law School

Wolters Kluwer
Law & Business

AUSTIN   BOSTON   CHICAGO   NEW YORK   THE NETHERLANDS

Aspen Publishers
Attn: Permissions Department
76 Ninth Avenue, 7th Floor
New York, NY 10011-5201

To contact Customer Care, e-mail customer.care@aspenpublishers.com,
call 1-800-234-1660, fax 1-800-901-9075, or mail correspondence to:

Aspen Publishers
Attn: Order Department
PO Box 990
Frederick, MD 21705

Printed in the United States of America.

1 2 3 4 5 6 7 8 9 0

ISBN 978-0-7355-6313-1

Library of Congress Cataloging-in-Publication Data

Allen, William T.
    Commentaries and cases on the law of business organization / William T.
Allen, Reinier Kraakman, Guhan Subramanian. — 2nd ed.
        p. cm.
    Includes index.
    ISBN 978-0-7355-6313-1
    1. Corporation law — United States — Cases. 2. Business enterprises — Law
and legislation — United States — Cases. I. Kraakman, Reinier H.
II. Subramanian, Guhan. III. Title.

KF1413.A435   2007
346.73'065 — dc22

                                                        2006037953

About Wolters Kluwer Law & Business

Wolters Kluwer Law & Business is a leading provider of research information and workflow solutions in key specialty areas. The strengths of the individual brands of Aspen Publishers, CCH, Kluwer Law International and Loislaw are aligned within Wolters Kluwer Law & Business to provide comprehensive, in-depth solutions and expert-authored content for the legal, professional and education markets.

CCH was founded in 1913 and has served more than four generations of business professionals and their clients. The CCH products in the Wolters Kluwer Law & Business group are highly regarded electronic and print resources for legal, securities, antitrust and trade regulation, government contracting, banking, pension, payroll, employment and labor, and health-care reimbursement and compliance professionals.

Aspen Publishers is a leading information provider for attorneys, business professionals and law students. Written by preeminent authorities, Aspen products offer analytical and practical information in a range of specialty practice areas from securities law and intellectual property to mergers and acquisitions and pension/benefits. Aspen's trusted legal education resources provide professors and students with high-quality, up-to-date and effective resources for successful instruction and study in all areas of the law.

Kluwer Law International supplies the global business community with comprehensive English-language international legal information. Legal practitioners, corporate counsel and business executives around the world rely on the Kluwer Law International journals, loose-leafs, books and electronic products for authoritative information in many areas of international legal practice.

Loislaw is a premier provider of digitized legal content to small law firm practitioners of various specializations. Loislaw provides attorneys with the ability to quickly and efficiently find the necessary legal information they need, when and where they need it, by facilitating access to primary law as well as state-specific law, records, forms and treatises.

Wolters Kluwer Law & Business, a unit of Wolters Kluwer, is headquartered in New York and Riverwoods, Illinois. Wolters Kluwer is a leading multinational publisher and information services company.

To those from whom I learned this subject:
the late S. Samuel Arsht of the Delaware bar and those still
contributing: Andrew B. Kirkpatrick of the Delaware bar; Martin
Lipton of the New York bar; Hon. Walter K. Stapleton of the Third
Circuit Court of Appeals; and my former colleagues on the Court of
Chancery of the State of Delaware, with my deep thanks.

—William T. Allen

To those who have made this casebook possible:
especially Victor Brudney, whose generous assistance with
materials rescued me during my first year of teaching corporate
law, and whose advice and criticism have been invaluable ever
since; and my wife, Catherine Krupnick, for her interest, sympathy,
and enthusiasm for this project over the years.

—Reinier Kraakman

To my mentors in corporate law, Lucian Bebchuk and
John Coates; and to my wife, Helen Clement, and
my parents, Narayanan and Padma Subramanian.

—Guhan Subramanian

Summary of Contents

CONTENTS

3

THE PROBLEM OF JOINT OWNERSHIP:
THE LAW OF PARTNERSHIP   **41**

6

7

8

Normal Governance: The Duty of Care   241

10

SHAREHOLDER LAWSUITS   369

11

TRANSACTIONS IN CONTROL   423

13

PUBLIC CONTESTS FOR CORPORATE CONTROL 525

PREFACE

This book represents our effort to assist students and non-specialist lawyers to achieve an understanding of the basic principles of law that undergird the legal structures within which business is conducted in the United States. Our approach in this effort is premised upon a functional perspective of law. Thus, we attempt to ask how these legal structures function to produce desired benefits to parties who enter into agreements and relationships, or how legal structures (or rules) add costs and can impede sensible business organization. In this second aspect, the analytical or critical perspective, our point of view is informed through our understanding of basic principles of economics. The book, however, requires of its readers no formal training or understanding of economics. The concepts are for the most part quite intuitive and easily grasped.

We have organized the book into two segments. The first (and shorter) of these segments — Chapters 1-5 — deals with the fundamentals of organizational law in a business setting. Here the briefest chapter — Chapter 1 — addresses the most basic questions: the role of efficiency as a yardstick for evaluating business law, and the fundamental tension between the perspectives of doctrine and policy analysis that most experts (including judges) bring to the analysis of business law. We place these topics first because they come first logically. This does not mean, however, that they must come first pedagogically. Some users of this casebook might wish to circle back to Chapter 1, as students become more familiar with the legal problems posed by business organizations.

Chapters 2-4 deal with the elemental forms of business organization. Chapter 2 focuses on agency law, which is no less a predicate for modern enterprises functioning in a market economy than contract or property law. Chapter 3 addresses the partnership form and its modern variants: the limited partnership, limited liability company, and limited liability partnership. Chapter 4 introduces the corporate form, explicitly contrasted against the partnership and its variants, such as the LLC.

Chapter 5 steps outside the usual progression of a text on business organizations to address rudimentary concepts in valuation. As with Chapter 1, our placement of Chapter 5 seems logical to us, but we recognize that it might also have come earlier or later in the book. On the one hand, valuation issues gain salience as the materials progress further into corporate law, which argues for a later discussion. On the other hand, the basic concepts in financial economics are arguably useful throughout, and so might come at the outset of a course. Again, we are confident that individual instructors can best decide when, and whether, to work through this brief valuation chapter.

The larger segment of the book, Chapters 6-14, addresses the legal regulation of a variety of actions, decisions, and transactions that involve or concern the modern public corporation. Chapter 6 explores relationships among shareholders, corporations, and corporate creditors. Chapters 7 and 8 explore what we term "normal governance" — that is, the legal framework that regulates the vast majority of the corporation's ordinary business activities. Chapter 7 addresses the routine functioning of the voting system, including the proxy rules. Chapter 8 explores the duty of care, together with the multiple legal devices that insulate corporate officers and directors from shareholder liability, including, most notably, the business judgment rule.

Chapters 9-13 are devoted to particular classes of corporate actions and related shareholder transactions that are subject to more specialized regulation by corporate law. Chapter 9 addresses self-dealing and other potential duty of loyalty issues arising from the conduct of corporate officers, directors, and controlling shareholders. Chapter 10 extends this discussion to issues of procedure and enforcement by reviewing the law and practice of shareholder derivative suits. Chapter 11 examines transactions in corporate control, including sales of control blocks and tender offers. Chapter 12 addresses the specialized legal treatment of so-called fundamental corporate actions, with special attention to merger and acquisition transactions. Chapter 13 turns to conflicts for corporate control, including hostile tender offers and proxy contexts. And finally, Chapter 14 examines the regulation of transactions in shares on the public markets, including such topics as insider trading and fraud on the market.

While we have structured these materials in a way that conforms to the simple insight that much of corporate law can be divided into general governance, on the one hand, and discrete areas of specialized governance on the other, we expect some teachers will present the materials in a different sequence. We have taken care to facilitate alternative approaches by recapping in later chapters points more exhaustively made in earlier ones and by supplying cross-references for further review.

The book contains a number of notes that are perhaps a bit longer and more openly explanatory than other authors prefer. In this we have been motivated by our experience as teachers to want to provide a rather full textual basis for a general understanding of each subject. Our aim is to provide for those happy occasions when class gets deeply involved in an interesting discussion. In this event we are comforted by the knowledge that we can move on to the next class knowing that all of the basic information and insights have been made available to the class in the reading assignment.

In the end, what makes this branch of law so interesting (and frustrating) to students, practitioners, and scholars alike is the vital role played in it by the open-textured concept of fiduciary duty. From the early study of agency, to its conclusion with corporate mergers and acquisitions, the field and these materials offer myriad puzzles arising from the admixture of morality and efficiency that is often encountered when courts are required to fill in the specifics of a fiduciary's obligations. In approaching this subject, the book places primary emphasis on the Delaware statute and decisions, as that law grows in its dominant importance for publicly financed corporations in the United States. Opinions by the Delaware Court of Chancery and the Delaware Supreme Court tend to outnumber cases from other jurisdictions.

This second edition includes developments in corporate law since 2003, among them excerpts from important decisions such as *Disney*, *In re Oracle*, and *Omnicare*. The second edition also provides citations to the rapidly growing empirical literature on corporate law issues (for example, examining the effects of the Sarbanes-Oxley Act of 2002), and adds more problems for students to work through. Finally, we introduce in this edition several sidebars throughout the book, which provide vivid real-world illustrations of the topics described in the main text, or background information on the principal players in certain cases. These sidebars can generally be viewed as optional, though often highly entertaining, reading for students. They seek to convey the inherently human element that only occasionally comes to the surface in the judicial opinions themselves. It is our hope that the sidebars will remind students that the law of business organization is about real people, often taking significant financial and personal risks, in an effort to create and distribute wealth in our economy.

We must offer very real thanks and appreciation to colleagues and friends who have taught from these materials for some years and who have been generous in their comments and suggestions. First among these are Victor Brudney, whose teaching materials provided the starting point for this book, and Henry Hansmann, who has commented so richly and so long that it would be difficult to exaggerate our gratitude. Other colleagues have made useful comments and supplied detailed guidance. Among these are Jennifer Arlen, Lucian Bebchuk, Bernard Black, John Coates, Rob Daines, Jill Fisch, Jesse Fried, Jon Hanson, Hon. Jack B. Jacobs, Marcel Kahan, Ehud Kamar, Vic Khanna, Stephen J. Lubben, Mark Roe, and Hon. Leo Strine. We acknowledge gladly our debt to them. We also thank Tim Poulin of the Maine Secretary of State's office for generously sharing his data on new business entity formation. In addition, numerous anonymous reviewers made very helpful comments, and we hope that they will find the book improved because of their efforts. Finally, we each owe a debt of gratitude to student researchers and secretarial associates. Among students, some especially stand out for their glad assistance: Alison Gooley, NYU, 1999, of the Bar of New South Wales; and Ronnie Deutch, NYU, 2002, of the New York bar. Special thanks to Melissa Anderson, HLS 2009, for her excellent work on the sidebars and data collection for the second edition. Susannah Atkins, Cara R. Conlin, Linell Hanover, Barbara Karasinski, Kimberly Peterson, and Paula Prather offered cheerful and highly competent assistance. Our gratitude extends to them all.

William T. Allen
Reinier Kraakman
Guhan Subramanian

December 2006

ACKNOWLEDGMENTS

We thank the authors and copyright holders of the following works for permitting their inclusion in this book:

Bebchuk, Kraakman, and Triantis, *Stock Pyramids, Cross-Ownership, and Dual Class Equity*, p. 295ff. in Randall K. Morck, ed., Concentrated Corporate Ownership (2000).

Black, Bernard S., *Next Steps in Proxy Reform*, 18 J. Corp. L. 1, 4-8 (1992).

Carney, Dan, Enron Shareholders Suits? Not So Fast. Reprinted from the February 12, 2002, of BusinessWeek by permission. Copyright 2002 by The McGraw-Hill Companies.

Chung, Juliet, and Daniel Gordon, At Elite prep School, Parents Do the Math: Rector Gets $524,000, Wall Street Journal, Eastern Edition, Aug. 25, 2003. Copyright 2003 by Dow Jones & Company, Inc. Reproduced with permission of Dow Jones & Company, Inc. in the format Textbook via Copyright Clearance Center.

Coffee, John C., Business Organization and Finance (3d ed. 1988), pgs. 53-54.

Easterbrook and Fischel, *Corporate Control Transactions*, 91 Yale L.J. 698, 715-719 (1982).

Easterbrook and Fischel, *Limited Liability and the Corporation*, 52 U. Chi. L. Rev. 89, 94-97 (1985).

Easterbrook and Fischel, *Voting in Corporate Law*, 26 J.L. & Econ. 395, 409-411 (1983).

Eisinger, Jesse, Long & Short: Icahu Cries Foul at Perry's No-Risk Play in Takeover Fight, Wall Street Journal, Eastern Edition, Dec. 15, 2004. Copyright 2007 by Dow Jones & Company, Inc. Reproduced with permission of Dow Jones & Company, Inc. in the format Textbook via Copyright Clearance Center.

Hansmann and Kraakman, *Toward Unlimited Shareholder Liability for Torts*, 100 Yale L.J. 1879 (1991).

Jenkins, Holman J. Jr, Google Baloney, Wall Street Journal, Eastern Edition, May 5, 2004. Copyright 2007 by Dow Jones & Company, Inc. Reproduced with permission of Dow Jones & Company, Inc. in the format Textbook via Copyright Clearance Center.

Kelly, Kate, Susanne Craig, and L. Jeanne Dugan, Grasso Quits NYSE Amid Pay Furor, Wall Street Journal, Eastern Edition, Sept. 18, 2003. Copyright 2003 by Dow Jones & Company, Inc. Reproduced with permission of Dow Jones & Company, Inc. in the format Textbook via Copyright Clearance Center.

Markon, Jerry, and Robert Frank, Five Adelphia Officials Arrested on Fraud Charges, Wall Street Journal, Eastern Edition, Jul. 25, 2002. Copyright 2007 by Dow Jones & Company, Inc. Reproduced with permission of Dow Jones & Company, Inc. in the format Textbook via Copyright Clearance Center.

Ng, Serena, Dennis Berman, and Kara Scannell, Are Deal Makers on Wall Street Leaking Secrets?, Wall Street Journal, Eastern Edition, Jul. 28, 2006. Copyright 2006 by Dow Jones & Company, Inc. Reproduced with permission of Dow Jones & Company, Inc. in the format Textbook via Copyright Clearance Center.

Ng, Serena, Dennis Berman, and Kara Scannell, *Djà vu: A 1920's Insider Trade Was Ruled by Court To Be Merely a Perk*, Wall Street Journal, Eastern Edition, Jul. 3, 2002. Copyright 2002 by Dow Jones & Company, Inc. Reproduced with permission of Dow Jones & Company, Inc. in the format Textbook via Copyright Clearance Center.

Ramirez, Anthony, A 93% Pay Cut, to Just 1 Million, Jul. 27, 1990. Copyright © 1990 by The New York Times Co. Reprinted with permission.

Staff Writer, Doing Good and Doing Well at Timberland, Wall Street Journal, Eastern Edition, Sept. 9, 2003. Copyright 2003 by Dow Jones & Company, Inc. Reproduced with permission of Dow Jones & Company, Inc. in the format Textbook via Copyright Clearance Center.

Staff Writer, Executives on Trial: Newest "Tyco Gone Wild" Video Is Out, Wall Street Journal, Eastern Edition, Nov. 26, 2003. Copyright 2003 by Dow Jones & Company, Inc. Reproduced with permission of Dow Jones & Company, Inc. in the format Textbook via Copyright Clearance Center.

Staff Writer, Getting Lord Black Off Hollinger's Tab, Wall Street Journal, Eastern Edition, Nov. 28, 2003. Copyright 2003 by Dow Jones & Company, Inc. Reproduced with permission of Dow Jones & Company, Inc. in the format Textbook via Copyright Clearance Center.

COMMENTARIES AND CASES ON THE LAW OF BUSINESS ORGANIZATION

1

INTRODUCTION TO THE LAW OF ENTERPRISE ORGANIZATION

In large measure, civil law is concerned with facilitating voluntary economic relationships. Property law and contract law are the legal bedrock of market economies, but other bodies of law are also important. Among these are the laws of security interests, money and credit, bankruptcy, intellectual property, and enterprise organization. This book deals with the last, but hardly the least, of these fields: the law of enterprise organization. In particular, we address the laws of agency, partnership (and related entities), and corporations.

Because the problems that people encounter in their cooperative economic relations are recurring, the law creates a useful menu of standard forms to govern business relations. Thus, the laws of agency, partnership, and corporations can be seen as offering parties related sets of standard legal relations. Most of these relations are essentially contractual in the sense that they are voluntarily created and may be customized or fine-tuned by express agreement. As we shall see, however, the laws of agency, partnership, and corporations have a "property" dimension in addition to the contractual dimension, since they alter the legal rights of third parties as well as the rights of the parties who enter these enterprise relationships.

We begin our study with the law of agency. The agency relationship can be thought of as the simplest form of business organization. It may be terminated at any time by either the principal or the agent. In agency law, however, we see prefigured many of the most basic and difficult problems of corporation law, most particularly those arising from the so-called fiduciary duty of loyalty. From agency, we move to a somewhat more stable form of relationship — the general partnership — which we may think of as the simplest form of jointly owned business firm. Here we define "firm" loosely to mean a form of business relation that has a temporal dimension, a social identity, and a separate pool of dedicated business assets. Partnerships are usually simple joint enterprises of individual partners, subject to dissolution at the whim of any partner in the absence of a contrary agreement. By contrast, the corporate form — our principal subject — is the most stable, complex, and socially important form of business organization.

Before we address the law of business organization, we use this introductory chapter to discuss a few very general points. Throughout these materials, we not only describe the rules of enterprise law but also attempt to evaluate them. In doing so, we often use the concept of "efficiency" as a standard. Efficiency is a slippery concept, however, and discussing it is therefore our first priority.

After exploring the concept of efficiency, we address the relationship between efficiency and "fairness" in the law of business organization. Fairness is rarely a topic in academic discussion of corporation law because it is usually thought to be too vague to be analytically useful. Efficiency is the dominant, if not the sole, criterion for academic evaluation of corporate law doctrines. Yet courts, which in this area of law are powerful generators of legal norms, frequently invoke the concept of fairness in their opinions and rarely address efficiency, at least in so many words. This odd disjunction requires some explanation, which we offer in §1.2 below.

Lastly, we provide a brief outline of the modern learning on the economics of the firm in this introductory chapter. This is truly summary in nature, but even a brief review may prove helpful to the student or practitioner who is unfamiliar with the literature. We especially want to introduce early on the modern economics concepts of agency theory and agency cost, since they are significant theoretical perspectives on modern corporation law.

1.1   EFFICIENCY AND THE SOCIAL SIGNIFICANCE OF ENTERPRISE ORGANIZATION

Wealth is an important ingredient of happiness for most of us. Money can't buy everything, as the saying goes, but it can satisfy real human needs, reduce suffering, and help people achieve their full potential. Greater wealth is not always deployed to advance total human welfare, but it does create greater power to do so. In all events, the modern law of organizational forms — most notably corporation law — is premised on the idea that facilitating individuals' efforts to create wealth is wise public policy.

As citizens, of course, we are concerned about far more than the creation of total wealth or even our share in it. We are concerned with the state of the world, the welfare of others, and the social policies that affect the distribution of wealth, although we might disagree about the particulars. But by and large, corporation law has been shaped within the classical liberal political paradigm as a field limited to only a slice of the human experience. Thus, legitimate political questions about, for example, the social distribution of wealth fall outside the competence of corporate law. The laws of taxation, education, environmental and labor policy, product safety, and other issues of health, safety, and welfare address the distribution of risks and rewards in society. Corporate law addresses the creation of economic wealth through the facilitation of voluntary, ongoing collective action.

1.1.1   Wealth Creation and the Corporate Form of Organization

Corporation law in particular deals with the creation and governance of the private legal entities that are the principal economic actors in the modern world. Thus, it deals with the control over vast aggregations of wealth and power. It addresses such important issues as how corporate enterprises are created and capitalized, how power over their internal affairs is distributed, how their economic performance is monitored, and what mechanisms exist to improve their performance.

Defined in this way, enterprise law is a practical subject. While there are no precise measures of the effect that organizational law has on economic productivity, we do have certain indicia of its significance. The bankruptcy of the old Soviet-style planned economy is exhibit one in an argument for the importance of incentives and the law of ownership, control structures, and legal protection of capital. Marxism doctrinally denied the productive contribution of capital to the collective effort to produce wealth. Anglo-American corporation law, on the other hand, recognized from the beginning the legitimate rights of the shareholders who contributed equity capital to business enterprise. The collapse of the Soviet economy and its political control system and the success of the Anglo-American model of legal regulation of large-scale enterprise suggest that an organization's internal governance affects its performance.

Additional evidence of the significance of the law of enterprise organization is the dominance of the corporate form throughout the world. The basic legal form of large-scale firms is remarkably similar in almost all economies. As we will see, their shared characteristics are the identifying characteristics of the corporate form. Naturally, there are differences, too, but they are concerned primarily with the sources of capital used to capitalize corporate enterprise in different countries. In some countries, like the United States and Great Britain, developed capital markets provide much of the equity (or risk) capital that flows to both new ventures and established ones. In others — such as Germany and Japan — financial intermediaries supply much of this capital. In these countries, banks, savings institutions, insurance companies, or other operating companies may be the dominant providers of capital. In still other jurisdictions, family groups may be the major source of equity capital. Thus, while the international differences are interesting, the similarities are more striking. The corporate form dominates in all instances where technology creates economies of scale.

1.1.2   What Do We Mean by Efficiency?

If we accept the classical liberal perspective that corporation law succeeds to the extent that it enables individuals to increase their utility, we implicitly agree that *economic efficiency* is the principal standard by which this law should be evaluated. Throughout this course, students will be required to grapple with the question of whether a given rule of law (or a principle or practice) is likely to be efficient. Thus, at the very beginning, we should pause to consider what such a question means.

Our intuitive notion of efficiency is probably something largely unexamined but likely something in the manner of, say, the minimization of waste or the production of maximum output from given inputs. Economists have developed concepts that are more specific but still consistent with these intuitions.

1.1.2.1 *Pareto Efficiency*

The most basic definition of economic efficiency is that of the late-nineteenth-century Italian economist and sociologist Vilfredo Pareto. Pareto reasoned that a given distribution of resources is efficient when, and only when, resources are distributed in such a way (within a given group or territory) that no reallocation of resources can make at least one person better off without making at least one other person worse off. Economists describe such a distribution as "Pareto-optimal." This does not mean, however, that any ordinary person would describe the state as "optimal" or even tolerable. Like most post-Enlightenment thinkers, Pareto believed that utility is a subjective state of well-being that cannot be accurately assessed by outside observers. The only person capable of determining when a change of circumstances makes an individual better off or worse off is that individual herself. Thus, it is only through voluntary exchange, in which individuals reveal their own preference for one outcome over another, that we can be sure that any transfer or redistribution yields a utility gain for both sides of the transaction. And it is only when all parties affected by a transfer experience a net utility gain (or, at a minimum, one party experiences a gain and no party experiences a loss) that we can be certain that there is a net utility gain from the transaction overall. Such a transaction is said to be "Pareto-efficient."

But while Pareto efficiency is important, it has serious drawbacks as a tool for evaluating legal policies. To begin with, it is agnostic about the legitimacy of the original distribution of assets within a society. Pareto-efficient transfers are those that are certain to increase social welfare starting from a fixed starting point — an original distribution of resources. But in real-life policy formation by legislatures or courts (or in legal criticism by scholars or citizens), the legitimacy of the existing distribution is often contested.

Even more important, it is virtually impossible for courts or legislatures to make important decisions that do *not* make someone worse off. Indeed, even voluntary agreements among private parties sometimes fail the Pareto efficiency test because, although they make all of their signatories better off, they also impose uncompensated costs on third parties. Consequently, almost all public policies and many private arrangements fail the test of Pareto efficiency for the seemingly technical reason that, however much good they do on balance, they make at least one person worse off. Odd as it sounds, for example, even a law punishing fraud would not be Pareto-efficient if it made the perpetrators of frauds worse off. It follows that Pareto efficiency is poorly suited to evaluating or criticizing the law of enterprise organization.

1.1.2.2 *Kaldor-Hicks Efficiency*

Another definition of efficiency that most people find more intuitive was developed by two English economists, Nicholas Kaldor and John R. Hicks. These authors sought to finesse the problem of externalities — that is, uncompensated costs imposed on parties without their consent. Under their definition, an act (or a rule) is efficient — i.e., leads to an overall improvement in social welfare — if at least one party would gain from it after all those who suffered a loss as a result of the transaction or policy were fully compensated. Note that *actual* payment of any compensation is not stipulated in this definition. The idea here is that, because information is imperfect and transactions are costly, it is generally impossible to compensate all persons who are negatively affected by an action. Professors Kaldor and Hicks, consequently, simply replace the Paretian distributional constraint with the weaker rule that holds actions to be welfare-improving — or "efficient" — if they lead to a *potential* improvement in the Pareto efficiency sense because the gainers from these actions could, in theory, make the losers whole. In the happy case in which all the gains and losses can be evaluated in monetary terms, this is equivalent to saying that a transaction is efficient if the aggregate monetary gains to the winners exceed the aggregate monetary losses to the losers — i.e., the total wealth of the affected parties increases. For this reason, the Kaldor-Hicks efficiency criterion is sometimes termed the rule of "wealth maximization."

To be sure, Kaldor-Hicks efficiency also has important limitations. Like the Paretian efficiency criterion, it has little to say about the legitimacy of initial distributions of wealth. Additionally, it can be criticized for ignoring the actual distributional *consequences* of policies and the difficulty of accurately measuring all of the negative (and positive) effects of third parties that follow a given action. Despite these limitations, however, Kaldor-Hicks efficiency has the decisive advantage of permitting lawyers and policy makers to compare the costs and benefits of a given action or legal change with the same metric. For this reason, it is vastly more workable than Pareto efficiency as a yardstick for policy makers. In particular, it has become a standard tool for evaluating enterprise law. Thus, when we speak of efficiency in these materials, we have Kaldor-Hicks efficiency in mind.

1.2 LAW FROM INSIDE AND OUT: SHARED MEANINGS AND SKEPTICISM

Another basic point we want to address before embarking on our review of the law concerns the analytical distinction between viewing law from the interior perspective of a legal actor and viewing it from the external perspective of a social scientist.

1.2.1 The Outside and the Inside

Consider first how one can look at law and legal institutions from the perspective of a social scientist. A scientist observes an interesting phenomenon (i.e., one that seems curious, that does not fit within the existing structure of her beliefs), postulates a hypothesis grounded in some theory to explain the pattern of occurrences of the phenomenon, and devises a means to test her hypothesis. If her hypothesis cannot be shown to be false, it continues to be a plausible "explanation" of the phenomenon and gains credibility as it survives further assaults.

Social science is especially difficult because it examines phenomena that are produced in part by "meanings" that actors attribute to their actions and the actions of others. These meanings are subjective states that are not directly observable, are deeply contextual, and are only problematically inferred. Despite this profound difference between social science and physical science, both systems of knowledge attempt to stand outside the phenomenon that they are trying to explain. Thus, to the extent empiricists study law, they do so from an external vantage. Such observers are officially agnostic about all normative issues, apart from their belief in science.

Practicing law can be considered to be a fundamentally different activity. The practicing judge and the lawyer were not operating outside the system — as agnostics with respect to its articulated statements. Rather, the judge and the lawyer were understood to be believers. Indeed, they were the high priest and the priest of the faith. For them, the articulated reason for some judicial act was not simply a concurrence but a cause. In this faith, law was all about the meaning of legal doctrines: statutes, court rules, administrative procedures, judicial precedents, and the rich body of professional learning that allows experienced lawyers to perform their professional functions. These meanings may be unclear at times, but the internal processes of law — trials, appellate review, and even much scholarship — are about clarifying legal meanings as well as determining their provenance in "authority" and the consistency of the entire body of meanings. This is the "interior" perspective on law.

Once, law schools were largely concerned with this interior perspective on law. But in a dynamic society, this perspective alone neither explains legal change nor provides a basis to criticize law (other than by criticizing it for apparent doctrinal inconsistencies). It should not be surprising that, in a time so dominated by changing technology, tastes, and demographics, legal change has come to dominate legal education — and the prominence of the interior perspective on law has diminished accordingly.

Today, legal education and scholarship combine the interior and exterior perspectives. There are, it seems, few remaining true believers in legal doctrine as the only basis for evaluating legal doctrine. But few in legal scholarship would deny the importance of understanding the hierarchy of principles and doctrine that constitute the interior perspective. Indeed, if one seeks to understand the operation of the legal system, one must master both perspectives on law, the interior, which is rooted in history, authority, and consistency, and the exterior, which is rooted in the practical need to produce a "good" society in a changing world.

1.2.2 Fairness and Efficiency

This takes us to the use of the social scientific concept of efficiency in organization law. So far, we have suggested that the search for efficiency is, and should be, at the core of organizational law. We have argued that judges and lawyers, as well as academic commentators, ought to use efficiency in the production of wealth as the principal standard for evaluating current law. But courts rarely use the efficiency concept to justify their decisions. How do we reconcile our view with this fact?

We offer the following explanation. It is generally said that courts apply — rather than create — law. But sophisticated observers know that this is only partly correct. Certainly, courts are bound by principle to apply existing law according to its terms. A judge does not possess a roving commission to make social policy under the banner of efficiency or anything else. But even a judge who is a strict constructionist occasionally finds that policy-making choices are inescapably thrust upon her. Linguistic ambiguity alone often requires judges to make choices. But in such situations — and they arise frequently in the law of enterprise organization — courts avoid using "exterior" concepts like efficiency to justify their choices, even if these concepts are central to evaluating the wisdom of the outcome reached. This may change over the years as more lawyers trained in economic analysis fill the profession, but it will not change any time soon. Efficiency will remain a controversial judicial standard, in part because determining what counts as a "cost" and what counts as a "benefit" in a world of incomplete markets, strategic behavior, and informational asymmetry inevitably involves guesswork. In corporate matters, therefore, courts are disinclined to acknowledge the policy rationale for their decisions, even though this rationale is decisive to our normative evaluation of the results courts reach.

How, then, *do* judges rationalize their choices when choice is forced upon them? For centuries, courts have used the language of moral reasoning when, having exhausted professional techniques to derive one clear answer to a problem they faced, they have inescapably been forced to choose. In such circumstances, courts often refer to "fairness," "good faith," "justifiable reliance," "loyalty," "candor," "exploitation," and "penalties." These broad, socially defined concepts are wellsprings of the creative role of common law courts in the Anglo-American legal tradition. They look not to the technical knowledge of economics for their meaning — a language to which only a small portion of the polity has access — but to the everyday notions of right conduct that courts assume most of the polity shares.

But if courts have an important role in creating the law of enterprise organization and yet do not actively employ the concept of efficiency in their work, how can we expect the legal system to even approximate a normative ideal of Kaldor-Hicks efficiency? A full answer must await our discussion of corporation law and especially the rights of shareholders. The short answer is that, when traditional corporation law addresses "fairness," it generally refers to fairness to shareholders. Because shareholders are the residual claimants to the corporation's income and assets, protection of their interests through a fairness norm is generally consistent with increasing total corporate wealth and with moving toward a Kaldor-Hicks efficient state.

1.3   DEVELOPMENT OF THE MODERN THEORY OF THE FIRM

Sophisticated business lawyers understand that they are in the business of structuring transactions to deal with forces that are largely economic or financial in nature. In business law, the lawyer who fails to understand the economics of a problem usually fails to find a satisfactory solution to the problem. Thus, in this section, we address the economic perspective on firms.

Curiously, economists were slow to ask why firms existed at all. In the eighteenth century, Adam Smith noted that firms facilitate specialization, allowing individuals to achieve greater productivity. But Smith also noted that joint stock companies offer an important disadvantage relative to sole proprietorships and small partnerships. They require hired managers, who, he posited, would work less diligently than would the owners themselves. Smith reasoned that owners of larger firms would have more difficulty in monitoring and controlling the behavior of managers and, therefore, that the corporate form (or the joint stock company, as it was then called) would remain little used. As we can see, this prediction was off the mark. Nevertheless, Smith's focus on the problems that arise from agents managing a firm's assets was prescient.

Economists were slow to take up Smith's implicit invitation to study the incentive effects of owners and managers of firms. For most of the twentieth century, economics focused on what happened between competitive firms rather than on what happened within them. Put differently, economists studied markets. In doing so, they tended to assume the existence of a complete set of markets in which many informed buyers and sellers sought to maximize their utility. The prices in these markets contained all the information that any trader might need, and buying and selling generally tended to move prices toward an efficient equilibrium.

Real economic activity, however, only sometimes resembles tradings in these hypothetical markets. Most obviously, much economic activity is accomplished within firms and is thus not the product of market transactions at all. For example, shoemakers do not bargain with lace makers on the factory floor; a supervisor directs the flow of laces to shoes by fiat. In addition, much of what happens in markets is accomplished not by individuals effecting simple buy/sell transactions but by firms entering into complex contracts. Oddly, or so it seems in retrospect, for a long time no one asked these questions: Why do these organizations exist? Are they efficient? And if they are, what is the source of that efficiency?

Economists were generally uninterested in a theory of firms. Scholarly investigation of large firms tended to focus instead on the way that they gained and exercised power over markets. Thus, studies of "market power," "concentration," "oligopolistic pricing," "monopoly power," "market definition," and other antitrust topics occupied the attention of many economists during much of the twentieth century. Until the 1970s, the internal organization and functioning of firms were largely ignored.

1.3.1 Ronald Coase's 1937 Insight

There is an important exception, however. In 1937, Ronald Coase published *The Nature of the Firm*.[1] In this paper, Coase observed that the assumption of neoclassical economics that informed markets costlessly bring together buyers and sellers at an equilibrium price simply ignores many of the problems that real economic activity must solve. Coase hypothesized that, in reality, costs associated with transactions between market participants were substantial. He suggested that firms exist because, in a world of positive transaction costs, it is sometimes more efficient to organize complex tasks within a hierarchical organization — with its established authority and compensation structures — than on a market. Certainly, complex tasks could be accomplished on markets through a series of individualized buy/sell transactions. But where many steps were involved, Coase asserted, market forms of transacting would be costly, in part because they might require extensive negotiation or wasted effort to discover the best prices. Therefore, firms could be seen as innovations that permitted transactions, especially complex and reiterated transactions, to be accomplished more cheaply than they could be effected on markets.

This insight gave rise to a series of further questions; most notably: How can an entrepreneur or a scholar tell which activities will be more efficiently accomplished on markets and which within firms? What factors define the efficient boundaries of the firm? And how are people best motivated or controlled within firms?

1.3.2 Transactions Cost Theory

Remarkably, other economists did not take up these interesting questions until thirty years after Coase's original 1937 insight. Today, however, the "theory of the firm," as it is termed, is a burgeoning field within economics. While we cannot survey all of the important developments in

---

1. Ronald H. Coase, *The Nature of the Firm*, 4 Economica 386 (1937).

this field, we should note two areas of ongoing research that are of particular significance in corporate law. The first of these areas—and the most direct application of Coase's insight—is found in the pioneering work of Professor Oliver Williamson and others who seek, in a more detailed way than did Coase, to explain the firm as a set of transactions cost-reducing relationships (or "governance structures," in Williamson's terminology).[2] In this view, owners of various resources are seen as committing to some "contractual" governance arrangement, such as the firm, in order to reduce their transactions costs and share the resulting efficiency gains.

1.3.3   Agency Cost Theory

Even more significant for students of corporation law, however, is the work of a second strain of modern economics that directly takes up implications of Adam Smith's observations on the incentives of non-owner managers. This is the work of the agency theorists (or "principal-agent" theorists). Rather than focus on buyers and sellers who interact directly on markets, agency theory addresses how the actions of one actor (the "agent") affect the interest of another (the "principal"), with whom she is tied by contract or otherwise. Agents in the economic sense typically act with respect to property that principals "own." The pervasive reliance on these agents in our economy gives rise to a specific form of transactions costs.

Agency theorists share the assumption that economic actors are rational, informed, utility maximizers. Nevertheless, they are more realistic than earlier neoclassicist economists insofar as they view agents as maximizers of their *own* interests rather than the interests of their principals. Thus, according to agency theorists, a transaction may be motivated, in part at least, to serve an interest of a controlling agent rather than the interest of her principal. All legal forms of business firms, including the corporate form, can be viewed through this principal-agent lens.

Building on the work of Professors Armen Alchian and Harold Demsetz,[3] a 1976 article by Professors Michael Jensen and William Meckling provided a clear statement of the nature of the firm under this perspective.[4] Jensen and Meckling assert that the firm could best be understood as a complex of "contracts" between owners of the various factors of production of the firm. In this view, management is seen as offering to investors a share of the utility that can arise from centralizing information and expertise in a single enterprise.

The basic insight of the agency approach is that, to the extent the incentives of the agent (i.e., the person or interest that possesses discretionary power over some aspect of the principal's investment in the rela-

---

2. See, e.g., Oliver E. Williamson, The Economic Institutions of Capitalism (1985).

3. E.g., Armen A. Alchian & Harold Demsetz, *Production, Information Costs, and Economic Organization*, 62 Am. Econ. Rev. 777 (1977).

4. Michael C. Jensen & William H. Meckling, *The Theory of the Firm: Managerial Behavior, Agency Costs, and Ownership Structure*, 3 J. Fin. Econ. 305 (1976).

tionship) differ from the incentives of the principal herself, a potential cost will arise that is termed an "agency cost." Thus, an agency cost is any cost — explicit or implicit — associated with the exercise of discretion over the principal's property by an agent. In the case of corporate managers, agency costs include obvious costs such as salaries or benefits. But they also include costs that are not so evident. For example, since managers are not owners, they cannot expect to receive all of the gains from investment decisions they make on behalf of the corporation, but they certainly bear some of the costs if they make poor investment choices. If, for example, the firm goes broke as a result, they will lose their jobs. Therefore, the risks and rewards of managers may be out of alignment with the interests of shareholders. At the margin, managers will inevitably fail to optimize firm value. Consider the following example.

PROBLEM

Proprietor Jonas, a rational utility maximizer, owns a thriving business that requires him and some of his employees to stay in New York for days at a time. Last year Jonas stayed in New York City for 46 nights, for a total hotel cost of $16,100; others stayed for a total of 16 nights, for a total of $3,200. Jonas sometimes has difficulty getting into the hotel of his choice and, all things considered, would prefer to stay in a comfortable apartment on Fifth Avenue, which his company could acquire at a net cost of about $70,000 a year. What will Jonas choose to do? Now, assume that Jonas sells 90 percent of the stock in the company in an initial public offering but continues to be CEO. Will he still make the same decision?

Professors Jensen and Meckling suggest three general sources of agency costs: monitoring costs, or costs that owners expend to ensure agent loyalty; bonding costs, or costs that agents expend to ensure owners of their reliability; and residual costs, or costs that arise from differences of interest that remain after monitoring and bonding costs are incurred. Jensen and Meckling's model assumes that the principal bears all of these costs. In the case of corporations, for example, the principal is the entrepreneur who originally sells shares at a price that reflects the market's expectations about the degree of opportunism that managers and controlling shareholders are likely to engage in. (This claim assumes an efficient primary market in shares, of course.)

Agency theory can also be employed to understand aspects of relationships beyond those of the owners or investors and the managers. From the perspective of agency theory, the corporation (and, indeed, all jointly owned business organizations) gives rise to agency problems. The first is the conflict between managers and investor/owners, which we addressed in the discussion above. The second agency problem arises from the ability of majority owners to control returns in a way that discriminates against minority owners. The third agency problem is that which exists between the firm and all other parties with whom it transacts, such as creditors of the firm. In fact, all parties who transact with the firm, and not just investors,

JONASES IN THE REAL WORLD?

Consider these two excerpts, published days apart in *The Wall Street Journal*. What would Jensen & Meckling's agency theory say about this behavior? What alternative explanations might there be?

Executives on Trial: Newest 'Tyco Gone Wild' Video is Out
Wall Street Journal (November 26, 2003)

Yesterday, jurors in the corporate-looting trial of former Tyco International Ltd. Chief Executive L. Dennis Kozlowski were shown a 15-minute video of Mr. Kozlowski's opulent, $18 million apartment on Fifth Avenue in Manhattan. Prosecutors contend most of the duplex apartment's furnishings, including a $15,000 umbrella stand, were improperly bought with Tyco assets. But it was the famous [$6,000] shower curtain that everyone was waiting to see. When news of the costly fabric first surfaced last year, it became a symbol of corporate excess, the butt of jokes by late-night TV comedians. The tape also featured still shots of artwork, such as paintings by French Impressionists Claude Monet and Pierre Auguste Renoir, that prosecutors say Mr. Kozlowski bought with Tyco money, without authorization from the company's board.

Getting Lord Black Off Hollinger's Tab
Wall Street Journal (November 28, 2003)

Lord Black, an imperious newspaper proprietor who climbed as high as the U.K.'s House of Lords, resigned as Hollinger International's chief executive last week after a board committee disclosed that he and other top officials received unauthorized payments totaling $32.2 million. . . . Hollinger has also grounded its air fleet. The plane used mostly by Lord Black — a leased Gulfstream IV — was recently refurbished at a cost of $3 million, according to company filings with the SEC. Improvements included a handcrafted table made of an exotic wood and a luxury sofa with a fold-out bed, according to one person who toured the plane. Meals prepared in the plane's galley are served with Christofle silverware. Mr. Badenhausen [a spokesman for Lord Black] says the renovation is "standard for corporate aircraft." According to a company official, Hollinger also is considering selling the papers that belonged to President Roosevelt, the subject of a recent book by Lord Black. The company hasn't publicly explained the reasons for the $8 million purchase. Asked by the Financial Times this summer why he didn't buy the papers himself, Lord Black responded: "$8 million was not something I was prepared to spend."

are likely to confront imperfections in contracting that expose them to the prospect of a firm's behaving opportunistically toward them. Unless the law or the parties craft protections from these risks, contracting parties (suppliers of equity capital, credit, labor, or other inputs) will demand higher returns to contract with the firm. (With respect to the agency problem faced by creditors, see Chapter 6.)

Using the metric of total assets, the corporation is the most important legal form of business organization. As we describe in Chapter 4, this form succeeds because it reduces the transactions costs of complex economic contracting. But the corporate form does so at the risk of creating agency problems that must be constrained if it is to succeed. Thus, a principal aim of corporation law is the reduction of agency costs of all sorts.

Before turning to the corporate form, however, it is useful to consider the role of the law in reducing transactions costs in two simpler contexts. Hence, Chapter 2 is dedicated to the law of agency, from which the economic concept of agency cost derives its name. (Note that the legal concept of agent is related to the economic concept but is narrower in scope.) Chapter 3 introduces the partnership form, which, apart from natural persons, is the simplest form of legal entity for conducting business and may be understood as a precursor and alternative to the corporate form.

ACTING THROUGH OTHERS: THE LAW OF AGENCY

2.1 INTRODUCTION TO AGENCY

The simplest form of joint economic undertaking occurs when one person extends the range of her own activity by engaging another to act for her and be subject to her control. This is the paradigm of the principal-agent relationship. Think of the successful sole proprietor hiring her first employee. Such a relationship is called an agency.

Together with property and contract law, agency law is one of the fundamental building blocks of market economies. Agency law is indispensable because it can create legal relationships between strangers — principals and the third parties with whom their agents interact. For this reason it must be part of the infrastructure established by legal fiat, and cannot be done through contract. While organizational economists often think about the corporate form as a "nexus of contracts," this point makes clear why the law of business organization is not merely a sub-field within contract law.

Many of the basic problems of corporation law are prefigured in the law of agency. Indeed, these problems are heightened in the context of a widely held public corporation because the putative "principal" — the class of dispersed shareholders — may be entirely unable to monitor its "agent" — the corporation's management. In the simpler agency context, the principal is typically an individual who is capable of actively monitoring her agent's activities to some extent. Despite this difference, however, many of the core problems of corporation law are fundamentally similar to those of agency law.

Law schools used to treat agency as an important course. Giants of the profession — Professor Warren Seavey at Harvard Law School and Professor Philip Mechem of the University of Pennsylvania School of Law, for example — dedicated much of their lives to explicating its interstices. Understanding agency remains fundamentally important to mastering the internal perspective on law, but it has been crowded out of the general curriculum by subjects thought to have greater relevance because they assist the understanding of the external perspective on law. Nowadays, agency appears only as an appetizer in the opening sections of a corporations course. Happily, the Restatement of the Law of Agency (Third),

15

finalized in 2006, is a masterful summary that can assist any student or practitioner in learning about the field.

Here we want to concentrate on those aspects of agency law that have the greatest relevance to a course on corporation law. That means that we will address three problems out of a much wider universe of issues that arise from agency relations. The first is the problem of formation and termination (or "entry" into and "exit" from agency): How are agency relationships formed and how are they dissolved? The second is the problem of the principal's relationship to third parties: What is the principal's responsibility for the agent's authorized and unauthorized contracts and for torts committed by the agent during the course of her service? And the third is the nature of the duties that the agent owes to the principal. Our discussion follows this three-part structure. References are made to Restatement (Third) Agency for further reading.

2.2   AGENCY FORMATION, AGENCY TERMINATION, AND PRINCIPAL'S LIABILITY

2.2.1   Formation

The Restatement (Third) Agency offers this definition: "Agency is the fiduciary relationship that arises when one person (a 'principal') manifests assent to another person (an 'agent') that the agent shall act on the principal's behalf and subject to the principal's control, and the agent manifests assent or otherwise consent so to act." Restatement (Third) Agency §1.01.

An agency is a consensual relationship between the principal, who grants authority to another to bind her in certain respects, and the agent, who accepts that responsibility. Thus, an agent is a holder of a power to affect the legal relations of the principal within the scope of the agent's agreed-on appointment (or "employment") and beyond this scope in some circumstances, Subject to the agent's consent, the principal can define or delimit the granted authority in any way that she pleases. Thus, agents may be *special agents* (i.e., the agency is limited to a single act or transaction), or they may be *general agents* (i.e., the agency contemplates a series of acts or transactions). Principals may be *disclosed* (i.e., when third parties transacting with the agent understand that the agent is acting on behalf of a particular principal), *undisclosed* (i.e., when third parties are unaware of a principal and believe that the agent herself is a principal), or *partially disclosed* (i.e., when third parties understand that they are dealing with an agent but do not know the identity of the principal).

The principal's right to control the agent is an essential aspect of an agency. But that right to control may vary substantially under the agreement. When a principal has a right under his deal with the agent to control the details of the way in which the agent goes about her task — for example, the order in which she addresses tasks or the precautions that she uses — the agent is called an *employee* or, more quaintly in the legal literature, a *servant*. When the principal's rights of control are significantly less extensive — for example, when the agent is a professional who is bound to provide independent judgment or when it is an established business that does not agree to minute control — such as a house contractor — the agent is described as an *independent contractor*.

2.2.2   Termination

Either the principal or the agent can terminate an agency at any time. If the contract between them fixes a set term of agency, then the principal's decision to *revoke* or the agent's decision to *renounce* gives rise to a claim for damages for breach of contract. In no event will an agency continue over the objection of one of the parties. The rule that either party may freely terminate is equivalent to restricting an agent or principal to monetary damages for breach of an agency contract. This rule seems unexceptional, since many agencies are employment contracts, and courts will not specifically enforce employment contracts against the wishes of either employees or employers. Doubtless you have addressed these policies before in your study of contract law. Nevertheless, these policies restrict the freedom to contract, and it is worth pondering whether the law's refusal to enforce irrevocable agency agreements (with certain minor exceptions) might not interfere with transactions that would make both parties better off.

The following is an example of an agreement that cannot be specifically enforced.

> P owns a resort hotel. P engages A to manage the hotel for a term of 10 years, in an agreement that expressly provides that P may not revoke A's authority except pursuant to mutual agreement. The agreement states that P's promise not to revoke A's authority constitutes security to A for A's interest in receiving the management fee specified in the agreement, which is three percent of gross revenues for the first five years, and five percent for the second five years.[1]

QUESTIONS

Should the law preclude P from committing herself to such an irrevocable arrangement by agreement? What is gained by removing this possible agreement from the array of other contracts that may be voluntarily undertaken? If the contract is not specifically enforceable, what if it is made anyway and breached: Should it be enforced for damages? Note that if a principal grants authority for a stated term, this authority expires automatically at the conclusion of the term. If no term is stated, authority terminates at the end of a reasonable term. A special agency terminates when the

---

1. Restatement (Third) Agency §3.12, illus. 3.

specific act contemplated is performed or after a "reasonable" time has elapsed. See generally Restatement (Third) Agency, ch. 3.

2.2.3   Parties' Conception Does Not Control

Agency relations may be implied even when the parties have not *explicitly* agreed to an agency relationship. An important context in which agency relationships are implied is when creditors assume "too much" control in relationships that ostensibly contain debtor-creditor relationships. Ask yourself: Why might courts be particularly concerned about debtor-creditor contracts? Consider the following case.

JENSON FARMS CO. v. CARGILL, INC.

309 N.W.2d 285 (Minn. 1981)

Plaintiffs, 86 individuals, partnerships or corporate farmers, brought this action against defendant Cargill, Inc. (Cargill) and defendant Warren Grain & Seed Co. (Warren) to recover losses sustained when Warren defaulted on the contracts made with plaintiffs for the sale of grain. After a trial by jury, judgment was entered in favor of plaintiffs, and Cargill brought this appeal. We affirm.

This case arose out of the financial collapse of defendant Warren Seed & Grain Co. . . . Warren operated a grain elevator and as a result was involved in the purchase of . . . grain from local farmers. The cash grain would be resold through the Minneapolis Grain Exchange or to the terminal grain companies directly. Warren also stored grain for farmers and sold chemicals, fertilizer and steel storage bins. . . .

[I]n 1964 [Warren applied] for financing from Cargill. Cargill's officials from the Moorhead regional office investigated Warren's operations and recommended that Cargill finance Warren.

Warren and Cargill thereafter entered into a security agreement which provided that Cargill would loan money for working capital to Warren on "open account" financing up to a stated limit, which was originally set as $175,000.[2] Under this contract, Warren would receive funds and pay its expenses by issuing drafts drawn on Cargill through Minneapolis banks. The drafts were imprinted with both Warren's and Cargill's names. Proceeds from Warren's sales would be deposited with Cargill and credited to its account. In return for this financing, Warren appointed Cargill as its grain agent for transaction with the Commodity Credit Corporation. Cargill was also given a right of first refusal to purchase market grain sold by Warren to the terminal market.

---

2. Loans were secured by a second mortgage on Warren's real estate and a first chattel mortgage on its inventories of grain and merchandise in the sum of $175,000 with 7 percent interest. . . .

A new contract was negotiated in 1967, extending Warren's credit line to $300,000 and incorporating the provisions of the original contract. It was also stated in the contract that Warren would provide Cargill with annual financial statements and that either Cargill would keep the books for Warren or an audit would be conducted by an independent firm. Cargill was given the right of access to Warren's books for inspection.

In addition, the agreement provided that Warren was not to make capital improvements or repairs in excess of $5,000 without Cargill's prior consent. Further, it was not to become liable as guarantor on another's indebtedness, or encumber its assets except with Cargill's permission. Consent by Cargill was required before Warren would be allowed to declare a dividend or sell and purchase stock.

Officials from Cargill's regional office made a brief visit to Warren shortly after the agreement was executed. They examined the annual statement and the accounts receivable, expenses, inventory, seed, machinery and other financial matters. Warren was informed that it would be reminded periodically to make the improvements recommended by Cargill. At approximately this time, a memo was given to the Cargill official in charge of the Warren account, Erhart Becker, which stated in part: "This organization (Warren) needs *very strong* paternal guidance."

In 1970, Cargill contracted with Warren and other elevators to act as its agent to seek growers for a new type of wheat called Bounty 208. Warren, as Cargill's agent for this project, entered into contracts for the growing of the wheat seed, with Cargill named as the contracting party. Farmers were paid directly by Cargill for the seed and all contracts were performed in full. In 1971, pursuant to an agency contract, Warren contracted on Cargill's behalf with various farmers for the growing of sunflower seeds for Cargill. . . .

During this period, Cargill continued to review Warren's operations and expenses and recommend that certain actions should be taken.[4] Warren purchased from Cargill various business forms printed by Cargill and received sample forms from Cargill which Warren used to develop its own business forms.

Cargill wrote to its regional office in 1970 expressing its concern that the pattern of increased use of funds allowed to develop at Warren was similar to that involved in two other cases in which Cargill experienced severe losses. Cargill did not refuse to honor drafts or call the loan, however. A new security agreement which increased the credit line to $750,000 was executed in 1972, and a subsequent agreement which raised the limit to $1,250,000 was entered into in 1976.

---

4. Between 1967 and 1973, Cargill suggested that Warren take a number of steps, including: (1) a reduction of seed grain and cash grain inventories; (2) improved collection of accounts receivable; (3) reduction or elimination of its wholesale seed business and its speciality grain operation; (4) marketing fertilizer and steel bins on consignment; (5) a reduction in withdrawals made by officers; (6) a suggestion that Warren's bookkeeper not issue her own salary checks; and (7) cooperation with Cargill in implementing the recommendations. These ideas were apparently never implemented, however.

Warren was at that time shipping Cargill 90% of its cash grain. When Cargill's facilities were full, Warren shipped its grain to other companies. Approximately 25% of Warren's total sales was seed grain which was sold directly by Warren to its customers.

As Warren's indebtedness continued to be in excess of its credit line, Cargill began to contact Warren daily regarding its financial affairs. Cargill headquarters informed its regional office in 1973 that, since Cargill money was being used, Warren should realize that Cargill had the right to make some critical decisions regarding the use of the funds. Cargill headquarters also told Warren that a regional manager would be working with Warren on a day-to-day basis as well as in monthly planning meetings. In 1975, Cargill's regional office began to keep a daily debit position on Warren. A bank account was opened in Warren's name on which Warren could draw checks in 1976. The account was to be funded by drafts drawn on Cargill by the local bank.

In early 1977, it became evident that Warren had serious financial problems. . . . In April 1977, an audit of Warren revealed that Warren was $4 million in debt. After Cargill was informed that Warren's financial statements had been deliberately falsified, Warren's request for additional financing was refused. . . .

After Warren ceased operations, it was found to be indebted to Cargill in the amount of $3.6 million. Warren was also determined to be indebted to plaintiffs in the amount of $2 million, and plaintiffs brought this action in 1977 to seek recovery of that sum. Plaintiffs alleged that Cargill was jointly liable for Warren's indebtedness as it had acted as principal for the grain elevator. . . .

The major issue in this case is whether Cargill, by its course of dealing with Warren, became liable as a principal on contracts made by Warren with plaintiffs. Cargill contends that no agency relationship was established with Warren. . . .

Agency is the fiduciary relationship that results from the manifestation of consent by one person to another that the other shall act on his behalf and subject to his control, and consent by the other so to act. . . .

In order to create an agency there must be an agreement, but not necessarily a contract between the parties. . . . An agreement may result in the creation of an agency relationship although the parties did not call it an agency and did not intend the legal consequences of the relation to follow. The existence of the agency may be proved by circumstantial evidence which shows a course of dealing between the two parties. . . . .

. . . We hold that all three elements of agency could be found in the particular circumstances of this case. By directing Warren to implement its recommendations, Cargill manifested its consent that Warren would be its agent. Warren acted on Cargill's behalf in procuring grain for Cargill as the part of its normal operations which were totally financed by Cargill.[7] . . .

---

7. Although the contracts with the farmers were executed by Warren, Warren paid for the grain with drafts drawn on Cargill. While this is not in itself significant . . . it is one factor to be taken into account in analyzing the relationship between Warren and Cargill.

A number of factors indicate Cargill's control over Warren, including the following:

(1) Cargill's constant recommendations to Warren by telephone;
(2) Cargill's right of first refusal on grain;
(3) Warren's inability to enter into mortgages, to purchase stock or to pay dividends without Cargill's approval;
(4) Cargill's right of entry onto Warren's premises to carry on periodic checks and audits;
(5) Cargill's correspondence and criticism regarding Warren's finances, officers salaries and inventory;
(6) Cargill's determination that Warren needed "strong paternal guidance";
(7) Provision of drafts and forms to Warren upon which Cargill's name was imprinted;
(8) Financing of all Warren's purchases of grain and operating expenses; and
(9) Cargill's power to discontinue the financing of Warren's operations.

We recognize that some of these elements, as Cargill contends, are found in an ordinary debtor-creditor relationship. However, these factors cannot be considered in isolation, but, rather, they must be viewed in light of all the circumstances surrounding Cargill's aggressive financing of Warren. . . .

The amici curiae assert that, if the jury verdict is upheld, firms and banks which have provided business loans to county elevators will decline to make further loans. The decision in this case should give no cause for such concern. We deal here with a business enterprise markedly different from an ordinary bank financing, since Cargill was an active participant in Warren's operations rather than simply a financier. Cargill's course of dealing with Warren was, by its own admission, a paternalistic relationship in which Cargill made the key economic decisions and kept Warren in existence.

Although considerable interest was paid by Warren on the loan, the reason for Cargill's financing of Warren was not to make money as a lender but, rather, to establish a source of market grain for its business. As one Cargill manager noted, "We were staying in there because we wanted the grain." . . .

On the whole, there was a unique fabric in the relationship between Cargill and Warren. . . . We conclude that, on the facts of this case, there was sufficient evidence from which the jury could find that Cargill was the principal of Warren within the definitions of agency set forth in Restatement (Second) of Agency §§1 and 140.

QUESTION ON JENSON FARMS CO. v. CARGILL, INC.

If Cargill exercised control over Warren to protect its loan, why should it matter that Cargill made the loan to preserve access to a supply of grain?

2.2.4 Liability in Contract

2.2.4.1 Actual and Apparent Authority

An agency is an arrangement that confers legal power on the agent and gives rise to duties by both the principal and the agent. Both parties must manifest their intention to enter an agency relationship. This manifestation need not necessarily be in writing, nor is it essential that it even be verbal. What is necessary is for the agent to *reasonably understand from the action or speech of the principal that she has been authorized to act on the principal's behalf.*

Thus, the scope of the *actual authority* conferred on the agent is that which a reasonable person in the position of A would infer from the conduct of P. Actual authority includes (unless specifically withheld) *incidental authority* — that is, the authority to do those implementary steps that are ordinarily done in connection with facilitating the authorized act. In addition to actual authority, there is another source of authority. *Apparent authority* is authority that a reasonable third party would infer from the actions or statements of P. Thus, apparent authority is in the nature of an equitable remedy designed to prevent fraud or unfairness to third parties who reasonably rely on P's actions or statements in dealing with A. This will be true even if, unbeknownst to the third party, P had quite explicitly limited the authority of A in a way that precluded A from engaging in that action. See generally Restatement (Third) Agency §2.03.

WHITE v. THOMAS

1991 LEXIS 109 (Ark. App. 1991)

CRACRAFT, Chief Judge.

Appellants Bradford White, Sr., and Northwest National Bank appeal from an order of the Washington County Chancery Court requiring White to specifically perform a contract to convey real estate to Stanley Thomas and Mary Thomas, and directing the bank to release the property from the lien of the mortgage it held. As we find sufficient merit in the argument that appellant White was not bound under the contract, we reverse the chancellor's decree.

The facts are not seriously in dispute. Appellant Bradford White had employed Betty Simpson on a part-time basis for nearly two years. During her employment, Ms. Simpson answered appellant's telephone, watched his house when he was out of town, did some typing, and "fixed up" two houses. She had once signed, on appellant's behalf and under a power of attorney, the closing papers on a piece of property appellant was purchasing.[†] She also had brought appellant information about other properties

---

† A Power of Attorney (POA) is a written instrument executed by the principal (or "grantor") designating the agent to perform specified acts on the principal's behalf. It is intended to provide written evidence of an agency relationship.–Eds.

for sale, but had never negotiated sales or purchases of land for appellant and had never before gone to an auction to buy property.

In December 1988, appellant White instructed Simpson to attend a land auction and bid, in his behalf, up to $250,000.00 on an entire 220-acre farm, except for the three acres on which a house sat. He signed a blank check for her to use in depositing the required ten percent of the bid. Simpson was given no other instructions, and White left for a trip to Europe before the sale was held.

Appellees attended the auction and were the successful bidders on the three-acre tract on which the residence was located. They also unsuccessfully bid on acreage adjoining the homesite. The 217-acre balance of the land, including that additional acreage in which appellees had shown an interest, was struck off and sold to Ms. Simpson for $327,500.00. When Ms. Simpson realized that her bid had exceeded the amount authorized by appellant, she approached appellees about purchasing from her some of the lands surrounding their house. She signed the agreement with the auctioneer to purchase the 217-acre tract. She then entered into an offer and acceptance with appellees in which she agreed to sell to appellees approximately forty-five acres of the land that she had just purchased for appellant White. The contract was signed by appellees and by "Betty Simpson, POA, Power of Attorney for Brad White."

Appellant White returned from Europe on Friday, December 9. The following Monday, Ms. Simpson told him that she had paid $327,500.00 for the property and he "almost had a heart attack. I was upset but I still went through with the closing." Ms. Simpson later told appellant White that appellees wanted to buy part of the property. This was the first information he had concerning it. He immediately repudiated Ms. Simpson's action in signing the offer and acceptance and so informed appellees. The following day, appellant White's purchase of the 217-acre tract was consummated in part with the proceeds of a purchase-money loan, secured by a lien on the real estate, from the appellant bank.

Appellees then began this action seeking specific performance of the contract and release of the land embraced in the contract from the mortgage. Appellant White and Simpson both denied that Simpson was expressly authorized to enter into a contract of sale on White's behalf, and appellees do not contend otherwise. The only relevant factual dispute centered around Simpson's representations as to her authority. Appellee Stanley Thomas testified that "[a]t one point in time, before the offer and acceptance, I asked Ms. Simpson whether she had the authority or something, and she said was the power of attorney [sic]. At some point in time, the question crossed my mind as to whether or not Ms. Simpson could convey the property, but I was satisfied with her statement that she had a power of attorney." Ms. Simpson, on the other hand, testified that the auctioneer asked her if she had a power of attorney and "I said, 'No.' Then he asked me if I would send one. There was no more conversation about it." It is undisputed that no such power of attorney actually existed.

At the conclusion of the evidence, the court found that Ms. Simpson had in fact informed appellees that she had a power of attorney granting her the authority she had exercised and that appellees had relied on

Ms. Simpson's representations as to her authority. The court concluded that the offer and acceptance was a valid and binding contract, complete in its terms, that the reliance by appellees on the representations of Ms. Simpson was reasonable, and that appellant White was estopped from denying the authority of Ms. Simpson and was legally bound to the terms of the contract as her principal and employer. The court also concluded that it would be inequitable to allow appellant White to ratify Ms. Simpson's act of purchasing the farm, despite her having exceeded his express instructions, but allow him to disaffirm her action in entering into the offer and acceptance with appellees. Finally, the court found that the appellant bank had actual and constructive notice of appellees' claim, and ordered it to release its mortgage lien as to that portion of the lands ordered to be conveyed to appellees. . . .

Although we review chancery cases de novo, we will not reverse a chancellor's findings unless they are clearly erroneous. . . .

Here, it is undisputed that Ms. Simpson was not expressly authorized to sell appellant White's property; she was expressly authorized only to purchase a 217-acre tract of land for her principal if she could do so for no more than $250,000.00. Nor did she have the implied authority to contract to sell to appellees a portion of the property that she had purchased, as that act was not necessary to accomplish her assigned task of purchasing the entire tract. Therefore, in order for appellant White to be liable for Simpson's actions in entering into the offer and acceptance with appellees, her actions must have fallen within the scope of her apparent authority. . . .

Here, it is undisputed that appellees knew that Simpson's actions at the auction were purportedly being taken on behalf of appellant White. While Simpson's possession of a blank check signed by White may have indicated some limited authority on her part to make a purchase for him, there is no evidence that White knowingly permitted Simpson to enter into a contract to sell or that he ever held her out as having such authority. Nor can we conclude that the two types of transactions, purchasing and selling, are so closely related that a third person could reasonably believe that authority to do the one carried with it authority to do the other. Indeed, appellees were sufficiently concerned about Simpson's authority to contract to sell White's property that they specifically asked her whether she was so authorized. Appellees made no attempt to contact White concerning Simpson's authority and did not even demand to see the alleged written power of attorney under which Simpson claimed to be acting. Instead, they chose to rely solely upon an admitted agent's own declarations as to her authority.

While the declarations of an alleged agent may be used to corroborate other evidence of the scope of agency, neither agency nor the extent of the agent's authority can be shown solely by his own declarations or actions in the absence of the party to be affected. From our review of the record, we cannot conclude that there is any evidence in this case to support Simpson's statements as to her authority to sell White's property. Therefore, we must conclude that the chancellor's conclusion that appellant White was bound under the contract due to Simpson's apparent authority to enter into it is clearly erroneous. There could be no basis for finding White estopped to deny Simpson's authority either, for, as noted above, there is no evidence that he knew or should have known of her action or declarations.

Nor do we find merit in the argument that because appellant White ratified Simpson's contract to purchase the 217-acre tract, it would be inequitable to allow him to deny the burdens of her action in agreeing to sell forty-five acres of it. . . . Simpson entered into two separate contracts involving different parties.

In view of our conclusion that appellant was not bound by the agreement to sell to appellees, we reverse the order of specific performance and the order that the appellant bank release the property from its mortgage lien. . . .

Reversed and dismissed.

2.2.4.2   *Inherent Authority*

In addition to actual authority, express or implied, and apparent authority, some courts have identified circumstances in which they find that individuals possess *inherent authority* to bind principals to contracts. Such power might better be described as *inherent power* in order to emphasize that it is not conferred on agents by principals but represents consequences imposed on principals by the law. See Restatement (Second) Agency §§8A, 161, 194. The 2006 Restatement (Third) of Agency no longer conceptualizes the field in this way. According to the reporter: "Other doctrines stated in this Restatement encompass the justifications underpinning §8A, including the importance of interpretation by the agent in the agent's relationship with the principal, as well as the doctrines of apparent authority, estoppel, and restitution." See Restatement (Third) Agency §2.01 comment b.

Inherent authority is perhaps easiest to understand in the context of an undisclosed principal transaction. Imagine, for example, that a principal allows an agent to manage property and hold herself out as its owner but that the principal privately restricts the agent's actual authority to deal with the property in some particular — say, she is not authorized to contract for improvements in excess of $3,000. If the agent makes a contract to clear some of the land for a price of $7,000, is the principal bound by the contract obligation to pay? The third party cannot invoke the doctrine of apparent authority, since she did not even know of the existence of the principal. Nevertheless, it seems plain that, since the principal can force the third party to complete the contract, the principal should not be able to walk away from her obligations. But how is this result obtained?

Under the traditional approach, the doctrine of inherent power gives a general agent the power to bind a principal, whether disclosed or undisclosed, to an unauthorized contract as long as a general agent would ordinarily have the power to enter such a contract and the third party does not know that matters stand differently in this case. See Restatement (Second) Agency §161, 194. The Restatement (Third) seems to provide the same result for the particular case of an undisclosed principal.

See Restatement (Third) Agency §2.06. More generally, the Restatement (Third) provides agency by estoppel and restitution. See Restatement (Third) Agency §§2.05, 2.07. Please review these provisions in your statutory supplement. Is the reporter of the Restatement (Third) correct in stating that these new provisions do the same work as previously done by Restatement (Second) §8A? Which approach do you prefer?

The following case addresses the nature of inherent authority.

GALLANT INS. CO. v. ISAAC

732 N.E.2d 1262 (Ind. App. 2000)

Riley, Judge

Plaintiff-Appellant, Gallant Insurance Company (Gallant), appeals from the trial court's grant of summary judgment in favor of Defendants-Appellees, Christina Isaac (Isaac) and Loretta Davis (Davis) (hereinafter referred to collectively as "Insured"), on its complaint for declaratory judgment regarding its insurance coverage of Isaac's accident.

Thompson-Harris is an independent insurance agent. Its authority includes the power to bind Gallant on new insurance policies, as well as interim policy endorsement such as adding a new driver, or changing and adding a vehicle insured under a policy. Although no written agreement describes the relation between Gallant and Thompson-Harris, the Record indicates Gallant became bound to provide insurance coverage at the time and date on which Thompson-Harris faxed or called the required information to Gallant's producing agent, and premiums were paid to Thompson-Harris.

On June 2, 1994, Gallant issued automobile insurance coverage on Isaac's 1986 Pontiac Fiero through its independent agent, Thompson-Harris. . . . The printed application form, which had been filled out by the agent, showed that Isaac's coverage was bound as of 2:06 p.m. on June 2, 1994 until December 2, 1994. . . . With regard to "CHANGES" made to its conditions, the policy states that an agent shall not waive or change any part of the policy, except by endorsement issued to form a part of the policy, which is signed by a duly authorized representative of the company. The policy also stated that the written policy embodied all agreements existing between the insured, the company and all agents relating to the insurance.

On the last day of her insurance coverage, Isaac traded her 1986 Pontiac Fiero for a 1988 Pontiac Grand Prix. To obtain the newly purchased car, the financing bank required Isaac to obtain full coverage on it. That same day, Isaac contacted Thompson-Harris to notify it that she was purchasing the new car, and to discuss enhancing the existing insurance policy to meet bank requirements. Isaac told a Thompson-Harris employee that she must obtain "full insurance coverage" as a condition to receiving a loan. She also told the employee at Thompson-Harris that her current coverage expires on December 3, 1994, the next day.

In response, the Thompson-Harris employee informed Isaac that because their agency was about to close for the weekend, she would immediately "bind" coverage on the 1988 Grand Prix. They decided that Isaac would come in to Thompson-Harris on Monday, December 5, 1994, to complete the paperwork and pay the down payment on the premium. The employee also informed Isaac that the new coverage on her Pontiac Grand Prix would include the same coverage existing from her Pontiac Fiero, along with additional coverage to comply with conditions set by the bank.

The next day, on December 3, 1994, a different employee completed the "Personal Policy Change Request." This form deleted the 1987 Pontiac Fiero from Isaac's Policy and replaced it with the 1988 Pontiac Grand Prix. It also added additional coverage to the policy as well as additional loss payee/lienholder. The Personal Policy Change Request listed the "Agency" and "Producer" as Thompson-Harris, and stated that the "effective date of change" was December 3, 1994. Towards the bottom of the form, the Thompson-Harris employee typed "[s]he will be in at 9:00 a.m. Monday, 12/5/94, to [sic] down [sic] on renewal. What is [sic] new rate? Thanks." This form, which requested the listed changes, was faxed to Insurance Brokers of Indiana, Inc., on December 3, 1994.

On December 4, 1994, while driving her Pontiac Grand Prix, Isaac collided with another car in which Davis was a passenger. The next day, as planned, Isaac went to Thompson-Harris and paid $133.00 down payment on the new insurance policy. She also reported the accident. Thompson-Harris completed an "Indiana Operator's Vehicle Crash Report," which notified the State Police that Isaac had insurance coverage at the time of the accident, on December, 4, 1994. Thompson-Harris completed that form on behalf of Gallant. Later, on or about December 22, 1994, Gallant renewed Isaac's insurance policy, with an effective period of December 6, 1994 to June 6, 1995.

Soon afterwards, Gallant brought its complaint for declaratory judgment regarding its insurance coverage of Isaac's accident. It sought a judgment that stated Gallant was not liable for any losses incurred because the policy was not in force. . . .

Gallant contends that Isaac's insurance coverage had lapsed at the time Isaac's accident occurred because the policy renewal premium was not paid as dictated in the policy. It is undisputed that Thompson-Harris is Gallant's independent insurance agent. However, Gallant insists that Thompson-Harris had no authority to renew the insurance policy or orally contract in a manner contrary to what the policy states without the approval of Gallant's producing agent, Insurance Brokers of Indiana, Inc. We disagree. . . .

Gallant argues that Thompson-Harris had no actual or apparent authority to renew the insurance policy or orally contract to do so. Specifically, Gallant contends that it, as a principal, did not manifest any act toward Thompson-Harris or Isaac, whether directly or indirectly, that may have granted such authority. However, because we find that neither an actual nor apparent authority theory applies to the particular facts of this case, we instead address *sua sponte* Thompson-Harris's authority to act as Gallant's agent under an inherent authority theory.

Inherent agency power indicates the power of an agent that is derived not from authority, apparent or estoppel, but from the agency relation itself. This inherent authority theory exists for the protection of persons harmed by or dealing with a principal's servant or agent. . . .

In the case at bar, Thompson-Harris's renewal of Isaac's insurance policy constitutes an act which usually accompanies or is incidental to insurance transactions that it is authorized to conduct. Examining Gallant and Thompson-Harris's agency relation reveals that, as an agent, Thompson-Harris *was authorized to bind Gallant* on new insurance policies, as well as interim policy endorsements, such as changing and adding new drivers, or changing or adding the vehicle insured. For example, Thompson-Harris "had authority to write an application." That application "had to be either called to [Insurance Brokers of Indiana, Inc.] or faxed to them to bind coverage." In general, the power to bind its principal came into being once Thompson-Harris faxed the necessary paperwork to Gallant's producing agent and payment was made.

Thompson-Harris also had a common practice of telling its insured that they were "bound" despite not receiving payment until later, violating instructions by Gallant and provisions found in the policy. For example, the Record indicates that Thompson-Harris would "orally tell the insured that the new schedule vehicle was bound for coverage." Thompson-Harris would then relay that communication on to Gallant, which would then issue the endorsement. We conclude that this common practice of binding coverage verbally, in violation of Gallant's orders, is similar to Thompson-Harris's authorized conduct, given expressly by Gallant, to bind coverage by fax or phone. Therefore, we find that Thompson-Harris acted within the usual and ordinary scope of its authority.

Next . . . a court looks to the *agent's* direct and indirect manifestations and determines whether the third party could have reasonably believed that the agent had authority to conduct the act in question. . . . Here, Isaac could have reasonably believed that Thompson-Harris had authority to orally bind coverage. Isaac's past dealings were all through Thompson-Harris, whether involving payment of premiums, changing or including a driver, or requesting a new estimate. Direct communication between Gallant and Isaac never occurred. Thus, it was reasonable for Isaac to take at face value Thompson-Harris's communication that coverage was bound, and that she could come in at the end of the weekend to pay for the policy renewal. The reasonableness of Isaac's belief is bolstered by the fact that Thompson-Harris completed all the paperwork necessary and faxed the "Personal Policy Change Request," requesting at the bottom of the page an estimate and noting that Isaac will be in on December 5th, after the weekend, to pay.

. . . Isaac had no reason to second guess a direct communication by Thompson-Harris stating coverage was bound, particularly since that was a common practice of Thompson-Harris. . . . As such, we find that Thompson-Harris's direct and indirect manifestation over time, and its direct verbal communication to Isaac that coverage was bound, lead Isaac to reasonably believe that Thompson-Harris had the authority to renew the insurance policy.

Isaac lacked notice that Thompson-Harris did not have authority to verbally bind coverage. . . . [T]he Record fails to indicate whether Isaac was aware that Thompson-Harris had limited authority. It does not mention whether Isaac knew of expressed limitations about the authority of Thompson-Harris to bind insurance coverage without actual payment . . . . Isaac had no reason to know that when Thompson-Harris bound coverage Gallant must still endorse that verbal binding. Therefore, we find Isaac did not have notice that Thompson-Harris was not authorized to verbally bind coverage, without payment. . . .

If Gallant or its producing agent *informed* insured individuals or potential clients that Thompson-Harris could not verbally bind coverage, or if Thompson-Harris was required to give such notice, Gallant would have satisfied the notice requirement. Instead, however, Thompson-Harris was left unsupervised to establish common practice in violation of Gallant's granted authority.

[W]e conclude that the Record supports the trial court's findings that Isaac's insurance policy was in full force and effect on December 3, 1994, because Thompson-Harris had the inherent authority to bind coverage by Gallant verbally.

Affirmed.

QUESTIONS ON WHITE & GALLANT

1. If we evaluate these cases from an ex ante perspective (meaning that we ask whether they articulate the right rule for governing the actions of similarly situated people in the future), what considerations should bear on our answer?

2. Inherent agency power has been criticized as an unwarranted shift in the traditional (and, it is argued, economically efficient) balance of monitoring costs between principals and third parties. See Steven A. Fishman, *Inherent Agency Power — Should Enterprise Liability Apply to Agents' Unauthorized Contracts?*, 19 Rut. L. Rev. 1 (1987). Do you agree?

3. Consider the apparent and inherent authority doctrines as implicit terms (rules of the road) in contracting between principals and third parties. Why should principals *ever* escape liability for contracts negotiated in their names by bona fide general agents? From an economic perspective, are principals always or usually the least costly monitors of their own agents?

Agency by Estoppel or Ratification. Finally, even where an agent's act is not authorized by the principal or is not within any inherent agency power of the agent, the principal may still be bound by the agent's acts by *estoppel* or by *ratification* (Restatement (Third) Agency §2.05, Ch 4). The elements of an estoppel are the customary ones: failure to act when knowledge and an opportunity to act arise plus reasonable change in position on the part of the third person (Restatement (Third) Agency

§2.05). Alternatively, accepting benefits under an unauthorized contract will constitute acceptance (affirmance, in the language of the section) of its obligations as well as its benefits (Restatement (Third) Agency §§4.01, 4.07). For an exposition on the doctrine of implied ratification, see Elliot Axelrod, *The Doctrine of Implied Ratification — Application and Limitations,* 35 Okla. L. Rev. 849-862 (1983).

2.2.5 Liability in Tort

In most circumstances, principals are liable for torts committed by a class of agents known as "employees," as distinguished from another class of agents (and nonagents) known as "independent contractors." Put differently, only a particular kind of agency relationship, the employer-employee relationship, ordinarily triggers vicarious liability for all torts committed within the agent's scope of employment. Please read Restatement (Third) Agency §2.04 and §7.07 in your Statutory Supplement.

QUESTIONS

Obviously, "right of control" is key for distinguishing between employees and independent contractors. What should "control" mean? Does your analysis fit the following two "gasoline station" cases?

HUMBLE OIL & REFINING CO. v. MARTIN
148 Tex. 175, 222 S.W.2d 995 (1949)

Garwood, J.:

Petitioners Humble Oil & Refining Company and Mrs. A. C. Love and husband complain here of the judgments of the trial court and the Court of Civil Appeals in which they were held liable in damages for personal injuries following a special issue verdict at the suit of respondent George F. Martin acting for himself and his two minor daughters. The injuries were inflicted on the three Martins . . . by an unoccupied automobile belonging to the petitioners Love, which, just prior to the accident, had been left by Mrs. Love at a filling station owned by petitioner Humble for servicing and thereafter, before any station employee had touched it, rolled by gravity off the premises into and obliquely across the abutting street, striking Mr. Martin and his children from behind as they were walking into the yard of their home, a short distance downhill from the station.

The trial court rendered judgment against petitioners Humble and Mrs. Love jointly and severally and gave the latter judgment over against Humble for whatever she might pay the respondents. The Court of Civil Appeals affirmed the judgment after reforming it to eliminate the judgment over in favor of Mrs. Love. . . . The petitioners here respectively complain of the judgment in favor of the Martins, and each seeks full indemnity (as distinguished from contribution) from the other.

The apparently principal contention of petitioner, Humble, is that it is liable neither to respondent Martin nor to petitioner Mrs. Love, since the station was in effect operated by an independent contractor, W. T. Schneider, and Humble is accordingly not responsible for his negligence nor that of W. V. Manis, who was the only station employee or representative present when the Love car was left and rolled away. In this connection, the jury convicted petitioner Humble of the following acts of negligence proximately causing the injuries in question: (a) Failure to inspect the Love car to see that the emergency brake was set or the gears engaged; (b) failure to set the emergency brake on the Love car; (c) leaving the Love car unattended on the driveway. The verdict also included findings that Mrs. Love "had delivered her car to the custody of the defendant Humble Oil & Refining Company, before her car started rolling from the position in which she had parked it"; that the accident was not unavoidable; and that no negligent act of either of petitioners was the sole proximate cause of the injuries in question. We think the Court of Civil Appeals properly held Humble responsible for the operation of the station, which admittedly it owned, as it did also the principal products there sold by Schneider under the so-called "Commission Agency Agreement" between him and Humble which was in evidence. The facts that neither Humble, Schneider nor the station employees considered Humble as an employer or master; that the employees were paid and directed by Schneider individually as their "boss," and that a provision of the agreement expressly repudiates any authority of Humble over the employees, are not conclusive against the master-servant relationship, since there is other evidence bearing on the right or power of Humble to control the details of the station work as regards Schneider himself and therefore as to employees which it was expressly contemplated that he would hire. . . . Even if the contract between Humble and Schneider were the only evidence on the question, the instrument as a whole indicates a master-servant relationship quite as much as, if not more than, it suggests an arrangement between independent contractors. For example, paragraph 1 includes a provision requiring Schneider "to make reports *and perform other duties in connection with the operation of said station that may be required of him from time to time by Company.*" (Emphasis supplied). And while paragraph 2 purports to require Schneider to pay all operational expenses, the schedule of commissions forming part of the agreement does just the opposite in its paragraph (F), which gives Schneider a 75% "commission" on "the net public utility bills paid" by him and thus requires Humble to pay three-fourths of one of the most important operational expense items. Obviously the main object of the enterprise was the retail marketing of Humble's products with title remaining in Humble until delivery to the consumer. This was done under a strict system of financial control and supervision by Humble, with little or no business discretion reposed in Schneider except as to hiring, discharge, payment and supervision of a few station employees of a more or less laborer status. Humble furnished the all important station location and equipment, the advertising media, the products and a substantial part of the current operating costs. The hours of operation were controlled by Humble. The "Commission Agency Agreement," which evidently was Schneider's only title to occupancy of the premise, was terminable at the will of Humble. The so-called "rentals" were, at least in part, based on the amount of Humble's products sold, being, therefore, involved with the matter of Schneider's remuneration and not rentals in the usual sense. And, as above shown, the agreement required Schneider in effect to do anything Humble might tell him to do. All in all, aside from the stipulation regarding Schneider's assistants, there is essentially little difference between his situation and that of a mere store clerk who happens to be paid a commission instead of a salary. The business was Humble's business, just as the store clerk's business would be that of the store owner. Schneider was Humble's servant, and so accordingly were Schneider's assistants who were contemplated by the contract. . . .

The evidence above discussed serves to distinguish the instant case from *The Texas Company v. Wheat*, 140 Texas 468, 168 S.W.(2d) 632, upon which petitioner Humble principally relies. In that case the evidence . . . clearly showed a "dealer" type of relationship in which the lessee in charge of the filling station purchased from his landlord, The Texas Company, and sold as his own, and was free to sell at his own price and on his own credit terms, the company products purchased, as well as the products of other oil companies. The contracts contained no provision requiring the lessee to perform any duty The Texas Company might see fit to impose on him, nor did the company pay any part of the lessee's operating expenses, nor control the working hours of the station. . . .

HOOVER v. SUN OIL CO.

212 A.2d 214 (Del. 1965)

CHRISTIE, J.:

This case is concerned with injuries received as the result of a fire on August 16, 1962 at the service station operated by James F. Barone. The fire started at the rear of plaintiff's car where it was being filled with gasoline and was allegedly caused by the negligence of John Smilyk an employee of Barone. Plaintiffs brought suit against Smilyk, Barone and Sun Oil Company (Sun) which owned the service station.

Sun has moved for summary judgment as to it on the basis that Barone was an independent contractor and therefore the alleged negligence of his employee could not result in liability as to Sun. The plaintiffs contend instead that Barone was acting as Sun's agent and that Sun may therefore be responsible for plaintiff's injuries.

Barone began operating this business in October of 1960 pursuant to a lease dated October 17, 1960. The station and all of its equipment, with the exception of a tire-stand and rack, certain advertising displays and miscellaneous hand tools, were owned by Sun. The lease was subject to termination by either party upon thirty days' written notice after the first six months and at the anniversary date thereafter. The rental was partially determined by the volume of gasoline purchased but there was also a minimum and a maximum monthly rental.

At the same time, Sun and Barone also entered into a dealer's agreement under which Barone was to purchase petroleum products from Sun and Sun was to loan necessary equipment and advertising materials. Barone was required to maintain this equipment and to use it solely for Sun products. Barone was permitted under the agreement to sell competitive products but chose to do so only in a few minor areas. As to Sun products, Barone was prohibited from selling them except under the Sunoco label and from blending them with products not supplied by Sun.

Barone's station had the usual large signs indicating that Sunoco products were sold there. His advertising in the classified section of the telephone book was under a Sunoco heading, and his employees wore uniforms with the Sun emblem, the uniforms being owned by Barone or rented from an independent company.

Barone, upon the urging of Robert B. Peterson, Sun's area sales representative, attended a Sun school for service station operators in 1961. The school's curriculum was designed to familiarize the station operator with bookkeeping and merchandising, the appearance and proper maintenance of a Sun station, and the Sun Oil products. The course concluded with the operator working at Sun's model station in order to gain work experience in the use of the policy and techniques taught at the school.

Other facts typifying the company-service station relationship were the weekly visits of Sun's sales representative, Peterson, who would take orders for Sun products, inspect the restrooms, communicate customer complaints, make various suggestions to improve sales and discuss any problems that Barone might be having. Besides the weekly visits, Peterson was in contact with Barone on other occasions in order to implement Sun's "competitive allowance system" which enabled Barone to meet local price competition by giving him a rebate on the gasoline in his inventory roughly equivalent to the price decline and a similarly reduced price on his next order of gasoline.

While Peterson did offer advice to Barone on all phases of his operation, it was usually done on request and Barone was under no obligation to follow the advice. Barone's contacts and dealings with Sun were many and their relationship intricate, but he made no written reports to Sun and he alone assumed the overall risk of profit or loss in his business operation. Barone independently determined his own hours of operation and the identity, pay scale and working conditions of his employees, and it was his name that was posted as proprietor.

Plaintiffs contend in effect that the aforegoing facts indicate that Sun controlled the day-to-day operation of the station and consequently Sun is responsible for the negligent acts of Barone's employee. Specifically, plaintiffs contend that there is an issue of fact for the jury to determine as to whether or not there was an agency relationship.

The legal relationships arising from the distribution systems of major oil-producing companies are in certain respects unique. As stated in an annotation collecting many of the cases dealing with this relationship:

In some situations traditional definitions of principal and agent and of employer and independent contractor may be difficult to apply to service station operations. But the undisputed facts of the case at bar make it clear that Barone was an independent contractor.

Barone's service station, unlike retail outlets for many products, is basically a one-company outlet and represents to the public, through Sunoco's national and local advertising, that it sells not only Sun's quality products but Sun's quality service. Many people undoubtedly come to the service station because of that latter representation.

However, the lease contract and dealer's agreement fail to establish any relationship other than landlord-tenant, and independent contractor. Nor is there anything in the conduct of the individuals which is inconsistent with that relationship so as to indicate that the contracts were mere subterfuge or sham. The areas of close contact between Sun and Barone stem from the fact that both have a mutual interest in the sale of Sun products and in the success of Barone's business. . . .

The facts of this case differ markedly from those in which the oil company was held liable for the tortious conduct of its service station operator or his employees. Sun had no control over the details of Barone's day-to-day operation. Therefore, no liability can be imputed to Sun from the allegedly negligent acts of Smilyk. Sun's motion for summary judgment is granted.

It is so ordered. . . .

QUESTIONS ON HUMBLE OIL AND SUN OIL

1. Both *Humble Oil* and *Sun Oil* involve distributorship relationships between gas station proprietors and oil companies. Why might oil companies prefer to establish such networks of semi-independent distributors instead of staffing stations with their own employees or selling through affiliated retail outlets?

2. Without doubt, Humble Oil reserved more contractual control over Schneider's station than Sun Oil retained over Barone's station. How important were these differences? Did they affect the ability of these two oil companies to prevent accidents?

3. Is Schneider in a better position than Humble Oil to supervise station attendants? If so, what are the consequences of shifting liability from Schneider to Humble Oil? Does it matter whether Schneider is wealthy? Judgment proof?

4. Suppose that, as a practical matter, neither Humble Oil nor Sunoco can exercise supervisory control over the negligent actions of service station attendants. Will imposing liability on Humble Oil affect safety precautions nonetheless? Does the same analysis apply to Sun Oil?

2.3   THE GOVERNANCE OF AGENCY (THE AGENT'S DUTIES)

2.3.1   The Nature of the Agent's Fiduciary Relationship

In common law, an agent is a fiduciary of her principal. When we say that a legal relationship is fiduciary in character, we generally mean that legal power over property (including information) held by the fiduciary is held for the sole purpose of advancing the aim of a relationship pursuant to which she came to control that property. In testamentary trusts, the purpose is to carry out the will of the deceased. In agencies, it is to advance the purposes of the principal. In corporations, it is for the directors to advance the purposes of the corporation. In each case, the fiduciary is bound to exercise her good-faith judgment in an effort to pursue, under future circumstances, the purposes established at the time of creation of the relationship.

While fiduciaries can have numerous specific duties in particular contexts, generally their duties can be said to fall into three categories. First is the *duty of obedience* to the documents creating the relationship (e.g., Restatement (Third) Agency §8.09). This is the duty to obey the principal's commands. Of course, if optimal use of the assets requires flexibility that cannot be perfectly defined at the time of the creation of the relationship, then the duty of obedience will be insufficient to fully inform the principal-agent relationship. The law of agency therefore incorporates two open-ended duties owed by the agent, the *duty of loyalty* and the *duty of care*. The duty of loyalty is the pervasive obligation always to exercise legal power over the subject of the relationship in a manner that the holder of the power believes in good faith is best to advance the interest or purposes of the principal or beneficiary and not to exercise such power for a personal benefit. The duty of care is the duty to act in good faith, as one believes a reasonable person would act, in becoming informed and exercising any agency or fiduciary power.

The materials that follow illustrate the duty of loyalty in the contexts of the principal-agent relationship and the beneficiary-trustee relationship. We will return to fiduciary duties in the partnership and corporate contexts in due course. The point here is to ask the broad questions: Why do these duties assume the form that they do? What remedy should follow if they are breached? And how should they differ according to the particular nature of the fiduciary relationship at issue?

2.3.2   The Agent's Duty of Loyalty to the Principal

QUESTIONS ON RESTATEMENT (THIRD) AGENCY §§8.01-8.03, 8.06

1. Please read these Restatement Agency (Third) sections. If your client learns after the fact that his real estate agent purchased his house on her own account — purportedly after making full disclosure — at 50 percent below the price of a similar house sold through another agent the next week, how confident are you that you will be able to void the deal?

2. More generally, why should self-dealing transactions that are not disclosed be voidable automatically under §8.03? Why not simply place the burden of proof on the agent to establish that the terms of such an undisclosed transaction were "fair" to the principal?

TARNOWSKI v. RESOP

51 N.W.2d 801 (Minn. 1952)

KNUTSON, J.:

Plaintiff desired to make a business investment. He engaged defendant as his agent to investigate and negotiate for the purchase of a route of coin-operated music machines. On June 2, 1947, relying upon the advice of defendant and the investigation he had made, plaintiff purchased such a business from Phillip Loechler and Lyle Mayer of Rochester, Minnesota, who will be referred to hereinafter as the sellers . . . . Plaintiff alleges that defendant represented to him that he had made a thorough investigation of the route; that it had 75 locations in operation; that one or more machines were at each location; that the equipment at each location was not more than six months old; and that the gross income from all locations amounted to more than $3,000 per month. As a matter of fact, defendant had made only a superficial investigation and had investigated only five of the locations. Other than that, he had adopted false representations of the sellers as to the other locations and had passed them on to plaintiff as his own. Plaintiff was to pay $30,620 for the business. He paid $11,000 down. About six weeks after the purchase, plaintiff discovered that the representations made to him by defendant were false, in that there were not more than 47 locations; that at some of the locations there were no machines and at others there were machines more than six months old, some of them being seven years old; and that the gross income was far less than $3,000 per month. Upon discovering the falsity of defendant's representations and those of the sellers, plaintiff rescinded the sale. He offered to return what he had received, and he demanded the return of his money. The sellers refused to comply, and he brought suit against them in the district court of Olmsted county. The action was tried, resulting in a verdict of $10,000 for plaintiff. Thereafter, the sellers paid plaintiff $9,500, after which the action was dismissed with prejudice pursuant to a stipulation of the parties.

In this action, brought in Hennepin county, plaintiff alleges that defendant, while acting as agent for him, collected a secret commission from the sellers for consummating the sale, which plaintiff seeks to recover under his first cause of action. In his second cause of action, he seeks to recover damages for (1) losses suffered in operating the route prior to rescission; (2) loss of time devoted to operation; (3) expenses in connection with rescission of the sale and his investigation in connection therewith; (4) nontaxable expenses in connection with prosecution of the suit against the sellers; and (5) attorneys' fees in connection with the suit. The case was tried to a jury, and plaintiff recovered a verdict of $5,200. This appeal is from the judgment entered pursuant thereto. . . .

1. With respect to plaintiff's first cause of action, the principle that all profits made by an agent in the course of an agency belong to the principal, whether they are the fruits of performance or the violation of an agent's duty, is firmly established and universally recognized.

It matters not that the principal has suffered no damage or even that the transaction has been profitable to him. . . .

The right to recover profits made by the agent in the course of the agency is not affected by the fact that the principal, upon discovering a fraud, has rescinded the contract and recovered that with which he parted. Restatement, Agency, §407(2). . . .

It follows that, insofar as the secret commission of $2,000 received by the agent is concerned, plaintiff had an absolute right thereto, irrespective of any recovery resulting from the action against the sellers for rescission.

2. Plaintiff's second cause of action is brought to recover damages for (1) losses suffered in the operation of the business prior to rescission; (2) loss of time devoted to operation; (3) expenses in connection with rescission of the sale and investigation therewith; (4) nontaxable expenses in connection with the prosecution of the suit against the sellers; and (5) attorneys' fees in connection with the suit.

. . . Our inquiry is limited to a consideration of the question whether a principal may recover of an agent who has breached his trust the items of damage mentioned after a successful prosecution of an action for rescission against the third parties with whom the agent dealt for his principal.

The general rule is stated in Restatement, Agency, §407(1), as follows:

If an agent has received a benefit as a result of violating his duty of loyalty, the principal is entitled to recover from him what he has so received, its value, or its proceeds, and also the amount of damage thereby caused, except that if the violation consists of the wrongful disposal of the principal's property, the principal cannot recover its value and also what the agent received in exchange therefor.

In Comment a on Subsection (1) we find the following:

. . . In either event, whether or not the principal elects to get back the thing improperly dealt with or to recover from the agent its value or the amount of benefit which the agent has improperly received, he is, in addition, entitled to be indemnified by the agent for any loss which has been caused to his interests by the improper transaction. . . .

So far as the right to recover attorneys' fees is concerned, the same may be said in this case. Plaintiff sought to return what had been received and demanded a return of his down payment. The sellers refused. He thereupon sued to accomplish this purpose, as he had a right to do, and was successful. His attorneys' fees and expenses of suit were directly traceable to the harm caused by defendant's wrongful act. As such, they are recoverable. . . .

QUESTIONS ON TARNOWSKI v. RESOP

Is the plaintiff overcompensated in this case? Why should he receive both damages and the agent's secret commission from the sellers? Has he not already recovered almost all of his down payment in a separate action against the sellers?

2.3.3   The Trustee's Duty to Trust Beneficiaries

The private trust is a legal device that allows a "trustee" to hold legal title to trust property, which the trustee is under a fiduciary duty to manage for the benefit of another person, the *trust beneficiary*. The trust resembles the agency relationship insofar as the trustee has obvious power to affect the interests of the beneficiary. The trust differs from agency, of course, insofar as the trustee is subject to the terms of the trust, as these have been fixed by the trust's *settlor* (or creator); the trustee is not ordinarily subject to the control of the beneficiary. Before considering the following case, please read Restatement (Second) of Trusts §§ 203, 205, 206.

IN RE GLEESON
124 N.E.2d 624 (Ill. App. 1954)

CARROLL, J.:

Mary Gleeson, who died testate on February 14, 1952, owned among other properties, 160 acres of farm land in Christian County, Illinois. By her will admitted to Probate March 29, 1952, she nominated Con Colbrook, petitioner-appellee (who will be referred to herein as petitioner) executor thereof. Petitioner was also appointed as trustee under the will and the residuary estate, including the aforesaid 160 acres of land, was devised to him in trust for the benefit of decedent's 3 children, Helen Black, Bernadine Gleeson, and Thomas Gleeson, an incompetent, who are respondents herein.

On March 1, 1950, the testatrix leased the 160 acres for the year ending March 1, 1951 to petitioner and William Curtin, a partnership. On March 1, 1951, she again leased the premises to said partnership for the year ending March 1, 1952. Upon the expiration of this latter lease the partnership held over as tenants under the provisions thereof and farmed the land until March 1, 1953, at which time petitioner leased the land to another tenant. While there is no written lease in evidence, the record indicates the terms thereof provided for payment to the lessor of $10 per acre cash rent and a share in the crops of 1/2 of the corn and 2/5 of the small grain.

The petitioner's appointment as trustee was confirmed by the Circuit Court of Christian County on April 29, 1953. On July 22, 1953, he filed his first semi-annual report. This report was not approved and petitioner was ordered to recast the same in accordance with certain directions of the Court. The recast report was filed December 5, 1953. To this report respondents filed certain objections. We are concerned here with only one of the said objections, which is as follows:

> 1. Report shows trustee was co-tenant of trust real estate but fails to account for share of profits received by trustee as co-tenant which by law should be repaid by him to trust estate. . . .

The Courts of this state have consistently followed a general principle of equity that a trustee cannot deal in his individual capacity with the trust property. . . .

Petitioner recognizes the existence of this general rule, but argues that because of the existence of the peculiar circumstances under which the petitioner proceeded, the instant case must be taken to constitute one of the rare exceptions to such rule. The circumstances alluded to as peculiar are pointed out as being the facts that the death of Mrs. Gleeson occurred on February 14, 1952, only 15 days prior to the beginning of the 1952 farm year; that satisfactory farm tenants are not always available, especially on short notice; that the petitioner had in the preceding fall of 1951 sown part of the 160 acres in wheat to be harvested in 1952; that the holding over by the trustee and his partner was in the best interests of the trust; that the same was done in an open manner; that the petitioner was honest with the trust; and that it suffered no loss as a result of the transaction.

Petitioner contends that since only 15 days intervened between the death of Mrs. Gleeson and the beginning of the farm year, and that good tenant farmers might not be available at such a time, it was in the interests of the trust that the petitioner continue to hold over for the year of 1952. No showing is made that petitioner tried to obtain a satisfactory tenant to replace Colbrook and Curtin on March 1, 1952. The record discloses that subsequent to the death of testatrix, petitioner discussed continuance of the farming operation with two of the beneficiaries under the trust and voluntarily raised the cash rent from $6 to $10 per acre. This evidence tending to show that petitioner was interested in continuing a tenancy under which he was leasing trust property to himself would seem to refute any contention that an effort to lease the property to anyone other than the partnership was made. The fact that the partners had sown wheat on the land in the fall of 1951 cannot be said to be a peculiar circumstance. It is not suggested that the trust would have suffered a loss if some one other than the petitioner had farmed the land in 1952 and harvested the wheat. It would appear that a satisfactory adjustment covering the matter of the wheat could have been made between the trust and the partnership without great difficulty.

The good faith and honesty of the petitioner or the fact that the trust sustained no loss on account of his dealings therewith are all matters which can avail petitioner nothing so far as a justification of the course he chose to take in dealing with trust property is concerned. . . .

[T]he petitioner herein, upon the death of the testatrix, instead of conferring with her beneficiaries concerning continuance of his tenancy of the trust property, should have then decided whether he chose to continue as a tenant or to act as trustee. His election was to act as trustee and as such he could not deal with himself.

This Court, therefore, reaches the conclusion that the Circuit Court erred . . . and that petitioner should have been required to recast his first semi-annual report and to account therein for all monies received by him personally as a profit by virtue of his being a co-tenant of trust property during the 1952 crop year, and to pay the amount of any such profit to the trust.

The judgment of the Circuit Court of Christian County is reversed. . . .

QUESTIONS ON IN RE GLEESON

1. If new tenants are hard to find on short notice, why expect Colbrook to look for one?

2. If the trustee relationship is analogized to the agency relationship, whom should we view as the principal in this case? The trust beneficiaries? Mary Gleeson?

3. Does the rule illustrated by this case differ from the parallel agency rule? Is there a functional explanation for why it should differ?

4. Who do you suppose first pressed for an action to challenge the trustee's report?

creditors should not expect to have an exclusive claim on the assets
needed to satisfy the obligations of the business without the aid of
property law or detailed...

3

THE PROBLEM OF JOINT OWNERSHIP: THE LAW OF PARTNERSHIP

3.1 INTRODUCTION TO PARTNERSHIP

The general partnership is the earliest and simplest form of a jointly owned and managed business. With respect to third parties, the law of partnership closely follows agency law: For example, each partner binds the partnership when acting in the usual course of business, and so on. With respect to the relations among partners, numerous common law rules deal with the internal problems of these small, jointly managed firms. These provisions are codified in the Uniform Partnership Act (UPA) and the Revised Uniform Partnership Act (RUPA), which many states have recently adopted.

Perhaps the most important conceptual step in the transition from agency law to partnership law is the rules that give distinct legal treatment to partnership property. Property held by the partnership is entitled in a special form: "tenancy in partnership." This form of tenancy provides that the partnership qua firm, rather than the individual partners, exercises true ownership rights over partnership property, and in practice, in the event of partnership bankruptcy or liquidation, this form of title gives creditors of the partnership first priority over the claims of the creditors of individual partners. This form of property ownership is a fundamental step toward the creation of a freestanding legal entity with a "personality" distinct from the investors who finance it. Because it owns assets, a partnership acting through a partner can contract on its own behalf and therefore can be a reliable counterparty for others.

This development in the property rights of the partnership, dating from at least the seventeenth century in the common law, was, we believe, a key step in the development of the law of legal business organizations (i.e., legal entities that carry on business in their own name rather than in the name of a natural person).[1] While the laws of property, contract, and agency alone permit one to construct a jointly owned business (consider a single agent who invests the funds of multiple principals), the creditors of

---

1. See Henry Hansmann & Reinier Kraakman, *The Essential Role of Organizational Law*, 110 Yale L.J. 387 (2000).

such a "firm" could not expect to have an exclusive claim on the assets of the business to satisfy the obligations of the business without the law of partnership. In the event of default by the "partnership," its creditors could enforce judgments only against property owned by any of the individual partners and thus would share priority with other creditors of that individual. This might be (would be) an impediment to contracting with a partnership. Do you see why tenancy in partnership makes contracting with a partnership more attractive?

Apart from the important matter of partnership property, the drafters of the UPA often wavered between conceptualizing the partnership as a loose association of co-owners and as a separate business entity in which partners invest. This makes for difficult reading. Perhaps the UPA has persisted (despite its awkwardness) because much of it is really a default partnership agreement that can be superseded by an express agreement among the partners. Regardless, reform is finally in the works. Your statutory supplement includes a Revised Uniform Partnership Act, which has been adopted in important commercial jurisdictions, such as New York and California, and is gradually displacing the UPA.

This chapter addresses the formation of partnerships, partner liability and creditor rights, partnership property, and the problems associated with the dissolution of partnerships. Read the following cases in conjunction with the relevant provisions of the UPA in your statutory supplement. We have included a set of questions drafted by Professor Victor Brudney that will help you think about the operation of the UPA. Look to the listed provisions of the Act, but don't be too sure that you will find clear answers. In some cases, it will be helpful to check the parallel provisions in the RUPA.

Before turning to these issues, however, it is worth inquiring into the reasons for joint ownership and the legal boundary between partnership assets and personal assets. In partnership, the primary agency problem is not the conflict between the agent or manager and the owner — the paradigmatic problem in the law of agency — but potential conflicts *among* the joint owners.

3.1.1   Why Have Joint Ownership?

So why have joint ownership at all? Even in the small-scale, intimate form of the general partnership? Why structure a business to invite conflict among multiple principals over business policies and the division of the profits, in addition to the agent-principal conflicts?

Your initial response to this question might be "capital." Perhaps partners go into business together because they cannot afford to finance the business on their own or, even if they can, they do not wish to risk the funds.

No doubt this answer is often correct. It does not, however, go very far. If an entrepreneur does not have the cash to finance her business, why doesn't she simply borrow it, as many sole proprietors do? To this you might respond that there is only so much that can be borrowed before creditors conclude that additional lending is too risky. Here you would be closer to a full answer: After a certain point, selling an *ownership* stake may simply be a cheaper way to raise capital than attempting to borrow more funds. Or, put another way, whatever the costs of co-ownership, after a certain point they may be lower than the agency costs of the debt contract. Co-ownership creates problems of its own, but it can also resolve contracting problems (such as those between entrepreneurs and creditors). Consider the following stylized story of the formation of a partnership driven by the need for capital.

WILLIAM KLEIN & JOHN C. COFFEE, THE NEED TO ASSEMBLE AT-RISK CAPITAL

Business Organization and Finance 54-56 (9th ed. 2004)

Let's begin with the kind of situation in which the co-owners will contribute capital rather than services. Imagine, for example, that a person, Pamela, has spotted what she regards as an attractive opportunity to buy an existing grocery store. Pamela is familiar with the retail grocery business but does not want to manage the store and is content to continue to employ the present manager, Morris. The total purchase price for the store is $200,000. The maximum amount of her own funds that Pamela is willing or able to invest is $20,000. She can raise $150,000 by borrowing nonrecourse from Walter, a wealthy individual, at an interest rate of 10 percent, if she gives Walter first claim on all assets in case of default. Walter is not willing to lend more because any additional investment would involve greater risk than he is willing to accept. Where and how will Pamela raise the additional $30,000?

Obviously, there will be a variety of institutional and individual sources for the kind of "venture capital" that Pamela seeks to raise. For simplicity, let's assume that Pamela has found two individuals, Abe and Bill, who have indicated that they might be interested in investing $15,000 in the enterprise if the terms are attractive enough to them. Imagine what might happen if Pamela sought simply to borrow the $30,000 (nonrecourse) from Abe and Bill. If it is assumed that Walter will have first claim on all assets in case of default (that is, that Walter's claim is "*senior*"), Abe and Bill would be subject to a higher risk of loss than Walter. If Abe and Bill were willing to take this risk, but if their expected gain were limited to interest on the $30,000, the rate of interest that they would demand would be significantly higher than that paid to Walter. Suppose (arbitrarily, but not unrealistically) that the required rate would be 20 percent, or $6,000, per year — that is, that they would be willing to lend at that rate but not at any lower rate. That $6,000 per year would be a *fixed obligation*, payable without regard to the success of the business. It would constitute a heavy burden for Pamela and would subject her own investment to a level of risk that she might find unacceptable. . . . Besides, even if Abe and Bill were willing to accept a high risk of loss in return for the high rate of interest, . . . Walter might object. The fixed obligation to Abe and Bill would create a significant additional risk of bankruptcy or of other legal proceedings associated with default. Such proceedings are costly and might adversely affect Walter's interests despite the seniority of his claim. Moreover, with a relatively small investment in the business, Pamela would have an incentive to engage in activities or adopt operating strategies involving high risks, with the thought that the gains would be hers and the losses would be borne mostly by the lenders. . . .

Assuming that some or all of these, and possibly other, considerations rule out the possibility of a loan from Abe and Bill, the alternative is some sort of arrangement in which Abe and Bill share in the risks of the business. Instead of a fixed return of 20 percent, Pamela might offer them a share of profits with a possible rate of return far greater than 20 percent but no guaranteed annual payment. There would be no fixed obligation and, therefore, no possibility of default. There could be a requirement of repayment of the $30,000 at the end of some specified time period, but suppose that the deal settled upon by the parties does not include any such guarantee. Suppose, that is, that the agreement reached is that Abe and Bill receive a share of the current earnings of the business, if any, and a share of any proceeds of its sale. Abe and Bill will be subject to the same risks of loss and will have the same prospects for return as Pamela. All three will have a *residual*, or *equity*, interest in the business. The interests of Abe and Bill would then be aligned with those of Pamela. But since Abe and Bill would be sharing in risks and returns, it would be natural for them to ask to share in control as well, and hard for Pamela to refuse.

Neither profit shares nor control, by the way, would of necessity be divided pro rata according to dollar contribution. That is, even though Abe and Bill contributed, together, $30,000, or 60 percent of a total equity of $50,000, they would not necessarily receive 60 percent of the profits or 60 percent control. Pamela might, for example, be able to insist on half the profits in return for her $20,000 contribution; or she might be required to settle for 30 percent . . . . The division of gain (and loss) and control, in other words, would be subject to negotiation, with the outcome dependent not so much on any identifiable notion of fairness or custom as on the relative bargaining positions of the parties.

QUESTIONS ON THE KLEIN-COFFEE EXCERPT

1. In the preceding story, Pamela, Abe, and Bill become partners. What other contracting problems besides the difficulty of borrowing capital beyond a certain point might lead an entrepreneur to sell an ownership interest and take on a partner? Consider *Vohland v. Sweet,* infra.

2. The partnership form (and also the corporate form) assigns ownership rights (control and residual profits) to the parties who provide capital (Pamela, et al.). Other assignments are possible: Ownership might go to workers, customers, or suppliers. For discussion of the assignment of

ownership rights as a device for reducing the costs of contracting among participants in the firm, see Henry Hansmann, *Ownership of the Firm*, 2 J.L. Econ. & Org. 267 (1988).

3.1.2   The Agency Conflict Among Co-Owners

Our discussion of the principal-agent relationship in Chapter 2 touched on two of the fundamental agency problems in the law of business organizations: the conflict between agents and principals and the conflict between principals and third parties, such as creditors. The partnership introduces the last of the basic agency problems of organizational law: the conflict between controlling and "minority" co-owners.
A good case for thinking about this conflict — and its relationship to the conflict between principal and agent — is the most famous American case in all of organizational law, including corporate law. The case concerns a joint venture between two "co-venturers," Salmon and Meinhard. This is, in effect, a circumscribed partnership limited to a single investment project. The issue concerns the scope of the duty of loyalty owed by the managing co-venturer (Salmon) to the passive co-venturer (Meinhard).

MEINHARD v. SALMON

164 N.E. 545 (N.Y. 1928)

CARDOZO, C.J.:
On April 10, 1902, Louisa M. Gerry leased to the defendant Walter J. Salmon the premises known as the Hotel Bristol at the northwest corner of Forty-Second street and Fifth Avenue in the city of New York. The lease was for a term of 20 years, commencing May 1, 1902, and ending April 30, 1922. The lessee undertook to change the hotel building for use as shops and offices at a cost of $200,000. Alterations and additions were to be accretions to the land.

Salmon, while in course of treaty with the lessor as to the execution of the lease, was in course of treaty with Meinhard, the plaintiff, for the necessary funds. The result was a joint venture with terms embodied in a writing. Meinhard was to pay to Salmon half of the moneys requisite to reconstruct, alter, manage, and operate the property. Salmon was to pay to Meinhard 40 percent of the net profits for the first five years of the lease and 50 percent for the years thereafter. If there were losses, each party was to bear them equally. Salmon, however, was to have sole power to "manage, lease, underlet and operate" the building. There were to be certain preemptive rights for each in the contingency of death.

The two were coadventurers, subject to fiduciary duties akin to those of partners. *King v. Barnes*, 109 N.Y. 267, 16 N.E. 332. As to this we are all agreed. The heavier weight of duty rested, however, upon Salmon. He was a coadventurer with Meinhard, but he was manager as well. During the early years of the enterprise, the building, reconstructed, was operated at a loss. If the relation had then ended, Meinhard as well as Salmon would have carried a heavy burden. Later the profits became large with the result that for each of the investors there came a rich return. For each the venture had its phases of fair weather and of foul. The two were in it jointly, for better or for worse.

When the lease was near its end, Elbridge T. Gerry had become the owner of the reversion. He owned much other property in the neighborhood, one lot adjoining the Bristol building on Fifth avenue and four lots on Forty-Second street. He had a plan to lease the entire tract for a long term to some one who would destroy the buildings then existing and put up another in their place. In the latter part of 1921, he submitted such a project to several capitalists and dealers. He was unable to carry it through with any of them. Then, in January, 1922, with less than four months of the lease to run, he approached the defendant Salmon. The result was a new lease to the Midpoint Realty Company, which is owned and controlled by Salmon, a lease covering the whole tract, and involving a huge outlay. The term is to be 20 years, but successive covenants for renewal will extend it to a maximum of 80 years at the will of either party. The existing buildings may remain unchanged for seven years. They are then to be torn down, and a new building to cost $3,000,000 is to be placed upon the site. The rental, which under the Bristol lease was only $55,000, is to be from $350,000 to $475,000 for the properties so combined. Salmon personally guaranteed the performance by the lessee of the covenants of the new lease until such time as the new building had been completed and fully paid for.

The lease between Gerry and the Midpoint Realty Company was signed and delivered on January 25, 1922. Salmon had not told Meinhard anything about it. Whatever his motive may have been, he had kept the negotiations to himself. Meinhard was not informed even of the bare existence of a project. The first that he knew of it was in February, when the lease was an accomplished fact. He then made demand on the defendants that the lease be held in trust as an asset of the venture, making offer upon the trial to share the personal obligations incidental to the guaranty. The demand was followed by refusal, and later by this suit. A referee gave judgment for the plaintiff, limiting the plaintiff's interest in the lease, however, to 25 percent. The limitation was on the theory that the plaintiff's equity was to be restricted to one-half of so much of the value of the lease as was contributed or represented by the occupation of the Bristol site. Upon cross-appeals to the Appellate Division, the judgment was modified so as to enlarge the equitable interest to one-half of the whole lease. With this enlargement of plaintiff's interest, there went, of course, a corresponding enlargement of his attendant obligations. The case is now here on an appeal by the defendants. . . .

Joint venturers, like copartners, owe to one another, while the enterprise continues, the duty of the finest loyalty. Many forms of conduct permissible in a workaday world for those acting at arm's length, are forbidden to those bound by fiduciary ties. A trustee is held to something stricter than the morals of the market place. Not honesty alone, but the punctilio of an honor the most sensitive, is then the standard of behavior.

As to this there has developed a tradition that is unbending and inveterate. Uncompromising rigidity has been the attitude of courts of equity when petitioned to undermine the rule of undivided loyalty by the "disintegrating erosion" of particular exceptions. . . . Only thus has the level of conduct for fiduciaries been kept at a level higher than that trodden by the crowd. It will not consciously be lowered by any judgment of this court.

The owner of the reversion, Mr. Gerry, had vainly striven to find a tenant who would favor his ambitious scheme of demolition and construction. Baffled in the search, he turned to the defendant Salmon in possession of the Bristol, the keystone of the project. He figured to himself beyond a doubt that the man in possession would prove a likely customer. To the eye of an observer, Salmon held the lease as owner in his own right, for himself and no one else. In fact he held it as a fiduciary, for himself and another, sharers in a common venture. If this fact had been proclaimed, if the lease by its terms had run in favor of a partnership, Mr. Gerry, we may fairly assume, would have laid before the partners, and not merely before one of them, his plan of reconstruction. The pre-emptive privilege, or, better, the pre-emptive opportunity, that was thus an incident of the enterprise, Salmon appropriated to himself in secrecy and silence. He might have warned Meinhard that the plan had been submitted, and that either would be free to compete for the award. If he had done this, we do not need to say whether he would have been under a duty, if successful in the competition, to hold the lease so acquired for the benefit of a venture then about to end, and thus prolong by indirection its responsibilities and duties. The trouble about his conduct is that he excluded his coadventurer from any chance to compete, from any chance to enjoy the opportunity for benefit that had come to him alone by virtue of his agency. This chance, if nothing more, he was under a duty to concede. The price of its denial is an extension of the trust at the option and for the benefit of the one whom he excluded.

No answer is it to say that the chance would have been of little value even if seasonably offered. Such a calculus of probabilities is beyond the science of the chancery. Salmon, the real estate operator, might have been preferred to Meinhard, the woolen merchant. On the other hand, Meinhard might have offered better terms, or reinforced his offer by alliance with the wealth of others. Perhaps he might even have persuaded the lessor to renew the Bristol lease alone, postponing for a time, in return for higher rentals, the improvement of adjoining lots. We know that even under the lease as made the time for the enlargement of the building was delayed for seven years. All these opportunities were cut away from him through another's intervention. . . .

Little profit will come from a dissection of the precedents. None precisely similar is cited in the briefs of counsel. What is similar in many, or so it seems to us, is the animating principle. Authority is, of course, abundant that one partner may not appropriate to his own use a renewal of a lease, though its term is to begin at the expiration of the partnership. *Mitchell v. Read*, 61 N.Y. 123, 19 Am. Rep. 252; Id., 84 N.Y. 556. The lease at hand with its many changes is not strictly a renewal. Even so, the standard of loyalty for those in trust relations is without the fixed divisions of a graduated scale. There is indeed a dictum in one of our decisions that a partner, though he may not renew a lease, may purchase the reversion if he acts openly and fairly. *Anderson v. Lemon,* 8 N.Y. 236; It is a dictum, and no more, for on the ground that he had acted slyly he was charged as a trustee. The holding is thus in favor of the conclusion that a purchase as well as a lease will succumb to the infection of secrecy and silence. Against the dictum in that case, moreover, may be set the opinion of Dwight, C., in *Mitchell v. Read,* where there is a dictum to the contrary. (61 N.Y. 123, at page 143) . . . .

We have no thought to hold that Salmon was guilty of a conscious purpose to defraud. Very likely he assumed in all good faith that with the approaching end of the venture he might ignore his coadventurer and take the extension for himself. He had given to the enterprise time and labor as well as money. He had made it a success. Meinhard, who had given money, but neither time nor labor, had already been richly paid. There might seem to be something grasping in his insistence upon more. Such recriminations are not unusual when coadventurers fall out. They are not without their force if conduct is to be judged by the common standards of competitors. That is not to say that they have pertinency here. Salmon had put himself in a position in which thought of self was to be renounced, however hard the abnegation. He was much more than a coadventurer. He was a managing coadventurer. *Clegg v. Edmondson,* 8 D. M. & G. 787, 807. For him and for those like him the rule of undivided loyalty is relentless and supreme. . . .

A question remains as to the form and extent of the equitable interest to be allotted to the plaintiff. The trust as declared has been held to attach to the lease which was in the name of the defendant corporation. We think it ought to attach at the option of the defendant Salmon to the shares of stock which were owned by him or were under his control. The difference may be important if the lessee shall wish to execute an assignment of the lease, as it ought to be free to do with the consent of the lessor. On the other hand, an equal division of the shares might lead to other hardships. It might take away from Salmon the power of control and management which under the plan of the joint venture he was to have from first to last. The number of shares to be allotted to the plaintiff should, therefore, be reduced to such an extent as may be necessary to preserve to the defendant Salmon the expected measure of dominion. To that end an extra share should be added to his half . . . .

ANDREWS, J. (dissenting) . . . . It may be stated generally that a partner may not for his own benefit secretly take a renewal of a firm lease to himself. . . .

Where the trustee, or the partner or the tenant in common, takes no new lease but buys the reversion in good faith a somewhat different question arises. Here is no direct appropriation of the expectancy of renewal. Here is no offshoot of the original lease. We so held in *Anderson v. Lemon,* 8 N.Y. 236, and although Judge Dwight casts some doubt on the rule in *Mitchell v. Reed,* it seems to have the support of authority. W. & T. Leading Cas. in Equity, p. 650; Lindley on Partnership (9th Ed.) p. 396; *Bevan v. Webb,* [1905] 1 Ch. 620. The issue, then, is whether actual fraud, dishonesty, or unfairness is present in the transaction. If so, the purchaser may well be held as a trustee. (*Anderson v. Lemon,* cited above.)

With this view of the law I am of the opinion that the issue here is simple. Was the transaction, in view of all the circumstances surrounding it, unfair and inequitable? I reach this conclusion for two reasons. There was no general partnership, merely a joint venture for a limited object, to end at a fixed time. The new lease, covering additional property, containing many new and unusual terms and conditions, with a possible duration of 80 years, was more nearly the purchase of the reversion than the ordinary renewal with which the authorities are concerned. . . .

ELDBRIDGE T. GERRY

Meinhard v. Salmon was not the first important case to involve Elbridge T. Gerry.

Gerry was named after his grandfather, who had served as Vice President of the United States from 1813 to 1814 under President James Madison. The elder Elbridge Gerry brought the family name into the dictionary when he presided over a controversial redrawing of Massachusetts electoral districts designed to keep the Jeffersonian party in power. The oddly shaped districts were declared to resemble salamanders. "Gerry" and "salamander" were soon combined to create the new word "gerrymander" describing the distorting of political district boundaries in order to gain an unfair advantage for one particular party.

An ardent reformer, the younger Gerry served as legal counsel to the American Society for the Prevention of Cruelty to Animals. In 1874, a Methodist church social worker came to the animal society with the story of a young girl locked in a dark tenement, frequently whipped, dressed in rags, and emaciated with starvation. The city police had refused to intervene for the child's welfare. Gerry developed a successful legal strategy to bring the child into court to testify against her guardians. Promptly removed from her guardians' care, the girl was placed in a comfortable home in upstate New York and her foster-mother was sentenced to one year in jail. The "Mary Ellen case" made national headlines as the first case to result in the punishment of a child abuser and the removal of a child from her home. Gerry went on to devote much of his life to advocating for laws protecting children from abusive homes and exploitative labor.

QUESTIONS ON MEINHARD

1. Imagine that Judge Cardozo is supplying a standard term in the joint venture agreements between the Salmons and Meinhards of this world. What does the term say? (What must an active co-venturer like Salmon share and what can he keep to himself?)

2. The case suggests alternative standard terms as well, including the one that Salmon presumably urged on the court. What do these terms say?

3. How would Salmon and Meinhard have evaluated these alternatives if they had negotiated explicitly about renewals and extensions? Which would they have probably adopted?

4. Meinhard was a forerunner of today's venture capitalists (VCs). Meinhard provided financing but no operational expertise, while Salmon invested his effort and had expertise in the hotel business. Today, venture capital agreements often provide the VC a "preemptive right" on the next stage of financing, meaning that the venture capitalist has the right, but not the obligation, to maintain his stake in the company by participating in subsequent financing on the same terms as other later-stage investors. (This kind of right is often called a "real option" in modern finance, because the asset that underlies the option is "real" (here, an investment opportunity), not a financial instrument.) Does this contract structure create the appropriate incentives for the entrepreneur? For the VC?

3.2 PARTNERSHIP FORMATION

VOHLAND v. SWEET

433 N.E.2d 860 (Ind. App. 1982)

NEAL, J.:

Plaintiff-appellee Norman E. Sweet (Sweet) brought an action for dissolution of an alleged partnership and for an accounting in the Ripley Circuit Court against defendant-appellant Paul Eugene Vohland (Vohland). From a judgment in favor of Sweet in the amount of $58,733, Vohland appeals . . . . The undisputed facts reveal that Sweet, as a youngster, commenced working in 1956 for Charles Vohland, father of Paul Eugene Vohland, as an hourly employee in a nursery operated by Charles Vohland and known as Clarksburg Dahlia Gardens. Upon the completion of his military service, which was performed from 1958 to 1960, he resumed his former employment. In approximately 1963 Charles Vohland retired, and Vohland commenced what became known as Vohland's Nursery, the business of which was landscape gardening. At that time Sweet's status changed. He was to receive a 20 percent share of the net profit of the enterprise after all of the expenses were paid . . . .

No partnership income tax returns were filed. Vohland and his wife, Gwenalda, filed a joint return in which the business of Vohland's Nursery was reported in Vohland's name on Schedule C. Money paid Sweet was listed as a business expense under "Commissions." Also listed on Schedule C were all of the expenses of the nursery, including investment credit and depreciation on trucks, tractors, and machinery. Sweet's tax returns declared that he was a self-employed salesman at Vohland's Nursery. He filed a self-employment Schedule C and listed as income the income received from the nursery; as expenses he listed travel, advertising, phone, conventions, automobile, and trade journals. He further filed a Schedule C-3 for self-employment Social Security for the receipts from the nursery.

Vohland handled all of the finances and books and did most of the sales. He borrowed money from the bank solely in his own name for business purposes, including the purchase of the interests of his brothers and sisters in his father's business, operating expenses, bid bonds, motor vehicles, taxes, and purchases of real estate. Sweet was not involved in those loans. Sweet managed the physical aspects of the nursery and supervised the care of the nursery stock and the performance of the contracts for customers. Vohland was quoted by one customer as saying Sweet was running things and the customer would have to see Sweet about some problem.

Evidence was contradictory in certain respects. The Vohland Nursery was located on approximately 13 acres of land owned by Charles Vohland. Sweet testified that at the commencement of the arrangement with Vohland in 1963, Charles Vohland grew the stock and maintained the inventory, for which he received 25 percent of the gross sales. In the late 1960's, because of age, Charles Vohland could no longer perform. The nursery stock became depleted to nearly nothing, and new arrangements were made. An extensive program was initiated by Sweet and Vohland to replenish and enlarge the inventory of nursery stock; this program continued until February, 1979. The cost of planting and maintaining the nursery stock was assigned to expenses before Sweet received his 20 percent. The nursery stock generally took up to ten years to mature for market. Sweet testified that at the termination of the arrangement there existed $293,665 in inventory which had been purchased with the earnings of the business. Of that amount $284,860 was growing nursery stock. Vohland, on the other hand, testified that the inventory of 1963 was as large as that of 1979, but the inventory became depleted in 1969. Vohland claimed that as part of his agreement with Charles Vohland he was required to replenish the nursery stock as it was sold, and in addition pay Charles Vohland 25 percent of the net profit from the operation. He contends that the inventory of nursery stock balanced out. However, Vohland conceded on cross-examination that the acquisition and enlargement of the existing inventory of nursery stock was paid for with earnings and, therefore, was financed partly with Sweet's money. He further stated that the consequences of this financial arrangement never entered his mind at the time.

Sweet's testimony, denied by Vohland, disclosed that, in a conversation in the early 1970's regarding the purchase of inventory out of earnings, Vohland promised to take care of Sweet. Vohland acknowledged that Sweet refused to permit his 20 percent to be charged with the cost of a truck unless his name was on the title. Sweet testified that at the outset of the arrangement Vohland told him, "he was going to take . . . me in and that . . . I wouldn't have to punch a time clock anymore, that I would be on a commission basis and that I would be, have more of an interest in the business if I had 'an interest in the business.' . . . He referred to it as a piece of the action." Sweet testified that he intended to enter into a partnership. Vohland asserts that no partnership was intended and that Sweet was merely an employee, working on a commission. There was no contention that Sweet made any contribution to capital, nor did he claim any interest in the real estate, machinery, or motor vehicles. The parties had never discussed losses . . . .

The principal point of disagreement between Sweet and Vohland is whether the arrangement between them created a partnership, or a contract of employment of Sweet by Vohland as a salesman on commission. It therefore becomes necessary to review briefly the principles governing the establishment of partnerships.

It has been said that an accurate and comprehensive definition of a partnership has not been stated; that the lines of demarcation which distinguish a partnership from other joint interests on one hand and from agency on the other, are so fine as to render approximate rather than exhaustive any attempt to define the relationship. *Bacon v. Christian,* (1916) 184 Ind. 517, 111 N.E. 628 . . . .

Under U.P.A. §7(4) receipt by a person of a share of the profits is prima facie evidence that he is a partner in the business. . . . Lack of daily involvement for one partner is not per se indicative of absence of a partnership. A partnership may be formed by the furnishing of skill and labor by others. The contribution of labor and skill by one of the partners may be as great a contribution to the common enterprise as property or money . . . . It is an established common law principle that a partnership can commence only by the voluntary contract of the parties . . . . In *Bond* it was said, "[t]o be a partner, one must have an interest with another in the profits of a business, as profits. There must be a voluntary contract to carry on a business with intention of the parties to share the profits as common owners thereof." . . . In *Bacon,* supra, in reviewing the law relative to the creation of partnerships, the court said:

> . . . [I]t is apparent to establish the partnership relation, as between the parties, there must be (1) a voluntary contract of association for the purpose of sharing the profits and losses, as such, which may arise from the use of capital, labor or skill in a common enterprise; and (2) an intention on the part of the principals to form a partnership for that purpose. But it must be borne in mind, however, that the intent, the existence of which is deemed essential, is an intent to do those things which constitute a partnership. Hence, if such an intent exists, the parties will be partners notwithstanding that they proposed to avoid the liability attaching to partners or [have] even expressly stipulated in their agreement that they were not to become partners. (Citation omitted.)" . . .

In the analysis of the facts, we are first constrained to observe that should an accrual method of accounting have been employed here, the enhancement of the inventory of nursery stock would have been reflected as profit, a point which Vohland, in effect, concedes. We further note that both parties referred to the 20 percent as "commissions." To us the term "commission," unless defined, does not mean the same thing as a share of the net profits. However, this term, when used by landscape gardeners and not lawyers, should not be restricted to its technical definition. "Commission" was used to refer to Sweet's share of the profits, and the receipt of a share of the profits is prima facie evidence of a partnership. Though evidence is conflicting, there is evidence that the payments were not wages, but a share of the profit of a partnership. As in *Watson,* supra, it can readily be inferred from the evidence most favorable to support the judgment that the parties intended a community of interest in any increment in the value of the capital and in the profit. As shown in *Watson,* absence of contribution to capital is not controlling, and contribution of labor and skill will suffice. There is evidence from which it can be inferred that the parties intended to do the things which amount to the formation of a partnership, regardless of how they may later characterize the relationship. *Bacon,* supra. From the evidence the court could find that part of the operating profits of the business, of which Sweet was entitled to 20 percent, were put back into it in the form of inventory of nursery stock. In the authorities cited above it seems the central factor in determining the existence of a partnership is a division of profits.

From all the circumstances we cannot say that the court erred in finding the existence of a partnership. . . .

Affirmed.

QUESTION AND NOTE ON VOHLAND v. SWEET

1. Why should the receipt of a share of the profits create a presumption of partnership under §7(4) of the UPA, while, under §7(3), the sharing of gross returns does not?

2. The usual case in which partnership is inferred by the courts despite the absence of an explicit partnership agreement involves a third-party action against the alleged partner for the tort or contract liabilities of the partnership. This takes us to the topic of creditor rights.

3.3   RELATIONS WITH THIRD PARTIES

Since the general partnership form includes unlimited personal liability for partners, partnership law is in large measure defined by the rights of creditors vis-à-vis the assets of (express or implied) partners. Three principal issues arise under the topic of creditor rights. First, who is a partner for purposes of personal liability to business creditors? (This is the creditors' side of the formation question, which is explored in Brudney's UPA problems below.) Second, when can an exiting or retiring partner escape liability for a partnership obligation? And, third, since a partner's liability on a partnership debt can be satisfied from a partner's nonpartnership property, how are such claims to an individual partner's personal assets to be balanced against the claims of other (nonpartnership) creditors of that person?

3.3.1   Who Is a Partner?

PROFESSOR BRUDNEY'S UPA PROBLEMS

1. Ars, Gratia, and Artis form and operate a business to distribute sporting goods and equipment at wholesale. The enterprise — whose

letterhead, billheads, and bank account are in the name Argrar — has built a warehouse for $200,000 (on land supplied by Gratia), which it depreciates to the tax advantage of the individual participants because it reports to the IRS as a partnership. Ars, who has no assets, has furnished his talents as an administrator and manages the internal operations of the business. Gratia contributed the use of his land, which he could have sold for $40,000, and has handled the firm's sales, and Artis contributed $30,000 in cash and has done the purchasing. The three men have agreed that Ars is, in all events, to receive the greater of $5,000 annually or one-third of the profits. During the first years of the business, the three men divided the annual profits equally among themselves. With the knowledge of the other two, Artis obtained half the cash from Mayer, to whom (unbeknownst to them) he has promised half his profits.

   (a) If a consumer is injured by equipment that Artis knew was defective, is Ars liable? Is Mayer?

   (b) If a customer loses foreseeable resales because Gratia fails to request timely delivery to the customer, is Artis liable? Ars? Mayer? Consider §§6, 7, 12-16, and 18 of the UPA.

   2. In a later year, Low, who is Ars's uncle and an investment banker, loaned the business $50,000 for ten years. Since the warehouse was mortgaged to the hilt, he could not get any security for his loan, and he insisted on interest in an amount equal to 25 percent of the profits and on a veto of expenditures of more than $10,000. The loan is repayable on demand but is not prepayable without Low's consent. Low also indicated that he would be available to give the others advice about how to finance transactions from time to time.

   The parties plan to obtain further necessary financing by a bank loan, which will be senior to Low's loan, and by as much credit as they can get from their suppliers.

   If Gratia tells the bank that Low has an interest in the business and the bank makes a loan to the firm and passes the word to suppliers that Low is interested in the business, is Low liable to the bank or any supplier who extends credit? Suppose he receives a bill from a supplier and forwards it to Ars with instructions to pay it and explain his status, and Ars pays but fails to explain.

3.3.2   Third-Party Claims Against Departing Partners

   Dissolution of a partnership does not itself affect a partner's individual liability on partnership debts. When a partner withdraws from a partnership but other partners continue the business, this continuing liability for existing obligations leaves the withdrawing partner in an uncomfortable situation. She is liable for partnership obligations incurred prior to her departure, but she no longer exercises control over the capacity of the continuing business to satisfy those obligations.

Sections 36(3) and 36(3) of the UPA are designed to make life easier for the departing partner. Section 36(2) releases the departing partner of partnership debts if the court can infer an agreement between the continuing partners and the creditor to release the withdrawing partner. Section 36(3) is usually applied to release the departing partner from personal liability when a creditor renegotiates his debt with the continuing partners after receiving notice of the departing partner's exit. See, e.g., *Munn v. Scalera*, 181 Conn. 527, 436 A.2d 18 (1990). From a policy perspective, these provisions attempt to strike a balance between competing concerns. On one hand, making it too easy for departing partners to escape partnership debts would create incentives for partners to leave when trouble appeared on the horizon. On the other hand, making it too difficult for departing partners to escape liability for partnership debts would allow the continuing partners to bind the departing partner who no longer has control over partnership decision-making—externalizing some of the risk of the partnership. These provisions seek to balance these competing concerns.

3.3.3 Third-Party Claims Against Partnership Property

Here we discuss a bit more fully tenancy in partnership. As we noted earlier, a fundamental characteristic of all business entities—including partnerships, trusts, and corporations—is a segregated pool of assets available to secure business debts. Without segregated business assets, all of the business and personal assets of investors would be available to *both* business and personal creditors. While this would not necessarily pose a problem for sole proprietorships,[2] it would create an increasingly severe problem as the number of co-owners increased. With an increasing number of investors, business creditors would soon be unable to monitor the claims of personal creditors with whom they would have to compete for assets in the event of insolvency. As a result, third parties would become increasingly unwilling to contract with the jointly owned business without security interests, high interest payments, or equivalent protections. Put differently, a segregated pool of assets is essential for contracting with jointly owned business entities of any significant size.

In Europe, at least, widespread legal recognition of segregated assets dedicated to business creditors seems first to have developed in medieval Italian city states.[3] By the late 17th century, the concept had become part of

2. It is even a problem with sole proprietorships in so far as business creditors must not only ascertain the sole proprietor's personal debt but also ensure that the proprietor does not incur additional personal debt in the futures. A simple contract limiting the amount of the proprietor's personal debt would not bind third-party personal creditors. Put differently, without some sort of prior claim on business assets, business creditors face what economists term a "moral hazard problem."

3. See Henry Hansmann, Reinier Kraakman & Richard Squire, *Law and the Rise of the Firm*, 119 Harv. L. Rev. 1333, 1356-1360 (2006).

English common law of partnership.[4] Despite these deep historical roots, however, the functional need to preserve a segregated pool of business assets conflicted with the traditional doctrinal view of partnership as an "aggregate," or association of partners. The aggregate theory implied that partnership property ought to be held not by the business but jointly, by the individual partners, as joint tenants or tenants in common. But such inchoate forms of joint ownership would have seriously compromised the availability of dedicated business assets for business creditors.

The UPA's solution to this dilemma was to recognize a peculiar form of joint ownership: partnership property owned by the partners as "tenants in partnership." UPA §25(1). The critical feature of this form of "joint owner- ship" is that it affords to individual partners virtually no power to dispose of partnership property, thus transforming this property into de facto busi- ness property. Under UPA §25(2), a partner cannot possess or assign rights in partnership property, a partner's heirs cannot inherit it, and a partner's creditors cannot attach or execute upon it. Indeed, the fiction of joint partner ownership of partnership property is so transparent that RUPA (1994) has abandoned it entirely in favor of straightforward entity owner- ship. RUPA §§501, 502.

If a partner does not own her partnership's assets in any ordinary sense, she nevertheless retains a transferable interest *in the profits arising from the use of partnership property* and the right to receive partnership distribu- tions. (It is these rights to cash flow that a creditor can attach or that an heir may succeed to.) Thus, a functional two-level ownership structure characterizes partnerships and all business entities: The contributors of equity capital do not "own" the assets themselves but rather own the rights to the net financial returns that these assets generate, as well as certain governance or management rights. See UPA §§26, 27; RUPA §§502, 503. As RUPA §503 makes clear, a partner's transferable interest can be transferred in most circumstances. RUPA §504 and UPA §28 permit individual creditors of partners (e.g., the bank that has made the partner a personal loan) to obtain a "charging order," which is a lien on the partner's transferable interest that is subject to foreclosure unless it is redeemed by repayment of the debt.

3.3.4   Claims of Partnership Creditors to Partner's Individual Property[5]

Another issue is the extent to which partnership creditors whose debts are not fully satisfied by partnership property can assert claims to the assets of individual partners. This question is important because, as you might expect, frequently a partnership's bankruptcy filing will trigger bankruptcy filings by its general partners. This may not happen when the bankruptcy proceeding is just a reorganization, but it is quite likely when the

---

4. See Craven v. Knight (1683) 21 Eng. Rep. 664 (Ch.).
5. We are grateful to Professor Jesse Fried for his revisions of this note.

partnership is insolvent and will have to be liquidated under Chapter 7. When both partners and their partnership are in bankruptcy, conflicts will arise concerning priority of claims between the partner's personal creditors and the creditors of the partnership. The common law rule that evolved during the nineteenth century and was codified in the Bankruptcy Act of 1898 — sometimes called the "jingle rule" — gave partnership creditors priority in all partnership assets and assigned first priority to the separate creditors of individual partners in the individual assets of those partners.[6]

The Bankruptcy Act of 1978 modified this approach. Today, §723 of the Bankruptcy Code (11 U.S.C. §723) contemplates a trustee in bankruptcy first administering the estate of the partnership (i.e., its partnership property) and then turning to the assets of general partners to the extent of any deficiency. Pending determination of any deficiency, the court may require a partner to provide indemnity for any deficiency or may "order any such partner ... not to dispose of property," §723(b). When there is a deficiency in the partnership assets, §723(c) provides that the trustee's claim against the assets of any general partner is on a parity with individual creditors of the partner. Thus, partnership creditors still have first priority in the assets of a partnership (as under the jingle rule). But under §723(c), partnership creditors (acting through the trustee in bankruptcy) are placed on parity with individual creditors in allocating the assets of an individual partner when the partnership is bankrupt under Chapter 7.

What happens when the partnership is not being liquidated under Chapter 7, but the estate of an individual partner is itself being administered in bankruptcy? If the partnership business is sound, there will typically not be a problem. Partnership creditors may be content to look to the partnership assets (and the credit of the other general partners) to protect their rights to payment. Nevertheless, any partnership creditor who has a mature claim could assert that claim in the partner's bankruptcy case. In that event, the question again arises of priority between individual creditors and partnership creditors. Here, bankruptcy law creates no special rule; rather, it distributes assets according to the applicable state law that determines the allocation of the partner's assets.

The UPA and RUPA diverge on the question of how an insolvent partner's assets should be distributed. The UPA follows the jingle rule, giving the partner's creditors priority over partnership creditors, while the RUPA follows the parity treatment rule codified in §723 of the Bankruptcy Code. Thus, the bankruptcy assets of a partner whose partnership is not in Chapter 7 will be distributed according to the jingle rule if the UPA applies and according to the parity rule if the RUPA applies. (Note that regardless of priority rules, if the estate of an insolvent partner were to be

---

6. The Jingle Rule evolved in the English equity courts at the end of the 17th and beginning of the 18th centuries. See, *e.g.*, Craven v. Knight (1683) 21 Eng. Rep. 664 (Ch.) (giving business creditors priority in business assets); Ex Parte Crowder (1715) 23 Eng. Rep. 1064 (Ch.) (giving personal creditors of partners priority in personal assets). In fact the first part of the Jingle Rule, giving business creditors first priority in business assets, dates back to the city states in medieval Italy. See generally Hansmann, Kraakman & Squire, *supra* note 10, at 1381.

required to satisfy a partnership obligation, the estate would have an action for subrogation against the solvent partnership or contribution against its partners in the event of its insolvency).

State partnership law also applies in cases where the assets of an insolvent partner or of an insolvent partnership are distributed outside of bankruptcy (e.g., in a state insolvency proceeding). Thus, when the assets belong to an insolvent partner, the distribution will depend on whether the UPA or RUPA applies. When the assets belong to the partnership (not the partner), both the UPA and the RUPA give partnership creditors first priority in the assets.

The following chart provides a visualization of the different approaches:

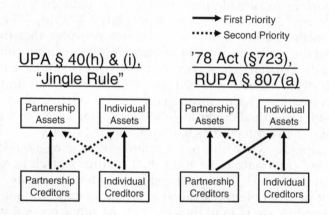

So, in all cases, partnership creditors get first priority in the assets of the partnership. As to claims against the individual assets of partners, however, partnership creditors are subordinated to the claims of a part-ner's creditors in the allocation of the partner's assets (as under the jingle rule) if (1) the UPA is controlling state law *and* (2) §723 does not apply (that is, the partnership is not in Chapter 7 or the individual partner is not in bankruptcy). But partnership creditors receive parity treatment if *either* (1) the RUPA is controlling state law *or* (2) §723 applies (the partnership is in Chapter 7 and the individual partner is in bankruptcy). If this sounds complicated, you now see one of the benefits of the corporate form, which we will come to in the next chapter.

QUESTION

What arguments justify the repeal of the second half of the old jingle rule, which makes partnership creditors more secure at the expense of unse-cured individual creditors? Note that the legislative history accompanying §723(c) of the 1978 Bankruptcy Act merely observed that the change would align bankruptcy with partnership law outside of bankruptcy.

3.4 PARTNERSHIP GOVERNANCE AND ISSUES OF AUTHORITY

NATIONAL BISCUIT CO. v. STROUD

249 N.C. 467 (1959)

PARKER, J.:

C. N. Stroud and Earl Freeman entered into a general partnership to sell groceries under the firm name of Stroud's Food Center. There is nothing in the agreed statement of facts to indicate or suggest that Freeman's power and authority as a general partner were in any way restricted or limited by the articles of partnership in respect to the ordinary and legitimate business of the partnership. Certainly, the purchase and sale of bread were ordinary and legitimate business of Stroud's Food Center during its continuance as a going concern.

Several months prior to February 1956 Stroud advised plaintiff that he personally would not be responsible for any additional bread sold by plaintiff to Stroud's Food Center. After such notice to plaintiff, it from 6 February 1956 to 25 February 1956, at the request of Freeman, sold and delivered bread in the amount of $171.04 to Stroud's Food Center.

In *Johnson v. Bernheim*, 76 N.C. 139, this Court said: "A and B are general partners to do some given business; the partnership is, by operation of law, a power to each to bind the partnership in any manner legitimate to the business. If one partner go to a third person to buy an article on time for the partnership, the other partner cannot prevent it by writing to the third person not to sell to him on time; or, if one party attempt to buy for cash, the other has no right to require that it shall be on time. And what is true in regard to buying is true in regard to selling. What either partner does with a third person is binding on the partnership. It is otherwise where the partnership is not general, but is upon special terms, as that purchases and sales must be with and for cash. There the power to each is special, in regard to all dealings with third persons at least who have notice of the terms." There is contrary authority. 68 C.J.S., Partnership, pp. 578-579. However, this text of C.J.S. does not mention the effect of the provisions of the Uniform Partnership Act.

The General Assembly of North Carolina in 1941 enacted a Uniform Partnership Act, which became effective 15 March 1941. G.S. Ch. 59, Partnership, Art. 2 . . . .

Freeman as a general partner with Stroud, with no restrictions on his authority to act within the scope of the partnership business so far as the agreed statement of facts shows, had under the Uniform Partnership Act "equal rights in the management and conduct of the partnership business." Under [UPA §18(h)] Stroud, his co-partner, could not restrict the power and authority of Freeman to buy bread for the partnership as a going concern, for such a purchase was an "ordinary matter connected with the partnership business," for the purpose of its business and within its scope, because in the very nature of things Stroud was not, and could not be, a majority of the partners. Therefore, Freeman's purchases of bread from plaintiff for Stroud's Food Center as a going concern bound the partnership and his co-partner Stroud. . . .

In Crane on Partnership, 2d Ed., p. 277, it is said: "In cases of an even division of the partners as to whether or not an act within the scope of the business should be done, of which disagreement a third person has knowledge, it seems that logically no restriction can be placed upon the power to act. The partnership being a going concern, activities within the scope of the business should not be limited, save by the expressed will of the majority deciding a disputed question; half of the members are not a majority." . . .

At the close of business on 25 February 1956 Stroud and Freeman by agreement dissolved the partnership. By their dissolution agreement all of the partnership assets, including cash on hand, bank deposits and all accounts receivable, with a few exceptions, were assigned to Stroud, who bound himself by such written dissolution agreement to liquidate the firm's assets and discharge its liabilities. It would seem a fair inference from the agreed statement of facts that the partnership got the benefit of the bread sold and delivered by plaintiff to Stroud's Food Center, at Freeman's request, from 6 February 1956 to 25 February 1956. But whether it did or not, Freeman's acts, as stated above, bound the partnership and Stroud.

The judgment of the court below is
Affirmed.

QUESTIONS ON NABISCO

1. *Nabisco* illustrates the majority rule that half of a two-person partnership is not a "majority" for purposes of making firm decisions within the ordinary course of business. But why not the reverse rule? If Stroud notifies Nabisco that he will not be bound by Freeman's purchases, why hold Stroud liable on the partnership transaction? More generally, why hold any partner liable who explicitly opts out of a transaction with a third party? How else could Stroud have attempted to halt Freeman's contracting?

2. Return to Professor Brudney's Argrar hypothetical, described above. After the firm (assume it is a partnership) has been in business for several years, the flow of unexpected business requires Ars, Artis, and Gratia to decide whether to make alterations in the building. The partners are in disagreement about how extensive the alterations should be. Gratia signs a contract with a construction company for the erection of a retail storefront addition to the building at a cost of $50,000.

   (a) Are the firm and its individual partners bound?

   (b) Even if Artis tells the construction company to stop before it begins actual work?

   (c) What are the construction company's obligations to inquire before entering into the transaction — whom should it ask for what?

Consider §§9, 12-16, and 18 of the Uniform Partnership Act.

3.5 TERMINATION (DISSOLUTION AND DISASSOCIATION)

Many of the most critical aspects of partnership law and partnership agreements deal with the dissolution and wind-up of partnerships. Both the statutes and the parties to partnership agreements analyze the dissolution problem with the aid of accounting categories. For this reason, it is helpful to review some simple accounting categories before examining the dissolution problem.

3.5.1 Accounting for Partnership's Financial Status and Performance

An evaluation of the financial *status* of a partnership begins with an inspection of its balance sheet — a simple statement of the assets that it holds, the liabilities that it owes, and the difference between the two, which is the equity that the partners have in the firm. Inspecting a balance sheet is just the first step in evaluating its financial status, but it is an important step.

Since a balance sheet is always reported as of a particular date, the first step in undertaking a current evaluation of a partnership is bringing it up to date. Next, one must appreciate that in almost all cases figures on a balance sheet representing the assets are stated at historical cost (minus a regular periodic charge or reduction for "depreciation" but more of that later). In some businesses (where there is a fast turnover of inventory, for example), the difference between historical costs and current values may not be great. In all events, with an ongoing business even the historical figures, if kept in a consistent way from one period to the next, will supply some information that is somewhat illuminating.

Sample Partnership Balance Sheet

Washington Square Pharmacia
Statement of Profit and Loss
December 31, 2006

Assets		Liabilities	
Cash	$ 5,400	Accounts Payable	$ 74,000
Accts Receivable	76,000	Notes Payable	136,000
Inventory	189,000	Mortgage Note	350,000
			$560,000
Real Estate	463,553	Partners' Capital	$173,953
Total Assets	**$733,953**	**Total Liabilities & Capital**	**$733,953**

Sample Partnership Income Statement

After the balance sheet, the second fundamental accounting statement is one that reflects the results of transactions in which the firm has engaged over a set period, often a year. This Income Statement is sometimes referred to as a Statement of Profit and Loss (or more accurately profit *or* loss). For our illustrative purposes we assume that this partnership keeps its books on a *cash basis.* Another and probably better technique is *accrual basis accounting.* In accrual, amounts paid are treated as expenses in the period to which they relate. So, for example, if Washington Square paid out $35,000 in November of 2006 to cover radio advertising for the next ten months, its 12/31/06 Income Statement would report only 2/10th of that cash outlay as an expense. The rest would not be reported on the Income Statement at all, but would be reported on the balance sheet as a prepaid expense. (We did not put it into our sample balance sheet, so don't look.)

Washington Square Pharmacia
Income Statement
December 31, 2006

Gross Sales	$632,550
Cost of Goods Sold	311,000
GROSS PROFIT	321,550
General Administration Expenses:	
Advertising	48,000
Mortgage (rent)	38,000
Salaries	168,000
Total Expenses	$254,000
NET PROFIT	$67,550
(Allocated to Partners' Accounts)	

Accounting for Partners' Capital

Finally, the third category of the balance sheet, the capital account, will have a report that records the effects on the partners' capital of the operations of the business over the year. For our imagined business on Washington Square, it might look like this.

Washington Square Pharmacia
Capital Accounts
December 31, 2006

	Opening Balance 1/1/06	Income FY2006	Withdrawals FY2006	Closing Balance 12/31/06
Allen	$140,000	$22,517	$64,666	$97,851
Kraakman	140,000	22,517	74,666	87,851
Subramanian	30,000	22,517	64,266	(11,749)

QUESTIONS ON THE SAMPLE BALANCE SHEET AND INCOME STATEMENT

1. If advertising expenses during 2006 had been $58,000 instead of $48,000 — and all else had remained the same — how would this affect the income statement? How would it affect the balance sheet, or can you say?

2. Suppose each of the three partners earned $40,000 in salary for the services they performed for the partnership during 2006. What are their taxable incomes from the partnership for 2006?

ADAMS v. JARVIS

127 N.W.2d 400 (Wis. 1964)

Action for declaratory judgment construing a medical-partnership agreement between three doctors. Plaintiff-respondent withdrew from the partnership seven years after it was formed.

The dispute concerns the extent of the plaintiff's right to share in partnership assets, specifically accounts receivable. The relevant portions of the agreement provide:

12. Books of Account. Proper books of account shall be kept by said partners and entries made therein of all matters, transactions, and things as are usually entered in books of account kept by persons engaged in the same or similar business. Such books and all partnership letters, papers and documents shall be kept at the firm's office and each partner shall at all times have access to examine, copy, and take extracts from the same.

13. Fiscal Year — Share of Profits and Losses. The partnership fiscal year shall coincide with the calendar year. Net profits and losses of the partnership shall be divided among the individual[s] in the same proportion as their capital interest in the partnership, except as hereinafter provided for partners who become incapacitated or have withdrawn from the partnership, or the estates of the deceased partners . . . .

15. Conditions of Termination. Partnership shall not terminate under certain conditions. The incapacity, withdrawal or death of a partner shall not terminate this partnership. Such partner, or the estate or heirs of a deceased partner shall continue to participate in partnership profits and losses, as provided in this agreement, but shall not participate in management, the making of partnership decisions, or any professional matters. On the happening of any of the above events, the books of the partnership shall not be closed until the end of the partnership fiscal year.

16. Withdrawal. No withdrawal from the firm shall be effective until at least thirty (30) days have elapsed from the date on which written notice of such intention is given the other partners by registered mail to their last known address. As used herein "withdrawal" shall refer to any situation in which a partner leaves the partnership, at a time when said partnership is not dissolving, pursuant to a written agreement of the parties to do so. The withdrawing partner shall be entitled to receive from the continuing partners the following:

(1) Any balance standing to his credit on the books of the partnership;

(2) That proportion of the partnership profits to which he was entitled by this agreement in the fiscal year of his withdrawal, which the period from the beginning of such year to the effective date of withdrawal shall bear to the whole of the then current fiscal year. Such figure shall be ascertained as soon as practicable after the close of the current fiscal year and shall be payable as soon as the amount thereof is ascertained. All drawings previously made during the then fiscal year shall be first charged against the share in net partnership profits as above computed. If there shall have been losses for

such fiscal year, or overdrawings, or losses and the whole of any overdrawings or loans, shall be determined and charged against his capital account, and if in excess thereof, shall be paid by him or his estate promptly after the close of the fiscal year, plus

(3) The amount of his capital account on the effective date of his withdrawal (after deduction of any losses required to be paid in subdivision (2) above). In the event such withdrawing partner dies prior to receiving any or all of the above payments, his personal representative, heirs or assigns shall receive the same payments at the same time as those to which he would have been entitled by the terms had he lived. Payment of the items set forth in subdivisions (1) and (3) above shall be made according to and evidenced by a promissory note, executed by the remaining partners, payable in twelve (12) equal quarterly installments, the first of which shall be payable at the end of the six (6) months following the effective date of such withdrawal. Acceleration of said note shall be permitted at the sole discretion of the remaining partners. Such note shall bear interest at Two (2) Per Cent, payable with each installment.

It is further agreed that in the event of the withdrawal of any partner or partners, any and all accounts receivable for any current year and any and all years past shall remain the sole possession and property of the remaining member or members of THE TOMAHAWK CLINIC.

18. Dissolution. Should this partnership be dissolved by agreement of the parties, all accounts and notes shall be liquidated and all firm assets sold or divided between the partners at agreed valuations. The books of the partnership shall then be closed and distribution made in proportion to the capital interests of the partners as shown by the partnership books. No drawings should be paid once the partnership has begun to wind up its affairs, although liquidating dividends based on estimates may be paid from time to time. No dissolution shall be effective until the end of the then fiscal year, and until ninety (90) days have elapsed from the date on which written agreement to such dissolution shall have been executed by the parties hereto.

This agreement shall be binding not only upon the parties hereto, but also upon their heirs, executors, administrators, successors, and assigns, and the wives of said partners have signed this agreement as witnesses, after being advised of the terms of this agreement.

The trial court decided that the withdrawal of the plaintiff worked a dissolution of the partnership under [UPA §§29, 30]; that the partnership assets should be liquidated and applied to the payment of partnership interests according to the scheme set forth in [UPA §38] for the reason that paragraphs 15 and 16 of the partnership agreement did not apply in the case of a statutory dissolution; that plaintiff's interest was one third of the net worth, including therein accounts receivable of the partnership as of May 31, 1961; that plaintiff should recover from defendants the value of his partnership interest; and gave judgment accordingly, but retained jurisdiction for supplementary proceedings. Defendants appeal.

OPINION: *BEILFUSS, J.*

1. Does a withdrawal of a partner constitute a dissolution of the partnership under [UPA §§29, 30], notwithstanding a partnership agreement to the contrary?

2. Is plaintiff, as withdrawing partner, entitled to a share of the accounts receivable?

The partnership agreement as set forth above (paragraph 15) specifically provides that the partnership shall not terminate by the withdrawal of a partner. We conclude the parties clearly intended that even though a partner withdrew, the partnership and the partnership business would continue for the purposes for which it was organized. Paragraph 18 of the agreement provides for a dissolution upon agreement of the parties in the sense that the partnership would cease to function as such subject to winding up of its affairs.

While the withdrawal of a partner works a dissolution of the partnership under the statute as to the withdrawing partner, it does not follow that the rights and duties of remaining partners are similarly affected. The agreement contemplates a partnership would continue to exist between the remaining partners even though the personnel constituting the partnership was changed.

Persons with professional qualifications commonly associate in business partnerships. The practice of continuing the operation of the partnership business, even though there are some changes in partnership personnel, is also common. The reasons for an agreement that a medical partnership should continue without disruption of the services rendered is self-evident. If the partnership agreement provides for continuation, sets forth a method of paying the withdrawing partner his agreed share, does not jeopardize the rights of creditors, the agreement is enforceable. The statute does not specifically regulate this type of withdrawal with a continuation of the business. The statute should not be construed to invalidate an otherwise enforceable contract entered into for a legitimate purpose.

The provision for withdrawal is in effect a type of winding up of the partnership without the necessity of discontinuing the day-to-day business. [UPA §38] contemplates a discontinuance of the day-to-day business but does not forbid other methods of winding up a partnership.

The agreement does provide that Dr. Adams shall no longer actively participate and further provides for winding up the affairs insofar as his interests are concerned. In this sense his withdrawal does constitute a dissolution. We conclude, however, that when the plaintiff, Dr. Adams, withdrew, the partnership was not wholly dissolved so as to require complete winding up of its affairs, but continued to exist under the terms of the agreement. The agreement does not offend the statute and is valid.

ACCOUNTS RECEIVABLE

[The court reviews UPA §38(1).]

The trial court concluded that the withdrawal constituted a statutory dissolution; that partnership assets shall be liquidated pursuant to the statute and that the plaintiff was entitled to a one-third interest in the accounts receivable.

[UPA §38(1)] applies only "unless otherwise agreed." The distribution should therefore be made pursuant to the agreement.

Paragraphs 15 and 16 of the contract as set forth above provide for the withdrawal of a partner and the share to which he is entitled. Subject to limitations not material here, paragraph 16 provides that a withdrawing partner shall receive (1) any balance to his credit on partnership books, (2) his proportionate share of profits calculated on a fiscal year basis, and (3) his capital account as of the date of his withdrawal. Paragraph 16 further provides that in event of withdrawal "any and all accounts receivable for any current year and any and all years past shall remain the sole possession and property of the remaining member or members of THE TOMAHAWK CLINIC."

The plaintiff contends that provision of the agreement denying him a share of the accounts receivable works a forfeiture and is void as being against public policy.

We conclude the parties to the agreement intended accounts receivable to be restricted to customer or patient accounts receivable.

The provision of the agreement is clear and unambiguous. There is nothing in the record to suggest the plaintiff's bargaining position was so unequal in the negotiations leading up to the agreement that the provision should be declared unenforceable upon the grounds of public policy. Legitimate business and goodwill considerations are consistent with a provision retaining control and ownership of customer accounts receivable in an active functioning professional medical partnership. We hold the provision on accounts receivable enforceable. . . .

Because of our determination that the partnership agreement is valid and enforceable the judgment of the trial court insofar as it decrees a dissolution of the partnership and a one-third division of the accounts receivable to the plaintiff must be reversed and remanded to the trial court with directions to enter judgment in conformity with this opinion.

The trial court properly retained jurisdiction for the purpose of granting supplementary relief to plaintiff to enforce a distribution to the plaintiff. The trial court may conduct such proceedings as are necessary to effectuate a distribution pursuant to the agreement.

The parties have stipulated that the plaintiff ceased to be an active partner as of June 1, 1961. The agreement provides that the partnership fiscal year shall coincide with the calendar year. It further provides that his share of the partnership profits upon withdrawal shall be calculated upon the whole year and in proportion to his participation of the whole fiscal year. He is, therefore, entitled to $5/12$ ths of $1/3$ d, or $5/36$ ths of the profits for the fiscal year ending December 31, 1961.

Such of the accounts receivable as were collected during the year 1961 do constitute a part of the profits for 1961. The plaintiff had no part of the management of the partnership after June 1, 1961; however, his eventual distributive share of profits is dependent, in some degree, upon the management of the business affairs and performance of the continuing partners for the remainder of the fiscal year. Under these circumstances the continuing partners stand in a fiduciary relationship to the withdrawing partner and are obligated to conduct the business in a good-faith manner including a good-faith effort to liquidate the accounts receivable consistent with good business practices.

Judgment reversed with directions to conduct supplementary proceedings to determine distributive share of plaintiff and then enter judgment in conformity with this opinion.

QUESTIONS ON ADAMS v. JARVIS

1. Paragraph 16 of the partnership agreement defines "withdrawal" as
"any situation in which a partner leaves the partnership, at a time when said
partnership is not dissolving." Compare UPA §29. What should paragraph
16 say?
2. Why did the plaintiff want the accounts receivable? Was the partnership agreement's provision for withdrawing partners unfair on its face (and
if so, why did the plaintiff agree to it)?
3. How would you draft a withdrawal provision for a plaintiff's law
firm that litigated large class actions and derivative suits, typically lasting
several years, in the hope of earning contingent fees?

DREIFUERST v. DREIFUERST

80 N.W.2d 335 (Wis. 1979)

BROWN, J.:
The plaintiffs and the defendant, all brothers, formed a partnership.
The partnership operated two feed mills, one located at St. Cloud, Wiscon-
sin and one located at Elkhart Lake, Wisconsin. There were no written
Articles of Partnership governing this partnership.

On October 4, 1975, the plaintiffs served the defendant with a notice
of dissolution and wind-up of the partnership. The action for dissolution
and wind-up was commenced on January 27, 1976. The dissolution complaint alleged that the plaintiffs elected to dissolve the partnership. There
was no allegation of fault, expulsion or contravention of an alleged agreement as grounds for dissolution. The parties were unable, however, to
agree to a winding-up of the partnership.

Hearings on the dissolution were held on October 18, 1976 and March
4, 1977. Testimony was presented regarding the value of the partnership
assets and each partner's equity. At the March 4, 1977 hearing, the defendant requested that the partnership be sold pursuant to [UPA §38(1)] and
that the court allow a sale, at which time the partners would bid on the
entire property. By such sale, the plaintiffs could continue to run the
business under a new partnership, and the defendant's partnership equity
could be satisfied in cash.

On February 20, 1978, the trial court, by written decision, denied the
defendant's request for a sale and instead divided the partnership assets in-
kind according to the valuation presented by the plaintiffs. The plaintiffs
were given the physical assets from the Elkhart Lake mill, and the defendant
was given the physical assets from the St. Cloud mill. The defendant
appeals this order and judgment dividing the assets in-kind . . . .

At the outset, we note, and the parties agree, that the appellant was not in contravention of the partnership agreement since there was no partnership agreement. The partnership was a partnership at will. They also agree there was no written agreement governing distribution of partnership assets upon dissolution and wind-up. The dispute, in this case, is over the authority of the trial court to order in-kind distribution in the absence of any agreement of the partners.

[UPA §38(1)] provides:

> When dissolution is caused in any way, except in contravention of the partnership agreement, each partner, as against his copartners and all persons claiming through them in respect to their interests in the partnership, *unless otherwise agreed,* may have the partnership property applied to discharge its liabilities, and the surplus applied to pay in cash the net amount owing to the respective partners. (Emphasis supplied.)

The appellant contends this statute grants him the right to force a sale of the partnership assets in order to obtain his fair share of the partnership assets in cash upon dissolution. He claims that in the absence of an agreement of the partners to in-kind distribution, the trial court had no authority to distribute the assets in-kind. He is entitled to an in-cash settlement after judicial sale.

The respondents contend the statute does not entitle the appellant to force a sale and grants the trial court the power to distribute the assets in-kind if in-kind distribution is equitably possible and doesn't jeopardize the rights of creditors.

We do not believe that the statute can be read in any way to permit in-kind distribution unless the partners agree to in-kind distribution or unless there is a partnership agreement calling for in-kind distribution at the time of dissolution and wind-up.

A partnership at will is a partnership which has no definite term or particular undertaking and can rightfully be dissolved by the express will of any partner. In the present case, the respondents wanted to dissolve the partnership. This being a partnership at will, they could rightfully dissolve this partnership with or without the consent of the appellant . . . .

Unless otherwise agreed, partners who have not wrongfully dissolved a partnership have a right to wind up the partnership. Winding-up is the process of settling partnership affairs after dissolution. Winding-up is often called liquidation and involves reducing the assets to cash to pay creditors and distribute to partners the value of their respective interests. Thus, lawful dissolution (or dissolution which is caused in any way except in contravention of the partnership agreement) gives each partner the right to have the business liquidated and his share of the surplus paid *in cash.* In-kind distribution is permissible only in very limited circumstances. If the partnership agreement permits in-kind distribution upon dissolution or wind-up or if, at any time prior to wind-up, all partners agree to in-kind distribution, the court may order in-kind distribution. While at least one court has permitted in-kind distribution, absent an agreement by all partners, *Rinke v. Rinke,* 330 Mich. 615, 48 N.W.2d 201 (1951), the court's holding in that case was limited. In *Rinke,* the court stated:

> The decree of the trial court provided for dividing the assets of the partnerships rather than for the sale thereof and the distribution of cash proceeds. Appellants insist that such method of procedure is erroneous and [not] contemplated by the Uniform Partnership Act. Attention is directed to §38 of said act. Construing together pertinent provisions of the statute leads to the conclusion that it was not the intention of the legislature in the enactment of the Uniform Partnership Act to impose a mandatory requirement that, under all circumstances, the assets of a dissolved partnership shall be sold and the money received therefore divided among those entitled to it, particularly so, as in the case at bar, where there are no debts to be paid from the proceeds. *The situation disclosed by the record in the present case is somewhat unusual in that no one other than the former partners is interested in the assets of the businesses. In view of this situation and of the nature of the assets,* we think that the trial court was correct in apportioning them to the parties. There is no showing that appellants have been prejudiced thereby. (Emphasis supplied.) 330 Mich. at 628, 48 N.W.2d at 207.

The Michigan court's holding was limited to situations where: (1) there were no creditors to be paid from the proceeds, (2) ordering a sale would be senseless since no one other than the partners would be interested in the assets of the business, and (3) an in-kind distribution was fair to all partners.

That is not the case here. There was no showing that there were no creditors who would be paid from the proceeds, nor was there a showing that no one other than the partners would be interested in the assets. These factors are important if an in-kind distribution is to be allowed. [Section 38] of the Uniform Partnership Act [is] intended to protect creditors as well as partners. In-kind distributions may affect a creditor's right to collect the debt owed since the assets of the partnership, as a whole, may be worth more than the assets once divided up. Thus, the creditor's ability to collect from the individual partners may be jeopardized. Secondly, if others are interested in the assets, a sale provides a more accurate means of establishing the market value of the assets and, thus, better assuring each partner his share in the value of the assets. Where only the partners are interested in the assets, a fair value can be determined without the necessity of a sale. The sale would be merely the partners bidding with each other without any competition. This process could be accomplished through negotiations or at trial with the court as a final arbitrator of the value of the assets. With these policy considerations in mind, we think the Michigan court's holding in *Rinke* was limited to the facts of that case. Those facts not being present in this case, we do not feel an in-kind distribution in this case was proper.

However, even assuming the respondents in this case can show that there are no creditors to be paid, no one other than the partners are interested in the assets, and in-kind distribution would be fair to all partners, we cannot read §38 of the Uniform Partnership Act or sec. 178.33(1), Stats. (the Wisconsin equivalent), as permitting an in-kind distribution under any circumstances, unless all partners agree. The statute and §38 of the Uniform Partnership Act are quite clear that if a partner may force liquidation, he is entitled to his share of the partnership assets, after creditors are paid *in cash.* To the extent that *Rinke v. Rinke,* supra, creates an exception to cash distribution, we decline to adopt that exception. We, therefore, must hold the trial court erred in ordering an in-kind distribution of the assets of the partnership.

The last question that arises is whether the appellant can force an actual sale of the assets or whether the trial court can determine the fair market value of the assets and order the respondents to pay the appellant in cash an amount equal to his share in the assets.

As discussed above, a sale is the best means of determining the true fair market value of the assets. Generally, liquidation envisions some form of sale. Since the statutes provide that, unless otherwise agreed, any partner who has not wrongfully dissolved the partnership has the right to wind up the partnership and force liquidation, he likewise has a right to force a sale, unless otherwise agreed. While judicial sales in some instances may cause economic hardships, these hardships can be avoided by the use of partnership agreements.

Judgment reversed and cause remanded for further proceedings not inconsistent with this opinion.

QUESTIONS ON DREIFUERST

1. Sections 402, 801, 802, and 804 of the RUPA (1994) codify the holding of *Dreifuerst.* Is the holding sound? Are there any circumstances in which payment in kind might generate more value for partners than a cash sale?

2. More generally, contrast the right of the withdrawing partner to force liquidation under UPA §38 (or RUPA 1994 §801) with the approach recommended by the ABA Committee on Partnerships and Unincorporated Associations: that of allowing a majority of the partners in an at-will partnership to continue the business without a winding up, providing that the majority repurchases the disassociating minority's interest at fair value as of the date of disassociation. Which approach is preferable?

For further discussion of these issues, see the excellent partnership notes in Charles R.T. O'Kelly and Robert B. Thompson, Corporations and Other Business Associations 57-144 (1992).

A LAST BRUDNEY QUESTION

After the Argrar partnership has continued for several years, Artis wants to resign and move across the continent. The business is worth, as a going concern, $700,000, but if it were liquidated and sold piece by piece, it would bring $400,000; and if it were sold intact to a related business that would not have to alter the warehouse, it would bring $500,000. A new person is needed to replace Artis as a purchasing agent. On what terms should Artis fairly leave and the newcomer enter?

Consider UPA §§17, 24-27, 36, 41, and 42 (and RUPA 1994 §701).

PAGE v. PAGE

359 P.2d 41 (Cal. 1961)

TRAYNOR, J.:

Plaintiff and defendant are partners in a linen supply business in Santa Maria, California. Plaintiff appeals from a judgment declaring the partnership to be for a term rather than at will.

The partners entered into an oral partnership agreement in 1949. Within the first two years each partner contributed approximately $43,000 for the purchase of land, machinery, and linen needed to begin the business. From 1949 to 1957 the enterprise was unprofitable, losing approximately $62,000. The partnership's major creditor is a corporation, wholly owned by plaintiff, that supplies the linen and machinery necessary for the day-to-day operation of the business. This corporation holds a $47,000 demand note of the partnership. The partnership operations began to improve in 1958. The partnership earned $3,824.41 in that year and $2,282.30 in the first three months of 1959. Despite this improvement plaintiff wishes to terminate the partnership.

The Uniform Partnership Act provides that a partnership may be dissolved "By the express will of any partner when no definite term or particular undertaking is specified." U.P.A. §31(1)(b). The trial court found that the partnership is for a term, namely, "such reasonable time as is necessary to enable said partnership to repay from partnership profits, indebtedness incurred for the purchase of land, buildings, laundry and delivery equipment and linen for the operation of such business. . . ." Plaintiff correctly contends that this finding is without support in the evidence.

Defendant testified that the terms of the partnership were to be similar to former partnerships of plaintiff and defendant, and that the understanding of these partnerships was that "we went into partnership to start the business and let the business operation pay for itself, put in so much money, and let the business pay itself out." There was also testimony that one of the former partnership agreements provided in writing that the profits were to be retained until all obligations were paid.

Upon cross-examination defendant admitted that the former partnership in which the earnings were to be retained until the obligations were repaid was substantially different from the present partnership. The former partnership was a limited partnership and provided for a definite term of five years and a partnership at will thereafter. Defendant insists, however, that the method of operation of the former partnership showed an understanding that all obligations were to be repaid from profits. He nevertheless concedes that there was no understanding as to the term of the present partnership in the event of losses. . . .

Viewing this evidence most favorably for defendant, it proves only that the partners expected to meet current expenses from current income and to recoup their investment if the business were successful.

Defendant contends that such an expectation is sufficient to create a partnership for a term under the rule of *Owen v. Cohen*, 19 Cal. 2d 147, 150, 119 P.2d 713. In that case we held that when a partner advances a sum of money to a partnership with the understanding that the amount contributed was to be a loan to the partnership and was to be repaid as soon as feasible from the prospective profits of the business, the partnership is for the term reasonably required to repay the loan. It is true that *Owen v. Cohen*, supra, and other cases hold that partners may impliedly agree to continue in business until a certain sum of money is earned (*Mervyn Investment Co. v. Biber*, 184 Cal. 637, 641-642, 194 P. 1037), or one or more partners recoup their investments (*Vangel v. Vangel*, 116 Cal. App. 2d 615, 625, 254 P.2d 919), or until certain debts are paid (*Owen v. Cohen*, supra, 19 Cal. 2d at page 150, 119 P.2d at page 714), or until certain property could be disposed of on favorable terms (*Shannon v. Hudson*, 161 Cal. App. 2d 44, 48, 325 P.2d 1022). In each of these cases, however, the implied agreement found support in the evidence. . . .

In the instant case, however, defendant failed to prove any facts from which an agreement to continue the partnership for a term may be implied. The understanding to which defendant testified was no more than a common hope that the partnership earnings would pay for all the necessary expenses. Such a hope does not establish even by implication a "definite term or particular undertaking" as required by U.P.A. §31(1)(b). All partnerships are ordinarily entered into with the hope that they will be profitable, but that alone does not make them all partnerships for a term and obligate the partners to continue in the partnerships until all of the losses over a period of many years have been recovered.

Defendant contends that plaintiff is acting in bad faith and is attempting to use his superior financial position to appropriate the now profitable business of the partnership. Defendant has invested $43,000 in the firm, and owing to the long period of losses his interest in the partnership assets is very small. The fact that plaintiff's wholly-owned corporation holds a $47,000 demand note of the partnership may make it difficult to sell the business as a going concern. Defendant fears that upon dissolution he will receive very little and that plaintiff, who is the managing partner and knows how to conduct the operations of the partnership, will receive a business that has become very profitable because of the establishment of Vandenberg Air Force Base in its vicinity. Defendant charges that plaintiff has been content to share the losses but now that the business has become profitable he wishes to keep all the gains.

There is no showing in the record of bad faith or that the improved profit situation is more than temporary. In any event these contentions are irrelevant to the issue whether the partnership is for a term or at will. Since, however, this action is for a declaratory judgment and will be the basis for future action by the parties, it is appropriate to point out that defendant is amply protected by the fiduciary duties of co-partners.

Even though the Uniform Partnership Act provides that a partnership at will may be dissolved by the express will of any partner (§31(1)(b)), this power, like any other power held by a fiduciary, must be exercised in good faith. . . .

[P]laintiff has the power to dissolve the partnership by express notice to defendant. If, however, it is proved that plaintiff acted in bad faith and violated his fiduciary duties by attempting to appropriate to his own use the new prosperity of the partnership without adequate compensation to his co-partner, the dissolution would be wrongful and the plaintiff would be liable [for damages for breach of partnership agreement] as provided by U. P.A. §38(2)(a) (rights of partners upon wrongful dissolution) for violation of the implied agreement not to exclude defendant wrongfully from the partnership business opportunity.

The judgment is reversed. . . .

QUESTIONS ON PAGE v. PAGE

1. Like *Meinhard v. Salmon*, which it resembles, *Page* has excited considerable commentary. See, e.g., Robert W. Hillman, *The Dissatisfied Participant in the Solvent Business Venture: A Consideration of the Relative Permanence of Partnerships and Close Corporations*, 67 Minn. L. Rev. 1, 33 (1982).

2. How should *Page* have been decided? Consider three possibilities: (1) by ruling that the partnership implied a term, as the trial court did; (2) by holding, with Justice Traynor, that the power to dissolve the partnership was constrained by fiduciary duty (what would violate this duty?); or (3) by ruling that the statutory power to wind up the partnership was unconstrained and absolute.

3.6 LIMITED LIABILITY MODIFICATIONS OF THE PARTNERSHIP FORM

The general partnership form has the bare minimum of features necessary to establish an investor-owned legal entity: (1) a dedicated pool of business assets, (2) a class of beneficial owners (the partners), and (3) a clearly delineated class of agents authorized to act for the entity (again, the partners). The separation between the partnership as a legal entity and the investors who finance it can be further increased by adding limited liability as a fourth element of the form. Limited liability means that business creditors cannot proceed against the personal assets of some or all of a firm's equity investors. Put differently, to the extent that investors enjoy limited liability, business creditors can rely on the assets of the partnership, but these are also the *only* assets on which they can rely.

3.6.1   The Limited Partnership

Traditionally, the partnership was modified to introduce limited liability for investors by adding to the general partnership so-called limited partners, who did not manage the business. Limited partners share in profits without incurring personal liability for business debts. Thus, all limited partnerships must have at least one general partner, with unlimited liability, in addition to one or more limited partners.

In the United States, limited partnerships are generally governed by the Uniform Limited Partnership Act (ULPA) or the Revised Uniform Limited Partnership Act (RULPA). The general partner in a limited partnership is treated almost exactly like a member of an ordinary partnership, e.g., the general partner is personally liable for partnership debts, may bind the partnership in dealings with third parties, and so forth. The limited partner, however, may participate in the profits of enterprise but enjoy liability limited to his or her partnership contribution. Limited partners may not participate in management or "control," beyond voting on major decisions such as dissolution. If limited partners do exercise management powers, they risk losing their limited liability protection as de facto general partners.

Limited partnerships have traditionally been popular because they combine the pass-through tax advantages of partnership — partnership income and losses are deemed to be those of the individual partners — with limited liability. Increasingly, the limited liability company (LLC), considered below, is encroaching on the traditional turf of limited partnerships, such as active investment companies, oil and gas ventures, real estate investment companies, and the like.

In addition, since 1987, any enterprise with publicly traded equity — whether limited partnership, limited liability company, or corporation — faces the same two-tier tax treatment as a corporation under subchapter C of the Internal Revenue Code (IRC). See IRC §7704(a); Treas. Reg. §301.7701-2(b)(7). That is, the enterprise is taxed on its entity income, and its investors are taxed again, at individual rates, when that income is distributed. The test for double taxation is whether or not ownership interests of the firm are traded either on an established securities market, such as the New York Stock Exchange, or on a secondary market or equivalent, such as the NASDAQ Stock Market. (The blanket rule of double taxation for entities with publicly traded equity has special exceptions for mutual funds, real estate investment trusts, and other entities that satisfy tests in the tax code. E.g., IRC §7704(c).)

NOTE ON "CONTROL" IN LIMITED PARTNERSHIPS

Following the common law, Section 7 of the original Uniform Limited Partnership Act established that the hallmark of a general partner in a limited partnership is that she "takes part in the control of the business." This principle — that limited partners who remain passive escape personal liability for partnership debts — finds its roots in the creditor protection rules developed in ancient Rome and the Middle Ages.[7] The theoretical explanation for the control test is that those who can actively shift assets out of the firm, or make risky decisions, should be held personally liable to prevent opportunism against partnership creditors. This opportunism concern does not apply to passive investors, who do not control the enterprise and cannot shift assets — hence we do not hold the limited partners liable for partnership debts.[8]

Despite the strong theoretical underpinnings for a control test, the evolution of the Uniform Limited Partnership Act over the past twenty years indicates a progression away from a "control" test for determining when limited partners will be held liable for partnership debts. Section 303 of the 1976 Revised Uniform Partnership Act adopts the control test, but adds the qualification that a limited partner who participates in the control of the business is liable "only to persons who transact business with the limited partnership reasonably believing, based on the limited partner's conduct, that the limited partner is a general partner." Section 303 of the 2001 Uniform Partnership Act entirely abandons the control test, stating that a limited partner is not personally liable for partnership liabilities "even if the limited partner participates in the management and control of the enterprise." The Comment to Section 303 of the 2001 Uniform Act states: "This section provides a full, status-based liability shield for each limited partner. . . . In a world with LLPs, LLCs, and, most importantly, LLLPs, the control rule has become an anachronism. This Act therefore takes the next logical step in the evolution of the limited partner's liability shield and renders the control rule extinct."

Although the control rule is now an anachronism, most LP agreements vest virtually complete control of the enterprise in the hands of its general partners.

QUESTION

Many venture capital and private equity funds are organized as limited partnerships. Under the typical terms, the fund is a limited partnership with a ten-year term. The limited partners give money to the VC for ten years. The general partners pick the investments. The general partners get 2% of the total funds under management each year, plus 20% of the profits at the end of the ten-year term. As funds have generally grown larger in recent years, the 2% annual management fee has become quite large at successful firms: in 2006, for example, private equity firms Kohlberg, Kravis & Roberts

---

7. See Henry Hansmann, Reinier Kraakman & Richard Squire, *Law and the Rise of the Firm*, 119 Harv. L. Rev. 1333 (2006). Under Roman law, the eldest male, or *pater familias*, of a wealthy aristocratic family could set aside funds to capitalize a business managed by a slave or by a son of the *pater familias*. Technically, these funds continued to belong to the *pater familias*. But as long as the *pater familias* did not exercise managerial control over the business, the *pater familias* could not be held liable on the debts of the business beyond the funds (called the *peculium*) that he had contributed to the business. See *id*. at 1358-60.

8. See id.

(KKR) and Texas Pacific Group (TPG) both announced $10 billion funds, which would give them each $200 million per year in management fees under the typical deal. Given that the limited partners exercise no control, what factors protect them from exploitation by the general partners at KKR or TPG? (Or, put more bluntly, why don't the KKR and TPG general partners take their $200 million each year for ten years and just sit on a beach?)

3.6.2   Limited Liability Partnerships and Companies

The search to combine partnership taxation with limited liability has produced two novel business entities in recent years: the registered limited liability partnership (LLP) and the limited liability company (LLC).

3.6.2.1   The Limited Liability Partnership

The limited liability partnership is just what the name implies: a general partnership in which partners retain limited liability, at least for certain liabilities and limited periods. Texas adopted the first LLP statute in 1991; since then all other states have followed suit. Most of the new statutes clearly intend to protect professionals such as lawyers and accountants. They limit liability only with respect to partnership liabilities arising from the negligence, malpractice, wrongful act, or misconduct of another partner or an agent of the partnership not under the partners' direct control. See, e.g., Delaware Limited Liability Partnership Act, §1515(b), in your statutory supplement. (*Query*: If you were to pick one form of liability protection for partners, would it be protection against "vicarious" liability for partnership torts as opposed to commercial debts?) By contrast, a few LLP statutes, including those of New York and Minnesota, extend liability protection to partnership contract debts as well as tort liabilities.

In addition, some LLP statutes establish minimum capitalization or insurance requirements. For example, Delaware requires at least $1,000,000 in insurance coverage or segregated assets available for creditors to substitute for the unlimited liability of partners for business torts. See Del. LLP Act, §1546(a) & (d). Is such a minimum capitalization requirement an adequate substitute for personal liability?

QUESTION

After New York passed its LLP statute in 1994, one study shows that 67% of law firms headquartered in New York City chose LLP status, while 13% remained general partnerships and the remaining 20% were split between PCs (professional corporations) and LLCs (discussed below). See Scott Baker & Kimberly D. Krawiec, *The Economics of Limited Liability: An Empirical Study of New York Law Firms*, 2005 U. Ill. L. Rev. 107 (2005). Is it clearly a mistake for a law firm to organize as a general partnership, when limited liability vehicles are now available? If not, what kinds of law firms do you think would be likely to make the jump from GP to LLP status?

3.6.2.2   The Limited Liability Company[9]

The LLC is more popular but less easily described than the LLP because, of the 50 state LLC statutes adopted since 1977, no two are exactly alike. Yet the general contours of this legal form are reasonably clear. Internal relations among investors in the LLC (known as "members") are to be governed more or less by general or limited partnership law: Members may operate the firm and serve as its agents, just as general partners do, or elect "managers" to do so, as in limited partnerships or corporations; the resignation of a member may or may not lead to dissolution; and so on. Like limited partnerships, LLCs must file a copy of their articles of organization with the secretary of state. Moreover, unlike limited partners, the members of an LLC enjoy limited liability even when they exercise control over the business in much the same way that a general partner would.

The rise of LLCs was primarily tax-driven, and until 1997, all LLC statutes were drafted with an eye toward qualifying for partnership (or pass-through) taxation under IRS regulations (repealed in 1997) that provided that an LLC would be taxed like a corporation if it possessed three or more of the following four corporate characteristics: (i) limited liability for the owners of the business, (ii) centralized management, (iii) freely transferable ownership interests, and (iv) continuity of life. During this era, LLC drafters relied on failing the corporate resemblance test by lacking both free transferability of interests and continuity of life.

Limits on continuity of life took the form of requirements that LLCs involuntary dissolve upon the happening of specified events. Restrictions on transfer took the form of a requirement that transferees of LLC interests not become members unless all or a specified percentage of remaining members consented, as provided in the LLC articles of organization. Transferees not approved by remaining members obtain only the distribution rights of the transferor. See ULLCA §503; Delaware LLCA §18-702. As noted above, the publicly traded partnership rules of IRC §7704 treat all publicly held LLCs as C corporations for tax purposes, so that transfer limitations are usually not a problem for LLCs; nevertheless, the legal right to transfer ownership interests freely can be important, even for non-publicly traded firms, to attract passive investment capital.

Unlike the usually benign features of transfer restrictions, limits on continuity of life raise concerns that should be familiar from our coverage of partnerships. The ULLCA addresses continuity, as does the UPA, by permitting members to designate in the articles of organization that the LLC is for a term; if no term is set, the LLC is an at-will LLC. See ULLCA §203(d). In an at-will company, the members have the power, and generally the right, to rightfully withdraw at any time. Upon

---

9. We are grateful to Professor John Coates for revising and updating this note on LLCs.

withdrawal, members are entitled to a payment of the fair value of their membership interest. In a term LLC, the members have the power to withdraw, but generally not the unlimited right to withdraw, and do not receive the fair value of their interest until the end of the stated duration in the articles of organization.

The rules changed significantly in 1997. After nearly every state had adopted an LLC statute, the Internal Revenue Service (IRS) proposed (in 1996) and adopted (in 1997) new rules (known as "check the box" regulations) that scrapped the four-factor test. The new rules allow all new unincorporated businesses (including general and limited partnerships, LLCs, and LLPs) to *choose* whether to be taxed as partnerships or corporations. The new "check the box" rules are in the statutory supplement. See IRS Reg. §§7701-1 through 7701-3; IRS Notice 95-14, 1995-14 IRB 7 (proposing "check the box" rules).

LLCs now can combine pass-through treatment for federal income tax purposes with limited liability, participation in control by members (without loss of limited liability), free transferability of interests, and continuity of life. In addition, LLC statutes generally offer more flexibility than corporate statutes in the form of near-complete freedom to "opt out" of default rules.

By contrast, closely held corporations that seek pass-through tax treatment must comply with the ownership limitations of subchapter S of the IRC, such as a single class of stock and 75 or fewer noncorporate shareholders. LLCs and other unincorporated entities also enjoy federal tax advantages beyond those available even to S corporations, such as the ability to pass entity-level debt through to members for income tax purposes and the ability to adjust the inside basis of a firm's assets upon the death of an owner, transfer of ownership interests, or distributions from the firm. See IRC §§752, 754.

Subchapter S still offers some benefits over LLCs and other unincorporated entities. "S corps" (but not LLCs or other firms taxed as partnerships) may participate in tax-free reorganizations with subchapter C corporations (which include all publicly held corporations). See IRC §1371(a). In addition, if managers of a new entity expect to sell stock to the public in the near future, incorporation may be the best choice, given that the IRC taxes all new publicly held business organizations as corporations, and many start-ups encounter minimal taxes prior to going public. Finally, even ten years after check-the-box made LLCs particularly attractive, there is still considerable uncertainty as to how courts will address issues such as authority, creditors' rights, fiduciary duties, and dissolution for LLCs—perhaps courts will apply partnership principles, perhaps they will apply close corporation principles, or perhaps they will devise yet another set of "gap-filling" rules.

The tiny state of Delaware is an early leader in the market for LLCs. The Delaware legislature passed its LLC statute in 1992,[10] and by 2005 approximately 7% of all new LLCs were chartered in Delaware, second only to

10. Delaware Limited Liability Company Act, 6 Del. C. 18-101, et. seq. (effective October 1, 1992).

Florida's 10%. Delaware's large share can be attributed, at least in part, to its dominance in corporate charters, which we will examine in Chapter 4. In addition, Delaware practitioners point to the flexibility of the Delaware LLC statute: for example, unlike LLCs in several other states, Delaware LLCs may provide professional services; unlike other states which prohibit the contribution of services, the Delaware statute permits members to contribute cash, property or services, or obligations to contribute any of these in in the future; and as a catch-all, the Delaware LLC statute explicitly provides that "[i]t is the policy of this chapter to give maximum effect to the principle of freedom of contract and to the enforceability of limited liability agreements."[11] Delaware practitioners also point to the confidentiality that is permitted in a Delaware LLC. Unlike some states that require the names of the initial managers and/or members of the LLC to be disclosed, the Certificate of Formation for a Delaware LLC does not.

Despite the flexibility inherent in Delaware's LLC statute, the emerging case law suggests that Delaware courts will still impose fiduciary duties on LLC members that go beyond what the LLC operating agreement requires — that is, freedom of contract cannot entirely replace traditional principles of fiduciary duty in LLCs. For example, in *Solar Cells, Inc. v. True North Partners, LLC*,[12] True North controlled three out of the five managers of First Solar, LLC, while Solar Cells controlled the other two. The True North managers secretly approved a merger with a wholly-owned subsidiary of True North, which would have diluted Solar Cells' stake in First Solar from 50% to 5%. In Delaware Chancery Court, the True North managers defended their actions based on the contractual limitations on their fiduciary duties in the First Solar operating agreement. Nevertheless, the court granted an injunction against the merger, on the grounds that the operating agreement still contained a requirement to act in good faith.

Of course, what would have happened without the good faith requirement in the First Solar operating agreement remains an open question in Delaware. But in the LP context, the Delaware Supreme Court has indicated in dicta that while a partner's fiduciary duties may be restricted, they may not be completely eliminated.[13] We examine fiduciary duties in the corporate form in Chapters 8 and 9. It will be interesting to see how the contours of fiduciary duty in LLCs borrow, or not, from corporate law principles.

In order to judge the success of LLCs relative to other organizational forms simply in terms of number of entities, the table on page 80 presents the number of new corporations, LLCs, and LLPs over the past ten years, for Delaware and two other leading business-entity jurisdictions.

The statistics reveal at least a few interesting patterns. First, Delaware's new corporate charter business has actually declined over the period, at an annualized rate of 4.3%. Second, Delaware has moved the most quickly into the LLC form, with almost half of its new entities during this period coming from LLCs. Third, California's share of new corporations has increased at an

---

11. 6 Del. C. 18-1101.
12. Solar Cells, Inc. v. True North Partners, LLC, 2002 WL 749173 (Del. Ch. 2002).
13. Gotham Partners v. Hallwood Realty Partners, 817 A.2d 160 (Del. 2002).

Formations of New Entities and Qualifications by Out-of-State Entities

State	Entity	1996	1997	1998	1999	2000	2001	2002	2003	2004	2005	CAGR 96-05	% of Total New Entities
Delaware	Corp.	51,272	52,184	48,074	53,687	59,071	39,289	36,256	32,180	33,047	34,377	-4.34%	46%
	LLC	10,888	15,967	30,793	40,131	48,041	43,434	47,726	49,551	69,136	87,792	26.10%	47%
	LP	5,125	5,826	6,301	6,827	7,821	5,647	5,740	5,572	7,812	8,742	6.11%	7%
California	Corp.	44,043	47,055	48,836	53,054	54,275	70,031	78,935	83,763	92,949	97,432	9.22%	62%
	LLC	12,151	17,979	23,190	27,987	29,675	32,344	37,429	45,724	58,097	70,024	21.48%	33%
	LP	5,213	5,552	5,478	4,659	5,035	5,161	4,893	5,560	5,734	5,775	1.06%	5%
New York	Corp.	73,866	74,397	72,568	75,276	75,992	73,410	77,650	78,104	79,231	76,999	0.46%	71%
	LLC	11,170	14,454	18,101	21,510	24,778	25,887	34,193	40,768	47,967	54,847	19.34%	28%
	LP	2,015	1,899	1,647	1,554	1,662	1,513	1,470	1,357	1,466	1,495	-3.26%	2%

Source: Annual Report of the Jurisdictions, 1996-2005

annualized rate of 9.2%. Note that the sharpest increase in California and sharpest decrease in Delaware come in 2000-01, suggesting that the Delaware and California trends may be related.

Perhaps most importantly, the chart shows that LLCs have grown at a much faster rate than either corporations or limited partnerships, with double-digit annual growth rates in all three jurisdictions examined. However, it is important to not lose sight of the fact that the primary engine for wealth generation in the United States (and all other developed economies) still resides in the corporate form. The following chart shows gross value added of corporate businesses in the United States as a percent of U.S. gross domestic product since the end of World War II.

Contribution of U.S. corporations to total GDP, 1947-2005

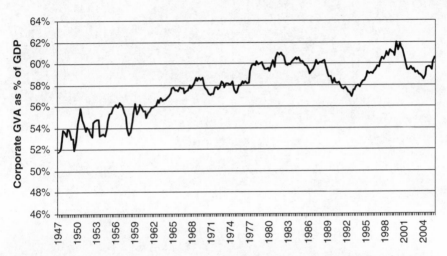

Source: U.S. Bureau of Economic Statistics. Corporations are defined as business entities that file Form 1120 with the IRS, and so includes LLCs that elect to be taxed as corporations.

This chart shows that the contribution of corporations to overall U.S. GDP has increased during the post-WWII era, from approximately 50% of GDP in 1947 to approximately 60% today. This 60% figure has remained relatively stable over the past ten years, even though the numbers of LLCs and other pass-through entities have increased dramatically during this period. These findings are consistent with conventional wisdom among practitioners that the growth of LLCs and LLPs has come primarily at the expense of LPs and GPs, and not corporations. It provides the motivation for a detailed analysis of the corporate form, which we turn to now.

THE CORPORATE FORM

4.1 INTRODUCTION TO THE CORPORATE FORM

From Delaware to Dushanbe, the corporation is the standard legal form adopted by large-scale private enterprises. Why? The answer lies in the contracting problems engendered by the UPA-type general partnership: personal liability of those who contribute capital, instability of the firm, illiquidity of an individual's investment, and cumbersome joint management. The basic characteristics of the corporate form offset all these weaknesses. These attributes are

1. legal personality with indefinite life
2. limited liability for investors
3. free transferability of share interests
4. centralized management
5. appointed by equity investors[1]

Historically, the corporation emerged as a response to the limitations of the partnership for financing the increasingly capital-intensive enterprises of the nineteenth century. Even today, while the limited partnership and the LLC forms ameliorate the limitations of the general partnership, the corporation remains a superior structure for capitalizing large firms. One reason is that the corporation's legal characteristics have strongly complementary qualities. Limited liability, for example, makes free transferability more valuable by reducing the costs associated with transfers of interest. (The value of shares is independent of the assets of their owners.) Free transferability permits the development of large capital (equity or stock) markets, which are also advanced by the presence of centralized management. (Again, if I must learn about how to manage a business in order to invest in it, I might not invest at all.) These characteristics combine to make the corporation a highly efficient legal form for enterprise organization. This is especially so where large aggregations

---

1. A similar list may be found in Robert Charles Clark, Corporate Law 4-24 (1986) and, prior to 1997, in the tax law. See Rev. Rul. 88-76 (1988) (recognizing pass-through taxation for certain LLCs). All commercial jurisdictions have at least one statutory form with these five features as default options.

of capital are required and complex operations demand specialized management.

Some Analytical Distinctions.   Although most corporations possess all of what we have termed "core features,"[2] there are at least two very basic distinctions among businesses organized as corporations. The first is between "public" corporations and "closely held," or "close," corporations. The second distinction is between corporations that are controlled by a single shareholder or a small group of affiliated persons (controlled corporations) and corporations that lack a controlling shareholder or control group. In the latter case, practical control over the affairs of the corporation resides with the company's incumbent managers.

Close Corporations.   Closely held corporations (so named because they have few shareholders) are often businesses that incorporate for tax or liability purposes rather than for capital-raising purposes. Because they tend to be small, their shareholders are also likely to be their officers and directors. (Indeed, in close corporations, shareholders often take their investment return as a tax-deductible salary rather than as a dividend.) Such firms frequently drop features of the corporate form that conflict with their status as "incorporated partnerships." For example, their charters (or associated shareholder agreements) may contain features such as restrictions on transfers of shares; "buy-sell agreements" allowing any shareholder to name a price at which she is willing to buy out her fellow shareholders or sell her own shares; or commitments to make further capital contributions to the business. By contrast, firms that incorporate because they foresee a need to raise capital in the public capital markets (aspiring "public" firms) tend to adopt all the basic characteristics of the corporate form.

Whether a particular closely held business adopts the corporate form or another legal form usually depends on tax objectives and, secondarily, on transaction costs. (Organizing a small business as a no-frills corporation costs about half as much as forming a partnership or LLC because the corporate form supplies a more elaborate set of default provisions and requires less drafting.)

Controlled Corporations.   The second analytical distinction relates to the corporation's ownership structure — how a company's stock is held and who controls its voting rights. In some corporations, a single shareholder or group of shareholders exercises control through its power to appoint the board (these are termed "controlled corporations"). Where there is no such person or group, control is said to be "in the market." In other words, anyone can purchase control of these companies in the market by buying enough stock, but until they do, no shareholder or

---

2. Corporations that lack one of the core characteristics noted above are sometimes encountered. Many close corporations, for example, lack freely transferable shares. Historically, specially chartered corporations in the earlier part of the nineteenth century frequently lacked limited liability, as did California corporations until 1931. No corporation, however, lacks the characteristic of legal personality; it is the most elemental characteristic of the form.

group exercises control. This describes the ownership structure of most large public corporations in the United States and a few other countries today.[3] As long as control is in the market, of course, practical control resides with the existing management of the firm.

The major problems in corporation law deal with the relations between "outside" investors, who lack power, and "insiders," who control the company's assets, whether as controlling shareholders or as autonomous managers. To state the obvious, powerful insiders who are not constrained by law, morality, or incentives will generally find a way to increase their share of the enterprise's net returns. In the case of controlled corporations, tensions between public and controlling shareholders arise most clearly in the form of self-dealing transactions or appropriations of corporate opportunities (both addressed in Chapter 9). Such inter-shareholder conflicts between "controlling" and "minority" shareholders are characteristic of both controlled public corporations and many close corporations. In cases of corporations with no controller — where, as a practical matter, the firm's management is almost self-perpetuating — parallel tensions arise between shareholders as a class and said management. These conflicts emerge most clearly in the areas of executive compensation and insider trading.

4.2 CREATION OF A FICTIONAL LEGAL ENTITY

The corporation is considered a separate person in the eyes of the law. This seemingly mundane legal characteristic is extraordinarily important. Consider, for example, the simple act of acquiring a plot of ground. As a buyer, the corporation, acting through its authorized agents, may sign binding contracts, close sales, and so take title in its own name. Thereafter, it may deal with the acquired property as its board of directors deems expedient. Because its principal investors need not execute the transaction or even agree to it, the information and coordination costs of closing the transaction are minimal. Consider, too, the way in which a corporation's ability to own assets as a legal entity enables it to enter into contracts, such as bank loans. Creditors need to know what stands behind any borrower's promise to pay interest and principal. Enabling corporations to own assets — including businesses — delimits the pool of assets upon which corporate creditors can rely for repayment. If there were no separate corporate entity, a large creditor would be forced to investigate the asset holdings and creditworthiness of all the joint venturers — i.e., the company's shareholders — on the loan. Thus, the doctrinal fiction of an artificial entity vastly reduces the costs of contracting for credit.[4]

---

3. See Rafael La Porta, Florencio Lopez-de-Silanes, Andrei Schleifer & Robert W. Vishny, *Corporate Ownership Around the World*, 54 J. Fin. 471 (1999).

4. See Henry Hansmann & Reinier Kraakman, *The Essential Role of Organizational Law*, 110 Yale L.J. 387 (2000). Evolution of the tenancy in partnership, which we touched upon in Chapter 3, serves an analogous transaction cost reducing function for modern partnerships.

In addition to economizing on the monitoring costs of creditors, the status of the corporation as a fictive legal entity allows it to have an indefinite "life." This enhances the stability of the corporate form. Even without complex drafting, the death or departure of a "principal" need not disturb the operation of a corporation, as it would a partnership. Entity status, although seemingly pedestrian, is vital to business continuity, and it also supports the other corporate characteristics of tradable shares, centralized management, and limited liability.

4.2.1   A Note on the History of Corporate Formation

Today, anyone can create a corporation as a matter of right, quickly and inexpensively. This was not always so, however, and in some parts of the world, it is not so today. The story of the evolution of U.S. law — from a system in which incorporation was a privilege to one in which it is freely available and easily customized — helps to put the regulation of the corporate form in perspective.

Before the nineteenth century, creating a corporation was seen as a significant public act to be undertaken only to achieve a special public advantage. Indeed, in the England of the seventeenth and eighteenth centuries, corporations were formed chiefly for political or charitable purposes rather than for business ones. As J. Willard Hurst observes, "[T]he first English treatise on corporations [published in 1794] has little to say, and scant authority to cite, concerning use of the corporation for economic enterprise."[5] Thus, we can safely pass over the law of royally chartered English joint-stock companies and begin with American corporation law, which branched out early in the nineteenth century to reflect a distinctly American mix of social forces and ideologies.

Federal-State Division of Jurisdiction.   In the United States, the creation of corporations has from our earliest days been seen as requiring governmental action. The states were held to have reserved the sovereign power to form corporations when they joined the federal union.[6] While the

5. See James Willard Hurst, The Legitimacy of the Business Corporation in the Law of the United States, 1780-1970, at 3 (1970); Edwin M. Dodd, *Dogma and Practice in the Law of Associations*, 42 Harv. L. Rev. 977 (1929). Curiously, all corporation-like entities with the power to own assets and contract in their own name prior to the seventeenth century appear to have been what we would today term "nonprofit corporations." They include the Roman *collegia* as well as the monasteries, charitable institutions, and religious orders of the Middle Ages.

6. During the constitutional debates, Madison twice proposed that the federal government be given the power to grant corporate charters, but each proposal was defeated. James Madison, Journal of the Federal Convention 549-550 (E. Scott ed., 1893); James Madison, The Debates in the Federal Convention of 1787, at 420, 557, 563-564, 570 (Gaillard Hunt & James Scott eds., 1920); John W. Brabner-Smith, *Federal Incorporation of Business*, 24 Va. L. Rev. 159 (1937). The federal power to grant such charters is restricted to those that are necessary and proper to accomplish some expressly granted power, such as the power "to coin money and regulate the value thereof." U.S. Const. art. I, §8. It is a fundamental characteristic of our federalism that the various states have reserved the power to form corporations.

national government also gained the power to form corporations pursuant to its delegated powers, the internal regulation of business corporations was, in general, a matter governed by state law from the Republic's beginning. Specifically, under the so-called internal affairs doctrine, the law of the state of incorporation governs the internal affairs of a corporation, including such matters as who votes, on what, and how often.[7]

Special Acts of Incorporation.   In the earliest years of our Republic, state legislatures established corporations by passing individual acts of incorporation ("special acts"), which constituted certain named persons as a corporation, with specific enumerated powers, for a stated term. At first, these corporations were typically formed in order to address public needs, such as the transportation or infrastructure.[8]

Demand for incorporation grew with the American economy in the early nineteenth century. Supply, however, was restricted by the system of special acts. The task of enacting special bills for corporations became a heavy burden for state legislatures. More important, rationing the incorporation power by means of special acts became increasingly controversial for two reasons.[9] The first was the suspicion that legislatures were creating artificial entities that would in time come to dominate the social landscape.[10] The second basis of criticism of the special chartering system was the more reasonable claim that it corrupted public life by opening the legislature to the possibility of favoritism. The rich or well-connected could, by one technique or another, get a corporate franchise that might otherwise be denied.

General Incorporation Statutes.   General laws of incorporation, under which the corporate form would be equally available to all citizens through a uniform administrative process, unburdened the legislative

---

7. *CTS Corp. v. Dynamics Corp. of America*, 481 U.S. 69, 94 (1987); *Hart v. General Motors Corp.*, 129 A.D.2d 179, 183-184, 517 N.Y.S.2d 490, 492-493 (1987); *Draper v. Gardner Defined Plan Trust*, 625 A.2d 859, 864-868 (Del. 1993).

8. Professor Hurst reports that, "of the 317 separate-enterprise special charters from 1780 to 1801 in the states, nearly two-thirds were for enterprises concerned with transport (inland navigation, turnpikes, toll bridges); another 20 percent were for banks or insurance companies; 10 percent were for the provision of local public services (mostly water companies); and less than 4 percent were for general business corporations." Hurst, supra note 5, at 17.

9. Lawrence M. Friedman, A History of American Law 197 (1985).

10. This possibility was deeply upsetting to the egalitarian sensibility of the Jacksonian Democrats of the early to mid-nineteenth century. One critic in 1833, for example, published the view that, "[a]gainst corporations of every kind, the objection may be brought that whatever power is given to them is so much taken from either the government or the people . . . . [T]he very existence of monied corporations is incompatible with equality of rights . . . " (William M. Gouge, Short History of Paper Money and Banking in the United States 17 (2d ed. 1835). See also Bray Hammond, Banks and Politics in America from the Revolution to the Civil War 54-63 (1957). This first level of criticism tended to conflate the legislative grant of a monopoly franchise with the legislative grant of a corporate franchise. While these two types of franchise may often have been awarded together — as in the case of banks, railroads, or ferries — with respect to increasingly important mercantile or manufacturing businesses, they were not logically tied to one another. See Hurst, supra note 5, at 33-42.

process and removed a source of corruption.[11] Although other states permitted incorporation early on for limited purposes,[12] New York led the way in 1811 with the first broadly available incorporation statute.[13] Connecticut followed in 1837 with a general statute that allowed incorporation for "any lawful purpose." Nevertheless, these early statutes failed to slow the flood of special incorporation acts. It was not until 1845, when Louisiana adopted a constitution that banned special corporations (except for political or municipal purposes), that an effective antidote to special legislative incorporation was found.[14] The movement toward exclusive general laws governing incorporation remained the dominant issue of nineteenth-century American corporation law until the 1880s, by which time general acts of incorporation had become the norm.

The Erosion of Regulatory Corporate Law.   If the dominant corporate law story of the nineteenth century is the movement toward general acts of incorporation, the dominant story of the twentieth century is the movement from the general statutes with mandatory governance terms to today's statutes, which are largely free of substantive regulation. Corporate managers and controlling shareholders drove this process. The fact that corporate law is state, rather than federal, law in the United States gave those who sought a more "liberal" corporate law an important means to their objective at the end of the nineteenth century. Chartering states that attracted new incorporations reaped franchise fees (a tax levied on the privilege of forming and maintaining a corporation). Moreover, lawyers in these states benefited from successful incorporations.

Of course, this evolution was not driven exclusively by the special interests of corporate managers and controlling shareholders. Larger forces were also at work. The arrival of a freely accessible corporate form tended to complement (or, if you prefer, was driven by) the same forces in the economy that promoted the development of complex new forms of industrial organization. Especially during the last quarter of the nineteenth century, the United States experienced phenomenal economic growth. Burgeoning populations, enormous infrastructural investments (railroads, telegraph lines, etc.), and rapidly evolving technologies created large markets and large economies of scale and scope, and thus opportunities for large-scale enterprise that favored the corporate form. In addition, the evolution of a new class of managers and the rise of liquid markets for stock favored the emergence of large corporate structures that could capture the new financial and technical economies.[15]

11. See, e.g., Henry N. Butler, *Nineteenth Century Jurisdictional Competition in the Granting of Corporate Privileges*, 14 J. Legal Stud. 129 (1985).

12. North Carolina, in 1795, and Massachusetts, in 1799, enacted such statutes for canal companies or aqueducts. See E. Merrick Dodd, American Business Corporations Until 1860, at 228 (1954).

13. Laws N.Y. ch. 47 (1811).

14. *Christopher v. Brusselback*, 302 U.S. 500, 502-503 (1938); *Bernheimer v. Converse*, 206 U.S. 516, 528-529 (1907); *Keehn v. Hodge Drive-It-Yourself, Inc.*, 64 N.E.2d 117, 120 (Ohio 1945).

15. Alfred D. Chandler, The Visible Hand: The Management Revolution in American Business (1977); Alfred D. Chandler, Scale and Scope: The Dynamics of Industrial Capitalism (1990).

New Jersey began the process of liberalizing incorporation statutes and rapidly attracted new incorporations as a result. By 1894, one commentator reported, "New Jersey is a favorite state for incorporation. Her laws seem to be framed with a special view to attracting incorporation fees and business fees . . . and she has largely succeeded."[16] New Jersey's statute contained many innovations, but among the most important was that it authorized corporations to own the stock of other corporations.[17] This permitted the holding company structure, which, in turn, made possible corporate joint ventures and networks of corporations related by ownership, sometimes called corporate groups.

States liberated the corporate form in other ways as well. Corporations could now have perpetual (or, more accurately, indefinite) existence. They could do business anywhere. They could be organized for any lawful purpose (with the general exception of banking). Capital requirements became more flexible: Corporations were not required to have a stated minimum capital or a limit on either their authorized equity capital or the debt they could issue. They could amend their certificates of incorporation, own and vote stock of other corporations, own land without limit, and merge with other corporations. While these changes may seem modest today, they raised howls of protest at the time.

States began to compete in a "race" to deregulate.[18] In 1890, New York abandoned its limitation on maximum authorized capital and, to a limited extent, permitted intercorporation ownership of stock.[19] Nevertheless, these changes failed to stem the flow of incorporation to New Jersey, and in 1892, New York amended its statute further to permit corporate ownership of stock without limitation. Other states soon got into the act. In 1899, Delaware adopted what was, in essence, the New Jersey statute as its general law of incorporation.[20] Although Maine and West Virginia did so as

16. Cook on Stock and Stockholders 1604-1605 (1894), quoted in *Liggett Co. v. Lee*, 288 U.S. 517, 558 n.34 (Brandeis, J., dissenting).

17. General Corporation Law of New Jersey, §51 (1896). The story of the politics behind the enactment of this first "modern" general corporation law is a fascinating one involving the legal talent and political skill of one of the leading Wall Street legal practitioners of his age.

18. One of the most long-standing and voluminous debates in corporate law is whether this regulatory competition constitutes a "race to the top" or a "race to the bottom." The first commentators on opposing sides of the debate were former SEC Commissioner William L. Cary and Ralph K. Winter. Compare William T. Cary, *Federalism and Corporate Law: Reflections upon Delaware*, 83 Yale L. J. 663 (1974) (describing "this race for the bottom, with Delaware in the lead") with Ralph K. Winter, Jr., *State Law, Shareholder Protection, and the Theory of the Corporation*, 6 J. Leg. Stud. 251 (1977) (arguing for a "race to the top"). For the leading modern commentators, compare Lucian Arye Bebchuk, *Federalism and the Corporation: The Desirable Limits on State Competition in Corporate Law*, 105 Harv. L. Rev. 1435, 1440 (1992) (arguing that "state competition produces a race for the top with respect to some corporate issues but a race for the bottom with respect to others") with Roberta Romano, The Genius of American Corporate Law 16 (1993) (stating that "the evidence supports the view that states do compete for the chartering business" and that this "benefits rather than harms shareholders").

19. New York Business Corporation Law, ch. 567 '12 (1890); see also *Liggett*, 288 U.S. at 560-565.

20. See Note, *Little Delaware Makes Bid for the Organization of Trusts*, 33 Am. L. Rev. 418 (1899).

well, it was tiny Delaware that took the lead. When New Jersey Governor and future U.S. President Woodrow Wilson cracked down on New Jersey's permissive corporate code in the 1910s, companies flocked to Delaware. Delaware quickly gained a dominant share and never looked back: by 1965, 35 percent of companies listed on the New York Stock Exchange (NYSE) were incorporated in Delaware; by 1973 this number had risen to 40 percent; and by 2000 approximately half of all NYSE companies were incorporated in Delaware.

As corporation statutes evolved over the twentieth century, most of the remaining mandatory regulation of internal corporate governance gradually fell away. More technical, but equally important, liberalizations include the disappearance of shareholder preemptive rights,[21] the broadening of lawful consideration for stock, the disappearance of par value as a minimum consideration for stock, and the repeated liberalization of merger law. The typical corporation statute of today, such as the Delaware General Corporation Law (DGCL), is a nonregulatory, "enabling" statute with few mandatory features. However, complementary evolutionary phenomena should also be mentioned. As corporate management's freedom to act grew under the enabling approach of modern statutes, and as shareholders of public companies also grew more numerous and disaggregated, courts came to give greater weight to the judicially created "fiduciary duty" of corporate directors and officers, and the federal government began to regulate public companies under the aegis of securities law, which has some of the rule-like, mandatory flavor of early corporation law. See generally Chapters 5, 9, and 14.

4.2.2   The Process of Incorporating Today

The process of incorporating today is nicely reflected in §§2.01 to 2.04 of the Revised Model Business Corporation Act (RMBCA). A flesh-and-blood individual (or other entity, since corporations and partnerships may themselves form new corporations) called an "incorporator" signs the requisite documents and pays the necessary fees. While incorporators create corporations initially, they are often clerks or secretaries who act in a purely ministerial capacity.[22] The incorporator drafts (or has prepared) and signs a document called either the articles of incorporation (under the RMBCA) or the certificate of incorporation (under the DGCL). In both instances, this foundational document is colloquially termed the corporation's "charter." The articles of incorporation state the purpose and powers of the corporation and define all of its special features, with great flexibility being afforded

---

21. Preemptive rights (conferred on shareholders either by statute or in the documents creating the corporation) allow a shareholder to buy stock in any future corporate offering of new stock, up to such amount as is required to permit a shareholder to maintain his or her proportionate interest in the corporation.

22. Recognition of the ministerial nature of the incorporator's role is reflected in the fact that, while statutes formerly required three or more such persons, one is sufficient under current statutes.

to the designer of the firm's legal structure. Today, the purposes of the corporation are typically put forth in an extremely broad statement, such as "to engage in any lawful act or activity for which corporations may be organized under this title." DGCL §102(a)(3). The company charter will contain any customized features of the new enterprise, such as a complex capital structure (discussed more fully in Chapter 5) or customized voting rights. More often, however, the charter is a generic document with few special features. After it is duly executed, the charter is filed with a designated public official, usually the secretary of state. This filing also identifies the corporation's principal office within the state or, if there is none, the name of an agent in the state upon whom process may be served.

Upon filing, a fee will be due, naturally. In Delaware, the fee may be calculated in part as a function of how many shares the new corporation is authorized to issue. This technique is a crude form of price discrimination because bigger businesses will tend to issue more shares and thus will be willing and able to pay a higher fee.[23] In Delaware, the corporation's legal life begins when its charter is filed. DGCL §106. After the articles are filed and the fee is paid, the secretary of state issues the corporation's charter, which is a copy of the articles attached to a certificate of good standing, signed by the secretary of state. In other jurisdictions, the corporation's existence begins only when the secretary of state issues a charter.

The first acts of business in a newly formed corporation are electing directors (if initial directors are not named in the charter), adopting bylaws, and appointing officers. These actions take place at an organizational meeting, which is called either by the incorporators, who elect the initial board of directors, or, when the initial board is named in the articles of incorporation, by the board members themselves. See DGCL §108; RMBCA §2.05. Sample bylaws and minutes of an organizational meeting of the board of directors are included in your statutory supplement. See also RMBCA §2.06.

4.2.3   The Articles of Incorporation, or "Charter"

The articles of incorporation (or charter) may contain any provision that is not contrary to law. Modern American corporation statutes mandate only a few terms in the charter. The charter must, for example, provide for voting stock, a board of directors, and shareholder voting for certain transactions. Contractual freedom is, however, the overriding concept. Thus, the corporate charter will contain the most important "customized" features of the corporation, should there be any. If the corporation is to have a special or limited purpose, it will be stated here. If it is to have some governance oddity — say, that one class of stock will elect 75 percent of the board and a second class will elect the balance — this condition must be spelled out in the charter.

---

23. See Marcel Kamar & Ehud Kahan, *The Myth of State Competition in Corporate Law*, 55 Stan. L. Rev. 679 (2003).

Additionally, the charter must name the original incorporators, state the corporation's name and (very broadly) its business, and fix its original capital structure. Thus, the charter defines how many shares and classes of shares the corporation will be authorized to issue and what the characteristics of those shares will be: Will all shares vote? On all issues? In one class or separately? Will any have enhanced voting rights? Will they have par value?[24] Be redeemable? Be convertible? Will they be cumulatively voted? Will any shares have a preference on liquidation? Will the board be given the power to issue preferred stock with whatever terms it deems expedient (so-called blank-check preferred)? All these capital structure questions are appropriately answered in the charter and will be explained as we proceed.

Finally, the charter may establish the size of the board or include other governance terms, such as whether directors shall have concurrent one-year terms or staggered three-year terms,[25] and the procedures for removing directors from office.[26] Beyond such essentials, the charter may as a legal matter contain any provisions that are not in contravention of law. For example, it may even assign shareholders liability for corporate debts,[27] although this rarely happens.

4.2.4 The Corporate Bylaws

The bylaws are the least fundamental of the corporation's "constitutional" documents, which means they must conform to both the corporation statute and the corporation's charter.[28] Generally, bylaws fix the operating rules for the governance of the corporation. They establish, for example, the existence and responsibilities of corporate offices. If the certificate of incorporation does not mandate the size of the board of directors (which it rarely does) or the manner in which the size of the board is to be established, the bylaws will do so. The bylaws will also establish an annual meeting date or a formula by which such a meeting date will be fixed. They may empower an officer to call a stockholders' meeting, and they may establish procedures for the functioning of the board, such as the board's committee structure or quorum requirements.

Under some statutes, shareholders have the inalienable right to amend the bylaws.[29] Others limit this power to the board of directors.[30]

---

24. Par value stock — i.e., stock with a stated face value — is now largely of historical interest only in U.S. corporation law. Historically, it represented an amount of capital that creditors could rely on having been originally contributed to the firm in exchange for its stock. Corporations could not, and still cannot, pay dividends from amounts in the capital account attributable to par value. The story of how and why this concept was eroded by U.S. law (while still taken seriously in many nations) is an interesting one. See generally, Bayless Manning, *A Concise Textbook on Legal Capital* (1977).

25. See DGCL §141(d).

26. Id. §145(k).

27. Id. §102(b)(6).

28. Id. §109(b).

29. See DGCL §109(b).

30. See, e.g., 18 Okla. Stat. §1013 (2001).

Where shareholders are able to amend the charter, however, several questions remain. First, what voting rules apply to these amendments? Can directors overrule a shareholder amendment where the board possesses power to make bylaws itself, and how far can bylaws themselves limit the power to amend the bylaws? Because directors owe a fiduciary duty of loyalty to the corporation and its shareholders, courts have sometimes reviewed the directors' exercise of the power to modify and invalidate bylaws as an abuse of that power.[31] A problem of this type is most likely to arise where directors are arguably amending bylaws in order to protect their incumbency.

A question of current interest (and one that we will touch on when we deal with hostile corporate takeovers) is this: What limits, if any, restrict the topics that shareholder-initiated bylaws can legitimately govern? One might ask why anything should limit the shareholders in this way (other than their own agreement to such a limit in the corporate charter). This issue underscores the basic tension between the shareholders' powers and the board's power to manage the firm's business.

4.2.5 Shareholders' Agreements

Formal agreements among shareholders play an important part in the legal governance structures of many close corporations and in some controlled public corporations (although not in widely held public companies). Shareholders' agreements typically address such questions as restrictions on the disposition of shares, buy/sell agreements, voting agreements,[32] and agreements with respect to the employment of officers or the payment of dividends. Generally, the corporation is a party to these contracts. Thus, courts will specifically enforce these agreements where all shareholders are parties as well. But where some shareholders are not parties, specific enforcement — especially against the corporation — may turn on whether the agreement is fair to shareholders who were not signatories.

Where the voting of corporate stock is the subject of a shareholders' agreement, the agreement may take an even more formal form. A voting trust is an arrangement in which shareholders publicly agree to place their shares with a trustee who then legally owns them and is to exercise voting power according to the terms of the agreement. This formal arrangement is subject to special statutory restrictions.[33]

---

31. E.g., *State ex rel. Brumley v. Jessup & Moore Paper Co.*, 77 A. 16 (Del. Ch. 1916).
32. See DGCL §218(c).
33. Id. §218(a).

4.3   Limited Liability

We now turn to another fundamental characteristic of the corporate form: limited liability. Although the phrase is not quite accurate, long-time usage prevails over fussy correctness. Technically, neither corporations nor shareholders have limited liability. Corporations have unlimited liability, and shareholders, by reason of their shareholder status alone, have no liability for the debts or obligations of the corporation. Limited liability simply means that shareholders cannot lose more than the amount they invest (absent some special circumstances, discussed more fully later), unlike the general partner, who, under traditional principles, is legally a party to all partnership agreements and thus liable under them. Of course, limited liability is nothing more than a default term in the corporate form; a shareholder can undertake by contract to be a corporate guarantor. One empirical study finds that, among a sample of small corporations that filed Chapter 11 petitions in 1998, the owners had personally guaranteed the corporation's debt in 56 percent of the cases.[34]

In some ways, limited liability looks like the mirror image of entity status. After all, if the corporation *is* legally a separate person, why ought another legal person (a shareholder) be liable for its debts? While this notion has some surface appeal, it is not a functional argument and, historically, not always a persuasive one. Separate entity status for corporations coexisted with "unlimited" shareholder liability for a substantial period — until the 1930s in California, for example. But limited liability ultimately emerged as the general default rule for corporations everywhere, and there are sound economic reasons for its prevalence. First, limited liability vastly simplifies the job of evaluating an equity investment. A corporate investor who would naturally be concerned about his own liability can, under a limited liability regime, ignore low-probability events that may bankrupt the firm and, without limited liability, would visit a large liability on her. Nor need she be concerned with the financial status of co-venturers (as in a partnership), since in no event will she end up being jointly and severally liable with her co-investors. This savings encourages capital investment in equity securities. Second, the ability of the corporate form to segregate assets may encourage risk-averse shareholders to invest in risky ventures, such as biotech firms designing new medicines. Finally, limited liability may also increase the incentive for banks or other expert creditors to monitor their corporate debtors more closely.

Because limited liability represented a radical break with the common law liability rules of agency and partnership, its development took time. Shareholders only gradually won the protection of limited liability for private business ventures in the United States during the first half of the nineteenth century.[35] Great Britain established it later, with the Limited Liability Act of 1855. Only gradually did limited liability come to be seen as a

---

34. See Douglas Baird & Edward R. Morrison, *Serial Entrepreneurs and Small Business Bankruptcies*, 105 Colum. L. Rev. 8 (Table 17) (2005).

35. E. Merrick Dodd, *The Evolution of Limited Liability in American Industry: Massachusetts*, 61 Harv. L. Rev. 1351 (1948).

device that assisted people in arranging voluntary contractual relations. The change in attitude toward limited liability over the nineteenth century is suggested by the following two views. First, an excerpt from an 1824 editorial from the *Times* of London:

> Nothing can be so unjust as for a few persons abounding in wealth to offer a portion of their excess for the information of a company, to play with that excess for the information of a company — to lend the importance of their whole name and credit to the society [i.e., the company], and then should the funds prove insufficient to answer all demands, to retire into the security of their unhazarded fortune, and leave the bait to be devoured by the poor deceived fish.[36]

By contrast, about a century later, the *Economist* took a deeper view:

> The economic historian of the future may assign to the nameless inventor of the principle of limited liability, as applied to trading corporations, a place of honour with Watt and Stephenson, and other pioneers of the Industrial Revolution. The genius of these men produced the means by which man's command of natural resources has multiplied many times over; the limited liability company the means by which huge aggregations of capital required to give effect to their discoveries were collected, organized and efficiently administered.[37]

Setting aside the theoretically troubling problem of tort creditors, the chief purpose of limited liability is to encourage investment in equity securities and thus to make capital more available for risky ventures.

Judge Frank Easterbrook and Daniel Fischel elaborate on these points in the following excerpt.

FRANK EASTERBROOK & DANIEL FISCHEL, LIMITED LIABILITY AND THE CORPORATION

52 U. Chi. L. Rev. 89, 94-97 (1985)

THE RATIONALE OF LIMITED LIABILITY

. . . The separation of investment and management requires firms to create devices by which these participants monitor each other and guarantee their own performance. Neither group will be perfectly trustworthy. Moreover, managers who do not obtain the full benefits of their own performance do not have the best incentives to work efficiently. The costs of the separation of investment and management (agency costs) may be substantial. Nonetheless, we know from the survival of large corporations that the costs generated by agency relations are outweighed by the gains

---

36. As quoted in Paul Halpern, Michael Trebilcock, & Stuart Turnbull, *An Economic Analysis of Limited Liability in Corporate Law*, 30 U. Toronto L. Rev. 117 (1980).

37. Id. (quoting *Economist*, Dec. 18, 1926).

from separation and specialization of function. Limited liability reduces the costs of this separation and specialization.

First, limited liability decreases the need to monitor [managers]. All investors risk losing wealth because of the actions of agents. They could monitor these agents more closely. The more risk they bear, the more they will monitor. But beyond a point more monitoring is not worth the cost. . . . Limited liability makes diversification and passivity a more rational strategy and so potentially reduces the cost of operating the corporation.

Of course, rational shareholders understand the risk that the managers' acts will cause them loss. They do not meekly accept it. The price they are willing to pay for shares will reflect the risk. Managers therefore find ways to offer assurances to investors without the need for direct monitoring; those who do this best will attract the most capital from investors. . . .

Second limited liability reduces the costs of monitoring other shareholders. Under a rule exposing equity investors to additional liability, the greater the wealth of other shareholders, the lower the probability that any one shareholder's assets will be needed to pay a judgment. Thus existing shareholders would have incentives to engage in costly monitoring of other shareholders to ensure that they do not transfer assets to others or sell to others with less wealth. Limited liability makes the identity of other shareholders irrelevant and thus avoids these costs.

Third, by promoting free transfer of shares, limited liability gives managers incentives to act efficiently. . . . So long as shares are tied to votes, poorly run firms will attract new investors who can assemble large blocs at a discount and install new managerial teams. This potential for displacement gives existing managers incentives to operate efficiently in order to keep share prices high.

Although this effect of the takeover mechanism is well known, the relation between takeovers and limited liability is not. Limited liability reduces the costs of purchasing shares. Under a rule of limited liability, the value of shares is determined by the present value of the income stream generated by a firm's assets. The identity and wealth of other investors is irrelevant. Shares are fungible; they trade at one price in liquid markets. Under a rule of unlimited liability, . . . shares would not be fungible. . . . An acquiror who wanted to purchase a control bloc of shares under a rule of unlimited liability might have to negotiate separately with individual shareholders, paying different prices to each.

Worse, the acquiror in corporate control transactions typically is much wealthier than the investors from which it acquires the shares. The anticipated cost of additional capital contributions would be higher to the [acquiror] than [to other shareholders]. This may be quite important to a buyer considering the acquisition of a firm in financial trouble, for there would be a decent chance of being required to contribute to satisfy debts if the plan for revitalization of the firm should go awry. . . .

Fourth, limited liability makes it possible for market prices to impound additional information about the value of firms. With unlimited liability, shares would not be homogeneous commodities, so they would no longer have one market price. Investors would therefore be required to expend greater resources analyzing the prospects of the firm in order to know whether "the price is right"....

Fifth, as Henry Manne emphasized, limited liability allows more efficient diversification. Investors can minimize risk by owning a diversified portfolio of assets.... Diversification would increase rather than reduce risk under a rule of unlimited liability. If any one firm went bankrupt, an investor could lose his entire wealth. The rational strategy under unlimited liability, therefore, would be to minimize the number of securities held. As a result, investors would be forced to bear risk that could have been avoided by diversification, and the cost to firms of raising capital would rise.

Sixth, limited liability facilitates optimal investment decisions. When investors hold diversified portfolios, managers maximize investors' welfare by investing in any project with a positive net present value. They can accept [risky] ventures (such as the development of new products) without exposing the investors to ruin. Each investor can hedge against the failure of one project by holding stock in other firms....

Both those who want to raise capital for entrepreneurial ventures, and society as a whole, receive benefits from limited liability.... So long as the rule of liability is known, investors will price shares accordingly. The choice of an inefficient rule [of unlimited shareholder liability], however, will shrink the pool of funds available for investment in projects that would subject investors to risk. The increased availability of funds for projects with positive net values is the real benefit of limited liability.

QUESTION

What problem does limited liability potentially raise respecting tort claimants, and why? What legal rules might ameliorate this problem?

4.4 TRANSFERABLE SHARES

Corporate law everywhere provides that equity investors in the corporate entity legally own something distinct from any part of the corporation's property: They own a share interest. This share, or stock, is their personal legal property, and generally (i.e., absent special restrictions imposed by charter or contract), such a share may be transferred together with all rights that it confers.[38] Transferability permits the firm to conduct business uninterruptedly as the identities of its owners change, which avoids the complications of dissolution and reformation, which can affect partnerships.

---

38. This is the general effect. It is possible for the certificate of incorporation to create a type of stock that, upon transfer, has altered legal characteristics. However, this is rarely done.

As Easterbrook and Fischel argue in the excerpt above, the transferability of shares is intimately tied to limited liability. Absent limited liability, the creditworthiness of the firm as a whole could change, perhaps fundamentally, as the identities of its shareholders changed. Consequently, the value of shares would be difficult for potential purchasers to judge. Perhaps more important, each seller of shares could impose a cost on her fellow shareholders by selling to a buyer with fewer assets. It is not surprising, therefore, that limited liability and transferable shares are complementary features of the corporate form. This is in contrast to the partnership form, which lacks both features.

Equally significant, the ability of investors to freely trade stock encourages the development of an active stock market. An active market, in turn, facilitates investment by providing liquidity and by facilitating the inexpensive diversification of the risk of any equity investment. These factors make investing in corporate stock more attractive to savers and so increase the ability of the firm to raise capital. For these reasons, all of the important jurisdictions provide for free transferability of shares as the default regime for at least one class of corporations (sometimes referred to as "open" corporations).

Free transferability is a default provision. If investors see value in agreeing to restrictions on transfer, all jurisdictions provide mechanisms for permitting agreements to that effect. Sometimes this is done by means of a separate statute, such as the special European statutes for closely held (or close) corporations; sometimes it is done by providing for restraints on transferability as an option under a single general corporation statute, as in the U.S.

Additionally (as Easterbrook and Fischel also point out), the free transferability of stock complements centralized management in the corporate form by serving as a potential constraint on the self-serving behavior of the managers of widely held companies.[39] If the stock market distrusts the current management of a company, its share price will fall, and its managers are more likely to be replaced — either because its existing shareholders will throw out the board of directors or because an acquirer will find it financially attractive to take over the company. (As we discuss below in Chapter 13, which deals with control offers, the threat of a takeover can be an important motivator for incumbent managers.) Antitakeover defenses that limit the ability of shareholders to sell their stock to would-be acquirors are controversial among scholars and other corporate governance experts, largely because these defenses restrict the power of the market to discipline managers by transferring control to a new management team.

---

39. Of course, partners in a general partnership have a different kind of protective "transfer" right that shareholders lack: the power to force dissolution and liquidation of the business. While free transferability is characteristic of corporate shares, it is not mandatory. Close corporations often restrict the free transfer of their stock, which U.S. corporate law allows as long as conspicuous notice appears on the face of the certificate evidencing the share of stock. See, e.g., DGCL §202.

4.5 CENTRALIZED MANAGEMENT

Effectively deploying complex technology in large competitive markets requires continuous investment in specialized information and skills. A great advantage of the corporate form is the creation of the institution of centralized management, which can achieve economies of scale in knowledge of the firm, its technologies and markets. Thus under modern corporate law shareholder designated boards of directors, not investors, are accorded the power to initiate corporate transactions and manage the day to day affairs of the corporation. But the powerful innovation of centralized management also gives rise to the principal problem of modern corporate governance for publicly financed firms. Freed of need to invest in information about the firm and protected by cheap diversification of risk, investors become rationally apathetic. Thus among the foundational problems for modern corporate law is the determination of the set of legal rules and remedies most likely to ensure that these managers will strive to advance the financial interests of investors *without* unduly impinging on management's ability to manage the firm productively.

There are at least three aspects of this problem. First, what can the law do to encourage managers to be diligent, given that shareholders — not judges — choose the directors who designate managers. Second, how can the law assist shareholders in acting collectively vis-à-vis managers, especially in the case of widely held companies with many small shareholders? Corporate law cannot eliminate this "collective action problem," as it is termed, but the law can mitigate it by specifying when shareholder votes are required, what information shareholders must be given,[40] and that shareholders must be able to vote in convenient ways that do not require physical attendance at a shareholders' meeting. Third, how can the law encourage companies to make investment decisions that are best for shareholders (and therefore, under most states of the world beneficial for society as a whole)?

Corporate law attempts to mitigate the agency problem in a number of ways. Its main technique is to require, as a default rule, that management be appointed by a board of directors that is elected by the holders of common stock in the company. This centralized directorate structure is, to be sure, a basic feature not only of corporations, but also of large firms generally. (It is typical of accounting partnerships, for example, and even large law firms.) Nevertheless, the corporate form is unique in two respects: First, it makes the centralization of management power in the board a strong default option for firms organized as corporations; and second, by contrast, it vests more power in the board than even large partnerships commonly do. Consider, for example, the typical statutory formulation set forth in §141 of the DGCL:

---

40. Thus, for example, the Securities and Exchange Act requires that certain financial information be publicly filed periodically by covered firms and that the financial data be audited by an independent auditor.

(a) The business and affairs of every corporation organized under this chapter shall be managed by or under the direction of a board of directors, except as may be otherwise provided in this chapter or in its certificate of incorporation.

As we previously stated, the details of the board's structure and decision-making procedure are found in a company's charter or bylaws. Generally, however, the board "acts" by adopting resolutions at duly called meetings that are recorded in the board's minutes. The board appoints a firm's officers and is therefore formally distinct from the operational managers of the company. Legally speaking, the corporate officers are agents of the company; on the other hand, corporate law often treats the board as if it were a quasi-principal of the company (although, of course, the board is often thought of as the *economic* agent of shareholders).

The formal distinction between a corporation's board and its management also permits a distinction between the approval of business decisions and their initiation and execution. As a practical matter, initiation and execution are the province of management, whereas monitoring and approval are the province of the board. This separation serves as a check on the quality of delegated decision making[41] and makes the board a convenient focus for control mechanisms based on the legal duties of directors.

The additional distinction between a corporation's board and its shareholders is, as we have already noted, principally a device for reducing the costs of corporate decision making. Between annual meetings and while in office, the board need not respond to shareholder concerns, which makes sense because, putting aside agency problems, boards in public companies are often much better informed than shareholders about the firm's business affairs. Also, empowering boards to act in opposition to the will of shareholder majorities can provide a check on opportunistic behavior by controlling shareholders vis-à-vis minority shareholders or other constituencies, such as employees or creditors.

Finally, the board is usually elected by the firm's shareholders. A U.S. corporation may issue nonvoting stock or, at the opposite extreme, accord voting rights to its bondholders. Nevertheless, few companies modify the general default rule that all stock votes at a ratio of one vote per share, and bondholders are never accorded voting rights except by contract when there is a default of interest payments. The obvious utility of restricting the franchise to holders of common stock is that it helps to ensure that the board will act in the interests of the company's owners, i.e., its residual claimants.

4.5.1   Legal Construction of the Board

4.5.1.1   *The Holder of Primary Management Power*

In the United States, corporate law makes the board the ultimate locus of managerial powers. More specifically, board members are not required

---

41. See Eugene F. Fama & Michael C. Jensen, *Agency Problems and Residual Claims*, 26 J.L. & Econ. 327 (1983).

by duty to follow the wishes of a majority shareholder; thus, the corporation has a republican form of government, but it is not a direct democracy. Is this what the shareholders want? Consider the following English case from early in the last century.

AUTOMATIC SELF-CLEANSING FILTER SYNDICATE CO., LTD. v. CUNNINGHAME

2 Ch. 34 (Eng. C.A. 1906)

[Plaintiff McDiarmid, who, together with his friends, held 55 percent of the shares of the Automatic Self-Cleansing Filter Syndicate Co., Ltd., wished to sell the company's assets. The articles of the company provided that "the management of the business and the control of the company shall be vested in the directors, subject nevertheless . . . to such regulations . . . as may from time to time be made by extraordinary resolution" (i.e., vote of 3/4 of the shareholders). At a special shareholders' meeting, a resolution to sell the company's assets failed by a vote of 55 percent in favor to 45 percent opposed. Plaintiff then asked the court to order the board to proceed with a sale of assets on specific terms. This request was denied.]

COLLINS, M.R.

. . . At a meeting of the company a resolution was passed by a majority — I was going to say a bare majority, but it was a majority [of shareholders] — in favor of a sale [of the company's assets] to a purchaser, and the directors, honestly believing, . . . that it was most undesirable in the interests of the company that that agreement should be carried into effect, refused to affix the seal of the company to it, or to assist in carrying out a resolution which they disapproved of; and the question is whether under the memorandum and articles of association here the directors are bound to accept, in substitution of their own view, the views contained in the resolution of the company. . . .

[I]n the matters referred to in article 97(1.) [of the company law], the view of the directors as to the fitness of the matter is made the standard; and furthermore, by article 96 they are given in express terms the full powers which the company has, except so far as they "are not hereby or by statute expressly directed or required to be exercised or done by the company," so that the directors have absolute power to do all things other than those that are expressly required to be done by the company, and then comes the limitation on their general authority — "subject to such regulations as may from time to time be made by extraordinary resolution." Therefore, if it is desired to alter the powers of the directors that must be done, not by a resolution carried by a majority at an ordinary meeting of the company, but by an extraordinary resolution. In these circumstances it seems to me that it is not competent for the majority of the shareholders at an ordinary meeting to affect or alter the mandate originally given to the directors, by the articles of association. It has been suggested that this is a mere question of principal and agent, and that it would be an absurd thing if a principal in appointing an agent should in effect appoint a dictator who is to manage him instead of his managing the agent.

I think that that analogy does not strictly apply to this case. No doubt for some purposes directors are agents. For whom are they agents? You have, no doubt, in theory and law one entity, the company, which might be a principal, but you have to go behind that when you look to the particular position of directors. It is by the consensus of all the individuals in the company that these directors become agents and hold their rights as agents. It is not fair to say that a majority at a meeting is for the purposes of this case the principal so as to alter the mandate of the agent. The minority also must be taken into account. There are provisions by which the minority may be over-borne, but that can only be done by special machinery in the shape of special resolutions. Short of that the mandate which must be obeyed is not that of the majority — it is that of the whole entity made up of all the shareholders. If the mandate of the directors is to be altered, it can only be under the machinery of the memorandum and articles themselves. I do not think I need say more.

[Judge Collins goes on to observe that there would be no point to requiring a "special resolution" — i.e., a 75 percent vote — for removal of directors in the company's charter if the company could be sold by majority vote at a general shareholders' meeting over the objection of the board.]

In a concurring opinion, COZENS-HARDY, L.J., said:

I am of the same opinion. It is somewhat remarkable that in the year 1906 this interesting and important question of company law should for the first time arise for decision, and it is perhaps necessary to go back to the root principle which governs these cases under the Companies Act, 1862. It has been decided that the articles of association are a contract between the members of the company *inter se.* That was settled finally by the case of *Browne v. La Trinidad,* 37 Ch. D. 1, if it was not settled before. We must therefore consider what is the relevant contract which these shareholders have entered into, and that contract, of course, is to be found in the memorandum and articles. I will not again read articles 96 and 97, but it seems to me that the shareholders have by their express contract mutually stipulated that their common affairs should be managed by certain directors to be appointed by the shareholders in the manner described by other articles, such directors being liable to be removed only by special resolution. If you once get a stipulation of that kind in a contract made between the parties, what right is there to interfere with the contract, apart, of course, from any misconduct on the part of the directors? There is no such misconduct in the present case.

. . . If you once get clear of the view that the directors are mere agents of the company, I cannot see anything in principle to justify the contention that the directors are bound to comply with the votes or the resolutions of a simple majority at an ordinary meeting of the shareholders. I do not think it is true to say that the directors are agents. I think it is more nearly true to say that they are in the position of managing partners appointed to fill that post by mutual arrangement between all the shareholders. So much for principle. On principle I agree entirely with what the Master of the Rolls has said, agreeing as he does with the conclusions of Warrington, J.

... For these reasons I think that the appeal must be dismissed. ...

QUESTIONS ON AUTOMATIC SELF-CLEANSING FILTER SYNDICATE

1. Are there good reasons why investors might prefer a rule that requires a supermajority vote in order to override a board decision? Do these reasons apply equally well to all types of decisions?

2. Could the majority of shareholders of a Delaware corporation sell the company's assets without the concurrence of the board? See DGCL §271. Note that, if the board thwarts the will of a majority of the shareholders, the shareholders have a variety of avenues open to them, including passage of a resolution to remove directors at a special shareholders' meeting — or, in some jurisdictions, by consent solicitation.

3. Even with shareholders' right to remove directors, the U.S. approach allocates more power to the board than most other jurisdictions, including the U.K. and most of Continental Europe.[42] Under many company law statutes, the general shareholder meeting is explicitly recognized as the "highest managerial organ," able to countermand the board on any decision.[43] Can this difference be explained by the fact that U.S. companies tend to be widely held, while European companies more often have concentrated shareholder ownership? And if so, how?

Although the board of directors has the primary power to direct or manage the business and affairs of the corporation (e.g., DGCL §141), it rarely exercises nitty-gritty management power. Instead, it designates managers or, more realistically, a chief executive officer, who, in turn, nominates other officers for board confirmation. But the managerial powers of directors, acting as a board, are extremely broad. Beyond the powers to appoint, compensate, and remove officers, they include the power to delegate authority to subcommittees of the board, to officers, or to others; the power to declare and pay dividends; the power to amend the company's bylaws; the exclusive power to initiate and approve certain extraordinary corporate actions, such as amendments to the articles of incorporation, mergers, sales of all assets, and dissolutions; and more generally, the power to make major business decisions, including deciding the products the company will offer, the prices it will charge, the wages it will pay, the financing agreements it will enter, and the like.

---

42. The primary exception is Germany, where the codetermination law allocates half of the board seats in large companies to employee representatives. In the case of a tie vote, the chair — a shareholder representative — is allowed a decisive second vote.

43. See Henry Hansmann & Reinier Kraakman, The Basic Governance Structure, in Reinier Kraakman et al., eds., *The Anatomy of Corporate Law: A Comparative and Functional Approach* (2004).

4.5.1.2   Structure of the Board

The charter sets forth the structure of the board in very general terms. In default of any special provisions in the charter, all members of the board are elected annually to one-year terms. The charter may provide that board seats are to be elected by certain classes of stock. For example, Class A common stock may elect one-third of the members of the board, while Class B elects the rest. In such situations, however, all directors still owe their fiduciary duty to the corporation as an entity and to *all* its shareholders: Specially elected directors do not owe a particular duty to the class that elected them. All directors have one vote on matters before the board.

The board has inherent power to establish standing committees for the effective organization of its own work, and it may delegate certain aspects of its task to these committees or to ad hoc committees. Insofar as committees are advisory, they may include nondirectors; should they exercise any part of the board's power, they must be composed entirely of directors. Under general practice (and New York Stock Exchange listing requirements), board committees include special committees on audit, nominations, and compensation. These committees are typically filled largely or entirely by "independent" directors.[44] Matters that by statute require board action cannot be delegated to a committee for final action.

While the statutory default in almost all states is that the entire board is elected for a one-year term, corporation statutes generally permit corporate charters to create staggered boards, in which directors are divided into classes that stand for election in consecutive years. Under Delaware law, there may be up to three such classes (DGCL §141(d)). Under the New York Business Corporation Law, there may be as many as four classes (§704).[45] Thus, under these provisions, an individual director might have a three-or four-year term of office. Since the early 1990s institutional shareholders have generally opposed staggered boards because they plainly enhance management's ability to resist hostile takeovers.[46] For this reason, established public corporations now rarely ask shareholders to approve the introduction of staggered boards. Interestingly, however, staggered boards are standard features of new companies that sell their shares in the public market for the first time, despite the fact that the institutional investors are also large buyers of their initial public offerings of stock.[47] Professor

---

44. The definition of "independence" for this purpose may vary. It means, at a minimum, that the director is not an employee or officer of the corporation or a family member of an employee or officer. For one fairly strict definition, see Report of Blue Ribbon Committee on Audit Practices, at www.sec.gov. Also see NYSE definition in its listing standards at www.nyse.com.

45. In New York, a staggered board may be established in the charter or by shareholder-enacted bylaw without board concurrence.

46. Empirical evidence confirms this intuition. See Lucian Arye Bebchuk, John C. Coates IV & Guhan Subramanian, *The Powerful Antitakeover Force of Staggered Boards: Theory, Evidence & Policy*, 54 Stan. L. Rev. 887 (2002).

47. See Robert Daines & Michael Klausner, *Do IPO Charters Maximize Firm Value? Anti-Takeover Provisions in IPOs*, 17 J.L. & Econ. 83 (2001); John C. Coates IV, *Explaining Variation in Takeover Defenses: Blame the Lawyers*, 89 Cal. L. Rev. 1301 (2001); Laura Casares Field & Jonathan M. Karpoff, *Takeover Defenses at IPO Firms*, 57 J. Fin. 1857 (2002).

Lucian Bebchuk puts forward several potential explanations for this apparent puzzle: for example, antitakeover protections at the IPO stage might be welfare-increasing because they induce pre-IPO owners to break up their control blocks; antitakeover protections might be welfare-reducing but nevertheless exist because of agency problems among pre-IPO shareholders; or, more simply, antitakeover arrangements might not get priced at the IPO stage because IPO investors may not have more important things to pay attention to (a "bounded attention" theory).[48]

4.5.1.3 Formality in Board Operation

As the *Automatic Self-Cleansing Filter Syndicate* case reflects, corporate directors are not legal agents of the corporation.[49] Governance power resides in the board of directors, not in the individual directors who constitute the board. Thus, it matters whether a majority of the directors find themselves discussing business at a company picnic or at a formal board meeting. At the picnic, they are powerless to act with respect to the corporation's affairs; in the boardroom, they have all of the power created by the firm's constitutional documents.

Legally speaking, directors act as a board only at a duly constituted board meeting and by majority vote (unless the corporate charter requires a supermajority vote on an issue) that is formally recorded in the minutes of the meeting. Proper notice of these meetings must be given and a quorum must be present. The bylaws of the corporation usually specify what constitutes proper notice and what constitutes a quorum. Statutes usually provide minimums. (See, e.g., DGCL §141(b).) Many states now provide that, in lieu of the traditional board action described above, a board may act without a meeting if the members give their unanimous written consent to the corporate action in question. (E.g., DGCL §141(f).)[50]

The law's insistence that corporate boards meet formally (or act by unanimous written consent) is an effort to discourage the manipulation of board decision making. Anyone experienced in group decision making recognizes the danger that a strong-willed individual can skew a group's collective decision by caucusing with group members individually and

48. See Lucian Arye Bebchuk, *Why Firms Adopt Antitakeover Arrangements*, 152 U. Penn. L. Rev. 713 (2003).

49. Like other individuals, directors may in their individual capacity enter into an agency relationship and may specifically do so with the corporation. Were a director to do so, however, such a contract would have to be fair to the corporation, since directors are fiduciaries for the corporation. The point in the text is that directors are not agents by reason of their being directors.

50. These provisions were enacted principally to accommodate the realities of practice in close corporations (i.e., corporations with very few shareholders and in which management and shareholders typically overlap). In these situations, the added costs of formality may mean that formality is less observed. Some statutes also permit directors to hold a meeting by telephone conference, but this is an acknowledgment of possibilities created by new technology rather than a repudiation of the notion that directors should act at a meeting.

extracting each member's consent, when the group meeting as a whole would have withheld its consent or decided differently. Consistent with this preference for group deliberation, corporate directors may not give proxies to others; rather, they must vote personally.

4.5.1.4 *A Critique of Boards*

American corporate law locates the center of energy and power of the corporate enterprise with the board of directors. In fact, most corporation statutes do not even mention the position of chief executive officer (CEO), the most important single organizational role in the large majority of corporations.

Unlike the CEO, most directors cannot in the time available consider the merits of any significant number of complex corporate decisions or second-guess the judgments of the corporation's full-time officers, who are intimately versed in the company's business affairs. In most instances, directors of a large corporation meet only for a single day (excluding an obligatory dinner) between four and eight times a year. Moreover, directors customarily receive their information about the corporation through the filter of documents and presentations put together by the corporation's officers. These practical limitations make the role of the "outside," or independent, director on the boards of major U.S. corporations one of the last great amateur roles in American life.

During the 1990s, many observers nevertheless placed faith in the monitoring abilities of corporate boards, in part because the percentage of outside directors on the boards of U.S. public companies had grown in tandem with the growth in stock ownership by large institutional investors.[51] However, the wave of scandals at Enron, WorldCom, and several other large public companies has, in the minds of many, cast doubt on whether traditional independent directors, constrained by their "day jobs" and friendship networks, are capable of discharging their monitoring tasks. Consider this excerpt from board experts Colin Carter and Harvard Business School professor Jay Lorsch:

> [T]here is a significant gap between what boards are expected to accomplish and the time and knowledge available to directors to do their work. Put simply, the job is difficult if not impossible to carry out in the time most directors can devote to it. Because of that limited time and the rapidity with which business events occur, most directors find it difficult to keep up with their companies. The more complex the company, the more likely a director is to fall behind the curve.[52]

51. According to figures compiled by the Institutional Investor Study sponsored by Columbia Law School, institutional investors owned over 50 percent of the equity in all U.S. public companies by 1990; one-fifth of the 1,000 largest companies had more than 60 percent of their stock in institutional hands. These institutional holdings mitigate the collective action problem faced by small shareholders. These numbers seem to have been fairly stable throughout the 2000s.

52. Colin B. Carter & Jay W. Lorsch, Back to the Drawing Board: Designing Corporate Boards for a Complex World 19-20 (2004).

Carter and Lorsch provide guidelines for effective board structure, but then focus most of their attention on the "soft stuff:" building and sustaining the right team; building knowledge and using it wisely; and using board time "behind closed doors" as effectively as possible. Well before the corporate scandals of the early 2000s, one of the authors of this book proposed that institutional investors consider funding a clearinghouse for "professional" directors, experts whose *only* job would be to sit on the boards of a half-dozen large companies to safeguard the interests of shareholders.[53]

4.5.2 Corporate Officers: Agents of the Corporation

Generally, the corporate charter empowers the board to appoint officers and remove them, with or without cause. By and large, the board has the power to delegate authority to corporate officers as it sees fit. The traditional officers are the president, vice presidents, treasurer, and secretary, although nowadays the most senior officer is frequently designated as the CEO. But this matter of names means very little; for legal purposes, a CEO might just as well be termed the company's Imperial Czar or Grand Pooh-Bah. The only important point is that the corporate officers, unlike directors, are unquestionable agents of the corporation and are therefore subject to the fiduciary duty of agents.

JENNINGS v. PITTSBURGH MERCANTILE CO.

202 A.2d 51 (Pa. 1964)

Cohen, J.:

Appellees, Dan R. Jennings, a Pittsburgh real estate broker, . . . instituted this action of assumpsit against Pittsburgh Mercantile Company (Mercantile) to recover a real estate brokerage commission for the alleged consummation of a sale and leaseback of all of Mercantile's real property. Mercantile appeals from the lower court's denial of its motion for judgment n.o.v. after jury verdict for appellees.

The principal issue in this appeal is whether there was sufficient evidence upon which the jury could conclude that Mercantile clothed its agent with the apparent authority to accept an offer for the sale and leaseback thereby binding it to the payment of the brokerage commission, the agent having had, admittedly, no actual authority to so do.

Mercantile is a publicly-held corporation with over 400 shareholders. It is managed by a nine-member board of directors. An executive committee, consisting of the three major officers, functions between the board's quarterly meetings.

---

53. See Ronald J. Gilson & Reinier Kraakman, *Reinventing the Outside Director: An Agenda for Institutional Investors*, 43 Stan. L. Rev. 863 (1991).

The facts in issue viewed in a light most favorable to appellees are as follows: In April, 1958, Frederick A. Egmore, Mercantile's vice-president and treasurer-comptroller, and Walter P. Stern, its financial consultant, met with Jennings, explained Mercantile's desire to raise cash for store modernization and provided Jennings with information concerning Mercantile's finances. Jennings was asked to solicit offers for a sale and leaseback.

At this meeting Egmore made the following representations: (1) the executive committee, of which Egmore was a member, controlled Mercantile and (2) would be responsible for determining whether the company would accept any of the offers produced by Jennings; (3) subsequent board of directors' approval of the acceptance would be automatic. Egmore promised the payment of a commission if Jennings succeeded in bringing in an offer on terms as to amount realized, annual rental, and lease duration acceptable to the executive committee. Egmore outlined preliminarily the terms of an acceptable offer.

In July and August, 1958, Jennings brought Egmore three offers. . . . The third offer came close to [Egmore's] original terms. On November 4, 1958, Jennings was informed by Stern that the executive committee had "agreed to the deal." However, within a week Egmore informed Jennings that the third offer had been rejected. Mercantile refused to pay Jennings' bill for commission of $32,000 and suit was thereafter instituted.

At the outset, we note that for Mercantile this proposed sale and leaseback was not a transaction in the ordinary course of business. Rather, it was unusual and unprecedented. The transaction envisaged Mercantile's relinquishment of ownership of all its real property, worth approximately $1.5 million, for a period of 30 years. Hence, the apparent authority which appellees seek to establish is the apparent authority to accept an offer for an extraordinary transaction.

Apparent authority is defined as that authority which, although not actually granted, the principal (1) knowingly permits the agent to exercise or (2) holds him out as possessing. . . .

Jennings strongly contends that Egmore's representations gave rise to the apparent authority asserted. We do not agree. . . . An agent cannot, simply by his own words, invest himself with apparent authority. Such authority emanates from the actions of the principal and not the agent. . . .

Jennings further argues that apparent authority arose by virtue of (1) certain prior dealings of Egmore and (2) the corporate offices held by Egmore. . . .

Focusing on the first of these factors, in order for a reasonable inference of the existence of apparent authority to be drawn from prior dealings, these dealings must have (1) a measure of similarity to the act for which the principal is sought to be bound, and, granting this similarity, (2) a degree of repetitiveness. . . . Although the required degree of repetitiveness might have been present here, the prior acts relied upon consisted solely of Egmore's provision of financial information to Jennings and other brokers with regard to the sale and leaseback, and Egmore's solicitation of offers through them. The dissimilarities between these acts and the act of accepting the offer in issue are self-evident, and apparent authority to do the latter act cannot be inferred from the doing of the former.

As to the second of the above factors, the corporate offices of vice-president and treasurer-comptroller, which Egmore held, do not provide the basis for a reasonable inference that Mercantile held out Egmore as having the apparent authority to accept the offers produced by Jennings. . . . We hold . . . any other conclusion would improperly extend the usual scope of authority which attaches to the holding of various corporate offices, and would greatly undercut the proper role of the board of directors in corporate decision-making by thrusting upon them determinations on critical matters which they have never had the opportunity to consider. . . .

Finally, the extraordinary nature of this transaction placed appellees on notice to inquire as to Egmore's actual authority, particularly since appellees were an experienced real estate broker and investment counselor-attorney team. . . . Had inquiry been made, appellees would have discovered that the board never considered any of the proposals and obviously did not delegate actual authority to accept offers.

Appellees having failed to produce sufficient evidence upon which the jury could reasonably have found the existence of apparent authority to accept an offer for the sale and leaseback of all of Mercantile's real property, appellant is entitled to judgment n.o.v.

NOTE

For an analogous Delaware case that looks to the corporation statute to limit the apparent/inherent authority of corporate officers, see *Grimes v. Alteon, Inc.*, 804 A.2d 256 (Del. 2002). In *Grimes,* a CEO was held to lack the authority to enter an oral contract to sell 10 percent of any new issue of stock to an existing shareholder who wished to maintain his proportionate shareholdings. The Delaware Supreme Court held that such a contract constituted a "right" in the company's securities and thus required board approval under DGCL §§152 and 157. While this construction might not have been compelling on the face of DGCL §§152 and 157 alone, it was, according to the court, required by the spirit animating a broader set of DGCL provisions as well as the fundamental social policies of protecting the board's power to regulate corporate capital structure and ensuring the certainty of property rights in corporate shares.

QUESTIONS ON JENNINGS

1. Why would extending apparent authority to Egmore, Mercantile's vice president and treasurer, undercut the role of the board?

2. As a member of Mercantile's Executive Committee, Egmore was a director as well as a high corporate officer. Should that fact affect the scope of Egmore's apparent authority?

3. Should the outcome differ if Mercantile's board had made a firm decision to enter a sale and leaseback transaction on the best terms available?

DEBT, EQUITY, AND ECONOMIC VALUE[1]

5.1 CAPITAL STRUCTURE

A business corporation raises capital to fund its operations. It does so by selling legal claims to its assets and prospective cash flows. Fundamentally, there are two types of long-term claims that a corporation may sell for this purpose. First, like any market participant, it may borrow money through the issuance of debt instruments. Second, it may sell ownership claims in the corporate entity by issuing equity securities. Although both of these sources of long-term capital can take a variety of forms, their fundamental differences are easy to grasp.

Usually, those who buy corporate debt have a contractual right to receive a periodic payment of interest and to be repaid their principal — the money they originally loaned — at a stated maturity date. If a corporation fails to make any of these payments, the creditor has legal remedies, which ordinarily include the basic right to sue the company and to have the sheriff seize the debtor's property for the creditor's benefit if the debtor corporation fails to pay. The creditor typically also gets a contractual right to "accelerate" payment of the principal amount if the debtor defaults (for long enough) in paying an interest payment. The debtor and creditor write this "acceleration clause" into their contract, the loan agreement. Moreover, the debtor generally must pay its creditors the amounts currently due to the creditors before the debtor can distribute funds or other things of value to equity owners.

Equity claims, the other source of long-term capital, may also be customized, although most equity claims on corporations take the form of common stock. What is particularly notable about common stock is the apparent fragility of its legal protections. Its holders have no right to any periodic payment, nor can they demand the return of their investment from the corporation. Nor, as we shall see in due course, can they typically tell the firm's managers what to do. They merely have a right to vote, as we will later explore. Common stockholders can expect to receive dividends, but they get those dividends only when the corporation's board of directors so

---

1. We owe special thanks in this chapter to Professor Marcel Kahan for most of the exercises that appear here and to Professor Mark Roe for numerous specific revisions.

111

declares. And stockholders cannot typically tell the board to declare those dividends.

The mix of long-term debt and equity claims that the corporation issues to finance its operations is generally termed its "capital structure." In this chapter, we describe the range of longer-term claims that corporations may issue in structuring their capital. In addition, we introduce the economic concept of value to acquaint those who need it with the rudiments of finance.

5.1.1   Legal Character of Debt

Debt securities are contracts. Typically, there is a loan agreement, filled with terms, often heavily negotiated. Even if the debt is represented by no more than an "I.O.U.," it is still a contract, just a very simple one. The debt contract — the loan agreement — has great flexibility in design. Some lawyers — those who spend their professional lives negotiating and drafting loan agreements — might even think of it as a higher form of art. The lawyers can construct whatever terms the parties desire, as long as these terms do not violate positive law in some respect. Thus, when we speak of the legal "characteristics" of debt, to a large extent we are talking about general patterns of contract terms — of the contractual terms that have become typical or customary (such as the acceleration clause we have just mentioned). For the most part, we are not speaking of definitional categories or mandatory terms that are strictly enforced. One can think of the loan agreement as allocating risks and responsibilities between the debtor and the creditor and, in more complex companies, among *each of several* classes of creditors. As such, the terms of a loan agreement can range from low risk for the creditor (we must be repaid come hell or high water, as one recurring contract phrase might have it) to high risk for the creditor — and, conversely, from lower risk for the equity holder (no need to repay in this or that circumstance) to higher risk.

Maturity Date.   The single most common characteristic of debt is a maturity date. That is, the issuer of debt will have (almost always) a legal obligation to repay at a stated date in the future. The repayment obligation is often to repay the principal amount (typically the amount the creditor originally lent) of the bond plus any outstanding interest not yet paid by the maturity date. Bonds typically bear interest at a stated rate (or according to a formula), which the debtor must pay periodically, often semiannually. As we said, terms can vary almost infinitely. Although most bonds pay interest semiannually, one type that became popular in recent decades has no obligation to pay interest. Instead, the debtor must repay at maturity an amount larger (usually much larger) than the amount the creditor originally lent it. (These are called "zero coupon" bonds.)

If any interest or principal is not paid when due (or upon the expiration of any grace period that the documents may create), bonds are said to be in default. The debtor is said to have defaulted on its debt. Ordinarily, a default in an interest payment, under the terms of the bond, allows the creditor to accelerate the payment of the principal from its original maturity date, perhaps deep in the future, to the current date. The creditor can demand, after the debtor's default on paying interest, that the debtor repay the principal amount in full — immediately. And the mechanisms for the creditor to use to sue the debtor are typically specified in the loan agreement.

Investors choose between investing in debt (as a creditor) by, say, lending the money to the debtor or (the equivalent) by buying a bond of the debtor. A critical advantage of bonds, from the perspective of investors, is that the investor generally faces less risk as a creditor than as an equity holder because creditors have a legal right to periodic payment of a return (interest) and, most important, a priority claim over the company's shareholders on corporate assets in the event that the corporation defaults. And if the creditors are not paid on time, they can do more than ask the company to pay them. They can sue on their contract. (Not so for the equity holders who are unhappy with paltry periodic dividends from the firm they own.) Moreover, bond agreements can be constructed to reduce the financial risk of default through devices such as protective covenants (discussed briefly below) or security interests in specific property that further assure repayment.

Tax Treatment. Tax is another important feature of debt as a source of finance. Interest paid by the borrower is a deductible cost of business when the firm calculates its taxable income. The corporation, like all taxpayers, pays tax only on its taxable income, which is roughly its net income after costs. Thus, the net cost to the corporation of capital that it arranges through borrowing is approximately half of the stated interest rate on the bonds that it sells: If the corporate tax rate is approximately 50 percent, then, for each dollar the corporation pays in interest, its taxable income is reduced by a dollar, and it saves $0.50 in taxes. By contrast, no deduction is available for dividends or distributions paid to the corporation's stockholders. Thus, in this respect the cost to the corporation of debt is less than that of equity. (Other factors besides the deductibility of interest, however, also bear on the relative cost of debt, including the higher risk of equity investments, the tax rates of investors in debt or equity and the costs of financial distress, which increase with a company's debt burden.)

5.1.2 Legal Character of Equity

Common Stock. The legal character of common stock can also be seen as essentially contractual in nature, but in this instance, the law fixes clear default rules on the contract. The most important of these rules are that owners of stock can vote to elect directors and that stock (again, almost always) carries one vote per share.

This then is what equity has: not the right to payment but (usually) the right to vote on certain important matters. Equity securities — specifically

common stock — generally possess *control rights* in the form of the power
to elect the board of directors. Any deviation from this one-vote-per-share
default rule must appear in the corporation's charter. Thus, the charter
contains the specifics of the firm's equity securities, including whether
there are multiple types of stock with different voting rights, preferences
upon liquidation (by which some stockholders get more than others if the
firm liquidates), or other terms that affect the company's stock.[2]

Residual Claims and Residual Control.   Common stock holds
both control rights, through its power to designate the board, and the
residual claim on the corporation's assets and income. Common stockholders elect the board. After the company has paid its expenses ("met its
payroll") and paid interest to those creditors whom we have considered in
the preceding section, whatever is left over can "belong" to the stockholders in the sense that it is available for the payment of dividends. If
the company has done well, by selling many widgets at a high markup,
those remaining moneys could be a lot. If the company's management has
not sold much and has barely covered the firm's expenses, then there is not
much left over for stockholders to be paid a dividend.

Preferred Stock.   Any equity security on which the corporate charter confers a special right, privilege, or limitation is referred to as a "preferred stock." Preferred stocks are just as malleable as bonds. Generally,
they carry a stated dividend, but unlike a bond "coupon" or interest rate
obligation, this dividend is payable only when it is declared by the board.
Payment of these dividends is usually enforced indirectly, by a provision in
the terms of the preferred stock stipulating that any unpaid dividends
accumulate and that all accumulated dividends must be paid to preferred
stockholders before any dividend can be paid to common stockholders.
Sometimes preferred stockholders also get votes, or designated board
seats, if the preferred stock dividend has been skipped for long enough.
Preferred stock is ordinarily less risky than common stock in the same
corporation because it typically has a preference over common stock in
liquidation as well as dividends. This means that, if the corporation fails
and plans to close, a designated amount of money must first be paid to the
preferred stockholders before the liquidating corporation can distribute
any property to holders of common stock.

2. Important examples of such "other terms" include the company's redemption and
call rights and the shareholder's exchange, conversion, and put rights. A *redeemable stock* is
one that the corporation may redeem on terms stated in the charter, either at the election of
the board or at some set time. An exchange right is a right to switch one security for another.
    Closely related is a *conversion right*, which is the right to convert one security into
another at a stated conversion rate. In this context, a *put right* is the shareholder's right to
force the company to buy her security at a fixed price, while a *call right* is the corporation's
option to force shareholders to surrender their stock at a fixed price. The difference
between a call right and a redemption right relates to the status of the security after the
right is exercised. Stock that is called becomes the company's "treasury" stock that continues to be issued but is no longer outstanding in the market. Stock that is redeemed is
cancelled and may not be reissued.

Ordinarily, preferred stock does not vote so long as its dividend is current. If its dividend is in default, however, it can sometimes elect a stated number (or all) of the directors (as provided by the corporation's charter). On certain fundamental matters, such as mergers in which their rights may be affected, holders of preferred stock are accorded a class vote under some statutes, which can mean that they exercise a veto right on the proposed deal. Under the Delaware statute, however, this right must be created specifically in the document creating and defining the preferred stock.

5.2 BASIC CONCEPTS OF VALUATION

The entrepreneur who assembles the inputs to operate a firm wants to attract capital at the lowest cost to the firm. But to do this, she must understand how to value the securities — or the outsiders' claims against the firm's revenue — that she will sell to finance the firm's operations. Thus, we must now turn to the economic concept of value. The four basic finance concepts that are important for understanding value, as it pertains to corporate law, are (1) the time value of money, (2) risk and return, (3) systematic risk and diversification, and (4) capital market efficiency.

5.2.1 The Time Value of Money

Intuitively, we understand that one dollar today is worth more than a promise (even a promise certain to be kept) of one dollar ten years from now. Why? Because you can use the money during the waiting period. If you have no use for it, you can put it aside. But if you use it (or lend it out to those who can use it even more profitably), you will make money by having that dollar now instead of ten years from now.

How much more valuable a payment, or sum of money, is today, rather than later, depends on the value of the use you have for it, or on the value you can get by finding someone who needs that dollar now for something valuable. That's the "time value" of money. We might think of the time value of money as a rental charge: $1 today is worth whatever $1 is worth ten years from now *plus* whatever you can get for "renting out" $1 for ten years. (Of course, since we are dealing with money, the vocabulary would shift to "lending" from "renting," but the concept is the same.)

The concepts of *present value* and *discount* flow from the time value of money. Present value is simply the value today of money to be paid at some future point. Thus, if $1 in ten years is worth what 38.5 cents is worth today, 38.5 cents is the present value (the value today) of receiving $1 in ten years. If the two are equal, then a typical investor will believe, or at least act as if, 38.5 cents today and $1 ten years from now are equivalent. I will trade my promise of $1 ten years from now for anything over 38.5 cents today. And I will trade away 38.5 cents today for anything a little over a sure promise to get $1 ten years from now.

The discount rate tells us how to calculate present values. The discount rate is the rate that is earned from renting money out for one year in the market for money. A discount rate of 10 percent means that you earn 10 cents for lending $1 for one year, in which case one year from now you will have $1.10. The present value of $1.10 one year from today, would in turn be $1.

What happens if you lend $1 for two years? After one year, you will get $1.10. Lending $1.10 for a second year at 10 percent gives you $1.21 (assuming the discount rate for the second year remains 10 percent). Thus, the present value of $1.21 two years from now (assuming a 10 percent discount rate) is also $1.

$$\$1.00 + 10\% \text{ of } \$1.00 = \$1.10 \text{ (for year 1)}$$

Then for year 2:

$$\$1.10 + 10\% \text{ of } \$1.10 = \$1.21 \text{ (at the end of year 2)}$$

Or for a period of one year:

$$\text{Equation 1}: PV + r(PV) = FV$$

where PV is the present value, r is the annual interest rate, and FV is the future value.

This last sequence is intuitive. It gets us from values today to values in the future. It is only a little more complicated to see how we get from values in the future to present value. How then is the discount rate used to calculate present value? Simple. If you want to calculate the present value of an amount of money one year from now, you divide that amount by the sum of 1 and the discount rate (this sum is called the discount factor). Stated in a formula:

$$\text{Equation 2}: PV = FV/(1+r)$$

where PV is the present value, FV is the amount that will be paid at the conclusion of one year, and r is the annual discount rate. Recalling a little basic high school algebra, we see that equation 2 rearranges the terms from equation 1.

Thus, if the discount rate is 10 percent, you calculate the present value of $1.10 one year from now by dividing $1.10 by 1.1. This yields $1. If you are dealing with amounts of money that are further away than one year, you simply repeat the same process. Thus, to calculate the present value of $1.21 two years from now, you divide $1.21 first by 1 + the discount rate for the second year and then by 1 + the discount rate for the first year. If both rates are 10 percent, you divide twice by 1.1 or, equivalently, once by 1.1^2 (or 1.21). Again, you get $1.

DISCOUNTING EXERCISES

1. What is the present value of $1.10 one year from now if the discount rate is 5 percent?

2. What is the present value of $1 ten years from now if the discount rate for each of the ten years is 10 percent?

3. What is the relationship between present value and discount rate? Will $100 one year from now have a higher present value if the discount rate is 7 percent or 8 percent? Can you tell the answer without calculating the present values?

4. If the present value of $150 one year from now is $120, what is the discount factor? What is the discount rate?

The above concepts of future value and present value, related to one another by an interest rate, are the basics. There are other concepts that float through finance, many of which are variations of present value and future value.

You may have encountered other kinds of rates. One is the rate of return: the percentage that you would earn if you invested in a particular project. For example, if you invested $1,000 a year ago and receive $1,200 today, your rate of return is 20 percent. This does *not* mean that the present value of $1,200 one year from now is $1,000. When you made the investment, you might have expected to make more, or less. But the return you actually got is 20 percent. For instance, if the discount rate was 10 percent, this was a great investment. But if the appropriate discount rate when you made the investment was, say, 25 percent, this investment was a loser when compared to other potential uses of the money.

Projects for which the present value of the amount invested ($1,000) is less than the present value of the amount received in return are called *positive net present value* projects. In more ordinary language, these are good, profitable projects. (*Net* present value is just the difference between the present value of the amounts invested and the present value of those received in return.) Investing in such projects is a good idea for investors: If they play out as expected, they will pay out more than is needed to compensate for the time value of money. Their rate of return (say, 20 percent) is higher than the market rate of return (say, a 10 percent rate demanded by investors for this kind of project).

"Interest" is the money you are promised when you lend out money or the amount you have to pay if you borrow money. (Think of interest as equivalent to a rental charge.) The interest rate is that amount expressed as a percentage of the amount lent. Thus, if you borrow $10,000 for one year and have to return, at the end of that year, the $10,000 borrowed plus $850 in interest, the rate of interest you have to pay is 8.5 percent.

Thus far, we have distinguished interest returns from other returns. But the same concepts used so far apply to stock and to debt. Stockholders expect a return and discount the future return (typically in the form of dividends) to present value, comparing that value to the value of the investment of buying the stock today.

A QUESTION ON NET PRESENT VALUE

What is the present value of the $10,850 you have to repay a year from now if the discount rate is 7 percent? If it is 8.5 percent? If it is 10 percent? What is the net present value of $10,000 borrowed at an 8.5 percent interest rate at each of these discount rates?

5.2.2   Risk and Return

So far, we have dealt with a world of certainty. But future returns on most investments are uncertain. Assessing that uncertainty is a big job. In some ways, it may be Wall Street's biggest job. So to evaluate risky investments — which is to say, nearly all investments — the investor has to consider the probability of their success or failure.

To attempt this rationally, an investor typically calculates what we now call the *expected return.* If a return a year from now on an investment will be either $2,000 or zero, each with equal likelihood, the expected return on the investment is $1,000. Thus, to calculate the present value of this investment opportunity, the investor will discount $1,000 to present value, not either $2,000 or zero.[3]

The expected return is a weighted average of the value of the investment. It is the sum of what the returns would be if an investment succeeded, multiplied by the probability of success, *plus* what the returns would be if the investment failed, multiplied by the probability of failure. If outcomes intermediate between success and failure are possible, they, too, must be multiplied by their probabilities and added in to calculate the expected return.

For example, consider the following array of potential outcomes of a risky investment of $1 million by XYZ Corporation. These estimates were made by XYZ's senior executives after exhaustive discussion by its management team. The investment is to be liquidated at the end of one year.

Returns During Year	Value at Termination	Total Return	Probability
50,000	300,000	350,000	10%
125,000	800,000	925,000	20%
200,000	1,300,000	1,500,000	30%
200,000	1,400,000	1,600,000	20%
500,000	1,400,000	1,900,000	10%
-0-	-0-	-0-	10%

What is the expected value of this investment opportunity? To calculate it, we must add the two forms of return for each probability, multiply the sum by the corresponding probability, and add the results for all

3. The investor could discount both $2,000.00 and zero to present value and take the average, which gives the same answer as discounting $1,000 to present value. But to our minds, this approach is not as logical.

probabilities together. In this instance, the expected (future) value of the investment would be $1.18 million.

Total Return	Probability	Expected Return
350,000	10%	35,000
925,000	20%	185,000
1,500,000	30%	450,000
1,600,000	20%	320,000
1,900,000	10%	190,000
-0-	10%	-0-
Total expected value:		**$1,180,000**

Of course, another step would be required to calculate the *present* expected value of this opportunity.

Now we introduce the concept of financial risk. Compare this array of expected returns with the hypothetical return on a $1 million one-year Treasury note issued at par bearing stated interest at 9 percent. Such an investment has no array of probable outcomes. Its expected (future) value is simply $1,090,000. Since there is no volatility in its return, we characterize this investment as riskless. (Finance-types will want to add some risk: maybe not that the United States of America will default on repaying its debt but that inflation will increase. Ignore the finance/inflation risk here. Think of this as a sure thing.) However, the XYZ project, as shown in the two tables, may have an *actual* return ranging from $0 to $1.9 million, although its expected future return in $1.18 million. The potential returns for XYZ are risky.

An investor is said to be *risk neutral* if all she is concerned about is the expected return of an investment — that is, if she is indifferent to receiving the $1.18 million in cash one year from now or receiving the returns from the XYZ investment project. Most investors are not risk neutral but are, instead, *risk averse*. This means that volatile payouts are worth less to them — they might well value the XYZ project and the Treasury note at the same price, or even prefer the Treasury note to the XYZ project, notwithstanding the fact that it has a lower future expected value.

Consider an even simpler investment opportunity, the right to purchase the outcome of a coin flip. Risk-averse investors — i.e., most investors — would prefer a coin flip that paid them $9,000 for tails and $11,000 for heads over a flip that paid them $5,000 for tails and $15,000 for heads. Although both flips have the same $10,000 expected value, the variance in the outcomes of the second is wider than that of the first. (True, some investors are risk preferring, but their number is small.) The additional amount that risk-averse investors demand for accepting higher-risk investments in the capital markets is termed the *risk premium*. Like almost everything else, risk has its market price.

The risk premium does *not* compensate the investor for the possible out-of-pocket losses associated with the probability that an investment might fail. Even a risk-neutral investor demands compensation for these losses because failure lowers the expected return of an investment. In our XYZ investment payout table, there is a 40 percent chance that the company will get back less than it invests, that the actual outcome of the investment will be a loss. Even risk-neutral investors care about these real losses and reduce the expected return on investments to account for these losses. But again, these reductions in the expected payout of an investment are not part of the risk premium. Instead, the risk premium is compensation for the intrinsic unpleasantness of volatile returns to the risk-averse investors who dominate market prices. Most investors like the $9K-$11K flip more than the $5K-$15K flip. Everyone takes the downside ($5K or $9K) and the upside ($11K or $15K) into account. Risk-averse investors have to be compensated for taking the $5K-$15K flip. Risk-neutral investors do not have to be paid to switch.

Let's tie this discussion of risk and return to the discussion of the time value of money. We noted earlier that future cash flows must be discounted to arrive at their present value. We now assert that most investors are risk averse and demand extra compensation for bearing risk. This means, in effect, that in order to calculate the present value of risky expected future cash flows (remember that we always discount *expected* cash flows), we need to discount these cash flows at a rate that reflects both the time discount value of money and the market price of the risk involved. We call this combined rate a risk-adjusted rate. By contrast, the rate at which we discount future cash flows that are certain is the risk-free rate. The difference between the risk-adjusted rate and the risk-free rate is the risk premium. More risk in expected future cash flows yields a higher risk premium and a higher risk-adjusted rate.

QUESTIONS ON RISK AND NET PRESENT VALUE

National Hotel Corporation wants to borrow $10,000,000 from First City Bank for one year. National Hotel Corporation offers to repay to First City Bank $11,300,000, as principal and interest, at the end of the one-year term. First City Bank believes that, if it extends the loan, it has a 95 percent chance of being repaid in full at the year's end and a 5 percent chance of receiving nothing because National Hotel Corporation will be bankrupt and worth nothing at all. The risk-free discount rate is 6.5 percent. But the risk-averse managers of First City Bank require a 2 percent risk premium to extend a loan to a borrower with the characteristics of National Hotel Corporation.

1. What is the nominal interest rate that National Hotel offers to pay for the loan?

2. Assuming National Hotel obtains a loan at the rate it demands, what is First City's expected return on the $10 million that it would lend?

3. What is the net present value of the loan extended on National Hotel's terms if investors are generally risk neutral? What discount rate would these investors use?

4. What is the net present value of the loan if First City's managers correctly assess the risk premium that most investors in the market would charge for the National Hotel loan? What discount rate does First City use in this case? Should it extend the loan on National Hotel's terms?

5.2.3 Diversification and Systematic Risk

There is, finally, one more twist to the basic intuition about risk premium. And it turns out to be an important one, not just in the world of investors but also in the world of corporate law and corporate takeovers.

Begin with this "riddle": Imagine that all investments are risky. And imagine that all investors are risk averse. That is, all of the investments are of the $9K or $11K type or the $5K or $15K type. Yet financial promoters figure out how to sell some of these investments—conceivably all of them—without having to put up with a risk premium.

How?

Consider a large class of $5K or $15K coin-flip-type investments. Let's say that, for investment A, the payout is $5K if the Democrats win the next election and $15K if the Republicans win. But for investment B, the payout if the Republicans win the next election is $5K, and if the Democrats win, it is $15K.

Now you see it. If the two investments can be packaged together, they turn into a $20K certain investment, or a $20K actual return no matter what the outcome of the election. The risk-averse investor who would demand a premium for either investment alone *desists from demanding any premium at all for a package of the two investments together.*

A somewhat different example of the same point is as follows. Suppose we flip a coin ten times and pay out $1,500 for each head and $500 for each tail. The expected value of a package of these ten coin flips (the "ten-pack") is $10K, just as it was for the single $15K/$5K coin flip. But a risk-averse investor will demand a much lower premium to invest in the ten-pack than she would to invest in the single big flip. Unlike the two-investment case we considered above, there is still some risk associated with the ten-pack, but this risk is much less than that associated with the single $15K/$5K investment. Think of it this way: While you might end up with $15,000 or $5,000 by investing in the ten-pack, you are much more likely to end up somewhere in between—say, with six heads and four tails or the other way around, which yield payouts of $11,000 and $9,000, respectively.[4]

The packaging of investments to reduce risk is a big business on Wall Street: It is the construction of mutual funds, the construction of a diversified portfolio.

Risk aversion means that investors are averse only to risks that they actually end up bearing. Thus, a risky investment held as part of a portfolio that includes other equally risky investments is likely to be worth more to its owner than it would be if it were held alone. The odds are that, even if one or two investments go sour, most of them will succeed. The investor is said to have *diversified* across a portfolio that has less total risk than its

---

4. In the two-investment case, investments A and B are said to be perfectly *negatively correlated* if, whenever one does well, the other fails, and vice versa. In the ten-pack coin flip investment, each coin flip is *uncorrelated* with the others. As the examples suggest, investments with negatively correlated outcomes are very efficient in eliminating risk. But uncorrelated investments are not far behind. Ten coin flips really do get rid of 90 percent of the risk associated with flipping coins by some measures. We do not explore how risk is measured here, but the intuition is easy to understand.

individual components. This is a fancy way of saying that risk-averse investors should not put all their eggs into one basket — unless, as always, they are paid to do so. But notice the implication: Since investors can hold portfolios, risky investments, such as stock, should be priced to reflect the fact that investors need not bear all the risk associated with holding a single investment.

If investors can hold very large portfolios, why must corporations pay them a risk premium to invest in risky stock? Why doesn't all stock sell at exactly its expected return? The reason is that not every risk is diversifiable — i.e., not every risk disappears if you hold a very large portfolio. While an increase in value for some investments correlates with a decline in value for other investments, there is always some level of risk (of, say, the entire economy going up or down) that even the most diversified investor must bear, and for which this risk-averse investor still demands a premium.

QUESTIONS ON SYSTEMATIC AND UNSYSTEMATIC RISK

Assume that a person living in Phantasia can invest only in the following four investment projects. She can loan money to the Phantasia government at an interest rate of 6 percent (in which case she is sure to be repaid). She can buy stock of either (or both) of Phantasia's two leading baseball teams. If the Phantasia Mets win the annual baseball championship, Mets stock will sell for $100 a share and the stock of the losing Phantasia Yankees will sell for $50 a share a year from now; if the Yankees win, Yankee stock will sell for $100 a share and Mets stock for $50 a share at that time. Assume that each team has a 50 percent chance of winning the championship. Finally, assume that our investor can buy stock of Phantasia Tourism Inc., a local hotel and restaurant operator. If Phantasia completes construction of its airport one year from now, tourists will start flocking in, and Phantasia Tourism stock will be worth $300 a share. However, if the airport is not completed one year from now, Phantasia Tourism stock will be worth only $30. The likelihood that the airport will be completed in time is 20 percent.

1. What is the expected value one year from now of (a) $1,000 of Phantasia government bonds, (b) one share of Mets stock, (c) one share of Yankee stock, and (d) one share of Phantasia Tourism stock?

2. Which of these investments involve risk? Which involve risk that is fully diversifiable? Which involve risk that is partly undiversifiable?

3. In light of your answer to question 2, what price would you expect Mets stock to sell for today? Yankee stock? Phantasia Tourism stock? (If you cannot figure out an exact price, can you estimate a range of reasonable prices?)

4. How would your answers to question 2 change if you learned that Phantasia's airport will definitely be completed by next year if the Mets win the pennant and that it definitely will not be completed if the Yankees win? (Notice that the probabilities of a completed airport and a Mets victory are now both 50 percent).

In the Phantasia problems above, we encountered risky projects that involved only diversifiable risk and risky projects that involved partly undiversifiable risk. In reality, most projects involve a combination of diversifiable and undiversifiable risk. For instance, the value of General Motors (GM) stock depends both on the quality of the new GM models compared to Ford, Toyota, and BMW models (diversifiable risk, since you could buy Ford, Toyota, and BMW stock) and on whether the world economy is going to enter a period of prolonged recession (undiversifiable risk). The appropriate risk premium and risk-adjusted discount rate, however, depend only on the undiversifiable portion of the risk. Thus, to modify our conclusion above, the greater the undiversifiable risk is, the greater the risk premium and the risk-adjusted discount rate are.

5.3 VALUING ASSETS

5.3.1. The Discount Cash Flow (DCF) Approach

A basic understanding of capital structure, time value of money, and the connection between risk and return give us all the building blocks we need to be able to value tangible and financial assets, such as stocks and bonds. These building blocks all come together in the "discounted cash flow" (DCF) approach to valuing assets. At the highest level, DCF valuation requires a prediction of all future cash flows, and a discount rate to bring those cash flows back to the present to yield a "net present value" (NPV).

Of course, this is easier said than done, and employing DCF valuation to estimate intrinsic value is a true art. Nevertheless, DCF analysis is sometimes the only rational way to estimate present values based on an uncertain future. It is routinely used, with a lot of prayer, by investment bankers in valuing takeovers and small businesses, by courts in valuing shares in closely held corporations, by bankruptcy courts in valuing plans for reorganizing businesses, and by managers in valuing corporate projects. We therefore present a basic conceptual approach to the valuation of assets. The goal of this brief overview is not to make you an expert in the valuation of assets — such an objective would take at least a semester and perhaps a lifetime to achieve — but rather to make you an educated "consumer" of valuations presented by others.

The first step in the DCF valuation process is the estimation of all future cash flows generated by the asset. Of course, as with any predictions about the future, this step is fraught with uncertainty. Adding further complexity is the fact that many assets typically have indefinite life, while cash flows can only be calculated for a finite number of periods. The solution that valuation experts often use is a "terminal value," which brings all cash flows from a future year (say, year 10) and going into perpetuity, into that future year (year 10). In many DCF valuations, this terminal value is a large fraction of the overall cash flows — sometimes 60 to 70 percent, depending on the discount rate used and the number of discrete cash flows periods that are available. As a result small changes in assumptions about what happens going in to perpetuity (for example, the growth rate of the cash flows) can make a big difference in the overall NPV.

The second step in a DCF valuation is the calculation of an appropriate discount rate. The simplest, perhaps most well-accepted, approach is to calculate a *weighted-average cost of capital* (WACC), which is calculated as the weighted average of the *cost of debt* and the *cost of equity*, where the weights are the relative amounts of debt and equity in the capital structure. The before-tax cost of debt for a firm is the interest rate that the firm would pay if it were to seek new debt financing today (i.e., not the historical interest rate on its existing debt). Of course, the after-tax cost of debt is usually significantly lower, because companies can deduct interest payments from their taxable income. If a company with a 50 percent marginal tax rate on its earnings has a 6 percent before-tax cost of debt, its after-tax cost of debt is only 3 percent as a first approximation.

The cost of equity is more complicated. Although equity does not have mandated payments like debt, equity plainly has a cost in the sense that investors must expect a return before they will make their funds available to the firm. A corporation that disappoints this expectation may be unable to access equity markets again. This expected return then is the cost of the equity. But how can one estimate this *implicit* cost of equity?

Perhaps the most well-accepted, conceptually pure, method for calculating a cost of equity is the *capital asset pricing model (CAPM)*, developed originally by Professor William Sharpe of Stanford University. This model is built on the insight that well-functioning markets will link risk and return. That is, risky ventures are required to pay a higher price for their capital (they have to offer a higher return) in order to compensate investors for their risk aversion. How then do we measure the degree of risk inherent in an equity investment in order to estimate its return (or implied cost)? The CAPM does this by linking securities risk to the *volatility* of the security prices.

In the real world of investments, investors have a price history by which they can estimate how the returns of a particular investment are likely to fare in response to future events. Risk from future events can be said to be of two types: systemwide, or *systematic,* risk and company-specific, or *unsystematic,* risk. The first kind is a risk that investors cannot get rid of, no matter how they construct their portfolio. The second kind is a risk that investors can get rid of (as by matching a $5K-$15K flip with a $15K-$5K flip).

Finance scholars have developed a measure of the systematic risk associated with securities. By looking at the trading history of the stock and how the stock price moves in relation to the stock market as a whole, these scholars believe that the amount of systemic risk in a stock's returns can be estimated. (The finance coefficient for this risk is beta, and the term "beta" has taken on a life of its own in the finance literature. But it means nothing more than the estimated systemic, nondiversifiable risk, measured as a proportion of the systematic risk of a diversified portfolio, such as a weighted portfolio of stocks in S&P 500 companies.)

There is another, down-and-dirty, technique for estimating the cost of equity. It is simpler, but, perhaps unsurprisingly, less precise than CAPM.

It is based on *historical average equity risk premia* data. It requires a calculation of the firm's before-tax cost of debt and recognizes that, historically, equity has been priced at a cost that is approximately 8 percent higher than the before-tax cost of debt on average. Although imprecise, this technique has the advantage of not requiring one to calculate equity betas.

5.3.2   The Relevance of Prices in the Securities Market

Traditional discounting concepts are a sturdy guide to the underlying logic of valuing assets. These concepts yield a theoretically satisfying notion of intrinsic value. To be sure, they are difficult to apply. Predicting future cash flow is problematic. Determining an appropriate risk premium for a risky investment is inherently problematic as well. Fortunately, for some assets such as stock and oil, an alternative mode of valuation is available. These assets are bought and sold in a well-functioning market with many traders. Thus, finding a market price for a share of stock or a barrel of Brent crude oil is easy. In the case of stock, we need only pick up the business section of almost any newspaper listing the closing prices of exchange-traded stocks from the preceding day. In the case of oil, we do not have to figure out the future cash flows from owning 100,000 barrels of oil. We can pick up the finance section of the paper and see how much a barrel of oil trades for. This raises an obvious question: How do the market prices of publicly traded stocks relate to possible estimates of stock value based on discounting their expected dividends?

It would be exceedingly convenient — not to say socially valuable — if the prices of securities reflected well-informed estimates, based on all available information, of the discounted value of the expected future payouts of corporate stocks and bonds. That is, it would simplify matters greatly if market prices aggregated the best estimates of the best-informed traders about the underlying present value of corporate assets — net of payments to creditors, taxes, and all the rest.

One of the core working hypotheses of modern financial economics is that the stock market manages to do just this. Much empirical research indicates that stock market prices rapidly reflect all public information bearing on the expected value of individual stocks. This is generally known as the efficient capital market hypothesis (ECMH). As you will see in Chapter 14, the ECMH has had an important influence on developments in securities law at the federal level. It has met with a more skeptical reception in corporate law developments at the state level, especially in Delaware.

In this book, we remain agnostic about the more aggressive claims that have been made on behalf of the ECMH. It is sufficient for us that prices in an informed market should be regarded as prima facie evidence of the true value of traded shares. Whether the market price of a company's shares also reflects, in a straightforward way, the value of the entire company (or all of its equity in aggregate) is a more complicated question that we will touch on in later chapters. We will also remind you periodically that the accuracy of market prices depends entirely on the quality of information that informs trading—which, in turn, depends on the integrity of all major actors in the market, including top corporate management, accounting firms, law firms, investment banks, security analysts, and even the portfolio managers who invest on behalf of institutional investors.

We close this chapter with a look at a real-world valuation. In this case, Vice-Chancellor (now Delaware Supreme Court Justice) Jack Jacobs was required to value the minority shares in a "freeze-out" merger. We return to freeze-out transactions in Chapter 12, but we include this excerpt from the opinion here in order to give you a flavor for the questions that arise in real-world valuation proceedings. We focus on the court's treatment of two issues: the calculation of the cost of equity, and the relevance of the market price of the Emerging Communications stock for valuation purposes.

IN RE EMERGING COMMUNICATIONS INC., SHAREHOLDER LITIGATION

2004 Del. Ch. LEXIS 70 (2004)

... Both Prof. Zmijewski and Mr. Bayston used the CAPM formula to calculate ECM's [Emerging Communication's] cost of equity. Using that standard approach, Zmijewski derived a cost of equity of 10.4% (for the years when the tax abatement would be in effect), and 10.3% (when the current tax abatement expires). Bayston's initial cost of equity was somewhat lower—9.9%—but Bayston then increased it to 14% by adding "premiums" totaling 4.1%. More specifically, Bayston added a "small stock premium" of 1.7% and a "company-specific premium" of 2.4%, the latter consisting of a 1 to 1.5% "super-small stock premium" and a .9 to 1.4% hurricane risk premium." Those "premiums" account for most of the difference between these two experts' cost of equity inputs. Accordingly, the issue becomes whether either of these premiums is appropriate in these circumstances. The party seeking to add the premium (here, the defendants) has the burden to establish that they are appropriate.

A.   *The 1.7% "Small Firm/Small Stock" Premium*

Although plaintiffs contend that there is no basis in the finance literature or theory for adding a "small firm/small stock" premium to the cost of equity, that is not entirely accurate. There is finance literature supporting the position that stocks of smaller companies are riskier than securities of large ones and, therefore, command a higher expected rate of return in the market. Our case law also recognizes the propriety of a small firm/small stock premium in appropriate circumstances. The issue, therefore, is not whether a small firm/small stock premium is permissible theoretically, but whether the defendants have shown that a premium of 1.7% is appropriate in this particular case. The Court concludes that the defendants have made that showing. ...

B. The 2.4% "Supersmall Firm" and "Hurricane Risk" Premium

Far more controversial, and less grounded in finance theory and legal precedent, is the additional 2.4% premium added by Bayston to account for what he determined was the incremental risk of ECM being both a "supersmall" firm and also subject to unusually hazardous weather risk, specifically, hurricanes. Bayston's justification for adding an incremental premium of 1%-1.5% to ECM due to its "supersmall" size occupies less than one page of defendants' 150 page brief. That justification boils down to an assertion that the 1.7% small firm premium reflected only Ibbotson's average premium for small firms, but that Ibbotson contains "more particularized data which permits an assessment of the appropriate premium for a company, such as [ECM] 'which is much smaller . . . than the average companies within the Ibbotson data.'" Other than to assert that that additional adjustment of the discount rate "reflects the reality of investment returns in such micro-cap companies" the defendants offer no analysis, discussion of specific data, reference to any finance text, or other rationale for their "supersmall" firm premium.

Defendants' support for an incremental premium that if accepted would further increase ECM's cost of capital, falls woefully short of the showing that is required. The defendants offer nothing to persuade the Court that ECM's risk profile fits what they contend is the "reality" of investment returns for micro-cap companies. ECM may be small, but it is also a utility that was unusually protected from the hazards of the marketplace. ECM was well established, it had no competition, it was able to borrow at below-market rates, and it was cushioned by regulators from extraordinary hazards (for example, by tax abatements). Implicit in the defendants' position, but nowhere straightforwardly argued, is the assumption that these advantages, however extraordinary, were not enough to offset the added risk created by ECM's "supersmall" size. It is the defendant's burden to support that assumption, and they have not done that.

By adding a second incremental premium to ECM's cost of equity to account for the risk of size, Bayston appears to have performed a mechanical exercise, rather than make a nuanced, textured judgment. Accordingly, the Court determines that the defendants have not established a credible justification for their incremental "supersmall" firm premium, and declines to add that premium to the cost-of-equity.

Apart from the "supersmall firm" premium, Bayston also added a company-specific incremental premium for hurricane risk. The effect was to increase the cost of equity by 1-1.5%, to increase the discount rate by a range of .7% to 1.05%, and to decrease enterprise value by $18 to $24 million (i.e., by $1.64 to $2.19 per share). Bayston's justification for this incremental premium was that (1) as a result of Hurricane Hugo in 1989 and Hurricane Marilyn in 1995, Vitelco (ATN) suffered losses, not reimbursed by insurance or Universal Service Fund revenues, of approximately $80 million; and (2) ECM's management believed that hurricanes would pose a significant risk to ECM's business in the future, in that future storm losses would not be reimbursable by insurance because (management was informed) coverage would no longer be available.

This analysis is faulty on factual and conceptual grounds. First, it overstates the amount of unreimbursed hurricane damage. That amount, Mr. Heying testified, totaled about $55 million for the entire 70 years preceding the merger. Second, defendants' claim that management knew as of the merger date that its hurricane insurance would not continue, relies entirely on Prosser's trial testimony, which is not corroborated by any contemporaneous document and is inconsistent with ECM's SEC filings and RTFC loan documents, none of which indicate any impending loss of hurricane loss coverage. Third, assuming that the risk of future storm losses should be accounted for in some way, the defendants have not supported their argument that the appropriate way to do that is by increasing the cost of equity. Defendants cite no finance literature supporting that approach, nor have they supported their argument empirically, such as (for example) by comparing ECM's company-specific weather-related risk (net of mitigation factors) to the "average" or "mean" weather-related risk for all companies, or even for all "small" companies.

The absence of theoretical and evidentiary support leaves this Court unpersuaded that the risk of unrecoverable hurricane damage loss is so embedded in ECM's business as to require a structural increase in ECM's cost of equity. Absent theoretical and empirical guidance, a more rational approach would be to factor that risk into ECM's cash flow projections such as (for example) by dividing the net hurricane-related loss by a statistically representative number of years to arrive at a loss deduction from projected cash flow for each forecast year. Unfortunately, neither side performed such a calculation. . . .

***

For the reasons previously discussed, the Court cannot accept in its entirety the DCF valuation of either side's expert. Although the Court accepts the plaintiffs' position that the projected cash flows and terminal value should be derived from the June projections, it has determined independently the disputed elements of the WACC and CAPM formulas from which the discount rate is computed. Based upon the Court's findings, the appropriate discount rate is determined to be 8.69%, and the fair value of ECM as of the merger date is determined to be $38.05 per share.

C.   What Weight Should Be Accorded to ECM's Market Price as Evidence of Fair Value?

To support their claim that the fair value of ECM on the merger date was no more than $10.38 per share, the defendants urge that "where, as here, the market for a publicly traded security is an active and efficient one, the market price [of ECM's common stock] is, at the least, important corroborative evidence of value. . . . " For that argument, the defendants rely upon the expert testimony of Professor Burton Malkiel of Princeton

University. Professor Malkiel opined that ECM's stock "was trade[d] in an efficient market with enough volume and a low enough bid-asked spread, and that it reflected news without delay; and these ... indicators led [Prof. Malkiel] to conclude that ECM was traded in an efficient market and that the [$7.00 per share] market price of ECM common stock prior to the buyout ... was a reasonable reflection of its value." Intending no disrespect to Professor Malkiel, the Court is unable to accept his conclusion in this specific case. However sound Professor Malkiel's market price-based theory may be in other circumstances, that theory is inapplicable to these facts because its premise is not supported by either the trial record or Delaware law.

Delaware law recognizes that, although market price should be considered in an appraisal, the market price of shares is not always indicative of fair value. Our appraisal cases so confirm.

Moreover, the record undermines any assertion that ECM's common stock was traded in an efficient market. Indeed, it was precisely because ECM's stock market price did not reflect ECM's underlying values that Prosser decided to abandon the proposed merger and instead acquire the ECM minority interest in the Privatization. Prosser himself told his fellow ECM directors that the ECM stock price had failed to reach the desired appreciation as a result of the small public float and the fact that the stock was not being followed by Wall Street analysts. Moreover, because Prosser always owned the majority interest, the market price of ECM stock always reflected a minority discount.

Professor Malkiel admitted that markets occasionally make errors, that the market could have been wrong about ECM, and that it is possible for a stock that trades even in an efficient market to be mispriced, especially in the short run. Professor Malkiel also conceded that the market may be inefficient if material information is withheld from it. In the case of ECM, while the stock was trading freely, (*i.e.*, before Prosser announced the Privatization), the market never had the benefit of any disclosed earnings or projections of future results, including the June Projections.

For these reasons, the Court rejects the defendants' argument that the market price of ECM stock corroborates the $10.25 price as the fair or intrinsic value of ECM on the date of the merger. In this case, ECM's unaffected stock market price merits little or no weight.

QUESTIONS ON EMERGING COMMUNICATIONS

1. The primary defendant in this case was the controlling shareholder of ECM (Jeffrey Prosser), who was trying to justify the $10.25 per share that he paid to the minority shareholders in his company. Why would the addition of a "small firm" premium and a "hurricane" premium to the cost of equity, if accepted by the court, help his position?

2. If the Court is correct that the intrinsic value of the minority shares was $38.05, why did 60% of the ECM minority shareholders approve of (by tendering) Prosser's freeze-out offer at $10.25 per share? We return to this question in Chapter 12.

THE PROTECTION OF CREDITORS

Fundamentally, the problems of corporate creditors are not different from those of any other creditors. Debtors can misrepresent their income or assets before they borrow. Alternatively, after they borrow, they can dilute the assets that secure their debts (by operating their business badly or by hiding or shifting assets so they are out of the reach of creditors), dilute the claims of their unsecured creditors (by taking on senior debt), or increase the riskiness of their debt (by altering investment policy). In addition, debtors can externalize costs to involuntary creditors such as tort victims by incurring liabilities that exceed the value of their assets.

Since all debtors can do these things, corporate creditors face the same qualitative risks as other creditors and naturally benefit from the protections offered by the general law of debtor-creditor relations. Nevertheless, corporate law does not leave creditor protection solely to this general law; it provides creditors with additional protections in all jurisdictions. Moreover, it does so even though it does not attempt to protect other classes of corporate stakeholders, such as employees, suppliers, or customers. An obvious first question is this: Why should corporate law be so solicitous toward creditors? The most plausible explanation is that lawmakers believe that the core corporate feature of limited liability greatly exacerbates the traditional problems of debtor-creditor relationships.[1]

Limited liability can have this effect in two ways. First, it opens opportunities for both express and tacit misrepresentation in transactions with voluntary creditors. Shareholders who employ the corporate form through which to contract with others may play a game of "bait and switch." They may, in effect, misrepresent the assets within the corporation and simply walk away if the business fails. Indeed, shareholders may contract through companies with no assets whatsoever, while at least implicitly representing otherwise. Second, limited liability makes it possible and sometimes attractive to shift assets out of the corporation after a creditor has extended credit to the corporation. It is a simple thing for shareholders to distribute assets to themselves, while leaving the debts with their corporation in violation of

---

1. A second reason may be that *all* stakeholders are at least potential creditors if the firm breaches its contractual obligations by, for example, failing to pay its employees, suppliers, etc.

an implicit representation to continue to operate a solvent business. Or more subtly, shareholders can undertake highly risky (volatile) investments or increase leverage in order to shift uncompensated risk onto the shoulders of both voluntary and involuntary creditors.

All of these opportunistic moves would lose much of their appeal if shareholders did not have the shield of limited liability to protect their personal assets from the consequences of contractual default on the part of the corporation.

Of course, creditors can minimize the costs of such forms of shareholder opportunism by exercising vigilance and negotiating for contractual protections. They can, for example, take security interests in particular corporate assets or negotiate specific covenants that give them early warning of credit problems. In the real world, most effective creditor protection for substantial creditors comes from contractually based protections of this sort. These protections are costly, however. Indeed, they are usually too costly for small creditors to afford. Moreover, some forms of debtor opportunism are so blatant that no amount of contracting can offer protection from them. It follows that special protections for corporate creditors are easily justified. In this chapter, we leave to the side contractual protections that creditors must negotiate for, but focus instead on the default provisions of law that protect all creditors regardless of their contract.

Corporate law generally pursues three basic strategies in its limited efforts to protect creditors. First, it can impose a more or less extensive mandatory disclosure duty on corporate debtors. Second, it can promulgate (usually de minimis) rules regulating the amount and disposition of corporate capital. Finally, it can impose duties to safeguard creditors on corporate participants, such as directors, creditors, and shareholders. We consider each of these strategies in turn.

6.1 MANDATORY DISCLOSURE

Insofar as debtor opportunism turns on misrepresentation, mandatory disclosure offers some promise of controlling it. Federal securities law imposes extensive mandatory disclosure obligations on public corporations (see Chapter 14 below), and creditors are among its beneficiaries. Indeed, public issues of debt are themselves occasions for extensive disclosure. State corporation law, however, generally makes little use of mandatory disclosure to protect creditors of closely held corporations. No U.S. state requires closely held corporations to prepare audited financial statements or to file financial statements — audited or not — with a commercial register or the attorney general's office.[2] In this respect, U.S. law contrasts with that of European Union (EU) jurisdictions, where at least "large" closely held companies are required to prepare audited financial

---

2. A few states, such as Michigan, require all corporations to prepare financial statements annually for distribution to shareholders, but these disclosures are not intended to benefit corporate creditors. See Mich. Bus. Corp. Act §901.

statements annually,[3] and even the smallest corporations are frequently required to file financial statements with public authorities that are open for creditor inspection. Whether the more extensive European requirements for small firm disclosure are worthwhile clearly depends on their costs and benefits. Arguably, credit bureau reports, which are generally available for small businesses as well as individuals in the United States, are more useful than financial statements for evaluating credit risks associated with close corporations. In any case, voluntary creditors are in a position to ask for both.

6.2 CAPITAL REGULATION

Regulation of the capital committed to the corporation — by, for example, requiring investors to contribute a minimum amount of capital to the corporation and restricting the removal of capital from the firm — is a very direct means by which the legal system can attempt to protect against some of the risks that creditors face. As we will see, neither of these strategies provides real protection to creditors (and probably should not provide strong protection) under U.S. corporate law. Nevertheless, a variety of rules do regulate corporate capital, some much more protective (and restrictive) than others, even among state corporation laws. In order to discuss these rules as they have traditionally evolved, we must first introduce the corporate balance sheet and the somewhat arcane concept of legal capital.

6.2.1 Financial Statements

Accounting is a standardized methodology for describing a firm's past financial performance. In the United States, generally accepted accounting principles (GAAP) are set by the Financial Accounting Standards Board (FASB), a self-regulatory body authorized by the Securities Exchange Commission to establish accounting standards.

It is important for novices to appreciate both the importance and the limitations of accounting reports. We start here with the corporate versions of the two principal accounting statements that we introduced in Chapter 3 in the context of a general partnership: the balance sheet and the income statement (sometimes called the profit and loss statement). The balance sheet represents the financial picture of a business organization as it stands on one particular day, in contrast to the income statement, which presents the results of the operation of the business over a specified period. A firm customarily presents the balance sheet and income statement figures for two or more years in order to show how the situation of the firm has changed over time.

3. Art. 2(1)(f), EU First Company Law Directive. Note that there has been quite some resistance to having smaller EU companies disclose their financial statements (see Case C-191/95, *Commission of the European Communities v. Federal Republic of Germany*, 1998 ECR-I 5485). Thus, in the United Kingdom, corporations with total sales in excess of 90,000 must present audited financial statements. See Companies Act, 1985, §§249A-249E (introduced in 1994).

Typical Corp.: Balance Sheet

ASSETS*	2006	2005
Current assets		
Cash	$ 51,000	$ 25,000
Marketable securities — cost		
(Market value: 2006 $71,400	$ 68,000	
2005 $57,800)		$ 54,400
Accounts receivable (less allowance for doubtful accounts):		
2006 $5,100.00	$ 265,200	
2005 $4,037.50		$ 246,500
Inventories	$ 326,000	$ 315,000
Prepaid expenses	$ 6,800	$ 5,100
Total current assets	$ 717,000	$ 646,000
Fixed assets		
Land	$ 51,000	$ 51,000
Buildings	$ 212,500	$ 201,450
Machinery	$ 365,500	$ 316,370
Office equipment	$ 35,500	$ 20,400
Total property, plant, and equipment	$ 664,500	$ 589,220
Less accumulated depreciation	$ 212,700	$ 164,900
Net fixed assets	$ 451,800	$ 424,320
Intangibles	$ 3,400	$ 3,400
TOTAL ASSETS	$1,172,200	$1,073,720
LIABILITIES	2006	2005
Current liabilities		
Accounts payable	$ 122,400	$ 117,300
Notes payable	$ 86,700	$ 103,700
Accrued expenses payable	$ 51,000	$ 61,200
Federal income taxes payable	$ 28,900	$ 25,500
Total current liabilities	$ 289,000	$ 307,700
Long-term liabilities		
Deferred income tax	$ 17,000	$ 15,300
Debentures 12.5%, due 2010	$ 231,200	$ 231,200
TOTAL LIABILITIES	$ 537,200	$ 554,200
STOCKHOLDERS' EQUITY	2006	2005
Preferred stock:		
($5.83 cumulative, $100 par value, authorized 60,000 shares, outstanding 60,000 shares)	$ 6,000	$ 6,000
Common stock:		
($5.00 par value, 20,000,000 shares authorized, outstanding 2006 15,000,000 shares, 2005 14,500,000 shares	$ 75,000	$ 72,500
Capital surplus	$ 27,200	$ 12,750
Accumulated retained earnings	$ 527,000	$ 428,270
Total stockholders' equity	$ 635,000	$ 519,520
TOTAL LIABILITIES & STOCKHOLDERS' EQUITY	$1,172,200	$1,073,720

* All sums in thousands of dollars.

The principal limitation of the entries on the balance sheet is that they typically reflect historical costs instead of current economic (market) values. Thus, each asset is listed at its acquisition cost (minus depreciation charges, which are only loosely correlated with deterioration in economic value). Book value (the value found on the balance sheet) may therefore differ quite a bit from the current economic value of an asset. A balance sheet might show a value for shareholder equity that is much more than shareholders could achieve upon the sale of the firm or, more likely in an inflationary period, a value that is much less than the firm's market value. Liabilities also reflect a historical approach to valuation rather than an economic (market value) one. Moreover, the income statement suffers limitations as well — mainly that its account of profit or loss does not reflect the actual amount of cash that a business throws off (or makes available to its owners) in the year. The figure accountants report as net profit may differ from the cash available for distribution for a number of reasons. For example, depreciation is a noncash charge reflected in the income statement; it reduces net profit, but it does not affect the amount of cash that can be made available that year to owners. On the other hand, some cash expenditures may reduce cash available to owners but not reduce net profit, since they are treated in accounting as capital investment. In sum, the income statement does not reflect the amount of cash available to owners, just as the balance sheet does not reflect current economic values. Despite these limitations, however, financial statements remain highly important to investors and others who wish to evaluate economic performance and estimate company values.

The balance sheet is particularly important in traditional corporation statutes. As the hypothetical statement above illustrates, a corporate balance sheet is divided into two columns: on the left side are the assets, while on the right side are the liabilities, which represent the debts of the business and stockholders' equity (or partners' capital if the business is organized as a partnership). In the example we provide above, we present the "asset" and "liability" columns sequentially, rather than simultaneously, for ease of presentation. But whether they are shown sequentially or in side-by-side columns, the asset and liability portions of the balance sheet are always in balance. Every element of the corporation's value (asset column) must be accounted for by an equivalent debt or equity claim on the liability column. The assets column includes all of a business' tangible property, intellectual property, goodwill, and even outstanding legal claims against third parties that have come to judgment but have not yet been collected. Under liabilities are listed all debts of the business payable to others. The stockholders' equity category is what brings the assets and liabilities into balance. It represents the difference between the asset values and the liability values. This is the amount of equity or the ownership stake that shareholders have in the business (although, of course, this does not determine the market values of equity).

Look first to the asset side of the balance sheet. Current assets include cash, marketable securities, accounts receivable, inventories, and prepaid expenses. These are the "working" assets of the corporation in the sense that they are constantly cycling through the firm's production process, from raw materials to inventory to receivables to cash. In contrast, fixed assets, which are sometimes referred to as "property, plant, and equipment" and sometimes as "capital assets," represent those assets not intended for sale, which are used for lengthy periods in order to manufacture, display, warehouse, and transport the product. Accordingly, this category includes land, buildings, machinery, equipment, furniture, and vehicles. Note again that under GAAP, the balance sheet fixes asset values at historical cost and adjusts these figures downward to reflect depreciation. The resulting valuation may bear little relationship to market value (or replacement cost), which is often much higher. An open question for the accounting profession is whether this accounting bias toward "objective" historical costs should continue or whether the profession ought to introduce some version of "mark to market" accounting. Since both approaches have difficulties, it is unlikely that a market-oriented standard will squeeze out historical costs any time soon.

Similarly, the liabilities side of the balance sheet divides into current liabilities (due within the year) and long-term liabilities (due over a longer period). A comparison of current assets with current liabilities gives a sense of the liquidity (or the capacity of noncash assets to be converted into cash) of a company's assets and the likelihood that it can pay its obligations or make new investments in the near future. To facilitate comparison, both current assets and current liabilities are listed in current dollars. Long-term liabilities also tend to be stated in units that approximate real economic dollars. Thus, if our hypothetical company has 12.5 percent debentures, with a principal value of $231.2 million, due in 2010, the true economic value of this liability may be in the neighborhood of $231.2 million if 12.5 percent is a reasonable risk-adjusted interest rate for the company at this time. If the company is currently significantly riskier (weaker) than when it issued the note, then the economic value of the note (liability) will be less than the principal amount the company is legally obligated to pay. (If you don't see why, ask in class.) In this event, a weak company will be able to buy its notes on the market at a price lower than its legal repayment obligation — that is, if it has the resources to do so.

The third major division of the corporate balance sheet is stockholders' equity. This is the book value of the owners' economic interests. Stockholders' equity is always a "plug figure"; i.e., it is the difference between corporate assets and liabilities. In our example, in 2006 the equity accounts equal the difference between total assets ($1,172,200) and total liabilities ($537,200), or $635,000. For both legal and accounting reasons, the stockholders' equity is divided into three accounts: stated (or legal) capital, capital surplus, and accumulated retained earnings (or earned surplus).

Stated capital is also known as capital stock, or the corporation's legal or nominal capital. This item represents all or a portion of the value that shareholders transferred to the corporation at the time of the original sale of the company's stock to its original shareholders. The amount of stated capital, expressed in dollars, is usually the product of the par value[4] of the

---

4. The par value of a stock is an arbitrary dollar amount stated in the articles of incorporation and on the stock certificate. It bears no relationship to the stock's economic (market) value.

stock multiplied by the number of issued and outstanding shares (although the board may fix a higher level). Alternatively, if a corporation chooses to issue "no par stock," which U.S. corporation statutes generally permit, the board of directors must set aside some (discretionary) portion of the sale price as the company's stated capital. See, e.g., DGCL §154. If the stock is sold for more than its par value, the excess is accounted for in a capital surplus or paid-in surplus account. Suppose, for example, Typical Co. has issued 15 million shares of common stock, with a par value of $5 a share, at an average price of $6.066 per share. In this case, Typical has received a total of $91,000,000 for its common stock, and on the balance sheet, it allocates $7.5 million to capital stock or legal capital and $83.5 million to capital surplus.

Finally, consider the third shareholder equity account: accumulated retained earnings, or earned surplus. Retained earnings are merely the amounts that a profitable corporation earns but has not distributed to its shareholders. (*Note:* When a company first starts in business, it has no accumulated retained earnings.) Undistributed amounts of net profit accumulate in the earned surplus or retained earnings account. E.g.:

Balance of retained earnings (end of year 1)	$ 50,000	
Net profit for year 2	$160,000	
Total available for dividends		$210,000
Less: All dividends paid year 2		$ 75,000
Accumulated retained earnings (end of year 2)		$135,000

6.2.2 Distribution Constraints

How does the balance sheet enter into capital regulation and the protection of creditors? One (rather primitive) idea might be to represent a particular fund on the balance sheet as "permanent capital" that could not be paid out to shareholders and upon which creditors could rely in extending credit. Such an account could be (and often is) called the legal capital or stated capital account. Thus most distribution restrictions look to the legal capital account in the corporate balance sheet. We will see as creditor protections, these restrictions are fairly weak.

New York Business Corporation Law §510 illustrates the structure of a traditional distribution constraint. Section 510(a) bars distributions that would render the corporation "insolvent," by which is meant insolvency in the equity sense of being unable to pay its immediate obligations as they come due. Section 510(b) is a balance sheet test or, more particularly, a capital surplus test: Dividends may be paid only out of surplus; they may not be paid out of stated capital. This test is much looser than it may seem, however, because the board of directors is entitled to restructure the capital account by shifting any portion of the stated capital account to the surplus account if it is authorized to do so by *shareholders*. See N.Y. Bus. Corp. Law §516(a)(4).

DGCL §170 employs a modified capital surplus test that is commonly referred to as a "nimble dividend" test. Under §170(a), the directors of a business corporation (but not a banking corporation) may pay dividends either out of capital surplus (as in New York) or, if there is no capital surplus, out of net profits in the current or preceding fiscal year. The motivation is apparently to permit boards to reward the shareholders of firms that, although not conspicuously healthy, may nevertheless be on an upward trajectory. Unlike in New York, moreover, the board of a Delaware corporation may freely transfer stated capital associated with no par stock into the surplus account on its own decision. Reducing the stated capital associated with par stock requires a charter amendment to reduce the par value of the stock, and therefore requires a shareholder vote. See DGCL §244(a)(4) (but once again as a creditor protection a shareholder vote is, of course, no help).

By contrast, California has promulgated a tighter two-part distribution test that explicitly attempts to give creditors meaningful protection. A corporation may pay dividends either out of its retained earnings or out of its assets, as long as those assets (on the balance sheet) remain at least 1.25 times greater than its liabilities and the current assets at least equal current liabilities. See Cal. Corp. Code §500. This test then is a modified retained earnings test.

Section 6.40 of the RMBCA is a traditional distribution test with a modern twist. Corporations may not pay dividends if, as a result of doing so, (a) they cannot pay their debts as they come due or (b) their assets are less than their liabilities plus the preferential claims of preferred shareholders. However, in determining whether assets suffice to make distributions under this test, the RMBCA permits boards to rely on either GAAP or "a fair valuation or other method that is reasonable in the circumstances." RMBCA §6.40(d). The latter clause invites a shift from accounting conventions to alternative measures of value that more accurately reflect economic reality, such as a DCF estimate of going concern value. See RMBCA §6.40 cmt. b.

Economic reality can impinge on the accounting conceptions of capital surplus in another way. If a corporation's assets are worth more (in economic value) than the amount at which they are carried on the firm's books, no law prevents the firm from adjusting its books to reflect that higher value. GAAP will allow it to account for its assets on this basis so long as the firm's revaluation is clearly disclosed and its outside auditors concur that the new value is a fair estimate of economic value. The additional value recognized upon such a revaluation will have to be balanced by an equal increase in the values on the other side of the firm's balance sheet. Since the write-up involves no increase in the firm's liabilities, the only account available to make this adjustment is some sort of capital surplus account, which we could call "revaluation surplus." Since it is a surplus account, dividends can be paid from it. See D.A. Drexler, L.S. Black, Jr., & A.G. Sparks, Delaware Corporation Law and Practice §20.03 [2] (2001). Thus, as a practical matter, under the DGCL and the RMBCA, the only real protection that creditors have against dividend payments (except for contractual restrictions that are often found in loan documents) is the restriction that we discuss below under the fraudulent transfers act.

QUESTIONS

Alpha Inc. has the following balance sheet at the end of 2006 (all numbers in millions of dollars):

Current assets		Liabilities	
Cash	1,000	Current liabilities	9,650
Securities	650	Long-term liabilities	5,000
Accounts receivable	6,000	Total liabilities	14,650
Inventory	5,000		
Property, plant, and equipment	3,000	Shareholders' equity	
		Stated capital	200
Total assets	15,650	Capital surplus	300
		Retained earnings	500
		Total shareholders' equity	1,000

Additionally, Alpha's net profit in 2005 was $400 million and, in 2006, $120 million. An investment banking firm has valued Alpha at $30 billion using a DCF methodology, while Alpha's market capitalization (the aggregate market value of its outstanding stock) is $15 billion.

1. What is the maximum dividend that Alpha can pay under the New York statute? The Delaware statute? The California statute? The RMBCA?

2. How can a capital surplus test protect corporate creditors if there is no minimum level of stated capital to serve as a creditor cushion?

3. Which distribution constraint do you prefer? Why?

6.2.3 Minimum Capital and Capital Maintenance Requirements

An obvious objection to distribution constraints based on accounting categories such as capital surplus is that they are easily avoided through the expedient of placing trivial sums in the "trust fund" of legal capital reserved for creditors. A response to this objection might be to require shareholders to commit a stated amount of capital to the firm: a mandatory minimum capital requirement. But within the United States, statutory minimum capital requirements are either truly minimal ($1,000) or entirely nonexistent. (Neither the DGCL nor the RMBCA requires a minimum capital amount as a condition of incorporation.) Internationally, minimum capital requirements have historically been significant but seem to be on the decline. Japan used to impose relatively high capital requirements on corporations[5] but abolished these requirements as of May 2006, though a Japanese corporation must now have 3 million yen in assets (~ $30,000)

---

5. See Art. 168-4, Japanese Commercial Code (about $100,000 for AGs, or open joint stock companies); Art. 9, Japanese GmbHG (about $30,000 for GmbHs, or closed corporations).

before it can distribute profits.[6] The European Union imposes a minimum capital requirement of approximately $25,000 for "open" corporations, but the European Commission is currently considering relaxing this requirement.[7] Even in jurisdictions where minimum capital requirements continue to exist, they are fixed at levels that seem to provide a form of de minimis screening rather than a substantial form of creditor protection.

One reason that minimum capital requirements cannot be an effective creditor protection is that this check, where it exists, is fixed at the date of organization of the corporation. But, even if companies cannot dip into minimum capital to pay shareholders, normal business activity can easily dissipate a company's capital, leaving nothing on the books or in the kitty for its creditors. For this reason, jurisdictions within the EU have traditionally adopted not only a minimum capital rule but also so-called capital maintenance rules. The main characteristic of these capital maintenance rules is that they accelerate the point at which failing corporations must file for insolvency: EU company law requires member states to mandate that larger companies call a shareholders' meeting to consider dissolution when there has been a serious loss of legal capital that causes the firm to violate capital maintenance standards.[8] In fact, many European jurisdictions go beyond the EU minimum. For example, German and Swiss company laws extend the duty to call a shareholders' meeting to smaller as well as larger companies and, in addition, require that directors immediately file for bankruptcy when legal capital is totally lost.[9] There are no such requirements in the United States.

QUESTIONS

What are the costs and benefits of tough minimum capital and capital maintenance requirements? Which do you prefer, the European regulation in the interest of creditors or the relatively deregulatory approach of U.S. jurisdictions? How does it assist creditors if EU law requires an early shareholders' meeting?

6.3 STANDARD-BASED DUTIES

Corporate law (and debtor-creditor law) typically subjects certain participants in the corporate enterprise to limited duties to protect the interests of creditors under specific circumstances. These participants are directors, fellow creditors, and — last but not least — shareholders.

6. See Law No. 86 of Japan ("Kaisha ho") (promulgated July 26, 2005).

7. See *Modernising Company Law and Enhancing Corporate Govvernance in the European Union — A Plan to Move Forward*, COM(2003)284 at 18.

8. Art. 17, EU Second Company Law Directive, applicable to société anonyme; Aktiengesellschaft; società per azioni; public company limited by shares.

9. See for Germany: AktG §92(2) and GmbHG §64(1); for Switzerland: OR Art. 725 and Art. 817.

6.3.1 Director Liability

Under certain circumstances, directors owe an obligation to creditors not to render the firm unable to meets its obligations to creditors by making distributions to shareholders or to others without receiving fair value in return. These obligations are chiefly established by the Uniform Fraudulent Transfers Act (discussed below), by statutory restrictions on the payment of dividends (discussed above), and to a lesser extent by common law. In a couple of interesting opinions, the Delaware Chancery Court has suggested that when a firm is insolvent (but no one has yet invoked the federal bankruptcy protections), its directors owe a duty to consider the interests of corporate creditors.

In fact, the courts have gone further on the strength of the fiduciary duty of directors to the corporation (and not only its shareholders). In one interesting case, the Court of Chancery opined that, when a corporation is "in the vicinity of insolvency," its directors in making business decisions should not consider shareholders' welfare alone but should consider the welfare of the community of interests that constitute the corporation. The court stated:

> The possibility of insolvency can do curious things to incentives, exposing creditors to risks of opportunistic behavior and creating complexities for directors. Consider, for example, a solvent corporation having a single asset, a judgment for $51 million against a solvent debtor. The judgment is on appeal and thus subject to modification or reversal. Assume that the only liabilities of the company are to bondholders in the amount of $12 million. Assume that the array of probable outcomes of the appeal is as follows:

> | Expected Value | | |
> | --- | --- | --- |
> | 25% chance of affirmance | ($51m) | $12.75 |
> | 70% chance of modification | ($ 4m) | 2.80 |
> | 5% chance of reversal | ($ 0m) | 0.00 |
> | Expected Value of Judgment on Appeal | | $15.55 |

Thus, the best evaluation is that the current value of the equity is $3.55 million. ($15.55 million expected value of judgment on appeal-12 million liability to bondholders). Now assume an offer to settle at $12.5 million (also consider one at $17.5 million). By what standard do the directors of the company evaluate the fairness of these offers? The creditors of this solvent company would be in favor of accepting either a $12.5 million offer or a $17.5 million offer. In either event they will avoid the 75 percent risk of insolvency and default. The stockholders, however, will plainly be opposed to acceptance of a $12.5 million settlement (under which they get practically nothing). More importantly, they very well may be opposed to acceptance of the $17.5 million offer under which the residual value of the corporation would increase from $3.5 to $5.5 million. This is so because the litigation alternative, with its 25 percent probability of a $39 million outcome to them ($51 million-$12 million = $39 million) has an expected value to the residual risk bearer of

$9.75 million ($39 million × 25 percent chance of affirmance), substantially greater than the $5.5 million available to them in the settlement. While in fact the stockholders' preference would reflect their appetite for risk, it is possible (and with diversified shareholders likely) that shareholders would prefer rejection of both settlement offers.

But if we consider the community of interests that the corporation represents it seems apparent that one should in this hypothetical accept the best settlement offer available providing it is greater than $15.55 million, and one below that amount should be rejected. But that result will not be reached by a director who thinks he owes duties directly to shareholders only. It will be reached by directors who are capable of conceiving of the corporation as a legal and economic entity. Such directors will recognize that in managing the business affairs of a solvent corporation in the vicinity of insolvency, circumstances may arise when the right (both the efficient and the fair) course to follow for the corporation may diverge from the choice that the stockholders (or the creditors, or the employees, or any single group interested in the corporation) would make if given the opportunity to act.[10]

If we look elsewhere, we note that, as with minimum capital and capital maintenance requirements, the duties of directors to protect the interests of creditors are more developed in EU jurisdictions than in the United States.[11] In particular, directors are responsible in many of these jurisdictions for ensuring that insolvent corporations enter bankruptcy rather than continuing to do business and accumulating further debt. In the United States, where management retains control when the company enters reorganization proceedings under Chapter 11, such duties are usually unnecessary because management often has an incentive to enter bankruptcy voluntarily in the hopes of engineering a successful recapitalization.

---

10. *Credit Lyonnais Bank Nederland v. Pathe Communications Corp.*, 1991 Del. Ch. LEXIS 215, at *109 n.55 (Del Ch. Dec. 30, 1991). Other Delaware Chancery Court precedents appear to hold that directors owe a direct duty to manage on behalf of creditors when the corporation is insolvent (but not yet in bankruptcy). See *Geyer v. Ingersoll Publications Co.*, C.A. No. 12,406, 1992 Del. Ch. LEXIS 132 (Del. Ch. June 18, 1992); Greg V. Varallo & Jesse A. Finkelstein, *Fiduciary Obligations of Directors of the Financially Troubled Company*, 48 Bus. Law. 239 (1992). This emergent fiduciary doctrine is newsworthy because, as our discussion in Chapter 9 of the fiduciary duty of loyalty will show, it is generally the shareholders who are regarded as the beneficiaries of the directors' business judgment and loyalty in American law. Just how far fiduciary duties should protect creditors in circumstances of near insolvency remains warmly contested. See Henry T. Hu, *Risk, Time, and Fiduciary Principles in Corporate Investment*, 38 UCLA L. Rev. 277 (1990); Laura Lin, *Shift of Fiduciary Duty upon Corporate Insolvency: Proper Scope of Directors' Duty to Creditors*, 46 Vand. L. Rev. 1485 (1993). For a challenging discussion of which creditors merit the protection of the board, see Alon Chaver & Jesse M. Fried, *Managers' Fiduciary Duty Upon the Firm's Insolvency: Accounting for Performance Creditors*, 55 Vand. L. Rev. 1813 (2002).

11. See for France: Arts 52 and 244, Loi de 1966; Art. 180, Loi de 1985; for Germany: GmbHG §§43, 93 and AktG §116. The approach is a rather recent one, as far as the United Kingdom is concerned: see Insolvency Act of 1986, §214(4); *Dorchester Finance Co. v. Stebbing*, [1989] Butterworths Company Law Cases 498; Christopher A. Riley, *The Company Director's Duty of Care and Skill: The Case for an Onerous but Subjective Standard*, 62 Mod. L. Rev. 697 (1999).

QUESTIONS

1. Consider the preceding hypothetical. Isn't it plain to see that, as a matter of policy, the directors ought to be legally compelled to reject the $12.5 million offer and to accept the $17.5 million offer? How would you articulate their duty in order to achieve that outcome?

2. What difficulties exist in delineating a zone of "near insolvency," in which the board's core duty of loyalty shifts from creating shareholder value to maximizing the pie for creditors and shareholders jointly?

One way of interpreting the result in *Credit Lyonnais Bank Nederlands* is that the court does not recognize a right in creditors but does recognize a privilege in the board of directors to be free of disloyalty claims by shareholders if it follows a course intended to maximize joint (debt and equity) wealth. Most commentators on the case neglect this interpretive possibility. Would it make sense as the legal rule?

6.3.2 Creditor Protection: Fraudulent Transfers

Fraudulent conveyance law (a general creditor remedy) imposes an effective obligation on parties contracting with an insolvent — or soon to be insolvent — debtor to give fair value for the cash or benefits they receive, or risk being forced to return those benefits to the debtor's estate. Fraudulent conveyance law is among the oldest creditor protections. It is designed to void transfers by a debtor that — speaking loosely — are made under circumstances that are unfair to creditors. More specifically, the statute provides a means to void any transfer made for the purpose of delaying, hindering, or defrauding creditors. The original fraudulent conveyance act was passed in 1571 by the English Parliament; modern state acts follow the model of the Uniform Fraudulent Conveyance Act (UFCA) or the updated Uniform Fraudulent Transfer Act (UFTA) (in your statutory supplement).

The UFCA and UFTA are substantially similar in their approach. Under either statute, creditors may attack a transfer on two grounds. First, "present or future creditors" may void transfers made with the "*actual intent* to hinder, delay, or defraud any creditor of the debtor." (emphasis added) UFTA §4(a)(1); UFCA §7. Second, "creditors" may void transfers made "without receiving a reasonably equivalent value" if the debtor is left with "remaining assets . . . unreasonably small in relation to [its] business," or the debtor "intended . . . believed . . . or reasonably should have believed he would incur debts beyond his ability to pay as they became due," or the debtor is insolvent after the transfer. UFTA §§4(a)(2), 5(a) & (b). Compare UFCA §§4-6. Most fraudulent transfer litigation today takes place today under Section 548 of the U.S. Bankruptcy Code, which takes a virtually identical approach as the UFCA and UFTA, or Section 544(b) of the Code, which invokes state law doctrine of fraudulent transfer.

Taken as a whole, fraudulent transfer doctrine permits creditors to void transfers by establishing that they were either actual or constructive frauds on creditors. Actual fraud is easy to understand as a basis for voiding a transfer. On constructive fraud, rather than understanding this test as an evidentiary presumption pointing to likely fraud, can it be understood to describe the reasonable expectations of creditors when negotiating with debtors — that is, as a conventional term in creditor-debtor contracts except where the parties explicitly opt out of it? Restated, don't business debtors implicitly represent that their assets, as affected by normal business (e.g., sales for fair value) or diminished by normal wear and tear and legal distributions, will be available to creditors in the event of default?

How easily *future* creditors can void transfers on the grounds that there was no equivalent value and the business was left with unreasonably small capital is unclear. One construction of the references to future creditors in the statute is that they can void transfers only in the event of actual fraud. Compare UFCA §4 with §§6, 7. In any event, future creditors who "knew or could easily have found out about" otherwise vulnerable transfers cannot void them. *Kupetz v. Wolf*, 845 F.2d 842, 846 n.16 (9th Cir. 1988).[12]

Modern Applications. First, apart from garden-variety fraud on creditors, fraudulent conveyance law has played an important corporate role in challenges to so-called leveraged buyouts (LBOs), which were common during the easy lending days of the late 1980s. See, e.g., Miller, *LBOs, Fraudulent Transfers Revisited*, Natl. L.J., Jan. 20, 1992, at 20.

A second context in which fraudulent conveyance norms may be implicated concerns proposals that large tobacco companies insulate assets from potential tort liability by placing these assets in subsidiaries and then distributing the stock of these subsidiaries to their shareholders. This maneuver is called a "spin-off." For example, in 1999 RJR Nabisco spun-off its tobacco company R.J. Reynolds to its shareholders, leaving behind its Nabisco food business. Could fraudulent conveyance law arguably reach such divestitures? If not, should it? It is interesting to note that the stock of Nabisco Group Holdings (renamed from RJR Nabisco) did poorly, in part because of this possibility. One year after the spin-off of the tobacco assets, the *Wall Street Journal* reported: "The stock of NGH, the holding company, has been a huge disappointment to shareholders because of what some investors call the 'tobacco taint.' This refers to the possibility that, even though the tobacco and food holding companies are separate now, tobacco-liability plaintiffs might try to go after the assets of the holding company should Reynolds ever go bankrupt because of adverse legal judgments."[13]

---

12. Professor Robert Clark has argued that fraudulent conveyance law ought to apply to corporate distributions to shareholders *in addition to* the strictures of the more particularistic dividend tests. Robert C. Clark, *Corporate Law*, §2.5, 86-92 (1986). As we note above, in fact dividend limitations function very much like the fraudulent conveyance act.

13. See Nikhil Deogun & Gordon Fairclough, *R.J. Reynolds Considers a Reunion with Nabisco*, Wall St. J. (May 5, 2000). In 2000, just eighteen months after the spin-off, Phillip Morris, another tobacco company, acquired Nabisco and integrated it into its Kraft food business. The acquisition merged powerhouse Kraft brands such as Maxwell House coffee, Oscar Mayer meats, and Philadelphia cream cheese with equally formidable Nabisco brands such as Oreo cookies, Ritz crackers, and Lifesavers candies. In 2001, Phillip Morris spun off the combined food business in an initial public offering. Kraft Foods trades on the New York Stock Exchange today.

6.3.3   Shareholder Liability

Shareholders may either find themselves liable to corporate creditors, or have any "loans" they have made to the company subordinated to other creditors under at least two legal doctrines, equitable subordination and corporate veil piercing.

6.3.3.1   Equitable Subordination

Courts of equity invoke the equitable subordination doctrine when they feel compelled, by considerations of equity, to recharacterize debt owed by the company to its controlling shareholders as equity. This remedy is sometimes known as the "Deep Rock doctrine," after the 1939 U.S. Supreme Court case that validated its application under the U.S. Bankruptcy Code. Today is it codified at Section 510(c)(1) of the U.S. Bankrupty Code, which permits subordination of a debt claim "under principles of equitable subordination." The doctrine is rarely invoked outside the bankruptcy context.

Equitable subordination is a means of protecting unaffiliated creditors by giving them rights to corporate assets superior to those of other creditors who happen to also be significant shareholders of the firm. The critical question is what set of circumstances will permit a court to impose this subordination on a shareholder-creditor. The first requirement is that the creditor be an equity holder and typically an officer of the company. (Do you recall the subordination rule for partners' claims against a partnership? See UPA §40(b).) In addition, this insider-creditor must have, in some fashion, behaved unfairly or wrongly toward the corporation and its outside creditors. Consider the following case.

COSTELLO v. FAZIO
256 F.2d 903 (9th Cir. 1958)

HAMLEY, Cir. J.:

Creditors' claims against the bankrupt estate of Leonard Plumbing and Heating Supply, Inc., were filed by J. A. Fazio and Lawrence C. Ambrose. The trustee in bankruptcy objected to these claims, and moved for an order subordinating them to the claims of general unsecured creditors. The referee in bankruptcy denied the motion, and his action was sustained by the district court. The trustee appeals.

The following facts are not in dispute: A partnership known as "Leonard Plumbing and Heating Supply Co." was organized in October, 1948. The three partners, Fazio, Ambrose, and B. T. Leonard, made initial capital contributions to the business aggregating $44,806.40. The capital contributions of the three partners, as they were recorded on the company books in September 1952, totaled $51,620.78, distributed as follows: Fazio, $43,169.61; Ambrose, $6,451.17; and Leonard, $2,000.

In the fall of that year, it was decided to incorporate the business. In contemplation of this step, Fazio and Ambrose, on September 15, 1952, withdrew all but $2,000 apiece of their capital contributions to the business. This was accomplished by the issuance to them, on that date, of partnership promissory notes in the sum of $41,169.61 and $4,451.17, respectively. These were demand notes, no interest being specified. The capital contribution to the partnership business then stood at $6,000— $2,000 for each partner.

The closing balance sheet of the partnership showed current assets to be $160,791.87, and current liabilities at $162,162.22. There were also fixed assets in the sum of $6,482.90, and other assets in the sum of $887.45. The partnership had cash on hand in the sum of $66.66, and an overdraft at the bank in the amount of $3,422.78.

Of the current assets, $41,357.76, representing "Accounts receivable — Trade," was assigned to American Trust Co., to secure $50,000 of its $59,000 in notes payable. Both before and after the incorporation, the business had a $75,000 line of credit with American Trust Co., secured by accounts receivable and the personal guaranty of the three partners and stockholders, and their marital communities.

The net sales of the partnership during its last year of operations were $389,543.72, as compared to net sales of $665,747.55 in the preceding year. A net loss of $22,521.34 was experienced during this last year, as compared to a net profit of $40,935.12 in the year ending September 30, 1951.

Based on the reduced capitalization of the partnership, the corporation was capitalized for six hundred shares of no par value common stock valued at ten dollars per share. Two hundred shares were issued to each of the three partners in consideration of the transfer to the corporation of their interests in the partnership. Fazio became president, and Ambrose, secretary-treasurer of the new corporation. Both were directors. The corporation assumed all liabilities of the partnership, including the notes to Fazio and Ambrose.

In June 1954, after suffering continued losses, the corporation made an assignment to the San Francisco Board of Trade for the benefit of creditors. On October 8, 1954, it filed a voluntary petition in bankruptcy. At this time, the corporation was not indebted to any creditors whose obligations were incurred by the preexisting partnership, saving the promissory notes issued to Fazio and Ambrose.

Fazio filed a claim against the estate in the sum of $34,147.55, based on the promissory note given to him when the capital of the partnership was reduced. Ambrose filed a similar claim in the sum of $7,871.17. The discrepancy between these amounts and the amounts of the promissory notes is due to certain setoffs and transfers not here in issue.

In asking that these claims be subordinated to the claims of general unsecured creditors, the trustee averred that the amounts in question represent a portion of the capital investment in the partnership. It was alleged that the transfer of this sum from the partnership capital account to an account entitled "Loans from Copartners," effectuated a scheme and plan to place copartners in the same class as unsecured creditors. The trustee further alleged, with respect to each claimant: . . . .

If said claimant is permitted to share in the assets of said bankrupt now in the hands of the trustee, in the same parity with general unsecured creditors, he will receive a portion of the capital invested which should be used to satisfy the claims of creditors before any capital investment can be returned to the owners and stockholders of said bankrupt.

A hearing was held before the referee in bankruptcy. In addition to eliciting the above recounted facts, three expert witnesses called by the trustee, and one expert witness called by the claimants, expressed opinions on various phases of the transaction.

Clifford V. Heimbucher, a certified public accountant and management consultant, called by the trustee, expressed the view that, at the time of incorporation, capitalization was inadequate. He further stated that, in incorporating a business already in existence, where the approximate amount of permanent capital needed has been established by experience, normal procedure called for continuing such capital in the form of common or preferred stock.

Stating that only additional capital needed temporarily is normally set up as loans, Heimbucher testified that " . . . the amount of capital employed in the business was at all times substantially more than the $6,000 employed in the opening of the corporation." He also expressed the opinion that, at the time of incorporation, there was "very little hope (of financial success) in view of the fact that for the year immediately preceding the opening of the corporation, losses were running a little less than $2,000 a month. . . . "

William B. Logan, a business analyst and consultant called by the trustee, expressed the view that $6,000 was inadequate capitalization for this company. John S. Curran, a business analyst, also called by the trustee, expressed the view that the corporation needed at least as much capital as the partnership required prior to the reduction of capital.

Robert H. Laborde, Jr., a certified public accountant, has handled the accounting problems of the partnership and corporation. He was called by the trustee as an adverse witness, pursuant to §21, sub. j of the Bankruptcy Act, 11 U.S.C.A. §44, sub. j. Laborde readily conceded that the transaction whereby Fazio and Ambrose obtained promissory notes from the partnership was for the purpose of transferring a capital account into a loan or debt account. He stated that this was done in contemplation of the formation of the corporation, and with knowledge that the partnership was losing money.

The prime reason for incorporating the business, according to Laborde, was to protect the personal interest of Fazio, who had made the greatest capital contribution to the business. In this connection, it was pointed out that the "liabilities on the business as a partnership were pretty heavy." There was apparently also a tax angle. Laborde testified that it was contemplated that the notes would be paid out of the profits of the business. He agreed that, if promissory notes had not been issued, the profits would have been distributed only as dividends, and that as such they would have been taxable. . . .

Laborde expressed no opinion as to the adequacy of proprietary capital put at the risk of the business. On the other hand, the corporate accounts and the undisputed testimony of three accounting experts demonstrate that stated capital was wholly inadequate.

On the evidence produced at this hearing, as summarized above, the referee found that the paid-in stated capital of the corporation at the time of its incorporation was adequate for the continued operation of the business. He found that while Fazio and Ambrose controlled and dominated the corporation and its affairs they did not mismanage the business. He further found that claimants did not practice any fraud or deception, and did not act for their own personal or private benefit and to the detriment of the corporation or its stockholders and creditors. The referee also found that the transaction which had been described was not a part of any scheme or plan to place the claimants in the same class as unsecured creditors of the partnership.

On the basis of these findings, the referee concluded that, in procuring the promissory notes, the claimants acted in all respects in good faith and took no unfair advantage of the corporation, or of its stockholders or creditors.

Pursuant to §39, sub. c of the Bankruptcy Act, 11 U.S.C.A. §67, sub. c, the trustee filed a petition for review of the referee's order. The district court, after examining the record certified to it by the referee, entered an order affirming the order of the referee.

On this appeal, the trustee advances two grounds for reversal of the district court order. The first of these is that claims of controlling shareholders will be deferred or subordinated to outside creditors where a corporation in bankruptcy has not been adequately or honestly capitalized, or has been managed to the prejudice of creditors, or where to do otherwise would be unfair to creditors.

As a basis for applying this asserted rule in the case before us, the trustee challenges most of the findings of fact noted above.

The district court and this court are required to accept the findings of the referee in bankruptcy, unless such findings are clearly erroneous. . . .

It does not require the confirmatory opinion of experts to determine from this data that the corporation was grossly undercapitalized. In the year immediately preceding incorporation, net sales aggregated $390,000. In order to handle such a turnover, the partners apparently found that capital in excess of $50,000 was necessary. They actually had $51,620.78 in the business at that time. Even then, the business was only "two jumps ahead of the wolf." A net loss of $22,000 was sustained in that year; there was only $66.66 in the bank; and there was an overdraft of $3,422.78.

Yet, despite this precarious financial condition, Fazio and Ambrose withdrew $45,620.78 of the partnership capital — more than eighty-eight percent of the total capital. The $6,000 capital left in the business was only one-sixty-fifth of the last annual net sales. All this is revealed by the books of the company.

But if there is need to confirm this conclusion that the corporation was grossly undercapitalized, such confirmation is provided by three of the four experts who testified. The fourth expert, called by appellees, did not express an opinion to the contrary.

We therefore hold that the factual conclusion of the referee, that the corporation was adequately capitalized at the time of its organization, is clearly erroneous.

The factual conclusion of the trial court, that the claimants, in withdrawing capital from the partnership in contemplation of incorporation, did not act for their own personal or private benefit and to the detriment of the corporation or of its stockholders and creditors, is based upon the same accounting data and expert testimony.

Laborde, testifying for the claimants, made it perfectly clear that the depletion of the capital account in favor of a debt account was for the purpose of equalizing the capital investments of the partners and to reduce tax liability when there were profits to distribute. It is therefore certain, contrary to the finding just noted, that, in withdrawing this capital, Fazio and Ambrose did act for their own personal and private benefit.

It is equally certain, from the undisputed facts, that in so doing they acted to the detriment of the corporation and its creditors. The best evidence of this is what happened to the business after incorporation, and what will happen to its creditors if the reduction in capital is allowed to stand. The likelihood that business failure would result from such under-capitalization should have been apparent to anyone who knew the company's financial and business history and who had access to its balance sheet and profit and loss statements. Three expert witnesses confirmed this view, and none expressed a contrary opinion.

Accordingly, we hold that the factual conclusion, that the claimants, in withdrawing capital, did not act for their own personal or private benefit and to the detriment of the corporation and creditors, is clearly erroneous.

Recasting the facts in the light of what is said above, the question which appellant presents is this:

Where, in connection with the incorporation of a partnership, and for their own personal and private benefit, two partners who are to become officers, directors, and controlling stockholders of the corporation, convert the bulk of their capital contributions into loans, taking promissory notes, thereby leaving the partnership and succeeding corporation grossly under-capitalized, to the detriment of the corporation and its creditors, should their claims against the estate of the subsequently bankrupted corporation be subordinated to the claims of the general unsecured creditors?

The question almost answers itself.

In allowing and disallowing claims, courts of bankruptcy apply the rules and principles of equity jurisprudence. . . . Where the claim is found to be inequitable, it may be set aside, or subordinated to the claims of other creditors. . . . [T]he question to be determined when the plan or transaction which gives rise to a claim is challenged as inequitable is "whether, within the bounds of reason and fairness, such a plan can be justified."

Where, as here, the claims are filed by persons standing in a fiduciary relationship to the corporation, another test which equity will apply is "whether or not under all the circumstances the transaction carries the earmarks of an arm's length bargain." *Pepper v. Litton,* supra, 308 U.S. at page 306 . . . .

Under either of these tests, the transaction here in question stands condemned.

Appellees argue that more must be shown than mere undercapitalization if the claims are to be subordinated. Much more than mere undercapitalization was shown here. Persons serving in a fiduciary relationship to the corporation actually withdrew capital already committed to the business, in the face of recent adverse financial experience. They stripped the business of eighty-eight percent of its stated capital at a time when it had a minus working capital and had suffered substantial business losses. This was done for personal gain, under circumstances which charge them with knowledge that the corporation and its creditors would be endangered. Taking advantage of their fiduciary position, they thus sought to gain equality of treatment with general creditors.

In . . . other cases, there was fraud and mismanagement present in addition to undercapitalization. Appellees argue from this that fraud and mismanagement must always be present if claims are to be subordinated in a situation involving undercapitalization.

This is not the rule. The test to be applied . . . is whether the transaction can be justified "within the bounds of reason and fairness."

The fact that the withdrawal of capital occurred prior to incorporation is immaterial. This transaction occurred in contemplation of incorporation. The participants then occupied a fiduciary relationship to the partnership; and expected to become controlling stockholders, directors, and officers of the corporation. This plan was effectuated, and they were serving in those fiduciary capacities when the corporation assumed the liabilities of the partnership, including the notes here in question.

Nor is the fact that the business, after being stripped of necessary capital, was able to survive long enough to have a turnover of creditors a mitigating circumstance. The inequitable conduct of appellees consisted not in acting to the detriment of creditors then known, but in acting to the detriment of present or future creditors, whoever they may be. . . .
Reversed and remanded for further proceedings not inconsistent with this opinion.

QUESTIONS ON COSTELLO v. FAZIO

1. Which creditors benefit from equitable subordination: old partnership creditors, new corporate creditors, or all creditors?

2. Suppose there had been no past history of partnership and the business had been started as a corporation with $6,000 in stated capital and $50,000 in loans from its shareholders. Would such a new firm have involved the same inequitable conduct? What result under the doctrine of equitable subordination?

3. What result if the business had limped along for five years on its capital before going under?

4. Would the case have had the same outcome under UFTA §4(a)?

6.3.3.2 *Piercing the Corporate Veil*

The most frequently invoked — and radical — form of shareholder liability in the cause of creditor protection is the equitable power of the court to set aside the entity status of the corporation ("piercing the veil") to hold its shareholders liable directly on contract or tort obligations. This, too, is an "equitable" device through which courts declare that they will not permit the attributes of the corporate form to be used to perpetrate a fraud.

As with all doctrines that are "equitable" in character (e.g., the equitable subordination doctrine), the guidelines for veil piercing are vague. One common formulation is the Lowendahl test, under which veil piercing requires that plaintiff shows the existence of a shareholder who completely dominates corporate policy and uses her control to commit a fraud or "wrong" that proximately causes plaintiff's injury. The domination required for this test ordinarily includes a failure to treat the corporation formality seriously. Another formulation of the test calls on courts to disregard the corporate form whenever recognition of it would extend the principle of incorporation "beyond its legitimate purposes and [would] produce injustices or inequitable consequences." *Krivo Industrial Supp. Co. v. National Distill. & Chem. Corp.*, 483 F.2d 1098, 1106 (5th Cir. 1973). All courts agree that veil piercing should be done sparingly; the question remains how sparingly. A number of factors may play a role in veil-piercing decisions: A disregard of corporate formalities, thin capitalization, small numbers of shareholders, and active involvement by shareholders in management are but a few.

Consider the basis for applying the veil-piercing doctrine in the two following contract cases.

SEA-LAND SERVICES, INC. v. THE PEPPER SOURCE
941 F.2d 519 (7th Cir. 1991)

BAUER, C.J.:

This spicy case finds its origin in several shipments of Jamaican sweet peppers. Appellee Sea-Land Services, Inc. ("Sea-Land"), an ocean carrier, shipped the peppers on behalf of The Pepper Source ("PS"), one of the appellants here. PS then stiffed Sea-Land on the freight bill, which was rather substantial. Sea-Land filed a federal diversity action for the money it was owed. On December 2, 1987, the district court entered a default judgment in favor of Sea-Land and against PS in the amount of $86,767.70. But PS was nowhere to be found; it had been "dissolved" in mid-1987 for failure to pay the annual state franchise tax. Worse yet for Sea-Land, even had it not been dissolved, PS apparently had no assets. With the well empty, Sea-Land could not recover its judgment against PS. Hence the instant lawsuit.

In June 1988, Sea-Land brought this action against Gerald J. Marchese and five business entities he owns: PS, Caribe Crown, Inc., Jamar Corp., Salescaster Distributors, Inc., and Marchese Fegan Associates. Marchese also was named individually. Sea-Land sought by this suit to pierce PS's corporate veil and render Marchese personally liable for the judgment owed to Sea-Land, and then "reverse pierce" Marchese's other corporations so that they, too, would be on the hook for the $87,000. Thus, Sea-Land alleged in its complaint that all of these corporations "are alter egos of each other and hide behind the veils of alleged separate corporate existence for the purpose of defrauding plaintiff and other creditors." Not only are the corporations alter egos of each other, alleged Sea-Land, but also they are alter egos of Marchese, who should be held individually liable for the judgment because he created and manipulated these corporations and their assets for his own personal uses. Count III, PP 9-10. (Hot on the heels of the filing of Sea-Land's complaint, PS took the necessary steps to be reinstated as a corporation in Illinois.)

In early 1989, Sea-Land filed an amended complaint adding Tie-Net International, Inc., as a defendant. Unlike the other corporate defendants, Tie-Net is not owned solely by Marchese: he holds half of the stock, and an individual named George Andre owns the other half. Sea-Land alleged that, despite this shared ownership, Tie-Net is but another alter ego of Marchese and the other corporate defendants, and thus it also should be held liable for the judgment against PS.

Through 1989, Sea-Land pursued discovery in this case, including taking a two-day deposition from Marchese. In December 1989, Sea-Land moved for summary judgment. In that motion — which, with the brief in support and the appendices, was about three inches thick — Sea-Land argued that it was "entitled to judgment as a matter of law, since the evidence including deposition testimony and exhibits in the appendix will show that piercing the corporate veil and finding the status of an alter ego is merited in this case." Marchese and the other defendants filed brief responses.

In an order dated June 22, 1990, the court granted Sea-Land's motion. The court discussed and applied the test for corporate veil-piercing explicated in *Van Dorn Co. v. Future Chemical and Oil Corp.*, 753 F.2d 565 (7th Cir. 1985). Analyzing Illinois law, we held in *Van Dorn:*

> [A] corporate entity will be disregarded and the veil of limited liability pierced when two requirements are met: [F]irst, there must be such unity of interest and ownership that the separate personalities of the corporation and the individual [or other corporation] no longer exist; and second, circumstances must be such that adherence to the fiction of separate corporate existence would sanction a fraud or promote injustice.

753 F.2d at 569-70 (quoting *Macaluso v. Jenkins*, 95 Ill. App. 3d 461, 420 N. E.2d 251, 255 (1981)) (other citations omitted). . . . As for determining whether a corporation is so controlled by another to justify disregarding their separate identities, the Illinois cases . . . focus on four factors: "(1) the failure to maintain adequate corporate records or to comply with corporate formalities, (2) the commingling of funds or assets, (3) undercapitalization, and (4) one corporation treating the assets of another corporation as its own." 753 F.2d at 570 (citations omitted). . . .

Following the lead of the parties, the district court in the instant case laid the template of *Van Dorn* over the facts of this case. The court concluded that both halves and all features of the test had been satisfied, and, therefore, entered judgment in favor of Sea-Land and against PS, Caribe Crown, Jamar, Salescaster, Tie-Net, and Marchese individually. These defendants were held jointly liable for Sea-Land's $87,000 judgment, as well as for post-judgment interest under Illinois law. From that judgment Marchese and the other defendants brought a timely appeal.

Because this is an appeal from a grant of summary judgment, our review is de novo. . . .

The first and most striking feature that emerges from our examination of the record is that these corporate defendants are, indeed, little but Marchese's playthings. Marchese is the sole shareholder of PS, Caribe Crown, Jamar, and Salescaster. He is one of the two shareholders of Tie-Net. Except for Tie-Net, none of the corporations ever held a single corporate meeting. (At the handful of Tie-Net meetings held by Marchese and Andre, no minutes were taken.) During his deposition, Marchese did not remember any of these corporations ever passing articles of incorporation, bylaws, or other agreements. As for physical facilities, Marchese runs all of these corporations (including Tie-Net) out of the same, single office, with the same phone line, the same expense accounts, and the like. And how he does "run" the expense accounts! When he fancies to, Marchese "borrows" substantial sums of money from these corporations — interest free, of course. The corporations also "borrow" money from each other when need be, which left at least PS completely out of capital when the Sea-Land bills came due. What's more, Marchese has used the bank accounts of these corporations to pay all kinds of personal expenses, including alimony and child support payments to his ex-wife, education expenses for his children, maintenance of his personal automobiles, health care for his pet — the list goes on and on. Marchese did not even have a personal bank account! (With "corporate" accounts like these, who needs one?)

And Tie-Net is just as much a part of this as the other corporations. On appeal, Marchese makes much of the fact that he shares ownership of Tie-Net, and that Sea-Land has not been able to find an example of funds flowing from PS to Tie-Net to the detriment of Sea-Land and PS's other creditors. So what? The record reveals that, in all material senses, Marchese treated Tie-Net like his other corporations: he "borrowed" over $30,000 from Tie-Net; money and "loans" flowed freely between Tie-Net and the other corporations; and Marchese charged up various personal expenses (including $460 for a picture of himself with President Bush) on Tie-Net's credit card. Marchese was not deterred by the fact that he did not hold all of the stock of Tie-Net; why should his creditors be?

In sum, we agree with the district court that there can be no doubt that the "shared control/unity of interest and ownership" part of the *Van Dorn* test is met in this case: corporate records and formalities have not been maintained; funds and assets have been commingled with abandon; PS, the offending corporation, and perhaps others have been undercapitalized; and corporate assets have been moved and tapped and "borrowed" without regard to their source. Indeed, Marchese basically punted this part of the inquiry before the district court by coming forward with little or no evidence in response to Sea-Land's extensively supported argument on these points. That fact alone was enough to do him in; opponents to summary judgment motions cannot simply rest on their laurels, but must come forward with specific facts showing that there is a genuine issue for trial. . . . Regarding the elements that make up the first half of the *Van Dorn* test, Marchese and the other defendants have not done so. Thus, Sea-Land is entitled to judgment on these points.

The second part of the *Van Dorn* test is more problematic, however. "Unity of interest and ownership" is not enough; Sea-Land also must show that honoring the separate corporate existences of the defendants "would sanction a fraud or promote injustice." *Van Dorn*, 753 F.2d at 570. This last phrase truly is disjunctive:

> Although an intent to defraud creditors would surely play a part if established, the Illinois test does not require proof of such intent. Once the first element of the test is established, *either* the sanctioning of a fraud (intentional wrongdoing) or the promotion of injustice, will satisfy the second element.

Id. (emphasis in original). Seizing on this, Sea-Land has abandoned the language in its two complaints that make repeated references to "fraud" by Marchese, and has chosen not to attempt to prove that PS and Marchese intended to defraud it — which would be quite difficult on summary judgment. Instead, Sea-Land has argued that honoring the defendants' separate identities would "promote injustice."

But what, exactly, does "promote injustice" mean, and how does one establish it on summary judgment? These are the critical, troublesome questions in this case. To start with, as the above passage from *Van Dorn* makes clear, "promote injustice" means something less than an affirmative showing of fraud — but how much less? In its one-sentence treatment of this point, the district court held that it was enough that "Sea-Land would be denied a judicially-imposed recovery." Sea-Land defends this reasoning on appeal, arguing that "permitting the appellants to hide behind the shield of limited liability would clearly serve as an injustice against appellee" because it would "impermissibly deny appellee satisfaction." Appellee's Brief at 14-15. But that cannot be what is meant by "promote injustice." The prospect of an unsatisfied judgment looms in every veil-piercing action; why else would a plaintiff bring such an action? Thus, if an unsatisfied judgment is enough for the "promote injustice" feature of the test, then every plaintiff will pass on that score, and *Van Dorn* collapses into a one-step "unity of interest and ownership" test.

Because we cannot abide such a result [How is that for candor! — Eds.] we will undertake our own review of Illinois cases to determine how the "promote injustice" feature of the veil-piercing inquiry has been interpreted. In *Pederson* [*v. Paragon Enterprises*, 214 Ill. App. 3d 815, 158 Ill. Dec. 371, 373, 547 N.E.2d 165, 167 (1st Dist. 1991)], . . . the court offered the following summary: "Some element of unfairness, something akin to fraud or deception or the existence of a compelling public interest must be present in order to disregard the corporate fiction." 214 Ill. App. 3d at 821,

158 Ill. Dec. at 375, 574 N.E.2d at 169. (The court ultimately refused to pierce the corporate veil in *Pederson,* at least in part because "[n]othing in these facts provides evidence of scheming on the part of defendant to commit a fraud on potential creditors [of the two defendant corporations]." *Id.* at 823, 158 Ill. Dec. at 376, 574 N.E.2d at 169.)

The light shed on this point by other Illinois cases can be seen only if we examine the cases on their facts. . . .

Generalizing from these cases, we see that the courts that properly have pierced corporate veils to avoid "promoting injustice" have found that, unless it did so, some "wrong" beyond a creditor's inability to collect would result: the common sense rules of adverse possession would be undermined; former partners would be permitted to skirt the legal rules concerning monetary obligations; a party would be unjustly enriched; a parent corporation that caused a sub's liabilities and its inability to pay for them would escape those liabilities; or an intentional scheme to squirrel assets into a liability-free corporation while heaping liabilities upon an asset-free corporation would be successful. Sea-Land, although it alleged in its complaint the kind of intentional asset-and-liability-shifting found in *Van Dorn,* has yet to come forward with evidence akin to the "wrongs" found in these cases. Apparently, it believed as did the district court, that its unsatisfied judgment was enough. That belief was in error, and the entry of summary judgment premature. We, therefore, reverse the judgment and remand the case to the district court.

On remand, the court should require that Sea-Land produce, if it desires summary judgment, evidence and argument that would establish the kind of additional "wrong" present in the above cases. For example, perhaps Sea-Land could establish that Marchese, like Roth in *Van Dorn,* used these corporate facades to avoid its responsibilities to creditors; or that PS, Marchese, or one of the other corporations will be "unjustly enriched" unless liability is shared by all. Of course, Sea-Land is not required fully to prove intent to defraud, which it probably could not do on summary judgment anyway. But it is required to show the kind of injustice to merit the evocation of the court's essentially equitable power to prevent "injustice." It may well be that, after more of such evidence is adduced, no genuine issue of fact exists to prevent Sea-Land from reaching Marchese's other pet corporations for PS's debt. Or it may be that only a finder of fact will be able to determine whether fraud or "injustice" is involved here. In any event, the record as it currently stands is insufficient to uphold the entry of summary judgment.

REVERSED and REMANDED with instructions.

NOTE ON SEA-LAND SERVICES

Sea-Land's substance is more traditional than its prose. This is a fair summary of Illinois law and probably reflects the majority view on when the veil should be pierced. Notably in this case, and in most cases where the piercing remedy is invoked, there is a failure to treat the corporate fiction seriously. Thus, as in *Sea-Land,* courts find it significant when parties fail to observe corporate formalities.

On remand, the district court entered a judgment for Sea-Land and against Marchese for $86,768 plus postjudgment interest of $31,365. To support its legal conclusion that maintaining the corporate veil would "sanction a fraud or promote injustice," the court relied on the fact that Marchese had committed blatant tax fraud and that Marchese had assured a Sea-Land representative that his freight bill would be paid, even though he was planning to "manipulate" the corporate funds "to insure there would not be funds to pay" Sea-Land's bills. The district court's decision to pierce was subsequently affirmed by the Seventh Circuit. *Sea-Land Services, Inc. v. The Pepper Source*, 993 F.2d 1309 (7th Cir. 1993).

QUESTIONS ON SEA-LAND SERVICES

1. What does "reverse piercing" mean in this case? And why isn't Sea-Land content to pierce through to Marchese's assets — won't it acquire the stock (and hence the value) of his other corporations if Marchese is found to be personally liable? Who might legitimately complain that this novel remedy is unfair to them (other than the expected whining of Marchese himself)?

2. Why doesn't a creditor's inability to collect "unjustly enrich" the owners of a defaulting corporation, and hence "promote injustice" under the test?

3. Is there a principle lurking behind the court's various examples of "injustice" that falls short of fraud? Can you generalize (as the court fails to do)?

KINNEY SHOE CORP. v. POLAN

939 F.2d 209 (4th Cir. 1991)

CHAPMAN, Senior Cir. J.:

Plaintiff-appellant Kinney Shoe Corporation ("Kinney") brought this action in the United States District Court for the Southern District of West Virginia against Lincoln M. Polan ("Polan") seeking to recover money owed on a sublease between Kinney and Industrial Realty Company ("Industrial"). Polan is the sole shareholder of Industrial. The district court found that Polan was not personally liable on the lease between Kinney and Industrial. Kinney appeals asserting that the corporate veil should be pierced, and we agree. . . .

The district court based its order on facts which were stipulated by the parties. In 1984 Polan formed two corporations, Industrial and Polan Industries, Inc., for the purpose of re-establishing an industrial manufacturing business. The certificate of incorporation for Polan Industries, Inc. was issued by the West Virginia Secretary of State in November 1984. The following month the certificate of incorporation for Industrial was issued. Polan was the owner of both corporations. Although certificates of incorporation were issued, no organizational meetings were held, and no officers were elected.

In November 1984 Polan and Kinney began negotiating the sublease of a building in which Kinney held a leasehold interest. The building was

owned by the Cabell County Commission and financed by industrial revenue bonds issued in 1968 to induce Kinney to locate a manufacturing plant
in Huntington, West Virginia. Under the terms of the lease, Kinney was
legally obligated to make payments on the bonds on a semi-annual basis
through January 1, 1993, at which time it had the right to purchase the
property. Kinney had ceased using the building as a manufacturing plant in
June 1983.

The term of the sublease from Kinney to Industrial commenced in
December 1984, even though the written lease was not signed by the
parties until April 5, 1985. On April 15, 1985, Industrial subleased part of
the building to Polan Industries, for fifty percent of the rental amount due
Kinney. Polan signed both subleases on behalf of the respective companies.

Other than the sublease with Kinney, Industrial had no assets, no
income and no bank account. Industrial issued no stock certificates because nothing was ever paid in to this corporation. Industrial's only income
was from its sublease to Polan Industries, Inc. The first rental payment to
Kinney was made out of Polan's personal funds, and no further payments
were made by Polan or by Polan Industries, Inc. to either Industrial or to
Kinney.

Kinney filed suit against Industrial for unpaid rent and obtained a
judgment in the amount of $166,400 on June 19, 1987. A writ of possession
was issued, but because Polan Industries, Inc. had filed for bankruptcy,
Kinney did not gain possession for six months. Kinney leased the building
until it was sold on September 1, 1988. Kinney then filed this action against
Polan individually to collect the amount owed by Industrial to Kinney.
Since the amount to which Kinney is entitled is undisputed, the only
issue is whether Kinney can pierce the corporate veil and hold Polan
personally liable.

The district court held that Kinney had assumed the risk of Industrial's
undercapitalization and was not entitled to pierce the corporate veil.
Kinney appeals, and we reverse. . . .

We have long recognized that a corporation is an entity, separate and
distinct from its officers and stockholders, and the individual stockholders
are not responsible for the debts of the corporation. . . . This concept,
however, is a fiction of the law "'and it is now well settled, as a general
principle, that the fiction should be disregarded when it is urged with an
intent not within its reason and purpose, and in such a way that its
retention would produce injustices or inequitable consequences.'" *"Laya v.
Erin Homes, Inc.,* 352 S.E.2d 93, 97-98 (W. Va. 1986). . . . Piercing the
corporate veil is an equitable remedy, and the burden rests with the party
asserting such claim. A totality of the circumstances test is used in determining whether to pierce the corporate veil, and each case must be decided
on its own facts. The district court's findings of facts may be overturned
only if clearly erroneous.

Kinney seeks to pierce the corporate veil of Industrial so as to hold
Polan personally liable on the sublease debt. The Supreme Court of
Appeals of West Virginia has set forth a two-prong test to be used in
determining whether to pierce the corporate veil in a breach of contract
case. This test raises two issues. First, is the unity of interest and ownership

such that the separate personalities of the corporation and the individual shareholder no longer exist; and second, would an inequitable result occur if the acts were treated as those of the corporation alone. In *Laya,* 352 S.E.2d at 99. Numerous factors have been identified as relevant in making this determination.

The district court found that the two prong test of *Laya* had been satisfied. The court concluded that Polan's failure to carry out the corporate formalities with respect to Industrial, coupled with Industrial's gross undercapitalization, resulted in damage to Kinney. We agree.

It is undisputed that Industrial was not adequately capitalized. Actually, it had no paid in capital. Polan had put nothing into this corporation, and it did not observe any corporate formalities. As the West Virginia court stated in *Laya,* "[i]ndividuals who wish to enjoy limited personal liability for business activities under a corporate umbrella should be expected to adhere to the relatively simple formalities of creating and maintaining a corporate entity."*Laya,* 352 S.E.2d at 100, n.6 . . . . This, the court stated, is "a relatively small price to pay for limited liability."*Id.* Another important factor is adequate capitalization. "[G]rossly inadequate capitalization combined with disregard of corporate formalities, causing basic unfairness, are sufficient to pierce the corporate veil in order to hold the shareholder(s) actively participating in the operation of the business personally liable for a breach of contract to the party who entered into the contract with the corporation." *Laya,* 352 S.E.2d at 101-02.

In this case, Polan bought no stock, made no capital contribution, kept no minutes, and elected no officers for Industrial. In addition, Polan attempted to protect his assets by placing them in Polan Industries, Inc. and interposing Industrial between Polan Industries, Inc. and Kinney so as to prevent Kinney from going against the corporation with assets. Polan gave no explanation or justification for the existence of Industrial as the intermediary between Polan Industries, Inc. and Kinney. Polan was obviously trying to limit his liability and the liability of Polan Industries, Inc. by setting up a paper curtain constructed of nothing more than Industrial's certificate of incorporation. These facts present the classic scenario for an action to pierce the corporate veil so as to reach the responsible party and produce an equitable result. Accordingly, we hold that the district court correctly found that the two prong test in *Laya* had been satisfied. In *Laya,* the court also noted that when determining whether to pierce a corporate veil a third prong may apply in certain cases. The court stated:

> When, under the circumstances, it would be reasonable for that particular type of a party [those contract creditors capable of protecting themselves] entering into a contract with the corporation, for example, a bank or other lending institution, to conduct an investigation of the credit of the corporation prior to entering into the contract, such party will be charged with the knowledge that a reasonable credit investigation would disclose. If such an investigation would disclose that the corporation is grossly undercapitalized, based upon the nature and the magnitude of the corporate undertaking, such party will be deemed to have assumed the risk of the gross undercapitalization and will not be permitted to pierce the corporate veil.

Laya, 352 S.E.2d at 100. The district court applied this third prong and concluded that Kinney "assumed the risk of Industrial's defaulting" and that "the application of the doctrine of 'piercing the corporate veil' ought not and does not [apply]." While we agree that the two prong test of *Laya* was satisfied, we hold that the district court's conclusion that Kinney had assumed the risk is clearly erroneous.

Without deciding whether the third prong should be extended beyond the context of the financial institution lender mentioned in *Laya,* we hold that, even if it applies to creditors such as Kinney, it does not prevent Kinney from piercing the corporate veil in this case. The third prong is permissive and not mandatory. This is not a factual situation that calls for the third prong, if we are to seek an equitable result. Polan set up Industrial to limit his liability and the liability of Polan Industries, Inc. in their dealings with Kinney. A stockholder's liability is limited to the amount he has invested in the corporation, but Polan invested nothing in Industrial. This corporation was no more than a shell — a transparent shell. When nothing is invested in the corporation, the corporation provides no protection to its owner; nothing in, nothing out, no protection. If Polan wishes the protection of a corporation to limit his liability, he must follow the simple formalities of maintaining the corporation. This he failed to do, and he may not relieve his circumstances by saying Kinney should have known better. . . .

For the foregoing reasons, we hold that Polan is personally liable for the debt of Industrial, and the decision of the district court is reversed and this case is remanded with instructions to enter judgment for the plaintiff.

REVERSED AND REMANDED WITH INSTRUCTIONS.

QUESTIONS ON KINNEY SHOE

1. Why should we feel sorry for Kinney Shoe? It had a rent obligation and was apparently desperate to get someone else in the premises. It took a substantial risk with a newly formed business. If there was no misrepresentation by Polan about putting minimum capital in Industries, why not conclude with the district court that Kinney "assumed the risk of Industrial's defaulting"?

2. Where was Polan's lawyer? Is this sort of deal one that we should try to prevent? If not, then what should Polan do next time to ensure that the veil will not be pierced?

3. Would the Seventh Circuit, applying the Illinois law of *Sea-Land,* reach the same result in *Kinney Shoe?* How would you characterize the difference between the *Sea-Land* test and the three-prong West Virginia test described in *Kinney Shoe?*

More generally, there is the question of what the courts should look to in considering veil-piercing claims by contract creditors. Dean Clark, in his treatise, attempts to organize veil-piercing law under the norms that he perceives as central to fraudulent conveyance law. Commentators in the law and economics tradition, however, tend to see the appropriate norm in simpler terms: Limited liability is merely a standard term in the contract between the real debtor (the shareholders-owners of the corporation) and the creditor. It follows that the term should be enforced unless there is an element of misrepresentation without which the deal would not have been done.

Note, however, that misrepresentation can come in "hard" and "soft" varieties. Hard misrepresentations are explicit lies. Soft misrepresentations include nondisclosure of facts that contradict the legitimate expectations of a creditor and the undertaking of actions that thwart these expectations.

One study examined all veil-piercing cases appearing in Westlaw through 1985. The study found that the corporate veil was pierced in 92 percent of the cases in which there was a judicial finding of misrepresentation, in 8 percent of the cases in which there was a finding of no misrepresentation, and in 33 percent of the remaining cases in which misrepresentation was not explicitly addressed by the court. Somewhat surprisingly, the study also found that courts were considerably more likely to pierce on behalf of contract creditors than on behalf of tort creditors — perhaps because the presence of explicit misrepresentation in many of the contract cases made the justification for piercing especially persuasive. See Robert B. Thompson, *Piercing the Corporate Veil: An Empirical Study,* 76 Cornell L. Rev. 1036 (1991).

6.4   VEIL PIERCING ON BEHALF OF INVOLUNTARY CREDITORS

Tort creditors of thinly capitalized corporations differ from contract creditors in at least two key respects. First, they probably do not rely on the creditworthiness of the corporation in placing themselves in a position to suffer a loss. Second, they generally cannot negotiate with a corporate tortfeasor ex ante for contractual protections from risk. Indeed, tort creditors may be unaware of the existence of the tortfeasor and much less able to monitor its capitalization or insurance coverage. These distinctions between tort and contract creditors are well established in the law of agency and partnership, and are generally recognized as important by commentators on corporate law. Nevertheless, until recently they received surprisingly little explicit recognition in veil-piercing doctrine. The leading tort case remains *Walkovszky v. Carlton,* reprinted below. The general rule of veil piercing remains: Thin capitalization alone is insufficient ground for piercing the corporate veil.

WALKOVSZKY v. CARLTON

223 N.E.2d 6 (N.Y. 1966)

FULD, J.:

This case involves what appears to be a rather common practice in the taxicab industry of vesting the ownership of a taxi fleet in many corporations, each owning only one or two cabs.

The complaint alleges that the plaintiff was severely injured four years ago in New York City when he was run down by a taxicab owned by the defendant Seon Cab Corporation and negligently operated at the time by the defendant Marchese. The individual defendant, Carlton, is claimed to be a stockholder of 10 corporations, including Seon, each of which has but two cabs registered in its name, and it is implied that only the minimum automobile liability insurance required by law (in the amount of $10,000) is carried on any one cab. Although seemingly independent of one another, these corporations are alleged to be "operated . . . as a single entity, unit and enterprise" with regard to financing, supplies, repairs, employees and garaging, and all are named as defendants. The plaintiff asserts that he is also entitled to hold their stockholders personally liable for the damages sought because the multiple corporate structure constitutes an unlawful attempt "to defraud members of the general public" who might be injured by the cabs.

The defendant Carlton has moved . . . to dismiss the complaint on the ground that as to him it "fails to state a cause of action." The court at Special Term granted the motion but the Appellate Division, by a divided vote, reversed, holding that a valid cause of action was sufficiently stated. The defendant Carlton appeals to us, from the nonfinal order, by leave of the Appellate Division on a certified question.

The law permits the incorporation of a business for the very purpose of enabling its proprietors to escape personal liability . . . but, manifestly, the privilege is not without its limits. Broadly speaking, the courts will disregard the corporate form, or, to use accepted terminology, "pierce the corporate veil," whenever necessary "to prevent fraud or to achieve equity." . . . [W]henever anyone uses control of the corporation to further his own rather than the corporation's business, he will be liable for the corporation's acts "upon the principle of respondeat superior applicable even where the agent is a natural person." . . . Such liability, moreover, extends not only to the corporation's commercial dealings . . . but to its negligent acts as well.

In the *Mangan* case (247 App. Div. 853 . . .), the plaintiff was injured as a result of the negligent operation of a cab owned and operated by one of four corporations affiliated with the defendant Terminal. Although the defendant was not a stockholder of any of the operating companies, both the defendant and the operating companies were owned, for the most part, by the same parties. The defendant's name (Terminal) was conspicuously displayed on the sides of all the taxis used in the enterprise and, in point of fact, the defendant actually serviced, inspected, repaired and dispatched them. These facts were deemed to provide sufficient cause for piercing the corporate veil of the operating company—the nominal owner of the cab which injured the plaintiff—and holding the defendant liable. The operating companies were simple instrumentalities for carrying on the business of the defendant without imposing upon it financial and other liabilities incident to the actual ownership and operation of the cabs. . . .

In the case before us, the plaintiff has explicitly alleged that none of the corporations "had a separate existence of their own" and, as indicated above, all are named as defendants. However, it is one thing to assert that a corporation is a fragment of a larger corporate combine which actually conducts the business. (See Berle, "The Theory of Enterprise Entity," 47 Col. L. Rev. 343, 348-350.) It is quite another to claim that the corporation is a "dummy" for its individual stockholders who are in reality carrying on the business in their personal capacities for purely personal rather than corporate ends. . . . Either circumstance would justify treating the corporation as an agent and piercing the corporate veil to reach the principal but a different result would follow in each case. In the first, only a larger corporate entity would be held financially responsible . . . while, in the other, the stockholder would be personally liable. . . .

At this stage in the present litigation, we are concerned only with the pleadings and, since CPLR §3014 permits causes of action to be stated "alternatively or hypothetically," it is possible for the plaintiff to allege both theories as the basis for his demand for judgment. . . . Reading the complaint in this case most favorably and liberally, we do not believe that there can be gathered from its averments the allegations required to spell out a valid cause of action against the defendant Carlton.

The individual defendant is charged with having "organized, managed, dominated and controlled" a fragmented corporate entity but there are no allegations that he was conducting business in his individual capacity. Had the taxicab fleet been owned by a single corporation, it would be readily apparent that the plaintiff would face formidable barriers in attempting to establish personal liability on the part of the corporation's stockholders. The fact that the fleet ownership has been deliberately split up among many corporations does not ease the plaintiff's burden in that respect. The corporate form may not be disregarded merely because the assets of the corporation, together with the mandatory insurance coverage of the vehicle which struck the plaintiff, are insufficient to assure him the recovery sought. If Carlton were to be held individually liable on those facts alone, the decision would apply equally to the thousands of cabs which are owned by their individual drivers who conduct their businesses through corporations organized pursuant to section 401 of the Business Corporation Law, . . . and carry the minimum insurance. . . . These taxi owner-operators are entitled to form such corporations . . . and we agree with the court at Special Term that, if the insurance coverage required by statute "is inadequate for the protection of the public, the remedy lies not with the courts but with the Legislature." It may very well be sound policy to require that certain corporations must take out liability insurance which will afford adequate compensation to their potential tort victims. However, the responsibility for imposing conditions on the privilege of incorporation has been committed by the Constitution to the Legislature. . . .

This is not to say that it is impossible for the plaintiff to state a valid cause of action against the defendant Carlton. However, the simple fact is that the plaintiff has just not done so here. While the complaint alleges that the separate corporations were undercapitalized and that their assets have been intermingled, it is barren of any "sufficiently particular(ized) statements" . . . that the defendant Carlton and his associates are actually doing business in their individual capacities, shuttling their personal funds in and out of the corporations "without regard to formality and to suit their

immediate convenience." *Weisser v. Mursam Shoe Corp.*, 127 F.2d 344 . . . .
Nothing of the sort has in fact been charged, and it cannot reasonably or
logically be inferred from the happenstance that the business of Seon Cab
Corporation may actually be carried on by a large corporate entity composed of many corporations which, under general principles of agency,
would be liable to each other's creditors in contract and in tort.[3]

In point of fact, the principle relied upon in the complaint to sustain
the imposition of personal liability is not agency but fraud. Such a cause of
action cannot withstand analysis. If it is not fraudulent for the owner-
operator of a single cab corporation to take out only the minimum required
liability insurance, the enterprise does not become either illicit or fraudulent merely because it consists of many corporations. The plaintiff's injuries
are the same regardless of whether the cab which strikes him is owned by a
single corporation or part of a fleet with ownership fragmented among
many corporations. Whatever rights he may be able to assert against parties
other than the registered owner of the vehicle come into being not because
he has been defrauded but because, under the principle of respondeat
superior, he is entitled to hold the whole enterprise responsible for the acts
of its agents.

In sum, then, the complaint falls short of adequately stating a cause of
action against the defendant Carlton in his individual capacity.

The order of the Appellate Division should be reversed, with . . . leave
to serve an amended complaint.

KEATING, J. (dissenting):
The defendant Carlton, the shareholder here sought to be held for the
negligence of the driver of a taxicab, was a principal shareholder and
organizer of the defendant corporation which owned the taxicab. The
corporation was one of 10 organized by the defendant, each containing
two cabs and each cab having the "minimum liability" insurance coverage
mandated by section 370 of the Vehicle and Traffic Law. The sole assets of
these operating corporations are the vehicles themselves and they are
apparently subject to mortgages.[*]

From their inception these corporations were intentionally undercapitalized for the purpose of avoiding responsibility for acts which were
bound to arise as a result of the operation of a large taxi fleet having cars
out on the street 24 hours a day and engaged in public transportation. And
during the course of the corporations' existence all income was continually
drained out of the corporations for the same purpose.

---

3. In his affidavit in opposition to the motion to dismiss, the plaintiff's counsel
claimed that corporate assets had been "milked out" of, and "siphoned off" from the
enterprise. Quite apart from the fact that these allegations are far too vague and conclusory,
the charge is premature. If the plaintiff succeeds in his action and becomes a judgment
creditor of the corporation, he may then sue and attempt to hold the individual defendants
accountable for any dividends and property that were wrongfully distributed (Business
Corporation Law, §§510, 719, 720).

* It appears that the medallions, which are of considerable value, are judgment proof.
(Administrative Code of the City of New York, §4362.0.)

The issue presented by this action is whether the policy of this State, which affords those desiring to engage in a business enterprise the privilege of limited liability through the use of the corporate device, is so strong that it will permit that privilege to continue no matter how much it is abused, no matter how irresponsibly the corporation is operated, no matter what the cost to the public. I do not believe that it is.

Under the circumstances of this case the shareholders should all be held individually liable to this plaintiff for the injuries he suffered. . . . At least, the matter should not be disposed of on the pleadings by a dismissal of the complaint. . . .

The policy of this State has always been to provide and facilitate recovery for those injured through the negligence of others. The automobile, by its very nature, is capable of causing severe and costly injuries when not operated in a proper manner. The great increase in the number of automobile accidents combined with the frequent financial irresponsibility of the individual driving the car led to the adoption of section 388 of the Vehicle and Traffic law which had the effect of imposing upon the owner of the vehicle the responsibility for its negligent operation. It is upon this very statute that the cause of action against both the corporation and the individual defendant is predicated.

In addition the Legislature, still concerned with the financial irresponsibility of those who owned and operated motor vehicles, enacted a statute requiring minimum liability coverage for all owners of automobiles. The important public policy represented by both these statutes is outlined in section 310 of the Vehicle and Traffic Law. That section provides that: "The legislature is concerned over the rising toll of motor vehicle accidents and the suffering and loss thereby afflicted. . . . "

The defendant Carlton claims that, because the minimum amount of insurance required by the statute was obtained, the corporate veil cannot and should not be pierced despite the fact that the assets of the corporation which owned the cab were "trifling compared with the business to be done and the risks of loss" which were certain to be encountered. I do not agree.

The Legislature is requiring minimum liability insurance of $10,000, no doubt intended to provide at least some small fund for recovery against those individuals and corporations who just did not have and were not able to raise or accumulate assets sufficient to satisfy the claims of those who were injured as a result of their negligence. It certainly could not have intended to shield those individuals who organized corporations, with the specific intent of avoiding responsibility to the public, where the operation of the corporate enterprise yielded profits sufficient to purchase additional insurance. . . .

The defendant contends that a decision holding him personally liable would discourage people from engaging in corporate enterprise.

What I would merely hold is that a participating shareholder of a corporation vested with a public interest, organized with capital insufficient to meet liabilities which are certain to arise in the ordinary course of the corporation's business, may be held personally responsible for such liabilities. Where corporate income is not sufficient to cover the cost of insurance premiums above the statutory minimum or where initially adequate finances dwindle under the pressure of competition, bad times or extraordinary and unexpected liability, obviously the shareholder will not be held liable. . . .

The only type of corporate enterprises that will be discouraged as a result of a decision allowing the individual shareholder to be sued will be those such as the one in question, designed solely to abuse the corporate privilege at the expense of the public interest.

For these reasons I would vote to affirm the order of the Appellate Division.

DESMOND, C.J., and VAN VOORHIS, BURKE and SCILEPPI, JJ., concur with FULD, J.

KEATING, J., dissents and votes to affirm in an opinion in which BERGAN, J., concurs.

Order reversed, etc.

NOTES AND QUESTIONS ON WALKOVSZKY v. CARLTON

1. Following the decision in *Walkovszky*, the plaintiff amended his complaint. The Appellate Division held that "the amended complaint sufficiently alleges a cause of action against appellant, i.e., that he and the other individual defendants were conducting the business of the taxicab fleet in their individual capacities." *Walkovszky v. Carlton,* 29 A.D.2d 763 (1968). The Court of Appeals affirmed, noting that the amended complaint "now meets the pleading requirements set forth in [our prior] opinion and states a valid cause of action." 244 N.E.2d 55 (1988).

2. Note that taxicab medallions, which are extremely valuable, are judgment proof in New York. Administrative Code §436-2.0. The cab industry in New York City has traditionally lobbied to protect medallions from foreclosure.

3. What precisely might the plaintiff have alleged in the amended complaint to keep Carlton and his associates in the litigation?

4. *Walkovszky* observes: "The law permits the incorporation of a business for the very purpose of enabling its proprietors to escape personal liability." Does this imply that the corporate veil is legitimately treated as a costless substitute for liability insurance? Might limited liability in tort be viewed as a form of socially subsidized liability insurance? Is mandatory liability insurance a more efficient way than unlimited liability to assure that an appropriate amount of assets is available to satisfy foreseeable damage claims?

5. Limited liability presumably encouraged Carlton to structure his cab empire as a "portfolio" of small companies rather than as a single large corporation. Easterbrook and Fischel observe:

> Taxi firms may incorporate each cab or put just a few cabs in a firm. If courts routinely pierced this arrangement and put the assets of the full enterprise at risk for the accidents of each cab, then "true" single-cab firms would have lower costs of operation because they alone could cut off liability. That would create a perverse incentive because . . . larger firms are apt to carry more

insurance. Potential tort victims would not gain from a legal rule that promoted corporate disintegration.[14]

Do you agree?

Involuntary creditors are not the only garden-variety victims of corporate torts. The U.S. Supreme Court has held that state veil-piercing law also
applies in actions to impose liability under the Comprehensive Environmental Response, Compensation, and Liability Act (CERCLA) on parent
companies for the polluting activities of their subsidiaries. See *United
States v. BestFoods,* 528 U.S. 810 (1999). Consider the following case,
arising in the aftermath of *Bestfoods.*

CARTER-JONES LUMBER CO. v. LTV STEEL

237 F.3d 745 (6th Cir. 2001)

. . . Dixie was incorporated in Ohio under the name Chain Corporation of America in 1963. Denune and two others acted as incorporators.
The corporation, under its new name, is still in good standing upon the
records of the office of the Ohio Secretary of State. Denune is the sole
shareholder.

In addition to its illegal business involving used electrical transformers
containing PCBs [polychlorinated biphenyls, a hazardous substance regulated by CERCLA], Dixie engaged in legitimate business. It sold motorcycle
parts and purchased machinery at auction for sale. It had between twenty
and twenty-five employees in Columbus and Springfield. While Denune
exercised significant control over the affairs of Dixie, some of Dixie's
employees handled the company's payroll and petty cash accounts and
the management of motorcycle parts sales.

The excerpts from Dixie's corporate notebook included in the joint
appendix shows that the corporation held annual meetings of its board of
directors and of its shareholders in every year from 1985 to 1999 and
several special meetings in 1995. Denune served as director through
1989. He did not commingle personal and corporate funds, and the corporation was sufficiently capitalized at the times Dixie engaged in the illegal
actions that created its liability under CERCLA. At the time the case was
tried in the district court, Dixie had a negative net worth of between $2,000
and $2,500.

While Denune did not control every aspect of Dixie's affairs or every
transaction, he clearly controlled the particular transactions that constituted the CERCLA violations for which Dixie was found liable. The invoice
for the ten transformers was sent to Dixie to the attention of Denune.
Denune wrote the check on Dixie's account in payment for the transformers. Denune signed an affidavit indicating he had been advised that the
transformers contained PCBs. According to Woody Underwood, who was
affiliated with Top Dollar Liquidators, the entity to which Denune sold the

14. Frank H. Easterbrook & Daniel R. Fischel, *Limited Liability and the Corporation,*
52 U. Chi. L. Rev. 89, 111 (1985).

transformers, Denune was personally involved in the scheme with James Henderson to hide the transformers from the EPA. He was present for some period of time on the night Henderson and Underwood illegally transported the transformers to a property on Marion Road and later to a property on Herndon Road. Denune misled the Ohio EPA inspector, Thomas Buchan, concerning the number of transformers containing PCBs he or Dixie owned. Denune personally checked on the trailers containing the PCB-laden transformers at least twice. He sold to Tracy Westfall three of the seven transformers he had already sold to Top Dollar. According to Westfall, Denune personally arranged for the transportation of four transformers from the Herndon Road property to a property in Columbus owned by Denune and leased by Westfall. When the Ohio EPA finally found those transformers, the serial numbers had been destroyed.

In their briefs, Dixie and Denune have identified no person affiliated with Dixie other than Denune who had anything to do with the PCB-filled transformers. Denune's attorney and Chester Tracy, apparently a Dixie employee, accompanied Buchan on his inspection of the corporation's property in Springfield. But their involvement was incidental and in any case after the fact. There is no indication that they took part in any of Denune's illegal activities. Denune argues in his brief that Dixie employees were involved in the transportation of the transformers from Columbus to Springfield, but at trial, Denune was unable to identify any such employees.

. . . In *Belvedere*, the Ohio Supreme Court announced a three-pronged test to determine if a shareholder is liable for the wrongdoing of the corporation of which he is an owner. The three prongs are:

1. control over the corporation by those to be held liable was so complete that the corporation had no separate mind, will, or existence of its own;

2. control over the corporation by those to be held liable was exercised in such a manner as to commit fraud or an illegal act against the person seeking to disregard the corporate entity; and

3. injury or unjust loss resulted to the plaintiff from such control and wrong.

In this case, there is no real argument about the second and third prongs. There is no dispute that Carter-Jones was harmed by Dixie's violation of CERCLA, or that Denune used his control over the corporation to cause it to violate the law. Denune focuses his attack on the first prong. He claims the district court erred by regarding control of the illegal transaction as sufficient . . . According to Denune, Ohio law requires courts to use a multi-factor test to determine whether a corporation is the alter ego of its shareholder. The factors he points to are: (1) under-capitalization; (2) failure to observe corporate formalities; (3) insolvency of the corporation at the time it incurs liability; (4) whether the shareholder held himself out as personally liable for the corporation's debts; (5) whether the shareholder diverted corporate funds to his own use; (6) failure to keep corporate records; and (7) whether "the corporation was a mere facade for the operations of the dominant shareholder." Here, however, he claims the district court considered only the extent of Denune's control of the illegal transaction at issue in the underlying lawsuit.

 . . . [B]ecause of the equitable nature of the veil-piercing doctrine, no list of factors can be exclusive or exhaustive. . . . Denune's argument, if we adopted it, would straightjacket the courts in situations where equity demands that the fiction of corporate personhood be ignored. Consider, for example, a case in which a corporation with a single shareholder kept immaculate corporate records, observed all the formalities required by corporate law, and was adequately capitalized. The shareholder never commingled funds, and never held himself out as personally liable for the corporation's debts. The corporation even does some legitimate business. Can it be that the shareholder is immunized from personal liability if he causes the corporation to commit an illegal act, no matter the degree of his control over the corporation with regard to the illegal act, no matter the harm to third parties, and no matter the other equities? Neither we nor the Ohio courts hold that such immunity exists.

 . . . For the foregoing reasons, the Court rejects Denune's argument that under Ohio law, mere control of a corporation, no matter how complete, is insufficient as a matter of law to trigger veil-piercing.

QUESTION ON CARTER-JONES LUMBER

Does it necessary follow that, as the court suggests, absence of veil piercing in this case will immunize the shareholder from liability? See U.S. v. Browning-Ferris Industries of Illinois, 195 F.3d 953 (7th Cir. 1999) (Posner. J.)

NOTE ON SUBSTANTIVE CONSOLIDATION

Substantive consolidation is an equitable remedy in bankruptcy that consolidates assets among corporate subsidiaries for the benefit of creditors of the various corporate subsidiaries. Substantive consolidation can be thought of as "horizontal" veil piercing, in which the corporate holding company structure is ignored for the purpose of distributing assets in bankruptcy. Adelphia Communications, Enron, Global Crossing, K-Mart, Owens-Corning, and WorldCom are prominent recent examples of substantive consolidation in bankruptcy proceedings. Professor William Widen finds that among 344 large public-company bankruptcies between 2000 and 2004, 12 percent of the cases involved substantive consolidation. Among the 21 largest bankruptcies in this sample, the incidence of substantive consolidation increases to 52 percent.[15]

 We are troubled by the prevalence of substantive consolidation as reported in Professor Widen's study. As a threshold matter, because bankruptcy law is primarily federal law, substantive consolidation represents yet another area where federal law undermines well-established state corporate law doctrine on veil piercing. But our concern goes beyond general federalism principles. If bankruptcy courts regularly collapse entities in an

---

15. See William H. Widen, *Prevalence of Substantive Consolidation in Large Bankruptcies from 2000 to 2004: Preliminary Results* (University of Miami working paper 2006).

exercise of their equitable powers (notably, without any statutory authority in the Bankruptcy Act to do so), the corporate form will lose its utility as a device for "asset partitioning" and risk allocation.[16] In addition, the prevalence of substantive consolidation hinders the development of "internal capital markets" that efficiently allocate capital within firms.[17] Of course, countervailing considerations of *ex post* fairness run strong and deep in bankruptcy proceedings. What do you think?

NOTE ON DISSOLUTION AND SUCCESSOR LIABILITY

The empirical literature suggests that many small firms such as chemical manufacturers undertaking dangerous activities are not only thinly capitalized but also likely to dissolve and liquidate before the full extent of their potential tort liability becomes known. See Reingleb & Wiggins, *Liability and Large-Scale, Long-Term Hazards*, 90 J. Pol. Econ. 574 (1990). For the liability of shareholders after the dissolution of the firm, see Del. §§278 and 282 and RMBCA §14.07(c)(3). Is this what you expected?

Although shareholders can eventually escape all liability through the simple act of dissolving the corporation and abandoning its assets, it may be more difficult to escape tort costs by selling the corporation's assets. As Professor Mark Roe wrote in the mid-1980s:

> Several state supreme courts have devised a doctrine of successor corporation liability. Under this doctrine, the buyer of the liquidating firm's product line picks up the tort liability of the seller, at least as that liability relates to the purchased product line. Anticipating the liability, the purchasing firm will reduce the offering price by the amount of the expected liability. Thus, the potential liquidator cannot escape liability through sale of the damage-causing product line and distribution of the proceeds. Only purchaser miscalculation or ignorance would make sale of the defective product line profitable for the liquidating shareholders.
>
> To avoid imposition of successor corporation liability, the purchasing firm must have no operation identifiable as continuous with the selling firm's product line. But when selling the defective product line, the seller usually must shatter some of its own operational going concern value to accomplish this result. The factories that made the offending product might have to be dismantled and sold off piece by piece, machine by machine; the sale force might have to be cut back; and trademarks might have to be destroyed.[18]

Professor Roe was writing at the height of successor liability, in the 1980s. Since then the doctrine has atrophied somewhat, though some commentators argue that there has been a recent resurgence. The Restatement (Third) of Torts: Product Liability states that the majority of jurisdictions maintain a traditionally restrictive approach to successor liability.[19] This is

16. See Henry Hansmann & Reinier Kraakman, *The Essential Role of Organizational Law*, 110 Yale L. J. 387 (2000).

17. See George G. Triantis, *Organizations as Internal Capital Markets: The Legal Boundaries of Firms, Collateral, and Trusts in Commercial and Charitable Enterprises*, 117 Harv. L. Rev. 1103 (2004).

18. Mark J. Roe, *Corporate Strategic Reaction to Mass Tort*, 72 Va. L. Rev. 1, 32 (1986).

19. Restatement (Third) of Torts: Products Liability, §12 cmt. b (1997).

disputed, though, by others who find a growing number of cases adopting broad principals of successor liability.[20] What are the pros and cons of a doctrine of successor liability? We return to this topic in Section 12.5, in the context of asset acquisitions.

6.5   CAN LIMITED LIABILITY IN TORT BE JUSTIFIED?

Consider the following excerpt:

HENRY HANSMANN & REINIER KRAAKMAN, TOWARD UNLIMITED SHAREHOLDER LIABILITY FOR CORPORATE TORTS

100 Yale L.J. 1879 (1991)

Limited liability in tort has been the prevailing rule for corporations in the United States, as elsewhere, for more than a century. This rule is generally acknowledged to create incentives for excessive risk-taking by permitting corporations to avoid the full costs of their activities. Nevertheless, these incentives are conventionally assumed to be the price of securing efficient capital financing for corporations. Although several authors have recently proposed curtailing limited liability for certain classes of tort claims or for certain types of corporations in order to control its worst abuses, even the most radical of these proposals retains limited shareholder liability as the general rule.

Surprisingly, given the widespread acceptance of the prevailing rule, the existing literature contains no comprehensive comparison of the consequences of limited and unlimited liability for corporate torts. We offer such an analysis here. We argue, contrary to the prevailing view, that limited liability in tort cannot be rationalized for either closely-held or publicly-traded corporations on the strength of the conventional arguments offered on its behalf. In fact, there may be no persuasive reasons to prefer limited liability over a regime of unlimited pro rata shareholder liability for corporate torts. The question remains open chiefly because the merits of limited liability depend, as we demonstrate, on empirical issues that are difficult to resolve on the basis of available evidence. At a minimum, however, we conclude that the burden is now on the proponents of limited liability to justify the prevailing rule.

The topic is timely and important. Changes in technology, knowledge, liability rules, and procedures for mass tort litigation have for the first time raised the prospect of tort claims that exceed the net worth of even very large corporations. Environmental harms, such as oil spills or the release of toxic materials, are one potential source of massive liability; hazardous products and carcinogens in the workplace are others. At the same time, the mergers and acquisitions movement of the past decade has converted

20. See Richard L. Cupp, Jr., *Redesigning Successor Liability*, 1999 U. Illinois L. Rev. 845 (1999).

many large corporations that were formerly publicly-traded into highly leveraged closely-held firms; these firms, which have proportionately small net assets and are under great pressure to maximize cash flow, have an unusually strong incentive to engage in excessively risky behavior.

Already, strong empirical evidence indicates that increasing exposure to tort liability has led to the widespread reorganization of business firms to exploit limited liability to evade damage claims. The method of evasion differs by industry. For example, placing hazardous activities in separate subsidiaries seems to be the dominant mode of insulating assets in the tobacco and hazardous waste industries. In contrast, disaggregating or downsizing firms seems to be the primary strategy for avoiding liability in the chemical industry and, more recently, in the oil transport industry. Indeed, one study finds that, over the past twenty-five years, a very large proportion of small firms entering all hazardous industries in the United States are motivated primarily by a desire to avoid liability for consumer, employee, and environmental harms. . . .

I.   CLOSELY HELD CORPORATIONS

For clarity of analysis and exposition, we begin by analyzing the consequences of limited liability for the simplest types of corporate structures and then proceed to examine progressively more complex cases.

A. CORPORATIONS WITH A SINGLE SHAREHOLDER

Consider first the situation in which a single person forms a corporation, of which she is the sole shareholder and manager, to exploit an investment opportunity. The shareholder in this case could be an individual or — more realistically and more importantly — another firm of which the corporation in question is a wholly-owned subsidiary. Suppose that undertaking the investment creates a risk of tort liability exceeding the corporation's net value. Assume, moreover, that the shareholder's personal assets are larger than any potential liability that the corporation might incur (an assumption we shall relax below).

1.   With Risk Neutrality

Finally, assume that the corporation's single shareholder is risk neutral — an assumption that is reasonable when the shareholder is a parent corporation, even if it is unrealistic when the shareholder is an individual.

Under these circumstances, it is easy to see that a rule of limited shareholder liability for corporate torts creates incentives for several forms of inefficient behavior.

a. Incentives to Misinvest

The most familiar inefficiency created by limited liability is the incentive it provides for the shareholder to direct the corporation to spend too little on precautions to avoid accidents. In contrast, a rule of unlimited liability induces the socially efficient level of expenditure on precautions by making the shareholder personally liable for any tort damages that the corporation cannot pay.

Further, limited liability encourages overinvestment in hazardous industries. Since limited liability permits cost externalization, a corporation engaged in highly risky activities can have positive value for its shareholder, and thus can be an attractive investment, even when its net present value to society as a whole is negative. Consequently, limited liability encourages excessive entry and aggregate overinvestment in unusually hazardous industries.

Finally, limited liability may induce the shareholder either to over-invest or to underinvest in her individual firm — that is, to pick either too large or too small a scale for the firm. This scale effect is ambiguous because investing in the firm under limited liability has two different consequences for potential tort liability that operate in opposite directions. On the one hand, limited liability partially externalizes the marginal increase in tort damages caused by expansion of the firm and thus creates an incentive for excessive investment. On the other hand, increased investment increases the value of the firm, and hence the amount that is available to pay damages to all tort claimants, including those who would have been injured even without the new investment. Consequently, limited liability also creates an incentive to minimize investment in order to reduce the exposure of the firm's owner to tort damages. Although in most cases the second effect is likely to dominate the first, and hence lead to too small a scale for the firm, there may also be situations in which the reverse is true. . . .

II.   PUBLICLY-TRADED CORPORATIONS

Limited liability gives the managers of publicly-traded corporations an incentive to assume too much risk, just as it does the shareholders of closely-held firms. However, the public corporation adds several novel elements to the comparison of liability regimes. In addition to a new class of hired managers, these include: (1) large numbers of passive shareholders; (2) a market for freely-trading stock; (3) substantial assets; and (4) potential tort liability that may not only exceed the firm's assets but that may not be fully insurable at any premium. The traditional view is that these elements — and especially the need to maintain an efficient market for shares — make unlimited liability even less appropriate for public firms than for closely-held firms.

The merits of this view turn principally on three issues. The first is the feasibility of administering unlimited liability when shareholders are numerous and trade frequently. The second is the potential burden that unlimited liability might impose on the securities market. And the third is whether unlimited liability imposed on public shareholders can improve the incentives of the managers who actually determine firm policy.

A. DESIGNING AN UNLIMITED LIABILITY RULE

. . .

1.   When Should Liability Attach to Shareholders?

An administrable rule of unlimited liability for the public must specify both a measure of shareholder liability and the point at which freely-traded stock imposes personal liability on its holders. For reasons that we have already outlined in discussing closely-held corporations, and that will become more apparent below, the most plausible measure of shareholder liability is a rule of pro rata liability for any excess tort damages that the firm's estate fails to satisfy. The more difficult problem is selecting the timing rule that determines which shareholders become liable after a tort occurs.

The choice of a timing rule in determining when excess liability attaches to shareholders inevitably involves a conflict between administrative complexity and opportunities for evasion. An "occurrence" rule, under which liability attaches to persons who are shareholders at the time a tort occurs, is the most difficult rule for shareholders to evade but also the most difficult to administer. A "judgment" rule that attaches residual liability only to those persons who are shareholders at the time of judgment is the simplest to administer but creates widespread opportunities for evasion. A variety of considerations suggest that a reasonable compromise is a modified version of a "claims-made" rule, which attaches liability to persons who are shareholders when — or somewhat before — the tort claim is filed. We style this modified claims-made rule an "information-based" rule. . . .

[W]e propose a modified form of the claims-made rule — an "information-based rule" — under which liability would attach to shareholders at the earliest of the following moments: (1) when the tort claims in question were filed; (2) when the corporation's management first became aware that, with high probability, such claims would be filed; or (3) when the corporation dissolved without leaving a contractual successor. This information-based rule would fix liability before shareholders could evade responsibility for tort damages, without creating the uncertainties and complexities that would attend an occurrence rule. . . .

2.   The Costs of Collection

A second inquiry bearing on the feasibility of unlimited liability is whether recovering from numerous public shareholders would be prohibitively costly even in the absence of opportunistic efforts to disperse share ownership. Very large collection costs would make unlimited liability less attractive not only because they would be wasteful, but also because they would lower settlement values and hence reduce the deterrent effect of tort rules. We believe that collection costs are unlikely to be prohibitive in this sense.

One reason is that shareholders would rarely be forced into insolvency. Equity holdings today are already highly concentrated in the hands of wealthy institutions and individuals. Beyond this, assessments against shareholders would seldom exceed the assets of even a modest investor. It seems unlikely that even a catastrophic liability judgment would impose costs exceeding a publicly-traded firm's value by more than, say, a multiple of five. Thus, an unlucky small shareholder who had placed 5% of a $100,000 portfolio in the stock of such a firm would stand to lose $25,000, or 25% of her portfolio's value, in a worst case scenario. A large institution with 0.2% of its assets invested in the same stock would lose 1% of its asset value. Although such losses would be serious, they would hardly be beyond the pale of ordinary market fluctuations.

Given that shareholders would be able to pay, the mechanics of collection need not be excessively costly. A court could clearly administer the collection effort: bankruptcy trustees already collect accounts receivable from hundreds or thousands of debtors of bankrupt firms. Since share ownership on the liability dates would presumably be the chief legal issue in most collection efforts, few shareholders could successfully contest their assessments. Wealthy individuals and institutions would have little to gain from litigating separately to contest their assessments because they would be pursued in any event. Moreover, even small shareholders might be induced to cooperate simply by adding collection costs to the assessment bill of shareholders who unsuccessfully sought to contest their assessments. . . .

B. Costs Imposed by Unlimited Liability on the Securities Market

The claim that unlimited liability might distort share prices or prevent shareholders from diversifying risk is persuasive only under a joint and several liability rule. Under a pro rata rule, shares would have the same expected value for all shareholders. Although individual stocks would be riskier under such a rule, the additional risk would be no more difficult to diversify than the risk of tort liability is today. It would simply be larger in absolute terms, which would increase the number of stocks in an optimally diversified portfolio as well as the risk of taking a large position in a single firm. Given that a pro rata rule would leave shares with the same expected value for all investors and also permit full diversification of tort risks, it should not affect the efficiency of market pricing. Risk-averse small investors with too little capital to diversify fully under an unlimited liability regime could shift their investments at very little cost to mutual funds or corporate debt. Moreover, the infrequency of catastrophic torts suggests that a pro rata rule would impose relatively small expected costs, even on undiversified investors, except when corporate activities are extremely risky—which is precisely when an unlimited liability regime is needed to prevent corporations from externalizing large costs.

It is sometimes argued that, regardless of how remote the probability of a substantial judgment against them, the mere prospect of unlimited personal liability would cause many individual stockholders to abandon the equity markets entirely in favor of fixed-return securities, with the arguable consequence of impairing the liquidity of the markets. But such behavior seems as unlikely as it would be irrational. For example, under current law, every time a person drives an automobile she exposes herself to unlimited tort liability. Yet nearly all adults regularly drive automobiles, and casual empiricism suggests that few individuals even feel it worthwhile to purchase liability insurance that has exceptionally high coverage limits.

QUESTIONS ON THE HANSMANN & KRAAKMAN EXCERPT

1. How, according to Hansmann and Kraakman, does limited liability induce firms to behave inefficiently? What concept of efficiency do they employ?

2. Would the alternative role proposed by Hansmann and Kraakman eliminate the incentive to behave inefficiently in public corporations as well as close corporations? What assumption is made about managerial behavior?

3. Is the proposed alternative feasible? Regardless of its feasibility, is it desirable?

4. What about the merits of other alternatives to limited liability that are less dramatic than the Hansmann-Kraakman proposal? Those most often discussed include mandating insurance coverage for risky firms, imposing criminal penalties on corporate decision makers who create unreasonable tort risks, and giving tort victims priority over other creditors in the event of a corporate bankruptcy. Are these alternatives likely to be less costly and/or more efficacious than a rule of pro rata shareholder liability?

5. Professor Joseph Grundfest argues that, if the Hansmann-Kraakman proposal were adopted, the flexibility inherent in the capital markets would allow investors to avoid personal liability by concentrating the ownership of high-risk firms in the hands of "attachment-proof" investors, such as foreign investors. The attachment-proof investors would then balance their portfolios through a derivative market designed for exchanging returns with conventional investors. See Joseph A. Grundfest, *The Limited Future of Unlimited Liability: A Capital Markets Perspective*, 102 Yale L. J. 387 (1992). Grundfest concludes that rational investors, in increasingly liquid global capital markets, would arbitrage away the perceived benefits that advocates of unlimited liability foresee. For the Hansmann-Kraakman response, see Henry Hansmann & Reinier Kraakman, *Do the Capital Markets Compel Limited Liability?*, 102 Yale L. J. 427 (1992).

NORMAL GOVERNANCE: THE VOTING SYSTEM[1]

7.1 THE ROLE AND LIMITS OF SHAREHOLDER VOTING

Much of the utility of the corporate form derives from the broad discretion that it delegates to a centralized management structure. Yet that discretion is not absolute. It is restricted by statute in several important ways and may be curtailed by the corporate charter (and perhaps by bylaws — a complicated subject that is reserved for later). But remarkably very few public companies do restrict the board's managerial power in their charters. Instead, equity investors in public corporations rely largely on the default terms built into corporation law to control the agency costs of management.

Dean Robert Clark has aptly summarized the default powers of shareholders as three: the right to vote, the right to sell, and the right to sue. Stated more fully, shareholders have the power to vote on the designation of the board and on certain fundamental corporate transactions, the power to sell their stock if they are disappointed with their company's performance, and the right to sue their directors for breach of fiduciary duty in certain circumstances. It is important to recognize, however, that each of these shareholder strategies for disciplining management interacts with the others. Thus, the investor's power to sell her stock may facilitate a hostile takeover of an underperforming firm, but the effectiveness of a takeover attempt may, in turn, depend on the ability to conduct a proxy fight for shareholder votes. Likewise, the effectiveness of a proxy fight may be impaired by management actions that shareholders can attack in court as a breach of fiduciary duty. Although we analyze these basic rights separately, in practice they work together.

In this chapter, we address the shareholders' most basic voting right: the right to elect the board of directors. We also touch on many associated topics, including calling annual meetings, affording information to shareholders, voting by proxy, and removing directors from office. In aggregate, these topics cover the "normal governance" machinery of the corporation. We reserve for later chapters detailed consideration of the law bearing on

---

1. We are grateful to Dorian Barag and Tibor Nagy for their extensive editorial suggestions and proposed problems for this chapter.

proxy contests and on shareholder rights to vote on fundamental transactions: for example, an amendment of the charter, a merger, a sale of all assets, or a dissolution.[2] These topics are addressed in Chapters 12 and 13.

The most important factor affecting shareholder voting is the collective action problem faced by shareholders in large public companies. Consider two extreme cases. In the first, the corporation is wholly owned by a single shareholder. There are no costs of collective shareholder action. Indeed the voting system is merely a formality because the shareholder appoints directors at her pleasure. Whether the corporation's managers enjoy any discretion depends entirely on how closely our shareholder-principal decides to monitor their performance. (A single owner who was temperamentally inclined to confer no discretion on agents would necessarily have to limit the size of her organization.)

In the second extreme case, assume that shares in the corporation are held by 100,000 shareholders, each with a $100 investment. In this case, informed shareholder action (vote) would require that some investment in information be made by a very large number of shareholders. This would be collectively and individually costly. Any one shareholder's prospective share of the potential benefit that informed action *might* produce would probably not justify her personal costs. But more importantly, any one shareholder's vote *is quite unlikely to affect the outcome* of the vote. Thus, a shareholder is likely to get the same proportionate share of any benefit, without regard to whether she invests in becoming informed and voting intelligently. Economically, her incentive is to remain passive. Conversely, the larger a shareholder's proportionate stake is, the greater the probability that her vote will affect the outcome and the less she suffers from this problem of "rational apathy." But for our stylized firm of 100,000 equal shareholders, the shareholder collective action problem would preclude informed shareholder action; rational shareholders would be highly unlikely to challenge board decisions or even inform themselves about the company's performance beyond following the price of its stock. Thus, in this polar case, too, the voting system might largely be seen as a formality.

In the past, commentators tended to treat most American corporations as representative of one or the other of these extremes. Indeed, since Professors Adolf Berle and Gardner Means first confirmed the rise of a seemingly autonomous managerial class in the 1930s,[3] the second case (that of the diffusely held company with a passive shareholder base) has been the conventional model of the large American public corporation. Commentators have not always thought this arrangement of passive shareholding was optimal, however, and attempts have been made to create a more active "shareholder democracy." Most notably, the 1934 Securities and Exchange Act sought to empower shareholders through forced disclosure of information (see the discussion of §14 of the 1934 Act below), and the courts have tended to aid this process by implying private remedies under that Act. The Securities and Exchange Commission (SEC), acting under the color of §14, has promulgated elaborate proxy rules designed

---

2. See, e.g., DGCL §242 (charter amendment), §251 (merger), §271 (sale of substantially all assets), and §275 (dissolution).

3. Adolf Berle & Gardner Means, The Modern Corporation and Private Property (1932).

to encourage informed shareholder voting. Ironically, until their amendment in 1992, these rules, by increasing the expense associated with shareholder communication, may have encouraged even greater voting passivity among shareholders.[4]

But not everyone agrees that mandated disclosure makes shareholders effective monitors. Some economically oriented commentators believe that the collective action problem is fatal in diffuse public capital markets no matter how much information is available. These commentators argue that managers are constrained not by shareholder votes but by the pressures exerted by multiple markets: the product market, the market for managerial services (including compensation incentives), the capital market (which must be accessed for funds), and most dramatically, the market for corporate control.[5]

Notwithstanding widespread academic pessimism about the inevitability of shareholder passivity, however, a new shareholders' rights movement led by institutional investors holding large blocks of shares emerged at the end of the 1980s. The new movement has had some notable successes. In the 1960s and 1970s, no one would have expected the governance upheavals of the 1990s, where, under pressure from institutional shareholders, boards of directors of such leading firms as General Motors, IBM, Sears, Westinghouse, and American Express fired their CEOs for poor performance. Institutional shareholder activism received a boost in 1992, when the SEC amended the proxy rules to allow large shareholders to communicate more easily with respect to a forthcoming corporate vote, without incurring the expense of filing proxy solicitation materials with the SEC.

The rise of the shareholder rights movement has sparked a literature of explanation, celebration, and criticism. The most important observation of this literature is that we no longer live in a world of extreme cases in which collective action costs are either nonexistent (because the corporation has a controlling shareholder) or preclusive (because stockholding is highly diffuse). Instead, growing institutional portfolios, cheaper costs of communication between institutions, and the evolution of new agents of shareholder organization (such as Institutional Shareholder Services[6]) have created ownership and coordination structures that fall between these two extremes. In today's modal public corporation, collective action costs may be large but perhaps not large enough to prevent shareholders from monitoring managerial performance. Thus, the regulation of shareholder voting and proxy solicitation really does matter for the typical public corporation today.

4. For a useful study of successive revisions to the proxy rules and their depressing effects on shareholder participation in governance, see John Pound, *Proxy Voting and the SEC*, 29 J. Fin. Econ. 241 (1991).

5. See, e.g., Eugene F. Fama, *Agency Problems and the Theory of the Firm*, 88 J. Pol. Econ. 288 (1980); Eugene F. Fama & Michael C. Jensen, *Separation of Ownership and Control*, 26 J.L. & Econ. 301 (1983).

6. Institutional Shareholder Services (ISS) has become a powerful for-profit organization that provides proxy voting advice to institutional shareholders and corporate governance advice to major companies, among other services. On hotly contested issues (e.g., takeover contests, or, more recently, majority voting proposals) ISS's recommendation can determine the outcome. For more information on ISS, see their Web site, www.issproxy.com.

7.2   ELECTING AND REMOVING DIRECTORS

7.2.1   Electing Directors

This is the foundational — and mandatory — voting right. Every corporation *must* have a board of directors, even if the "board" has only a single member. DGCL §141(a). And every corporation must have at least one class of voting stock. Indeed, in the absence of any customization in the charter, each share of stock has one vote — no more, no less. DGCL §212 (a). However, the legal mandate that there be *some* voting stock is in fact a trivial constraint on governance design. It is possible to create nonvoting common stock and a single class of voting stock containing a single share. Of course, such one-class, one-share voting stock is never encountered in practice. Rather, in publicly financed corporations, most equity takes the form of voting common stock.

Why does almost all common stock carry voting rights? The sensible explanation is that the right to appoint the board of directors is more valuable to common stock investors than to any other class of investors. Their security has no maturity date and no legal right to periodic payments. Thus, they have a greater need for the default protection of voting rights than other investors in the enterprise. Bondholders are protected by a hard contractual right to interest payments and to the return of their principal, usually on a stated maturity date and sometimes secured with property of the debtor. It follows that the default right to choose or replace the board is much more important for common stock to possess than for bondholders or other investors in the corporation. In those uncommon cases in which one class of common stock is nonvoting, its holders must in effect free ride on the governance incentives of the voting common stock.

Another mandatory feature of the voting system is the *annual* election of directors.[7] Each year, holders of voting stock elect either the whole board, when there is a single class of directors, or some fraction of the board. For example, shareholders elect one-third of the board annually when the charter provides for a "staggered" or "classified" board made up of three "classes" of directors, each serving three-year terms. See DGCL §141(d).

Corporate law facilitates the election of directors by creating a flexible framework for holding the annual meeting of shareholders. Generally, the state statutes fix a minimum and maxi-mum notice period (e.g., 10-60 days, DGCL §222(b)) and a quorum requirement for the general meeting (e.g., DGCL §216). The statutes also establish a minimum and maximum period for the board to fix a so-called "record date." Shareholders who are registered as of the record date are legal shareholders entitled to vote at the meeting (e.g., DGCL §211(c)). Within the range of alternatives permitted by statute, a corporation's actual notice period, quorum requirement, and record date will be established by the charter or in a bylaw.

---

7. See DGCL §211. In non-U.S. jurisdictions, directors' terms are frequently longer; for example, four years in Germany and six years in France. Closely held private corporations in the United Kingdom occasionally elect directors *for life*. In all of these cases, however, shareholders retain a mandatory right to remove directors.

CUMULATIVE VOTING

The usual voting regime is that each shareholder gets one vote for each share of voting stock owned and may cast it for each directorship (or board position) that is to be filled at the election. Thus, if there are seven places on the board to be filled each year, an owner of one share casts one vote for a candidate for each office. This allows the holder of a 51 percent voting block to designate the complete membership of the board of directors, while the holder of a sizable minority block of stock (say, 49 percent) can be entirely excluded from representation on the board. To some, this seems undesirable.

An alternative technique for voting first sprang up late in the nineteenth century. This technique, called *cumulative voting,* is designed to increase the possibility for minority shareholder representation on the board of directors. In a cumulative voting regime, each shareholder may cast a total number of votes equal to the number of directors for whom she is entitled to vote, multiplied by the number of voting shares that she owns, with the top overall vote getters getting seated on the board.

To see how cumulative voting can work, consider a simple example. Family Corp. has 300 shares outstanding. Shareholder A owns 199 shares and Shareholder B owns 101 shares. Family Corp. has a three-person board elected to annual terms. Assume that shareholders A and B support different candidates for the board. Under "straight" voting, A would win each seat 199 to 101. Under cumulative voting, B could cast 303 votes (= 101 shares × 3 seats up for election) all for a single candidate. Thus B would be guaranteed to get one seat on the board, because A's 597 votes (= 199 shares × 3 seats) cannot be divided three ways so that all three of A's candidates receive more than 303 votes. This example illustrates how cumulative voting can allow significant minority shareholders to get board representation roughly in proportion to their shareholdings.

While cumulative voting was popular among certain shareholders during the first half of the twentieth century, it was never popular with managers, who argued that boards are collegial organizations that function best cooperatively. Boards with divided shareholder allegiances were said to be too adversarial. Thus, few companies have adopted cumulative voting during the last 50 years, even as a default option.[8] Where a corporate charter does mandate cumulative voting, however, it affects the exercise of the shareholder removal rights (since it obviously makes little sense to permit a straight majority vote to remove a director without cause when he or she was elected by a cumulative vote).

7.2.2   Removing Directors

State corporate law governs not only the right to elect directors, but also the right to remove them. At common law, shareholders could remove a director only "for cause." The leading case, *Campbell v. Loew's Inc.,*[9] establishes that a director is entitled to certain due process rights when he

8. See Jeffrey N. Gordon, *Institutions as Relational Investors: A New Look at Cumulative Voting,* 94 Colum. L. Rev. 124 (1994).
9. 134 A.2d 852 (Del. Ch. 1957).

or she is removed for cause, although just what these rights include, and who decides when they are violated, remains unclear. Equally important, it is not clear what constitutes "good cause." Certainly, fraud or unfair self-dealing is cause to remove a director, but what about abysmal business judgment? If one views the directorship as a sort of property right, which seems to be predicate of the "cause" requirement, then poor business judgment, without additional faults, would not constitute cause for removal. See DGCL §141(k), conferring broad removal power on shareholders.

State law in all jurisdictions bars directors from removing fellow directors, for cause or otherwise, in the absence of express shareholder authorization. This means, for example, that a board cannot adopt a bylaw that purports to authorize it to exercise a removal power. Some statutes, however, do permit shareholders to grant the board power to remove individual directors for cause. See, e.g., NYBCL §706. In all events, if the board uncovers cause for removal, it can petition a court of competent jurisdiction to remove the director from office. Although some courts have expressed doubt about their power to remove a director during her term, it is generally conceded that any court of equity supervising the performance of any fiduciary has an inherent power to remove for cause. Ordinarily, state courts of the jurisdiction of incorporation must exercise this power because the law of the state of incorporation governs a corporation's internal affairs. However, federal courts have this authority as well when the corporation is publicly traded, and therefore registered under the Securities and Exchange Act of 1934.

Shareholder removal is more difficult when a board is classified. DGCL §141(k) provides that when the board is classified directors can be removed only "for cause," unless the charter provides otherwise.

PROBLEM: THE UNFIREABLE CEO

Village, Inc., is a corporation engaged in the business of providing online fashion advice and consulting services to male law students and young lawyers. The firm had its initial public offering (IPO) two years ago, and after a meteoric rise, the stock has fallen steadily since then. GianCarlo Revesz, who is Village's CEO, owns 25 percent of its single class of stock. The balance of the stock is widely held. Revesz's block has allowed him to control the outcome of board elections. The word on the street, however, is that the nosedive of the stock has sparked the interest of others in gaining control. Under these circumstances, Revesz initiates the following actions.

First, the board recommends and the shareholders approve an amendment of the Village charter to provide that the power to amend the bylaws shall be vested exclusively in the directors and to provide for cumulative voting. The directors then amend the bylaws to provide that the number of directors shall be fixed at nine and divided into three equal classes, each of whose term shall expire in successive years. At the next annual meeting of the shareholders, nine directors are elected to the staggered board. All of them happen to believe that Revesz is the best leader a fashion e-company could have, even if the stock price is now quite low.

Six months later a well-known takeover artist, Qwen Vicious Kagan, purchases 51 percent of the outstanding Village, Inc. stock from numerous holders and consults you to devise some method of immediately assuming and exercising actual control over company policy. Kagan has been told that she is powerless for three full years. What advice would you give her (a) under Delaware law; (b) under the (old) Illinois Act, assuming provisions similar to Delaware with one exception, which reads as follows:

> The power to make, alter, amend, or repeal the bylaws of the corporation shall be vested in the board of directors, unless reserved to the shareholders by the articles of incorporation.

Consider in this connection Ms. Kagan's ability to use the following possible actions to advance her plan: (1) amending the certificate of incorporation, (2) amending the bylaws; (3) increasing the size of the board, (4) removing one or more directors, and (5) dissolving the company and distributing its assets.

Are there other facts that you must know before giving your opinion? Suppose that, instead of amending the bylaws, Revesz had managed to insert all of the above changes in the certificate of incorporation. How could he?

NOTE ON STAGGERED BOARDS

As the preceding problem illustrates, a staggered board makes it more difficult for a shareholder — even a shareholder who holds 51 percent of the stock — to gain control of the board of directors. Under a "unitary" board, in which all directors are elected annually, a shareholder has a clean shot at electing a full board once a year. But when the board is staggered, a shareholder must win two elections, which can be as long as thirteen to fifteen months apart, in order to gain majority control (specifically, two-thirds of the seats) on the board.

It is important to note that a shareholder may have ways to "disassemble" a staggered board to avoid the two-election problem. For example, a shareholder might be able to "pack" the board with new directors, or remove directors without cause and replace them with new directors. But if a staggered board is "effective" (nonevadable), then a shareholder who wants control of the board must wait at least one year and perhaps as long as two years, depending on when the challenge is launched relative to the annual meeting date.

This difference between unitary and staggered boards becomes most relevant in the context of a hostile takeover bid. As we shall see in Chapter 13, the invention of the "poison pill" in the mid-1980s made control of the board a prerequisite for acquiring a company's shares. A staggered board makes board control more difficult. Sure enough, empirical work shows that targets of hostile takeover bids are significantly more likely to remain independent when they have a staggered board than when they have a unitary board.[10] The data further shows that targets that remain independent do not, on average, achieve the same returns for their shareholders as they would have received by accepting the hostile takeover bid.[11] Putting these facts together suggests that staggered boards, on average, "entrench" boards and managers in ways that deter value-increasing hostile takeover bids. Consistent with this conclusion, a subsequent empirical study finds that companies with staggered boards had lower total shareholder returns than companies with unitary boards during the 1990s.[12] What countervailing benefits might staggered boards provide that are not captured by the empirical studies?

7.3   SHAREHOLDER MEETINGS AND ALTERNATIVES

In addition to the election of the board at the annual meeting, shareholders may consider other business. Thus, shareholders may also vote to adopt, amend, and repeal bylaws; to remove directors; and to adopt shareholder resolutions that may ratify board actions or request the board to take certain actions. Should the board fail to convene an annual meeting within 13 months of the last meeting, courts will entertain a shareholder's petition and promptly require that a meeting be held in a summary action. See, e.g., DGCL §211.

Special Meetings.   Special meetings of shareholders are those other than the annual meeting called for special purposes. Often they are called to permit shareholders to vote on fundamental transactions. Additionally, in most jurisdictions, a special meeting is the only way that shareholders can initiate action (such as, the amendment of bylaws or the removal from office of directors) between annual meetings. Therefore, who may call a special meeting and how a special meeting is called are matters of considerable importance.

If you were designing an ideal corporate governance structure, when would you permit shareholders to call a special meeting over the objection of the board? Presumably, the more that investors monitor corporate management, *ceteris paribus*, the lower wasteful agency costs will be, and to that extent, the lower the firm's cost of capital will be. This factor weighs in favor of permitting shareholders to call special meetings easily, where, for example, they might act to remove directors. Yet shareholder meetings are costly, especially for public companies. Their costs involve not

---

10. See Lucian Arye Bebchuk, John C. Coates IV & Guhan Subramanian, *The Powerful Antitakeover Force of Staggered Boards: Theory, Evidence & Policy*, 54 Stan. L. Rev. 887 (2002); Lucian Arye Bebchuk, John C. Coates IV & Guhan Subramanian, *The Powerful Antitakeover Force of Staggered Boards: Further Findings and a Reply to Symposium Participants*, 55 Stan. L. Rev. 885 (2002).

11. See Bebchuk, Coates & Subramanian, *Further Findings, supra* note 10.

12. See Lucian Arye Bebchuk & Alma Cohen, *The Cost of Entrenched Boards*, 78 J. Fin. Econ. 409 (2005).

only financial expenditures, but also the lost time of senior executives. Thus, like many issues of corporate law, we can easily state the general principle (maximize the value of the firm), but we cannot apply it without controversy to the choice of a rule. Either encouraging special meetings (and accepting the costs) or discouraging them (and allowing bad directors to stay in office) may increase or decrease the value of the firm.

Putting the matter of meetings in the corporate charter allows corporate planners to decide for themselves in particular cases. The Revised Model Business Corporation Act (RMBCA) offers a typical solution. Under §7.02, a corporation must hold a special meeting of stockholders if (i) such a meeting is called by the board of directors or a person authorized in the charter or bylaws to do so, or (ii) the holders of at least 10 percent of all votes entitled to be cast demand such a meeting in writing. Delaware law provides that special meetings may be called by the board or by such persons as are designated in the charter or bylaws. It does not contain the mandatory 10 percent provision that is found in many state (and foreign) statutes. See DGCL §211(d). Thus, absent a provision in the charter or bylaws, even a 10 percent shareholder cannot call a special meeting on her own authority in Delaware.

Shareholder Consent Solicitations. Shareholders may have an alternative to special meetings in the form of a statutory provision permitting them to act in lieu of a meeting by filing written consents. Delaware was an innovator in establishing this alternative technique for shareholder action, although at the time it was adopted, it was thought to be little more than a cost-reducing measure for small corporations. As we will see later, however, this technique, which was originally developed to facilitate decision making in close corporations, can also assist in hostile takeovers where acquirers wish to displace the boards of public companies.

The stockholder consent statute in Delaware provides that *any action* that may be taken at a meeting of shareholders (e.g., amendment of bylaws or removal of directors from office) may also be taken by the written concurrence of the holders of the number of voting shares required to approve that action at a meeting attended by all shareholders. See DGCL §228. Other states are less "liberal." The RMBCA, for example, requires unanimous shareholder consent. See §7.04(a).

7.4 PROXY VOTING AND ITS COSTS

Shareholder meetings require a quorum to act. Given the widely dispersed share ownership of most publicly financed corporations, public shareholders are unlikely to actually attend shareholder meetings. As a result, in order to gather a quorum, the board and its officers are permitted to collect voting authority from shareholders in the form of proxies. In doing so, management acts on behalf of and at the expense of the corporation. In short, proxy voting is fundamental to corporate governance in publicly financed corporations. State corporation law establishes its validity as well as the legal structure in which proxies are given, exercised, and revoked. See, e.g., DGCL §212(b); NYBCL §609.

There is no single form that is mandated for a valid proxy. Generally, proxies must record the designation of the proxy holder by the shareholder and authenticate the grant of the proxy. In traditional terms, this was, and most often still is, a signed "proxy card." Modern statutes do recognize that electronic communications may also be used to designate a proxy, so long as sufficient evidence of authenticity is supplied. See DGCL §212(c)(2). A proxy holder is bound to exercise the proxy as directed. This requires a list of the specific nominees and specific issues on which the proxy holder proposes to vote. In most cases, however, proxy holders may exercise independent judgment on issues arising at the shareholder meeting for which they have not received specific instruction. Proxies, like all agency relationships, are revocable unless the holder has contracted for the proxy as a means to protect a legal interest or property, such as an interest in the shares themselves. See DGCL §212(e); *Haft v. Haft*, 671 A.2d 413 (Del. Ch. 1995) (proxy held by CEO was irrevocable because of proxy holder's interest as officer of the corporation).

While state law governs the basic duties of proxy holders as agents, federal law governs the solicitation and exercise of proxies under §14 of the Securities and Exchange Act of 1934, which we discuss later in this chapter.

While proxy voting allows public shareholders to "meet," it does not remedy their collective action problem. In particular, proxy voting relies on one or more persons to incur the initial expenses of soliciting proxies. Since these costs are substantial, shareholders face a serious impediment to collective action.

On one hand, the costs of soliciting proxies are a matter of normal governance because subsidizing these costs from the corporate treasury is essential for the operation of annual shareholder meetings. In the normal governance setting, management must be allowed to expend corporate funds to call annual meetings and solicit proxies. *Hall v. Trans-Lux Daylight Picture Screen Corp.*, 171 A. 226 (Del. 1934) (otherwise shareholder rational passivity would make annual meetings impossible). On the other hand, authorizing the board to expend corporate funds on its own re-election seems to permit a kind of self-dealing. Specifically, in proxy fights for corporate control (see Chapter 13) it gives the board a financial advantage over others. This raises the question whether the law ought to encourage insurgent shareholders to solicit proxies by reimbursing their reasonable expenses as well. Under current law, such expenses are not reimbursed unless the insurgents are victorious in their proxy fight, in which case they can vote to reimburse themselves. What are the risks of such a reform and what benefits might we hope for?

In November 2005, the SEC proposed general reforms that would allow companies and insurgents to post proxy materials on a website rather than through paper mailings, a move that could dramatically reduce the costs of proxy solicitations. As of August 2006 the SEC has not yet put forward a specific proposal, suggesting that the problem of proxy costs will not be overcome through technological advances anytime soon.

PROBLEM: ONLY INCUMBENTS AND WINNERS GET FREE
PROXIES

A group of dissident shareholders controls 20 percent of the voting shares
of IncumbentAir, a poorly run airline catering to corporate executives.
Suppose that the dissidents believe they stand a 50 percent chance of
winning a proxy fight and that they will spend $2 million in mobilizing
shareholder support, as will the incumbent managers. Assume that management can use the corporate purse to pay the costly expenses of the
proxy battle.

If the dissidents have to pay their own legal and other proxy expenses
out of pocket, under what circumstances will they actually go through with
the proxy fight (assuming they are risk-neutral, rational profit-maximizers)?
What is the total gross gain in corporate value that the dissidents must
expect before they will initiate a proxy contest? What effect would there be
if the dissidents were reimbursed for their proxy expenses regardless of the
outcome?

ROSENFELD v. FAIRCHILD ENGINE & AIRPLANE CORP.

128 N.E.2d 291 (N.Y. 1955)

Froessel, J.:

In a stockholder's derivative action brought by plaintiff, an attorney,
who owns 25 out of the company's over 2,300,000 shares, he seeks to
compel the return of $261,522, paid out of the corporate treasury to
reimburse both sides in a proxy contest for their expenses. The Appellate
Division has unanimously affirmed a judgment of an Official Referee dismissing plaintiff's complaint on the merits, and we agree. Exhaustive opinions were written by both courts below, and it will serve no useful
purpose to review the facts again.

Of the amount in controversy $106,000 were spent out of corporate
funds by the old board of directors while still in office in defense of their
position in said contest; $28,000 were paid to the old board by the new
board after the change of management following the proxy contest, to
compensate the former directors for such of the remaining expenses of
their unsuccessful defense as the new board found was fair and reasonable;
payment of $127,000, representing reimbursement of expenses to mem-
bers of the prevailing group, was expressly ratified by a 16 to 1 majority vote
of the stockholders.

The essential facts are not in dispute. . . .

By way of contrast with the findings here, in *Lawyers' Adv. Co. v.
Consolidated Ry. Lighting & Refrig. Co.* (187 N.Y. 395), which was an action
to recover for the cost of publishing newspaper notices not authorized by
the board of directors, it was expressly found that the proxy contest there
involved was "by one faction in its contest with another for the control
of the corporation . . . a contest for the perpetuation of their offices and
control" (p. 399). We there said by way of dicta that under such

circumstances the publication of certain notices on behalf of the management faction was not a corporate expenditure which the directors had the power to authorize.

Other jurisdictions and our own lower courts have held that management may look to the corporate treasury for the reasonable expenses of soliciting proxies to defend its position in a bona fide policy contest. . . .

If directors of a corporation may not in good faith incur reasonable and proper expenses in soliciting proxies in these days of giant corporations with vast numbers of stockholders, the corporate business might be seriously interfered with because of stockholder indifference and the difficulty of procuring a quorum, where there is no contest. In the event of a proxy contest, if the directors may not freely answer the challenges of outside groups and in good faith defend their actions with respect to corporate policy for the information of the stockholders, they and the corporation may be at the mercy of persons seeking to wrest control for their own purposes, so long as such persons have ample funds to conduct a proxy contest. The test is clear. When the directors act in good faith in a contest over policy, they have the right to incur reasonable and proper expenses for solicitation of proxies and in defense of their corporate policies, and are not obliged to sit idly by. The courts are entirely competent to pass upon their bona fides in any given case, as well as the nature of their expenditures when duly challenged.

It is also our view that the members of the so-called new group could be reimbursed by the corporation for their expenditures in this contest by affirmative vote of the stockholders. With regard to these ultimately successful contestants, as the Appellate Division below has noted, there was, of course, "no duty . . . to set forth the facts, with corresponding obligation of the corporation to pay for such expense." However, where a majority of the stockholders chose — in this case by a vote of 16 to 1 — to reimburse the successful contestants for achieving the very end sought and voted for by them as owners of the corporation, we see no reason to deny the effect of their ratification nor to hold the corporate body powerless to determine how its own moneys shall be spent.

The rule then which we adopt is simply this: In a contest over policy, as compared to a purely personal power contest, corporate directors have the right to make reasonable and proper expenditures, subject to the scrutiny of the courts when duly challenged, from the corporate treasury for the purpose of persuading the stockholders of the correctness of their position and soliciting their support for policies which the directors believe, in all good faith, are in the best interests of the corporation. The stockholders, moreover, have the right to reimburse successful contestants for the reasonable and bona fide expenses incurred by them in any such policy contest, subject to like court scrutiny. That is not to say, however, that corporate directors can, under any circumstances, disport themselves in a proxy contest with the corporation's moneys to an unlimited extent. Where it is established that such moneys have been spent for personal power, individual gain or private advantage, and not in the belief that such expenditures are in the best interests of the stockholders and the corporation, or where the fairness and reasonableness of the amounts allegedly expended are duly and successfully challenged, the courts will not hesitate to disallow them.

The judgment of the Appellate Division should be affirmed, without costs. . . .

———————————

Despite a vigorous dissent, Judge Froessel's opinion for the court has carried the day. The doctrine is that, win or lose, incumbent managers are reimbursed for expenses that are reasonable in amount and can be attributed to deciding issues of principle or policy. As a practical matter, any disagreement (including "I am a better manager than you are") tends to satisfy the difference in policy requirement for reimbursement. Insurgents, on the other hand, stand a good chance of being reimbursed only if they win. See, e.g., *Steinberg v. Adams,* 90 F. Supp. 604 (S.D.N.Y. 1950). The rationale is that, when dissidents triumph, shareholders have decided that their expenses were made in a good-faith effort to advance a corporate interest. Without shareholder ratification, however, reimbursements to successful dissidents might be attacked as self-dealing. See *Heineman v. Datapoint Corp.,* 611 A.2d 950 (Del. 1992).

But does the Froessel rule fix the right incentives for proxy contests? If not, should the courts perhaps instead adopt a "super-Froessel" rule: Reimburse both sides for expenses, regardless of whether they win or lose? Or perhaps a pro rata rule in which each side is reimbursed in proportion to the votes they receive? Or finally, a rule in which neither side is reimbursed? What are the incentive effects of these alternatives? What kind of world is best regulated by a Froessel rule? For an analysis of incentives to mount proxy contests, see Lucian A. Bebchuk and Marcel Kahan, *A Framework for Analyzing Legal Policy Toward Proxy Contests,* 78 Cal. L. Rev. 1073 (1990).

7.5 CLASS VOTING

Voting regimes always present the risk that majority blocks will advance their private interests. In the political sphere, the problem of majority coalitions is mitigated by the fact that voters typically have a range of cross-cutting identifications — geographic, economic, ethnic or racial, professional, religious, etc. — and a variety of shifting and sometimes inconsistent interests. In the corporate sphere, however, narrow economic interests prevail. Thus, to the extent the interests of classes of shareholders diverge, as they may, for example, between preferred and common stock, the minority needs structural protection against exploitation by the majority. This protection is offered by the class voting requirement. A transaction that is subject to class voting simply means that a majority (or such higher proportion as may be fixed) of the votes in every class that is entitled to a separate class vote must approve the transaction for its authorization. Class votes sometimes occur in the normal governance context: when the charter creates rights of special classes to elect designated seats on the board. For example, the charter may provide that the Class A common stock will elect five directors and the Class B common stock will elect two. Of course, regardless of such differences, all corporate directors owe fiduciary loyalty to the corporation and to all of its shareholders equally, even when they are elected by a separate class of stock.

The more interesting class voting problems arise not in normal governance but in voting on fundamental transactions such as mergers and charter amendments. Here it may be necessary to protect the interests of separate classes of shares to ensure that the transaction is fair not only to shareholders in the aggregate but also to those subgroups. The Revised Model Business Corporation Act provides a fairly clear statutory scheme for doing so. See RMBCA §§10.04, 11.04(f). But notice that conferring class votes also gives each class a veto right; such rights can themselves be used opportunistically.

One can generalize to a limited extent about the class voting provisions of various state corporation laws. The general idea is easily stated: If a proposed charter amendment adversely affects the legal rights of a class of stock or disadvantages them in some other respect, then it should be adopted only with the concurrence of a majority of the voting power of that class voting separately. The RMBCA is probably the most coherently structured set of provisions governing class voting. Notice that RMBCA §10.04 avoids concepts such as whether proposed change to the charter "adversely affects" the rights of the stock. The RMBCA requires a vote whenever an amendment will "change" certain things, thus avoiding argument over whether a change is adverse or beneficial. (Compare DGCL §242 (b)(2), above). Moreover, the Model Act, along with most other corporation statutes, protects the economic interests of shareholders and not just their legal rights. Thus, for example, holders of the existing preferred stock have the right to vote on a charter amendment that creates a new class of preferred stock senior to the existing preferred in terms of either dividend preference or liquidation rights. See RMBCA §10.04(5) and §10.04(6); NYBCL §804(a)(3). The Delaware statute is more limited. It seems to require a separate vote only if an amendment would alter the legal rights of the existing security. This leaves open the possibility under Delaware law of inserting a senior security into the firm's capital structure without affording existing preferred stock a class vote. Because the Delaware statute on class votes is narrow (for example, mergers do not require class votes under the statute), lawyers must build in class vote protections when they design a preferred stock. The document that defines the rights of the preferred stock (the Certificate of Special Rights, Limitations and Preferences), therefore, generally defines these rights under Delaware law.

PROBLEM: WHEN THE PREFERRED STOCK PREFERS NOT

Avonex Corp. has two classes of stock: 5 million shares of no par common stock and 500,000 shares of 6 percent cumulative preferred with a par value of $10 million. Business has not been good recently. Last year the firm had a net after-tax income of only $745,000. No dividend was paid on the common stock, but the preferred dividend was paid. Avonex has an interesting, if somewhat risky, new project. The company's lines of credit with banks are exhausted, and the banks will not lend more unless the firm raises additional equity. Management proposes that Avonex amend its charter to permit it to issue a new class of a stock: an 11 percent senior cumulative preferred stock. In particular, it proposes that Avonex privately place $5 million worth of this new security. The money raised by the new issue will permit the company to invest in the new project, which, if it succeeds, will begin to throw off cash in about two years. Projections indicate that, in five years, the new project will generate more than $1 million per year of net cash flow.

Of course, the charter must be amended before the new issue can proceed. You are the lawyer to whom holders of the preferred stock come for advice. They do not like the proposal — why not, do you suppose?

Assume Avonex is a New York corporation. Can the preferred stock vote to prevent the transaction? See NYBCL §804.

What if, instead, Avonex proposed to issue 1 million additional shares of the 6 percent cumulative preferred at a large discount and all that management's proposal required was a vote to increase the number of shares authorized in the existing charter? Would the preferred stock have a class vote?

Now assume Avonex is a Delaware corporation. Would it yield the same result?

7.6 SHAREHOLDER INFORMATION RIGHTS

Shareholders must be informed in order to vote intelligently. State corporate law in the United States leaves the function of informing shareholders largely to the market. State law mandates neither an annual report nor any other financial statement. By contrast, federal securities law and the rules promulgated by the Securities and Exchange Commission mandate extensive disclosure for publicly traded securities. We discuss those requirements in later chapters. Now we focus on the limited state corporation law rights to information.

At common law, shareholders were recognized to have a right to inspect the company's books and records for a proper purpose. This right is codified in modern statutes. See, e.g., DGCL §220; RMBCA §§16.02-.03; NYBCL §624. Each statutory scheme differs, but the elements are similar. The Delaware statute provides, in part, as follows:

(b) Any stockholder. . . shall upon written demand under oath stating the purpose thereof, have the right during the usual hours of business to inspect for any proper purpose, the corporation's stock ledger, a list of its stockholders and its other books and records, and to make copies and extracts there from. A proper purpose shall mean a purpose reasonably related to such person's interests as a stockholder.[13]

In administering this statutory right of access to information for a proper purpose, the Delaware courts recognize two fundamentally different types of requests: a request for a "stock list" and a request for inspection of "books and records" of the corporation. These two applications for judicial assistance have different consequences for the corporation and are treated differently by the courts, even though both hinge on demonstrating a "proper purpose."

The Stock List.   A corporate stock list discloses the identity, ownership interest, and address of each registered owner of company stock. Since the stock list does not contain proprietary information and is easy to produce, the law makes this list readily available to registered owners of the corporation's stock. "Proper purpose" for acquiring the stock list is broadly construed, and once it is shown, the court will not consider whether the shareholder has additional, "improper" purposes.[14] As a practical matter, Delaware courts permit only very limited discovery in litigation in which the stock list is sought. These cases are brought quickly to trial (in a matter of weeks) and ordinarily settle prior to trial, since, if the plaintiff is in fact a shareholder, she will ordinarily prevail.

In today's practice, a stock list is unlikely to be a mere piece of paper listing the names and addresses of the corporation's shareholders. First, it will be digitally stored and delivered. Second, a corporation that is required to produce a stock list will also be required to produce related, identifying information. Thus, an order to produce the stock list will carry with it an obligation to update this list, to produce a second list of stock brokerage firms whose stock is registered in the name of the Depository Trust Co., and to furnish daily trading information. Of importance is the fact that the order will often require the company to also furnish a "non-objecting beneficial owners" (NOBO) list, if the company has such a list.[15] The NOBO list is important to those who want to communicate directly with the real owners (and voters) of the stock.

---

13. DGCL §220.

14. See *Bureau Reports, Inc. v. Credit Bureau of St. Paul, Inc.*, 290 A.2d 691 (Del. 1972) (requiring a corporation to disclose the stockholder list even thought it was sought to solicit proxies to force management to deal more favorably with suppliers, one of whom was the plaintiff stockholder); and *Food and Allied Service Trades Dept., AFL-CIO v. Wal-Mart Stores, Inc.*, 1992 Del. Ch. LEXIS 108 (stock list requested to inform shareholders that imported goods were made with prison labor was a proper purpose). But see *State ex Rel. Pillsbury v. Honeywell, Inc.*, 191 N.W.2d 406 (Minn. 1971) (purpose to communicate to shareholders concerning company's production of war material was not proper under Delaware law).

15. *Shamrock Associates v. Texas American Energy Corp.*, 517 A.2d 658 (Del. Ch. 1986).

Inspection of Books and Records. After requests for the shareholder list, the second kind of informational petition a court entertains is a request to examine a company's books and records. Here a plaintiff may allege the need for very broad access to the company's records in order to uncover suspected wrongdoing. Such a request, however, places the legitimate interests of the corporation at risk. Meeting such a request is far more expensive than furnishing a stock list. In addition, an inspection of books and records may jeopardize proprietary or competitively sensitive information. It follows that these requests are reviewed with care. Under Delaware law, this is reflected formally by requiring plaintiffs to carry the burden of showing a proper purpose and, informally, by carefully screening plaintiff's motives and the likely consequences of granting her request. Consider, for example, the different considerations bearing upon the granting or denial of relief in *Thomas & Betts Corp. v. Leviton Manufacturing Co., Inc.,* 685 A.2d 702 (Del. Ch. 1995) (scope of inspection right carefully delineated by court in a books and records case).

New York balances the value of shareholder access to corporate information against the corporate interest in confidentiality in a different way. New York law accords shareholders a statutory right to inspect the key financial statements, the balance sheet, and the income statement. Stock lists and meeting minutes are also available for inspection unless the company can show that the shareholder lacks a proper purpose. Beyond this, the New York statute simply provides that courts retain the common law power to compel inspection in a proper case.

GENERAL TIME CORP. v. TALLEY INDUSTRIES, INC.

240 A.2d 755 (Del. 1968)

WOLCOTT, C.J.:

The suit below was instituted under §220 by Talley Industries, Inc., a stockholder of General Time Corporation, to obtain a list of General Time's stockholders. . . . Talley Industries complied with the provisions of §220 respecting the form and manner of making demand for inspection of the list. When such is the fact, §220(c) prescribes that the burden of proof shall be upon the corporation to establish that the stockholder desires the list for an improper purpose.

General Time noticed the deposition of the President of Talley Industries. At the deposition he was asked a series of questions directed to the acquisition of General Time stock allegedly in furtherance of an illegal conspiracy and in violation of the Investment Company Act of 1940 and the Securities and Exchange Act of 1934. Upon the instructions of his counsel, Talley Industries' President refused to answer these questions on the ground that they were not directed to the primary purpose for which the list was desired, which was the soliciting of proxies to be used to oust the management of General Time.

The questions which were refused to be answered at the deposition related to (1) what other persons or entities, known to the officers of Talley Industries, owned stock in General Time; (2) whether the funds with which

Talley Industries purchased General Time stock were borrowed; and (3) whether Talley Industries desires to effect a merger with General Time and, if so, when the idea was first conceived. All of these questions presumably related to the charge of conspiracy and violation of the Investment Company Act and the Securities and Exchange Act.

There can be no question but that the desire to solicit proxies for a slate of directors in opposition to management is a purpose reasonably related to the stockholder's interest as a stockholder. It has been held in this State that such a purpose is directly related to stockholder status and, as such, proper. . . . [A]ny further or secondary purpose in seeking the list is irrelevant. Once the status of a stockholder is established under §220, he is entitled to the list if his primary purpose is reasonably related to that status. . . .

In short, we are of the opinion that when a stockholder establishes his status as such, and seeks production of a stockholders' list for a purpose germane to that status, such as a proxy solicitation, he is entitled to its production. It might well be asked what circumstances then would constitute a defense to the demand. Each case must depend upon its particular facts, but we point out that in the *Theile* case an individual owning one share of stock was denied a list when it appeared that his purpose was to sell it for a "sucker list."

7.7   TECHNIQUES FOR SEPARATING CONTROL FROM CASH FLOW RIGHTS

It is ordinarily good policy to award voting rights to the investors who claim the corporation's residual returns. In this way, managers are selected by the corporate constituency with the strongest interest in maximizing corporate value. This constituency generally is the class of common stockholders. Nevertheless, the law's policy of aligning control with residual returns is sometimes frustrated. For example, capital structures with dual-class voting, which misalign control rights and return rights, are not prohibited by law, although they are discouraged by stock exchange listing requirements. The law does proscribe some devices that misalign incentives — most notably a statutory prohibition against a corporation voting shares owned by the corporation directly or indirectly. But other structures are possible by which a corporation's capital may be used to affect ownership and voting of its own shares.

7.7.1   Circular Control Structures

Imagine, for a moment, a moderately bad person (MBP) who gains control of a corporation as its CEO. MBP is incapable of murder, rape, or mayhem, but he is lazy, greedy, and conspiratorial. If the corporation is large, MBP can live very well, so long as he has control of the corporate treasury. Naturally, MBP wants to keep this control. (At least he is not aimless!) One way to do so would be to use the corporate treasury to buy the corporation's stock and control its voting rights. This plan is too direct, however. The law prohibits management from voting stock owned by the corporation. As a result, MBP must come up with something a bit more complicated — a subsidiary or a joint venture — in which his company owns only a minority interest.

PROBLEM: ROUND AND ROUND THE VOTES GO

MBP is CEO of ExploitCorp, a Delaware corporation that manufactures law textbooks. ExploitCorp's shares are owned by the general public (45 percent), Follow Inc. (45 percent), and MBP himself (10 percent). Recently, a group of dissatisfied shareholders met to discuss MBP's wasteful management style, including the yearly renovations of MBP's office, the use of corporate jets to fly MBP's children to law school, and the purchase of luxury cars for senior executives. A representative of the dissatisfied shareholders, who collectively hold 35 percent of ExploitCorp's shares, met with MBP and threatened to launch a proxy fight for control of the company, should MBP continue his lavish spending. Angered by the challenge to his authority, MBP responded, "Don't even think about a proxy fight. To succeed, you'll need Follow Inc.'s votes, and you'll never get them." Soon after, the shareholder representative discovered that ExploitCorp owns 30 percent of Follow Inc. and MBP is a Follow Inc. director.

Could MBP rely on Follow Inc.'s 45 percent stake in ExploitCorp, together with his own 10 percent, in a proxy fight? Would your answer change if ExploitCorp controlled 51 percent of Follow Inc.? See DGCL 160(c).

SPEISER v. BAKER

525 A.2d 1001 (Del. Ch. 1987)

Allen, C.:

The present action is brought under Section 211(c) of our corporation law and seeks an order requiring the convening of an annual meeting of shareholders of Health Med Corporation, a Delaware corporation. The Answer admits that no annual meeting of stockholders of that corporation has been held for several years, but attempts to allege affirmative defenses to the relief sought. In addition, that pleading asserts an affirmative right to a declaratory judgment unrelated, in my opinion, to the annual meeting.

Pending is a motion by plaintiff seeking (1) judgment on the pleadings and (2) dismissal of defendant's affirmative claim for relief. That motion raises two distinct legal issues. The first relates to plaintiff's Section 211 claim: it is whether defendant, having admitted facts that constitute a *prima facie* case for such relief, has pleaded facts which, if true, would constitute an equitable defense to the claim.

The second issue is raised by plaintiff's motion to dismiss claims asserted by defendant as cross-claims and counterclaims. It is whether the circular ownership of stock among the companies involved in this litigation violates Section 160(c) of our general corporation law. Stated generally, Section 160(c) prohibits the voting of stock that belongs to the issuer and prohibits the voting of the issuer's stock when owned by another corporation if the issuer holds, directly or indirectly, a majority of the shares entitled to vote at an election of the directors of that second corporation.

Plaintiff is Marvin Speiser, the owner of 50% of Health Med's common stock. Mr. Speiser is also president of Health Med and one of its two directors. Named as defendants are the company itself and Leon Baker, who owns the remaining 50% of Health Med's common stock and is Health Med's other director. Because of the particular quorum requirements set forth in Health Med's certificate, Baker, as the owner of the other 50% of Health Med's common stock, is able to frustrate the convening of an annual meeting by simply not attending. Thus, the need for the Section 211 action.

Despite the admission of facts constituting a *prima facie* case under Section 211, Baker asserts that a meeting should not be ordered. He contends, in a pleading denominated as "Second Affirmative Defense and Cross-Counterclaim" (hereafter simply the counterclaim), that the meeting sought is intended to be used as a key step in a plan by Mr. Speiser to cement control of Health Med in derogation of his fiduciary duty to Health Med's other shareholders. For his part, to thwart an allegedly wrongful scheme Baker seeks a declaratory judgment that shares of another Delaware corporation — Health Chem (hereafter "Chem") — held by Health Med may not be voted by Health Med. The prohibition of Section 160(c) is asserted as the legal authority for this affirmative relief.

I conclude that Mr. Speiser is now entitled to judgment on his claim seeking to compel the holding of an annual meeting by Health Med, but that plaintiff's motion to dismiss the counterclaim must be denied. The legal reasoning leading to these conclusions is set forth below, after a brief recitation of the admitted facts.

I

The facts of the corporate relationships involved here are complex even when simplified to their essentials.

There is involved in this case a single operating business — Chem, a publicly traded company (American Stock Exchange). On its stock ledger, Chem's stockholders fall into four classes: the public (40%), Mr. Speiser (10%), Mr. Baker (8%) and Health Med (42%). In fact, however, Health Med is itself wholly owned indirectly by Chem and Messrs. Speiser and Baker. Thus, the parties interested in this matter (as owners of Chem's equity) are Speiser, Baker and Chem's public shareholders.

How the circular ownership here involved came about is not critical for present purposes. What is relevant is that Chem (through a wholly owned subsidiary called Medallion Corp.) owns 95% of the equity of Health Med.[1] However, Chem's 95% equity ownership in Health Med is not represented by ownership of 95% of the current voting power of Health Med. This is because what Chem owns is an issue of Health Med

---

1. Health Med's stock interest in Chem is treated as treasury stock on Chem's books.

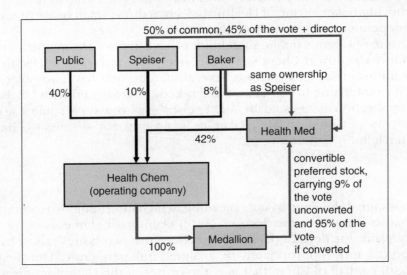

convertible preferred stock which, while bearing an unqualified right to be converted immediately into common stock of Health Med representing 95% of Health Med's voting power, in its present unconverted state, carries the right to only approximately 9% of Health Med's vote. In its unconverted state the preferred commands in toto the same dividend rights (i.e., 95% of all dividends declared and paid) as it would if converted to common stock.

Speiser and Baker own the balance of Health Med's voting power. Each presently votes 50% of Health Med's only other issue of stock, its common stock. This circular structure was carefully constructed as a means to permit Messrs. Speiser and Baker to control Chem while together owning less than 35% of its equity. It has functioned in that way successfully for some years. Speiser has served as president of all three corporations. When Speiser and Baker's mutual plan required shareholder votes, Speiser apparently directed the vote of Health Med's holdings of Chem stock (its only substantial asset) in a way that together with the vote of Speiser and Baker's personal Chem holdings, assured that their view would prevail.

The conversion of Chem's (Medallion's) preferred stock in Health Med would result in the destruction of the Baker-Speiser control mechanism. Under Section 160(c) of the Delaware corporation law (quoted and discussed below), in that circumstance, Health Med would certainly be unable to vote its 42% stock interest in Chem. As a result, the other shareholders of Chem (i.e., the owners of the real equity interest in Chem) would have their voting power increased to the percentages shown on the above chart, that is, the voting power of the public stockholders of Chem would increase from 40% to 65.6%.

For reasons that are not important for the moment, Speiser and Baker have now fallen out. Control of Health Med and the vote of its Chem stock thus has now become critical to them. Mr. Speiser, by virtue of his office as President of Medallion and of Health Med, is apparently currently in a position to control Health Med and its vote. Baker asserts, not implausibly,

that Speiser now seeks a Health Med stockholders meeting for the purpose
of removing Baker as one of Health Med's two directors in order to remove
his independent judgment from the scene.

   None of Chem's public shareholders have heretofore complained that
the failure to convert Chem's (Medallion's) preferred stock in Health Med
to common constituted a wrong. Several shareholders have, however, now
moved to intervene in this action and asked to be aligned with Mr. Baker.
This application is resisted by Mr. Speiser—who asserts some estoppel
arguments personal to Mr. Baker as a ground for dismissing Baker's
counterclaim.

II

   Despite defendant Baker's pleading, which intermingles aspects of his
affirmative defense to the Section 211(c) claim with elements of his affirmative claim for declaratory relief, I believe the two issues raised by this
motion can most appropriately be analyzed independently. The allegedly
wrongful control of Chem that is at the center of the claim for affirmative
relief is not a matter that will be voted upon at (nor be significantly affected
by) a Health Med stockholder meeting. The Section 160 claim is not that
Chem (Medallion) ought not to be permitted to vote its stock at a Health
Med meeting, but that Health Med is precluded from exercising rights as a
Chem shareholder. Thus, while the two claims are factually related, they
are, in my opinion, essentially independent claims legally. I therefore
analyze them separately and turn first to Speiser's motion for judgment
on the pleadings with respect to his Section 211(c) claim.

   Section 211(b) of our corporation law contains a mandatory requirement that every Delaware corporation "shall" hold an "annual meeting of
stockholders . . . for the election of directors." . . .

   . . . The facts alleged to flesh out this conclusory statement do state a
claim, as I hold below, for relief, but what seems clear is that they allege no
wrong to Health Med or its shareholders that will occur by reason of the
holding of Health Med's annual meeting statutorily required by subsection
(b) of Section 211. All that is really alleged with respect to Health Med is
that Baker will likely be voted out of office as a Health Med director and the
company will fall under the complete domination of Speiser. The answer to
that, of course, is if the votes entitled to be cast at the meeting are cast so as
to obtain that result, so be it.

III

   I turn now to Speiser's motion to dismiss the counterclaim seeking a
declaratory judgment that Health Med may not vote its 42% stock interest in
Chem. The prohibition contained in Section 160 of our corporation law is
asserted as the principal basis for such relief.

   The pertinent language of the statute is as follows:

Shares of its own capital stock belonging to the corporation or to another corporation, if a majority of the shares entitled to vote in the election of directors of such other corporation is held directly or indirectly, by the corporation, shall neither be entitled to vote nor counted for quorum purposes.

The statutory language of Section 160(c) which Baker relies upon, when read literally does not, in my opinion, proscribe the voting of Health Med's stock in Chem. That is, I cannot conclude that Chem (or its Medallion subsidiary) presently "holds," even indirectly, a majority of the stock "entitled to vote" in Health Med's election of directors. The stock entitled to vote in such an election, and the extent of its voting power, is technically defined in Health Med's certificate of incorporation. In its unconverted state, Medallion's holding of preferred simply does not represent a majority of the voting power of Health Med.

However, acceptance of Speiser's argument does not end the matter. The clause the parties argue over, even when read as Speiser reads it, does not purport to confer a right to vote stock not falling within its literal terms; it is simply a restriction. More importantly, other statutory words may be read to extend Section 160(c) prohibition to the voting of Health Med's Chem holdings. Specifically, the principal prohibition of the statute is directed to shares of its own capital stock "belonging to the corporation." This phrase is not a technically precise term whose literal meaning is clear; it requires interpretation. I turn then to the analysis of these statutory words that leads me to conclude that they do reach the facts pleaded in the counterclaim. . . .

[We] then begin our inquiry into what the legislature meant and intended by the words "belonging to," as used in Section 160(c). . . .

Almost from the earliest stirrings of a distinctive body of law dealing with corporations, courts have been alert to the dangers posed by structures that permit directors of a corporation, by reason of their office, to control votes appurtenant to shares of the company's stock owned by the corporation itself or a nominee or agent of the corporation.

The rule that finds its first expression in these cases can be said to be of common law origin in the sense that it arose as a judicial gloss on the statutory right to vote shares. The reason for the rule is not mysterious. Such structures deprive the true owners of the corporate enterprise of a portion of their voice in choosing who shall serve as directors in charge of the management of the corporate venture. . . .

. . . The first general incorporation law of this State of which I am aware, the Act of 1883, contained such a prohibition. See 17 Del. Laws 212, 225 (1883). The predecessor of our present general corporation law statute, first adopted in 1899, contained an expression of the rule typical for that period:

Section 24. Shares of stock of the corporation belonging to the corporation shall not be voted upon directly or indirectly.

21 Del. Laws 453 (1899).

[However, the mischief that this rule dealt with reemerged in corporate subsidiary structures. The first case in which the courts addressed subsidiary share ownership—] *Italo Petroleum Corp. v. Producers Oil Corporation,* Del. Ch., 174 A. 276—construed a version of the statutory prohibition not materially different from the section of the 1899 Act quoted above. Chancellor Wolcott there rejected the argument that stock belonging to a 99% owned subsidiary was not stock "belonging to the [parent] corporation" because it was owned legally by the subsidiary. Thus, he construed the statutory prohibition against voting (directly or indirectly) stock belonging to the corporation as a prohibition against voting stock belonging (directly or indirectly) to the corporation. In so holding, this court was motivated by the same concerns that underlay the pre-statute cases and the statutory codification itself:

> It seems to me to be carrying the doctrine of distinct corporate entity to an unreasonable extreme to say that, in a contest over control of a corporation those in charge of it should be allowed to have votes counted in their favor which are cast by a subsidiary stockholder wholly owned, controlled, dominated and therefore dictated to by themselves as the spokesmen of the parent. . . .

The statutory language construed in *Italo* remained substantially unchanged until 1967 when a version similar to the current version of Section 160(c) was enacted.[6] . . . One knowledgeable commentator has referred to the 1967 amendment as codifying the result of *Italo Petroleum.* . . . Actually, it did that and something more; it specified instances in which stock owned by a subsidiary would be conclusively presumed to be stock "belonging to" its parent. The critical question is, however, did the 1967 amendment intend to do the obverse? Did it intend to create a conclusive statutory presumption that, in no event would stock owned by another corporation that did not satisfy the new test (a majority of shares entitled to vote, etc.) be deemed to be stock "belonging to the corporation?"

There is no hint in the legislative words that such a result was intended and I think that (given the surprising fact that the underlying problem can — as this case attests — arise in situations in which the parent does not hold a majority of the stock entitled to vote at the election of the subsidiary's directors) the policy of the statute would require a clear expression of such an intention before it could be found. Moreover, there seems slight reason relating to the purpose of the statute for the legislature to have intended to create a safe harbor for entrenchment schemes implemented through the use of corporate subsidiaries while leaving all other agencies through which such plans could be executed governed by the general language "belonging to."

Accordingly, attempting to read these words in a sensible way consistent with the underlying purpose of the enactment, I conclude that stock held by a corporate "subsidiary" may, in some circumstances, "belong to" the issuer and thus be prohibited from voting, even if the issuer does not hold a majority of shares entitled to vote at the election of directors of the subsidiary.

---

6. The 1967 version did not include the "directly or indirectly" language, which was restored in 1970. See 57 Del. Laws, Ch. 649 (1970).

Assuming the truth of the facts alleged in the counterclaim, I am of the view that this is such a case. Here the substantial ownership of Chem in Health Med is not simply large, it is — at 95% — practically complete. . . .

The facts alleged exemplify the very problem Section 160(c) was intended to resolve. That is, here the capital of one corporation (Chem) has been invested in another corporation (Health Med) and that investment, in turn, is used solely to control votes of the first corporation. The principal (indeed the sole) effect of this arrangement is to muffle the voice of the public shareholders of Chem in the governance of Chem as contemplated by the certificate of incorporation of that corporation and our corporation law. In purpose and effect the scheme here put in place is not materially different from the schemes repeatedly struck down for more than one hundred fifty years by American courts. See, e.g., *Italo Petroleum Corp. v. Producers Oil Corporation*, Del. Ch., 174 A. 276 (1934) and cases cited supra.

For the foregoing reason, the motion to dismiss the counterclaim will be denied.

7.7.2 Vote Buying

It is often said that a shareholder may not sell her vote, by which it is meant that she may or may not sell her vote other than as part of a transfer of the underlying share.[16] The obverse is true as well. A court of equity will be inclined to require a transferor, who sells stock after a record date, to give his transferee a proxy to vote the stock — unless the transferor specifically retains the voting right to protect a legal interest in the stock or the corporation is strong enough to support the grant of an irrevocable proxy.[17] But why limit the separation of control rights (the vote) over cash flow rights (the dividends)? Isn't a stock investment just an economic decision with a single, profit-maximizing purpose? If so, why shouldn't investors be permitted to split up share rights in any way that they deem profitable? What supports this apparent preference for keeping votes and cash flow rights together?

Consider the following account of the common law prohibition of vote buying.

FRANK EASTERBROOK & DANIEL FISCHEL, VOTING IN CORPORATE LAW

26 J.L. & Econ. 395, 409-411 (1983)

It is not [legally] possible to separate the voting right from the equity interest. [*Warning:* This is a simplification that is not wholly true in all cases. — EDS.] Someone who wants to buy a vote must buy the stock too. The restriction on irrevocable proxies, which are possible only when

16. E.g., *Hall v. Isaacs*, 146 A.2d 602 (Del. Ch. 1958).
17. E.g., *Commonwealth Assocs. v. Providence Health Care*, 641 A.2d 155 (Del. Ch. 1993); *In re Giant Portland Cement Co.*, 21 A.2d 697 (Del. Ch. 1941).

coupled with a pledge of the stock, also ensures that votes go with the equity interest. [*Warning:* This is not true either; interests other than pledges may support an irrevocable proxy, but let us stop quibbling with our authors. — EDS.]

These rules are, at first glance, curious limits on the ability of investors to make their own arrangements. Yet they are understandable on much the same basis as the equal-weighting rule. Attaching the vote firmly to the residual equity interest ensures that an unnecessary agency cost will not come into being. Separation of shares from votes introduces a disproportion between expenditure and reward.

For example, if the owner of 20 percent of the residual claims acquires all of the votes, his incentive to take steps to improve the firm (or just to make discretionary decisions) is only one-fifth of the value of those decisions. The holder of the votes will invest too little. And he will also have an incentive to consume excessive leisure and perquisites and to engage in other non-profit-maximizing behavior because much of the cost would be borne by the other residual claimants. The risk of such shirking would reduce the value of investments in general, and the risk can be eliminated by tying votes to shares.

One possible response is that the agency costs created would be eliminated if the owner of 20 percent of the residual claims could obtain returns disproportionate to his equity interest. So long as there is a market in votes that parallels the market in shares, competition among vote-buyers could be sufficient to compensate equity investors for the value of the dilution of their interests.

This is intriguing but, we think, unsatisfactory. Transactions in votes would present difficult problems of valuation and create other costs without conferring any apparent benefit over transactions in votes tied to shares. Moreover, the collective choice problem would exert a strong influence over the market price of votes. Because no voter expects to influence the outcome of the election, he would sell the vote (which to him is unimportant) for less than the expected dilution of his equity interest. He would reason that if he did not sell, others would; he would then lose on the equity side but get nothing for the vote. Thus any nonzero price would persuade him to sell.

Competition among those bidding for votes might drive the price up, but not ordinarily all the way to the value of the expected equity dilution. Each person bidding for votes would be concerned that he would end up with less than a majority, and unless he obtained a majority he would have nothing at all. Thus he would offer less than the prospective value of the equity dilution. One cannot exclude the possibility that competition among buyers of votes would fully compensate the sellers. In that event, however, the bidders would see no difference between buying votes and buying shares, which, after the votes had been cast, could be held or resold to their former owners. The only time buying the votes without the shares is advantageous is when the buyer is planning to dilute the interests of the other equity owners. As we have argued elsewhere, investors would agree to prohibit such dilutions in order to ensure that all control changes are value increasing. Thus the legal rules tying votes to shares increase the efficiency of corporate organization.

SCHREIBER v. CARNEY

447 A.2d 17 (Del. Ch. 1982)

[Plaintiff, a shareholder in Texas International Airlines, Inc., challenged the propriety of the company's loan to defendant Jet Capital Corporation ("Jet"), which owned 35 percent of Texas International's

---

FRANK LORENZO

Born into a family of Spanish immigrants, Frank Lorenzo graduated from Columbia University and Harvard Business School. As CEO of Texas International Airlines during the 1970s, he honed his cost-cutting skills through innovations such as the "peanut flight," a low-fare, off-peak flight that offered peanuts instead of a full meal. Not content with the Texas market, in 1980 Lorenzo formed New York Air and launched a hostile takeover bid for Continental Airlines. Continental's employees attempted to purchase majority ownership in the company through an Employee Stock Purchase Plan, in a dramatic but unsuccessful effort to prevent the takeover. Once in control of Continental, Lorenzo realized the employees' worst fears by demanding severe wage cuts and benefit reductions. When the unions refused to comply, Lorenzo filed for Chapter 11 bankruptcy as a strategy to keep labor costs low. In 1986 Lorenzo acquired Eastern Airlines and similarly plunged it into bankruptcy, making him the only person in U.S. history to bankrupt two airlines. During the Eastern bankruptcy proceedings, Lorenzo was declared "unfit" to run the airline. He resigned his position as CEO and sold his ownership.

When Lorenzo again attempted to found an airline in 1993, his petition was refused by the U.S. Department of Transportation. The U.S. Centennial of Flight Commission, known for its celebration of individuals who contributed to air travel, referred to Lorenzo as "one of the most notorious players in the history of commercial aviation in the United States."[18]

---

common stock. Jet held an effective veto over a proposed merger between Texas International and Texas Air and had threatened to use it, because of adverse tax consequences for Jet, unless Jet were to exercise certain warrants it held in Texas International prior to the merger. Jet Capital claimed that it lacked the funds necessary to exercise these warrants and that borrowing funds from a third-party lender was too expensive.]

HARTNETT, V.C.:

In order to overcome this impasse, it was proposed that Texas International and Jet Capital explore the possibility of a loan by Texas

---

18. U.S. Centennial of Flight Commission, www.centennialofflight.gov/essay/Dictionary/lorenzo.htm

International to Jet Capital in order to fund an early exercise of the warrants. Because Texas International and Jet Capital had several common directors, the defendants recognized the conflict of interest and endeavored to find a way to remove any taint or appearance of impropriety. It was, therefore, decided that a special independent committee would be formed to consider and resolve the matter. The three Texas International directors who had no interest in or connection with Jet Capital were chosen to head up the committee. After its formation, the committee's first act was to hire independent counsel. Next, the committee examined the proposed merger and, based upon advice rendered by an independent investment banker, the merger was again found to be both a prudent and feasible business decision. The committee then confronted the "Jet Capital obstacle" by considering viable options for both Texas International and Jet Capital and, as a result, the committee determined that a loan was the best solution.

After negotiating at arm's length, both Texas International and Jet Capital agreed that Texas International would loan to Jet Capital $3,335,000 at 5% interest per annum for the period up to the scheduled 1982 expiration date for the warrants. After this period, the interest rate would equal the then prevailing prime interest rate. The 5% interest rate was recommended by an independent investment banker as the rate necessary to reimburse Texas International for any dividends paid out during this period. Given this provision for anticipated dividends and the fact that the advanced money would be immediately paid back to Texas International upon the exercise of the warrants, the loan transaction had virtually no impact on Texas International's cash position. . . .

The directors of Texas International unanimously approved the proposal as recommended by the committee and submitted it to the stockholders for approval — requiring as a condition of approval that a majority of all outstanding shares *and* a majority of the shares voted by the stockholders other than Jet Capital or its officers or directors be voted in favor of the proposal. After receiving a detailed proxy statement, the shareholders voted overwhelmingly in favor of the proposal. . . .

The complaint attacks the loan transaction on two theories. First, it is alleged that the loan transaction constituted vote-buying and was therefore void. Secondly, the complaint asserts that the loan was corporate waste. In essence, plaintiff argues that even if the loan was permissible and even if it was the best available option, it would have been wiser for Texas International to have loaned Jet Capital only $800,000 — the amount of the increased tax liability — because this would have minimized Texas International's capital commitment and also would have prevented Jet Capital from increasing its control in Texas International on allegedly discriminatory and wasteful terms. . . .

[Plaintiff contends] that vote-buying existed and, therefore, the entire transaction including the merger was void because Jet Capital, in consideration for being extended an extremely advantageous loan, withdrew its opposition to the proposed merger. . . . The critical inquiry, therefore, is whether the loan in question was in fact vote-buying and, if so, whether vote-buying is illegal, per se.

It is clear that the loan constituted vote-buying as that term has been defined by the courts. Vote-buying, despite its negative connotation, is simply a voting agreement supported by consideration personal to the stockholder, whereby the stockholder divorces his discretionary voting power and votes as directed by the offeror. The record clearly indicates that Texas International purchased or "removed" the obstacle of Jet Capital's opposition. Indeed, this is tacitly conceded by the defendants. However, defendants contend that the analysis of the transaction should not end here because the legality of vote-buying depends on whether its object or purpose is to defraud or in some manner disenfranchise the other stockholders. . . . Whether this is valid depends upon the status of the law.

The Delaware decisions dealing with vote-buying leave the question unanswered. . . . In each [decision], the Court [has] summarily voided the challenged votes as being purchased and thus contrary to public policy and in fraud of the other stockholders. However, the facts in each case indicated that fraud or disenfranchisement was the obvious purpose of the vote-buying. . . .

The present case presents a peculiar factual setting in that the proposed vote-buying consideration was conditional upon the approval of a majority of the disinterested stockholders after a full disclosure to them of all pertinent facts and was purportedly for the best interests of all Texas International stockholders. It is therefore necessary to do more than merely consider the fact that Jet Capital saw fit to vote for the transaction after a loan was made to it by Texas International. . . .

. . . There are essentially two principles which appear in these cases. The first is that vote-buying is illegal per se if its object or purpose is to defraud or disenfranchise the other stockholders. A fraudulent purpose is as defined at common law, as a deceit which operates prejudicially upon the property rights of another.

The second principle which appears in these old cases is that vote-buying is illegal per se as a matter of public policy, the reason being that each stockholder should be entitled to rely upon the independent judgment of his fellow stockholders. Thus, the underlying basis for this latter principle is again fraud but as viewed from a sense of duty owed by all stockholders to one another. The apparent rationale is that by requiring each stockholder to exercise his individual judgment as to all matters presented, "[t]he security of the small stockholders is found in the natural disposition of each stockholder to promote the best interests of all, in order to promote his individual interests." *Cone v. Russell,* 48 N.J. Eq. 208, 21 A. 847, 849 (1891). In essence, while self interest motivates a stockholder's vote, theoretically, it is also advancing the interests of the other stockholders. Thus, any agreement entered into for personal gain, whereby a stockholder separates his voting right from his property right was considered a fraud upon this community of interests.

The often cited case of *Brady v. Bean,* 221 Ill. App. 279 (1921), is particularly enlightening. In that case, the plaintiff—an apparently influential stockholder—voiced his opposition to the corporation's proposed sale of assets. The plaintiff feared that his investment would be wiped out because the consideration for the sale appeared only sufficient enough to satisfy the corporation's creditors. As a result and without the knowledge of the other stockholders, the defendant, also a stockholder as well as a director and substantial creditor of the company, offered to the plaintiff in exchange for the withdrawal of his opposition, a sharing in defendant's claims against the corporation. In an action to enforce this contract against the defendant's estate, the Court refused relief stating:

> Appellant being a stockholder in the company, any contract entered into by him whereby he was to receive a personal consideration in return for either his action or his inaction in a matter such as a sale of all the company's assets, involving, as it did, the interests of all the stockholders, was contrary to public policy and void, it being admitted that such contract was not known by or assented to by the other stockholders. *The purpose and effect of the contract was apparently to influence appellant, in his decision of a question affecting the rights and interests of his associate stockholders, by a consideration which was foreign to those rights and interests and would likely to induce him to disregard the consideration he owed them and the contract must, therefore, be regarded as a fraud upon them.* Such an agreement will not be enforced, as being against public policy. . . .

In addition to the deceit obviously practiced upon the other stockholders, the Court was clearly concerned with the rights and interests of the other stockholders. Thus, the potential injury or prejudicial impact which might flow to other stockholders as a result of such an agreement forms the heart of the rationale underlying the breach of public policy doctrine.

An automatic application of this rationale to the facts in the present case, however, would be to ignore an essential element of the transaction. The agreement in question was entered into primarily to further the interests of Texas International's other shareholders. Indeed, the shareholders, after reviewing a detailed proxy statement, voted overwhelmingly in favor of the loan agreement. Thus, the underlying rationale for the argument that vote-buying is illegal per se, as a matter of public policy, ceases to exist when measured against the undisputed reason for the transaction.

Moreover, the rationale that vote-buying is, as a matter of public policy, illegal per se is founded upon considerations of policy which are now outmoded as a necessary result of an evolving corporate environment. According to 5 Fletcher Cyclopedia Corporation (Perm. Ed.) §2066:

> The theory that each stockholder is entitled to the personal judgment of each other stockholder expressed in his vote, and that any agreement among stockholders frustrating it was invalid, is obsolete because it is both impracticable and impossible of application to modern corporations with many widely scattered stockholders, and the courts have gradually abandoned it. . . .

Recently, in *Oceanic Exploration Co. v. Grynberg,* Del. Supr., 428 A.2d 1 (1981), the Delaware Supreme Court applied this approach to voting trusts. The Court also indicated, with approval, the liberal approach to all contractual arrangements limiting the incidents of stock ownership. Significantly, *Oceanic* involved the giving up of voting rights in exchange for personal gain. There, the stockholder, by way of a voting trust, gave up his right to vote on all corporate matters over a period of years in return for "valuable benefits including indemnity for large liabilities."

Given the holdings in *Ringling* and *Oceanic*, it is clear that Delaware has discarded the presumptions against voting agreements. Thus, under our present law, an agreement involving the transfer of stock voting rights without the transfer of ownership is not necessarily illegal and each arrangement must be examined in light of its object or purpose. To hold otherwise would be to exalt form over substance. As indicated in *Oceanic* more than the mere form of an agreement relating to voting must be considered and voting agreements in whatever form, therefore, should not be considered to be illegal per se unless the object or purpose is to defraud or in some way disenfranchise the other stockholders. This is not to say, however, that vote-buying accomplished for some laudable purpose is automatically free from challenge. Because vote-buying is so easily susceptible of abuse it must be viewed as a voidable transaction subject to a test for intrinsic fairness. . . .

. . . I therefore hold that the agreement, whereby Jet Capital withdrew its opposition to the proposed merger in ex-

---

CARL ICAHN AT MYLAN LABORATORIES

Consider the following excerpt:

Long & Short: Icahn Cries Foul at Perry's No-Risk Play in Takeover Fight
Wall Street Journal (December 15, 2004)

. . . Here's how it works: Perry [a hedge fund] owns 9.9% of Mylan, or 26.6 million shares. But the firm has no economic interest in the stock, having entered into hedging transactions for its entire position. While Perry was buying all that stock, it had a cooperative brokerage firm (or firms) short an equal amount of Mylan stock — selling shares borrowed from shareholders. At the same time, Perry got the right to sell its shares back to the brokerage, while the brokerage received the right to call the stock back from Perry — all at the same price. The result is a wash. That means Perry is indifferent to the price of Mylan, having no economic interest in it. Nevertheless, it retains nearly 10% of Mylan's voting rights, becoming one of its most powerful shareholders.

Why would Perry go through all this trouble? Because the hedge fund owns seven million shares of King and wants Mylan's takeover bid to go through, boosting the value of Perry's stake in King.

Question: To what extent are Perry's maneuverings de facto vote buying? To what extent should corporate law regulate such behavior? (And if so, how might corporate law accomplish this?)

---

change for a loan to fund the early exercise of its warrants was not void per se because the object and purpose of the agreement was not to defraud or disenfranchise the other stockholders but rather was for the purpose of furthering the interest of all Texas International stockholders. The agreement, however, was a voidable act. Because the loan agreement was voidable it was susceptible to cure by shareholder approval. *Michelson v.*

Duncan, Del. Supr., 407 A.2d 211 (1979). Consequently, the subsequent ratification of the transaction by a majority of the independent stock-holders, after a full disclosure of all germane facts with complete candor precludes any further judicial inquiry of it. . . .

NOTE ON SCHREIBER v. CARNEY

Schreiber deals with the birth of Texas Air, a holding company that for a period owned Eastern and Continental, among other airlines. The point of the proposed merger was to leave Texas International as a wholly owned subsidiary of Texas Air, which would then be free to acquire other airlines as operating subsidiaries.

Jet served as a kind of venture capitalist, which had financed Texas International from its outset. As a result, Jet held both convertible preferred stock and warrants in Texas International. (Warrants, like options, are rights to purchase stock at a fixed exercise price.) In *Schreiber,* the warrants were quite valuable because the market price of Texas International common stock far exceeded its exercise price. The preferred stock was also valuable for much the same reason: Texas International was successful, and Jet Capital's pre-ferred stock could be converted into common stock. In addition, its preferred stock gave Jet Capital a veto right over the proposed merger by virtue of a provision in Texas International's certificate, allowing class votes on funda-mental changes such as mergers.

Given the transactional background, what would Jet Capi-tal have done if the *Schreiber* court had declared the loan transaction void?

As *Schreiber* notes, the traditional rule that shareholders cannot agree to sell their votes has been significantly eroded by the wide latitude share-holders enjoy to enter voting agreements and voting trusts in exchange for personal consideration. Given these developments, why shouldn't vote buying always be permitted? What distinguishes circumstances in which vote buying is not permitted? Didn't the agreement in *Schreiber* disenfran-chise shareholders who wished to vote against the merger?

Schreiber deals with a transaction that may be recast as possible vote buying. But recently the question of vote buying comes up in new ways that often the other shareholders may never learn about. This is shown, for example, by the sidebar on the Mylan Pharmaceutical matter above. Today many types of derivative financial contracts are available in more or less standard forms that allow the legal owner of shares to trade away the economic risk of an investment (or a slice of it) while maintaining legal title to the shares (and thus the legal right to vote them). When this occurs we may have a person with a legal right to vote with no economic interest in the outcome of the vote, or what may be worse, a person with a net short position and thus an economic interest in the stock's price falling voting shares. The law has not yet begun to grapple with this new phenomenon, but at the very least the rise in hedge funds and the growth in derivative markets suggest that greater disclosure of contracts whose value will turn on the value of the firm's shares should be required to be disclosed. See

Henry T.C. Hu & Bernard Black, *The New Vote Buying: Empty Voting and Hidden (Morphable) Ownership*, 79 So. Cal. L. Rev. 811 (2006).

7.7.3 Controlling Minority Structures

Vote buying and circular voting structures are not the only way to separate control rights from cash flow rights. There are three much more widely accepted structures that accomplish the same thing. They are dual class share structures, stock pyramids, and cross-ownership ties. We term these patterns of ownership "controlling minority structures" (CMSs) because they permit a shareholder to control a firm while holding only a fraction of its equity.

LUCIAN A. BEBCHUK, REINIER KRAAKMAN & GEORGE G. TRIANTIS, STOCK PYRAMIDS, CROSS-OWNERSHIP, AND DUAL CLASS EQUITY

Concentrated Corporate Ownership 295 (R. Morck ed., 2000)

CMS structures are common outside the U.S., particularly in countries whose economies are dominated by family-controlled conglomerates.[1] Because these structures can radically distort their controllers' incentives, however, they put great pressure on non-electoral mechanisms of corporate governance, ranging from legal protections for minority shareholders to reputational constraints on controlling families. . . .

Each of the three basic CMS forms firmly entrench minority control. In each case, the CMS form can be used in principle to separate cash flow rights from control rights, to any desired extent. We denote the degree of separation induced by a CMS structure between control and cashflow rights by α, which represents the fraction of the firm's equity cash flow rights held by the controlling-minority shareholder. . . .

The most straightforward CMS form is a single firm that has issued two or more classes of stock with differential voting rights. . . . Calibrating the separation of cash flow and control rights in a dual-class equity structure is child's play. A planner can simply attach all voting rights to the fraction of shares that are assigned to the controller, while attaching no voting rights to the remaining shares that are distributed to the public or other shareholders.[2] . . .

---

1. LaPorta, et al., who conduct a comprehensive survey of ownership structures around the world, demonstrate that controlling minority shareholder structures, and particularly stock pyramids, are widespread. [See LaPorta, Lopez-de-Silanes & Shleifer, *Corporate Ownership Around the World*, 54 J. Fin. 47 (1999). — EDS.]

2. In their sample of U.S. dual class firms, De Angelo and De Angelo (1985) found that insiders held a median of 56.9% of the voting rights but only 24% of the common stock claims to cash flow.

Despite its simplicity, however, dual class equity is not the most common CMS structure worldwide (although it is the most common in the U.S.). Presumably, the corporate law of many jurisdictions restricts both the voting ratio between high-and low-vote shares, and the numerical ratio between high-and low-vote shares that a firm is permitted to issue. Such restrictions would implicitly mandate a lower bound on the size of α. Yet, any such legal restrictions could not wholly explain the lagging popularity of differential voting rights. . . . Even in jurisdictions where shares with differential voting rights are common, CMS companies rarely reduce the fraction of controller ownership α to the legal minimum.[18]

[The most popular structure for erecting CMS structures worldwide is the corporate pyramid structure.] In a pyramid of two companies, a controlling minority shareholder holds a controlling stake in a holding company that, in turn, holds a controlling stake in an operating company. In a three-tier pyramid, the primary holding company controls a second-tier holding company that in turn controls the operating company. . . .

For any fraction α, however small, there is a pyramid that permits a controller to completely control a company's assets without holding more than α of the company's cash flow rights. [To take a concrete example of how rapidly pyramiding separates equity from control, consider a three-tier pyramid in which the controlling minority shareholder holds 50% of the shares at each level. Here, the minority investor controls the firm with only 12.5% of its cash flow rights. — Eds.]

In contrast to pyramids, companies in cross-ownership structures are linked by horizontal cross-holdings of shares that reinforce and entrench the power of central controllers. Thus, cross-holding structures differ from pyramids chiefly in that the voting rights used to control the corporate group are distributed over the entire group rather than concentrated in the hands of a single company or shareholder. . . . Like pyramiding, however, cross-ownership permits a controller to exercise complete control over a corporation with an arbitrarily small claim on its cash flow rights. More-over, cross-holdings have the advantage of making the locus of control over a company group less transparent, which is said to be a reason for their popularity in Asia.[19]

Neither pyramids nor cross-ownership are popular in the U.S. or the U.K. One reason for their paucity in the U.S. is that we impose an income tax on inter-corporate dividends. Thus, there is a significant tax penalty on moving corporate distributions through two or more levels of corporate structure. A second reason is the Investment Company Act of 1940, which imposes stringent regulatory and reporting requirements on group struc-tures tied together by webs of minority holdings. It follows that the only ownership structure suitable for separating cash flow from ownership in the U.S is dual class common stock.

---

18. LaPorta et al., supra note 1.

19. Murray Weidenbaum, *The Chinese Family Business Enterprise*, 38 Cal. Mgmt. Rev. 141 (1996).

American corporate law does not require all shares to have voting rights, nor does it require all voting shares to have equal voting rights.[19] Thus, most U.S. jurisdictions permit super-voting stock. Some economically oriented scholars believe that a dual-class voting stock may be the most effective (and most obvious) device for separating voting rights from cash flow rights and entrenching an individual or group as a controlling minority shareholder. The controversial character of dual-class stock in the United States raises several interesting questions. For example, how many of these firms are there really? Why were they created? Finally, are these structures really as inefficient as theory suggests they are likely to be?

Some answers are clear, some are not. To begin, dual-class share structures are rare among public companies (closely held companies are another matter). Some commentators suggest a historical explanation for this. For many years, the New York Stock Exchange (NYSE) would not list common stock that did not possess equal rights.[20] Since access to the NYSE was essential for public companies, firms simply did not adopt dual-class structures. (But would they have acted differently without the dual-class Exchange rule?)

Some economically oriented scholars believe that NYSE Rule 313.00 is unnecessary, given how a corporation's capital structure is formed. At the IPO stage, when the firm has few or no agency problems, corporate planners have an incentive to construct the best capital structure (i.e., the one the market will value most highly). Arguably, there may be some corporations in which a disjunction between control rights and rights to return is desirable. The case of newspapers is occasionally cited. These firms often have family control (a family controls *The New York Times* in a dual-class corporation), and that control is thought by some to add value by credibly committing the firm to a particular editorial approach. In all events, whether or not dual-class voting structures are efficient, economists conventionally assume that IPO pricing is efficient. Thus, if IPO entrepreneurs sell low-vote stock, public investors who discount accordingly will always get what they pay for.

Dual-class structures are more problematic, however, when they are adopted in "midstream," after the firm is already publicly trading. They can be adopted midstream only by a charter amendment requiring a shareholder vote. But such a vote might not protect public shareholders who face a collective action problem.[21] Those proposing a dual-class voting structure can exploit the collective action problem by offering public shareholders a minor benefit in consideration for accepting diluted voting power. For example, the corporation might exchange one share of the old common stock for one share of new Class A common stock or one share of new Class B common stock. The Class A will have all of the rights of the old common stock plus its holders will receive a one-time special dividend (say, 50 cents

---

19. See, e.g., DGCL §151(a); NYBCA §613. Note that some non-U.S. jurisdictions, such as Germany, have adopted a mandatory one-share, one-vote rule.

20. New York Stock Exchange Listed Company Manual §313.00.

21. See Jeffrey N. Gordon, *Ties That Bond: Dual Class Common Stock and the Problem of Shareholder Choice*, 76 Cal. L. Rev. 1 (1988); Ronald J. Gilson, *Evaluating Dual Class Common Stock: The Relevance of Substitutes*, 73 Va. L. Rev. 807 (1987).

a share). The new Class B stock will have those same rights except (1) it has
no right to a special dividend, (2) it has ten votes per share, and (3)
whenever it is transferred (except by death or inter vivos gift to a family
member), it will automatically be converted into the same number of Class
A common shares.[22] The result, of course, is that management soon accu-
mulates control over the company. Might such a transaction be efficient?
Perhaps so, although one suspects that most managers who propose midstream charter amendments hope to extract value from shareholders.

In 1986, in response to NASDAQ listing requirements that permitted dual-class structures, the NYSE proposed to amend its rules to permit such structures as well. A howl of
protest met the proposal, and the SEC, under its statutory au-
thority to regulate securities exchanges, enacted Rule 19c-4, which effectively prohibited
both the NYSE and NASDAQ from listing shares with un-
equal voting rights unless initi-
ally offered to the market in that structure. The D.C. Circuit
Court of Appeals subsequently struck down Rule 19c-4 (as
constituting unauthorized regu-
lation of internal corporate governance matters). See *Business Roundtable v. SEC*, 905 F.2d 406 (D.C. Cir. 1990). The
matter was thereafter resolved by an informal agreement
among the NYSE, NASDAQ, and SEC to amend listing
rules to proscribe securities that limit the voting rights of
existing securities but to per-
mit initial public offerings of low-vote or no-vote stock that
do not control the rights of existing stock.

GOOGLE BALONEY

Holman W. Jenkins Jr., in the Wall Street Journal (May 5, 2004)

[In addition to the Dutch auction process for allocating IPO shares,] [w]hat else set tongues a-flapping was Google's decision to issue two classes of stock, giving its founders, Larry Page and Sergey Brin, as well as CEO Eric Schmidt, super-voting shares worth 10 times the voting weight of an ordinary share. As the prospectus frankly states, the goal is to entrench insiders in control of the company. . . .

The Googlers don't mention the $800 heated toilet seats. Investors will have to judge whether such bennies are genuine productivity builders — or whether they count as "on-the-job consumption," one of the "private benefits of control" that academic economists traditionally regard as the motive for voting-power lockups. To translate, that's a nice way of saying insiders are living it up at shareholder's expense. . . .

Dual-share companies have become more common lately as founders seek to entrench themselves after going public.

---

22. See, e. g., *Lacos Land Company v. Arden Group, Inc.*, 517 A.2d 271 (Del. Ch. 1986)
(injunction against shareholder vote on management's effort to amend charter in a similar
way; basis was that management wrongfully coerced the vote by threatened breach of duty if
approval was not forthcoming). Compare *Blasius Corp v. Atlas*, infra, Chapter 13.

QUESTION

While agency theory seems to imply that control and cash flow rights should be aligned, can you think of reasons why it may be efficient for some firms to adopt dual-voting structure as Google has done? Note that among the firms with this structure is Berkshire Hathaway, which is controlled by famed investor Warren Buffett. Might the market believe that the particular controllers of these two firms are uniquely capable of creating value? In many entrepreneurial firms that go public with a dual-class voting structure, the charter mandates that high vote shares will convert to one-share/one-vote stock if the "original holder" (the entrepreneur) transfers them to a third party. This was the case, for example, in the *Omnicare* case discussed in Chapter 13 *infra*.

7.8   THE COLLECTIVE ACTION PROBLEM

The fact that public shareholders often approved devices that entrenched minority shareholders in the 1980s, such as dual-class recapitalizations, points to the public shareholders' collective action problem. Even a one-share, one-vote rule cannot protect shareholders who habitually approve management proposals. Early academic commentators stressed the severity of the collection problem, and consequently saw shareholder voting as a mere adjunct to the takeover marketplace. Subsequent commentators found potential solutions with institutional investors, if legal restrictions were loosened, while others were skeptical that institutions could ever play an active role in corporate governance. The latest commentators point to hedge funds as the solution to the collective action problem. The following excerpts follow the evolution of the thinking on this core problem in corporate law.

FRANK EASTERBROOK & DANIEL FISCHEL, VOTING IN CORPORATE LAW

26 J.L. & Econ. 395 (1983)

Because voting is expensive, the participants in the venture will arrange to conserve on its use. It could be employed from time to time to select managers and set the ground rules for their performance and not used again unless the managers' performance were seriously inadequate. Indeed, the collective choice problems that attend voting in corporations with large numbers of contracting parties suggest that voting would rarely have any function except in extremis. When many are entitled to vote, none of the voters expects his votes to decide the contest. Consequently none of the voters has the appropriate incentive at the margin to study the firm's affairs and vote intelligently.

If, for example, a given election could have a $1,000 effect on each voter, then each voter's optimal investment in information is zero if each is sure that the election will come out the same way whether or not he participates. And even if a voter thinks his vote will be dispositive, so that an investment up to $1,000 is warranted, that may be insufficient. If there are 1,000 voters, the effect on them as a group will be $1 million. An investment in $1,000 worth of information may be quite insufficient to make a $1 million decision; worse still, 1,000 people investing $1,000 each may mean that all of them are acting on inadequate information, even though a single investment in $10,000 worth of knowledge might be adequate. Now voters are not fungible. Those who have more shares, such as investment companies, pension trusts, and some insiders, do not face the collection action problem to the same extent. Nonetheless, no shareholder, no matter how large his stake, has the right incentives at the margin unless that stake is 100 percent.

These collective action problems may be overcome by aggregating the shares (and the attached votes) through acquisitions, such as mergers and tender offers. We expect voting to serve its principal role in permitting those who have aggregated equity claims to exercise control. Short of aggregating, however, some sort of collective information-generating agency is necessary. In a firm, the managers serve this function, and consequently, it is unlikely that voters would think themselves able to decide issues for themselves with greater insight than the managers do. No wonder voters delegate extensively to managers and almost always endorse their decisions. But this acquiescence should not obscure the fact that managers exercise authority delegated by voters.

BERNARD S. BLACK, NEXT STEPS IN PROXY REFORM

18 J. Corp. L. 1, 4-8 (1992)

American institutions are kept passive by a complex web of federal and state rules. A shareholder who owns a large percentage stake in a company will do more monitoring than a shareholder who owns a small stake. But legal rules keep financial institutions smaller than they would otherwise be, and discourage the institutions from acting together. Legal rules channel institutional investments into debt instead of equity. Legal rules push each institution to hold small percentage stakes in a huge number of companies, instead of large stakes in a limited number of companies. Legal rules make it especially dangerous for shareholders to intervene in companies in financial trouble, which might most need outside help; make it especially difficult to enter the boardroom, where oversight might be most effective; and let corporate managers largely control the shareholder voting agenda. In contrast, rules that encourage shareholder oversight of corporate managers are few and weak. Money manager cultural norms and conflicts of interest reinforce the legal disincentives for oversight; legal rules don't do much to control the conflicts. In a different legal environment, financial intermediaries could monitor the actions of corporate managers. In other countries, they do.

[In the United States,] [b]anks, insurers, and mutual funds face legal limits on their ability to hold large percentage stakes; banks and insurers are limited in their ability to own equity at all; banks are kept small by interstate banking restrictions; pension funds are encouraged by law to take diversification to ridiculous extremes. Active five percent shareholders must file a disclosure form under section 13(d) of the Securities Exchange Act. Ten percent shareholders are subject to short-swing profit forfeiture under Exchange Act section 16(b). An influential shareholder may be considered a control person, with severe consequences under securities, bankruptcy, and other laws. No shareholder can cross the trigger percentage for a firm's poison pill, often only ten to fifteen percent, without management approval. Most of these rules apply to shareholder groups as well as individual shareholders.

The list goes on. Tax rules discourage corporate crossholdings; accounting rules disfavor crossholdings under twenty percent; active shareholders risk antitrust entanglements; under some state antitakeover statutes, shareholders who wage a voting campaign can lose their voting power or become obliged to offer to buy everyone else's stock at a premium to market. Legal obstacles are especially great if shareholders want to choose even a minority of directors instead of rubberstamping the incumbents' choices. In many areas, the law is uncertain. That creates legal risk, which discourages oversight by institutional fiduciaries, who face personal risk on the downside while their beneficiaries get most of the upside. State corporate law lets managers exert substantial control over the shareholder voting agenda. Managers can control the voting of some shares they don't own; for example, they . . . can park stock in friendly hands, even in the middle of a proxy contest.

Will financial institutions hold large stakes and become active monitors if legal rules permit them to? We can't definitively answer that counterfactual question, but comparative analysis provides some clues. Banks are powerful in Japan and Germany; insurers are influential in Great Britain. American insurers and banks were once powerful, before politics clipped their wings.

Moreover, institutions own over half of the equity in American public companies—a percentage that continues to grow. It is common for a company's fifteen largest institutional shareholders to own twenty percent or so of its stock, despite the rules that create incentives for the institutions to limit their stakes in any one company. That is already enough to create some incentives to monitor. If legal restrictions were loosened, the percentage stakes held by the largest institutions would likely grow, and monitoring incentives would be correspondingly stronger. The institutions would surely do *more* monitoring if legal rules changed; perhaps they would do much more.

ROBERT C. POZEN, INSTITUTIONAL INVESTORS: THE RELUCTANT ACTIVISTS

Harvard Business Review (Jan/Feb 1994)

Most institutional investors do not set out to become activist share-holders, nor do they want to get involved with a company's operational issues. For most institutions, the approach to shareholder activism is straightforward: to decide whether and when to become active, an institutional investor compares the expected costs of a course of action with the expected benefits. The costs of activism depend primarily on the tools with which an institution exerts influence, from the high cost of waging a formal proxy fight to the low cost of holding informal discussions with management. The benefits depend partly on the probability of success and partly on the issue at hand, with more potential benefit from proposals directly affecting stock price and less from proposals for procedural reforms. . . .

Most advisory contracts require money managers to perform normal proxy activity: reading proxy statements, making careful voting decisions, and sending reports to an oversight board. These contracts typically do not address the question of who pays for proxy activism undertaken by the institutional investor on behalf of its clients. In some cases, a money manager may justify imposing a charge on the clients' fund in addition to the advisory fee that clients pay to the money manager. For example, proxy activism may require hiring outside experts, such as appraisers who will evaluate mineral rights held by a company proposing to go private. In other cases, such as travel expenses for meetings with company directors, the cost of activism is typically covered by the advisory fee.

Most such fees, however, are set on the assumption that institutional investors will usually function as passive money managers rather than as activists. The advisory fees of equity mutual funds average around 70 basis points (0.7%) per year, with a maximum performance fee of 10 to 20 basis points (0.1% to 0.2%). In other words, the fees do not cover heavy intervention on the part of the money manager. In contrast, advisory fees for a venture capital fund are typically composed of a 1% or 2% base fee plus 10% to 20% of all profits. This much higher fee is based on the assumption that venture fund managers will be actively involved with most of their portfolio companies.

MARCEL KAHAN & EDWARD B. ROCK, HEDGE FUNDS IN CORPORATE GOVERNANCE AND CORPORATE CONTROL

Working paper, May 2006

Hedge funds are emerging as the most dynamic and most prominent shareholder activists. On the bright side, this generates the possibility that hedge funds will, in the course of making profits for their own investors, help overcome the classic agency problem of publicly held corporations by dislodging underperforming managers, challenging ineffective strategies, and making sure that merger and control transactions make sense for target and acquirer shareholders. In doing so, the bright side holds, hedge funds would enhance the value of the companies they invest in for the benefit of both their own investors and their fellow shareholders. . . . But the bright side story of hedge funds, as large and sophisticated investors standing up to management for the benefit of shareholders at large — has an element of déjà vu. Twenty years ago, similar stories were told about another set of large and sophisticated investors: mutual funds, public pension funds, private pension funds, insurance companies, or "institutional investors" as they became called. But while, on the whole, the rise of these traditional institutional investors has probably been beneficial, they have hardly proved to be a silver bullet.

Are there reasons to think that newly prominent hedge funds will prove to be more effective? . . . The incentives to monitor by hedge funds differ in several important respects from those of traditional institutional investors. First, hedge fund managers are highly incentivized to maximize the returns to fund investors. The standard hedge fund charges a base fee equal to 1-2% of the assets under management and a significant incentive fee, typically 20% of the profits earned. This fee structure gives hedge fund managers very significant stakes in the financial success of the fund's investments. These stakes are even higher when, as is frequently the case, a hedge fund manager has invested a significant portion of her personal wealth in the hedge fund.

Secondly, many hedge funds strive to achieve high absolute returns, rather than returns relative to a benchmark. In particular, the industry-standard 20% incentive fee is usually based on a fund's absolute performance. And while a few funds use a hurdle rate before the incentive fee is payable, this hurdle rate is generally a rate based on the yield of debt securities, not a rate based on the performance of a market index or an index of hedge funds with similar investment objectives.

Thus, unlike mutual funds, hedge funds benefit directly and substantially from achieving high absolute returns. For successful managers, the resulting profits can be extraordinary high. Thus, the average take home pay for the top 25 hedge fund managers in 2003 was $207 million; and the lowest paid manager in that group still earned a respectable $65 million. For 2004, the average was $251 and the lowest paid received $100 million.

7.9   THE FEDERAL PROXY RULES

Nowhere are one's views on the severity of the collective action problem more salient than in an evaluation of the effects of the federal proxy rules on the operation of the voting system in public companies.

The federal proxy rules originate with the provisions of the Securities Exchange Act of 1934 (the Exchange Act or sometimes the '34 Act), chiefly §14(a)-(c), which regulate virtually every aspect of proxy voting in public

companies. These provisions support an array of rules subsequently promulgated and enforced by the Securities and Exchange Commission (SEC).

The federal proxy rules consist of four major elements:

1. Disclosure requirements and a mandatory vetting regime that
    permit the SEC to assure the disclosure of relevant information
    and to protect shareholders from misleading communications;
2. Substantive regulation of the process of soliciting proxies from
    shareholders;
3. A specialized "town meeting" provision (Rule 14a-8) that permits
    shareholders to gain access to the corporation's proxy materials
    and to thus gain a low-cost way to promote certain kinds of
    shareholder resolutions; and
4. A general antifraud provision (Rule 14a-9) that allows courts to
    imply a private shareholder remedy for false or misleading proxy
    materials.

In this section, we present, in plain English, a brief overview of the
federal proxy rules adopted by the SEC under §14 of the '34 Act. We then
present two of the rules in greater detail — Rule 14a-8, the town meeting
rule, and Rule 14a-9, the antifraud rule.

7.9.1   Rules 14a-1 Through 14a-7: Disclosure and Shareholder Communication

Unlike company law in EU jurisdictions, corporate law in most U.S.
states has never imposed an affirmative obligation on corporations to
inform shareholders of the state of the company's business or even to
distribute a balance sheet and income statement.[23] At most, shareholders
could demand stock lists and sometimes gain access to detailed books and
records. Presumably, in an earlier age, the power to replace the board was
seen in the United States as a sufficient inducement for firms to disclose.
Matters changed, however, after the Great Depression when federal legislation adopted the core strategy of mandating public disclosure. While
much of this legislation was designed to inform investors in the initial
offer and secondary markets, some of it — in particular, §14(a) of the
Securities and Exchange Act of 1934 — addressed disclosure in connection
with the solicitation of proxies.

Section 14(a) made it unlawful for any person, in contravention of any
rule that the commission may adopt, to "solicit" any "proxy" to vote any
"security" registered under §12 of the Act. The SEC soon gave each of these
terms — "solicit," "proxy," and "security" — a very broad interpretation in
Regulation 14A. The basic scheme of the Regulation was (and is) to state
with great detail the types of information that any person must provide

---

23. There are a few exceptions to this generalization. See, e.g., Mich. Bus. Corp. Act
§901, which requires corporations to distribute financial statements to shareholders.

when seeking a proxy to vote a covered security. These rules were drafted to force disclosure by corporations to the shareholders from whom they sought proxies. These rules, however, apply not only to an issuing corporation but also to a third party who might seek to oust incumbent management by a proxy fight. Thus, they had the unintended consequence of discouraging proxy fights. The 1966 case of *Studebaker Corporation v. Gittlin*[24] illustrates the point. In that case, a request to forty-two stockholders of a large public company to join in a request to inspect the shareholders' list (necessary because, under state law, the list was available only on the demand of more than 5 percent of the company's stock) was held to constitute a "solicitation" of a "proxy" requiring the preparation, filing, and distribution of a proxy statement. By 1990, the risks and expense that the proxy rules imposed on governance activities became the subject of widespread criticism. Consider the following excerpt from an op-ed by Professor Mark Roe:

> "Today [December 1991], if a dozen shareholders want to talk to one another about the company that they own, they must file a proxy statement with the SEC, informing it of what they want to say, and usually letting SEC staffers edit their statement. Even a simple newspaper ad usually requires clearance from the SEC. If stockholders have doubts about the quality of their management, they must act publicly, in costly, stilted, potentially embarrassing ways. Publicity instills silence. Why stick your neck out and publicly question management if no one else is going to go along? Before testing whether the water is over your head, you must commit to jumping in. . . . It might seem incredible if during a presidential election, voters could not talk to one another, other than through a formal statement filed with a government agency. But this is the situation in corporate elections."[25]

In 1992, the SEC responded by amending the rules in several important ways. In general, the 1992 amendments to Regulation 14A limited the term "solicitation" in Rule 14(a)-1(l) and created new exemptions under Rule 14(a)-2, which released institutional shareholders, in limited circumstances, from the requirement to file a disclosure form before they could communicate with other shareholders about a corporation. Prior to these amendments, institutional investors who communicated with other investors about a company ran a serious risk of being deemed to have solicited a proxy, which would have required them to file a costly proxy statement.

Rule 14a-3 contains the central regulatory requirement of the proxy rules. No one may be solicited for a proxy unless they are, or have been, furnished with a proxy statement "containing the information specified in Schedule 14A." When the solicitation is made on behalf of the company itself (the "registrant") and relates to an annual meeting for the election of directors, it must include considerable information about the company, including related party transactions (see Schedule 14A, Item 6) and detailed information about the compensation of top managers (see Item D). When the proxy statement is filed by anyone other than management, it

---

24. 360 F.2d 692 (2d Cir. 1966).
25. Mark Roe, *Free Speech for Shareholders?*, Wall Street Journal (Dec. 18, 1991).

requires detailed disclosure of the identity of the soliciting parties, as well as their holdings and the financing of the campaign.

Rule 14a-3 raises the central question of what constitutes a "proxy" and a "solicitation." Rule 14a-1 provides sweeping definitions of these terms — a "proxy," for example, can be any solicitation or consent whatsoever. Rule 14a-2 provides important exemptions from these broad definitions. Rule 14a-2(b)(2) provides an exemption for solicitations to less than 10 shareholders. Rule 14a-2(b)(1), added in 1992, provides an exemption for ordinary shareholders who wish to communicate with other shareholders but do not themselves intend to seek proxies. In addition, Rule 14a-1(l)(2)(iv) provides that announcements by shareholders on how they intend to vote, even if such announcement include the shareholders' reasoning, are not subject to the proxy rules. Of course, the SEC 1992 Release made clear that these exemptions did not exempt investors from Rule 14a-9 (discussed below), which prohibits false or misleading statements in connection with written or oral solicitations.[26]

Rules 14a-4 and 14a-5 regulate the form of the proxy — in effect, the actual "vote" itself — and the proxy statement, respectively. For example, the proxy must instruct shareholders that they can withhold support for a particular director on the solicitor's slate of candidates by crossing through her name (Rule 4(b)(2)(ii)). Similarly, subsection (c)(4) deals with circumstances under which a dissident can solicit votes for some but not all of management's candidates for the board (the so-called short-slate rule).

Rule 14a-6 lists formal filing requirements, not only for preliminary and definitive proxy materials but also for solicitation materials and Notices of Exempt Solicitations. Rule 14a-12 contains special rules applicable to contested directors — or, more specifically, solicitations opposing anyone else's (usually management's) candidates for the board. In particular, Rule 14a-12(a) permits dissident solicitations prior to the filing of a written proxy statement as long as dissidents disclose their identities and holdings, and do not furnish a proxy card to security holders. Finally, Rule 14a-12(b) deals with the treatment and filing of proxy solicitations made prior to the delivery of a proxy statement.

Rule 14a-7 sets forth the list-or-mail rule under which, upon request by a dissident shareholder, a company must either provide a shareholders' list or undertake to mail the dissident's proxy statement and solicitation materials to record holders (i.e., the intermediaries) in quantities sufficient to assure that all beneficial holders can receive copies.

PROBLEM: THE PROXY RULES MEET THE ACTIVE
INSTITUTIONAL SHAREHOLDER: TarPERS

You are counsel to the Texarkana Public Employees' Retirement System (TarPERS). TarPERS holds 1 percent of the outstanding shares of HLS, Inc. Since TarPERS has long been dissatisfied with HLS's lackluster

---

26. Regulation of Communications Among Shareholders, Release No. 34-31326, 52 S. E.C. Docket 2028, Release No. IC-19031 (1992).

management, TarPERS is considering a proxy campaign to elect three reputable business professors to HLS's nine-member board. Before initiating a
campaign, however, TarPERS wishes to test the waters by circulating a
memo outlining the prospective campaign to 15 other institutions that
hold a total of 15 percent of HLS's outstanding stock. If its sister institutions
respond favorably, TarPERS plans to file a proxy statement, distribute materials in support of its nominees to all HLS shareholders, and seek a public
endorsement of its nominees from Institutional Shareholder Services (ISS),
a nonprofit shareholder rights group.

Advise the TarPERS trustees on the difficulties they may expect to
confront. Is there a problem with nominating only three candidates? Who
must file what, with whom, and when? At what points can the SEC intervene? Can TarPERS expect to incur any litigation costs? What access does
TarPERS have under Rule 14a-7 to the HLS shareholder list? What access
does it have under DGCL §219 or §220? Under which provision would you
recommend TarPERS to proceed?

Consider, in this regard, the proxy rules under Regulation 14A and
Schedule 14A, all in your statutory supplement. Look closely at the following rules in connection with the TarPERS query: 14a-1(f) & (l); 14a-2(a)(6),
(b)(1), (b)(2), & (b)(3); 14a-3(a); 14a-6(a) to (c); 14a-7(a) & (e); 14a-9; and
14a-12(a) & (b). Please do *not* explore every clause of the proxy rules in
thinking about this question.

Whether the proxy rules or other legal barriers impede collective
action by shareholders depends not only on the rules themselves but also
on the identity of the shareholders. Large, passive institutions (such as
TarPERS) might well be deterred by the prospect of a lawsuit when scrappy
value investors, hedge funds, and other activist shareholders are not. For an
excellent analysis of this point and an exposition of the proxy rules from the
perspective of the professional insurgent, see Thomas W. Briggs, *Shareholder Activism and Insurgency Under the New Proxy Rules*, 50 Bus. Law
99 (1994).

NOTE ON THE RISE AND FALL OF RULE 14A-11, THE "SHAREHOLDER PROXY ACCESS RULE"

In October 2003, the SEC proposed a new Rule 14a-11, which would
have allowed long-term shareholders the power to place their own nominees in a public company's proxy materials under certain limited circumstances. The proposed rule would have permitted a 5 percent or more
shareholder or group of shareholders who have held their stock for at
least two years to nominate one, two, or three directors[27] upon the occurrence of one of two triggering circumstances. One trigger was a withhold

---

27. According to whether the company board had less than nine, between nine and
twenty, or more than twenty directors, respectively.

vote of 35 percent or more for a director nominee on the board's slate during the prior year. The second trigger was passage of a shareholder resolution during the prior year requesting shareholder nominees, proposed by a shareholder or group of shareholders holding 1 percent or more of the company's stock.

The so-called Shareholder Access Rule elicited more comment letters than any other SEC proposal in recent history. On one hand, opponents of the rule argued that it would likely shift a dangerous amount of power into the hands of institutional shareholders and other institutions that did not necessarily have the best interests of the corporation at heart. Union pension funds, public pension funds with political agendas, and Institutional Shareholder Services — a for-profit company that advises institutional shareholders on voting policy — were frequently mentioned as institutions with questionable motives that would gain in influence if the Rule were adopted. On the other hand, proponents of the rule pointed out that no shareholder directors could be elected without receiving a majority shareholder vote, and that shareholder nominees would be willing to survive the arduous triggering conditions, year long wait, and subsequent shareholder vote only if corporate performance were truly terrible and in strong need of shareholder intervention. Certainly, the rule appeared only mildly reformist from the standpoint of foreign jurisdictions, such as the U. K., where corporate law has traditionally accorded shareholders a much stronger legal role in the governance of the company.

In the end, the powerful Business Roundtable and its allies won. By early 2005, after more than a year of debate on the rule, the SEC issued a series of no-action letters permitting companies to omit shareholder proposals based on the proposed Rule 14a-11. Shareholder access seems to be dead, at least for now.

7.9.2   Rule 14a-8: Shareholder Proposals

Rule 14a-8 — the town meeting rule — entitles shareholders to include certain proposals in the company's proxy materials. From the perspective of a shareholder, this has the advantage of low costs: She can advance a proposal for vote by her fellow shareholders without filing with the SEC or mailing her own materials out to shareholders.

From the perspective of corporate management, Rule 14a-8 is at best a costly annoyance and at worst an infringement on management's autonomy. Management has a legitimate interest in excluding some materials from the proxy statement. The length of the proxy statement affects its intelligibility. Loyal agents would desire the proxy statement to be as concise as is consistent with effective communication of material matters and compliance with law. But management may also have other motives for excluding shareholder materials from the proxy statement. Management prefers to control the content of communications made by a corporation to its shareholders. Thus, access to the proxy statement is an important issue that, in the world of events, demands a great deal of attention from corporate counsel.

Regulation 14A provides a number of specific grounds to permit corporations to exclude shareholder-requested matter from the corporation's proxy solicitation materials. First, shareholder proposals must satisfy certain formal criteria: They must state the identity of the shareholder (Rule 14a-8(b)(1)), the number of proposals (Rule 14a-8(c)), the length of the supporting statement (Rule 14a-8(d)), and the subject matter of the proposal (Rule 14a-8(i)). Second, and more important, Rule 14a-8(i) lists 13 grounds that permit firms to exclude proposals from the company's solicitation materials. They include 14a-8(i)(1) — approval of the proposal would be improper under state law — and 8(i)(7) — the proposal relates to a matter of ordinary business. Matters of ordinary business, which you might suppose would be of interest to shareholders, are correctly regarded as the province of the board under the design of the corporate form.

Take a minute to go through these rules. How severe are the limitations? What may have been the rationale for Rules 14a-8(i)(8) and (9)?

Most Rule 14a-8 shareholder proposals fall into one of two categories. They deal with either corporate governance or matters of general social responsibility. Professors Randall Thomas and James Cotter find 72 percent corporate governance proposals and 28 percent social responsibility proposals among a large sample of 14a-8 proposals submitted in 2002-04.[28] The governance proposals address issues ranging from executive compensation (27 percent of the Thomas and Cotter sample) to "internal" governance proposals such as the separation of the chairman and CEO roles (19 percent of the sample) to "external" governance proposals such as dismantling poison pill or staggered board takeover defenses (23 percent of the sample). These proposals, which are often brought by labor unions or institutional investors, are now common and frequently win significant shareholder votes. For example, shareholders have had real success recently in encouraging boards to eliminate staggered boards of directors and redeem so-called poison pill stock rights plans.

Before 1985, however, the issue that dominated shareholder proposals was corporate social responsibility, which embraced topics ranging from environmental policies to personnel practices. Many such corporate responsibility proposals are still brought each year, although they rarely win more than 10 percent of the shareholder vote.

Companies that wish to exclude a shareholder proposal generally seek SEC approval. See Rule 14a-8(j). The SEC's approval of such a request is called a "no-action letter," since it takes the form of a letter stating that the SEC's Division of Corporate Finance will not recommend disciplinary action against the company if the proposal is omitted. The shareholder proponent has the opportunity to respond to the request for a no-action letter.

Corporate Governance Proposals. An important governance question today is the extent of the shareholders' ability to enact bylaws

---

28. Randall S. Thomas & James F. Cotter, *Shareholder Proposals Post-Enron: What's Changed, What's the Same?* (Table 2) (working paper Dec. 2005).

that limit the range of options open to the board in managing the firm. This question relates importantly to Rule 14a-8 because the SEC will not mandate access to the company's proxy statement if, inter alia, the matter on which shareholder action is sought is not a proper subject of shareholder action under state law. We return to the issue of constraining the board's discretion by shareholder bylaw proposals in greater detail at the end of this section, and again in our discussion of management's latitude to defend against hostile takeovers in Chapter 13.

Less controversial corporate governance proposals often urge bylaw amendments on shareholders that would impose structural reforms on the board. We provide an example below: a Rule 14a-8 request by the Carpenters' Pension Fund (CPF) to Hewlett-Packard (HP), requesting that the HP directors initiate a process to amend the charter and bylaws so that directors are elected by majority (rather than plurality) vote.

CARPENTERS' PENSION FUND PROPOSAL AND SUPPORTING STATEMENT

October 7, 2005
BE IT RESOLVED: That the shareholders of Hewlett-Packard Company hereby request that the Board of Directors initiate the appropriate process to amend the Company's governance documents (certificate of incorporation or bylaws) to provide that director nominees shall be elected by the affirmative vote of the majority of votes cast at an annual meeting of shareholders.
SUPPORTING STATEMENT: . . . Our Company presently uses the plurality vote standard to elect directors. This proposal requests that the Board initiate a change in the Company's director election vote standard to provide that nominees for the board of directors must receive a majority of the vote cast in order to be elected or re-elected to the Board.

We believe that a majority vote standard in director elections would give shareholders a meaningful role in the director election process. Under the Company's current standard, a nominee in a director election can be elected with as little as a single affirmative vote, even if a substantial majority of the votes cast are "withheld" from the nominee. The majority vote standard would require that a director receive a majority of the vote cast in order to be elected to the Board. . . .

Some companies have adopted board governance policies requiring director nominees that fail to receive majority support from shareholders to tender their resignations to the board. We believe that these policies are inadequate for they are based on continued use of the plurality standard and would allow director nominees to be elected despite only minimal shareholder support. We contend that changing the legal standard to a majority vote is a superior solution that merits shareholder support.

Our proposal is not intended to limit the judgment of the Board in crafting the requested governance change. For instance, the Board should address the status of incumbent director nominees who fail to receive a majority vote under a majority vote standard and whether a plurality vote standard may be appropriate in director elections when the number of director nominees exceeds the available board seats.

We urge your support for this important director election reform.

On November 2nd, 2005, HP announced a new policy related to the election of its board, "in a continuing effort to enhance its corporate governance procedures": "Under the policy, any nominee for director who receives a greater number of votes 'withheld' from his or her election than votes 'for' such election will tender his or her resignation by the nominating and governance committee of HP's board of directors. The board's nominating and governance committee will then recommend to the board the action to be taken with respect to such offer of resignation."

On November 4th, HP, through its outside counsel, wrote a "no-action letter request" to the SEC, seeking to exclude the CPF proposal from the company proxy on the grounds that the CPF proposal had already been "substantially implemented" and therefore excludable under Rule 14a-8(i)(10):

HEWLETT-PACKARD NO-ACTION LETTER REQUEST

November 4, 2005
. . . Under Delaware law and under HP's Certificate of Incorporation, directors serve until the next annual meeting of stockholders and thereafter until their successors are duly elected and qualified, unless they earlier resign or are removed by stockholders. Thus, an incumbent director who is not re-elected, regardless of whether the company uses a plurality or a majority voting standard, continues to serve as a director under Delaware law. . . . If a majority voting standard were implemented in the manner preferred by the Proponent, an incumbent director nominee who did not receive a majority vote of the shares cast would continue to serve as a director until the next election of directors. In contrast, under the HP Majority Voting Policy, if an incumbent director does not receive a majority of the votes cast, he or she would tender his or her resignation for consideration by the HP Board. If the Board accepted the resignation, then the director would no longer serve on the board. If the Board rejected the resignation, the result would be the same as would occur under the procedure preferred by the Proponent — the director would continue to serve until the next election of directors. In this context, therefore, the result obtained under HP's Majority Voting Policy can be more effective in giving stockholders a meaningful role in the direction election process than the result obtained under the procedure preferred by the Proponent, because the HP Majority Voting Policy provides a process under which that individual may cease to serve as a director if he or she does not receive the affirmative vote of the majority of votes cast at an annual meeting. In contrast, under the Proponent's preferred approach, the director would continue to serve because the board cannot remove directors under Delaware law.

CARPENTERS' RESPONSE

December 8, 2005
. . . The Company's entire argument rests on a flawed assumption that misconstrues the intent of the Proposal and the role prescribed for the Board in the requested implementation of the Proposal. It argues that an informal governance policy, which presumably the Board could revise at any time, requiring that a director nominee who receives a majority "withhold" vote in a director election must tender his resignation produces essentially the same outcome as the Fund's Proposal requests. However, the clear focus of the Proposal is a Board-initiated process to amend HP's bylaws or certificate of incorporation to change its legal director election vote standard from a

plurality vote standard to a majority of votes cast standard. The Proposal does not seek to prescribe any particular post-election treatment of directors that fail to receive the requisite vote. . . . [Under the Proposal,] [d]irector nominees that fail to receive a majority of the vote cast would not be elected or re-elected. The Company's adoption of a post-election policy calling for the resignation of a director legally elected despite receiving a "withhold" vote under a plurality vote standard is a fundamentally different proposition. The Proposal intends exactly what it says, that the legal standard for director elections be a majority vote. The director resignation policy fails to accomplish that end. . . .

On January 5th, 2006, the SEC declined HP's request for a no-action letter: "We are unable to concur in your view that HP may exclude the proposal under Rule 14a-8(i)(10). Accordingly, we do not believe that HP may omit the proposal from its proxy materials in reliance on Rule 14a-8(i)(10)."

HP accordingly placed the resolution on its proxy statement for the annual meeting scheduled for March 15, 2006. In response to the Carpenters' Supporting Statement (above), HP published the following:

MANAGEMENT STATEMENT IN OPPOSITION TO SHAREHOLDER PROPOSAL: . . .

As announced on November 2, 2005, HP has adopted a policy whereby any director nominee who receives a greater number of votes "withheld" from his or her election than votes "for" such election will tender his or her resignation for consideration by the Nominating and Governance Committee. HP believes that this policy is effective in giving stockholders a meaningful role in the election of directors and in removing a director opposed by stockholders. Under HP's policy, a nominee and incumbent director who receives a majority of withheld votes would tender his or her resignation and could be removed from the Board. By contrast, the majority voting standard requested by the proposal only addresses the voting requirement for being elected to the Board. It does not remove incumbent directors who have not received a majority vote because under Delaware law, an incumbent director who is not re-elected "holds over" and continues to serve with the same voting rights and powers until his or her successor is elected and qualified. Therefore, even if the proposal were adopted, HP could not force a director who failed to receive a majority vote to leave the Board until the next annual meeting.
The HP policy also gives stockholders a meaningful role in the director election process without interfering with cumulative voting. The ability to cumulate votes in director elections is universally recognized as protecting stockholder rights. A majority voting standard may raise difficult issues in the context of cumulative voting. While the rules governing plurality voting are well understood, majority voting at companies that have cumulative voting presents technical and legal issues for which there is no precedent. These difficulties have led the American Bar Association Committee on Corporate Laws, the Council of Institutional Investors and the Institutional Shareholder Services Institute for Corporate Governance to indicate that majority voting should not apply to companies that allow cumulative voting. HP's voting system must be a reliable process for the election of qualified directors to represent the interests of all of our stockholders. In the absence of uniform, workable standards that can be consistently applied by all companies and that take into account the special circumstances of companies with cumulative

voting, HP believes it would be inappropriate to adopt a majority voting standard.

For the reasons described above, the Board recommends a vote AGAINST this proposal.

At the HP annual meeting on March 15, 2006, 43.5 percent of HP shareholders voted for the proposal; 53.0 percent voted against; and 3.5 percent abstained.

QUESTIONS

1. In view of the close vote, the outcome may have turned on the omission of language specifying precisely what would happen if a director did not receive a majority of the votes cast. Consider a potential "Part B" to the resolution, as drafted by New York City law firm Wachtell, Lipton, Rosen & Katz: "If a nominee for director who is an incumbent director is not elected and no successor has been elected at such meeting, the director shall promptly tender his or her resignation to the Board of Directors. The [Nominating and Corporate Governance] Committee shall make a recommendation to the Board of Directors as to whether to accept or reject the tendered resignation, or whether other action should be taken. . . ."[29] Would this provision have addressed the concerns raised by Hewlett-Packard in its statement in opposition to the proposal?

2. For the 2006 proxy season, the Wachtell study finds that 86 percent (24 out of 28) majority voting proposals passed where a company did not already have a formal majority voting governance policy in place (like the one that Hewlett-Packard adopted), while only 18 percent (8 out of 44) passed where a company had adopted such a governance policy. The Hewlett-Packard outcome is consistent with this overall pattern. How would you advise a public-company board of directors on how to handle the majority-voting issue? The Wachtell study concludes that "[m]ajority voting proposals will continue to figure heavily in the 2007 proxy season."

3. In 2006, shortly after the HP shareholder meeting, the Delaware legislature amended its corporate code to facilitate majority voting bylaws amendments and to clarify some of the issues raised by the HP board in its statement of opposition. See DGCL §§ 141(b) and 216. What problems do these amendments solve with respect to majority voting bylaws?

The SEC has effectively encouraged shareholders to frame corporate governance resolutions in a precatory form — that is, as recommendations to the board of directors for adoption. The majority-vote proposal at HP is an example of such a precatory resolution. Precatory resolutions sidestep questions concerning the scope of shareholder authority under state law.

29. Martin Lipton, Gregory E. Ostling & David M. Adlerstein, Majority Voting — A Look Back at the 2006 Proxy Season (memorandum to clients June 12, 2006) at Annex C: Model Majority Voting and Director Qualification By-Law.

See the note following Rule 14a-8(i)(1). Since a large affirmative shareholder vote often has a dramatic effect even when a resolution is only precatory, shareholders may not have to give up much by adopting precatory language. Management may hesitate to offend a shareholder majority, even if its will is not binding.

We will return to 14a-8 proposals in Chapter 13, in the context of precatory and mandatory resolutions to redeem (eliminate) poison pills.

Corporate Social Responsibility Proposals.   When should share-holders have a federal right to place proposals in the corporation's proxy statement that are in opposition to lawful (but disapproved) activities of the firm? Generally, Regulation 14A permits management to exclude matters that fall within the ordinary business of the corporation (Rule 14a-8 (i)(7)). Suppose, for example, that the corporation decides to buy from the cheapest available source, a foreign supplier. Assume that this source is suspected of using prison labor and that a shareholder group believes this is immoral and bad business. (They argue the corporation will suffer long-term reputational damage.) Can these shareholders include a precatory resolution in the company's proxy demanding that it cease doing business with the foreign source under Regulation 14A?

While the SEC has generally supported governance proposals, it has waffled on social responsibility proposals. In 1991, it strayed from its earlier policy, under which the (then current) Rule 14a-8(c)(7) required issuers to include proposals that related to "matters which have significant policy, economic or other implications in them." In a 1991 no-action letter to the Cracker Barrel Old Country Store, Inc., the SEC agreed that Cracker Barrel could omit a shareholder proposal calling on the board to prohibit employment discrimination based on sexual orientation. The SEC asserted that it could not easily determine which employment-related matters fell within the "ordinary business exclusion" and would therefore permit the exclusion of all such proposals.

However, in July 1997, the SEC proposed changes to Rule 14a-8, including a reversal of its *Cracker Barrel* policy and a return to its previous interpretation of the "ordinary business" exclusion with respect to a company's personnel policies. Consider the SEC's explanation.

THE INTERPRETATION OF RULE 14a-8(c)(7): THE "ORDINARY BUSINESS" EXCLUSION

When adopted in 1953, the "ordinary business" exclusion had a fairly straightforward mission: to "relieve the management of the necessity of including in its proxy material security holder proposals which relate to matters falling within the province of management."

That mission became more complicated with the emergence of proposals focusing on social policy issues beginning in the late 1960s. As drafted, the rule provided no guidance on how to analyze proposals relating simultaneously to both an "ordinary business" matter and a significant social policy issue.

In 1976, the Commission considered revisions to the "ordinary business" exclusion, hoping to fashion more workable language distinguishing between "mundane" business matters and "important" ones. It declined to adopt the new language after commentators expressed concern that the new language might be overly restrictive and difficult to apply. In lieu of adopting revisions, the Commission stated that it would apply the exclusion in a "somewhat more flexible manner."

In applying the "ordinary business" exclusion to proposals relating to social policy issues, the Division applies the most well-reasoned standards possible, given the complexity of the task. From time to time, in light of experience dealing with proposals in particular subject areas, it adjusts its approach. Over the years, for instance, the Division has in several instances reversed its position on the excludability of proposals involving plant closings, the manufacture of tobacco products, executive compensation, and golden parachutes.

Another of these interpretive adjustments is a subject of today's proposals. In a 1992 no-action letter issued to the Cracker Barrel Old Country Stores, Inc., the Division announced that the fact that a shareholder proposal concerning a company's employment policies and practices for the general workforce is tied to a social issue will no longer be viewed as removing the proposal from the realm of ordinary business operations of the registrant. Rather, determinations with respect to any such proposals are properly governed by the employment-based nature of the proposal. . . .

The *Cracker Barrel* interpretation has been controversial since it was announced.[71] While the reasons for adopting the *Cracker Barrel* interpretation continue to have some validity, as well as significant support in the corporate community,[72] we believe that reversal of the position is warranted in light of the broader package of reforms proposed today. Reversal will require companies to include proposals in their proxy materials that some shareholders believe are important to companies and fellow shareholders. . . . That is, employment-related proposals focusing on significant social policy issues could not automatically be excluded under the "ordinary business" exclusion.

Under this proposal, the "bright line" approach for employment-related proposals established by the *Cracker Barrel* position would be replaced by the case-by-case analysis that prevailed previously. Return to a case-by-case approach should redress the concerns of shareholders interested in submitting for a vote by fellow shareholders employment-related proposals raising significant social issues. . . .

Despite return to a case-by-case, analytical approach, some types of proposals raising social policy issues may continue to raise difficult interpretive questions. For instance, reversal of the *Cracker Barrel* position would

71. Shortly after its announcement, the New York City Employees Retirement System unsuccessfully challenged the Commission's authority to adopt the position. See *New York City Employees' Retirement System v. SEC*, 843 F. Supp. 858, *rev'd* 45 F.3d 7 (2d Cir. 1995). The Amalgamated Clothing and Textiles Union successfully challenged Wal-Mart's decision to exclude an affirmative action proposal after the Division concurred that the proposal could be excluded. See *Amalgamated Clothing and Textile Workers Union v. Wal-Mart Stores, Inc.*, 821 F. Supp. 877 (S.D.N.Y. 1993). During the last proxy season, we declined proponents' requests that we review three Division no-action responses implicating the interpretation, and concerning companies' affirmative action policies and practices. Commissioner Wallman dissented, and issued a dissenting statement.

72. In response to the Questionnaire, 91% of companies favored excluding employment-related shareholder proposals raising significant social policy issues under the *Cracker Barrel* interpretation. 86% percent of shareholders thought such proposals should be included.

not automatically result in the inclusion of proposals focusing on wage and other issues for companies' operations in the Maquiladora region of Mexico, or on "workplace practices."

Finally, we believe that it would be useful to summarize the principal considerations in the Division's application of the "ordinary business" exclusion. These considerations would continue to impact our reasoning even if the proposals are adopted. The general underlying policy of this exclusion is consistent with the policy of most state corporate laws: to confine the resolution of ordinary business problems to management and the board of directors since it is impracticable for shareholders to decide how to solve such problems. . . .

The policy underlying the rule includes two central considerations. The first relates to the subject matter of the proposal. Certain tasks are so fundamental to management's ability to run a company on a day-to-day basis that they could not, as a practical matter, be subject to direct shareholder oversight. Examples include the management of the workforce, such as the hiring, promotion and termination of employees, decisions on production quality and quantity, and the retention of suppliers. However, proposals relating to such matters but focusing on significant social policy issues generally would not be considered to be excludable, because such issues typically fall outside the scope of management's prerogative.

The second consideration relates to the degree to which the proposal seeks to "micro manage" the company by probing too deeply into "matters of a complex nature that shareholders, as a group, would not be qualified to make an informed judgment on, due to their lack of business expertise and lack of intimate knowledge of the (company's) business." This consideration may come into play in a number of circumstances, such as where the proposal seeks intricate detail, or seeks to impose specific time-frames or methods for implementing complex policies . . .

In 1998, the SEC adopted the proposed amendments described above and withdrew the *Cracker Barrel* no-action letter. Thus, the commission returned to a "case-by-case analytic" for determining whether issues relating to employment practices were excludable as ordinary business matters or whether they were sufficiently important to the company to be an appropriate subject of a Rule 14a-8 resolution. See SEC Release No. 34-40018, Fed. Sec. L. Rep. (CCH) ¶86,018.

7.9.3   Rule 14a-9: The Antifraud Rule

As we will see in later chapters, private suits by investors alleging injury as a result of a violation of the federal securities laws have, over the last 40 years, emerged as an important device for enforcing these laws. Congress did not create most of the provisions of private rights of action that are important today. Only the SEC is expressly authorized to enforce the securities acts and the rules adopted under them. The federal courts, however, have implied private rights of action under the securities acts, starting modestly in 1946 (see the *Kardon* case, implying a private right of action under Rule 10b-5, discussed in Chapter 14) and accelerating markedly in the 1960s. The Supreme Court of the United States addressed the question of whether a private right of action arose under §14(a) and Rule 14a-9 in the 1964 case of *J.I. Case v. Borak*, 337 U.S. 426. The Court held that such a right of action exists and began the process of delineating all of its elements.

The golden age of implied private rights of action under the federal securities laws ended when the Supreme Court established a more restrictive test for implying such private remedies in *Cort v. Ash*, 422 U.S. 66 (1975). Under this test, an implied right must satisfy three criteria: "First is the plaintiff one of the class for whose *especial* benefit the statute was enacted?... Second, is there any indication of legislative intent, explicit or implicit, either to create such a remedy or deny one?... And finally, is the cause of action one traditionally relegated to state law, in an area basically the concern of the States, so that it would be inappropriate to infer a cause of action based solely on federal law." *Id.* at 78. Since *Cort*, the Supreme Court has been ambivalent toward implied private rights of action. This ambivalence is especially clear in cases construing private remedies under Rule 10b-5, which we address at length in Chapter 14, but it also marks litigation under Rule 14a-9 — the antifraud rule governing proxy solicitations.

Proxy Rule 14a-9 is the SEC's general proscription against false or misleading proxy solicitations. It is one of the half-dozen antifraud rules in federal securities legislation that supports much of the plaintiff's bar and an enormous edifice of federal case law. (We encounter two other such rules later in dealing with tender offers (Chapter 12) and misrepresentation generally (Chapter 14).)

As with any implied right of action, recognizing the right is only a first step. The devil is in the details of working out the elements of the right and limiting the scope of the new action without legislative guidance. In the case of Rule 14(a)-9, a series of Supreme Court decisions has established the key elements, roughly following the pattern of common law fraud. These elements include the following:

a. *Materiality.* A misrepresentation or omission in a proxy solicitation can trigger liability only if it is "material," that is, "there is a substantial likelihood that a reasonable shareholder would consider it important in deciding how to vote." *TSC Indus., Inc. v. Northway, Inc.*, 426 U.S. 438, 449 (1976).

b. *Culpability.* The Supreme Court has not yet determined a standard of culpability under Rule 14a-9. The Second and Third Circuits have adopted a negligence standard. See, e.g., *Gerstle v. Gamble-Skogmo, Inc.*, 478 F.2d 1281 (2d Cir. 1973) (Friendly, J.); *Herskowitz v. Nutri/System, Inc.*, 857 F.2d 179 (3d Cir.), *cert. denied*, 489 U.S. 1054 (1988) (bank). The Sixth Circuit has required proof of scienter (intentionality or extreme recklessness). See *Adams v. Standard Knitting Mills, Inc.*, 623 F.2d 422 (6th Cir.), *cert. denied sub nom. Adams v. Peat Marwick, Mitchell & Co.*, 449 U.S. 1067 (1980).

c. *Causation and Reliance.* The Supreme Court has ruled that, unlike a traditional case of fraud, a plaintiff need not prove actual reliance on a misrepresentation to complete a Rule 14a-9 cause of action. Instead, causation of injury is presumed if a misrepresentation is material and the proxy solicitation "was an *essential link* in the accomplishment of the transaction." *Mills v. Electric Auto-Lite Co.*, 396 U.S. 375, 385 (1970) (emphasis added).

d. *Remedies.* The *Mills* Court contemplated that courts might award injunctive relief, rescission, or monetary damages. See Robert C. Clark, *Corporate Law*, §9.4.5, pp. 387-388 (1986).

Two of these elements — materiality and causation — are addressed in the *Virginia Bankshares* decision, which is the Supreme Court's most recent effort to articulate the limits of Rule 14a-9. In reading the opinion consider whether the Court's arguments are sound. Does the holding advance the purposes of Rule 14a-9, or is it undermining its effectiveness?

VIRGINIA BANKSHARES, INC. v. SANDBERG

501 U.S. 1083 (1990)

SOUTER, J.:

In *J.I. Case Co. v. Borak*, 377 U.S. 426 (1964), we first recognized an implied private right of action for the breach of §14(a) as implemented by SEC Rule 14a-9, which prohibits the solicitation of proxies by means of materially false or misleading statements.

The questions before us are whether a statement couched in conclusory or qualitative terms purporting to explain directors' reasons for recommending certain corporate action can be materially misleading within the meaning of Rule 14a-9, and whether causation of damages compensable under §14(a) can be shown by a member of a class of minority shareholders whose votes are not required by law or corporate bylaw to authorize the corporate action subject to the proxy solicitation. We hold that knowingly false statements of reasons may be actionable even though conclusory in form, but that respondents have failed to demonstrate the equitable basis required to extend the §14(a) private action to such shareholders when any indication of congressional intent to do so is lacking.

I

In December 1986, First American Bankshares, Inc., (FABI), a bank holding company, began a "freeze-out" merger, in which the First American Bank of Virginia (Bank) eventually merged into Virginia Bankshares, Inc., (VBI), a wholly owned subsidiary of FABI. VBI owned 85% of the Bank's shares, the remaining 15% being in the hands of some 2,000 minority shareholders. FABI hired the investment banking firm of Keefe, Bruyette & Woods (KBW) to give an opinion on the appropriate price for shares of the minority holders, who would lose their interests in the Bank as a result of the merger. Based on market quotations and unverified information from FABI, KBW gave the Bank's executive committee an opinion that $42 a share would be a fair price for the minority stock. The executive committee approved the merger proposal at that price, and the full board followed suit.

Although Virginia law required only that such a merger proposal be submitted to a vote at a shareholders' meeting, and that the meeting be preceded by circulation of a statement of information to the shareholders, the directors nevertheless solicited proxies for voting on the proposal at the annual meeting set for April 21, 1987. In their solicitation, the directors urged the proposal's adoption and stated they had approved the plan because of its opportunity for the minority shareholders to achieve a "high" value, which they elsewhere described as a "fair" price, for their stock.

Although most minority shareholders gave the proxies requested, respondent Sandberg did not, and after approval of the merger she sought damages in the United States District Court for the Eastern District of Virginia from VBI, FABI, and the directors of the Bank. She pleaded two counts, one for soliciting proxies in violation of §14(a) and Rule 14a-9, and the other for breaching fiduciary duties owed to the minority shareholders under state law. Under the first count, Sandberg alleged, among other things, that the directors had not believed that the price offered was high or that the terms of the merger were fair, but had recommended the merger only because they believed they had no alternative if they wished to remain on the board. . . .

The jury's verdicts were for Sandberg on both counts, after finding violations of Rule 14a-9 by all defendants and a breach of fiduciary duties by the Bank's directors. The jury awarded Sandberg $18 a share, having found that she would have received $60 if her stock had been valued adequately. . . .

On appeal, the United States Court of Appeals for the Fourth Circuit affirmed the judgments. . . .

II

The Court of Appeals affirmed petitioners' liability for two statements found to have been materially misleading in violation of §14(a) of the Act, one of which was that "The Plan of Merger has been approved by the Board of Directors because it provides an opportunity for the Bank's public shareholders to achieve a high value for their shares." App. to Pet. for Cert. 53a. Petitioners argue that statements of opinion or belief incorporating indefinite and unverifiable expressions cannot be actionable as misstatements of material fact within the meaning of Rule 14a-9, and that such a declaration of opinion or belief should never be actionable when placed in a proxy solicitation incorporating statements of fact sufficient to enable readers to draw their own, independent conclusions.

A

We consider first the actionability per se of statements of reasons, opinion or belief. Because such a statement by definition purports to express what is consciously on the speaker's mind, we interpret the jury verdict as finding that the directors' statements of belief and opinion were made with knowledge that the directors did not hold the beliefs or opinions expressed, and we confine our discussion to statements so made.

That such statements may be materially significant raises no serious question. The meaning of the materiality requirement for liability under §14(a) was discussed at some length in *TSC Industries, Inc. v. Northway, Inc.*, 426 U.S. 438 (1976), where we held a fact to be material "if there is a substantial likelihood that a reasonable shareholder would consider it important in deciding how to vote." *Id.*, at 449. We think there is no room to deny that a statement of belief by corporate directors about a recommended course of action, or an explanation of their reasons for recommending it, can take on just that importance. . . .

B

But, assuming materiality, the question remains whether statements of reasons, opinions, or beliefs are statements "with respect to . . . material facts" so as to fall within the strictures of the Rule. . . .

[D]irectors' statements of reasons or belief . . . are factual in two senses: as statements that the directors do act for the reasons given or hold the belief stated and as statements about the subject matter of the reason or belief expressed. In neither sense does the proof or disproof of such statements implicate the concerns expressed in *Blue Chip Stamps.* The root of those concerns was a plaintiff's capacity to manufacture claims of hypothetical action, unconstrained by independent evidence. Reasons for directors' recommendations or statements of belief are, in contrast, characteristically matters of corporate record subject to documentation, to be supported or attacked by evidence of historical fact outside a plaintiff's control.

In this case, whether $42 was "high," and the proposal "fair" to the minority shareholders depended on whether provable facts about the Bank's assets, and about actual and potential levels of operation, substantiated a value that was above, below, or more or less at the $42 figure, when assessed in accordance with recognized methods of valuation.

Respondents adduced evidence for just such facts in proving that the statement was misleading about its subject matter and a false expression of the directors' reasons. Whereas the proxy statement described the $42 price as offering a premium above both book value and market price, the evidence indicated that a calculation of the book figure based on the appreciated value of the Bank's real estate holdings eliminated any such premium. . . . There was, indeed, evidence of a "going concern" value for the Bank in excess of $60 per share of common stock, another fact never disclosed. However conclusory the directors' statement may have been, then, it was open to attack by garden-variety evidence, subject neither to a plaintiff's control nor ready manufacture, and there was no undue risk of open-ended liability or uncontrollable litigation in allowing respondents the opportunity for recovery on the allegation that it was misleading to call $42 "high." . . .

The question arises whether disbelief, or undisclosed belief or motivation, standing alone, should be a sufficient basis to sustain an action under §14(a), absent proof by the sort of objective evidence described above that the statement also expressly or impliedly asserted something false or misleading about its subject matter. We think that proof of mere disbelief or belief undisclosed should not suffice for liability under §14(a), and if nothing more had been required or proven in this case we would reverse for that reason. . . .

III

The second issue before us, left open in *Mills v. Electric Auto-Lite Co.*, 396 U.S., at 385, n.7, is whether causation of damages compensable through the implied private right of action under §14(a) can be demonstrated by a member of a class of minority shareholders whose votes are not required by law or corporate bylaw to authorize the transaction giving rise to the claim. . . .

. . . The *Mills* Court . . . held that causation of damages by a material proxy misstatement could be established by showing that minority proxies necessary and sufficient to authorize the corporate acts had been given in accordance with the tenor of the solicitation, and the Court described such a causal relationship by calling the proxy solicitation an "essential link in the accomplishment of the transaction." . . .

In this case, respondents address *Mills'* open question by proffering two theories that the proxy solicitation addressed to them was an "essential link" under the *Mills* causation test. They argue, first, that a link existed and was essential simply because VBI and FABI would have been unwilling to proceed with the merger without the approval manifested by the minority shareholders' proxies, which would not have been obtained without the solicitation's express misstatements and misleading omissions. On this reasoning, the causal connection would depend on a desire to avoid bad shareholder or public relations, and the essential character of the causal link would stem not from the enforceable terms of the parties' corporate relationship, but from one party's apprehension of the ill will of the other.

In the alternative, respondents argue that the proxy statement was an essential link . . . because it was the means to satisfy a state statutory requirement of minority shareholder approval, as a condition for saving the merger from voidability resulting from a conflict of interest on the part of one of the Bank's directors, Jack Beddow, who voted in favor of the merger while also serving as a director of FABI. . . . On this theory, causation would depend on the use of the proxy statement for the purpose of obtaining votes sufficient to bar a minority shareholder from commencing proceedings to declare the merger void. . . .

A

Blue Chip Stamps set an example worth recalling as a preface to specific policy analysis of the consequences of recognizing respondents' first theory, that a desire to avoid minority shareholders' ill will should suffice to justify recognizing the requisite causality of a proxy statement needed to garner that minority support. It will be recalled that in *Blue Chip Stamps* we raised concerns about the practical consequences of allowing recovery, under §10(b) of the Act and Rule 10b-5, on evidence of what a merely hypothetical buyer or seller might have done on a set of facts that never occurred, and foresaw that any such expanded liability would turn on "hazy" issues inviting self-serving testimony, strike suits, and protracted discovery, with little chance of reasonable resolution by pretrial process. . . . These were good reasons to deny recognition to such claims in the absence of any apparent contrary congressional intent.

The same threats of speculative claims and procedural intractability are inherent in respondents' theory of causation linked through the directors' desire for a cosmetic vote. Causation would turn on inferences about what the corporate directors would have thought and done without the minority shareholder approval unneeded to authorize action. . . .

B

The theory of causal necessity derived from the requirements of Virginia law dealing with postmerger ratification seeks to identify the essential character of the proxy solicitation from its function in obtaining the minority approval that would preclude a minority suit attacking the merger. . . . [T]his theory of causation rests upon the proposition . . . that §14(a) should provide a federal remedy whenever a false or misleading proxy statement results in the loss under state law of a shareholder plaintiff's state remedy for the enforcement of a state right. Respondents agree with the suggestions of counsel for the SEC and FDIC that causation be recognized, for example, when a minority shareholder has been induced by a misleading proxy statement to forfeit a state-law right to an appraisal remedy by voting to approve a transaction. . . .

This case does not, however, require us to decide whether §14(a) provides a cause of action for lost state remedies, since there is no indication . . . that the proxy solicitation resulted in any such loss. The contrary appears to be the case. Assuming the soundness of respondents' characterization of the proxy statement as materially misleading, the very terms of the Virginia statute indicate that a favorable minority vote induced by the solicitation would not suffice to render the merger invulnerable to later attack on the ground of the conflict. The statute bars a shareholder from seeking to avoid a transaction tainted by a director's conflict if, inter alia, the minority shareholders ratified the transaction following disclosure of the material facts of the transaction and the conflict. Va. Code §13.1-691(A)(2) (1989). Assuming that the material facts about the merger and Beddow's interests were not accurately disclosed, the minority votes were inadequate to ratify the merger under state law, and there was no loss of state remedy to connect the proxy solicitation with harm to minority shareholders irredressable under state law. . . .

KENNEDY, J. (concurring in part and dissenting in part). . . .

The severe limits the Court places upon possible proof of nonvoting causation in a §14(a) private action are justified neither by our precedents nor any case in the courts of appeals.

To the extent the Court's analysis considers the purposes underlying §14(a), it does so with the avowed aim to limit the cause of action and with undue emphasis upon fears of "speculative claims and procedural intractability." Ante, at 20. The result is a sort of guerrilla warfare to restrict a well-established implied right of action. . . .

The Court seems to assume, based upon the footnote in *Mills* reserving the question, that [the respondent] bears a special burden to demonstrate causation because the public shareholders held only 15 percent of the Bank's stock. . . .

The Court's distinction presumes that a majority shareholder will vote in favor of management's proposal even if proxy disclosure suggests that the transaction is unfair to minority shareholders or that the board of directors or majority shareholder are in breach of fiduciary duties to the minority. . . . Of course, when the majority shareholder dominates the voting process, as was the case here, it may prefer to avoid the embarrassment of voting against its own proposal and so may cancel the meeting of shareholders at which the vote was to have been taken. For practical purposes, the result is the same: because of full disclosure the transaction does not go forward and the resulting injury to minority shareholders is avoided. The Court's distinction between voting and nonvoting causation does not create clear legal categories. . . .

There is no authority whatsoever for limiting §14(a) to protecting [only] those minority shareholders whose numerical strength could permit them to vote down a proposal. One of Section 14(a)'s "chief purposes is 'the protection of investors.'" *J.I. Case Co. v. Borak*, 377 U.S., at 432. Those who lack the strength to vote down a proposal have all the more need of disclosure. The voting process involves not only casting ballots but also the formulation and withdrawal of proposals, the minority's right to block a vote through court action or the threat of adverse consequences, or the negotiation of an increase in price. The proxy rules support this deliberative process. These practicalities can result in causation sufficient to support recovery.

The facts in the case before us prove this point. [The respondent] argues that had all the material facts been disclosed, FABI or the Bank likely would have withdrawn or revised the merger proposal. The evidence in the record . . . meets any reasonable requirement of specific and nonspeculative proof.

FABI wanted a "friendly transaction" with a price viewed as "so high that any reasonable shareholder will accept it." App. 99. Management expressed concern that the transaction result in "no loss of support for the bank out in the community, which was important." *Id.*, at 109. . . .

The theory that FABI would not have pursued the transaction if full disclosure had been provided and the shareholders had realized the inadequacy of the price is supported not only by the trial testimony but also by notes of the meeting of the Bank's board which approved the merger. . . .

. . . Directors of the Bank testified they would not have voted to approve the transaction if the price had been demonstrated unfair to the minority. Further, approval by the Bank's board of directors was facilitated by FABI's representation that the transaction also would be approved by the minority shareholders.

These facts alone suffice to support a finding of causation, but here . . . more evidence [was available] to link the nondisclosure with completion of the merger. FABI executive Robert Altman and Bank Chairman Drewer met on the day before the shareholders meeting when the vote was taken. Notes produced by petitioners suggested that Drewer, who had received some shareholder objections to the $42 price, considered postponing the meeting and obtaining independent advice on valuation. Altman persuaded him to go forward without any of these cautionary measures. . . .

Though I would not require a shareholder to present such evidence of causation, this case itself demonstrates that nonvoting causation theories are quite plausible where the misstatement or omission is material and the damage sustained by minority shareholders is serious. . . .

The majority avoids the question whether a plaintiff may prove causation by demonstrating that the misrepresentation or omission deprived her of a state law remedy. I do not think the question difficult, as the whole point of federal proxy rules is to support state law principles of corporate governance. Nor do I think that the Court can avoid this issue if it orders judgment for petitioners. The majority asserts that respondents show no loss of a state law remedy, because if "the material facts of the transaction and Beddow's interest were not accurately disclosed, then the minority votes were inadequate to ratify the merger under Virginia law." Ante, at 22. This theory requires us to conclude that the Virginia statute governing director conflicts of interest, Va. Code §13.1-691(A)(2) (1989), incorporates the same definition of materiality as the federal proxy rules. I find no support for that proposition. If the definitions are not the same, then Sandberg may have lost her state law remedy. For all we know, disclosure to the minority shareholders that the price is $42 per share may satisfy Virginia's requirement. If that is the case, then approval by the minority without full disclosure may have deprived Sandberg of the ability to void the merger. . . .

I would affirm the judgment of the Court of Appeals.

7.10   STATE DISCLOSURE LAW: FIDUCIARY DUTY OF CANDOR

In Chapter 9, we dilate on the directors' and officers' fiduciary duty of loyalty to the corporation and, in some circumstances, to its shareholders. Among the aspects of loyalty is, naturally enough, the obligation not to lie to one to whom the duty extends. Until recently, state law did not go beyond this in regulating communications between directors and shareholders (at least where there was no conflicting interest between the corporation and the director). Thus, state law has traditionally done little to regulate proxy solicitation by management. A plaintiff could always charge the common law tort of fraud if she could prove all of its difficult elements — a knowingly false statement of a material fact, relied upon, with the effect of causing injury. But corporate law itself offered no real assistance to shareholders when their own management sought to solicit their proxies.

Now, however, matters stand differently. Corporation law has evolved since the enactment of the Securities Exchange Act in 1934. Throughout the twentieth century, two large themes stand out. The first is the gradual disappearance of substantive regulation: no more par value for stock, no more required shareholder preemption rights, and no more right to continue an equity interest in the corporation or its successor in a merger. These and similar developments have rendered the corporate form more flexible (or, from a different perspective, more empty). The second theme is the growing importance of fiduciary duties. Courts have gradually become more willing to insert themselves ex post into disputes between shareholders and corporate managers. One example of this is a new, duty-based law of corporate disclosure.

In 1976, the Delaware Supreme Court held that a controlling shareholder making a cash tender offer for stock held by minority shareholders had a fiduciary duty to make full disclosure of all germane facts. See *Lynch v. Vickers Energy Corp.*, 383 A.2d 278 (Del. 1977). There followed a long series of cases applying this principle to corporate directors (e.g., *In re Anderson Clayton Shareholders Litigation*, 519 A.2d 680, 688 (Del. Ch. 1986)) as well as controlling shareholders. The principle was applied to proxy solicitations as well as tender offers. See, e.g., *Kahn v. Roberts*, 679 A.2d 460 (Del. 1996) (collecting cases).

Until recently, most of the Delaware cases minimized potential conflict between state corporate law and the massive body of federal regulatory and judicial law governing corporate disclosure. They did so in two ways. First, they crafted the state law duty of candor to look like the federal law that preceded it. The basic obligation is the same — to make full disclosure of all material facts, with materiality being similarly defined. Of course, this basic similarity does not ensure identical legal duties in all cases. See Lawrence A. Hamermesh, *Calling Off the Lynch Mob: A Corporate Director's Fiduciary Duty to Disclose*, 49 Vand. L. Rev. 1087 (1996).

Second, the Court of Chancery minimized potential conflict with federal law by limiting the fiduciary duty of candor to circumstances in which a corporation (or a controlling shareholder) asked shareholders to take action of some sort. This meant that mere press releases or other public statements by corporate directors or officers, without a concomitant call for shareholder action, did not violate the duty of candor. The rationale for this limitation was that the state law was concerned with the governance of the corporation, not with disclosures to the market. That is the subject of the federal securities laws.

However, in *Malone v. Brincat*, 722 A.2d 5 (Del. 1998), the Delaware Supreme Court abandoned this limitation. *Malone* was pleaded as a case involving a long-term fraud in which the directors made (or permitted the corporation to make) false filings with the SEC and distributed false financial statements to shareholders. These false statements were alleged to have caused the complete ruin of the company. The Court of Chancery dismissed the suit in deference to SEC regulation of fraud in the public markets. The Delaware Supreme Court affirmed the dismissal of the complaint but stated a different view of the merits that permitted the plaintiffs to replead. In its decision, the Supreme Court asserted: "Whenever directors communicate publicly or directly with shareholders about the corporation's affairs, with or without request for shareholder actions directors have a fiduciary duty . . . to exercise care, good faith and loyalty. . . . [T]he sine qua non of director's fiduciary duty is honesty." 722 A.2d 10. Thus, the Court held that a claim could be stated on the *Malone* facts. Plaintiffs were given right to replead their claim as a derivative claim or an individual claim.

The court was mindful of the potential overlap with federal law that its ruling might entail. It cited an earlier case in which it declined to recognize a "fraud on the market" theory of recovery for shareholders. More important though, it implied that the cause of action that it recognized in *Malone* was restricted to plaintiffs who still held their shares. Since these shareholders did not sell their shares, the Delaware court stated that they would not be protected by SEC Rule 10b-5 — the principal federal antifraud provision regulating misleading disclosure in the public markets. Thus, the court attempted to minimize conflict between its holding and federal law.

8

NORMAL GOVERNANCE: THE DUTY OF CARE

8.1 INTRODUCTION TO THE DUTY OF CARE

The shareholders' right to elect directors is not the law's only strategy for corporate governance. Fiduciary standards also play a role in normal governance, just as they do in agency and partnership law.[1] The duties of a fiduciary—whether a trustee, a partner, or a corporate director—are essentially three. The first and most basic, sometimes called the "duty of obedience," is that a fiduciary must act consistently with the legal documents that create her authority.[2] Thus, if a corporation's charter charges its directors with certain tasks, such as holding an annual meeting on a fixed date, these directors may face liability for failing to do as they are asked, even if they act in good faith.

The other two duties of fiduciaries in general are the judicially created duties of loyalty and care (or attention). The duty of loyalty (which we address in Chapter 9) requires that corporate fiduciaries exercise their authority in a good-faith attempt to advance corporate purposes. In particular, it bars corporate officers and directors from competing with the corporation; from appropriating its property, information, or business opportunities; and especially from transacting business with it on unfair terms. These requirements account for much of the mandatory content of U.S. corporate law.

---

1. As we noted in Chapter 2, examples of fiduciary relationships in the law include the relationship between a trustee and *cestui que trust* (i.e., the beneficiary), between a guardian and her ward, and between an executor and the estate. These relationships may be regarded as classical or pure fiduciary relationships because they involve both the exercise of legal power by one over property that he or she does not equitably own and relationships of dependency. For example, the settlor of a trust may well be dead and the beneficiary may be not legally of age or may be incompetent when the opportunity to misbehave presents itself to the trustee. In the case of a decedent's estate, those legally entitled to succeed to the decedent's property may not even know they are beneficiaries of a will. Another class of relationships that have traditionally been treated as fiduciary in character may not have the same degree of dependency, but they still present the same condition of trust. These relationships include the agent's relationship with his principal, the relationship between partners, and the relationship between directors and the corporation.

2. See Restatement Agency (Third) §§8.07, 8.09.

By contrast, the duty of care reaches every aspect of an officer's or director's conduct, since, in its classic formulation, it requires these parties to act with "the care of an ordinarily prudent person in the same or similar circumstances." Despite its sweeping scope, however, the duty of care is litigated much less than the duty of loyalty, primarily because the law insulates officers and directors from liability based on negligence (as opposed to knowing misconduct) in order to avoid inducing risk-averse management of the firm. In this chapter, we address both the duty of care and the insulating law that mitigates its effects on directors and officers. First, however, we offer a brief excursus on the evolution of fiduciary duties at common law.

8.2 THE DUTY OF CARE AND THE NEED TO MITIGATE DIRECTOR RISK AVERSION

From the beginnings of Anglo-American corporate law, courts have maintained that a corporate director must do more than pursue the corporation's interests in good faith; she also has the duty to act as a reasonable person would in overseeing the company's operations.

An English Court of Chancery case decided in 1742 evidences the foundational nature of the duty of care. The report relates that the King chartered the Charitable Company in the early eighteenth century as a stock company, "to assist poor persons with sums of money by way of loans, and to prevent their falling into the hands of pawnbrokers, &c."[3] It appears that the chief administrative officer of the corporation, with two confederates, soon began to defraud the company by "lending [] more money upon old pledges, without calling in the first sum lent." "The loss which ensued from this mismanagement [was] prodigious ... not less than 350,000 [pounds]." The liability of those actively engaged in the fraud was easily established by the Lord Chancellor. The more subtle question concerned the possible liability of the "committee-men" (directors), who had not participated in the wrongs, but whose inattention had permitted them to occur. As to them, the Lord Chancellor held that "by accepting of a trust of this sort a person is obligated to execute it with fidelity and reasonable diligence; and it is no excuse to say that they had no benefit from it. . . ."[4] Although we do not know if the directors were forced to pay damages, we do know that the Chancellor appointed a master to determine whether they had acted with reasonable diligence. This much establishes that a director's duty of "reasonable diligence" has been a feature of corporate law for a long time.[5]

---

3. *The Charitable Company v. Sutton*, 2 Atk. 400, 406 (Ch. 1742), 26 Eng. Reps. 642 (1742).

4. Id., 26 Eng. Reps. at 645.

5. See, e.g., *Godbold v. Branch Bank*, 11 Ala. 191 (1847); *Hodges v. New England Screw* Co., 1 R.I. 312 (1850); *Bates v. Dresser*, 251 U.S. 524 (1920) (Holmes, J.). It is notable that *Sutton* is not a case in which a loss resulted from a board decision; rather, it was a neglect of attention case. The cases of inattention, rather than poor judgment, are the cases in which one would traditionally find directors liable for breach of care.

How does the law currently express this basic obligation? According to the American Law Institute's (ALI's) Principles of Corporate Governance, a corporate director or officer is required to perform his or her functions (1) in good faith, (2) in a manner that he or she reasonably believes to be in the best interests of the corporation, and (3) with the care that an ordinarily prudent person would reasonably be expected to exercise in a like position and under similar circumstances.[6] The core of this standard is the level of care that we expect would be exercised by an ordinarily prudent person.[7] This formulation appears to make the duty of care into a negligence rule like any other negligence rule in tort law. However, the duty of care is not just another negligence rule. As we discuss below, there is an important policy reason why a business loss cannot be analogized to a traffic accident or a slip on a banana peel. The reason, bluntly stated, is that corporate directors and officers invest other people's money. They bear the full costs of any personal liability, but they receive only a small fraction of the gains from a risky decision. Liability under a negligence standard therefore would predictably discourage officers and directors from undertaking valuable but risky projects.

Consider the following excerpt from a Delaware Court of Chancery opinion.

GAGLIARDI v. TRIFOODS INTERNATIONAL, INC.

683 A.2d 1049 (Del. Ch. 1996)

ALLEN, C.:

Currently before the Court is a motion to dismiss a shareholders action against the directors of TriFoods International, Inc. . . . In broadest terms the motion raises the question, what must a shareholder plead in order to state a derivative claim to recover corporate losses allegedly sustain[ed] by reason of "mismanagement" unaffected by directly conflicting financial interests? . . .

I start with what I take to be an elementary precept of corporation law: in the absence of facts showing self-dealing or improper motive, a corporate officer or director is not legally responsible to the corporation for losses that may be suffered as a result of a decision that an officer made or that directors authorized in good faith. There is a theoretical exception to this general statement that holds that some decisions may be so "egregious" that liability for losses they cause may follow even in the absence of proof of conflict of interest or improper motivation. The exception,

---

6. See ALI, Principles of Corporate Governance §4.01 (1994). See also RMBCA §8.30.

7. As of 2005, forty jurisdictions required that a corporate director discharge the duties of that office in good faith and with a stated standard of care, usually phrased in terms of the care that an ordinarily prudent person would exercise under similar circumstances. Thirty-five of these jurisdictions also expressly required that a director perform these duties in a manner that she reasonably believes to be in the best interests of the corporation. See 3 Model Bus. Corp. Act Annot. §8.30, at 8-178 (2005).

however, has resulted in no awards of money judgments against corporate officers or directors in this jurisdiction. . . .

The rule could rationally be no different. Shareholders can diversify the risks of their corporate investments. Thus, it is in their economic interest for the corporation to accept in rank order all positive net present value investment projects available to the corporation, starting with the highest risk adjusted rate of return first. Shareholders don't want (or shouldn't rationally want) directors to be risk averse. . . .

[But] directors of public companies typically have a very small proportionate ownership interest in their corporations and little or no incentive compensation. Thus, they enjoy (as residual owners) only a very small proportion of any "upside" gains earned by the corporation on risky investment projects. If, however, corporate directors were to be found liable for a corporate loss from a risky project on the ground that the investment was too risky (foolishly risky! stupidly risky! egregiously risky! — you supply the adverb), their liability would be joint and several for the whole loss (with I suppose a right of contribution). Given the scale of operation of modern public corporations, . . . only a very small probability of director liability based on "negligence", "inattention", "waste", etc., could induce a board to avoid authorizing risky investment projects to any extent! Obviously, it is in the shareholders' economic interest to offer sufficient protection to directors from liability for negligence, etc., to allow directors to conclude that, as a practical matter, there is no risk that, if they act in good faith and meet minimal proceduralist standards of attention, they can face liability as a result of a business loss.

The law protects shareholder investment interests against the uneconomic consequences that the presence of such second-guessing risk would have on director action and shareholder wealth in a number of ways. It authorizes corporations to pay for director and officer liability insurance and authorizes corporate indemnification in a broad range of cases, for example. But the first protection against a threat of sub-optimal risk acceptance is the so-called business judgment rule. That "rule" in effect provides that where a director is independent and disinterested, there can be no liability for corporate loss, unless the facts are such that no person could possibly authorize such a transaction if he or she were attempting in good faith to meet their duty. . . .

As *Gagliardi* states, the law protects corporate officers and directors from liability for breach of the duty of care in many ways, some statutory and some judicial. First, the statutory law authorizes corporations to *indemnify the expenses* (including in some cases the judgment costs) incurred by officers or directors who are sued by reason of their corporate activities. See, e.g., DGCL §145. Second, the statutory law authorizes corporations to purchase liability insurance for their directors and officers, which may even cover some risks that are not subject to indemnification. Third, courts have long evolved the protection of the so-called business judgment rule, as we discuss below. And last, when in 1985 it was seen that the protection of the business judgment rule was not as far reaching as had been thought,[8] legislatures across the country followed Delaware's lead by specifically authorizing companies to waive director (and sometimes officer) liability for acts of negligence or gross negligence. We discuss these statutes, such as DGCL §102(b)(7), below.

8.3   STATUTORY TECHNIQUES FOR LIMITING DIRECTOR AND OFFICER RISK EXPOSURE

The judge-made business judgment rule, which we discuss in §8.4, is the most fundamental protection against liability for simple mistakes of judgment. But the statutory power to indemnify losses of corporate officers or directors for expenses (including attorneys' fees and even in some cases judgments), as well as the statutory authority allowing corporations to purchase insurance for directors and officers, provides officers and directors with the most reliable protection.

8.3.1   Indemnification

Consider indemnification first: Most corporate statutes prescribe mandatory indemnification rights for directors and officers and allow an even broader range of elective indemnification rights. Generally, these statutes authorize corporations to commit to reimburse any agent, employee, officer, or director for reasonable expenses for losses of any sort (attorneys' fees, investigation fees, settlement amounts, and in some instances judgments) arising from any actual or threatened judicial proceeding or investigation. The only limits are that the losses must result from actions undertaken on behalf of the corporation in good faith and that they cannot arise from a criminal conviction. See DGCL §145 (a), (b), (c).

WALTUCH v. CONTICOMMODITY SERVICES, INC.

88 F.3d 87 (2nd Cir. 1996)

JACOBS, Cir. J.:

Famed silver trader Norton Waltuch spent $2.2 million in unreimbursed legal fees to defend himself against numerous civil lawsuits and an enforcement proceeding brought by the Commodity Futures Trading Commission (CFTC). In this action under Delaware law, Waltuch seeks indemnification of his legal expenses from his former employer. The district court denied any indemnity, and Waltuch appeals.

As vice-president and chief metals trader for Conticommodity Services, Inc., Waltuch traded silver for the firm's clients, as well as for his

---

8. The case of *Smith v. Van Gorkom*, discussed below, was the occasion for this realization.

NORTON WALTUCH

Norton Waltuch graduated from New Jersey's Fairleigh Dickinson University in the mid-1950s. As a young finance clerk, he became fascinated with the growing futures market and, determined to learn every aspect of the business, took an entry-level position with a futures trading firm.[9] He rose through the ranks of the futures industry and by 1970, at the age of 37, was managing the New York office of ContiCommodity Services. In 1979, Waltuch began placing large bets on the silver futures market on behalf of himself and his wealthy Saudi Arabian clients. His animated behavior on the floor of the New York Commodity Exchange (COMEX) brought attention to his dramatic bids. At the same time, billionaire oil heirs Bunker and Herbert Hunt were also making large investments in silver futures. Together, the Hunts and Waltuch pushed the price of silver to dizzying heights. In a few months, the price of silver climbed from under $10 to an astonishing $50 per ounce. As with many commodities markets, silver futures are vulnerable to the possibility of a speculator illegally "cornering" the market by purchasing a large enough quantity of contracts. Authorities began to suspect that the Hunt brothers and Waltuch were colluding in an effort to corner the silver market. In 1980, COMEX instituted strict trading regulations designed to force the Hunt brothers to sell their investments. The market's subsequent collapse culminated in a 50 percent decline in value on March 27, 1980, a date known as "Silver Thursday."

The silver bubble financially ruined many hapless investors and sent tremors through the banking industry. The Hunt brothers declared bankruptcy and Bunker Hunt was convicted of conspiring to manipulate the market. Norton Waltuch, however, survived criminal investigations and congressional hearings relatively unscathed. Always the savvy investor, he had exited the market before the crash with a $20 million profit.

---

own account. In late 1979 and early 1980, the silver price spiked upward as the then-billionaire Hunt brothers and several of Waltuch's foreign clients bought huge quantities of silver future contracts. Just as rapidly, the price fell until (on a day remembered in trading circles as "Silver Thursday") the silver market crashed. Between 1981 and 1985, angry silver speculators filed numerous lawsuits against Waltuch and Conticommodity, alleging fraud, market manipulation, and antitrust violations. All of the suits eventually settled and were dismissed with prejudice, pursuant to settlements in which Conticommodity paid over $35 million to the various suitors. Waltuch himself was dismissed from the suits with no settlement contribution. His unreimbursed legal expenses in these actions total approximately $1.2 million.

Waltuch was also the subject of an enforcement proceeding brought by the CFTC, charging him with fraud and market manipulation. The proceeding was settled, with Waltuch agreeing to a penalty that included a $100,000 fine and a six-month ban on buying or selling futures contracts from any exchange floor. Waltuch spent $1 million in unreimbursed legal fees in the CFTC proceeding.

Waltuch brought suit in the United States District Court for the Southern District of New York against Conticommodity and its parent company,

9. Paul Sarnoff, *Silver Bulls* (1980).

Continental Grain Co. (together "Conti"), for indemnification of his unreimbursed expenses. Only two of Waltuch's claims reach us on appeal.

Waltuch first claims that Article Ninth of Conticommodity's articles of incorporation requires Conti to indemnify him for his expenses in both the private and CFTC actions. Conti responds that this claim is barred by subsection (a) of §145 of Delaware's General Corporation Law, which permits indemnification only if the corporate office acted "in good faith," something that Waltuch has not established. Waltuch counters that subsection (f) of the same statute permits a corporation to grant indemnification rights outside the limits of subsection (a), and that Conticommodity did so with Article Ninth (which has no stated good-faith limitation). The district court held that, notwithstanding §145(f), Waltuch could recover under Article Ninth only if Waltuch met the "good faith" requirement of §145 (a). On the factual issue of whether Waltuch had acted "in good faith," the court denied Conti's summary judgment motion and cleared the way for trial. The parties then stipulated that they would forgo trial on the issue of Waltuch's "good faith," agree to an entry of final judgment against Waltuch on his claim under Article Ninth and §145(f), and allow Waltuch to take an immediate appeal of the judgment to this Court. Thus, as to Waltuch's first claim, the only question left is how to interpret §§145(a) and 145(f), assuming Waltuch acted with less than "good faith." . . .

Waltuch's second claim is that subsection (c) of §145 requires Conti to indemnify him because he was "successful on the merits or otherwise" in the private lawsuits. . . .

I

Article Ninth, on which Waltuch bases his first claim, is categorical and contains no requirement of "good faith":

> The Corporation shall indemnify and hold harmless each of its incumbent or former directors, officers, employees and agents . . . against expenses actually and necessarily incurred by him in connection with the defense of any action, suit or proceeding threatened, pending or completed, in which he is made a party, by reason of his serving in or having held such position or capacity, except in relation to matters as to which he shall be adjudged in such action, suit or proceeding to be liable for negligence or misconduct in the performance of duty.

Conti argues that §145(a) of Delaware's General Corporation Law, which does contain a "good faith" requirement, fixes the outer limits of a corporation's power to indemnify; Article Ninth is thus invalid under Delaware law, says Conti, to the extent that it requires indemnification of officers who have acted in bad faith.

. . . Waltuch argues that §145(a) is not an exclusive grant of indemnification power, because §145(f) expressly allows corporations to indemnify officers in a manner broader than that set out in §145(a). Waltuch contends

that the "nonexclusivity" language in §145(f) is a separate grant of indemnification power, not limited by the good faith clause that governs the
power granted in §145(a). Conti on the other hand contends that §145(f)
must be limited to "public policies," one of which is that a corporation may
indemnify its officers only if they act in "good faith." ...

No Delaware court has decided the very issue presented here; but the
applicable cases tend to support the proposition that a corporation's grant
of indemnification rights cannot be inconsistent with the substantive statutory provisions of §145, notwithstanding §145(f). ...

The "consistency" rule suggested by [the] Delaware cases is reinforced by our reading of §145 as a whole. Subsections (a) (indemnification
for third-party actions) and (b) (similar indemnification for derivative suits)
expressly grant a corporation the power to indemnify directors, officers,
and others, if they "acted in good faith and in a manner reasonably believed
to be in or not opposed to the best interest of the corporation." These
provisions thus limit the scope of the power that they confer. They are
permissive in the sense that a corporation may exercise less than its full
power to grant the indemnification rights set out in these provisions. By the
same token, subsection (f) permits the corporation to grant additional
rights: the rights provided in the rest of §145 "shall not be deemed exclusive of any other rights to which those seeking indemnification may be
entitled." But crucially, subsection (f) merely acknowledges that one seeking indemnification may be entitled to "other rights" (of indemnification or
otherwise); it does not speak in terms of corporate power, and therefore
cannot be read to free a corporation from the "good faith" limit explicitly
imposed in subsections (a) and (b).

An alternative construction of these provisions would effectively force
us to ignore certain explicit terms of the statute. §145(a) gives Conti the
power to indemnify Waltuch "if he acted in good faith and in a manner
reasonably believed to be in or not opposed to the best interest of the
corporation." This statutory limit must mean that there is no power to
indemnify Waltuch if he did not act in good faith. ...

When the Legislature intended a subsection of §145 to augment the
powers limited in subsection (a), it set out the additional powers expressly.
Thus subsection (g) explicitly allows a corporation to circumvent the "good
faith" clause of subsection (a) by purchasing a directors and officers liability
insurance policy. Significantly, that subsection is framed as a grant of
corporate power:

> A corporation shall have power to purchase and maintain insurance on
> behalf of any person who is or was a director, officer, employee or
> agent of the corporation ... against any liability asserted against him
> and incurred by him in any such capacity, or arising out of his status as
> such, *whether or not the corporation would have the power to indem-
> nify him against such liability under this section.*

The italicized passage reflects the principle that corporations have the
power under §145 to indemnify in some situations and not in others. Since
§145(f) is neither a grant of corporate power nor a limitation on such

power, subsection (g) must be referring to the limitations set out in §145(a) and the other provisions of §145 that describe corporate power. . . .

Waltuch argues . . . that reading §145(a) to bar the indemnification of officers who acted in bad faith would render §145(f) meaningless. This argument misreads §145(f). . . . Delaware commentators have identified various indemnification rights that are "beyond those provided by statute," . . . and that are at the same time consistent with the statute:

> . . . For example, indemnification agreements or by-laws could provide for: (i) mandatory indemnification unless prohibited by statute; (ii) mandatory advancement of expenses, which the indemnitee can, in many instances, obtain on demand; (iii) accelerated procedures for the "determination" required by section 145(d) to be made in the "specific case"; (iv) litigation "appeal" rights of the indemnitee in the event of an unfavorable determination; (v) procedures under which a favorable determination will be deemed to have been made under circumstances where the board fails or refuses to act; [and] (vi) reasonable funding mechanisms. (E. Norman Veasey, et al., *Delaware Supports Directors With a Three-Legged Stool of Limited Liability, Indemnification, and Insurance*, 42 Bus. Law. 399, 415 (1987).)

We . . . conclude that §145(f) is not rendered meaningless . . . by the conclusion that a Delaware corporation lacks power to indemnify an officer or director "unless [he] 'acted in good faith and in a manner reasonably believed to be in or not opposed to the best interest of the corporation.'" As a result, . . . Conti's Article Ninth, which would require indemnification of Waltuch even if he acted in bad faith, is inconsistent with §145(a) and thus exceeds the scope of a Delaware corporation's power to indemnify. Since Waltuch has agreed to forgo his opportunity to prove . . . good faith, he is not entitled to indemnification under Article Ninth.

II

Unlike §145(a), which grants a discretionary indemnification power, §145(c) affirmatively requires corporations to indemnify its officers and directors for the "successful" defense of certain claims.

Waltuch argues that he was "successful on the merits or otherwise" in the private lawsuits, because they were dismissed with prejudice without any payment or assumption of liability by him. Conti argues that the claims against Waltuch were dismissed only because of Conti's $35 million settlement payments, and that this payment was contributed, in part, "on behalf of Waltuch." . . .

No Delaware court has applied §145(c) in the context of indemnification stemming from the settlement of civil litigation. One lower court, however, has applied that subsection to an analogous case in the criminal context, and has illuminated the link between "vindication" and the statutory phrase, "successful on the merits or otherwise." In *Merritt-Chapman & Scott Corp. v. Wolfson*, 321 A.2d 138 (Del.

Super. Ct. 1974), the corporation's agents were charged with several counts of criminal conduct. A jury found them guilty on some counts, but deadlocked on the others. The agents entered into a "settlement" with the prosecutor's office by pleading nolo contendere to one of the counts in exchange for the dropping of the rest. *Id.* at 140. The agents claimed entitlement to mandatory indemnification under §145(c) as to the counts that were dismissed. . . .

The court in *Merritt-Chapman & Scott Corp. v. Wolfson,* held that:

> The statute requires indemnification to the extent that the claimant "has been successful on the merits or otherwise." *Success is vindication.* In a criminal action, any result other than conviction must be considered success. *Going behind the result,* as [the corporation] attempts, is neither authorized by subsection (c) nor consistent with the presumption of innocence. *Id.* at 141 (emphasis added).

. . . Under *Merritt*'s holding, then, vindication, when used as a synonym for "success" under §145(c) does not mean moral exoneration. Escape from an adverse judgment or other detriment, for whatever reason, is determinative. According to *Merritt,* the only question a court may ask is what the result was, not why it was.

Conti's contention that, because of its $35 million settlement payments, Waltuch's settlement without payment should not really count as settlement without payment, is inconsistent with the rule in *Merritt.* Here, Waltuch was sued, and the suit was dismissed without his having paid a settlement. Under the approach taken in *Merritt,* it is not our business to ask why this result was reached. Once Waltuch achieved his settlement gratis, he achieved success "on the merits or otherwise." And as we know from *Merritt,* success is sufficient to constitute vindication (at least for the purposes of §145(c)). Waltuch's settlement thus vindicated him. . . .

This conclusion comports with the reality that civil judgments and settlements are ordinarily expressed in terms of cash rather than moral victory. . . .

For all of these reasons, we agree with Waltuch, that he is entitled to indemnification under §145(c) for his expenses pertaining to private lawsuits. . . .

QUESTION

As a matter of statutory construction, this result seems a bit of a stretch. DGCL §145(f) is textually quite independent of §145(a) according to its terms. Yet as a matter of good policy, this certainly seems like the right result. Was there another way to reach this result? For example, might the court have reasonably implied a requirement that indemnifiable actions must be taken in good-faith pursuit of the corporate interests *directly* into the company's bylaw?

8.3.2   Directors and Officers Insurance

The second important aspect of legislation designed to insulate officers and directors from liability is the provisions authorizing corporations to pay the premia on directors and officers liability insurance. See, e.g., DGCL §145(f); RMBCA §8.57. These group policies, financed by the corporation, place the financial muscle of an insurance company behind the company's pledge to make whole those directors who suffer losses as a result of their good-faith decisions.

These provisions pose an interesting question: Why do corporations purchase insurance for directors and officers rather than raising salaries and board fees and then allowing directors and officers to take the money and purchase insurance on their own accounts? We suppose, as in many aspects of this field, the answer lies in the transaction costs of contracting and in other institutional details of the environment in which this contracting occurs. While we do not claim to know the answer, we offer here some possibilities. First, D&O (directors and officers) insurance might be cheaper if the company acts as a central bargaining agent for all of its officers and directors. Second, and related, uniformity may have value in that it standardizes directors' individual risk profiles in decision-making, and avoids potentially negative signaling that would arise from directors having different levels of coverage. Third, tax law may favor firm-wide insurance coverage, since D&O insurance is a deductible expense for corporations. Or fourth, directors may under-invest in D&O insurance if left to themselves, because shareholders also benefit from D&O insurance. Of course, there is a less benign explanation as well: it may simply be that corporate purchase of D&O insurance helps to disguise the total amount of management compensation.

In early 2005, directors of WorldCom and Enron made headlines by paying out of their own pockets to settle shareholder lawsuits arising under federal securities laws. At Worldcom, the independent directors agreed to pay $18 million (20 percent of their collective net worth) toward a $54 million settlement for their role in WorldCom's $11 billion accounting fraud. At Enron, ten directors agreed to pay $13 million toward a $168 million settlement for their role in Enron's fraudulent accounting practices (but had collectively made $250 million (pre-tax) on the sale of their Enron shares). The natural question arises: where was the D&O insurance? Most academic commentators and practitioners agree that out-of-pocket liability arose in these two cases due to a "perfect storm" set of facts: both companies were bankrupt and so could not indemnify the directors; both companies had well-documented paper trails of director inattention and inaction; activist pension funds such as the New York State retirement fund were intent on making examples out of these two companies, which were the largest (WorldCom) and second-largest (Enron) bankruptcies in U.S. history; and the enormous potential liabilities in both cases could have easily exceeded the companies' D&O policies. Consistent with this "perfect storm" conclusion, Professors Black, Chefffins and Klausner report only one other case (*Van Gorkom*) in which directors actually paid out-of-pocket for either damages or legal expenses under U.S. securities law or corporate law;[10] and even this case is not really an example of out-of-pocket liability, for reasons described below.

8.4 JUDICIAL PROTECTION: THE BUSINESS JUDGMENT RULE

Long before legislatures acted to protect directors and officers from liability arising from breach of the duty of care, courts fashioned their own protection. Over roughly the past 150 years, U.S. courts have evolved the so-called business judgment rule.[11] Because corporate law is state law, there is no canonical statement of the "business judgment rule." The core idea, however, is universal: Courts should not second-guess good-faith decisions made by independent and disinterested directors. Put differently, the business judgment rule means that courts will not decide (or allow a jury to decide) whether the decisions of corporate boards are either substantively reasonable by the "reasonable prudent person" test or sufficiently well informed by the same test. In the following case, the shareholder plaintiffs had a pretty good argument that the board's decision was not "reasonably prudent." Nevertheless, the court refused to inquire whether an ordinarily prudent person would have made this same decision.

KAMIN v. AMERICAN EXPRESS CO.

54 A.2d 654 (N.Y. 1976)

GREENFIELD, J.:
In this stockholders' derivative action, the individual defendants, who are the directors of the American Express Company, move for an order dismissing the complaint for failure to state a cause of action ... and alternatively, for summary judgment. ... The complaint is brought derivatively by two minority stockholders of the American Express Company, asking for a declaration that a certain dividend in kind is a waste of corporate assets, directing the defendants not to proceed with the distribution, or, in the alternative, for monetary damages. ... It is the defendants' contention that, conceding everything in the complaint, no viable cause of action is made out.

[T]he complaint alleges that in 1972 American Express acquired for investment 1,954,418 shares of common stock of Donaldson, Lufken and Jenrette, Inc. (hereafter DLJ), a publicly traded corporation, at a cost of $29.9 million. It is further alleged that the current market value of those shares is approximately $4.0 million. On July 28, 1975, it is alleged, the Board of Directors of American Express declared a special dividend to all stockholders of record pursuant to which the shares of DLJ would be

10. Bernard S. Black, Brian R. Cheffins & Michael D. Klausner, *Outside Director Liability*, 58 Stan. L. Rev.1055 (2006).
11. See generally S. Samuel Arsht, *The Business Judgment Rule Revisited*, 8 Hofstra L. Rev. 93 (1979).

distributed in kind. Plaintiffs contend further that if American Express were to sell the DLJ shares on the market, it would sustain a capital loss of $25 million, which could be offset against taxable capital gains on other investments. Such a sale, they allege, would result in tax savings to the company of approximately $8 million, which would not be available in the case of the distribution of DLJ shares to stockholders. . . .

It is apparent that all the previously-mentioned allegations of the complaint go to the question of the exercise by the Board of Directors of business judgment in deciding how to deal with the DLJ shares. The crucial allegation which must be scrutinized to determine the legal sufficiency of the complaint is paragraph 19, which alleges:

> All of the defendant Directors engaged in or acquiesced in or negligently permitted the declaration and payment of the Dividend in violation of the fiduciary duty owed by them to Amex to care for and preserve Amex's assets in the same manner as a man of average prudence would care for his own property. . . .

[T]here is no claim of fraud or self-dealing, and no contention that there was any bad faith or oppressive conduct. The law is quite clear as to what is necessary to ground a claim for actionable wrongdoing. In actions by stockholders, which assail the acts of their directors or trustees, courts will not interfere unless the powers have been illegally or unconscientiously executed; or unless it be made to appear that the acts were fraudulent or collusive, and destructive of the rights of the stockholders. Mere errors of judgment are not sufficient as grounds for equity interference, for the powers of those entrusted with corporate management are largely discretionary. . . .

More specifically, the question of whether or not a dividend is to be declared or a distribution of some kind should be made is exclusively a matter of business judgment for the Board of Directors.

. . . Courts will not interfere with such discretion unless it be first made to appear that the directors have acted or are about to act in bad faith and for a dishonest purpose. It is for the directors to say . . . when and to what extent dividends shall be declared. . . . The statute confers upon the directors this power, and the minority stockholders are not in a position to question this right, so long as the directors are acting in good faith. . . .

Thus, a complaint must be dismissed if all that is presented is a decision to pay dividends rather than pursuing some other course of conduct. . . . Courts have more than enough to do in adjudicating legal rights and devising remedies for wrongs. The directors' room rather than the courtroom is the appropriate forum for thrashing out purely business questions which will have an impact on profits, market prices, competitive situations, or tax advantages. . . .

It is not enough to allege, as plaintiffs do here, that the directors made an imprudent decision, which did not capitalize on the possibility of using a potential capital loss to offset capital gains. More than imprudence or mistaken judgment must be shown.

Nor does this appear to be a case in which a potentially valid cause of action is inartfully stated. . . . The affidavits of the defendants and the exhibits annexed thereto demonstrate that the objections raised by the plaintiffs to the proposed dividend action were carefully considered and unanimously rejected by the Board at a special meeting called precisely for that purpose at the plaintiffs' request. The minutes of the special meeting indicate that the defendants were fully aware that a sale rather than a distribution of the DLJ shares might result in the realization of a substantial income tax saving. Nevertheless, they concluded that there were countervailing considerations primarily with respect to the adverse effect such a sale, realizing a loss of $25 million, would have on the net income figures in the American Express financial statement. Such a reduction of net income would have a serious effect on the market value of the publicly traded American Express stock. This was not a situation in which the defendant directors totally overlooked facts called to their attention. They gave them consideration, and attempted to view the total picture in arriving at their decision. While plaintiffs contend that according to their accounting consultants the loss on the DLJ stock would still have to be charged against current earnings even if the stock were distributed, the defendants' accounting experts assert that the loss would be a charge against earnings only in the event of a sale, whereas in the event of distribution of the stock as a dividend, the proper accounting treatment would be to charge the loss only against surplus. While the chief accountant for the SEC raised some question as to the appropriate accounting treatment of this transaction, there was no basis for any action to be taken by the SEC with respect to the American Express financial statement.

The only hint of self-interest which is raised . . . is that four of the twenty directors were officers and employees of American Express and members of its Executive Incentive Compensation Plan. Hence, it is suggested, by virtue of the action taken earnings may have been overstated and their compensation affected thereby. Such a claim . . . standing alone can hardly be regarded as sufficient to support an inference of self-dealing. There is no claim or showing that the four company directors dominated and controlled the sixteen outside members of the Board. Certainly, every action taken by the Board has some impact on earnings and may therefore affect the compensation of those whose earnings are keyed to profits. That does not disqualify the inside directors, nor does it put every policy adopted by the Board in question. All directors have an obligation, using sound business judgment, to maximize income for the benefit of all persons having a stake in the welfare of the corporate entity. . . . The directors are entitled to exercise their honest business judgment on the information before them, and to act within their corporate powers. That they may be mistaken, that other courses of action might have differing consequences, or that their action might benefit some shareholders more than others presents no basis for the superimposition of judicial judgment, so long as it appears that the directors have been acting in good faith. The question of to what extent a dividend shall be declared and the manner in which it shall be paid is ordinarily subject only to the qualification that the dividend be paid out of surplus (Business Corporation Law Section 510, subd. b). The Court will not interfere unless a clear case is made out of fraud, oppression, arbitrary action, or breach of trust.

... Accordingly, the motion by the defendants for summary judgment and dismissal of the complaint is granted. . . .

QUESTIONS

1. Assuming the board acted in good faith in *Kamin*, what is the board's view about the efficiency of the capital markets? If the capital markets are very highly efficient in fact, what does the *Kamin* transaction imply about the wealth-creating impact of this action?

2. The empirical literature in finance suggests that alternative accounting characterizations do not affect share price if they are made publicly and are well understood. Corporate directors and managers typically care a great deal about accounting changes that might lower reported earnings or revenues. If the studies are correct and the market sees through accounting treatments, why might businesspeople act in this way?

3. Would *Kamin* have been decided differently under §4.01(c) of ALI, Principles of Corporate Governance?

8.4.1 Understanding the Business Judgment Rule

Upon reflection, the so-called business judgment rule comes to seem a bit more mysterious than it first appears. More precisely, there are three mysteries. The first mystery is this: What exactly *is* this "rule"?

There is, as we have said, no single canonical statement of the business judgment rule. The closest one can come may be the formulation contained in the American Bar Association's Corporate Director's Guidebook, where it is said that a *decision* constitutes a valid business judgment (and gives rise to no liability for ensuing loss) when it (1) is made by *financially disinterested directors* or officers (2) who have become *duly informed* before exercising judgment and (3) who exercise judgment in a *good-faith* effort to advance corporate interests.[12] In some formulations, it is also said that the business judgment rule does not protect "irrational" or "egregious behavior."[13] However, we interpret this additional stricture as a restatement of the requirement that directors must act in good faith to enjoy the protections of the business judgment rule. Since the law cannot order directors to make correct decisions by fiat, it follows, in our view, that disinterested directors who act deliberately and in good faith should never be liable for a resulting loss, no matter how stupid their decisions may seem ex post.

---

12. See American Bar Assn., Corporate Director's Guidebook (2d ed. 1994); ALI, Corporate Governance Project §4.01(c) (1994); RMBCA §8.30.

13. E.g., ALI, Corporate Governance Project §4.01(c) (1994).

A more difficult mystery associated with the business judgment rule is why it is necessary at all. After all, if a director has no conflicting interest, is reasonably informed, and makes a good-faith judgment (by which we mean an honest judgment seeking to advance the corporation's interests), what possible basis for liability exists? The answer, we think, is that there is none — not because the business judgment rule exists but because there is no breach of directorial duty. So why have a special "business judgment rule" in the first place?

There are two reasons, we believe. The first is procedural. When courts invoke the business judgment rule, they are, in effect, converting what would otherwise be a question of fact — whether the financially disinterested directors who authorized this money-losing transaction exercised the same care as would a reasonable person in similar circumstances — into a question of law for the court to decide. Recall that courts decide questions of law, while juries ordinarily decide questions of fact. So the business judgment rule insulates disinterested directors from jury trials, which encourages the dismissal of some claims before trial and allows judicial resolution of the remaining case-based claims that go to trial.

In addition to this procedural reason, a second reason for the business judgment rule is to convert the question "Was the standard of care breached?" into the related, but different questions of whether the directors were truly disinterested and independent and whether their actions were not so extreme, unconsidered, or inexplicable as not to be an exercise of good-faith judgment. In most circumstances, courts are extremely reluctant to infer that directors lack good faith based on the outcome of board decisions.[14]

Thus, there are two ways in which the business judgment rule can be said to insulate directors from duty-of-care liability, one procedural and the other substantive. But why *should* the law have evolved to provide this additional insulation that is not available to other classes of defendants in negligence cases? Here we fall back on the analysis of directorial incentives that was introduced above in the *Gagliardi* case.

Directors who risk liability for making unreasonable decisions — or even for failing to become reasonably informed or engaging in appropriate deliberation before acting — are likely to behave in a risk-averse manner that harms shareholders. This is the reason why, once a court concludes that the case before it involves fully disinterested directors, the business judgment rule will be said to apply, and the case will be dismissed unless there is some very unusual feature that suggests possible suspect motivation.

This account of the practical effect of the business judgment rule, which we believe to be substantially correct, leads to the final mystery associated with the rule: Why bother with the duty of care at all? Why *announce* a legal duty to behave as a reasonable director would behave but *apply* a rule that *no good-faith decision* gives rise to liability as long as no financial conflict of interest is involved?

---

14. There is an exception in cases involving a change in corporate control, where directors may have an "entrenchment interest."

The answer must be that there is social value to announcing a standard ("you must act as a reasonable person would act") that is not enforced with a liability rule. But how? We suggest that when corporate lawyers charge directors with their legal duty of care, most board members will decide how to act based on several considerations, not on their risk of personal liability alone. Nonlegal sanctions such as personal reputation may affect some directors, but many more, we suspect, will be motivated by a simple desire to do the right thing without regard to self-interest. For such people, articulating the standard of care has the pedagogic function of informing them just what "doing the right thing" means under the circumstances.

8.4.2   The Duty of Care in Takeover Cases: A Note on
Smith v. Van Gorkom

One of the most interesting features of corporation law over the period 1985-2000 has been the evolution of the law of directors' and officers' duties in the context of hostile takeover attempts. This story is told in Chapter 13 but will be prefaced here. It begins with an unusual 3-2 Delaware Supreme Court decision in 1985, *Smith v. Van Gorkom*, which was met with considerable consternation by the corporate bar.[15] Most corporate law casebooks include an edited version of *Van Gorkom* in their materials on the duty of care because it treats the directors' decision to sign a merger agreement as a breach of their duty of care. Thus, the opinion announces itself to be one about the duty of care — and a unique one at that, insofar as it holds financially disinterested directors personally liable for the consequences of their business decision. By contrast, we believe that subsequent developments have shown *Smith v. Van Gorkom* to be the first in a series of cases in which the Delaware courts struggled to work out a new corporate law of corporate takeovers. Thus, *Van Gorkom* has little to teach about the duty of care in ordinary business decisions of the sort addressed by *Kamin* and *Gagliardi*. Nevertheless, because *Van Gorkom* is an important case that employs the vocabulary of the duty of care, we briefly describe it here.

Van Gorkom arose from an agreement between the Trans Union Corporation and a corporation controlled by the Pritzker family of Chicago. Trans Union had among its assets a substantial net operating loss (NOL) that, under the tax law of the day, could be carried forward for only a limited number of years. During that period, however, the loss could be used to reduce current taxable income. Unhappily, Trans Union was not producing enough net income to use up the carry forward, and thus a valuable asset (the NOL) was being wasted. Trans Union was managed by a board comprised of senior business luminaries from the Chicago area and had as a CEO Jerome Van Gorkom, who had headed the firm for a long time and was now looking toward retirement. The stock had been selling at about $35 per share. Van Gorkom, with little outside advice (no investment

---

15. 488 A.2d 858 (Del. 1985).

banker, no outside lawyer) and little advice from senior staff, set about to arrange a merger agreement with Mr. Pritzker's entity. He discussed the matter with Mr. Jay Pritzker, the leader of the family's business, and Pritzker offered Van Gorkom the cash price that Van Gorkom asked for, $55 per share. At a quickly called board meeting, the board approved the transaction and approved certain "deal protection" features in the merger agreement (see §13.6 below). No director was alleged to have any financial relationship to Mr. Pritzker or his companies.

A Trans Union shareholder sued, alleging that the directors had breached their duty of care in approving the Pritzker offer. While the price represented a large premium over the market price of the company's stock, it was alleged that the board had not acted in an informed manner in agreeing to the deal. A year earlier the Delaware court had addressed the duty-of-care liability standard in a decision involving self-dealing and management compensation and had declared that directors breached their duty of care only if they were "grossly negligent."[16] Extending this holding against all expectations at the time, the *Van Gorkom* court held that the Trans Union directors had been grossly negligent in their decision making and therefore could not claim the protections of the business judgment rule.

The case was remanded to the Chancery Court for a determination of the value of the Trans Union shares at the time of the board's decision, and for an award of damages to the extent that the fair value exceeded $55 per share. The case was settled prior to this determination for an additional $1.87 per share, or $23.5 million in total. The Trans Union D&O policy covered the first $10 million, which was the policy limit, and nearly all of the remaining $13.5 million was paid by the Pritzker family, apparently motivated by the view that Van Gorkom and the Trans Union board had done nothing wrong.

Van Gorkom was the first Delaware case to actually hold directors liable for breach of the duty of care in a case in which the board had made a business decision. The very few previous cases that had imposed liability for breach of the duty of care had done so in cases in which the board had failed to prevent a corporate fraud. *Van Gorkom* was a shocking result at the time and led to immediate revision in statutory law, to which we now turn. A fuller understanding of the case must await our discussion of the law of mergers and acquisitions.

8.4.3 Additional Statutory Protection: Authorization for Charter Provisions Waiving Liability for Due Care Violations

The immediate reaction to the *Van Gorkom* case was, first, a dramatic rise in the level of premia charged by insurance companies for director and

---

16. *Aronson v. Lewis*, 473 A.2d 805, 812 (Del. 1984). The gross negligence standard, by the way, can be understood as one more way in which courts can articulate a duty of "reasonable care" but enforce a more director protective standard.

officer (D&O) liability policies and, second, the enactment of §102(b)(7) of the Delaware General Corporation Law. Section 102(b)(7) validated charter amendments that provide that a corporate director has no liability for losses caused by transactions in which the director had no conflicting financial interest or otherwise was alleged to violate a duty of loyalty.

Between 1985 and 1995, approximately 40 other states followed Delaware's lead in authorizing the release of damage claims for breach of a duty of care. In Delaware, well over 90 percent of public corporations in a large sample had, by 1990, passed charter provisions eliminating liability to the full extent permitted by the statute.[17] Professor Roberta Romano provides an astute analysis of the explosion of D&O liability premia in the mid-1980s (occasioned in part by Delaware case law) and the consequent popularity of liability-limiting statutes in state legislatures. Among other interesting points, Romano reports that insurance companies did not lower premia in response to the passage of §102(b)(7) and that the plaintiffs' bar did not oppose the new legislation.[18] Does this suggest that §102(b)(7) is ineffective? If so, it is news to institutional investors, who generally support charter amendments waiving directorial liability, presumably because, as sophisticated investors, they understand that their self-interest lies in encouraging risk taking by directors.

QUESTIONS

1. Does Delaware's director liability statute raise issues different from those raised by the latitude Delaware firms enjoy to purchase personal liability insurance for their directors and officers? See DGCL §145(g). Could DGCL §102(b)(7) be viewed as simply allowing firms to "self-insure" directors against personal liability arising from gross negligence?

2. Is there reason to distrust a charter amendment, duly approved by shareholders, that eliminates director liability for gross negligence? Why might fully informed investors vote for such an amendment if it were not in their own interests? If the fact of informed shareholder approval of such a liability waiver might be consistent either with the advancement of shareholder economic interests or with a collective action disability of some sort, what might be an empirical methodology to estimate which interpretation of such approval is more likely correct?

3. Statutes such as DGCL §102(b)(7) can be viewed as a device for screening out some or all shareholder suits based on duty of care allegations. Is there reason to believe that such actions might be systematically less likely to increase shareholder welfare than duty of loyalty (i.e., conflict of interest) suits? Why?

4. How does the strategy of the Delaware statute compare to that of the Ohio statute reproduced below? Which statute provides more protection to directors?

17. Roberta Romano, *Corporate Governance in the Aftermath of the Insurance Crisis,* 39 Emory L.J. 1155, 1160-1161 (1990).
18. *Id.*

OHIO GENERAL CORPORATION LAW

§1701.59 Authority of directors; bylaws. . . .

(B) [A statement of the duty] A director shall perform his duties as a director, including his duties as a member of any committee of the directors upon which he may serve, in good faith, in a manner he reasonably believes to be in or not opposed to the best interests of the corporation, and with the care that an ordinarily prudent person in a like position would use under similar circumstances. . . .

(C) [A statement of an evidentiary and the liability standard] For purposes of division (B) of this section:

(1) A director shall not be found to have violated his duties under division (B) of this section unless it is proved by clear and convincing evidence that the director has not acted in good faith, in a manner he reasonably believes to be in or not opposed to the best interests of the corporation, or with the care that an ordinarily prudent person in a like position would use under similar circumstances. . . .

(D) [Mental state condition for monetary damages] A director shall be liable in damages for any action he takes or fails to take as a director only if it is proved by clear and convincing evidence in a court of competent jurisdiction that his action or failure to act involved an act or omission undertaken with deliberate intent to cause injury to the corporation or undertaken with reckless disregard for the best interests of the corporation. . . .

As we observed in the preceding section, the Delaware legislature responded to the surprising holding of *Van Gorkom* by passing the statutory provision authorizing a liability waiver for directors who act in good faith and without a conflict of interest. See DGCL §102(b)(7). Following the enactment of §102(b)(7), the very great majority of public corporations incorporated under Delaware law amended their certificates of incorporation, with, of course, shareholder concurrence, to remove duty of care liability to the extent the statute permits. Of course, the significance of this waiver provision depends, at least in part, on how it is now read by the Delaware courts. We now turn to this important question.

8.5 DELAWARE'S UNIQUE APPROACH TO ADJUDICATING DUE CARE CLAIMS AGAINST CORPORATE DIRECTORS: FROM *TECHNICOLOR* TO *EMERALD PARTNERS*

Section 102(b)(7) waivers are directed to damage claims. The directors' duty of care still can be the basis for an equitable order, such as an injunction. Thus, it is still possible for shareholders to seek to enjoin a transaction as a result of a breach of care by disinterested directors, and should they do so, Delaware has adopted a unique approach to adjudicating such claims. The story begins with a disputed transaction that predates both DGCL §102(b)(7) and the *Van Gorkom* opinion.

That transaction was considered in *Cede & Co. v. Technicolor, Inc.,*[19] with facts strikingly similar to those of *Van Gorkom.* In *Cede,* a takeover entrepreneur, Ronald O. Perelman, acquired Technicolor in a transaction characterized by arguable breaches of the duty of care by Technicolor's board of directors. The Delaware Chancery Court (Allen, C.) noted these possible lapses of care but held that Technicolor's plaintiff shareholders had failed to prove any injury in their liability action against Technicolor's board. The court, citing *Barnes v. Andrews,* a well-recognized case authored by Judge Learned Hand, had found no evidence that the board's action had caused injury, since Technicolor shareholders had apparently received full value for their stock. Indeed, an earlier appraisal proceeding (appraisal actions are explained in Chapter 12) had placed fair value for Technicolor somewhat *below* the price paid by Perelman. Thus, the Chancery Court reasoned that any arguable lapses of care by Technicolor's board could not have caused an injury.

The Delaware Supreme Court reversed: "This Court has consistently held that the breach of the duty of care, without any requirement of proof of injury, is sufficient to rebut the business judgment rule. . . . A breach of either the duty of loyalty or the duty of care rebuts the presumption that the directors have acted in the best interests of the shareholders, and requires the directors to prove that the transaction was entirely fair."[20] On remand, the Chancery Court, working within the doctrinal framework that the Supreme Court had innovated, found that the *Technicolor* defendants had carried their burden of showing entire fairness to the plaintiffs.[21] As the Chancery Court also resolved certain disclosure allegations in the defendants' favor, plaintiffs were again denied recovery and again turned to the Supreme Court for vindication. This time, the Supreme Court affirmed, although it did not relinquish the innovative doctrinal approach that it laid out in its 1993 opinion.[22]

The result is a complicated interplay between §102(b)(7), which seeks to insulate directors from liability, and the *Technicolor* line of cases, which has the effect of increasing director liability exposure. At the center of this interplay lies a simple question: How soon in the litigation process can a court dismiss directors from litigation charging them with liability in a transaction in which they had no conflicting financial interest? At the pleadings stage, the Delaware Supreme Court held in *Malpiede v. Townson*

---

19. 634 A.2d 345 (Del. 1993) ("Cede I").

20. *Cede & Co. v. Technicolor,* 634 A.2d 345, 370-371 (Del. 1993) ("Cede II").

21. 663 A.2d 1134 (Del. Ch. 1994).

22. *Cinerama, Inc. v. Technicolor, Inc.,* 663 A.2d 1156 (Del. 1995) ("Cede III"). This was not the end of the litigation over the Technicolor deal. The Delaware Supreme Court subsequently reversed the Court of Chancery's judgment in the appraisal action paralleling the personal liability action. *Cede & Co. v. Technicolor, Inc.,* 684 A.2d 289 (Del. 1996). An excerpt of this final chapter is reproduced in the appraisal section of Chapter 12.

that when a corporation has a §102(b)(7) provision in its charter and the plaintiff files a complaint that contains only a duty of care claim, the court should dismiss the complaint.[23] Put differently, a complaint must allege a breach of the duty of loyalty in order to survive a motion to dismiss, when the company has a §102(b)(7) provision in its charter. But not just any breach of the duty of loyalty will do. In *McMillan v. InterCargo Corp.*,[24] the plaintiffs alleged that the target's CEO agreed to a low acquisition price so that he could keep his job following the merger. Under ordinary pleading rules for a motion to dismiss (e.g., Fed. R. Civ. P. 12), a court assumes the truth of well-pleaded facts, and all inferences should be drawn in the pleader's favor. Nevertheless, the Chancery Court dismissed the complaint, seemingly on the grounds that such generic allegations are too easy to make. Unless particularized facts supporting duty of loyalty claims are alleged, goes the logic, the principal purpose of §102(b)(7) would be denied by allowing such claims to proceed to trial.

Once the plaintiffs have overcome the presumptions of the business judgment rule, however, Section 102(b)(7) offers less protection to defendant directors. *Emerald Partners v. Berlin,* 787 A.2d 85 (Del. 2001). *Emerald Partners* arose from a "roll-up" transaction, in which May Petroleum, a public corporation with a controlling shareholder, entered into transactions in which it acquired through merger thirteen corporations owned or dominated by this controlling shareholder. The transactions were negotiated and approved by the independent directors of May (although the controlling shareholder, who was also a director, remained in the room while they considered the transactions). Emerald Partners, a minority shareholder in May, sued all of May's directors, claiming that the resulting transactions were unfair to May. Certainly, as to the controlling shareholder, these were interested transactions, and as we will learn in Chapter 9, the controlling shareholder was obligated to prove that they were fair. But what about the other "independent, outside" directors? As to them, arguably, the mergers were not self-dealing transactions. Their only duty, presumably, was to exercise their reasonable best efforts to try in good faith to approve only beneficial transactions. As to them, might the case be dismissed on the ground that May's charter waived director liability for breaches of due care?

The case had a complex procedural history. Most notably, May's controlling shareholder declared personal bankruptcy during its pendency, and his respective liabilities arising from the *Emerald Partners* litigation were released by the Bankruptcy Court. Thus, when the case was tried, the only remaining defendants were the "disinterested" directors. After trial, the trial court dismissed the complaint against these outside directors on the theory that they had no conflicting interest, they were not shown to have conspired with the controlling shareholder, and the corporation had a waiver of liability for breaches of due care under §102(b)(7). The court did not bother to determine whether the transactions were "entirely fair" to the corporation.

---

23. See *Malpiede v. Townson*, 780 A.2d 1071 (Del. 2001).
24. 768 A.2d 492 (Del. Ch. 2000).

The Delaware Supreme Court reversed. It held that the correct standard of review for a transaction in which a controlling shareholder is
interested is objective fairness or, in the phrase popular with these courts,
"entire fairness." Moreover, under the *Technicolor* rule, the director defendants had the burden to prove entire fairness, so it was a mistake for the
court to render judgment in their favor without addressing this issue. On
remand, in a process strikingly reminiscent of the *Technicolor* end-game,
the Chancery Court found that the transaction was entirely fair to the
minority shareholders.[25] On appeal again, the Delaware Supreme Court,
as in *Technicolor*, affirmed the judgment.[26]

The doctrinal puzzle arises in the counter-factual, where the Delaware
Chancery Court would have found that the defendant directors had *not* met
their burden of demonstrating the fairness of the transaction. In that
scenario, according to the Delaware Supreme Court, "[t]he director defendants can avoid personal liability for paying monetary damages only if they
have established that their failure to withstand an entire fairness analysis is
exclusively attributable to a violation of the duty of care."[27] While judicial
efficiency concerns would suggest resolving the duty of care versus duty of
loyalty question first (as the Chancery Court tried to do) in order to avoid a
burdensome fairness hearing, the Supreme Court, following *Technicolor*,
rejected this approach. Do you find this puzzling? We do (but then again,
we may be biased).

8.6 THE BOARD'S DUTY TO MONITOR: LOSSES "CAUSED"
BY BOARD PASSIVITY

So far, we have discussed the possible liability of directors for failing to take
reasonable care in making business decisions that lead to financial losses.
We now turn to the related question: What is the scope of director liability
for losses that arise not from business choices but rather from causes that
the board might arguably have deflected? The business judgment rule
protects boards that have made *decisions*. In fact, however, the relatively
few cases that actually impose liability on directors for breach of the duty of
care are not cases in which a decision proved disastrously wrong but cases,
like the Enron collapse of 2001, in which directors simply failed to do
anything under circumstances in which it is later determined that a reasonably alert person would have taken action.[28]

Directors' incentives are far less likely to be distorted by liability
imposed for passive violations of the standard of care than for liability

---

25. *Emerald Partners v. Berlin*, 2003 WL 21003437 (Del. Ch. 2003).
26. *Emerald Partners v. Berlin*, C.A. 9700 (Del. 2003).
27. Emerald Partners, 787 A.2d 85, 98.
28. Recall that the earliest case we find is the 1741 decision *Sutton v. Charitable
Hospitable Case*, noted above, in which the board was charged with failing to uncover a
fraud. See also the often-cited U.S. Supreme Court case of *Briggs v. Spaulding*, 141 U.S. 132
(1891).

imposed for erroneous decisions. We should not be surprised that actual liability is more likely to arise from a failure to supervise or detect fraud than from an erroneous business decision. Nevertheless, given the disjunction between the scale of operations of many public corporations and the scale of the personal wealth of typical individual directors, the risk of liability for inactivity may still deter talented persons from serving on corporate boards. Despite this danger, the astonishingly rapid collapse of the Enron Corporation in 2001 suggested to many observers that boards may generally be too easily manipulated by company officers. As a corrective, some of these observers believe that the sharp prod of potential liability ought to be more in evidence. But liability for losses in these huge enterprises is a crude ex post method to enforce attention. Losses in the Enron case were in the many tens of billions of dollars. Liability for the smallest percentage of this loss would financially destroy corporate directors and would make board service to others desperately unappealing. How then are incentives for director attention to be created that do not deter service? We can, at least, say it cannot be done scientifically.

In this section, we review four cases dealing with directors who are charged with breaching their duty of care by not sufficiently monitoring the corporation and thus by not preventing a loss that the corporation incurred.

FRANCIS v. UNITED JERSEY BANK

432 A.2d 814 (N.J. 1981)

[Pritchard & Baird, Inc., was a reinsurance broker that arranged contracts between insurance companies that wrote large policies and other companies in order to share the risks of those policies. In this industry, the company that sells insurance to the client pays a portion of the premium to the reinsurance broker, who deducts its commission and forwards the balance to the reinsuring company. The broker thus handles large amounts of money as a fiduciary for its clients.

As of 1964, all the stock of Pritchard & Baird was owned by Charles Pritchard, Sr., one of the firm's founders, and his wife and two sons, Charles, Jr., and William. They were also the four directors. Charles, Sr., dominated the corporation until 1971, when he became ill and the two sons took over management of the business. Charles, Sr., died in 1973, leaving Mrs. Pritchard and the sons the only remaining directors.

Contrary to the industry practice, Pritchard & Baird did not segregate its operating funds from those of its clients, depositing all in the same account. From this account Charles, Sr., had drawn "loans" that correlated with corporate profits and were repaid at the end of each year. After his death, Charles, Jr., and William began to draw ever larger sums (still characterizing them as "loans") that greatly exceeded profits. They were able to do so by taking advantage of the "float" available to them during the period between the time they received a premium and the time they had to forward it (less commission) to the reinsurer.

. By 1975, the corporation was bankrupt. This action was brought by the trustees in bankruptcy against Mrs. Pritchard and the bank as administrator of her husband's estate. As to Mrs. Pritchard, the principal claim was that she had been negligent in the conduct of her duties as a director of the corporation. She died during the pendency of the proceedings, and her executrix was substituted as defendant.]

POLLOCK, J.:

The "loans" were reflected on financial statements that were prepared annually as of January 31, the end of the corporate fiscal year. Although an outside certified public accountant prepared the 1970 financial statement, the corporation prepared only internal financial statements from 1971-1975. In all instances, the statements were simple documents, consisting of three or four 8 1/2 × 11 inch sheets. . . .

	Working Capital Deficit	*Shareholders Loans*	*Net Brokerage Income*
70	$ 389,022	$ 508,941	$ 807,229
71	NOT AVAILABLE	NOT AVAILABLE	NOT AVAILABLE
72	$ 1,684,298	$ 1,825,911	$ 1,546,263
73	$ 3,506,460	$ 3,700,542	$ 1,736,349
74	$ 6,939,007	$ 7,080,629	$ 876,182
75	$10,176,419	$10,298,039	$ 551,598

The statements of financial condition from 1970 forward demonstrated: Mrs. Pritchard was not active in the business of Pritchard & Baird and knew virtually nothing of its corporate affairs. She briefly visited the corporate offices in Morristown on only one occasion, and she never read or obtained the annual financial statements. She was unfamiliar with the rudiments of reinsurance and made no effort to assure that the policies and practices of the corporation, particularly pertaining to the withdrawal of funds, complied with industry custom or relevant law. Although her husband had warned her that Charles, Jr. would "take the shirt off my back," Mrs. Pritchard did not pay any attention to her duties as a director or to the affairs of the corporation. . . .

After her husband died in December 1973, Mrs. Pritchard became incapacitated and was bedridden for a six-month period. She became listless at this time and started to drink rather heavily. Her physical condition deteriorated, and in 1978 she died. The trial court rejected testimony seeking to exonerate her because she "was old, was grief-stricken at the loss of her husband, sometimes consumed too much alcohol and was psychologically overborne by her sons." . . . That court found that she was competent to act and that the reason Mrs. Pritchard never knew what her sons "were doing was because she never made the slightest effort to discharge any of her responsibilities as a director of Pritchard & Baird." 162 N.J. Super. at 372. . . .

III

Individual liability of a corporate director for acts of the corporation is a prickly problem. Generally directors are accorded broad immunity and are not insurers of corporate activities. The problem is particularly nettlesome when a third party asserts that a director, because of nonfeasance, is liable for losses caused by acts of insiders, who in this case were officers, directors and shareholders. Determination of the liability of Mrs. Pritchard requires findings that she had a duty to the clients of Pritchard & Baird, that she breached that duty and that her breach was a proximate cause of their losses. . . .

As a general rule, a director should acquire at least a rudimentary understanding of the business of the corporation. Accordingly, a director should become familiar with the fundamentals of the business in which the corporation is engaged. . . . Because directors are bound to exercise ordinary care, they cannot set up as a defense lack of the knowledge needed to exercise the requisite degree of care. If one "feels that he has not had sufficient business experience to qualify him to perform the duties of a director, he should either acquire the knowledge by inquiry, or refuse to act." . . .

Directors are under a continuing obligation to keep informed about the activities of the corporation. . . . Directorial management does not require a detailed inspection of day-to-day activities, but rather a general monitoring of corporate affairs and policies. Accordingly, a director is well advised to attend board meetings regularly. Indeed, a director who is absent from a board meeting is presumed to concur in action taken on a corporate matter, unless he files a "dissent with the secretary of the corporation within a reasonable time after learning of such action." N.J.S.A. 14A:6-13 (Supp. 1981-1982). . . .

While directors are not required to audit corporate books, they should maintain familiarity with the financial status of the corporation by a regular review of financial statements. In some circumstances, directors may be charged with assuring that bookkeeping methods conform to industry custom and usage. The extent of review, as well as the nature and frequency of financial statements, depends not only on the customs of the industry, but also on the nature of the corporation and the business in which it is engaged. Financial statements of some small corporations may be prepared internally and only on an annual basis; in a large publicly held corporation, the statements may be produced monthly or at some other regular interval. Adequate financial review normally would be more informal in a private corporation than in a publicly held corporation.

Of some relevance in this case is the circumstance that the financial records disclose the "shareholders' loans." Generally directors are immune from liability if, in good faith, they rely upon the opinion of counsel for the corporation or upon written reports setting forth financial data concerning the corporation and prepared by an independent public accountant or certified public accountant or firm of such accountants or upon financial statements, books of account or reports of the corporation represented to them to be correct by the president, the officer of the corporation having charge of its books of account, or the person presiding at a meeting of the board.

The review of financial statements, however, may give rise to a duty to inquire further into matters revealed by those statements. . . . Upon discovery of an illegal course of action, a director has a duty to object and, if the corporation does not correct the conduct, to resign. . . .

[In this case, Mrs. Pritchard] should have realized [from those statements] that, as of January 31, 1970, her sons were withdrawing substantial trust funds under the guise of "Shareholders' Loans." The financial statements for each fiscal year commencing with that of January 31, 1970, disclosed that the working capital deficits and the "loans" were escalating in tandem. Detecting a misappropriation of funds would not have required special expertise or extraordinary diligence; a cursory reading of the financial statements would have revealed the pillage. . . .

Nonetheless, the negligence of Mrs. Pritchard does not result in liability unless it is a proximate cause of the loss. . . .

Cases involving nonfeasance present a much more difficult causation question than those in which the director has committed an affirmative act of negligence leading to the loss. Analysis in cases of negligent omissions calls for determination of the reasonable steps a director should have taken and whether that course of action would have averted the loss.

Usually a director can absolve himself from liability by informing the other directors of the impropriety and voting for a proper course of action. . . . Conversely, a director who votes for or concurs in certain actions may be "liable to the corporation for the benefit of its creditors or shareholders, to the extent of any injuries suffered by such persons, respectively, as a result of any such action." N.J.S.A. 14A:6-12 (Supp. 1981-1982). A director who is present at a board meeting is presumed to concur in corporate action taken at the meeting unless his dissent is entered in the minutes of the meeting or filed promptly after adjournment. N.J.S.A. 14:6-13. In many, if not most, instances an objecting director whose dissent is noted in accordance with N.J.S.A. 14:6-13 would be absolved after attempting to persuade fellow directors to follow a different course of action. . . .

In this case, the scope of Mrs. Pritchard's duties was determined by the precarious financial condition of Pritchard & Baird, its fiduciary relationship to its clients and the implied trust in which it held their funds. Thus viewed, the scope of her duties encompassed all reasonable action to stop the continuing conversion. Her duties extended beyond mere objection and resignation to reasonable attempts to prevent the misappropriation of the trust funds. . . .

A leading case discussing causation where the director's liability is predicated upon a negligent failure to act is *Barnes v. Andrews*, 298 F. 614 (S.D.N.Y. 1924). In that case the court exonerated a figurehead director who served for eight months on a board that held one meeting after his election, a meeting he was forced to miss because of the death of his mother. Writing for the court, Judge Learned Hand distinguished a director who fails to prevent general mismanagement from one such as Mrs. Pritchard who failed to stop an illegal "loan":

> When the corporate funds have been illegally lent, it is a fair
> inference that a protest would have stopped the loan, and that

the director's neglect caused the loss. But when a business fails from general mismanagement, business incapacity, or bad judgment, how is it possible to say that a single director could have made the company successful, or how much in dollars he could have saved? (*Id.* at 616-617) . . .

. . . The wrongdoing of her sons, although the immediate cause of [Pritchard & Baird's] loss, should not excuse Mrs. Pritchard from her negligence which also was a substantial factor contributing to the loss. . . . Her sons knew that she, the only other director, was not reviewing their conduct; they spawned their fraud in the backwater of her neglect. Her neglect of duty contributed to the climate of corruption; her failure to act contributed to the continuation of that corruption. . . .

Analysis . . . is especially difficult . . . where the allegation is that nonfeasance of a director is a proximate cause of damage to a third party. . . . Nonetheless, where it is reasonable to conclude that the failure to act would produce a particular result and that result has followed, causation may be inferred. We conclude that even if Mrs. Pritchard's mere objection had not stopped the depredations of her sons, her consultation with an attorney and the threat of suit would have deterred them. That conclusion flows as a matter of common sense and logic from the record. Whether in other situations a director has a duty to do more than protest and resign is best left to case-by-case determinations. In this case, we are satisfied that there was a duty to do more than object and resign. Consequently, we find that Mrs. Pritchard's negligence was a proximate cause of the misappropriations.

To conclude, by virtue of her office, Mrs. Pritchard had the power to prevent the losses sustained by the clients of Pritchard & Baird. With power comes responsibility. She had a duty to deter the depredation of the other insiders, her sons. She breached that duty and caused plaintiffs to sustain damages.

The judgment of the Appellate Division is affirmed.

NOTE

Although an odd case in some respects, *Francis* reflects the majority view that there is a minimum objective standard of care for directors — that directors cannot abandon their office but must make a good-faith attempt to do a proper job. The case law is divided on whether the minimum standard is the same for all directors or whether sophisticated directors (e.g., lawyers and investment bankers) ought to be held to a higher standard.

QUESTIONS

1. What would have been the result if Mrs. Pritchard had spotted her sons' activities; if they had responded: "Don't worry, Mama. We were stealing, but we'll stop now and establish a segregated fund for our clients'

moneys"; and if her sons had continued to steal as before but pacified their mother with a false financial statement?

2. Courts are reluctant to impose a duty on directors who suspect wrongful activity to do more than protest and resign. Ought the corporation law impose something tough, such as a whistle-blowing duty (i.e., to go to prosecutors or disclose to shareholders)?

In general, boards of public companies have a particular obligation to monitor their firm's financial performance, the integrity of its financial reporting, its compliance with the law, its management compensation, and its succession planning. Because of the large scale of modern public corporations, the board must monitor largely through reports from others, whether outside auditors, other professionals, or corporate officers. The board authorizes only the most significant corporate acts or transactions: mergers, changes in capital structure, fundamental changes in business, etc. The lesser decisions that are made by officers and employees within the interior of the organization can, however, vitally affect the welfare of the corporation. Recent business history has graphically demonstrated that the failure of appropriate controls can result in extraordinary losses to even very large public companies. Even before the Enron and WorldCom scandals, large losses following monitoring failures resulted in the displacement of senior management and much of the board of Salomon, Inc.;[29] the replacement of senior management of Kidder, Peabody;[30] and extensive financial loss and reputational injury to Prudential Insurance arising from misrepresentations in connection with the sale of limited partnership interests.[31] Financial disasters of this sort raise this question: What is the board's responsibility to assure that the corporation functions within the law to achieve its purposes?

GRAHAM v. ALLIS-CHALMERS MANUFACTURING CO.

188 A.2d 125 (Del. 1963)

WOLCOTT, J.:

This is a derivative action on behalf of Allis-Chalmers against its directors and four of its non-director employees. The complaint is based upon indictments of Allis-Chalmers and the four non-director employees named as defendants herein who, with the corporation, entered pleas of guilty to the indictments. The indictments, eight in number, charged violations of the Federal anti-trust laws. The suit seeks to recover damages which Allis-Chalmers is claimed to have suffered by reason of these violations.

29. See, e.g., *Rotten at the Core*, The Economist, Aug. 17, 1991, at 69-70; Mike McNamee et al., *The Judgment of Salomon: An Anticlimax*, Bus. Week, June 1, 1992, at 106.

30. See Terence P. Pare, *Jack Welch's Nightmare on Wall Street*, Fortune, Sept. 5, 1994, at 40-48.

31. Michael Schroeder & Leah N. Spiro, *Is George Ball's Luck Running Out?*, Bus. Week, Nov. 8, 1993, at 74-76.

The hearing and depositions produced no evidence that any director had any actual knowledge of the anti-trust activity, or had actual knowledge of any facts which should have put them on notice that anti-trust activity was being carried on by some of their company's employees. The plaintiffs, appellants here, thereupon shifted the theory of the case to the proposition that the directors are liable as a matter of law by reason of their failure to take action designed to learn of and prevent anti-trust activity on the part of any employees of Allis-Chalmers.

By this appeal the plaintiffs seek to have us reverse the Vice Chancellor's ruling of non-liability of the defendant directors upon this theory. . . .

Allis-Chalmers is a manufacturer of a variety of electrical equipment. It employs in excess of 31,000 people, has a total of 24 plants, 145 sales offices, 5000 dealers and distributors, and its sales volume is in excess of $500,000,000 annually. The operations of the company are conducted by two groups, each of which is under the direction of a senior vice president. One of these groups is the Industries Group under the direction of Singleton, director defendant. This group is divided into five divisions. One of these, the Power Equipment Division, produced the products, the sale of which involved the anti-trust activities referred to in the indictments. The Power Equipment Division, presided over by McMullen, non-director defendant, contains ten departments, each of which is presided over by a manager or general manager.

The operating policy of Allis-Chalmers is to decentralize by the delegation of authority to the lowest possible management level capable of fulfilling the delegated responsibility. Thus, prices of products are ordinarily set by the particular department manager, except that if the product being priced is large and special, the department manager might confer with the general manager of the division. Products of a standard character involving repetitive manufacturing processes are sold out of a price list which is established by a price leader for the electrical equipment industry as a whole.

Annually, the Board of Directors reviews group and departmental profit goal budgets. On occasion, the Board considers general questions concerning price levels, but because of the complexity of the company's operations the Board does not participate in decisions fixing the prices of specific products.

The Board of Directors of fourteen members, four of whom are officers, meets once a month, October excepted, and considers a previously prepared agenda for the meeting. Supplied to the Directors at the meetings are financial and operating data relating to all phases of the company's activities. The Board meetings are customarily of several hours duration in which all the Directors participate actively. Apparently, the Board considers and decides matters concerning the general business policy of the company. By reason of the extent and complexity of the company's operations, it is not practicable for the Board to consider in detail specific problems of the various divisions.

The indictments to which Allis-Chalmers and the four non-director defendants pled guilty charge that the company and individual non-director defendants, commencing in 1956, conspired with other manufacturers and their employees to fix prices and to rig bids to private electric utilities and governmental agencies in violation of the anti-trust laws of the United States. None of the director defendants in this cause were named as defendants in the indictments. Indeed, the Federal Government acknowledged that it had uncovered no probative evidence which could lead to the conviction of the defendant directors.

The first actual knowledge the directors had of anti-trust violations by some of the company's employees was in the summer of 1959 from newspaper stories that TVA proposed an investigation of identical bids. Singleton, in charge of the Industries Group of the company, investigated but unearthed nothing. Thereafter, in November of 1959, some of the company's employees were subpoenaed before the Grand Jury. Further investigation by the company's Legal Division gave reason to suspect the illegal activity and all of the subpoenaed employees were instructed to tell the whole truth.

Thereafter, on February 8, 1960, at the direction of the Board, a policy statement relating to anti-trust problems was issued, and the Legal Division commenced a series of meetings with all employees of the company in possible areas of anti-trust activity. The purpose and effect of these steps was to eliminate any possibility of further and future violations of the antitrust laws.

As we have pointed out, there is no evidence in the record that the defendant directors had actual knowledge of the illegal anti-trust actions of the company's employees. Plaintiffs, however, point to two FTC decrees of 1937 as warning to the directors that anti-trust activity by the company's employees had taken place in the past. It is argued that they were thus put on notice of their duty to ferret out such activity and to take active steps to insure that it would not be repeated.

The decrees in question were consent decrees entered in 1937 against Allis-Chalmers and nine others enjoining agreements to fix uniform prices on condensers and turbine generators. The decrees recited that they were consented to for the sole purpose of avoiding the trouble and expense of the proceeding.

The director defendants and now officers of the company either were employed in very subordinate capacities or had no connection with the company in 1937. At the time, copies of the decrees were circulated to the heads of concerned departments and were explained to the Managers Committee.

In 1943, Singleton, officer and director defendant, first learned of the decrees upon becoming Assistant Manager of the Steam Turbine Department, and consulted the company's General Counsel as to them. He investigated his department and learned the decrees were being complied with and, in any event, he concluded that the company had not in the first place been guilty of the practice enjoined.

Stevenson, officer and director defendant, first learned of the decrees in 1951 in a conversation with Singleton about their respective areas of the company's operations. He satisfied himself that the company was not then and in fact had not been guilty of quoting uniform prices. . . .

Scholl, officer and director defendant, learned of the decrees in 1956 in a discussion with Singleton on matters affecting the Industries Group. He was informed that no similar problem was then in existence in the company.

Under the circumstances, we think knowledge by three of the directors that in 1937 the company had consented to the entry of decrees enjoining it from doing something they had satisfied themselves it had never done, did not put the Board on notice of the possibility of future illegal price fixing.

Plaintiffs are thus forced to rely solely upon the legal proposition advanced by them that directors of a corporation, as a matter of law, are liable for losses suffered by their corporations by reason of their gross inattention to the common law duty of actively supervising and managing the corporate affairs. . . .

The precise charge made against these director defendants is that, even though they had no knowledge of any suspicion of wrongdoing on the part of the company's employees, they still should have put into effect a system of watchfulness which would have brought such misconduct to their attention in ample time to have brought it to an end. However, the *Briggs* case expressly rejects such an idea. On the contrary, it appears that directors are entitled to rely on the honesty and integrity of their subordinates until something occurs to put them on suspicion that something is wrong. If such occurs and goes unheeded, then liability of the directors might well follow, but absent cause for suspicion there is no duty upon the directors to install and operate a corporate system of espionage to ferret out wrongdoing which they have no reason to suspect exists.

The duties of the Allis-Chalmers Directors were fixed by the nature of the enterprise which employed in excess of 30,000 persons, and extended over a large geographical area. By force of necessity, the company's Directors could not know personally all the company's employees. The very magnitude of the enterprise required them to confine their control to the broad policy decisions. That they did this is clear from the record. . . .

In the last analysis, the question of whether a corporate director has become liable for losses to the corporation through neglect of duty is determined by the circumstances. If he has recklessly reposed confidence in an obviously untrustworthy employee, has refused or neglected cavalierly to perform his duty as a director, or has ignored either willfully or through inattention obvious danger signs of employee wrongdoing, the law will cast the burden of liability upon him. This is not the case at bar, however, for as soon as it became evident that there were grounds for suspicion, the Board acted promptly to end it and prevent its recurrence.

Plaintiffs say these steps should have been taken long before, even in the absence of suspicion, but we think not, for we know of no rule of law which requires a corporate director to assume, with no justification whatsoever, that all corporate employees are incipient law violators who, but for a tight checkrein, will give free vent to their unlawful propensities.

We therefore affirm the Vice Chancellor's ruling. . . .

QUESTIONS

1. There is evidence that the exceptionally decentralized operating policy of Allis-Chalmers was accompanied by enormous pressure on the company's semiautonomous units to show steadily growing profits. If this was the management style approved by the Allis-Chalmers board, should there be any implications for the board's duty of care?

2. What function would imposing liability for breach of the duty of care serve in *Allis-Chalmers*? When might it be in the narrow economic interests of shareholders, and when might it not be in the interests of shareholders?

3. To the extent that one is tempted to impose liability on the board for purposes of enforcing the antitrust laws, what alternative enforcement strategies might be available? What about increasing penalties against the company itself?

Beam v. Martha Stewart provides a recent, if "novel," application of the *Allis-Chalmers* "red flag" doctrine. *Beam* involved the board of directors of Martha Stewart Omnimedia (Omnimedia), Inc., a Delaware corporation. In a highly publicized trial, Martha Stewart, founder and former CEO of Omnimedia, was tried and convicted for matters arising out of certain trading of the stock of another corporation, ImClone Systems, Inc. Announcement of Stewart's indictment caused the Omnimedia stock to plunge, as the market was concerned that her image as the master home-maker would suffer a severe blemish that would affect the business. The business itself also suffered declines in sales.

Were these losses somehow the responsibility of the Omnimedia board? Given Stewart's extraordinary business importance to the welfare of the company, should the board have taken steps to protect against this sort of risk? Should Stewart herself be held to have violated a fiduciary duty in engaging in behavior that ultimately caused large stock value losses to the public shareholder of the corporation? The Delaware Chancery Court dealt with this issue on a motion to dismiss a derivative suit brought by an Omnimedia shareholder in the following excerpt.

BEAM v. MARTHA STEWART

833 A.2d 961 (Del. Ch. 2003)

CHANDLER, Chancellor:

Defendant Martha Stewart ("Stewart") is a director of the company and its founder, chairman, chief executive officer, and by far [the] majority shareholder [of Martha Stewart Omnimedia (MSO)]. MSO's common stock is comprised of Class A and Class B shares. Class A shares are traded on the New York Stock Exchange and are entitled to cast one vote per share on matters voted upon by common stockholders. Class B shares are not publicly traded and are entitled to cast ten votes per share on all matters voted upon by common stockholders. Stewart owns or beneficially holds 100% of the B shares in conjunction with a sufficient number of A shares that she controls roughly 94.4% of the shareholder vote. Stewart, a former stockbroker, has in the past twenty years become a household icon, known for her advice and expertise on virtually all aspects of cooking, decorating, entertaining, and household affairs generally. . . .

A. STEWART'S IMCLONE TRADING

The market for MSO products is uniquely tied to the personal image and reputation of its founder, Stewart. MSO retains "an exclusive, world-wide, perpetual royalty-free license to use [Stewart's] name, likeness, image, voice and signature for its products and services." In its initial public offering prospectus, MSO recognized that impairment of Stewart's services to the company, including the tarnishing of her public reputation, would have a material adverse effect on its business. The prospectus distinguished Stewart's importance to MSO's business success from that of other executives of the company noting that, "Martha Stewart remains the personification of our brands as well as our senior executive and primary creative force." In fact, under the terms of her employment agreement, Stewart may be terminated for gross misconduct or felony conviction that results in harm to MSO's business or reputation but is permitted discretion over the management of her personal, financial, and legal affairs to the extent that Stewart's management of her own life does not compromise her ability to serve the company.

Stewart's alleged misadventures with ImClone arise in part out of a longstanding personal friendship with Samuel D. Waksal ("Waksal"). Waksal is the former chief executive officer of ImClone as well as a former suitor of Stewart's daughter. . . . The speculative value of ImClone stock was tied quite directly to the likely success of its application for FDA approval to market the cancer treatment drug Erbitux. On December 26 [, 2001], Waksal received information that the FDA was rejecting the application to market Erbitux. The following day, December 27, he tried to sell his own shares and tipped his father and daughter to do the same. Stewart also sold her shares on December 27. . . . After the close of trading on December 28, ImClone publicly announced the rejection of its application to market Erbitux. The following day the trading price closed slightly more than 20% lower than the closing price on the date that Stewart had sold her shares. By mid-2002, this convergence of events had attracted the interest of the *New York Times* and other news agencies, federal prosecutors, and a committee of the United States House of Representatives. Stewart's publicized attempts to quell any suspicion were ineffective at best because they were undermined by additional information as it came to light and by the other parties' accounts of the events. Ultimately Stewart's prompt efforts to turn away unwanted media and investigative attention failed. Stewart eventually had to discontinue her regular guest appearances on CBS' *The Early Show* because of questioning during the show about her sale of ImClone shares. After barely two months of such adverse publicity, MSO's stock price had declined by slightly more than 65%. In August 2002, James Follo, MSO's chief financial officer, cited uncertainty stemming from the investigation of Stewart in response to questions about earnings prospects in the future.

***

Count II of the amended complaint alleges that the director defendants and defendant Patrick [President and Chief Operating Officer of MSO] breached their fiduciary duties by failing to ensure that Stewart would not conduct her personal, financial, and legal affairs in a manner that would harm the Company, its intellectual property, or its business.

The "duty to monitor" has been litigated in other circumstances, generally where directors were alleged to have been negligent in monitoring the activities of the corporation, activities that led to corporate liability. Plaintiff's allegation, however, that the Board has a duty to monitor the personal affairs of an officer or director is quite novel. That the Company is "closely identified" with Stewart is conceded, but it does not necessarily follow that the Board is required to monitor, much less control, the way Stewart handles her *personal* financial and legal affairs.

In *Graham v. Allis-Chalmers Manufacturing Co.*, the Delaware Supreme Court held that "absent cause for suspicion there is no duty upon the directors to install and operate a corporate system of espionage to ferret out wrongdoing which they have no reason to suspect exists." Despite this statement's implication that a duty to monitor may arise when the board has reason to suspect wrongdoing, it does not burden MSO's Board with a duty to monitor Stewart's *personal* affairs.

First, plaintiff does not allege facts that would give MSO's Board any reason to monitor Stewart's activities before mid-2002 when the allegations regarding her divestment of ImClone stock became public. Second, the quoted statement from *Graham* refers to wrongdoing *by the corporation*. Regardless of Stewart's importance to MSO, she is not the corporation. And it is unreasonable to impose a duty upon the Board to monitor Stewart's personal affairs because such a requirement is neither legitimate nor feasible. Monitoring Stewart by, for example, hiring a private detective to monitor her behavior is more likely to generate liability *to* Stewart under some tort theory than to protect the Company from a decline in its stock price as a result of harm to Stewart's public image.

Even if I accept that the board knew that Stewart's personal actions could result in harm to MSO, it seems patently unreasonable to expect the Board, as an exercise of its supervision *of the Company*, to preemptively thwart a personal call from Stewart to her stockbroker or to fully control her handling of the media attention that followed as a result of her *personal* actions, especially where her statements touched on matters that could subject Stewart to criminal charges. Plaintiff has not cited any case to support this new "duty" to monitor personal affairs. Since the defendant directors had no duty to monitor Stewart's personal actions, plaintiff's allegation that the directors breached their duty... by failing to monitor

Stewart because they were "beholden" to her is irrelevant. Count II is dismissed for failure to state a claim.

NOTE: THE DUTY TO MONITOR GONE AWRY AT HEWLETT PACKARD

In *Beam,* the court notes that monitoring Martha Stewart "is more likely to generate liability *to* Stewart . . . than to protect the Company from a decline in its stock price." This language foreshadowed the bizarre "pretexting" scandal three years later at Hewlett-Packard. In order to determine the source of boardroom leaks, board chairwoman Patricia Dunn authorized an investigation in which private investigators obtained phone records by pretending to be the users of particular phone accounts. Ms. Dunn resigned from the HP board as a result of the scandal, even though it seems that she had gotten assurances from her legal counsel that the investigation was perfectly legal. The California attorney general also brought criminal charges against Dunn and others at HP who were involved in the investigation.

State corporate law is not the only legal source of a director's duty of care. Securities law and the SEC also impose negligence-based duties on directors in a variety of contexts. *In the Matter of Michael Marchese,* below, is a particularly aggressive assertion of a breach in an outside director's duty to monitor a firm's financial statements. In the present regulatory enviroment, conventional wisdom has it that outside directors are at least as concerned about SEC enforcement actions as they are about shareholder suits under state law.

IN THE MATTER OF MICHAEL MARCHESE

Release Nos. 34-47732; AAER-1764; Administrative Proceeding File No. 3-11092 (April 24, 2003)

BACKGROUND

Respondent Marchese became an outside director of Chancellor in December 1996. He was an acquaintance of Brian Adley, who was Chancellor's controlling shareholder, chairman and chief executive officer. Chancellor reported in public filings that Marchese was a member of the company's audit committee from 1996 to May 1999. Marchese never reviewed Chancellor's accounting procedures or internal controls. He generally deferred to Adley when board action was required.

1. CHANCELLOR PREMATURELY CONSOLIDATED AN ACQUIRED SUBSIDIARY'S REVENUE

On August 10, 1998, Chancellor entered into a letter of intent to acquire MRB, a seller of used trucks. A final closing took place on January 29, 1999. When preparing its financial reports for 1998, Chancellor improperly designated August 1, 1998, as the MRB acquisition date for accounting purposes. Chancellor designated that date based on its claim that a preexisting written agreement between Chancellor and MRB gave Chancellor effective control of MRB's operations as of August 1, 1998. When Chancellor's auditors began the audit of Chancellor's year-end 1998 financial statements, they reviewed the agreement and informed Chancellor's management that it did not give Chancellor sufficient control of MRB during 1998 to justify consolidating the two companies' financial statements for accounting purposes. The auditors sent a memorandum to Adley and Marchese in February 1999 setting forth their position that GAAP required a 1999 consolidation date.

During February 1999, Adley directed Chancellor's acting CFO to create and backdate to August 1998 a purported amended management agreement with MRB to provide additional support to justify an August 1, 1998 acquisition date for accounting purposes. This document, however, did not cause the auditors to change their position with respect to the correct acquisition date.

On February 25, 1999, Adley dismissed Chancellor's auditors. Adley did not identify the difference of opinion about the accounting date for the MRB acquisition as a reason for the dismissal. As a director, Respondent Marchese approved the decision to dismiss Chancellor's auditors. He was aware of the disagreement between Chancellor's management and the auditors regarding the appropriate MRB acquisition date for accounting purposes. He knew that the disagreement formed part of the reason for the auditors' dismissal.

After dismissing its prior auditors, Chancellor engaged Metcalf, Rice, Fricke and Davis (now BKR Metcalf Davis)("Metcalf Davis") to conduct the independent audit of its 1998 financial statements. Respondent Marchese approved the engagement. During spring 1999, in connection with the Metcalf Davis audit, Chancellor's CEO Adley caused Chancellor's president and acting CFO to fabricate documents in order to support the 1998 acquisition date. The fabricated documents included letters and memoranda designed to demonstrate Chancellor's control of MRB during 1998. These documents were provided to Metcalf Davis.

In April 1999, after conducting its audit, Metcalf Davis personnel met with Marchese, another outside director, and Chancellor's top management. In the meeting, Metcalf Davis indicated that it would provide an unqualified audit report for Chancellor's 1998 year-end financial statements. For accounting purposes, Metcalf Davis approved an August 1998 acquisition date for MRB.

Marchese knew that Chancellor's prior auditors had disagreed with Chancellor's management and had stated that a 1998 acquisition date did not comport with GAAP. Marchese, however, made no inquiry into the reasons for Metcalf Davis's contrary view. Nor did he determine whether there was any factual support for the 1998 acquisition date.

2. CHANCELLOR IMPROPERLY RECORDED A $3.3 MILLION FEE

In connection with Chancellor's acquisition of MRB, Adley caused Chancellor to record $3.3 million in fees to Vestex Capital Corporation ("Vestex"), a private entity he owned. The fees were purportedly for consulting services including identifying, negotiating and closing the MRB acquisition. In fact, no significant consulting services were rendered to Chancellor by Vestex in connection with the acquisition. In order to substantiate the fees to Vestex, Adley directed Chancellor personnel to fabricate numerous documents and provide them to Metcalf Davis while the firm was conducting its audit of Chancellor's 1998 financial results. In addition, at Adley's direction, Chancellor recorded as an asset on its balance sheet the $3.3 million in unsupported Vestex fees rather than recording them as an expense on its income statement. This was inconsistent with GAAP, which provides that costs payable to an outside consultant in business combinations may be capitalized only if the consultant has no affiliation with the companies involved in the acquisition.

The year before, in connection with the preparation of Chancellor's year-end results for 1997, Chancellor's auditors had required the company to write off $1.14 million in related party payments to Adley-controlled entities because there was no substantiation for the payments. Although Marchese knew of the 1997 write-off of payments to Adley's entities, he took no steps to determine whether the $3.3 million MRB acquisition fee to Vestex recorded in 1998 was substantiated. He did not ask Metcalf Davis or Adley any questions about related party transactions.

3. MARCHESE SIGNED A MISLEADING FORM 10-KSB FILED BY CHANCELLOR

On April 16, 1999, Chancellor filed a Form 10-KSB for the year ended December 31, 1998. Adley, Chancellor's president, Chancellor's controller, Marchese and another outside director signed the Form 10-KSB. The Form 10-KSB was materially misleading in several respects.

First, in the financial statements included in its 1998 Form 10-KSB, Chancellor accounted for its acquisition of MRB as of August 1, 1998, and consolidated its financial results with those of MRB. As a result, Chancellor reported annual revenues of $29,639,000, 177% higher than the $10,708,000 revenue figure for Chancellor without the MRB consolidation. It also reported assets of $29,569,000 rather than $8,186,000 (261% higher). The accounting treatment did not comply with GAAP because during 1998 Chancellor did not have the effective control of MRB needed to justify accounting for MRB's acquisition.

Chancellor's Form 10-KSB also falsely represented that Adley's Vestex entity had handled the acquisition of MRB and provided consulting, financing and other services in connection with the acquisition, earning a fee payable of $3.3 million. The fee, for which no significant services in fact had been rendered, was improperly capitalized rather than reported as an expense. As a result, Chancellor reported net income of $850,000 rather than the $2.45 million loss which would have been reported had the fee been expensed, and its assets were overstated by 12%.

Marchese did not seek re-election as a director in 1999. He ceased to be a director of Chancellor on June 25, 1999. In August 1999, Marchese wrote a letter to the Commission staff expressing concern about Chancellor's financial reporting.

D. VIOLATIONS

1. MARCHESE VIOLATED AND CAUSED CHANCELLOR'S VIOLATION OF SECTION 10(B) OF THE EXCHANGE ACT AND RULE 10B-5 THEREUNDER

Marchese violated and caused Chancellor's violation of Section 10(b) of the Exchange Act and Rule 10b-5 thereunder when he signed Chancellor's 1998 Form 10-KSB. He was reckless in not knowing that it contained materially misleading statements. Marchese knew that the Form 10-KSB reflected a 1998 MRB acquisition date. He also knew that Chancellor's original audit firm had been fired, with his approval, due in part to its disagreement with the 1998 date. Nevertheless, he recklessly failed to make any inquiry into the circumstances leading to the new audit firm's approval of a 1998 MRB acquisition date, or whether it was correct. In addition, Marchese knew that in the previous year Chancellor had written off $1.14 million in related-party fees to Adley entities. However, he recklessly failed to make any inquiry into the basis for the reported $3.3 million in fees payable to an entity owned by Chancellor's CEO which were included in Chancellor's 1998 Firm 10-KSB. Marchese failed to make any inquiry into the existence of documents substantiating the services for which the fees were purportedly due.

2. MARCHESE CAUSED CHANCELLOR'S VIOLATIONS OF SECTIONS 13(A), 13(B)(2)(A) AND 13(B)(2)(B) OF THE EXCHANGE ACT AND RULES 12B-20 AND 13A-1 THEREUNDER

Marchese caused Chancellor's violations of Sections 13(a), 13(b)(2) (A) and 13(b)(2)(B) of the Exchange Act and Rules 12b-20 and 13a-1 thereunder. Section 13(a) of the Exchange Act and Rule 13a-1 require issuers of registered securities to file annual reports with the Commission. The information provided in those reports must be accurate. . . .

Section 13(b)(2)(A) of the Exchange Act requires every reporting company to make and keep books, records and accounts that accurately and fairly reflect the issuer's transactions. Section 13(b)(2)(B) requires a company to devise and maintain a system of internal controls sufficient to provide reasonable assurances that transactions are recorded as necessary to permit the preparation of financial statements in conformity with GAAP. These provisions require an issuer to employ and supervise reliable personnel, to maintain reasonable assurances that transactions are executed as authorized and to properly record transactions on an issuer's books. *SEC v. World-Wide Coin Investments, Ltd.*, 567 F. Supp. 724, 750 (N.D.Ga. 1983). A violation of Section 13(b)(2)(A) or 13(b)(2)(B) does not require a showing of scienter. *Id.* at 751.

Marchese's conduct caused Chancellor's violations of Sections 13(a) and 13(b)(2)(A) and Rules 12b-20 and 13a-1. He was reckless in not knowing that Chancellor's Form 10-KSB for 1998 contained materially misleading statements. Further, he signed Chancellor's Form 10-KSB for 1998 without making any inquiry into the basis for the reported fees payable to Adley's company or the basis for the new audit firm's approval of a 1998 MRB acquisition date.

Marchese also caused Chancellor's violations of Section 13(b)(2)(B) of the Exchange Act. He never attempted to determine the reason for Chancellor's varying accounting treatments of the MRB acquisition and related fees to Vestex, and whether these demonstrated a lack of internal controls to ensure accurate financial reporting and prevent improper transfers to related parties. Marchese never reviewed Chancellor's accounting procedures or determined whether in fact there were any internal controls.

***

ACCORDINGLY, IT IS ORDERED:

Pursuant to Section 21C of the Exchange Act, that Respondent Marchese shall cease and desist from committing or causing any violations and any future violations of Section 10(b) of the Exchange Act and Rule 10b-5 promulgated thereunder, and from causing any violations and any future violations of Sections 13(a), 13(b)(2)(A) and 13(B)(2)(B) of the Exchange Act and Rules 12b-20 and 13a-1 promulgated thereunder.

By the Commission.

Jonathan G. Katz

Secretary

QUESTION

Ever since the enactment of the Securities Enforcement and Penny Stock Reform Act of 1990, SEC enforcement actions have been a powerful and frequently used weapon to secure compliance with the federal securities laws. The case against Michael Marchese generated a great deal of practitioner commentary. In the aftermath of the settlement, then-SEC enforcement director Stephen Cutler stated: "[W]e intend to continue following closely in our investigations on whether outside directors have lived up to their role as guardians of the shareholders they serve. As with the *Chancellor* case, we will exercise particular scrutiny in considering the role of directors in approving or acquiescing in transactions by company management."[32] Imagine that a public-company board of directors has asked you to advise them on the implications of the Chancellor case on their duty to monitor obligations. How would you advise then? More specifically, to what extent, if at all, does the SEC enforcement action against Marchese go beyond existing "red flag" doctrine under state corporate law?

NOTE ON THE FEDERAL ORGANIZATIONAL SENTENCING GUIDELINES

The United States has begun to sometimes treat lapses from statutory or administratively mandated standards of business conduct as criminal matters.[33] Federal statutory law has been a powerful engine of this movement. The Comprehensive Environmental Response, Compensation, and Liability Act (CERCLA),[34] for example, opens up potential civil and criminal liabilities for both corporations and "persons in charge," who may be officers or low-level employees.[35] The Resource Conservation and Recovery Act (RCRA) imposes criminal liability on "any person" who knowingly transports hazardous waste to an unpermitted facility or treats, stores, or disposes of any hazardous waste without a permit.[36] Similarly, the Clean Water Act[37] and the Clean Air Act include criminal penalties applicable to any "person" including "any responsible corporate officer"[38] who violates those Acts. Environmental laws are simply one category of substantive federal regulation in which the criminal law is deployed to promote corporate compliance with regulation. The Occupational Safety and Health Act (OSHA);[39] the Food, Drug, and Cosmetics Act;[40] the antitrust acts; the Foreign Corrupt Practices Act (FCPA);[41] and the acts regulating federally chartered or insured depository institutions[42] and securities markets[43] all

---

32. Stephen M. Cutler, *The Themes of Sarbanes-Oxley as Reflected in the Commission's Enforcement Program.* Speech at UCLA Law School, Los Angeles, California (Sept. 20, 2004).

33. E.g., Flom, *U.S. Prosecutors Take a Tough Line,* Finan. Times, Oct. 31, 1991, at 21.

34. 42 U.S.C.A. §§9601 et seq.

35. E.g., *United States v. Mexico Seed & Feed Co.*, 764 F. Supp. 565, *rev'd in part*, 980 F.2d 473 (8th Cir. 1992).

36. 42 U.S.C. §6928(d), (e).

37. 33 U.S.C. §§1319(c), 1362(5), 1321(b)(5) (specifically including "any responsible corporate officer").

38. 42 U.S.C. §§7602(e), 7413(c)(6).

39. 21 U.S.C. §333.

40. 21 U.S.C.A. §§301 et seq.

41. 15 U.S.C. §§ 78m et seq.

42. E.g., Financial Institutions Reform, Recovery, and Enforcement Act of 1989, Pub. L. No. 101-429, 104 Stat. 931 (1990).

43. E.g., Securities Enforcement Remedies and Penny Stock Act of 1990, Pub. L. No. 101-429, 104 Stat. 931 (1990).

authorize substantial civil or criminal fines against corporations and their officers or employees.

In 1991, pursuant to the Sentencing Reform Act of 1984, the United States Sentencing Commission[44] adopted Organizational Sentencing Guidelines, which set forth a uniform sentencing structure for organizations convicted of federal criminal violations and provided for penalties that generally exceed those previously imposed on corporations.[45] The Guidelines offer powerful incentives for firms to put compliance programs in place, to report violations of law promptly, and to make voluntary remediation efforts. Under the Organizational Sentencing Guidelines, a convicted organization that has satisfied these conditions will receive a much lower fine. For example, the Guidelines will reduce the "base fine of a fully compliant firm"[46] by up to 95 percent, while they quadruple the base fine of firms with the highest culpability rating.[47] Since the maximum base fine under the Guidelines is $72.5 million, the culpability score could cause a variation in a fine from $3.6 million to $290 million for the same offense, depending on the circumstances.

Designing corporate compliance programs has developed into a new legal subspecialty. The enormous potential fines at stake today make it less likely than it was in 1963 that a court construing the duties of corporate directors would pass over a board's failure to implement a legal compliance program as blithely as was done in *Allis-Chalmers.*

IN RE CAREMARK INTERNATIONAL INC. DERIVATIVE LITIGATION

698 A.2d 959 (Del. Ch. 1996)

ALLEN, C.:

Pending is a motion pursuant to Chancery Rule 23.1 to approve as fair and reasonable a proposed settlement of a consolidated derivative action on behalf of Caremark International, Inc. ("Caremark"). The suit involves claims that the members of Caremark's board of directors (the "Board") breached their fiduciary duty of care to Caremark in connection with alleged violations by Caremark employees of federal and state laws and regulations applicable to health care providers. As a result of the alleged violations, Caremark was subject to an extensive four year investigation. . . . In 1994 Caremark was charged in an indictment with multiple felonies. It thereafter entered into a number of agreements with the Department of Justice and others. Those agreements included a plea agreement in which Caremark pleaded guilty to a single felony of mail fraud and agreed to pay civil and criminal fines. Subsequently, Caremark agreed to make reimbursements to

44. See Sentencing Reform Act of 1984, Pub. L. No. 98-473.
45. See United States Sentencing Commission, Guidelines Manual, ch. 8 (Nov. 1994) (www.ussc.gov/2002guid/2002guid.pdf).
46. *Id.* §8C2.4.
47. *Id.* §8C2.5.

various private and public parties. In all, the payments that Caremark has been required to make total approximately $250 million.

This suit was filed in 1994, purporting to seek on behalf of the company recovery of these losses from the individual defendants who constitute the Board of Directors of Caremark.[1] The parties now propose that it be settled and, after notice to Caremark shareholders, a hearing on the fairness of the proposal was held on August 16, 1996.

A motion of this type requires the court to assess the strengths and weaknesses of the claims asserted in light of the discovery record and to evaluate the fairness and adequacy of the consideration offered to the corporation in exchange for the release of all claims made or arising from the facts alleged. . . .

Legally, evaluation of the central claim made entails consideration of the legal standard governing a board of directors' obligation to supervise or monitor corporate performance. For the reasons set forth below I conclude, in light of the discovery record, that there is a very low probability that it would be determined that the directors of Caremark breached any duty to appropriately monitor and supervise the enterprise. . . .

I.   BACKGROUND

. . . I regard the following facts . . . as material. Caremark . . . was created in November 1992. . . . The business practices that created the problem pre-dated the spin-off. During the relevant period Caremark was involved in two main health care business segments, providing patient care and managed care services. . . .

A substantial part of the revenues generated by Caremark's businesses is derived from third party payments, insurers, and Medicare and Medicaid reimbursement programs. The latter source of payments is subject to the terms of the Anti-Referral Payments Law ("ARPL") which prohibits health care providers from paying any form of remuneration to induce the referral of Medicare or Medicaid patients. From its inception, Caremark entered into a variety of agreements with hospitals, physicians, and health care providers for advice and services, as well as distribution agreements with drug manufacturers, as had its predecessor prior to 1992. Specifically, Caremark did have a practice of entering into contracts for services (e.g., consultation agreements and research grants) with physicians at least some of whom prescribed or recommended services or products that Caremark provided to Medicare recipients and other patients. Such contracts were not prohibited by the ARPL but they obviously raised a possibility of unlawful "kickbacks."

As early as 1989, Caremark's predecessor issued an internal "Guide to Contractual Relationships" ("Guide") to govern its employees in entering into contracts with physicians and hospitals. . . . Each version of the Guide stated as Caremark's and its predecessor's policy that no payments would

---

1. Thirteen of the Directors have been members of the Board since November 30, 1992. Nancy Brinker joined the Board in October 1993.

be made in exchange for or to induce patient referrals. But what one might deem a prohibited quid pro quo was not always clear. Due to a scarcity of court decisions interpreting the ARPL, however, Caremark repeatedly publicly stated that there was uncertainty concerning Caremark's interpretation of the law. . . .

In August 1991, the HHS [Health and Human Service] Office of the Inspector General ("OIG") initiated an investigation of Caremark's predecessor. Caremark's predecessor was served with a subpoena requiring the production of documents, including contracts between Caremark's predecessor and physicians (Quality Service Agreements ("QSAs")). Under the QSAs, Caremark's predecessor appears to have paid physicians fees for monitoring patients under Caremark's predecessor's care, including Medicare and Medicaid recipients. Sometimes apparently those monitoring patients were referring physicians, which raised ARPL concerns. . . .

The first action taken by management, as a result of the initiation of the OIG investigation, was an announcement that as of October 1, 1991, Caremark's predecessor would no longer pay management fees to physicians for services to Medicare and Medicaid patients. . . .

During this period, Caremark's Board took several additional steps . . . to assure compliance with company policies concerning the ARPL and the contractual forms in the Guide. In April 1992, Caremark published a fourth revised version of its Guide apparently designed to assure that its agreements either complied with the ARPL and regulations or excluded Medicare and Medicaid patients altogether. In addition, in September 1992, Caremark instituted a policy requiring its regional officers, Zone Presidents, to approve each contractual relationship entered into by Caremark with a physician.

Although there is evidence that inside and outside counsel had advised Caremark's directors that their contracts were in accord with the law, Caremark recognized that some uncertainty respecting the correct interpretation of the law existed. . . .

Throughout the period of the government investigations, Caremark had an internal audit plan designed to assure compliance with business and ethics policies. In addition, Caremark employed Price Waterhouse as its outside auditor. On February 8, 1993, the Ethics Committee of Caremark's Board received and reviewed an outside auditors report by Price Waterhouse which concluded that there were no material weaknesses in Caremark's control structure. Despite the positive findings of Price Waterhouse, however, on April 20, 1993, the Audit & Ethics Committee adopted a new internal audit charter requiring a comprehensive review of compliance policies and the compilation of an employee ethics handbook concerning such policies.

The Board appears to have been informed about this project and other efforts to assure compliance with the law. For example, Caremark's management reported to the Board that Caremark's sales force was receiving an ongoing education regarding the ARPL and the proper use of Caremark's form contracts which had been approved by in-house counsel. On July 27, 1993, the new ethics manual, expressly prohibiting payments in exchange for referrals and requiring employees to report all illegal conduct to a toll free confidential ethics hotline, was approved and allegedly disseminated.[5] The record suggests that Caremark continued these policies in subsequent years, causing employees to be given revised versions of the ethics manual and requiring them to participate in training sessions concerning compliance with the law. . . .

On August 4, 1994, a federal grand jury in Minnesota issued a 47 page indictment charging Caremark, two of its officers (not the firm's chief officer), an individual who had been a sales employee of Genentech, Inc., and David R. Brown, a physician practicing in Minneapolis, with violating the ARPL over a lengthy period. According to the indictment, over $1.1 million had been paid to Brown to induce him to distribute Protropin, a human growth hormone drug marketed by Caremark. . . .

In reaction to the Minnesota Indictment . . . [m]anagement reiterated the grounds for its view that the contracts were in compliance with law.

Subsequently, five stockholder derivative actions were filed in this court and consolidated into this action. . . .

On September 21, 1994, a federal grand jury in Columbus, Ohio issued another indictment alleging that an Ohio physician had defrauded the Medicare program by requesting and receiving $134,600 in exchange for referrals of patients whose medical costs were in part reimbursed by Medicare in violation of the ARPL. . . . Caremark was the health care provider who allegedly made such payments. . . .

II. LEGAL PRINCIPLES . . .

The complaint charges the director defendants with breach of their duty of attention or care in connection with the on-going operation of the corporation's business. The claim is that the directors allowed a situation to develop and continue which exposed the corporation to enormous legal liability and that in so doing they violated a duty to be active monitors of corporate performance. The complaint thus does not charge . . . loyalty-type problems. . . .

1. *Potential liability for directoral decisions:* Director liability for a breach of the duty to exercise appropriate attention may, in theory, arise in two distinct contexts. First, such liability may be said to follow from a board decision that results in a loss because that decision was ill advised or "negligent". . . . What should be understood . . . is that compliance with a director's duty of care can never appropriately be judicially determined by reference to the content of the board decision that leads to a corporate loss, apart from consideration of the good faith or rationality of the process employed. . . .

---

5. Prior to the distribution of the new ethics manual, on March 12, 1993, Caremark's president had sent a letter to all senior, district, and branch managers restating Caremark's policies that no physician be paid for referrals, that the standard contract forms in the Guide were not to be modified, and that deviation from such policies would result in the immediate termination of employment.

2. *Liability for failure to monitor:* The second class of cases in which
director liability for inattention is theoretically possible entail circumstances in which a loss eventuates not from a decision, but from
unconsidered inaction. Most of the decisions that a corporation,
acting through its human agents, makes are, of course, not the subject of director attention. . . . As the facts of this case graphically
demonstrate, ordinary business decisions that are made by officers
and employees deeper in the interior of the organization can . . .
vitally affect the welfare of the corporation. . . . [They] raise the
question, what is the board's responsibility with respect to the organization and monitoring of the enterprise to assure that the corporation functions within the law to achieve its purposes?

Modernly this question has been given special importance by an
increasing tendency, especially under federal law, to employ the criminal
law to assure corporate compliance with external legal requirements,
including environmental, financial, employee and product safety as well
as assorted other health and safety regulations. In 1991, pursuant to the
Sentencing Reform Act of 1984, the United States Sentencing Commission
adopted Organizational Sentencing Guidelines which impact importantly
on the prospective effect these criminal sanctions might have on business
corporations. The Guidelines set forth a uniform sentencing structure for
organizations to be sentenced for violation of federal criminal statutes and
provide for penalties that equal or often massively exceed those previously
imposed on corporations. The Guidelines offer powerful incentives for
corporations today to have in place compliance programs to detect violations of law, promptly to report violations to appropriate public officials
when discovered, and to take prompt, voluntary remedial efforts.

In 1963, the Delaware Supreme Court in *Graham v. Allis-Chalmers
Mfg. Co.*, addressed the question of potential liability of board members for
losses experienced by the corporation as a result of the corporation having
violated the anti-trust laws of the United States. There was no claim in that
case that the directors knew about the behavior of subordinate employees
of the corporation that had resulted in the liability. Rather, as in this case,
the claim asserted was that the directors ought to have known of it. . . . The
Delaware Supreme Court concluded that, under the facts as they appeared,
there was no basis to find that the directors had breached a duty to be
informed of the ongoing operations of the firm. . . .

How does one generalize this holding today? Can it be said today,
absent some ground giving rise to suspicion of violation of law, that
corporate directors have no duty to assure that corporate information
gathering and reporting systems exists which represents a good faith
attempt to provide senior management and the Board with information
respecting . . . compliance with applicable statutes and regulations? I
certainly do not believe so. . . .

[I]n recent years the Delaware Supreme Court has made it clear —
especially in its jurisprudence concerning takeovers . . . — the seriousness
with which the corporation law views the role of the corporate board.
Secondly, I note the elementary fact that relevant and timely information
is an essential predicate for satisfaction of the board's supervisory and

monitoring role under [DGCL] Section 141. . . . Thirdly, I note the potential impact of the federal organizational sentencing guidelines on any business organization. Any rational person attempting in good faith to meet an organizational governance responsibility would be bound to take into account this development and the enhanced penalties and the opportunities for reduced sanctions that it offers.

[I]t would . . . be a mistake to conclude . . . that corporate boards may satisfy their obligation to be reasonably informed concerning the corporation, without assuring themselves that information and reporting systems exist in the organization that are reasonably designed to provide to senior management and to the board itself timely, accurate information sufficient to allow management and the board, each within its scope, to reach informed judgments concerning both the corporation's compliance with law and its business performance.

Obviously the level of detail that is appropriate for such an information system is a question of business judgment. And obviously too, no rationally designed information and reporting system will remove the possibility that the corporation will violate laws or regulations. . . . But it is important that the board exercise a good faith judgment that the corporation's information and reporting system is in concept and design adequate to assure the board that appropriate information will come to its attention in a timely manner as a matter of ordinary operations, so that it may satisfy its responsibility. . . .

III.   ANALYSIS OF THIRD AMENDED COMPLAINT AND SETTLEMENT

A. THE CLAIMS

On balance, . . . I conclude that this settlement is fair and reasonable. In light of the fact that the Caremark Board already has a functioning committee charged with overseeing corporate compliance, the changes in corporate practice that are presented as consideration for the settlement do not impress one as very significant. Nonetheless, that consideration appears fully adequate to support dismissal of the derivative claims of director fault asserted, because those claims find no substantial evidentiary support in the record and quite likely were susceptible to a motion to dismiss in all events. . . .

2. *Failure to monitor:* Since it does appear that the Board was to some extent unaware of the activities that led to liability, I turn to a consideration of the other potential avenue to director liability that the pleadings take: director inattention or "negligence". Generally where a claim of directorial liability for corporate loss is predicated upon ignorance of liability creating activities within the corporation, . . . only a sustained or systematic failure of the board to exercise oversight . . . will establish the lack of good faith that is a necessary condition to liability. . . .

Here the record supplies essentially no evidence that the director defendants were guilty of a sustained failure to exercise their oversight function. To the contrary, . . . the corporation's information systems appear to have represented a good faith attempt to be informed of relevant facts. If the directors did not know the specifics of the activities that led to the indictments, they cannot be faulted. . . .

NOTES FOLLOWING CAREMARK

Among the various provisions of the Sarbanes-Oxley Act of 2002, §404 requires that the CEO and the CFO of firms with securities regulated under the Securities Exchange Act of 1934 periodically certify that they have disclosed to the company's independent auditor all deficiencies in the design or operation, or any material weakness, of the firm's internal controls for financial reporting. Among all of the debate surrounding "SOX" (alternatively, "Sarbox"), §404 has generated the most discussion and controversy. Critics have complained that §404 compliance costs have far exceeded predictions, are irrationally high, and have pushed many companies, particularly smaller companies, out of the public markets.[48] More recently, it is noted that initial public offers of stock are, post SOX, moving to London, Hong Kong, and other financial centers and away from the New York Stock Exchange. Judging from public statements, Section 404 is not the only cause of this, but it is believed to be a very major part of the perceived problem. Proponents, on the other hand, argue that §404 forces companies to take a hard look at their control systems, which has long-term benefits that they suppose outweigh the costs. Since 2002, among companies with more than $1 billion in market capitalization, 2 percent have disclosed material weaknesses under §404.[49] Two studies find that companies disclosing weaknesses under §404 suffer a 2 percent market-adjusted decline in their stock price, on average.[50]

In the event that a firm's internal controls fail to prevent a loss and the CEO *did not* identify any weakness in the control system to the auditors, cases such as *Kamin v. American Express Co.*, above, indicate that state law imposes little risk of directorial liability — unless, under *Caremark*, the board's failure to prevent a loss resulted from a systematic failure to attempt to control potential liabilities. Does §404 of Sarbanes-Oxley change that prediction in any way? What are the arguments, pro and con?

In 2005, the U.S. Supreme Court struck down the federal sentencing guidelines for individuals as a violation of a criminal defendant's Sixth Amendment right to a jury trial.[51] As a result, the federal sentencing guidelines are now advisory, not mandatory, with respect to individual criminal defendants. The status of the organizational sentencing guidelines remains murkier, however, because the extent to which Sixth Amendment jury trial

48. Professors Ehud Kamar, Pinar Karaca-Mandic, and Eric Talley present empirical evidence supporting the view that small U.S. public companies are more likely to go private due to the burdens imposed by Sarbanes-Oxley compliance. See Ehud Kamar et al., *Going-Private Decisions and the Sarbanes-Oxley Act of 2002: A Cross-Country Analysis* (USC Center in Law, Economics & Organization Research Paper No. C05-12) (2006).

49. Christine Dunn, *Effective Controls, Clean Opinions Rule the Roost*, Compliance Week (June 2, 2006).

50. Messod Daniel Beneish et al., *Internal Control Weaknesses and Information Uncertainty* (working paper April 2006); Gus De Franco et al., *The Wealth Change and Redistribution Effects of Sarbanes-Oxley Internal Control Disclosures* (working paper April 2005).

rights extend to corporate defendants is not clear. Even if the organizational sentencing guidelines are deemed to be only advisory, a 2003 Department of Justice memorandum entitled "Principles of Federal Prosecution of Business Organizations" (a.k.a. the "Thompson Memo," after then-Deputy Attorney General Larry Thompson) directs U.S. Attorneys to consider the depth and quality of a company's compliance program in connection with charging decisions. As a result, the logic that underlies *Caremark* remains important under federal law as well.[52]

In any event, it is clear that some combination of *Caremark*, the federal sentencing guidelines, SOX §404, and the Thompson memo (as well as other factors, no doubt) has made corporate compliance programs a booming practice area within law firms and general counsels' offices. Today, enforcement actions for inadequate controls, not substantive regulations, are the most common federal mechanisms for the regulation of public corporations.

8.7 "KNOWING" VIOLATIONS OF LAW

In *Caremark*, the court says that directors have a duty to take reasonable steps to see that the corporation has in place an information and control structure designed to offer reasonable assurance that the corporation is in compliance with the law. But does that mean every aspect of our public policy should be deployed to this end? Specifically, in addition to the incentives provided in the federal Organizational Sentencing Guidelines above, should corporate law also command obedience to positive law? When we ask this question, are we necessarily asking whether shareholders should be able to sue directors to recover any loss the corporation may suffer (as in *Caremark*) by reason of a knowing violation of the law? Are there issues present in such a question in addition to whether we want augmented enforcement?

MILLER v. A.T.&T.

507 F.2d 759 (3rd Cir. 1974)

SEITZ, C.J.:

Plaintiffs, stockholders in American Telephone and Telegraph Company ("AT&T"), brought a stockholders' derivative action ... against

---

51. *U.S. v. Booker*, 543 U.S. 220 (2005).

52. In 2006, the Delaware Supreme Court endorsed and clarified the *Caremark* standard, stating that: "We hold that *Caremark* articulates the necessary conditions predicate for director oversight liability: (a) the directors utterly failed to implement any reporting or information system or controls; *or* (b) having implemented such a system or controls, consciously failed to monitor or oversee its operations thus disabling themselves from being informed of risks or problems requiring their attention. In either case, imposition of liability requires a showing that the directors knew that they were not discharging their fiduciary obligations." Stone v. Ritter, C.A. No. 1570-N (Del. Nov. 6, 2006).

AT&T and all but one of its directors. The suit centered upon the failure of AT&T to collect an outstanding debt of some $1.5 million owed to the company by the Democratic National Committee ("DNC") for communications services provided by AT&T during the 1968 Democratic national convention. Federal diversity jurisdiction was invoked under 28 U.S.C. §1332.

Plaintiffs' complaint alleged that "neither the officers or directors of AT&T have taken any action to recover the amount owed" from on or about August 20, 1968, when the debt was incurred, until May 31, 1972, the date plaintiffs' amended complaint was filed. The failure to collect was alleged to have involved a breach of the defendant directors' duty to exercise diligence in handling the affairs of the corporation, to have resulted in affording a preference to the DNC in collection procedures in violation of §202(a) of the Communications Act of 1934, . . . and to have amounted to AT&T's making a "contribution" to the DNC in violation of a federal prohibition on corporate campaign spending, 18 U.S.C. §610 (1970). . . .

The pertinent law on the question of the defendant directors' fiduciary duties in this diversity action is that of New York, the state of AT&T's incorporation. . . . The sound business judgment rule, the basis of the district court's dismissal of plaintiffs' complaint, expresses the unanimous decision of American courts to eschew intervention in corporate decision-making if the judgment of directors and officers in uninfluenced by personal considerations and is exercised in good faith. . . .

Had plaintiffs' complaint alleged only failure to pursue a corporate claim, application of the sound business judgment rule would support the district court's ruling that a shareholder could not attack the directors' decision. . . . Where, however, the decision not to collect a debt owed the corporation is itself alleged to have been an illegal act, different rules apply. When New York law regarding such acts by directors is considered in conjunction with the underlying purposes of the particular statute involved here, we are convinced that the business judgment rule cannot insulate the defendant directors from liability if they did in fact breach 18 U.S.C. §610, as plaintiffs have charged.

Roth v. Robertson, 64 Misc. 343, 118 N.Y.S. 351 (Sup. Ct. 1909), illustrates the proposition that even though committed to benefit the corporation, illegal acts may amount to a breach of fiduciary duty in New York. In *Roth,* the managing director of an amusement park company had allegedly used corporate funds to purchase the silence of persons who threatened to complain about unlawful Sunday operation of the park. Recovery from the defendant director was sustained on the ground that the money was an illegal payment. . . .

The plaintiffs' complaint in the instant case alleges a similar "waste" of $1.5 million through an illegal campaign contribution. . . .

The alleged violation of the federal prohibition against corporate political contributions not only involves the corporation in criminal activity but similarly contravenes a policy of Congress clearly enunciated in 18 U.S. C. §610. That statute and its predecessor reflect congressional efforts: (1) to destroy the influence of corporations over elections through financial contributions and (2) to check the practice of using corporate funds to benefit political parties without the consent of the stockholders. . . .

The fact that shareholders are within the class for whose protection the statute was enacted gives force to the argument that the alleged breach of that statute should give rise to a cause of action in those shareholders to force the return to the corporation of illegally contributed funds. Since political contributions by corporations can be checked and shareholder control over the political use of general corporate funds is effectuated only if directors are restrained from causing the corporation to violate the statute, such a violation seems a particularly appropriate basis for finding breach of the defendant directors' fiduciary duty to the corporation. Under such circumstances, the directors cannot be insulated from liability on the ground that the contribution was made in the exercise of sound business judgment.

Since plaintiffs have alleged actual damage to the corporation from the transaction in the form of the loss of a $1.5 million increment to AT&T's treasury, we conclude that the complaint does state a claim upon which relief can be granted sufficient to withstand a motion to dismiss.

II

We have accepted plaintiffs' allegation of a violation of 18 U.S.C. §610 as a shorthand designation of the elements necessary to establish a breach of that statute. . . . That such a designation is sufficient for pleading purposes does not, however, relieve plaintiffs of their ultimate obligation to prove the elements of the statutory violation as part of their proof of breach of fiduciary duty. At the appropriate time, plaintiffs will be required to produce evidence sufficient to establish three distinct elements comprising a violation of 18 U.S.C. §610: that AT&T (1) made a contribution of money or anything of value to the DNC (2) in connection with a federal election (3) for the purpose of influencing the outcome of that election. . . .

The order of the district court will be reversed and the case remanded for further proceedings consistent with this opinion.

PROBLEM

Knowing violations of law are conceptually distinct from the duty of care topics that are addressed in the prior sections of this chapter. To see why, consider a board that deliberates with the utmost care to authorize an action that they know to be illegal. As the *Miller* court tells us, the business judgment rule will not immunize their decision from judicial scrutiny.[53] For this reason the duty to obey the law can be seen as a judge-created

---

53. See also *Metro Communications Corp. BVI v. Advanced Mobilecomm Technologies, Inc.*, 854 A.2d 121, 131 (Del. Ch. 2004) ("Under Delaware law, a fiduciary may not choose to manage an entity in an illegal fashion, even if the fiduciary believes that the illegal activity will result in profits for the entity.").

positive overlay on the overall fiduciary duty structure. This imposition seems unproblematic in the case of definite violations of the law, but what about the far more common situation where the legal advice is "some likelihood" or "substantial risk" of violating the law? Could it be the case that the corporate law prevents directors from taking any risk of violating the law? Or is a balance of the probabilities test required, in which the directors have to know only that it is more likely than not lawful? (in which case they must do a rational calculation of profit minus fines, discounted by the risk of being caught?) To make the question concrete, consider the following problem:

The board of Acme, Inc. is asked to approve the use of Grade II fuel instead of Grade I fuel in operating a large plant. The board is told that using the lower grade of fuel will cause the company to run an 85 percent risk that the plant will exceed Clean Air Act standards at least once a month, and the best estimate is that it will cause this to happen on average 3.5 times per month. If such a violation were detected and prosecuted, a fine could be levied that would be no more than $10,000 for each violation. Using the lower grade fuel would save more than $80,000 per month at current prices. While this decision would not ordinarily require board action, in this case senior management brings the question to the board because it does involve a possible violation of government regulations.

1. Consider that you are the general counsel of the company. What would you tell the board about its fiduciary duty to the corporation, and what would you say about the corporation's obligation to obey the law and the directors' obligation to cause it to do so?

2. Would it matter if the probability of violation were 1 percent instead of 85 percent, but the sanction for causing a knowing violation of the standard was incarceration for any person in control of the violator (including directors)?

3. You are personal counsel to one of the outside directors. This action is taken, and the corporation is later determined to have violated applicable clean air standards and fined. What sources of potential risks to your client do you see, and what arguments in her favor exist?

CONFLICT TRANSACTIONS: THE DUTY OF LOYALTY

The core of fiduciary doctrine is the duty of loyalty. In Chapters 7 and 8, we examined the relatively mild legal controls on the board's discretion to make ordinary business decisions: the duty of care and the shareholders' right to appoint directors. These controls are "weak" in the sense that they do not limit the board's discretion to enter specific transactions — nor could they without sacrificing the efficiencies that arise from the delegation of managerial power to the board. But there are some specific corporate actions over which it may be sensible to limit board discretion. Indeed, the corporate law in every jurisdiction imposes specific controls on two classes of corporate actions: those in which a director or controlling shareholder has a personal financial interest and those that are considered integral to the continued existence or identity of the company. In this chapter, we address the first class of interested corporate actions. These actions naturally include self-dealing transactions between the company and its directors, but they also extend to other transactions, such as appropriations of "corporate opportunities," compensation of officers and directors, and even relations between controlling shareholders and minority shareholders. In U.S. corporate law, all of these interested transactions are regulated first and foremost by the fiduciary duty of loyalty. In Chapter 12, we explore the second class of corporate actions for which the law imposes specific limitations on board discretion, including such fundamental changes as corporate mergers, dissolutions, and sales of substantially all assets.

The duty of loyalty requires a corporate director, officer, or controlling shareholder to exercise her institutional power over corporate processes or property (including information) in a good-faith effort to advance the interests of the company. Stated negatively, the duty of loyalty requires such a person who transacts with the corporation to fully disclose all material facts to the corporation's disinterested representatives and to deal with the company on terms that are intrinsically fair in all respects. Thus, corporate officers, directors, and controlling shareholders may not deal with the corporation in any way that benefits themselves at its expense.

The importance of this default obligation is greater in the corporation than in the simple agency relationship because corporate directors and officers (like trustees) tend to exercise greater discretion than do ordinary agents. In addition, the duty of loyalty is more complex in the corporate context for two reasons. First, although the corporation is a fictional legal entity, real people invest in it. Some invest financial assets by buying the corporation's debt or equity, while others invest human capital over their years of employment. Communities may invest in the corporation with roads, schools, tax abatements, etc. Thus, when we say that directors owe a duty of loyalty, the logical first question is, "Loyalty to whom?" The second reason relates to the question how to enforce this duty of loyalty — to whomever it is owed. The enforcement problem is especially pressing in large public corporations, where most constituencies — but especially shareholders — tend to be fragmented and unorganized.

9.1   DUTY TO WHOM?

To whom do directors owe loyalty? The short answer is that they owe their duty to the corporation as a legal entity.[1] Yet the meaning of that answer is still disputed today. The "corporation" has multiple constituencies with conflicting interests, including stockholders, creditors, employees, suppliers, and customers. To say that directors owe loyalty to the corporation masks conflicts among these constituencies. Happily, in most cases, these conflicts can be reconciled in practice. When a solvent corporation pursues its regular business activities, the interests of its management, creditors, employees, and stockholders are largely congruent with the interests of its equity investors. Thus, it makes no difference whether managers think of themselves as furthering long-term shareholder interests or furthering a multiconstituency interest in long-term corporate welfare.

The question of whose interests ultimately count is of principal importance when the corporation faces insolvency (when by definition there may not be enough corporate assets to satisfy all of the corporation's obligations to all constituencies) or when it contemplates a terminal transaction for equity investors, such as a cash merger (when equity investors will no longer have an interest in the future welfare of the corporation or its other constituencies). In such cases the question of "Duty to whom?" may be acute.

9.1.1   The Shareholder Primacy Norm

That director loyalty to the "corporation" is, ultimately, loyalty to equity investors is an important theme of U.S. corporate law. Shareholders, after all, elect the boards of directors in U.S. corporations, as they do in almost all other jurisdictions. But exactly what additional weight the norm of shareholder primacy carries is not always clear.

---

1. In some circumstances, directors deal with stockholders directly, as when they disclose information about a transaction that requires shareholder approval. In these cases, directors owe a duty directly to shareholders. See *In re Cencom Cable Income Partners, L.P. Litigation*, 2000 Del. Ch. LEXIS 10.

In fact, shareholder priority more closely resembles a deep but implicit value in American corporate law than a legal rule in any normal sense. In 1919, the Supreme Court of Michigan recognized this value explicitly as a rule in the case *Dodge v. Ford Motor Co.*[2] The Dodge brothers, who held 10 percent of the shares in Ford Motor Company, had sued to force Ford's board to declare a dividend out of a large pool of earnings that had been retained to fund new projects and to "finance" price reductions on Ford products. Henry Ford, Ford's controlling shareholder, explained his decision to eliminate special dividends on the grounds that Ford had an obligation to share its success "with the public" through price reductions. Taking this claim at face value, the Dodge brothers alleged that Ford's directors had wrongfully subordinated shareholder interests to those of consumers by holding back dividends. The court agreed and affirmed the primacy of the shareholders' interests.

> [I]t is not within the lawful powers of a board to shape and conduct the affairs of a corporation for the merely incidental benefit of shareholders and for the primary purpose of benefiting others, and no one will contend that, if the avowed purpose of the defendant directors was to sacrifice the interests of shareholders, it would not be the duty of the courts to interfere.[3]

Dodge, however, is one of few decisions by a U.S. court to enforce shareholder primacy as a rule of law. Moreover, it is an old opinion. A board's decision today to use retained earnings to fund investments, price reductions, or even increased employee wages would easily be justified as a device to increase long-term corporate earnings and, as such, would be immune from shareholder attack. A question of loyalty would arise only in the odd circumstance that the board claimed to advance nonshareholder interests over those of shareholders. Thus, *Dodge v. Ford Motor Co.* is unique precisely because Mr. Ford announced that he was acting in the interests of nonshareholders.

Although the norm of shareholder primacy currently dominates discussion of U.S. corporate law, it has not fully eclipsed a competing norm: the view that directors must act to advance the interests of all constituencies in the corporation, not just the shareholders.[4] From this perspective, the

---

2. 204 Mich. 459, 170 N.W. 668 (1919).

3. *Id.* at 507.

4. The classic discussion of this subject is the Depression-era debate between Professor E. Merrick Dodd of Harvard and Professor Adolf Berle of Columbia. See Adopf A. Berle, *Corporate Powers as Powers in Trust*, 44 Harv. L. Rev. 1049 (1931); E. Merrick Dodd, *For Whom Are Corporate Managers Trustees*, 45 Harv. L. Rev. 1145 (1932); Adolf A. Berle, *For Whom Corporate Managers Are Trustees: A Note*, 45 Harv. L. Rev. 1365 (1932). The literature on this subject is voluminous. For a recap of the issue in the age of hostile takeovers, see William T. Allen, *Our Schizophrenic Conception of the Business Corporation*, 14 Cardozo L. Rev. 261 (1992). For a law-and-economics defense of the Merrick Dodd position that directors must reconcile the interests of disparate corporate constituencies, see Margaret M. Blair & Lynn A. Stout, *A Team Production Theory of Corporate Law*, 85 Va. L. Rev. 247 (1999). For a contrasting view that shareholder primacy is likely to dominate the future development of corporate law, see Henry Hansmann & Reinier H. Kraakman, *The End of History for Corporate Law*, 89 Geo. L.J. 439 (2001).

corporation is more than a private contract; the state bestows the status of legal entity, including limited liability, on the corporation in order to advance the public interest by enabling the board to protect all corporate constituencies, not just shareholders. Of course, sophisticated proponents of the shareholder primacy goal agree that the state is entitled to craft the duty of directors in any way it chooses. They argue, however, that framing the board's mission as maximizing shareholder welfare also serves to maximize the welfare of other corporate constituencies and society as a whole. (Or vice versa — see sidebar: Doing Good and Doing Well at Timberland.)

Before the leveraged buyout wave of the 1980s, conflict between these different conceptions of director loyalty occurred chiefly in the context of corporate charitable giving, where this question arose: How can directors *ever* justify giving away the corporation's profits to worthy causes if their principal duty is owed to shareholders? Unsurprisingly, when faced with defendant directors who, unlike Henry Ford, justified their actions by reference to long-term corporate benefits, courts have deferred to director action. The following excerpt deals with a small grant to Princeton University by the A.P. Smith Manufacturing Company.

> ### Doing Good and Doing Well at Timberland
> #### Wall Street Journal (Sept. 9, 2003)
>
> Nestled in this sleepy community north of Boston, 30-year old Timberland Co. is almost as well known for its corporate altruism as for its fashionable footwear and cutting-edge outdoor apparel. Timberland allows workers to take a full work week off each year, with pay, to help local charities. It also offers four paid sabbaticals each year to workers who agree to work full-time for up to six months at a nonprofit. And it shuts down operations for a day each year so its 5,400 workers can take part in various company-sponsored philanthropic projects. In the past few years, Timberland workers have helped in the cleanup and construction of community centers, camps, playgrounds, hiking trails, beaches, and homeless shelters.
>
> But Timberland's generosity isn't entirely altruistic. Company officials say offering its employees a chance to be good Samaritans helps it attract and retain valuable talent. That became even more evident after Sept. 11, 2001, when job applications spiked and many of the applicants cited the company's social awareness as a lure. "People like to feel good about where they work and what they do," says Jeffrey Swartz, Timberland's chief executive.

A.P. SMITH MANUFACTURING CO. v. BARLOW

98 A.2d 581 (N.J. 1953)

Jacobs, J.:

The objecting stockholders have not disputed any of the foregoing testimony nor the showing of great need by Princeton and other private institutions of higher learning and the important public service being rendered by them for democratic government and industry alike. Similarly, they have acknowledged that for over two decades there has been state legislation on our books which expresses a strong public policy in favor of corporate contributions such as that being questioned by them. Nevertheless, they have taken the position that (1) the plaintiff's certificate of incorporation does not expressly authorize the contribution and under common-law principles the company does not possess any implied or incidental power to make it, and (2) the New Jersey statutes which expressly authorize the contribution may not constitutionally be applied to the plaintiff, a corporation created long before their enactment. . . .

In his discussion of the early history of business corporations Professor Williston refers to a 1702 publication where the author stated flatly that "The general intent and end of all civil incorporations is for better government." And he points out that the early corporate charters, particularly their recitals, furnish additional support for the notion that the corporate object was the public one of managing and ordering the trade as well as the private one of profit for the members. . . . However, with later economic and social developments and the free availability of the corporate device for all trades, the end of private profit became generally accepted as the controlling one in all businesses other than those classed broadly as public utilities. Cf. E. Merrick Dodd, Jr., *For Whom Are Corporate Managers Trustees?*, 45 Harv. L. Rev. 1145, 1148 (1932). As a concomitant the common-law rule developed that those who managed the corporation could not disburse any corporate funds for philanthropic or other worthy public cause unless the expenditure would benefit the corporation. . . . *Dodge v. Ford Motor Co.*, 204 Mich. 459 (Sup. Ct. 1919). . . . [C]ourts while adhering to the terms of the common-law rule, have applied it very broadly to enable worthy corporate donations with indirect benefits to the corporations. . . . When the wealth of the nation was primarily in the hands of individuals they discharged their responsibilities as citizens by donating freely for charitable purposes. With the transfer of most of the wealth to corporate hands and the imposition of heavy burdens of individual taxation, [these individuals have] . . . turned to corporations to assume the modern obligations of good citizenship in the same manner as humans do. . . .

More and more [corporations] have come to recognize that their salvation rests upon [a] sound economic and social environment which in turn rests . . . upon free and vigorous nongovernmental institutions of learning. It seems to us that just as the conditions prevailing when corporations were originally created required that they serve public as well as private interests, modern conditions require that corporations acknowledge and discharge social as well as private responsibilities as members of the communities within which they operate. Within this broad concept there is no difficulty in sustaining, as incidental to their proper objects and in aid of the public welfare, the power of corporations to contribute corporate funds within reasonable limits in support of academic institutions. But even if we confine ourselves to the terms of the common-law-rule, . . . such expenditures may likewise readily be justified as being for the benefit of the corporation; indeed, if need be the matter may be viewed strictly in terms of actual survival of the corporation in a free enterprise system. . . .

In 1930 a statute was enacted in our State which expressly provided that any corporation could cooperate with other corporations and natural persons in the creation and maintenance of community funds and charitable, philanthropic or benevolent instrumentalities conducive to public welfare, and could for such purposes expend such corporate sums as the directors "deem expedient and as in their judgment will contribute to the protection of the corporate interests." . . . In 1950 . . . the Legislature declared that it shall be the public policy of our State . . . that encouragement be given to the creation and maintenance of institutions engaged in . . . the betterment of social and economic conditions, and it expressly empowered corporations . . . to contribute reasonable sums to such institutions, provided, however, that . . . the contribution shall not exceed 1% of capital and surplus unless . . . authorized by the stockholders. . . . It may [also] be noted that statutes relating to charitable contributions by corporations have now been passed in 29 states. . . .

The appellants contend that the foregoing New Jersey statutes may not be applied to corporations created before their passage. Fifty years before the incorporation of The A.P. Smith Manufacturing Company our Legislature provided that every corporate charter thereafter granted "shall be subject to alteration, suspension and repeal, in the discretion of the legislature." L.1846, p. 16; R.S. 14:2-9. A similar reserved power was placed into our State Constitution in 1875 (Art. IV, Sec. VII, par. 11), and is found in our present Constitution. . . .

In the light of all of the foregoing we have no hesitancy in sustaining the validity of the donation by the plaintiff. There is no suggestion that it was made indiscriminately or to a pet charity of the corporate directors in furtherance of personal rather than corporate ends. On the contrary, it was made to a preeminent institution of higher learning, was modest in amount and well within the limitations imposed by the statutory enactments, and was voluntarily made in the reasonable belief that it would aid the public welfare and advance the interests of the plaintiff as a private corporation and as part of the community in which it operate. . . .

QUESTIONS ON SMITH v. BARLOW

1. How far does *Barlow*'s holding reach? Can the long-term benefit of the corporation support a financial contribution to a controversial political cause (say, a contraception manufacturer wanting to make a donation to a pro-choice organization)? What about to the favorite charity of a corporate customer or a director? Does it matter which?

2. More fundamentally, what, precisely, is the connection between the observation that the corporation should serve the public interest and the claim that directors ought to have the power to contribute to charity? Could the law deny directors this power in the name of public interest, too?

9.1.2 Constituency Statutes

In most cases, the scope of the board's discretion to make charitable contributions is economically unimportant because the sums at stake are small. By contrast, the question "To whom do directors owe loyalty?" had much more economic import in the leveraged buyout transactions of the 1980s. In these transactions, buyers would typically offer shareholders a high premium price for their shares and then, when they had control, sell off significant assets, lay off workers, increase debt on the company's balance sheet, and replace senior management. Thus these transactions left creditors and employees to face an increased risk of default and bankruptcy.[5] In most cases, these changes increased the value of target companies, partly at the cost of imposing uncompensated losses on nonshareholder constituencies.

In some buyout transactions, financial buyers recruited incumbent senior managers as joint venturers in their deals. But in others, financial buyers were "hostile," and senior managers found themselves in the same precarious position as other nonshareholder stakeholders. Naturally, these managers often resisted being taken over, but in justifying their resistance to high-premium cash offers, they could not persuasively resort to a vision of maximizing long-term economic value of shareholders (as managers had long done for making charitable contributions). Thus, managerial advocates turned to the rationale that directors owe loyalty to something apart from the shareholders alone: the corporation, understood as a combination of all its stakeholders — creditors, shareholders, managers, workers, suppliers, and customers.

With remarkable speed, state legislatures attempted to ride to the rescue of managers and other nonshareholder constituencies by enacting statutes that provided, in varying terms, that directors have the power (but not the obligation) to balance the interests of nonshareholder constituencies against the interests of shareholders in setting corporate policy.[6] These statutes may or may not break with our venerable legal tradition of shareholder primacy. A conservative reading of them might be that they merely reassert the board's traditional freedom to deal with nonshareholder constituencies in whatever manner it believes best in order to advance the long-term interests of the corporate shareholders. By contrast, the Corporation Law Committee of the American Bar Association has refused to include a constituency provision in the Model Business Corporation Act on the grounds that this would break sharply with the tradition of U.S. corporate law and would undermine much of the established case law.[7] We deal with the constituency problem in greater depth in Chapter 13, in the context of hostile corporate takeovers.

5. See Andrei Shleifer & Lawrence H. Summers, *Breach of Trust in Hostile Takeovers*, in Corporate Takeovers: Causes and Consequences, pp. 33-56 (Alan J. Auerbach ed., 1988).

6. Delaware has *not* adopted a constituency statute. However, the Delaware Supreme Court has stated that, in creating takeover defenses, the board may consider the interests of corporate constituencies other than shareholders as long as these have some relationship to long-term shareholder value. *Unocal Corp. v. Mesa Petroleum Co.*, 493 A.2d 946 (Del. 1985). For an argument that the Delaware takeover cases implicitly adopt a paternalistic form of the shareholder primacy norm, see Bernard S. Black & Reinier H. Kraakman, *Delaware's Takeover Law: The Uncertain Search for Hidden Value*, 96 Nw. L. Rev. 521, 527-528 (2002).

7. Corporation Law Committee of the American Bar Association, *Report: Other Constituencies Statutes*, 45 Bus. Law. 2253 (1990).

9.2   SELF-DEALING TRANSACTIONS

If the legal primacy of shareholder interests over those of other constituencies remains uncertain in some cases, what is quite clear is that directors and corporate officers may not benefit financially at the expense of the corporation in self-dealing transactions. The danger in such transaction is apparent, but how should the law deal with it? The law might simply prohibit all (direct or indirect) transactions between directors or officers and the corporation. This would obviously eliminate the opportunity for insider opportunism, but it would do so at the cost of deterring some mutually beneficial transactions, as when directors are more confident about a corporation's prospects than are banks or outside investors. An alternative approach then would be to permit interested transactions that are "fair" but to proscribe those that are not.

In rationally choosing between these alternatives, we also must consider the costs of administering the rule chosen. Ideally, the legal regime should be simple (like the preclusion alternative) but discriminating (like the screening alternative), and it should operate without requiring (or inviting) litigation in every such transaction. The evolution of fiduciary law of director self-dealing mirrors the interplay among these competing goals.

9.2.1   Early Regulation of Fiduciary Self-Dealing

In the late eighteenth and early nineteenth centuries, American and English courts looked to the law of trusts for guidance in adjudicating disputes over the duties of corporate directors.[8] The trust's division of ownership into legal ownership (with control) and beneficial interest (without control) provided an obvious analogue for the division of ownership powers between the board and the minority shareholders in the widely held corporation.

Early trust law flatly prohibited a trustee from dealing with trust property on his own account or with the trust beneficiary.[9] Such transactions could be set aside at the insistence of any interested party, without regard to their terms. But with time, the law recognized that a trustee could deal with a beneficiary with respect to trust property,[10] at least if the beneficiary was competent, the trustee made full disclosure, and the transaction was fair.[11] If any of these conditions was not met, the transaction between a beneficiary and a trustee was voidable. But transactions with beneficiaries were not flatly prohibited, as were transactions between the trustee and the trust itself.[12]

---

8. *Ex parte Holmes*, 5 Cow. 426 (N.Y. Sup. Ct. 1826); Lawrence E. Mitchell, *Fairness in Trust in Corporate Law*, 43 Duke L.J. 425 (1993).

9. *Ex parte Holmes*, 5 Cow. 426.

10. *Smith v. Lancing*, 22 N.Y. 520 (1860).

11. *U.S. Rolling Stock Co. v. The Atlantic and Great Western Railroad Co.*, 34 Ohio St. 450 (1878).

12. See, e.g., *In re Gleeson*, 124 N.E.2d 624 (Ill. App 1954).

Some commentators argue that, by 1880, the trust rule (as opposed to the trust beneficiary rule) had become the general rule of corporation law; conflicted director transactions were simply void.[13] Other commentators dispute this claim.[14] All agree, however, that, beginning in the early twentieth century, courts would uphold a contract between a director and the corporation if it was (1) fair and (2) approved by a board comprised of a majority of disinterested directors. A contract that did not meet *both* tests was voidable, meaning that it would be set aside on the application of any party with an interest in the contract.

The practical impact of this approach lay in the requirement that transactions be approved by a majority of disinterested directors. Under early twentieth-century law, an interested director's attendance at a board meeting could not be counted toward a quorum on a question in which he was interested.[15] This rule meant that a corporation could not act to authorize a contract in which a majority of the board was personally interested. Of course, corporate officers could authorize minor contracts within the scope of their inherent authority. But major contracts requiring board approval simply could not be authorized when a majority of directors were financially interested in it.

There was, however, good reason to make some of these contracts binding; knowledgeable directors might sometimes offer the company better terms than anyone else. One response was for shareholders to put into the corporation's charter a provision allowing an interested director to be counted toward a quorum. Courts upheld the validity of these provisions, and this innovation thus permitted interested transactions involving a majority of the board to be accomplished.[16] Nevertheless, courts continued to require directors to prove that such transactions were fair — that is, these transactions remained voidable following "interested" approval but only if they were unfair or inadequately disclosed. This was essentially the nineteenth-century trust beneficiary rule, applied to the corporation.

The next stage in the development of the law of director conflict occurred in the mid-twentieth century, with the movement to enact legislative provisions governing director conflict transactions.[17] These provisions were, in effect, a statutory embodiment of earlier charter provisions

---

13. See Harold Marsh Jr., *Are Directors Trustees,* 22 Bus. Law. 35 (1966). Professor Marsh's interpretation has been widely accepted. See, e.g., 2 Model Business Corp. Act Annot. §8.60, at 8-406 (3d ed. 1994). ("[A]s late as the end of the nineteenth century the rule appeared settled that the corporation had the power to avoid all such transactions without regard to the fairness of the transaction or the manner in which it was originally approved by the corporation.")

14. Professor Norwood Brevenridge urges that, at times in the nineteenth century, judges were willing to permit interested director transactions to stand if they found them fair in all respects. See Norwood P. Brevenridge, Jr, *The Corporate Director's Fiduciary Duty of Loyalty: Understanding the Self-Interested Director Transaction,* 41 DePaul L. Rev. 655 (1992) (Professor Marsh was completely wrong; the rule was opposite of that which he asserts: If an interested contract was fair, it was sustained (citing the leading treatise, 1 V. Morowitz, *The Law of Public Corporations* 214 (2d ed. 1843))).

15. See *Blish v. Thompson Automatic Arms Corp.,* 64 A.2d 602 (Del. 1948).

16. E.g., *Sterling v. Mayflower Hotel Corp.,* 93 A.2d 107, 117 (Del. 1952).

17. See, e.g., Cal. Corp. Code §310; DGCL §144; NYBCL §713; RMBCA §8.60.

that sought to ensure that interested transactions would not be void per se. But read literally, which courts have been exceptionally slow to do, they may go further. These "safe harbor" statutes are discussed below.

9.2.2   The Disclosure Requirement

Valid authorization of a conflicted transaction between a director and her company requires the interested director to make full disclosure of all material facts of which she is aware at the time of authorization. But how far does this disclosure obligation reach?

STATE EX REL. HAYES OYSTER CO. v. KEYPOINT OYSTER CO.

391 P.2d 979 (Wash. 1964)

DENNEY, J.:

Verne Hayes was CEO, director, and 23 percent shareholder of Coast Oyster Co., a public company that owned several large oyster beds. Verne's employment contract barred him from taking part in any business that would compete with Coast except for his activities in Hayes Oyster Co., a family corporation in which he owned 25 percent of the shares and his brother, Sam, owned 75 percent. In the spring of 1960, when Coast was badly in need of cash to satisfy creditors, Hayes suggested that Coast sell its Allyn and Poulsbo oyster beds. Hayes then discussed with Engman, a Coast employee, how Hayes Oyster might help Engman finance the purchase.

On August 11, 1960, Coast's board approved Hayes's plan to sell the Allyn and Poulsbo beds to Keypoint Oyster Co., a corporation to be formed by Engman, for $250,000, payable $25,000 per year, with 5 percent interest, thus improving Coast's cash position and relieving it of the expenses of harvesting the oysters in those beds. On September 1, 1960, Hayes and Engman agreed that Keypoint's shares would be owned half by Engman and half by Hayes Oyster. At a Coast shareholders' meeting on October 21, 1960, the shareholders approved the sale to Keypoint—Hayes voting his Coast shares and others for which he held proxies (in total constituting a majority) in favor. At none of these times did any person connected with Coast (other than Hayes and Engman) know of Hayes's or Hayes Oyster's interest in Keypoint.

In 1961 and 1962, Hayes sold his Coast shares and executed a settlement agreement with respect to his Coast employment contract. Shortly thereafter, Coast's new managers brought suit against Verne and Sam Hayes for their Keypoint shares and all profits obtained by Hayes as a result of the transaction. The trial court absolved Hayes of any breach of duty to Coast.

Coast does not seek a rescission of the contract with Keypoint, nor does it question the adequacy of the consideration which Keypoint agreed to pay for the purchase of Allyn and Poulsbo, nor does Coast claim that it suffered any loss in the transaction. It does assert that Hayes, Coast's president, manager and director, acquired a secret profit and personal advantage to himself in the acquisition of the Keypoint stock by Hayes or Hayes Oyster in the side deal with Engman; and that such was in violation of his duty to Coast, and that, therefore, Hayes or Hayes Oyster should disgorge such secret profit to Coast.

Certain basic concepts have long been recognized by courts throughout the land on the status of corporate officers and directors. They occupy a fiduciary relation to a private corporation and the shareholders thereof akin to that of a trustee, and owe undivided loyalty, and a standard of behavior above that of the workaday world. . . .

Directors and other officers of a private corporation cannot directly or indirectly acquire a profit for themselves or acquire any other personal advantage in dealings with others on behalf of the corporation. . . .

Respondent [Hayes] is correct in his contention that this court has abolished the mechanical rule whereby any transaction involving corporate property in which a director has an interest is voidable at the option of the corporation. Such a contract cannot be voided if the director or officer can show that the transaction was fair to the corporation. However, nondisclosure by an interested director or officer is, in itself, unfair. This wholesome rule can be applied automatically without any of the unsatisfactory results which flowed from a rigid bar against any self-dealing. . . .

The trial court found that any negotiations between Hayes and Engman up to . . . September 1, 1960, resulted in no binding agreement that Hayes would have any personal interest for himself or as a stockholder in Hayes Oyster in the sale of Allyn and Poulsbo. The undisputed evidence, however, shows that Hayes knew he might have some interest in the sale. It would have been appropriate for Hayes to have disclosed his possible interest at the informal meeting in Long Beach on August 4, 1960, and particularly at the meeting of Coast's board of directors on August 11, 1960. It is not necessary, however, for us to decide this case on a consideration of Hayes' obligation to Coast under the circumstances obtaining at that time.

Subsequent to the agreement with Engman, Hayes attended the meeting of Coast stockholders on October 21, 1960, recommended the sale, and voted a majority of the stock, including his own, in favor of the sale to Keypoint. On the same day, . . . he signed the contract which, among other things, required Keypoint to pay 10 monthly payments amounting to $25,000 per year, to pay interest on [a] deferred balance at 5 percent, to make payments on an option agreement which Coast had with one Smith, to plant sufficient seed to produce 45,000 gallons of oysters per year, inform Coast of plantings, furnish annual reports to Coast, operate the oysterlands in good workmanlike manner, keep improvements in repair, pay taxes, refrain directly or indirectly from engaging in growing, processing or marketing dehydrated oysters or oyster stew, give Coast first refusal on purchase of Keypoint oysters of 10,000 gallons per year or one-fourth of Keypoint's production. Title was reserved in Coast until payment in full of the purchase price of $250,000. . . .

At this juncture, Hayes was required to divulge his interest in Keypoint. His obligation to do so [arose] from the possibility, even probability, that some controversy might arise between Coast and Keypoint relative to the numerous provisions of the executory contract. Coast share-holders and directors had the right to know of Hayes' interest in Keypoint in order to intelligently determine the advisability of retaining Hayes as president and manager under the circumstances, and to determine whether or not it was wise to enter into the contract at all, in view of Hayes' conduct. In all fairness, they were entitled to know that their president and director might be placed in a position where he must choose between the interest of Coast and Keypoint in conducting Coast's business with Keypoint.

Furthermore, after receipt of the Keypoint stock, Hayes instructed the treasurer of Coast to make a payment on the Smith lease-option agreement which Keypoint was required to pay under the provisions of the contract. This action by Hayes grew out of a promise which Hayes made to Engman during their negotiations before the sale to reduce the sale price because of mortality of oysters on Allyn and Poulsbo. There was a clear conflict of interest.

The cases relied upon by respondent are not opposed to the rule condemning secrecy when an officer or director of a corporation may profit in the sale of corporate assets. In *Leppaluoto v. Eggleston,* 57 Wash. 2d 393, 357 P.2d 725, Eggleston secretly chartered his own equipment to a corpo-ration in which he had one-half interest, for $25,000, without the knowl-edge of the owner of the remaining stock. We held that Eggleston was not required to return the $25,000 to the corporation because there was no proof that the charter arrangement was unfair or unreasonable and no proof that Eggleston made any profit on the transaction and that, absent proof of loss to the corporation or profit to Eggleston, no recovery could be had. In the case before us, profit to Hayes or Hayes Oyster in acquiring 50 percent of Keypoint stock is clear and undisputed. . . .

It is true that Hayes hypothecated his stock in Coast to one of Coast's creditors in early August, 1960. Undoubtedly, this aided Coast in placating its creditors at that time and showed absence of an intent to defraud Coast. It is not necessary, however, that an officer or director of a corporation have an intent to defraud or that any injury result to the corporation for an officer or director to violate his fiduciary obligation in secretly acquiring an interest in corporate property. . . .

Actual injury is not the principle upon which the law proceeds in condemning such contracts. Fidelity in the agent is what is aimed at, and as a means of securing it, the law will not permit the agent to place himself in a situation in which he may be tempted by his own private interest to disregard that of his principal. . . .

Respondent asserts that action by Coast shareholders was not neces-sary to bind Coast to the sale because it had already been approved by Coast's board of directors. Assuming this to be true, Hayes' fiduciary status with Coast did not change. He could not place himself in an adverse position to Coast by acquiring an interest in the executory contract before the terms of said contract had been performed by Keypoint. Coast had the option to affirm the contract or seek rescission. It chose the former and can successfully invoke the principle that whatever a director or officer acquires by virtue of his fiduciary relation, except in open dealings with the company, belongs not to such director or officer, but to the company. . . .

This rule appears to have universal application. . . .

The trial court's finding that Hayes acted on behalf of Hayes Oyster in all of his negotiations with Engman subsequent to July, 1960, does not alter the situation. Sam Hayes knew that Verne Hayes was president and manager of Coast and owed complete devotion to the interests of Coast at the time Verne Hayes first approached him on the subject of sharing with Engman in the purchase of Allyn and Poulsbo. Sam Hayes knew and agreed that any interest of Verne Hayes or Hayes Oyster in Keypoint was to be kept secret and revealed to no one, including Coast. Sam Hayes authorized Verne Hayes to proceed with the deal on behalf of Hayes Oyster on this basis. Verne Hayes became the agent of Hayes Oyster in negotiating with Engman.

. . . Every sound consideration of equity affects Hayes Oyster as well as Verne Hayes. Neither can profit by the dereliction of Verne Hayes. . . .

The decree and judgment of the trial court . . . is reversed with direction to order Keypoint Oyster Company to issue a new certificate for 250 shares of its stock to Coast Oyster Company and cancel the certificates heretofore standing in the name of or assigned to Hayes Oyster Company. . . .

QUESTIONS ON STATE EX REL. HAYES OYSTER CO. v. KEYPOINT OYSTER CO.

Why is nondisclosure per se unfair? Why shouldn't Hayes be granted the opportunity to show that the consideration received for the oyster beds was fair? After all, Hayes Oyster is not attempting to rescind the sale.

NOTES ON DISCLOSURE OF CONFLICTED TRANSACTIONS

Requiring a corporate fiduciary to disclose his or her interest in a proposed transaction with the corporation is only the first step. The difficult question is just what must be disclosed beyond the simple fact of self-interest. For example, if a director (call him Jones) offers to buy 50 acres of the corporation's land at a price that he regards as fair, must he disclose his intended use of the property? What if Jones's cousin is a developer who has informed him of a large residential development in the neighborhood, which will make the property more valuable? Does Jones have to disclose his cousin's plans? Does Jones have to disclose the highest price that he is willing to pay? What principle answers these questions?

The fiduciary's role in negotiating a conflicted transaction with his corporation is not an easy one. Recall the singing phrases of Judge Cardozo in *Meinhard v. Salmon*: Some forms of behavior open to traders in the market are not available to fiduciaries. Among these forms is a range of disingenuous actions that fall short of fraud. The Delaware court's legal standard for disclosure by a conflicted fiduciary is that a director or controlling shareholder must disclose *all* material information relevant to the transaction.[18] In our example, a literal application of this language would require Jones to disclose both what he learned from his cousin and the highest price he would pay. But the question of disclosure is more complicated. The Delaware Supreme Court has encouraged the use of special committees of independent directors to simulate arm's-length negotiations. See *Weinberger v. UOP, Inc.*, 457 A.2d 701 (Del. 1983) (en banc). But negotiations never entail one party being required to disclose this information. Some Delaware cases indicate that a fiduciary is not required to state the best price that he would pay or accept.[19]

Finally, note that federal securities laws also regulate disclosure of self-dealing transactions in public corporations. Given that Coast Oyster is a public company, would Verne be compelled to disclose his interest in the oyster bed sale under Regulation S-K, Item 404(a) (in your statutory supplement) if he were to undertake the same transaction with Engman today?[20]

9.2.3 Controlling Shareholders and the Fairness Standard

It is a short step from the fiduciary duties of a shareholder director to those of a controlling shareholder. Corporation law has long recognized a fiduciary duty on the part of controlling shareholders to the company and its minority shareholders.[21] Control in this context should be determined by a practical test rather than a formalistic one. A shareholder with less than 50 percent of the outstanding voting power of the firm may have a fiduciary obligation by reason of the exercise of corporate control. A shareholder with 50 percent or more of the vote will probably owe such a duty, despite evidence that it did not in fact exercise control.

Despite the judicial consensus (in the United States) that controlling shareholders owe a duty of fairness to minority shareholders in the exercise of corporate powers, an additional consideration complicates the articulation of the controller's duty. This consideration is that the controller is also a shareholder, after all, and is therefore entitled to pursue her own investment interests. Thus, two values collide. The dominant value (at least in

---

18. See *Rosenblatt v. Getty Oil Co.*, 493 A.2d 929 (Del. 1985); *Lynch v. Vickers Energy Corp.*, 383 A.2d 278 (Del. 1978).

19. See *Kahn v. Tremont Corp.*, 694 A.2d 422 (Del. 1997). See generally Hammermesh, *Calling Off the Lynch Mob: The Corporate Director's Fiduciary Disclosure Duty*, 49 Vand. L. Rev. 1087 (1996).

20. Note that the disclosure required of the issuer for "related party" transactions must be made in the Form 10-K Annual Report (filed with the SEC) and the annual statement that public companies must distribute to shareholders.

21. *Sterling v. Mayflower Hotel Corp.*, 93 A.2d 107, 109-110 (Del. 1952); *Allied Chemical & Dye Corp. v. Steel & Tube Co.*, 120 A. 486, 491 (Del. Ch. 1923); *Jones v. Missouri-Edison Electrical Co.*, 144 F. 765, 771 (8th Cir. 1906); *May v. Midwest Refining Co.*, 121 F.2d 431, 439 (1st Cir. 1941).

Delaware law) is that a controlling shareholder's power over the corporation, and the resulting power to affect other shareholders, gives rise to a duty to consider their interests fairly whenever the corporation enters into a contract with the controller or its affiliate. The subsidiary value is the entitlement of all shareholders—even controlling shareholders—to vote in their own interests.[22]

The first principle clearly governs when a controlling shareholder engages in a conflicted transaction with the corporation. But what about situations in which a controller exercises influence without authorizing a conflicted transaction? For example, what if a controlling shareholder causes the board to launch a risky new product that results in a substantial loss? Directors are protected by the business judgment rule, but might the controlling shareholder be liable for the resulting loss? What if the controller believes the company is too large and replaces the board at the next annual meeting to reduce its size? Has the controller breached any duty to others? Do minority shareholders have a cognizable injury if the controller influences the board to declare dividends because it wants the money, even if others would prefer new investments? The next case provides a useful structure for thinking about situations in which a controlling shareholder's interest is not a direct conflict-of-interest transaction.

SINCLAIR OIL CORP. v. LEVIEN.

280 A.2d 717 (Del. 1971)

WOLCOTT, C.J.:

This is an appeal by the defendant, Sinclair Oil Corporation (hereafter Sinclair), from an order of the Court of Chancery, 261 A.2d 911, in a derivative action requiring Sinclair to account for damages sustained by its subsidiary, Sinclair Venezuelan Oil Company (hereafter Sinven), organized by Sinclair for the purpose of operating in Venezuela, as a result of dividends paid by Sinven, the denial to Sinven of industrial development, and a breach of contract between Sinclair's wholly-owned subsidiary, Sinclair International Oil Company, and Sinven.

Sinclair, operating primarily as a holding company, is in the business of exploring for oil and of producing and marketing crude oil and oil products. At all times relevant to this litigation, it owned about 97% of Sinven's stock. The plaintiff owns about 3000 of 120,000 publicly held shares of Sinven. Sinven, incorporated in 1922, has been engaged in petroleum operations primarily in Venezuela and since 1959 has operated exclusively in Venezuela.

Sinclair nominates all members of Sinven's board of directors. The Chancellor found as a fact that the directors were not independent of

---

22. *Tanzer v. International General Industries, Inc.,* 379 A.2d 1121, 1124 (Del. 1977); *Thorpe v. CERBCO, Inc.,* 676 A.2d 436 (Del. 1996) (controller can vote against sale of all assets that public shareholders regard as advantageous without having to justify fairness because this is purely exercising power as shareholder).

Sinclair. Almost without exception, they were officers, directors, or employees of corporations in the Sinclair complex. By reason of Sinclair's domination, it is clear that Sinclair owed Sinven a fiduciary duty. . . . Sinclair concedes this.

The Chancellor held that because of Sinclair's fiduciary duty and its control over Sinven, its relationship with Sinven must meet the test of intrinsic fairness. The standard of intrinsic fairness involves both a high degree of fairness and a shift in the burden of proof. Under this standard the burden is on Sinclair to prove, subject to careful judicial scrutiny, that its transactions with Sinven were objectively fair. . . .

Sinclair argues that the transactions between it and Sinven should be tested, not by the test of intrinsic fairness with the accompanying shift of the burden of proof, but by the business judgment rule. . . . A board of directors enjoys a presumption of sound business judgment, and its decisions will not be disturbed if they can be attributed to any rational business purpose. A court under such circumstances will not substitute its own notions of what is or is not sound business judgment.

We think, however, that Sinclair's argument in this respect is misconceived. When the situation involves a parent and a subsidiary, with the parent controlling the transaction and fixing the terms, the test of intrinsic fairness, with its resulting shifting of the burden of proof, is applied. . . . The basic situation for the application of the rule is the one in which the parent has received a benefit to the exclusion and at the expense of the subsidiary. . . .

A parent does indeed owe a fiduciary duty to its subsidiary when there are parent-subsidiary dealings. However, this alone will not evoke the intrinsic fairness standard. This standard will be applied only when the fiduciary duty is accompanied by self-dealing—the situation when a parent is on both sides of a transaction with its subsidiary. Self-dealing occurs when the parent, by virtue of its domination of the subsidiary, causes the subsidiary to act in such a way that the parent receives something from the subsidiary to the exclusion of, and detriment to, the minority stockholders of the subsidiary.

We turn now to the facts. The plaintiff argues that, from 1960 through 1966, Sinclair caused Sinven to pay out such excessive dividends that the industrial development of Sinven was effectively prevented, and it became in reality a corporation in dissolution.

From 1960 through 1966, Sinven paid out $108,000,000 in dividends ($38,000,000 in excess of Sinven's earnings during the same period). The Chancellor held that Sinclair caused these dividends to be paid during a period when it had a need for large amounts of cash. Although the dividends paid exceeded earnings, the plaintiff concedes that the payments were made in compliance with 8 Del. C. §170, authorizing payment of dividends out of surplus or net profits. However, the plaintiff attacks these dividends on the ground that they resulted from an improper motive—Sinclair's need for cash. The Chancellor, applying the intrinsic fairness standard, held that Sinclair did not sustain its burden of proving that these dividends were intrinsically fair to the minority stockholders of Sinven.

Since it is admitted that the dividends were paid in strict compliance with 8 Del. C. §170, the alleged excessiveness of the payments alone would not state a cause of action. Nevertheless, compliance with the applicable statute may not, under all circumstances, justify all dividend payments. If a plaintiff can meet his burden of proving that a dividend cannot be grounded on any reasonable business objective, then the courts can and will interfere with the board's decision to pay the dividend.

Sinclair contends that it is improper to apply the intrinsic fairness standard to dividend payments even when the board which voted for the dividends is completely dominated. In support of this contention, Sinclair relies heavily on *American District Telegraph Co. (ADT) v. Grinnell Corp.*, (N.Y. Sup. Ct. 1969) *aff'd*, 33 A.D.2d 769, 306 N.Y.S.2d 209 (1969). Plaintiffs were minority stockholders of ADT, a subsidiary of Grinnell. The plaintiffs alleged that Grinnell, realizing that it would soon have to sell its ADT stock because of a pending anti-trust action, caused ADT to pay excessive dividends. Because the dividend payments conformed with applicable statutory law, and the plaintiffs could not prove an abuse of discretion, the court ruled that the complaint did not state a cause of action. . . .

We do not accept the argument that the intrinsic fairness test can never be applied to a dividend declaration by a dominated board, although a dividend declaration by a dominated board will not inevitably demand the application of the intrinsic fairness standard. . . .

If such a dividend is in essence self-dealing by the parent, then the intrinsic fairness standard is the proper standard. For example, suppose a parent dominates a subsidiary and its board of directors. The subsidiary has outstanding two classes of stock, X and Y. Class X is owned by the parent and Class Y is owned by minority stockholders of the subsidiary. If the subsidiary, at the direction of the parent, declares a dividend on its Class X stock only, this might well be self-dealing by the parent. It would be receiving something from the subsidiary to the exclusion of and detrimental to its minority stockholders. This self-dealing, coupled with the parent's fiduciary duty, would make intrinsic fairness the proper standard by which to evaluate the dividend payments.

Consequently it must be determined whether the dividend payments by Sinven were, in essence, self-dealing by Sinclair. The dividends resulted in great sums of money being transferred from Sinven to Sinclair. However, a proportionate share of this money was received by the minority shareholders of Sinven. Sinclair received nothing from Sinven to the exclusion of its minority stockholders. As such, these dividends were not self-dealing. We hold therefore that the Chancellor erred in applying the intrinsic fairness test as to these dividend payments. The business judgment standard should have been applied.

We conclude that the facts demonstrate that the dividend payments complied with the business judgment standard and with 8 Del. C. §170. The motives for causing the declaration of dividends are immaterial unless the plaintiff can show that the dividend payments resulted from improper motives and amounted to waste. The plaintiff contends only that the dividend payments drained Sinven of cash to such an extent that it was prevented from expanding.

The plaintiff proved no business opportunities which came to Sinven independently and which Sinclair either took to itself or denied to Sinven. As a matter of fact, with two minor exceptions which resulted in losses, all of Sinven's operations have been conducted in Venezuela, and Sinclair had a policy of exploiting its oil properties located in different countries by subsidiaries located in the particular countries.

From 1960 to 1966 Sinclair purchased or developed oil fields in Alaska, Canada, Paraguay, and other places around the world. The plaintiff contends that these were all opportunities which could have been taken by Sinven. The Chancellor concluded that Sinclair had not proved that its denial of expansion opportunities to Sinven was intrinsically fair. He based this conclusion on the following findings of fact. Sinclair made no real effort to expand Sinven. The excessive dividends paid by Sinven resulted in so great a cash drain as to effectively deny to Sinven any ability to expand. During this same period Sinclair actively pursued a company-wide policy of developing through its subsidiaries new sources of revenue, but Sinven was not permitted to participate and was confined in its activities to Venezuela.

However, the plaintiff could point to no opportunities which came to Sinven. Therefore, Sinclair usurped no business opportunity belonging to Sinven. Since Sinclair received nothing from Sinven to the exclusion of and detriment to Sinven's minority stockholders, there was no self-dealing. Therefore, business judgment is the proper standard by which to evaluate Sinclair's expansion policies.

Since there is no proof of self-dealing on the part of Sinclair, it follows that the expansion policy of Sinclair and the methods used to achieve the desired result must, as far as Sinclair's treatment of Sinven is concerned, be tested by the standards of the business judgment rule. Accordingly, Sinclair's decision, absent fraud or gross overreaching, to achieve expansion through the medium of its subsidiaries, other than Sinven, must be upheld.

Even if Sinclair was wrong in developing these opportunities as it did, the question arises, with which subsidiaries should these opportunities have been shared? No evidence indicates a unique need or ability of Sinven to develop these opportunities. The decision of which subsidiaries would be used to implement Sinclair's expansion policy was one of business judgment with which a court will not interfere absent a showing of gross and palpable overreaching. . . .

We will therefore reverse that part of the Chancellor's order that requires Sinclair to account to Sinven for damages sustained as a result of dividends paid between 1960 and 1966, and by reason of the denial to Sinven of expansion during that period.

QUESTIONS AND NOTES ON SINCLAIR OIL

1. Is plaintiff's complaint in this case really about self-dealing or an alleged misappropriation of corporate opportunity? How can the pro rata payment of dividends be a basis for either complaint?

2. Do you think that Sinclair would have forced Sinven to pay such large dividends if additional drilling opportunities had been available in Venezuela? How would *Sinclair Oil* have been decided under ALI Principles of Corporate Governance §5.12 (in your statutory supplement)?

3. One commentator notes that *Sinclair* establishes a threshold test for applying the fairness norm to parent-subsidiary transactions: Fairness review is required only if the parent "receives something from the subsidiary to the exclusion of, and detriment to, minority shareholders of the subsidiary." *Sinclair*, 280 A.2d at 720. See Mary Siegel, *The Erosion of the Law of Controlling Shareholders*, 24 Del. J. Corp. L. 27 (1999). Professor Siegel notes, however, that the *Sinclair* threshold test has fallen into disuse in recent years, largely in favor of reviewing *all* majority actions under an entire fairness test. *Id.* at 69. Should the courts return to *Sinclair*'s "benefit-detriment" test as a threshold for fairness review? Why should it matter?

For recent examples of cases in which controllers are said to face fairness scrutiny for engineering corporate decisions that, as a formal matter, treat all shareholders equally, see *McMullin v. Beran*, 765 A.2d 910 (Del. 2000); and *In re Digex Inc. Shareholder Litigation*, 789 A.2d 1176 (Del. Ch. 2000).

4. The body of law dealing with parent-subsidiary transactions in particular was reenergized in the 1983 case of *Weinberger v. UOP, Inc.*, 457 A.2d 701 (Del. 1983). While parent-subsidiary dealings can take a wide range of forms, much of the litigation challenging these transactions arises from cash-out mergers. The same general rule applies to all transactions that are between a controlling person — a parent — and its subsidiary: There must be full disclosure of relevant facts, and the deal must be substantively and procedurally fair.

9.3   THE EFFECT OF APPROVAL BY A DISINTERESTED PARTY

A student reading thus far might conclude that litigation about conflicted transactions would focus solely on the adequacy of disclosure or, if the insider actions were fully disclosed, on the intrinsic fairness of their terms. However, that is not the case, either generally or under Delaware law. We noted in our earlier discussion of the law of fiduciary self-dealing that approval by disinterested directors or shareholders began to play a key role in the defense of self-dealing transactions beginning in the early twentieth century. This role was codified in the so-called safe harbor statutes, adopted by states from the mid-twentieth century, and was further developed by the courts since. The principal legal questions raised by disinterested review mechanisms concern the standard of judicial review *after* disinterested review and approval. For example, is it cursory review under the business judgment standard? Or is it more searching review under some sort of "fairness-lite" standard? And should it matter whether directors or shareholders approve the transaction? (A related issue is, What if the transaction is only disclosed *after* the fact but is then ratified by disinterested directors?)

We explore these issues below, beginning with the effects of safe harbor statutes.

9.3.1 The Safe Harbor Statutes

As we indicate above, the safe harbor statutes initially sought to permit boards to authorize transactions in which a majority of directors had an interest. Most U.S. jurisdictions now have such statutes. Almost all of these statutes provide that a director's self-dealing transaction is not voidable *solely* because it is interested, so long as it is adequately disclosed and approved by a majority of disinterested directors or shareholders, or it is fair. See, e.g., DGCL §144; NYBCL §713; Cal. Corp. Code §310. However, these statutes might also be interpreted to mean that a conflict transaction is *never* voidable if it is fully disclosed and authorized or approved by the board and shareholders in good faith *or* if it is fair to the corporation at the time it is authorized. However, courts have resisted such a broad reading. Consider the following case.

COOKIES FOOD PRODUCTS v. LAKES WAREHOUSE

430 N.W.2d 447 (Iowa 1988)

NEUMAN, Justice.

This is a shareholders' derivative suit brought by the minority shareholders of a closely held Iowa corporation specializing in barbecue sauce, Cookies Food Products, Inc. (Cookies). The target of the lawsuit is the majority shareholder, Duane "Speed" Herrig and two of his family-owned corporations, Lakes Warehouse Distributing, Inc. (Lakes) and Speed's Automotive Co., Inc. (Speed's). Plaintiffs alleged that Herrig, by acquiring control of Cookies and executing self-dealing contracts, breached his fiduciary duty to the company and fraudulently misappropriated and converted corporate funds. Plaintiffs sought actual and punitive damages. Trial to the court resulted in a verdict for the defendants, the district court finding that Herrig's actions benefited, rather than harmed, Cookies. We affirm. . . .

L. D. Cook of Storm Lake, Iowa, founded Cookies in 1975 to produce and distribute his original barbeque sauce. Searching for a plant site in a community that would provide financial backing, Cook met with business leaders in seventeen Iowa communities, outlining his plans to build a growth-oriented company. He selected Wall Lake, Iowa, persuading thirty-five members of that community, including Herrig and the plaintiffs, to purchase Cookies stock. All of the investors hoped Cookies would improve the local job market and tax base. The record reveals that it has done just that.

Early sales of the product, however, were dismal. After the first year's operation, Cookies was in dire financial straits. At that time, Herrig was one of thirty-five shareholders and held only two hundred shares. He was also the owner of an auto parts business, Speed's Automotive, and Lakes

Warehouse Distributing, Inc., a company that distributed auto parts from Speed's. Cookies' board of directors approached Herrig with the idea of distributing the company's products. It authorized Herrig to purchase Cookies' sauce for twenty percent under wholesale price, which he could then resell at full wholesale price. Under this arrangement, Herrig began to market and distribute the sauce to his auto parts customers and to grocery outlets from Lakes' trucks as they traversed the regular delivery route for Speed's Automotive.

In May 1977, Cookies formalized this arrangement by executing an exclusive distribution agreement with Lakes. Pursuant to this agreement, Cookies was responsible only for preparing the product; Lakes, for its part, assumed all costs of warehousing, marketing, sales, delivery, promotion, and advertising. Cookies retained the right to fix the sales price of its products and agreed to pay Lakes thirty percent of its gross sales for these services.

Cookies' sales have soared under the exclusive distributorship contract with Lakes. Gross sales in 1976, the year prior to the agreement, totaled only $20,000, less than half of Cookies' expenses that year. In 1977, however, sales jumped five-fold, then doubled in 1978, and have continued to show phenomenal growth every year thereafter. By 1985, when this suit was commenced, annual sales reached $2,400,000.

As sales increased, Cookies' board of directors amended and extended the original distributorship agreement. In 1979, the board amended the original agreement to give Lakes an additional two percent of gross sales to cover freight costs for the ever expanding market for Cookies' sauce. In 1980, the board extended the amended agreement through 1984 to allow Herrig to make long-term advertising commitments. Recognizing the role that Herrig's personal strengths played in the success of the joint endeavor, the board also amended the agreement that year to allow Cookies to cancel the agreement with Lakes if Herrig died or disposed of the corporation's stock.

In 1981, L. D. Cook, the majority shareholder up to this time, decided to sell his interest in Cookies. He first offered the directors an opportunity to buy his stock, but the board declined to purchase any of his 8100 shares. Herrig then offered Cook and all other shareholders $10 per share for their stock, which was twice the original price. Because of the overwhelming response to these offers, Herrig had purchased enough Cookies stock by January 1982 to become the majority shareholder. His investment of $140,000 represented fifty-three percent of the [outstanding shares]. . . .

Shortly after Herrig acquired majority control he replaced four of the five members of the Cookies' board with members he selected. . . . Subsequent changes made in the corporation under Herrig's leadership formed the basis for this lawsuit.

First, under Herrig's leadership, Cookies' board has extended the term of the exclusive distributorship agreement with Lakes and expanded the scope of services for which it compensates Herrig and his companies. In April 1982, when a sales increase of twenty-five percent over the previous year required Cookies to seek additional short-term storage for the peak summer season, the board accepted Herrig's proposal to compensate Lakes at the "going rate" for use of its nearby storage facilities. . . .

Second, Herrig moved from his role as director and distributor to take on an additional role in product development. This created a dispute over a royalty Herrig began to receive. . . . Herrig developed a recipe [for taco sauce] because he recognized that taco sauce, while requiring many of the same ingredients needed in barbeque sauce, is less expensive to produce. . . . In August 1982, Cookies' board approved a royalty fee to be paid to Herrig for this taco sauce recipe. This royalty plan was similar to royalties the board paid to L. D. Cook for the barbeque sauce recipe. That plan gives Cook three percent of the gross sales of barbeque sauce; Herrig receives a flat rate per case. Although Herrig's rate is equivalent to a sales percentage slightly higher than what Cook receives, it yields greater profit to Cookies because this new product line is cheaper to produce.

Third, since 1982 Cookies' board has twice approved additional compensation for Herrig. In January 1983, the board authorized payment of a $1000 per month "consultant fee" in lieu of salary, because accelerated sales required Herrig to spend extra time managing the company. Averaging eighty-hour work weeks, Herrig devoted approximately fifteen percent of his time to Cookies and eighty percent to Lakes business. In August, 1983, the board authorized another increase in Herrig's compensation. Further, at the suggestion of a Cookies director who also served as an accountant for Cookies, Lakes, and Speed's, the Cookies board amended the exclusive distributorship agreement to allow Lakes an additional two percent of gross sales as a promotion allowance to expand the market for Cookies products outside of Iowa. As a direct result of this action, by 1986 Cookies regularly shipped products to several states throughout the country.

As we have previously noted, however, Cookies' growth and success has not pleased all its shareholders. The discontent is motivated by two factors that have effectively precluded shareholders from sharing in Cookies' financial success: the fact that Cookies is a closely held corporation, and the fact that it has not paid dividends. Because Cookies' stock is not publicly traded, shareholders have no ready access to buyers for their stock at current values that reflect the company's success. Without dividends, the shareholders have no ready method of realizing a return on their investment in the company. This is not to say that Cookies has improperly refused to pay dividends. The evidence reveals that Cookies would have violated the terms of its loan with the Small Business Administration had it declared dividends before repaying that debt. That SBA loan was not repaid until the month before the plaintiffs filed this action.

Unsatisfied with the status quo, a group of minority shareholders commenced this equitable action in 1985. Based on the facts we have detailed, the plaintiffs claimed that the sums paid Herrig and his companies have grossly exceeded the value of the services rendered, thereby substantially reducing corporate profits and shareholder equity. Through the exclusive distributorship agreements, taco sauce royalty, warehousing fees, and consultant fee, plaintiffs claimed that Herrig breached his fiduciary duties to the corporation and its shareholders because he allegedly negotiated for these arrangements without fully disclosing the benefit he would gain. The plaintiffs sought recovery for lost profits, an accounting to determine the full extent of the damage, attorneys fees, punitive damages, appointment of a receiver to manage the company properly, removal of Herrig from control, and sale of the company in order to generate an appropriate return on their investment.

Having heard the evidence presented on these claims at trial, the district court filed a lengthy ruling that reflected careful attention to the testimony of the twenty-two witnesses and myriad of exhibits admitted. The court concluded that Herrig had breached no duties owed to Cookies or to its minority shareholders. . . .

II.   FIDUCIARY DUTIES

Herrig, as an officer and director of Cookies, owes a fiduciary duty to the company and its shareholders. . . . Herrig concedes that Iowa law imposed the same fiduciary responsibilities based on his status as majority stockholder. . . . Conversely, before acquiring majority control in February 1982, Herrig owed no fiduciary duty to Cookies or plaintiffs. . . . Therefore, Herrig's conduct is subject to scrutiny only from the time he began to exercise control of Cookies. . . .

[T]he legislature enacted section 496A.34, . . . that establishes three sets of circumstances under which a director may engage in self-dealing without clearly violating the duty of loyalty:

> No contract or other transaction between a corporation and one or more of its directors or any other corporation, firm, association or entity in which one or more of its directors are directors or officers or are financially interested, shall be either void or voidable because of such relationship or interest . . . if any of the following occur:
>
> 1.   The fact of such relationship or interest is disclosed or known to the board of directors or committee which authorizes, approves, or ratifies the contract or transaction . . . without counting the votes . . . of such interested director.
> 2.   The fact of such relationship or interest is disclosed or known to the shareholders entitled to vote [on the transaction] and they authorize . . . such contract or transaction by vote or written consent.
> 3.   The contract or transaction is fair and reasonable to the corporation.

Some commentators have supported the view that satisfaction of any *one* of the foregoing statutory alternatives in and of itself, would prove that a director has fully met the duty of loyalty. . . . We are obliged, however, to interpret statutes in conformity with the common law wherever statutory language does not directly negate it. . . . Because the common law and section 496A.34 require directors to show "good faith, honesty, and fairness" in self-dealing, we are persuaded that satisfaction of any one of these three alternatives under the statute would merely preclude us from rendering the transaction void or voidable *outright* solely on the basis "of such [director's] relationship or interest." . . . We thus require directors who engage in self-dealing to establish the additional element that they have acted in good faith, honesty, and fairness. . . .

. . . The crux of appellants' claim is that the [trial] court should have focused on the fair market value of Herrig's services to Cookies rather than on the success Cookies achieved as a result of Herrig's actions.

We agree with appellants' contention that corporate profitability should not be the sole criteria by which to test the fairness and reasonableness of Herrig's fees. . . .

Given an instance of alleged director enrichment at corporate expense . . . the burden to establish fairness resting on the director requires not only a showing of "fair price" but also a showing of the fairness of the bargain to the interests of the corporation. . . . Applying such reasoning to the record before us, however, we cannot agree with appellants' assertion that Herrig's services were either unfairly priced or inconsistent with Cookies corporate interest.

There can be no serious dispute that the four agreements in issue — for exclusive distributorship, taco sauce royalty, warehousing, and consulting fees — have all benefited Cookies, as demonstrated by its financial success. Even if we assume Cookies could have procured similar services from other vendors at lower costs, we are not convinced that Herrig's fees were therefore unreasonable or exorbitant. Like the district court, we are not persuaded by appellants' expert testimony that Cookies' sales and profits would have been the same under agreements with other vendors. As Cookies' board noted prior to Herrig's takeover, he was the driving force in the corporation's success. Even plaintiffs' expert acknowledged that Herrig has done the work of at least five people — production supervisor, advertising specialist, warehouseman, broker, and salesman. While eschewing the lack of internal control, for accounting purposes, that such centralized authority may produce, the expert conceded that Herrig may in fact be underpaid for all he has accomplished. We believe the board properly considered this source of Cookies' success when it entered these transactions, as did the district court when it reviewed them. . . .

[T]he record before us aptly demonstrates that all members of Cookies' board were well aware of Herrig's dual ownership in Lakes and Speed's. We are unaware of any authority supporting plaintiffs' contention that Herrig was obligated to disclose to Cookies' board or shareholders the extent of his profits resulting from these distribution and warehousing agreements; nevertheless, the exclusive distribution agreement with Lakes authorized the board to ascertain that information had it so desired. Appellants cannot reasonably claim that Herrig owed Cookies a duty to render such services at no profit to himself or his companies. Having found that the compensation he received from these agreements was fair and reasonable, we are convinced that Herrig furnished sufficient pertinent information to Cookies' board to enable it to make prudent decisions concerning the contracts. . . .

AFFIRMED.

SCHULTZ, J. (dissenting). . . .

Much of Herrig's evidence concerned the tremendous success of the company. I believe that the trial court and the majority opinion have been so enthralled by the success of the company that they have failed to examine whether these matters of self-dealing were fair to the stock-holders. While much credit is due to Herrig for the success of the company, this does not mean that these transactions were fair to the company.

I believe that Herrig failed on his burden of proof by what he did not show. He did not produce evidence of the local going rate for distribution contracts or storage fees outside of a very limited amount of self-serving testimony. He simply did not show the fair market value of his services or expense for freight, advertising and storage cost. He did not show that his taco sauce royalty was fair. This was his burden. He cannot succeed on it by merely showing the success of the company.

The shareholders, on the other hand, . . . have put forth convincing testimony that Herrig has been grossly overcompensated for his services based on their fair market value. . . .

9.3.2   Approval by Disinterested Members of the Board

Reading the law to require fairness in addition to approval by a disinterested board after full disclosure seems to strain the language of the Iowa statute in the *Cookies* case ("if any of the following occur"). Nevertheless, this interpretation conforms to other judicial interpretations of safe harbor statutes such as DGCL §144(a), NYBCL §713, and Cal. Corp. Code §310. Under the conventional interpretation of these statutes, the approval of an interested transaction by a fully informed board has the effect only of authorizing the transaction, not of foreclosing judicial review for fairness.[23]

This narrow judicial interpretation is plausible when a conflicted transaction is between the controlling shareholder and the corporation (as in the *Cookies* case), since there are grounds to suppose that even "disinterested" directors are not fully independent from a controlling shareholder who, under Delaware law, can cast his votes to ratify the transaction he proposes. Under established Delaware law, for example, approval by disinterested directors merely shifts the burden of proving fairness in a controlled transaction to the plaintiff challenging the deal; it does not transform the standard of review to business judgment. See *Kahn v. Lynch Communication Systems*, in Chapter 12.

But an interested transaction between the company and a single director who is neither a top manager nor a controlling shareholder does not pose the same dangers—or at least not to the same degree. Here full disclosure and approval by disinterested directors can arguably protect shareholder interests. Thus, in this context, courts can be expected to be more deferential to the decision of an independent board, even if the legal doctrine it employs will be the same.

Professor Melvin Eisenberg, a principal reporter of the ALI's Principles of Corporate Governance, argues strongly in the following excerpt that

23. See, e.g., *Fliegler v. Lawrence*, 361 A.2d 218 (Del. 1976); *Kahn v. Lynch Communication Systems*, 638 A.2d 1110 (Del. 1994); *Gaillard v. Natomas Co.*, 256 Cal. Rptr. 702, 208 Cal. App. 3d 1250 (Ct. App. 1989); *Cohen v. Ayers*, 596 F.2d 733 (7th Cir. 1979).

disinterested director review should *not* lead courts to relinquish substantive review under the fairness standard. Section 5.01 of the Principles of Corporate Governance naturally reflects Professor Eisenberg's view.

MELVIN EISENBERG, SELF-INTERESTED TRANSACTIONS IN CORPORATE LAW

13 J. Corp. L. 997, 997-1008 (1988)

[W]hy isn't fairness of price enough without full disclosure? . . .

[A] rule that fairness of price was enough without full disclosure would in effect remove decision making from the corporation's hands and place it in the hands of the court. Many or most self-interested transactions involve differentiated commodities. . . . In the case of commodities that are differentiated, . . . prices are invariably negotiated. The market may set outside limits on the price — at some point, the price the seller demands is so high that the buyer would prefer a market substitute, or the price the buyer insists upon is so low that the seller would prefer to market his commodity to someone else — but within those limits the price will be indeterminable prior to negotiation. Therefore, if by a "fair price" we mean the price that would have been arrived at by a buyer and a seller dealing at arm's length, in the case of a self-interested transaction involving a differentiated commodity, a court attempting to determine whether the price was fair can do no more than to say that the price was or was not within the range at which parties dealing at arm's length would have concluded a deal. . . .

The real question . . . is whether a self-interested transaction that has been approved by disinterested directors after full disclosure will still be subject to a test of fairness, or will [be accorded the protection of the business judgment rule].

There are two reasons why such a transaction should be subject to some sort of fairness test. First, directors, by virtue of their collegial relationships, are unlikely to treat one of their number with the degree of wariness with which they would approach a transaction with a third party. Second, it is difficult if not impossible to utilize a legal definition of disinterestedness in corporate law that corresponds with factual disinterestedness. A factually disinterested director would be one who had no significant relationship of any kind with . . . the subject matter of the self-interested transaction. . . .

. . . A review of the fairness of price of a self-interested transaction may be thought of as a surrogate for a review of the fairness of process by which the transaction was approved. . . . If a self-interested transaction that has been approved by "disinterested" directors is substantively unfair, it can normally be inferred that either the approving directors were not truly disinterested, or that they were not as wary as they should have been because they were dealing with a colleague.[24] . . .

24. Professor Eisenberg continues by observing that, under ALI's Principles of Corporate Governance §5.02, approval by disinterested directors serves to insulate a self-interested transaction, even if it does not accord it the ultimate protection of the business judgment

NOTES AND QUESTIONS

Do you agree with Professor Eisenberg? For simplicity, take the case of a single director (Jones, again) who is personally interested in a transaction that a corporation proposes to enter. Recall that Jones offered to buy 50 acres of land adjacent to the company's main plant. Assume further that Jones fully disclosed his interest to the other directors (as we discussed above) and withdrew from deliberation over the transaction as well as from voting on it. (While withdrawal from discussion is not technically required, it is helpful in persuading a reviewing court that the corporate interest was protected.) Finally, assume that the board, after due deliberation, approved the proposed transaction as in the corporation's best interests. What effect, if any, should this procedure have on a derivative suit claiming that the transaction constituted a breach of loyalty if Jones was not an employee or a controlling shareholder?

There are several possibilities. First, the derivative suit might be dismissed for failing to state a claim in light of the board's approval, unless the shareholder could plead fraud. This would be a literal application of the statutory safe harbor language, and it is quite close to the approach adopted by the RMBCA (§§8.61 et seq.). Second, a court might apply the business judgment rule to the substance of the transaction — i.e., the transaction is not actionable so long as it is not irrational or egregious.[25] Finally, a court could give the approval a more modest effect by following the approach advocated by Professor Eisenberg and the ALI: that is, simply shifting the burden of proving fairness from the defendant to the plaintiff and possibly also stretching the fairness category to include "a reasonable belief in fairness."

Which of these three positions most closely resembles the view of the Delaware Court of Chancery? Consider the following decision.

COOKE v. OOLIE

2000 Del. Ch. LEXIS 89 (May 24, 2000)

CHANDLER, C.:

This case involves a dispute between two directors of The Nostalgia Network, Inc. ("TNN" or the "Company"), Sam Oolie and Morton Salkind, and TNN's shareholders. . . .

[In an earlier opinion,] I granted shareholder plaintiffs further discovery on the sole issue of whether the two director defendants, Oolie and Salkind, breached their fiduciary duty of loyalty by electing to pursue a particular acquisition proposal that allegedly best protected their personal

---

rule. In particular, such approval shifts the burden of proof to the plaintiff (as it does for self-dealing transactions by controlling shareholders under Delaware law). In addition, disinterested approval raises the proof threshold, i.e., the plaintiff "must show that disinterested directors 'could not [have] reasonably . . . believed' the transaction to be fair." — EDS.

25. One of us interprets this language to mean "not a good faith exercise of judgment"; see *In re RJR Nabisco, Inc. Shareholders Litigation*, 1989 Del. Ch. LEXIS 9, at 41.

interests as TNN creditors, rather than pursue other proposals that allegedly offered superior value to TNN's shareholders. . . .

The Court begins with the presumption that the business judgment rule applies to Oolie's and Salkind's decision to pursue the USA acquisition proposal. . . . The plaintiffs bear the burden of rebutting the presumption that the business judgment rule applies to Oolie and Salkind.

To do so, the plaintiffs allege that the defendants failed to act with disinterest and independence and, therefore, do not deserve the protection of the business judgment rule. The USA deal, argue the plaintiffs, provided the greatest benefit to Oolie and Salkind as individuals, but did not necessarily provide the best option for all shareholders in general. . . .

Even assuming that the facts supported the plaintiffs' claim, the two disinterested directors voted to pursue the USA proposal, which removes the alleged taint of disloyalty. Although [DGCL §144] does not explicitly apply,[39] I recognize the policy rationale behind the provision's safe harbor. Under §144(a)(1), this Court will apply the business judgment rule to the actions of an interested director, who is not the majority shareholder, if the interested director fully discloses his interest and a majority of the disinterested directors ratify the interested transaction. The disinterested directors' ratification cleanses the taint of interest because the disinterested directors have no incentive to act disloyally and should be only concerned with advancing the interests of the corporation. The Court will presume, therefore, that the vote of a disinterested director signals that the interested transaction furthers the best interests of the corporation despite the interest of one or more directors.

Although Oolie's and Salkind's actions do not fall explicitly within §144, the rationale behind the Legislature's creation of the safe harbor is on all fours. . . . The disinterested directors' vote to pursue the same proposal that Oolie and Salkind voted to pursue provides strong evidence to the Court that Oolie and Salkind acted in good faith and with the interests of TNN and its shareholders in mind.[40] If the USA deal favored Oolie and Salkind to the detriment of the other shareholders, then presumably the independent directors would not have voted to pursue the USA deal. As such, the disinterested directors' votes present the Court with another reason why the business judgment rule remains the appropriate standard with which to review Oolie's and Salkind's actions. . . .

In addition to the arguments discussed above, the plaintiffs [fail] . . . to offer any evidence or argument on the issue of whether Oolie and Salkind attempted to derive an improper personal benefit by voting to

---

39. Section 144 does not apply . . . for two reasons. First, the statute [only] applies to transactions between a corporation and its directors or another corporation in which the directors have a financial interest. Although a potential conflict exists between Oolie and Salkind as directors and Oolie and Salkind as creditors of TNN, they neither sit on both sides of the potential USA transaction nor do they have a financial interest in USA. Second, §144 applies to a "contract or transaction," but, in this case, no transaction has occurred. The plaintiffs merely challenge defendants' decision to pursue a transaction which ultimately never took place.

40. Additionally, DLJ, the investment bank advising TNN's board, expressed the view that the board should pursue the USA proposal.

pursue the USA proposal. . . . Because the facts do not support the plaintiffs' claim, the disinterested directors voted to pursue the USA deal, and the plaintiffs themselves abandoned this claim at oral argument, I grant summary judgment for the defendants. . . .

NOTE ON COOKE v. OOLIE AND THE DELAWARE SUPREME COURT

Cooke v. Oolie must be read (or generalized) with care. There is, we believe, a detectable difference in philosophy on the subject of review of director-interested transactions between the Court of Chancery and the Supreme Court of Delaware when determining the effect of added procedures in interested transactions. Where the existing precedents leave room for discretionary judgments, the Chancery judges — who, of course, are the ones who must make the actual valuations of "fair prices" — seem more willing to defer to substitute process if it seems to have integrity. These judges understand from practice that valuation decisions are often impossible to make with confidence. The concept of the "intrinsic value" of a company is slippery to the point of indeterminacy. There may be no "there" there — or at least "there" is not a point but a wide range of possible values. Gross disparities can be detected with some confidence, but subtle ones are impossible to detect. And the adversarial process itself may make valuation more difficult. For example, in the valuation aspect of the first *Cede v. Technicolor, Inc.* trial, the defendant's expert offered a valuation of about $13 a share for the company, while the plaintiff's expert offered a valuation of about $65 a share.

Chancery judges, who personally face the daunting task of valuation, seem institutionally inclined to avoid it wherever they can do so responsibly. Thus, the Chancery cases have invoked business judgment-like review where it seems fair.[26] The Delaware Supreme Court, however, is not exposed to the same institutional pressures because it can simply remand cases for valuation. The Delaware Supreme Court may be more receptive to judicial valuation because it is less exposed to the weaknesses of the process.

In *Kahn v. Lynch Communications Corp.*,[27] the Supreme Court cabined the tendency to invoke business judgment review by Chancery judges in cases involving controlled mergers. In related areas, however, the judges of the Court of Chancery still seem to seek interstitially to avoid substantive review of prices where possible. For example, in *In re Siliconix Shareholders Litigation*,[28] the Court of Chancery held that a controlling shareholder has no obligation to pay a fair price in a noncoercive tender

26. See, e.g., *In re TransWorld Airlines, Inc. Shareholders Litigation*, 14 Del. J. Corp. L. 870 (1989); William T. Allen, Jack B. Jacobs & Leo E. Strine, Jr., *Function over Form: A Reassessment of Standards of Review in Delaware Corporation Law*, 56 Bus. Law. 1287 (2001).

27. 630 A.2d 1110 (Del. 1994).

28. 2001 WL 716787 (Del. Ch. 2001).

offer to minority shareholders. Similarly, in *In re Western National Corporation Shareholders Litigation*,[29] the Court of Chancery applied business judgment review to a merger between two corporations, both controlled by the same shareholder, after investigating in detail the independence of the target's board and its special committee of independent directors, and finding that its minority shareholders had approved the merger on full information.

How then is the Court of Chancery likely to review an interested transaction between a company and one or two of its directors who are not affiliated with a controlling shareholder? It will employ business judgment review, we believe, as long as the remaining disinterested directors who approve the transaction cannot be shown to be misinformed, dominated, or manipulated in some fashion. The question is closest when the interested director is also the company's CEO because in this setting it will be easier for a plaintiff to allege domination or manipulation of the disinterested directors. If such allegations cannot be proven, however, we would expect the Court of Chancery to apply business judgment review even in this case.

Of course, the Chancery Court's natural attraction to business judgment review in cases involving a single interested director will not override its historical commitment to remedying apparent breaches of fiduciary duty. Thus, if the terms of a deal are sufficiently egregious to raise strong suspicions in their own right (that is, they carry what older cases referred to as a "badge of fraud"), the Court of Chancery can be expected to require the defendant to explain the transaction as one that represents a fair deal to the company. As long as the Delaware Supreme Court perceives that the Court of Chancery is mindful of this historical responsibility, moreover, we would not expect it to block the Chancery Court from deploying business judgment review where the conflict is between a single director and the corporation.

In other words, notwithstanding a difference in doctrine, the difference in outcomes between Professor Eisenberg's approach and that of the Delaware courts may be small.

9.3.3   Approval by a Special Committee of Independent Directors

There is now a standard template — not a mandatory template but one that is widely employed — for controlled transactions between a subsidiary corporation and its parent or affiliates that involve the greatest risk of overreaching.[30] Parent companies have a clear obligation to treat their subsidiaries fairly and can expect shareholder lawsuits to trigger judicial

---

29. 2000 Del. Ch. LEXIS 82 (2000).
30. Some jurisdictions, such as Germany, dedicate an entire subfield of corporate law to protecting minority shareholders and creditors from the risk of exploitation in such intragroup transactions.

scrutiny of large transactions with their subsidiaries. Therefore, techniques that assure the appearance as well as the reality of a fair deal are useful. As we noted earlier, the special committee of disinterested independent directors is the most common such technique. Two aspects of this technique deserve mention: the operation of the special committee and its effects, if it is well executed.

To be given effect under Delaware law, a special committee must be properly charged by the full board, comprised of independent members, and vested with the resources to accomplish its task. The charge is critical. Committee members must understand that their mission is not only to negotiate a fair deal but also to obtain the best available deal. Therefore, a special committee's conclusion that a deal is merely within a range of fairness will not serve to shift the burden of proof if the deal is attacked.[31] Moreover, a committee must "just say no" when a controlling shareholder refuses to consider advantageous alternatives unless the controller proposes terms that are their financial equivalent. Make no mistake, a committee has real bargaining power in this context because the courts are likely to be skeptical of any deal forced on the minority shareholders without the committee's approval.

Every aspect of the operation of the special committee is important in assuring that its recommendation receives judicial respect. Almost universally, the committee will retain outside investment bankers and lawyers to advise it. The choice of such firms and, in the case of bankers, the method of their compensation may be important. Since the principal reason for appointing a special committee is to assume the appearance of honest, independent judgment, it is a mistake to allow any shadow to fall on that process.[32]

Difficulties do arise in special committee cases, of course. For example, must the "buyer" in a cash-out merger reveal its reservation price to the special committee with which it is negotiating? Presumably not. Does it have to disclose why it seeks the transaction? And how is a fair price to be determined? Is it a proportion of the entire change in control value of the firm? Is it the market capitalization of the public block or perhaps the market capitalization plus some sharing of synergy gains? But what is the principle of sharing?[33]

Moreover, even if the committee process is done well, it only shifts the burden of proving fairness from the defendant to the plaintiff (that is, the plaintiff must now show "unfairness") in a controlled transaction.[34] Is this worth the substantial expense and delay of the special committee process? Reasonable minds may differ, but consider also that the shareholder plaintiff who attacks the transaction will bear a substantial evidentiary burden if the process is well executed.

31. See *In re First Boston Shareholders Litigation,* 1990 Del. Ch. LEXIS 206 (1990).

32. See, e.g., *Kahn v. Tremont Corp.,* 694 A.2d 422, 429 (Del. 1997).

33. See *id.*; Jeffery L. Brudney, Eighth Annual Baron de Hirsch Meyer Lecture Series: ALI Corporate Governance Project: *The Role of the Board of Directors: The ALI and Its Critics,* 37 U. Miami L. Rev. 223, 224 (1996).

34. See *Kahn v. Lynch Communications* below, in Chapter 12.

9.3.4   Shareholder Ratification of Conflict Transactions

In agency law, a principal can adopt an agent's unauthorized acts through ratification.[35] In corporate law, shareholders may ratify acts of the board, too, but because shareholders are a collectivity, their ratification involves issues not present in the agency model. In particular, the law must limit the power of an interested majority of shareholders to bind a minority that is disinclined to ratify a submitted transaction. See ALI, Principals of Corporate Governance §5.02(a)(2)(D). In addition, the power of shareholders to affirm self-dealing transactions is limited by the corporate "waste" doctrine, which holds that even a majority vote cannot protect wildly unbalanced transactions that, on their face, irrationally dissipate corporate assets. See, e.g., ALI, Principles of Corporate Governance §5.02(a)(2)(D).

The following excerpt from a Delaware Court of Chancery opinion indicates why shareholder ratification is not treated as a full answer to a complaint that the deal is unfair.

LEWIS v. VOGELSTEIN

699 A.2d 327 (Del. Ch. 1997)

ALLEN, Chancellor. . . .

Ratification is a concept deriving from the law of agency which contemplates the ex post conferring upon or confirming of the legal authority of an agent in circumstances in which the agent had no authority or arguably had no authority. RESTATEMENT (SECOND) OF AGENCY §82 (1958). To be effective, of course, the agent must fully disclose all relevant circumstances with respect to the transaction to the principal prior to the ratification. . . . Beyond that, since the relationship between a principal and agent is fiduciary in character, the agent in seeking ratification must act not only with candor, but with loyalty. Thus an attempt to coerce the principal's consent improperly will invalidate the effectiveness of the ratification. . . .

Application of these general ratification principles to shareholder ratification is complicated by three other factors. First, most generally, in the case of shareholder ratification there is of course no single individual acting as principal, but rather a class or group of divergent individuals — the class of shareholders. This aggregate quality of the principal means that decisions to affirm or ratify an act will be subject to collective action disabilities (see Robert C. Clark, Corporate Law at 181-182); that some portion of the body doing the ratifying may in fact have conflicting interests in the transaction; and some dissenting members of the class may be able to assert more or less convincingly that the "will" of the principal is wrong, or even corrupt and ought not to be binding on the class. In the case of individual ratification these issues won't arise, assuming that the principal does not suffer from multiple personality disorder. . . . The second, mildly complicating factor present in shareholder ratification is the fact that in

---

35. Restatement (Third) Agency §§4.01, 4.03-4.04.

corporation law the "ratification" that shareholders provide will often not be directed to lack of legal authority of an agent but will relate to the consistency of some authorized director action with the equitable duty of loyalty. Thus shareholder ratification sometimes acts not to confer legal authority—but as in this case—to affirm that action taken is consistent with shareholder interests. [The third complicating factor arises because] when what is "ratified" is a director conflict transaction, the statutory law—in Delaware Section 144 of the Delaware General Corporation Law—may bear on the effect [of ratification]. . . .

These [complicating factors] lead to a difference in the effect of a valid ratification in the shareholder context. The principal novelty added to ratification law generally by the shareholder context, is . . . that . . . shareholder ratification [may be held to be] . . . ineffectual (1) because a majority of those affirming the transaction had a conflicting interest with respect to it or (2) because the transaction that is ratified constituted a corporate waste. As to the second of these, it has long been held that shareholders may not ratify a waste except by a unanimous vote. *Saxe v. Brady,* Del. Ch., 184 A.2d 602, 605 (1962). The idea behind this rule is apparently that a transaction that satisfies the high standard of waste constitutes a gift of corporate property and no one should be forced against their will to make a gift of their property. In all events, informed, uncoerced, disinterested shareholder ratification of a transaction in which corporate directors have a material conflict of interest has the effect of protecting the transaction from judicial review except on the basis of waste. . . .

The judicial standard for determination of corporate waste is well developed. Roughly, a waste entails an exchange of corporate assets for consideration so disproportionately small as to lie beyond the range at which any reasonable person might be willing to trade. . . . Most often the claim is associated with a transfer of corporate assets that serves no corporate purpose; or for which no consideration at all is received. . . .

A somewhat different formulation of the effects of shareholder ratification is offered by the following opinion, in which the Delaware Court of Chancery indicates that a conflicted transaction that is approved by a shareholder vote is subject to business judgment review by the courts.

IN RE WHEELABRATOR TECHNOLOGIES, INC.

663 A.2d 1194 (Del. Ch. 1995)

[This derivative action was brought by shareholders of Wheelabrator Technologies, Inc. (WTI), whose company was bought by Waste Management, Inc. (Waste), in a merger transaction. The claim was that the WTI directors breached their duties of care and loyalty. Although 4 of WTI's 11 directors were officers of Waste (which owned 22 percent of WTI's stock), the court found that Waste did not control WTI. Nevertheless, the sale of

WTI to Waste was an interested-director transaction for purposes of DGCL §144. Even so, the Court held informed approval by WTI's non-Waste shareholders meant that the transaction was subject only to business judgment review.]

JACOBS, V.C.:

To repeat: in only two circumstances has the Delaware Supreme Court held that a fully-informed shareholder vote operates to extinguish a claim: (1) where the board of directors takes action that, although not alleged to constitute ultra vires, fraud, or waste, is claimed to exceed the board's authority; and (2) where it is claimed that the directors failed to exercise due care to adequately inform themselves before committing the corporation to a transaction. In no case has the Supreme Court held that stockholder ratification automatically extinguishes a claim for breach of the directors' duty of loyalty. Rather, the operative effect of shareholder ratification in duty of loyalty cases has been either to change the standard of review to the business judgment rule, with the burden of proof resting upon the plaintiff, or to leave "entire fairness" as the review standard, but shift the burden of proof to the plaintiff. . . .

The ratification decisions that involve duty of loyalty claims are of two kinds: (a) "interested" transaction cases between a corporation and its directors . . . and (b) [interested] transaction[s] between the corporation and its controlling shareholder.

Regarding the first category, [DGCL] §144(a)(2) pertinently provides that an "interested" transaction of this kind will not be voidable if it is approved in good faith by a majority of disinterested stockholders. Approval by fully informed, disinterested shareholders pursuant to §144 (a)(2) invokes "the business judgment rule and limits judicial review to issues of gift or waste with the burden of proof upon the party attacking the transaction." *Marciano v. Nakash*, Del. Supr., 535 A.2d 400, 405 n.3 (1987). The result is the same in "interested" transaction cases not decided under §144. . . .

The second category concerns . . . transactions between the corporation and its controlling stockholder. Those cases involve primarily parent-subsidiary mergers that were conditioned upon receiving "majority of the minority" stockholder approval. In a parent-subsidiary merger, the standard of review is ordinarily entire fairness, with the directors having the burden of proving that the merger was entirely fair. . . . But where the merger is conditioned upon approval by a "majority of the minority" stockholder vote, and such approval is granted, the standard of review remains entire fairness, but the burden of demonstrating that the merger was unfair shifts to the plaintiff. . . .

. . . I conclude that in duty of loyalty cases arising out of transactions with a controlling shareholder, our Supreme Court would reject the proposition that the Delaware courts will have no reviewing function in cases where the challenged transaction is approved by an informed shareholder vote. . . . Even if the ratified transaction does not involve a controlling stockholder, the result would not be to extinguish a duty of loyalty claim. In such cases the Supreme Court has held that the effect of shareholder ratification is to make business judgment the applicable review standard and shift the burden of proof to the plaintiff stockholder. None of these authorities holds that shareholder ratification operates automatically to extinguish a duty of loyalty claim. . . .

The participation of the controlling interested stockholder is critical to the application of the entire fairness standard because . . . the potential for process manipulation by the controlling stockholder, and the concern that the controlling stockholder's continued presence might influence even a fully informed shareholder vote, justify the need for the exacting judicial scrutiny. . . .

In this case, there is no contention . . . that Waste, a 22% stockholder of WTI, exercised de jure or de facto control over WTI. . . . Accordingly, the review standard applicable to this merger is business judgment, with the plaintiffs having the burden of proof.

9.4 DIRECTOR AND MANAGEMENT COMPENSATION

A different type of self-dealing transaction is the payment of compensation to officers and directors. Technically speaking, compensation paid to corporate directors or officers who are directors is a conflicted, "self-dealing" transaction, just like any other. But, of course, compensation is different, since a corporation must naturally compensate its managers and directors. Compensation, then, is a necessary form of self-interested transaction. Compensation plans that are wisely structured and closely monitored can better align the interests of managers and shareholders, and thus reduce the agency costs of management. As the following discussion points out, however, incentive compensation schemes also create agency problems of their own.

Traditionally, employee compensation is a core matter of business judgment for the board. It becomes problematic principally in the case of a company's directors and senior officers. The most valuable "asset" of a senior manager is his skill and his specialized knowledge of his firm. But managers, like other employees, cannot easily diversify their "investment" in the firm. This fact will tend to make managers risk averse. Compensation structures must respond to this fact. A substantial part of manager compensation should take the form of fixed, short-term claims, i.e., salary commitments. This will reduce the amount that a manager has at risk at any moment. But there are real drawbacks to salary-based compensation plans for managers and directors. In particular, a fixed salary is unlikely to do enough to induce a manager to accept risky projects that nevertheless are valuable from a long-term shareholder perspective. Motivated at least in part by this reasoning, Section 162(m) of the Internal Revenue Code (introduced in the Revenue Reconciliation Act of 1993) prevents public companies from taking a tax deduction for annual compensation to the CEO or four other top employees in excess of $1 million, unless the compensation is "performance-based."

The conventional alternative (or complement) to fixed salaries is high-powered incentive compensation based on the performance of individual managers or, where this cannot be monitored, on the performance of the company as a whole. But this solution also has its problematic side. It is rarely possible to match long-term compensation, except in the crudest way, to the contributions of a manager (even a CEO) to the value of a company. Not only is it difficult to measure those contributions, but also managers are more likely to "game" incentive pay schemes as the monetary stakes increase, just as athletes are more likely to use performance-enhancing drugs as the monetary returns for victory increase. Thus, incentive compensation, including the traditional stock-option plan, is an antidote to management slack, but it is also a source of additional agency costs. Designing a system that balances the productivity gains resulting from high-powered incentives against the additional monitoring and governance costs that these incentives impose is a task that demands great expertise.

9.4.1   Perceived Excessive Compensation

The past fifteen years has been among the best of economic times in the United States. Price stability, decreasing unemployment and capital costs, and increasing domestic production, investment, and technological innovation sustained extraordinarily high growth rates. From this perspective, it is not surprising that the total compensation for CEOs of Fortune 500 companies grew rapidly over the period 1993 to 2003. The following chart shows the trend in CEO pay during this period.

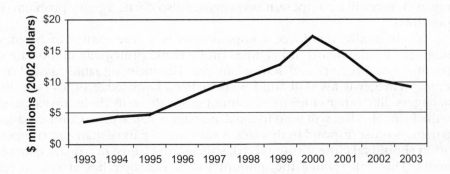

The trend in executive compensation roughly tracks the increase and subsequent decline of the stock market overall during this period. However, Professors Lucian Bebchuk and Yaniv Grinstein calculate that share price performance, industry effects, and increases in firm size can explain only half of the overall growth.[36] Bebchuk and Grinstein further report that

---

36. Lucian Bebchuk & Yaniv Grinstein, *The Growth of Executive Pay*, 21 Oxford Review of Economic Policy 283 (2005).

aggregate compensation to the top five managers increased from 5 percent of corporate profits in 1993 to approximately 10 percent in 2003.[37] In a similar vein, Professor Kevin J. Murphy calculates that in 1970 the average pay of a CEO in a public company was more than 25 times greater than the average worker's pay, but by 1996, that ratio had increased to over 200 times![38] These findings suggest a fundamental change in the underlying mechanisms that set top executive pay in the 1990s and early 2000s.

Whatever the explanation for this data, the astonishing payments made to certain CEOs by their companies are a frequent source of concern. In addition, shareholder advocates attack many common features of top executive compensation, including its overall level (for being too high), its form (for not sufficiently punishing failure), the procedures used for setting compensation (for being insufficiently disinterested), and the common sweeteners in compensation contracts, such as "golden parachutes," that reward executives for standing aside gracefully in the sale of their companies.

It is difficult to determine whether any particular CEO, or even CEOs as a class, receives excessive pay, partly because it is difficult to estimate the market price for unique executive talent.[39] Senior officers are not fungible. One might suspect, as many do, that the process that sets their compensation does not produce a true reading of the market, but suspicion is a frail basis for judicial review.[40] Moreover, the recent period of high growth in CEO compensation has also been a time of substantially greater CEO turnover, much of it forced.[41] CEOs get fired more often today than before, and economic theory suggests that increases in the riskiness of future payments will reduce the present value of the flow of funds. Thus, we would expect CEO compensation to rise in response to reduced job security.

Consider the following excerpts from news articles about specific CEO pay packages. What arguments might justify the packages in each case? What arguments suggest more nefarious (i.e., socially undesirable) forces instead?

ANTHONY RAMIREZ, REEBOK CHIEF FACING 93% PAY CUT

N.Y. Times, July 27, 1990, at D1

Paul B. Fireman, whose salary and bonus of $14.6 million last year as chairman and chief executive of Reebok International made him one of the

---

37. Id.

38. Kevin J. Murphy, *Executive Compensation,* in Handbook of Labor Economics, fig. 15 (Orley Ashenfelter & David Card eds., 1999).

39. One can say, however, that CEOs of U.S. public companies are paid far more than their counterparts in other countries, and far more in 2002 than in 1992.

40. A consultant makes a report to a board committee, recommending a future compensation proposal. Typically, the compensation firm is selected by management and is permissibly retained serially.

41. See Steven N. Kaplan & Bernadette A. Minton, *How Has CEO Turnover Changed? Increasingly Performance Sensitive Boards and Increasingly Uneasy CEOs* (working paper May 2006).

highest-paid heads of a publicly held company, has agreed to take one of the biggest pay cuts ever, the company said yesterday.

As a result, Mr. Fireman's earnings next year could drop 93 percent from their 1989 level.

Under a new contract that takes effect next January, Mr. Fireman's base salary will be $1 million plus a possible maximum bonus of $1 million. His 1990 salary will not be determined until year-end results are in. . . .

Forbes magazine recently listed Mr. Fireman as the best-compensated chief executive, in terms of salary and bonus, of a publicly owned American corporation, in 1989. When stock value increases are counted, however, *Forbes* said Craig O. McCaw, the head of McCaw Cellular, was on top over all, with $53.9 million in total compensation. . . .

Support for Mr. Fireman's compensation may have waned among Reebok's board with the falling out between Mr. Fireman and Pentland Group P.L.C., Reebok's largest shareholder. Pentland recently put up for sale its 31.5 percent Reebok stake, citing longstanding disputes over marketing, production and other corporate strategies.

Stephen Rubin, Pentland's chairman and vice chairman of Reebok, had negotiated Mr. Fireman's original compensation agreement when Pentland bought 60 percent of Reebok in 1982.

Under a new five-year arrangement, Mr. Fireman has agreed to a base salary of $1 million and a bonus of up to $1 million, depending on whether Reebok reaches profit objectives to be set annually by the board. Mr. Fireman will also get stock options for 2.5 million common shares, exercisable over 10 years. . . .

Mr. Fireman's salary began to draw attention in 1984, when investment bankers preparing to take Reebok public said he was being paid too much. The initial 1982 pay pact was originally designed to minimize Pentland's risk by paying Mr. Fireman a low salary — then $65,000 annually — but an unlimited incentive of 10 percent of pretax earnings over $100,000.

Despite the objections of investment bankers and Mr. Fireman's offer to reduce the compensation, Pentland's Mr. Rubin had said a deal was a deal. Under the 1986 five-year agreement, which expires next January, Mr. Fireman was paid a relatively modest base salary — $350,000 — and 5 percent of pretax earnings over $20 million.

As Reebok's earnings exploded, so did Mr. Fireman's earnings. He made $1.2 million in 1984, $5.5 million in 1985, $13.1 million in 1986, $15.4 million in 1987, $11.4 million in 1988 and $14.6 million last year.

GRASSO QUITS NYSE AMID PAY FUROR

Wall Street Journal (September 18, 2003)

Yesterday, Mr. Grasso, 57 years old, was pressured to step down after a public outcry over a $139.5 million retirement-pay package that he had built up over 36 years at the NYSE. The resignation, after an emergency NYSE board meeting yesterday, followed calls for Mr. Grasso to resign in recent days by a growing chorus of Big Board directors, floor traders, institutional investors and politicians. Critics were especially furious over his pay package because the markets are just now recovering from an unprecedented period of corporate scandal that included shockingly high compensation for some executives.

[Grasso] has favored the Big Board's position as a secretive club run by Wall Street insiders — and has had his pay set by directors whose firms Mr. Grasso regulates. But he became a casualty of the public's revulsion over 1990s-style corporate excess. He was paid like a big-time Wall Street chief executive, rather than a regulator. The National Association of Securities Dealers, by contrast, pays its CEO about $2 million a year. And Securities and Exchange Commission Chairman William Donaldson — whose total annual pay when he served as Big Board chairman in the early 1990s was about $1.5 million — now makes$142,500 a year.

AT ELITE PREP SCHOOL, PARENTS DO THE MATH: RECTOR GETS $524,000

Wall Street Journal (August 25, 2003)

Last year Mr. Anderson, whose official title is "rector," made $524,000 in salary, benefits and deferred compensation—more than most college presidents. That doesn't include the seven-bedroom, 14,062-square-foot mansion that St. Paul's provides for him or the $32,000 stipend for his wife to assist in his official duties.

That compensation package has sparked an ugly fight at this genteel boarding school, where gossip usually revolves around the crew team's chances in the Royal Henley Regatta and who will get into Harvard. Some alumni, parents and donors, outraged at Mr. Anderson's salary, are campaigning for his ouster. They are also pushing for new faces on the 24-member board of trustees, which sets his pay.

The complaints don't stop there. Critics have attacked the school's vice rector, Sharon Hennessy, for her $316,400 in total compensation and the perks of her position, including a stipend for her spouse, membership in the upscale Canyon Ranch spa and an annual two-week summer sojourn on the French Riviera.

The school acknowledges Mr. Anderson's compensation is at or near the top of headmasters at comparable prep schools. But trustees say a simple fact underlies the hefty salaries: Mr. Anderson and Ms. Hennessy have received overtures from other schools, and generous rewards are needed to keep them from defecting. They say the pay also reflects stellar performance. Since Mr. Anderson and Ms. Hennessy arrived at the school in 1997, St. Paul's has boosted donations to $25 million a year from $6.2 million, while the financial aid doled out annually has roughly doubled to $4.4 million. The school's yield, or the proportion of accepted applicants who matriculate, has risen to 64% from 58%.

9.4.2   Option Grants and the Law of Director and Officer Compensation

Shareholders or disinterested directors often ratify the compensation of the CEO and other board members to provide an extra measure of legal insulation, even though compensation agreements are not subject to the ordinary law of director conflicts. There are two reasons for doing so. First, corporations must pay compensation; they are not like universities, art museums, orphanages, or other nonprofit organizations that attract volunteers. Second, courts are poorly equipped to determine fair salaries because of the unique character of particular managers — and the wide range of returns that comparably skilled managers command on the market.

In the legal history of management compensation, nothing has caused the Delaware courts more difficulty than the introduction of option[42] compensation plans following World War II. Early Delaware opinions were hostile to stock option grants because courts had been on guard against the threat of controllers issuing themselves cheap stock. From this perspective, option grants seemed troubling, and the Delaware courts initially policed them closely under a standard of review that was said to be the waste doctrine but was in fact stricter than the waste standard. Later, as the courts grew comfortable with option grants to managers, shareholders probed the use of options to compensate directors, as in the *Lewis v. Vogelstein* case excerpted below.[43] The particular compensation plan at issue in *Lewis* was, at the time of granting, unusually generous to the board of directors. The *Lewis* complaint attacked the plan, inter alia, on the ground that its approval by shareholders was invalid because the grant itself constituted a waste of corporate assets.

LEWIS v. VOGELSTEIN

699 A.2d 327 (Del. Ch. 1997)

ALLEN, C.:

The early Delaware cases on option compensation established that, even in the presence of informed [shareholder] ratification, in order for stock option grants to be valid a two part test had to be satisfied. First it was seen as necessary that the court conclude that the grant contemplates that the corporation will receive "sufficient consideration." E.g., *Kerbs*, at 90 A.2d 652, 656 (1952). . . .

Secondly it was held early on that, in addition, the plan or the circumstances of the grant must include "conditions or the existence of

---

42. A stock option in this context (technically a "call" option) is the right to purchase a share of stock from the company for a fixed price, which is generally the market price of the stock at the time the grant is made. Options granted by corporations for compensation purposes generally have much longer exercise periods than option that trade in the financial markets; i.e., they can ordinarily be exercised at any time over a ten-year period.

43. Other portions of this opinion were excerpted above, in §9.3.

circumstances *which may be expected to insure* that the contemplated consideration will in fact pass to the corporation." *Kerbs* at 656 (emphasis added). . . .

In all events, these tests were in fact operationally very problematic. Valuing an option grant (as part of a reasonable relationship test) is quite difficult, even under today's more highly developed techniques of financial analysis. This would be especially true where, as this case exemplifies, the options are tied to and conditioned upon a continued status as an officer or director. Even more problematic is valuing — or judicially reviewing a judgment of equivalency of value of — the future benefits that the corporation hopes to obtain from the option grant. There is no objective metric to gauge ex ante incentive effects of owning options by officers or directors. Beyond this operational problem, the approach of these early option cases may be thought to raise the question, why was it necessary for the court reviewing a stock option grant to conclude that the circumstances "insure" that the corporation will receive the benefits it seeks to achieve. . . .

In *Beard v. Elster,* Del. Supr., 160 A.2d 731 (1960), the Delaware Supreme Court. . . rejected the [condition]. . . that the corporation had to have (or insure receipt of) legally cognizable consideration in order to make an option grant valid. The court also. . . held that what was necessary to validate an officer or director stock option grant was a finding that a reasonable board could conclude from the circumstances that the corporation may reasonably expect to receive a proportionate benefit. A good faith determination by a disinterested board or committee to that effect, at least when ratified by a disinterested shareholder vote, entitled such a grant to business judgment protection (i.e., classic waste standard). . . .

A substantive question that remains, however [is]: whether in practice the waste standard that is utilized where informed shareholders ratify a grant of options [that is] recommended by a *self-interested board* is the classical waste test (i.e., no consideration; gift; no person of ordinary prudence could possibly agree, etc.) or whether, in fact, it is a species of intermediate review in which the court assesses reasonableness in relationship to perceived benefits. [Emphasis added.]

The Supreme Court has not expressly deviated from the "proportionality" approach to waste of its earlier decision, although in recent decades it has had few occasions to address the subject. [Nevertheless, in] *Michelson v. Duncan,* Del. Supr., 407 A.2d 211 (1979), a stock option case in which ratification had occurred, . . . the court repeatedly referred to the relevant test where ratification had occurred as that of "gift or waste" and plainly meant by waste, the absence of *any* consideration [emphasis added]. . . .

The Court of Chancery has [also recently] interpreted the waste standard in the ratified option context as invoking . . . the traditional waste standard. . . .

In according substantial effect to shareholder ratification these more recent cases are not unmindful of the collective action problem faced by shareholders in public corporations. [However,] in this age in which institutional shareholders have grown strong and can more easily communicate, . . . [shareholder] assent, is, I think, a more rational means to monitor compensation than judicial determinations of the "fairness," or sufficiency of consideration. . . . In all events, the classic waste standard does afford some protection against egregious cases of "constructive fraud." . . .

[The Court next rejected the defendant's motion to dismiss the complaint, invoking classic waste doctrine to do so.]

Giving the pleader the presumptions to which he is entitled on this motion, I cannot conclude that no set of facts could be shown that would permit the court to conclude that the grant of these options, particularly focusing upon the one-time options, constituted an exchange to which no reasonable person not acting under compulsion and in good faith could agree. . . . I do not mean to suggest . . . that these grants are suspect, only that one time option grants to directors of this size seem at this point sufficiently unusual to require the court to refer to evidence before making an adjudication of their validity and consistency with fiduciary duty. . . .

NOTE ON CORPORATE LOANS TO OFFICERS AND DIRECTORS: BACK TO THE FUTURE?

The corporate statutes of an earlier era restricted the ability of boards to authorize loans of corporate funds to directors or senior officers or to guarantee loans to these managers made by third parties. Most often these statutes required shareholder approval of any such loan, but some statutes flatly prohibited interested loans.[44] The gradual "liberalization" of the corporate law, however, led to a relaxation of these restrictions. Delaware led the way. Section 143 of the DGCL provides that the board may authorize such loans when it finds "that the loan or guarantee benefits the corporation." Moreover, with such apparent statutory encouragement, the practice grew. Indeed, there is anecdotal evidence that, during the boom of the late 1990s, loans to some CEOs grew scandalously large. For example, the board of WorldCom, Inc., authorized loans to its CEO, Bernie Ebbers, totaling more than $350 million — loans that remained outstanding 18 months later when WorldCom declared bankruptcy.

If judges cannot distinguish legitimate from wasteful compensation except in egregious cases (even the author of *Lewis* would have gagged at a $350 million unsecured loan), and if disaggregated public shareholders cannot monitor boards effectively, *and* if the problem is grave enough, then perhaps there is no alternative except to prohibit companies from making loans to their officers and directors. This appears to be the reasoning behind §402 of the federal Sarbanes-Oxley Act of 2002, which prohibits any corporation whose shares trade on a national exchange or NASDAQ, or the subsidiary of such a corporation, from directly or indirectly extending any credit to any director or executive officer of the corporation. This remarkable federal intervention into the law of executive compensation thus cancels a conventional compensation provision in state corporation statutes and may bar a number of common corporation practices, such as advancing managers funds to buy stock, exercise options, or even

---

44. See Douglas M. Branson, Corporate Governance §8.21 (1993); Jayne W. Barnard, *Corporate Loans to Directors and Officers: Every Business Now a Bank?*, 1988 Wis. L. Rev. 237.

finance legal fees prior to the resolution of shareholder suits. Put differently, the federal ban on corporate loans to executives injects a mandatory
prohibition into an area of corporate law in which similar prohibitions had
disappeared nearly 70 years earlier.

QUESTION

Under indemnification statutes such as DGCL §145, when an officer or
director is sued for any action she arguably took in furtherance of her
corporate duties, the corporation may "advance" reasonable defense
costs even before it is determined that the expenses are properly indemnifiable under the corporate bylaws. Is this common practice made unlawful
under §402? Are there arguments under which it may continue?

9.4.3   Corporate Governance and SEC Regulatory Responses

The compensation committee of the board of directors generally sets
the compensation of the CEO and top officers in public corporations.
Institutional investors need information if they are to take a role in constraining excessive compensation. In 1993, the SEC took steps to provide
that information by enhancing disclosure rules. These rules required corporations to make far more detailed public disclosures about the compensation of their top five corporate officers. Three elements were particularly
noteworthy. First, companies had to disclose, in a standardized Summary
Compensation Table, the annual compensation (salary, bonus, etc.), long-
term compensation (restricted stock awards, option awards, etc.), and all
other compensation for the top five employees in the company. Second,
the 1993 reforms required a narrative description of all employment contracts with top executives, and disclosure of a Compensation Committee
report explaining the committee's compensation decisions. Finally, the
reforms required a graph showing the company's cumulative shareholder
returns for the previous five years, along with a broad-based market index
and a peer-group index for the same period.

The net effect of these reforms was increased transparency, the implicit goal of which was (presumably) to "shame" corporations into "reasonable" compensation for their top executives. But as the graph at the
beginning of this section indicates, executive compensation took off over
the following decade. While the dramatic gains in the stock market during
the 1990s are of course part of the explanation, are there reasons
one might think that the disclosure rules themselves helped fuel the
increase?

In 2006, the SEC, under the leadership of Chairman Christopher Cox,
returned to the issue of executive compensation. As in 1993, the focus of
the 2006 reforms was increased disclosure of executive compensation. The
new SEC rule requires a single number that captures all compensation for

each of the top executives, as well as improved disclosures on retirement payouts, perquites, directors' pay, and related-party transactions. The SEC proposed requiring disclosure of compensation paid to up to three employees who were not executives, but who were more highly compensated than at least one executive officer of the company. The proposed requirement, dubbed the "Katie Couric" rule after the famed news reporter who now anchors the CBS Evening News, received criticism from Hollywood and Wall Street, as many entertainers, athletes, and investment bankers would have fallen into this category. The SEC's currently proposed version of this rule will make an exception for employees who do not have policy-making roles within the company.

Chairman Cox has argued that these changes would further improve transparency for investors and the public at large. On one hand, increased transparency might pressure directors to keep all forms of compensation "reasonable." On the other hand, increased transparency might accelerate compensation growth rates even further, or push compensation into other, even more difficult to detect, forms. What do you think?

NOTE ON ACCOUNTING FOR STOCK OPTIONS

While there are various financial measures of a corporation's performance, the single measure followed most closely is earnings per share (EPS). Cash compensation is, of course, a business expense and is deducted from revenues before net profit is determined. Thus, cash compensation reduces earnings and EPS. Options have value when they are granted, even when they can be exercised only at a price greater than current market price. For a long time, the Financial Standards Accounting Board (FASB)[45] accounting standards did not require corporations to treat the granting of options as an expense unless these options were "in of the money" when granted (i.e., afford the right to buy stock at a price *below* the current market value). Instead, companies needed only disclose the terms of such grants in the notes to their financial statements, without reducing earnings or EPS by the value of these option grants. If capital markets are informationally efficient, this alternative form of providing information should not affect stock price. Yet American businesses acted as if it did matter.

After the Enron debacle, the Financial Accounting Standards Board (FASB) successfully pushed through a revised Rule 123 on accounting for stock options, which now requires U.S. companies to expense the fair value of stock options granted to employees. Although Rule 123 does not require a specific method for valuing the options, the vast majority of U.S. companies have announced their intention to use the Black-Scholes option pricing formula. Critics complain that the Black-Scholes formula overstates the value of options on the income statement; among other reasons, the Black-Scholes formula assumes that the option-holder is perfectly diversified,

---

45. The FASB is the private body charged by the SEC with developing generally accepted accounting principles (GAAP).

which is not the case for managers who are over-invested in their own companies. (Even if their financial portfolios were perfectly diversified, managers' "human capital" is invested 100 percent in the company, and cannot be diversified.) For most companies 2006 is the first year of expensing stock options, which means that the first wave of financial results under Rule 123 will be reported in early 2007.[46]

9.4.4 The *Disney* Decision

In the aftermath of Enron and the resulting public focus on perceived deficiencies in corporate controls, the judicial urge to correct perceived governance excesses became irresistible. Few areas of corporate governance had drawn more attention during the booming 1990s than executive compensation. Therefore, it is perhaps not surprising that the next area of corporate governance to witness erosion of the business judgment rule was executive compensation. The case in which this development burst forth arose from astonishing facts involving a payment of compensation valued at approximately $140 million to Michael Ovitz upon his termination by the Walt Disney Company after a bit more than one year of service.

The story begins with the accidental death of Frank Wells in 1994. Wells had been number two to Disney's CEO Michael Eisner for ten years, and together the management team had been highly successful. There were no acceptable inside candidates for Wells's job and for the time being Eisner assumed these duties. About a year later, Eisner had a health scare, and the board insisted that succession planning be addressed. Michael Ovitz had started a talent agency in 1974 with Ron Meyer and others called Creative Artists Agency (CAA). He represented many of the biggest stars in Hollywood and was an effective negotiator. Eisner and Ovitz had been personal friends for twenty-five years, and Eisner had approached Ovitz several times (unsuccessfully) to have him join Disney's management team.

In July 1995, after Meyer left CAA to join MCA, Eisner sensed that the time might be ripe to approach Ovitz again. Ovitz's income at this time was $20-$25 million per year, and in the ensuing negotiations with Eisner and Disney he insisted on substantial "downside protection" in order to give up his 55 percent interest in CAA. Eisner and Irwin Russell, chairman of Disney's compensation committee, led the negotiations for Disney. Russell recruited Graef Crystal, an executive compensation

---

46. The New York Stock Exchange and NASDAQ listing standards now require listed companies to seek shareholder approval for *all* stock option plans except those that are offered as an inducement to new employees or in connection with a merger or acquisition. See www.nyse.com/pdfs/finalruletext303A.pdf;nasd.complinet.com/nasd/display/index.html (Rule 4350-5). Formerly, the NYSE and NASDAQ excluded "broadly based" option plans from required shareholder votes. In addition, all issuers must obtain shareholder approval of stock option plans in order to qualify for favorable federal tax treatment, including exemption from the limits on deductibility under §162(m) of the IRC and special tax treatment for incentive stock options (ISOs).

consultant, and Raymond Watson, a former Disney board chairman, to help evaluate the financial terms of Ovitz's employment agreement. In August 1995, Ovitz accepted the job as President of Walt Disney, and joined the Disney board. Disney's stock price rose 4.4 percent on the day of the announcement, increasing Disney's market capitalization by more than $1 billion.

It rapidly became clear that Ovitz was a poor fit for Disney.[47] In November 1996 Eisner asked Sanford Litvack, Disney's general counsel, whether Ovitz could be fired "for cause," which would have avoided the "non-fault termination" ("NFT") payments that were built in to Ovitz's employment agreement. After studying the facts and consulting with others in Disney's legal department, Litvack concluded that Ovitz could not be fired for cause, though Litvack did not personally conduct any legal research or request an outside opinion on the issue. In December 1996, the Disney board fired Ovitz "without cause," thus triggering approximately $38 million in cash severance payments and accelerated vesting of options under Ovitz's employment agreement. When all the dust had settled, Ovitz had received approximately $140 million in compensation for fifteen months of service as president of Disney. In both the hiring and firing of Michael Ovitz, the extensive factual record made clear that the directors other than Eisner and, secondarily, Russell were only marginally involved in the decision-making processes.

Shareholder plaintiffs brought suit on behalf of the corporation claiming, among other things, that the Disney directors breached their duty of care in approving Ovitz's employment agreement, and that the severance payment to Ovitz constituted waste. The Disney charter contained a 102(b)(7) waiver, which meant that the plaintiffs had to assert that the board had not acted in "good faith." In October 1998, the Delaware Chancery Court dismissed the complaint on the grounds that the board was made up of a majority of independent directors who had no interest in the transaction. Chancellor Chandler wrote: "Just as the 85,000-ton cruise ships Disney Magic and Disney Wonder are forced by science to obey the same laws of buoyancy as Disneyland's significantly smaller Jungle Cruise ships, so is a corporate board's extraordinary decision to award a $140 million severance package governed by the same corporate law principles as its everyday decision to authorize a loan." *In re Walt Disney Co. Derivative Litigation*, 731 A.2d 342, 351 (Del. Ch. 1998). On appeal, the Supreme Court of Delaware reversed in part and directed that plaintiff be given an opportunity to replead. *Brehm v. Eisner*, 746 A.2d 244 (Del 2000). When reviewing the repleaded complaint on remand, the Chancellor sustained the complaint in the following opinion.

---

47. For a fascinating exposition of this point, see James B. Stewart, *DisneyWar* (2004).

IN RE THE WALT DISNEY COMPANY
DERIVATIVE LITIGATION

825 A.2d 275 (Del. Ch. 2003)

CHANDLER, Chancellor.

In this derivative action . . . plaintiffs allege that the defendant directors breached their fiduciary duties when they blindly approved an employment agreement with defendant Michael Ovitz and then, again without any review or deliberation, ignored defendant Michael Eisner's dealings with Ovitz regarding his non-fault termination. Plaintiffs seek rescission and/or money damages from defendants and Ovitz, or compensation for damages allegedly sustained by Disney and disgorgement of Ovitz's unjust enrichment.

The matter is now before the Court [on a motion to dismiss the complaint].

According to the new complaint, Eisner unilaterally made the decision to hire Ovitz, even in the face of internal documents warning of potential adverse publicity and with three members of the board of directors initially objecting to the hiring when Eisner first broached the idea in August 1995. No draft employment agreements were presented to the compensation committee or to the Disney board for review before the September 26, 1995 meetings. The compensation committee met for less than an hour on September 26, 1995, and spent most of its time on two other topics, including the compensation of director Russell for helping secure Ovitz's employment. With respect to the employment agreement itself, the committee received only a summary of its terms and conditions. No questions were asked about the employment agreement. No time was taken to review the documents for approval. Instead, the committee approved the hiring of Ovitz and directed Eisner, Ovitz's close friend, to carry out the negotiations with regard to certain still unresolved and significant details. The allegation that Eisner and Ovitz had been close friends for over twenty-five years is not mentioned to show self-interest or domination. Instead, the allegation is mentioned because it casts doubt on the good faith and judgment behind the Old and New Boards' decisions to allow two close personal friends to control the payment of shareholders' money to Ovitz.*

---

* Throughout the Disney opinions, "Old Board" refers to the Disney board at the time that Ovitz was hired, in October 1995. The "New Board" refers to the Disney board at the time that Ovitz was fired, in December 1996. The "Old Board" consisted of Eisner, Stephen F. Bollenbach, Reveta F. Bowers, Roy E. Disney, Stanley P. Gold, Sanford M. Litvack, Ignacio E. Lozano, Jr., George J. Mitchell, Richard A. Nunis, Sidney Poitier, Irwin E. Russell, Robert A. M. Stern, E. Cardon Walker, Raymond L. Watson, and Gary L. Wilson. The New Board consisted of these same people other than Bollenbach, plus Leo J. O'Donovan and Thomas S. Murphy. Disney's compensation committee at all relevant times consisted of Russell (chair), Lozano, Poitier, and Watson. –EDS.

The Old Board met immediately after the committee did. Less than one and one-half pages of the fifteen pages of Old Board minutes were devoted to discussions of Ovitz's hiring as Disney's new president. . . . No presentations were made to the Old Board regarding the terms of the draft agreement. No questions were raised, at least so far as the minutes reflect. At the end of the meeting, the Old Board authorized Ovitz's hiring as Disney's president. No further review or approval of the employment agreement occurred. Throughout both meetings, no expert consultant was present to advise the compensation committee or the Old Board. Notably, the Old Board approved Ovitz's hiring even though the employment agreement was still a "work in progress." The Old Board simply passed off the details to Ovitz and his good friend, Eisner.

Negotiation over the remaining terms took place solely between Eisner, Ovitz, and attorneys representing Disney and Ovitz. The compensation committee met briefly in October to review the negotiations, but failed again to actually consider a draft of the agreement or to establish any guidelines to be used in the negotiations. The committee was apparently not otherwise involved in the negotiations. . . .

Eisner and Ovitz reached a final agreement on December 12, 1995. They agreed to backdate the agreement, however, to October 1, 1995 [when Ovitz had actually commenced his services as President]. The final employment agreement also differed substantially from the original draft, but evidently no further committee or board review of it ever occurred. The final version of Ovitz's employment agreement was signed (according to the new complaint) without any board input beyond the limited discussion on September 26, 1995.

From the outset, Ovitz performed poorly as Disney's president. In short order, Ovitz wanted out, and, once again, his good friend Eisner came to the rescue, agreeing to Ovitz's request for a non-fault termination. Disney's board, however, was allegedly never consulted in this process. No board committee was ever consulted, nor were any experts consulted. Eisner and Litvack alone granted Ovitz's non-fault termination, which became public on December 12, 1996. Again, Disney's board did not appear to question this action, although affirmative board action seemed to be required. On December 27, 1996, Eisner and Litvack, without explanation, accelerated the effective date of the non-fault termination, from January 31, 1997, to December 27, 1996. Again, the board apparently took no action; no questions were asked as to why this was done.

Disney had lost several key executives in the months before Ovitz was hired. Moreover, the position of president is obviously important in a publicly owned corporation. But the Old Board and the compensation committee (it is alleged) each spent less than an hour reviewing Ovitz's possible hiring. According to the new complaint, neither the Old Board nor the compensation committee reviewed the actual draft employment agreement. Nor did they evaluate the details of Ovitz's salary or his severance provisions. No expert presented the board with details of the agreement, outlined the pros and cons of either the salary or non-fault termination provisions, or analyzed comparable industry standards for such agreements. Notwithstanding this alleged information vacuum, the Old Board and the compensation committee approved Ovitz's hiring, appointed Eisner to negotiate with Ovitz directly in drafting the unresolved terms of his employment, never asked to review the final terms, and were never voluntarily provided those terms.

During the negotiation over the unresolved terms, the compensation committee was involved only once, at the very early stages in October 1995. The final agreement varied significantly from the draft agreement in the areas of both stock options and the terms of the non-fault termination. Neither the compensation committee nor the Old Board sought to review, nor did they review, the final agreement. In addition, both the Old Board and the committee failed to meet in order to evaluate the final agreement before it became binding on Disney. . . .

The new complaint, fairly read, also charges the New Board with a similar ostrich-like approach regarding Ovitz's non-fault termination. Eisner and Litvack granted Ovitz a non-fault termination on December 12, 1996, and the news became public that day. Although formal board approval appeared necessary for a non-fault termination, the new complaint alleges that no New Board member even asked for a meeting to discuss Eisner's and Litvack's decision. On December 27, 1996, when Eisner and Litvack accelerated Ovitz's non-fault termination by over a month, with a payout of more than $38 million in cash, together with the three million "A" stock options, the board again failed to do anything. Instead, it appears from the new complaint that the New Board played no role in Eisner's agreement to award Ovitz more than $38 million in cash and the three million "A" stock options, all for leaving a job that Ovitz had allegedly proven incapable of performing.

The New Board apparently never sought to negotiate with Ovitz regarding his departure. Nor, apparently, did it consider whether to seek a termination based on fault. During the fifteen-day period between announcement of Ovitz's termination and its effective date, the New Board allegedly chose to remain invisible in the process. The new complaint alleges that the New Board: (1) failed to ask why it had not been informed; (2) failed to inquire about the conditions and terms of the agreement; and (3) failed even to attempt to stop or delay the termination until more information could be collected. If the board had taken the time or effort to review these or other options, perhaps with the assistance of expert legal advisors, the business judgment rule might well protect its decision. In this case, however, the new complaint asserts that the New Board directors refused to explore any alternatives, and refused to even attempt to evaluate the implications of the non-fault termination-blindly allowing Eisner to hand over to his personal friend, Ovitz, more than $38 million in cash and the three million "A" stock options.

These facts, if true, do more than portray directors who, in a negligent or grossly negligent manner, merely failed to inform themselves or to deliberate adequately about an issue of material importance to their corporation. Instead, the facts alleged in the new complaint suggest that the defendant directors consciously and intentionally disregarded their responsibilities, adopting a "we don't care about the risks" attitude concerning a material corporate decision. Knowing or deliberate indifference by a director to his or her duty to act faithfully and with appropriate care is conduct, in my opinion, that may not have been taken honestly and in good faith to advance the best interests of the company. Put differently, all of the alleged facts, if true, imply that the defendant directors knew that they were making material decisions without adequate information and without adequate deliberation, and that they simply did not care if the decisions caused the corporation and its stockholders to suffer injury or loss. Viewed in this light, plaintiffs' new complaint sufficiently alleges a breach of the directors' obligation to act honestly and in good faith in the corporation's best interests for a Court to conclude, if the facts are true, that the defendant directors' conduct fell outside the protection of the business judgment rule.

Where a director consciously ignores his or her duties to the corporation, thereby causing economic injury to its stockholders, the director's actions are either "not in good faith" or "involve intentional misconduct." [citing Section 102(b)(7)(ii)]. Thus, plaintiffs' allegations support claims that fall outside the liability waiver provided under Disney's certificate of incorporation.

CONCLUSION

It is of course true that after-the-fact litigation is a most imperfect device to evaluate corporate business decisions, as the limits of human competence necessarily impede judicial review. But our corporation law's theoretical justification for disregarding honest errors simply does not apply to intentional misconduct or to egregious process failures that implicate the foundational directoral obligation to act honestly and in good faith to advance corporate interests. Because the facts alleged here, if true, portray directors consciously indifferent to a material issue facing the corporation, the law must be strong enough to intervene against abuse of trust. Accordingly, all three of plaintiffs' claims for relief concerning fiduciary duty breaches and waste survive defendants' motions to dismiss.

The trial consumed 37 days of testimony. On August 9, 2005, Chancellor Chandler issued a 174-page decision exhaustively reviewing the testimony and concluding that plaintiffs bore the burden of proof on their claims against all defendants, including Ovitz, and that they had failed to carry that burden.

IN RE THE WALT DISNEY COMPANY
DERIVATIVE LITIGATION

2005 WL 2056651 (Del. Ch. 2005)

The outcome of this case is determined by whether the defendants complied with their fiduciary duties in connection with the hiring and termination of Michael Ovitz. At the outset, the Court emphasizes that the best practices of corporate governance include compliance with fiduciary duties. Compliance with fiduciary duties, however, is not always enough to meet or to satisfy what is expected by the best practices of corporate governance.

The fiduciary duties owed by directors of a Delaware corporation are the duties of due care and loyalty. Of late, much discussion among the bench, bar, and academics alike, has surrounded a so-called third fiduciary duty, that of good faith. Of primary importance in this case are the fiduciary duty of due care and the duty of a director to act in good faith. Other than to the extent that the duty of loyalty is implicated by a lack of good faith, the only remaining issues to be decided herein with respect to the duty of loyalty are those relating to Ovitz's actions in connection with his own termination. These considerations will be addressed *seriatim*, although issues of good faith are (to a certain degree) inseparably and necessarily intertwined with the duties of care and loyalty, as well as a principal reason the distinctness of these duties make a difference — namely § 102(b)(7) of the Delaware General Corporation Law. . . .

Decisions from the Delaware Supreme Court and the Court of Chancery are far from clear with respect to whether there is a separate fiduciary duty of good faith. Good faith has been said to require an "honesty of purpose," and a genuine care for the fiduciary's constituents, but, at least in the corporate fiduciary context, it is probably easier to define bad faith rather than good faith. This may be so because Delaware law presumes that directors act in good faith when making business judgments. Bad faith has been defined as authorizing a transaction "for some purpose *other than* a genuine attempt to advance corporate welfare or [when the transaction] is *known to constitute* a violation of applicable positive law." In other words, an action taken with the intent to harm the corporation is a disloyal act in bad faith. A similar definition was used seven years earlier, when Chancellor Allen wrote that bad faith (or lack of good faith) is when a director acts in a manner "unrelated to a pursuit of the corporation's best interests." It makes no difference the reason why the director intentionally fails to pursue the best interests of the corporation. . . .

Upon long and careful consideration, I am of the opinion that the concept of *intentional dereliction of duty, a conscious disregard for one's responsibilities,* is an appropriate (although not the only) standard for determining whether fiduciaries have acted in good faith. Deliberate indifference and inaction *in the face of a duty to act* is, in my mind, conduct that is clearly disloyal to the corporation. It is the epitome of faithless conduct.

To act in good faith, a director must act at all times with an honesty of purpose and in the best interests and welfare of the corporation. The presumption of the business judgment rule creates a presumption that a director acted in good faith. In order to overcome that presumption, a plaintiff must prove an act of bad faith by a preponderance of the evidence. To create a definitive and categorical definition of the universe of acts that would constitute bad faith would be difficult, if not impossible. And it would misconceive how, in my judgment, the concept of good faith operates in our common law of corporations. Fundamentally, the duties traditionally analyzed as belonging to corporate fiduciaries, loyalty and care, are but constituent elements of the overarching concepts of allegiance, devotion and faithfulness that must guide the conduct of every fiduciary. The good faith required of a corporate fiduciary includes not simply the duties of care and loyalty, in the narrow sense that I have discussed them above, but all actions required by a true faithfulness and devotion to the interests of the corporation and its shareholders. A failure to act in good faith may be shown, for instance, where the fiduciary intentionally acts with a purpose other than that of advancing the best interests of the corporation, where the fiduciary acts with the intent to violate applicable positive law, or where the fiduciary intentionally fails to act in the face of a known duty to act, demonstrating a conscious disregard for his duties. There may be other examples of bad faith yet to be proven or alleged, but these three are the most salient. As evidenced by previous rulings in this case both from this Court and the Delaware Supreme Court, issues of the Disney directors' good faith (or lack thereof) are central to the outcome of this action. With this background, I now turn to applying the appropriate standards to defendants' conduct.

ANALYSIS

Stripped of the presumptions in their favor that have carried them to trial, plaintiffs must now rely on the evidence presented at trial to demonstrate by a preponderance of the evidence that the defendants violated their fiduciary duties and/or committed waste. More specifically, in the area of director action, plaintiffs must prove by a preponderance of the evidence that the presumption of the business judgment rule does not apply either because the directors breached their fiduciary duties, acted in bad faith or that the directors made an "unintelligent or unadvised judgment," by failing to inform themselves of all material information reasonably available to them before making a business decision.

If plaintiffs cannot rebut the presumption of the business judgment rule, the defendants will prevail. If plaintiffs succeed in rebutting the presumption of the business judgment rule, the burden then shifts to the defendants to prove by a preponderance of the evidence that the challenged transactions were entirely fair to the corporation.

As it relates to director inaction, plaintiffs will prevail upon proving by a preponderance of the evidence that the defendants breached their fiduciary duties by not acting. In order to invoke the protections of the provision in the Company's certificate of incorporation authorized by 8 Del. C. §102(b)(7), the defendants must prove by a preponderance of the evidence that they are entitled to the protections of that provision.

THE OLD BOARD'S DECISION TO HIRE OVITZ AND THE COMPENSATION COMMITTEE'S APPROVAL OF THE OEA [ORIGINAL EMPLOYMENT AGREEMENT] WAS NOT GROSSLY NEGLIGENT AND NOT IN BAD FAITH

The members of the "Old Board" (Eisner, Bollenbach, Litvack, Russell, Roy Disney, Gold, Nunis, Poitier, Stern, Walker, Watson, Wilson, Bowers, Lozano and Mitchell) were required to comply with their fiduciary duties on behalf of the Company's shareholders while taking the actions that brought Ovitz to the Company. For the future, many lessons of what not to do can be learned from defendants' conduct here. Nevertheless, I conclude that the only reasonable application of the law to the facts as I have found them, is that the defendants did not act in bad faith, and were at most ordinarily negligent, in connection with the hiring of Ovitz and the approval of the OEA. In accordance with the business judgment rule (because, as it turns out, business judgment was exercised), ordinary negligence is insufficient to constitute a violation of the fiduciary duty of care. I shall elaborate upon this conclusion as to each defendant.

EISNER

Eisner was clearly the person most heavily involved in bringing Ovitz to the Company and negotiating the OEA. He was a long-time friend of Ovitz and the instigator and mastermind behind the machinations that resulted in Ovitz's hiring and the concomitant approval of the OEA. In that aspect, Eisner is the most culpable of the defendants. He was pulling the strings; he knew what was going on. On the other hand, at least as the duty of care is typically defined in the context of a business judgment (such as a decision to select and hire a corporate president), of all the defendants, he was certainly the most informed of all reasonably available material information, making him the least culpable in that regard.

As a general rule, a CEO has no obligation to continuously inform the board of his actions as CEO, or to receive prior authorization for those actions. Nevertheless, a reasonably prudent CEO (that is to say, a reasonably prudent CEO with a board willing to think for itself and assert itself against the CEO when necessary) would not have acted in as unilateral a manner as did Eisner when essentially committing the corporation to hire a second-in-command, appoint that person to the board, and provide him with one of the largest and richest employment contracts ever enjoyed by a non-CEO. I write, "essentially committing," because although I conclude that legally, Ovitz's hiring was not a "done deal" as of the August 14 OLA [Original Letter Agreement], it was clear to Eisner, Ovitz, and the directors who were informed, that as a practical matter, it certainly was a "done deal."

Notwithstanding the foregoing, Eisner's actions in connection with Ovitz's hiring should not serve as a model for fellow executives and fiduciaries to follow. His lapses were many. He failed to keep the board as informed as he should have. He stretched the outer boundaries of his authority as CEO by acting without specific board direction or involvement. He prematurely issued a press release that placed significant pressure on the board to accept Ovitz and approve his compensation package in accordance with the press release. To my mind, these actions fall far short of what shareholders expect and demand from those entrusted with a fiduciary position. Eisner's failure to better involve the board in the process of Ovitz's hiring, usurping that role for himself, although not in violation of law, does not comport with how fiduciaries of Delaware corporations are expected to act.

Despite all of the legitimate criticisms that may be leveled at Eisner, especially at having enthroned himself as the omnipotent and infallible monarch of his personal Magic Kingdom, I nonetheless conclude, after carefully considering and weighing all the evidence, that Eisner's actions were taken in good faith. That is, Eisner's actions were taken with the subjective belief that those actions were in the best interests of the Company — he believed that his taking charge and acting swiftly and decisively to hire Ovitz would serve the best interests of the Company notwithstanding the high cost of Ovitz's hiring and notwithstanding that two experienced executives who had arguably been passed over for the position (Litvack and Bollenbach) were not completely supportive. . . .

[The Court then examined the actions of all of the other Disney directors individually, and reached the same conclusion with respect to each.]

EISNER AND LITVACK DID NOT ACT IN BAD FAITH IN CONNECTION WITH OVITZ'S TERMINATION, AND THE REMAINDER OF THE NEW BOARD HAD NO DUTIES IN CONNECTION THEREWITH

The New Board was likewise charged with complying with their fiduciary duties in connection with any actions taken, or required to be taken, in connection with Ovitz's termination. The key question here becomes whether the board was under a duty to act in connection with Ovitz's termination, because if the directors were under no duty to act, then they could not have acted in bad faith by not acting, nor would they have failed to inform themselves of all material information reasonably available before making a decision, because no decision was required to be made. Furthermore, the actions taken by the Company's officers (namely Eisner and Litvack) in connection with Ovitz's termination must be viewed through the lens of whether the board was under a duty to act. If the board was under no such duty, then the officers are justified in acting alone. If the board was under a duty to act and the officers improperly usurped that authority, the analysis would obviously be different.

THE NEW BOARD WAS NOT UNDER A DUTY TO ACT

[Having reviewed Disney's governing documents,] I come to the following conclusions: 1) the board of directors has the sole power to elect the officers of the Company; 2) the board of directors has the sole power to determine the "duties" of the officers of the Company (either through board resolutions or bylaws); 3) the Chairman/CEO has "general and active management, direction, and supervision over the business of the Corporation and over its officers," and that such management, direction and supervision is subject to the control of the board of directors; 4) the Chairman/CEO has the power to manage, direct and supervise the lesser officers and employees of the Company; 5) the board has the *right*, but not the *duty* to remove the officers of the Company with or without cause, and that right is non-exclusive; and 6) because that right is non-exclusive, and because the Chairman/CEO is affirmatively charged with the management, direction and supervision of the officers of the Company, together with the powers and duties incident to the office of chief executive, the Chairman/CEO, subject to the control of the board of directors, also possesses the *right* to remove the inferior officers and employees of the corporation.

The New Board unanimously believed that Eisner, as Chairman and CEO, possessed the power to terminate Ovitz without board approval or intervention. Nonetheless, the board was informed of and supported Eisner's decision. The board's simultaneous power to terminate Ovitz, reserved to the board by the certificate of incorporation, did not divest Eisner of the authority to do so, or vice-versa. Eisner used that authority, and terminated Ovitz — a decision, coupled with the decision to honor the OEA, that resulted in the Company's obligation to pay the NFT. Because Eisner unilaterally terminated Ovitz, as was his right, the New Board was not required to act in connection with Ovitz's termination.

Therefore, the fact that no formal board action was taken with respect to Ovitz's termination is of no import. . . . For these reasons, the members of the New Board (other than Eisner and Litvack, who will be discussed individually below) did not breach their fiduciary duties and did not act in bad faith in connection with Ovitz's termination and his receipt of the NFT benefits included in the OEA.

EISNER

Having concluded that Eisner alone possessed the authority to terminate Ovitz and grant him the NFT, I turn to whether Eisner acted in accordance with his fiduciary duties and in good faith when he terminated Ovitz. As will be shown hereafter, I conclude that Eisner did not breach his fiduciary duties and did act in good faith in connection with Ovitz's termination and concomitant receipt of the NFT.

When Eisner hired Ovitz in 1995, he did so with an eye to preparing the Company for the challenges that lay ahead, especially in light of the CapCities/ABC acquisition and the need for a legitimate potential successor to Eisner. To everyone's regret, including Ovitz, things did not work out as blissfully as anticipated. Eisner was unable to work well with Ovitz, and Eisner refused to let Ovitz work without close and constant supervision. Faced with that situation, Eisner essentially had three options: 1) keep Ovitz as President and continue trying to make things work; 2) keep Ovitz at Disney, but in a role other than President; or 3) terminate Ovitz.

In deciding which route to take, Eisner, consistent with his discretion as CEO, considered keeping Ovitz as the Company's President an unacceptable solution. Shunting Ovitz to a different role within the Company would have almost certainly entitled Ovitz to the NFT, or at the very least, a costly lawsuit to determine whether Ovitz was so entitled. Eisner would have also rightly questioned whether there was another position within the Company where Ovitz could be of use. Eisner was then left with the only alternative he considered feasible — termination. Faced with the knowledge that termination was the best alternative and knowing that Ovitz had not performed to the high expectations placed upon him when he was hired, Eisner inquired of Litvack on several occasions as to whether a for-cause termination was possible such that the NFT payment could be avoided, and then relied in good faith on the opinion of the Company's general counsel. . . . In the end, however, he bit the bullet and decided that the best decision would be to terminate Ovitz and pay the NFT.

After reflection on the more than ample record in this case, I conclude that Eisner's actions in connection with the termination are, for the most part, consistent with what is expected of a faithful fiduciary. . . .

CONCLUSION

For the reasons set forth in the Court's Opinion of this date, judgment is hereby entered in the above captioned action against plaintiffs and in favor of defendants on all counts. The parties shall bear their own costs. IT IS SO ORDERED.

NOTE ON DISNEY AND THE DIRECTOR'S DUTY OF GOOD FAITH

Plaintiffs appealed once again to the Delaware Supreme Court. In June 2006, the Supreme Court affirmed. Perhaps the most important part of the Court's opinion is not the holding, which was doctrinally unremarkable and widely expected among practitioners and commentators, but rather the guidance that the Court provides in dicta on the "duty of good faith." Writing for the Court, Justice Jack Jacobs provided a spectrum of behavior for identifying "bad faith" conduct. On one end of the spectrum, fiduciary conduct that is "motivated by an actual intent to do harm" constitutes "classic, quintessential bad faith."[48] On the other end of the spectrum, grossly negligent conduct, without any malevolent intent, cannot

48. Slip op. at 65.

constitute bad faith.[49] In between lies conduct that involves "intentional dereliction of duty, a conscious disregard for one's responsibilities." The Court concluded that "such misconduct is properly treated as a non-exculpable, non-indemnifiable violation of the fiduciary duty to act in good faith."[50] While the Court clarified a good deal of ground, in a footnote it left open one of the big questions: "[W]e do not reach or otherwise address the issue of whether the fiduciary duty to act in good faith is a duty that, like the duties of care and loyalty, can serve as an independent basis for imposing liability upon corporate officers and directors."[51]

How, then, are we to understand the conceptual structure of directors' duties today? That is, how do these three terms — care, loyalty, and good faith — relate to each other and, operationally, what if anything does recognition of the obligation of good faith add to the conventional conception of appropriate director conduct? In some ways, the most basic duty of every fiduciary may be said to be the duty to exercise good faith in an effort to understand and to satisfy the obligations of the office. The obligations of the office will vary depending on the purposes for which the institution was created. A trustee of an express trust may have a high responsibility to attempt to preserve capital, for example, while a director of a business corporation must exercise due care both to preserve assets and monitor the acceptance of risk in the informed hope of capital appreciation. But while the specifics required of the fiduciary may vary depending on the institution and the circumstances, the generalities of the duties can be stated. All fiduciary offices require that the fiduciary to avoid unfair self-dealing and to exercise power for the purpose of the institution and not for the fiduciary's personal benefit. And all require reasonable attention to the role. Thus, the predicate duty of good faith may be seen as simply a higher level of abstraction of the fiduciary obligations of care and loyalty. So, for example, the Director Mrs. Pritchard may be said to have violated her duty of care and attention by not attending meetings of the corporation's board and not otherwise taking any steps to monitor her sons' fraudulent activities. But she could just as easily have been said to violate her duty of good faith since she did not even try to do her job. Indeed, while the Disney directors were not as "out of it" as Mrs. Pritchard seems to have been, of the cases often read in introductory law school courses on director liabilities, her case may be closest to theirs. But if Mrs. Pritchard violated her duty of care, we do not need to recur to any obligation of "good faith" to impress liability upon her. Why then do we need this concept for the Disney directors?

The answer comes from some unfortunately broad statutory drafting in §102(b)(7) of the Delaware statute, which is quoted by the court in *Disney*. So here we see the problem: §102(b)(7) was enacted in 1985 following the surprising result in *Smith v. Van Gorkom*. It provides that a corporate charter may waive director liability to the corporation for damages except for, among other things, damages in connection with a breach of loyalty (here the lawyers drafting the statute were apparently thinking of loyalty in a

---

49. Id. at 70.
50. Id.
51. Id. at 73 n.112.

narrow financial conflict sense) and for acts or omissions "not in good faith." Under most conceptions of loyalty, acts not in good faith would constitute a breach of loyalty, so at best this exception seems to create a redundancy. But as *Disney* shows it does more than that.

After the *Disney* case (and before it for thoughtful corporate lawyers), one cannot offer to directors the broad assurance that §102(b)(7) presumably intended. *Disney* establishes that there can be a level of director neglect or inattention that might lead a court to find that the directors were not seriously trying to meet their duty, in which event the protection of the charter amendment authorized by §102(b)(7) may not offer protection. One cannot say very much at present concerning what constitutes that level of inattention. Certainly as a general matter allowing the CEO to negotiate the terms of the employment (and termination) of his second in command subject to rather general board oversight and review does not itself or in general seem like an abandonment of board responsibilities. The spectacular amounts involved in the Ovitz matter of course provide strong coloration in that instance.

But the more basic question is: why should shareholders be able to waive damages for director "gross negligence" in the charter, but not even grosser negligence? In fact, one might take the view that what should be excepted from the waiver authorized by §102(b)(7) are only (i) breaches of loyalty, including any act authorized for an inappropriate purpose or for which a director received an improper personal benefit (ii) knowingly illegal acts or (iii) for distributions that violate §174. In other words, §102 (b)(7) should be amended to give it the effect that it was thought to have created. Liability for bad judgments, where no financial conflict is involved or for losses caused by a failure to prevent conduct that causes a loss — should be waivable *ex ante* by the shareholders. What arguments can you imagine in support of and in opposition to such a proposed amendment to Section 102(b)(7)?

We close with an attempt to synthesize the big picture. Post-*Disney*, Delaware law apparently reflected the following formal structure of director liability for inattention. First, mere director negligence — lacking that degree of attention that a reasonable person in the same or similar situation would be expected to pay to a decision — does not give rise to liability. In this circumstance the business judgment rule forecloses liability and generally permits dismissal at the motion to dismiss phase of the litigation. See *Gagliardi* and *American Express, supra*. Second, facts that establish gross negligence may (as in *Smith v. Van Gorkom*) be the basis for a breach of duty finding and result in liability for any losses that result. However, under §102(b)(7) such liability for gross negligence alone can be waived (and in most public companies has been waived) through a shareholder approved amendment to the corporate charter. Third, such waivers however *may not* waive liability that rests in part upon breach of the duty of loyalty and, under the statutory language, that inability to waive damages is extended to acts (or omissions) not done in "good faith." Therefore, there is a conceptually a third level of inattention — we could call it abandonment of office as some old cases did — in which a director's inattention is so profound that the court concluded that the directors lacked "good faith." In the event of this extreme level of inattention, neither the business judgment rule nor the waiver authorized by 102(b)(7) will protect the defendant from liability.

This structure may be criticized as being overly developed and perhaps incoherent. What is the line between gross negligence, liability for which the legislature permits shareholder waiver, and inattention so profound as to constitute lack of good faith that may not be waived? More importantly, what is the social advantage in attempting to draw such a line?

9.5 CORPORATE OPPORTUNITY DOCTRINE

A distinctive branch of the duty of loyalty involves the question of when a fiduciary may pursue a business opportunity on her own account if this opportunity might arguably "belong" to the corporation. The corporate opportunity cases tend to focus on the rules of recognition; i.e., when is an opportunity "corporate" rather than personal and hence off-limits to the corporation's managers? This is in contrast to the typical self-dealing case, where the usual issue is whether a self-dealing transaction violates the duty of loyalty rather than whether a given transaction is "interested" in the first instance.

Because the corporate opportunity doctrine is a special application of the duty of loyalty, it is better described with standards than with tightly drawn rules (although many courts still try to formulate business opportunity problems in rule-like language). The chief questions that arise in the corporate opportunity context concern whether an opportunity is corporate, the circumstances under which a fiduciary may take a corporate opportunity, and the remedies that are available when a fiduciary has taken a corporate opportunity illegitimately.

9.5.1 Determining Which Opportunities "Belong" to the Corporation

There are three general lines of corporate opportunity doctrine. The first includes those cases that tend to give the narrowest protection to the corporation by applying an "expectancy or interest" test. As applied by the leading case of *Lagarde v. Anniston Lime & Stone Inc.*, 28 So. 199 (Ala. 1900), the expectancy or interest must grow out of an existing legal interest, and the appropriation of the opportunity will in some degree "balk the corporation in effecting the purpose of its creation." *Id.* at 201. This language dates from an era in which corporations frequently had a single business purpose. Today, corporations are generally formed for all legal business activities. Thus, more recent cases applying the expectancy or interest test look to the firm's practical business expectancy or interest. Yet this test is still relatively narrow.

The second test, known as the "line of business" test, classifies any opportunity falling within a company's line of business as its corporate opportunity. In other words, anything that a corporation could be reasonably expected to do is a corporate opportunity. Factors affecting this determination include (1) how this matter came to the attention of the director, officer, or employee; (2) how far removed from the "core economic activities" of the corporation the opportunity lies; and (3) whether corporate information is used in recognizing or exploiting the opportunity. *Guft v. Loft, Inc.*, 5 A.2d 503, 511 (Del. 1939), is perhaps the most cited case applying the line of business test.

Finally, some courts employ a more diffuse test that relies on multiple factors—a "fairness" test—to identify corporate opportunities. A court employing the fairness test will look into factors such as how a manager learned of the disputed opportunity, whether he or she used corporate assets in exploiting the opportunity, and other fact-specific indicia of good faith and loyalty to the corporation, in addition to a company's line of business.[52]

9.5.2 When May a Fiduciary Take a Corporate Opportunity?

Some courts have held that a fiduciary may take an opportunity if the corporation is not in a financial position to do so.[53] Incapacity is related to disinterest and implies that a corporation's board has determined not to accept the opportunity. In either event, it is reasoned, a fiduciary should be free to take the opportunity. What is critical in these cases, as in other instances of fiduciary analysis, is whether the board has evaluated the question of whether to accept the opportunity in good faith. Financial inability may seem an odd reason for a public corporation to reject an opportunity, at least if the opportunity promises a return that implies a positive net present value and exceeds the corporation's implicit costs of capital. Similarly, a board's decision to permit one of its directors to take a profitable opportunity might be regarded as inherently suspicious. Nevertheless, most courts accept a board's good-faith decision not to pursue an opportunity as a complete defense to a suit challenging a fiduciary's acceptance of a corporate opportunity on her own account.[54] Of course, this defense is effective only if a court is persuaded that the decision to reject a valuable opportunity on financial grounds is the genuine business judgment of a disinterested decision maker. The fiduciary who takes the opportunity bears the burden of establishing this defense.[55]

What if the director never presented a business opportunity to the board, in the good faith belief that it was not a corporate opportunity?

---

52. For a critical review of the competing common law doctrines, see Victor Brudney & Robert C. Clark, *A New Look at Corporate Opportunities*, 94 Harv. L. Rev. 997 (1981).

53. See *Miller v. Miller*, 202 N.W.2d 71 (Minn. 1974) (recognizing company's "financial incapacity" to exploit opportunity as a defense).

54. In the past, many courts refused to accept the financial incapacity defense. Thus, in *Irving Trust Co. v. Deutsch*, 75 F.2d 121 (2d Cir. 1934), the court framed a rigid rule forbidding directors of solvent corporations to take over for their own profit a corporate contract on the plea of the corporation's financial inability to perform.

55. See *Klinicki v. Lundgren*, 695 P.2d 906 (Or. 1985).

While presenting the opportunity to the board seems clearly the safer practice for the fiduciary and the better corporate governance practice, it is not required under Delaware law. In *Broz v. Cellular Information Systems, Inc.*, 673 A.2d 148, 157 (Del. 1996), the Delaware Supreme Court stated: "It is not the law of Delaware that presentation to the board is a necessary prerequisite to a finding that a corporate opportunity has not been usurped." Instead, the Court stated that presenting an opportunity to the board "simply provides a kind of 'safe harbor' for the director, which removes the specter of a *post hoc* judicial determination that the director or officer has improperly usurped a corporate opportunity." See *id.*

IN RE EBAY, INC. SHAREHOLDERS LITIGATION

2004 Del. Ch. LEXIS 4 (2004)

CHANDLER, Chancellor

The facts, as alleged in the complaint, are straightforward. In 1995, defendants Pierre M. Omidyar and Jeffrey Skoll founded nominal defendant eBay, a Delaware corporation, as a sole proprietorship. eBay is a pioneer in online trading platforms, providing a virtual auction community for buyers and sellers to list items for sale and to bid on items of interest. In 1998, eBay retained Goldman Sachs and other investment banks to underwrite an initial public offering of common stock. Goldman Sachs was the lead underwriter. The stock was priced at $18 per share. Goldman Sachs purchased about 1.2 million shares. Shares of eBay stock became immensely valuable during 1998 and 1999, rising to $175 per share in early April 1999. Around that time, eBay made a secondary offering, issuing 6.5 million shares of common stock at $170 per share for a total of $1.1 billion. Goldman Sachs again served as lead underwriter. Goldman Sachs was asked in 2001 to serve as eBay's financial advisor in connection with an acquisition by eBay of PayPal, Inc. For these services, eBay has paid Goldman Sachs over $8 million.

During this same time period, Goldman Sachs "rewarded" the individual defendants by allocating to them thousands of IPO shares, managed by Goldman Sachs, at the initial offering price. Because the IPO market during this particular period of time was extremely active, prices of initial stock offerings often doubled or tripled in a single day. Investors who were well-connected, either to Goldman Sachs or to similarly situated investment banks serving as IPO underwriters, were able to flip these investments into instant profit by selling the equities in a few days or even in a few hours after they were initially purchased.

The essential allegation of the complaint is that Goldman Sachs provided these IPO share allocations to the individual defendants to show appreciation for eBay's business and to enhance Goldman Sachs' chances of obtaining future eBay business. In addition to co-founding eBay, defendant Omidyar has been eBay's CEO, CFO and President. He is eBay's largest stockholder, owning more than 23% of the company's equity. Goldman Sachs allocated Omidyar shares in at least forty IPOs at the initial offering price. Omidyar resold these securities in the public market for millions of dollars in profit. Defendant Whitman owns 3.3% of eBay stock and has been President, CEO and a director since early 1998. Whitman also has been a director of Goldman Sachs since 2001. Goldman Sachs allocated Whitman shares in over a 100 IPOs at the initial offering price. Whitman sold these equities in the open market and reaped millions of dollars in profit. Defendant Skoll, in addition to co-founding eBay, has served in various positions at the company, including Vice-President of Strategic Planning and Analysis and President. He served as an eBay director from December 1996 to March 1998. Skoll is eBay's second largest stockholder, owning about 13% of the company. Goldman Sachs has allocated Skoll shares in at least 75 IPOs at the initial offering price, which Skoll promptly resold on the open market, allowing him to realize millions of dollars in profit. Finally, defendant Robert C. Kagle has served as an eBay director since June 1997. Goldman Sachs allocated Kagle shares in at least 25 IPOs at the initial offering price. Kagle promptly resold these equities, and recorded millions of dollars in profit.

. . . Plaintiffs have stated a claim that defendants usurped a corporate opportunity of eBay. Defendants insist that Goldman Sachs' IPO allocations to eBay's insider directors were "collateral investments opportunities" that arose by virtue of the inside directors status as wealthy individuals. They argue that this is not a corporate opportunity within the corporation's line of business or an opportunity in which the corporation had an interest or expectancy. These arguments are unavailing.

First, no one disputes that eBay financially was able to exploit the opportunities in question. Second, eBay was in the business of investing in securities. The complaint alleges that eBay "consistently invested a portion of its cash on hand in marketable securities." According to eBay's 1999 10-K, for example, eBay had more than $550 million invested in equity and debt securities. eBay invested more than $181 million in "short-term investments" and $373 million in "long-term investments." Thus, investing was "a line of business" of eBay. Third, the facts alleged in the complaint suggest that investing was integral to eBay's cash management strategies and a significant part of its business. Finally, it is no answer to say, as do defendants, that IPOs are risky investments. It is undisputed that eBay was never given an opportunity to turn down the IPO allocations as too risky.

Defendants also argue that to view the IPO allocations in question as corporate opportunities will mean that every advantageous investment opportunity that comes to an officer or director will be considered a corporate opportunity. On the contrary, the allegations in the complaint in this case indicate that unique, below-market price investment opportunities were offered by Goldman Sachs to the insider defendants as financial inducements to maintain and secure corporate business. This was not an instance where a broker offered advice to a director about an investment in a marketable security. The conduct challenged here involved a large investment bank that regularly did business with a company steering highly lucrative IPO allocations to select insider directors and officers at that company, allegedly both to reward them for past business and to induce them to direct future business to that investment bank. This is a far cry from the defendants' characterization of the conduct in question as merely "a broker's investment recommendations" to a wealthy client.

Nor can one seriously argue that this conduct did not place the insider defendants in a position of conflict with their duties to the corporation. One can realistically characterize these IPO allocations as a form of commercial discount or rebate for past or future investment banking services. Viewed pragmatically, it is easy to understand how steering such commercial rebates to certain insider directors places those directors in an obvious conflict between their self-interest and the corporation's interest. It is noteworthy, too, that the Securities and Exchange Commission has taken the position that "spinning" practices violate the obligations of broker-dealers under the "Free-riding and Withholding Interpretation" rules. As the SEC has explained, "the purpose of the interpretation is to protect the integrity of the public offering system by ensuring that members make a bona fide public distribution of 'hot issue' securities and do not withhold such securities for their own benefit or use the securities to reward other persons who are in a position to direct future business to the member."

Finally, even if one assumes that IPO allocations like those in question here do not constitute a corporate opportunity, a cognizable claim is nevertheless stated on the common law ground that an agent is under a duty to account for profits obtained personally in connection with transactions related to his or her company. The complaint gives rise to a reasonable inference that the insider directors accepted a commission or gratuity that rightfully belonged to eBay but that was improperly diverted to them. Even if this conduct does not run afoul of the corporate opportunity doctrine, it may still constitute a breach of the fiduciary duty of loyalty. Thus, even if one does not consider Goldman Sachs' IPO allocations to these corporate insiders-allocations that generated millions of dollars in profit-to be a corporate opportunity, the defendant directors were nevertheless not free to accept this consideration from a company, Goldman Sachs, that was doing significant business with eBay and that arguably intended the consideration as an inducement to maintaining the business relationship in the future. [Citing RESTATEMENT (SECOND) OF AGENCY § 388 (1957)].

CONCLUSION

For all of the above reasons, I deny the defendants' motions to dismiss the complaint in this consolidated action.

NOTE ON CORPORATE OPPORTUNITY DOCTRINE

In 2000, the Delaware legislature added §122(17) to the Delaware corporate code, which explicitly authorizes waiver in the charter of the corporate opportunity constraints for officers, directors, or share-holders. The amendment was motivated, at least in part, by the growing culture of "interlocking" boards at Silicon Valley companies, in which entrepreneurs from closely related businesses would sit on each others' boards. Waiver of corporate opportunity doctrine, it was argued, was needed in order to induce these entrepreneurs to serve as directors.

As an example from another West Coast industry, consider Dream-Works Animation SKG, a collaboration among entertainment moguls Steven Spielberg, Jeffery Katzenberg, and David Geffen. Since its inception in 1994, DreamWorks has produced blockbuster movies such as *American Beauty*, *Gladiator*, *Chicken Run*, and *Shrek*. When DreamWorks went public in October 2004, its charter contained the following provision:

> None of the Founding Stockholders [Spielberg, Katzenberg, and Geffen] or any director, officer, member, partner, stockholder or employee of any Founding Stockholder (each a "Specified Party"), independently or with others, shall have any duty to refrain from engaging directly or indirectly in the same or similar business activities or lines of business as the Corporation and that might be in direct or indirect competition with the Corporation. In the event that any Founding Stockholder or Specified Party acquires knowledge of a potential transaction or matter that may be a corporate opportunity for any Founding Stockholder or Specified Party, as applicable, and the Corporation, none of the Founding Stockholders or Specified Parties shall have any duty to communicate or offer such corporate opportunity to the Corporation, and any Founding Stockholder and Specified Party shall be entitled to pursue or acquire such corporate opportunity for itself or to direct such corporate opportunity to another person or entity and the Corporation shall have no right in or to such corporate opportunity or to any income or proceeds derived therefrom.

Why would DreamWorks put such a clause in its charter? What questions and concerns would arise for potential investors, reading this clause?

9.6   THE DUTY OF LOYALTY IN CLOSE CORPORATIONS

Virtually all of the legal characteristics of the corporate form, including limited liability, may fail to capture significant features of the "bargain" among the small numbers of equity participants in closely held corporations. European jurisdictions have long recognized the close or private corporation as a distinct form. France has the *società responsibility limité* (S.A.R.L.), Germany has the *Gesellschaft mit beschränkte Haftung* (G.m.b. H.), and England provides customized statutory treatment for private companies.

In the United States, explicit statutory and judicial recognition of the unique features of the private corporation (with overlapping management and ownership) did not emerge until the late 1960s. Today, however, American corporate statutes allow legal planners enormous latitude in customizing the form of the close corporation. Most often, this new flexibility is characterized by a "unified" corporations statute, which explicitly permits planners to contract around statutory provisions through either general opt-out clauses ("unless otherwise provided in the charter") or opt-out provisions restricted to close corporations. See, e.g., RMBCA §8.01(b); F. Hodge O'Neal & Robert Thompson, O'Neal's Close Corp. §1.14 (3d ed. 1971). Other states, by contrast, provide specialized close corporation statutes, which companies meeting the statutory criteria of a close corporation can elect to be governed by, in lieu of general corporation law. Here DGCL §§341-356 are an excellent illustration. (DGCL §342 defines eligible close corporations as those that have, inter alia, 30 or fewer shareholders.)

Notwithstanding the great freedom that business planners now have to customize the form of a close corporation, problems arise, since every contingency cannot be anticipated when the corporation is established. As in the case of dissolving partnerships, shareholder disputes in close corporations often raise questions about the proper role of courts in superintending ongoing businesses. The difference, of course, is that equity participants in close corporations have selected the corporate form — with its associated characteristics of permanence, centralized management, etc. — to frame their long-term deal.

DONAHUE V. RODD ELECTROTYPE CO.

328 N.E.2d 505 (Mass. 1975)

TAURO, C.J.:

The plaintiff, Euphemia Donahue, a minority stockholder in the Rodd Electrotype Company of New England, Inc. ("Rodd Electrotype"), a Massachusetts corporation, brings this suit against the directors of Rodd Electrotype, Charles H. Rodd, Frederick I. Rodd and Mr. Harold E. Magnuson, against Harry C. Rodd, a former director, officer and controlling stockholder of Rodd Electrotype and against Rodd Electrotype (hereinafter called "defendants"). The plaintiff seeks to rescind Rodd Electrotype's purchase of Harry Rodd's shares in Rodd Electrotype and to compel Harry Rodd "to repay to the corporation the purchase price of said shares, $36,000, together with interest from the date of purchase." The plaintiff alleges that the defendants caused the corporation to purchase the shares in violation of their fiduciary duty to her, a minority stockholder of Rodd Electrotype.[4]

---

4. In form, the plaintiff's bill of complaint presents, at least in part, a derivative action, brought on behalf of the corporation, and, in the words of the bill, "on behalf of . . . [the] stockholders" of Rodd Electrotype. Yet the plaintiff's bill, in substance, was one seeking redress because of alleged breaches of the fiduciary duty owed to *her*, a minority stockholder, by the controlling stockholders.

We treat that bill of complaint (as have the parties) as presenting a proper cause of suit in the personal right of the plaintiff.

The trial judge, after hearing oral testimony, . . . found that the purchase was without prejudice to the plaintiff and implicitly found that the transaction had been carried out in good faith and with inherent fairness. . . .

[Briefly, the facts were as follows: In the mid-1930s Harry Rodd and Joseph Donahue were employees of Royal Electrotype, (Rodd Electrotype's predecessor). Donahue had never participated in the management of the business, but Rodd advanced rapidly within the company, and in 1946, he became general manager and treasurer. Subsequently, Rodd acquired 200 of the corporation's 1,000 shares, and Donahue (at Rodd's suggestion) acquired 50 shares. In 1955, Rodd became president of the company, and the company itself repurchased 750 of its shares, so that Rodd and Donahue became Royal's sole shareholders, owning 80 percent and 20 percent of its stock, respectively. In 1960, the corporation was renamed Rodd Electrotype, and Harry Rodd's two sons, Charles and Frederick, soon became managers. In 1965, Charles succeeded his father as president and general manager.

In 1970, Harry Rodd was 77 years old and not in good health, and he was contemplating retirement. He had already distributed 117 of his 200 shares equally among his two sons and his daughter, and he had returned 2 shares to the corporate treasury. Before retiring, he wished to dispose of the remaining 81 shares. Accordingly, Charles, acting for the company, offered to repurchase 45 of Harry's shares for $800/share — a price that, Charles testified, reflected book and liquidating value. The company's board — then consisting of Charles, Frederick, and a lawyer — authorized the repurchase in July 1970. Subsequently, Harry Rodd sold 2 shares to each of his three children at $800/share and gave each child 10 shares as a gift. Meanwhile, Donahue had died, and his 50 shares had passed to his wife and son. When the Donahues learned of the repurchase of Harry Rodd's shares, they offered to sell their shares to the company on the same terms, but their offer was rejected.[10]

In her argument before this court, the plaintiff has characterized the corporate purchase of Harry Rodd's shares as an unlawful distribution of corporate assets to controlling shareholders. She urges that the distribution constitutes a breach of the fiduciary duty owed by the Rodds, as controlling shareholders, to her, a minority stockholder in the enterprise, because the Rodds failed to accord her an equal opportunity to sell her shares to the corporation. . . . For the reasons hereinafter noted, we agree with the plaintiff and reverse the decree of the Superior Court. However, we limit the applicability of our holding to "close corporations," as hereinafter defined. Whether the holding should apply to other corporations is left for decision in another case, on a proper record.

A. Close Corporations.   In previous opinions, we have alluded to the distinctive nature of the close corporation but have never defined

---

10. Between 1965 and 1969, the company offered to purchase the Donahue shares for amounts between $2,000 and $10,000 ($40 to $200 a share). The Donahues rejected these offers.

precisely what is meant by a close corporation. There is no single, generally accepted definition. Some commentators emphasize an "integration of ownership and management" . . . in which the stockholders occupy most management positions. Others focus on the number of stockholders and the nature of the market for the stock. In this view, close corporations have few stockholders; there is little market for corporate stock. . . . We accept aspects of both definitions. We deem a close corporation to be typified by: (1) a small number of stockholders; (2) no ready market for the corporate stock; and (3) substantial majority stockholder participation in the management, direction and operations of the corporation.

As thus defined, the close corporation bears striking resemblance to a partnership. Just as in a partnership, the relationship among the stockholders must be one of trust, confidence and absolute loyalty if the enterprise is to succeed. . . .

Although the corporate form provides advantages for the stockholders (limited liability, perpetuity, and so forth), it also supplies an opportunity for the majority stockholders to oppress or disadvantage minority stockholders. The minority is vulnerable to a variety of oppressive devices, termed "freezeouts," which the majority may employ. An authoritative study of such "freezeouts" enumerates some of the possibilities: "The squeezers . . . may refuse to declare dividends; they may drain off the corporation's earnings in the form of exorbitant salaries and bonuses to majority shareholder-officers and perhaps to their relatives, or in the form of high rent by the corporation for property leased from majority shareholders; they may deprive minority shareholders of corporation offices and of employment by the company. . . ."

The minority can, of course, initiate suit against the majority and their directors. Self-serving conduct by directors is proscribed by the director's fiduciary obligation to the corporation. However, in practice, the plaintiff will find difficulty in challenging dividend or employment policies. Such policies are considered to be within the judgment of the directors. . . . [G]enerally, plaintiffs who seek judicial assistance against corporate dividend or employment policies do not prevail. . . .

Thus, when these types of "freezeouts" are attempted by the majority stockholders, the minority shareholders, cut off from all corporation-related revenues, must either suffer their losses or seek a buyer for their shares. Many minority stockholders will be unwilling or unable to wait for an alteration in majority policy. Typically, the minority stockholder in a close corporation has a substantial percentage of his personal assets invested in the corporation. The stockholder may have anticipated that his salary from his position with the corporation would be his livelihood. Thus, he cannot afford to wait passively. He must liquidate his investment in the close corporation in order to reinvest the funds in income-producing enterprises.

At this point, the true plight of the minority stockholder in a close corporation becomes manifest. He cannot easily reclaim his capital. In a large public corporation, the oppressed or dissident minority stockholder could sell his stock in order to extricate some of his invested capital. By definition, this market is not available for shares in the close corporation.

In a partnership, a partner who feels abused by his fellow partners may cause dissolution by his "express will . . . at any time" and recover his share of partnership assets and accumulated profits. By contrast, the stockholder in the close corporation or "incorporated partnership" may achieve dissolution and recovery of his share of the enterprise assets only by compliance with the rigorous terms of the applicable chapter of the General Laws.

Thus, in a close corporation, the minority stockholders may be trapped in a disadvantageous situation. No outsider would knowingly assume the position of the disadvantaged minority. The outsider would have the same difficulties. To cut losses, the minority stockholder may be compelled to deal with the majority. This is the capstone of the majority plan. Majority "freezeout" schemes which withhold dividends are designed to compel the minority to relinquish stock at inadequate prices. When the minority stockholder agrees to sell out at less than fair value, the majority has won.

Because of the fundamental resemblance of the close corporation to the partnership, the trust and confidence which are essential to this scale and manner of enterprise, and the inherent danger to minority interests in the close corporation, we hold that stockholders[17] in the close corporation owe one another substantially the same fiduciary duty in the operation of the enterprise[18] that partners owe to one another. In our previous decisions, we have defined the standard of duty owed by partners to one another as the "utmost good faith and loyalty." *Cardullo v. Landau,* 329 Mass. 5, 8, 105 N.E.2d 843 (1952). . . . Stockholders in close corporations must discharge their management and stockholder responsibilities in conformity with this strict good faith standard. They may not act out of avarice, expediency or self-interest in derogation of their duty of loyalty to the other stockholders and to the corporation.

We contrast this strict good faith standard with the somewhat less stringent standard of fiduciary duty to which directors and stockholders of all corporations must adhere in the discharge of their corporate responsibilities. . . .

The more rigorous duty of partners and participants in a joint adventure, here extended to stockholders in a close corporation, was described by then Chief Judge Cardozo of the New York Court of Appeals in *Meinhard v. Salmon.* . . . "Joint adventurers, like copartners, owe to one another, while the enterprise continues, the duty of the finest loyalty. Many forms of conduct permissible in a workaday world for those acting at arm's length, are forbidden to those bound by fiduciary ties. . . . Not honesty alone, but the punctilio of an honor the most sensitive, is then the standard of behavior." . . . 164 N.E. at 546.

17. We do not limit our holding to majority stockholders. In the close corporation, the minority may do equal damage through unscrupulous and improper "sharp dealings" with an unsuspecting majority. . . .

18. We stress that the strict fiduciary duty which we apply to stockholders in a close corporation in this opinion governs *only* their actions relative to the operations of the enterprise and the effects of that operation on the rights and investments of other stockholders. We express no opinion as to the standard of duty applicable to transactions in the shares of the close corporation when the corporation is not a party to the transaction. . . .

B. Equal Opportunity in a Close Corporation.   Under settled Massachusetts law, a domestic corporation, unless forbidden by statute, has the power to purchase its own shares. An agreement to reacquire stock "[is] enforceable, subject, at least, to the limitations that the purchase must be made in good faith and without prejudice to creditors and stockholders." When the corporation reacquiring its own stock is a close corporation, the purchase is subject to the additional requirement, in the light of our holding in this opinion, that the stockholders, who, as directors or controlling stockholders, caused the corporation to enter into the stock purchase agreement, must have acted with the utmost good faith and loyalty to the other stockholders.

To meet this test, if the stockholder whose shares were purchased was a member of the controlling group, the controlling stockholders must cause the corporation to offer each stockholder an equal opportunity to sell a ratable number of his shares to the corporation at an identical price. Purchase by the corporation confers substantial benefits on the members of the controlling group whose shares were purchased. These benefits are not available to the minority stockholders if the corporation does not also offer them an opportunity to sell their shares. The controlling group may not, consistent with its strict duty to the minority, utilize its control of the corporation to obtain special advantages and disproportionate benefit from its share ownership. . . .

The purchase also distributes corporate assets to the stockholder whose shares were purchased. Unless an equal opportunity is given to all stockholders, the purchase of shares from a member of the controlling group operates as a *preferential* distribution of assets. In exchange for his shares, he receives a percentage of the contributed capital and accumulated profits of the enterprise. The funds he so receives are available for his personal use. The other stockholders benefit from no such access to corporate property and cannot withdraw their shares of the corporate profits and capital in this manner unless the controlling group acquiesces. Although the purchase price for the controlling stockholder's shares may seem fair to the corporation and other stockholders under the tests established in the prior case law . . . , the controlling stockholder whose stock has been purchased has still received a relative advantage over his fellow stockholders, inconsistent with his strict fiduciary duty — an opportunity to turn corporate funds to personal use.

The rule of equal opportunity in stock purchases by close corporations provides equal access to these benefits for all stockholders. We hold that, in any case in which the controlling stockholders have exercised their power over the corporation to deny the minority such equal opportunity, the minority shall be entitled to appropriate relief. . . .

C. Application of the Law to This Case.   We turn now to the application of the learning set forth above to the facts of the instant case.

The strict standard of duty is plainly applicable to the stockholders in Rodd Electrotype. Rodd Electrotype is a close corporation [under the test set out above]. . . .

In testing the stock purchase from Harry Rodd against the applicable strict fiduciary standard, we treat the Rodd family as a single controlling group. . . . From the evidence, it is clear that the Rodd family was a close-knit one with strong community of interest. . . .

Moreover, a strong motive of interest requires that the Rodds be considered a controlling group. When Charles Rodd and Frederick Rodd were called on to represent the corporation in its dealings with their father, they must have known that further advancement within the corporation and benefits would follow their father's retirement and the purchase of his stock. . . .

On its face, then, the purchase of Harry Rodd's shares by the corporation is a breach of the duty which the controlling stockholders, the Rodds, owed to the minority stockholders, the plaintiff and her son. The purchase distributed a portion of the corporate assets to Harry Rodd, a member of the controlling group, in exchange for his shares. The plaintiff and her son were not offered an equal opportunity to sell their shares to the corporation. In fact, their efforts to obtain an equal opportunity were rebuffed by the corporate representative. As the trial judge found, they did not, in any manner, ratify the transaction with Harry Rodd.

Because of the foregoing, we hold that the plaintiff is entitled to relief. Two forms of suitable relief are set out hereinafter. The judge below is to enter an appropriate judgment. The judgment may require Harry Rodd to remit $36,000 with interest at a legal rate from July 15, 1970, to Rodd Electrotype in exchange for forty-five shares of Rodd Electrotype treasury stock. This, in substance, is the specific relief requested in the plaintiff's bill of complaint. Interest is manifestly appropriate. . . . In the alternative, the judgment may require Rodd Electrotype to purchase all of the plaintiff's shares for $36,000 without interest. In the circumstances of this case, we view this as the equal opportunity which the plaintiff should have received. Harry Rodd's retention of thirty-six shares, which were to be sold and given to his children within a year of the Rodd Electrotype purchase, cannot disguise the fact that the corporation acquired one hundred percent of that portion of his holdings (forty-five shares) which he did not intend for his children to own. The plaintiff is entitled to have one hundred percent of her forty-five shares similarly purchased. . . .

WILKINS, J. (concurring).

I agree with much of what the Chief Justice says in support of granting relief to the plaintiff. However, I do not join in any implication (see, e.g., footnote 18 and the associated text) that the rule concerning a close corporation's purchase of a controlling stockholder's shares applies to all operations of the corporation as they affect minority stockholders. That broader issue, which is apt to arise in connection with salaries and dividend policy, is not involved in this case. The analogy to partnerships may not be a complete one.

FRANK EASTERBROOK & DANIEL FISCHEL, CLOSE CORPORATIONS AND AGENCY COSTS

38 Stan. L. Rev. 271 (1986)

C. STRICT STANDARDS OF FIDUCIARY DUTY

Minority shareholders who believe those in control have acted wrongfully may bring an action for breach of fiduciary duty. Because the parties cannot anticipate every contingency, contractual arrangements of any complexity necessarily will be incomplete. Fiduciary duties serve as implicit standard terms in contractual agreements that lower the cost of contracting. Properly interpreted, fiduciary duties should approximate the bargain the parties themselves would have reached had they been able to negotiate at low cost.

The usefulness of fiduciary duties as a guide for conduct is limited, however, because it is often difficult for a court to determine how the parties would have contracted had they anticipated this contingency. Because of this and other problems with liability rules as a means for assuring contractual performance, the parties have incentives to adopt governance mechanisms to resolve problems that cannot be anticipated. . . .

The same rule could be applied in [publicly held and] closely held corporations, but its application would vary because of differences between the two types of firms. For example, the decision to terminate an employee in a publicly held corporation is a classic example of the exercise of business judgment that a court would not second guess. In a closely held corporation, by contrast, termination of an employee can be a way to appropriate a disproportionate share of the firm's earnings. It makes sense, therefore, to have greater judicial review of terminations of managerial (or investing) employees in closely held corporations than would be consistent with the business judgment rule. The same approach could be used with salary, dividend, and employment decisions in closely held corporations where the risks of conflicts of interests are greater. . . .

If a court is unavoidably entwined in a dispute, it must decide what the parties would have bargained for had they written a complete contingent contract. The difficulties that result when a court misses this point are illustrated by the much applauded case of *Donahue v. Rodd Electrotype Co.* . . .

Grave reflections on the plight of minority investors in closely held corporations and stirring proclamations of the fiduciary duty of the majority fill the opinion. Completely overlooked in all of this rhetoric was any consideration of the basic question—which interpretation of fiduciary duties would the parties have selected had they contracted in anticipation of this contingency? Although no one can answer such a question with certainty (precisely because the parties did not), it is most unlikely that they would have selected a rule requiring an equal opportunity for all. Buy-out arrangements on contingencies such as retirement are common in closely held corporations. Such agreements provide some liquidity and ensure that the identity of the managers and the investors remains the same, reducing agency problems. At the same time, [limiting buy-out rights to managers or employees] minimizes the costs of requiring cash payouts or disrupting hard-won patterns of investment. In comparable corporations, a commonly used agreement requires a firm to purchase all shares if it buys any. Firms often undertake to buy the shares of all who retire, and the court might have made something of this. The plaintiff was the widow of a long-time employee whose shares were not purchased when he died. Among the firms that have written explicit contracts concerning the repurchase of shares, some allow selective repurchases from departing employees and some make repurchase mandatory. It would have been difficult to determine into which category a firm such as Rodd best fit. The court did not pursue this line, however, and it did not suggest that anything turned on the employment history of the current owners of the shares.

Several states seem to follow *Donahue* in imposing a fiduciary duty running directly from shareholder to shareholder in close corporations.[56] The Delaware Supreme Court however, seems to endorse Easterbrook and Fischel's analytical approach to the problem. See *Nixon v. Blackwell*, 626 A.2d 1366 (Del. 1993) (quoting Easterbrook and Fischel in support of reversing a Chancery Court ruling that had required close corporations to provide similar insurance benefits to all shareholders). Even Massachusetts seems to cut back on the *Donahue* rule somewhat. One year after *Donahue*, in *Wilkes v. Springside Nursing Home, Inc.*,[57] the Supreme Judicial Court of Massachusetts qualified the duty of "utmost good faith and loyalty" with a balancing test that recognized the controlling shareholder's right of "selfish ownership." Specifically, if the controlling shareholder can demonstrate a "legitimate business purpose" for its actions, then there is no breach of fiduciary duty unless the minority shareholder can demonstrate "that the same legitimate objective could have been achieved through an alternative course of action less harmful to the minority's interest."[58]

SMITH v. ATLANTIC PROPERTIES, INC.

422 N.E.2d 798 (Mass. App. 1981)

CUTTER, J.:

In December 1951, Dr. Louis E. Wolfson agreed to purchase land in Norwood for $350,000, with an initial cash payment of $50,000. . . . Dr. Wolfson offered a quarter interest each in the land to Mr. Paul T. Smith, Mr. Abraham Zimble, and William H. Burke. Each paid to

---

56. See Douglas K. Moll, *Shareholder Oppression and "Fair Value": Of Discounts, Dates, and Dastardly Deeds in the Close Corporation*, 54 Duke L. J. 293, 305 (2004).

57. 353 N.E.2d 657 (Mass. 1976).

58. *Id.* at 663.

Dr. Wolfson $12,500, one quarter of the initial payment. Mr. Smith, an attorney, organized the defendant corporation (Atlantic) in 1951 to operate the real estate. Each of the four subscribers received twenty-five shares of stock. Mr. Smith included, both in the corporation's articles of organization and in its by-laws, a provision reading, "No election, appointment or resolution by the Stockholders and no election, appointment, resolution, purchase, sale, lease, contract, contribution, compensation, proceeding or act by the Board of Directors or by any officer or officers shall be valid or binding upon the corporation until effected, passed, approved or ratified by an affirmative vote of eighty percent (80%) of the capital stock issued outstanding and entitled to vote." This provision (hereinafter referred to as the 80% provision) was included at Dr. Wolfson's request and had the effect of giving to any one of the four original shareholders a veto in corporate decisions.

Atlantic purchased the Norwood land. Some of the land and other assets were sold for about $220,000. Atlantic retained twenty-eight acres on which stood about twenty old brick or wood mill-type structures, which required expensive and constant repairs. After the first year, Atlantic became profitable and showed a profit every year prior to 1969, ranging from a low of $7,683 in 1953 to a high of $44,358 in 1954. The mortgage was paid in 1958 and Atlantic has incurred no long-term debt thereafter.

Salaries of about $25,000 were paid only in 1959 and 1960. Dividends in the total amount of $10,000 each were paid in 1964 and 1970. By 1961, Atlantic had about $172,000 in retained earnings, more than half in cash.

For various reasons, which need not be stated in detail, disagreements and ill will soon arose between Dr. Wolfson, on the one hand, and the other stockholders as a group.[3] Dr. Wolfson wished to see Atlantic's earnings devoted to repairs and possibly some improvements in its existing buildings and adjacent facilities. The other stockholders desired the declaration of dividends. Dr. Wolfson fairly steadily refused to vote for any dividends. Although it was pointed out to him that failure to declare dividends might result in the imposition by the Internal Revenue of a penalty under the Internal Revenue Code, I.R.C. §531 et seq. (relating to unreasonable accumulation of corporate earnings and profits), Dr. Wolfson persisted in his refusal to declare dividends. The other shareholders did agree over the years to making at least the most urgent repairs to Atlantic's buildings, but did not agree to make all repairs and improvements which were recommended in a 1962 report by an engineering firm retained by Atlantic to make a complete estimate of all repairs and improvements which might be beneficial.

The fears of an Internal Revenue Service assessment of a penalty tax were soon realized. Penalty assessments were made in 1962, 1963, and 1964. These were settled by Dr. Wolfson for $11,767.71 in taxes and interest. Despite this settlement, Dr. Wolfson continued his opposition to declaring dividends. The record does not indicate that he developed any

---

3. At least one cause of ill will on Dr. Wolfson's part may have been the refusal of the other shareholders to consent to his transferring his shares in Atlantic to the Louis E. Wolfson Foundation, a charitable foundation created by Dr. Wolfson.

specific and definitive schedule or plan for a series of necessary or desirable repairs and improvements to Atlantic's properties. At least none was proposed which would have had a reasonable chance of satisfying the Internal Revenue Service that expenditures for such repairs and improvements constituted "reasonable needs of the business," I.R.C. §534(c), a term which includes (see I.R.C. §537) "the reasonably anticipated needs of the business." Predictably, despite further warnings by Dr. Wolfson's shareholder colleagues, the Internal Revenue Service assessed further penalty taxes for the years 1965, 1966, 1967, and 1968. These taxes were upheld by the United States Tax Court . . . , and on appeal in 519 F.2d 1233 (1st Cir. 1975). . . . [T]hese decisions make it apparent that Atlantic has incurred substantial penalty taxes and legal expense largely because of Dr. Wolfson's refusal to vote for the declaration of sufficient dividends to avoid the penalty, a refusal which was (in the Tax Court and upon appeal) attributed in some measure to a tax avoidance purpose on Dr. Wolfson's part.

On January 23, 1967, the shareholders, other than Dr. Wolfson, initiated this proceeding in the Superior Court, later supplemented to reflect developments after the original complaint. The plaintiffs sought a court determination of the dividends to be paid by Atlantic, the removal of Dr. Wolfson as a director, and an order that Atlantic be reimbursed by him for the penalty taxes assessed against it and related expenses. . . .

The trial judge made findings (but in more detail) of essentially the facts outlined above and concluded that "Dr. Wolfson's obstinate refusal to vote in favor of . . . dividends was . . . caused more by his dislike for other stockholders and his desire to avoid additional tax payments than . . . by any genuine desire to undertake a program for improving . . . [Atlantic] property." She also determined that Dr. Wolfson was liable to Atlantic for taxes and interest amounting to "$11,767.11 plus interest from the commencement of this action, plus $35,646.14 plus interest," from the date of the First Circuit decision affirming the second penalty tax assessment. The latter amount includes an attorney's fee of $7,500 in the Federal tax cases. She also ordered the directors of Atlantic to declare "a reasonable dividend at the earliest practical date and reasonable dividends annually thereafter consistent with the good business practice." In addition, the trial judge directed that jurisdiction of the case be retained in the Superior Court "for a period of five years to [e]nsure compliance." . . .

The trial judge, in deciding that Dr. Wolfson had committed a breach of his fiduciary duty to other stockholders, relied greatly on broad language in *Donahue v. Rodd Electrotype Co.*, in which the Supreme Judicial Court afforded to a minority stockholder in a close corporation equality of treatment (with members of a controlling group of shareholders) in the matter of the redemption of shares. The court (at 592-593, 328 N.E.2d 505) relied on the resemblance of a close corporation to a partnership and held that [stockholders owe a duty to one another in the operation of the enterprise of] "utmost good faith and loyalty." [They] . . . "may not act out of avarice, expediency or self-interest in derogation of their duty of loyalty to the other stockholders and to the corporation." Similar principles were stated in *Wilkes v. Springside Nursing Home, Inc.*, but with some modifications, . . . of the sweeping language of the *Donahue* case. . . .

In the *Donahue* case, . . . the court recognized that cases may arise in which, in a close corporation, majority stockholders may ask protection from a minority stockholder. Such an instance arises in the present case because Dr. Wolfson has been able to exercise a veto concerning corporation action on dividends by the 80% provision (in Atlantic's articles of organization and by-laws) already quoted. The 80% provision may have substantially the effect of reversing the usual roles of the majority and the minority shareholders. The minority, under the provision, becomes an ad hoc controlling interest.[6]

It does not appear to be argued that this 80% provision is not authorized by G.L. c. 156B [which] . . . was intended to provide desirable flexibility in corporate arrangements. The provision is only one of several methods which have been devised to protect minority shareholders in close corporations from being oppressed by their colleagues and, if the device is used reasonably, there may be no strong public policy considerations against its use. . . . In the present case, Dr. Wolfson testified that he requested the inclusion of the 80% provision "in case the people [the other shareholders] whom I knew, but not very well, ganged up on me." The possibilities of shareholder disagreement on policy made the provision seems a sensible precaution.[8] A question is presented, however, concerning the extent to which such a veto power possessed by a minority shareholder may be exercised as its holder may wish, without a violation of the "fiduciary duty" referred to in the *Donahue* case. . . .

With respect to the past damage to Atlantic caused by Dr. Wolfson's refusal to vote in favor of any dividends, the trial judge was justified in finding that his conduct went beyond what was reasonable. The other stockholders shared to some extent responsibility for what occurred by failing to accept Dr. Wolfson's proposals with much sympathy, but the inaction on dividends seems the principal cause of the tax penalties. Dr. Wolfson had been warned of the dangers of an assessment under the Internal Revenue Code, I.R.C. §531 et seq. He had refused to vote dividends in any amount adequate to minimize that danger and failed to bring forward, within the relevant taxable years, a convincing, definitive program

---

6. The majority shareholders, in the event of a deadlock, at least may seek dissolution of the corporation if forty percent of the voting power can be mustered, whereas a single stockholder with only twenty-five percent of the stock may not do so. See G.L. c. 156B, §99(b), as amended by St. 1969, c. 392, §23.

8. Dr. Wolfson himself had discovered the business opportunity which led to the formation of Atlantic, had made the initial $50,000 payment which made possible the Norwood purchase, and had given the other shareholders an opportunity to share with him in what looked like a probably profitable enterprise. It was reasonably foreseeable that there might be differences of opinion between Dr. Wolfson, a man with substantial income likely to be in a high income tax bracket, and less affluent shareholders on such matters of policy as dividend declarations, salaries, and investment in improvements in the property. The other shareholders, two of whom were attorneys, should have known that it was as open to Dr. Wolfson reasonably to exercise the veto provided to him by the 80% provision in favor of a policy of reinvestment of earnings in Atlantic's properties, which would probably avoid taxes and increase the value of the corporate assets, as it was for them (possessed of the same veto) to use reasonably their voting power in favor of a more generous dividend and salary policy.

of appropriate improvements which could withstand scrutiny by the Internal Revenue Service. Whatever may have been the reason for Dr. Wolfson's refusal to declare dividends (and even if in any particular year he may have gained slight, if any tax advantage from withholding dividends) we think that he recklessly ran serious and unjustified risks of precisely the penalty taxes eventually assessed, risks which were inconsistent with any reasonable interpretation of a duty of "utmost good faith and loyalty." The trial judge (despite the novelty of the situation) was justified in charging Dr. Wolfson with the out-of-pocket expenditure incurred by Atlantic for the penalty taxes and related counsel fees of the tax cases.[10] . . .

QUESTION ON SMITH v. ATLANTIC PROPERTIES

Does the fact that the minority protection device at issue in *Smith* was clearly bargained for undermine a contractualist rationale for invoking a fiduciary remedy? What about the fact that the majority in *Smith* could have forced a statutory dissolution? See note 6 in *Smith*.

---

10. We do not now suggest that the standard of "utmost good faith and loyalty" may require some relaxation when applied to a minority ad hoc controlling interest, created by some device, similar to the 80% provision, designed in part to protect the selfish interests of a minority shareholder. This seems to us a difficult area of the law best developed on a case-by-case basis . . . .

SHAREHOLDER LAWSUITS

We now turn from the content of the fiduciary duties of directors and officers to the legal procedures that facilitate their enforcement. In considering shareholder lawsuits, we address a unique feature of Anglo-American law — one that has an importance in American law, in particular, that is without parallel in any other jurisdiction.

There are two principal forms of shareholder suits: *derivative suits* and direct actions, which are customarily brought as *class actions*. A class action is simply a gathering together of many individual or direct claims that share some important common aspects. (See Fed. R. Civ. P. 23.) The claim in such a suit is to recover damages suffered by individuals directly (or to prevent injury to these individuals) because they are shareholders. The derivative suit, on the other hand, is an assertion of a *corporate claim* against an officer or director (or third party), which charges them with a wrong to the corporation. Such an injury only indirectly (or "derivatively") harms shareholders. Thus, the derivative suit is said to represent two suits in one. The first suit is against the directors, charging them with *improperly* failing to sue on the existing corporate claim. The second suit is the underlying claim of the corporation itself. These suits typically allege that the corporation's directors have failed to vindicate its claims because they themselves are the wrongdoers and so would be the defendants in the resulting suit.

Both class suits and derivative suits have their roots in the English Court of Chancery and in the Rules of Equity Practice, which preceded the modern Rules of Federal Civil Procedure. Both of these legal actions are important features of American corporate law. As we will see, academics disagree about just how useful these devices are. Suffice it to say, however, that fiduciary duties can deter misconduct only if the shareholders can bring claims of fiduciary breach to court. The virtue of class actions and derivative suits is that they bring claims of fiduciary breach to court on behalf of disaggregated shareholders; the vice of these actions is that they may encourage the plaintiff's bar to bring too many, or the wrong sort of, fiduciary claims to court.

10.1 DISTINGUISHING BETWEEN DIRECT AND DERIVATIVE CLAIMS

Since, technically speaking, directors owe their loyalty principally to the corporation itself, alleged breaches of corporate law obligations by directors and officers most often arise in the context of derivative suits. However, the numerous suits arising under the federal securities laws are direct actions; the injury alleged is to a personal interest, such as the right to vote shares, rather than to a corporate interest. Often the same behavior that gives rise to a derivative suit can also support a class action alleging securities fraud (for example, a failure to disclose the fact that the transaction was a self-dealing transaction). Depending on the circumstances, the plaintiffs' attorneys may bring one or both kinds of actions.

The distinction between derivative suits and class actions is important for several reasons. On the most basic level, it is important because the derivative suit advances a corporate claim, which implies that any recovery that results *should go directly to the corporation* itself. Occasionally, courts approve direct payment to minority shareholders in derivative litigation,[1] but this offends the formal character of corporate law and, more important, may be unfair to corporate creditors. If, for example, minority shareholders successfully sue a controlling shareholder for looting, the company's creditors will very much prefer to have the resulting recovery go to the corporation, which owes them money, rather than to the minority shareholders, who do not. Procedural law supplies a second reason why characterization of a shareholders' suit as derivative or individual/class may be important. As we shall shortly see, derivative suits have a number of special procedural hurdles designed to protect the board of directors' role as the primary guardian of corporate interests. A suit that is correctly characterized as a derivative suit may be dismissed if it does not satisfy the provisions of Rule 23.1 of the Federal Rules of Civil Procedure (or similar rules in state court systems).

Although the class action and the derivative suit differ in concept (and to some extent in procedure), they share important commonalities. Both require plaintiffs to give notice to the absent interested parties; both permit other parties to petition to join in the suit; both provide for settlement and release only after notice, opportunity to be heard, and judicial determination of fairness of the settlement; and in both actions, successful plaintiffs are customarily compensated from the fund that their efforts produce. Compare Fed. R. Civ. P. 23 (class actions) and Fed. R. Civ. P. 23.1 (derivative actions).

Professors Robert Thompson and Randall Thomas provide a comprehensive review of the Delaware Chancery Court's caseload in 1999-2000. Among 1,716 complaints filed, Professors Thompson and Thomas find that they break down as follows:

---

1. See ALI, Principles of Corporate Governance §7.01(d) (1992).

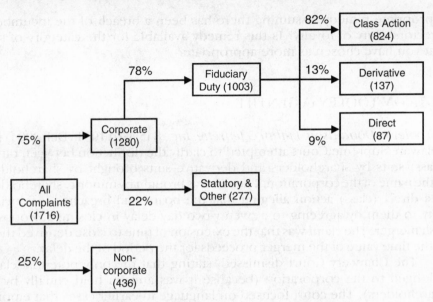

Source: Robert Thompson & Randall Thomas, *The New Look of Shareholder Litigation: Acquisition-Oriented Class Actions*, 57 Vand. L. Rev. 133, 166-18 (2004) (Tables 1A, 1B & 2). The breakdown of class action, derivative, and direct claims is greater than the total number of fiduciary duty claims because a few suits have multiple kinds of counts, e.g., direct and derivative counts.

In terms of numbers alone, these statistics indicate that the class action lawsuit and direct claims are far more important than derivative claims in Delaware. But number of filings alone may not be a very good measure of significance. In any case, we will pay a good deal of attention to derivative complaints in this chapter, where the procedural requirements are more intricate and the conceptual issues more challenging. Of course, the difference between derivative and direct (class action) claims is reasonably clear in theory, but is often problematic in practice. Consider the following problem.

PROBLEM: A FRIEND IN DEED IS A FRIEND IN NEED

The board of directors of Friendlier, Inc., defeated a coalition of insurgents at the annual shareholders' meeting by issuing a 15 percent block of common stock to the Friendship Investment Company shortly before the meeting. The CEO of Friendship assured the CEO of Friendlier that if he got a 10 percent discount from the market price of Friendlier's stocks, he would vote for the incumbent board for at least two election cycles. The newly issued stock was voted in favor of the incumbent directors and proved to be their margin of victory. The stock was issued at a price that was 10 percent below market.

Should a disgruntled public shareholder who knows these facts bring a derivative suit or a direct suit and seek class certification? What is the appropriate remedy, assuming there has been a breach of the incumbent directors' duty of loyalty? Is this remedy available for the category of suit that you have chosen as more appropriate?

NOTE ON TOOLEY & GENTILE

In *Tooley v. Donaldson, Lufkin & Jenrette, Inc.*, 845 A.2d 1031 (Del. 2004) the Delaware Supreme Court attempted to clarify the distinction between direct (class) suits by shareholders and derivative suits brought by shareholders in the name of the corporation. The suit was brought by minority shareholders as a direct (class) action alleging that the board had breached a fiduciary duty to them by agreeing to a twenty-two day delay in closing a proposed cash merger. The claim was that the extension of time to close deprived them of the time value of the merger proceeds for the period of the delay.

The Chancery Court dismissed, stating that the only potential claim belonged to the corporation (because it was a claim held equally by all shareholders). The court focused on language in earlier cases that emphasized that a shareholder had to suffer some special injury in order to state a direct claim. The Supreme Court affirmed the dismissal, but in doing so restated the test for determining whether a suit is to be treated as derivative or direct: "We set forth in this Opinion the law to be applied henceforth in determining whether a stockholder's claim is derivative or direct. That issue must turn *solely* on the following questions: (1) who suffered the alleged harm (the corporation or the suing shareholders); and (2) who would receive the benefit of any recovery or other remedy (the corporation or the stockholders individually)?"[2] Thus the Supreme Court removed from the analysis the question of special injury as being the mark of a direct claim.

In *Tooley*, the Supreme Court held that no claim was stated by the complaint, because the shareholders had no individual right to have the merger occur at all. From the corporation's perspective as well, there was no wrong alleged. Nevertheless, if there had been a claim stated, it would have been direct.

This case shows the limited utility of the special injury concept. Here, while the claim (such as it was) was shared by all shareholders and thus was not "special" it was nevertheless individual (if a legal right had been asserted at all). The restatement in *Tooley* is clarifying, but does not constitute a change in the law.

The recent case of *Gentile v. Rossette*[3] illustrates the malleability of the direct/derivative distinction. In *Gentile*, SinglePoint's CEO and Director Pasquale Rossette owned 61 percent of the shares and held $3 million in convertible debt in SinglePoint. In March 2000, Rossette negotiated with the only other board member at the time, Douglas Bachelor, to change the conversion ratio for the debt from $0.50 of debt per share to $0.05 of debt per share. Rossette and Bachelor then called a special meeting of shareholders to approve an increase in the number of authorized shares from

---

2. 845 A.2d 1031, 1033 (Del. 2004) (emphasis in original).
3. C.A. No. 20213 (Del. Aug. 17, 2006).

10 million to 60 million, in order to enable a conversion at the new ratio, but the minority shareholders were not informed of this underlying purpose. After shareholders approved the increase in the number of authorized shares, Rossette converted $2.2 million of his debt into SinglePoint equity, thereby increasing his stake in SinglePoint from 61 percent to 93 percent.

Minority shareholders brought suit claiming breach of fiduciary duty by Rossette and Bachelor. Citing *Tooley*, the Delaware Chancery Court granted summary judgment to the defendants, on the grounds that the plaintiffs' claim was solely derivative, and the plaintiffs had lost standing after SinglePoint had been merged into Cofiniti in October 2000. Surprisingly, in our view, the Delaware Supreme Court reversed, holding that the plaintiffs' claim was both direct and derivative. In addition to the obvious derivative claim, the Court found a direct claim from "an extraction from the public shareholders, and a redistribution to the controlling shareholder, of a portion of the economic value and voting power embodied in the minority interest. As a consequence, the public shareholders are harmed, uniquely and individually, to the same extent that the controlling shareholder is (correspondingly) benefited."[4] What do you think?

10.2 SOLVING A COLLECTIVE ACTION PROBLEM: ATTORNEYS' FEES AND THE INCENTIVE TO SUE

The fundamental problem in the governance of publicly financed corporations is the collective action problem associated with dispersed share ownership. Where all investors hold small stakes in the enterprise, no single investor has a strong incentive to invest time and money in monitoring management. Nor will derivative or class suits prove to be practical if shareholders have no individual economic incentive to expend the time and money necessary to prosecute them. Of course, if minority shareholders own large fractions of company shares, as is common in closely held companies, the economic benefits of a shareholder suit alone may suffice to induce minority shareholders to litigate. But if the shareholder suit is to be plausible for enforcing fiduciary duties in widely held corporations, the law must construct an incentive system to reward small shareholders for prosecuting meritorious claims. Such a system has evolved out of the court of equity's practice of awarding attorneys' fees to plaintiffs whose litigation created a common fund that benefited others as well as plaintiff herself. Consequently, the large majority of shareholder suits against the directors and officers of public companies are initiated by the plaintiffs' bar. In fact, the attorneys who bring shareholder suits seeking to earn fees from a positive outcome are the real parties in interest in these actions. Plaintiffs' attorneys are paid — or not — by order of the court or as part of a settlement at the conclusion of the litigation. In form, these attorneys are the economic agents of their shareholder-clients. In substance, they are legal entrepreneurs motivated by the prospect of attorneys' fees.

---

4. Id. at 17.

Whether an attorney for the plaintiff in a shareholder action receives a fee at all turns on whether the suit is dismissed or a judgment is entered in the suit, either through litigation (rare) or settlement (common). The plaintiffs' attorney receives nothing when a derivative suit is dismissed because there is no recovery and no benefit. When a derivative suit succeeds on the merits or settles (the usual outcome), the corporation is said to benefit from any monetary recovery or governance change resulting from the litigation. However, the corporation and its insurer also generally bear the bulk of litigation costs on both sides. The company is likely to have advanced the cost of defense to its managers, and it must usually pay the plaintiff a sum for "costs" that ranges, in the case of monetary recoveries, that ranges from a couple of percent (where the financial benefit is very large) to up to as much as 30 percent in some cases. While the formulas used to calculate contingent fees differ by jurisdiction and suit, the percentage of the recovery awarded for legal costs remains surprisingly stable.[5]

FLETCHER v. A.J. INDUSTRIES, INC.

72 Cal. Rptr. 146, 266 Cal. App. 2d 313 (1968)

RATTIGAN, A.J.:

This appeal is from certain orders entered in a stockholders' derivative action against appellant A.J. Industries, Inc. (hereinafter called the "corporation," or "AJ"). . . . The named defendants included the corporation; respondents Ver Halen and Malone . . . [and other members of AJ's board of directors].

The complaint alleged generally that . . . Ver Halen had dominated and controlled the board and the management of the corporation . . . and that, in consequence, the corporation had been damaged in the various transactions . . . . The complaint prayed for several forms of relief on behalf of the corporation, including a money judgment against Ver Halen for $134,150 and one against all the individual defendants in the amount of $1,000,000. . . .

During the course of a protracted hearing . . . a settlement of the action was negotiated. . . .

The "executory provisions" of the stipulation included these agreements: Four incumbent directors were to be replaced by persons acceptable to plaintiffs, to Ver Halen, and to the corporation; failing their agreement, the new directors were to be appointed by the trial court. The corporation agreed to employ a new officer who would be in charge of its "operations," and who would be one of the four new directors. In the election of future directors, Ver Halen's voting powers as a stockholder were to be limited so as to permit him to elect only two of the board's nine members. His employment contract was to be amended to provide that he could be employed as president of the corporation or, at the board's

---

5. See Roberta Romano, *The Shareholder Suit: Litigation Without Foundation?*, 7 J.L. Econ. & Org. 55 (1991).

option, as chairman of the board. Malone was to be one of the directors replaced, and he was to resign as the corporation's treasurer.

Several of the specific charges alleged in plaintiffs' complaint related to claimed mismanagement of the corporation due to Ver Halen's "domination" of its affairs; to Malone's allegedly excessive salary; and to Ver Halen's asserted breach of his employment contract. The stipulated agreements summarized above apparently disposed of these matters.

Most of the other charges made in the complaint related to specific transactions in which plaintiffs asserted misconduct on the part of Ver Halen. In other "executory provisions" of the stipulation it was agreed that these would be referred to arbitration. . . .

Whether the corporation was entitled to monetary recovery in any respect was, thus, to be determined in the future. In contrast, the stipulated agreements — providing for the reorganization of the corporation's board of directors and its management, the ouster of Malone, and the amendment of Ver Halen's contract of employment — were to be performed immediately.

The stipulation further provided that the arbitrator could award attorneys' fees, to be paid by the corporation, to any counsel who appeared in the arbitration proceeding, except that plaintiffs' attorneys could be awarded fees only in the event the corporation received a monetary award. The parties acknowledged (1) that plaintiffs' . . . attorneys intended to apply to the trial court — as distinguished from the future arbitrator — for fees and costs to be paid to them by the corporation "in connection with this action," but (2) that the corporation could take "any position in connection with such applications that it may choose." . . .

In its order granting plaintiffs' application for attorneys' fees and costs, the trial court found that they had employed their attorneys to prosecute the derivative action, in good faith, on behalf of themselves and the other stockholders of the corporation, and that the corporation was able to pay the fees and costs incurred. The court also found that by reason of the action, and its settlement, "substantial benefits have been conferred" upon the corporation.[2] Based upon these findings, the court ordered the corporation to pay plaintiffs' attorneys' fees ($64,784) and costs ($2,179.26).

. . . Under the general rule in California and in most American jurisdictions, the party prevailing in an action may not recover attorneys' fees unless a statute expressly permits such recovery. . . .

---

2. [I]n the following particulars, to wit:

a) That by reason of the settlement of said action, and without regard to whether plaintiffs or defendants would have been successful in the ultimate outcome thereof, the defendant A.J. Industries, Inc., a corporation, has been saved substantial expenditures for attorneys' fees, costs, and the loss of valuable time of valued employees by reason of the fact that the settlement and compromise obviates the necessity of a trial of this cause on its merits. Probable expenditures by the corporation, aforesaid, have been estimated by witnesses offered by defendants to be in excess of the sum of $200,000.00.

b) That by reason of said settlement the rights of the defendant corporation, if any, to recover from the defendant C. J. Ver Halen monies . . . has been fully protected and reserved in that a fair and equitable arbitration proceeding is provided for as a part of the terms of said settlement. . . .

An exception to the general rule is found, however, in the so-called common-fund doctrine. . . . "It is a well-established doctrine of equity jurisprudence that where a common fund exists to which a number of persons are entitled and in their interest successful litigation is maintained for its preservation and protection, an allowance of counsel fees may properly be made from such fund. By this means *all* of the beneficiaries of the fund pay their share of the expense necessary to make it available to them. [Citations.]" . . .

Under the "substantial benefit" rule, a variant of the common-fund doctrine as applied more recently in other jurisdictions, the successful plaintiff in a stockholder's derivative action may be awarded attorneys' fees against the corporation if the latter received "substantial benefits" from the litigation, although the benefits were not "pecuniary" and the action had not produced a fund from which they might be paid. . . .

In the present case, some of the causes of action alleged in plaintiffs' complaint might have produced a "common fund" in the form of a money judgment against appellant corporation. None, however, did: they were referred to an arbitration proceeding which was to be conducted in the future. For the obvious reason that no fund existed, the trial court applied the substantial-benefit rule . . . under which the award of attorneys' fees is charged directly against the corporation. . . .

[W]e conclude, that under the California rule (1) an award of attorneys' fees to a successful plaintiff may properly be measured by, and paid from, a common fund where his derivative action on behalf of a corporation has recovered or protected a fund in fact; but (2) the existence of a fund is not a prerequisite of the award itself. . . .

The stockholder's derivative suit . . . is an effective means of policing corporate management. [It] should not be inhibited by a doctrine which limits the compensation of successful attorneys to cases which produce a monetary recovery: the realization of substantial, if nonpecuniary, benefits by the corporation should [also] be the criterion. . . .

The final question . . . is whether the benefits realized by the corporation were sufficiently "substantial" to warrant the award. To find that they were, . . . [i]t will suffice if the [trial] court finds, upon proper evidence, that the results of the action "maintain the health of the corporation and raise the standards of 'fiduciary relationships and of other economic behavior,'" or "*prevent* an abuse which would be prejudicial to the rights and interests of the corporation or affect the enjoyment or protection of an essential right to the stockholder's interest." [Citation omitted.] . . .

It is not significant that the "benefits" found were achieved by settlement of plaintiffs' action rather than by final judgment. The authorities recognizing the substantial-benefit rule have permitted attorneys' fee awards in settled cases. . . . This is in keeping with the law's general policy favoring settlements . . . and in a stockholder's derivative action the trial court is in a position to scrutinize the fairness of a settlement because the court alone can authorize the action's dismissal. . . .

Some of the "benefits" found by the trial court in the present case related to the comparative economy to be realized by proceeding in arbitration rather than in conventional adversary litigation. Other "benefits," though, were realized in the form of immediate changes in the corporate management. The corporation argues that some of these had been under consideration by its board of directors before plaintiffs sued and settled, and that the real value of others is speculative. But the trial court found that the changes were substantial as benefits to the corporation and, in effect, that plaintiffs' action had brought them about. The finding is supported by ample evidence, and it is decisive on the appeal. We therefore affirm the award of attorneys' fees.

CHRISTIAN, J. (dissenting in part).
... The majority opinion refers to certain considerations of policy which appear to indicate that it would be a good thing to allow attorneys' fees against a corporation when one of its shareholders succeeds in a derivative action and substantial benefit to the corporation results. ... But countervailing policy arguments are not lacking: for example, if the existence of a "common fund" ... is not prerequisite to the allowance of fees the officers and directors [of the corporation] may well be faced with a liquidation of assets to pay fees, even though resulting harm to the corporation might be disproportionate to the "substantial benefits" derived from the lawsuit. Considerations of this character can better be appraised in the legislative process than by the [courts]. Moreover, it appears likely that the new enlargement of the "common fund" exception to the rule laid down in the statute may greatly outweigh in practical importance the court-created exception on which it is to be grafted. The variety of shareholders' actions in which "substantial benefit" to the corporation may be found is literally boundless. ...

QUESTIONS ON FLETCHER v. A. J. INDUSTRIES, INC.

1. What was the "substantial benefit" conferred on the corporation by the derivative suit in this litigation?
2. The rationale for shifting from the traditional common fund doctrine to the substantial benefit test for attorneys' fees is obvious. Is there a counterargument as well? What new risk is introduced by the substantial benefit test? How do you imagine courts deal with that risk?
3. Should the avoidance of litigation costs figure among the "benefits" conferred by the settlement of a derivative suit?

NOTE ON AGENCY COSTS IN SHAREHOLDER LITIGATION

The role of lawyer as bounty hunter creates an obvious agency problem in its own right. Legally, the plaintiffs' lawyers are agents of shareholders, just as the corporate defendants are fiduciaries charged with acting for the corporation and, ultimately, for its shareholders. But both sides have important financial interests at stake: fees for the lawyers and potential liability for corporate officers and directors. Much of the law of derivative suits is an effort to deal with the crosscutting agency problems that arise on the side of the plaintiffs' lawyers, on the one hand, and on that of the corporate managers, on the other. One such problem is that plaintiffs' lawyers may initiate so-called strike suits, or suits without merit, simply to extract a settlement by exploiting the nuisance value of litigation and the personal fears of liability — even if unfounded — of officers and directors. A second problem is that the corporate defendants may be too eager to settle because they bear at least some of the costs of litigation personally (e.g., the pain of depositions and the risk of personal liability), but they do not bear the cost of settling, which is borne by the corporation or its insurer. Strike suits have long been a concern of the corporate bar and are widely discussed in the literature.[6] One controversial article has even argued that the merits of litigation are unrelated to settlement amounts in the related context of securities class actions.[7]

Agency problems also arise when shareholder litigation is meritorious and corporate managers face a serious prospect of liability. In this case, plaintiffs' attorneys and corporate defendants — if these defendants remain in control of the corporations — have an incentive to settle on terms that are mutually advantageous but that allow the defendants to fully escape personal liability for their conduct.

Finally, the legal system itself can generate agency problems by structuring attorneys' fees in dysfunctional ways. For example, awarding plaintiffs' attorneys a percentage of the recovery may encourage the premature settlement. The chief alternative fee rule, the so-called lodestar formula sometimes used in federal securities litigation, pays attorneys a base hourly fee for the reasonable time expended on a case, inflated by a multiplier to compensate for unusual difficulty or risk. By decoupling attorneys' fees from the recovery amount, this rule eliminates the incentives of attorneys to settle too soon, but it creates the opposite incentive to spend too much time litigating relative to the likely settlement outcomes.[8] Finally, as a reaction to the evident weaknesses in both techniques for the awarding of attorneys' fees, some courts have experimented with auctioning the rights to represent the corporation (or the class of shareholders) to the law firm that makes the best bid. But even this technique is vulnerable to "gaming" by plaintiffs' attorneys. The incentives of bidding firms may, for example, lead to low bids that permit a lawyer to control the case in order to negotiate a settlement.[9]

6. See, e.g., Roberta Romano, *The Shareholder Suit: Litigation Without Foundation?*, 7 J.L. Econ. & Org. 55 (1991); John C. Coffee, Jr., *Understanding the Plaintiff's Attorney: The Implications for Private Enforcement of Law Through Class and Derivative Actions*, 86 Col. L. Rev. 669 (1986).

7. Janet C. Alexander, *Do the Merits Matter? A Study of Settlements in Securities Class Actions*, 43 Stan. L. Rev. 497 (1991). For criticism of this initial study, see, *e.g.*, Leonard B. Simon & William S. Dato, *Legislating on a False Foundation: The Erroneous Academic Underpinnings of the Private Securities Litigation Reform Act of 1995*, 33 San Diego L. Rev. 959, 964 (1996). For more recent empirical work on this question, *compare* Marilyn F. Johnson, Karen K. Nelson & A.C. Pritchard, *Do the Merits Matter More? The Impact of the Private Securities Litigation Reform Act*, 23 J. L. Econ. & Org. (forthcoming 2007) (finding a "closer relation between factors related to fraud and the filing of securities class actions after the passage of the PSLRA") with Stephen J. Choi, *Do the Merits Matter Less After the Private Securities Litigation Reform Act?*, 23 J. L. Econ. & Org. (forthcoming 2007) (reporting some evidence that meritorious suits were deterred by the PSLRA).

8. See, e.g., Coffee, supra note 3; John C. Coffee, *The Unfaithful Champion: The Plaintiff as Monitor of Shareholder Litigation*, 48 L. & Contemp. Probs. 5 (1985).

9. See Third Circuit Task Force Report on Selection of Class Counsel, 74 Temple L. Rev. 685 (2001).

Thus, while paying bounties to plaintiffs' lawyers mitigates the shareholders' collective action problem in widely held corporations, it also gives rise to new risks and challenges for the legal system. Much of what follows in this chapter — specifically the law of presuit demand and the law of dismissal by independent board committees — can be understood as judicially created measures intended to fine-tune the power and incentives of plaintiffs' lawyers to prosecute shareholder suits.

In addition to these judicial innovations, there have been several statutory responses to the agency problems of fee-driven litigation. Beginning in the 1940s, a number of states adopted "security for expenses" statutes, which permitted corporate defendants to require plaintiffs (or their attorneys) to post a bond to secure coverage of the company's anticipated expenses in the litigation. See, e.g., NYBCL §627; Cal. Corp. Code §800. The purpose of these statutes was to add a stick to the carrot of the attorneys' fees — to engineer a fee rule that would discourage strike suits as well as encourage meritorious litigation. But however attractive this approach seems in theory, it appears to have failed in practice. Savvy plaintiffs' attorneys, reluctant defendants, and sympathetic judges together ensure that plaintiffs are rarely forced to post bonds and are virtually never charged with the litigation costs of corporate defendants.[10]

General dissatisfaction with the growth in the number of securities class actions led to enactment of the federal Private Securities Litigation Reform Act (PSLRA) of 1995.[11] That statute embraces a variety of devices to discourage nonmeritorious suits, such as particularized pleading requirements and changes in substantive law, and to encourage institutional shareholders to assume control of shareholder litigation under the "most adequate plaintiff" rule considered below. The following chart shows the number of securities class actions filed since 1994, the year before the PSLRA was passed.

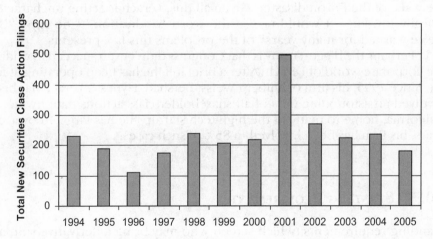

Source: Stanford Law School Securities Class Action Clearinghouse (last updated July 14, 2006).

10. See Robert Clark, Corporate Law §15.5.
11. Pub. L. No. 104-67, 109 Stat. 737 (1995) (codified throughout 15 U.S.C. §§77-78).

As shown, new securities fraud filings decreased after the PSLRA was passed, but only for one year. Filings then returned to their 1994 level of approximately 200 new cases per year, then exploded in 2001, coincident with the wave in corporate scandals led by Enron and WorldCom. The conventional wisdom is that the PSLRA provides a minor speed-bump for plaintiffs' lawyers on the way to the courthouse, but that "fundamentals" such as stock market volatility (which increases litigation) and good corporate governance (which, arguably, reduces litigation) are more important drivers of overall litigation actvity.[12] With this background consider the following excerpt, focusing on the most prominent plaintiffs' attorney today, Bill Lerach of Lerach, Coughlin, Stoia, Geller, Rudman & Robbins (formerly of Milberg Weiss, Bershad, Hynes & Lerach).

ENRON SHAREHOLDER SUITS? NOT SO FAST

Business Week Online (February 12, 2002)

For most of the 1990s, Bill Lerach, the whirling dervish of securities litigators, was Corporate America's Public Enemy No. 1. His mass production of shareholder class actions, filed against just about any company that had suffered a big drop in its stock price, made him "lower than pond scum" in the eyes of business... In 1995, Lerach's enemies helped persuade Congress to enact the Private Securities Litigation Reform Act. The idea was to shield "decent" executives, accountants, and lawyers from Lerach's type of all-purpose lawsuit.

Probably no one anticipated, however, how quickly the let's-get-Lerach legislation might backfire. Thanks to that law, it's now going to be much more difficult than before for shareholders to exact any satisfaction in the wake of the Enron disaster. Given all this, Lerach is acting uncharacteristically low-key. "I wouldn't use the word 'vindication,'" he says. "But we've warned for many years" of the problems this law presents.

Perhaps the biggest irony is that Congress didn't even succeed in ridding the corporate world of Lerach. After a brief lull, he has been operating at full tilt. Since 1995, his firm of Milberg Weiss, Bershad, Hynes & Lerach has been involved an astounding 60% of all shareholder class-actions nationwide. In California, home to many of the high-tech startups he has targeted over the years, his firm has been involved in 85% of such cases. . . .

10.3 STANDING REQUIREMENTS

Standing requirements, which screen who may bring a derivative suit, are established both by statute and by court rule. See, e.g., 10 Del. Code Com. §327; Fed. R. Civ. P. 23.1. They are premised on the assumption that

---

12. See, e.g., Cornerstone Research, Securities Class Action Case Filings: 2005.

screening for qualified litigants increases the quality of shareholder litigation, i.e., that some potential litigants have better incentives to sue than others. (Compare, from this perspective, the various standing requirements for derivative suits in your statutory supplement: Fed. R. Civ. P. 23.1; RMBCA §7.41; and ALI, Principles of Corporate Governance §7.02).

Federal Rule 23.1, which Delaware also follows, typifies standing rules for derivative actions. First, the plaintiff must be a shareholder for the duration of the action. (Why? What shapes the incentives of a plaintiff who sues on behalf of a company in which she no longer has any financial interest?) Second, the plaintiff must have been a shareholder at the time of the alleged wrongful act or omission (the "contemporaneous ownership rule"). This requirement reflects the traditional bias of courts against plaintiffs who "buy a lawsuit." In public companies, however, this rule is not very important, since shareholders are easy to find. Third, the plaintiff must be able to "fairly and adequately" represent the interests of shareholders, meaning in practice that there are no obvious conflicts of interest. Finally, the complaint must specify what action the plaintiff has taken to obtain satisfaction from the company's board (a requirement that forms the basis of the "demand requirement") or state with particularity the plaintiff's reason for not doing so.

Do these standing rules screen out strike suits — or are they obstacles to otherwise meritorious derivative suits? The answer in most cases is "neither." The requirement that a plaintiff remain a shareholder during the course of litigation, which arises from judicial construction of "fair and adequate" representation under Rule 23.1, has bite chiefly in the context of corporate mergers and dissolutions, where plaintiffs may cease to be shareholders because the corporations in which they held shares disappear.[13] The contemporaneous ownership rule is the most restrictive of the pure standing requirements. But how much bite is it likely to have in the case of widely held companies? (In the case of close corporations, your answer will be different, but should it be?)

QUESTIONS ON THE POLICY RATIONALE FOR DERIVATIVE ACTIONS

1. From an incentive standpoint, do you think the contemporaneous ownership requirement makes sense? Current ownership of shares might affect a plaintiff's incentive, but why should past ownership matter?

2. Should the law try to structure attorneys' fees to ensure that every meritorious derivative suit is brought? Why or why not?

3. Evaluate the following proposals for new "standing" rules to govern the right to bring derivative litigation (or class actions):

---

13. See, e.g., *Basch v. Talley Industries, Inc.*, 53 F.D.R. 9 (S.D.N.Y. 1971). What policy might be invoked to justify this rule? What if the plaintiff received stock in the surviving corporation?

a. A rule limiting standing to shareholders holding 2 percent or $500,000 worth of company shares.

b. A rule assigning the right to control derivative litigation to the largest (nonconflicted) shareholder willing to intervene in the litigation, on the ground that this shareholder is the "most adequate plaintiff." Note that a provision of the Private Securities Litigation Reform Act of 1995 adopts precisely this rule for assigning control over class actions alleging violations of the federal securities laws. See Pub. L. No. 104-67, 109 Stat. 737 (1995).[14]

c. A rule permitting judges to auction standing to bring derivative actions to the highest bidder — with the proceeds of the auction going to the corporation, a finder's fee to the attorney who filed the initial complaint, and any recovery to the winning bidder who prosecutes the suit.[15]

10.4 BALANCING THE RIGHTS OF BOARDS TO MANAGE THE CORPORATION AND SHAREHOLDERS' RIGHTS TO OBTAIN JUDICIAL REVIEW

An important set of legal doctrines is intended to balance the rights of boards to manage their companies (including deciding which of its potential claims are litigated) against the rights of shareholder-plaintiffs to obtain judicial review of alleged corporate claims. Just when a shareholder-plaintiff should be empowered to take a corporate claim out of the hands of the board, against the will of management, is an issue that can arise in several contexts. First, it arises when a company moves to dismiss a derivative suit on the ground that the shareholder-plaintiff has made a presuit demand on the board, as contemplated by Rule 23.1, but the board has refused to bring the suit. Here the court must decide whether or not to defer to the board's business judgment in electing not to prosecute the action. The issue of deference to the board also arises when the shareholder-plaintiff does *not* make demand on the board, on the ground that the board could not exercise disinterested business judgment. Here the court must pass on the validity of the plaintiff's excuse for not making presuit demand. In

---

14. For an empirical assessment of this provision, see Stephen J. Choi, Jill E. Fisch & A. C. Pritchard, *Do Institutions Matter? The Impact of the Lead Plaintiff Provision of the Private Securities Litigation Reform Act*, 83 Wash. U. L. Q. 869 (2005) (finding that public pension funds have participated more frequently as lead plaintiff since 1995, but overall institutional participation remains unchanged in four-year samples pre-and post-PSLRA).

15. There is a lively controversy about the policy merits of auctioning shareholder suits. See Jonathan R. Macey & Geoffrey P. Miller, *The Plaintiff's Attorney's Role in Class Action and Derivative Litigation: Economic Analysis and Recommendations for Reform*, 58 U. Chi. L. Rev. 1 (1991). Compare Randall S. Thomas & Robert G. Hansen, *Auctioning Class Action and Derivative Lawsuits: A Critical Analysis*, 87 Nev. L. Rev. 423 (1993); Jonathan R. Macey & Geoffrey P. Miller, *Auctioning Class Action and Derivative Suits: A Rejoinder*, 87 Nev. L. Rev. 458 (1993).

addition, the question of board deference arises when the board seeks to terminate a derivative suit at a later point in the litigation, after the suit has already survived the company's initial motion to dismiss. That is, even if the company's board was disqualified from dismissing the suit at the time the complaint was filed, it may be that the board has subsequently become capable of exercising its business judgment over the action — usually because new directors have joined the board. In this case, the board should arguably be able to reclaim its power to direct the company's litigation strategy.[16]

Finally, the need for courts to balance the rights of management and shareholders in the derivative context arises in connection with settlements of shareholder suits, and especially in the rare case in which a derivative case is settled over the objection of a derivative plaintiff. We discuss settlements in the next section.

10.4.1 The Demand Requirement of Rule 23

The demand requirement originates in the traditional rule that a derivative complaint must "allege with particularity the efforts, if any, made by the plaintiff to obtain the action he desires from the directors or comparable authority . . . or the grounds for not making the effort." Fed. R. Civ. P. 23.1 (Delaware has the identical rule). But what precisely are the circumstances in which the complaint may be dismissed once the plaintiff does — or does not — make a demand on the board? The answer is a matter of common law.

LEVINE v. SMITH

591 A.2d 194 (Del. 1991)

[Shareholders of the General Motors Corporation (GM) brought several derivative actions involving a transaction by which Ross Perot — a director of GM, and as holder of 0.8 percent of its stock, GM's largest shareholder — and a few associates sold back to GM their holdings of GM Class E stock in exchange for $743 million. This repurchase was in response to disagreements between Perot and GM senior management concerning the management of GM's EDS subsidiary and its automobile business as

---

16. While this may sound like the derivative plaintiff is apt to get the runaround, in fact there are some circumstances when this step is clearly appropriate. Imagine, for example, that a hostile takeover follows the initiation of a derivative suit. Even though the old board may have been implicated in the matter sued on, the new board is not and therefore should be given its rights to manage the company's claim in litigation. The matter becomes far less clear when the company's newfound ability to make a valid business judgment comes not from a complete turnover of the board but from the appointment of one or two new directors, who thereafter are appointed to a special committee to review the matter. This is the situation presented in the well-known Delaware case of *Zapata Corp. v. Maldanodo*, set forth below.

well. By the time of the repurchase, GM was in the awkward position of
facing accusations by its director and target shareholder, Ross Perot, that it
sold "second rate cars." A committee of outside directors negotiated the
buy-back transaction for GM, which was subsequently approved by the full
board at a meeting that Perot did not attend. Part of the consideration on
Perot's side was a covenant not to compete with GM and a promise not to
publicly criticize the company. The suit named all directors and Perot as
defendants, and claimed that the transaction paid Perot a premium for his
shares for no reason other than stopping his criticisms.]

HORSEY, J.:
 ... The directors of a corporation and not its shareholders manage the
business and affairs of the corporation. . . and accordingly, the directors
are responsible for deciding whether to engage in derivative litigation. . . .
    The demand requirements of Rule 23.1 represent a procedural
restatement of these bedrock principles. . . . Rule 23.1's alternative
requirements of pleading, demand futility or wrongful refusal of demand,
are designed to strike a balance between a shareholder's claim of right to
assert a derivative claim and a board of directors' duty to decide whether to
invest the resources of the corporation in pursuit of the shareholder's claim
of corporate wrong. . . . Both the requirements of demand futility and
wrongful refusal of demand are predicated upon and "inextricably bound
to issues of business judgment and the standards of that doctrine's applicability." *Aronson,* 473 A.2d at 812. Thus, the correct application of the
business judgment rule is crucial to a determination of the sufficiency of
a derivative complaint to withstand a Rule 23.1 motion in both a demand
excused and a demand refused context. . . .
    . . . In determining the sufficiency of a complaint to withstand dis-
missal under Rule 23.1 based on a claim of demand futility, the controlling
legal standard is well established. The trial court is confronted with two
related but distinct questions: (1) whether threshold presumptions of
director disinterest or independence are rebutted by well-pleaded facts;
and, if not, (2) whether the complaint pleads particularized facts sufficient
to create a reasonable doubt that the challenged transaction was the product of a valid exercise of business judgment. . . .
    The premise of a shareholder claim of futility of demand is that a
majority of the board of directors either has a financial interest in the
challenged transaction or lacks independence or otherwise failed to exercise due care. . . . On either showing, it may be inferred that the Board is
incapable of exercising its power and authority to pursue the derivative
claims directly. When lack of independence is charged, a plaintiff must
show that the Board is either dominated by an officer or director who is
the proponent of the challenged transaction or that the Board is so under
his influence that its discretion is "sterilize[d]." . . .
    Assuming a plaintiff cannot prove that directors are interested or
otherwise not capable of exercising independent business judgment, a
plaintiff in a demand futility case must plead particularized facts creating
a reasonable doubt as to the "soundness" of the challenged transaction
sufficient to rebut the presumption that the business judgment rule

attaches to the transaction. The point is that in a claim of demand futility, there are two alternative hurdles, either of which a derivative shareholder complainant must overcome to successfully withstand a Rule 23.1 motion.

In addressing plaintiffs' restated claim of demand futility, the Vice Chancellor correctly limited his threshold analysis to the issue of director independence. We decline to revisit plaintiffs' . . . allegation that the GM Directors, in approving the Perot buy-out, acted out of motives of entrenchment or financial self-interest. We also decline to reconsider plaintiffs' allegations that the buy-out represented a waste of corporate assets. . . .

Plaintiffs' remaining allegations, offered to sustain a claim of demand futility, are that the GM outside directors lacked independence because they were deceived or misled by management or inside directors concerning the true purpose of the Perot buy-out and the substantial progress that had been made in resolving the ongoing disputes between GM and EDS. Plaintiffs claim that the GM outside directors were so manipulated, misinformed and misled that they were subject to management's control and unable to exercise independent judgment. Plaintiffs assert that their restated complaint pleads with sufficient particularity the manner in which the GM outside directors, though they comprise the majority of the Board, were dominated and controlled by its management directors. As a result, plaintiffs allege that the outside directors' "independence was thereby destroyed and they were effectively dominated by the management directors."[4]

The Court of Chancery found that plaintiffs' restated claim of demand futility failed to plead particularized facts sufficient to create a reasonable doubt as to the independence of a majority of the GM Board. The court found that plaintiffs' claims based on newly discovered evidence implicated, at most, only two of GM's fourteen outside directors, thereby leaving at least twelve of the twenty-one directors (excluding Perot) independent and

---

4. The crux of plaintiffs' claim of demand excused is found in the following allegations of the Second Amended Complaint:

56. Demand upon the GM Board is excused. The approval by the GM Board of the Perot Buy Out was not approval by an independent or disinterested Board. . . . The outside directors knew or should have known that Smith [GM's CEO — EDS.] and his fellow management directors had a direct personal and financial interest in seeing that Perot's objections were silenced because, if voiced and if convincing, Perot's objections could result in the loss of hundreds of thousands of dollars to the management directors.

57. The management directors' personal financial interest in maintaining their high salaries, bonuses and perquisites caused them to conceal material information from many of the outside directors, including members of the Oversight Committee, concerning the pivotal fact that the prior disputes between Perot and EDS over auditing, pricing and compensation were already substantially resolved. The outside directors had good reason to question and investigate the expressed justification for the Buy Out. Had they done so, they could have discovered that material facts were being concealed from them. Instead, members of the Oversight Committee and members of the full Board allowed themselves to be misinformed and uninformed. . . .

"capable of impartially considering a demand." The court also found any alleged deception concerning the placement of blame for the GM/EDS disputes immaterial to the fundamental decision of severing the GM-Perot relationship. Hence, the court found plaintiffs' Second Amended Complaint to have inadequately pleaded a claim of futility of demand. . . .

We affirm the Vice Chancellor's findings. . . . Plaintiffs' conclusory allegations that the outside directors' independence was compromised by the inside directors' misleading, manipulative and deceptive conduct are unsupported by particularized facts. Such allegations of improper conduct by management are also inadequate to establish Board domination or control of GM's outside directors sufficient to find the latter lacking in "independence," in the customary definition of the term. See *Aronson,* 473 A.2d at 815-816. . . . Plaintiffs' allegations detailed in paragraphs 56 and 57 of their restated complaint more appropriately relate to the issue of director due care and the business judgment rule's application to the challenged transaction. Indeed, plaintiffs plead virtually the same averments for both purposes.

The question then becomes whether the restated Grobow complaint otherwise pleads particularized facts sufficient to rebut the presumption that the Perot buy-back was the product of a valid exercise of business judgment. . . .

Plaintiffs allege that GM's "outside" directors acted with such haste and were so misled by management as to reach an uninformed decision in approving the Perot buy-out. In [a previous decision], we carefully addressed plaintiffs' original allegations of the GM Board's lack of procedural due care. *Grobow I,* 539 A.2d at 190-191. We reviewed the role of the GM "Special Review Committee," and we especially noted the absence of any allegations "that the GM directors, and in particular its outside directors, were dominated or controlled by GM's management. . . . " *Id.* at 191. In their restated complaint, plaintiffs delete reference to GM's Special Review Committee and the exclusive role played by GM's outside directors in reviewing the challenged transaction. Instead, plaintiffs now contend that a majority of GM's outside directors were uninformed because: (a) they were allegedly misled concerning the gravity of the disputes between senior management and Perot, and (b) the deposition testimony of two of GM's fourteen outside directors, Evans and Wyman (suggesting that they had misimpressions concerning the buy-out), is sufficient to defeat the presumption otherwise attached to an approval of a transaction by a board consisting of a majority of independent and disinterested directors.

. . . We have previously found wanting plaintiffs' allegations that GM's outside directors lacked independence because they were manipulated, misinformed or misled by management. . . . [T]hese findings with respect to director independence have equal application to the issue of director due care. In summary, we agree with the Court of Chancery that plaintiffs' restated complaint fails to plead particularized facts sufficient to raise a reasonable doubt that a majority of the GM Board acted in so uninformed a manner as to fail to exercise due care. . . .

H. ROSS PEROT

Ross Perot will long be remembered for his feisty third-party political campaigns in the 1992 and 1996 U.S.presidential elections. His outspoken career, however, had begun well before he came to political prominence. As a child in Depression-era Texas, Perot honed his entrepreneurial instincts by selling newspapers, garden supplies, and farm animals. He graduated from the U.S. Naval Academy in 1953 and, after four years in the navy, joined IBM's sales department. Soon the company's top computer sales representative, Perot tried unsuccessfully to convince IBM's management that selling technology servicing contracts, in addition to hardware, was the trend of the future.[17] When IBM wasn't convinced, he resigned in 1962 to form Electronic Data Services (EDS) with $1,000 in capital. In 1968, the company's wildly successful initial public offering made Perot a billionaire.

General Motors purchased EDS for $2.4 billion in 1984, retaining Ross Perot as CEO of the EDS division and giving him a seat on the GM board. Perot soon became disenchanted, but his demand for a change in GM's corporate culture clashed with GM CEO Roger Smith's autocratic management style and explosive temper. Perot took his case to the public, criticizing GM and Smith's management in interviews with prominent business publications. "Revitalizing GM is like teaching an elephant to tap dance," he told *Business Week.* "You find the sensitive parts and start poking."[18] In 1986, Smith orchestrated a $743 million purchase of Perot's ownership, hoping to be rid of his critic. Perot had the last word, however, when at a news conference he implied that the buyout deal he had reluctantly accepted was a waste of stockholder funds.

NOTE ON PRESUIT DEMAND

Levine and the case it interprets, *Aronson v. Lewis,* raise many issues. The most fundamental of these was taken up by the ALI in its Principles of Corporate Governance project: Is the traditional equity rule of presuit demand, with its exception for futility, the best way to adjudicate the board's colorable disability to claim sole right to control the adjudication of corporate claims? The drafters of the ALI's Principles concluded that the answer was "no." Instead, the ALI proposed a rule of universal demand, under which a plaintiff would be required to always make a demand, and if, as is likely, she was not satisfied with the board's response to her demand, she could institute suit. If the defendants thereafter sought dismissal of the suit, the court would review the board's exercise of business judgment in making its response. If the court concluded that the board was in a position to exercise a valid business judgment on the question whether suit should be brought, then it would dismiss the suit. Otherwise, the suit would continue to its merits. See ALI, Principles of Corporate Governance §7.04.

In an odd way, the Delaware Supreme Court has promulgated a rule that is the mirror image of the ALI rule: a rule of "universal nondemand." It has done so through its practice of inferring that, whenever a plaintiff actually does make a presuit demand, she automatically concedes that the

17. Doron Levin, *Irreconcilable Differences: Ross Perot Versus General Motors* (1989).
18. Id.

board is independent and disinterested with respect to the question to be litigated. If independence is conceded by making demand, then the only prong of the *Aronson-Levine* test that the plaintiff is left to contest in the event that the demand is denied (as it usually is) is the test's second prong, which asks whether bad faith or gross negligence may be inferred from the decision itself. See *Speigel v. Buntrock*, 571 A.2d 767 (Del. 1990).[19] Thus, although there is some ex post plausibility in the reasoning of the Delaware courts, the practical effect of this rule is to discourage any presuit demand at all. The real policy question then is whether we prefer a universal demand rule or a universal nondemand rule. In either event the court will ultimately have to pass upon the board's ability to fairly deal with the issue the litigation presents. The ALI approach allows it to do so with more information (but would entail more time and cost by the board).

The *Levine* case itself employs a relaxed modification of the business judgment rule to screen derivative suits: Do the facts alleged "creat[e] a *reasonable doubt* of the 'soundness' of the challenged transaction"? (Emphasis added.) This is presumably because the court is conscious that it is addressing a pleading standard and does not want to prejudge the merits of the claim. Nevertheless, the *Levine* case might be accused of confusing matters because it focuses in part on the identity of the directors at the time of the occurrence of the alleged delict. What is really relevant, however, is the board's capacity to decide at the time that the suit is brought. That question may, but need not logically, relate to the composition of the board at the time of the wrong. In the following case, the court struggles to overcome this bit of confusion.

RALES v. BLASBAND

634 A.2d 927 (Del. 1993)

VEASEY, C.J.:

[Before the court on certification from the United States District Court.] . . .

[Shareholder-plaintiff] Blasband is currently a stockholder of Danaher Corp. Prior to 1990 Blasband owned 1100 shares of Easco Hand Tools, Inc., a Delaware corporation ("Easco"). Easco entered into a [stock for stock] merger agreement with Danaher in February 1990 whereby Easco became a wholly-owned subsidiary of Danaher (the "Merger").

Steven M. Rales and Mitchell P. Rales (the "Rales brothers") have been directors, officers, or stockholders of Easco and Danaher at relevant times. Prior to the Merger, the Rales brothers were directors of Easco, and together owned approximately 52 percent of Easco's common stock. They continued to serve as directors of Easco after the Merger.

The Rales brothers also own approximately 44 percent of Danaher's

---

19. The holding that plaintiffs concede board independence by making demand appears to have been partly qualified by a more recent case, although just how much is difficult to say. See *Scattered Corp. v. Chicago Stock Exchange, Inc.*, 701 A.2d 70 (Del. 1997).

common stock. Prior to the Merger, Mitchell Rales was President and Steven Rales was Chief Executive Officer of Danaher. The Rales brothers resigned their positions as officers of Danaher in early 1990, but continued to serve as members of the Board. The Board consists of eight members. The other six members are Danaher's President and Chief Executive Officer, George Sherman ("Sherman"), Donald E. Ehrlich ("Ehrlich"), Mortimer Caplin ("Caplin"), George D. Kellner ("Kellner"), A. Emmett Stephenson, Jr. ("Stephenson"), and Walter Lohr ("Lohr"). A number of these directors have business relationships with the Rales brothers or with entities controlled by them.

The central focus of the amended complaint is the alleged misuse by the Easco board of the proceeds of a sale of that company's 12.875% Senior Subordinated Notes due 1998 (the "Notes"). On or about September 1, 1988, Easco sold $100 million of the Notes in a public offering (the "Offering"). The prospectus for the Offering stated that the proceeds from the sale of the Notes would be used for (1) repaying outstanding indebtedness, (2) funding corporate expansion, and (3) general corporate purposes. The prospectus further stated that "pending such uses, the Company will invest the balance of the net proceeds from this offering in government and other marketable securities

MICHAEL MILKEN

While an MBA student at the University of Pennsylvania's Wharton School, Michael Milken studied the academic literature regarding debt financing and became fascinated with the investment potential of low-grade, high-yield bonds. After graduating in 1970, he traded securities in investment bank Drexel Burnham's low-grade bond department and quickly rose through the ranks to lead the department. He became so adept at promoting and selling "junk bonds," convertible debt issuances with low ratings and high yields, that Drexel Burnham's name became synonymous with the product. Milken was especially skilled at building networks of investors and borrowers for financing deals. Borrowers working with Milken often took a larger loan than necessary and invested the excess in other junk bonds offered by Milken. In the 1980s, Milken financed many of the decade's hostile takeovers with junk bonds, enabling mid-sized companies to make bids for much larger and more established institutions. One of these upstart companies was Danaher, an investment holdings company owned by brothers Steven and Mitchell Rales.[20] The Rales brothers used junk bond financing to fund numerous hostile takeovers, which led to financial success for their company and made them billionaires. Like many of Milken's beneficiaries, they felt a strong sense of loyalty to Michael Milken.

Milken soon became embroiled in controversy as the public became increasingly outraged by the perceived corruption of Wall Street bankers and the greed of corporate raiders. In 1986, U.S. District Attorney Rudolph Giuliani began a two-year investigation of Milken and Drexel Burnham for insider-trading and stock manipulation, which culminated in a ten-year prison sentence for Milken.

20. Colfax Corporation Company History, www.fundinguniverse.com/company-histories/Colfax-Corporation-Company-history.html.

which are expected to yield a lower rate of return than the rate of interest borne by the Notes."

Blasband alleges that the defendants did not invest in "government and other marketable securities," but instead used over $61.9 million of the proceeds to buy highly speculative "junk bonds" offered through Drexel Burnham Lambert Inc. ("Drexel"). Blasband alleges that these junk bonds were bought by Easco because of the Rales brothers' desire to help Drexel at a time when it was under investigation and having trouble selling such bonds. The amended complaint describes the prior business relationship between the Rales brothers and Drexel in the mid-1980s, including Drexel's assistance in the Rales brothers' expansion of Danaher through corporate acquisitions and the role played by Drexel in the Rales brothers' attempt to acquire Interco, Inc. Moreover, Drexel was the underwriter of the Offering of Easco's Notes.

The amended complaint alleges that these investments have declined substantially in value, resulting in a loss to Easco of at least $14 million. Finally, Blasband complains that the Easco and Danaher boards of directors refused to comply with his request for information regarding the investments. . . .

The certified question . . . calls upon this Court to decide whether Blasband's amended complaint establishes that demand is excused under the "substantive law of the State of Delaware." It is therefore necessary for this Court to determine what the applicable "substantive law" is before we can decide whether demand on the Board should be excused. . . .

The stockholder derivative suit is an important . . . feature of corporate governance. In such a suit, a stockholder asserts a cause of action belonging to the corporation. . . . In a double derivative suit, such as the present case, a stockholder of a parent corporation seeks recovery for a cause of action belonging to a subsidiary corporation. . . . Because directors are empowered to manage, or direct the management of, the business and affairs of the corporation, 8 Del. C. §141(a), the right of a stockholder to prosecute a derivative suit is limited to situations where the stockholder has demanded that the directors pursue the corporate claim and they have wrongfully refused to do so or where demand is excused because the directors are incapable of making an impartial decision regarding such litigation. *Levine*, 591 A.2d at 200. Fed. R. Civ. P. 23.1, like Chancery Court Rule 23.1, constitutes the procedural embodiment of this substantive principle of corporation law.[7] . . .

Because . . . derivative suits challenge the propriety of decisions made by directors pursuant to their managerial authority, we have repeatedly held that the stockholder plaintiffs must overcome the powerful presumptions of the business judgment rule before they will be permitted to pursue the derivative claim. . . . Our decision in *Aronson* enunciated the test for determining a derivative plaintiff's compliance with this fundamental threshold obligation: "whether, under the particularized facts alleged, a reasonable doubt is created that: (1) the directors are disinterested and

---

7. The United States Supreme Court has recognized that the demand requirements for a derivative suit are determined by the law of the state of incorporation in *Kamen v. Kemper Fin. Servs., Inc.*, 500 U.S. 90, 111 S. Ct. 1711, 114 L. Ed. 2d 152 (1991). . . .

independent [or] (2) the challenged transaction was otherwise the product of a valid exercise of business judgment." 473 A.2d at 814.

Although these standards are well-established, they cannot be applied in a vacuum. Not all derivative suits fall into the paradigm addressed by *Aronson* and its progeny. The essential predicate for the *Aronson* test is the fact that a decision of the board of directors is being challenged in the derivative suit. . . .

Under the unique circumstances of this case, an analysis of the Board's ability to consider a demand requires a departure here from the standards set forth in *Aronson*. The Board did not approve the transaction which is being challenged by Blasband in this action. In fact, the Danaher directors have made no decision relating to the subject of this derivative suit. Where there is no conscious decision by directors to act or refrain from acting, the business judgment rule has no application. *Aronson*, 473 A.2d at 813. The absence of board action, therefore, makes it impossible to perform the essential inquiry contemplated by *Aronson* — whether the directors have acted in conformity with the business judgment rule in approving the challenged transaction.

Consistent with the context and rationale of the *Aronson* decision, a court should not apply the *Aronson* test for demand futility where the board that would be considering the demand did not make a business decision which is being challenged in the derivative suit. This situation would arise in three principal scenarios: (1) where a business decision was made by the board of a company, but a majority of the directors making the decision have been replaced; (2) where the subject of the derivative suit is not a business decision of the board; and (3) where, as here, the decision being challenged was made by the board of a different corporation.

Instead, it is appropriate in these situations to examine whether the board that would be addressing the demand can impartially consider its merits without being influenced by improper considerations. Thus, a court must determine whether or not the particularized factual allegations of a derivative stockholder complaint create a reasonable doubt that, as of the time the complaint is filed, the board of directors could have properly exercised its independent and disinterested business judgment in responding to a demand. If the derivative plaintiff satisfies this burden, then demand will be excused as futile.

In so holding, we reject the defendants' proposal that, for purposes of this derivative suit and future similar suits, we adopt either a universal demand requirement or a requirement that a plaintiff must demonstrate a reasonable probability of success on the merits. The defendants seek to justify these stringent tests on the need to discourage "strike suits" in situations like the present one. This concern is unfounded.

A plaintiff in a double derivative suit is still required to satisfy the *Aronson* test in order to establish that demand on the subsidiary's board is futile. The *Aronson* test was designed, in part, with the objective of preventing strike suits by requiring derivative plaintiffs to make a threshold showing, through the allegation of particularized facts, that their claims have some merit. *Aronson*, 473 A.2d at 811-12. Moreover, defendants' proposal of requiring demand on the parent board in all double derivative cases, even where a board of directors is interested, is not the appropriate protection against strike suits. While defendants' alternative suggestion of requiring a plaintiff to demonstrate a reasonable probability of success is more closely related to the prevention of strike suits, it is an extremely onerous burden to meet at the pleading stage without the benefit of discovery.[10] Because a plaintiff must satisfy the *Aronson* test in order to show that demand is excused on the subsidiary board, there is no need to create an unduly onerous test for determining demand futility on the parent board simply to protect against strike suits.

In order to determine whether the Board could have impartially considered a demand at the time Blasband's original complaint was filed, it is appropriate to examine the nature of the decision confronting it. A stockholder demand letter would, at a minimum, notify the directors of the nature of the alleged wrongdoing and the identities of the alleged wrong-doers. The subject of the demand in this case would be the alleged breaches of fiduciary duty by the Easco board of directors in connection with Easco's investment in Drexel "junk bonds." The allegations of the amended complaint, which must be accepted as true in this procedural context, claim that the investment was made solely for the benefit of the Rales brothers, who were acting in furtherance of their business relation-ship with Drexel and not with regard to Easco's best interests. Such con-duct, if proven, would constitute a breach of the Easco directors' duty of loyalty. . . .

The task of a board of directors in responding to a stockholder demand letter is a two-step process. First, the directors must determine the best method to inform themselves of the facts relating to the alleged wrongdoing and the considerations, both legal and financial, bearing on a response to the demand. If a factual investigation is required,[11] it must be conducted reasonably and in good faith. . . . Second, the board must weigh the alternatives available to it, including

---

10. Although derivative plaintiffs may believe it is difficult to meet the particularization requirement of *Aronson* because they are not entitled to discovery to assist their compliance with Rule 23.1, see *Levine,* 591 A.2d at 208-10, they have many avenues available to obtain information bearing on the subject of their claims. For example, there are a variety of public sources from which the details of a corporate act may be discovered, including the media and governmental agencies such as the Securities and Exchange Commission. In addition, a stockholder who has met the procedural requirements and has shown a specific proper purpose may use the summary procedure embodied in 8 Del. C. §220 to investigate the possibility of corporate wrongdoing. *Compaq Computer Corp. v. Horton,* Del. Supr., 631 A.2d 1 (1993). Surprisingly, little use has been made of section 220 as an information-gathering tool in the derivative context. Perhaps the problem arises in some cases out of an unseemly race to the court house, chiefly generated by the "first to file" custom seemingly permitting the winner of the race to be named lead counsel. The result has been a plethora of superficial complaints that could not be sustained. . . .

11. In most instances, a factual investigation is appropriate so that the board can be fully informed about the validity, if any, of the claims of wrongdoing contained in the demand letter. Nevertheless, a formal investigation will not always be necessary because the directors may already have sufficient information regarding the subject of the demand to make a decision in response to it. See *Levine,* 591 A.2d at 214. In such a case, the minutes or other writing of the Board may properly reference that information in a summary manner.

the advisability of implementing internal corrective action and commencing legal proceedings. . . . In carrying out these tasks, the board must be able to act free of personal financial interest and improper extraneous influences.[12] We now consider whether the members of the Board could have met these standards. . . .

The members of the Board at the time Blasband filed his original complaint were Steven Rales, Mitchell Rales, Sherman, Ehrlich, Caplin, Kellner, Stephenson, and Lohr. The Rales brothers and Caplin were also members of the Easco board of directors at the time of the alleged wrongdoing. Blasband's amended complaint specifically accuses the Rales brothers of being the motivating force behind the investment in Drexel "junk bonds." The Board would be obligated to determine whether these charges of wrongdoing should be investigated and, if substantiated, become the subject of legal action.

A director is considered interested where he or she will receive a personal financial benefit from a transaction that is not equally shared by the stockholders. Directorial interest also exists where a corporate decision will have a materially detrimental impact on a director, but not on the corporation and the stockholders. In such circumstances, a director cannot be expected to exercise his or her independent business judgment without being influenced by the adverse personal consequences resulting from the decision.

We conclude that the Rales brothers and Caplin must be considered interested in a decision of the Board in response to a demand addressing the alleged wrongdoing described in Blasband's amended complaint. Normally, "the mere threat of personal liability for approving a questioned transaction, standing alone, is insufficient to challenge either the independence or disinterestedness of directors. . . . " *Aronson*, 473 A.2d at 815. Nevertheless, the Third Circuit has already concluded that "Blasband has pleaded facts raising at least a reasonable doubt that the [Easco board's] use of proceeds from the Note Offering was a valid exercise of business judgment." *Blasband I*, 971 F.2d at 1052. This determination is part of the law of the case, *Blasband II*, 979 F.2d at 328, and is therefore binding on this Court. Such determination indicates that the potential for liability is not "a mere threat" but instead may rise to "a substantial likelihood."[13]

Therefore, a decision by the Board to bring suit against the Easco directors, including the Rales brothers and Caplin, could have

12. Where a demand has actually been made, the stockholder making the demand concedes the independence and disinterestedness of a majority of the board to respond. *Spiegel*, 571 A.2d at 777; *Levine*, 591 A.2d at 212-13. In the present context, however, no demand has been made and the Court must determine whether the Board could have considered a demand without being affected by improper influences. See *Aronson*, 473 A.2d at 816.

13. We emphasize that this assessment of potential liability is based solely on the presumed truthfulness of the allegations of Blasband's amended complaint and the Third Circuit's conclusions thereon, all of which must be accepted by this Court in the present procedural posture. No portion of our decision should be interpreted as a prediction regarding the outcome of this litigation since the Easco defendants have not had the opportunity to rebut Blasband's allegations of wrongdoing.

potentially significant financial consequences for those directors. Common sense dictates that, in light of these consequences, the Rales brothers and Caplin have a disqualifying financial interest that disables them from impartially considering a response to a demand by Blasband.

Having determined that the Rales brothers and Caplin would be interested in a decision on Blasband's demand, we must now examine whether the remaining Danaher directors are sufficiently independent to make an impartial decision despite the fact that they are presumptively disinterested. . . . To establish lack of independence, Blasband must show that the directors are "beholden" to the Rales brothers or so under their influence that their discretion would be sterilized. . . . We conclude that the amended complaint alleges particularized facts sufficient to create a reasonable doubt that Sherman and Ehrlich, as members of the Board, are capable of acting independently of the Rales brothers.

Sherman is the President and Chief Executive Officer of Danaher. His salary is approximately $1 million per year. Although Sherman's continued employment and substantial remuneration may not hinge solely on his relationship with the Rales brothers, there is little doubt that Steven Rales' position as Chairman of the Board of Danaher and Mitchell Rales' position as Chairman of its Executive Committee place them in a position to exert considerable influence over Sherman. In light of these circumstances, there is a reasonable doubt that Sherman can be expected to act independently considering his substantial financial stake in maintaining his current offices.

Ehrlich is the President of Wabash National Corp. ("Wabash"). His annual compensation is approximately $300,000 per year. Ehrlich also has two brothers who are vice presidents of Wabash. The Rales brothers are directors of Wabash and own a majority of its stock through an investment partnership they control. As a result, there is a reasonable doubt regarding Ehrlich's ability to act independently since it can be inferred that he is beholden to the Rales brothers in light of his employment.

Therefore, the amended complaint pleads particularized facts raising a reasonable doubt as to the independence of Sherman and Ehrlich. Because of their alleged substantial financial interest in maintaining their employment positions, there is a reasonable doubt that these two directors are able to consider impartially an action that is contrary to the interests of the Rales brothers.

We conclude that, under the "substantive law" of the State of Delaware, the *Aronson* test does not apply in the context of this double derivative suit because the Board was not involved in the challenged transaction. Nevertheless, we do not agree with the defendants' argument that a more stringent test should be applied to deter strike suits. Instead, the appropriate inquiry is whether Blasband's amended complaint raises a reasonable doubt regarding the ability of a majority of the Board to exercise properly its business judgment in a decision on a demand had one been made at the time this action was filed. Based on the existence of a reasonable doubt that the Rales brothers and Caplin would be free of a financial interest in such a decision, and that

Sherman and Ehrlich could act independently in light of their employment with entities affiliated with the Rales brothers, we conclude that the allegations of Blasband's amended complaint establish that DEMAND IS EXCUSED on the Board.

QUESTIONS ON RALES v. BLASBAND

The court describes this case as "special" and distinguishes as inapplicable here earlier statements indicating that it is the independence and good faith of the board that made the decision attacked that is relevant for passing on the validity of an alleged exemption from presuit demand. But is this case special in an important way? Which board's decision should the court review: the decision by the board to approve a disputed transaction or the decision by a later board to refuse to bring or to dismiss the suit? Does the court agree with you?

NOTE AND QUESTIONS ON ABA AND ALI PROPOSALS FOR REFORM

Both the American Bar Association and the American Law Institute have proposed wholesale — and in some respects similar — revisions of the common law screening doctrines developed by the Delaware courts. Read over RMBCA §§7.42-7.44, and compare these provisions to ALI, Principles of Corporate Governance §§7.03, 7.08, and 7.10.

   1.   How would you contrast the common approach of the ALI and the RMBCA to the demand requirement with that of the Delaware courts? Which approach do you prefer?
   2.   How do the approaches of the ALI and the RMBCA differ? Which places more faith in the corporate board?
   3.   Will either reform proposal significantly improve shareholder litigation incentives?

10.4.2   Special Litigation Committees

In contrast to the demand requirement, which is embedded in Rule 23.1 of the Federal Rules of Civil Procedure, there is no basis in positive law for a procedure under which a court, upon the motion of a special committee of disinterested directors, may dismiss a derivative suit that is already under way. Nevertheless, many state courts adopted such a special litigation procedure under the pressure of growing numbers of shareholder suits in the 1970s and 1980s.[21] The special litigation committee is now a standard feature of derivative suit doctrine even though it is not triggered in

---

21. See Robert Clark, Corporate Law, at pp. 645-649.

every case (unlike the demand requirement). Different jurisdictions treated the question differently. The chief divide is between those jurisdictions that follow Delaware's lead in the 1981 case of *Zapata Corp. v. Maldonado*, reviewed below, in giving a role to the court itself to judge the appropriateness of a special litigation committee's decision to dismiss a derivative suit and those jurisdictions, such as New York, that apply a rule that, if the committee is independent and informed, its action is entitled to business judgment deference without any further judicial second-guessing. See *Auerbach v. Bennett*, 393 N.E.2d 994 (N.Y. 1979).

ZAPATA CORP. v. MALDONADO

430 A.2d 779 (Del. 1981)

QUILLEN, J.:

In June, 1975, William Maldonado, a stockholder of Zapata, instituted a derivative action in the Court of Chancery on behalf of Zapata against ten officers and/or directors of Zapata, alleging, essentially, breaches of fiduciary duty. Maldonado did not first demand that the board bring this action, stating instead such demand's futility because all directors were named as defendants and allegedly participated in the acts specified. . . .

By June, 1979, four of the defendant-directors were no longer on the board, and the remaining directors appointed two new outside directors to the board. The board then created an "Independent Investigation Committee" (Committee), composed solely of the two new directors, to investigate Maldonado's actions, as well as a similar derivative action then pending in Texas, and to determine whether the corporation should continue any or all of the litigation. The Committee's determination was stated to be "final, . . . not . . . subject to review by the Board of Directors and . . . in all respects . . . binding upon the Corporation."

Following an investigation, the Committee concluded, in September, 1979, that each action should "be dismissed forthwith as their continued maintenance is inimical to the Company's best interests. . . ."[15] Consequently, Zapata moved for dismissal or summary judgment. . . .

[W]e turn first to the Court of Chancery's conclusions concerning the right of a plaintiff stockholder in a derivative action. We find that its determination that a stockholder, once demand is made and refused, possesses an independent, individual right to continue a derivative suit

---

15. As reasons for dismissal, the Committee stated: "(1) the asserted claims appeared to be without merit; (2) costs of litigation, exacerbated by likelihood of indemnification; (3) wasted senior management time and talents on pursuing litigation; (4) damage to company from publicity; (5) that no material injury appeared to have been done to company; (6) impairment of current director-defendants' ability to manage; (7) the slight possibility of recurrence of violations; (8) lack of personal benefit to current director-defendants from alleged conduct; (9) that certain alleged practices were continuing business practices, intended to be in company's best interests; (10) legal question whether the complaints stated a cause of action; (11) fear of undermining employee morale; (12) adverse effects on the company's relations with employees and suppliers and customers." *Maldonado v. Flynn*, 485 F. Supp. 274, 284 n.35 (S.D.N.Y. 1980). — Eds.

for breaches of fiduciary duty over objection by the corporation, . . . is erroneous. . . . *McKee v. Rogers*, Del. Ch., 156 A. 191 (1931), stated "as a general rule" that "a stockholder cannot be permitted . . . to invade the discretionary field committed to the judgment of the directors and sue in the corporation's behalf when the managing body refuses. This rule is a well settled one." 156 A. at 193.

The *McKee* rule, of course, should not be read so broadly that the board's refusal will be determinative in every instance. Board members, owing a well-established fiduciary duty to the corporation, will not be allowed to cause a derivative suit to be dismissed when it would be a breach of their fiduciary duty. Generally disputes pertaining to control of the suit arise in two contexts.

Consistent with the purpose of requiring a demand, a board decision to cause a derivative suit to be dismissed as detrimental to the company, after demand has been made and refused, will be respected unless it was wrongful.[10] . . . A claim of a wrongful decision not to sue is thus the first exception and the first context of dispute. Absent a wrongful refusal, the stockholder in such a situation simply lacks legal managerial power. . . .

But it cannot be implied that, absent a wrongful board refusal, a stockholder can never have an individual right to initiate an action. For, as is stated in *McKee*, a "well settled" exception exists to the general rule. "[A] stockholder may sue in equity in his derivative right to assert a cause of action in behalf of the corporation, *without prior demand* upon the directors to sue, when it is apparent that a demand would be futile, that the officers are under an influence that sterilizes discretion and could not be proper persons to conduct the litigation." . . . A demand, when required and refused (if not wrongful), terminates a stockholder's legal ability to initiate a derivative action. But where demand is properly excused, the stockholder does possess the ability to initiate the action on his corporation's behalf.

These conclusions, however, do not determine the question before us. Rather, they merely bring us to the question to be decided. . . . : When, if at all, should an authorized board committee be permitted to cause litigation, properly initiated by a derivative stockholder in his own right, to be dismissed? As noted above, a board has the power to choose not to pursue litigation when demand is made upon it, so long as the decision is not wrongful. If the board determines that a suit would be detrimental to the company, the board's determination prevails. Even when demand is excusable, circumstances may arise when continuation of the litigation would not be in the corporation's best interests. Our inquiry is whether, under such circumstances, there is a permissible procedure under §141(a) by which a corporation can rid itself of detrimental litigation. If there is not,

---

10. In other words, when stockholders, after making demand and having their suit rejected, attack the board's decision as improper, the board's decision falls under the "business judgment" rule and will be respected if the requirements of the rule are met. . . . That situation should be distinguished from the instant case, where demand was not made, and the *power* of the board to seek a dismissal, due to disqualification, presents a threshold issue. . . . We recognize that the two contexts can overlap in practice.

a single stockholder in an extreme case might control the destiny of the entire corporation. . . .

Section 141(c) allows a board to delegate all of its authority to a committee. Accordingly, a committee with properly delegated authority would have the power to move for dismissal or summary judgment if the entire board did.

Even though demand was not made in this case and the initial decision of whether to litigate was not placed before the board, Zapata's board, it seems to us, retained all of its corporate power concerning litigation decisions. If Maldonado had made demand on the board in this case, it could have refused to bring suit. Maldonado could then have asserted that the decision not to sue was wrongful and, if correct, would have been allowed to maintain the suit. The board, however, never would have lost its statutory managerial authority. The demand requirement itself evidences that the managerial power is retained by the board. When a derivative plaintiff is allowed to bring suit after a wrongful refusal, the board's authority to choose whether to pursue the litigation is not challenged although its conclusion reached through the exercise of that authority is not respected since it is wrongful. Similarly, Rule 23.1, by excusing demand in certain instances, does not strip the board of its corporate power. It merely saves the plaintiff the expense and delay of making a futile demand resulting in a probable tainted exercise of that authority in a refusal by the board or in giving control of litigation to the opposing side. But the board entity remains empowered under §141(a) to make decisions regarding corporate litigation. The problem is one of member disqualification, not the absence of power in the board.

The corporate power inquiry then focuses on whether the board, tainted by the self-interest of a majority of its members, can legally delegate its authority to a committee of two disinterested directors. We find our statute clearly requires an affirmative answer to this question. As has been noted, under an express provision of the statute, §141(c), a committee can exercise all of the authority of the board to the extent provided in the resolution of the board. . . .

We do not think that the interest taint of the board majority is per se a legal bar to the delegation of the board's power to an independent committee composed of disinterested board members. The committee can properly act for the corporation to move to dismiss derivative litigation that is believed to be detrimental to the corporation's best interest.

Our focus now switches to the Court of Chancery which is faced with a stockholder assertion that a derivative suit, properly instituted, should continue for the benefit of the corporation and a corporate assertion, properly made by a board committee acting with board authority, that the same derivative suit should be dismissed as inimical to the best interests of the corporation.

At the risk of stating the obvious, the problem is relatively simple. If, on the one hand, corporations can consistently wrest bona fide derivative actions away from well-meaning derivative plaintiffs through the use of the committee mechanism, the derivative suit will lose much, if not all, of its generally-recognized effectiveness as an intra-corporate means of policing boards of directors. . . . If, on the other hand, corporations are unable to rid themselves of meritless or harmful litigation and strike suits, the derivative action, created to benefit the corporation, will produce the opposite, unintended result. . . . It thus appears desirable to us to find a balancing point where bona fide stockholder power to bring corporate causes of action cannot be unfairly trampled on by the board of directors, but the corporation can rid itself of detrimental litigation.

[T]he question has been treated by other courts as one of the "business judgment" of the board committee. If a "committee, composed of independent and disinterested directors, conducted a proper review of the matters before it, considered a variety of factors and reached, in good faith, a business judgment that [the] action was not in the best interest of [the corporation]," the action must be dismissed. . . . The issues become solely independence, good faith, and reasonable investigation. The ultimate conclusion of the committee, under that view, is not subject to judicial review.[11] . . .

We are not satisfied, however, that acceptance of the "business judgment" rationale at this stage of derivative litigation is a proper balancing point. While we admit an analogy with a normal case respecting board judgment, it seems to us that there is sufficient risk in the realities of a situation like the one presented in this case to justify caution beyond adherence to the theory of business judgment.

The context here is a suit against directors where demand on the board is excused. We think some tribute must be paid to the fact that the lawsuit was properly initiated. It is not a board refusal case. Moreover, this complaint was filed in June of 1975 and, while the parties undoubtedly would take differing views on the degree of litigation activity, we have to be concerned about the creation of an "Independent Investigation Committee" four years later, after the election of two new outside directors. Situations could develop where such motions could be filed after years of vigorous litigation for reasons unconnected with the merits of the lawsuit.

Moreover, notwithstanding our conviction that Delaware law entrusts the corporate power to a properly authorized committee, we must be mindful that directors are passing judgment on fellow directors in the same corporation and fellow directors, in this instance, who designated them to serve both as directors and committee members. The question naturally arises whether a "there but for the grace of God go I" empathy might not play a role. And the further question arises whether inquiry as to independence, good faith and reasonable investigation is sufficient safeguard against abuse, perhaps subconscious abuse.

. . . There is some analogy to a settlement in that there is a request to terminate litigation without a judicial determination of the merits. . . . "In determining whether or not to approve a proposed settlement of a derivative stockholders' action [when directors are on both sides of the transaction], the Court of Chancery is called upon to exercise its own business judgment." *Neponsit Investment Co. v. Abramson,* Del. Supr., 405 A.2d 97,

---

11. The leading case is *Auerbach v. Bennett,* . . . 393 N.E.2d 994 . . . (1979).

100 (1979) and cases therein cited. In this case, the litigating stockholder plaintiff facing dismissal of a lawsuit properly commenced ought, in our judgment, to have sufficient status for strict Court review. . . .

Whether the Court of Chancery will be persuaded by the exercise of a committee power resulting in a summary motion for dismissal of a derivative action, where a demand has not been initially made, should rest, in our judgment, in the independent discretion of the Court of Chancery. We thus steer a middle course between those cases which yield to the independent business judgment of a board committee and this case as determined below which would yield to unbridled plaintiff stockholder control. In pursuit of the course, we recognize that "[t]he final substantive judgment whether a particular lawsuit should be maintained requires a balance of many factors ethical, commercial, promotional, public relations, employee relations, fiscal as well as legal." *Maldonado v. Flynn,* supra, 485 F. Supp. at 285. But we are content that such factors are not "beyond the judicial reach" of the Court of Chancery which regularly and competently deals with fiduciary relationships, disposition of trust property, approval of settlements and scores of similar problems. We recognize the danger of judicial overreaching but the alternatives seem to us to be outweighed by the fresh view of a judicial outsider. Moreover, if we failed to balance all the interests involved, we would in the name of practicality and judicial economy foreclose a judicial decision on the merits. At this point, we are not convinced that is necessary or desirable.

After an objective and thorough investigation of a derivative suit, an independent committee may cause its corporation to file a pretrial motion to dismiss in the Court of Chancery. The basis of the motion is the best interests of the corporation, as determined by the committee. The motion should include a thorough written record of the investigation and its findings and recommendations. Under appropriate Court supervision, akin to proceedings on summary judgment, each side should have an opportunity to make a record on the motion. As to the limited issues presented by the motion noted below, the moving party should be prepared to meet the normal burden under Rule 56 that there is no genuine issue as to any material fact and that the moving party is entitled to dismiss as a matter of law. The Court should apply a two-step test to the motion.

First, the Court should inquire into the independence and good faith of the committee and the bases supporting its conclusions. Limited discovery may be ordered to facilitate such inquiries. The corporation should have the burden of proving independence, good faith and a reasonable investigation, rather than presuming independence, good faith and reasonableness.[17] If the Court determines either that the committee is not independent or has not shown reasonable bases for its conclusions, or, if the Court is not satisfied for other reasons relating to the process, including but not limited to the good faith of the committee, the Court shall deny the corporation's motion. If, however, the Court is satisfied under   . . .

---

17. Compare *Auerbach v. Bennett,* 393 N.E.2d 994 (1979). Our approach here is analogous to and consistent with the Delaware approach to "interested director" transactions, where the directors, once the transaction is attacked, have the burden of establishing its "intrinsic fairness" to a court's careful scrutiny. . . .

[summary judgment] standards that the committee was independent and showed reasonable bases for good faith findings and recommendations, the Court may proceed, in its discretion, to the next step.

The second step provides, we believe, the essential key in striking the balance between legitimate corporate claims as expressed in a derivative stockholder suit and a corporation's best interests as expressed by an independent investigating committee. The Court should determine, applying its own independent business judgment, whether the motion should be granted.[18] This means, of course, that instances could arise where a committee can establish its independence and sound bases for its good faith decisions and still have the corporation's motion denied. The second step is intended to thwart instances where corporate actions meet the criteria of step one, but the result does not appear to satisfy its spirit, or where corporate actions would simply prematurely terminate a stockholder grievance deserving of further consideration in the corporation's interest. The Court of Chancery of course must carefully consider and weigh how compelling the corporate interest in dismissal is when faced with a non-frivolous lawsuit. The Court of Chancery should, when appropriate, give special consideration to matters of law and public policy in addition to the corporation's best interests.

If the Court's independent business judgment is satisfied, the Court may proceed to grant the motion, subject, of course, to any equitable terms or conditions the Court finds necessary or desirable.

. . . [Reversed and remanded.]

NOTES AND QUESTIONS ON ZAPATA v. MALDONADO

1. If, as *Zapata* holds, a court may second-guess the board's evaluation of a derivative action when demand is excused, why shouldn't a court be able to do the same in cases in which demand was required but the board rejected suit? Academic commentary has generally criticized the "demand required/demand excused" distinction,[22] arguing that courts should be able to exercise their own judgment in both classes of cases. As one might expect, corporate counsel have criticized this distinction in the name of *Auerbach v. Bennett* and have urged that the board's business judgment should prevail in both classes of cases.

2. What elements should be included in an appraisal of the corporation's "best interests" in the second step of the *Zapata* test? In particular, what "matters of law and public policy" — if any — should a court consider in addition to the corporation's economic best interests? Would a court's decision to weigh matters other than the company's economic interests be consistent with viewing the derivative suit as an

18. This step shares some of the same spirit and philosophy of the statement by the Vice Chancellor: "Under our system of law, courts and not litigants should decide the merits of litigation." 413 A.2d at 1263.

22. E.g., Reporters Notes to ALI, Principles of Corporate Governance §7.03 (1994).

asset "belonging to" the corporation? (One former Delaware Chancery Court judge was heard to confide about the second level of *Zapata* inquiry, "I have no business judgment. If I had I wouldn't be a judge.")

3. In the later case of *Kaplan v. Wyatt*, 499 A.2d 1184 (Del. 1988), the Delaware Supreme Court held that whether to proceed to the second step of the *Zapata* test, and how much discovery to accord derivative plaintiffs, lies entirely within the discretion of the Chancery Court.

In re Oracle Corp. Derivative Litigation demonstrates the highly individualized inquiry that the Chancery Court may pursue in probing the independence of a Special Litigation Committee that requests the dismissal of a shareholder derivative action.

IN RE ORACLE CORP. DERIVATIVE LITIGATION

824 A.2d 917 (Del. Ch. 2003)

STRINE, V.C.:

In this opinion, I address the motion of the special litigation committee ("SLC") of Oracle Corporation to terminate this action, "the Delaware Derivative Action," and other such actions pending in the name of Oracle against certain Oracle directors and officers. These actions allege that these Oracle directors engaged in insider trading while in possession of material, non-public information showing that Oracle would not meet the earnings guidance it gave to the market for the third quarter of Oracle's fiscal year 2001. The SLC bears the burden of persuasion on this motion and must convince me that there is no material issue of fact calling into doubt its independence. This requirement is set forth in *Zapata Corp. v. Maldonado* and its progeny....

The question of independence "turns on whether a director is, *for any substantial reason,* incapable of making a decision with only the best interests of the corporation in mind."... That is, the independence test ultimately "focus[es] on impartiality and objectivity."... In this case, the SLC has failed to demonstrate that no material factual question exists regarding its independence....

Ellison is Oracle's Chairman, Chief Executive Officer, and its largest stockholder, owning nearly twenty-five percent of Oracle's voting shares. By virtue of his ownership position, Ellison is one of the wealthiest men in America. By virtue of his managerial position, Ellison has regular access to a great deal of information about how Oracle is performing on a week-to-week basis.

Henley is Oracle's Chief Financial Officer, Executive Vice President, and a director of the corporation. Like Ellison, Henley has his finger on the pulse of Oracle's performance constantly.

Lucas is a director who chairs Oracle's Executive Committee and its Finance and Audit Committee....

Boskin is a director, Chairman of the Compensation Committee, and a member of the Finance and Audit Committee. As with Lucas, Boskin's access to information was limited mostly to historical financials and did not include the week-to-week internal projections and revenue results that Ellison and Henley received.

According to the plaintiffs, each of these Trading Defendants [Ellison, Henley, Lucas and Boskin] possessed material, non-public information demonstrating that Oracle would fail to meet the earnings and revenue guidance it had provided to the market in December 2000. . . . In addition, the plaintiffs contend more generally that the Trading Defendants received material, non-public information that the sales growth for Oracle's other products was slowing in a significant way, which made the attainment of the earnings and revenue guidance extremely difficult. This information grew in depth as the quarter proceeded, as various sources of information that Oracle's top managers relied upon allegedly began to signal weakness in the company's revenues. These signals supposedly included a slowdown in the "pipeline" of large deals that Oracle hoped to close during the quarter and weak revenue growth in the first month of the quarter.

During the time when these disturbing signals were allegedly being sent, the Trading Defendants engaged in the following trades:

- On January 3, 2001, Lucas sold 150,000 shares of Oracle common stock at $30 per share, reaping proceeds of over $4.6 million. These sales constituted 17% of Lucas's Oracle holdings.
- On January 4, 2001, Henley sold one million shares of Oracle stock at approximately $32 per share, yielding over $32.3 million. These sales represented 7% of Henley's Oracle holdings.
- On January 17, 2001, Boskin sold 150,000 shares of Oracle stock at over $33 per share, generating in excess of $5 million. These sales were 16% of Boskin's Oracle holdings.
- From January 22 to January 31, 2001, Ellison sold over 29 million shares at prices above $30 per share, producing over $894 million. Despite the huge proceeds generated by these sales, they constituted the sale of only 2% of Ellison's Oracle holdings.

Into early to mid-February, Oracle allegedly continued to assure the market that it would meet its December guidance. Then, on March 1, 2001, the company announced that rather than posting 12 cents per share in quarterly earnings and 25% license revenue growth as projected, the company's earnings for the quarter would be 10 cents per share and license revenue growth only 6%. The stock market reacted swiftly and negatively to this news, with Oracle's share price dropping as low as $15.75 before closing at $16.88—a 21% decline in one day. These prices were well below the above $30 per share prices at which the Trading Defendants sold in January 2001. . . .

B. THE PLAINTIFFS' CLAIMS IN THE DELAWARE DERIVATIVE ACTION

The plaintiffs make two central claims in their amended complaint in the Delaware Derivative Action. First, the plaintiffs allege that the Trading Defendants breached their duty of loyalty by misappropriating inside information and using it as the basis for trading decisions. This claim rests its legal basis on the venerable case of *Brophy v. Cities Service Co.* Its factual foundation is that the Trading Defendants were aware (or at least possessed information that should have made them aware) that the company would miss its December guidance by a wide margin and used that information to their advantage in selling at artificially inflated prices.

Second, as to the other defendants—who are the members of the Oracle board who did not trade—the plaintiffs allege a *Caremark* violation, in the sense that the board's indifference to the deviation between the company's December guidance and reality was so extreme as to constitute subjective bad faith. . . .

D. THE FORMATION OF THE SPECIAL LITIGATION COMMITTEE

On February 1, 2002, Oracle formed the SLC in order to investigate the Delaware Derivative Action and to determine whether Oracle should press the claims raised by the plaintiffs, settle the case, or terminate it. Soon after its formation, the SLC's charge was broadened to give it the same mandate as to all the pending derivative actions, wherever they were filed.

The SLC was granted full authority to decide these matters without the need for approval by the other members of the Oracle board.

E. THE MEMBERS OF THE SPECIAL LITIGATION COMMITTEE

Two Oracle board members were named to the SLC. Both of them joined the Oracle board on October 15, 2001, more than a half a year after Oracle's 3Q FY 2001 closed. The SLC members also share something else: both are tenured professors at Stanford University.

Professor Hector Garcia-Molina is Chairman of the Computer Science Department at Stanford and holds the Leonard Bosack and Sandra Lerner Professorship in the Computer Science and Electrical Engineering Departments at Stanford. . . .

The other SLC member, Professor Joseph Grundfest, is the W.A. Franke Professor of Law and Business at Stanford University. He directs the University's well-known Directors' College[8] and the Roberts Program in Law, Business, and Corporate Governance at the Stanford Law School. Grundfest is also the principal investigator for the Law School's Securities Litigation Clearinghouse. Immediately before coming to Stanford,

---

8. In the interests of full disclosure, I spoke at the Directors' College in spring 2002.

Grundfest served for five years as a Commissioner of the Securities and Exchange Commission. Like Garcia-Molina, Grundfest's appointment at Stanford was a homecoming, because he obtained his law degree and performed significant post-graduate work in economics at Stanford. . . .

For their services, the SLC members were paid $250 an hour, a rate below that which they could command for other activities, such as consulting or expert witness testimony. Nonetheless, during the course of their work, the SLC members became concerned that (arguably scandal-driven) developments in the evolving area of corporate governance as well as the decision in *Telxon v. Meyerson*, . . . might render the amount of their compensation so high as to be an argument against their independence. Therefore, Garcia-Molina and Grundfest agreed to give up any SLC-related compensation if their compensation was deemed by this court to impair their impartiality.

The SLC members were recruited to the board primarily by defendant Lucas, with help from defendant Boskin. . . . The wooing of them began in the summer of 2001. Before deciding to join the Oracle board, Grundfest, in particular, did a good deal of due diligence. His review included reading publicly available information, among other things, the then-current complaint in the Federal Class Action.

The SLC's investigation was, by any objective measure, extensive. The SLC reviewed an enormous amount of paper and electronic records. SLC counsel interviewed seventy witnesses, some of them twice. SLC members participated in several key interviews, including the interviews of the Trading Defendants.

Importantly, the interviewees included all the senior members of Oracle's management most involved in its projection and monitoring of the company's financial performance, including its sales and revenue growth. These interviews combined with a special focus on the documents at the company bearing on these subjects, including e-mail communications.

The SLC also asked the plaintiffs in the various actions to identify witnesses the Committee should interview. The Federal Class Action plaintiffs identified ten such persons and the Committee interviewed all but one, who refused to cooperate. The Delaware Derivative Action plaintiffs and the other derivative plaintiffs declined to provide the SLC with any witness list or to meet with the SLC.

During the course of the investigation, the SLC met with its counsel thirty-five times for a total of eighty hours. In addition to that, the SLC members, particularly Professor Grundfest, devoted many more hours to the investigation.

In the end, the SLC produced an extremely lengthy Report totaling 1,110 pages (excluding appendices and exhibits) that concluded that Oracle should not pursue the plaintiffs' claims against the Trading Defendants or any of the other Oracle directors serving during the 3Q FY 2001. . . . I endeavor a rough attempt to capture the essence of the Report in understandable terms, . . .

. . . [T]he SLC concluded that even a hypothetical Oracle executive who possessed all information regarding the company's performance in December and January of 3Q FY 2001 would not have possessed material, non-public information that the company would fail to meet the earnings and revenue guidance it provided the market in December. Although there were hints of potential weakness in Oracle's revenue growth, especially starting in mid-January 2001, there was no reliable information indicating that the company would fall short of the mark, and certainly not to the extent that it eventually did.

Consistent with its Report, the SLC moved to terminate this litigation. The plaintiffs were granted discovery focusing on three primary topics: the independence of the SLC, the good faith of its investigative efforts, and the reasonableness of the bases for its conclusion that the lawsuit should be terminated. Additionally, the plaintiffs received a large volume of documents comprising the materials that the SLC relied upon in preparing its Report.

III. THE APPLICABLE PROCEDURAL STANDARD

In order to prevail on its motion to terminate the Delaware Derivative Action, the SLC must persuade me that: (1) its members were independent; (2) that they acted in good faith; and (3) that they had reasonable bases for their recommendations. If the SLC meets that burden, I am free to grant its motion or may, in my discretion, undertake my own examination of whether Oracle should terminate and permit the suit to proceed if I, in my oxymoronic judicial "business judgment," conclude that procession is in the best interests of the company. This two-step analysis comes, of course, from *Zapata*. . . .

. . . I begin with certain features of the record — as I read it — that are favorable to the SLC. Initially, I am satisfied that neither of the SLC members is compromised by a fear that support for the procession of this suit would endanger his ability to make a nice living. Both of the SLC members are distinguished in their fields and highly respected. Both have tenure, which could not have been stripped from them for making a determination that this lawsuit should proceed.

Nor have the plaintiffs developed evidence that either Grundfest or Garcia-Molina have fundraising responsibilities at Stanford. . . .

Defendant Michael J. Boskin is the T.M. Friedman Professor of Economics at Stanford University. During the Administration of President George H.W. Bush, Boskin occupied the coveted and important position of Chairman of the President's Council of Economic Advisors. He returned to Stanford after this government service, continuing a teaching career there that had begun many years earlier.

During the 1970s, Boskin taught Grundfest when Grundfest was a Ph.D. candidate. Although Boskin was not Grundfest's advisor and although they do not socialize, the two have remained in contact over the years, speaking occasionally about matters of public policy. . . .

As noted in the SLC Report, the SLC members admitted knowing that Lucas was a contributor to Stanford. They also acknowledged that he had donated $50,000 to Stanford Law School in appreciation for Grundfest having given a speech at his request. About half of the proceeds were allocated for use by Grundfest in his research.

But Lucas's ties with Stanford are far, far richer than the SLC Report lets on. To begin, Lucas is a Stanford alumnus, having obtained both his undergraduate and graduate degrees there. By any measure, he has been a very loyal alumnus.

In showing that this is so, I start with a matter of some jousting between the SLC and the plaintiffs. Lucas's brother, Richard, died of cancer and by way of his will established a foundation. Lucas became Chairman of the Foundation and serves as a director along with his son, a couple of other family members, and some non-family members. A principal object of the Foundation's beneficence has been Stanford. The Richard M. Lucas Foundation has given $11.7 million to Stanford since its 1981 founding. Among its notable contributions, the Foundation funded the establishment of the Richard M. Lucas Center for Magnetic Resonance Spectroscopy and Imaging at Stanford's Medical School. Donald Lucas was a founding member and lead director of the Center.

The SLC Report did not mention the Richard M. Lucas Foundation or its grants to Stanford. In its briefs on this motion, the SLC has pointed out that Donald Lucas is one of nine directors at the Foundation and does not serve on its Grant Review Committee. Nonetheless, the SLC does not deny that Lucas is Chairman of the board of the Foundation and that the board approves all grants.

Lucas's connections with Stanford as a contributor go beyond the Foundation, however. From his own personal funds, Lucas has contributed $4.1 million to Stanford, a substantial percentage of which has been donated within the last half-decade. . . . From these undisputed facts, it is inarguable that Lucas is a very important alumnus of Stanford and a generous contributor to [the school]. . . .

With these facts in mind, it remains to enrich the factual stew further, by considering defendant Ellison's ties to Stanford. There can be little doubt that Ellison is a major figure in the community in which Stanford is located. The so-called Silicon Valley has generated many success stories, among the greatest of which is that of Oracle and its leader, Ellison. One of the wealthiest men in America, Ellison is a major figure in the nation's increasingly important information technology industry. Given his wealth, Ellison is also in a position to make—and, in fact, he has made—major charitable contributions.

Some of the largest of these contributions have been made through the Ellison Medical Foundation, which makes grants to universities and laboratories to support biomedical research relating to aging and infectious diseases. Ellison is the sole director of the Foundation. Although he does not serve on the Foundation's Scientific Advisory Board that sifts through grant applications, he has reserved the right—as the Foundation's sole director—to veto any grants, a power he has not yet used but which he felt it important to retain. The Scientific Advisory Board is comprised of distinguished physicians and scientists from many institutions, but not including Stanford.

Although it is not represented on the Scientific Advisory Board, Stanford has nonetheless been the beneficiary of grants from the Ellison Medical Foundation — to the tune of nearly $10 million in paid or pledged funds. Although the Executive Director of the Foundation asserts by way of an affidavit that the grants are awarded to specific researchers and may be taken to another institution if the researcher leaves, . . . the grants are conveyed under contracts between the Foundation and Stanford itself and purport by their terms to give Stanford the right (subject to Foundation approval) to select a substitute principal investigator if the original one becomes unavailable. . . .

During the time Ellison has been CEO of Oracle, the company itself has also made over $300,000 in donations to Stanford. Not only that, when Oracle established a generously endowed educational foundation — the Oracle Help Us Help Foundation — to help further the deployment of educational technology in schools serving disadvantaged populations, it named Stanford as the "appointing authority," which gave Stanford the right to name four of the Foundation's seven directors. . . . Stanford's acceptance reflects the obvious synergistic benefits that might flow to, for example, its School of Education from the University's involvement in such a foundation, as well as the possibility that its help with the Foundation might redound to the University's benefit when it came time for Oracle to consider making further donations to institutions of higher learning.

Taken together, these facts suggest that Ellison (when considered as an individual and as the key executive and major stockholder of Oracle) had, at the very least, been involved in several endeavors of value to Stanford.

The SLC contends that even together, these facts regarding the ties among Oracle, the Trading Defendants, Stanford, and the SLC members do not impair the SLC's independence. In so arguing, the SLC places great weight on the fact that none of the Trading Defendants have the practical ability to deprive either Grundfest or Garcia-Molina of their current positions at Stanford. Nor, given their tenure, does Stanford itself have any practical ability to punish them for taking action adverse to Boskin, Lucas, or Ellison — each of whom, as we have seen, has contributed (in one way or another) great value to Stanford as an institution. As important, neither Garcia-Molina nor Grundfest are part of the official fundraising apparatus at Stanford; thus, it is not their on-the-job duty to be solicitous of contributors, and fundraising success does not factor into their treatment as professors.

In so arguing, the SLC focuses on the language of previous opinions of this court and the Delaware Supreme Court that indicates that a director is not independent only if he is dominated and controlled by an interested party, such as a Trading Defendant. . . .

More subtly, the SLC argues that university professors simply are not inhibited types, unwilling to make tough decisions even as to fellow professors and large contributors. What is tenure about if not to provide professors with intellectual freedom, even in non-traditional roles such as special litigation committee members? No less ardently—but with no record evidence that reliably supports its ultimate point—the SLC contends that Garcia-Molina and Grundfest are extremely distinguished in their fields and were not, in fact, influenced by the facts identified heretofore. Indeed, the SLC argues, how could they have been influenced by many of these facts when they did not learn them until the post-Report discovery process? If it boils down to the simple fact that both share with Boskin the status of a Stanford professor, how material can this be when there are 1,700 others who also occupy the same position?

The plaintiffs confronted these arguments with less nuance than was helpful. Rather than rest their case on the multiple facts I have described, the plaintiffs chose to emphasize barely plausible constructions of the evidence, such as that Grundfest was lying when he could not recall being asked to participate in the Ellison Scholars Program. From these more extreme arguments, however, one can distill a reasoned core that emphasizes what academics might call the "thickness" of the social and institutional connections among Oracle, the Trading Defendants, Stanford, and the SLC members. . . . Taken in their totality, the plaintiffs contend, these connections simply constitute too great a bias-producing factor for the SLC to meet its burden to prove its independence.

———————————

Having framed the competing views of the parties, it is now time to decide.

I begin with an important reminder: the SLC bears the burden of proving its independence. It must convince me.

. . . Delaware law should not be based on a reductionist view of human nature that simplifies human motivations on the lines of the least sophisticated notions of the law and economics movement. *Homo sapiens* is not merely *homo economicus.* We may be thankful that an array of other motivations exist that influence human behavior; not all are any better than greed or avarice, think of envy, to name just one. But also think of motives like love, friendship, and collegiality, think of those among us who direct their behavior as best they can on a guiding creed or set of moral values. . . .

Nor should our law ignore the social nature of humans. To be direct, corporate directors are generally the sort of people deeply enmeshed in social institutions. Such institutions have norms, expectations that, explicitly and implicitly, influence and channel the behavior of those who participate in their operation. . . . Some things are 'just not done,'' or only at a cost, which might not be so severe as a loss of position, but may involve a loss of standing in the institution. In being appropriately sensitive to this factor, our law also cannot assume—absent some proof of the point—that corporate directors are, as a general matter, persons of unusual social bravery, who operate heedless to the inhibitions that social norms generate for ordinary folk.

In examining whether the SLC has met its burden to demonstrate that there is no material dispute of fact regarding its independence, the court must bear in mind the function of special litigation committees under our jurisprudence. . . .

Special litigation committees are permitted as a last chance for a corporation to control a derivative claim in circumstances when a majority of its directors cannot impartially consider a demand. By vesting the power of the board to determine what to do with the suit in a committee of independent directors, a corporation may retain control over whether the suit will proceed, so long as the committee meets the standard set forth in *Zapata.*

In evaluating the independence of a special litigation committee, this court must take into account the extraordinary importance and difficulty of such a committee's responsibility. It is, I daresay, easier to say no to a friend, relative, colleague, or boss who seeks assent for an act *(e.g.,* a transaction) that has not yet occurred than it would be to cause a corporation to sue that person. . . .

The difficulty of making this decision is compounded in the special litigation committee context because the weight of making the moral judgment necessarily falls on less than the full board. A small number of directors feels the moral gravity—and social pressures—of this duty alone. . . .

I conclude that the SLC has not met its burden to show the absence of a material factual question about its independence. I find this to be the case because the ties among the SLC, the Trading Defendants, and Stanford are so substantial that they cause reasonable doubt about the SLC's ability to impartially consider whether the Trading Defendants should face suit. . . . In so concluding, I necessarily draw on a general sense of human nature. It may be that Grundfest is a very special person who is capable of putting these kinds of things totally aside. But the SLC has not provided evidence that that is the case. In this respect, it is critical to note that I do not infer that Grundfest would be less likely to recommend suit against Boskin than someone without these ties. Human nature being what it is, it is entirely possible that Grundfest would in fact be tougher on Boskin than he would on someone with whom he did not have such connections. The inference I draw is subtly, but importantly, different. What I infer is that a person in Grundfest's position would find it difficult to assess Boskin's conduct without pondering his own association with Boskin and their mutual affiliations. Although these connections might produce bias in either a tougher or laxer direction, the key inference is that these connections would be on the mind of a person in Grundfest's position, putting him in the position of either causing serious legal action to be brought against a person with whom he shares several connections (an awkward thing) or not doing so (and risking being seen as having engaged in favoritism toward his old professor . . .).

The same concerns also exist as to Lucas. . . . [F]or both Grundfest and Garcia-Molina, service on the SLC demanded that they consider whether an extremely generous and influential Stanford alumnus should be sued by Oracle for insider trading. Although they were not responsible for fundraising, as sophisticated professors they undoubtedly are aware of how important large contributors are to Stanford, and they share in the benefits that come from serving at a university with a rich endowment. A reasonable professor giving any thought to the matter would obviously consider the effect his decision might have on the University's relationship with Lucas, it being (one hopes) sensible to infer that a professor of reasonable collegiality and loyalty cares about the well-being of the institution he serves. . . .

In view of the ties involving Boskin and Lucas alone, I would conclude that the SLC has failed to meet its burden on the independence question. The tantalizing facts about Ellison merely reinforce this conclusion. The SLC, of course, argues that Ellison is not a large benefactor of Stanford personally, that Stanford has demonstrated its independence of him by rejecting his child for admission, and that, in any event, the SLC was ignorant of any negotiations between Ellison and Stanford about a large contribution. For these reasons, the SLC says, its ability to act independently of Ellison is clear.

I find differently. The notion that anyone in Palo Alto can accuse Ellison of insider trading without harboring some fear of social awkwardness seems a stretch. That being said, I do not mean to imply that the mere fact that Ellison is worth tens of billions of dollars and is the key force behind a very important social institution in Silicon Valley disqualifies all persons who live there from being independent of him. Rather, it is merely an acknowledgement of the simple fact that accusing such a significant person in that community of such serious wrongdoing is no small thing.

Before closing, it is necessary to address two concerns. The first is the undeniable awkwardness of opinions like this one. By finding that there exists too much doubt about the SLC's independence for the SLC to meet its *Zapata* burden, I make no finding about the subjective good faith of the SLC members, both of whom are distinguished academics at one of this nation's most prestigious institutions of higher learning. . . . Nothing in this record leads me to conclude that either of the SLC members acted out of any conscious desire to favor the Trading Defendants or to do anything other than discharge their duties with fidelity. But that is not the purpose of the independence inquiry.

That inquiry recognizes that persons of integrity and reputation can be compromised in their ability to act without bias when they must make a decision adverse to others with whom they share material affiliations. To conclude that the Oracle SLC was not independent is not a conclusion that the two accomplished professors who comprise it are not persons of good faith and moral probity, it is solely to conclude that they were not situated to act with the required degree of impartiality. *Zapata* requires independence to ensure that stockholders do not have to rely upon special litigation committee members who must put aside personal considerations that are ordinarily influential in daily behavior in making the already difficult decision to accuse fellow directors of serious wrongdoing.

The SLC's motion to terminate is DENIED. IT IS SO ORDERED.

NOTES & QUESTIONS ON IN RE ORACLE

1. The plaintiffs subsequently dropped their claims against defendants Lucas and Boskin. In November 2004, Vice Chancellor Strine granted summary judgment for defendants Ellison and Henley[23] — thereby reaching precisely the same conclusion on the merits of the plaintiffs' case that Grundfest and Garcia-Molinas had reached more than a year earlier. With the benefit of hindsight, then, does this conclusion call into question the Court's reasoning in allowing the case to proceed?

2. Consider the problem that a board now faces in the aftermath of *In re Oracle*. *Zapata* makes clear that the power to appoint an SLC comes from DGCL §141(c), which means that the SLC must consist entirely of directors. But wouldn't any current director inevitably consider the "'thickness' of the social and institutional connections" between themselves and the defendant directors? And if so, would a board be forced to add new directors whenever it wished to establish an SLC? How would you advise a board that wanted to establish an SLC without expanding, but also staying within the constraints imposed by *In re Oracle*?

3. In *Beam v. Martha Stewart*, considered already in Chapter 8 in the context of the board's duty to monitor, plaintiffs claimed that demand was futile against the board of Martha Stewart Omnimedia (MSO) for claims arising from Stewart's trading in ImClone stock, because a majority of the MSO board was not independent of Martha Stewart. Chancellor Chandler, applying the test for demand futility articulated in *Rales v. Blasband*, held that demand was not excused, even though there were "relationships," "friendships," and "inter-connections" between Martha Stewart and the other MSO board members reminiscent of *In re Oracle*.[24] The Delaware Supreme Court affirmed, and, noting the apparent tension between *Beam* and *Oracle*, drew a distinction between the SLC context and the demand excused context: "Unlike the demand-excusal context, where the board is presumed to be independent, the SLC has the burden of establishing its own independence by a yardstick that must be 'like Caesar's wife' — 'above reproach.'"[25] As a policy matter, do you find this distinction justifiable?

HOW DOES THE COURT EXERCISE ITS BUSINESS JUDGMENT?

What does it mean to exercise business judgment about whether litigation should go forward? Is litigation "like" an investment in a factory? And does the business judgment of a court resemble the business judgment of a corporate manager, or must the court weigh matters of public interest as

---

23. In re Oracle Corp. Derivative Litigation, C.A. No. 18751 (Nov. 24, 2004).
24. Beam v. Martha Stewart, 833 A.2d 961, 984 (Del. Ch. 2003).
25. Beam v. Martha Stewart, 845 A.2d 1040, 1055 (Del. 2004).

well as the private interest of the firm? Consider the following excerpt from a well-known case.

JOY v. NORTH

692 F.2d 880 (2d Cir. 1982)

[In a diversity case, the court predicted that Connecticut would adopt the *Zapata* approach to derivative suits and, exercising its business judgment, rejected a special litigation committee's motion to dismiss.]

WINTER, J.:

[The dissent] is correct in anticipating difficulties in judicial review of the recommendations of special litigation committees. These difficulties are not new, however, but have confronted every court which has scrutinized the fairness of corporate transactions involving a conflict of interest.

Moreover, the difficulties courts face in evaluation of business decisions are considerably less in the case of recommendations of special litigation committees. The relevant decision—whether to continue litigation—is at hand and the danger of deceptive hindsight simply does not exist. Moreover, it can hardly be argued that terminating a lawsuit is an area in which courts have no special aptitude. Citytrust's Special Litigation Committee concluded that there was "no reasonable possibility" that 23 outside defendants would be held liable. A court is not ill-equipped to review the merits of that conclusion. Even when the Committee recommendation arises from the fear of further damage to the corporation, for example, the distraction of key personnel, the cost of complying with discovery, and the possible indemnification of defendants out of the corporate treasury, courts are not on unfamiliar terrain. The rule we predict Connecticut would establish emphasizes matters such as probable liability and extent of recovery. For these reasons we hold that the wide discretion afforded directors under the business judgment rule does not apply when a special litigation committee recommends dismissal of a suit. . . .

In cases such as the present one, the burden is on the moving party, as in motions for summary judgment generally, to demonstrate that the action is more likely than not to be against the interests of the corporation. This showing is to be based on the underlying data developed in the course of discovery and of the committee's investigation and the committee's reasoning, not simply its naked conclusions. The weight to be given certain evidence is to be determined by conventional analysis, such as whether testimony is under oath and subject to cross-examination. Finally, the function of the court's review is to determine the balance of probabilities as to likely future benefit to the corporation, not to render a decision on the merits, fashion the appropriate legal principles or resolve issues of credibility. Where the legal rule is unclear and the likely evidence in conflict, the court need only weigh the uncertainties, not resolve them. The court's function is thus not unlike a lawyer's determining what a case is "worth" for purposes of settlement.

Where the court determines that the likely recoverable damages discounted by the probability of a finding of liability are less than the costs to the corporation in continuing the action, it should dismiss the case. The costs which may properly be taken into account are attorney's fees and other out-of-pocket expenses related to the litigation and time spent by corporate personnel preparing for and participating in the trial. The court should also weigh indemnification which is mandatory under corporate bylaws, private contract or Connecticut law, discounted of course by the probability of liability for such sums. We believe indemnification the corporation may later pay as a matter of discretion should not be taken into account since it is an avoidable cost. The existence or non-existence of insurance should not be considered in the calculation of costs, since premiums have previously been paid. The existence of insurance is relevant to the calculation of potential benefits.

Where, having completed the above analysis, the court finds a likely net return to the corporation which is not substantial in relation to shareholder equity, it may take into account two other items as costs. First, it may consider the impact of distraction of key personnel by continued litigation. Second, it may take into account potential lost profits which may result from the publicity of a trial.

Judicial scrutiny of special litigation committee recommendations should thus be limited to a comparison of the direct costs imposed upon the corporation by the litigation with the potential benefits. We are mindful that other less direct costs may be incurred, such as a negative impact on morale and upon the corporate image. Nevertheless, we believe that such factors, with the two exceptions noted, should not be taken into account. Quite apart from the elusiveness of attempting to predict such effects, they are quite likely to be directly related to the degree of wrongdoing, a spectacular fraud being generally more newsworthy and damaging to morale than a mistake in judgment as to the strength of consumer demand. . . .

CARDAMONE, Cir. J. dissented in part:

[T]he majority goes beyond [*Zapata*] by requiring that the court *must* proceed to apply its own business judgment, rather than leaving the decision to resort to the second step within the trial court's discretion. . . .

Under [*Zapata*'s] two-step analysis . . . unanswered questions abound. For example, . . . under what circumstances can the trial court conclude that the director's decision [has not satisfied *Zapata*'s criteria]; will evidence be considered by the court that was not before the independent committee; in the exercise of its "business judgment" will the court consider facts not in the record; will the court need to appoint its own experts?

The majority proposes a calculus in an attempt to resolve additional issues engendered by its analysis. This calculus is so complicated, indefinite and subject to judicial caprice as to be unworkable. For example, how is a court to determine the inherently speculative costs of future attorneys' fees and expenses related to litigation, time spent by corporate personnel preparing for trial, and mandatory indemnification "discounted of course by the probability of liability for such sums." How is a court to quantify corporate goodwill, corporate morale and "the distraction of key personnel" in cases in which it "finds a likely net return to the corporation which is not substantial in relation to shareholder equity?" Should a court also take into account the potential adverse impact of continuing litigation upon the corporation's ability to finance its operations? Should future costs be discounted to present value and, if so, at what rate? Must the income tax ramifications of expected future costs be considered and, if so, how? This veritable Pandora's box of unanswered questions raises more problems than it solves.

Even more fundamentally unsound is the majority's underlying premise that judges are equipped to make business judgments. It is a truism that judges really are not equipped either by training or experience to make business judgments. . . . Reasons of practicality and good sense strongly suggest that business decisions be left to businessmen. Whether to pursue litigation is not a judicial decision, rather, it is a business choice.

My colleagues . . . contend that director committees simply cannot be expected to act independently. Where a special litigation committee does not act independently and in good faith, its decision to terminate derivative litigation will not survive judicial scrutiny under *Auerbach*. Thus the contention that director committees will not act independently and in good faith does not support the conclusion that the *Auerbach* standard is inadequate to protect shareholder rights. [In addition, my colleagues argue] that limiting judicial review to the *Auerbach* test would effectively eliminate the fiduciary obligations of directors and officers because the sole method of enforcing these obligations, shareholder derivative suits, could be eliminated upon the recommendation of persons appointed by the officers and directors whose conduct is being challenged. Even if shareholder derivative suits are the only effective method of enforcing the fiduciary obligations of officers and directors, this second objection to *Auerbach* again assumes that director committees reviewing derivative litigation will not act independently and in good faith. Since *Auerbach* will require judicial intervention if the director committees do not so act this second objection to the use of the *Auerbach* standard is similarly without merit. . . .

QUESTIONS FOLLOWING JOY v. NORTH

1. How does the court's exercise of business judgment in *Joy* compare to the calculus that a 100 percent shareholder (a "sole owner") might use in deciding whether to sue after discovering managerial misconduct? How does the *Joy* rule compare to the calculus of an absolutely loyal and dispassionate director charged with considering whether to sue after discovering managerial misconduct?

2. The *Joy* dissent argues that the decision to pursue a derivative claim is a business decision for the board, just like any other business decision that it might make. Is that right? For a loyal board, is this decision no different than, say, a decision to build a new widget factory?

3. Does the majority in *Joy* disagree that the litigation decision is fundamentally an investment decision?

4. How does *Joy*'s balancing test compare to the considerations that a Delaware court may weigh in applying the second step of the *Zapata* two-step test to a board's motion to dismiss a derivative action? Which test is the more restrictive?

——————————————

For board skeptics and reformers, an alternative to the *Zapata* rule might be a more rigorous effort to ensure the independence of the directors who sit on the special litigation committee. Consider Michigan's efforts in this regard.

MICHIGAN COMPILED LAWS

§450.1107

"Independent director" means a director who meets all of the following requirements:

(a) Is elected by the shareholders.

(b) Is designated as an independent director by the board or the shareholders.

(c) Has at least [five] years of business, legal, or financial experience, or other equivalent experience. . . .

(d) Is not and during the [three] years prior to being designated as an independent director has not been any of the following:

(i) An officer or employee of the corporation or any affiliate of the corporation.

(ii) Engaged in any business transaction for profit or series of transactions for profit, including banking, legal, or consulting services, involving more than $10,000.00 with the corporation or any affiliate of the corporation.

(iii) An affiliate, executive officer, general partner, or member of the immediate family of any person that had the status or engaged in a transaction described in subparagraph (i) or (ii). . . .

(f) Does not have an aggregate of more than [three] years of service as a director of the corporation, whether or not as an independent director.

§495

(1) The court shall dismiss a derivative proceeding if, on motion by the corporation, the court finds that [one] of the groups specified in subsection (2) has made a determination in good faith after conducting a reasonable

investigation . . . that the maintenance of the derivative proceeding is not in the best interests of the corporation. . . . If the determination is made . . . [by a court-appointed panel or by Michigan independent directors], the plaintiff shall have the burden of proving that the determination was not made in good faith or that the investigation was not reasonable.

10.5 SETTLEMENT AND INDEMNIFICATION

10.5.1 Settlement by Class Representatives

The parties are strongly driven to settle in the typical derivative (or class action) suit. From the perspective of plaintiffs' attorneys, litigation becomes increasingly costly as a suit progresses through discovery, and the prospect of a trial imposes the further risk that all suit costs will be lost in the end. Similar considerations shape the dynamics of the defendants. Directors will generally have a right under a company's bylaws to the indemnification of reasonable defense costs, including any amounts paid if the action settles. By contrast, if an action goes to trial, there is a risk of personal liability that can be indemnified only with court approval. Thus, trial imposes an uncompensated risk on defendants that settlement avoids. Similarly, a director's directors and officers (D&O) insurance coverage will typically exclude losses that arise from "fraud" or self-dealing, while settlement allows the proceeds of the D&O insurance policy to be used.

DGCL §145(b) accords a corporation broad latitude to indemnify corporate officers, directors, and agents for costs in derivative and share-holder suits. Upon a favorable determination of disinterested board members or outside counsel, a director or officer can be indemnified for any payment made to settle a derivative action as well as for all of her litigation expenses. In the very rare event that the litigation is not settled prior to adjudication, the corporation cannot indemnify officers and directors who are "adjudged to be liable to [it] — except to the extent authorized by the Court of Chancery." However, it can purchase liability insurance for its officers, directors, and agents to cover claims arising out of their status with the corporation, "whether or not the corporation would have the power to indemnify [them] against such liability." DGCL §145(g).

In practice, virtually all public corporations purchase D&O insurance. The standard policy divides into two parts: The first part provides coverage to the corporation for its expenses in defending and indemnifying its officers and directors; the second part provides coverage directly to officers and directors when the corporation does not or cannot indemnify them. In addition, the standard D&O policy excludes criminal penalties and civil recoveries for fraud or fiduciary breach that resulted in a personal gain for officers and directors.[26] A scholarly analysis of several hundred shareholder

---

26. See generally John F. Olsen & Josiah O. Hatch, Director and Officer Liability: Indemnification and Insurance (1991).

suits finds (1) that most suits settle and lead to an award of attorneys' fees; (2) that, of the settling suits, about half result in monetary recovery; (3) that D&O insurance pays for most or all of the settlement fund in most cases; and (4) that officers and directors never — in this large sample — face out-of-pocket costs.[27]

Settlement procedures in derivative actions are largely determined by the rules of civil procedure. After the lawyers negotiate a settlement, the court approves the form of the notice of settlement that is conveyed to the shareholders. This notice must describe the claims, the defenses, the settlement consideration, the attorneys' fees sought, and the nature of the release that the settlement gives to the defendants as well as the time and place of a hearing on the fairness of the settlement. While shareholders are thus formally invited to participate in considering the settlement's merits, few ever do in public companies (which is hardly surprising, since shareholder stakes are usually small). Occasionally, however, an institutional shareholder may object to the terms of a settlement or, more likely, to the size of an attorneys' fee application.

10.5.2   Settlement by Special Committee

In theory, committees of independent directors might be employed not only to consider whether derivative actions ought to be dismissed but also to take control of derivative suits in order to settle them. In practice, the use of independent committees is rare. Nevertheless, it happens, and sometimes it succeeds. Consider the following case.

CARLTON INVESTMENTS v. TLC BEATRICE INTERNATIONAL HOLDINGS, INC.

1997 WL 305829 (Del. Ch. May 30, 1997)

ALLEN, C.:

Pending is a motion pursuant to Chancery Court Rule 23.1 for approval of a Special Litigation Committee ("SLC") proposed settlement of a derivative action on behalf of TLC Beatrice International Holdings, Inc., ("TLC Beatrice"). The action was brought on January 4, 1995, by Carlton Investments ("Carlton"), a very substantial stockholder of TLC Beatrice. The complaint alleged that certain past and present directors and officers of TLC Beatrice had engaged in conduct constituting breach of fiduciary duty, corporate waste, fraud, and conspiracy. At the core of this action is the claim that individual defendants breached their fiduciary duties in connection with the board's approval of an approximately $19.5 million compensation package awarded to the company's former CEO, Reginald F. Lewis, on

---

27. See Roberta Romano, *The Shareholder Suit: Litigation Without Foundation?*, 7 J. L. Econ. & Org. 55 (1991).

REGINALD LEWIS

Reginald Lewis's intense determination and strong work ethic were evident even during his youth. As a high school student he vowed not to be a "burden" to his working-class family and worked long hours after school in addition to starring on the football team and diligently reading business publications such as *The Wall Street Journal*. Despite his efforts, he was told by a teacher that "he would never amount to anything more than a carpenter."[28] The prejudice he experienced as an African-American in racially segregated Baltimore, and throughout his life, only intensified his determination to reach his lofty goals.

He attended Virginia State College on a football scholarship and graduated from Harvard Law School in 1968. After two years in a large New York law firm, he left to form his own law firm specializing in providing services to the many African-American owned businesses in New York. This was a risky step for a young lawyer, but his rigorous work ethic, strong networking skills, and keen business instincts made his firm a financial success. He expanded to include clients from across the country and became involved in increasingly complex business deals. In 1984, Lewis acquired McCall Pattern Company in a highly leveraged transaction. His innovative ideas, such as using idle equipment to produce greeting cards and hiring celebrities to model McCall designs, greatly increased McCall's profits.[29] In 1987, when he sold the company, its market value had tripled. That same year, he acquired Beatrice International, an international food processing and distributing company, for $985 million in a transaction financed with junk bonds. The acquisition brought Lewis to national attention, although he was often dismayed by the news media's tendency to focus on his ethnic background rather than his accomplishments. Cancer brought his life to an untimely end at the age of 50. In his short life, he had accomplished much and inspired many.

December 24, 1992. The case has been strongly contested on both sides.

[A]fter more than a year of extensive discovery and several contested motions, the board of directors of TLC Beatrice unanimously voted to add two new directors and to constitute them as the SLC, empowering it to investigate the allegations of misconduct and determine the best course of action for the company with regard to this litigation. After a five month investigation of eleven principal claims alleged by Carlton in its Second Amended Complaint, the SLC entered into a proposed settlement with the Estate of Reginald Lewis ("Estate"), the principal defendant in this action. Pursuant to a stipulation of settlement, ... the Estate has agreed ... to pay TLC Beatrice a total of $14,932,000 plus interest, in installment payments over the next seven years. ... [T]he parties differ somewhat on the present value of this obligation. Carlton, for example, claims that in no event could it be worth more than $13,032,926 presently ... [and] as the plaintiff, warmly resists this proposed settlement. ...

---

28. Reginald Lewis & Blair Walker, *Why Should White Guys Have All the Fun: How Reginald Lewis Created a Billion-Dollar Business Empire* (1995).
29. Id.

Before discussing the proposed settlement itself, it is appropriate to note the role of the court under Delaware law in reviewing proposed settlements generally, and to note several unique issues presented in this particular case. As a general rule, in evaluating a proposed settlement, this court does not attempt to make substantive determinations concerning disputed facts or the merits of the claims alleged. . . . Instead, the court considers whether the proposed settlement is fair and reasonable in light of the factual support for the alleged claims and defenses in the discovery record before it . . . .

Since this proposed settlement was negotiated by an SLC, the parties have agreed that under Delaware law, it is to be reviewed under the two step approach set forth in *Zapata Corp. v. Maldonado.* . . .

After carefully reviewing the investigation and negotiation process of the SLC, the evidentiary basis for the conclusions reached by the SLC, and the terms of the proposed settlement, I have reached the following conclusions. First, the SLC and its counsel proceeded in good faith throughout the investigation and negotiation of the proposed settlement. Second, the conclusions reached by the SLC, which formed the basis for the amount of the proposed settlement, were well informed by the existing record. Third, the proposed settlement falls within a range of reasonable solutions to the problem presented. Finally, to the extent I am required by the second step of *Zapata,* uncomfortably, to exercise some form of independent judgment concerning the merits of the settlement, I cannot conclude that it is badly off the mark. It is true that in some respects the claims that Carlton asserts on behalf of TLC Beatrice appear strong. But the settlement proposed offers substantial consideration for their release. As to the conceptually difficult second step of the *Zapata* technique, it is difficult to rationalize in principle; but it must have been designed to offer protection for cases in which, while the court could not consciously determine on the first leg of the analysis that there was no want of independence or good faith, it nevertheless "felt" that the result reached was "irrational" or "egregious" or some other such extreme word. My opinion is that courts should not make such judgments but for reasons of legitimacy and for reasons of shareholder welfare. . . . But if I am directed to exercise my own "business judgment" by the second step of *Zapata,* I must conclude that this settlement represents one reasonable compromise of the claims asserted. . . .

10.6   WHEN ARE DERIVATIVE SUITS IN SHAREHOLDERS' INTERESTS?[30]

When should a shareholder wish a derivative suit to be brought against a corporate manager who has violated her fiduciary duty? Presumably, a shareholder (and society as a whole) would prefer a suit to be brought

---

30. This subsection borrows from a more extensive discussion in Reiner H. Kraakman, Hyun Park, & Steven M. Shavell, *When Are Shareholder Suits in Shareholder Interests?,* 82 Geo. L. J. 1733 (1994)

only when it increases corporate value, i.e., when its benefits outweigh its costs to the company.

A derivative suit can increase corporate value in two ways. First, the suit may confer something of value on the corporation. Thus, the corporation benefits if it recovers compensation for the past harms inflicted by an errant manager. More subtly, the corporation can benefit in a similar way if a derivative suit forces a governance change that prevents the same manager from inflicting harm on the company in the future (as when, say, the introduction of an independent audit prevents future manipulation of the books). Second, a derivative suit (or, more precisely, the prospect of suit) can add to corporate value by deterring wrongdoing that might otherwise happen in the future. In this second case, unlike the first, the suit adds value only in the contingent sense that it serves to make future would-be wrongdoers *believe* that they will be the target of *another* suit should they also breach their fiduciary duties. Correlatively, any change in circumstances that makes a future suit less likely also reduces the deterrent value of *today's* derivative suit.

As with the benefits of suit, the costs of a derivative suit to the company can be resolved into two categories. First, litigation imposes direct costs on a company. The corporation must pay the price of both defending and (as a practical matter) prosecuting successful derivative suits — in time and energy as well as dollars. As a legal matter, shareholder-plaintiffs (or their attorneys) bear their own costs if they lose, and culpable managers may be charged with defense costs if they lose. See DGCL §145(b). In practice, however, most derivative suits settle, after which the company's liability insurer picks up the costs of both sides in the suit. The insurer, in turn, passes these settlement costs back to the corporation in the form of insurance premia.

Second, shareholder suits impose a variety of indirect costs on the corporation and its shareholders. The corporation must pay in advance for at least some of the prospective costs of managerial liability. In particular, corporate officers and directors must be compensated ex ante for their expected litigation costs or, alternatively, insulated from bearing these costs in the first instance. Again, the legal system facilitates insulation through a variety of mechanisms, the most important of which is the institution of D&O insurance. Derivative suits that are not dismissed generally settle, and settlement costs as well as litigation costs are almost always paid by D&O insurers, who anticipate their own costs in the insurance premia they charge corporations ex ante.

QUESTIONS ON COSTS AND BENEFITS

1. Because D&O insurers generally pay settlement costs, managers are rarely forced to pay out of pocket for alleged breaches of fiduciary duty. So how can anyone claim that the prospect of a derivative suit deters misconduct?

2. Consider the position of a corporation *before* its officers and directors face a derivative suit. Can the company benefit, on an expected value basis, from the certain knowledge that its D&O insurer will make good any

losses it suffers if its officers and directors breach their fiduciary duties and are sued as a result? Remember that the company must pay insurance premia, and the insurance corporation is no dummy. Do you have to know how closely underwritten D&O policies are?

3. Consider the following fanciful proposal for reform of the rules for plaintiffs' attorneys: "Attorneys' fees shall be available in settlements of derivative suits only if one of the following criteria is met: (1) The settlement imposes an *uncompensated* financial penalty on alleged wrongdoers; or (2) the settlement results in a monetary recovery in excess of the requested attorneys' fees that is *not* funded, directly or indirectly, by the company or its insurer."

4. Could shareholders validly approve a charter amendment that precludes the institution of derivative suits by shareholders? Are there good policy reasons in favor of or opposed to such an idea?

TRANSACTIONS IN CONTROL

Unlike self-dealing transactions initiated by corporate insiders, transactions in shares have traditionally escaped regulation by corporate law. What shareholders do with their own property—their shares—has been seen as their own business and of no concern to the corporation or other shareholders. Over the past 50 years, however, corporate law has come to recognize that share transactions on the market cannot be wholly isolated from the core agency problems of corporate law. For example, trading on nonpublic information by corporate insiders (see Chapter 14) closely parallels the traditional fiduciary problems that gave rise to the corporate opportunity doctrine. Exchanging or aggregating blocks of shares large enough to control corporations—the topic addressed in this chapter— can be thought to raise problems that resemble those arising from self-dealing and appropriations of business opportunities. Share for share, controlling blocks of stock inevitably sell in negotiated transactions at a premium over market price of non-control shares.

Why are buyers willing to pay a premium for control? The academic literature refers to several possible explanations. The most popular explanation posits that the premium is a payment for "private benefits of control," by which is meant a range of possible sources of value, from the power to capture salary, perks, and perhaps self-dealing opportunities, to the prestige value of being the company's indisputable boss. Just how controllers extract extra value is important, of course. (For an egregious— and illegal—illustration of how controllers can extract extra value, see the sidebar on the Rigas clan at Adelphia.) But no matter how controllers extract private benefits, these benefits are non-pro rata distributions of value from corporate assets.

Other theorists suggest that control premia are paid not by those seeking to harvest private benefits, but from buyers who have (or believe they have) a superior business plan that will increase the value of the stock in their hands. We might call this "shared" or "public" benefits of control. Still others hold that a control premium is simply a function of the nature of capital markets: Anyone attempting to accumulate a control block of stock from many trades will drive up the price of the stock (all other factors staying the same) and thus will have to pay a premium over the market price. Since control blocks are costly to create, they command a premium on sale.

Each of these theories may explain some part of any control premium. But which one you find most powerful may affect what you think of as good corporate law policy with respect to control share transactions.

Other than vigilantly policing conflicted corporate decisions, there is, as a practical matter, little the law can do to regulate controllers' private benefits in the day-to-day operation of the company. But control transactions are more visible and occur less often, so the law could feasibly monitor them more closely if it were thought useful to do so. But whatever policy position one advances on this question, it will have both costs and benefits — there is no unambiguously preferable policy position on the regulation of control transactions.

Consider that investors can acquire control over corporations in two ways, each of which present different regulatory issues. The first is by purchasing a controlling block of shares from an existing control shareholder. In such a sale of control, the incumbent controller will demand a premium over the price of the publicly traded stock for her control block. The acquirer may expect to finance this control premium by extracting larger private benefits than the incumbent controller already does (in the extreme, by looting the company), by putting the company's assets to more profitable uses, or by doing both. Therefore, any regulatory measure that hinders the purchase of control at a premium price will both mitigate the risks of opportunistic transfers of control to "bad" acquirers,

---

ADELPHIA

Five Adelphia Officials Arrested on Fraud Charges
Wall Street Journal (July 25, 2002)

Three members of the Rigas family that founded Adelphia Communications Corp., and two other company executives, were arrested early yesterday morning and charged with looting the nation's sixth-largest cable-television company "on a massive scale." . . . Adelphia also filed suit yesterday seeking more than $1 billion against the entire Rigas family. . . . The suit accuses the family of a violation of the Racketeer Influenced and Corrupt Organizations Act, breaching its fiduciary duties, wasting corporate assets, abusing control, breaching its contracts and other violations.

The Rigases used company jets for private jaunts — including an African safari — borrowed billions of dollars for their closely held companies and used $252 million of company funds to meet margin calls on their private stock, the complaint alleged. After John J. Rigas racked up a personal debt of more than $66 million by early 2001, he was withdrawing so much money from the company for personal use that his son Timothy had to limit him to $1 million a month — which he duly withdrew for 12 months, even as public filings listed his annual compensation at less than $1.9 million, the complaint said. The Rigases also spent $12.8 million of company funds to start construction of a golf course. . . . The company also paid for two apartments in Manhattan — one used rent-free by John's daughter and son-in-law, according to the complaint. (The son-in-law was a member of the board at the time.)

and hinder the efficient transfer of control to acquirers who will use company assets in more profitable ways. In either case, an incumbent controller who already extracts private gains from a company has no incentive to sell out, except at a premium price that capitalizes his own private benefits.[1]

The second way in which an acquirer might take control of a corporation is by purchasing the shares of numerous smaller shareholders. Here a similar trade-off exists between the law's ambition to protect shareholders from opportunism and its ambition to foster efficient transfers of control. In the absence of ex ante regulation, antitakeover defenses, or ex post derivative litigation, a looter could exploit the collective action problem of disaggregated shareholders by buying 51 percent of a target corporation at a high price and later appropriating a large part of the value of the remaining 49 percent as a private benefit. A variety of regulatory measures directed at acquiring companies — from minimum tender offer periods to mandatory cash-out rights for minority shareholders — mitigate the collective action problem of target shareholders and thereby reduce the risk of inefficient takeovers — but, again, they do so only at the price of also reducing the number of efficient control transfers. Similarly, managers who control preclusive defensive tactics have a great deal of leverage to bargain on behalf of their shareholders with would-be acquirers, but can also use that power to block efficient transfers for selfish reasons. Managers could abuse such power by, for example, selling the firm to an inefficient acquirer who offers a side deal, or refusing to sell the firm regardless of a potential buyer's price. We consider the latitude of managers to defend the company against a hostile tender offer in Chapter 13.

11.1   SALES OF CONTROL BLOCKS: THE SELLER'S DUTIES

Control blocks in public companies are costly to aggregate and valuable to have. But what rules govern the sale of a control block once it is obtained? We explore three traditional aspects of this issue here: (1) the extent to which the law should regulate premia from the sale of control (i.e., the difference between the market price of minority shares and the price obtained in the sale of a control block); (2) the law's response to sales of managerial power over the corporation that appear to occur *without* transferring a controlling block of stock (i.e., a "sale of corporate office"); and (3) the seller's duty of care to screen out buyers who are potential looters.

1. See Marcel Kahan, *Sales of Corporate Control*, 9 J.L. Econ. & Org. 368 (1993); Lucian Arye Bebchuk, *Efficient and Inefficient Sales of Corporate Control*, 109 Q.J. Econ. 957 (1994).

11.1.1   The Regulation of Control Premia

While some non-U.S. jurisdictions have statutes that require any acquirer of a control block to offer to acquire all shares at the same price paid
in the control transaction, U.S. jurisdictions do not afford to minority
shareholders such a right to sell their own stock alongside the controlling
shareholder, nor a right to sell their stock back to the company, as they
would in a corporate merger. The *Zetlin* case, below, illustrates the common law rule, which we call the "market rule," following Professor Lucian
Bebchuk's terminology, i.e., sale of control is a market transaction that
creates rights and duties between the parties, but does not confer rights on
other shareholders.

A critical tradition of academic commentary, beginning with Professor
Adolf A. Berle in the 1950s and extending to Dean Robert Clark's treatise
Corporate Law, attacks both the fairness and the efficiency of the market
rule and proposes in its place a variety of premia-sharing alternatives.[2]
Perhaps the best known of these alternatives is the "equal opportunity
rule," proposed by Professor William Andrews,[3] under which minority
shareholders would be entitled to sell their shares to a buyer of control
on the same terms as the seller of control. For a careful review of the
literature and case law on sales of control, see Einer R. Elhauge, *The
Triggering Function of Sale of Control Doctrine*, 59 U. Chi. L. Rev. 1465
(1992).

Proponents of minority shareholder interests have looked to a handful
of cases, including the classic case of *Perlman v. Feldmann*, excerpted
below, as legal support for according minority shareholders a claim on
control premia. Before examining the interesting facts of *Perlman*, consider the baseline rule, articulated in the classic case of *Zetlin v. Hanson
Holdings*.

ZETLIN v. HANSON HOLDINGS, INC.

397 N.E.2d 387 (N.Y. 1979)

Memorandum:

Plaintiff Zetlin owned approximately 2% of the outstanding shares of
Gable Industries, Inc., with defendants Hanson Holdings, Inc., and Sylvestri,
together with members of the Sylvestri family, owning 44.4% of Gable's
shares. The defendants sold their interests to Flintkote Co. for a premium
price of $15 per share, at a time when Gable stock was selling on the open
market for $7.38 per share. It is undisputed that the 44.4% acquired by
Flintkote represented effective control of Gable.

---

2. Robert C. Clark, Corporate Law at 491-497 (1986); Adolf A. Berle, Jr., *"Control"
in Corporate Law*, 58 Colum. L. Rev. 1212 (1958).
3. William D. Andrews, *The Stockholder's Right to Equal Opportunity in the Sale of
Shares*, 78 Harv. L. Rev. 505 (1965).

Recognizing that those who invest the capital necessary to acquire a dominant position in the ownership of a corporation have the right of controlling that corporation, it has long been settled law that, absent looting of corporate assets, conversion of a corporate opportunity, fraud or other acts of bad faith, a controlling stockholder is free to sell, and a purchaser is free to buy, that controlling interest at a premium price. . . .

Certainly, minority shareholders are entitled to protection against such abuse by controlling shareholders. They are not entitled, however, to inhibit the legitimate interests of the other stockholders. It is for this reason that control shares usually command a premium price. The premium is the added amount an investor is willing to pay for the privilege of directly influencing the corporation's affairs.

In this action plaintiff Zetlin contends that minority stockholders are entitled to an opportunity to share equally in any premium paid for a controlling interest in the corporation. This rule would profoundly affect the manner in which controlling stock interests are now transferred. It would require, essentially, that a controlling interest be transferred only by means of an offer to all stockholders, i.e., a tender offer. This would be contrary to existing law and if so radical a change is to be effected it would best be done by the Legislature.

Chief Judge COOKE and Judges JASEN, GABRIELLI, JONES, WACHTLER, FUCHSBERG and MEYER concur in memorandum.

PERLMAN v. FELDMANN

219 F.2d 173 (2d Cir. 1955), cert. denied, 349 U.S. 952 (1955)

CLARK, C.J.:

This is a derivative action brought by minority stockholders of Newport Steel Corporation to compel accounting for, and restitution of, allegedly illegal gains which accrued to defendants as a result of the sale in August, 1950, of their controlling interest in the corporation. The principal defendant, C. Russell Feldmann, who represented and acted for the others, members of his family,[1] was at that time not only the dominant stockholder, but also the chairman of the board of directors and the president of the corporation. Newport, an Indiana corporation, operated mills for the production of steel sheets for sale to manufacturers of steel products, first at Newport, Kentucky, and later also at other places in Kentucky and Ohio. The buyers, a syndicate organized as Wilport Company, a Delaware corporation, consisted of end-users of steel who were interested in securing a source of supply in a market becoming ever tighter in the Korean War. Plaintiffs contend that the consideration paid for the stock included

---

1. The stock was not held personally by Feldmann in his own name, but was held by the members of his family and by personal corporations. The aggregate of stock thus had amounted to 33% of the outstanding Newport stock and gave working control to the holder. The actual sale included 55,552 additional shares held by friends and associates of Feldmann, so that a total of 37% of the Newport stock was transferred.

compensation for the sale of a corporate asset, a power held in trust for the corporation by Feldmann as its fiduciary. This power was the ability to control the allocation of the corporate product in a time of short supply, through control of the board of directors; and it was effectively transferred in this sale by having Feldmann procure the resignation of his own board and the election of Wilport's nominees immediately upon consummation of the sale.

. . . Jurisdiction below was based upon the diverse citizenship of the parties. Plaintiffs argue . . . that in the situation here disclosed the vendors must account to the non-participating minority stockholders for that share of their profit which is attributable to the sale of the corporate power. Judge Hincks denied the validity of the premise, holding that the rights involved in the sale were only those normally incident to the possession of a controlling block of shares, with which a dominant stockholder, in the absence of fraud or foreseeable looting, was entitled to deal according to his own best interests. Furthermore, he held that plaintiffs had failed to satisfy their burden of proving that the sales price was not a fair price for the stock per se. . . .

The essential facts found by the trial judge are not in dispute. Newport was a relative newcomer in the steel industry with predominantly old installations which were in the process of being supplemented by more modern facilities. Except in times of extreme shortage Newport was not in a position to compete profitably with other steel mills for customers not in its immediate geographical area. Wilport, the purchasing syndicate, consisted of geographically remote end-users of steel who were interested in buying more steel from Newport than they had been able to obtain during recent periods of tight supply. The price of $20 per share was found by Judge Hincks to be a fair one for a control block of stock, although the over-the-counter market price had not exceeded $12 and the book value per share was $17.03. But this finding was limited by Judge Hincks' statement that "[what] value the block would have had if shorn of its appurtenant power to control distribution of the corporate product, the evidence does not show." It was also conditioned by his earlier ruling that the burden was on plaintiffs to prove a lesser value for the stock.

Both as director and as dominant stockholder, Feldmann stood in a fiduciary relationship to the corporation and to the minority stockholders as beneficiaries thereof. . . . Although there is no Indiana case directly in point, the most closely analogous one emphasizes the close scrutiny to which Indiana subjects the conduct of fiduciaries when personal benefit may stand in the way of fulfillment of trust obligations. . . . Directors of a corporation are its agents, and they are governed by the rules of law applicable to other agents, and, as between themselves and their principal, the rules relating to honesty and fair dealing in the management of the affairs of their principal are applicable. They must not, in any degree, allow their official conduct to be swayed by their private interest, which must yield to official duty.

In Indiana, then as elsewhere, the responsibility of the fiduciary is not limited to a proper regard for the tangible balance sheet assets of the corporation, but includes the dedication of his uncorrupted business judgment for the sole benefit of the corporation, in any dealings which may adversely affect it. *Meinhard v. Salmon*, . . . 164 N.E. 545. . . . Although the Indiana case is particularly relevant to Feldmann as a director, the same rule should apply to his fiduciary duties as majority stockholder, for in that capacity he chooses and controls the directors, and thus is held to have assumed their liability. *Pepper v. Litton*, supra, 308 U.S. 295, 60 S. Ct. 238. This, therefore, is the standard to which Feldmann was by law required to conform in his activities here under scrutiny.

It is true . . . that this is not the ordinary case of breach of fiduciary duty. We have here no fraud, no misuse of confidential information, no outright looting of a helpless corporation. But on the other hand, we do not find compliance with that high standard which we have just stated and which we and other courts have come to expect and demand of corporate fiduciaries. In the often-quoted words of Judge Cardozo: "Many forms of conduct permissible in a workaday world for those acting at arm's length, are forbidden to those bound by fiduciary ties. A trustee is held to something stricter than the morals of the market place. Not honesty alone, but the punctilio of an honor the most sensitive, is then the standard of behavior. As to this there has developed a tradition that is unbending and inveterate. Uncompromising rigidity has been the attitude of courts of equity when petitioned to undermine the rule of undivided loyalty by the 'disintegrating erosion' of particular exceptions." *Meinhard v. Salmon*, supra, . . . 164 N.E. 545, 546. . . . The actions of defendants in siphoning off for personal gain corporate advantages to be derived from a favorable market situation do not betoken the necessary undivided loyalty owed by the fiduciary to his principal.

The corporate opportunities of whose misappropriation the minority stockholders complain need not have been an absolute certainty in order to support this action against Feldmann. If there was possibility of corporate gain, they are entitled to recover. . . . [I]n *Irving Trust Co. v. Deutsch*, supra, 2 Cir., 73 F.2d 121, 124, an accounting was required of corporate directors who bought stock for themselves for corporate use, even though there was an affirmative showing that the corporation did not have the finances itself to acquire the stock. . . .

This rationale is equally appropriate to a consideration of the benefits which Newport might have derived from the steel shortage. In the past Newport had used and profited by its market leverage by operation of what the industry had come to call the "Feldmann Plan." This consisted of securing interest-free advances from prospective purchasers of steel in return for firm commitments to them from future production. The funds thus acquired were used to finance improvements in existing plants and to acquire new installations. In the summer of 1950 Newport had been negotiating for cold-rolling facilities which it needed for a more fully integrated operation and a more marketable product, and Feldmann plan funds might well have been used toward this end.

Further, as plaintiffs alternatively suggest, Newport might have used the period of short supply to build up patronage in the geographical area in which it could compete profitably even when steel was more abundant. Either of these opportunities was Newport's, to be used to its advantage only. Only if defendants had been able to negate completely any possibility of gain by Newport could they have prevailed. It is true that a trial court finding states: "Whether or not, in August, 1950, Newport's position was such that it could have entered into 'Feldmann Plan' type transactions to procure funds and financing for the further expansion and integration of its steel facilities and whether such expansion would have been desirable for Newport, the evidence does not show." This, however, cannot avail the defendants, who — contrary to the ruling below — had the burden of proof on this issue, since fiduciaries always have the burden of proof in establishing the fairness of their dealings with trust property. . . .

Defendants seek to categorize the corporate opportunities which might have accrued to Newport as too unethical to warrant further consideration. It is true that reputable steel producers were not participating in the gray market brought about by the Korean War and were refraining from advancing their prices, although to do so would not have been illegal. But Feldmann Plan transactions were not considered within this self-imposed interdiction; the trial court found that around the time of the Feldmann sale Jones & Laughlin Steel Corporation, Republic Steel Company, and Pittsburgh Steel Corporation were all participating in such arrangements. In any event, it ill becomes the defendants to disparage as unethical the market advantages from which they themselves reaped rich benefits.

We do not mean to suggest that a majority stockholder cannot dispose of his controlling block of stock to outsiders without having to account to his corporation for profits or even never do this with impunity when the buyer is an interested customer, actual or potential, for the corporation's product. But when the sale necessarily results in a sacrifice of this element of corporate good will and consequent unusual profit to the fiduciary who has caused the sacrifice, he should account for his gains. So in a time of market shortage, where a call on a corporation's product commands an unusually large premium, in one form or another, we think it sound law that a fiduciary may not appropriate to himself the value of this premium. Such personal gain at the expense of his coventurers seems particularly reprehensible when made by the trusted president and director of his company. In this case the violation of duty seems to be all the clearer because of this triple role in which Feldmann appears, though we are unwilling to say, and are not to be understood as saying, that we should accept a lesser obligation for any one of his roles alone.

Hence to the extent that the price received by Feldmann and his codefendants included such a bonus, he is accountable to the minority stockholders who sue here. . . . And plaintiffs, as they contend, are entitled to a recovery in their own right, instead of in right of the corporation (as in the usual derivative actions), since neither Wilport nor their successors in interest should share in any judgment which may be rendered. . . . Defendants cannot well object to this form of recovery, since the only alternative, recovery for the corporation as a whole, would subject them to a greater total liability.

The case will therefore be remanded to the district court for a determination of the question expressly left open below, namely, the value of defendants' stock without the appurtenant control over the corporation's output of steel. We reiterate that on this issue, as on all others relating to a breach of fiduciary duty, the burden of proof must rest on the defendants. . . .

SWAN, Cir. J. (dissenting).
. . . My brothers' opinion does not specify precisely what fiduciary duty Feldmann is held to have violated or whether it was a duty imposed upon him as the dominant stockholder or as a director of Newport. Without such specification I think that both the legal profession and the business world will find the decision confusing and will be unable to foretell the extent of its impact upon customary practices in the sale of stock.

The power to control the management of a corporation, that is, to elect directors to manage its affairs, is an inseparable incident to the ownership of a majority of its stock, or sometimes, as in the present instance, to the ownership of enough shares, less than a majority, to control an election. Concededly a majority or dominant shareholder is ordinarily privileged to sell his stock at the best price obtainable from the purchaser. In so doing he acts on his own behalf, not as an agent of the corporation. If he knows or has reason to believe that the purchaser intends to exercise to the detriment of the corporation the power of management acquired by the purchase, such knowledge or reasonable suspicion will terminate the dominant shareholders' privilege to sell and will create a duty not to transfer the power of management to such purchaser. The duty seems to me to resemble the obligation which everyone is under not to assist another to commit a tort rather than the obligation of a fiduciary. But whatever the nature of the duty, a violation of it will subject the violator to liability for damages sustained by the corporation. Judge Hincks found that Feldmann had no reason to think that Wilport would use the power of management it would acquire by the purchase to injure Newport, and that there was no proof that it ever was so used. Feldmann did know, it is true, that the reason Wilport wanted the stock was to put in a board of directors who would be likely to permit Wilport's members to purchase more of Newport's steel than they might otherwise be able to get. But there is nothing illegal in a dominant shareholder purchasing from his own corporation at the same prices it offers to other customers. That is what the members of Wilport did, and there is no proof that Newport suffered any detriment therefrom.

My brothers say that "the consideration paid for the stock included compensation for the sale of a corporate asset," which they describe as "the ability to control the allocation of the corporate product in a time of short supply, through control of the board of directors; and it was effectively transferred in this sale by having Feldmann procure the resignation of his own board and the election of Wilport's nominees immediately upon consummation of the sale." The implications of this are not clear to me. If it means that when market conditions are such as to induce users of a corporation's product to wish to buy a controlling block of stock in order to be able to purchase part of the corporation's output at the same mill list prices as are offered to other customers, the dominant stockholder is under a fiduciary duty not to sell his stock, I cannot agree. For reasons already stated, in my opinion Feldmann was not proved to be under any fiduciary duty as a stockholder not to sell the stock he controlled.

Feldmann was also a director of Newport. Perhaps the quoted statement means that as a director he violated his fiduciary duty in voting to elect Wilport's nominees to fill the vacancies created by the resignations of the former directors of Newport. As a director Feldmann was under a fiduciary duty to use an honest judgment in acting on the corporation's behalf. A director is privileged to resign, but so long as he remains a director he must be faithful to his fiduciary duties and must not make a personal gain from performing them. Consequently, if the price paid for Feldmann's stock included a payment for voting to elect the new directors, he must account to the corporation for such payment, even though he honestly believed that the men he voted to elect were well qualified to serve as directors. He can not take pay for performing his fiduciary duty. There is no suggestion that he did do so, unless the price paid for his stock was more than its value. So it seems to me that decision must turn on whether finding 120 and conclusion 5 of the district judge are supportable on the evidence. They are set out in the margin.[1]

Judge Hincks went into the matter of valuation of the stock with his customary care and thoroughness. He made no error of law in applying the principles relating to valuation of stock. Concededly a controlling block of stock has greater sale value than a small lot. While the spread between $10 per share for small lots and $20 per share for the controlling block seems rather extraordinarily wide, the $20 valuation was supported by the expert testimony of Dr. Badger, whom the district judge said he could not find to be wrong. I see no justification for upsetting the valuation as clearly erroneous. Nor can I agree with my brothers that the $20 valuation "was limited" by the last sentence in finding 120. The controlling block could not by any possibility be shorn of its appurtenant power to elect directors and through them to control distribution of the corporate product. It is this "appurtenant power" which gives a controlling block its value as such block. What evidence could be adduced to show the value of the block "if shorn" of such appurtenant power, I cannot conceive, for it cannot be shorn of it.

The opinion also asserts that the burden of proving a lesser value than $20 per share was not upon the plaintiffs but the burden was upon the defendants to prove that the stock was worth that value. Assuming that this might be true as to the defendants who were directors of Newport, they did show it, unless finding 120 be set aside. Furthermore, not all the defendants were directors; upon what theory the plaintiffs should be relieved

---

1. "120. The 398,927 shares of Newport stock sold to Wilport as of August 31, 1950, had a fair value as a control block of $20 per share. What value the block would have had if shorn of its appurtenant power to control distribution of the corporate product, the evidence does not show."

"5. Even if Feldmann's conduct in cooperating to accomplish a transfer of control to Wilport immediately upon the sale constituted a breach of a fiduciary duty to Newport, no part of the moneys received by the defendants in connection with the sale constituted profits for which they were accountable to Newport."

from the burden of proof as to defendants who were not directors, the opinion does not explain.

The final conclusion of my brothers is that the plaintiffs are entitled to recover in their own right instead of in the right of the corporation. This appears to be completely inconsistent with the theory advanced at the outset of the opinion, namely, that the price of the stock "included compensation for the sale of a corporate asset." If a corporate asset was sold, surely the corporation should recover the compensation received for it by the defendants. . . .

NOTES AND QUESTIONS ON ZETLIN AND PERLMAN

1. Feldmann sold his control stake for $20/share when the market price was $12/share. Upon remand, the district court determined that the pro rata value of Newport's stock, based on the underlying value of the company's assets, was $14.67/share. This left Feldmann with a premium of $5.33/share, which he was ordered to share pro rata with his fellow shareholders. See *Perlman v. Feldmann,* 154 F. Supp. 436 (D. Conn. 1957). Does *Perlman* support a general rule of equal sharing in sales of control blocks, as some have argued, or does its holding turn on the unique circumstances of the case? Put differently, can *Perlman* be reconciled with *Zetlin*?

2. In a parallel case, an earlier panel of the Second Circuit determined that Feldmann had turned down an offer to sell the entire company that would have benefited all of Newport's shareholders and, shortly thereafter, had sold his own shares to the Wilport Group for a slightly higher cash price. Does this fact strengthen the court's holding? Is it conclusive? See *Birnbaum v. Newport Steel Corp.*, 193 F.2d 461, 462 (2d Cir. 1952), *cert. denied*, 343 U.S. 956.

3. In the district court's opinion in *Perlman*, written almost two years after the sale of Feldmann's stock, the court found that the Wilport Group had made substantial improvements in Newport's facilities, that Newport had sold substantial quantities of steel to Wilport at the same prices at which it had sold steel to other customers, and that there was simply no evidence of any sort that Wilport had inflicted economic harm on Newport. See 129 F. Supp. 162, 175-176 (D. Conn. 1952). Does this finding alter your view of the case?

11.1.2 A Defense of the Market Rule in Sales of Control

FRANK H. EASTERBROOK & DANIEL R. FISCHEL, CORPORATE CONTROL TRANSACTIONS

91 Yale L.J. 698, 715-719 (1982)

Investors' welfare is maximized by a legal rule that permits unequal division of gains from corporate control changes, subject to the constraint that no investor be made worse off by the transaction. In essence, this is a straightforward application of the Pareto principle of welfare economics. . . .

A. SALES OF CONTROL BLOCS

Sales of controlling blocs of shares provide a good example of transactions in which the movement of control is beneficial. The sale of control may lead to new offers, new plans, and new working arrangements with other firms that reduce agency costs and create other gains from new business relationships. The premium price received by the seller of the control bloc amounts to an unequal distribution of the gains. . . . [H]owever, this unequal distribution reduces the costs to purchasers of control [because the purchaser need only buy the control bloc and not all shares at the higher price — EDS.], thereby increasing the number of beneficial control transfers, and increasing the incentive for inefficient controllers to relinquish their positions.

Numerous academic commentators, however, argue for some form of sharing requirement. Adolph Berle, for example, has argued that control is a "corporate asset" requiring that premiums paid for control go into the corporate treasury. Another well-known proposal is the "equal opportunity" rule advocated by Professors Jennings and Andrews. This proposal would entitle the minority shareholders to sell their shares on the same terms as the controlling shareholder.

Both of these proposed treatments of the control premium would stifle transfers of control. If the premium must be paid into the corporate treasury, people may not consent to the sale of a controlling bloc; if minority shareholders may sell on the same terms as the controlling shareholder, bidders may have to purchase more shares than necessary, possibly causing the transaction to become unprofitable. Minority shareholders would suffer under either rule, as the likelihood of improvements in the quality of management declined.

[T]he legal treatment of control sales is largely along the lines of wealth maximization. Sales at a premium are lawful, and the controlling shareholder generally has no duty to spread the bounty. The rhetoric of the cases, however, is not uniform. In particular, the famous case of *Perlman v. Feldmann* suggests that the gains may have to be shared in some circumstances.

In *Perlman* the president and chairman (Feldmann) of the board of Newport Steel, a producer of steel sheets, sold his controlling bloc of shares for $20 per share at a time when the market price was less than $12 per share. The purchasers, a syndicate organized as Wilport Company, consisted of end-users of steel from across the country who were interested in a secure source of supply during a period of shortage attributable to the Korean War.

Because of the war, steel producers were prohibited from raising the price of steel. The "Feldmann Plan," adopted by Newport and some other steel producers, effectively raised the price of steel to the market-clearing price. . . .

The Second Circuit held in *Perlman* that the seller of the control bloc had a duty to share the control premium with other shareholders. The court's holding that Feldmann could not accept the premium paid by Wilport without violating his fiduciary duty was based on a belief that the steel shortage allowed Newport to finance needed expansion via the "Plan," and that the premium represented an attempt by Wilport to divert a corporate opportunity — to secure for itself the benefits resulting from the shortage. . . .

There are several problems with this treatment. Foremost is its assumption that the gain resulting from the "Plan" was not reflected in the price of Newport's stock. Newport stock was widely traded, and the existence of the Feldmann Plan was known to investors. The going price of Newport shares prior to the transaction therefore reflected the full value of Newport, including the value of advances under the Feldmann Plan. The Wilport syndicate paid some two-thirds more than the going price and thus could not profit from the deal unless (a) the sale of control resulted in an increase in the value of Newport, or (b) Wilport's control of Newport was the equivalent of looting. To see the implications of the latter possibility, consider the following simplified representation of the transaction. Newport has only 100 shares, and Wilport pays $20 for each of 37 shares. The market price of shares is $12, and hence the premium over the market price is $8 \times 37 = $296. Wilport must extract more than $296 from Newport in order to gain from the deal; the extraction comes at the expense of the other 63 shares, which must drop approximately $4.75 each, to $7.25.

Hence the court's proposition that Wilport extracted a corporate opportunity from Newport — the functional equivalent of looting — has testable implications. Unless the price of Newport's outstanding shares plummeted, the Wilport syndicate could not be extracting enough to profit. In fact, however, the value of Newport's shares rose substantially after the transaction. Part of this increase may have been attributable to the rising market for steel companies at the time, but even holding this factor constant, Newport's shares appreciated in price.[43] The sale to the Wilport syndicate took place on August 31, 1950. This pattern of prices certainly

---

43. Charles Cope has computed changes in the price of Newport shares using the market model, well developed in the finance literature. . . . Cope found a significant positive [positive abnormal returns] for Newport in the month of the sale to Wilport. . . . The raw price data are no less telling. The $12 price to which the *Perlman* court referred was the highest price at which shares changed hands before the sale of control. The average monthly bid prices for Newport stock during 1950 were:

July: 6 3/4

August: 8 1/2

September: 10 7/8

October: 12 1/2

November: 12 3/8

December: 12

[Recall that the sale to Wilport took place on August 31. — EDS.]

does not suggest that the 63% interest excluded from the premium perceived any damage to Newport. The data refute the court's proposition that Wilport appropriated a corporate opportunity of Newport.

It seems, then, that the source of the premium in *Perlman* is the same as the source of the gains for the shares Wilport did not buy: Wilport installed a better group of managers and, in addition, furnished Newport with a more stable market for its products. The gains from these changes must have exceeded any loss from abolition of the Feldmann Plan.

Doubtless not all public shareholders have the same good fortune as those who held Newport Steel. Looting is a profitable transaction under some circumstances. Existing holders of control, no less than prospective purchasers, however, have an incentive to put their hands in the till, and a proposal to ban sales of control at a premium as an antidote to looting is like a proposal to ban investments in common stocks as an antidote to bankruptcy.

If it were feasible to detect looters in advance, it might make sense to put the sellers of control blocs under a duty not to allow shares to pass to the knaves — certainly the sellers of control can detect knavery at a lower cost than the public shareholders who are not parties to the transaction. Indeed, some cases have held that a seller of a control bloc can be liable for failing to investigate adequately a prospective purchaser of control. The wisdom of such holdings is suspect, however, because it is difficult if not impossible to detect looters as they approach. A looter takes the money and runs, and looting is by nature a one-time transaction. . . . Any requirement that owners of control blocs investigate buyers and not sell to suspected looters is equivalent to a program of preventive detention for people who have never robbed banks but have acquisitive personalities.

Although sellers could spend substantial sums investigating buyers . . . and the result of some investigations would be a refusal to sell, almost all of these refusals would be false positives. . . .

We do not suggest that the legal system should disregard looting, but we think it likely that the best remedies are based on deterrence rather than prior scrutiny. Looters, when caught, could be heavily fined or imprisoned, taking into account the frequency with which looting escapes detection. . . . The costs of deterrence are probably much lower than the costs of dealing with looting through a system of prior scrutiny that would scotch many valuable control shifts as a byproduct.

QUESTIONS ON THE EASTERBROOK AND FISCHEL EXCERPT

1. Why do Easterbrook and Fischel conclude that the control premium at issue in *Feldmann* must have resulted from efficiency gains rather than from Wilport's power to extract the value of the Feldmann plan?

2. Some commentators[4] observe that incumbent controllers can extract private benefits from a corporation in many ways, ranging from excessive salaries and perks to low-visibility self-dealing. Even the power to hobnob

---

4. See, e.g., Bebchuk, supra note 1; Kahan, supra note 1.

with professional athletes at sports events or chair the art museum's board of trustees can be tallied as private benefits of control in some cases.

These ongoing benefits to an incumbent controller of a company imply that a would-be purchaser of control must offer a price for the incumbent's shares that reflects the capitalized value of her private benefits. The buyer can pay this premium price only if he expects to increase cash flows by managing the corporation more efficiently *or* if he expects to extract even greater non-pro rata private benefits from the corporation than the seller has done—or both. The first of these plans is socially valuable; the second, wasteful.

Assuming this analysis of the seller's premia is correct, what implications follow for the choice between the market rule and the equal opportunity rule? Which rule will deter more *inefficient* control transactions (i.e., control sales that reduce the value of the corporation)? Which rule will deter more *efficient* control transactions? Will all efficient transactions occur under either rule? Will all inefficient transactions be prevented under either rule?

NOTE: BACK TO THE REAL WORLD: HOW MUCH DO THE DELAWARE COURTS REALLY BELIEVE IN THE CONTROLLER'S RIGHT TO A CONTROL PREMIUM?

The market rule is black-letter law in the United States: A controlling shareholder can keep what she gets from the sale of her stock. But how far do modern courts really support this black-letter doctrine? In Delaware, at least, the answer is "not as far as is often thought."

Of course, all modern U.S. courts still treat the simple sale of a controlling block of stock, unconnected to any corporate activity, as free of any duty to minority shareholders.[5] But such sales are rare. A controller often requires corporate action of some sort to facilitate the sale of a control block, from a waiver of Section 203 (discussed in Chapter 13) and to information disclosure by the firm. These actions could provide a doctrinal hook for a duty on the part of the board to try to help the minority benefit from the control transaction. Arguably whenever the corporate board is asked to take action, it should do so only when it believes that it is beneficial to the corporation and all its shareholders to do so. Thus it might be argued that the corporation's independent directors have a duty to bargain with the controller to extract part of the control premium for minority shareholders.

---

5. There is a minor, and obvious, qualification to this point when the controller has made a contractual commitment to not sell his control block. In *Hollinger Intl. v. Black*, 844 A.2d 1022 (Del. Ch. 2004) the Delaware Chancery Court upheld the Hollinger board's use of a poison pill to prevent Conrad Black from selling his control block in Hollinger to the Barclay brothers, because the Court found that such a sale would violate a formal contract that Black had made with the Hollinger board. We return to this case in Chapter 12. For present purposes, *Hollinger* would seem to present an exceptional case that does not undermine the controller's fundamental right to sell his stake.

In re Digex, Inc. Shareholders Litigation[6] draws a sharp formal distinction between the controller's "shareholder right" to exercise her voting power for her private benefit and her management duty to exercise corporate power for the benefit of all shareholders. In *Digex*, an acquirer first approached the board of the partly held subsidiary of the controller with a lucrative offer. The controller arranged to sell itself to the acquirer in lieu of selling the subsidiary, thereby excluding the subsidiary's minority shareholders from a premium deal. The court ruled that the controller was entitled to use its voting power as a shareholder to block a deal between the subsidiary and the acquirer. But the controller nevertheless violated a duty of fairness to minority public shareholders when, in the course of selling itself, it pressured the subsidiary's board to waive the applicability of §203 of the DGCL in order to facilitate its sale. Section 203 prevents a party who purchases control of a Delaware corporation from pursuing a cash-out merger to eliminate minority shareholders (inter alia) for a period of three years unless the company's board approves ex ante or certain other technical requirements are met.

The rationale for *Digex* appears to be that the board may waive the §203 constraint only for the benefit of the corporation and all of its shareholders — not just its controlling shareholder. As a generality, this statement is surely correct. But if it is vigorously construed, this norm seriously weakens a controlling shareholder's entitlement to the whole of a control premium. A controller who wishes to receive premium value for her shares will typically ask the board to waive §203 protections unless the board has already done so. Thus, if such a waiver must be justified on the basis of a corporate benefit, the board must either conclude that the transfer itself is good for the corporation or must extract some benefit from the controller to justify the cooperation. Even when §203 is not at issue, boards are commonly asked to cooperate with potential buyers of control in other respects, such as providing access to nonpublic information about the company's operations. Here, too, a decision to cooperate with the controlling shareholder arguably requires a benefit for the corporation itself or the minority shareholders.

11.2 SALE OF CORPORATE OFFICE

How should we analyze the sale of a relatively small block of stock in a widely held firm at a premium price by the CEO or managing directors, who simultaneously promise to resign from the board in favor of the buyer's appointees upon conclusion of the sale? Compare the following cases. In *Carter v. Muscat*, 21 A.D.2d 543 (1st Dept. N.Y. 1964), the board of the Republic Corporation appointed a new slate of directors as part of a transaction in which the company's management sold a 9.7 percent block of its stock to a new "controlling" person at a price slightly above market. Despite a shareholder challenge, the court upheld the *re-election* of new directors at the annual shareholders meeting.

6. 789 A.2d 1176 (Del. Ch. 2000).

By contrast, in *Brecher v. Gregg,* 392 N.Y.S.2d 776 (1975), Gregg, the CEO of a public company, received a 35 percent control premium on the sale of his 4 percent block of stock, in exchange for his promise to secure the appointment of the buyer's candidate as the company's new CEO and the election of two of the buyer's candidates to the board of directors. Gregg temporarily delivered on his promise, but the company's board soon rebelled and fired the buyer's handpicked CEO. The would-be buyer of control then sued Gregg, unsuccessfully, for a refund of the premium it had paid for his stock. Shortly thereafter, however, a stockholder of the company successfully sued Gregg derivatively and forced him to disgorge his control premium to the company. The New York court observed, inter alia, that paying a premium for control while purchasing only 4 percent of a company's outstanding shares is "contrary to public policy and illegal."

QUESTIONS ON CARTER AND BRECHER

What is the functional argument for requiring sellers of corporate office to disgorge the premia they receive from the sale of their shares to the corporation? Isn't the efficiency argument for allowing the seller to keep her control premium equally strong whether she holds 4 percent of the company's shares or 40 percent? If not, why not?

11.3 LOOTING

Another important qualification of the controller's right to take whatever the market will bear for her control stake is the duty that the law imposes to screen against selling control to a looter.

HARRIS v. CARTER

582 A.2d 222 (Del. Ch. 1990)

[Through a 52 percent stock position, the Carter Group controlled Atlas Energy Corporation, which was a Delaware corporation in the oil and gas exploration business. Carter Group was induced by Mascolo to enter an agreement to transfer its stock position to Mascola in return for stock in Insuranshares of America, Inc. (ISA) a corporation controlled by Mascola that was purportedly in the insurance business. The contract called for the resignation from the Atlas board of directors by the Carter designees in such a way as to permit Mascola and his confederates to assume these board positions. The contract of sale was induced by a great many false statements about ISA and its subsidiaries

Upon assuming control of Atlas, Mascola and his designees authorized a number of complex transactions that, at the end of the day, had the effect of increasing Mascola's ownership of Atlas to 78 percent and of diverting a great deal of the value of Atlas from Atlas to Mascola and his friends. Atlas shareholders brought suit to try to recover on behalf of the corporation the looted funds. Mascola himself was at the time of suit thought to be judgment proof and therefore the Carter Group was added as a defendant, as well. Carter of course had been duped by Mascola and had essentially already lost the value of its 52 percent investment in Atlas. Carter moved to dismiss the complaint on the ground that the complaint failed to state any claim of wrongdoing on its part.]

ALLEN, C.:

* * * *

The gist of plaintiff's claim against the Carter defendants is the allegation that those defendants had reason to suspect the integrity of the Mascolo group, but failed to conduct even a cursory investigation into any of several suspicious aspects of the transaction: the unaudited financial statement, the mention of LICA [a claimed ISA subsidiary] in negotiations but not in the representations concerning ISA's subsidiaries, and the ownership of the subsidiaries themselves.[6] Such an investigation, argues plaintiff, would have revealed the structure of ISA to be fragile indeed, with minimal capitalization and no productive assets.

The charges against the Mascolo defendants are that the Mascolo defendants caused the effectuation of self-dealing transactions designed to benefit members of the Mascolo group, at the expense of Atlas.

* * * *

Finally, I turn to the Carter defendants motion to dismiss for failure to state a claim upon which relief may be granted. This motion raises novel questions of Delaware law. Stated generally the most basic of these questions is whether a controlling shareholder or group may under any circumstances owe a duty of care to the corporation in connection with the sale of a control block of stock. If such a duty may be said to exist under certain circumstances the questions in this case then become whether the facts alleged in the amended complaint would permit the finding that such a duty arose in connection with the sale to the Mascolo group and was breached. In this inquiry one applies the permissive standard appropriate for motions to dismiss. . . .

A number of cases may be cited in support of the proposition that when transferring control of a corporation to another, a controlling shareholder may, in some circumstances, have a duty to investigate the bona fides of the buyer — that is, in those circumstances, to take such steps as a reasonable person would take to ascertain that the buyer does not intend or is unlikely to plan any depredations of the corporation. The circumstance to which these cases refer is the existence of facts that would give rise to suspicion by a reasonably prudent person. The leading case is *Insuranshares Corporation,* 35 F. Supp. 22 (E.D. Pa. 1940).

In that case defendants, who comprised the entire board of directors of the corporation involved, sold their 27% stock interest in the corporation and resigned as directors. The resignations were done seriatim, in a way that permitted the designation of the buyers as successor directors. The buyers proceeded to loot the corporation.

As here, the sellers contended that they could have no liability for the wrongs that followed their sale. They merely sold their stock and resigned. These were acts that they were privileged to do, they claimed. Judge Kirkpatrick rejected this position:

> Those who control a corporation, either through majority stock owner-ship, ownership of large blocks of stock less than a majority, officeholding, management contracts, or otherwise, owe some duty to the corporation in respect of the transfer of the control to outsiders. The law has long ago reached the point where it is recognized that such persons may not be wholly oblivious of the interest of everyone but themselves, even in the act of parting with control, and that, under certain circumstances, they may be held liable for whatever injury to the corporation made possible by the transfer. Without attempting any general definition, and stating the duty in minimum terms as applicable to the facts of this case, it may be said that the owners of control are under a duty not to transfer it to outsiders if the circumstances surrounding the proposed transfer are such as to awaken suspicion and put a prudent man on his guard — unless a reasonably adequate investigation discloses such facts as would convince a reasonable person that no fraud is intended or likely to result. 35 F. Supp. at 25. . . .

Although there are few cases applying the principle of the *Insuranshares* case that do fix liability on a seller, it is the principle of *Insuranshares* and not the actual notice rule of *Levy* that has commanded the respect of later courts. . . .

While Delaware law has not addressed this specific question, one is not left without guidance from our decided cases. Several principles deducible from that law are pertinent. First, is the principle that a shareholder has a right to sell his or her stock and in the ordinary case owes no duty in that connection to other shareholders when acting in good faith.

Equally well established is the principle that when a shareholder presumes to exercise control over a corporation, to direct its actions, that shareholder assumes a fiduciary duty of the same kind as that owed by a director to the corporation. . . . A sale of controlling interest in a corpora-tion, at least where . . . that sale is coupled with an agreement for the sellers to resign from the board of directors in such a way as to assure that the buyer's designees assume that corporate office, does, in my opinion, in-volve or implicate the corporate mechanisms so as to call this principle into operation.

More generally, it does not follow from the proposition that ordinarily a shareholder has a right to sell her stock to whom and on such terms as she deems expedient, that no duty may arise from the particular circumstances to take care in the exercise of that right. It is established American legal doctrine that, unless privileged, each person owes a duty to those who may foreseeably be harmed by her action to take such steps as a reasonably prudent person would take in similar circumstances to avoid such harm to others. While this principle arises from the law of torts and not the law of corporations or of fiduciary duties, that distinction is not, I think, significant unless the law of corporations or of fiduciary duties somehow privileges a selling shareholder by exempting her from the reach of this principle. The principle itself is one of great generality and, if not negated by privilege, would apply to a controlling shareholder who negligently places others foreseeably in the path of injury.

That a shareholder may sell her stock (or that a director may resign his office) is a right that, with respect to the principle involved, is no different, for example, than the right that a licensed driver has to operate a motor vehicle upon a highway. The right exists, but it is not without conditions and limitations, some established by positive regulation, some by common-law. Thus, to continue the parallel, the driver owes a duty of care to her passengers because it is foreseeable that they may be injured if, through inattention or otherwise, the driver involves the car she is operating in a collision. In the typical instance a seller of corporate stock can be expected to have no similar apprehension of risks to others from her own inattention. But, in some circumstances, the seller of a control block of stock may or should reasonably foresee danger to other shareholders; with her sale of stock will also go control over the corporation and with it the opportunity to misuse that power to the injury of such other shareholders. Thus, the reason that a duty of care is recognized in any situation is fully present in this situation. I can find no universal privilege arising from the corporate form that exempts a controlling shareholder who sells corporate control from the wholesome reach of this common-law duty. . . .

Thus, I conclude that while a person who transfers corporate control to another is surely not a surety for his buyer, when the circumstances would alert a reasonably prudent person to a risk that his buyer is dishonest or in some material respect not truthful, a duty devolves upon the seller to make such inquiry as a reasonably prudent person would make, and generally to exercise care so that others who will be affected by his actions should not be injured by wrongful conduct. . . .

One cannot determine [on this motion] whether Mr. Carter and those who acted with him were in fact negligent in a way that proximately caused injury to the corporation. Indeed one cannot determine now whether the circumstances that surrounded the negotiations with Mascolo were such as to have awakened suspicion in a person of ordinary prudence. . . . [But it] is sufficient to require denial of this motion to dismiss that I cannot now say as a matter of law that under no state of facts that might be proven could it be held that a duty arose, to the corporation and its other shareholders, to make further inquiry and was breached. . . .

That Mr. Carter may well have been misled to his own detriment may be a factor affecting the question whether a duty to inquire arose, as Carter might be assumed to be a prudent man when dealing with his own property. But that assumption is essentially evidentiary and can be given no weight on this motion. . . .

QUESTIONS ON HARRIS v. CARTER

1. What standard ought to govern the sale of control to potential looters? Should the same standard have applied if the Carter group had merely sold its stock and not agreed to have its representatives on the board replaced by Mascolo? Why not instead deter looting by imposing greater penalties on looters?

2. Could a minority shareholder be liable when she tenders her shares to a potential looter in a tender offer and the looter gains control of the company through the tender offer? Should she be?

3. Upon the facts alleged, do you believe that the Carter group violated its duty? Can the size of a control premium by itself have alerted the seller to potential looting? Should the fact that Carter himself appears to have suffered a major financial loss at the hands of the Mascolo group be prima facie evidence that Carter acted as a reasonable man and thus complied with his duties to his fellow shareholders?

11.4   TENDER OFFERS: THE BUYER'S DUTIES

Unlike corporations in most of the world, large public companies in the United States generally do not have a controlling shareholder. This means that an investor who wishes to purchase a control stake in a widely held company must do so by aggregating the shares of many small shareholders. In theory, at least, there are two ways to do this. The buyer might approach the largest of the small shareholders singly, or the buyer might make a general offer — a tender offer — that is open to all shareholders.

More precisely, a tender offer is an offer of cash or securities to the shareholders of a public corporation in exchange for their shares at a premium over market price. In most cases, a tender offeror aims at acquiring a control block in a diffusely held corporation that lacks a dominant shareholder or shareholder group. The premium paid by the offeror is often analogized to the control premium paid to a controlling shareholder.

Before the passage of the Williams Act in 1967, cash tender offers were unregulated. Offerors could — and sometimes did — make "Saturday Night Special" offers that left public shareholders only 24 or 48 hours to decide whether to tender their shares, without providing any information about the identity or plans of the offeror. The Williams Act sought to provide shareholders sufficient time and information to make an informed decision about tendering their shares and to warn the market about an impending offer. Arguably, it was also intended to assure shareholders an equal opportunity to participate in offer premia and to discourage hostile tender offers on the margin.

The Williams Act did not define "tender offer," partly because Congress did not wish to be underinclusive and partly because tender offers were an easily recognized market phenomenon, even by 1967. Nevertheless, it is worth asking why, in 1967 and today, efforts to aggregate control usually take the form of public offers for shares rather than long-term gradual efforts to buy shares on the stock market or through negotiated transactions with individual shareholders in "creeping tender offers"?

The regulatory structure of the Williams Act, as amplified by the SEC, has four principal elements. The first of these elements is an "early warning system" under §13(d), which alerts the public and the company's managers whenever anyone acquires more than 5 percent of the company's voting stock. The SEC rules promulgated under §13(d) include the following.[7]

Rule 13d-1(a) requires investors to file a 13D report within 10 days of acquiring 5+ percent beneficial ownership, although Rule 13d-1(b) allows certain "qualified institutional investors" to file a shortened 13G report (in lieu of the 13D report) within 45 days of year-end; Rule 13d-1(c) permits passive but nonqualifying investors to file a 13G report (in lieu of the 13D report) within 10 days of acquiring their holdings; Rule 13d-2 requires shareholders to amend their 13D and 13G reports annually, or upon acquiring 10+ percent of an issuer's shares; and finally, Rule 13d-5 defines a §13(d) group, subject to §13(d) rules, as multiple shareholders who act together to buy, vote, or sell stock.

The second principal element of Williams Act regulation is §14(d)(1) (as well as related provisions under §§13 and 14 of the Securities Exchange Act and their associated rules), which mandates disclosure of the identity, financing, and future plans of a tender offeror, including plans for any subsequent going-private transaction. The regulations under these provisions include Rule 14d-3, which requires bidders to file and keep current 14D-1 reports for tender offers; Rule 14e-2, which requires the target's board to comment on the tender offer; Rule 13e-4, which requires companies to make much the same disclosures as third-party offerors when these companies tender for their *own* shares; and Rule 13e-3, which mandates particularly strict disclosure when insiders (including controlling shareholders) plan going-private transactions that would force public shareholders out of the company.

The third element of the Williams Act is §14(e), an antifraud provision that prohibits misrepresentations, nondisclosures, and "any fraudulent, deceptive, or misrepresentative" practices in connection with a tender offer. The rules promulgated under this section of the Act include Rule 14e-3, which bars trading on insider information in connection with a tender offer.

Finally, the fourth element of the Williams Act, which builds largely on §§14(d)(4)-(7) and 14(e) of the Act, is a dozen rules that regulate the substantive terms of tender offers, including matters such as how long offers must be left open, when shareholders can withdraw previously tendered shares, and how bidders must treat shareholders who tender. Among the more important of these are Rule 14e-1, which mandates that tender offers be left open for a minimum of 20 business days, and Rule 14d-10, which requires bidders to open their tender offers to *all shareholders* and pay all who tender the same "best" price.

---

7. We thank Professor John Coates for contributing this overview of the Williams Act rules.

QUESTION ON §13(d) OF THE WILLIAMS ACT

Section 13(d) serves as a disclosure provision and an early warning system for target management. But how does §13(d) (or any parallel disclosure requirement) affect the *proportion* of the value in a premium tender offer that public shareholders are likely to capture? Put differently, if there were no requirement to disclose shareholdings beyond the 5 percent level, and no obstacles to accumulating shares, how would a bidder divide her efforts to accumulate shares between open market purchases and a tender offer? What are the consequences for the total amount she must pay to acquire control?

NOTE: WHAT EXACTLY IS A TENDER OFFER, ANYWAY?

Curiously, the Williams Act does not define "tender offer," the subject of its regulations. One reason may have been that conventional tender offers were unmistakable and self-identifying, even before the Williams Act. A second reason may have been that unconventional "tender offers" are not easy to define. The absence of a definition in the Act has led to case law on "de facto tender offers." Consider the following case.

BRASCAN LTD. v. EDPER EQUITIES LTD.

477 F. Supp. 773 (S.D.N.Y. 1979)

[Over two days, Edper purchased 24 percent of Brascan, a Canadian company trading in Canada, in the United Kingdom, and on the American Stock Exchange. As a Canadian company, Brascan was not subject to the rules promulgated under §§13(d) and 14(d) of the Williams Act. However, §14(e) of the Act was applicable if Edper's open market purchases on the American Stock Exchange amounted to a de facto tender offer. Edper already held a 5 percent stake in Brascan and had proposed a friendly acquisition, which Brascan had rebuffed. To increase its influence over Brascan, Edper decided to purchase an additional 3 million Brascan shares, and to do so through the American Stock Exchange to avoid Canadian regulations. Edper asked Connacher, president of Gordon Securities Ltd., to advise it. On April 30, 1979, after some initial difficulties in purchasing shares on the American Stock Exchange, Edper informed Connacher that it might purchase up to three million shares at a premium price if these were available. Gordon Securities contacted between 30 and 50 institutional investors and 10 to 15 individual investors, who held large blocks of Brascan shares, telling them that Edper might be willing to purchase three or four million shares at 22¾ (which was several dollars above the trading price).

On April 30, Connacher informed Edper that approximately 1.5 million shares of Brascan might be available at 22¾ per share. Edper authorized its broker to purchase 2.5 million shares at 22¾. Edper's broker on the Exchange floor found very little stock available below 22⅜, but when it raised the bid to 22¾, it suddenly acquired 2.4 million shares (2 million of which were offered by Gordon Securities on behalf of the shareholders it had just solicited). By the end of the day, Edper had purchased 3.1 million shares. Edper announced, in response to a demand from Canadian officials, that it had no plans to buy any more shares at that time. Nevertheless, on May 1, without further public announcement, Edper resumed its buying activity, and Gordon Securities again solicited large holders of Brascan. This time Edper managed to purchase 3.2 million shares at 22¾ or slightly higher, almost half of which came from Gordon Securities or its customers.

Brascan sued Edper, seeking to require Edper to divest itself of the shares it had bought, claiming that the failure to announce that it was making further purchases violated §14(e) of the Williams Act and Rule 10b-5 (the general antifraud provision under the securities acts). Judge Leval found Edper in violation of Rule 10b-5, but he did not find a violation of §14(e). The judge held that Edper did not make a de facto tender offer within the meaning of the Williams Act.]

LEVAL, J.:

. . . Edper's conduct had very little similarity to what is commonly understood as a tender offer and what was described as a tender offer in the context of the hearings leading to the passage of the Williams Act. Edper did not engage in widespread solicitation of stockholders. Indeed, it scrupulously avoided any solicitation upon the advice of its lawyers. Its purchasing was not contingent on a minimum fixed number of shares being offered, it did not put out an offer at a fixed price and the form of the transaction did not provide for tenders by the selling shareholders to be held for some period of time by the purchaser or a depositary, as is customary in tender offers. What Edper did was to acquire a large amount of stock in open market purchases, bidding cautiously so as to avoid bidding up the price of the stock to excessive levels unless there was large volume available at such prices. This is not a tender offer, even if a large volume of stock is accumulated in such fashion. . . .

Brascan argues that Edper made Connacher its agent so that all of Connacher's and his firm's activity in lining up potential sellers is attributable to Edper in determining whether or not Edper engaged in a tender offer. I do not find this contention supported by the evidence. . . .

Of course Connacher and Edper necessarily had interests in common. A seller's broker always has interests in common with the buyer. If the buyer does not buy, the seller's broker will not earn his commission. Thus, if Connacher as a seller's broker were capable of rounding up a large volume of shares for sale at a price that Edper was willing to pay, Edper's objectives would be satisfied and Connacher would make money. That did not make Connacher Edper's agent for the solicitation of sellers' shares.

Even if Connacher were deemed to have been Edper's agent in the solicitation of shares for sale, still the transaction would not constitute a tender offer within the meaning of the Williams Act. All that Connacher and his firm did was to scout between 30 and 50 large institutional holders of Brascan stock, plus about a dozen large individual investors, to collect a large block for Edper to purchase at a price agreeable to both sides of the transaction. He and his firm did this in the conventional methods of privately negotiated block trades. Such privately negotiated block trading is done on a daily basis in the U.S. securities markets without anyone's ever suspecting that what is being practiced might be a tender offer. . . .

A small number of District Court cases have held that the Williams Act should be deemed applicable to such large scale accumulations. The general thrust of the reasoning is that since the Williams Act was designed to remedy certain problems often found in tender offers, and since similar problems are to be found in other forms of stock accumulation, the Williams Act should be deemed to cover such other forms of stock accumulation even though they are not what is conventionally understood as a tender offer.

There are serious problems with this form of statutory interpretation. First of all the legislative history of the Williams Act shows that it was passed with full awareness of the difference between tender offers and other forms of large scale stock accumulations. . . .

Further the regulatory scheme established by Congress in the Williams Act is incompatible with its application to a program of market purchasing. . . . The consequence of bringing such large scale open market and privately negotiated purchases within the scope of the Williams Act would be to rule, in effect, that no large scale acquisition program may be lawfully accomplished except in the manner of a conventional tender offer. While this may be a sensible legislative provision . . . there is nothing in the legislative history or the text of the Williams Act which suggests that it intended to bring about such consequences.

The Securities Exchange Commission, at this Court's request, submitted a brief amicus curiae. The Commission takes no position as to whether the acts of Edper constituted a tender offer, but lists eight factors which authorities have considered in determining whether acquisitions constitute a tender offer under the Williams Act. The SEC refrains from specifying which of the eight factors or how many must be met or how clearly before an acquisition will be considered a tender offer. I have doubts as to whether this view constitutes either a permissible or a desirable interpretation of the statute. . . .

But more important for purposes of this decision, I find that even if the Commission's eight criteria represented the authorized interpretation of the Williams Act, Edper's actions, even as supplemented by Connacher's, do not sufficiently meet these criteria to come within the definition of a tender offer.

The first criterion calling for "active and widespread solicitation of public shareholders" is clearly not met. The solicitations were directed to only approximately 50 of Brascan's 50,000 shareholders, each of the 50 being either an institution or a sophisticated individual holder of large blocks of Brascan shares.

The third criterion calling for "a premium over the prevailing market price" is met, but only to a slight degree. Edper was unable to purchase large amounts at 21½. Its broker, Balfour, did not encounter sizeable blocks until it went as high as 22⅜. The price at which it accomplished its major volume, ¾, was only ⅜ of a point above what any purchaser would have had to pay for any significant volume.

Criterion number four that "the terms of the offer are firm rather than negotiable" was not met. Edper, Gordon, and the sellers were feeling their way to find a level at which large volume purchasing could be done. The fact that Gordon spoke to potential sellers during the morning of the likelihood of a price of $26 Cdn. (22¾ U.S.) did not represent a firm bid. I find that it represented Connacher's well educated guess as to where a deal might be put together based on his knowledge of the market and of the buyer's and sellers' desires. He and his traders repeatedly denied to their customers the existence of any firm bid.

The fifth criterion, "whether the offer is contingent on the tender of a fixed minimum number of shares," is met only to a slight degree. It is true that Edper was not interested in bidding up the price too high without acquiring a large number of shares in doing so. And it is true that Connacher advised his customers that he didn't believe a transaction would go through unless sufficient volume were achieved. But these conditions were general, fluid and negotiable. They were not fixed as part of the terms of any offer to purchase shares.

The sixth condition, "whether the offer is open only for a limited period of time," is not met. Since there was no open offer, there was certainly no assurance that any offer would remain open for any period of time. Nor was there any statement to the effect that an offer temporarily available would soon disappear. What was said to the potential sellers by Gordon was that a buyer was interested in accumulating a large volume. Thus the situation did not carry with it the kind of potential pressure which, coupling a high premium with the threat that the offer will disappear as of a certain time, places an offeree under pressure to decide. That is the kind of pressure which the Williams Act was designed to alleviate, by providing information on which to base a decision. That was not present here.

I find that the seventh criterion, "whether the offerees are subjected to pressure to sell their stock," was not met. The offerees were experienced professionals, in most cases institutional portfolio managers. Even assuming that such professional investors can be susceptible to "pressure" in the sense in which the Williams Act is concerned, no such pressures were applied.

Finally, the eighth criterion, "whether public announcements of a purchasing program . . . precede or accompany a rapid accumulation," was not met. Edper had made some public announcements in early April when it was contemplating differently structured programs of acquisition. It announced its application on April 18 to the Ontario Securities Commission for permission to make a conditional circular offering. When permission was refused on April 20, Edper announced the refusal to the public and indicated that it had no specific further plans at that time. No further public statement was made by Edper until the close of business on April 30.

In short, the only one of the SEC's eight criteria which is clearly and solidly met is number two, that "the solicitation is made for a substantial percentage of the issuer's stock." While one might have no disagreement with legislation which imposed pre-acquisition disclosure requirements, comparable to those required by §13(d), whenever a purchaser intended to acquire by any means a large specified percentage of any publicly held stock, that is not what the Williams Act now requires. It is not in my view within the power of a court to so rewrite its provisions.

NOTES AND QUESTIONS ON BRASCAN LTD.

1. In the *Wellman* case, mentioned by *Brascan,* a corporate acquirer solicited the sale of stock in a target company from 30 large institutional shareholders and 9 wealthy individuals. The solicitations were made in simultaneous phone calls to the prospective sellers by 30 agents. The offers were made at a fixed price substantially above market price and were left open for only one hour. The solicitees had been told beforehand to expect a phone solicitation but had not been told the offering price. By this method, the acquirer managed to purchase 34 percent of the outstanding stock of its target in a single afternoon. The federal district court, however, ruled that the solicitation campaign was a de facto tender offer subject to the requirements of the Williams Act — each of the eight factors was present except "widespread solicitation." *Wellman v. Dickinson,* 475 F. Supp. 783 (S.D.N.Y. 1979), *aff'd on other grounds,* 682 F.2d 355 (2d Cir. 1982).

2. What distinguishes *Wellman* from *Brascan*? Was it important that the *Brascan* purchases were effected over the market rather than as private purchases as in *Wellman*? Should it have been important? Should the fact that none of the selling institutions in *Wellman* complained have weighed against the court's decision? Who was really injured in *Wellman*?

11.5   THE HART-SCOTT-RODINO ACT WAITING PERIOD

Apart from the Williams Act, a second legal constraint on the immediate acquisition of control of large U.S. companies is the Hart-Scott-Rodino Antitrust Improvements Act of 1976 (HSR Act), which was intended to give the Federal Trade Commission (FTC) and the Department of Justice (DOJ) the proactive ability to block deals that violate the antitrust laws. If there are no antitrust issues, the HSR Act affects only the timing of transactions. In most friendly acquisitions, the HSR Act does not even delay a deal because the HSR waiting period is shorter than those imposed by other legal requirements such as the proxy rules and the Williams Act.

Precisely when a filing is required under the HSR Act is a surprisingly complex question. Suffice to say here that a filing is always required for transactions in excess of $212 million in value, and often when they are smaller. Initial filings are relatively short, although the antitrust agencies may later request more information about the deal or the parties.

From the standpoint of corporate law (as opposed to antitrust law), the real significance of the HSR Act lies in the waiting periods it imposes *before* a bidder can commence her offer. The effect is something like that of §13(d), only more so, since HSR filings must be disclosed immediately to target companies, and bidders may not close a deal until the relevant waiting period has elapsed. Waiting periods under the HSR Act vary by category of transaction. For cash tender offers, acquirers must wait 15 calendar days after filing before closing; for regulated open market purchases, acquirers must wait 30 days after filing; for mergers, asset deals, and other negotiated acquisitions, both parties must wait 30 days after filing.[8]

QUESTION ON THE HSR ACT

What would be the effect if the HSR waiting periods had been in place at the time of the *Wellman* transaction? What would have been the effect in the case of the *Brascan* transaction, assuming Brascan and Edper had been U.S. companies?

NOTE ON THE AUCTION DEBATE AND THE SHAREHOLDER COLLECTIVE ACTION PROBLEM

Until the late 1980s, one of the most important effects of the Williams Act was to create a de facto auction period of at least four weeks, which allowed target management to build its defenses and permitted other acquirers to look over the firm. In this way, the Williams Act led directly to broader questions: How should the law structure the purchase of control from disaggregated shareholders? Should it assist shareholders in overcoming their collective action problem by facilitating the highest bid, or should it protect discovery values by facilitating a successful acquisition by the first bidder?

Academic commentators lined up on both sides of this issue. Judge Frank Easterbrook and Professor Daniel Fischel argued strongly that auctioneering is likely to reduce the total number of value-increasing takeovers.[9] Professors Ronald Gilson and Lucian Bebchuk countered that an auction regime enhances the efficiency of individual takeovers, while

8. If a second request is made, further waiting periods apply (10 days from the acquiring person's compliance for tender offers; 20 days from both parties' compliance for open market purchases or negotiated acquisitions). In addition, the antitrust agencies have effective power to extend waiting periods indefinitely if they believe parties have not complied with information requests. In each case, the agencies may grant "early termination" of the applicable waiting period, and generally will do so if the deal raises no competitive concerns.

9. See, e.g., Frank H. Easterbrook & Daniel R. Fischel, *The Proper Role of a Target's Management in Responding to a Tender Offer*, 94 Harv. L. Rev. 1161 (1981).

having relatively little impact on the number of value-enhancing trans-actions.[10] The empirical evidence on this question is mixed: on one hand studies showed that returns to U.S. acquirers in tender offers were lower in the 1970s than they were in the 1960s;[11] on the other hand there is no evidence that acquisition activity declined in the 1970s due to the de facto auction period imposed by the Williams Act.

The legal import of the auction debate reaches well beyond the Williams Act. A related question was how much latitude target managers ought to enjoy under state law to "shop" the company by searching for a higher bidder after a hostile first bid. The auction debate thus feeds into a parallel controversy over the proper role for target management when confronted with a hostile bid. We address this debate in Chapter 13.

10. E.g., Ronald J. Gilson, *Seeking Competitive Bids Versus Pure Passivity in Tender Offer Defense*, 35 Stan. L. Rev. 51 (1982); Lucian Arye Bebchuk, *The Case for Facilitating Competing Tender Offers*, 95 Harv. L. Rev. 1028 (1982); Lucian Arye Bebchuk, *The Case for Facilitating Competing Tender Offers: A Reply and Extension*, 35 Stan. L. Rev. 23 (1984).

11. See, e.g., M. Bradley, A. Desai, & E.H. Kim, *Synergistic Gains from Corporate Acquisitions and Their Division Between the Stockholders of Target and Acquiring Firms*, 21 J. Fin. Econ. 3 (1988); (average returns to acquirers declined to 1.3 percent during the 1970s compared to 4.1 percent in the 1960s).

FUNDAMENTAL TRANSACTIONS: MERGERS AND ACQUISITIONS

12.1 INTRODUCTION

Among the most important transactions in corporate law are those that pool the assets of separate companies into either a single entity or a dyad of a parent company and a wholly owned subsidiary (which is practically the same thing, only better). There are three legal forms for such transactions: the merger, the purchase (or sale) of all assets, and—in RMBCA jurisdictions—the compulsory share exchange. A merger is a legal event that unites two existing corporations with a public filing of a certificate of merger, usually with shareholder approval. Ordinarily, one of the two companies absorbs the other and is termed the "surviving corporation."[1] This company subsequently owns all of the property and assumes all of the obligations of both parties to the merger. An RMBCA share exchange, as we describe below, closely resembles certain kinds of mergers in its legal effects. Finally, "acquisitions" comprise a generic class of "nonmerger" techniques for combining companies, which generally involve the purchase of the assets or shares of one firm by another. Following an acquisition, the acquiring corporation may or may not assume liability for the obligations of the acquired corporation, as we discuss below.

Mergers and acquisitions by public companies (M&A transactions) are among the most complex of business transactions. They implicate diverse legal questions[2] and, at least potentially, profoundly alter the characteristics of shareholder investments. In this chapter, we first examine economic motives for M&A transactions and then turn to specific protections that the law accords shareholders in these transactions. In particular, M&A transactions provide a useful platform for revisiting two fundamental questions of policy in corporate law: the role of shareholders in checking the board's discretion and the role of fiduciary duty in checking the power of controlling shareholders.

1. A merger in which both parties disappear and are survived by a new third corporation is technically called a consolidation. See, e.g., DGCL §251(a).
2. Even the simplest M&A transaction involving public companies typically raises issues of securities law, tax law, compensation law, and quite possibly competition law, in addition to corporate law, of course. See Martin D. Ginsburg & Jack S. Levin, Mergers, Acquisitions and Buyouts (2006).

12.2   ECONOMIC MOTIVES FOR MERGERS

Like other legal forms of enterprise, the corporate form partitions business assets into discrete pools under the management of particular management teams.[3] There is, however, no guarantee that the initial match among assets, managers, and companies is the right one or that it continues to be the right one in an economy subject to continuous change. The law of M&A transactions provides (relatively) quick and inexpensive ways to reform the partitioning and management of corporate assets. We begin by surveying motives, value increasing or not, for combining corporate assets.

12.2.1   Integration as a Source of Value

Gains from integrating corporate assets arise from what economists term economies of "scale," "scope," and "vertical integration." Economies of scale result when a fixed cost of production — such as the investment in a factory — is spread over a larger output, thereby reducing the average fixed cost per unit of output. Consider two companies, each with a widget factory that operates at half capacity. If the companies merge, the "surviving" company might be able to close down one factory and meet the combined demand for its products at a much lower cost. This source of efficiency often explains so-called horizontal mergers between firms in the same industry.

Economies of scope provide a similar source of efficiency gains. Here mergers reduce costs not by increasing the scale of production but instead by spreading costs across a broader range of related business activities. For example, a business might merge with another company that manufactures a product that can be efficiently marketed through the first company's sales force. In theory, at least, even the talents of a company's management team could be a source of economies of scope if a merger could extend its talents to a larger asset base.[4]

Vertical integration, a special form of economies of scope, may sometimes arise by merging a company backward, toward its suppliers, or forward, toward its customers. Buying a component on the market has advantages, but so, too, does buying the factory that makes the component. Contracting through the market can be expensive if the component is highly specialized. Moreover, even if a supplier is found, it may begin to behave

---

3. See our discussion of asset partitioning in Chapter 3.

4. Thus, a management team with superior "general management" skills could attempt to wring added value from its skills by expanding the asset base over which it exercises its judgment. Something like this idea was a popular rationale for mergers during the "conglomerate merger" movement of the 1960s. Those mergers, however, did not generally prove to be efficient. See, e.g., Ronald W. Melichner & David F. Rush, *The Performance of Conglomerate Firms: Recent Risk and Return Experience*, 28 J. Fin. 381 (1973); David J. Ravenscraft & F. M. Scherer, Mergers, Sell-Offs and Economic Efficiency (1987). Indeed, many commentators believe that the "bust-up" takeover movement of the 1980s was largely about the unwinding of these inefficient mergers of two decades before. See, e.g., Andrei Shleifer & Robert W. Vishny, *The Takeover Wave of the 1980s*, 249 Sci. 745 (Aug. 17, 1990).

opportunistically once it determines that its customers are dependent on it. Thus, it may be cheaper to merge with the supplier than to buy the product.[5]

12.2.2   Other Sources of Value in Acquisitions: Tax, Agency Costs, and Diversification

Apart from integration gains, M&A transactions are often said to generate value for at least three other reasons, relating to tax, agency costs, and diversification. Consider tax first. Corporations with tax losses (i.e., deductible expenses greater than income during the tax year) may set those losses off against income in subsequent years for up to twenty years. This ability to carry a net operating loss (NOL) forward is itself a valuable asset — but only if its owner has sufficient taxable income to absorb it. Since an NOL cannot be sold directly, a corporation that lacks sufficient income might prefer to find a wealthy merger partner rather than waste its NOL. In this transaction, the shareholders of the NOL's owner and its merger partner would implicitly share the NOL's present value.[6]

A very different economic motive for M&A transactions is the replacement of an underperforming management team that has depressed the company's stock price. As a company's stock price declines because the market anticipates that its incumbent managers will mismanage *in the future*, it becomes more likely that an outside buyer can profit by purchasing a controlling block of stock and replacing the incumbent managers.[7] Of course, acquiring a controlling block of stock, by means of a tender offer or otherwise, is usually enough to displace the target company's managers. The point is not merely to depose bad managers, however, but also to realize the maximum economic returns from doing so. Realizing maximum

5. See generally F. M. Scherer & David Ross, Industrial Market Structures and Economic Performance (3d ed. 1990). Professors Brealey and Myers, the finance mavens, offer the following illustration of how integration through ownership can increase efficiency. Suppose that airlines rented their planes on short-term leases but owned their brand names, operated airport gates, advertised, sold tickets, etc. The administrative cost of matching the supply of rented planes with the published schedule of flights would be enormous. Intuitively, any airline that switched to either owning its own planes or leasing them for long periods (which is economically quite similar) could realize huge savings. Thus, we would expect airlines to move to vertical integration — either owning or leasing the vital aircraft input for long periods. Nevertheless, a good thing can be overdone. Professors Brealey and Myers also note that, in the late 1980s, the Polish State Airline owned not only its own planes but also its own hog farms to supply meat to its customers and employees. See Richard A. Brealey & Stewart C. Myers, Principles of Corporate Finance (7th ed. 2003). Of course, our intuition is that it is cheaper for an airline to buy sausages on the market than to make them itself. At least, we hope that this is true in a developed market economy like our own, even if it might not have been true in socialist Poland.

6. See Ginsburg & Levin, supra note 2, at ch. 12. The Internal Revenue Service not only bars the sale of NOLs but also disallows their deduction if the merger appears to have been structured solely to capture their value. Thus, the surviving company in a tax-driven merger must generally continue to operate the assets acquired from the NOL's owner, at least for a period.

7. See Reinier Kraakman, *Taking Discounts Seriously: The Implications of "Discounted" Share Prices as an Acquisition Motive*, 88 Colum. L. Rev. 891 (1981).

returns will generally require that the target company merge with a subsidiary of the acquiring company.

In the 1980s, most transactions to displace underperforming managers appear to have been hostile. As we discuss in Chapter 13, an acquirer would first bid for a controlling block of stock in a public tender offer and then, when successful, would arrange for a merger to cash out minority shareholders. Once in control, the acquirer would be free to discipline or fire management. Although hostile takeovers have been less common in recent years, the desire to improve management may also motivate friendly acquisitions. Why would poorly performing managers leave if they were not forced to do so? The answer is money, of course. As a matter of fact, poor managers (or good managers) can be bought off as part of the premium that a new investor must pay to acquire the corporation's assets. One device for sharing takeover premia with managers is the "golden parachute" contract, which provides senior managers with a generous payment upon certain triggering events, typically a change in the ownership of a controlling interest in the corporation or a change in the membership of its board. A second compensation technique is a stock option plan, which allows options that would otherwise vest over a four- to six-year period to become immediately exercisable upon a change in control.

Yet a third way in which M&A transactions are sometimes said to increase corporate value is by diversifying a company's business projects, thus smoothing corporate earnings over the business cycle. For example, the managers of an air conditioner company might wish to merge with a snowblower company to ensure stable year-round earnings. Just why this sort of merger should increase the value of corporate assets is unclear, since investors can "smooth" corporate earnings at less cost merely by diversifying their *own* investment portfolios. Nevertheless, such "smoothing" is frequently offered as a rationale for mergers. The reason may be that such mergers simply make life more comfortable for managers,[8] or it may be that they actually can increase company value for some reason as yet undiscovered by financial economists.[9]

12.2.3   Suspect Motives for Mergers

The discussion thus far has emphasized positive or neutral motives for mergers that increase the value of corporate assets without making anyone else worse off (except the government in tax-driven deals). There are,

8. See Yakov Amihud & Baruch Lev, *Risk Reduces Managerial Motive for Conglomerate Mergers*, 12 Bell J. Econ. 605 (1981).

9. See Ronald J. Gilson & Bernard S. Black, The Law and Finance of Corporate Acquisitions 312-357 (2d ed. 1995). Wholly apart from smoothing earnings, product diversification can add efficiency by combining complementary assets, as when an acquirer can use its distribution channels to sell a target's products. A merger between a snowblower company and an air conditioner company makes good sense if the combined firm can use shared physical facilities or the same trained workers. Economies of scope such as these do increase the real value of the target's assets, and thus the value of the surviving corporation's stock.

however, also opportunistic motives to enter mergers that increase share-holder value or management compensation at the expense of another corporate constituency. One example is a squeeze-out merger, in which a controlling shareholder acquires all of a company's assets at a low price, at the expense of its minority shareholders. Another form of opportunistic merger is one that creates market power in a particular product market, and thus allows the postmerger entity to charge monopoly prices for its output. (Of course, the government also attempts to block anticompetitive mergers under the elaborate federal framework of antitrust statutes.[10])

Finally, in addition to opportunistic M&A transactions, there is a last class of mergers that destroy value, perhaps even more so than opportunistic mergers. These are "mistaken" mergers that occur because their planners misjudge the difficulties of realizing merger economies. Common errors of judgment include underestimating the costs of overcoming disparate firm cultures; neglecting intangible costs, such as the labor difficulties that might follow wholesale layoffs; and failing to anticipate the added coordination costs that result merely from increasing the size of a business organization.[11]

12.2.4 Do Mergers Create Value?

There is a vast empirical literature on the wealth effects of mergers. While the magnitude of the result varies widely from study to study, the general weight of the evidence indicates that, measured by immediate stock market price reaction to the merger's announcement, on average, mergers do create value.[12] In one frequently cited study, Professors Gregor Andrade, Mark Mitchell, and Erik Stafford examine 3,688 deals over the period 1973–1998 and find an increase in combined (target and acquirer) wealth of 1.8 percent in the window around the announcement of

10. Phillip Areeda & Donald F. Turner, Antitrust Law, 5 vols. (1978, 1980); Thomas W. Brunner, Mergers in the New Antitrust Era (1985). The Sherman Antitrust Act, the Clayton Act, and the Federal Trade Commission Act are the three most notable such statutes.

11. While there are often advantages to a larger scale, there is also a special burden that large-scale organizations must bear. That burden is reflected in minor part by the costs of determining transfer prices within large firms and, in a more important way, by the imperfections in these transfer prices. The firm loses market discipline by assigning internal costs that differ from true market prices. This problem is small where the input has a comparable market price, in which case internal pricing can be based on an actual price. But as the organization grows large and its inputs become specialized, the costs assigned to them grow unreliable. As a result, the firm comes to lack critical information about the relative efficiency of different aspects of its operations. See Ludwig von Mises, Human Action: A Treatise on Economics (1949); and Socialism: An Economic and Sociological Analysis (1922) (J. Kahane trans., 1951). In addition, large-scale organizations typically require complex compensation schemes to encourage team cooperation and motivate individual performance. Such plans grow increasingly difficult to design and operate as the scale and complexity of the firm increase. Correlatively, smaller firms are better able to monitor worker productivity and create functional incentives.

12. For a comprehensive recent survey of the empirical evidence, see Robert F. Bruner, Applied Mergers and Acquisitions 47-49 (2004) (summarizing the results from 24 studies and concluding that "M&A does pay the investors in the combined buyer and target firms").

the deal.[13] This value, however, is not evenly distributed: studies find that targets generally win, while acquirers break even, or lose on average. Andrade, Mitchell, and Stafford, for example, report that targets in their sample experienced positive abnormal returns of 16.0 percent, on average, while acquirers experienced negative abnormal returns of 0.7 percent.[14] (The combined effect is only modestly positive because acquirers are generally much larger than targets.)

Using a more recent M&A sample and employing the same market price methodology, Professors Sara Moeller, Frederick Schlingemann, and Rene Stulz report an acceleration in acquirers' losses from acquisition: between 1998 and 2001 acquiring firm shareholders lost 12 cents at deal announcement for every dollar spent, for a total loss of $240 billion during this period, compared to a loss of just 1.6 cents per dollar spent, or a total loss of $7 billion, during all of the 1980s.[15] The authors note that their results for the 1998-2001 period are driven by a small number of acquisition announcements with extremely large losses. In addition, these and all other empirical studies of the question must be interpreted with caution because we do not have the counter-factual — what would have happened to acquirers if they had not engaged in acquisition activity? If acquisitions are effective in mitigating losses, then we cannot conclude that acquisition activity, on average, destroys value for acquirers.

12.3   THE EVOLUTION OF THE U.S. CORPORATE LAW OF MERGERS

The history of U.S. merger law is one of constantly loosening constraints, driven by dynamic markets and technological change. It begins in a world without any mergers at all and ends in a world in which mergers can force shareholders to divest all of their stock in a company. The fundamental move in this evolution occurred when the law became willing to treat equity investors as a class of interests that could, except where fiduciaries duties were triggered, be adequately protected by majority vote and a right to a statutory appraisal of fair value. For convenience, we can divide the history of merger law into two periods.

12.3.1   When Mergers Were Rare

The first period is the era when mergers were rare, which covers the history of U.S. corporate law until roughly 1890. Until about 1840,

---

13. Gregor Andrade, Mark Mitchell, & Erik Stafford, *New Evidence and Perspectives on Mergers*, 15 J. Econ. Persp. 103, 110 (Table 3) (2001).
14. See *id.*
15. Sara B. Moeller, Frederick P. Schlingemann, & Rene M. Stulz, *Wealth Destruction on a Massive Scale? A Study of Acquiring-Firm Returns in the Recent Merger Wave*, 60 J. Fin. 757 (2005).

corporate charters were acts of the sovereign, in theory and in actuality. Legislatures created business corporations by special acts of incorporation, often to facilitate projects with a public purpose: the construction of canals or railroads, the creation of financial intermediaries (banks and insurance firms), or, more rarely, the establishment of manufacturing enterprises. Shareholders naturally lacked the power to amend these legislative charters, and thus, mergers could not occur except by intervention of state legislatures. Beginning around 1840, however, the enactment of general incorporation statutes permitted shareholders to incorporate on their own initiative with a charter of their own design. But until around 1890, state incorporation law uniformly barred shareholders from amending their charters (which a merger would require) without unanimous consent, in order to protect investors who had contributed funds in reliance on the charter. Thus, in this respect, the mid-nineteenth-century corporate form looked rather like the general partnership form.

12.3.2   The Modern Era

Technological change in the last decades of the nineteenth century increased the efficiency scale of many industries. Nevertheless, mergers could not become an economical way to restructure businesses into larger units as long as they required the unanimous consent of shareholders, which created crippling hold-up problems at the hands of minority shareholders. Thus, toward the end of the nineteenth century, corporation statutes were amended to permit mergers and charter amendments that received less than unanimous shareholder approval, providing that they were recommended by the board and approved by a majority (at first a supermajority) of a company's shareholders. Class vote provisions were sometimes added to assure fairness to subgroups of shareholders. Today, Delaware and many other states allow mergers to proceed with the approval of only a bare majority of the outstanding shares of each class of stock that is entitled to vote on them. In addition, a second innovation introduced at the turn of the century was the establishment of the shareholders' right to dissent from a proposed merger and demand an "appraisal" — or judicial determination of the cash value of her shares — as an alternative to continuing as a shareholder in the new, merged enterprise.

Conditioning mergers on majority (originally supermajority) shareholder approval rather than unanimous approval introduced the most important element of modern merger laws at the turn of the twentieth century. A second important element of merger law in the modern era followed some 50 years later, when, in the mid-twentieth century, states greatly liberalized the permissible forms of merger consideration. Originally, shareholders of a merging company could receive only equity in the surviving company in exchange for their old shares. Under the mid-century statutes, the range of possible forms of consideration moved beyond securities in the surviving corporation to include all forms of property — most notably cash. Thus, from at least mid-century onward, it has been possible under state law to construct a "cash-out" merger, in which shareholders can be forced to exchange their shares for cash as long as the procedural requirements for a valid merger are met.

12.4   THE ALLOCATION OF POWER IN FUNDAMENTAL TRANSACTIONS

Today, the merger is the most prominent among a handful of corporate decisions that require shareholder approval.[16] Of course, those who formulate the corporation's original charter could shape additional shareholder voice in almost any way thought useful. Charters could create shareholder veto power, for example, in the sale of certain assets or in order to leave or enter certain lines of business. But as far as we are aware, no charters of public companies contain such provisions. All rely strictly on the provisions of the statutes to allocate power between the board and shareholders.

So, why does the law usually require shareholder consent for mergers and certain other transactions? Or put differently, how *should* the law draw the line between transactions that are completely delegated to the board and those that also must be approved by shareholders?

To explore this question, consider first the universal requirement that shareholders approve material amendments of the articles of incorporation, the basic "charter" of the corporation. Investors buy shares subject to the terms of the charter, and the board of directors exercises its management powers subject to these same terms. Thus, if it is useful for investors to be able to rely on any constraint in the charter, then the law must preclude unilateral amendment of the charter by the board. In fact, the law in all jurisdictions does this.[17] Moreover, to protect investors' reasonable expectations, the law must provide a shareholder veto over all transactions that might effectively amend the charter. Thus, shareholders must approve both corporate dissolution, which nullifies the corporate charter, and corporate mergers, in which the surviving corporation's charter may be amended. But the power to change the charter cannot be the only criterion for determining which transactions require a shareholder vote. Other transactions that do not change the charter also require shareholder approval. Specifically, a sale of substantially all of a corporation's assets may not occur unless it has been approved by a vote of the company's shareholders, even though no change in the company's charter occurs.[18] In some non-U.S. jurisdictions, shareholders must approve other transactions

---

16. In most U.S. jurisdictions, the other corporate decisions that require shareholder approval include sales of substantially all assets, charter amendments, and voluntary dissolutions. Some states and foreign jurisdictions add other classes of decisions to the shortlist of fundamental decisions requiring shareholder approval.

17. See, e.g., DGCL §242(b); RMBCA §§10.03, 10.04.

18. E.g., DGCL §271; RMBCA §12.02.

as well, such as large share issues and asset purchases.[19] (While in the United States these transactions do not require shareholder approval as a matter of corporation law, the listing rules of the major securities exchanges do require companies to obtain shareholder approval if they issue 20 percent or more of their outstanding stock in a single transaction.[20])

As a general matter, two major considerations ought to determine the allocation of decision-making power within organizations: who has the best information, and who has the best incentives. At least in large companies, the answers to these questions are not always the same. Managers will generally have much better information regarding a company's business and all of its proposed transactions. But managers may have incentive problems — the most obvious example is the decision to sell the company, which may cost them their job. So the boundary case of complete managerial authority does not seem socially optimal, and shareholders should reserve some decisions for themselves. We suggest that, rationally, principals will reserve power to veto those matters that are most economically significant and in which they have some capacity to exercise informed judgment. In the corporate context, these criteria suggest that dispersed shareholders will wish to decide at most only very large issues (those that affect their entire investment) and will wish to decide only issues that they can be expected to decide with some competence ("investment-like" decisions rather than "business" decisions).

The general contours of corporate law follow this logic. Bet-the-company operational decisions (take, for example, Microsoft's decision to develop Microsoft Windows; or Boeing's decision to develop the 747 wide-body jet) do not require a shareholder vote. Even though such decisions are of supreme economic importance, shareholders generally lack the ability and information to make them, relative to the alternative decision maker, the board and top managers. Likewise very small acquisitions (sometimes called "whale-minnow" acquisitions) do not require a shareholder vote, because shareholders would be rationally apathetic about evaluating the merits of the transaction. Far better to leave both of these kinds of decisions to the board.

What about large-scale M&A? Depending on your intuition about shareholder competence (or information) you might conjecture either that shareholders should vote on *all* large M&A transactions — including mergers, large asset sales and purchases, and share exchanges — or none. The benefits of avoiding errors might be large for such transactions, and shareholders might plausibly think they are likely to possess the expertise necessary to evaluate them.

United States law, however, does not quite conform to this logic in which shareholders would reserve the right to approve all or none of these transactions. Mergers require a shareholder vote on the part of both the target and the acquiring company, except the acquiring company's

19. Theodor Baums & Eddy Wymeersch, Shareholder Voting Rights and Practices in Europe and the United States (1999).

20. E.g. NYSE Listed Co. Rule 312.03(c); ASE Co. Guide §712(b).

shareholders do not vote when the acquiring company is much larger than the target (DGCL §251(b)). Sales of substantially all assets require a vote by the target's shareholders (DGCL §271), but purchases of assets do not require them to do so. Thus, even if the seller of substantially all assets is much larger than the buyer, the buyer's shareholders lack any statutory right of approval. What accounts for the different treatment of a very large purchase of assets that transforms the business and a merger that has a similar effect? It cannot be the magnitude of these transactions (and hence the size of potential management error), as both transactions are equally large. Nor can it be the likely quality and cost of shareholder decision making, since similar transactions can be structured in either way. However, there is a third factor bearing on optimal delegation that may have some role here: the potential severity of the agency problem between the principal (top shareholders) and the agent (the board).

By and large, the M&A transactions that require shareholder approval are those that change the board's relationship to its shareholders most dramatically, reducing the ability of shareholders to displace their managers after the transaction is completed. This is true for example of both corporations in a stock-for-stock merger between equally sized corporations because the shareholders of each constituent corporation will be very substantially diluted by the transaction. It is also true when the board proposes to sell substantially all of the corporation's assets because the company is likely to dissolve after the deal, leaving management to go its own way (perhaps to the purchaser of the assets) with no further ties to the target's shareholders. By contrast, a purchase of assets for cash does not alter the power of shareholders to displace their managers.[21] The purchase of assets for shares is another matter, and it is puzzling why American corporate law does not generally require shareholder votes to authorize large-scale share issues. One (unsatisfying) explanation might be that shareholders have already approved the corporate charter that authorizes such issues. But the major U.S. stock exchanges do require shareholders to authorize large-scale stock issues (20 percent or more).

For these reasons, it seems possible that concerns relating to shareholder future control over managers, rather than size or shareholder competence, are the binding functional determinants of when the law requires a shareholder vote. But we can easily see how other jurisdictions might delineate a wider or narrower class of corporate decisions that require shareholder approval.

12.5   OVERVIEW OF TRANSACTIONAL FORM

How is the acquisition of a business to be structured? As we noted above, there are three principal legal forms of acquisitions: (1) The acquirer can buy the target company's assets, (2) the acquirer can buy all of the target

---

21. This point is developed in Ronald H. Gilson & Bernard Black, The Law of Finance of Corporate Acquisitions 714-722 (1995).

corporation's stock, or (3) the acquirer can merge itself or a subsidiary corporation with the target on terms that ensure its control of the surviving entity. In each of these transactional forms, the acquirer can use cash, its own stock, or any other agreed-upon form of consideration. Each form, moreover, has particular implications for the acquisition's transactions costs (including its speed), potential liability costs, and tax consequences. Here we focus on the transactions costs and liability implications of transactional forms. We put off to §12.7 consideration of the tax aspects of mergers — which, as you might guess, play an important part in choosing the transactional form.

12.5.1 Asset Acquisition

The acquisition of a business through the purchase of its assets has a relatively high transaction cost (but a low liability cost). The purchase of assets — any assets — presents a standard set of contracting problems. One must identify the assets to be acquired, conduct due diligence with respect to these assets (e.g., investigate quality of title and existence of liens or other interests that may exist in the assets by others), establish the representations and warranties that both parties must make respecting the assets or themselves, negotiate covenants to protect the assets prior to closing, fix the price and terms of payment, and establish the conditions of closing. Titled assets, such as land and automobiles, must be transferred formally through documents of title and, frequently, by filing with an appropriate state office. Each of these individual steps is costly, and in the case of purchasing a large firm, aggregate acquisitions can be quite large.[22]

Finally, as we have just discussed, a sale of substantially all assets is a fundamental transaction for the selling company, which requires shareholder approval under all U.S. corporate law statutes. See, e.g., DGCL §271; RMBCA §12.02. But neither the meaning of "all or substantially all" assets nor the policy intent behind these words is always clear. Consider the following excerpt.

KATZ v. BREGMAN

431 A.2d 1274 (Del. Ch. 1981)

MARVEL, C.:

. . . The complaint alleges that during the last six months of 1980, the board of directors of Plant Industries, Inc., . . . embarked on a course of action which resulted in the disposal of several unprofitable subsidiaries of the corporate defendant located in the United States, namely Louisiana Foliage, Inc., a horticultural business, Sunaid Food Products, Inc., a Florida

---

22. See generally American Bar Association, Business Law Section, Negotiated Acquisition Committee, Model Asset Purchase Agreement with Commentary (Draft 1999).

packaging business, and Plant Industries (Texas), Inc., a business concerned with the manufacture of woven synthetic cloth. As a result of these sales Plant Industries, Inc. by the end of 1980 had disposed of a significant part of its unprofitable assets.

According to the complaint, [Plant CEO] Bregman thereupon proceeded on a course of action designed to dispose of a subsidiary of the corporate defendant knows as Plant National (Quebec) Ltd., a business which constitutes Plant Industries, Inc.'s entire business operation in Canada and has allegedly constituted Plant's only income producing facility during the past four years. The professed principal purpose of such proposed sale is to raise needed cash and thus improve Plant's balance sheets. And while interest in purchasing the corporate defendant's Canadian plant was thereafter evinced not only by Vulcan Industrial Packaging, Ltd., but also by Universal Drum Reconditioning Co., which latter corporation originally undertook to match . . . and . . . to top Vulcan's bid, a formal contract was entered into between Plant Industries, Inc. and Vulcan on April 2, 1981 for the purchase and sale of Plant National (Quebec) despite the constantly increasing bids for the same property being made by Universal. One reason advanced by Plant's management for declining to negotiate with Universal is that, a firm undertaking having been entered into with Vulcan, the board of directors of Plant may not legally or ethically negotiate with Universal. . . .

In seeking injunctive relief, as prayed for, plaintiff relies on two principles, one that found in 8 Del. C. §271 to the effect that a decision of a Delaware corporation to sell " . . . all or substantially all of its property and assets . . ." requires not only the approval of such corporation's board of directors but also a resolution adopted by a majority of the outstanding stockholders of the corporation entitled to vote thereon at a meeting duly called upon at least twenty days' notice. . . .

According to Plant's 1980 10K form, it appears that at the end of 1980, Plant's Canadian operations represented 51% of Plant's remaining assets. Defendants also concede that National represents 44.9% of Plant's sales' revenues and 52.4% of its pre-tax net operating income. Furthermore, such report by Plant discloses, in rough figures that while National made a profit in 1978 of $2,900,000, the profit from the United States businesses in that year was only $770,000. In 1979, the Canadian business profit was $3,500,000 while the loss of the United States businesses was $344,000. Furthermore, in 1980, while the Canadian business profit was $5,300,000, the corporate loss in the United States was $4,500,000. And while these figures may be somewhat distorted by the allocation of overhead expenses and taxes, they are significant. In any event, defendants concede that " . . . National accounted for 34.9% of Plant's pre-tax income in 1976, 36.9% in 1977, 42% in 1978, 51% in 1979 and 52.4% in 1980." . . .

In the case at bar, I am first of all satisfied that historically the principal business of Plant Industries, Inc. has not been to buy and sell industrial facilities but rather to manufacture steel drums for use in bulk shipping as well as for the storage of petroleum products, chemicals, food, paint, adhesives and cleaning agents, a business which has been profitably performed by National of Quebec. Furthermore, the proposal, after the sale of

National, to embark on the manufacture of plastic drums represents a radical departure from Plant's historically successful line of business, namely steel drums. I therefore conclude that the proposed sale of Plant's Canadian operations, which constitute over 51% of Plant's total assets and in which are generated approximately 45% of Plant's 1980 net sales, would, if consummated, constitute a sale of substantially all of Plant's assets. By way of contrast, the proposed sale of Signal Oil in *Gimbel v. Signal Companies, Inc.,* . . . represented only about 26% of the total assets of Signal Companies, Inc. And while Signal Oil represented 41% of Signal Companies, Inc. total net worth, it generated only about 15% of Signal Companies, Inc. revenue and earnings.

I conclude that because the proposed sale of Plant National (Quebec) Ltd. would, if consummated, constitute a sale of substantially all of the assets of Plant Industries, Inc., as presently constituted, . . . an injunction should issue preventing the consummation of such sale at least until it has been approved by a majority of the outstanding stockholders of Plant Industries, Inc., entitled to vote at a meeting duly called on at least twenty days' notice. Compare *Robinson v. Pittsburg Oil Refining Company,* Del. Ch., 126 A. 46 (1933).

In light of this conclusion it will be unnecessary to consider whether or not the sale here under attack, as proposed to be made, is for such an inadequate consideration, viewed in light of the competing bid of Universal, as to constitute a breach of trust on the part of the directors of Plant Industries, Inc. . . .

Being persuaded for the reasons stated that plaintiff has demonstrated a reasonable probability of ultimate success on final hearing in the absence of stockholder approval of the proposed sale of the corporate assets here in issue to Vulcan, a preliminary injunction against the consummation of such transaction, at least until stockholder approval is obtained, will be granted. . . .

NOTE ON KATZ v. BREGMAN *AND THE MEANING OF* "*SUBSTANTIALLY ALL*"

Students may wonder how 51 percent of the assets, producing 45 percent of the income, can reasonably be called "substantially all" of the assets? Others have wondered as well, and no later court has approached this level of liberality in interpreting these words. Indeed, the drafters of the Revised Model Business Corporation Act have gone out of their way to indicate that "substantially all" is intended to have a literal interpretation. See RMBCA §12.02.

The result in *Katz v. Bregman* can be explained, we think, as an early precursor to the cases decided in 1985 that revolutionized mergers and acquisition law. Specifically, in *Katz* the court is struggling to protect an active bidding contest for control of Plant National (Quebec) Ltd. The same task was more aggressively undertaken by the Delaware Supreme Court in its famous *Revlon* case of 1985 (which we take up in Chapter 13). In *Katz,* the court apparently thought either that management had agreed to sell too early (before a higher bidder came along) or that there was something inherently suspect about selecting a lower price over a higher one. Plaintiff's claim was that management was guilty of a "studied refusal to consider a potentially higher bid for the assets in question."[23]

Thus, for historians of corporation law (a small set for sure) and for students seeking to uncover the true motivation of courts in reaching decisions (a large set, we believe), *Katz* is an interesting case. We suggest that it represents a court taking up the tools at hand (§271) to reach a result that it thought fairness to shareholders required. For the legal doctrinalist, this case marks the outer boundary of the meaning of the statutes that mandate shareholder votes on sales of assets.

Further guidance may be derived from the 1996 case *Thorpe v. CERBCO.*[24] CERBCO was a holding company with three subsidiaries, including Insituform East, Inc. CERBCO's stock in Insituform comprised 68 percent of its assets and was CERBCO's primary income-generating asset. CERBCO's public shareholders wanted CERBCO to sell Insituform. The controlling shareholders of CERBCO, however, wanted to sell *their* controlling interest in CERBCO instead. An issue was whether the controlling shareholders (who were also directors and officers of CERBCO) had a right in their capacity as shareholders to veto any CERBCO sale of Insituform. Put differently, would sale of CERBCO's Insituform stock constitute a sale of "substantially all of CERBCO's assets," thereby assuring CERBCO's controlling shareholders power to block such a sale?

The Delaware Supreme Court applied the following test: "[T]he need for shareholder approval is to be measured not by the size of the sale alone, but also on the qualitative effect upon the corporation. Thus, it is relevant to ask whether a transaction is out of the ordinary course and substantially affects the existence and purpose of the corporation." *Thorpe v. CERBCO*, 676 A.2d at 446. In this case, the Court held, a sale of the Insituform shares, comprising 68 percent of CERBCO's assets, would have been subject to a shareholder vote under DGCL §271.

The most recent interpretation of the "substantially all" test under DGCL §271 arises in *Hollinger, Inc. v. Hollinger Intl.*[25] The question presented in that case was whether the sale of the *Telegraph* Group of newspapers (consisting of various newspapers associated with the London-based *Daily Telegraph*) constituted "substantially all" of the assets of Hollinger International ("International"), which in addition to

<hr />

23. The court twice cites *Thomas v. Kempner*, which was an unreported 1973 case on preliminary injunction in which Chancellor Marvel, the author of *Katz*, granted an injunction against the closing of an asset sale of substantially all assets when a higher price emerged after contract signing but before closing. While a contract entered on imperfect information is not rescindable for that reason alone, if the early contract represents an effort to favor one buyer over another for private reasons, it will constitute a breach of duty. The court also cites *Robinson v. Pittsburg Oil Refining Company*, 126 A. 46 (Del. 1933), an old case that stands for the proposition that a fiduciary must sell for more rather than less cash where price is the only material difference between bidders.

24. 676 A.2d 444 (Del. 1996).

25. 858 A.2d 342 (Del. Ch. 2004).

the *Telegraph* Group also held the *Chicago* Group of newspapers (consisting of more than 100 newspapers in the Chicago area, including the *Chicago Sun-Times*). International's controlling shareholder, Lord Conrad Black, claimed that a shareholder vote was required under the "substantially all" test, which would have allowed him to block the sale.

Examining relative revenue contributions, profitability, and other financial measures, Vice Chancellor Leo Strine found that the *Telegraph* Group accounted for 56 to 57 percent of International's value, with the *Chicago* Group accounting for the rest. In his characteristically direct (and often entertaining) way, V.C. Strine held that the sale of the *Telegraph* Group did not constitute "substantially all" of International's assets:

> Has the judiciary transmogrified the words "substantially all" in §271 of the [DGCL] into the words "approximately half"? . . . I begin my articulation of the applicable legal principles with the words of the statute itself. There are two key words here: "substantially" and "all." Although neither word is particularly difficult to understand, let's start with the easier one. "All" means "all," or if that is not clear, all, when used before a plural noun such as "assets," means "[t]he entire or unabated amount or quantity of." . . . "Substantially" conveys the same meaning as "considerably" and "essentially." . . . A fair and succinct equivalent to the term "substantially all" would therefore be "essentially everything."[26]

By 2004, then, it would seem that the Delaware courts have moved quite a bit back from *Katz v. Bregman*.

NOTE ON ASSET ACQUISITIONS AND POTENTIAL LIABILITY

As we noted above, the chief drawback of asset acquisition as a method of acquiring a company is that it is costly and very time consuming to transfer all of the individual assets of a large business. Offsetting this drawback, it might seem, is that an acquirer accedes only to the assets, and not the liabilities, of the target. In theory, this is true so long as an asset purchase is at arm's length and does not violate the Fraudulent Conveyances Act (discussed in Chapter 6). However, when the assets at issue constitute an integrated business, courts have identified circumstances in which a purchaser of assets may become responsible for liability associated with those assets. The best-known examples of this doctrine of "successor liability" involve tort claims as a result of defective products manufactured in plants now owned by different owners. They also tend to be cases in which the culpable previous owners of the assets — the plants — have dissolved and paid out a liquidating distribution to their shareholders, leaving no one else to sue but the asset's new owners.[27] Note, however, that courts are less likely to invoke successor liability today than they were in the innovative decades of the 1970s and 1980s.

---

26. 858 A.2d 342, 377.

27. See, e.g., *Ray v. Alad Corp.*, 506 P.2d 3 (Cal. 1977). See generally Michael D. Green, *Successor Liability*, 72 Cornell L. Rev. 17 (1986).

A different legal risk that attends asset acquisition is liability for environmental cleanup expenses that are imposed under various federal statutes on "owners" or "operators" of acquired assets. Thus, the purchase of assets that constitute hazardous environmental conditions may make the new owner jointly liable for cleanup expenses. In response to the risk of successor liability and environmental liability, business planners find it prudent to make acquisitions through separately incorporated subsidiaries, even when they plan to purchase only the assets of a target firm. Courts have not generally "pierced" the corporate existence of this separate legal buyer itself, absent independent grounds to do so.[28]

12.5.2   Stock Acquisition

A second transactional form for acquiring an incorporated business is through the purchase of all, or a majority of, the company's stock. As we discussed in Chapter 11, a company that acquires a controlling block of stock in another has, in a practical sense, "acquired" the controlled firm. Thus, tender offers and the purchase of a controlling block of stock may be thought of as acquisition transactions. In a technical sense, however, the purchase of control by an acquirer is merely a shareholder transaction that does not alter the legal identity of the corporation. Something more is needed beyond the purchase of control to result in a full-fledged acquisition.

To acquire a corporation in the full sense of obtaining complete dominion over its assets, an acquirer must purchase 100 percent of its target's stock, not merely a control block. As a practical matter, moreover, acquirers typically do not want a small minority of public shares outstanding. There are costs to being a public company, including the costs of complying with SEC regulations and the implicit costs of assuring that all transfers among controlled entities are fair to the public minority. Corporate law recognizes the legitimacy of the desire to eliminate a small public minority by creating the easy-to-execute short-form merger statutes, which allow a 90 percent shareholder to simply cash out a minority unilaterally.[29] Also, some states take the additional step of offering acquirers and willing targets the statutory device of a compulsory "share exchange" transaction. This is, in effect, a tender offer negotiated with the target board of directors that, after approval by the requisite majority of shareholders, becomes compulsory for all shareholders. The acquiring company's stock (or other tender offer consideration) is then distributed to the target's shareholders pro rata, while the acquirer becomes the sole owner of all of the stock of the target. The result is a form of acquisition that receives the tax treatment of a tender offer without the attendant holdup problems of a true tender offer or the awkward residue of a minority of public shareholders.[30] Thus, the

---

28. See *United States v. BestFoods, Inc.*, 524 U.S. 51 (1998) (refusal to pierce the corporate veil to impose CERCLA liability on parent of wholly owned subsidiary).

29. See, e.g., DGCL §253.

30. See RMBCA §12.02.

compulsory share exchange is yet another example of the malleability of share interests in modern corporate law.

Delaware has no compulsory share exchange statute. Nevertheless, corporate lawyers have developed a perfectly serviceable hybrid acquisition form under Delaware law that produces almost the same result as the compulsory share exchange. This is the "two-step" merger, in which the boards of the target and the acquirer negotiate two linked transactions in a single package. The first transaction is a tender offer for most or all of the target's shares at an agreed-upon price, which the target board promises to recommend to its shareholders. The second transaction is a merger between the target and a subsidiary of the acquirer, which is to follow the tender offer and remove minority shareholders who failed to tender their shares (often at the same price as the tender offer). Sometimes the second-step consideration will be cash, in which case this step is called a "cash-out" merger. Occasionally, this two-step merger is accomplished through the triangular merger form described below. But before exploring triangular mergers, we first discuss mergers more generally as an acquisition technique.

12.5.3 Mergers

A merger legally collapses one corporation into another; the corporation that survives with its legal identity intact is, not surprisingly, termed the "surviving corporation."[31] A management team that wishes to acquire another company in a merger typically researches the target and initiates negotiations over the terms of a merger itself. A merger requires the approval of the board, too, of course. But just *when* a CEO raises a proposed merger with the board and *how involved* the board will be are not dictated by law. Good practice dictates, however, that outside directors should be involved earlier and more intensively when the merger transaction is significant relative to the assets of the corporation. In all events, the management teams of the corporations, aided by lawyers and often by investment bankers, prepare a merger agreement for board approval. (We provide an excerpted example below.) After the board formally authorizes the execution of this agreement, the board will in most instances call a shareholders' meeting to obtain shareholder approval of the merger.

In most states, a valid merger requires a majority vote by the outstanding stock of each constituent corporation that is entitled to vote.[32] The

---

31. A less common transaction, a "consolidation," collapses two corporations into a new legal entity, the "resulting corporation." In most respects, corporation statutes treat mergers and consolidations identically.

Note that civil law jurisdictions generally have not only a merger transaction but also its statutory inverse, a statutory "separation" transaction, in which a portion of the assets and liabilities of a single large company are *assigned* to a new corporate entity. In the United States, separation is generally accomplished by dropping a portion of a company's assets into a subsidiary and distributing the shares of this subsidiary to the original company's shareholders.

32. See, e.g., DGCL §251(c).

default rule is that all classes of stock vote on a merger unless the certificate of incorporation expressly states otherwise.[33] Oddly, the Delaware merger statute, DGCL §251, does not also protect preferred stock with the right to a class vote in most circumstances.[34] Of course, the Delaware statute does give class-voting rights to preferred stock if their rights are adversely affected by a charter amendment. See DGCL §242(b)(2). But this narrow right is triggered only when a charter amendment alters the *formal* rights of the preferred stock, not when it reduces the economic value of the stock.[35] Thus, under Delaware law, the most important source of preferred voting rights on a merger is the charter itself.[36]

The voting common stock of the "target" or collapsed corporation always have voting rights. The voting stock of the surviving corporation is generally afforded statutory voting rights on a merger *except* when three conditions are met: (1) The surviving corporation's charter is not modified, (2) the security held by the surviving corporation's shareholders will not be exchanged or modified, and (3) the surviving corporation's outstanding common stock will not be increased by more than 20 percent.[37] The rationale for this exemption from the usual requirement that shareholders of both companies approve a merger is that mergers satisfying these conditions have too little impact on the surviving corporation's shareholders to justify the delay and the expense of a shareholder vote.

Of course, higher or special voting requirements for mergers may also be established by the corporate charter or by state takeover statutes (e.g., DGCL §203). Moreover, the stock exchanges and the NASDAQ require a listed corporation to hold a shareholder vote on any transaction or series of related transactions that result in the issuance of common stock (or convertible preferred stock) sufficient to increase outstanding shares by 20 percent. Unlike corporate statutes, the stock exchange rules require approval of 50 percent of shares voting on the matter (a "simple majority"), as opposed to 50 percent of outstanding shares (an "absolute majority"). Thus, if the acquisition contemplates the issuance of more than 20 percent of the acquirer's common stock, shareholders of the acquirer, as

---

33. E.g., DGCL §212(a). Generally, all common stock votes, although nonvoting common is possible. The voting rights of preferred stock are typically more limited. Most commonly, preferred has no right to vote at all except in stated circumstances (e.g., when a preferred dividend has been skipped). But when preferred stock has a right to vote, it is generally the right to a class vote, since preferred votes would otherwise ordinarily be swamped by the votes of common stock if they voted together.

34. Compare RMBCA §§11.03, 11.04. Thus, under Delaware law, preferred stockholders are heavily dependent on the terms of their security for their protection and receive scant help from Delaware corporate law. There is interesting history here for the specialist. See *Federal United Corp. v. Havender*, 11 A.2d 331 (Del. 1940).

35. *Shanik v. White Sewing Machine Corp.*, 19 A.2d 831 (Del. 1941). Compare RMBCA §10.04(a)(6) (contra).

36. By contrast, the RMBCA creates parallel class-voting tests for charter amendments and mergers. Under these provisions, any special effect on a class of security holders (even stock that is made expressly nonvoting in the charter) will give that class of security holders a right to vote as a class. See RMBCA §§10.04, 11.04(f). Other statutes, including the California and Connecticut codes, give nonvoting preferred stock the right to vote on a merger even if the merger does not affect the legal rights of the holders.

37. See, e.g., DGCL §251(f); RMBCA §12.03; Cal. Corp. Code §1201 (b), (d).

well as those of the target, must approve the transaction, regardless of how it is structured.[38]

Following an affirmative shareholder vote, a merger is effectuated by filing a certificate of merger with the appropriate state office. The governance structure of the surviving corporation may be restructured in the merger through the adoption of an amended certificate of incorporation (or articles of incorporation) and bylaws, which will have been approved by the shareholders as part of the merger vote. Shareholders who disapprove of the terms of the merger must dissent from it in order to seek, as an alternative, a judicial appraisal of the fair value of their shares. (Generally, if they have no right to vote on the merger, they will not have appraisal rights for similar reasons.)

12.5.4 Triangular Mergers

As we have noted, the surviving corporation in a merger assumes the liabilities of both constituent corporations by operation of law. But to expose the acquirer's assets to the (imperfectly known) liabilities of a new acquisition is inevitably a risky step. Thus, the acquirer has a strong incentive to preserve the liability shield that the target's separate incorporation confers. This can easily be done by merging the target into a wholly owned subsidiary of the acquirer (or reversing this, by merging the subsidiary into the target). And this is precisely what is done. Preserving the liability protection that separate incorporation provides to the acquirer is almost always a highly desirable business goal. Most mergers are accomplished in a way that permits two separate corporate entities to survive the merger.

This maintenance of the liability shield is the premise for the *triangular merger* form. In this structure, the acquirer (A) forms a wholly owned subsidiary (call it NewCo). Imagine that A transfers the merger consideration to NewCo in exchange for all of NewCo's stock. Then Target will merge into NewCo (or NewCo will merge into Target). In either event, at the time of the merger, the merger consideration will be distributed to Target shareholders, and their Target stock will be canceled. The stock of A in Target, if it owned any, will also be canceled. Thus, after the merger, A will own all of the outstanding stock of NewCo, which, in turn, will own all of Target's assets and liabilities. If NewCo is the surviving corporation, the merger is referred to as a "forward triangular merger." If Target is the surviving corporation (its shareholders nevertheless having their shares converted into the merger consideration), the merger is said to be a "reverse triangular merger." Of course, if NewCo is the surviving company,

---

38. It is possible, for example, that the approval of the buyer-parent's shareholders may be required in a reverse triangular stock merger under the NYSE rules even though no vote of parent shareholders would be required under the DGCL. See NYSE Listed Co. Manual ¶B12.03(C), at www.nyse.com. (This situation, in fact, arose in the planned stock acquisition of Warner Communications by Time, Inc., in 1989.) See *Paramount Communications, Inc. v. Time, Inc.*, 1989 Westlaw 79880, Fed. Sec. L. Rep. 94,514, 15 Del. J. Corp. L. 700 (Del. Ch. 1989).

it can immediately change its name to Target, Inc., after the merger and thus preserve the value of Target's brands and goodwill. But no matter which company — NewCo or Target — is the survivor, its charter can be restated (and typically is restated) at the merger to include the governance terms and capital structure that the parties deem desirable. The merger agreement will be entered into by all three parties — A, Target, and Newco. In practice, the merger consideration — cash or shares of A typically — will not be transferred first to Newco, as in our example, but will be distributed at the closing of the transaction directly from A to the holders of Target shares in consideration of the cancellation of those shares.

12.6   STRUCTURING THE M&A TRANSACTION

To choose the right structure for an M&A transaction, the lawyer, banker, and client must consider the interaction of many variables. Costs, speed, liabilities, information known and unknown, accounting treatment, regulatory hurdles, and threats from alternative acquirers are the more obvious considerations bearing on this choice. In this section, we briefly address a number of the concerns that are faced by lawyers structuring and documenting an M&A transaction. These topics are, in several instances, treated at greater length elsewhere. In particular, tax is dealt with separately in §12.7.

Since merger and other acquisition agreements are commercial contracts, they contain the customary provisions found in such contracts. As in all such contracts, issues of timing, cost, and risk will affect the choice of the deal structure. There will also be terms identifying the property subject to the contract, specifying obligations, setting forth the nature and times of performance, and making whatever representations, warranties, and covenants the parties may require. In addition, however, merger agreements may contain specialized provisions not found elsewhere. Two types of provisions are particularly important: (1) "lock-up" provisions, which are designed to protect friendly deals from hostile interlopers, and (2) "fiduciary out" provisions. There may also be *standstill agreements*, which bar hostile activity before the agreement is closed, as well as *confidentiality provisions*. We explore these provisions further in Chapter 13. In this section, we address a range of the concerns that will face a lawyer selecting a transaction structure and drafting an appropriate contract for an M&A transaction.

12.6.1   Timing

Consider first timing. Speed is almost always desirable in acquisition transactions. In dynamic markets, the conditions that make an agreement advantageous may suddenly change. Since each side wants the deal to occur on present information and since neither can predict future market movements, it is rational, once a deal is reached, for business people to be impatient to close it.

An all-cash, multistep acquisition is usually the fastest way to lock up a target and assure its complete acquisition. An all-cash tender offer may be consummated 20 business days after commencement under the Williams Act, as discussed in Chapter 11. By contrast, a merger will generally require a shareholder vote of at least the target shareholders, which, in turn, will involve several months for clearance of the proxy materials with the SEC and solicitation of proxies under the proxy rules.

However, if stock constitutes any part of the deal consideration, the two-step structure generally does not provide a significant timing advantage because — regardless of which transaction structure is used — the stock to be issued generally must be registered with the SEC pursuant to Rule 145 under the Securities Act. This is a process that takes several months to complete (the Securities Act and the SEC registration process are beyond the scope of these materials). Thus, most deals using 100 percent stock consideration are structured as one-step direct or triangular mergers. Likewise, if lengthy regulatory procedures must be completed before a first-step tender offer can be closed (as is the case in bank acquisitions), a multistep structure may have no timing advantage, even in an all-cash deal, and a one-step merger may be the best choice.

12.6.2 Regulatory Approvals, Consents, and Title Transfers

Timing considerations also turn on mechanical aspects of a transaction, such as regulatory approvals, consents, and title transfers. Title transfers are not a matter of concern in a merger, since all assets owned by either corporation vest as a matter of law in the surviving corporation without further action. In a sale of assets, however, title transfers may impose substantial cost and delay. Thus, reverse triangular mergers are the cheapest and easiest methods of transfer because they leave both preexisting operating corporations intact. Stock purchases entail stock transfers and the corresponding costs of documentation (stock certificates, stock powers), but they are nevertheless much simpler to conclude than asset purchases.

Governmental approval and third-party consents vary with the form of transaction. Planners will attempt to choose a structure that minimizes the cost of obtaining regulatory approvals or consents under contracts (e.g., real estate leases, bank loans, service agreements) needed to close the transaction. In addition, planners will wish to make the transfer of corporate assets as cheap as possible.

12.6.3 Planning Around Voting and Appraisal Rights

From the planner's perspective, shareholder votes and appraisal rights are costly and potentially risky. Sometimes planners may voluntarily condition transactions on shareholder approval or provide appraisal rights, even when this is not technically required. (Why might they do this?) But ordinarily, they will choose a structure that avoids or minimizes such requirements. Planners are particularly wary of structures that trigger class votes for holders of preferred (or nonvoting common) stock, since these votes may enable the holders of such securities to extract a "holdup" payment in exchange for allowing the deal to proceed.[39]

12.6.4   Due Diligence, Representations and Warranties, Covenants, and Indemnification

In any deal, the buyer will wish to acquire reliable information about the target. In many deals involving public companies, acquiring this information is made much easier by public SEC filings and the availability of financial statements audited by an independent public accountant. This is especially true in highly regulated industries such as banking. "Hostile" transactions, of course, are incompatible with due diligence from the target itself. Even if and when such deals turn "friendly," hostile takeovers will rarely provide much opportunity for due diligence. Risk and uncertainty will accordingly be greater.

In negotiated transactions, the representations and warranties contained in a merger agreement will facilitate the due diligence process by forcing the disclosure of all of the target's assets and liabilities.[40] They establish conditions necessary for closing the transaction as well as allocating between the parties the risks arising from the property subject to the transaction. Target warranties and representations are particularly useful when there is a solvent corporation or individual to stand behind them. When the target is a public corporation, there are generally fewer such provisions because information about these companies is already relatively good, and more important there is no easy way to enforce a breach of warranty against the persons who will have the acquirer's money. It follows that warranties and representations have their greatest use in private deals — that is, where control is acquired through any method from a single entity or small group.[41]

39. See, e.g., *Schreiber v. Carney*, 447 A.2d 17. (Del. Ch. 1982); *Warner Communications, Inc. v. Chris Craft Industries, Inc.*, 583 A.2d 962 (Del. Ch. 1989). (Chris Craft alleged that it was the sole holder of a class of preferred stock that had a right to a class vote in the Time-Warner merger.)

40. The most important function of warranties and representations is to force the disclosure of information respecting the target's property and liabilities. To learn about a target's business, an acquirer commonly asks for broad warranties concerning properties owned or potential liabilities. The acquirer then learns about the business by discussing why such warranties are impractical or what aspect must be excepted from any such warranties. The process is similar with representations. The target must carefully shape each representation on which the acquirer will rely, which teaches the acquirer about the firm.

41. In this context, it is also customary for the acquisition agreement to contain detailed representations concerning the organization of the seller/target, its capital structure, its good standing and the authority to enter into the transaction in question, its financial statements, its tax payments; its licenses, etc., necessary to conduct its businesses; its title to intellectual property and real property; and its insurance and environmental

Covenants in merger agreements are another tool for controlling risk. A typical covenant offered by a target in a merger agreement will provide that the business will be operated only in the normal course from the date of the signing of the agreement to the closing and may, for example, require the target to confer with the acquirer before undertaking material transactions. Another typical covenant will require the target to notify the buyer if it learns of any event or condition that constitutes a breach of any representation or warranty. A third standard covenant is a pledge by the target to use its best efforts to cause the merger agreement to close. This often will include a covenant that the board will recommend approval of the merger agreement by the corporation's stockholders (subject usually to a "fiduciary out," discussed in Chapter 13).

In addition, the parties will customarily indemnify each other for any damages arising from any misrepresentation or breach of warranty. This indemnification has the effect of making every representation a covenant to hold harmless. Thus, the agreement will effectively allocate the burden of undiscovered noncompliance to the party making the representation (ordinarily the seller). Of course, this sort of protection is generally not feasible in a public company acquisition unless it can be negotiated from a large block holder.

12.6.5 Deal Protections and Termination Fees

The period beginning in 1985 witnessed a revolution in the corporate law of mergers and acquisitions. That revolution was initiated by a quartet of surprising Delaware Supreme Court opinions. Those opinions — *Smith v. Van Gorkom, Unocal, Revlon,* and *Moran v. Household* — and their progeny are treated in Chapter 13, which deals with hostile changes in corporate control. Today, in light of the changes that this revolution wrought, among the most important terms of a friendly merger agreement are those terms that are designed to assure a prospective buyer that its investment in negotiating in good faith with a target will result in a closable transaction. Any discussion of these "deal protection" terms requires an understanding of the doctrine that emerged from the revolutionary cases, and therefore, we take up these provisions in the next chapter.

12.6.6 Accounting Treatment

Under current standards for the accounting for mergers, in a direct merger the surviving corporation will typically record the assets acquired at their fair market value. To the extent the merger consideration exceeds the total of the fair market value of the assets (as it ordinarily will, since the

---

liabilities. While the seller/target will be giving most of the representations and warranties, the buyer/acquirer may be asked to make representations that will go to its ability to close the transaction.

business organization and intangible assets of the target will contribute value to it), the survivor will record this excess as an intangible asset, "goodwill." Under current rules, the value of this goodwill need not be amortized against earnings so long as it continues to represent this economic value. This asset must, however, be periodically evaluated to ensure that the goodwill account continues to be a reasonable approximation of the intangible value embedded in the firm. If it is not, then the goodwill account will be reduced by taking a charge against earnings (a noncash expense) in the amount of its impairment.

12.6.7   A Case Study: Excerpt from Timberjack Agreement and Plan of Merger

AGREEMENT AND PLAN OF MERGER ("Agreement") dated as of this 13th day of April, 1989, by and among RAUMA-REPOLA OY ("Parent"), a corporation organized under the laws of Finland; RAUMA ACQUISITION CORPORATION ("Purchaser"), a Delaware corporation and a direct, wholly owned subsidiary of Parent; and TIMBERJACK CORPORATION ("Company"), a Delaware corporation.

WITNESSETH

WHEREAS, the respective Boards of Directors of Parent, Purchaser and the Company have approved the acquisition of the Company by Purchaser pursuant to the terms and subject to the conditions set forth in this Agreement;

WHEREAS, as an integral part of such acquisition, Purchaser will make a cash tender offer for all shares of the issued and outstanding common stock, par value $0.01 per share, of the Company (the "Common Stock"), upon the terms and subject to the conditions set forth in this Agreement;

WHEREAS, the Board of Directors of the Company has approved the Offer and has recommended that the stockholders of the Company tender their shares of Common Stock pursuant to the Offer;

WHEREAS, in order to induce Parent and Purchaser to enter into this Agreement, the Company has entered into a Cancellation Fee Agreement with Parent and Purchaser, dated as of an even date herewith (the "Fee Agreement");

NOW, THEREFORE, in consideration of the premises and the representations, warranties, covenants and agreements contained herein and in the Fee Agreement, and intending to be legally bound hereby, Parent, Purchaser and the Company hereby agree as follows:

ARTICLE I
THE OFFER

1.01. *The Offer.* Provided this Agreement has not been terminated pursuant to Section 6.01 hereof, Purchaser shall, as soon as practicable after the date hereof, and in any event within five (5) business days after the date on which Purchaser's intention to make the Offer is first publicly announced, commence a tender offer to acquire any and all issued and outstanding shares of the Common Stock, at a price of $25.00 per share net to the seller in cash (the "Offer"). Subject to the conditions to the Offer set forth in Annex I hereto, including the condition that a minimum amount of at least 70% of the issued and outstanding shares of Common Stock be tendered and available for acquisition (the "Minimum Amount"), Purchaser (a) shall not extend the Offer beyond midnight, New York City time, on the twentieth business day from the date of commencement of the Offer and (b) shall purchase by accepting for payment, and shall pay for, all Common Stock validly tendered and not withdrawn promptly after expiration of the Offer; *provided, however,* that (i) if, as of the then-scheduled expiration of the Offer, in excess of 50%, but less than 90% of the Common Stock have been validly tendered and not withdrawn, Purchaser may, at its sole option, extend the Offer for a period not to extend beyond an additional ten business days in order to qualify for a "short-form merger" in accordance with Section 253 of the Delaware General Corporation Law (the "Delaware Law"), (ii) Purchaser may, at its sole option, extend the Offer with the consent of the Company, (iii) Purchaser may, at its sole option, extend and reextend the Offer for reasonable periods of time, not to exceed ten business days in any instance, in order to allow a condition to the Offer specified in Annex I to be satisfied that is reasonably likely to be satisfied within the period of such extension and (iv) Purchaser, at its sole option, reserves the right to waive any condition to the Offer set out in Annex I, to purchase fewer than the Minimum Amount and to increase the price per share pursuant to the Offer.

ARTICLE II
THE MERGER

2.01 *The Merger.*

  (a) Subject to the terms and conditions hereof, at the Effective Date (as such term is defined in Section 2.01(b)), Purchaser will be merged with and into the Company (the "Merger") in accordance with Delaware Law, the separate existence of Purchaser (except as may be continued by operation of law) shall cease and the Company shall continue as the surviving corporation in the Merger ("the Surviving Corporation").

  (b) As soon as practicable after satisfaction or waiver of the conditions set forth in Article V, the parties hereto shall cause the Merger to be consummated by filing with the Secretary of State of Delaware appropriate articles of merger (the "Articles of Merger") in such form as is required by, and executed in accordance with, the relevant provisions of Delaware law, and with this Agreement (the date and time of such filing being referred to herein as the "Effective Date"). . . .

  2.02 *Conversion of Shares.* Subject to the terms and conditions of this Agreement, at the Effective Date, by virtue of the Merger and without any action on the part of the Purchaser, the Company or the holder of any of the following securities:

(a) Each share of Common Stock then issued and outstanding, other than (i) shares then held, directly or indirectly, by Parent, Purchaser or any direct or indirect subsidiary of Parent, or (ii) shares held in the Company's treasury, or (iii) Dissenting Shares (as such term is defined in Section 2.03), shall be converted into and represent the right to receive (as provided in Section 2.04) $25.00 net in cash, without any interest thereon (such amount of cash or such higher amount as shall be paid pursuant to the Offer, being referred to herein as the "Merger Consideration"), subject only to reduction for any applicable federal backup withholding or stock transfer taxes which shall be payable by the holder of such Common Stock.

(b) Each share of Common Stock then held, directly or indirectly, by Parent, Purchaser or any direct or indirect subsidiary of Parent shall be canceled and retired without payment of any consideration therefor.

(c) Each share of Common Stock held in the Company's treasury shall be canceled and retired without payment of any consideration therefor.

(d) Each issued and outstanding share of common stock, par value $1.00 per share, of Purchaser shall be converted into and become one validly issued, fully paid and nonassessable share of common stock of the Surviving Corporation. . . .

2.07 *Certificate of Incorporation.* The Restated Articles of Incorporation of the Company in effect immediately prior to the Effective Date (except as such Restated Articles of Incorporation may be amended pursuant to the Articles of Merger) shall be the Articles of Incorporation of the Surviving Corporation until thereafter amended as provided therein and under Delaware Law.

2.08 *By-laws.* The By-laws of the Purchaser, as in effect immediately prior to the Effective Date, shall be the By-laws of the Surviving Corporation until thereafter amended as provided therein and under Delaware Law.

2.09 *Directors.* The directors of Purchaser immediately prior to the Effective Date shall be the initial directors of the Surviving Corporation and will hold office from the Effective Date until their successors are duly elected or appointed and qualified in the manner provided in the Certificate of Incorporation and the By-laws of the Surviving Corporation, or as otherwise provided by law.

2.10 *Officers.* The officers of the Company immediately prior to the Effective Date shall be the initial officers of the Surviving Corporation and will hold office from the Effective Date until their successors are duly elected or appointed and qualified in the manner provided in the Certificate of Incorporation and the By-laws of the Surviving Corporation, or as otherwise provided by law. . . .

ARTICLE III
REPRESENTATIONS AND WARRANTIES

3.02 *Representations and Warranties of the Company.* The Company hereby represents and warrants to Parent and Purchaser that:

(a) *Organization.* The Company and each of its Subsidiaries (as such term is defined in Section 3.02(c)) is a corporation duly organized, validly existing and in good standing (or, with respect to any Subsidiaries organized under the Laws of Canada, subsisting) under the laws of its jurisdiction of incorporation and has all requisite corporate power and authority to own, lease and operate its properties and to carry on its business as now being conducted. The Company and each of its Subsidiaries is duly qualified as a foreign corporation to do business, and is in good standing, in each jurisdiction in which the property owned, leased or operated by it or the nature of the business conducted by it makes such qualification necessary, except where the failure to be so qualified would not have a Material Adverse Effect on the Company and its Subsidiaries. The Company has made available to Purchaser true, correct and complete copies of the Articles of Incorporation and By-laws of the Company and its Subsidiaries, and any amendments thereto. . . .

(d) *Authorization and Validity of Agreements.* The Company has all requisite corporate power and authority to enter into this Agreement and the Documents contemplated to be executed hereunder, including, without limitation, the Fee Agreement, and to perform all of its obligations hereunder and under all documents contemplated to be executed hereunder (subject, in the case of performance of this Agreement, to obtaining the necessary approval of its stockholders if required under Delaware Law). The execution, delivery and performance by the Company of this Agreement and the documents executed hereunder, including, without limitation, the Fee Agreement, and the consummation by it of the transactions contemplated hereby and under all documents executed hereunder, have been duly authorized by the Board of Directors and no other corporate action on the part of the Company is necessary to authorize the execution and delivery by the Company of this Agreement. . . .

(f) *Legal Proceedings.* Except as set forth in the Company Commission Filings (as such term is defined in Section 3.01(g)) or as previously disclosed to Parent or Purchaser in writing, there is no claim, suit, action, proceeding, grievance or investigation pending, or to the Company's best knowledge, threatened against or involving the Company or properties or rights of the Company or its Subsidiaries which, if adversely determined, would have, either individually or in the aggregate, a Material Adverse Effect on the Company and its Subsidiaries. . . .

(h) *Absence of Certain Changes or Events.* Since December 31, 1988, except as disclosed in writing to Parent or Purchaser or in the Company Commission Filings, or as contemplated in this Agreement, the Company and its Subsidiaries have conducted their business only in the ordinary course and in a manner consistent with past practice and have not made any material change in the conduct of the business or operations of the Company and its Subsidiaries taken as a whole, and there has not been (a) any event resulting in any Material Adverse Effect with respect to the Company and its Subsidiaries; (b) any strike, picketing, unfair labor practice, refusal to work, work slowdown or other labor disturbance involving the Company or any of its Subsidiaries; (c) any damage, destruction or loss (whether or not covered by insurance) with respect to any of the assets of the Company or any of its Subsidiaries resulting in any Material Adverse Effect on the Company or any of its Subsidiaries; (d) any redemption or other acquisition of Common Stock by the Company or any of its Subsidiaries or any declaration or payment of any dividend or other distribution in cash, stock or property with respect to Common Stock, other than regularly scheduled cash dividends; (e) any entry into any material commitment or transaction including, without limitation, any material borrowing or material capital expenditure) other than in the ordinary course of business or as contemplated by this Agreement; (f) any transfer of, or any transfer of rights granted under, any material leases, licenses, agreements, patents, trademarks, trade names or copyrights, other than those transferred or granted in the ordinary course of business and consistent with past practice; (g) any mortgage, pledge, security interest or imposition of lien or other encumbrance on any asset of the Company or any of its Subsidiaries that when viewed in the aggregate with all such other encumbrances is material to the business, financial condition or operations of the company and its Subsidiaries taken as a whole; (h) any change in the Certificate of Incorporation or By-laws or equivalent organizational documents of the Company or any Subsidiary; or (i) any change by the Company in accounting principles or methods except insofar as may have been required by a change in generally accepted accounting principles. . . .

(i) *Title to Property.*

(a) The Company and its Subsidiaries have good and marketable title, or valid leasehold rights in the case of leased property, to all real and personal property purported to be owned or leased by them and material to the business and operations of the Company and its Subsidiaries taken as a whole, free and clear of all material liens, security interests, claims, encumbrances and charges, excluding (i) liens securing any revolving term loan with any bank; (ii) liens for fees, taxes, levies, imports, duties or other governmental charges of any kind which are not yet delinquent or are being contested in good faith by appropriate proceedings which suspend the collection thereof; (iii) liens for mechanics, materialmen, laborers, employees, suppliers or similar liens arising by operation of law for sums which are not yet delinquent or are being contested in good faith by appropriate proceedings; (iv) liens created in the ordinary course of business in connection with the leasing or financing of operating assets, including, without limitation, vehicles and office computer and related equipment and supplies and (v) liens, encumbrances or defects in title or leasehold rights that, in the aggregate, do not have a Material Adverse Effect on the Company and its Subsidiaries.

(b) Consummation of the Offer and the Merger will not result in any breach of or constitute a default (or an event which with notice or lapse of time or both would constitute a default) under, or give to others any rights of termination or cancellation of, or require the consent of others under, any material lease under which the Company is a lessee, except for such breaches or defaults which in the aggregate would not have a Material Adverse Effect on the Company and its Subsidiaries. . . .

QUESTIONS ON TIMBERJACK MERGER AGREEMENT

1. What course of events is envisioned by the merger agreement?
2. What happens to the shares of Timberjack upon the merger? Why are all shares not treated in the same way? What will be the charter and the bylaws, and who will be the officers and directors of the surviving corporation?
3. What is the purpose of the provisions in Article III? In what other kind of agreement would you find similar provisions?

12.7 TAXATION OF CORPORATE COMBINATIONS

Tax is always important, even if it is rarely the prime driver of a corporate control transaction. The taxation of acquisition transactions is too complex for a comprehensive summary here, yet too important to ignore. We therefore offer only an abbreviated sketch of the basics of tax-free reorganizations.[42] For those looking for deep understanding of the subject, we recommend the outstanding treatise by Professor Martin Ginsburg of Georgetown Law School and Mr. Jack Levin, of the firm of Kirkland & Ellis.[43]

12.7.1 Basic Concepts

In the United States, federal taxes are levied on income, which includes gains in the value of investments as they are realized and recognized. Gain is sensibly calculated as the excess of the net amount realized on sale over the taxpayer's adjusted cost *basis.* The adjusted cost basis of an asset is its cost (which may include the transaction costs of acquiring it), after reduction for the depreciation or amortization charges made against the asset's cost in calculating annual income taxes. The "realization" of gain (or loss) generally occurs when the investment is sold, while "recognition" refers to the legal rules that determine whether taxes will be due at the time that gain is realized. Thus, for example, the shareholders of the target corporation (T) will generally realize a gain or a loss upon the sale or exchange of their stock in either an individual transaction or a corporate transaction (such as a share exchange). Therefore, an important aspect of tax planning for M&A transactions is to attempt to defer the recognition of any realized shareholder gain.[44] Similarly, T itself will realize gains (or losses) upon the sale or exchange of any of its property, including a sale

---

42. Thanks to Deborah Paul, Esq., and Josh Holmes, Esq., of Wachtell, Lipton, Rosen & Katz for their guidance in fashioning this summary.

43. See Ginsburg & Levin, supra note 2.

44. If T's shareholders are required to recognize gain, they may qualify for the installment method of tax computation if the consideration they received included notes and T's stock is not traded on an established securities market. This level of detail, however, is already beyond our scope.

of substantially all of its assets. Whether these gains or losses are recognized for tax purposes will depend on the terms and structure of the deal.

Gains or losses are recognized either as capital gains or losses or as ordinary income or loss. Capital gains or losses may be either long term or short term. Gains or losses on investments held for less than one year count as short-term capital gains or losses under current (2006) law. For individuals, but not corporations, long-term capital gain is currently eligible for taxation at a reduced rate: as of this writing, the top rate for long-term capital gains is generally 15 percent, while the top rate for ordinary income (and short-term capital gains) is generally 35 percent.[45] Of importance for transactional lawyers is the fact that the federal income tax code contains specific provisions defining the characteristics of tax-free reorganizations. Compliance with these provisions makes these transactions nonrecognition events.[46]

12.7.2   Tax-Free Corporate Reorganizations

Although tax inevitably affects economic activities, tax law ought to interfere with capital allocation in the market no more than is necessary. This is why the Code does not recognize taxable gain for transactions that, in economic substance, merely reorganize ownership interests without fundamentally changing the identity of the owners. But while this principle is clear, its administration is not. Section 368 of the Internal Revenue Code (IRC) provides a safe harbor for tax-free reorganizations that is further implemented in numerous regulations and letter rulings.[47] (In addition, §351 of the IRC specifies when an exchange of corporate control with another corporation controlled by the transferor will be nontaxable.)

Section 368 delineates three ways of obtaining control over a business: purchase of its assets, purchase of a controlling stock interest in the corporation that owns the business, and a merger. Because the concept that drives the §368 safe harbor is continuity of ownership, the consideration that A uses to acquire control must be solely or predominantly stock.[48]

1. Subsection 368(a)(1)(A) exempts statutory mergers in which a sufficient proportion of the consideration is stock.
2. Subsection 368(a)(1)(B) exempts transactions in which at least 80 percent of all shares of voting stock (and 80 percent of each

---

45. For tax years beginning before January 1, 2009, the Jobs and Growth Tax Relief Reconciliation Tax Act of 2003 has reduced the maximum tax rate applicable to long-term capital gains and "qualified dividend income" of individuals to 15 percent.

46. See Ginsburg & Levin, supra note 2, at §106.3. Here we do not touch on §351 of the Internal Revenue Code, which authorizes an alternative technique to achieve tax-free reorganizations: for example, the exchange of target stock for NewCo stock where, after the transaction, old T shareholders hold 80 percent of the voting stock of NewCo. *Id.*, ch. 9.

47. See, e.g., Ginsburg & Levin, supra note 2, at §610.2.

48. In a reverse triangular merger, this may be the voting stock of the parent company.

class of nonvoting stock) of Target are acquired in exchange solely for voting stock of the acquirer.

3. Subsection 368(a)(1)(C) exempts reorganizations in which A acquires assets solely in exchange for voting stock of A.

Qualifying a transaction as a tax-free reorganization under one of these provisions generally means that there is no recognition of gain by sellers except to the extent they receive "boot" (permissible consideration other than stock of A). Sellers will take a carryover cost basis in the stock they receive. Moreover, buyers, too, will not be taxed on any gain that may be said to be realized on the exchange. They assume the carryover basis of their transferors in the target stock or assets they acquire.

Thus, §368 provides a number of possible transaction forms for non-recognition of gain. For example, three types of B reorganizations are possible.[49] In the standard B reorganization, A acquires, in exchange solely for its voting stock, at least 80 percent of the voting power of T and at least 80 percent of each class of any T nonvoting equity. In the subsidiary B reorganization, A acts through a first-tier subsidiary that uses not its own voting securities but solely those of A. Finally, in the forced B reorganization, there is a reverse triangular merger of a transitory subsidiary of A with and into T in which T's shareholders receive A's voting stock. The only problem in this form is that A must learn from T's shareholders what basis it carries forward in T's stock.

Similarly, the C reorganization — the acquisition of substantially all of the target's assets solely for voting stock — has three common forms. In the standard C reorganization, A acquires substantially all of T's assets solely in exchange for its voting stock. Here we do not encounter the range of opinion on what constitutes "substantially all" of the target's assets as we do in the corporate law doctrine. The advance ruling guidelines of the Internal Revenue Service provide that, in all events, the acquisition of 90 percent of the fair value of T's net assets and at least 70 percent of T's gross assets constitutes the acquisition of substantially all of T's assets.[50] The requirement that the exchange be solely for voting stock of A does not, however, quite mean "solely."[51] Section 368(a)(2)(B) permits the inclusion in the consideration of "boot" (any nonvoting stock consideration) to the extent of 20 percent of the total. In calculating the percentage of consideration that is not voting stock, A must include any T liabilities assumed by A, plus the fair market value of any T property not transferred to A. Since 1997, there has been another form of consideration that, while not disqualifying a transaction from C reorganization status, will nonetheless be treated as "boot" in the hands of T's shareholders. That is voting nonqualifying preferred securities of A. (See §§351(g)(2), 356(e) and 354(a)(2)(c)).

The second common form of the C reorganization is the forward triangular merger form: A's subsidiary, S, acquires substantially all of T's assets in exchange "solely" for voting stock of A. Assuming that S is a firm

49. See Ginsburg & Levin, supra note 2.
50. Rev. Proc. 77-37, §3.01, 1977-2 568.
51. See Ginsburg & Levin, supra note 2, at §702.6.

formed for this transaction, A's basis in its S stock will thereafter be the basis that T had in its assets.[52]

A third qualifying C reorganization is a forward triangular merger in which T merges into S and T's shareholders receive only A voting stock.[53] This ruling reflects the tax maxim that substance, not form, governs. The economic substance of such a transaction is the same as the purchase of T's assets for A stock, so it receives the same tax treatment. Since 1968, however, IRC §368(a)(2)(D) has rendered this form of transaction largely unnecessary.

Finally, we look briefly at a third form of tax-free reorganization: a statutory merger or consolidation, the so-called A reorganization. This form of transaction has no requirement that consideration be solely for stock, that any stock used be "voting" stock, or that substantially all assets be acquired.[54] Thus, it offers great flexibility to the corporate planner. An A reorganization must meet three principal requirements in addition to being a merger or consolidation under state law. These requirements are that there is a business purpose, not merely a tax avoidance purpose for the transaction; that it satisfies a continuity of interests test; and that it satisfies the continuity of business enterprise requirements.[55] The A reorganization can be accomplished in a triangular form as well.[56]

12.8   THE APPRAISAL REMEDY

12.8.1   History and Theory

Modern corporation law has abandoned the nineteenth-century idea that shareholders possess "vested rights" in the form of their investment. The introduction of the shareholder non-unanimity rule for authorization of mergers established that shareholder interests are held subject to the exercise of collective shareholder judgment.[57] Today, the shareholder vote (including the right to a class vote created by statute or in charters) is the shareholders' principal protection against unwise or disadvantageous mergers or other fundamental transactions. Through the vote, shareholders can replace an underperforming board or reject a fundamental transaction that requires their authorization. But what if you are a shareholder in a

---

52. *Id.* at §702.12

53. See Rev. Rul. 2003-99, 2003-34 I.R.B. 388.

54. Of course, by action of law all assets are acquired in a statutory merger, but tax policy in other reorganization contexts will collapse transactions that are carried out pursuant to a single plan. Thus, it is conceivable that a tax-free merger might contain a requirement that it include all or substantially all assets, and courts might interpret such a requirement to disqualify mergers in which substantial T assets were disposed of prior to the merger.

55. See Ginsburg & Levin, supra note 2, at §§609, 610, and 611, for a discussion of the law respecting each of these requirements.

56. See *id.* at §§802, 803.

57. See, e.g., *Federal United Corp. v. Havender,* 11 A.2d 331 (Del. 1940).

corporation in which the other shareholders have deplorable business judgment? If those shareholders vote to approve a foolish transaction over your objection, should you have a right to require them to buy you out (at a fair price determined by a court) as a condition of their accomplishing their silly deal?

In the United States, corporate law has provided that right — the right to a judicial appraisal of the fair value of one's shares — for more than one hundred years. Every U.S. jurisdiction provides an appraisal right to shareholders who dissent from qualifying corporate mergers (more in a minute on which mergers qualify). Most states provide appraisal for shareholders who dissent from a sale of substantially all of the corporation's assets, and in about half of the states, an amendment of a corporate charter gives rise to an appraisal. The Delaware corporate law statute mandates appraisal only in connection with corporate mergers and then only in certain circumstances. See DGCL §262.

This pattern of appraisal statutes raises a basic question: Why do we provide this protection against majority judgment? Only if we know the purpose of appraisal can we determine whether that statute ought to be interpreted narrowly or broadly, or what the measure of "fair value" for dissenting shareholders should be.

It is often said that the appraisal remedy was granted as a quid pro quo when legislatures first permitted the authorization of mergers to be effectuated with less than unanimous shareholder approval.[58] The stock-for-stock merger was the only form of merger contemplated at that point, and equity markets were not yet well developed. Thus, a merger might very well have meant that a shareholder would have been forced to accept an illiquid investment in a new company in which she had no desire to invest. A judicial appraisal was a way to provide a liquidity event for such a shareholder, who previously could have prevented the alteration of her investment simply by vetoing a proposed merger.[59] Of course, our equity markets today are very liquid, at least for securities traded on a national securities exchange or through the NASDAQ market, which implies that for public companies the costs of an appraisal procedure are no longer justified by a liquidity rationale. The question then is whether there are other justifications for this remedy that gives it continuing utility for publicly traded firms.

QUESTIONS ON APPRAISAL RIGHTS

1. Many aspects of our lives are subject to the judgments of democratic majorities or institutions subject to majority control. Our land, for example, may be rezoned, but as long as basic procedural norms are observed

58. See, e.g., Elliott J. Weiss, *The Law of Take Out Mergers: A Historical Perspective*, 56 N.Y.U. L. Rev. 624 (1981); Hideki Kanda & Saul Levmore, *The Appraisal Remedy and the Goals of Corporate Law*, 32 UCLA L. Rev. 429 (1985).

59. The arguments that show the incoherence of the rationales offered for appraisal actions have been masterfully marshaled by Bayless Manning. See Bayless Manning, *The Shareholder's Appraisal Remedy: An Essay for Frank Coker*, 72 Yale L.J. 223 (1962).

upon a change in zoning status, we have no right to be paid the fair value of our land. Why should stock in corporations be different?

2. The Delaware statute permits, but does not require, an appraisal remedy when the corporation's charter is amended or when substantially all of its assets are sold. See DGCL §262(c). Yet charters rarely provide an appraisal remedy in these circumstances. If the market for corporate charters responds to investors' economic interests, what inferences do you draw from this observation? Is there a convincing "market failure" story that might account for this fact?

12.8.2   The Appraisal Alternative in Interested Mergers

Modernly, in this era of cash mergers and large security markets, the liquidity explanation for the function of appraisal remedy makes little sense in the case of public companies. Today the appraisal remedy tends to be invoked either in nonpublicly traded firms or in transactions in which shareholders have structural reasons to think that the merger consideration may not be "fair value." In our view, there is little reason to believe that dissenters will often be right in challenging the terms of a transaction negotiated at arm's length by the board and approved by an absolute majority of shareholders. In fact, the appraisal remedy is rarely invoked in arm's-length mergers. This may be because the remedy is costly and inefficient, as some commentators suppose.[60] It is more likely, however, that, without conflicts of interest, most arm's-length mergers achieve something close to market price and that remaining disagreements about value are too small to justify the costs of seeking judicial valuation. Thus, in our view, the appraisal remedy is never justified in an arm's-length transaction, in which the consideration is either cash or a publicly traded security.

Matters stand very differently, however, where there is a controlling shareholder or some other reason to doubt that the shareholder vote fairly reflects the independent business judgment of a majority of disinterested public shareholders. In these circumstances, some judicial remedy to assure fairness is necessary. A minority shareholder ought not to be at the mercy of a shareholder vote that is either controlled or potentially manipulated by an interested party, as in a parent-subsidiary merger or even a management-sponsored buyout. Thus, the parent-subsidiary merger (or any merger involving a self-interested controlling shareholder) continues to provide a compelling justification for the appraisal remedy or something like it, at least in the case of public firms.[61]

As the discussion of the duties of controlling shareholders in Chapter 9 indicated, the law has provided an equitable remedy in the form of fairness review when minority shareholders challenge the self-interested transaction. So should the law then provide *both* an appraisal action and a fairness

---

60. See 2 ALI, Principles of Corporate Governance §7.21 reporter's note at 298.

61. Where the acquiring company's stock is not publicly traded, an appraisal will provide a liquidity event at a time in which a sudden dramatic change in the firm may make it seem unfair to "force" a dissenting shareholder to continue her investment.

action for controlling mergers? And if so, how should these actions relate to each other? As it happens, this issue remains problematic in Delaware law.[62] To a considerable extent, these two actions overlap. In some aspects, an appraisal action is the easier for shareholders to bring, since the plaintiff need only establish her bona fides as a dissenting shareholder to seek appraisal and need not show that the board or a controlling shareholder breached a fiduciary duty.

In most other respects, however, an action alleging breach of entire fairness seems more favorable to plaintiffs. Under the statutory standard, a plaintiff in an appraisal proceeding is entitled to claim only a pro rata share of the fair value of the company *without regard to any gain caused by the merger or its expectation.* By contrast, in a fiduciary "fairness" action against a controlling shareholder, the defendant must prove that a self-dealing transaction was fair in all respects. See *Weinberger v. UOP Inc.,* below. If the defendant fails in this, the possible remedies are very broad and may include rescission or "rescissory damages." (Rescissory damages are the financial equivalent to what rescission would bring, were it feasible.) Still more important, plaintiffs — or, more likely, their attorneys — can bring a fairness action as a class action on behalf of *all* affected shares and not just the small minority who will typically dissent from the merger and seek appraisal. Put differently, the class action procedure gives to plaintiffs the great leverage that results from a large "opt-out" class of shares.

Traditional law dealt with the overlap between an appraisal and a suit for breach of fiduciary duty by making appraisal the exclusive remedy of shareholders who complained that the merger consideration was inadequate or unfair.[63] Recently, the Delaware Supreme Court returned to this old-time religion in a limited class of cases by decreeing that appraisal is the *exclusive* remedy of minority shareholders cashed out in a §253 short-form merger. See *Glassman v. Unocal Exploration Corp.,* 777 A.2d 242 (Del. 2001).

In long-form mergers, however, the course of doctrinal development has been different. In *Weinberger v. UOP, Inc.,* 457 A.2d 701 (Del. 1983), the Delaware Supreme Court "modernized" the appraisal remedy by approving the use of modern valuation techniques and by attempting to somehow unite the appraisal remedy and the equitable action against a fiduciary. Before we turn to review that effort by the Supreme Court in §12.10, below (and putting aside our bias against appraisal actions in public company contexts), we focus briefly on the "market-out" rule, which precludes appraisal as an available remedy in an important class of mergers: the stock-for-stock mergers of most public companies.

---

62. Compare *Weinberger v. UOP, Inc.,* excerpted below, and *Rabkin v. Phillip A. Hunt Chemical Corp.,* noted below.

63. See, e.g., *Stauffer v. Standard Brands, Inc.,* 187 A.2d 78 (Del. 1962); RMBCA §13.02(d).

12.8.3   The Market-Out Rule

Section 262 of the Delaware statute is by no means simple to read. After granting the right of judicial appraisal to all qualifying shares of any class in a merger effectuated under the general merger statute (i.e., §251), the Delaware appraisal statute and others (e.g., RMBCA §13.02(b)) go on to deny this remedy when shares of target corporations are traded on a national security exchange or held of record by 2,000 registered holders. In addition, an appraisal is denied if the shareholders were not required to vote on the merger. Then, notwithstanding this, the statute restores the appraisal remedy if target shareholders receive as consideration anything *other than* (i) stock in the surviving corporation, (ii) any other shares traded on a national security exchange, (iii) cash in lieu of fractional shares, or (iv) a combination of those items. This is the so-called market out. See DGCL §262(b)(2).

Thus, shareholders in a privately traded firm (with fewer than 2,000 shareholders) will always have appraisal rights in a merger if they are required to vote on it. But consistent with the liquidity rationale of appraisal rights, shareholders in a public company with more than 2,000 shareholders have no appraisal rights in a stock-for-stock merger. The theory, we suppose, is that, if one gets traded stock in the merger, then one will not be "forced" to make an investment against one's will. This is a fine theory, but it does not explain why shareholders who receive cash for their shares *do* have appraisal rights. Nor does it acknowledge a role for appraisal as a check on the amount of consideration a shareholder receives (the only plausible rationale for appraisal when the consideration is cash). So how can withholding appraisal in stock-for-stock mergers when shares are publicly traded be reconciled with granting appraisal rights in cash-out mergers? You tell us.

12.8.4   The Nature of "Fair Value"

The appraisal right is a put option — an opportunity to sell shares back to the firm at a price equal to their "fair value" immediately prior to the transaction triggering the right. Thus, there are two dimensions to appraisals: (1) the definition of the shareholder's claim (i.e., what it is specifically that the court is supposed to value) and (2) the technique for determining value. For a long time, courts, including Delaware's, remained vague about both dimensions of appraisal rights.

Today, however, Delaware law has resolved uncertainty about the first of these dimensions. It clearly defines the dissenting shareholder's claim as a pro rata claim on the value of the firm as a going concern. The Delaware appraisal statute explicitly seeks to measure the fair value of dissenting shares, free of any element of value that might be attributed to the merger. The Delaware Supreme Court has made it clear, however, that such value is to include all elements of future value that were present at the time of the merger, excluding only speculative elements of value. See, e.g., *Glassman v. Unocal Exploration Corporation*, 777 A.2d 242 (Del. 2001).

The last 20 years or so have seen significant change in the second dimension of the appraisal remedy, namely, how claims are measured. Traditionally, Delaware law determined fair value for appraisal purposes by a technique known as the Delaware block method. This technique examined a number of factors relating to a firm's value: earnings of the firm and price earnings multiples in the industry, asset values, and share market prices. Because courts sought a value untainted by the merger itself, they eschewed looking to comparative transactions and relied on historical data to determine value. Of course, market participants who were estimating values for investment purposes did try to take knowledgeable estimates of future cash flows into account. But the Delaware block technique considered this information to be too speculative.

This traditional valuation methodology, as well as the concept of fair value itself, was transformed by the 1983 case of *Weinberger v. UOP, Inc.*, discussed below. After *Weinberger*, the discounted cash flow (DCF) methodology (see Chapter 5) became the most common valuation technique in appraisal cases. In the typical case today, each side presents through an expert a detailed evaluation of the firm, with a projection of future cash flows and an estimate of the appropriate cost of capital for discounting those expected cash flows to present value. This technique produces judicial records with exceptionally wide differences in value. The case of *Cede v. Technicolor Inc.* was not exceptional in this respect. Technicolor's stock had been trading at between $9 and $11 a share prior to the merger negotiations. The deal price was $23 a share. In the appraisal action that followed the merger, the company's expert witnesses valued the stock as low as $13 a share, while the plaintiff's expert valued it at above $60 a share. For a judge untrained in valuation methodologies, such testimony is less than helpful. Recently, courts have begun appointing their own expert witnesses in appraisal cases to pass on the battle of the experts.

Excerpted below is an interesting, but atypical, appraisal valuation case. A number of factors make this case unusual. Most important, the company was on the brink of bankruptcy at the time of the merger. In bankruptcy, the firm's stock would be worth little or nothing. The merger was both an effort to salvage the business and a self-dealing transaction in which a large credit-or-shareholder refinanced the enterprise and cashed out the public minority. As in every appraisal, the key issue was the "fair value" of the company's equity.

IN RE VISION HARDWARE GROUP, INC.

669 A.2d 671 (Del. Ch. 1995)

[Better Vision (Vision) was born in a 1988 leveraged buyout in which shareholders invested $500,000. Vision never made any money, and the company ultimately accumulated debt in excess of $125 million. By late 1993, it had run out of cash and any source of additional financing, and it was on the verge of bankruptcy. Trust Company of the West (TCW), a so-called vulture fund investing in distressed companies, negotiated a transaction with Vision's creditors and its board of directors under which TCW purchased all of Vision's debt (at a deep discount), acquired warrants to purchase 51 percent of Vision's stock and — with the support of Vision's board — was implementing a merger agreement that cashed out Vision's public shareholders for total consideration of $125,000. The merger was negotiated by Vision's old board, which had no association with TCW, but the shareholder vote that approved the merger was dominated by TCW's newly issued shares. A group of minority share-holders countered in an appraisal proceeding that the fair value of their shares was really $15 million — a figure they reached by subtracting the deeply discounted *market value* of Vision's debt (i.e., not the face value of the debt) from the underlying value of Vision's assets.]

ALLEN, C.:

The principal issue presented is how one values the debt of a finan-cially strapped company that is on the brink of bankruptcy for purposes of Section 262. Both of the experts presented by the parties employed the discounted cash flow technique to estimate the enterprise value of the Company.[10] The inputs for the discounted cash flow models used by the experts varied. Nevertheless, the outcomes of their analyses were not vastly dissimilar. Mr. DiNapoli, the Company's expert, estimated the Company's enterprise value immediately before the merger to be approx-imately $86 million and within a range of $82 to $102 million. Share-holders' expert Mr. Kevin Dages' valuation of $95.9 million falls within that range. The two experts markedly diverged, however, in their opi-nions of the valuation of Better Vision's outstanding debt at the time of the merger. Mr. DiNapoli testified that, in this context, the appropriate valuation of the Company's senior debt was its face amount or $125.8 million and $10 million for the subordinated debt. As the value of the senior debt alone exceeds his estimate of the value of the enterprise, Mr.DiNapoli concluded that Better Vision's equity had no value.

Mr. Dages, on the other hand, was of the view that the deduction from enterprise value for debt should be estimated by using the market value of the debt. Mr. Dages claimed that the prices paid by TCW . . . to purchase Better Vision's senior and subordinated debts were reliable indications of the market value. As the total price paid by TCW for all of Better Vision's senior and subordinated debts amounted to approximately $56 million, Mr. Dages calculated the going concern value of Better Vision to be $39.9 million ($95.9 million of enterprise value less $56 million of debt) or $2.54 per share of common or junior preferred stock. . . .

The objective of this appraisal proceeding is to provide the dissenting shareholders the value of their shares at the time of the merger from which they dissented, affording them, however, no "element of value arising from the accomplishment or expectation of the merger." 8 Del. C. §262(h). In doing so the Delaware courts will attempt to value the whole enterprise as a going concern, *Bell v. Kirby Lumber Corporation*, Del. Supr., 413 A.2d 137,

---

10. Enterprise value as used by the witnesses in this case is an estimate of the value of the company without considering the existence of liabilities used to finance it.

141 (1980) and will afford dissenting shareholders their pro-rata portion free of any "minority discount."

Generally, shareholders are entitled to their proportionate share of the synergies created by the current deployment of assets and the good will of the firm. In determining the fair value of stock, even for financially troubled companies such as Better Vision, the court appraises such stock on a going concern and not on a liquidation basis. . . . But this principle is usually applied in a setting in which, but for the merger, there would still be a going concern.

In this instance the evidence shows conclusively that but for the TCW proposal and its effectuation, Better Vision was a going concern heading immediately into bankruptcy and, unless new credit was made available, liquidation. This fact has very basic importance in determining the fair value of Better Vision stock. . . .

. . . I find that Better Vision was an insolvent company that was in default on substantial obligations, with an even greater obligation falling due in its immediate future. . . . The record demonstrates that without new capital Better Vision was on a track leading to further losses and ultimately liquidation. Better Vision was saved from that fate only by TCW's proposal under which TCW purchased all of the outstanding debt of the Company at deep discounts and advanced new money to the firm. . . .

One way to understand the position of the dissenting shareholders is that they claim that the creditors of Better Vision — who held debt which the dissenters claim was worth $56 million — would ultimately have been forced to agree to a re-financing of the debt to a much lower face amount and that in that process the recognition of loss by the lenders would result in the realization of gain by the holders of equity. The problem is that the evidence does not show that it is likely that the lenders would be forced to refinance the company by writing off a major part of the legal liability that they were owed. To the contrary the holder of the debt by the time of the merger (TCW) had the right to enforce the legal liability and to force the company into bankruptcy. . . .

For the foregoing reasons I conclude that on the facts of this case the appropriate valuation of the company's debt, for purposes of Section 262, is the dollar value of the legal claim that that debt represented. Thus, I conclude that the shares held by the public shareholders excluding value attributable to the merger and its cash infusion, had no substantial value. They had nuisance value no greater than the amount paid in fact.

NOTES AND QUESTIONS FOLLOWING BETTER VISION

1. What should the value of debt be in most appraisal proceedings — the legal liability of the firm or the market value of the debt if sold by its holder? See *Rapid-American Corp. v. Harris,* 603 A.2d 796 (Del. 1992) (trial court committed no error in valuing debt at market value for appraisal purposes). If market value is generally relevant, is there a good reason to value it differently when the company is on the verge of bankruptcy?

2. Placing Better Vision in bankruptcy (Chapter 11) would have likely imposed costs and delays, and further reduced the value of the enterprise. Despite the rule of absolute priority in bankruptcy (i.e., all senior claimants must be fully paid before junior claimants are entitled to participate), even underwater equity sometimes has sufficient leverage to extract some value in a bankruptcy proceeding through its power to impose expense and delay.[64] If the creditors had been required to use bankruptcy to refinance Better Vision instead of the merger, plaintiffs might have succeeded in extracting some additional value in trade for their cooperation. Should the court, in determining the fair value of the equity in this case, have recognized this possible "holdup" value? The theory would be that only in bankruptcy could the debt be valued at face value, but in bankruptcy, equity could exercise a holdup right with which it could extract real value. Are such considerations worthy of judicial recognition?

3. Midway was a troubled airline. Without an injection of new capital, it would soon be bankrupt. GoodAero, Inc., agreed to inject $22 million into Midway in exchange for common stock if (1) Midway's majority shareholder would forgive its substantial loans to Midway and would inject new equity capital into the firm and (2) other creditors would also grant Midway substantial concessions, including more attractive terms on future transactions. Once the parties agreed to this recapitalization, Midway entered a merger transaction that cashed out the public shareholders for $.01 per share, left GoodAero with 67 percent of the equity, left the former Midway majority shareholder with 22 percent, and left other parties (presumably creditors) with the balance. Public holders of the old common stock object to receiving almost nothing for their shares and now seek appraisal. What argument supports their contention that they did not receive the fair value of their shares? See *Allenson v. Midway Airlines Corp.*, 789 A.2d 572 (Del. Ch. 2001).

4. For an interesting discussion of *Vision Hardware's* implications for transactional practice see Michael J. Sage & Mark E. Palmer, *Don't Pay Old Equity That Is Truly 'Underwater'!*, Bankruptcy Strategist (April 2003).

12.9   THE DE FACTO MERGER DOCTRINE

Should a "merger" be regarded as a functional concept (as implied in §12.4) or a formal or technical concept precisely defined by the corporation statute? Might there be functional reasons for treating the concept of a "merger" formally?

Consider, for example, a sale of substantially all assets by one corporation in exchange for stock of the buyer, followed by dissolution of the seller and distribution of buyer's stock to seller's shareholders. In effect, this resembles a stock-for-stock merger, with buyer as the surviving entity that owns all the assets and the investors in both companies owning buyer's

---

64. See Lynn M. LoPucki & William C. Whitford, *Bargaining over Equity's Share in Bankruptcy Reorganization at Large, Publicly Held Companies*, 139 U. Pa. L. Rev. 125 (1990).

stock. Should shareholder sellers be able to seek appraisal of the fair value of their shares from buyer, as they could in a merger? Some U.S. courts have adopted a functionalist approach to questions of this type and have accorded shareholder voting and appraisal rights to all corporate combinations that resemble mergers in effect. These courts have reasoned that when a de facto merger has the same economic effect as a de jure merger, shareholders should have the same protection. Outside of the United States, similar reasoning has been used to extend voting rights to shareholders, especially under German law, where the seminal *Holzmuller* decision extended voting rights in the 1980s to protect an entire class of fundamental transactions.[65]

There is, of course, a (functional) counterargument to such a functionalist approach. Corporate law contains a large element of formalism. Corporations exist as entities because certain formal steps are taken. Incorporators sign incorporation documents containing designated information, they hold an organizational meeting at which designated acts are performed, they file a charter in a prescribed form, they make a small payment, and—voila!—a legal person is born.[66] Still other formalities carry the corporation forward in its new life. Boards meet and vote, shareholders elect directors annually (usually), and filings are made. And finally, mergers are consummated by filing with the appropriate state office. All of this is not "mere formality"; it is a source of utility. It permits people to accurately predict the legal consequences of their activities.

Delaware courts, together with most other U.S. courts, take the formalist side of the argument, at least with respect to the range of statutory protections that are available to shareholders in a corporate combination. The provisions of the Delaware statute are said to have "equal dignity" or "independent legal significance." A self-identified sale of assets that results in exactly the same economic consequences as a merger will nonetheless be governed by the (lesser) shareholder protections associated with a sale of assets, and not the full panoply of merger protections. A well-known formulation of this position is *Hariton v. Arco Electronics, Inc.*, excerpted below.[67]

HARITON v. ARCO ELECTRONICS, INC.

182 A.2d 22 (Del. Ch. 1962), aff'd, 188 A.2d 123 (Del. 1963)

SHORT, V.C.:

Plaintiff is a stockholder of defendant Arco Electronics, Inc., a Delaware corporation. The complaint challenges the validity of the purchase by Loral

65. BGHZ, Zivilsenat, II ZR 174/80Y (1980) (German judicial decisions extending shareholder voting rights to apparently fundamental corporate transaction).

66. If corporate organizers get it wrong, courts of equity may resort to a number of devices, such as corporation by estoppel, to try to reach fair outcomes, but if the firm is not formally created, the separate personality does not exist. Frank William McIntyre, *Note and Comment: De Facto Merger in Texas: Reports of Its Death Have Been Greatly Exaggerated,* 2 Tex. Wesleyan L. Rev. 593 (Spring 1996).

67. A noted American formulation of the opposite position, the de facto merger doctrine, is *Farris v. Glen Alden Corp.,* 393 Pa. 427, 143 A.2d 25 (1958). We do not reproduce the *Farris* decision—partly because its continuing authority is suspect but principally because the underlying issue is identical to that in the *Hariton* case.

Electronics Corporation, a New York corporation, of all the assets of Arco. Two causes of action are asserted, namely (1) that the transaction is unfair to Arco stockholders, and (2) that the transaction constituted a de facto merger and is unlawful since the merger provisions of the Delaware law were not complied with. . . .

Plaintiff now concedes that he is unable to sustain the charge of unfairness. The only issue before the court, therefore, is whether the transaction was by its nature a de facto merger with a consequent right of appraisal in plaintiff.

Prior to the transaction of which plaintiff complains Arco was principally engaged in the business of the wholesale distribution of components or parts for electronics and electrical equipment. It had outstanding 486,500 shares of Class A common stock and 362,500 shares of Class B common stock. The rights of the holders of the Class A and Class B common stock differed only as to preferences in dividends. Arco's balance sheet as of September 30, 1961 shows total assets of $3,013,642. Its net income for the preceding year was $273,466.

Loral was engaged, primarily, in the research, development and production of electronic equipment. Its balance sheet shows total assets of $16,453,479. Its net income for the year ending March 31, 1961 was $1,301,618.

In the summer of 1961 Arco commenced negotiations with Loral with a view to the purchase of all of the assets of Arco in exchange for shares of Loral common stock. I think it fair to say that the record establishes that the negotiations which ultimately led to the transaction involved were conducted by the representatives of the two corporations at arm's length. There is no suggestion that any representative of Arco had any interest whatever in Loral, or vice versa. In any event, Arco rejected two offers made by Loral of a purchase price based upon certain ratios of Loral shares for Arco shares. Finally, on October 12, 1961, Loral offered a purchase price based on the ratio of one share of Loral common stock for three shares of Arco common stock. This offer was accepted by the representatives of Arco on October 24, 1961 and an agreement for the purchase was entered into between Loral and Arco on October 27, 1961. This agreement provides, among other things, as follows:

> Arco will convey and transfer to Loral all of its assets and property of every kind, tangible and intangible; and will grant to Loral the use of its name and slogans.
>
> Loral will assume and pay all of Arco's debts and liabilities.
>
> Loral will issue to Arco 283,000 shares of its common stock.
>
> Upon the closing of the transaction Arco will dissolve and distribute to its shareholders, pro rata, the shares of the common stock of Loral.
>
> Arco will call a meeting of its stockholders to be held December 21, 1961 to authorize and approve the conveyance and delivery of all the assets of Arco to Loral.
>
> After the closing date Arco will not engage in any business or activity except as may be required to complete the liquidation and dissolution of Arco.

Pursuant to its undertaking in the agreement for purchase and sale Arco caused a special meeting of its stockholders to be called for December 27, 1961. The notice of such meeting set forth three specific purposes therefor: (1) to vote upon a proposal to ratify the agreement of purchase and sale, a copy of which was attached to the notice; (2) to vote upon a proposal to change the name of the corporation; and (3) if Proposals (1) and (2) should be adopted, to vote upon a proposal to liquidate and dissolve the corporation and to distribute the Loral shares to Arco shareholders. . . .

Plaintiff contends that the transaction, though in form a sale of assets of Arco, is in substance and effect a merger, and that it is unlawful because the merger statute has not been complied with, thereby depriving plaintiff of his right of appraisal.

Defendant contends that since all the formalities of a sale of assets pursuant to 8 Del. C. §271 have been complied with the transaction is in fact a sale of assets and not a merger. In this connection it is to be noted that plaintiffs nowhere allege or claim that defendant has not complied to the letter with the provisions of said section. . . .

The right of appraisal accorded to a dissenting stockholder by the merger statutes is in compensation for the right which he had at common law to prevent a merger. . . . The Legislatures of many states have seen fit to grant the appraisal right to a dissenting stockholder not only under the merger statutes but as well under the sale of assets statutes. Our Legislature has seen fit to expressly grant the appraisal right only under the merger statutes. This difference in treatment of the rights of dissenting stock-holders may well have been deliberate, in order "to allow even greater freedom of action to corporate majorities in arranging combinations than is possible under the merger statutes." 72 Harv. L. Rev. 1232, *The Right of Shareholders Dissenting From Corporate Combinations To Demand Cash Payment For Their Shares.*

While plaintiff's contention that the doctrine of de facto merger should be applied in the present circumstances is not without appeal, the subject is one which, in my opinion, is within the legislative domain. Moreover it is difficult to differentiate between a case such as the present and one where the reorganization plan contemplates the ultimate dissolution of the selling corporation but does not formally require such procedure in express terms. . . .

Arco continued in existence as a corporate entity following the exchange of securities for its assets. The fact that it continued corporate existence only for the purpose of winding up its affairs by the distribution of Loral stock is, in my mind, of little consequence. . . . The right of the corporation to sell all of its assets for stock in another corporation was expressly accorded to Arco by §271 of Title 8, Del. C. The stockholder was, in contemplation of law, aware of this right when he acquired his stock. He was also aware of the fact that the situation might develop whereby he would be ultimately forced to accept a new investment, as would have been the case here had the resolution authorizing dissolution followed consummation of the sale. . . . Inclusion of the condition in the sale agreement does not in any way add to his position to complain.

There is authority in decisions of courts of this state for the proposition that the various sections of the Delaware Corporation Law conferring authority for corporate action are independent of each other and that a given result may be accomplished by proceeding under one section which is not possible, or is even forbidden under another. . . .

I conclude that the transaction complained of was not a de facto merger, either in the sense that there was a failure to comply with one or more of the requirements of §271 of the Delaware Corporation Law, or that the result accomplished was in effect a merger entitling plaintiff to a right of appraisal.

NOTE AND QUESTIONS

1. The Revised Model Business Corporation Act removes the issue of de facto mergers by giving shareholders a right to dissent and seek appraisal every time a restructuring is authorized. See RMBCA §13.02(3).

2. Was *Hariton* rightly decided? Should courts provide identical protections to minority shareholders involved in economically identical transactions? If not, should legislatures do so? Does the value you attach to appraisal rights in arm's-length transactions matter to your answer (as it would to ours)?

12.10   THE DUTY OF LOYALTY IN CONTROLLED MERGERS

As we discussed in Chapter 9, U.S. corporate law generally provides that controlling shareholders owe to the corporation and its minority shareholders a fiduciary duty of loyalty whenever they exercise any aspect of their control over corporate actions and decisions.[68] All shareholders, however, have the right to vote their shares in their own best interests.[69] Thus, there is some tension between a controlling shareholder's exercise of voting rights, which can arguably reflect her own "selfish" self-interest, and her exercise of "control" over the corporation or its property, which cannot. What precisely is the exercise of control that gives rise to an obligation of fairness? It is best defined as the de facto power to do what other shareholders cannot, such as the controller's power to access non-public corporate information or influence the board to approve a transaction (e.g., a merger) with another company in which the controller is financially interested.

---

68. *Weinberger v. UOP, Inc.*, 457 A.2d 701 (Del. 1983); *Sinclair Oil Corp. v. Levien*, 280 A.2d 717 (Del. 1971) (*Sinclair Oil* is the source of a particular test for invoking the entire fairness burden: that the corporate transaction under scrutiny treats the controller differently than the other shareholders before the obligation to prove its fairness arises. Of course, this test is typically met in freeze-out mergers).

69. *Tanzer v. International General Industries, Inc.*, 379 A.2d 1221 (Del. 1977).

Controlled mergers, including parent-subsidiary mergers, expose minority shareholders to an acute risk of exploitation. Today, we describe most of these mergers as "cash-out," "freeze-out," or "going-private" mergers. But since fully arm's-length mergers may be effectuated through a two-step transaction, with a (new) majority shareholder in the second stage, the concept of a parent-subsidiary merger extends even to transactions that, at their outset, are fully arm's-length in character.[70]

A merger is not the only technique for accomplishing a cash-out or freeze-out. Asset sales and reverse stock splits can also be freeze-out techniques. For example, a controlling shareholder can cause the company to sell all of its assets to his wholly owned firm, in exchange for cash, which may then be distributed to the company's shareholders in a liquidation. Alternatively, a controlling shareholder can cause the company to radically decrease its number of shares and pay off minority shareholders in cash for fractional shares. If the reverse split is dramatic enough, only one shareholder will be left after it is completed.[71]

12.10.1   Cash Mergers or Freeze-Outs

Nineteenth-century corporation lawyers would have been horrified (or maybe delighted) by the cash-out merger. Even after the repudiation of the unanimity rule allowed a qualified majority of shareholders to impose a merger against the will of a disagreeing minority, all shareholders had the

---

70. In *Cede and Co. v. Technicolor, Inc.*, 1991 Westlaw 111134 (Del. Ch. 1991), *rev'd*, 634 A.2d 345 (Del. 1993), the Delaware Court of Chancery held that a two-step merger that was an arm's-length transaction when negotiated with the target board did not become an interested transaction when the second-step merger was effectuated, provided there were no material changes in the business or the industry in the intervening period. The Delaware Supreme Court rejected that holding. Thus, under Delaware law, a two-step merger would seem to give rise to duties of loyalty to the public minority prior to the cash-out merger.

71. To better understand a reverse stock split, first consider a normal stock split. In a normal stock split, either the company pays a stock dividend on its outstanding shares, so that each shareholder receives more stock for each share already held, or the company amends its charter to provide that each share is "reclassified" into more than one share. Of course, the company's expected cash flows and earnings are unaffected by simply changing the number of shares outstanding, and the only other certain result of a split is to reduce the company's stock price in proportion (or nearly so) to the split. Typical stock splits are 2-for-1 or 3-for-1 and are used to decrease the per-share price to a "normal" range ($10 to $200). Lower absolute stock prices reduce an investor's threshold investment: Stock is generally traded in round lots of 100 shares, and purchases of smaller ("odd") lots usually involve higher transaction costs. Well-timed splits may thus have the real economic effect of increasing the liquidity of a stock and so may (modestly) increase the total value of outstanding shares.

In a reverse stock split, the opposite effect is achieved. A controlling shareholder amends the corporate charter to provide for the combination of some large number of shares into a single share (e.g., 1-for-10, 1-for-100, etc.). Cash is provided to shareholders holding less than a single share ("fractional share") after the reverse split, pursuant to statute. See DGCL §155. The reverse split ratio is set large enough to insure that only the controlling shareholder ends up with one or more whole shares of stock; all other shareholders end up with fractional shares (and thus cash).

right to continue as shareholders of the surviving entity. Indeed, this is still the rule in most non-U.S. jurisdictions.

Nevertheless, by the 1920s, the idea of cashing out minority share-holders through the merger device no longer shocked the consciences of U.S. corporate lawyers. Florida led the way by amending its statute in 1925 to permit cash consideration in a merger. Other states followed. Delaware was uncustomarily slow, since it did not authorize the use of cash in short-form mergers until 1957 and not in long-form mergers until 1967. The MBCA followed in 1968 and 1969, respectively.[72] Cash-out mergers (or freeze-outs) reemerged as a controversial topic during the 1960s and 1970s, when a period of low stock market prices followed after a boom in public offerings of stock. The low stock values allowed many controlling shareholders to cash out public shareholders at prices sub-stantially below the prices that these investors had paid for the same shares a short time before. This raised complaints about unfairness. Critics argued, among other things, that such transactions often occurred when the pro rata value of the assets held by these companies far exceeded the market value of their minority shares. A "cashout" even at a premium price allowed controlling shareholders to capture a dispro-portionate share of the company's value. In a much-publicized speech given at the University of Notre Dame in November 1974, SEC Commis-sioner A.A. Sommer said:

> Daily we read of companies which are offering to buy out all, or sub-stantially all, of their shareholders, thus enhancing the control of the controlling shareholders and freeing the corporation of the "burdens" of being publicly-held. In other instances clever and indeed most imagi-native devices are used to afford the small shareholders little, if any, choice in the matter. What is happening is, in my estimation, serious, unfair, and sometimes disgraceful, a perversion of the whole process of public financing, and a course that inevitably is going to make the individual shareholder even more hostile to American corporate mores and the securities markets than he already is.[73]

At the federal level, the SEC adopted Rule 13e-3 under the Williams Act specifically to require uniquely extensive disclosure in going-private transactions. At the state level, courts in Delaware and elsewhere wrestled with the task of protecting minority shareholders without banning freeze-outs altogether. The next case, *Weinberger v. UOP*, gives some of the history of Delaware's freeze-out case law and sets forth the core of its current law on freeze-outs and other controlled transactions.

---

72. See generally Elliott J. Weiss, *The Law of Take Out Mergers: A Historical Perspec-tive*, 56 N.Y.U. L. Rev. 624, 632 (1981); Arthur M. Borden, *Going Private—Old Tort, New Tort or No Tort?*, 49 N.Y.U. L. Rev. 987 (1974).

73. A.A. Sommer, Jr., Law Advisory Council Lecture, Notre Dame Law School (Nov. 1974) in [1974-75 Transfer Binder] Fed. Sec. L. Rep. (CCH) 80,010, at 84,695 (Nov. 20, 1974).

WEINBERGER v. UOP, INC.

457 A.2d 701 (Del. 1983)

MOORE, J.:

This post-trial appeal was reheard en banc from a decision of the Court of Chancery. It was brought by the class action plaintiff below, a former shareholder of UOP, Inc., who challenged the elimination of UOP's minority shareholders by a cash-out merger between UOP and its majority owner, The Signal Companies, Inc. . . .

Signal is a diversified, technically based company operating through various subsidiaries. Its stock is publicly traded on the New York, Philadelphia and Pacific Stock Exchanges. UOP, formerly known as Universal Oil Products Company, was a diversified industrial company. . . . Its stock was publicly held and listed on the New York Stock Exchange. [In 1974, Signal acquired 50.5 percent of UOP at $21 per share when UOP shares had traded at $14 per share.] . . .

Although UOP's board consisted of thirteen directors, Signal nominated and elected only six. Of these, five were either directors or employees of Signal. The sixth, a partner in the banking firm of Lazard Freres & Co., had been one of Signal's representatives in the negotiations and bargaining with UOP concerning the tender offer and purchase price of the UOP shares.

However, the president and chief executive officer of UOP retired during 1975, and Signal caused him to be replaced by James V. Crawford, a long-time employee and senior executive vice president of one of Signal's wholly-owned subsidiaries. Crawford succeeded his predecessor on UOP's board of directors and also was made a director of Signal.

By the end of 1977 Signal basically was unsuccessful in finding other suitable investment candidates for its excess cash, and by February 1978 considered that it had no other realistic acquisitions available to it on a friendly basis. Once again its attention turned to UOP.

The trial court found that at the instigation of certain Signal management personnel, including William W. Walkup, its board chairman, and Forrest N. Shumway, its president, a feasibility study was made concerning the possible acquisition of the balance of UOP's outstanding shares. This study was performed by two Signal officers, Charles S. Arledge, vice president (director of planning), and Andrew J. Chitiea, senior vice president (chief financial officer). Messrs. Walkup, Shumway, Arledge and Chitiea were all directors of UOP in addition to their membership on the Signal board.

Arledge and Chitiea concluded that it would be a good investment for Signal to acquire the remaining 49.5% of UOP shares at any price up to $24 each. Their report was discussed between Walkup and Shumway who, along with Arledge, Chitiea and Brewster L. Arms, internal counsel for Signal, constituted Signal's senior management. In particular, they talked about the proper price to be paid if the acquisition was pursued, purportedly keeping in mind that as UOP's majority shareholder, Signal owed a fiduciary responsibility to both its own stockholders as well as to UOP's minority. It was ultimately agreed that a meeting of Signal's Executive Committee would be called to propose that Signal acquire the remaining outstanding stock of UOP through a cash-out merger in the range of $20 to $21 per share.

The Executive Committee meeting was set for February 28, 1978. As a courtesy, UOP's president, Crawford, was invited to attend, although he was not a member of Signal's executive committee. On his arrival, and prior to the meeting, Crawford was asked to meet privately with Walkup and Shumway. He was then told of Signal's plan to acquire full ownership of UOP and was asked for his reaction to the proposed price range of $20 to $21 per share. Crawford said he thought such a price would be "generous", and that it was certainly one which should be submitted to UOP's minority shareholders for their ultimate consideration. He stated, however, that Signal's 100% ownership could cause internal problems at UOP. He believed that employees would have to be given some assurance of their future place in a fully-owned Signal subsidiary. Otherwise, he feared the departure of essential personnel. Also, many of UOP's key employees had stock option incentive programs which would be wiped out by a merger. Crawford therefore urged that some adjustment would have to be made, such as providing a comparable incentive in Signal's shares, if after the merger he was to maintain his quality of personnel and efficiency at UOP.

Thus, Crawford voiced no objection to the $20 to $21 price range, nor did he suggest that Signal should consider paying more than $21 per share for the minority interests. . . .

Thus, it was the consensus that a price of $20 to $21 per share would be fair to both Signal and the minority shareholders of UOP. Signal's executive committee authorized its management "to negotiate" with UOP "for a cash acquisition of the minority ownership in UOP, Inc., with the intention of presenting a proposal to [Signal's] board of directors . . . on March 6, 1978." Immediately after this February 28, 1978 meeting, Signal issued a press release stating [that Signal and UOP were negotiating for the cash purchase of the 49.5 percent of UOP that Signal did not presently own, without reference to the price. Nevertheless, the announcement referred to UOP's closing market price of $14.50/share. — EDS.]

Two days later, on March 2, 1978, Signal issued a second press release stating that its management would recommend a price in the range of $20 to $21 per share for UOP's 49.5% minority interest. This announcement referred to Signal's earlier statement that "negotiations" were being conducted for the acquisition of the minority shares.

Between Tuesday, February 28, 1978 and Monday, March 6, 1978, a total of four business days, Crawford spoke by telephone with all of UOP's non-Signal, i.e., outside, directors. Also during that period, Crawford retained Lehman Brothers to render a fairness opinion as to the price offered the minority for its stock. He gave two reasons for this choice. First, the time schedule between the announcement and the board meetings was short (by then only three business days) and since Lehman Brothers had been acting as UOP's investment banker for many years, Crawford felt that it would be in the best position to respond on such brief notice. Second, James W. Glanville, a long-time director of UOP and a partner in Lehman Brothers, had acted as a financial advisor to UOP for many years. Crawford believed that Glanville's familiarity with UOP, as a member of its board, would also be of assistance in enabling Lehman Brothers to render a fairness opinion within the existing time constraints.

. . . Glanville's immediate personal reaction was that a price of $20 to $21 [for UOP shares] would certainly be fair, since it represented almost a 50% premium over UOP's market price. Glanville sought a $250,000 fee for Lehman Brothers' services, but Crawford thought this too much. After further discussions Glanville finally agreed that Lehman Brothers would render its fairness opinion for $150,000. . . .

[T]he Lehman Brothers team concluded that "the price of either $20 or $21 would be a fair price for the remaining shares of UOP". They telephoned this impression to Glanville, who was spending the weekend in Vermont.

On Monday morning, March 6, 1978, Glanville and the senior member of the Lehman Brothers team flew to Des Plaines to attend the scheduled UOP directors meeting. Glanville looked over the assembled information during the flight. The two had with them the draft of a "fairness opinion letter" in which the price had been left blank. Either during or immediately prior to the directors' meeting, the two-page "fairness opinion letter" was typed in final form and the price of $21 per share was inserted.

On March 6, 1978, both the Signal and UOP boards were convened to consider the proposed merger. Telephone communications were maintained between the two meetings. Walkup, Signal's board chairman, and also a UOP director, attended UOP's meeting with Crawford in order to present Signal's position and answer any questions that UOP's non-Signal directors might have. Arledge and Chitiea, along with Signal's other designees on UOP's board, participated by conference telephone. . . .

First, Signal's board unanimously adopted a resolution authorizing Signal to propose to UOP a cash merger of $21 per share. . . . This proposal required that the merger be approved by a majority of UOP's outstanding minority shares voting at the stockholders meeting at which the merger would be considered, and that the minority shares voting in favor of the merger, when coupled with Signal's 50.5% interest would have to comprise at least two-thirds of all UOP shares. Otherwise the proposed merger would be deemed disapproved.

UOP's board then considered the proposal. Copies of the agreement were delivered to the directors in attendance. . . . In addition they had Lehman Brothers' hurriedly prepared fairness opinion letter finding the price of $21 to be fair. Glanville, the Lehman Brothers partner, and UOP director, commented on the information that had gone into preparation of the letter.

Signal also suggests that the Arledge-Chitiea feasibility study, indicating that a price of up to $24 per share would be a "good investment" for Signal, was discussed at the UOP directors' meeting. The Chancellor made no such finding, and our independent review of the record, detailed infra, satisfies us by a preponderance of the evidence that there was no discussion of this document at UOP's board meeting. Furthermore, it is clear beyond peradventure that nothing in that report was ever disclosed to UOP's minority shareholders prior to their approval of the merger.

After consideration of Signal's proposal, Walkup and Crawford left the meeting to permit a free and uninhibited exchange between UOP's non-Signal directors. Upon their return a resolution to accept Signal's offer was then proposed and adopted. . . .

On March 7, 1978, UOP sent a letter to its shareholders advising them of the action taken by UOP's board with respect to Signal's offer. . . .

Despite the swift board action of the two companies, the merger was not submitted to UOP's shareholders until their annual meeting on May 26, 1978. In the notice of that meeting and proxy statement sent to shareholders in May, UOP's management and board urged that the merger be approved. The proxy statement also advised:

> The price was determined after *discussions* between James V. Crawford, a director of Signal and Chief Executive Officer of UOP, and officers of Signal which took place during meetings on February 28, 1978, and in the course of several subsequent telephone conversations. (Emphasis added.)

In the original draft of the proxy statement the word "negotiations" had been used rather than "discussions". However, when the Securities and Exchange Commission sought details of the "negotiations" as part of its review of these materials, the term was deleted and the word "discussions" was substituted. . . .

As of the record date for UOP's annual meeting, there were 12,488,302 shares of UOP common stock outstanding, 5,688,302 of which were owned by the minority. At the meeting only 56%, or 3,208,652, of the minority shares were voted. Of these, 2,953,812, or 51.9% of the total minority, voted for the merger, and 254,840 voted against it. When Signal's stock was added to the minority shares voting in favor, a total of 76.2% of UOP's outstanding shares approved the merger while only 2.2% opposed it.

By its terms the merger became effective on May 26, 1978, and each share of UOP's stock held by the minority was automatically converted into a right to receive $21 cash. . . .

A primary issue mandating reversal [of the Court of Chancery's judgment] is the preparation by two UOP directors, Arledge and Chitiea, of their feasibility study for the exclusive use and benefit of Signal. This document was of obvious significance to both Signal and UOP. Using UOP data, it described the advantages to Signal of ousting the minority at a price range of $21-24 per share. Mr. Arledge, one of the authors, outlined the benefits to Signal:

PURPOSE OF THE MERGER

1. Provides an outstanding investment opportunity for Signal — (Better than any recent acquisition we have seen.)
2. Increases Signal's earnings.
3. Facilitates the flow of resources between Signal and its subsidiaries — (Big factors — works both ways.)

4.   Provides cost savings potential for Signal and UOP.
5.   Improves the percentage of Signal's "operating earnings" as opposed to "holding company earnings."
6.   Simplifies the understanding of Signal.
7.   Facilitates technological exchange among Signal's subsidiaries.
8.   Eliminates potential conflicts of interest.

Having written those words, solely for the use of Signal, it is clear from the record that neither Arledge nor Chitiea shared this report with their fellow directors of UOP. We are satisfied that no one else did either. This conduct hardly meets the fiduciary standards applicable to such a transaction. . . .

The Arledge-Chitiea report speaks for itself in supporting the Chancellor's finding that a price of up to $24 was a "good investment" for Signal. It shows that a return on the investment at $21 would be 15.7% versus 15.5% at $24 per share. This was a difference of only two-tenths of one percent, while it meant over $17,000,000 to the minority. Under such circumstances, paying UOP's minority shareholders $24 would have had relatively little long-term effect on Signal, and the Chancellor's findings concerning the benefit to Signal, even at a price of $24, were obviously correct. . . .

Certainly, this was a matter of material significance to UOP and its shareholders. Since the study was prepared by two UOP directors, using UOP information for the exclusive benefit of Signal, and nothing whatever was done to disclose it to the outside UOP directors or the minority shareholders, a question of breach of fiduciary duty arises. This problem occurs because there were common Signal-UOP directors participating, at least to some extent, in the UOP board's decision-making processes without full disclosure of the conflicts they faced.[7] . . .

Given the absence of any attempt to structure this transaction on an arm's length basis, Signal cannot escape the effects of the conflicts it faced, particularly when its designees on UOP's board did not totally abstain from participation in the matter. There is no "safe harbor" for such divided loyalties in Delaware. When directors of a Delaware corporation are on both sides of a transaction, they are required to demonstrate their utmost good faith and the most scrupulous inherent fairness of the bargain. . . .

There is no dilution of this obligation where one holds dual or multiple directorships, as in a parent-subsidiary context. . . . The record demonstrates that Signal has not met this obligation.

---

7. Although perfection is not possible, or expected, the result here could have been entirely different if UOP had appointed an independent negotiating committee of its outside directors to deal with Signal at arm's length. . . . Since fairness in this context can be equated to conduct by a theoretical, wholly independent, board of directors acting upon the matter before them, it is unfortunate that this course apparently was neither considered nor pursued. . . . Particularly in a parent-subsidiary context, a showing that the action taken was as though each of the contending parties had in fact exerted its bargaining power against the other at arm's length is strong evidence that the transaction meets the test of fairness. . . .

The concept of fairness has two basic aspects: fair dealing and fair price. The former embraces questions of when the transaction was timed, how it was initiated, structured, negotiated, disclosed to the directors, and how the approvals of the directors and the stockholders were obtained. The latter aspect of fairness relates to the economic and financial considerations of the proposed merger, including all relevant factors: assets, market value, earnings, future prospects, and any other elements that affect the intrinsic or inherent value of a company's stock. However, the test for fairness is not a bifurcated one as between fair dealing and price. All aspects of the issue must be examined as a whole since the question is one of entire fairness. However, in a non-fraudulent transaction we recognize that price may be the preponderant consideration outweighing other features of the merger. Here, we address the two basic aspects of fairness separately because we find reversible error as to both.

Part of fair dealing is the obvious duty of candor required by *Lynch I*, supra. Moreover, one possessing superior knowledge may not mislead any stockholder by use of corporate information to which the latter is not privy. . . . With the well-established Delaware law on the subject, . . . it is inevitable that the obvious conflicts posed by Arledge and Chitiea's preparation of their "feasibility study", derived from UOP information, for the sole use and benefit of Signal, cannot pass muster.

The Arledge-Chitiea report is but one aspect of the element of fair dealing. How did this merger evolve? It is clear that it was entirely initiated by Signal. The serious time constraints under which the principals acted were all set by Signal. It had not found a suitable outlet for its excess cash and considered UOP a desirable investment, particularly since it was now in a position to acquire the whole company for itself. For whatever reasons, and they were only Signal's, the entire transaction was presented to and approved by UOP's board within four business days. . . .

. . . So far as negotiations were concerned, it is clear that they were modest at best. Crawford, Signal's man at UOP, never really talked price with Signal, except to accede to its management's statements on the subject, and to convey to Signal the UOP outside directors' view that as between the $20-$21 range under consideration, it would have to be $21. The latter is not a surprising outcome, but hardly arm's length negotiations. Only the protection of benefits for UOP's key employees and the issue of Lehman Brothers' fee approached any concept of bargaining.

As we have noted, the matter of disclosure to the UOP directors was wholly flawed by the conflicts of interest raised by the Arledge-Chitiea report. . . .

This cannot but undermine a conclusion that this merger meets any reasonable test of fairness. The outside UOP directors lacked one material piece of information generated by two of their colleagues, but shared only with Signal. True, the UOP board had the Lehman Brothers' fairness opinion, but that firm has been blamed by the plaintiff for the hurried task it performed, when more properly the responsibility for this lies with Signal. There was no disclosure of the circumstances surrounding the rather cursory preparation of the Lehman Brothers' fairness opinion. Instead, the impression was given UOP's minority that a careful study had been made, when in fact speed was the hallmark, and Mr. Glanville, Lehman's partner in charge of the matter, and also a UOP director, having spent the weekend in Vermont, brought a draft of the "fairness opinion letter" to the UOP directors' meeting on March 6, 1978 with the price left blank. We can only conclude from the record that the rush imposed on Lehman Brothers by Signal's timetable contributed to the difficulties under which this investment banking firm attempted to perform its responsibilities. Yet, none of this was disclosed to UOP's minority.

Finally, the minority stockholders were denied the critical information that Signal considered a price of $24 to be a good investment. Since this would have meant over $17,000,000 more to the minority, we cannot conclude that the shareholder vote was an informed one. Under the circumstances, an approval by a majority of the minority was meaningless. . . .

Turning to the matter of price, plaintiff also challenges its fairness. His evidence was that on the date the merger was approved the stock was worth at least $26 per share. In support, he offered the testimony of a chartered investment analyst who used two basic approaches to valuation: a comparative analysis of the premium paid over market in ten other tender offer-merger combinations, and a discounted cash flow analysis. . . .

While the Chancellor rejected plaintiff's discounted cash flow method of valuing UOP's stock, as not corresponding with "either logic or the existing law" (426 A.2d at 1360), it is significant that this was essentially the focus, i.e., earnings potential of UOP, of Messrs. Arledge and Chitiea in their evaluation of the merger. Accordingly, the standard "Delaware block" or weighted average method of valuation, formerly employed in appraisal and other stock valuation cases, shall no longer exclusively control such proceedings. We believe that a more liberal approach must include proof of value by any techniques or methods which are generally considered acceptable in the financial community and otherwise admissible in court, subject only to our interpretation of 8 Del. C. §262(h), infra. . . .

The basic concept of value under the appraisal statute is that the stockholder is entitled to be paid for that which has been taken from him, viz., his proportionate interest in a going concern. By value of the stockholder's proportionate interest in the corporate enterprise is meant the true or intrinsic value of his stock which has been taken by the merger. In determining what figure represents this true or intrinsic value, the appraiser and the courts must take into consideration all factors and elements which reasonably might enter into the fixing of value. Thus, market value, asset value, dividends, earning prospects, the nature of the enterprise and any other facts which were known or which could be ascertained as of the date of merger and which throw any light on *future prospects* of the merged corporation are not only pertinent to an inquiry as to the value of the dissenting stockholders' interest, *but must be considered* by the agency fixing the value. (Emphasis added.) . . .

It is significant that section 262 now mandates the determination of "fair" value based upon "all relevant factors." Only the speculative elements of value that may arise from the "accomplishment or expectation" of the merger are excluded. We take this to be a very narrow exception to the appraisal process, designed to eliminate use of pro forma data and projections of a speculative variety relating to the completion of a merger. But elements of future value, including the nature of the enterprise, which are known or susceptible of proof as of the date of the merger and not the product of speculation, may be considered. When the trial court deems it appropriate, fair value also includes any damages, resulting from the taking, which the stockholders sustain as a class. . . .

The plaintiff has not sought an appraisal, but rescissory damages. . . . On remand the plaintiff will be permitted to test the fairness of the $21 price by the standards we herein establish, in conformity with the principle applicable to an appraisal — that fair value be determined by taking "into account all relevant factors" [see 8 Del. C. §262(h), supra]. In our view this includes the elements of rescissory damages if the Chancellor considers them susceptible of proof and a remedy appropriate to all the issues of fairness before him. To the extent that *Lynch II* . . . purports to limit the Chancellor's discretion to a single remedial formula for monetary damages in a cash-out merger, it is overruled.

While a plaintiff's monetary remedy ordinarily should be confined to the more liberalized appraisal proceeding herein established, we do not intend any limitation on the historic powers of the Chancellor to grant such other relief as the facts of a particular case may dictate. The appraisal remedy we approve may not be adequate in certain cases, particularly where fraud, misrepresentation, self-dealing, deliberate waste of corporate assets, or gross and palpable overreaching are involved. . . . Under such circumstances, the Chancellor's powers are complete to fashion any form of equitable and monetary relief as may be appropriate, including rescissory damages. Since it is apparent that this long completed transaction is too involved to undo, and in view of the Chancellor's discretion, the award, if any, should be in the form of monetary damages based upon entire fairness standards, i.e., fair dealing and fair price. . . .

Finally, we address the matter of business purpose. . . .

In view of the fairness test which has long been applicable to parent-subsidiary mergers, . . . the expanded appraisal remedy now available to shareholders, and the broad discretion of the Chancellor to fashion such relief as the facts of a given case may dictate, we do not believe that any additional meaningful protection is afforded minority shareholders by the business purpose requirement of the trilogy of *Singer, Tanzer, Najjar,* and their progeny. Accordingly, such requirement shall no longer be of any force or effect. . . .

QUESTIONS ON WEINBERGER

1. What is the significance of the fact that, at $24 per share, UOP stock would have been a good investment for Signal? Must a controlling shareholder inform minority shareholders of the top price it is willing or able to pay? If so, how could the negotiating committee device, endorsed in footnote 7, work in practice? If not, why did the court lay emphasis on the fact that Signal could have rationally paid more? See *Kahn v. Tremont Corp.,* 694 A.2d 422 (Del. 1997).

2. Regarding the negotiating committee idea mentioned in footnote 7, how much protection to the minority would that device offer even if undertaken in good faith? Specifically, what is the source of negotiating leverage that such a committee might have? See *Kahn v. Lynch Communication*, below (i.e., "the power to say no").

3. To what extent does this result represent disapproval by the court of an apparent failure to observe proper and formal corporate governance practices? Did Arledge and Chitiea use confidential data for Signal's purposes? If they had not been UOP directors and had only used public information, would the case have been decided differently? Why the speed to get UOP board approval when no external force drove the schedule?

4. What is *Weinberger* saying about the exclusivity of the appraisal proceeding? Before answering, take a look at the following note.

NOTES ON WEINBERGER, RABKIN, AND TECHNICOLOR: *ON THE BLURRING OF ANALYTICAL CATEGORIES*

1. *Weinberger*'s attempt to establish the "new" appraisal as the exclusive remedy for shareholder complaints about merger consideration was short lived. In *Rabkin v. Phillip A. Hunt Chemical Corp.*, 498 A.2d 701 (Del. 1985), the court permitted a nonappraisal attack on a cash-out merger action to proceed. Here the buyer of a control block contracted with the seller that, if the buyer — the new controlling shareholder — completed a cash-out merger within 12 months of purchasing control, it would pay the minority shareholders no less per share than it had paid to acquire its control stake. The buyer then waited a bit longer than 12 months and then cashed out the minority at a lower price. Rather than seek appraisal, the minority shareholders complained of a breach of fiduciary duty because the controlling shareholder knew within 12 months that it would effectuate the cash-out transaction but it deliberately waited longer to avoid paying the agreed-upon minimum price. Defendant moved to dismiss the complaint on the theory that the "new" post-*Weinberger* appraisal action was the exclusive remedy for complaints about the adequacy of price in a merger. The Delaware Supreme Court denied the motion. Henceforth, it ruled, cases could continue to be litigated where the claim was that a fiduciary duty between the parties had been breached. (Just why complying with the letter of a contract constituted an obvious breach of fiduciary duty to the *Rabkin* court remains mysterious to us even today.) In all events, following *Rabkin*, entire fairness actions rather than appraisals have been the principal means of attacking the fairness of price in a self-dealing merger.

2. One of *Weinberger*'s lasting and important contributions was to introduce a more realistic approach to valuation in the Delaware courts. Today, discounted cash flow analysis is the most common technique for estimating asset values, although evidence of comparative transaction values is also used. *Weinberger* also introduced the view that in "new" appraisal actions, the fair value to which a dissenter is entitled includes a

fair share of synergy gains that are available in the merger (or from an alternative merger partner). The Delaware appraisal statute clearly states that such gains are *not* to be included in the "fair value," which is said to be "exclusive of any element of value arising from the accomplishment or expectation of the merger." DGCL §262(h). The statutory idea then is that a dissenting shareholder is entitled to a pro rata share of the value of the corporation as it exists *prior* to the merger. But if the appraisal remedy is understood as it was by the *Weinberger* court — as a protection against self-dealing — then a measure of recovery that looks to a fair deal price begins to make sense. After all, the going concern value of a controlled firm will reflect the policies of its controlling shareholder. One might nevertheless ask whether the Delaware Supreme Court overstepped its power by refashioning the statute in this way.

3. Mandating that the measure of recovery in an appraisal remedy under *Weinberger* is to be the same as the measure of recovery available in an entire fairness claim against a controlling shareholder blurs an important distinction between the two actions. Where controlling shareholder transactions are involved, this blurring is harmless. In a later case, however, the Delaware Supreme Court blurred the line between arm's-length mergers and parent-subsidiary mergers.

Cede v. Technicolor, Inc., 684 A.2d 289 (Del. 1996), which we have already addressed in Chapter 8, arose out of a two-step, arm's-length cash merger between a corporation controlled by Ronald Perelman and Technicolor, Inc., a public company with no controlling shareholder. The Technicolor board negotiated a cash price that represented about a 100 percent premium over Technicolor's predeal market price. The first-step tender offer was fully subscribed. As agreed in the merger agreement, the second-step merger was accomplished at the same price as the tender offer and occurred, as contemplated, a few months after the tender offer closed. During the interim period, the acquirer caused the target to take preliminary steps to effectuate his business plan, which called for the selling off of assets and the reorganization of remaining activities. A substantial minority shareholder dissented from the merger and brought an appraisal action. As the appraisal action progressed, the shareholder uncovered what he thought of as evidence of board misbehavior.[74] He then brought a second suit — this one charging multiple breaches of fiduciary duties by the Technicolor directors and Mr. Perelman.

Thus, the question presented was whether Mr. Perelman — or more correctly, the entity through which he effectuated these transactions — owed a fiduciary duty to pay a fair price to the minority shareholders in the second-step merger. The Delaware Court of Chancery concluded that, while Perelman might be said to owe such a duty to the public shareholders of Technicolor, following the closing of step one, the facts that (1) the merger price had been fixed in arm's-length negotiations with an

---

74. The misbehavior charged was that the board had not voted in favor of the Perelman deal by the requisite supermajority because one director had voted against it but was recorded as voting in favor. Ultimately, at trial, this evidence was disbelieved, and the claim was rejected.

independent board and (2) no important new information bearing on value since the date of the merger agreement had emerged meant that the negotiated price would be deemed fair. The Delaware Supreme Court reversed. It held that Perelman, as a controlling shareholder, had a burden to establish that the price paid to minority shareholders was fair and that this burden could not be satisfied by looking at the results of the negotiations with the Technicolor board, since Perelman had begun to implement his new business plan by the time of the cash-out merger. The case was remanded for a determination of the fairness of the merger price. What are the ex ante effects of this ruling likely to be?

With respect to the appraisal remedy, the *Technicolor* court concluded that plaintiff could simultaneously pursue both his appraisal action and his claim for breach of fiduciary duty, and need not choose at any point prior to judgment which remedy he would elect. Therefore, this holding makes clear what *Rabkin* implied: Where there is a claim that the defendant owes fiduciary duties to the public shareholders — as in a parent-subsidiary merger or even a two-tier cash-out merger by a third party — appraisal is not the exclusive remedy for complaints concerning price. But where there is a straight (one-step) cash or stock merger between firms with no shared ownership interest (an arm's-length merger), complaints about price alone may be relegated to the appraisal remedy.

If the appraisal remedy provides the same measure of recovery post-*Weinberger* as the entire fairness or fiduciary claim and if the appraisal remedy does not require that the court find a breach of fiduciary duty, one might suppose that appraisal would now be the favored means for a disappointed shareholder to challenge merger consideration. This apparently was the intention of the *Weinberger* court. Whatever the intention, however, fairness actions still predominate. There are several reasons for this that have been touched on in our earlier discussion. First, appraisal may not be available because of the "market-out" provisions of the statute. See, e.g., DGCL §262(b)(1), (2).[75] Second, unlike an appraisal suit, an action claiming a breach of fiduciary duty can be brought *before* the effectuation of the merger, which provides to plaintiff an opportunity to request a preliminary injunction — an application that can significantly increase the plaintiff's settlement leverage. Third, suits for breach of fiduciary duty can be, and most often are, brought as class actions, which affords counsel a means to get paid from the class settlement or the corporation, in the event that any good consequence can be claimed to follow from the initiation of the suit. And, also important, the class is composed of all public shareholders of the target corporation. By comparison, the appraisal class is limited to a much smaller class of shareholders who have affirmatively opted out of the merger. The size of the group represented has a great impact on both the negotiating leverage that the lawyer will possess and the fee that she may expect to earn. Thus, from the perspective of the lawyers who stand behind most shareholder litigation,

---

75. Since, however, cash mergers always have the appraisal remedy available to target shareholders, this explanation is probably not important.

the appraisal remedy is a much less attractive venture than a class action for breach of fiduciary duty.

12.10.2   What Constitutes Control and Exercise of Control

Recall from our discussion of safe harbor statutes that self-dealing fiduciaries have two principal devices for easing the burden of proving entire fairness: shareholder ratification and independent director approval. These same devices are available in controlled mergers, but controlled mergers may raise some distinctive issues. The first is whether the practical context of a parent-subsidiary merger (i.e., the fact that the parent is not simply a fiduciary but also a controller) offers reasons for the legal system to be even more suspicious of the efficacy of these procedural devices. As we will see, judicial opinion has deferred a bit on this. The second issue is what a well-functioning special committee of independent directors entails. What powers, what advisors, and what degree of independence should such a committee have? The third issue is what effect is to be accorded the act of a well-functioning special committee in a controlled merger context.

KAHN v. LYNCH COMMUNICATION SYSTEMS, INC.

638 A.2d 1210 (Del. 1994)

[Alcatel U.S.A. Corporation (Alcatel), a holding company, is an indirect subsidiary of Compagnie Generale d'Electricite (CGE), a French corporation. In 1981, Alcatel acquired 30.6 percent of the common stock of Lynch Communication Systems, Inc. (Lynch) pursuant to a stock purchase agreement.]

HOLLAND, J.:

By the time of the merger which is contested in this action, Alcatel owned 43.3 percent of Lynch's outstanding stock; designated five of the eleven members of Lynch's board of directors; two of three members of the executive committee; and two of four members of the compensation committee.

In the spring of 1986, Lynch determined that in order to remain competitive in the rapidly changing telecommunications field, it would need to obtain fiber optics technology to complement its existing digital electronic capabilities. Lynch's management identified a target company, Telco Systems, Inc. ("Telco"), which possessed both fiber optics and other valuable technological assets. The record reflects that Telco expressed interest in being acquired by Lynch. Because of the supermajority voting provision, which Alcatel had negotiated when it first purchased its shares, in order to proceed with the Telco combination Lynch needed Alcatel's consent. In June 1986, Ellsworth F. Dertinger ("Dertinger"), Lynch's CEO and chairman of its board of directors, contacted Pierre Suard ("Suard"), the chairman of Alcatel's parent company, CGE, regarding the acquisition of Telco by Lynch. Suard expressed Alcatel's opposition to Lynch's acquisition of Telco. Instead, Alcatel proposed a combination of Lynch and Celwave Systems, Inc. ("Celwave"), an indirect subsidiary of CGE engaged in the manufacture and sale of telephone wire, cable and other related products.

Alcatel's proposed combination with Celwave was presented to the Lynch board at a regular meeting held on August 1, 1986. Although several directors expressed interest in the original combination which had been proposed with Telco, the Alcatel representatives on Lynch's board made it clear that such a combination would not be considered before a Lynch/Celwave combination. According to the minutes of the August 1 meeting, Dertinger expressed his opinion that Celwave would not be of interest to Lynch if Celwave was not owned by Alcatel.

At the conclusion of the meeting, the Lynch board unanimously adopted a resolution establishing an Independent Committee, consisting of Hubert L. Kertz ("Kertz"), Paul B. Wineman ("Wineman"), and Stuart M. Beringer ("Beringer"), to negotiate with Celwave and to make recommendations concerning the appropriate terms and conditions of a combination with Celwave. On October 24, 1986, Alcatel's investment banking firm, Dillon, Read & Co., Inc. ("Dillon Read") made a presentation to the Independent Committee. Dillon Read expressed its views concerning the benefits of a Celwave/Lynch combination and submitted a written proposal of an exchange ratio of 0.95 shares of Celwave per Lynch share in a stock-for-stock merger.

However, the Independent Committee's investment advisors, Thomson McKinnon Securities Inc. ("Thomson McKinnon") and Kidder, Peabody & Co. Inc. ("Kidder Peabody"), reviewed the Dillon Read proposal and concluded that the 0.95 ratio was predicated on Dillon Read's overvaluation of Celwave. Based upon this advice, the Independent Committee determined that the exchange ratio proposed by Dillon Read was unattractive to Lynch. The Independent Committee expressed its unanimous opposition to the Celwave/Lynch merger on October 31, 1986.

Alcatel responded to the Independent Committee's action on November 4, 1986, by withdrawing the Celwave proposal. Alcatel made a simultaneous offer to acquire the entire equity interest in Lynch, constituting the approximately 57 percent of Lynch shares not owned by Alcatel. The offering price was $14 cash per share.

On November 7, 1986, the Lynch board of directors revised the mandate of the Independent Committee. It authorized Kertz, Wineman, and Beringer to negotiate the cash merger offer with Alcatel. At a meeting held that same day, the Independent Committee determined that the $14 per share offer was inadequate. The Independent's Committee's own legal counsel, Skadden, Arps, Slate, Meagher & Flom ("Skadden Arps"), suggested that the Independent Committee should review alternatives to a cash-out merger with Alcatel, including a "white knight" third party acquirer, a repurchase of Alcatel's shares, or the adoption of a shareholder rights plan.

On November 12, 1986, Beringer, as chairman of the Independent Committee, contacted Michiel C. McCarty ("McCarty") of Dillon Read, Alcatel's representative in the negotiations, with a counteroffer at a price of $17 per share. McCarty responded on behalf of Alcatel with an offer of $15 per share. When Beringer informed McCarty of the Independent Committee's view that $15 was also insufficient, Alcatel raised its offer to $15.25 per share. The Independent Committee also rejected this offer. Alcatel then made its final offer of $15.50 per share.

At the November 24, 1986 meeting of the Independent Committee, Beringer advised its other two members that Alcatel was "ready to proceed with an unfriendly tender at a lower price" if the $15.50 per share price was not recommended by the Independent Committee and approved by the Lynch board of directors. Beringer also told the other members of the Independent Committee that the alternatives to a cash-out merger had been investigated but were impracticable. After meeting with its financial and legal advisors, the Independent Committee voted unanimously to recommend that the Lynch board of directors approve Alcatel's $15.50 cash per share price for a merger with Alcatel. The Lynch board met later that day. With Alcatel's nominees abstaining, it approved the merger. . . .

Alcatel held a 43.3 percent minority share of stock in Lynch. Therefore, the threshold question to be answered by the Court of Chancery was whether, despite its minority ownership, Alcatel exercised control over Lynch's business affairs. Based upon the testimony and the minutes of the August 1, 1986 Lynch board meeting, the Court of Chancery concluded that Alcatel did exercise control over Lynch's business decisions.

At the August 1 meeting, Alcatel opposed the renewal of compensation contracts for Lynch's top five managers. According to Dertinger, Christian Fayard ("Fayard"), an Alcatel director, told the board members, "you must listen to us. We are 43 percent owner. You have to do what we tell you."

Although Beringer and Kertz, two of the independent directors, favored renewal of the contracts, according to the minutes, the third independent director, Wineman, admonished the board as follows:

> Mr. Wineman pointed out that the vote on the contracts is a "watershed vote" and the motion, due to Alcatel's "strong feelings," might not carry if taken now. Mr. Wineman clarified that "you [management] might win the battle and lose the war." With Alcatel's opinion so clear, Mr. Wineman questioned "if management wants the contracts renewed under these circumstances." He recommended that management "think twice." Mr. Wineman declared: "I want to keep the management. I can't think of a better management." Mr. Kertz agreed, again advising consideration of the "critical" period the company is entering.

The minutes reflect that the management directors left the room after this statement. The remaining board members then voted not to renew the contracts.

At the same meeting, Alcatel vetoed Lynch's acquisition of the target company, which, according to the minutes, Beringer considered "an immediate fit" for Lynch. Dertinger agreed with Beringer, stating that the "target company is extremely important as they have the products that Lynch needs now." Nonetheless, Alcatel prevailed. The minutes reflect that Fayard advised the board: "Alcatel, with its 44% equity position, would not approve such an acquisition as it does not wish to be diluted from being the main shareholder in Lynch." From the foregoing evidence, the Vice Chancellor concluded:

> . . . Alcatel did control the Lynch board, at least with respect to the matters under consideration at its August 1, 1986 board meeting. . . .

The record supports the Court of Chancery's underlying factual finding that "the non-Alcatel [independent] directors deferred to Alcatel because of its position as a significant stockholder and not because they decided in the exercise of their own business judgment that Alcatel's position was correct." The record also supports the subsequent factual finding that, notwithstanding its 43.3 percent minority shareholder interest, Alcatel did exercise actual control over Lynch by dominating its corporate affairs. . . .

A controlling or dominating shareholder standing on both sides of a transaction, as in a parent-subsidiary context, bears the burden of proving its entire fairness. . . .

The logical question raised by this Court's holding in *Weinberger* was what type of evidence would be reliable to demonstrate entire fairness. That question was not only anticipated but also initially addressed in the *Weinberger* opinion. *Id.* at 709-10 n.7. This Court suggested that the result "could have been entirely different if UOP had appointed an independent negotiating committee of its outside directors to deal with Signal at arm's length," because "fairness in this context can be equated to conduct by a theoretical, wholly independent, board of directors." *Id.* Accordingly, this Court stated, "a showing that the action taken was as though each of the contending parties had in fact exerted its bargaining power against the other at arm's length is strong *evidence* that the transaction meets the test of fairness." *Id.* (emphasis added).

. . . In *Weinberger*, this Court recognized that it would be inconsistent with its holding [to abolish the business purpose requirement] to apply the business judgment rule in the context of an interested merger transaction which, by its very nature, did not require a business purpose. Consequently, [an informal vote by a majority of the minority shareholders merely shifts the burden of proof as to proving unfairness. — EDS.] . . .

Even where no coercion is intended, [minority] shareholders voting on a parent subsidiary merger might perceive that their disapproval could risk retaliation of some kind by the controlling stockholder. For example, the controlling stockholder might decide to stop dividend payments or to effect a subsequent cash out merger at a less favorable price, for which the remedy would be time consuming and costly litigation. At the very least, the potential for that perception, and its possible impact upon a shareholder vote, could never be fully eliminated. . . .

Once again, this Court holds that the exclusive standard of judicial review in examining the propriety of an interested cash-out merger transaction by a controlling or dominating shareholder is entire fairness. . . . The initial burden of establishing entire fairness rests upon the party who stands on both sides of the transaction. . . . However, an approval of the transaction by an independent committee of directors or an informed majority of minority shareholders shifts the burden of proof on the issue of fairness from the controlling or dominating shareholder to the challenging shareholder-plaintiff. . . .

[However, t]he mere existence of an independent special committee does not itself shift the burden. At least two factors are required. First, the majority shareholder must not dictate the terms of the merger. . . . Second, the special committee must have real bargaining power that it can exercise with the majority shareholder on an arm's length basis. . . .

[T]he performance of the Independent Committee merits careful judicial scrutiny to determine whether Alcatel's demonstrated pattern of domination was effectively neutralized. . . . The fact that the same independent directors had submitted to Alcatel's demands on August 1, 1986 was part of the basis for the Court of Chancery's finding of Alcatel's domination of Lynch. Therefore, the Independent Committee's ability to bargain at arm's length with Alcatel was suspect from the outset.

The Independent Committee's second assignment was to consider Alcatel's proposal to purchase Lynch. The Independent Committee proceeded on that task with full knowledge of Alcatel's demonstrated pattern of domination. The Independent Committee was also obviously aware of Alcatel's refusal to negotiate with it on the Celwave matter.

The Court of Chancery gave credence to the testimony of Kertz, one of the members of the Independent Committee, to the effect that he did not believe that $15.50 was a fair price but that he voted in favor of the merger because he felt there was no alternative.

The Court of Chancery also found that Kertz understood Alcatel's position to be that it was ready to proceed with an unfriendly tender offer at a lower price if Lynch did not accept the $15.50 offer, and that Kertz perceived this to be a threat by Alcatel. . . .

According to the Court of Chancery, the Independent Committee rejected three lower offers for Lynch from Alcatel and then accepted the $15.50 offer "after being advised that [it] was fair and after considering the absence of alternatives." . . .

Nevertheless, based upon the record before it, the Court of Chancery found that the Independent Committee had "appropriately simulated a third-party transaction, where negotiations are conducted at arm's length and there is no compulsion to reach an agreement." . . .

The Court of Chancery's determination . . . is not supported by the record. . . . [T]he ability of the Committee effectively to negotiate at arm's length was compromised by Alcatel's threats to proceed with a hostile tender offer if the $15.50 price was not approved by the Committee and the Lynch board. The fact that the Independent Committee rejected three initial offers, which were well below the Independent Committee's estimated valuation for Lynch and were not combined with an explicit threat that Alcatel was "ready to proceed" with a hostile bid, cannot alter the conclusion that any semblance of arm's length bargaining ended when the Independent Committee surrendered to the ultimatum that accompanied Alcatel's final offer.

Accordingly, the judgment of the Court of Chancery is reversed. This matter is remanded for further proceedings consistent herewith, including a redetermination of the entire fairness of the cash-out merger to Kahn and the other Lynch minority shareholders with the burden of proof remaining on Alcatel, the dominant and interested shareholder.

QUESTIONS ON KAHN v. LYNCH COMMUNICATION SYSTEMS

1. Do you think that Alcatel breached its duty of fair dealing with the corporation and its public shareholders? Why? If Alcatel had simply extended a tender offer at the price it was interested in paying, would it have breached its duty? If it had done so, what might the board have done? What error did the independent directors make?

2. What factors should determine the legal effect of a well-functioning committee of independent directors? Should it matter whether the merger consideration is cash? What about stock? Should it matter whether the merger is with a majority shareholder affiliate or with a controller who controls with less than majority ownership? How does the effect that director committees are accorded in parent-subsidiary or controlling party mergers compare with the effect given to the approval of independent directors of regular self-dealing or recommendations to dismiss a derivative suit? If there is a difference, what justifies it?

12.10.3 Special Committees of Independent Directors in Controlled Mergers

Assuming a properly constituted, diligent, and well-advised special committee of independent directors, what effect should courts give to its decision to approve an interested transaction? There are two possible responses. The first is to treat the special committee's decision as that of a disinterested and independent board, which merits review under the deferential business judgment rule.[76] This approach assumes that courts are better judges of the integrity of the process than of the merits of a deal. Alternatively, the second possible response is to continue to apply the entire fairness test, even if the committee appears to have acted with integrity, since a court cannot easily evaluate whether subtle pressure or feelings of solidarity have unduly affected the outcome of the committee's deliberation.[77] One might think that *Kahn v. Lynch Communication Systems, Inc.* concluded this debate in Delaware. Recall that *Lynch* held that an independent committee's approval of a transaction with a 43 percent shareholder had no effect at all, given the controlling shareholder's conduct. The *Lynch* court stated in dicta that even a truly independent

---

76. See, e.g., *In re Trans World Airlines, Inc. Shareholders Litigation*, 1988 Westlaw 111271, 14 Del. J. Corp. L. 870 (Del. Ch. 1988).

77. See *Citron v. E.I. DuPont DeNemours & Co.*, 584 A.2d 490 (Del. Ch. 1990).

committee decision could only shift the burden of proving the unfairness of the transaction to the plaintiffs.

Yet the intuition that a well-functioning committee of independent directors deserves greater judicial recognition than that reflected in *Kahn v. Lynch* has not been altogether banished from Delaware.[78] Consider, for example, the case of *In re Western National Corp. Shareholders Litigation*, 2000 Westlaw 710192, 26 Del. J. Corp. L. 806 (Del. Ch. 2000), in which the shareholder plaintiffs attacked the fairness of a merger between Western National Corporation and American General Corporation, a 46 percent shareholder of Western National. The value of the merger consideration offered for Western National's public shares was $29.75 a share; the preannouncement market price of Western's stock was $28.19. Notably, American General was party to a standstill agreement with Western National that limited it to the nomination of two of the corporation's eight directors. (Three of the remaining directors were officers of Western National and three were unaffiliated outside directors.) According to the court, the three nonaffiliated directors suggested that Western should be sold. American General responded that it would not vote for any sale transaction (or, obviously, tender into any stock offer). Thus, the independent directors were left with a single potential buyer, American General, with whom they subsequently negotiated a merger that was the subject of the litigation.

Shareholders attacked the deal as unfair, which is not surprising, since the deal offered almost no market premium. The Delaware chancellor, however, granted summary judgment to the defendants, holding that the business judgment rule applied to judicial review of the case, since, in the court's view, American General was not a controlling shareholder. Thus, the court gave to the action of the independent board committee the respect that it would accord an action approving an arm's-length transaction.[79] One teaching from *Western National* may be that standstill agreements can determine whether a large shareholder will be treated as a controlling shareholder when a court assesses the action of independent director committees.[80]

---

78. The Delaware chancery judges are the ones who have to judicially determine what a "fair price" might be, and not surprisingly, their familiarity with that practice seems to make them institutionally more open to procedural solutions to problems of self-dealing. See William T. Allen, Jack B. Jacobs, & Leo E. Strine, Jr., *Function over Form: A Reassessment of Standards of Review in Delaware Corporation Law*, 56 Bus. Law. 1287 (2001).

79. The court cited in support the 1971 case of *Puma v. Marriott.*, 283 A.2d 693 (Del. Ch. 1971), where the Delaware Chancery Court applied business judgment review to a transaction between a corporation and its 46 percent shareholder. In *Puma*, only a minority of the directors were affiliated with the dominant shareholder. *Puma* reflects the "old time religion" of the Delaware law. Its holding, while occasionally cited, has not been in the spirit of the evolution of that law post 1985. The chancery court distinguished *Kahn v. Lynch* on the basis that "a 43% shareholder's veto of a proposed merger between the subsidiary and a third party was evidence of [the shareholder's] control of [the subsidiary]." It is, however, difficult to see how American General's veto of a third-party sale of Western National is any less revealing of control.

80. See, e.g., *Ivanhoe Partners v. Newmont Mining Corp.*, 535 A.2d 1334 (Del. 1987) (no change in corporate control where Consolidated Gold Fields, Plc, increased its ownership percentage of Newmont from 26 percent to 49 percent because a written governance

12.10.4   Controlling Shareholder Fiduciary Duty on the First Step of a Two-Step Tender Offer

A controlling shareholder who sets the terms of a transaction and effectuates it through his control of the board has a duty of fairness to pay a fair price. But what if the controlling shareholder does not "force" a transaction on the board through the actions of his board appointees but merely "offers" the transaction to the board, which then acts to accept the offer through its independent directors. According to *Kahn v. Lynch Communication Systems, Inc.*, the controlling shareholder must still pay a fair price, although the burden lies with an objecting shareholder to prove its price unfair. The next question then is, What is the duty of a controlling shareholder who skips the board altogether and "offers" a transaction directly to the public shareholders in the form of a tender offer? Does he have a duty to pay an objectively fair price?

Of course, the shareholder has a duty under both corporate law (*Lynch v. Vickers Energy Corp.*, 383 A.2d 278 (Del. 1977)) and federal securities laws (§14(e) of the 1934 Act) to disclose all material information respecting the offer. But there is no federal law duty to pay a "fair" price. Is there such a duty under fiduciary principles? Under the theory recently articulated by the Delaware Court of Chancery, the answer is no. The court held that, as long as such an offer is not "coercive"—as, for example, it would be if the controller threatened to discontinue paying dividends—entering such a transaction is voluntary on the part of minority shareholders. If these shareholders do not like the price on offer, they can remain shareholders in the company and force the controller to cash them out, in which event they will have the protection of an appraisal action. See *In re Siliconix Incorporated Shareholder Litigation*, 2001 WL 716787 (Del. Ch. 2001).

IN RE PURE RESOURCES, INC., SHAREHOLDERS LITIGATION

808 A.2d 421 (2002)

[In this case, plaintiffs sought to enjoin an exchange offer by Unocal Corporation, the holder of 65 percent of the shares of Pure Resources, Inc. ("Pure"), for Pure's remaining shares. Pure's CEO, Jack Hightower, held 6.1 percent of its shares; Pure's managers, in aggregate, held between a quarter and a third of its non-Unocal stock. A voting agreement among the principal shareholders ensured that Pure's 8-member board had five Unocal designees, two Hightower designees, and one joint designee. In addition, if Unocal obtained more than 85 percent of Pure's shares,

---

agreement restricted Gold Fields' ability to exercise control). See also *Cooke v. Oolie*, 2000 Westlaw 710199, 26 Del. J. Corp. L. 609 (Del. Ch. 2000) (business judgment review is appropriate in all cases of interested transactions unless interested party is a majority shareholder).

Pure's management shareholders had certain put rights that other minority shareholders did not have.

Tension between Pure's management and Unocal over the company's growth plans led Unocal to initiate a surprise exchange offer for Pure's minority shares at a 27 percent premium to market price, contingent upon increasing Unocal's ownership to 90 percent of Pure's shares. The offer was announced by letter to Pure's board, and followed by an oral presentation by Ling and Chessum, Pure directors who were also Unocal's President and Treasurer, respectively. Pure responded by creating a Special Committee comprised of Covington (the joint designee to the board) and Williamson (the only Unocal designee with no material ties to Unocal). The Special Committee, in turn, hired the investment banking firms of Credit Suisse First Boston ("First Boston") and Petrie Parkman & Co., Inc. ("Petrie") to advise it. It also retained the law firms of Baker Botts and Potter Anderson & Corroon.

For reasons that are not entirely clear, the Special Committee's responsibilities were narrowly drawn. It was to study the offer, negotiate with Unocal, and make a Rule 14D-9 recommendation to Pure's minority shareholders. In particular, the Special Committee neither sought nor obtained a poison pill that might have given it a veto power over Unocal's exchange offer. Nevertheless, the Special Committee vigorously sought a higher exchange ratio than the ratio that Unocal had originally proposed. When Unocal refused to increase its proffered consideration, the Special Committee voted *not* to recommend Unocal's offer to Pure's minority shareholders, based on the advice of its financial advisors. Unocal, meanwhile, decided to launch its offer, even in the face of opposition by Pure's Special Committee.

Pure minority shareholders sued for an injunction to block Unocal's offer.]

STRINE, V.C.:

. . . Distilled to the bare minimum, the plaintiffs argue that the Offer should be enjoined because: (i) the Offer is subject to the entire fairness standard and the record supports the inference that the transaction cannot survive a fairness review; (ii) in any event, the Offer is actionably coercive and should be enjoined on that ground; and (iii) the disclosures provided to the Pure stockholders in connection with the Offer are materially incomplete and misleading. . . .

The primary argument of the plaintiffs is that the Offer should be governed by the entire fairness standard of review. In their view, the structural power of Unocal over Pure and its board, as well as Unocal's involvement in determining the scope of the Special Committee's authority, make the Offer other than a voluntary, non-coercive transaction. In the plaintiffs' mind, the Offer poses the same threat of (what I will call) "inherent coercion" that motivated the Supreme Court in *Kahn v. Lynch Communication Systems, Inc.* to impose the entire fairness standard of review on any interested merger involving a controlling stockholder, even when the merger was approved by an independent board majority, negotiated by an independent special committee, and subject to a majority of the minority vote condition. . . .

This case therefore involves an aspect of Delaware law fraught with doctrinal tension: what equitable standard of fiduciary conduct applies when a controlling shareholder seeks to acquire the rest of the company's shares? . . .

At present, the Delaware case law has two strands of authority that answer these questions differently. In one strand [the *Lynch* line of cases], which deals with situations in which controlling stockholders negotiate a merger agreement with the target board to buy out the minority, our decisional law emphasizes the protection of minority stockholders against unfairness. In the other strand [a line of cases beginning with *Solomon v. Pathe Communications*, 672 A.2d 35 (Del. 1996)], which deals with situations when a controlling stockholder seeks to acquire the rest of the company's shares through a tender offer followed by a short-form merger under 8 Del. C. §253, Delaware case precedent facilitates the free flow of capital between willing buyers and willing sellers of shares, so long as the consent of the sellers is not procured by inadequate or misleading information or by wrongful compulsion. . . .

[In the context of a tender offer freeze-out such as the present case,] the preferable policy choice is to continue to adhere to the more flexible and less constraining *Solomon* approach, while giving some greater recognition to the inherent coercion and structural bias concerns that motivate the *Lynch* line of cases. Adherence to the *Solomon* rubric as a general matter, moreover, is advisable in view of the increased activism of institutional investors and the greater information flows available to them. . . .

To the extent that my decision to adhere to *Solomon* causes some discordance between the treatment of similar transactions to persist, that lack of harmony is better addressed in the *Lynch* line, by affording greater liability-immunizing effect to protective devices such as majority of minority approval conditions and special committee negotiation and approval.[43]

To be more specific about the application of *Solomon* in these circumstances, it is important to note that the *Solomon* line of cases does not eliminate the fiduciary duties of controlling stockholders or target boards in connection with tender offers made by controlling stockholders. Rather, the question is the contextual extent and nature of those duties, a question I will now tentatively, and incompletely, answer.

The potential for coercion and unfairness posed by controlling stockholders who seek to acquire the balance of the company's shares by acquisition requires some equitable reinforcement, in order to give proper effect to the concerns undergirding *Lynch*. In order to address the prisoner's dilemma problem, our law should consider an acquisition tender offer by a controlling stockholder non-coercive only when: (1) it is subject to a non-waivable majority of the minority tender condition; (2) the controlling stockholder promises to consummate a prompt §253 merger at the same

43. A slight easing of the *Lynch* rule would help level the litigation risks posed by the different acquisition methods, and thereby provide an incentive to use the negotiated merger route. At the very least, this tailoring could include providing business judgment protection to mergers negotiated by a special committee and subject to majority of the minority protection. This dual method of protection would replicate the third-party merger process under 8 Del. C. §251.

price if it obtains more than 90% of the shares; and (3) the controlling stockholder has made no retributive threats. Those protections — also stressed in this court's recent *Aquila* decision — minimize the distorting influence of the tendering process on voluntary choice. . . .

The informational and timing advantages possessed by controlling stockholders also require some countervailing protection if the minority is to truly be afforded the opportunity to make an informed, voluntary tender decision. In this regard, the majority stockholder owes a duty to permit the independent directors on the target board both free rein and adequate time to react to the tender offer, by (at the very least) hiring their own advisors, providing the minority with a recommendation as to the advisability of the offer, and disclosing adequate information for the minority to make an informed judgment. For their part, the independent directors have a duty to undertake these tasks in good faith and diligently, and to pursue the best interests of the minority.

When a tender offer is non-coercive in the sense I have identified and the independent directors of the target are permitted to make an informed recommendation and provide fair disclosure, the law should be chary about superimposing the full fiduciary requirement of entire fairness upon the statutory tender offer process. Here, the plaintiffs argue that the Pure board breached its fiduciary duties by not giving the Special Committee the power to block the Offer by, among other means, deploying a poison pill. . . .

That argument has some analytical and normative appeal, embodying as it does the rough fairness of the goose and gander rule.[49] I am reluctant, however, to burden the common law of corporations with a new rule that would tend to compel the use of a device that our statutory law only obliquely sanctions and that in other contexts is subject to misuse, especially when used to block a high value bid that is not structurally coercive. When a controlling stockholder makes a tender offer that is not coercive in the sense I have articulated, therefore, the better rule is that there is no duty on its part to permit the target board to block the bid through use of the pill. Nor is there any duty on the part of the independent directors to seek blocking power. . . .

Turning specifically to Unocal's Offer, I conclude that the application of these principles yields the following result. The Offer, in its present form, is coercive because it includes within the definition of the "minority" those stockholders who are affiliated with Unocal as directors and officers. It also includes the management of Pure, whose incentives are skewed by their employment, their severance agreements, and their Put Agreements. This is, of course, a problem that can be cured if Unocal amends the Offer to condition it on approval of a majority of Pure's unaffiliated stockholders.

---

49. Management-side lawyers must view this case, and the recent *Digex* case, see *In re Digex, Inc. S'holders Litig.*, 789 A.2d 1176 (Del. Ch. 2000), as boomerangs. Decades after their invention, tools designed to help management stay in place are now being wielded by minority stockholders. I note that the current situation can be distinguished from *Digex*, insofar as in that case the controlling stockholder forced the subsidiary board to take action only beneficial to it, whereas here the Pure board simply did not interpose itself between Unocal's Offer and the Pure minority.

Requiring the minority to be defined exclusive of stockholders whose independence from the controlling stockholder is compromised is the better legal rule (and result). Too often, it will be the case that officers and directors of controlled subsidiaries have voting incentives that are not perfectly aligned with their economic interest in their stock and who are more than acceptably susceptible to influence from controlling stockholders. Aside, however, from this glitch in the majority of the minority condition, I conclude that Unocal's Offer satisfies the other requirements of "non-coerciveness." Its promise to consummate a prompt §253 merger is sufficiently specific, and Unocal has made no retributive threats.

Although Unocal's Offer does not altogether comport with the above-described definition of non-coercive, it does not follow that I believe that the plaintiffs have established a probability of success on the merits as to their claim that the Pure board should have blocked that Offer with a pill or other measures. Putting aside the shroud of silence that cloaked the board's (mostly, it seems, behind the scenes) deliberations, there appears to have been at least a rational basis to believe that a pill was not necessary to protect the Pure minority against coercion, largely, because Pure's management had expressed adamant opposition to the Offer. Moreover, the board allowed the Special Committee a free hand: to recommend against the Offer — as it did; to negotiate for a higher price — as it attempted to do; and to prepare the company's 14D-9 — as it did.

For all these reasons, therefore, I find that the plaintiffs do not have a probability of success on the merits of their attack on the Offer, with the exception that the majority of the minority condition is flawed.

C. THE PLAINTIFFS' DISCLOSURE CLAIMS

As their other basis for attack, the plaintiffs argue that neither of the key disclosure documents provided to the Pure stockholders — the S-4 Unocal issued in support of its Offer and the 14D-9 Pure filed in reaction to the Offer — made materially complete and accurate disclosure. The general legal standards that govern the plaintiffs' disclosure claims are settled. . . .

First and foremost, the plaintiffs argue that the 14D-9 is deficient because it does not disclose *any* substantive portions of the work of First Boston and Petrie Parkman on behalf of the Special Committee, even though the bankers' negative views of the Offer are cited as a basis for the board's own recommendation not to tender. . . .

This is a continuation of an ongoing debate in Delaware corporate law, and one I confess to believing has often been answered in an intellectually unsatisfying manner. . . .

[The two sides of the debate] were manifested recently in two Supreme Court opinions. In one, *Skeen v. Jo-Ann Stores, Inc.,*[61] the Court was inclined towards the view that a summary of the bankers' analyses and conclusions was not material to a stockholders' decision whether to seek

---

61. 750 A.2d 1170 (Del. 2000).

appraisal. In the other, *McMullin v. Beran*,[62] the Court implied that information about the analytical work of the board's banker could well be material in analogous circumstances.

In my view, it is time that this ambivalence be resolved in favor of a firm statement that stockholders are entitled to a fair summary of the substantive work performed by the investment bankers upon whose advice the recommendations of their board as to how to vote on a merger or tender rely. . . . [C]ourts must be candid in acknowledging that the disclosure of the banker's "fairness opinion" alone and without more, provides stockholders with nothing other than a conclusion, qualified by a gauze of protective language designed to insulate the banker from liability.

The real informative value of the banker's work is not in its bottom-line conclusion, but in the valuation analysis that buttresses that result. This proposition is illustrated by the work of the judiciary itself, which closely examines the underlying analyses performed by the investment bankers when determining whether a transaction price is fair or a board reasonably relied on the banker's advice. Like a court would in making an after-the-fact fairness determination, a Pure minority stockholder engaging in the before-the-fact decision whether to tender would find it material to know the basic valuation exercises that First Boston and Petrie Parkman undertook, the key assumptions that they used in performing them, and the range of values that were thereby generated. After all, these were the very advisors who played the leading role in shaping the Special Committee's finding of inadequacy.

The need for this information is heightened here, due to the Pure board's decision to leave it up to the stockholders whether to "say no." . . .

Although there are other reasons why I find this type of information material, one final policy reason will suffice for now. When controlling stockholders make tender offers, they have large informational advantages that can only be imperfectly overcome by the special committee process, which almost invariably involves directors who are not involved in the day-to-day management of the subsidiary. The retention of financial advisors by special committees is designed to offset some of this asymmetry, and it would seem to be in full keeping with that goal for the minority stockholders to be given a summary of the core analyses of these advisors in circumstances in which the stockholders must protect themselves in the voting or tender process. That this can be done without great burden is demonstrated by the many transactions in which meaningful summary disclosure of bankers' opinions are made, either by choice or by SEC rule. . . .

This court has recognized that irreparable injury is threatened when a stockholder might make a tender or voting decision on the basis of materially misleading or inadequate information. Likewise, the possibility that structural coercion will taint the tendering process also gives rise, in my view, to injury sufficient to support an injunction. The more tailored relief of an injunction also has the advantage of allowing a restructured Offer to proceed, potentially obviating the need for a complex, after-the-fact, damages case. . . .

62. 765 A.2d 910 (Del. 2000).

[A]lthough I recognize that this court rightly hesitates to deny stockholders an opportunity to accept a tender offer, I believe that the risks of an injunction are outweighed by the need for adequate disclosure and to put in place a genuine majority of the *unaffiliated* minority condition. Thus, I conclude that the balance of the hardships favors the issuance of a preliminary injunction.

QUESTIONS

1. Vice Chancellor Strine here suggests a resolution for the doctrinal tension that is present in the Delaware law of cash-out mergers. Do you think that this suggestion adequately protects the interests of minority shareholders? What would be gained by such a modification and what would be risked?

2. Empirical evidence indicates that minority shareholders have received less (measured by shareholder abnormal returns) in tender offer freeze-outs than in merger freeze-outs in the four years following *Siliconix*.[81] One potential response is: so what? Professor Adam Pritchard argues that investors will simply pay less for a minority stake if they know that they will be cashed out at a lower price in a freeze-out down the road.[82] Why, then, is Vice Chancellor Strine concerned about reconciling the doctrinal disconnect between the *Lynch* and *Solomon* line of cases, beyond simply doctrinal purity? For an efficiency justification for reconciling the competing doctrinal strands, see Guhan Subramanian, *Fixing Freeze-outs*, 115 Yale L.J. 2 (2005).

---

81. Guhan Subramanian, *Post*-Siliconix *Freeze-outs: Theory & Evidence*, 36 J. Leg. Stud. (forthcoming 2007).

82. Adam Pritchard, *Tender Offers by Controlling Shareholders: The Specter of Coercion and Fair Price*, 1 Berkeley Bus. L.J. 83 (2004).

13

PUBLIC CONTESTS FOR CORPORATE CONTROL

13.1 INTRODUCTION

Control contests occupy a central place in the theory of U.S. corporate governance. Stock prices fall when companies fail to perform well, and cheap stock presents an opportunity to those who believe they could do better than the incumbent managers, driven by any of the several motivations for acquisitions that we reviewed in Chapter 12. Thus, control contests create important opportunities. They give acquiring managers the opportunity to capitalize on the new value created by different plans or better skills, and they give target shareholders the opportunity to share in this new value. The flip side, however, is that control contests are profoundly unpleasant for incumbent managers. But for this very reason, the threat of a takeover has the salutary effect of encouraging all managers to deliver shareholder value. Thus, control contests are an important potential constraint on manager-shareholder agency costs generally.[1]

Law is one of the principal determinants of the scope of the takeover market. Traditionally, Anglo-American law opened two avenues for initiating a hostile change in control. The first was the proxy contest — the simple expedient of running an insurgent slate of candidates for election to the

---

1. Credit for first articulating the key governance role of control costs must go to Henry Manne. See Henry Manne, *Mergers and the Market for Corporate Control*, 73 J. Pol. Econ. 110 (1965). For subsequent development of the governance role of control contests, see two classic articles from the early 1980s: Frank H. Easterbrook & Daniel R. Fischel, *The Proper Role of a Target's Management in Responding to Hostile Takeovers*, 94 Harv. L. Rev. 1161 (1981); and Ronald J. Gilson, *A Structural Approach to Corporations: The Case Against Defensive Tactics in Tender Offers*, 33 Stan. L. Rev. 819 (1981). Hostile takeovers grew less important in the United States during the 1990s, even while the overall incidence of M&A transactions increased dramatically. Worldwide, however, hostile takeovers grew more important. For example, the largest hostile takeover ever is the acquisition of a German public company, Mannesmann, A.G., by a British upstart, Vodafone, PLC, in 1999. After Vodafone acquired Mannesmann, the German Parliament passed significant new antitakeover legislation. Ask yourself, as you read through this chapter, how far this European development recapitulates the American experience.

board. Although the proxy contest was costly and often unsuccessful (at least at first),[2] it was nevertheless the only insurgent technique employed during the infrequent contests for control over widely-held companies prior to the 1960s. Moreover, the proxy contest has returned with the rise of hedge funds—large pools of unregulated investment money—in the hands of activist investors who are using proxy fights as an important tool. For hedge funds, however, the most common strategy is not to pursue a complete takeover but rather a partial slate of directors who will promote change through "constructive engagement" with the other members of the board.

The second technique was the tender offer—the even simpler expedient of purchasing enough stock oneself to obtain voting control rather than soliciting the proxies of others. Widespread use of this technique dates from the 1960s, and it has remained important ever since. Clearly, a tender offer is even costlier than a proxy contest, but it also has a great comparative advantage in capturing the attention of stockholders with its promise of cash up front rather than promises of future performance. In recent years, moreover, the proxy contest and the tender offer have often merged into a single hybrid form of hostile takeover, as the law's acceptance of increasingly potent defensive tactics has made it difficult to pursue either avenue alone.

The law of corporate control contests has developed in tandem with the steep rise in the number of M&A transactions in the U.S. economy over the past 30 years. At the outset of this period, courts reviewed the board's response to a contest for control just as they would review any other corporate action. If the response were self-interested in an immediate financial way, the board would be required to demonstrate that it was intrinsically fair;[3] otherwise, it would be reviewed under the business judgment standard.[4] From a practical perspective, however, this approach worked poorly for mergers or other acquisition-of-control transactions— and, by extension, for efforts to foreclose hostile takeovers. Management and the board are never truly disinterested in the efforts to acquire control over the corporation (and hence over their positions). Nevertheless, responses to takeover offers are not "self-interested" to the same extent as a self-dealing transaction. These offers are immensely complicated business propositions that can expose shareholders to serious risks of exploitation by third-party bidders.

The Delaware Supreme Court first began to grapple seriously with the complexities of the board's duties in contests for corporate control in a series of three cases argued during 1985, which together set the framework for the analysis of directors' fiduciary duties in M&A transactions and for

2. Even in those instances in which incumbent managers defeat a proxy fight, history shows that there is a relatively strong probability that incumbent management will be changed within the following year.

3. *Sterling v. Mayflower Hotel Corp.*, 93 A.2d 107 (Del. 1952); *Weinberger v. UOP, Inc.*, 457 A.2d 701 (Del. 1983).

4. *Painter v. Marshall Field & Co.*, 646 F.2d 271, 293-295 (7th Cir.), *cert. denied*, 454 U.S. 1092 (1981); *Johnson v. Trueblood*, 629 F.2d 287, 292-293 (3d Cir. 1980) (Seitz, C.J.); *Treadway Cos. v. Care Corp.*, 638 F.2d 357, 382-383 (2d Cir. 1980).

defenses against hostile takeovers. Each of these cases involved a different doctrinal question, but all concerned changes in corporate control. The wisdom of hindsight suggests that they were all aspects of a single effort to bring meaningful judicial review to control transactions. The first case was *Smith v. Van Gorkom*,[5] which arose out of a friendly two-step acquisition, consisting of a cash tender offer followed by a cash-out merger. On its face, *Van Gorkom* appears to be chiefly about the corporate director's duty of care. Nevertheless, *Van Gorkom* held an entire board liable for "gross negligence" under circumstances in which most experts would have said its directors *had* met their standard of care; i.e., they had attended all meetings and deliberated about the key corporate decisions at issue. To better understand this surprising case, we suggest looking at it in the context of the law of mergers. Later cases make clear that during this period the Delaware Supreme Court began a project of redefining the role of the corporate board in corporate control transactions.

The second major decision was *Unocal Corp. v. Mesa Petroleum Co.*,[6] which is excerpted below. It dealt with the Unocal board's efforts to defend against a hostile tender offer. *Unocal* articulated for the first time a standard of judicial review intermediate between lax business judgment review and tough entire fairness review to address board efforts to defend against a threatened change-in-control transaction.

The third significant case argued in 1985 was *Revlon v. MacAndrews and Forbes Holdings, Inc.*[7] *Revlon* also addressed the efforts of an incumbent board to resist an unwelcome takeover. Revlon's board, however, attempted to resist by pursuing an alternative transaction, which is the focus of the case. Again, the court adopted a form of heightened review short of intrinsic fairness. For want of better terminology, lawyers and judges came to talk of "*Revlon* duties," "*Revlon*land," and "*Revlon* mode" for those times when similar duties arose. Yet no one was certain when a board had entered *Revlon*land or exactly what the new *Revlon* duties required.

Although these 1985 cases appeared revolutionary to some, they had precursors: two earlier cases that sought to introduce flexibility into the business judgment rule/entire fairness dichotomy. The first was *Cheff v. Mathes*,[8] a 1964 Delaware Supreme Court opinion in which shareholders attacked a corporate repurchase at a premium price of all the stock belonging to a dissident shareholder/director. The court agreed that the repurchase had the effect of securing the directors in control but held that, as long as the board's *primary purpose* was to advance business policies, the buyback did not violate the board's fiduciary duty.[9] The second precursor

---

5. 488 A.2d 858 (Del. 1985). See the discussion in Chapter 8.
6. 493 A.2d 946 (Del. 1985).
7. 506 A.2d 173 (Del. 1986).
8. 199 A.2d 548 (Del. 1964).
9. The shareholder attacked the corporation marketing strategy, which management defended as a source of real value. The board resolved the disagreement by causing the company to repurchase the dissident's stock at a premium over market price. Plaintiff shareholders claimed that this purchase was wasteful, since the company paid a premium to market price, and that the repurchase was made to entrench the directors in office.

was *Schnell v. Chris-Craft Industries*[10] (excerpted in §13.8.), which, in contrast to *Cheff*, did find a breach of fiduciary duty when a "disinterested" board advanced the date of the company's annual meeting, as it was permitted to do by statute, solely in order to make a hostile proxy solicitation impossible to mount.[11]

Although *Cheff* and *Schnell* dealt intelligently with a board's use of corporate power to maintain control, neither case afforded useful doctrinal tools for examining entrenchment measures more generally. However, the extraordinary growth in the number of M&A transactions — and especially hostile tender offers — in the late 1970s and early 1980s made the question of a director's fiduciary duty in the face of a takeover bid inescapable. The courts addressed this question, and so did other institutions. State legislatures passed antitakeover statutes and promulgated standards for evaluating defensive action undertaken by boards. And more important still, private legal innovation, particularly the so-called poison pill, dramatically altered the law governing changes in control of public companies. In fact, this private innovation (together with copious case law that it has stimulated) has made most state takeover legislation as well as much of the Williams Act (as discussed previously in Chapter 11) very much less significant.

NOTE ON THE EUROPEAN UNION TAKEOVER DIRECTIVE

Controversy over the regulation of hostile takeovers in general — and of management defensive tactics in particular — is by no means limited to the United States. The European Union promulgated its long-awaited Takeover Directive in December 2003, after 14 years of negotiation. The Directive was adopted only after the E.U. Member States reached the radical compromise of making its two most important provisions optional — a decision that naturally limits the extent to which the Directive can impose uniformity on takeover policy in the E.U.

The first of these key provisions is Article 9 of the Directive, which prohibits target companies from taking defensive actions to defeat hostile bids without a shareholder vote. This rule of managerial passivity in the face of a hostile takeover reflects the policy of the British City Code. For firms in member states that do not opt out, it is a mandatory rule of shareholder choice rather than board decision making, which is precisely the reverse of the approach that Delaware courts have adopted, at least as a default rule. As of June 2006 France, Spain, and the U.K. have opted in to Article 9, while

---

10. 285 A.2d 437 (Del. 1971).

11. Upon receiving word that the insurgents had filed the proposed proxy solicitation materials, the board advanced the meeting date to a new date, as the corporation statute permitted. Yet the new date was a fatal blow to the insurgents, who were legally prohibited from soliciting proxies until the SEC had cleared their materials. Thus, a lawful board action had the practical effect of ending the insurgents' proxy contest. In a brief opinion, the Delaware Supreme Court struck down the corporate action on the ground that the board's statutory authority was superceded by its fiduciary duty. A court of equity will not permit the board's legal powers to be deployed "inequitably" against the interests of shareholders. *Id.*

Germany and the Netherlands have opted out, among the larger EU member states.

The second key provision of the Takeover Directive is the so-called breakthrough rule embodied in Article 11. Under the breakthrough rule, a hostile acquirer that obtains more than 75 percent of voting equity of a target company could remove the board of directors, regardless of any restrictions on the voting rights in the charter (including differential voting rights among multiple classes of stock) and any restrictions on the transfer of securities. All shares vote equally on charter amendments proposed by such an acquirer. In addition, multiple voting class structures and restrictions on shareholder votes are unenforceable under Article 11 against the bidder in a takeover, and do not apply to target shareholders who must vote on defensive measures. Most EU members (e.g., France, Germany, the Netherlands, Spain, UK) have opted out of Article 11; as of June 2006 only Italy seems likely to opt-in.

In terms of social welfare maximization, why might Article 9 be more attractive than Article 11? See John C. Coates IV, *Ownership, Takeovers, and EU Law: How Contestable Should EU Corporations Be?*, in E. Wymeersch & G. Ferrarini, eds., Company and Takeover Law in Europe (2003).

13.2   DEFENDING AGAINST HOSTILE TENDER OFFERS

UNOCAL CORP. v. MESA PETROLEUM CO.

493 A.2d 946 (Del. 1985)

MOORE, J.:

We confront an issue of first impression in Delaware — the validity of a corporation's self-tender for its own shares which excludes from participation a stockholder making a hostile tender offer for the company's stock. . . .

On April 8, 1985, Mesa, the owner of approximately 13% of Unocal's stock, commenced a two-tier "front loaded" cash tender offer for 64 million shares, or approximately 37%, of Unocal's outstanding stock at a price of $54 per share. The "back-end" was designed to eliminate the remaining publicly held shares by an exchange of securities purportedly worth $54 per share. However, pursuant to an order entered by the United States District Court for the Central District of California on April 26, 1985, Mesa issued a supplemental proxy statement to Unocal's stockholders disclosing that the securities offered in the second-step merger would be highly subordinated, and that Unocal's capitalization would differ significantly from its present structure. Unocal has rather aptly termed such securities "junk bonds."

Unocal's board consists of eight independent outside directors and six insiders. It met on April 13, 1985, to consider the Mesa tender offer. Thirteen directors were present, and the meeting lasted nine and one-half hours. The directors were given no agenda or written materials prior to the session. However, detailed presentations were made by legal counsel regarding the board's obligations under both Delaware corporate law and the federal securities laws. The board then received a presentation from Peter Sachs on behalf of Goldman Sachs & Co. (Goldman Sachs) and Dillon, Read & Co. (Dillon Read) discussing the bases for their opinions that the Mesa proposal was wholly inadequate. Mr. Sachs opined that the minimum cash value that could be expected from a sale or orderly liquidation for 100% of Unocal's stock was in excess of $60 per share. . . .

Mr. Sachs also presented various defensive strategies available to the board if it concluded that Mesa's two-step tender offer was inadequate and should be opposed. One of the devices outlined was a self-tender by Unocal for its own stock with a reasonable price range of $70 to $75 per share. The cost of such a proposal would cause the company to incur $6.1-6.5 billion of additional debt, and a presentation was made informing the board of Unocal's ability to handle it. The directors were told that the primary effect of this obligation would be to reduce exploratory drilling, but that the company would nonetheless remain a viable entity.

The eight outside directors, comprising a clear majority of the thirteen members present, then met separately with Unocal's financial advisors and attorneys. Thereafter, they unanimously agreed to advise the board that it should reject Mesa's tender offer as inadequate, and that Unocal should pursue a self-tender to provide the stockholders with a fairly priced alternative to the Mesa proposal. . . .

On April 15, the board met again. . . . Unocal's Vice President of Finance and its Assistant General Counsel made a detailed presentation of the proposed terms of the exchange offer. A price range between $70 and $80 per share was considered, and ultimately the directors agreed upon $72. . . . The board's decisions were made in reliance on the advice of its investment bankers. . . . Based upon this advice, . . . the directors unanimously approved the exchange offer. Their resolution provided that if Mesa acquired 64 million shares of Unocal stock through its own offer (the Mesa Purchase Condition), Unocal would buy the remaining 49% outstanding for an exchange of debt securities having an aggregate par value of $72 per share. The board resolution also stated that the offer would be subject to other conditions. . . .

Legal counsel advised that under Delaware law Mesa could only be excluded for what the directors reasonably believed to be a valid corporate purpose. The directors' discussion centered on the objective of adequately compensating shareholders at the "back-end" of Mesa's proposal, which the latter would finance with "junk bonds." To include Mesa would defeat that goal, because under the proration aspect of the exchange offer (49%) every Mesa share accepted by Unocal would displace one held by another stockholder. Further, if Mesa were permitted to tender to Unocal the latter would in effect be financing Mesa's own inadequate proposal. . . .

[Unocal's board subsequently waived the Mesa Purchase Condition as to 50 million shares (roughly 30 percent of outstanding shares), five days after the commencement of its April 17 exchange offer. This waiver—in effect, a self-tender for 30 percent of Unocal — was meant to placate institutional shareholders who correctly anticipated that Unocal's offer would defeat Mesa's bid and feared that it would also lead stock prices to decline to the $30 level, where they had languished prior to Mesa's bid.]

We begin with the basic issue of the power of a board of directors of a Delaware corporation to adopt a defensive measure of this type. . . .

The board has a large reservoir of authority upon which to draw. Its duties and responsibilities proceed from the inherent powers conferred by 8 Del. C. §141(a), respecting management of the corporation's "business and affairs." Additionally, the powers here being exercised derive from 8 Del. C. §160(a), conferring broad authority upon a corporation to deal in its own stock. From this it is now well established that in the acquisition of its shares a Delaware corporation may deal selectively with its stockholders, provided the directors have not acted out of a sole or primary purpose to entrench themselves in office. *Cheff v. Mathes,* Del. Supr., 199 A.2d 548, 554 (1964). . . .

Finally, the board's power to act derives from its fundamental duty and obligation to protect the corporate enterprise, which includes stockholders, from harm reasonably perceived, irrespective of its source. . . .

When a board addresses a pending takeover bid it has an obligation to determine whether the offer is in the best interest of the corporation and its shareholders. In that respect a board's duty is no different from any other responsibility it shoulders, and its decisions should be no less entitled to the respect they otherwise would be accorded in the realm of business judgment. . . . There are, however, certain caveats to a proper exercise of this function. Because of the omnipresent specter that a board may be acting primarily in its own interests, rather than those of the corporation and its shareholders, there is an enhanced duty which calls for judicial examination at the threshold before the protections of the business judgment rule may be conferred. . . .

In the face of this inherent conflict directors must show that they had reasonable grounds for believing that a danger to corporate policy and effectiveness existed because of another person's stock ownership. . . .

[C]orporate directors have a fiduciary duty to act in the best interests of the corporation's stockholders. . . . As we have noted, their duty of care extends to protecting the corporation and its owners from perceived harm whether a threat originates from third parties or other shareholders.[10] But such powers are not absolute. A corporation does not have unbridled discretion to defeat any perceived threat by any Draconian means available.

The restriction placed upon a selective stock repurchase is that the directors may not have acted solely or primarily out of a desire to perpetuate themselves in office . . . [or take] inequitable action. . . .

---

10. It has been suggested that a board's response to a takeover threat should be a passive one. Easterbrook & Fischel, supra, 36 Bus. Law. at 1750. However, that clearly is not the law of Delaware, and as the proponents of this rule of passivity readily concede, it has not been adopted either by courts or state legislatures. Easterbrook & Fischel, supra, 94 Harv. L. Rev. at 1194 (1981).

A further aspect is the element of balance. If a defensive measure is to come within the ambit of the business judgment rule, it must be reasonable in relation to the threat posed. This entails an analysis by the directors of the nature of the takeover bid and its effect on the corporate enterprise. Examples of such concerns may include: inadequacy of the price offered, nature and timing of the offer, questions of illegality, the impact on "constituencies" other than shareholders (i.e., creditors, customers, employees, and perhaps even the community generally), the risk of non-consummation, and the quality of securities being offered in the exchange. See Lipton and Brownstein, *Takeover Responses and Directors' Responsibilities: An Update*, p. 7, ABA National Institute on the Dynamics of Corporate Control (December 8, 1983). While not a controlling factor, it also seems to us that a board may reasonably consider the basic stockholder interests at stake, including those of short term speculators, whose actions may have fueled the coercive aspect of the offer at the expense of the long term investor.[11] Here, the threat posed was viewed by the Unocal board as a grossly inadequate two-tier coercive tender offer coupled with the threat of greenmail.

Specifically, the Unocal directors had concluded that the value of Unocal was substantially above the $54 per share offered in cash at the front end. Furthermore, they determined that the subordinated securities to be exchanged in Mesa's announced squeeze out of the remaining shareholders in the "back-end" merger were "junk bonds" worth far less than $54. It is now well recognized that such offers are a classic coercive measure designed to stampede shareholders into tendering at the first tier, even if the price is inadequate, out of fear of what they will receive at the back end of the transaction. Wholly beyond the coercive aspect of an inadequate two-tier tender offer, the threat was posed by a corporate raider with a national reputation as a "greenmailer."[13]

In adopting the selective exchange offer, the board stated that its objective was either to defeat the inadequate Mesa offer or, should the offer still succeed, provide the 49% of its stockholders, who would otherwise be forced to accept "junk bonds", with $72 worth of senior debt. We find that both purposes are valid.

However, such efforts would have been thwarted by Mesa's participation in the exchange offer. First, if Mesa could tender its shares, Unocal would effectively be subsidizing the former's continuing effort to buy Unocal stock at $54 per share. Second, Mesa could not, by definition, fit

---

11. There has been much debate respecting such stockholder interests. One rather impressive study indicates that the stock of over 50 percent of target companies, who resisted hostile takeovers, later traded at higher market prices than the rejected offer price, or were acquired after the tender offer was defeated by another company at a price higher than the offer price. See Marton Lipton, [*Takeover Bids in the Target's Boardroom*, 35 Bus.Law. 101 (1979)] at 106-109, 132-133. Moreover, an update by Kidder Peabody & Company of this study, involving the stock prices of target companies that have defeated hostile tender offers during the period from 1973 to 1982 demonstrates that in a majority of cases the target's shareholders benefited from the defeat. . . .

13. The term "greenmail" refers to the practice of buying out a takeover bidder's stock at a premium that is not available to other shareholders in order to prevent the takeover. . . .

within the class of shareholders being protected from its own coercive and inadequate tender offer.

Thus, we are satisfied that the selective exchange offer is reasonably related to the threats posed. . . . Thus, the board's decision to offer what it determined to be the fair value of the corporation to the 49% of its shareholders, who would otherwise be forced to accept highly subordinated "junk bonds", is reasonable and consistent with the directors' duty to ensure that the minority stockholders receive equal value for their shares.

Mesa contends that it is unlawful, and the trial court agreed, for a corporation to discriminate in this fashion against one shareholder. It argues correctly that no case has ever sanctioned a device that precludes a raider from sharing in a benefit available to all other stockholders. However, as we have noted earlier, the principle of selective stock repurchases by a Delaware corporation is neither unknown nor unauthorized. . . . The only difference is that heretofore the approved transaction was the payment of "greenmail" to a raider or dissident posing a threat to the corporate enterprise. All other stockholders were denied such favored treatment, and given Mesa's past history of greenmail, its claims here are rather ironic.

However, our corporate law is not static. It must grow and develop in response to, indeed in anticipation of, evolving concepts and needs. . . .

[A]s the sophistication of both raiders and targets has developed, a host of other defensive measures to counter such ever mounting threats have evolved and received judicial sanction. These include defensive charter amendments and other devices bearing some rather exotic, but apt, names: Crown Jewel, White Knight, Pac Man, and Golden Parachute. Each has highly selective features, the object of which is to deter or defeat the raider.

Thus, while the exchange offer is a form of selective treatment, given the nature of the threat posed here the response is neither unlawful nor unreasonable. If the board of directors is disinterested, has acted in good faith and with due care, its decision in the absence of an abuse of discretion will be upheld as a proper exercise of business judgment. . . .

In conclusion, there was directorial power to oppose the Mesa tender offer, and to undertake a selective stock exchange made in good faith and upon a reasonable investigation pursuant to a clear duty to protect the corporate enterprise. Further, the selective stock repurchase plan chosen by Unocal is reasonable in relation to the threat that the board rationally and reasonably believed was posed by Mesa's inadequate and coercive two-tier tender offer. Under those circumstances the board's action is entitled to be measured by the standards of the business judgment rule. Thus, unless it is shown by a preponderance of the evidence that the directors' decisions were primarily based on perpetuating themselves in office, or some other breach of fiduciary duty such as fraud, overreaching, lack of good faith, or being uninformed, a Court will not substitute its judgment for that of the board.

If the stockholders are displeased with the action of their elected representatives, the powers of corporate democracy are at their disposal to turn the board out. . . .

QUESTIONS AND NOTES ON UNOCAL

1. What does it mean to characterize the Mesa offer as "coercive"? How can Mesa's two-tier offer be coercive if the prebid market price for Unocal shares was, say, $33/share, Pickens's cash price for 37 percent of Unocal was $55/share, and Pickens's back-end cash-out price for the remaining 50 percent of Unocal's shares was around $45/share (the likely market value of junk bonds with a face value of $55/share)? Even the "back end" of the Pickens offer was generally acknowledged to be worth a lot more than Unocal's prebid market price.

2. Was the Unocal exchange offer also coercive? Which offer would you have valued more as a shareholder?

3. What was the logical relevance of Mesa's reputation as a greenmailer to the court's analysis?

4. What are we to make of a discriminatory self-tender? Is it any different from greenmail, which the Delaware Supreme Court had authorized to protect corporate policies since the *Cheff* case? The SEC presumably thought so, since it effectively overruled this aspect of *Unocal* by promulgating Rule 13e-4, which bars discriminatory self-tenders. No SEC rule bars greenmail.

5. Is Justice Moore abandoning shareholder primacy in this opinion? Is the fundamental duty of boards to further the interests of shareholders, to balance the interests of all corporate "constituencies," or to do something in between?

6. In footnote 11 of its opinion the Court cites empirical evidence from Martin Lipton and Kidder Peabody indicating that targets remaining independent achieve higher returns for their shareholders than targets that sell to the hostile bidder. The Court does not cite Professor Ronald Gilson, who points out several flaws in Lipton's study, including no adjustment for market effects or the time value of money. When these and other factors are considered, Gilson states that "Lipton's data refute his own conclusion."[12] A more recent study, examining targets that remained independent between 1996 and 2002, shows that shareholders received lower returns than they would have received if the company had been sold to the initial bidder or to a white knight[13] — the opposite of what Lipton and Kidder Peabody found 20 years earlier. In general, how should courts utilize empirical evidence in formulating their opinions? For one judge's perspectives on this "meta-question," see Jack B. Jacobs, *Comments on Contestability*, 54 U. Miami L. Rev. 847 (2000).

7. *Unocal* announces a new standard for reviewing defensive tactics — what the Delaware Supreme Court refers to as "enhanced business judgment review." To earn the protection of the business judgment rule, the board must show that its defensive tactic was "reasonable in relation to the

---

12. See Gilson, *supra* note 1, at 857-58.
13. Lucian Arye Bebchuk, John C. Coates IV & Guhan Subramanian, *The Powerful Antitakeover Force of Staggered Boards: Further Findings and a Reply to Symposium Participants*, 55 Stan. L. Rev. 885 (2002).

threat posed." How different is this standard from old-fashioned business judgment review? See Gilson & Kraakman, *Delaware's Intermediate Standard for Defensive Tactics: Is There Substance to Proportionality Review?*, 44 Bus. Law. 247 (1989).

———————————

In the 1995 case *Unitrin v. American General Corp.*,[14] the Delaware Supreme Court clarified to some extent what "reasonable in relation to the threat posed" means. The case involved a hostile tender offer by American General Corp. (AmGen) for Unitrin at $50 3/8 per share, a substantial premium to market price. Unitrin's board was comprised of seven persons, who collectively owned 23 percent of the company's stock.

After concluding that AmGen's offer was inadequate, Unitrin's board sought to defend by implementing a poison pill, an advance-notice bylaw,[15] and a tender offer to repurchase 5 million, or 20 percent, of its outstanding shares. Unitrin's directors announced that they would not participate in this buyback, which, if successful, would increase their proportional share ownership to 28 percent of Unitrin's outstanding stock. Unitrin's charter mandated that any transaction with an entity controlled by or affiliated with a person owning 15 percent of Unitrin's stock required approval by 75 percent of the outstanding stock.

The Chancery Court held that the AmGen offer represented a threat of "substantive coercion."[16] This Orwellian phrase meant that (the board believed) shareholders might be "coerced" because they would not fully understand the value of their stock or the inadequacy of the consideration offered. Applying *Unocal*, the court held that the pill was a proportional response to this threat but that the repurchase program was not. Increasing the management block from 23 percent to 28 percent of the shares by repurchases would, according to the court, preclude a change in control as a practical matter. The court concluded that this response was "unnecessary" in light of what was only a "mild" threat.

On appeal, the Delaware Supreme Court reversed. Justice Holland held that "if the board of directors' defensive response is not draconian (preclusive or coercive) and is within a 'range of reasonableness,' a court

———————————

14. 651 A.2d 1361 (Del. 1995).

15. Advance-notice bylaws generally require any stockholder who intends to nominate an insurgent slate at the next annual shareholders' meeting to give certain information to the corporation concerning the identity of such persons well in advance of the meeting. Sometimes the mandated time is 90 days, but often it is longer, 120 days or more. Obviously, as the period increases, so does the constraint on proxy contests. Some such bylaws will be validly subject to a claim that they constitute a manipulation foreclosed by the *Schnell* principle.

16. This phrase was coined in Ronald J. Gilson & Reinier Kraakman, *Delaware's Intermediate Standard for Defensive Tactics: Is There Substance to Proportionality Review?*, 44 Bus. Law. 247, 267 (1989). Although the article advocated "a meaningful proportionality test" when a board alleged substantive coercion, the *Unitrin* Court seems to have adopted the term "substantive coercion" without the accompanying hard look at "how — and when — management expects a target's shareholders to do better." Id. at 268. See also *Chesapeake v. Shore*, 771 A.2d 293, 329 (Del. Ch. 2000) (Strine, V.C.) (noting the tension).

must not substitute its judgment for the board's." The Court found that neither the poison pill nor the repurchase program was coercive or preclusive, because AmGen could run a proxy contest to replace the Unitrin board. The Court then remanded the case to the Chancery Court for a determination as to whether the pill and the repurchase program were within the range of reasonable defenses (with the burden on the Unitrin directors). If the defendant directors *did* establish that the board action was proportionate and within a range of reasonableness, the burden would then shift back to the plaintiffs to prove that the defensive action was not otherwise a breach of the duty; for instance, by being primarily motivated to maintain the board in office.

Unitrin reflects the almost Byzantine complexity of the Delaware corporate law of hostile takeovers. One might think that, if a court concludes that directors have taken an action that was proportionate to a threat and within a range of reasonable responses, the challenge to the action should be at an end. But under *Unitrin*, such a finding does not justify a dismissal of the complaint — it simply shifts the burden back to the plaintiff. Analogous consequences follow if the defendant directors do *not* establish that a defensive action is proportionate (i.e., if the action *is* deemed either coercive/preclusive or outside the range of reasonableness). Here, too, Delaware law does not simply say that such actions violate a board's fiduciary duty. Rather, according to the cases, it is open to defendants to prove the fairness of the action. See, e.g., *Shamrock Holdings, Inc. v. Polaroid Corp.*, 559 A.2d 278 (Del. Ch. 1989).

Unitrin also clarifies the *Unocal* test. In doing so, it makes clear how limited an "enhancement" to the business judgment rule *Unocal* really is.[17] In this regard, *Unitrin* boils down to three things. First, under *Unocal/Unitrin*, the target's directors, not the plaintiff, bear the burden of going forward with evidence to show that the defensive action was proportionate to a threat. Second, substantively, action that is "preclusive" or "coercive" will fail to satisfy *Unocal*'s test. Third, assuming that a defensive measure passes the preclusive/coercive test (in *Unitrin*'s language, that it is not "draconian"), then it will satisfy *Unocal* so long as it is "within a range of reasonable action." Properly understood, this last aspect of the test is operationally similar to the business judgment rule: An action will be sustained if it is attributable to *any* reasonable judgment. It will not matter if the court would have regarded some other action as more reasonable. Taken together, these three aspects of "enhanced" business judgment in the end may be thought to provide more smoke than warmth. But see *Omnicare v. NCS Healthcare*, at § 13.6.2.

13.3   PRIVATE LAW INNOVATION: THE POISON PILL

We turn now to a most remarkable innovation in corporate law, the shareholders' rights plan or "poison pill." This was an audacious invention that

---

17. A prominent New York City practitioner commented to one of us after *Unitrin*: "So it looks like we're back to business judgment review, aren't we?"

has proven to be remarkably effective, although it continues to be highly controversial. In this section, we describe these colloquially named "poison pills" and set forth yet another vital 1985 case of the Delaware Supreme Court, *Moran v. Household International, Inc.*,[18] which validated the poison pill technique. Judicial acceptance of shareholders' rights plans was a major evolutionary step in U.S. corporate law. The invention of the pill was not quite like a technological innovation such as the cell phone because whether or not the pill "worked" depended largely on whether it could capture the sympathy of the Delaware courts. Nevertheless, the technical elegance of the pill, as it was perfected by New York's preeminent takeover law specialists, doubtlessly enhanced its attractiveness to the courts.

Although academic commentators and institutional investors generally believe that hostile tender offers are a useful device for disciplining corporate management, managers themselves believe that vulnerability to hostile bids is a profound weakness in the corporate governance structure because it exposes disaggregated and disorganized shareholders to abusive tender-offer tactics. They argue that they cannot protect shareholders without the tools to defeat inadequate tender offers. Moreover, in the late 1970s and early 1980s, the practices of certain takeover entrepreneurs made management's arguments plausible. "Front-end loaded, two-tier" tender offers could unquestionably lead shareholders to sell, even if they were offered a price less than what they believed their shares were worth. This much was confirmed by the most rigorous academic research.[19] And although the academics did not make the point, to managers the implication was clear: Only a loyal bargaining agent — namely, the board — could remedy the bargaining infirmities of dispersed shareholders.

Imagine that you are a corporate lawyer representing one of the corporations whose management and board were worried about abusive tender offers in the early 1980s. You search for a way to empower the board to act as a bargaining agent for shareholders in tender offers. The answer to your prayers is the shareholders' rights plan or "poison pill." Shareholders' rights plans take the form of capital instruments: rights to buy a capital asset, such as a bond, common share, or preferred share. Yet their only real function is to alter the allocation of power between shareholders and boards. The most common form of rights plans today functions rather like the Mesa exclusion in *Unocal.* Rights to buy the company's stock at a discounted price are "distributed" to all shareholders. (Shareholders do not literally receive a new piece of paper; the rights trade with the stock.) These rights are triggered — i.e., become exercisable to actually buy discounted stock — only if someone acquires more than a certain percentage of the company's outstanding stock — say, 10 percent or 15 percent — without first receiving the target board's blessing. Moreover (and this is the key), the person whose stock acquisition triggers the exercise of the rights is herself (or in the case of a corporation, itself) excluded from

18. 500 A.2d 1346 (Del. 1985).
19. See, e.g., Lucian Arye Bebchuk, *Toward Undistorted Choice and Equal Treatment in Corporate Takeovers,* 98 Harv. L. Rev. 1639 (1985).

buying discounted stock. Thus, her holdings are severely diluted; she will end up losing the greatest part, perhaps most, of her investment in the company stock. The result is that buying a substantial block of stock without the prior consent of the target's board will be ruinously expensive. This effect gives the board the practical power to veto a tender offer, just as it is able to veto a merger or asset sale under the corporation law.

Here is a simple example: T Corp. distributes as a dividend to shareholders Rights. Each Right purports to be a right to buy 1/100 of a share of the company's common stock in the future for an extravagant, "out of the money" price: say, $50 (or $5,000 per share) when the common stock is selling for $75 a share. Given its terms, no one really expects this Right ever to be exercised (although the company's lawyers might argue that the Right's high exercise price represents the hidden long-term value of the company's stock). The Rights do not trade separately at this point but are embedded in the common stock on which the dividend is paid. However, should a "triggering event" occur, the Rights detach and are tradable separately. Today, a triggering event might be the acquisition of 10 percent of the company's stock by any single entity or an affiliated group of persons, or the announcement of a tender offer for 10 percent or more of the company's stock.[20]

If a person or group did acquire a 10 percent block, then under a "flip-in" pill, each outstanding Right would "flip-into" a right to acquire some number of shares of the target's common stock at one half of the market price for that stock. In other words, the Right's holder would be able to buy stock from the company at half price. Now, if every Right holder bought stock at half price, the aggregate effect is to increase the proportionate holdings of all shareholders *except* the "triggering person," whose Right would be canceled upon the occurrence of the triggering event and who, as a result, would only own a much smaller interest in the company than that for which she initially paid.

The original rights plans were not "flip-in" plans, but "flip-over" plans. They purported when triggered to create a right to buy some number of shares of stock *in the corporation whose acquisition of target stock had triggered the right.* In this plan, a triggering event (when followed by a merger or sale of more than 50 percent of the target's assets to the triggering shareholder or an affiliate) results in the rights being exercisable. How can that be done? How can the target's board create a right that requires a third party to sell its stock at half price to the target's shareholders? Well, we are not certain that it can be done, since the question whether a *triggering* shareholder must respect an obligation created by a flip-over plan has yet to be litigated. The reason these plans are *supposed* to work, however, is that they purport to compel the target's board to put terms in any merger

---

20. When rights plans were first introduced in the 1980s, triggering events typically involved 30 percent of the company's stock. The size of the triggering threshold has steadily receded, however, and since 1990, triggers have been typically 10 percent. Once the rights are triggered, they are no longer redeemable by the company, and ten days later they are exercisable. For a recent commentary that examines pill design choices with respect to redeemability, see Guhan Subramanian, *Bargaining in the Shadow of PeopleSoft's (Defective) Poison Pill*, Harv. Neg. L. Rev. (forthcoming 2007).

agreement (or asset sale agreement, etc.) with the acquirer that will force the acquirer to recognize flip-over rights.[21]

Flip-over plans may be thought to be less effective than flip-in rights because a hostile party may acquire a large block of target stock but propose no self-dealing transaction which would trigger the rights. It may wait to elect a new board. Indeed, this weakness was demonstrated in one instance and flip-in pills, which did not require the hostile acquirer to take any second step in order to execute the punishing dilution, were designed in response.

Rights plans were, and to some extent remain, controversial. One can easily see how they could be beneficial to shareholders, but it is just as easy to see ways in which they might be misused to protect the status quo. Institutional investors generally dislike them, mainly because boards do not need shareholder approval to adopt rights plans and generally do not seek it. (Of course, the corporation's charter must authorize enough shares to cover the exercise of the rights in the wholly unimaginable event that they were ever exercised in their untriggered state.) When rights plans were first introduced, it was fairly clear that the charters of most corporations — and the corporation law — authorized boards to issue rights resembling those created by rights plans. It was less clear, however, that these rights could be issued solely as a defense against takeovers rather than to raise capital. This issue surfaced in the 1985 case involving Household International, Inc.

MORAN v. HOUSEHOLD INTERNATIONAL, INC.

500 A.2d 1346 (Del. 1985)

McNEILLY, J.:

This case presents to this Court for review the most recent defensive mechanism in the arsenal of corporate takeover weaponry — the Preferred Share Purchase Rights Plan ("Rights Plan" or "Plan"). The validity of this mechanism has attracted national attention. . . .

In a detailed opinion, the Court of Chancery upheld the Rights Plan as a legitimate exercise of business judgment by Household. *Moran v. Household International, Inc.*, Del. Ch., 490 A.2d 1059 (1985). We agree, and therefore, affirm the judgment below. . . .

On August 14, 1984, the Board of Directors of Household International, Inc. adopted the Rights Plan by a fourteen to two vote.[2] The intricacies of the Rights Plan are contained in a 48-page document entitled "Rights

---

21. If the second-step transaction were a sale of assets, the theory would likely be the same. The target's board cannot agree to the sale unless the triggering shareholder agrees to respect the flip-over rights. How good is this theory?

2. Household's Board has ten outside directors and six who are members of management. Messrs. Moran (appellant) and Whitehead voted against the Plan. The record reflects that Whitehead voted against the Plan not on its substance but because he thought it was novel and would bring unwanted publicity to Household.

Agreement." Basically, the Plan provides that Household common stock-holders are entitled to the issuance of one Right per common share under certain triggering conditions. There are two triggering events that can activate the Rights. The first is the announcement of a tender offer for 30 percent of Household's shares ("30% trigger") and the second is the acquisition of 20 percent of Household's shares by any single entity or group ("20% trigger").

If an announcement of a tender offer for 30 percent of Household's shares is made, the Rights are issued and are immediately exercisable to purchase 1/100 share of new preferred stock for $100 and are redeemable by the Board for $.50 per Right. If 20 percent of Household's shares are acquired by anyone, the Rights are issued and become non-redeemable and are exercisable to purchase 1/100 of a share of preferred. If a Right is not exercised for preferred, and thereafter, a merger or consolidation occurs, the Rights holder can exercise each Right to purchase $200 of the common stock of the tender offeror for $100. This "flip-over" provision of the Rights Plan is at the heart of this controversy.

Household is a diversified holding company with its principal subsidiaries engaged in financial services, transportation and merchandising. HFC, National Car Rental and Vons Grocery are three of its wholly-owned entities.

Household did not adopt its Rights Plan during a battle with a corporate raider, but as a preventative mechanism to ward off future advances. The Vice-Chancellor found that as early as February 1984, Household's management became concerned about the company's vulnerability as a takeover target. . . .

In the meantime, appellant Moran, one of Household's own Directors and also Chairman of the Dyson-Kissner-Moran Corporation ("D-K-M") which is the largest single stockholder of Household, began discussions concerning a possible leveraged buy-out of Household by D-K-M. D-K-M's financial studies showed that Household's stock was significantly under-valued in relation to the company's break-up value. It is uncontradicted that Moran's suggestion of a leveraged buy-out never progressed beyond the discussion stage.

Concerned about Household's vulnerability to a raider in light of the current takeover climate, Household secured the services of Wachtell, Lipton, Rosen and Katz ("Wachtell, Lipton") and Goldman, Sachs & Co. ("Goldman, Sachs") to formulate a takeover policy for recommendation to the Household Board at its August 14 meeting. . . .

Representatives of Wachtell, Lipton and Goldman, Sachs attended the August 14 meeting. The minutes reflect that Mr. Lipton explained to the Board that his recommendation of the Plan was based on his understanding that the Board was concerned about the increasing frequency of "bust-up"[4] takeovers, the increasing takeover activity in the financial service industry . . . and the possible adverse effect this type of activity could have on employees and others concerned with and vital to the continuing

---

4. "Bust-up" takeover generally refers to a situation in which one seeks to finance an acquisition by selling off pieces of the acquired company.

successful operation of Household even in the absence of any actual bust-up takeover attempt. Against this factual background, the Plan was approved.

Thereafter, Moran and the company of which he is Chairman, D-K-M, filed this suit. . . . The primary issue here is the applicability of the business judgment rule as the standard by which the adoption of the Rights Plan should be reviewed. . . .

[But] the business judgment rule can only sustain corporate decision making or transactions that are within the power or authority of the Board. Therefore, before the business judgment rule can be applied it must be determined whether the Directors were authorized to adopt the Rights Plan. . . .

While appellants contend that no provision of the Delaware General Corporation Law authorizes the Rights Plan, Household contends that the Rights Plan was issued pursuant to 8 Del. C. §§151(g) and 157. It explains that the Rights are authorized by §157[7] and the issue of preferred stock underlying the Rights is authorized by §151. . . .[8]

[First, a]ppellants contend that §157 is a corporate financing statute, and that nothing in its legislative history suggests a purpose that has anything to do with corporate control or a takeover defense. Appellants are unable to demonstrate that the legislature, in its adoption of §157, meant to limit the applicability of §157 to only the issuance of Rights for the purposes of corporate financing. Without such affirmative evidence, we decline to impose such a limitation upon the section that the legislature has not. . . .

Secondly, appellants contend that §157 does not authorize the issuance of sham rights such as the Rights Plan. They contend that the Rights were designed never to be exercised, and that the Plan has no economic value. . . .

Appellants' sham contention fails in both regards. As to the Rights, they can and will be exercised upon the happening of a triggering mechanism, as we have observed during the current struggle of Sir James Goldsmith to take control of Crown Zellerbach. See *Wall Street Journal*,

---

7. [DGCL] §157 . . . provides in relevant part:

Subject to any provisions in the certificate of incorporation, every corporation may create and issue, whether or not in connection with the issue and sale of any shares of stock or other securities of the corporation, rights or options entitling the holders thereof to purchase from the corporation any shares of its capital stock . . . as shall be approved by the board of directors.

8. [DGCL] §151(g) provides in relevant part:

When any corporation desires to issue any shares of stock of any class . . . of which the voting powers, designations, preferences and relative, participating, optional or other rights . . . shall not have been set forth in the certificate of incorporation . . . but shall be provided for in a resolution . . . adopted by the board of directors pursuant to authority expressly vested in it by the provisions of the certificate of incorporation . . . a certificate setting forth a copy of such resolution . . . and the number of shares of stock of such class or series shall be executed, acknowledged, filed, recorded, and shall become effective, in accordance with §103 of this title.

July 26, 1985, at 3, 12. As to the preferred shares, we agree with the Court of Chancery that they are distinguishable from sham securities. . . . The Household preferred, issuable upon the happening of a triggering event, have superior dividend and liquidation rights.

Third, appellants contend that §157 authorizes the issuance of Rights "entitling holders thereof to purchase from the corporation any shares of *its* capital stock of any class . . . " (emphasis added). Therefore, their contention continues, the plain language of the statute does not authorize Household to issue rights to purchase another's capital stock upon a merger or consolidation.

. . . We find no merit to such a distinction. We have already rejected appellants' similar contention that §157 could only be used for financing purposes. We also reject that distinction here.

"Anti-destruction" clauses generally ensure holders of certain securities of the protection of their right of conversion in the event of a merger by giving them the right to convert their securities into whatever securities are to replace the stock of their company. . . . The fact that the rights here have as their purpose the prevention of coercive two-tier tender offers does not invalidate them.

Fourth, [a]ppellants contend that the lack of [a strong Delaware anti-takeover statute] indicates a legislative intent to reject anything which would impose an impediment to the tender offer process. Such a contention is a non sequitur. The desire to have little state regulation of tender offers cannot be said to also indicate a desire to also have little private regulation. Furthermore, as we explain infra, we do not view the Rights Plan as much of an impediment on the tender offer process. . . .

Having concluded that sufficient authority for the Rights Plan exists in 8 Del. C. §157, we note the inherent powers of the Board conferred by 8 Del. C. §141(a), concerning the management of the corporation's "business and *affairs*" (emphasis added), also provides the Board additional authority upon which to enact the Rights Plan. . . .

Appellants contend that the Board is unauthorized to usurp stockholders' rights to receive tender offers by changing Household's fundamental structure. We conclude that the Rights Plan does not prevent stockholders from receiving tender offers, and that the change of Household's structure was less than that which results from the implementation of other defensive mechanisms upheld by various courts.

Appellants' contention that stockholders will lose their right to receive and accept tender offers seems to be premised upon [a mis]understanding of the Rights Plan. . . .

[L]ook at the recent takeover of Crown Zellerbach, which has a similar Rights Plan, by Sir James Goldsmith. *Wall Street Journal*, July 26, 1985, at 3, 12. The evidence at trial also evidenced many methods around the Plan ranging from tendering with a condition that the Board redeem the Rights, tendering with a high minimum condition of shares and Rights, tendering and soliciting consents to remove the Board and redeem the Rights, to acquiring 50% of the shares and causing Household to self-tender for the Rights. One could also form a group of up to 19.9% and solicit proxies for consent to remove the Board and redeem the Rights. These are but a few of the methods by which Household can still be acquired by a hostile tender offer. . . .

The Rights Plan does not destroy the assets of the corporation. The implementation of the Plan neither results in any outflow of money from the corporation nor impairs its financial flexibility. It does not dilute earnings per share and does not have any adverse tax consequences for the corporation or its stockholders. The Plan has not adversely affected the market price of Household's stock.

Comparing the Rights Plan with other defensive mechanisms, it does less harm to the value structure of the corporation than do the other mechanisms. . . .

. . . Appellants contend that the "20% trigger" effectively prevents any stockholder from first acquiring 20% or more shares before conducting a proxy contest and further, it prevents stockholders from banding together into a group to solicit proxies if, collectively, they own 20% or more of the stock.

. . . In essence, the Rights Agreement provides that the Rights are triggered when someone becomes the "beneficial owner" of 20% or more of Household stock. Although a literal reading of the Rights Agreement definition of "beneficial owner" would seem to include those shares which one has the right to vote, it has long been recognized that the relationship between grantor and recipient of a proxy is one of agency, and the agency is revocable by the grantor at any time. . . . Therefore, the holder of a proxy is not the "beneficial owner" of the stock. As a result, the mere acquisition of the right to vote 20% of the shares does not trigger the Rights.

The issue, then, is whether the restriction upon individuals or groups from first acquiring 20% of shares before waging a proxy contest fundamentally restricts stockholders' right to conduct a proxy contest.

. . . Evidence at trial established that many proxy contests are won with an insurgent ownership of less than 20%, and that very large holdings are no guarantee of success. There was also testimony that the key variable in proxy contest success is the merit of an insurgent's issues, not the size of his holdings. . . .

There are no allegations here of any bad faith on the part of the Directors' action in the adoption of the Rights Plan. There is no allegation that the Directors' action was taken for entrenchment purposes. Household has adequately demonstrated . . . that the adoption of the Rights Plan was in reaction to what it perceived to be the threat in the market place of coercive two-tier tender offers. . . .

In conclusion, the Household Directors receive the benefit of the business judgment rule in their adoption of the Rights Plan. . . .

The Directors adopted the Plan in the good faith belief that it was necessary to protect Household from coercive acquisition techniques. The Board was informed as to the details of the Plan. In addition, Household has demonstrated that the Plan is reasonable in relation to the threat posed. . . .

While we conclude for present purposes that the Household Directors are protected by the business judgment rule, that does not end the matter. The ultimate response to an actual takeover bid must be judged by the

Directors' actions at that time, and nothing we say here relieves them of their basic fundamental duties to the corporation and its stockholders. . . . Their use of the Plan will be evaluated when and if the issue arises.

QUESTIONS AND NOTES ON MORAN

1. What effect should poison pills have on shareholder value? Most commentators agree that, in the hands of absolutely loyal managers, the pill benefits shareholders by providing the managers with the power to bargain on their behalf and so overcome their chronic collective action problem. Thus, the pill might have the effect of increasing corporate value, or at least the size of takeover premia. But in the hands of disloyal managers, the pill might be used to entrench managers or to increase their private benefits. In this case, the pill undoubtedly lowers corporate value. Will it also lower takeover premia — or just decrease the likelihood of takeovers?

Testing the effects of pills on corporate value is not easy, in part because every Delaware company might be said to have a pill. Companies that do not presently have a pill can adopt one in a matter of days (if not hours) if they are threatened by an impending takeover bid. All that is required to adopt a pill is a board meeting, after all, not a shareholder vote. See John C. Coates IV, *Takeover Defenses in the Shadow of the Pill: A Critique of the Scientific Evidence*, 79 Tex. L. Rev. 271 (2000).

2. The Delaware Supreme Court was careful in *Moran* to state that corporate directors continue to exercise power subject to their fiduciary duty after adoption of a stock rights plan. In particular, the court noted that, under *Unocal*, a board might have a duty to redeem rights issued under its rights plan if their effect no longer appears reasonable in relation to the threat posed by an uninvited tender offer. But exactly when must a pill be redeemed? Is the board entitled to keep rights outstanding only long enough to complete an important company transaction, such as a recapitalization, that serves as an alternative to the bidder's offer? Or is the board entitled to "just say no" to a hostile bidder indefinitely, even without proposing an alternative to its shareholders?

Should the distinction between doing nothing and offering a management alternative to a hostile offer matter? The courts have sometimes acted as if it did. The cases in which the Delaware Court of Chancery forced boards to redeem their pills were ones in which the pills were used to protect company-sponsored alternatives to all-cash tender offers. In *City Capital Associates Ltd. Partnership v. Interco, Inc.*, 551 A.2d 787 (Del. Ch. 1988), the court ordered Interco, Inc., to redeem a stock rights plan that the company used to protect its recapitalization alternative to a hostile all-cash, all-shares tender offer.[22] Similarly, in *Grand Metropolitan Public Ltd.*

22. After reviewing the company's own restructuring plan, the court concluded that the hostile all-cash, all-shares offer did not constitute a sufficient threat to Interco or its shareholders to justify foreclosing the shareholders indefinitely from choosing to accept the offer.

Co. v. Pillsbury Co., 558 A.2d 1049 (Del. Ch. 1988), the court required Pillsbury to redeem its rights plan after concluding that Pillsbury's own restructuring proposal compared unfavorably in value to a hostile all-cash, all-shares offer from Grand Met. To be sure, these cases were expressly disapproved by the Delaware Supreme Court in dicta in the *Time-Warner* case excerpted below. Despite such disapproval, however, the Supreme Court continues to assert that boards have an ongoing fiduciary obligation to redeem the pill if it is no longer reasonable in relationship to the threat of an acquisition offer.

NOTE ON THE JAPANESE GUIDELINES ON TAKEOVER DEFENSE

In September 2004, Japan's Ministry of Economy, Trade, and Industry convened a group of experts and business representatives, chaired by Professor Hideki Kanda of the University of Tokyo, to propose a governmental response to the hostile takeovers that were beginning to appear on the Japanese corporate landscape. After extensive study and consultation with takeover experts around the world, the Corporate Value Study Group published its report in March 2005. Two months later, METI and the Japanese Ministry of Justice jointly promulgated "guidelines" that adopted the general approach and many of the specific recommendations from the report.[23] On one hand, the Guidelines follow Delaware by allowing Japanese boards to adopt poison pills without a shareholder vote, and, more generally, requiring that defenses be "necessary and reasonable in relation to the threat posed." (Sound familiar?) On the other hand, the Guidelines indicate that defenses can only be used to maximize shareholder value, not to protect other constituencies as suggested in *Unocal*. In addition, the Guidelines suggest a more stringent form of reasonableness review than the Delaware courts have historically applied. For example, in order to be reasonable a board-adopted poison pill must provide a mechanism for shareholders to eliminate it, such as through an annual election of all the directors, or a sunset provision.

Taken as a whole, Japan seems to have adopted a middle-ground approach somewhere between Delaware and the EU Takeover Directive. Of course, the Guidelines only provide general principles, and it will take at least a few years of judicial interpretation to see how they play out in practice. For an insightful commentary on these developments, see Curtis J. Milhaupt, *In the Shadow of Delaware? The Rise of Hostile Takeovers in Japan*, 105 Colum. L. Rev. 2171 (2005).

---

23. Ministry of Economy, Trade and Industry & Ministry of Justice, Guidelines Regarding Takeover Defense for the Purposes of Protection and Enhancement of Corporate Value and Shareholders' Common Interests (May 27, 2005).

13.4 CHOOSING A MERGER OR BUYOUT PARTNER: REVLON, ITS SEQUELS, AND ITS PREQUELS

The board's entrenchment interest can affect not only its takeover defenses but also its choice of a merger or buyout partner. Management can obtain a variety of benefits in "friendly" deals, ranging from a place on the surviving corporation's board to a cascade of consulting contracts, termination payments, and other compensation-related benefits. Traditionally, corporate law treated decisions to initiate merger proposals as business judgments as long as management did not have a conflicting ownership interest. In its third revolutionary takeover opinion of the 1985-1986 season, the Delaware Supreme Court addressed the board's fiduciary duty in arranging for the "sale" of a company. The case was *Revlon, Inc. v. MacAndrews and Forbes Holdings, Inc.*, 506 A.2d 173 (Del. 1986). Even before *Revlon*, however, the Delaware Supreme Court signaled its concern about the possibility that incumbent managers might sell their company at a low price to a favored bidder in the remarkable case of *Smith v. Van Gorkom*, 488 A.2d 858 (Del. 1985). At the time it was issued, the *Smith* opinion was believed to be an aggressive articulation of the board's general duty of care. (Accordingly, we also discuss it in Chapter 8 above.) In hindsight, however, *Smith* has come to seem much more like a precursor of the great Delaware takeover cases of the mid-1980s, and especially of *Revlon.* We reproduce portions of this very lengthy opinion below.

SMITH v. VAN GORKOM

488 A.2d 858 (Del. 1985)

HORSEY, J.:

This appeal from the Court of Chancery involves a class action brought by shareholders of the defendant Trans Union Corporation ("Trans Union" or "the Company"), originally seeking rescission of a cash-out merger of Trans Union into . . . a wholly-owned subsidiary of the defendant, Marmon Group, Inc. ("Marmon"). Alternate relief in the form of damages is sought against the defendant members of the Board of Directors of Trans Union. . . .

Speaking for the majority of the Court, we conclude that both rulings of the Court of Chancery are clearly erroneous. Therefore, we reverse and direct that judgment be entered in favor of the plaintiffs and against the defendant directors for the fair value of the plaintiffs' stockholdings in Trans Union. . . .

Trans Union was a publicly-traded, diversified holding company, the principal earnings of which were generated by its railcar leasing business. During the period here involved, the Company had a cash flow of hundreds of millions of dollars annually. However, the Company had difficulty in generating sufficient taxable income to offset increasingly large investment tax credits (ITCs). Accelerated depreciation deductions had decreased available taxable income against which to offset accumulating ITCs. . . .

[At a senior management meeting on September 5, 1980, Trans Union's CFO and COO discussed a leveraged buyout as a solution to the ITC problem.] . . . They did not "come up" with a price for the Company. They merely "ran the numbers" at $50 a share and at $60 a share with the "rough form" of their cash figures at the time. Their "figures indicated that $50 would be very easy to do but $60 would be very difficult to do under those figures." This work did not purport to establish a fair price for either the Company or 100% of the stock. It was intended to determine the cash flow needed to service the debt that would "probably" be incurred in a leveraged buy-out. . . .

. . . Van Gorkom [Trans Union's CEO for more than 17 years] stated that he would be willing to take $55 per share for his own 75,000 shares. [Nevertheless, h]e vetoed the suggestion of a leveraged buy-out by Management . . . as involving a potential conflict of interest for Management. . . . It is noteworthy in this connection that he was then approaching 65 years of age and mandatory retirement.

For several days following the September 5 meeting, Van Gorkom pondered the idea of a sale. He had participated in many acquisitions as a manager and director of Trans Union and as a director of other companies. He was familiar with acquisition procedures, valuation methods, and negotiations; and he privately considered the pros and cons of whether Trans Union should seek a privately or publicly-held purchaser.

Van Gorkom decided to meet with Jay A. Pritzker, a well-known corporate takeover specialist and a social acquaintance. However, rather than approaching Pritzker simply to determine his interest in acquiring Trans Union, Van Gorkom assembled a proposed per share price for sale of the Company and a financing structure by which to accomplish the sale. Van Gorkom did so without consulting either his Board or any members of Senior Management except one: Carl Peterson, Trans Union's Controller. Telling Peterson that he wanted no other person on his staff to know what he was doing, but without telling him why, Van Gorkom directed Peterson to calculate the feasibility of a leveraged buy-out at an assumed price per share of $55. Apart from the Company's historic stock market price,[5] and Van Gorkom's long association with Trans Union, the record is devoid of any competent evidence that $55 represented the per share intrinsic value of the Company. . . .

Van Gorkom arranged a meeting with Pritzker at the latter's home on Saturday, September 13, 1980. Van Gorkom prefaced his presentation by stating to Pritzker: "Now as far as you are concerned, I can, I think, show how you can pay a substantial premium over the present stock price and pay off most of the loan in the first five years. . . . If you could pay $55 for this Company, here is a way in which I think it can be financed." . . .

[Pritzker subsequently made a cash offer for Trans Union at $55/share. The offer was to remain open for a period of 90 days, during which Trans

---

5. The common stock of Trans Union was traded on the New York Stock Exchange. Over the five year period from 1975 through 1979, Trans Union's stock had traded within a range of a high of $39½ and a low of $24¼. Its high and low range for 1980 through September 19 (the last trading day before announcement of the merger) was $38 ¼–$29½.

Union could accept a higher offer. But this "market test" was defective in the Court's view.] ...

On Friday, September 19 [1980], Van Gorkom called a special meeting of the Trans Union Board for noon the following day. ...

Ten directors served on the Trans Union Board, five inside ... and five outside. ... Of the outside directors, four were corporate chief executive officers and one was the former Dean of the University of Chicago Business School. None was an investment banker or trained financial analyst. All members of the Board were well informed about the Company and its operations as a going concern. They were familiar with the current financial condition of the Company, as well as operating and earnings projections reported in the recent Five Year Forecast. The Board generally received regular and detailed reports and was kept abreast of the accumulated investment tax credit and accelerated depreciation problem.

Van Gorkom began the Special Meeting of the Board with a twenty-minute oral presentation. Copies of the proposed Merger Agreement were delivered too late for study before or during the meeting. He reviewed the Company's ITC and depreciation problems and the efforts theretofore made to solve them. He discussed his initial meeting with Pritzker and his motivation in arranging that meeting. Van Gorkom did not disclose to the Board, however, the methodology by which he alone had arrived at the $55 figure, or the fact that he first proposed the $55 price in his negotiations with Pritzker.

Van Gorkom outlined the terms of the Pritzker offer as follows ... for a period of 90 days, Trans Union could receive, but could not actively solicit, competing offers; the offer had to be acted on by the next evening, Sunday, September 21; Trans Union could only furnish to competing bidders published information, and not proprietary information; the offer was subject to Pritzker obtaining the necessary financing by October 10, 1980; if the financing contingency were met or waived by Pritzker, Trans Union was required to sell to Pritzker one million newly-issued shares of Trans Union at $38 per share.

Van Gorkom took the position that putting Trans Union "up for auction" through a 90-day market test would validate a decision by the Board that $55 was a fair price. He framed the decision before the Board not as whether $55 per share was the highest price that could be obtained, but as whether the $55 price was a fair price that the stockholders should be given the opportunity to accept or reject. ...

On Monday, September 22, the Company issued a press release announcing that Trans Union had entered into a "definitive" Merger Agreement with an affiliate of the Marmon group, Inc., a Pritzker holding company. Within 10 days of the public announcement, dissent among Senior Management over the merger had become widespread. Faced with threatened resignations of key officers, Van Gorkom met with Pritzker who agreed to several modifications of the Agreement. Pritzker was willing to do so provided that Van Gorkom could persuade the dissidents to remain on the Company payroll for at least six months after consummation of the merger. ...

The next day, October 9, Trans Union issued a press release announcing: (1) that Pritzker had obtained "the financing commitments necessary to consummate" the merger with Trans Union; (2) that Pritzker had acquired one million shares of Trans Union common stock at $38 per share; (3) that Trans Union was now permitted to actively seek other offers and had retained Salomon Brothers for that purpose; and (4) that if a more favorable offer were not received before February 1, 1981, Trans Union's shareholders would thereafter meet to vote on the Pritzker proposal. . . .

Salomon Brothers' efforts over a three-month period from October 21 to January 21 produced only one serious suitor for Trans Union — General Electric Credit Corporation ("GE Credit"), a subsidiary of the General Electric Company. However, GE Credit was unwilling to make an offer for Trans Union unless Trans Union first rescinded its Merger Agreement with Pritzker. When Pritzker refused, GE Credit terminated further discussions with Trans Union in early January. . . .

On February 10, the stockholders of Trans Union approved the Pritzker merger proposal. Of the outstanding shares 69.9% were voted in favor of the merger; 7.25% were voted against the merger; and 22.85% were not voted. . . .

On [this] record . . . , we must conclude that the Board of Directors did not reach an informed business judgment on September 20. . . . [T]he Board based its September 20 decision to approve the cash-out merger primarily on Van Gorkom's representations. None of the directors, other than Van Gorkom and Chelberg, had any prior knowledge that the purpose of the meeting was to propose a cash-out merger of Trans Union. No members of Senior Management were present, other than Chelberg, Romans and Peterson; and the latter two had only learned of the proposed sale an hour earlier. Both general counsel Moore and former general counsel Browder attended the meeting, but were equally uninformed as to the purpose of the meeting and the documents to be acted upon.

Without any documents before them concerning the proposed transaction, the members of the Board were required to rely entirely upon Van Gorkom's 20-minute oral presentation of the proposal. No written summary of the terms of the merger was presented; the directors were given no documentation to support the adequacy of $55 price per share for sale of the Company; and the Board had before it nothing more than Van Gorkom's statement of his understanding of the substance of an agreement which he admittedly had never read, nor which any member of the Board had ever seen. . . .

A substantial premium may provide one reason to recommend a merger, but in the absence of other sound valuation information, the fact of a premium alone does not provide an adequate basis upon which to assess the fairness of an offering price. . . .

The parties do not dispute that a publicly-traded stock price is solely a measure of the value of a minority position and, thus, market price represents only the value of a single share. Nevertheless, on September 20, the Board assessed the adequacy of the premium over market, offered by Pritzker, solely by comparing it with Trans Union's current and historical stock price. . . .

Indeed, as of September 20, the Board had no other information on which to base a determination of the intrinsic value of Trans Union as a going concern. As of September 20, the Board had made no evaluation of the Company designed to value the entire enterprise, nor had the Board ever previously considered selling the Company or consenting to a buy-out merger. Thus, the adequacy of a premium is indeterminate unless it is assessed in terms of other competent and sound valuation information that reflects the value of the particular business. . . .

This brings us to the post-September 20 "market test" upon which the defendants ultimately rely to confirm the reasonableness of their September 20 decision to accept the Pritzker proposal. . . .

Again, the facts of record do not support the defendants' argument. There is no evidence: (a) that the Merger Agreement was effectively amended [on September 20] to give the Board freedom to put Trans Union up for auction sale to the highest bidder; or (b) that a public auction was in fact permitted to occur. . . .

We conclude that Trans Union's Board was grossly negligent in that it failed to act with informed reasonable deliberation in agreeing to the Pritzker merger proposal on September 20. . . .

The October 10 amendments to the Merger Agreement did authorize Trans Union to solicit competing offers, but the amendments had more far-reaching effects. The most significant change was in the definition of the third-party "offer" available to Trans Union as a possible basis for withdrawal from its Merger Agreement with Pritzker. Under the October 10 amendments, a better *offer* was no longer sufficient to permit Trans Union's withdrawal. Trans Union was now permitted to terminate the Pritzker Agreement and abandon the merger only if, prior to February 10, 1981, Trans Union had either consummated a merger (or sale of assets) with a third party or had entered into a "definitive" merger agreement more favorable than Pritzker's and for a greater consideration — subject only to stockholder approval. Further, the "extension" of the market test period to February 10, 1981 was circumscribed by other amendments which required Trans Union to file its preliminary proxy statement on the Pritzker merger proposal by December 5, 1980 and use its best efforts to mail the statement to its shareholders by January 5, 1981. Thus, the market test period was effectively reduced, not extended. . . .

The October 9 press release, coupled with the October 10 amendments, had the clear effect of locking Trans Union's Board into the Pritzker Agreement. . . .

Finally, we turn to the Board's meeting of January 26, 1981 . . . [which] was the first meeting following the filing of the plaintiffs' suit in mid-December and the last meeting before the previously-noticed shareholder meeting of February 10. . . .

The defendants characterize the Board's Minutes of the January 26 meeting as a "review" of the "entire sequence of events" from Van Gorkom's initiation of the negotiations on September 13 forward. The defendants . . . argue that whatever information the Board lacked to make a deliberate and informed judgment on September 20, or on October 8, was fully divulged to the entire Board on January 26. Hence, the argument goes, the Board's vote on January 26 to again "approve" the Pritzker merger must be found to have been an informed and deliberate judgement. . . .

We must conclude from the foregoing that the Board was mistaken as a matter of law regarding its available courses of action on January 26, 1981. . . . [T]he Board had but two options: (1) to proceed with the merger and the stockholder meeting, with the Board's recommendation of approval; *or* (2) to rescind its agreement with Pritzker, withdraw its approval of the merger, and notify its stockholders that the proposed shareholder meeting was canceled. There is no evidence that the Board gave any consideration to these, its only legally viable alternative courses of action.

But the second course of action would have clearly involved a substantial risk — that the Board would be faced with suit by Pritzker for breach of contract based on its September 20 agreement as amended October 10. As previously noted, under the terms of the October 10 amendment, the Board's only ground for release from its agreement with Pritzker was its entry into a more favorable definitive agreement to sell the Company to a third party. Thus, in reality, the Board was not "free to turn down the Pritzker proposal". . . . Clearly, the Board was not "free" to withdraw from its agreement with Pritzker on January 26 by simply relying on its self-induced failure to have reached an informed business judgment at the time of its original agreement. . . .

The defendants ultimately rely on the stockholder vote of February 10 for exoneration. The defendants contend that the stockholders' "overwhelming" vote approving the Pritzker Merger Agreement had the legal effect of curing any failure of the Board to reach an informed business judgment in its approval of the merger. . . .

[W]e find that Trans Union's stockholders were not fully informed of all facts material to their vote on the Pritzker Merger and that the Trial Court's ruling to the contrary is clearly erroneous. . . .

We conclude that the Board acted in a grossly negligent manner on October 8 [in addition to acting in a grossly negligent manner at the initial meeting on September 20 — Eds.]; and that Van Gorkom's representations on which the Board based its actions do not constitute "reports" under §141(e) on which the directors could reasonably have relied. . . .

NOTE ON SMITH v. VAN GORKOM

As noted above, *Smith v. Van Gorkom* is on its own terms a case about the extent of the directors' duty of care. Yet as argued in Chapter 8, courts generally refuse to examine the reasonableness of decisions made by disinterested directors in the board's regular decision-making process. (Recall the *Kamin* case in particular.) *Smith v. Van Gorkom* was a jolting break with this tradition — so much so that we are persuaded it is something other than the simple application of duty of care doctrine to special

JAY PRITZKER & JEROME VAN GORKOM

Jay Pritzker was born into a family already prominent in Chicago's business circles. His grandfather, a Ukrainian immigrant, had arrived in Chicago at the turn of the century with little money and no knowledge of the English language, but had risen to become partner in the law firm Pritzker & Pritzker and patriarch of the close-knit, business-minded Pritzker family. The Pritzkers, through skillful networking and shrewd investing, had proceeded to build a sizeable fortune.

At the precocious age of fourteen, Jay Pritzker graduated from high school and began his studies at Northwestern University. After obtaining a law degree from Northwestern and performing military service during World War II, he returned home to help manage the family investments. He formed what would become The Marmon Group in 1953 with his brother Robert in order to purchase underperforming industrial companies. Jay Pritzker was known for his ability to swiftly evaluate business deals and his preference for quick and simple transactions. As he told the *Wall Street Journal*, "We've bought a lot of things on just a handshake or a paragraph or two. We're the least legal-minded people you'll ever meet."[24] His investment made him and his family billionaires.

While vacationing at a ski chalet in the Swiss Alps, Pritzker met Jerome Van Gorkom, CEO of Trans Union. Both men were active in the Chicago business community and became friends while working together to rescue the Chicago public school system from severe financial difficulties. Their relationship would lead to a merger of their respective companies and to a groundbreaking legal decision in *Smith v. Van Gorkom*.

facts.[25] In particular, we recommend the interpretation offered by Professors Jonathan Macey and Geoffrey Miller that *Van Gorkom* should be understood *not* as a director negligence case (although the court presented it this way) but rather as the first of several important cases in which the court struggled to construct a new standard of judicial review for "change in control" transactions such as mergers.[26]

NOTE: INTRODUCING THE REVLON DECISION

The opinion that gave full cry to the courts' desire to modify the business judgment rule in the context of transactions that involved a change in control was the *Revlon* decision, which was handed down the year after *Van Gorkom*. The bidder in *Revlon* was Ronald O. Perelman, a

24. Quoted in William Owen, *Autopsy of a Merger* (1986).

25. We are unaware of any prior nonbanking case in which directors who have no conflicting interests and who attend meetings and deliberate before authorizing a transaction are held personally liable for breach of a duty of care, let alone a case in which they are held liable for approving a sale of the company at a 50 percent premium to market price.

26. Jonathan R. Macey & Geoffrey P. Miller, *Trans Union Reconsidered*, 98 Yale L.J. 127, 138 (1988). We stand behind our conviction by locating an excerpt from *Van Gorkom* in this chapter, rather than Chapter 8, although, of course, we do not object if some of our readers wish to read *Van Gorkom* in conjunction with Chapter 8.

well-known takeover entrepreneur and the chairman of Pantry Pride, Inc. Revlon's management opposed the Perelman/Pantry Pride offer with two defensive tactics. First, it adopted a form of flip-in rights plan as described above, and second, it repurchased 20 percent of Revlon's stock with unsecured debt (the Notes) at a premium price. This repurchase had two useful effects from the standpoint of Revlon's embattled management. First, these Notes clouded Revlon's balance sheet and thus made it harder for Perelman to find financing to support his buyout. Second, the Notes gave management a vehicle for inserting a covenant that barred Revlon from selling or encumbering its assets without the approval of its independent directors. Again, such a covenant would make it more difficult for Perelman to borrow against Revlon's assets and subsequently pay down his debt by selling assets in typical leveraged buyout fashion.[27]

Perelman proved to be a formidable opponent, however. He countered management's moves by raising his bid price! Soon shareholder pressure on Revlon's board to act became overwhelming. At this point, Revlon's management attempted to reverse course by soliciting a competing bid from a "white knight," or friendly bidder, Forstmann Little & Co., a financial firm in the leveraged buyout business. The board's new strategy aimed at giving shareholders the cash they were demanding by selling Revlon to a friendly buyer (Forstmann and themselves) rather than to Perelman. But for the new strategy to succeed, Revlon had to remove the restrictive covenant contained in the Notes that it had exchanged with its shareholders, since this covenant not only interfered with Perelman's financing but also precluded Forstmann from financing the new alternative transaction. Yet one thing leads to another. Stripping the restrictive covenant from the Notes sharply lowered their value. Within days, lawyers representing Revlon's noteholders (who were erstwhile shareholders) were threatening to sue the board for bad faith and breach of duty.

Forstmann was persuaded to enter the fray and make a bid, but Perelman vowed to beat whatever price Forstmann would offer. Revlon then concluded a final deal with Forstmann: Revlon would assure Forstmann's victory by giving it a "lock-up option" to purchase Revlon's most valuable assets at a bargain price if another bidder (i.e., Perelman) were to acquire more than 40 percent of Revlon's stock. In exchange, Forstmann would increase its offer for Revlon's stock (to $57.25) and support the price of Revlon's Notes (thus satisfying any claims of noteholders).

In response to the new Revlon-Forstmann deal, Pantry Pride increased its offer to $58/share conditional on the lock-up being rescinded or declared invalid. It sought to enjoin Forstmann's lock-up option as well as its agreement not to assist buyers other than Forstmann in the Delaware courts. The Delaware Supreme Court (per Justice Moore) firmly rejected what it considered to be Revlon's attempt to "rig" the bidding.

We pick up here with the Delaware Supreme Court opinion after the court approved Revlon's original defensive tactics that were designed to

27. A leveraged buyout is a transaction in which a buyer borrows cash that will be used to buy the equity of the target corporation. Repayment of the borrowing comes from sale of the target's assets (breakup) or is secured by the target's assets.

maintain its independence (the poison pill and the exchange offer). Justice Moore now turns to Revlon's decision to sell to Forstmann and the lock-up option.

REVLON, INC. v. MACANDREWS AND FORBES HOLDINGS, INC.

506 A.2d 173 (Del. 1986)

MOORE, J.:

[The Revlon board's focus on its agreement with Forstmann on] shoring up the sagging market value of the Notes in the face of threatened litigation . . . was inconsistent with . . . the directors' responsibilities at this stage of the developments. The impending waiver of the Notes covenants had caused the value of the Notes to fall, and the board was aware of the noteholders' ire as well as their subsequent threats of suit. The directors thus made support of the Notes an integral part of the company's dealings with Forstmann, even though their primary responsibility at this stage was to the equity owners.

The original threat posed by Pantry Pride — the break-up of the company — had become a reality which even the directors embraced. Selective dealing to fend off a hostile but determined bidder was no longer a proper objective. Instead, obtaining the highest price for the benefit of the stockholders should have been the central theme guiding director action. Thus, the Revlon board could not make the requisite showing of good faith by preferring the noteholders and ignoring its duty of loyalty to the shareholders. The rights of the former already were fixed by contract. . . . The noteholders required no further protection, and when the Revlon board entered into an auction-ending lock-up agreement with Forstmann on the basis of impermissible considerations at the expense of the shareholders, the directors breached their primary duty of loyalty.

The Revlon board argued that it acted in good faith in protecting the noteholders because *Unocal* permits consideration of other corporate constituencies. Although such considerations may be permissible, there are fundamental limitations upon that prerogative. A board may have regard for various constituencies in discharging its responsibilities, provided there are rationally related benefits accruing to the stockholders. *Unocal*, 493 A.2d at 955. However, such concern for non-stockholder interests is inappropriate when an auction among active bidders is in progress, and the object no longer is to protect or maintain the corporate enterprise but to sell it to the highest bidder.

Revlon also contended that . . . it had contractual and good faith obligations to consider the noteholders. However, any such duties are limited to the principle that one may not interfere with contractual relationships by improper actions. Here, the rights of the noteholders were fixed by agreement, and there is nothing of substance to suggest that any of those terms were violated. The Notes covenants specifically contemplated a waiver to permit sale of the company at a fair price. The Notes were accepted by the holders on that basis, including the risk of an adverse market effect stemming from a waiver. Thus, nothing remained for Revlon to legitimately protect, and no rationally related benefit thereby accrued to the stockholders. Under such circumstances we must conclude that the merger agreement with Forstmann was unreasonable in relation to the threat posed.

A lock-up is not per se illegal under Delaware law. . . . Current economic conditions in the takeover market are such that a "white knight" like Forstmann might only enter the bidding for the target company if it receives some form of compensation to cover the risks and costs involved. . . . However, while those lock-ups which draw bidders into the battle benefit shareholders, similar measures which end an active auction and foreclose further bidding operate to the shareholders' detriment. . . .

Recently, the United States Court of Appeals for the Second Circuit invalidated a lock-up on fiduciary duty grounds similar to those here. *Hanson Trust PLC, et al. v. ML SCM Acquisition Inc., et al.*, 781 F.2d 264 (2d Cir. 1986). . . .

In *Hanson Trust*, the bidder, Hanson, sought control of SCM by a hostile cash tender offer. SCM management joined with Merrill Lynch to propose a leveraged buy-out of the company at a higher price, and Hanson in turn increased its offer. Then, despite very little improvement in its subsequent bid, the management group sought a lock-up option to purchase SCM's two main assets at a substantial discount. The SCM directors granted the lock-up without adequate information as to the size of the discount or the effect the transaction would have on the company. Their action effectively ended a competitive bidding situation. The *Hanson* Court invalidated the lock-up because the directors failed to fully inform themselves about the value of a transaction in which management had a strong self-interest. . . .

The Forstmann option had a similar destructive effect on the auction process. Forstmann had already been drawn into the contest on a preferred basis, so the result of the lock-up was not to foster bidding, but to destroy it. The board's stated reasons for approving the transaction were: (1) better financing, (2) noteholder protection, and (3) higher price. As the Court of Chancery found, and we agree, any distinctions between the rival bidders' methods of financing the proposal were nominal at best, and such a consideration has little or no significance in a cash offer for any and all shares. The principal object, contrary to the board's duty of care, appears to have been protection of the noteholders over the shareholders' interests.

While Forstmann's $57.25 offer was objectively higher than Pantry Pride's $56.25 bid, the margin of superiority is less when the Forstmann price is adjusted for the time value of money. In reality, the Revlon board ended the auction in return for very little actual improvement in the final bid. The principal benefit went to the directors, who avoided personal liability to a class of creditors to whom the board owed no further duty under the circumstances. Thus, when a board ends an intense bidding contest on an insubstantial basis, and where a significant by-product of that action is to protect the directors against a perceived threat of personal liability for consequences stemming from the adoption of previous defensive measures, the action cannot withstand the enhanced scrutiny which *Unocal* requires of director conduct. See *Unocal*, 493 A.2d at 954-55.

In addition to the lock-up option, the Court of Chancery enjoined the no-shop provision as part of the attempt to foreclose further bidding by Pantry Pride. *MacAndrews & Forbes Holdings, Inc. v. Revlon, Inc.*, 501 A.2d at 1251. The no-shop provision, like the lock-up option, while not per se illegal, is impermissible under the *Unocal* standards when a board's primary duty becomes that of an auctioneer responsible for selling the company to the highest bidder. The agreement to negotiate only with Forstmann ended rather than intensified the board's involvement in the bidding contest.

It is ironic that the parties even considered a no-shop agreement when Revlon had dealt preferentially, and almost exclusively, with Forstmann throughout the contest. After the directors authorized management to negotiate with other parties, Forstmann was given every negotiating advantage that Pantry Pride had been denied: cooperation from management, access to financial data, and the exclusive opportunity to present merger proposals directly to the board of directors. Favoritism for a white knight to the total exclusion of a hostile bidder might be justifiable when the latter's offer adversely affects shareholder interests, but when bidders make relatively similar offers, or dissolution of the company becomes inevitable, the directors cannot fulfill their enhanced *Unocal* duties by playing favorites with the contending factions. Market forces must be allowed to operate freely to bring the target's shareholders the best price available for their equity. Thus, as the trial court ruled, the shareholders' interests necessitated that the board remain free to negotiate in the fulfillment of that duty.

The court below similarly enjoined the payment of the cancellation fee, pending a resolution of the merits, because the fee was part of the overall plan to thwart Pantry Pride's efforts. We find no abuse of discretion in that ruling. ...

In conclusion, the Revlon board was confronted with a situation not uncommon in the current wave of corporate takeovers. A hostile and determined bidder sought the company at a price the board was convinced was inadequate. The initial defensive tactics worked to the benefit of the shareholders, and thus the board was able to sustain its *Unocal* burdens in justifying those measures. However, in granting an asset option lock-up to Forstmann, we must conclude that under all the circumstances the directors allowed considerations other than the maximization of shareholder profit to affect their judgment, and followed a course that ended the auction for Revlon, absent court intervention, to the ultimate detriment of its shareholders. No such defensive measure can be sustained when it represents a breach of the directors' fundamental duty of care. See *Smith v. Van Gorkom*, Del. Supr., 488 A.2d 858, 874 (1985). In that context the board's action is not entitled to the deference accorded it by the business judgment rule. The measures were properly enjoined. ....

RONALD PERELMAN & TED FORSTMANN

Born into a wealthy Philadelphia family, Ron Perelman sat in on his father's board meetings as a child and pored over financial statements in his teenage years. After graduating from the University of Pennsylvania's Wharton School, he learned the art of dealmaking while working for his father. In 1978, he moved to Manhattan with no job, but big ambitions. He started by acquiring Hatfield Jewelers and turning it around by selling off many of its underperforming assets. His investment holding company, MacAndrews & Forbes, proceeded to acquire several other companies, including Marvel Comics, First Nationwide Bank, Panavision, and (as already discussed in Chapter 8) Technicolor. Early on he developed a relationship with "junk bond king" Michael Milken, who financed many of his acquisitions, including Revlon. By installing new management, disposing of assets, and then selling firms at a profit, he became a billionaire. On Wall Street, he was known for his exceptionally aggressive style.

Ted Forstmann graduated from Yale and Columbia Law School, and eventually formed Forstmann Little in 1978. The firm, an innovator in leveraged buyouts, became enormously profitable by buying and selling companies such as Dr. Pepper Co. When junk bonds became popular, however, Forstmann increasingly found himself losing out on deals because he could not raise as much money as junk-bond financed competitors. Forstmann publicly extolled his "old-fashioned" approach to business, which involved avoiding junk bond financing and maintaining good relations with the management of acquired companies. In a column for the *Wall Street Journal* in 1988, he attacked the junk bond industry, writing that "today's financial age has become a period of unbridled excess with accepted risk soaring out of proportion to possible reward."

QUESTIONS AND NOTES ON REVLON

1. What fiduciary duty did Revlon's board violate — a duty of care or a duty of loyalty?

2. According to the Court in *Revlon*, what must a board do when it is committed to enter an acquisition transaction with one of two suitors who are locked in a competitive bidding contest? Does your answer imply that Delaware law is ultimately committed to shareholder primacy in board decision making, notwithstanding the dicta in *Unocal* allowing boards to consider nonshareholder interests in evaluating the threat posed by a hostile takeover?

3. Consider the potential free-rider problem introduced by the Court's holding, illustrated by commentary from Stephen Fraidin of Fried, Frank, Harris, Shriver & Jacobson on the deal:

> I represented Forstmann Little. At one point there was a negotiation between the parties to try to settle the situation, and my client tells Perelman, "We have a big advantage: we have confidential information, you don't have any. We know what to bid and you do not." Perelman, who was a smart man, said, "Actually, I have even better information than you have because I know what you're bidding. And once I know what you're bidding and I know how smart

you are and I know that you have all the confidential information, I know I can bid a nickel more and still have a good deal." And he was absolutely right.[28]

Despite claims that the *Revlon* decision would deter first bidders due to this free rider problem, the empirical evidence does not suggest that *Revlon* reduced deal activity.[29] The watering down of *Revlon* requirements over time (see below) may be part of the answer.

4. In *Barkan v. Amsted Industries, Inc.*,[30] the Delaware Supreme Court attempted to clarify the substantive requirements imposed by *Revlon*. The clearest case occurs when two bidders are already engaged in a bidding contest for the target. Here, as in *Revlon* itself, "the directors may not use defensive tactics that destroy the auction process. [F]airness forbids directors from using defensive mechanisms to thwart an auction or to favor one bidder over another."[31] But what about if there is only a single bidder at the table? Before signing up the deal, the board must engage in a so-called market check to see if a higher bid is available, unless "the directors possess a body of reliable evidence with which to evaluate the fairness of a transaction."[32]

5. In *In re Pennaco Energy, Inc.*,[33] the board negotiated exclusively with Marathon Oil and reached an agreement at $19 cash per share, with a 3 percent breakup fee and a right for Marathon to match any competing offer that might appear post-announcement. Despite the lack of any pre-announcement shopping, the Delaware Chancery Court found that the target board had fulfilled its *Revlon* duties, on the theory that the relatively modest deal protection would allow a third-party to enter if it could pay more than $19: "While one would not commend the Pennaco board's actions as a business school model of value maximization, the process the directors used to sell the company cannot be characterized as unreasonable."[34] While the breakup fee in *Pennaco* was relatively modest, how might the combination of the breakup fee and the "match right" deter competition?

6. When are *Revlon* duties triggered? Arguably, decisions "to sell the company" are made in many contexts other than bidding contexts. What range of other transactions triggers *Revlon* duties? How does the substance of these duties change, if at all, when they are triggered outside the context of a bidding contest? What does it mean to sell the company, anyway? Is a stock for stock merge a "sale"?

---

28. Quoted in Guhan Subramanian, *The Drivers of Market Efficiency in* Revlon *Transactions*, 28 J. Corp. L. 691, 700 (2000).
29. See id.
30. 567 A.2d 1279 (Del. 1989).
31. *Id.* at 1286-87.
32. *Id.* at 1287.
33. 787 A.2d 691 (Del. 2001).
34. *Id.* at 705.

In particular, the questions of what *Revlon* duties are and when they are triggered continue to haunt Delaware law. The distinction between transactions in which the company is sold and those in which the board merely defends against a hostile takeover bid is not always clear. Consider, for example, a situation in which, in response to a hostile LBO-type cash tender offer, management uses its control over company assets to initiate a very similar transaction by (1) selling a large group of company assets, (2) borrowing extensively against the company's remaining assets, and (3) using the proceeds to fund a premium-priced self-tender for a large percentage of the company's stock. After this transaction, shareholders are left with cash and an equity interest in a smaller and more highly leveraged business. Assume, in addition, that, as between the two similar transactions, one prepared by management and one by the "raider," a reasonable investor might well prefer the raider's all-cash offer. In reviewing management's preference for its own plan, should a court assume that the target's board has a *Revlon* duty to get the highest current value for the shareholders? Or does the court use the *Unocal* standard of "reasonable in relation to a threat"? See *AC Acquisitions Corp. v. Anderson Clayton & Co.*, 519 A.2d 103 (Del. Ch. 1986).

13.5 PULLING TOGETHER *UNOCAL* AND *REVLON*

A much-discussed Delaware Supreme Court decision of the late eighties, *Paramount Communications, Inc. v. Time, Inc.*, addressed both the question of whether the board has a duty to redeem its poison pill and the issue of what triggers *Revlon* duties. Discussion of the first issue was dicta, since Time, Inc., the corporate defendant, had not relied on its poison pill to defend against a hostile attack by Paramount Communications, Inc. That characterization, however, detracts little from the force of the court's statements.

PARAMOUNT COMMUNICATIONS, INC. v. TIME, INC.

571 A.2d 1140 (Del. 1989)

[Paramount Communications' unsuccessful bid for Time, Inc., was perhaps the most famous hostile takeover attempt of the 1980s. In brief, Paramount launched its bid after Time had already initiated a friendly merger transaction with Warner Communications. Time succeeded in thwarting Paramount by transforming its original merger deal into a tender offer by Time for Warner, thereby making itself too large (and debt-ridden) to be an attractive target for Paramount. Prior to Time's tender offer, both Paramount and several groups of Time's shareholders sought to enjoin the tender offer in order to give Time's shareholders an opportunity to choose between this offer and Paramount's bid. The Delaware Court of Chancery recognized that Time's shareholders apparently preferred the higher price offered by the Paramount deal but nonetheless refused to enjoin Time's tender offer, on the grounds that, since Time's board was not under a *Revlon* duty to optimize Time's current stock value, the board had acted reasonably in pursuing its long-term plan to create business value.

The facts of the case were as follows. Time's long-term business strategy was to expand from a publishing company into a diversified multimedia and entertainment company. Pursuant to this strategy, Time initiated merger negotiations with Warner Communications. As both companies were in the $10-12 billion range, the proposed combination was to be a "merger of equals." The negotiations were protracted. The chief sticking points were the management structure of the combined company and the role that Steven Ross, Warner's extraordinarily successful CEO, would play in the new entity.

On March 3, 1989, the parties signed a stock-for-stock merger agreement that cast Time in the role of the surviving corporation but would have transferred 62 percent of Time's common stock to Warner shareholders at an exchange ratio reflecting the current market price of the shares in the two firms (i.e., Warner had a somewhat larger market capitalization). The agreement also provided that the surviving corporation would be renamed Time-Warner Corporation, would have an expanded board to be divided equally between the old Time and Warner directors, and would have shared management with a succession plan. Under the management arrangement, there would be co-CEOs for a period of five years. One would be from the Time organization (Nicholas) and one from the Warner organization (Ross). After the five-year period, Ross would retire and Nicholas would continue as the sole CEO. Ross received a compensation package valued at roughly $200 million. Thus, Time bargained hard to assure the ultimate ascendancy of its managers in the combined firm. A final provision of the agreement gave each party the option to trigger a share exchange in which Time would receive 9.4 percent of Warner's stock and Warner would receive 11.1 percent of Time's stock. The purpose of this option was to deter third-party bids for Time or Warner prior to the merger vote.

On June 7, 1989, Paramount announced a $175 per share cash bid for all of Time's shares, contingent on the termination of the share exchange agreement, the redemption of Time's poison pill, and the resolution of legal difficulties attending the transfer of Time properties to Paramount. Paramount's offer came two weeks before Time's shareholders were scheduled to vote on the Warner merger. Time's shares had traded at a high of $50 prior to the Warner merger agreement and $122 prior to Paramount's offer. After Paramount's offer, they jumped to a high of $188/share.

Time's board rejected Paramount's price as grossly inadequate and concluded that the Warner deal was a better vehicle for Time's strategic goals. On June 16, Wasserstein, Perella, Time's investment banker, informed Time's board that a "control market value" for Time would exceed $250/share, although an earlier Wasserstein valuation conducted in connection with the Time-Warner agreement had valued Time at between $189 and $212 per share. In addition, Wasserstein estimated that Time's stock would trade at between $106 and $188 if the Time-Warner combination succeeded.

Having rejected Paramount's offer, however, Time's management faced a dilemma: It had planned the stock-for-stock merger that required a shareholder vote. But if Time's shareholders were to vote, they would almost certainly reject the proposed merger in the hope of tendering into the higher Paramount offer. Therefore, Time and Warner abandoned their merger agreement and agreed that Time would make a friendly cash tender offer to Warner shareholders and that, following the closing of that offer, a merger between Time and Warner would be effectuated. The governance terms in the new Time-Warner agreement were identical to those in the old agreement. The chief difference was that Time was forced to borrow $10 billion to purchase Warner shares at a 56 percent cash premium over their preagreement market price.

As a result of various delays that were caused by Paramount getting regulatory approval to acquire Time's programming and cable TV franchises, Paramount could not pursue its offer for Time immediately. On June 22, Paramount increased its cash offer to $200/share in the hope of dissuading Time from buying Warner, but to no avail. Paramount then sought to enjoin Time's offer in the Delaware Chancery Court, where it was joined by several groups of Time shareholders also seeking to block Time's maneuver. It was clear that if Time's offer went forward, Paramount would lack the incentive and the resources to bid for the heavily indebted Time-Warner entity that would emerge.

Here we pick up the Delaware Supreme Court's opinion after the statement of facts.]

HORSEY, J.:

The Shareholder Plaintiffs first assert a *Revlon* claim. They contend that the March 4 Time-Warner [Original Stock-for-Stock Merger] agreement effectively put Time up for sale, triggering *Revlon* duties, requiring Time's board to enhance short-term shareholder value and to treat all other interested acquirers on an equal basis. The Shareholder Plaintiffs base this argument on two facts: (i) the ultimate Time-Warner exchange ratio of .465 favoring Warner, resulting in Warner shareholders' receipt of 62% of the combined company; and (ii) the subjective intent of Time's directors as evidenced in their statements that the market might perceive the Time-Warner merger as putting Time up "for sale" and their adoption of various defensive measures.

The Shareholder Plaintiffs further contend that Time's directors, in structuring the original merger transaction to be "takeover-proof," triggered *Revlon* duties by foreclosing their shareholders from any prospect of obtaining a control premium. In short, plaintiffs argue that Time's board's decision to merge with Warner imposed a fiduciary duty to maximize immediate share value and not erect unreasonable barriers to further bids. . . .

Paramount asserts only a *Unocal* claim in which the shareholder plaintiffs join. Paramount contends that the Chancellor, in applying the first part of the *Unocal* test, erred in finding that Time's board had reasonable grounds to believe that Paramount posed both a legally cognizable threat to Time shareholders and a danger to Time's corporate policy and effectiveness. Paramount also contests the court's finding that Time's board made a reasonable and objective investigation of Paramount's offer so as to be informed before rejecting it. Paramount further claims that the court erred in applying *Unocal*'s second part in finding Time's response to be "reasonable." Paramount points primarily to the preclusive effect of the revised agreement which denied Time shareholders the opportunity both to vote on the agreement and to respond to Paramount's tender offer. Paramount argues that the underlying motivation of Time's board in adopting these defensive measures was management's desire to perpetuate itself in office.

The Court of Chancery posed the pivotal question presented by this case to be: Under what circumstances must a board of directors abandon an in-place plan of corporate development in order to provide its shareholders with the option to elect and realize an immediate control premium? . . .

While we affirm the result reached by the Chancellor, we think it unwise to place undue emphasis upon long-term versus short-term corporate strategy. Two key predicates underpin our analysis. First, Delaware law imposes on a board of directors the duty to manage the business and affairs of the corporation. 8 Del. C. §141(a). This broad mandate includes a conferred authority to set a corporate course of action, including time frame, designed to enhance corporate profitability. Thus, the question of "long-term" versus "short-term" values is largely irrelevant because directors, generally, are obliged to charter a course for a corporation which is in its best interest without regard to a fixed investment horizon. Second, absent a limited set of circumstances as defined under *Revlon*, a board of directors, while always required to act in an informed manner, is not under any per se duty to maximize shareholder value in the short term, even in the context of a takeover. In our view, the pivotal question presented by this case is: "Did Time, by entering into the proposed merger with Warner, put itself up for sale?" A resolution of that issue through application of *Revlon* has a significant [b]earing upon the resolution of the derivative *Unocal* issue. . . .

We first take up plaintiffs' principal *Revlon* argument, summarized above. In rejecting this argument, the Chancellor found the original Time-Warner merger agreement not to constitute a "change of control" and concluded that the transaction did not trigger *Revlon* duties. The Chancellor's conclusion is premised on a finding that "[b]efore the merger agreement was signed, control of the corporation existed in a fluid aggregation of unaffiliated shareholders representing a voting majority — in other words, in the market." The Chancellor's findings of fact are supported by the record and his conclusion is correct as a matter of law. However, we premise our rejection of plaintiffs' *Revlon* claim on different grounds, namely, the absence of any substantial evidence to conclude that Time's board, in negotiating with Warner, made the dissolution or breakup of the corporate entity inevitable, as was the case in *Revlon*.

Under Delaware law there are, generally speaking and without excluding other possibilities, two circumstances which may implicate *Revlon* duties. The first, and clearer one, is when a corporation initiates an active bidding process seeking to sell itself or to effect a business reorganization involving a clear break-up of the company. . . . However, *Revlon* duties may also be triggered where, in response to a bidder's offer, a target abandons its long-term strategy and seeks an alternative transaction also involving the breakup of the company. Thus, in *Revlon,* when the board responded to Pantry Pride's offer by contemplating a "bust-up" sale of assets in a leveraged acquisition, we imposed upon the board a duty to maximize immediate shareholder value and an obligation to auction the company fairly. If, however, the board's reaction to a hostile tender offer is found to constitute only a defensive response and not an abandonment of the corporation's continued existence, *Revlon* duties are not triggered, though *Unocal* duties attach. . . .

Finally, we do not find in Time's recasting of its merger agreement with Warner from a share exchange to a share purchase a basis to conclude that Time had either abandoned its strategic plan or made a sale of Time inevitable. The Chancellor found that although the merged Time-Warner company would be large (with a value approaching approximately $30 billion), recent takeover cases have proven that acquisition of the combined company might nonetheless be possible. The legal consequence is that *Unocal* alone applies to determine whether the business judgment rule attaches to the revised agreement. . . .

We turn now to plaintiffs' *Unocal* claim. . . .

. . . Time's decision in 1988 to combine with Warner was made only after what could be fairly characterized as an exhaustive appraisal of Time's future as a corporation. After concluding in 1983-84 that the corporation must expand to survive, and beyond journalism into entertainment, the board combed the field of available entertainment companies. By 1987 Time had focused upon Warner; by late July 1988 Time's board was convinced that Warner would provide the best "fit" for Time to achieve its strategic objectives. The record attests to the zealousness of Time's executives, fully supported by their directors, in seeing to the preservation of Time's "culture," i.e., its perceived editorial integrity in journalism. We find ample evidence in the record to support the Chancellor's conclusion that the Time board's decision to expand the business of the company through its March 3 merger with Warner was entitled to the protection of the business judgment rule. . . .

The Chancellor reached a different conclusion in addressing the Time-Warner transaction as revised three months later. He found that the revised agreement was defense-motivated. . . . Thus, the court . . . analyzed the Time board's June 16 decision under *Unocal.* The court ruled that *Unocal* applied to all director actions taken, following receipt of Paramount's hostile tender offer, that were reasonably determined to be defensive. Clearly that was a correct ruling. . . .

Unocal involved a two-tier, highly coercive tender offer. In such a case, the threat is obvious: shareholders may be compelled to tender to avoid being treated adversely in the second stage of the transaction. . . .

Since Paramount's offer was [not two-tier, but all-shares and] all-cash, the only conceivable "threat," plaintiffs argue, was inadequate value. We disapprove of such a narrow and rigid construction of *Unocal*, for the reasons which follow.

Plaintiffs' position represents a fundamental misconception of our standard of review under *Unocal* principally because it would involve the court in substituting its judgment as to what is a "better" deal for that of a corporation's board of directors. To the extent that the Court of Chancery has recently done so in certain of its opinions, we hereby reject such approach as not in keeping with a proper *Unocal* analysis. See, e.g., *Interco*, 551 A.2d 787, and its progeny. . . .

The usefulness of *Unocal* as an analytical tool is precisely its flexibility in the face of a variety of fact scenarios. *Unocal* is not intended as an abstract standard; neither is it a structured and mechanistic procedure of appraisal. Thus, we have said that directors may consider, when evaluating the threat posed by a takeover bid, the "inadequacy of the price offered, nature and timing of the offer, questions of illegality, the impact on 'constituencies' other than shareholders, the risk of nonconsummation and the quality of securities being offered in the exchange." 493 A.2d at 955. The open-ended analysis mandated by *Unocal* is not intended to lead to a simple mathematical exercise: that is, of comparing the discounted value of Time-Warner's expected trading price at some future date with Paramount's offer and determining which is the higher. Indeed, in our view, precepts underlying the business judgment rule militate against a court's engaging in the process of attempting to appraise and evaluate the relative merits of a long-term versus a short-term investment goal for shareholders. To engage in such an exercise is a distortion of the *Unocal* process and, in particular, the application of the second part of *Unocal*'s test, discussed below.

In this case, the Time board reasonably determined that inadequate value was not the only legally cognizable threat that Paramount's all-cash, all-shares offer could present. Time's board concluded that Paramount's eleventh hour offer posed other threats. One concern was that Time shareholders might elect to tender into Paramount's cash offer in ignorance or a mistaken belief of the strategic benefit which a business combination with Warner might produce. Moreover, Time viewed the conditions attached to Paramount's offer as introducing a degree of uncertainty that skewed a comparative analysis. Further, the timing of Paramount's offer to follow issuance of Time's proxy notice was viewed as arguably designed to upset, if not confuse, the Time stockholders' vote. Given this record evidence, we cannot conclude that the Time board's decision of June 6 that Paramount's offer posed a threat to corporate policy and effectiveness was lacking in good faith or dominated by motives of either entrenchment or self-interest. . . .

We turn to the second part of the *Unocal* analysis. . . . As applied to the facts of this case, the question is whether the record evidence supports the Court of Chancery's conclusion that the restructuring of the Time-Warner transaction, including the adoption of several preclusive defensive measures, was a reasonable response in relation to a perceived threat.

Paramount argues that, assuming its tender offer posed a threat, Time's response was unreasonable in precluding Time's shareholders from accepting the tender offer or receiving a control premium in the immediately foreseeable future. Once again, the contention stems, we believe, from a fundamental misunderstanding of where the power of corporate governance lies. Delaware law confers the management of the corporate enterprise to the stockholders' duly elected board representatives. The fiduciary duty to manage a corporate enterprise includes the selection of a time frame for achievement of corporate goals. That duty may not be delegated to the stockholders. Directors are not obliged to abandon a deliberately conceived corporate plan for a short-term shareholder profit unless there is clearly no basis to sustain the corporate strategy. See, e.g., Revlon, 506 A.2d 173.

Although the Chancellor blurred somewhat the discrete analyses required under *Unocal*, he did conclude that Time's board reasonably perceived Paramount's offer to be a significant threat to the planned Time-Warner merger and that Time's response was not "overly broad." . . .

. . . Time's responsive action to Paramount's tender offer was not aimed at "cramming down" on its shareholders a management-sponsored alternative, but rather had as its goal the carrying forward of a pre-existing transaction in an altered form. Thus, the response was reasonably related to the threat. The Chancellor noted that the revised agreement and its accompanying safety devices did not preclude Paramount from making an offer for the combined Time-Warner company or from changing the conditions of its offer so as not to make the offer dependent upon the nullification of the Time-Warner agreement. Thus, the response was proportionate. We affirm the Chancellor's rulings as clearly supported by the record. . . .

QUESTIONS AND NOTES ON TIME-WARNER

1. Under *Time-Warner*'s restatement of the *Unocal* doctrine, can a hostile bidder ever force management to redeem a poison pill that is said to protect a company's existing business plan? Does it matter whether the business plan is clearly a defensive response to a hostile takeover effort, such as those in *AC Acquisitions* and *Interco*? Does it matter whether the plan was in place prior to the offer?

2. In reaching out to disapprove the Court of Chancery's *Interco* decision, the Delaware Supreme Court in *Time-Warner* suggests that courts are not authorized to substitute their judgment for the target board's judgment to retain the pill. Arguably, however, the supreme court mischaracterized *Interco*, since, in that case, the chancery court did not make a business decision itself but ruled that the *shareholders* ought to be permitted to decide between management's recapitalization transaction and the hostile bidder's all-cash deal. Thus, the chancery court ruling addressed the legal allocation of decision-making power between boards and shareholders — a fundamental subject of corporate law and, a fortiori, an appropriate subject for courts deciding issues of corporate law.

3. *Time-Warner* might be read to imply that a board may maintain a pill defense indefinitely whenever it fears that shareholders might "wrongly" conclude that a hostile offer is fairly priced, despite the board's contrary view. However, since *Time-Warner* repudiates *Interco* (in which the board pursued an alternative recapitalization transaction), another interpretation of *Time-Warner* is that the pill may sometimes — but not always — be used to protect new or defensive transactions.[35] These two interpretations are consistent in the sense that it is logically possible to bar the chancery court from pulling the pill, while permitting it to enjoin disproportionate alternative responses to hostile tender offers. In other words, it is logically possible to allow the court to bar management's "disproportionate" business plans, while refusing to allow shareholders to pass on these plans by removing the pill. Is there irony here in light of the court's rationale for disapproving the *Interco* result?

4. Does a board's fiduciary duty to be informed require it to negotiate with every plausible acquirer that approaches the corporation with a take-over proposal? At least when the suitor appears to be financially responsible, the duty of care might be construed to require the board to make *some* inquiry before rejecting unsolicited offers. Such a rule would impose real costs, however. Once the public learns of discussions with a would-be acquirer (and this sort of information regularly tends to leak out), the price of a target company's stock inevitably rises in anticipation of a control payment. Short-term investors (arbitrageurs) buy into the target stock, and risk-averse, long-term investors sell as prices rise. The new stockholders will exert pressure on management to either accept a deal or propose an alternative. Since the dominant view among practitioners, managers, and politicians during the 1980s was that there were too many takeovers,[36] it is hardly surprising that the Delaware courts did not construe the duty of care or the duty to be informed to require the board to investigate every merger proposal. That is, a board that had decided that its company was not for sale could "just say no" without negotiating with would-be acquirers.[37]

5. On the *Revlon* side of the *Unocal-Revlon* doctrinal dichotomy, the *Time-Warner* court appears to reject the change-of-control test as the trigger for invoking judicial scrutiny. But stay tuned — the moving hand writes, and having written, sometimes writes again. The next chapter in Delaware's law of corporate takeovers, the *QVC* case, which follows, returns to the sale-of-control test for *Revlon* duties.

---

35. The *Time-Warner* court added at the end of the excerpt reproduced above that "we have found that even in light of a valid threat, management actions that are coercive in nature or force upon shareholders a management-sponsored alternative to a hostile offer may be struck down as unreasonable and nonproportionate responses" (citing *Mills Acquisition Co. v. Macmillan, Inc.,* 559 A.2d 1261 (Del. 1989), and *AC Acquisition Corp.,* 519 A.2d 103 (Del. Ch. 1986).

36. This was not, of course, the dominant view among financial economists or corporate law professors.

37. That is, boards have the legal power to "just say no" under Delaware case law. As managers in both *Unocal* and *Revlon* learned, however, as a practical matter it may be impossible to say no without offering shareholders an alternative transaction designed to give value comparable to what the acquirer offers.

PARAMOUNT COMMUNICATIONS, INC. v. QVC NETWORK, INC.

637 A.2d 34 (Del. 1994)

VEASEY, C.J.:

In this appeal we review an order of the Court of Chancery ... , preliminarily enjoining certain defensive measures designed to facilitate a so-called strategic alliance between Viacom Inc. ("Viacom") and Paramount Communications Inc. ("Paramount") approved by the board of directors of Paramount ... and to thwart an unsolicited, more valuable, tender offer by QVC Network Inc. ("QVC"). In affirming, we hold that the sale of control in this case, which is at the heart of the proposed strategic alliance, implicates enhanced judicial scrutiny of the conduct of the Paramount Board under [*Unocal* and *Revlon*]. ...

... Paramount owns and operates a diverse group of entertainment businesses, including motion picture and television studios, book publishers, professional sports teams and amusement parks.

There are 15 persons serving on the Paramount Board. Four directors are officer-employees.... Paramount's 11 outside directors are distinguished and experienced business persons who are present or former senior executives of public corporations or financial institutions.

... Viacom is controlled by Sumner M. Redstone ("Redstone"), its Chairman and Chief Executive Officer, who owns indirectly approximately 85.2 percent of Viacom's voting Class A stock and approximately 69.2 percent of Viacom's nonvoting Class B stock. ... Viacom has a wide range of entertainment operations, including a number of well-known cable television channels such as MTV, Nickelodeon, Showtime, and The Movie Channel. ...

... Barry Diller ("Diller"), [is] the Chairman and Chief Executive Officer of QVC, [and] is also a substantial stockholder. QVC sells a variety of merchandise through a televised shopping channel. ...

Beginning in the late 1980s, Paramount investigated the possibility of acquiring or merging with other companies in the entertainment, media, or communications industry. Paramount considered such transactions to be desirable, and perhaps necessary, in order to keep pace with competitors in the rapidly evolving field of entertainment and communications. Consistent with its goal of strategic expansion, Paramount made a tender offer for Time Inc. in 1989, but was ultimately unsuccessful. ...

Although Paramount had considered a possible combination of Paramount and Viacom as early as 1990, recent efforts to explore such a transaction began at a dinner meeting between Redstone and Davis on April 20, 1993. ...

On September 12, 1993, the Paramount Board ... unanimously approved the Original Merger Agreement whereby Paramount would merge with and into Viacom. The terms of the merger provided that each share of Paramount common stock would be converted into 0.10 shares of Viacom Class A voting stock, 0.90 shares of Viacom Class B nonvoting stock, and $9.10 in cash. In addition, the Paramount Board agreed to amend its "poison pill" Rights Agreement to exempt the proposed merger with Viacom. The Original Merger Agreement also contained several provisions designed to make it more difficult for a potential competing bid to succeed. We focus, as did the Court of Chancery, on three of these defensive provisions: a "no-shop" provision (the "No-Shop Provision"), the Termination Fee, and the Stock Option Agreement.

First, under the No-Shop Provision, the Paramount Board agreed that Paramount would not solicit, encourage, discuss, negotiate, or endorse any competing transaction unless: (a) a third party "makes an unsolicited written, bona fide proposal, which is not subject to any material contingencies relating to financing"; and (b) the Paramount Board determines that discussions or negotiations with the third party are necessary for the Paramount Board to comply with its fiduciary duties.

Second, under the Termination Fee provision, Viacom would receive a $100 million termination fee if: (a) Paramount terminated the Original Merger Agreement because of a competing transaction; (b) Paramount's stockholders did not approve the merger; or (c) the Paramount Board recommended a competing transaction.

The third and most significant deterrent device was the Stock Option Agreement, which granted to Viacom an option to purchase approximately 19.9 percent (23,699,000 shares) of Paramount's outstanding common stock at $69.14 per share if any of the triggering events for the Termination Fee occurred. In addition to the customary terms that are normally associated with a stock option, the Stock Option Agreement contained two provisions that were both unusual and highly beneficial to Viacom: (a) Viacom was permitted to pay for the shares with a senior subordinated note of questionable marketability instead of cash, thereby avoiding the need to raise the $1.6 billion purchase price (the "Note Feature"); and (b) Viacom could elect to require Paramount to pay Viacom in cash a sum equal to the difference between the purchase price and the market price of Paramount's stock (the "Put Feature"). Because the Stock Option Agreement was not "capped" to limit its maximum dollar value, it had the potential to reach (and in this case did reach) unreasonable levels.

After the execution of the Original Merger Agreement and the Stock Option Agreement on September 12, 1993, Paramount and Viacom announced their proposed merger. In a number of public statements, the parties indicated that the pending transaction was a virtual certainty. Redstone described it as a "marriage" that would "never be torn asunder" and stated that only a "nuclear attack" could break the deal. . . .

Despite these attempts to discourage a competing bid, Diller sent a letter to Davis on September 20, 1993, proposing a merger in which QVC would acquire Paramount for approximately $80 per share, consisting of 0.893 shares of QVC common stock and $30 in cash. QVC also expressed its eagerness to meet with Paramount to negotiate the details of a transaction. When the Paramount Board met on September 27, it was advised by Davis that the Original Merger Agreement prohibited Paramount from having discussions with QVC (or anyone else) unless certain conditions were satisfied. In particular, QVC had to supply evidence that its proposal was not subject to financing contingencies. . . .

[After] QVC provided Paramount with evidence of QVC's financing, [t]he Paramount Board ... decided to authorize management to meet with QVC. Davis also informed the Paramount Board that Booz-Allen & Hamilton ("Booz-Allen"), a management consulting firm, had been retained to assess, inter alia, the incremental earnings potential from a Paramount-Viacom merger and a Paramount-QVC merger. Discussions proceeded slowly, however, due to a delay in Paramount signing a confidentiality agreement. In response to Paramount's request for information, QVC provided two binders of documents to Paramount on October 20.

On October 21, 1993, QVC filed this action and publicly announced an $80 cash tender offer for 51 percent of Paramount's outstanding shares (the "QVC tender offer"). Each remaining share of Paramount common stock would be converted into 1.42857 shares of QVC common stock in a second-step merger. The tender offer was conditioned on, among other things, the invalidation of the Stock Option Agreement. . . .

Confronted by QVC's hostile bid, which on its face offered over $10 per share more than the consideration provided by the Original Merger Agreement, Viacom realized that it would need to raise its bid in order to remain competitive. . . . In effect, the opportunity for a "new deal" with Viacom was at hand for the Paramount Board. With the QVC hostile bid offering greater value to the Paramount stockholders, the Paramount Board had considerable leverage with Viacom.

At a special meeting on October 24, 1993, the Paramount Board approved the Amended Merger Agreement and an amendment to the Stock Option Agreement. The Amended Merger Agreement was, however, essentially the same as the Original Merger Agreement, except that it included a few new provisions. One provision related to an $80 per share cash tender offer by Viacom for 51 percent of Paramount's stock, and another changed the merger consideration so that each share of Paramount would be converted into 0.20408 shares of Viacom Class A voting stock, 1.08317 shares of Viacom Class B nonvoting stock, and 0.20408 shares of a new series of Viacom convertible preferred stock. The Amended Merger Agreement also added a provision giving Paramount the right not to amend its Rights Agreement to exempt Viacom if the Paramount Board determined that such an amendment would be inconsistent with its fiduciary duties because another offer constituted a "better alternative." Finally, the Paramount Board was given the power to terminate the Amended Merger Agreement if it withdrew its recommendation of the Viacom transaction or recommended a competing transaction.

Although the Amended Merger Agreement offered more consideration to the Paramount stockholders and somewhat more flexibility to the Paramount Board ..., the defensive measures designed to make a competing bid more difficult were not removed or modified. . . .

On November 6, 1993, Viacom unilaterally raised its tender offer price to $85 per share in cash and offered a comparable increase in the value of the securities being proposed in the second-step merger. At a telephonic meeting held later that day, the Paramount Board agreed to recommend Viacom's higher bid to Paramount's stockholders.

QVC responded to Viacom's higher bid on November 12 by increasing its tender offer to $90 per share and by increasing the securities for its second-step merger by a similar amount. . . .

At its meeting on November 15, 1993, the Paramount Board determined that the new QVC offer was not in the best interests of the stockholders. The purported basis for this conclusion was that QVC's bid was excessively conditional. The Paramount Board did not communicate with QVC regarding the status of the conditions because it believed that the No-Shop Provision prevented such communication in the absence of firm financing. . . .

Under normal circumstances, neither the courts nor the stockholders should interfere with the managerial decisions of the directors. . . .

Nevertheless, there are rare situations which mandate that a court take a more direct and active role in overseeing the decisions made and actions taken by directors. In these situations, a court subjects the directors' conduct to enhanced scrutiny to ensure that it is reasonable.[9] The decisions of this Court have clearly established the circumstances where such enhanced scrutiny will be applied. . . . The case at bar implicates two such circumstances: (1) the approval of a transaction resulting in a sale of control, and (2) the adoption of defensive measures in response to a threat to corporate control.

When a majority of a corporation's voting shares are acquired by a single person or entity, or by a cohesive group acting together, there is a significant diminution in the voting power of those who thereby become minority stockholders. Under the statutory framework of the General Corporation Law, many of the most fundamental corporate changes can be implemented only if they are approved by a majority vote of the stockholders. . . . Because of the overriding importance of voting rights, this Court and the Court of Chancery have consistently acted to protect stockholders from unwarranted interference with such rights.

In the absence of devices protecting the minority stockholders, stockholder votes are likely to become mere formalities where there is a majority stockholder. For example, minority stockholders can be deprived of a continuing equity interest in their corporation by means of a cash-out merger. *Weinberger,* 457 A.2d at 703. Absent effective protective provisions, minority stockholders must rely for protection solely on the fiduciary duties owed to them by the directors and the majority stockholder, since the minority stockholders have lost the power to influence corporate direction through the ballot. The acquisition of majority status and the consequent privilege of exerting the powers of majority ownership come at a price. That price is usually a control premium which recognizes not only the value of a control block of shares, but also compensates the minority stockholders for their resulting loss of voting power.

In the case before us, the public stockholders (in the aggregate) currently own a majority of Paramount's voting stock. Control of the

---

9. By November 15, 1993, the value of the Stock Option Agreement had increased to nearly $500 million based on the $90 QVC bid. See Court of Chancery Opinion, 635 A.2d at 1260.

corporation is not vested in a single person, entity, or group, but vested in the fluid aggregation of unaffiliated stockholders. In the event the Paramount-Viacom transaction is consummated, the public stockholders will receive cash and a minority equity voting position in the surviving corporation. Following such consummation, there will be a controlling stockholder who will have the voting power to: (a) elect directors; (b) cause a break-up of the corporation: (c) merge it with another company; (d) cashout the public stockholders: (e) amend the certificate of incorporation; (f) sell all or substantially all of the corporate assets; or (g) otherwise alter materially the nature of the corporation and the public stockholders' interests. Irrespective of the present Paramount Board's vision of a long-term strategic alliance with Viacom, the proposed sale of control would provide the new controlling stockholder with the power to alter that vision.

Because of the intended sale of control, the Paramount-Viacom transaction has economic consequences of considerable significance to the Paramount stockholders. Once control has shifted, the current Paramount stockholders will have no leverage in the future to demand another control premium. As a result, the Paramount stockholders are entitled to receive, and should receive, a control premium and/or protective devices of significant value. There being no such protective provisions in the Viacom-Paramount transaction, the Paramount directors had an obligation to take the maximum advantage of the current opportunity to realize for the stockholders the best value reasonably available.

. . . In the sale of control context, the directors must focus on one primary objective — to secure the transaction offering the best value reasonably available for the stockholders — and they must exercise their fiduciary duties to further that end. . . .

. . . Moreover, the role of outside, independent directors becomes particularly important because of the magnitude of a sale of control transaction and the possibility, in certain cases, that management may not necessarily be impartial. . . .

[The] *Barkan* [decision] teaches some of the methods by which a board can fulfill its obligation to seek the best value reasonably available to the stockholders. 567 A.2d at 1286-87. . . . They include conducting an auction, canvassing the market, etc. Delaware law recognizes that there is "no single blueprint" that directors must follow. . . .

In determining which alternative provides the best value for the stockholders, a board of directors is not limited to considering only the amount of cash involved . . . Where stock or other non-cash consideration is involved, the board should try to quantify its value, if feasible, to achieve an objective comparison of the alternatives. . . . While the assessment of these factors may be complex, the board's goal is straightforward: Having informed themselves of all material information reasonably available, the directors must decide which alternative is most likely to offer the best value reasonably available to the stockholders.

Board action in the circumstances presented here is subject to enhanced scrutiny. Such scrutiny is mandated by: (a) the threatened diminution of the current stockholders' voting power; (b) the fact that an asset belonging to public stockholders (a control premium) is being sold and may never be available again[;] and (c) the traditional concern of Delaware courts for actions which impair or impede stockholder voting rights. . . .

The key features of an enhanced scrutiny test are: (a) a judicial determination regarding the adequacy of the decisionmaking process employed by the directors, including the information on which the directors based their decision; and (b) a judicial examination of the reasonableness of the directors' action in light of the circumstances then existing. The directors have the burden of proving that they were adequately informed and acted reasonably.

Although an enhanced scrutiny test involves a review of the reasonableness of the substantive merits of a board's actions,[17] a court should not ignore the complexity of the directors' task in a sale of control. There are many business and financial considerations implicated in investigating and selecting the best value reasonably available. The board of directors is the corporate decisionmaking body best equipped to make these judgments. Accordingly, a court applying enhanced judicial scrutiny should be deciding whether the directors made a reasonable decision, not a perfect decision. If a board selected one of several reasonable alternatives, a court should not second-guess that choice even though it might have decided otherwise or subsequent events may have cast doubt on the board's determination. Thus, courts will not substitute their business judgment for that of the directors, but will determine if the directors' decision was, on balance, within a range of reasonableness. . . .

The Paramount defendants and Viacom assert that the fiduciary obligations and the enhanced judicial scrutiny discussed above are not implicated in this case in the absence of a "break-up" of the corporation, and that the order granting the preliminary injunction should be reversed. This argument is based on their erroneous interpretation of our decisions in *Revlon* and *Time-Warner*. . . .

Although [the earlier] *Macmillan* and *Barkan* [decisions] are clear in holding that a change of control imposes on directors the obligation to obtain the best value reasonably available to the stockholders, the Paramount defendants have interpreted our decision in *Time-Warner* as requiring a corporate break-up in order for that obligation to apply. The facts in *Time-Warner*, however, were quite different from the facts of this case. . . . In *Time-Warner*, the Chancellor held that there was no change of control in the original stock-for-stock merger between Time and Warner because Time would be owned by a fluid aggregation of unaffiliated stockholders both before and after the merger. . . .

In our affirmance of the Court of Chancery's well-reasoned decision, this Court held that "The Chancellor's findings of fact are supported by the record and *his conclusion is correct as a matter of law.*" 571 A.2d at 1150 (emphasis added). Nevertheless, the Paramount defendants here have

---

17. It is to be remembered that, in cases where the traditional business judgment rule is applicable and the board acted with due care, in good faith, and in the honest belief that they are acting in the best interests of the stockholder (which is not this case), the Court gives great deference to the substance of the directors' decision and will not invalidate the decision. . . .

argued that a break-up is a requirement and have focused on the following language in our Time-Warner decision:

> However, we premise our rejection of plaintiffs' *Revlon* claim on different grounds, namely, the absence of any substantial evidence to conclude that Time's board, in negotiating with Warner, made the dissolution or break-up of the corporate entity inevitable, as was the case in *Revlon.*
>
> Under Delaware law there are, generally speaking and without excluding other possibilities, two circumstances which may implicate *Revlon* duties. The first, and clearer one, is when a corporation initiates an active bidding process seeking to sell itself or to effect a business reorganization involving a clear breakup of the company. However, *Revlon* duties may also be triggered where, in response to a bidder's offer, a target abandons its long-term strategy and seeks an alternative transaction involving the breakup of the company. *Id.* at 1150 (emphasis added) (citation and footnote omitted).

The Paramount defendants have misread the holding of *Time-Warner.* Contrary to their argument, our decision in *Time-Warner* expressly states that the two general scenarios discussed in the above-quoted paragraph are not the only instances where "*Revlon* duties" may be implicated. The Paramount defendants' argument totally ignores the phrase "without excluding other possibilities." Moreover, the instant case is clearly within the first general scenario set forth in *Time-Warner.* The Paramount Board, albeit unintentionally, had "initiated an active bidding process seeking to sell itself" by agreeing to sell control of the corporation to Viacom in circumstances where another potential acquirer (QVC) was equally interested in being a bidder.

The Paramount defendants' position that both a change of control and a break-up are required must be rejected. Such a holding would unduly restrict the application of *Revlon,* is inconsistent with this Court's decisions in *Barkan* and *Macmillan,* and has no basis in policy. There are few events that have a more significant impact on the stockholders than a sale of control or a corporate break-up. Each event represents a fundamental (and perhaps irrevocable) change in the nature of the corporate enterprise from a practical standpoint. It is the significance of each of these events that justifies: (a) focusing on the directors' obligation to seek the best value reasonably available to the stockholders; and (b) requiring a close scrutiny of board action which could be contrary to the stockholders' interests.

Accordingly, when a corporation undertakes a transaction which will cause: (a) a change in corporate control; or (b) a break-up of the corporate entity, the directors' obligation is to seek the best value reasonably available to the stockholders. This obligation arises because the effect of the Viacom-Paramount transaction, if consummated, is to shift control of Paramount from the public stockholders to a controlling stockholder, Viacom. Neither *Time-Warner* nor any other decision of this Court holds that a "break-up" of the company is essential to give rise to this obligation where there is a sale of control. . . .

We now turn to duties of the Paramount Board under the facts of this case and our conclusions as to the breaches of those duties that warrant injunctive relief. . . .

Under the facts of this case, the Paramount directors had the obligation: (a) to be diligent and vigilant in examining critically the Paramount-Viacom transaction and the QVC tender offers; (b) to act in good faith; (c) to obtain, and act with due care on, all material information reasonably available, including information necessary to compare the two offers to determine which of these transactions, or an alternative course of action, would provide the best value reasonably available to the stockholders; and (d) to negotiate actively and in good faith with both Viacom and QVC to that end.

Having decided to sell control of the corporation, the Paramount directors were required to evaluate critically whether or not all material aspects of the Paramount-Viacom transaction (separately and in the aggregate) were reasonable and in the best interests of the Paramount stockholders in light of current circumstances, including: the change of control premium, the Stock Option Agreement, the Termination Fee, the coercive nature of both the Viacom and QVC tender offers,[18] the No-Shop Provision, and the proposed disparate use of the Rights Agreement as to the Viacom and QVC tender offers, respectively.

These obligations necessarily implicated various issues, including the questions of whether or not those provisions . . . : (a) adversely affected the value provided to the Paramount stockholders; (b) inhibited or encouraged alternative bids; (c) were enforceable contractual obligations in light of the directors' fiduciary duties; and (d) in the end would advance or retard the Paramount directors' obligation to secure for the Paramount stockholders the best value reasonably available under the circumstances.

The Paramount defendants contend that they were precluded by certain contractual provisions including the No-Shop Provision, from negotiating with QVC or seeking alternatives. Such provisions, whether or not they are presumptively valid in the abstract, may not validly define or limit the directors' fiduciary duties under Delaware law or prevent the Paramount directors from carrying out their fiduciary duties under Delaware law. To the extent such provisions are inconsistent with those duties, they are invalid and unenforceable. . . .

Since the Paramount directors had already decided to sell control, they had an obligation to continue their search for the best value reasonably available to the stockholders. This continuing obligation included the responsibility, at the October 24 board meeting and thereafter, to evaluate critically both the QVC tender offers and the Paramount-Viacom transaction to determine if: (a) the QVC tender offer was, or would continue to be, conditional; (b) the QVC tender offer could be improved; (c) the Viacom tender offer or other aspects of the Paramount-Viacom transaction could be improved; (d) each of the respective offers would be reasonably likely to come to closure, and under what circumstances; (e) other material

---

18. Both the Viacom and the QVC tender offers were for 51 percent cash and a "back-end" of various securities, the value of each of which depended on the fluctuating value of Viacom and QVC stock at any given time. Thus, both tender offers were two-tiered, front-end loaded, and coercive. Such coercive offers are inherently problematic and should be expected to receive particularly careful analysis by a target board. See *Unocal*, 493 A.2d at 956.

information was reasonably available for consideration by the Paramount directors; (f) there were viable and realistic alternative courses of action; and (g) the timing constraints could be managed so the directors could consider these matters carefully and deliberately. . . .

When entering into the Original Merger Agreement, and thereafter, the Paramount Board clearly gave insufficient attention to the potential consequences of the defensive measures demanded by Viacom. The Stock Option Agreement had a number of unusual and potentially "draconian"[19] provisions, including the Note Feature and the Put Feature. Furthermore, the Termination Fee, whether or not unreasonable by itself, clearly made Paramount less attractive to other bidders, when coupled with the Stock Option Agreement. Finally, the No-Shop Provision inhibited the Paramount Board's ability to negotiate with other potential bidders, particularly QVC which had already expressed an interest in Paramount.

Throughout the applicable time period, and especially from the first QVC merger proposal on September 20 through the Paramount Board meeting on November 15, QVC's interest in Paramount provided the opportunity for the Paramount Board to seek significantly higher value for the Paramount stockholders than that being offered by Viacom. . . .

The Paramount directors had the opportunity in the October 23-24 time frame, when the Original Merger Agreement was renegotiated, to take appropriate action to modify the improper defensive measures as well as to improve the economic terms of the Paramount-Viacom transaction. Under the circumstances existing at that time, it should have been clear to the Paramount Board that the Stock Option Agreement, coupled with the Termination Fee and the No-Shop Clause, were impeding the realization of the best value reasonably available to the Paramount stockholders. Nevertheless, the Paramount Board made no effort to eliminate or modify these counterproductive devices, and instead continued to cling to its vision of a strategic alliance with Viacom. Moreover, based on advice from the Paramount management, the Paramount directors considered the QVC offer to be "conditional" and asserted that they were precluded by the No-Shop Provision from seeking more information from, or negotiating with, QVC.

By November 12, 1993, the value of the revised QVC offer on its face exceeded that of the Viacom offer by over $1 billion at then current values. This significant disparity of value cannot be justified on the basis of the directors' vision of future strategy, primarily because the change of control would supplant the authority of the current Paramount Board to continue to hold and implement their strategic vision in any meaningful way. Moreover, their uninformed process had deprived their strategic vision of much of its credibility. . . .

When the Paramount directors met on November 15 to consider QVC's increased tender offer, they remained prisoners of their own

19. The Vice Chancellor so characterized the Stock Option Agreement. Court of Chancery Opinion, 635 A.2d at 1272. We express no opinion whether a stock option agreement of essentially this magnitude, but with a reasonable "cap" and without the Note and Put Features, would be valid or invalid under other circumstances. . . .

misconceptions and missed opportunities to eliminate the restrictions they had imposed on themselves. Yet, it was not "too late" to reconsider negotiating with QVC. . . . Nevertheless, the Paramount directors remained paralyzed by their uninformed belief that the QVC offer was "illusory." This final opportunity to negotiate on the stockholders' behalf and to fulfill their obligation to seek the best value reasonably available was thereby squandered. . . .

Viacom argues that it had certain "vested" contract rights with respect to the No-Shop Provision and the Stock Option Agreement. In effect, Viacom's argument is that the Paramount directors could enter into an agreement in violation of their fiduciary duties and then render Paramount, and ultimately its stockholders, liable for failing to carry out an agreement in violation of those duties. Viacom's protestations about vested rights are without merit. This Court has found that those defensive measures were improperly designed to deter potential bidders, and that such measures do not meet the reasonableness test to which they must be subjected. They are consequently invalid and unenforceable under the facts of this case.

The No-Shop Provision could not validly define or limit the fiduciary duties of the Paramount directors. To the extent that a contract, or a provision thereof, purports to require a board to act or not act in such a fashion as to limit the exercise of fiduciary duties, it is invalid and unenforceable. . . .

Viacom, a sophisticated party with experienced legal and financial advisors, knew of (and in fact demanded) the unreasonable features of the Stock Option Agreement. It cannot be now heard to argue that it obtained vested contract rights by negotiating and obtaining contractual provisions from a board acting in violation of its fiduciary duties. . . .

The realization of the best value reasonably available to the stockholders became the Paramount directors' primary obligation under these facts in light of the change of control. That obligation was not satisfied, and the Paramount Board's process was deficient. The directors' initial hope and expectation for a strategic alliance with Viacom was allowed to dominate their decisionmaking process to the point where the arsenal of defensive measures established at the outset was perpetuated (not modified or eliminated) when the situation was dramatically altered. QVC's unsolicited bid presented the opportunity for significantly greater value for the stockholders and enhanced negotiating leverage for the directors. Rather than seizing those opportunities, the Paramount directors chose to wall themselves off from material information which was reasonably available and to hide behind the defensive measures as a rationalization for refusing to negotiate with QVC or seeking other alternatives. Their view of the strategic alliance likewise became an empty rationalization as the opportunities for higher value for the stockholders continued to develop.

For the reasons set forth herein, the . . . Order of the Court of Chancery has been AFFIRMED, and this matter has been REMANDED for proceedings consistent herewith. . . .

BARRY DILLER & SUMNER REDSTONE

Barry Diller dropped out of UCLA in 1961 to begin his career in the mailroom of talent agency William Morris. He eventually joined television network ABC and by 1968, at the age of twenty-six, had become Vice President for prime-time programming. His innovative ideas, such as television miniseries and made-for-television movies, brought ABC enormous success. He actively sought rising talent, hiring young unknowns such as Steven Spielberg and Aaron Spelling to create his movies and Michael Eisner and Jeffrey Katzenberg to assist with operations.[38] In 1978, he became CEO of Paramount Pictures and proceeded to triple the studio's profits. After a decade at Paramount, he moved to Fox, Inc. and transformed the industry with edgy shows such as *Married . . . With Children* and *The Simpsons*. In 1992, the media titan shocked the entertainment world by leaving the glamour of Hollywood for small-town Pennsylvania to manage and partially own home-shopping television company QVC. Diller, however, saw QVC as a launching point for a profitable partnership between cable television and Hollywood studios and in 1993 began planning the acquisition of his former employer, Paramount Pictures.

He met his match in Sumner Redstone. Redstone, a Harvard Law School graduate, had by his thirtieth birthday served as a World War II army decoder, worked for the Department of Justice, and argued a tax case before the United States Supreme Court.[39] In 1953, he took control of his family's movie theatre chain and eventually began making investments in Hollywood studios, while teaching courses at Harvard Law School in his spare time. His hard-fought hostile takeover of Viacom in 1971 and subsequent acquisitions brought him a cable, television, and radio empire. The one missing piece was the movie industry, and Redstone found himself in a bitter fight with his former friend, Barry Diller, over the future of Paramount Pictures.

QUESTIONS AND NOTES ON PARAMOUNT v. QVC

1. Suppose Viacom had been widely held, without Sumner Redstone as its controlling shareholder. Would an acquisition agreement between Viacom and Paramount that provided for Viacom to make a cash tender offer for 51 percent of Paramount's shares, followed by a merger in which Paramount's remaining shareholders received Viacom stock, trigger *Revlon* duties on the part of Paramount's board?

2. What is the policy justification for imposing *Revlon* duties on a target's board when a merger shifts control to a controlling shareholder, as in *Paramount v. QVC*, but not when control remains in a dispersed body of shareholders, as in *Time-Warner*? Suppose, as *QVC* suggests, that minority shareholders are, postmerger, in a vulnerable position when there is a controlling shareholder in the combined company. Why can't the target's board anticipate this fact ex ante and demand commensurately favorable

---

38. George Mair, *The Barry Diller Story* (1997).
39. Sumner Redstone & Peter Knobler, *A Passion to Win* (2001).

merger terms? And if the target's board concludes that its shareholders will be adequately compensated for the hardships of investing in a controlled company, why must it maximize short-term shareholder value in this case but not in a plain vanilla merger?

3. What consequences follow from allowing managers more discretion to defend the corporation's independence under *Unocal* than to choose its acquirer under *Revlon*? Or is this characterization of the case law inaccurate?

4. In *Paramount v. QVC*, the Delaware Supreme Court adopted a "change-in-corporate control" trigger to distinguish between *Revlon* and non-*Revlon* deals. That is, it drew the line at the point at which public shareholders are excluded from meaningful participation in governance in the combined company, by a controlling shareholder or otherwise. In applying this principle, courts might look to a de jure or de facto definition of control. In fact, the formation of a 30 percent block of voting stock probably represents the creation of a controlling shareholder in the combined company. Legally, however, control is not certain unless a large shareholder holds more than 50 percent of the company's outstanding stock. Since *QVC*'s analysis rests heavily on policy considerations, we would expect Delaware courts to gravitate toward a practical test for control rather than a formal one. Thus, *Revlon* duties are likely to be triggered when mergers create shareholdings with between 30 and 35 percent of the voting rights in widely held companies.

5. While far from completely clear, the change-in-control test carries a number of specific implications. The most obvious of these is that a stock-for-stock merger between two public companies with no controlling shareholders should not trigger *Revlon* duties. Instead, such a merger ought to be reviewed by courts under some form of the business judgment standard. The Delaware Supreme Court affirmed this principle explicitly in *In re Santa Fe Pacific Corp. Shareholder Litigation*, 669 A.2d 59 (Del. 1995). But is that review "plain vanilla" business judgments or "enhanced" business judgment of *Unocal*?

6. A second implication of the change-in-control test is that a cash merger generally triggers *Revlon* duties unless there is *already* a majority shareholder in the target company.[40] In a merger in which all, or a majority, of the public shareholders are cashed out of the enterprise, these public shareholders cannot participate in the long-term strategic value of the combination, no matter how successful it proves to be. Thus, the target's board must have a duty to maximize shareholder value today, not in the future.

---

40. A majority shareholder has no obligation to sell her stock. See *Bershad v. Curtis Wright Corp.*, 535 A.2d 840 (Del. 1987). And a controller's desire to accomplish a cash-out of the minority does not obligate it to sell to one willing to pay more than it offers. *Mendel v. Carroll*, 651 A.2d 297(Del. Ch. 1994). But cf. *McMullin v. Beran*, 765 A.2d 910 (Del. 2000) (where controller negotiated a merger that paid all shareholders—itself and small public minority—the same amount, target board's duty was to be informed concerning alternatives for shareholders).

7. *Paramount/QVC* is unclear about how to evaluate board conduct when merger consideration is mixed. For example, suppose a target's board is offered 70 percent of the merger consideration in stock and 30 percent in cash (or the other way around). May the board accept such a deal and "lock it up" (see the next note on lock-ups) without meeting its *Revlon* duties? More basically, what principle distinguishes those cases in which the board should exercise its own business judgment about long-term synergistic benefits and those in which the board must maximize current value?

PROBLEM

The stock of T Corp., a producer of audio components, sells for $12 a share on NASDAQ. It has a million shares outstanding and annual sales of $200 million. The stock of Xenor, Inc., a large conglomerate with total sales of $13 billion and sales in its audio division of $500 million, recently traded on the NYSE in the range of $40-45 per share. Xenor has offered to acquire T in a merger. For each share of T, Xenor has offered the following consideration with an approximate total value of $14 per T share: 1/10 of a share of Xenor common stock, 1/4 of a share of a new redeemable preferred stock with a 5 percent dividend to be valued at $20 a share at issuance, and $4.50 in cash. Xenor has also offered T's CEO a position in its top management that she finds quite interesting.

Must T's board treat Xenor's proposal as a *Revlon* transaction? Cash represents only 33 percent of the total consideration—but the preferred stock portion of the merger consideration is redeemable and nonvoting. On the other hand, Xenor itself is publicly owned, with no controlling shareholder.

Suppose further that T's board decides that *Revlon* does not apply and votes to protect the Xenor merger agreement with a large lock-up. Shortly thereafter a competitor, SoundsaLot, Inc., offers $15 cash per share for T shares, which T's board rejects because it finds the Xenor deal to be a better long-term "fit." Would you expect the court to hold that the board has an obligation to optimize present value in a shareholder suit seeking an injunction?

AN APPROACH TO THE PROBLEM

Consider the following approach to this problem. In our view, the rules that underlie *Revlon* duties turn on the assumption that, in most circumstances, boards of directors are better able to value companies than are shareholders—*but* in some circumstances, as when shareholders are or might be cashed out of the postmerger enterprise, boards must maximize short-term value, since this is the only value that shareholders are likely to receive.[41] Courts believe (implicitly) that, in an all-stock deal between two

---

41. For an elaboration and critique of this account of the judicial theory behind *Revlon* duties, see Bernard S. Black & Reinier H. Kraakman, *Delaware's Takeover Law: The Uncertain Search for Hidden Value*, 96 Nw. U. L. Rev. 521 (2002).

companies of the same size, the board has a substantial advantage over shareholders (and the market) in evaluating the long-term value of the surviving company as well as the long-term value of the merger consideration. Thus, courts defer to the views of boards in these cases. A focus on informational advantage implies that the more the value of merger consideration depends on synergies between the target and the acquiring company (about which the directors have superior information), the more courts will defer to the judgment of T's directors. In cash deals, courts will not defer; in stock-for-stock mergers of equals, they will defer a great deal.

Put differently, judicial deference to a target board's choice is a trade-off. The more opportunity there is for a directorial informational advantage, the more deference is likely. But judges are realists, too. They understand that the agency problem exists. Thus, the greater the "hidden" value is that a board must assert to defend its choice of a transaction partner, the more likely a skeptical court is to cite *Revlon* and require the board to seek the highest current value. These two trade-offs create a pragmatic structure for judicial review, not a rule of decision. In the end, the courts must evaluate the bona fides of board judgment.

To return to our problem, when the T board's claim that a Xenor merger would give shareholders better long-term value is evaluated, a court is likely to ask itself how much value can reasonably be attributed to the T directors' informational advantage, given that only 25 percent of the value of the merger consideration is common stock and that this will be stock in a huge company, most of which will be unaffected by the acquisition of target. In the real world, we suppose that this case would be decided on the basis of whether the context would permit the court to decide that, in choosing a deal apparently worth 7 percent or so less, the board was making a good-faith judgment about achievable future value. Unlike a plain business judgment case, here the board would have to be prepared to explain its decision.

In our view, consideration of the Xenor problem points to the conclusion that the dichotomy between a *Revlon* test and a business judgment test is unstable and will ultimately prove unhelpful in deciding many cases. As between two cash bids, a simple injunction to "take more rather than less" decides the winner (if there are no other relevant considerations).[42] But in most cases, the choice is not so clear because the deal consideration is not so easily valued. This ambiguity is not a reason to invoke the traditional business judgment rule, however, because M&A transactions are simply too important to target shareholders for such a rule of wholesale delegation. Ultimately, the test for deciding whether a board's decision to select a merger partner should be respected must be whether the board has shown that it decided in an informed manner and made a good-faith effort to advance the interests of the corporation and its shareholders. Of course, whether a board's decision satisfies such a test is not an easy question to answer. When a transaction is very important — a friendly merger in the face of a hostile alternative, for example — a court must examine the

---

42. This is also an old rule of trust and corporate law; see, e.g., *Robinson v. Pittsburg Oil Refining Corp.*, 126 A. 46 (Del. Ch. 1924).

board's bona fides very closely, keeping in mind all of the soft conflicts of interest that the deciding incumbents are likely to have in the matter.

For these reasons, we believe that the *Revlon*/non-*Revlon* dichotomy is too rigid, both normatively and descriptively. What courts should do — and do in fact — in reviewing authorized corporate action is to accord corporate boards degrees of deference along a continuum. Where, as in *Revlon* itself, the merger consideration is cash, courts will not defer to the board's judgment. Thus, in such instances, any "deal protection" accorded to the favored merger partner will be closely reviewed to assure it represents a good-faith effort to get the best current price. By contrast, where, as in *Santa Fe*, the consideration is stock of a company of approximately equal size (that is, a situation in which the synergy contribution of the target is greatest and thus directors' private information is most valuable to target shareholders), deal protections will receive the greatest deference. In the middle range (where the merger represents mixed consideration or the target is vastly smaller than the survivor), courts will inevitably assess deal-protective terms by evaluating the good faith of the corporate directors who approve these terms.

13.6 PROTECTING THE DEAL

The question of what *Revlon* duties mean generally arises in the context of negotiating or enforcing "deal protection" provisions, which could include "lock-ups" and termination payments.[43] A lock-up is a colloquial term for any contract, collateral to an M&A transaction, that is designed to increase the likelihood that the parties will be able to close the deal. Although many forms of contracts can have a lock-up effect, the two major categories of lock-ups are options to a target's assets and its stock.[44] Asset lock-ups create rights to acquire specific corporate assets that become exercisable after a triggering event, such as a target shareholder vote disapproving a merger or a target board's decision to sign an alternative merger agreement. Thus, should a third party disrupt the parties' favored transaction, the target corporation will lose, pursuant to the terms of the "lock-up," some of its more attractive assets through the exercise of the lock-up rights. Asset lock-

43. In the next section, we discuss "no shops" and "no talks," which are another species of deal protection provisions.

44. An example of a nonfinancial form of lock-up is an a agreement providing that, if the target shareholders do not approve the favored merger, the target board will not enter into any other control transaction for a period of, say, 18 months. Such a provision is designed to suppress alternative transactions and pressure shareholders to approve the recommended deal. (Courts in dicta have expressed some skepticism about such provisions.) Note, too, that the term "lock-up" is also used to describe a contract between a large shareholder of a target and the acquirer. See infra. Section 13.6.2. Such a contract may commit the shareholder to sell in a tender offer or give to the acquirer a proxy to vote his shares. Of course, because these lock-ups are given individually, they are fundamentally different from lock-ups that involve corporate, not individual, contracting. Nevertheless, they are extremely important to reducing the risks of failure for a friendly bidder.

ups have been virtually non-existent since *Revlon*, which as you will recall struck down an asset lock-up granted to Forstmann Little.[45]

Stock lock-ups, which during the 1990s were more common than asset lock-ups, are options to buy a block of securities of the target company's stock (often 19.9 percent of the currently outstanding shares) at a stated price. The exercise price of the option is typically the deal price in the "protected transaction." Should a third party disturb the favored transaction, the lock-up provides that the jilted acquirer can participate in the increased value of the target to the extent of its proportionate share in the company's diluted equity (e.g., 19.9 percent).[46] Stock lock-ups were popular in the 1980s and 1990s, in part because their exercise could force less favorable "purchase" accounting — rather than more favorable "pooling" accounting — on the interloper that snatched the target from the arms of its initial partner. After the Financial Accounting Standards Board eliminated pooling of interest accounting in 2001, stock lock-ups have virtually disappeared. The Thomson Financial M&A database indicates virtually no stock option lock-ups (<0.1% incidence) since 2002 in U.S. public-company deals larger than $50 million.

By 2006, then, we seem to be left primarily with "termination fees," or "breakup fees," which are cash payments in the event that the seller elects to terminate the merger or otherwise fails to close. Termination fees are often justified as necessary to compensate a friendly buyer for spending the time, money, and reputation to negotiate a deal with a target when a third party ultimately wins the target. Courts have long approved reasonable payments for this purpose, even when the target was in an auction mode and subject to *Revlon* duties. Lump-sum termination payments no larger than 3 to 4 percent of the deal price are easily rationalized as a means to assure that a would-be acquirer will recover its transaction expenses (including opportunity costs) if the favored contract does not close.[47]

The second basic justification for termination fees, or lock-ups more generally, is that the boards of the target and acquiring companies see unique benefits from the favored transaction that the target's shareholders may not recognize, and that these boards therefore wish to minimize the possibility that a third party might break up the deal. This justification might support a lock-up of any magnitude, including one that would

---

45. See John C. Coates IV & Guhan Subramanian, *A Buy-Side Model of M&A Lockups: Theory & Evidence*, 53 Stan. L. Rev. 307, 326-28 (2000).

46. Stock option lock-ups may also contain provisions relating to the funding of the exercise of the stock option in the event that rights under the agreement are triggered. See, e.g., *Paramount Communications, Inc. v. QVC Network Inc.*, 637 A.2d 34 (Del. 1994). For example, the lock-up may, in the event of exercise of the rights, simply contemplate a cash payment to the holder of the option in the per share amount equal to the difference between the option price and the per share deal price of the transaction that forecloses the favored transaction.

47. There have been indications, however, that courts will question the bona fides of amounts beyond a certain range (perhaps 4 to 5 percent of the deal price). See *Phelps Dodge Corp. v. Cyprus Amax Minerals Co.*, 1999 WL 1054255 (Del. 1999) (dicta: "I think 6.3 percent certainly seems to stretch the definition of range of reasonableness and probably stretches the definition beyond its breaking point").

entirely preclude any competing offer. Not surprisingly, courts reject this second justification for lock-ups in transactions that trigger *Revlon* duties.

Query, however, whether a lock-up that is preclusive, or nearly so, is permissible to protect a merger of equals? Should such a lock-up receive business judgment review? In theory, when no change in control is involved in an M&A transaction, the board, acting in good faith, is free to choose a facially lower-value merger over a higher-value deal if it concludes that it is in the best interest of the corporation to do so. It follows that, technically, a court should review even a termination fee protecting such a transaction under the traditional business judgment rule. In all likelihood, however, the Delaware courts will not use business judgment review, but will use the *Unocal* version of the business judgment review instead, since the protective provision — like the pill itself — serves an obvious defensive function.

By contrast, in determining whether a lock-up is consistent with the board's duties in a *Revlon* transaction, courts will weigh such considerations as how early in the process the lock-up was given and the value-enhancing nature of its specific terms. Standard deal protection that the board grants after completing an auction or other process dedicated to maximizing shareholder value may very well survive heightened review under *Revlon/QVC*, while a similar option granted very early in the process (or at a time when the board has only thin information about market values) is more susceptible to ex post attack. In evaluating the specific terms of lock-ups, it might seem that courts should always view a lock-up ex ante, from the board's perspective of the time it was authorized, rather than ex post, according to how much it eventually paid out. But where a lock-up pays out a very large sum ex post (relative to the deal price), its sheer size may lead a skeptical court to suspect that it might be either an uninformed or a bad-faith attempt to tilt the playing field, and hence unenforceable.[48]

A final issue concerns the range of legitimate triggers for lock-ups and termination fees. Buyers rights under "deal protective" provisions are commonly triggered by (1) a failure of the board to recommend a negotiated deal to shareholders in light of the emergence of a higher offer (thus employing a "fiduciary out," which is discussed in the next section), (2) a rejection of the negotiated deal by a vote of the target's shareholders, or (3) a later sale of assets to another firm. A board decision *not* to recommend a negotiated acquisition is an accepted trigger for a termination payment. Indeed, §251(c) of the DGCL was amended in 1998 to validate contracts that require the board to submit a merger proposal to shareholders for a vote even if there is a better offer now on the table — a so-called "force the vote" provision (thus reversing another aspect of *Smith v. Van Gorkom*).[49]

---

48. See *Paramount Communications, Inc. v. QVC Network, Inc.* It should be noted that a substantial lock-up payment will not affect the top price that an alternative bidder will pay, but it does affect how that payment will be distributed among the target shareholders and the lock-up option holder.

49. Prior to the amendment, in the event of a later higher-value merger proposal from a third party, target directors could be placed in an untenable position by a contractual provision that requires the corporation to recommend the deal to its shareholders, in light of their fiduciary duty of loyalty (specifically, candor).

Since then, shareholders have found it easier than before to reject friendly deals. While the first rationale for termination payments (compensation) is still valid in this setting, the second rationale (deal protection) is far weaker when the lock-up seeks to "protect the deal" from an adverse shareholder vote. It would seem evident that the board of directors has no legitimate interest in "protecting a deal" from an informed shareholder vote, at least where the corporate law grants shareholders a right to vote on the transaction.

13.6.1   "No Shops/No Talks" and "Fiduciary Outs"

Every buyer of an asset wants assurances that her deal will close and she will obtain the asset on the terms agreed. For acquirers in corporate mergers, however, the legal requirement that the target's shareholders vote approval introduces an irreducible contingency into merger contracts. Something might happen — for example, a second bidder might offer a higher price — before the shareholders vote and the deal closes. Buyers protect against this risk in two ways. First, they may seek a large lock-up, as described above. Second, they may seek certain covenants from the seller that will protect their deal. For example, a target board will be asked to covenant (a) not to shop for alternative transactions or supply confidential information to alternative buyers (or more extreme, not to talk at all to others interested in a transaction), (b) to submit the merger agreement (and no other agreement) to the shareholders for approval, and (c) to recommend that shareholders approve this agreement. Such terms are often found in merger agreements, and it is important to recognize that they can serve the interests of target shareholders as well as those of acquirers. Without them, prospective buyers would invest fewer resources in searching for deals and might offer less generous prices.

But what happens to the directors' fiduciary duties when, despite these covenants, a third party makes a better offer before the shareholders can vote on the original offer? The Delaware Supreme Court held in *Smith v. Van Gorkom* that a target's board of directors had no fiduciary right (as opposed to power) to breach a contract. That is, even if the directors' fiduciary duty required them to breach, the corporation was not privileged to do so and consequently would be liable for damages. Consider, for example, a covenant to recommend a deal to the shareholders. This is a perfectly reasonable provision for the buyers and sellers to negotiate. But what happens when the better deal arrives before the shareholders vote? Can the target's board members continue to recommend the less attractive original deal without violating their duty of loyalty? Clearly not, so the board is well advised to breach its contract. But then the company faces contractual damages, which is not a good thing either. To cut through this catch-22, counsel for targets have devised the "fiduciary out" clause, which specifies that, if some triggering event occurs (such as a better offer or an opinion from outside counsel that the board has a fiduciary duty to abandon the original deal), then the target's board can avoid the contract without breaching it.

Buyers resist fiduciary outs, since they crave certainty. But where a transaction triggers *Revlon* duties, target counsel typically admonish that the legal risk of failing to have a fiduciary-out clause is unacceptable. And if a deal is not subject to *Revlon* duties? If there is no legal duty to sell for the highest price, can target directors safely tie their own hands by leaving out a fiduciary out? In theory, they probably may, but it would still be imprudent to covenant to make a recommendation to shareholders in a way that left no room for second thoughts at the point, months later, when the shareholders actually had to vote.

Properly understood, fiduciary outs constitute much ado about not so much. Today, they are heavily negotiated in all friendly merger agreements. But in fact, if *Revlon* duties apply, no contract term can protect a negotiated deal from an alternative buyer who is willing to pay significantly more. If nothing else, target shareholders will refuse to approve a merger if an alternative buyer has sufficient information to announce a significantly higher price. Thus, a fiduciary out has little practical importance in such a deal. Indeed, since the Delaware Supreme Court has seemed to declare contracts unenforceable that violate a fiduciary duty, contract damages may not ever be available against a corporation that abandons a transaction subject to *Revlon* duties on the grounds that a better deal is available. But there is still uncertainty about this point, so the fiduciary out continues to be treated as a material aspect of M&A transactions.

13.6.2 Shareholder Lock-ups

If one were to derive general principles from the analysis thus far, it would seem that, whether or not a transaction constitutes a "change in control," if the board's process is deliberate and informed and the board is truly independent, the law must let the board make business decisions without fear of being second-guessed. When the transaction does constitute a "change in control" that deference will be expressed in some form of heightened scrutiny (reasonableness in relation to something); when the transaction is not a *Revlon* transaction, that deference may indeed be expressed in the language of the business judgment rule. That is, the corporation law — or at least the Delaware courts in construing it — does not seem to mandate specific terms of merger agreements, but requires a process that is informed and honestly pursued in the interests of the corporation and its shareholders. The Delaware Supreme Court's 3-2 decision in *Omnicare v. NCS Healthcare* provides a recent, and important, exception to this general approach.

OMNICARE, INC., v. NCS HEALTHCARE, INC.,

818 A.2d 914 (Del. 2003)

HOLLAND, Justice, for the majority:

NCS Healthcare, Inc. ("NCS"), a Delaware corporation, was the object of competing acquisition bids, one by Genesis Health Ventures, Inc. ("Genesis"), a Pennsylvania corporation, and the other by Omnicare, Inc. ("Omnicare"), a Delaware corporation. . . .

FACTUAL BACKGROUND

. . . . Beginning in late 1999, changes in the timing and level of reimbursements by government and third-party providers adversely affected market conditions in the health care industry. As a result, NCS began to experience greater difficulty in collecting accounts receivables, which led to a precipitous decline in the market value of its stock. NCS common shares that traded above $20 in January 1999 were worth as little as $5 at the end of that year. By early 2001, NCS was in default on approximately $350 million in debt, including $206 million in senior bank debt and $102 million of its 5 3/4 % Convertible Subordinated Debentures (the "Notes"). After these defaults, NCS common stock traded in a range of $0.09 to $0.50 per share until days before the announcement of the transaction at issue in this case.

NCS began to explore strategic alternatives . . . . NCS retained UBS Warburg, L.L.C. . . . UBS Warburg contacted over fifty different entities to solicit their interest in a variety of transactions with NCS. . . . By October 2000, NCS had only received one non-binding indication of interest valued at $190 million, substantially less than the face value of NCS's senior debt. This proposal was reduced by 20% after the offeror conducted its due diligence review.

In April 2001, NCS received a formal notice of default and acceleration from the trustee for holders of the Notes. As NCS's financial condition worsened, the Noteholders formed a committee to represent their financial interests (the "Ad Hoc Committee"). At about that time, NCS began discussions with various investor groups regarding a restructuring in a "prepackaged" bankruptcy. NCS did not receive any proposal that it believed provided adequate consideration for its stakeholders. At that time, full recovery for NCS's creditors was a remote prospect, and any recovery for NCS stockholders seemed impossible.

On July 20, Joel Gemunder, Omnicare's President and CEO, sent [Kevin B.] Shaw [President, CEO and director of NCS] a written proposal to acquire NCS in a bankruptcy sale under Section 363 of the Bankruptcy Code. This proposal was for $225 million subject to satisfactory completion of due diligence. NCS asked Omnicare to execute a confidentiality agreement so that more detailed discussions could take place.[3]

---

3. Discovery had revealed that, at the same time, Omnicare was attempting to lure away NCS's customers through what it characterized as the "NCS Blitz." The "NCS Blitz"

In August 2001, Omnicare increased its bid to $270 million, but still proposed to structure the deal as an asset sale in bankruptcy. Even at $270 million, Omnicare's proposal was substantially lower than the face value of NCS's outstanding debt. It would have provided only a small recovery for Omnicare's Noteholders and no recovery for its stockholders. In October 2001, NCS sent Glen Pollack of Brown Gibbons [a banker representing NCS] to meet with Omnicare's financial advisor, Merrill Lynch, to discuss Omnicare's interest in NCS. Omnicare responded that it was not interested in any transaction other than an asset sale in bankruptcy.

There was no further contact between Omnicare and NCS between November 2001 and January 2002. Instead, Omnicare began secret discussions with Judy K. Mencher, a representative of the Ad Hoc Committee. In these discussions, Omnicare continued to pursue a transaction structured as a sale of assets in bankruptcy. In February 2002, the Ad Hoc Committee notified the NCS board that Omnicare had proposed an asset sale in bankruptcy for $313,750,000.

In January 2002, Genesis was contacted by members of the Ad Hoc Committee concerning a possible transaction with NCS. Genesis executed NCS's standard confidentiality agreement and began a due diligence review. Genesis had recently emerged from bankruptcy because, like NCS, it was suffering from dwindling government reimbursements.

Genesis [had] previously lost a bidding war to Omnicare in a different transaction. This led to bitter feelings between the principals of both companies. More importantly, this bitter experience for Genesis led to its insistence on exclusivity agreements and lock-ups in any potential transaction with NCS.

NCS's [financial] performance improved. The NCS directors began to believe that it might be possible for NCS to enter into a transaction that would provide some recovery for NCS stockholders. . . . In March 2002, NCS . . . formed an independent [board] committee . . . (the "Independent Committee"). The NCS board thought this was necessary because, due to NCS's precarious financial condition, it felt that fiduciary duties were owed to the enterprise as a whole rather than solely to NCS stockholders. Sells and Osborne were selected as the members of the committee, and given authority to consider and negotiate possible transactions for NCS. The entire four member NCS board, however, retained authority to approve any transaction. The Independent Committee retained the same legal and financial counsel as the NCS board.

The Independent Committee met for the first time on May 14, 2002. At that meeting Pollack suggested that NCS seek a "stalking-horse merger partner" to obtain the highest possible value in any transaction. The Independent Committee agreed with the suggestion.

Two days later, on May 16, 2002, Scott Berlin of Brown Gibbons, Glen Pollack and [NCS board member] Boake Sells met with George Hager, CFO

---

was an effort by Omnicare to target NCS's customers. Omnicare has engaged in an "NCS Blitz" a number of times, most recently while NCS and Omnicare were in discussions in July and August 2001.

of Genesis, and Michael Walker, who was Genesis's CEO. At that meeting, Genesis made it clear that if it were going to engage in any negotiations with NCS, it would not do so as a "stalking horse." As one of its advisors testified, "We didn't want to be someone who set forth a valuation for NCS which would only result in that valuation . . . being publicly disclosed, and thereby creating an environment where Omnicare felt to maintain its competitive monopolistic positions, that they had to match and exceed that level." Thus, Genesis "wanted a degree of certainty that to the extent [it] w[as] willing to pursue a negotiated merger agreement . . . , [it] would be able to consummate the transaction [it] negotiated and executed."

In June 2002, Genesis proposed a transaction that would take place outside the bankruptcy context. Although it did not provide full recovery for NCS's Noteholders, it provided the possibility that NCS stockholders would be able to recover something for their investment. As discussions continued, the terms proposed by Genesis continued to improve. On June 25, the economic terms of the Genesis proposal included repayment of the NCS senior debt in full, full assumption of trade credit obligations, an exchange offer or direct purchase of the NCS Notes providing NCS Noteholders with a combination of cash and Genesis common stock equal to the par value of the NCS Notes (not including accrued interest), and $20 million in value for the NCS common stock. Structurally, the Genesis proposal continued to include consents from a significant majority of the Noteholders as well as support agreements from stockholders owning a majority of the NCS voting power.

NCS's financial advisors and legal counsel met again with Genesis and its legal counsel on June 26, 2002, to discuss a number of transaction-related issues. At this meeting, Pollack asked Genesis to increase its offer to NCS stockholders. . . . Genesis agreed to offer a total of $24 million in consideration for the NCS common stock, or an additional $4 million, in the form of Genesis common stock.

At the June 26 meeting, Genesis's representatives demanded that, before any further negotiations take place, NCS agree to enter into an exclusivity agreement with it. As Hager from Genesis explained it: "[I]f they wished us to continue to try to move this process to a definitive agreement, that they would need to do it on an exclusive basis with us. We were going to, and already had incurred significant expense, but we would incur additional expenses . . . , both internal and external, to bring this transaction to a definitive signing. We wanted them to work with us on an exclusive basis for a short period of time to see if we could reach agreement." On June 27, 2002, Genesis's legal counsel delivered a draft form of exclusivity agreement for review and consideration by NCS's legal counsel.

The Independent Committee met on July 3, 2002, to consider the proposed exclusivity agreement. Pollack presented a summary of the terms of a possible Genesis merger, which had continued to improve. The then-current Genesis proposal included (1) repayment of the NCS senior debt in full, (2) payment of par value for the Notes (without accrued interest) in the form of a combination of cash and Genesis stock, (3) payment to NCS stockholders in the form of $24 million in Genesis stock, plus (4) the assumption, because the transaction was to be structured as a merger, of additional liabilities to trade and other unsecured creditors.

NCS director Sells testified [that] Pollack told the Independent Committee at a July 3, 2002 meeting that Genesis wanted the Exclusivity Agreement to be the first step towards a completely locked up transaction that would preclude a higher bid from Omnicare. . . .

After NCS executed the exclusivity agreement, Genesis provided NCS with a draft merger agreement, a draft Noteholders' support agreement, and draft voting agreements for Outcalt and Shaw, who together held a majority of the voting power of the NCS common stock.

Genesis and NCS negotiated the terms of the merger agreement over the next three weeks. During those negotiations, the Independent Committee and the Ad Hoc Committee persuaded Genesis to improve the terms of its merger.

The parties were still negotiating by July 19, and the exclusivity period was automatically extended to July 26. At that point, NCS and Genesis were close to executing a merger agreement and related voting agreements. Genesis proposed a short extension of the exclusivity agreement so a deal could be finalized. On the morning of July 26, 2002, the Independent Committee authorized an extension of the exclusivity period through July 31.

By late July 2002, Omnicare came to believe that NCS was negotiating a transaction, possibly with Genesis or another of Omnicare's competitors, that would potentially present a competitive threat to Omnicare. Omnicare also came to believe, in light of a run-up in the price of NCS common stock, that whatever transaction NCS was negotiating probably included a payment for its stock. Thus, the Omnicare board of directors met on the morning of July 26 and, on the recommendation of its management, authorized a proposal to acquire NCS that did not involve a sale of assets in bankruptcy.

On the afternoon of July 26, 2002, Omnicare faxed to NCS a letter outlining a proposed acquisition. The letter suggested a transaction in which Omnicare would retire NCS's senior and subordinated debt at par plus accrued interest, and pay the NCS stockholders $3 cash for their shares. . . . Late in the afternoon of July 26, 2002, NCS representatives received voicemail messages from Omnicare asking to discuss the letter. The exclusivity agreement prevented NCS from returning those calls. In relevant part, that agreement precluded NCS from "engag[ing] or particpat[ing] in any discussions or negotiations with respect to a Competing Transaction or a proposal for one." The July 26 letter from Omnicare met the definition of a "Competing Transaction."

Despite the exclusivity agreement, the Independent Committee met to consider a response to Omnicare. It concluded that discussions with Omnicare about its July 26 letter presented an unacceptable risk that Genesis would abandon merger discussions. The Independent Committee believed that, given Omnicare's past bankruptcy proposals and unwillingness to consider a merger, as well as its decision to negotiate exclusively with the Ad Hoc Committee, the risk of losing the Genesis proposal was too substantial. Nevertheless, the Independent Committee instructed Pollack to use Omnicare's letter to negotiate for improved terms with Genesis.

On July 27, Genesis proposed substantially improved terms. First, it proposed to retire the Notes in accordance with the terms of the indenture, thus eliminating the need for Noteholders to consent to the transaction. This change involved paying all accrued interest plus a small redemption premium. Second, Genesis increased the exchange ratio for NCS common stock to one-tenth of a Genesis common share for each NCS common share, an 80% increase. Third, it agreed to lower the proposed termination fee in the merger agreement from $10 million to $6 million. In return for these concessions, Genesis stipulated that the transaction had to be approved by midnight the next day, July 28, or else Genesis would terminate discussions and withdraw its offer.

The Independent Committee and the NCS board both scheduled meetings for July 28. The committee met first. Although that meeting lasted less than an hour, the Court of Chancery determined the minutes reflect that the directors were fully informed of all material facts relating to the proposed transaction. After concluding that Genesis was sincere in establishing the midnight deadline, the committee voted unanimously to recommend the transaction to the full board.

The full board met thereafter. After receiving similar reports and advice from its legal and financial advisors, the board concluded that "balancing the potential loss of the Genesis deal against the uncertainty of Omnicare's letter, results in the conclusion that the only reasonable alternative for the Board of Directors is to approve the Genesis transaction."

The board first voted to authorize the voting agreements with Outcalt and Shaw, for purposes of Section 203 of the Delaware General Corporation Law ("DGCL"). The board was advised by its legal counsel that "under the terms of the merger agreement and because NCS shareholders representing in excess of 50% of the outstanding voting power would be required by Genesis to enter into stockholder voting agreements contemporaneously with the signing of the merger agreement, and would agree to vote their shares in favor of the merger agreement, shareholder approval of the merger would be assured even if the NCS Board were to withdraw or change its recommendation. *These facts would prevent NCS from engaging in any alternative or superior transaction in the future.*" (emphasis added).

After listening to a summary of the merger terms, the board then resolved that the merger agreement and the transactions contemplated thereby were advisable and fair and in the best interests of all the NCS stakeholders. The NCS board further resolved to recommend the transactions to the stockholders for their approval and adoption. A definitive merger agreement between NCS and Genesis and the stockholder voting agreements were executed later that day. . . .

Among other things, the NCS/Genesis merger agreement provided the following:

- NCS stockholders would receive 1 share of Genesis common stock in exchange for every 10 shares of NCS common stock held;
- NCS stockholders could exercise appraisal rights under 8 Del. C. § 262;

- NCS would redeem NCS's Notes in accordance with their terms;
- NCS would submit the merger agreement to NCS stockholders regardless of whether the NCS board continued to recommend the merger;
- NCS would not enter into discussions with third parties concerning an alternative acquisition of NCS, or provide non-public information to such parties, unless (1) the third party provided an unsolicited, bona fide written proposal documenting the terms of the acquisition; (2) the NCS board believed in good faith that the proposal was or was likely to result in an acquisition on terms superior to those contemplated by the NCS/Genesis merger agreement; and (3) before providing non-public information to that third party, the third party would execute a confidentiality agreement at least as restrictive as the one in place between NCS and Genesis; and
- If the merger agreement were to be terminated, under certain circumstances NCS would be required to pay Genesis a $6 million termination fee and/or Genesis's documented expenses, up to $5 million.

VOTING AGREEMENTS

Outcalt and Shaw, in their capacity as NCS stockholders, entered into voting agreements with Genesis. NCS was also required to be a party to the voting agreements by Genesis.

Those agreements provided, among other things, that:

- Outcalt and Shaw were acting in their capacity as NCS stockholders in executing the agreements, not in their capacity as NCS directors or officers;
- Neither Outcalt nor Shaw would transfer their shares prior to the stockholder vote on the merger agreement;
- Outcalt and Shaw agreed to vote all of their shares in favor of the merger agreement; and
- Outcalt and Shaw granted to Genesis an irrevocable proxy to vote their shares in favor of the merger agreement.
- The voting agreement was specifically enforceable by Genesis.

OMNICARE'S SUPERIOR PROPOSAL

On July 29, 2002, hours after the NCS/Genesis transaction was executed, Omnicare faxed a letter to NCS restating its conditional proposal and attaching a draft merger agreement. Later that morning, Omnicare issued a press release publicly disclosing the proposal.

On August 1, 2002, Omnicare filed a lawsuit attempting to enjoin the NCS/Genesis merger, and announced that it intended to launch a tender offer for NCS's shares at a price of $3.50 per share. On August 8, 2002,

Omnicare began its tender offer. By letter dated that same day, Omnicare expressed a desire to discuss the terms of the offer with NCS. Omnicare's letter continued to condition its proposal on satisfactory completion of a due diligence investigation of NCS.

On August 8, 2002, and again on August 19, 2002, the NCS Independent Committee and full board of directors met separately to consider the Omnicare tender offer in light of the Genesis merger agreement. NCS's outside legal counsel and NCS's financial advisor attended both meetings. The board was unable to determine that Omnicare's expressions of interest were likely to lead to a "Superior Proposal," as the term was defined in the NCS/Genesis merger agreement.

On September 10, 2002, NCS requested and received a waiver from Genesis allowing NCS to enter into discussions with Omnicare without first having to determine that Omnicare's proposal was a "Superior Proposal."

On October 6, 2002, Omnicare irrevocably committed itself to a transaction with NCS. Pursuant to the terms of its proposal, Omnicare agreed to acquire all the outstanding NCS Class A and Class B shares at a price of $3.50 per share in cash. As a result of this irrevocable offer, on October 21, 2002, the NCS board withdrew its recommendation that the stockholders vote in favor of the NCS/Genesis merger agreement. NCS's financial advisor withdrew its fairness opinion of the NCS/Genesis merger agreement as well.

GENESIS REJECTION IMPOSSIBLE

The Genesis merger agreement permits the NCS directors to furnish non-public information to, or enter into discussions with, "any Person in connection with an unsolicited bona fide written Acquisition Proposal by such person" that the board deems likely to constitute a "Superior Proposal." That provision has absolutely no effect on the Genesis merger agreement. Even if the NCS board "changes, withdraws or modifies" its recommendation, as it did, it must still submit the merger to a stockholder vote.

A subsequent filing with the Securities and Exchange Commission ("SEC") states: "the NCS independent committee and the NCS board of directors have determined to withdraw their recommendations of the Genesis merger agreement and recommend that the NCS stockholders vote against the approval and adoption of the Genesis merger." In that same SEC filing, however, the NCS board explained why the success of the Genesis merger had already been predetermined. "Notwithstanding the foregoing, the NCS independent committee and the NCS board of directors recognize that (1) the existing contractual obligations to Genesis currently prevent NCS from accepting the Omnicare irrevocable merger proposal; and (2) the existence of the voting agreements entered into by Messrs. Outcalt and Shaw, whereby Messrs. Outcalt and Shaw agreed to vote their shares of NCS Class A common stock and NCS Class B common stock in favor of the Genesis merger, ensure NCS stockholder approval of the Genesis merger."

This litigation was commenced to prevent the consummation of the inferior Genesis transaction.

LEGAL ANALYSIS

The Court of Chancery concluded that, because the stock-for-stock merger between Genesis and NCS did not result in a change of control, the NCS directors' duties under *Revlon* were not triggered by the decision to merge with Genesis. . . .

After concluding that the *Revlon* standard of enhanced judicial review was completely inapplicable, the Court of Chancery then held that it would examine the decision of the NCS board of directors to approve the Genesis merger pursuant to the business judgment rule standard. After completing its business judgment rule review, the Court of Chancery held that the NCS board of directors had not breached their duty of care by entering into the exclusivity and merger agreements with Genesis. The Court of Chancery also held, however, that "even applying the more exacting *Revlon* standard, the directors acted in conformity with their fiduciary duties in seeking to achieve the highest and best transaction that was reasonably available to [the stockholders]."

The Court of Chancery's decision to review the NCS board's decision to merge with Genesis under the business judgment rule rather than the enhanced scrutiny standard of *Revlon* is not outcome determinative for the purposes of deciding this appeal. We have assumed arguendo that the business judgment rule applied to the decision by the NCS board to merge with Genesis. We have also assumed arguendo that the NCS board exercised due care when it: abandoned the Independent Committee's recommendation to pursue a stalking horse strategy . . . ; executed an exclusivity agreement with Genesis; acceded to Genesis' twenty-four hour ultimatum for making a final merger decision; and executed a merger agreement that was summarized but never completely read by the NCS board of directors.

DEAL PROTECTION DEVICES REQUIRE ENHANCED SCRUTINY

The dispositive issues in this appeal involve the defensive devices that protected the Genesis merger agreement. The Delaware corporation statute provides that the board's management decision to enter into and recommend a merger transaction can become final only when ownership action is taken by a vote of the stockholders. Thus, the Delaware corporation law expressly provides for a balance of power between boards and stockholders which makes merger transactions a shared enterprise and ownership decision. Consequently, a board of directors' decision to adopt defensive devices to protect a merger agreement may implicate the stockholders' right to effectively vote contrary to the initial recommendation of the board in favor of the transaction. . . . A board's decision to protect its decision to enter a merger agreement with defensive devices against uninvited competing transactions that may emerge is analogous to a board's decision to protect against dangers to corporate policy and effectiveness when it adopts defensive measures in a hostile takeover contest. . . . The latitude a board will have in either maintaining or using the defensive devices it has adopted to protect the merger it approved will vary according to the degree of benefit or detriment to the stockholders' interests that is presented by the value or terms of the subsequent competing transaction.

GENESIS' ONE DAY ULTIMATUM

The record reflects that two of the four NCS board members, Shaw and Outcalt, were also the same two NCS stockholders who combined to control a majority of the stockholder voting power. Genesis gave the four person NCS board less than twenty-four hours to vote in favor of its proposed merger agreement. Genesis insisted the merger agreement include a Section 251(c) clause, mandating its submission for a stockholder vote even if the board's recommendation was withdrawn. Genesis further insisted that the merger agreement omit any effective fiduciary out clause.

Genesis also gave the two stockholder members of the NCS board, Shaw and Outcalt, the same accelerated time table to personally sign the proposed voting agreements. These voting agreements committed them irrevocably to vote their majority power in favor of the merger and further provided in Section 6 that the voting agreements be specifically enforceable. Genesis also required that NCS execute the voting agreements.

Genesis' twenty-four hour ultimatum was that, unless both the merger agreement and the voting agreements were signed with the terms it requested, its offer was going to be withdrawn. According to Genesis' attorneys, these "were unalterable conditions to Genesis' willingness to proceed."

Genesis insisted on the execution of the interlocking voting rights and merger agreements because it feared that Omnicare would make a superior merger proposal. The NCS board signed the voting rights and merger agreements, without any effective fiduciary out clause, to expressly guarantee that the Genesis merger would be approved, even if a superior merger transaction was presented from Omnicare or any other entity. . . .

These Deal Protection Devices Unenforceable: In this case, the Court of Chancery correctly held that the NCS directors' decision to adopt defensive devices to completely "lock up" the Genesis merger mandated "special scrutiny" under the two-part test set forth in *Unocal*. . . . The record does not, however, support the Court of Chancery's conclusion that the defensive devices adopted by the NCS board to protect the Genesis merger were reasonable and proportionate to the threat that NCS perceived from the potential loss of the Genesis transaction.

Pursuant to the judicial scrutiny required under *Unocal*'s two-stage analysis, the NCS directors must first demonstrate "that they had reasonable grounds for believing that a danger to corporate policy and effectiveness existed . . . . " To satisfy that burden, the NCS directors are required to show they acted in good faith after conducting a reasonable investigation. The threat identified by the NCS board was the possibility of losing the Genesis offer and being left with no comparable alternative transaction.

The second stage of the *Unocal* test requires the NCS directors to demonstrate that their defensive response was "reasonable in relation to the threat posed." This inquiry involves a two-step analysis. The NCS directors must first establish that the merger deal protection devices adopted in response to the threat were not "coercive" or "preclusive," and then demonstrate that their response was within a "range of reasonable responses" to the threat perceived. A response is "preclusive" if it deprives stockholders of the right to receive all tender offers or precludes a bidder from seeking control by fundamentally restricting proxy contests or otherwise. This aspect of the *Unocal* standard provides for a disjunctive analysis. If defensive measures are either preclusive or coercive they are draconian and impermissible. In this case, the deal protection devices of the NCS board were both preclusive and coercive.

In this case, the Court of Chancery did not expressly address the issue of "coercion" in its *Unocal* analysis. It did find as a fact, however, that NCS's public stockholders (who owned 80% of NCS and overwhelmingly supported Omnicare's offer) will be forced to accept the Genesis merger because of the structural defenses approved by the NCS board.

Consequently, the record reflects that any stockholder vote would have been robbed of its effectiveness by the impermissible coercion that predetermined the outcome of the merger without regard to the merits of the Genesis transaction at the time the vote was scheduled to be taken. Deal protection devices that result in such coercion cannot withstand *Unocal*'s enhanced judicial scrutiny standard of review because they are not within the range of reasonableness.

EFFECTIVE FIDUCIARY OUT REQUIRED

The defensive measures that protected the merger transaction are unenforceable not only because they are preclusive and coercive but, alternatively, they are unenforceable because they are invalid as they operate in this case. Given the specifically enforceable irrevocable voting agreements, the provision in the merger agreement requiring the board to submit the transaction for a stockholder vote and the omission of a fiduciary out clause in the merger agreement completely prevented the board from discharging its fiduciary responsibilities to the minority stockholders when Omnicare presented its superior transaction. "To the extent that a [merger] contract, or a provision thereof, purports to require a board to act or not act in such a fashion as to limit the exercise of fiduciary duties, it is invalid and unenforceable."[74]

Under the circumstances presented in this case, where a cohesive group of stockholders with majority voting power was irrevocably

---

74. [*Paramount Communications Inc. v. QVC Network Inc.*], 637 A.2d 34, 51 (Del.1993) (citation omitted). Restatement (Second) of Contracts §193 explicitly provides that a "promise by a fiduciary to violate his fiduciary duty or a promise that tends to induce such a violation is unenforceable on grounds of public policy." The comments to that section indicate that "[d]irectors and other officials of a corporation act in a fiduciary capacity and are subject to the rule stated in this Section." Restatement (Second) of Contracts §193 (1981).

committed to the merger transaction, "[e]ffective representation of the financial interests of the minority shareholders imposed upon the [NCS board] an affirmative responsibility to protect those minority shareholders' interests." The NCS board could not abdicate its fiduciary duties to the minority by leaving it to the stockholders alone to approve or disapprove the merger agreement because two stockholders had already combined to establish a majority of the voting power that made the outcome of the stockholder vote a foregone conclusion.

The Court of Chancery noted that Section 251(c) of the Delaware General Corporation Law now permits boards to agree to submit a merger agreement for a stockholder vote, even if the Board later withdraws its support for that agreement and recommends that the stockholders reject it. The Court of Chancery also noted that stockholder voting agreements are permitted by Delaware law. In refusing to certify this interlocutory appeal, the Court of Chancery stated "it is simply nonsensical to say that a board of directors abdicates its duties to manage the 'business and affairs' of a corporation under Section 141(a) of the DGCL by agreeing to the inclusion in a merger agreement of a term authorized by §251(c) of the same statute."[80]

Taking action that is otherwise legally possible, however, does not *ipso facto* comport with the fiduciary responsibilities of directors in all circumstances.

Genesis admits that when the NCS board agreed to its merger conditions, the NCS board was seeking to assure that the NCS creditors were paid in full and that the NCS stockholders received the highest value available for their stock. In fact, Genesis defends its "bulletproof" merger agreement on that basis. We hold that the NCS board did not have authority to accede to the Genesis demand for an absolute "lock-up."

The directors of a Delaware corporation have a continuing obligation to discharge their fiduciary responsibilities, as future circumstances develop, after a merger agreement is announced. Genesis anticipated the likelihood of a superior offer after its merger agreement was announced and demanded defensive measures from the NCS board that completely protected its transaction.

Instead of agreeing to the absolute defense of the Genesis merger from a superior offer, however, the NCS board was required to negotiate a fiduciary out clause to protect the NCS stockholders if the Genesis transaction became an inferior offer. By acceding to Genesis' ultimatum for complete protection in futuro, the NCS board disabled itself from exercising its own fiduciary obligations at a time when the board's own judgment is most important, i.e. receipt of a subsequent superior offer.

Any board has authority to give the proponent of a recommended merger agreement reasonable structural and economic defenses,

---

80. Section 251(c) was amended in 1998 to allow for the inclusion in a merger agreement of a term requiring that the agreement be put to a vote of stockholders whether or not their directors continue to recommend the transaction. Before this amendment, Section 251 was interpreted as precluding a stockholder vote if the board of directors, after approving the merger agreement but before the stockholder vote, decided no longer to recommend it. See *Smith v. Van Gorkom*, 488 A.2d 858, 887-88 (Del. 1985).

incentives, and fair compensation if the transaction is not completed. To the extent that defensive measures are economic and reasonable, they may become an increased cost to the proponent of any subsequent transaction. Just as defensive measures cannot be draconian, however, they cannot limit or circumscribe the directors' fiduciary duties. Notwithstanding the corporation's insolvent condition, the NCS board had no authority to execute a merger agreement that subsequently prevented it from effectively discharging its ongoing fiduciary responsibilities. . . .

In the context of this preclusive and coercive lock up case, the protection of Genesis' contractual expectations must yield to the supervening responsibility of the directors to discharge their fiduciary duties on a continuing basis. The merger agreement and voting agreements, as they were combined to operate in concert in this case, are inconsistent with the NCS directors' fiduciary duties. To that extent, we hold that they are invalid and unenforceable.

VEASEY, Chief Justice, with whom STEELE, Justice, joins dissenting.

The process by which this merger agreement came about involved a joint decision by the controlling stockholders and the board of directors to secure what appeared to be the only value-enhancing transaction available for a company on the brink of bankruptcy. The Majority adopts a new rule of law that imposes a prohibition on the NCS board's ability to act in concert with controlling stockholders to lock up this merger. The Majority reaches this conclusion by analyzing the challenged deal protection measures as isolated board actions. The Majority concludes that the board owed a duty to the NCS minority stockholders to refrain from acceding to the Genesis demand for an irrevocable lock-up notwithstanding the compelling circumstances confronting the board and the board's disinterested, informed, good faith exercise of its business judgment.

Because we believe this Court must respect the reasoned judgment of the board of directors and give effect to the wishes of the controlling stockholders, we respectfully disagree with the Majority's reasoning that results in a holding that the confluence of board and stockholder action constitutes a breach of fiduciary duty. The essential fact that must always be remembered is that this agreement and the voting commitments of Outcalt and Shaw concluded a lengthy search and intense negotiation process in the context of insolvency and creditor pressure where no other viable bid had emerged. Accordingly, we endorse the Vice Chancellor's well-reasoned analysis that the NCS board's action before the hostile bid emerged was within the bounds of its fiduciary duties under these facts.

We share with the Majority and the independent NCS board of directors the motivation to serve carefully and in good faith the best interests of the corporate enterprise and, thereby, the stockholders of NCS. It is now known, of course, after the case is over, that the stockholders of NCS will receive substantially more by tendering their shares into the topping bid of Omnicare than they would have received in the Genesis merger, as a result of the post-agreement Omnicare bid and the injunctive relief ordered by the Majority of this Court. Our jurisprudence cannot, however, be seen as turning on such ex post felicitous results. Rather, the NCS board's good faith decision must be subject to a real-time review of the board action before the NCS-Genesis merger agreement was entered into.

AN ANALYSIS OF THE PROCESS LEADING TO THE LOCK-UP REFLECTS A QUINTESSENTIAL, DISINTERESTED AND INFORMED BOARD DECISION REACHED IN GOOD FAITH

The Majority has adopted the Vice Chancellor's findings and has assumed arguendo that the NCS board fulfilled its duties of care, loyalty, and good faith by entering into the Genesis merger agreement. Indeed, this conclusion is indisputable on this record. The problem is that the Majority has removed from their proper context the contractual merger protection provisions. The lock-ups here cannot be reviewed in a vacuum. A court should review the entire bidding process to determine whether the independent board's actions permitted the directors to inform themselves of their available options and whether they acted in good faith.

Going into negotiations with Genesis, the NCS directors knew that, up until that time, NCS had found only one potential bidder, Omnicare. Omnicare had refused to buy NCS except at a fire sale price through an asset sale in bankruptcy. Omnicare's best proposal at that stage would not have paid off all creditors and would have provided nothing for stockholders. The Noteholders, represented by the Ad Hoc Committee, were willing to oblige Omnicare and force NCS into bankruptcy if Omnicare would pay in full the NCS debt. Through the NCS board's efforts, Genesis expressed interest that became increasingly attractive. . . .

Situations will arise where business realities demand a lock-up so that wealth-enhancing transactions may go forward. Accordingly, any bright-line rule prohibiting lock-ups could, in circumstances such as these, chill otherwise permissible conduct.

OUR JURISPRUDENCE DOES NOT COMPEL THIS COURT TO INVALIDATE THE JOINT ACTION OF THE BOARD AND THE CONTROLLING STOCKHOLDERS

The Majority invalidates the NCS board's action by announcing a new rule that represents an extension of our jurisprudence. That new rule can be narrowly stated as follows: A merger agreement entered into after a market search, before any prospect of a topping bid has emerged, which locks up stockholder approval and does not contain a "fiduciary out" provision, is per se invalid when a later significant topping bid emerges. As we have noted, this bright-line, per se rule would apply regardless of (1) the circumstances leading up to the agreement and (2) the fact that stockholders who control voting power had irrevocably committed themselves, as stockholders, to vote for the merger. Narrowly stated, this new rule is a judicially-created "third rail" that now becomes one of the given "rules of the game," to be taken into account by the negotiators and drafters of merger agreements. In our view, this new rule is an unwise extension of existing precedent.

Although it is debatable whether *Unocal* applies — and we believe that the better rule in this situation is that the business judgment rule should apply[102] — we will, nevertheless, assume arguendo — as the Vice Chancellor did — that *Unocal* applies. Therefore, under *Unocal* the NCS directors had the burden of going forward with the evidence to show that there was a threat to corporate policy and effectiveness and that their actions were reasonable in response to that threat. The Vice Chancellor correctly found that they reasonably perceived the threat that NCS did not have a viable offer from Omnicare — or anyone else — to pay off its creditors, cure its insolvency and provide some payment to stockholders. The NCS board's actions — as the Vice Chancellor correctly held — were reasonable in relation to the threat because the Genesis deal was the "only game in town," the NCS directors got the best deal they could from Genesis and — but-for the emergence of Genesis on the scene — there would have been no viable deal.

In our view, the Majority misapplies the *Unitrin* concept of "coercive and preclusive" measures to preempt a proper proportionality balancing. Thus, the Majority asserts that "in applying enhanced judicial scrutiny to defensive devices designed to protect a merger agreement, ... a court must ... determine that those measures are not preclusive or coercive. ... " Here, the deal protection measures were not adopted unilaterally by the board to fend off an existing hostile offer that threatened the corporate policy and effectiveness of NCS. They were adopted because Genesis — the "only game in town" — would not save NCS, its creditors and its stockholders without these provisions.

The Majority — incorrectly, in our view — relies on *Unitrin* to advance its analysis. The discussion of "draconian" measures in *Unitrin* dealt with unilateral board action, a repurchase program, designed to fend off an existing hostile offer by American General. In *Unitrin* we recognized the need to police preclusive and coercive actions initiated by the board to delay or retard an existing hostile bid so as to ensure that the stockholders can benefit from the board's negotiations with the bidder or others and to exercise effectively the franchise as the ultimate check on board action.

---

102. The basis for the Unocal doctrine is the "omnipresent specter" of the board's self-interest to entrench itself in office. *Unocal Corp. v. Mesa Petroleum Co.*, 493 A.2d 946, 954 (Del.1985). NCS was not plagued with a specter of self-interest. Unlike the Unocal situation, a hostile offer did not arise here until after the market search and the locked-up deal with Genesis.

Unitrin polices the effect of board action on existing tender offers and proxy contests to ensure that the board cannot permanently impose its will on the stockholders, leaving the stockholders no recourse to their voting rights.

The very measures the Majority cites as "coercive" were approved by Shaw and Outcalt through the lens of their independent assessment of the merits of the transaction. The proper inquiry in this case is whether the NCS board had taken actions that "have the effect of causing the stockholders to vote in favor of the proposed transaction for some reason other than the merits of that transaction."[109]

Outcalt and Shaw were fully informed stockholders. As the NCS controlling stockholders, they made an informed choice to commit their voting power to the merger. The minority stockholders were deemed to know that when controlling stockholders have 65% of the vote they can approve a merger without the need for the minority votes.

Moreover, to the extent a minority stockholder may have felt "coerced" to vote for the merger, which was already a fait accompli, it was a meaningless coercion—or no coercion at all—because the controlling votes, those of Outcalt and Shaw, were already "cast." Although the fact that the controlling votes were committed to the merger "precluded" an overriding vote against the merger by the Class A stockholders, the pejorative "preclusive" label applicable in a *Unitrin* fact situation has no application here.

Therefore, there was no meaningful minority stockholder voting decision to coerce.

In applying *Unocal* scrutiny, we believe the Majority incorrectly preempted the proportionality inquiry. In our view, the proportionality inquiry must account for the reality that the contractual measures protecting this merger agreement were necessary to obtain the Genesis deal. The Majority has not demonstrated that the director action was a disproportionate response to the threat posed. Indeed, it is clear to us that the board action to negotiate the best deal reasonably available with the only viable merger partner (Genesis) who could satisfy the creditors and benefit the stockholders, was reasonable in relation to the threat, by any practical yardstick.

AN ABSOLUTE LOCK-UP IS NOT A PER SE VIOLATION
OF FIDUCIARY DUTY

We respectfully disagree with the Majority's conclusion that the NCS board breached its fiduciary duties to the Class A stockholders by failing to negotiate a "fiduciary out" in the Genesis merger agreement. What is the practical import of a "fiduciary out?" It is a contractual provision, articulated in a manner to be negotiated, that would permit the board of

---

109. [Williams v.] Geier, 671 A. 2d [1368] at 1382-83.

the corporation being acquired to exit without breaching the merger agreement in the event of a superior offer.

In this case, Genesis made it abundantly clear early on that it was willing to negotiate a deal with NCS but only on the condition that it would not be a "stalking horse." Thus, it wanted to be certain that a third party could not use its deal with NCS as a floor against which to begin a bidding war.

As a result of this negotiating position, a "fiduciary out" was not acceptable to Genesis. The Majority Opinion holds that such a negotiating position, if implemented in the agreement, is invalid per se where there is an absolute lock-up. We know of no authority in our jurisprudence supporting this new rule, and we believe it is unwise and unwarranted.

One hopes that the Majority rule announced here—though clearly erroneous in our view—will be interpreted narrowly and will be seen as sui generis. By deterring bidders from engaging in negotiations like those present here and requiring that there must always be a fiduciary out, the universe of potential bidders who could reasonably be expected to benefit stockholders could shrink or disappear.

Nevertheless, if the holding is confined to these unique facts, negotiators may be able to navigate around this new hazard.

Accordingly, we respectfully dissent.

[Justice Steele also filed a separate dissent.]

NOTES & QUESTIONS

1. The Court finds that the NCS Board went wrong by not negotiating for an effective fiduciary out in the Genesis transaction. What would have happened, do you think, if the NCS Board had tried to do what the Court insisted on?

2. In holding that a fiduciary out must be included in the merger agreements undertaking to call a meeting, the majority quotes the Restatement (Second) of Contracts §193 which provides that a "promise by a fiduciary to violate his fiduciary duty or a promise that tends to induce such a violation is unenforceable on grounds of public policy." The comments to that section indicate that "[d]irectors and other officials of a corporation act in a fiduciary capacity and are subject to the rule stated in this Section." Can you identify a duty that the members of the board violated (or promised to violate) on July 28th?

3. Applying a *Unocal/Unitrin* analysis to the execution of the Genesis agreement, what would you identify as the risk that the Board sought to protect against? What in the view of the majority makes the board's choice "unreasonable"? Does the majority opinion in effect hold that *the law required the board to accept the business risk* that Genesis would walk if

it did not get the deal protections it sought? How can you support this result from a policy perspective?

4. In applying *Unocal/Unitrin*, the Court states: "The latitude a board will have in either maintaining or using the defensive devices it has adopted to protect the merger it approved will vary according to the degree of benefit or detriment to the stockholders' interests that is presented by the value or terms of the subsequent competing transaction." The Court seems to be saying that a target board will have less latitude to protect the deal if a higher bid emerges later; that is, the Court will assess lockups with 20-20 hindsight. In the words of one observer, does the Court's holding in *Omnicare* require directors to be omniscient? See *Orman v. Cullman* (described below), 2004 WL 2348395 at*8 n.98 ("As formulated, the [*Omnicare*] test would appear to result in judicial invalidation of negotiated contractual provisions based on the advantages of hindsight.").

5. Do you think the majority's analysis was affected by the fact that the controlling shareholders did not represent a majority of the equity capital? (The Court notes that the public shareholders represented 80% of the equity and that, according to the Court, they wanted the Omincare deal.) Is this a legitimate consideration in your opinion?

6. Did Genesis have any obligation *not* to ask for the controller's irrevocable proxy, or for the merger term mandating the calling of a shareholder meeting at which the merger would be voted upon (authorized by §251(c)) or to refrain from giving the seller a 24-hour deadline? If these positions did not violate a duty of any sort what is the significance to the majority of its taking these positions?

7. In January 2000, Swedish Match agreed to buy out the minority shareholders of General Cigar for $15.25 per share cash, such that Swedish Match would own 64 percent and the controlling Cullman family would own 36% of General Cigar (with the Cullmans retaining control by virtue of their high-vote stock). The merger agreement contained: (1) no breakup fee; (2) a fiduciary out that allowed General Cigar to consider an unsolicited superior proposal; (3) a class vote of the A and B shares separately; and (4) a majority-of-the-minority approval condition from the Class A shareholders. In addition, the Cullman family agreed to vote their controlling interest for the Swedish Match transaction, and against any alternative acquisition proposal for 18 months after any termination of the merger. Putting it all together, the minority shareholders could veto the deal, but if they did so they would not be able to see another deal for 18 months. Chancellor Chandler of the Delaware Chancery Court upheld the shareholder lockup agreement: "In [*Omnicare*], the challenged action was the directors' entering into a contract in their capacity as *directors*. The Cullmans entered into the voting agreement *as shareholders*. ... [Unlike *Omnicare*,] the public shareholders were free to reject the proposed deal, even though, permissibly, their vote may have been influenced by the existence of the

50. *Orman v. Cullman*, 2004 WL 2348395 at*7 (Del. Ch. Oct. 20, 2004) (emphasis in original).

deal protection measures."[50] Do you find the distinction persuasive? How would you structure a shareholder lockup in the aftermath of *Omnicare* and *Orman v. Cullman?*

13.7   STATE ANTITAKEOVER STATUTES[51]

13.7.1   First- and Second-Generation Antitakeover Statutes (1968-1987)

Although poison pills were the decisive legal development of the hostile takeover era, the states were also active before and after the advent of the pill. State legislation, which came in waves, was generally an attempt by the forces of the status quo to limit the disruption that accompanied hostile takeovers. The first wave of statutes followed the enactment in 1968 of what may be thought of as the first federal antitakeover legislation, the Williams Act.[52] Over the following 13 years, approximately 37 states enacted some version of "first-generation" antitakeover legislation.[53]

The first generation of antitakeover statutes addressed both disclosure and fairness concerns and was generally limited to attempted takeovers of companies with a connection to the enacting state.[54] An example is the Illinois Business Takeover Act of 1979, which required any offer for the shares of qualifying target companies to be registered with the secretary of state, after which the offer entered a 20-day waiting period and then became registered unless, during that period, the secretary called a hearing to adjudicate the substantive fairness of the offer. The secretary exercised discretionary power to call a hearing to protect the shareholders of the target company, but she was required to do so if requested by a majority of the target's outside directors or by Illinois shareholders who owned 10 percent of the class of securities subject to the offer. The secretary was required to deny registration if a tender offer failed to "provide full and fair disclosure to the offerees of all material information concerning the take-over offer" or was "inequitable or would work or tend to work a fraud or deceit upon the offerees." In 1982, the U.S. Supreme Court struck down the Illinois Act[55] as preempted by the federal Williams Act and thus in

---

51. We thank Allison Gooley for her research and drafting assistance on this section.

52. Recall from Chapter 11 that, by creating an auction period and forcing disclosure of takeover plans, the Williams Act raised the costs of takeovers and shifted transaction gains from acquirers to target shareholders. See Easterbrook & Fischel, supra note 1.

53. See Roberta Romano, *Law as a Product: Some Pieces in the Incorporation Puzzle*, 1 J.L. Econ. & Org. 225 (1985).

54. For example, the Illinois Business Takeover Act of 1979 applied to target corporations in which Illinois shareholders held 10 percent or more of the shares subject to the tender offer and to target corporations who satisfied any two of three conditions in an alternative test for local interest: having its principal executive office in Illinois; being organized under the laws of Illinois; or having at least 10 percent of its stated capital and paid-in surplus represented within the state.

55. *Edgar v. MITE Corp.*, 457 U.S. 624 (1982).

violation of the Supremacy Clause (and — it seems likely — the Commerce Clause).

After the first generation of antitakeover statutes was invalidated, a second generation of statutes attempted to avoid preemption by the Williams Act by maintaining an appropriate balance between the interests of the offerors and the targets within the overarching policy of investor protection. One example is the "fair price statute," which deters coercive two-tier takeovers by requiring that minority shareholders who are frozen out in the second step of such a takeover receive no less for their shares than the shareholders who tendered in the first step of the takeover. Typically, this result is achieved by requiring a very high supermajority vote to approve a freeze-out merger unless the merger provides shareholders with a statutory "fair price" that equals or exceeds the original tender offer price.[56]

Another example of a second-generation antitakeover statute is the "control share statute," which resists hostile takeovers by requiring a disinterested shareholder vote to approve the purchase of shares by any person crossing certain levels of share ownership in the company that are deemed to constitute "acquisition of control" (usually 20 percent, 33.33 percent, and 50 percent of outstanding shares). Ohio enacted such a statute in 1982 that became the model for other states.[57] Indiana's control share acquisition statute varied the Ohio model by allowing the bidder to cross the relevant ownership thresholds without obtaining shareholder approval but with an automatic loss of voting rights. The offeror could regain voting rights only upon gaining approval from a majority of disinterested shareholders. Indiana's statute was upheld by the United States Supreme Court in the following case.

CTS CORP. v. DYNAMICS CORP. OF AMERICA

481 U.S. 69 (1987)

POWELL, J.:

[The Indiana Control Share Acquisition Act applies to "issuing public corporations."] An "issuing public corporation" is defined as:

    (A) a corporation that has:

        (1) "one hundred (100) or more shareholders;

        (2) "its principal place of business, its principal office, or substantial assets within Indiana; and

        (3) "either:

            (A) "more than ten percent (10%) of its shareholders resident in Indiana;

            (B) "more than ten percent (10%) of its shares owned by Indiana residents; or

---

56. Maryland adopted a fair price statute in 1986. Md. Gen. Corp. L. §§3-601 to 3-603 (1986), and several other states followed suit. See, e.g., Conn. Stock Corp. Act §§33-374a to 33-374c (1986); Ga. Bus. Corp. L. §§232-234 (1985).

57. Ohio Gen. Corp. L. §1701.32.

(C) "ten thousand (10,000) shareholders resident in Indiana."
§23-1-42-4(a).

The Act focuses on the acquisition of "control shares" in an issuing public corporation. Under the Act, an entity acquires "control shares" whenever it acquires shares that, but for the operation of the Act, would bring its voting power in the corporation to or above any of three thresholds: 20%, 33 1/3%, or 50%. §23-1-42-1. An entity that acquires control shares does not necessarily acquire voting rights. Rather, it gains those rights only "to the extent granted by resolution approved by the shareholders of the issuing public corporation." §23-1-42-9(a). Section 23-1-42-9 (b) requires a majority vote of all disinterested[2] shareholders holding each class of stock for passage of such a resolution. The practical effect of this requirement is to condition acquisition of control of a corporation on approval of a majority of the pre-existing disinterested shareholders.

The shareholders decide whether to confer rights on the control shares at the next regularly scheduled meeting of the shareholders, or at a specially scheduled meeting. The acquirer can require management of the corporation to hold such a special meeting within 50 days if it files an "acquiring person statement," requests the meeting, and agrees to pay the expenses of the meeting. . . .

B

On March 10, 1986, appellee Dynamics Corporation of America (Dynamics) owned 9.6% of the common stock of appellant CTS Corporation, an Indiana corporation. . . . Dynamics announced a tender offer for another million shares in CTS; purchase of those shares would have brought Dynamics' ownership interest in CTS to 27.5%. . . . On March 27, the board of directors of CTS . . . elected to be governed by the provisions of the Act, see §23-1-17-3.

Four days later, on March 31, Dynamics moved for leave to amend [an existing] complaint to allege that the Act is pre-empted by the Williams Act . . . and violates the Commerce Clause. . . .
[The first question in these cases is whether the Williams Act preempts the Indiana Act.] Because it is entirely possible for entities to comply with both the Williams Act and the Indiana Act, the state statute can be pre-empted only if it frustrates the purposes of the federal law. . . .

The Indiana Act differs in major respects from the Illinois statute that the Court considered in *Edgar v. MITE Corp.* . . .

[The MITE plurality, per Justice White] identified three offending features of the Illinois statute. . . . [First, it] noted that the Illinois statute provided for a 20-day precommencement period. During this time,

---

2. "Interested shares" are shares with respect to which the acquirer, an officer, or an inside director of the corporation "may exercise or direct the exercise of the voting power of the corporation in the election of directors." §23-1-42-3. If the record date passes before the acquirer purchases shares pursuant to the tender offer, the purchased shares will not be "interested shares" within the meaning of the Act. . . .

management could disseminate its views on the upcoming offer to share-holders, but offerors could not publish their offers. The plurality found that this provision gave management "a powerful tool to combat tender offers." . . . [Second] was a provision for a hearing on a tender offer that, because it set no deadline, allowed management " 'to stymie indefinitely a takeover,' ". . . . [Third] was [the] requirement that the fairness of tender offers would be reviewed by the Illinois Secretary of State. Noting that "Congress intended for investors to be free to make their own decisions," the plurality concluded that " '[t]he state thus offers investor protection at the expense of investor autonomy — an approach quite in conflict with that adopted by Congress." ' *Id.*, at 639-640. . . .

As the plurality opinion in *MITE* did not represent the views of a majority of the Court, we are not bound by its reasoning. We need not question that reasoning, however, because we believe the Indiana Act passes muster even under the broad interpretation of the Williams Act articulated by [the plurality]. [T]he overriding concern of the *MITE* plurality was that the Illinois statute . . . operated to favor management against offerors, to the detriment of shareholders. By contrast, the statute now before the Court protects the independent shareholder. . . .

The Indiana Act operates on the assumption, implicit in the Williams Act, that independent shareholders faced with tender offers often are at a disadvantage. By allowing such shareholders to vote as a group, the Act protects them from the coercive aspects of some tender offers . . . [which] furthers the federal policy of investor protection.

. . . Unlike the *MITE* statute, the Indiana Act does not give either management or the offeror an advantage in communicating with the share-holders about the impending offer. The Act also does not impose an indefinite delay on tender offers. Nothing in the Act prohibits an offeror from consummating an offer on the 20th business day, the earliest day permitted under applicable federal regulations . . . Nor does the Act allow the state government to interpose its views of fairness between willing buyers and sellers of shares of the target company. Rather, the Act allows shareholders to evaluate the fairness of the offer collectively. . . .

The Court of Appeals based its finding of pre-emption on its view that the practical effect of the Indiana Act is to delay consummation of tender offers until 50 days after the commencement of the offer. . . .

[But t]he Act does not impose an absolute 50-day delay on tender offers. . . . If the offeror fears an adverse shareholder vote under the Act, it can make a conditional tender offer, offering to accept shares on the condition that the shares receive voting rights within a certain period of time. The Williams Act permits tender offers to be conditioned on the offeror's subsequently obtaining regulatory approval. . . .

Even assuming that the Indiana Act imposes some additional delay, nothing in *MITE* suggested that any delay imposed by state regulation, however short, would create a conflict with the Williams Act. . . .

Finally, we note that the Williams Act would pre-empt a variety of state corporate laws of hitherto unquestioned validity if it were construed to pre-empt any state statute that may limit or delay the free exercise of power after a successful tender offer. State corporate laws commonly permit corporations to stagger the terms of their directors. . . . By staggering the terms of directors, and thus having annual elections for only one class of directors each year, corporations may delay the time when a successful offeror gains control of the board of directors. Similarly, state corporation laws commonly provide for cumulative voting. . . .

As an alternative basis for its decision, the Court of Appeals held that the Act violates the Commerce Clause . . . [in] that [it] discriminate[s] against interstate commerce. . . .

[N]othing in the Indiana Act imposes a greater burden on out-of-state offerors than it does on similarly situated Indiana offerors[. Therefore,] we reject the contention that the Act discriminates against interstate commerce. . . .

This Court's recent Commerce Clause cases . . . have invalidated statutes that may adversely affect interstate commerce by subjecting activities to inconsistent regulations. . . . [But t]he Indiana Act poses no such problem. So long as each State regulates voting rights only in the corporations it has created, each corporation will be subject to the law of only one State. No principle of corporation law and practice is more firmly established than a State's authority to regulate domestic corporations, including the authority to define the voting rights of shareholders. . . .

[Every state regulates the governance of domestic corporations.] These regulatory laws may affect directly a variety of corporate transactions. Mergers are a typical example. In view of the substantial effect that a merger may have on the shareholders' interests in a corporation, many States require supermajority votes to approve mergers. . . . By requiring a greater vote for mergers than is required for other transactions, these laws make it more difficult for corporations to merge. State laws also may provide for "dissenters' rights" under which minority shareholders who disagree with corporate decisions to take particular actions are entitled to sell their shares to the corporation at fair market value. . . . By requiring the corporation to purchase the shares of dissenting shareholders, these laws may inhibit a corporation from engaging in the specified transactions.

It thus is an accepted part of the business landscape . . . for States to create corporations, to prescribe their powers, and to define the rights that are acquired by purchasing their shares. A State has an interest in promoting stable relationships among parties involved in the corporations it charters, as well as in ensuring that investors in such corporations have an effective voice in corporate affairs.

There can be no doubt that the Act reflects these concerns. The primary purpose of the Act is to protect the shareholders of Indiana corporations. It does this by affording shareholders, when a takeover offer is made, an opportunity to decide collectively whether the resulting change in voting control of the corporation, as they perceive it, would be desirable. . . .

On its face, the Indiana Control Share Acquisitions Chapter evenhandedly determines the voting rights of shares of Indiana corporations. The Act does not conflict with the provisions or purposes of the Williams Act. To the limited extent that the Act affects interstate commerce, this is justified by the State's interests in defining the attributes of shares in its corporations and in protecting shareholders. Congress has never questioned the need for state regulation of these matters. Nor do we think such regulation offends the Constitution. Accordingly, we reverse the judgment of the Court of Appeals. . . .

13.7.2　Third-Generation Antitakeover Statutes (1987-2000)

After the Supreme Court's approval of the Indiana statute, numerous states adopted "third-generation" antitakeover statutes — third generation because they followed, logically and chronologically, from the Supreme Court's holding in *CTS* that state antitakeover legislation is consistent with both the Williams Act and the Commerce Clause if it allows a bidder to acquire shares, even if it makes such acquisition less attractive in some circumstances. A prominent example is the "business combination statute," also referred to as the moratorium statute. This type of statute prohibits a corporation from engaging in a "business combination" (variously defined) within a set time period after a shareholder acquires more than a threshold level of share ownership. In some statutes, an exception allows a merger to proceed in that time period if a statutory "fair price" is paid in the merger. Such statutes thus act as a ban on immediate liquidation of an acquired entity but not as bar to takeovers where the acquirer will continue to operate the business of the target. New York adopted the first moratorium statute in 1985, NYBCL §912 (1985), and was followed by other states, including Delaware, DGCL §203 (1988).[58]

NOTE ON DGCL §203

The full text of DGCL §203 is available in your statutory supplement. Like other business combination statutes, DGCL §203 is meant to deter "junk bond"-financed "bust-up" takeovers by preventing acquirers from getting their hands on the assets of target firms. There are two "outs" that may affect the planning of an acquisition. First, the statute's restriction does not apply if the bidder can acquire 85 percent of the outstanding voting stock in a single transaction (on the apparent premise that this level of unity implies a lack of coercion). Second, its restrictions will not be imposed if, after acquiring more than 15 percent, but less than 85 percent, a bidder can secure a two-thirds vote from the remaining shareholders (other than itself) as well as board approval. Obviously, the 85 percent exclusion chills partial

---

58. The constitutionality of these statutes was upheld, albeit unenthusiastically, by the Court of Appeals for the Seventh Circuit in *Amanda Acquisition Corp. v. Universal Foods Corp.*, 877 F.2d 496 (7th Cir. 1989) ("Wisconsin's law may well be folly; we are confident that it is constitutional"); see also *BNS, Inc. v. Koppers Co.*, 683 F. Supp 458 (D. Del. 1988); and *City Capital Assocs. Ltd. Partnership v. Interco, Inc.*, 696 F. Supp. 1551 (D. Del. 1988), both upholding the Delaware statute.

bids and low-premium takeovers. The two-thirds vote exception may have a more curious and even paradoxical impact because the more shares a successful bidder gains (short of achieving 85 percent), the greater will be the voting power of any intransigent minority that does not tender. Suppose, for example, that a bidder acquires 80 percent of the voting stock (thus failing to come within the 85 percent exemption in §203(a)(2)). Now, it must secure a two-thirds vote from this remaining 20 percent if it is to escape a three-year moratorium. Thus, if 1/3 of 20 percent or 6.6 percent of the stock is opposed (or wants to hold up the acquirer) or if that percentage simply does not vote (since the statute requires 2/3 of outstanding shareholders to vote affirmatively), the §203(a)(3) exception is not satisfied. Potentially, this could create an incentive to make a partial bid for only 50 percent (if the bidder is uncertain about its ability to acquire 85 percent and it fears falling just short of that level). Alternatively, the bidder could protect itself by specifying an 85 percent minimum tender condition to its obligation to close its tender offer.

Unlike the New York business combination statute, which bars any substantial sale of assets or merger for five years after the threshold is crossed without prior approval, DGCL §203(c)(3) defines the term "business combination" narrowly so as to cover only transactions between the target and the bidder or its affiliates. Thus, a takeover entrepreneur could still seek to acquire control of a company having a liquidation value substantially in excess of its stock market value in order to sell those assets — either piecemeal or in a single sale — to others, and it could then pay out the proceeds of this sale as a pro rata dividend to all remaining shareholders.[59]

QUESTIONS ON DGCL §203

1. How difficult do you suppose it is to acquire 85 percent of the stock in a diffusely held corporation through a tender offer?
2. If you wished to exploit one of the two loopholes in DGCL §203 in a hostile offer, which would you choose? Could you choose both? What might management do to thwart you?
3. How does DGCL §203 work? Why do acquirers need to get their hands on corporate assets within three years? Isn't it enough to be a controlling shareholder?

A second example of the post-*CTS* statutes is the disgorgement statute, which has been adopted by Pennsylvania, 15 Pa. Consol. Stat. Ann.

---

59. Although the content of the Delaware statute is fairly mild as antitakeover statutes go, its coverage is extraordinarily broad. It has been estimated that the passage of the Delaware statute by itself extended the protective mantle of a state takeover statute to 80 percent of the business capital in the United States from a prior level of 20 percent. See D. Bandow, *Curbing Raiders Is Bad for Business,* N. Y. Times, Feb. 7, 1988, at F-2.

§§2561-2567, and Ohio, Ohio Rev. Code Ann. §1707.043. These statutes mandate the disgorgement of profits made by bidders upon the sale of either stock in the target or assets of the target. Any bidder who acquires a fixed percentage of voting rights, including (in some acts) voting rights acquired by proxy solicitation, is subject to this statute. Thus, under the Pennsylvania statute, any profit realized by a "controlling person" from the sale of any equity security of the target within 18 months of becoming a "controlling person" belongs to the target. A "controlling person" includes any person or group who has acquired, offered to acquire, or publicly disclosed the intent to acquire over 20 percent of the total voting rights. Since the emphasis is on voting rights, a solicitation of proxies triggers the disgorgement provision. The Ohio statute is more circumscribed, providing safe harbors to management proxy solicitations. It also provides safe harbors to insurgent solicitations made in accordance with federal proxy rules where the solicitation of the voting right is limited to the matters described in the proxy statement and constrained by the instructions of the proxy giver. The constitutionality of these statutes remains untested.

A third example of new antitakeover legislation is the "redemption rights statute," which allows shareholders to bring an appraisal action not merely for freeze-out mergers but also whenever a person makes a "controlling share acquisition," defined as acquisition of 30 percent of a corporation's stock. The court, in calculating the "fair value" of the stock of petitioning shareholders, is required to include a pro rata allocation of the control premium the acquirer paid for the "controlling share acquisition." Again, this statute has not yet been challenged.

"Constituency statutes" comprise the last major class of third-generation statutes.[60] They allow, or in some states require, the board of a target corporation to consider the interests of constituencies other than the shareholders when determining what response to take to a hostile takeover offer. These statutes deter takeovers by releasing directors from some of the fiduciary constraints imposed by case law in the takeover context, thus allowing the board to use a broader range of potential justifications for taking defensive measures. Ohio adopted its statute in 1988, Ohio Gen. Corp. L. §1701.59 (1988), and Indiana in 1989, Ind. Code §23-1-26-5. The Indiana statute, excerpted below, also alters the content of and judicial scrutiny applied to directors' duties, explicitly rejecting Delaware's imposition of enhanced scrutiny and referring solely to "good faith exercise of . . . business judgment after reasonable investigation" as the measure of a director's duty.

---

60. There are other, more idiosyncratic antitakeover statutes as well. The less common statutes include those that prohibit targets from adopting golden parachutes for their executives or paying greenmail without shareholder approval, Ariz. Rev. Stat. §§1202, 1204; authorize the adoption of discriminatory rights plans without shareholder approval, NYBCL §§501, 505; or require appraisals in management-led buyouts, Cal. Gen. Corp. L. §§181, 1001, 1101.

INDIANA CODE

§23-1-35-1   [Standards of Conduct; Liability; Reaffirmation of Corporate Governance Rules; Presumption]

(a) A director shall, based on facts then known to the director, discharge the duties as a director, including the director's duties as a member of a committee:

(1) In good faith;

(2) With the care an ordinarily prudent person in a like position would exercise under similar circumstances; and

(3) In a manner the director reasonably believes to be in the best interests of the corporation. . . .

(d) A director may, in considering the best interests of a corporation, consider the effects of any action on shareholders, employees, suppliers, and customers of the corporation, and communities in which offices or other facilities of the corporation are located, and any other factors the director considers pertinent.

(e) A director is not liable for any action taken as a director, or any failure to take any action, unless:

(1) The director has breached or failed to perform the duties of the director's office in compliance with this section; and

(2) The breach or failure to perform constitutes willful misconduct or recklessness.

(f) In enacting this article, the general assembly established corporate governance rules for Indiana corporations, including in this chapter, the standards of conduct applicable to directors of Indiana corporations, and the corporate constituent groups and interests that a director may take into account in exercising the director's business judgment. The general assembly intends to reaffirm certain of these corporate governance rules to ensure that the directors of Indiana corporations . . . are not required to approve a proposed corporate action if the directors in good faith determine, after considering and weighing as they deem appropriate the effects of such action on the corporation's constituents, that such action is not in the best interests of the corporation. In making such determination, directors are not required to consider the effects of a proposed corporate action on any particular corporate constituent group or interest as a dominant or controlling factor. Without limiting the generality of the foregoing, directors are not required to render inapplicable any of the provisions of IC 23-1-43, to redeem any rights under or to render inapplicable a shareholder rights plan adopted pursuant to IC 23-1-26-5, or to take or decline to take any other action under this article, solely because of the effect such action might have on a proposed acquisition of control of the corporation or the amounts that might be paid to shareholders under such an acquisition. Certain judicial decisions in Delaware and other jurisdictions, which might otherwise be looked to for guidance in interpreting Indiana corporate law, including decisions relating to potential change of control ... are inconsistent with the proper application of the business judgment rule under this article. Therefore, the general assembly intends:

> (1) To reaffirm that this section allows directors the full discretion to weigh the factors enumerated in subsection (d) as they deem appropriate; and
>
> (2) To protect both directors and the validity of corporate action taken by them in the good faith exercise of their business judgment after reasonable investigation.
>
> (g) In taking or declining to take any action, ... a board of directors may ... consider both the short term and long term best interests of the corporation, taking into account, and weighing as the directors deem appropriate, the effects thereof on the corporation's shareholders and the other corporate constituent groups and interests listed or described in subsection (d) as well as any other factors deemed pertinent by the directors under subsection (d). If a determination is made with respect to the foregoing with the approval of a majority of the disinterested directors of the board of directors, that determination shall conclusively be presumed to be valid unless it can be demonstrated that the determination was not made in good faith after reasonable investigation. . . .

QUESTIONS ON INDIANA CODE §§23-1-26-5 ET SEQ.

1. How fundamental is the change imposed by the Indiana statute? Can we still speak of shareholders as the owners of Indiana corporations?

2. What effect do you think the Indiana statute will have on the behavior of corporations toward nonshareholder constituencies? Can we analogize this statute to one that requires direct constituency representation on the board (for example, labor or community directors)?

13.8   PROXY CONTESTS FOR CORPORATE CONTROL

In a world in which a board may unilaterally adopt a poison pill, those seeing opportunity in a change of management have only two alternatives. The first is to negotiate with the incumbent board. In some cases, board leadership might be convinced that a change-in-control transaction is a good thing. A cynic might say that the odds of persuasion are increased by lucrative inducements for CEOs, such as consultation agreements or other compensation. While an incumbent director who permits her business judgment to be tainted by personal benefit undoubtedly breaches her fiduciary duties, the enforcement of these duties is imperfect. Therefore, one might predict that, as the Delaware Supreme Court has become more willing to permit boards to leave poison pills in place indefinitely, the number of "friendly deals," in which controlling management captures (in the form of compensation payments or otherwise) a larger share of the transaction gains, will increase.[61]

The second alternative for displacing management is the hostile option of running both a proxy contest and a tender offer simultaneously. In this case, closing the tender offer is conditioned on electing the acquirer's nominees to the board and the board's redemption of the target's poison pill. See, e.g., *Hilton Hotels, Inc. v. ITT Corp.*, 978 F. Supp. 1342 (D. Nev. 1997). Contests of this type leave open a variety of further defensive steps that the target may attempt to take. For example, the target board may attempt to affect the outcome of the proxy fight by issuing stock into friendly hands; it may move the meeting date; it may sell assets that the "raider" presumably treasures — and it may sell them to a friendly party for high-vote stock; it may put covenants in new loan agreements that impede the takeover, etc. In other words, a target board may engage in a wide variety of actions that are designed to impede an insurgent from gathering enough support to oust the current board through a shareholder vote. The following cases address the legal test for evaluating board actions that affect proxy contests.

SCHNELL v. CHRIS-CRAFT INDUSTRIES, INC.

285 A.2d 437 (Del. 1971)

HERRMANN, J.:

This is an appeal from the denial by the Court of Chancery of the petition of dissident stockholders for injunctive relief to prevent management from advancing the date of the annual stockholders' meeting from January 11, 1972, as previously set by the by-laws, to December 8, 1971. . . .

In our view, [the conclusions of the Court below] amount to a finding that management has attempted to utilize the corporate machinery and the Delaware Law for the purpose of perpetuating itself in office; and, to that end, for the purpose of obstructing the legitimate efforts of dissident stockholders in the exercise of their rights to undertake a proxy contest against management. These are inequitable purposes, contrary to established principles of corporate democracy. The advancement by directors of the by-law date of a stockholders' meeting, for such purposes, may not be permitted to stand. Compare *Condec Corporation v. Lunkenheimer Company*, Del. Ch., 230 A.2d 769 (1967).

When the by-laws of a corporation designate the date of the annual meeting of stockholders, it is to be expected that those who intend to contest the reelection of incumbent management will gear their campaign to the by-law date. It is not to be expected that management will attempt to advance the date in order to obtain an inequitable advantage in the contest.

---

61. See, e.g., Marcel Kahan & Edward B. Rock, *How I Learned to Stop Worrying and Love the Pill: Adaptive Responses to Takeover Law*, 69 U. Chi. L. Rev. 871 (2002).

Management contends that it has complied strictly with the provisions of the new Delaware Corporation Law in changing the by-law date. The answer to that contention, of course, is that inequitable action does not become permissible simply because it is legally possible. . . .

We are unable to agree with the conclusion of the Chancery court that the stockholders' application for injunctive relief here was tardy and came too late. The stockholders learned of the action of management unofficially on Wednesday, October 27, 1971; they filed this action on Monday, November 1, 1971. Until management changed the date of the meeting, the stockholders had no need of judicial assistance in that connection. There is no indication of any prior warning of management's intent to take such action; indeed, it appears that an attempt was made by management to conceal its action as long as possible. Moreover, stockholders may not be charged with the duty of anticipating inequitable action by management, and of seeking anticipatory injunctive relief to foreclose such action, simply because the new Delaware Corporation Law makes such inequitable action legally possible.

Accordingly, the judgment below must be reversed and the cause remanded. . . .

WOLCOTT, C.J. (dissenting):

I do not agree with the majority of the Court in its disposition of this appeal. The plaintiff stockholders concerned in this litigation have, for a considerable period of time, sought to obtain control of the defendant corporation. These attempts took various forms.

In view of the length of time leading up to the immediate events which caused the filing of this action, I agree with the Vice Chancellor that the application for injunctive relief came too late.

I would affirm the judgment below on the basis of the Vice Chancellor's opinion. . . .

Schnell v. Chris-Craft Industries expresses the most fundamental "rule" of the fiduciary duty of loyalty. Legal power held by a fiduciary may not be deployed in a way that is *intended* to treat a beneficiary of the duty unfairly. The case law reflecting this broad equitable superintendence of fiduciary power predates the classic academic recognition of this practice. See Adolf Berle, *Corporate Powers as Powers in Trust*, 44 Harv. L. Rev. 1049 (1931). Delaware courts have been willing to use this power, as in *Schnell*, to protect the integrity of the shareholder franchise. It may seem natural that the franchise deserves special protection, but our colleagues Ron Gilson and Alan Schwartz have asked why the right to sell stock should be regarded as a less sacred value than the right to participate in the designation of board members.[62] The following case offers one justification, but what do you think?

62. See Ronald J. Gilson & Alan Schwartz, *Sales & Elections as Methods for Transferring Corporate Control*, 2 Theor. Inq. in L. 783 (2000).

BLASIUS INDUSTRIES, INC. V. ATLAS CORP.

564 A.2d 651 (Del. Ch. 1988)

[Blasius Industries, the owner of about 9 percent of the stock of the Atlas Corporation, proposed a restructuring to Atlas's management that would have resulted in a major sale of Atlas assets, an infusion of new debt financing, and the disbursement of a very large cash dividend to Atlas's shareholders. When management rejected the restructuring proposal, Blasius announced that it would pursue a campaign to obtain shareholder consents to increase Atlas's board from 7 to 15 members, the maximum size allowed by Atlas's charter, and to fill the new board seats with Blasius's nominees. The Atlas board, however, preempted Blasius's campaign by immediately amending the bylaws to add two new board seats and filling these seats with its own candidates. (Remember the Village, Inc., exercise in Chapter 7? The Atlas board was classified, needless to say.)]

ALLEN, C.:

THE MOTIVATION OF THE INCUMBENT BOARD IN EXPANDING THE BOARD AND APPOINTING NEW MEMBERS.

In increasing the size of Atlas' board by two and filling the newly created positions, the members of the board realized that they were thereby precluding the holders of a majority of the Company's shares from placing a majority of new directors on the board through Blasius' consent solicitation, should they want to do so. Indeed the evidence establishes that that was the principal motivation in so acting.

The conclusion that, in creating two new board positions on December 31 and electing Messrs. Devaney and Winters to fill those positions the board was principally motivated to prevent or delay the shareholders from possibly placing a majority of new members on the board, is critical to my analysis of the central issue posed by the first filed of the two pending cases. If the board in fact was not so motivated, but rather had taken action completely independently of the consent solicitation, which merely had an incidental impact upon the possible effectuation of any action authorized by the shareholders, it is very unlikely that such action would be subject to judicial nullification. . . . The board, as a general matter, is under no fiduciary obligation to suspend its active management of the firm while the consent solicitation process goes forward. . . .

I conclude that, while the addition of these qualified men would, under other circumstances, be clearly appropriate as an independent step, such a step was in fact taken in order to impede or preclude a majority of the shareholders from effectively adopting the course proposed by Blasius. . . .

Plaintiff attacks the December 31 board action as a selfishly motivated effort to protect the incumbent board from a perceived threat to its control of Atlas. Their conduct is said to constitute a violation of the principle, applied in such cases as *Schnell v. Chris Craft Industries,* Del. Supr., 285 A.2d 437 (1971), that directors hold legal powers subjected to a supervening duty to exercise such powers in good faith pursuit of what they reasonably believe to be in the corporation's interest. . . .

On balance, I cannot conclude that the board was acting out of a self-interested motive in any important respect on December 31. I conclude rather that the board saw the "threat" of the Blasius recapitalization proposal as posing vital policy differences between itself and Blasius. It acted, I conclude, in a good faith effort to protect its incumbency, not selfishly, but in order to thwart implementation of the recapitalization that it feared, reasonably, would cause great injury to the Company.

The real question the case presents, to my mind, is whether, in these circumstances, the board, even if it is acting with subjective good faith (which will typically, if not always, be a contestable or debatable judicial conclusion), may validly act for the principal purpose of preventing the shareholders from electing a majority of new directors. The question thus posed is not one of intentional wrong (or even negligence), but one of authority as between the fiduciary and the beneficiary (not simply legal authority, i.e., as between the fiduciary and the world at large).

It is established in our law that a board may take certain steps — such as the purchase by the corporation of its own stock — that have the effect of defeating a threatened change in corporate control, when those steps are taken advisedly, in good faith pursuit of a corporate interest, and are reasonable in relation to a threat to legitimate corporate interests posed by the proposed change in control. See *Unocal Corp. v. Mesa Petroleum Co.,* Del. Supr., 493 A.2d 946 (1985). . . . Does this rule — that the reasonable exercise of good faith and due care generally validates, in equity, the exercise of legal authority even if the act has an entrenchment effect — apply to action designed for the primary purpose of interfering with the effectiveness of a stockholder vote? Our authorities, as well as sound principles, suggest that the central importance of the franchise to the scheme of corporate governance, requires that, in this setting, that rule not be applied and that closer scrutiny be accorded to such transaction. . . .

The shareholder franchise is the ideological underpinning upon which the legitimacy of directorial power rests. Generally, shareholders have only two protections against perceived inadequate business performance. They may sell their stock (which, if done in sufficient numbers, may so affect security prices as to create an incentive for altered managerial performance), or they may vote to replace incumbent board members.

It has, for a long time, been conventional to dismiss the stockholder vote as a vestige or ritual of little practical importance. It may be that we are now witnessing the emergence of new institutional voices and arrangements that will make the stockholder vote a less predictable affair than it has been. Be that as it may, however, whether the vote is seen functionally as an unimportant formalism, or as an important tool of discipline, it is clear that it is critical to the theory that legitimates the exercise of power by some (directors and officers) over vast aggregations of property that they do not own. Thus, when viewed from a broad, institutional perspective, it can be seen that matters involving the integrity of the shareholder voting process involve consideration not present in any other context in which directors exercise delegated power.

The distinctive nature of the shareholder franchise context also appears when the matter is viewed from a less generalized, doctrinal point of view. From this point of view, as well, it appears that the ordinary considerations to which the business judgment rule originally responded are simply not present in the shareholder-voting context.[2] That is, a decision by the board to act for the primary purpose of preventing the effectiveness of a shareholder vote inevitably involves the question who, as between the principal and the agent, has authority with respect to a matter of internal corporate governance. That, of course, is true in a very specific way in this case which deals with the question who should constitute the board of directors of the corporation, but it will be true in every instance in which an incumbent board seeks to thwart a shareholder majority. A board's decision to act to prevent the shareholders from creating a majority of new board positions and filling them does not involve the exercise of the corporation's power over its property, or with respect to its rights or obligations; rather, it involves allocation, between shareholders as a class and the board, of effective power with respect to governance of the corporation. This need not be the case with respect to other forms of corporate action that may have an entrenchment effect — such as the stock buybacks present in *Unocal, Cheff* or *Kors v. Carey*. Action designed principally to interfere with the effectiveness of a vote inevitably involves a conflict between the board and a shareholder majority. Judicial review of such action involves a determination of the legal and equitable obligations of an agent towards his principal. This is not, in my opinion, a question that a court may leave to the agent finally to decide so long as he does so honestly and competently; that is, it may not be left to the agent's business judgment. . . .

2. Delaware courts have long exercised a most sensitive and protective regard for the free and effective exercise of voting rights. This concern suffuses our law, manifesting itself in various settings. For example, the perceived importance of the franchise explains the cases that hold that a director's fiduciary duty requires disclosure to shareholders asked to authorize a transaction of all material information in the corporation's possession, even if the transaction is not a self-dealing one. See, e.g., *Smith v. Van Gorkom*, Del. Supr., 488 A.2d 858 (1985). . . . A similar concern, for credible corporate democracy, underlies those cases that strike down board action that sets or moves an annual meeting date upon a finding that such action was intended to thwart a shareholder group from effectively mounting an election campaign. See, e.g., *Schnell v. Chris Craft*. . . . The cases invalidating stock issued for the primary purpose of diluting the voting power of a control block also reflect the law's concern that a credible form of corporate democracy be maintained. . . . Similarly, a concern for corporate democracy is reflected (1) in our statutory requirement of annual meetings (8 Del. C. §211), and in the cases that aggressively and summarily enforce that right. . . .

QUESTIONS AND NOTES ON SCHNELL AND BLASIUS

1. Which of the following actions by the board may be prohibited under the *Schnell* and *Blasius* rationales? Under what circumstances?

a. During a heated proxy context for control of the board, the incumbent board purchases stock selectively from a large shareholder who is otherwise likely to vote for the insurgents.

b. Under the same circumstances, the incumbent board issues a large block of additional stock at the market price to shareholders who are likely to support the incumbent board.

c. Under the same circumstances, the incumbent board delays the annual meeting after the meeting date is set when its initial proxy returns suggest that the insurgents may win.

2. Is it ever a useful policy to permit a court to invalidate board actions undertaken in good faith and in the honest belief (by the board) that they are in the best interests of the corporation and its shareholders?

3. *Blasius* addressed the vital importance of the franchise just as it seemed that hostile tender offers would be legally restrained (both by constituency statutes and judicial decisions) and as the growing assertiveness of institutional investors increased the practical importance of the franchise.

4. Two commentators state that, "[w]ithin its realm," judicial review under the *Schnell-Blasius* line of cases "is perhaps the most exacting in corporate law. It unequivocally reverses the business judgment presumption. Director action that interferes with the voting process is presumptively inequitable." Dale A. Oesterle & Alan R. Palmiter, *Judicial Schizophrenia in Shareholder Voting Cases,* 79 Iowa L. Rev. 485, 535 (1994). Yet it is not easy to fortify the vote with strong fiduciary protections. Since manipulations of the voting process can often be characterized as "defensive," courts may apply the *Unocal* test to them: Review under *Unocal* is less demanding than review under *Blasius.* The structure of analysis under either review standard, however, is the same. In both instances, directors have the burden to establish compliance with a standard, and in both instances, the standard is a relative one. In *Unocal,* the action must be reasonable in light of something else (a threat that the act is directed against). Under *Blasius,* the justification for the act must be deemed compelling in light of something else (the threat that the act is directed against). The substantive difference is one of emphasis. *Blasius* requires a very powerful justification to thwart a shareholder franchise for an extended period. But where a board delays a shareholder vote for a week or two, a less compelling justification may suffice.[63]

---

63. For example, in two later cases involving board action intended to affect the franchise process, the Delaware Court of Chancery did not issue an injunction. See *Stahl v. Apple Bancorp, Inc.,* 579 A.2d 1115 (Del. Ch. 1989) (*Stahl I*) (when a board postponed a shareholder meeting after fixing the record date in order to frustrate a would-be acquirer); Fed. Sec. L. Rep. (CCH) ¶95,412 (Del. Ch. 1990) (*Stahl II*). See also *Kidsco Inc. v. Dinsmore,* 670 A.2d 1338 (Del. Ch.), *aff'd,* 674 A.2d 483 (Del. 1995) (moving meeting held not to violate *Unocal* in the circumstances).

There is, however, one critical difference between review under *Unocal* and review under *Blasius.* The Delaware Supreme Court's *Time-Warner* opinion seems to authorize a target board to take defensive action if the company is threatened by what the court terms "substantive coercion." This, in the end, is simply the board's belief that the tender offer is inadequate and that the shareholders do not understand that fact. Under *Blasius*, however, corporate action to defeat a proxy contest cannot be justified by a parallel belief that the voters simply do not understand the foolishness of voting for the insurgent slate.

In the Delaware case law today, *Blasius* continues to be a significant precedent where board action specifically attempts to impede a shareholder vote. In fact, however, *Blasius* is not a radical departure from prior case law; it is just a special case evaluating board conduct under the general principles of fiduciary duty. *Blasius* is useful for courts and practitioners who wish to underscore the importance of shareholder voting, but it is not revolutionary.

5. *Liquid Audio v. MM Companies, Inc.*[64] is a recent case that lies at the intersection of *Unocal* and *Blasius.* Liquid Audio (LA) was yet another victim of the dot-com bubble, reaching $48 per share at its peak but down to less than $3 per share by 2001. The *Wall Street Journal* reported that LA's business strategy suffered because rivals "offer[ed] similar services free of charge." (How's that for a business problem?) LA rejected a cash offer from MM Companies in favor of a stock-for-stock merger with Alliance Entertainment. MM then forced LA to hold its annual meeting, at which MM planned to: (1) challenge the two incumbent directors who were up for re-election; and (2) propose a bylaw amendment expanding the board from five to nine members. In August 2002, LA added two directors, increasing the board size from five to seven. At the annual meeting one month later, shareholders elected the two MM candidates to replace the LA incumbents, but rejected the MM proposal to add four more board seats. MM brought suit alleging *Blasius* and *Unocal* violations. Vice Chancellor Jack Jacobs upheld LA's defensive tactics under *Unocal*, and declined to apply *Blasius* because LA's actions would not have prevented MM from achieving board control had its board expansion amendment succeeded.[65] The Delaware Supreme Court reversed, holding that *Blasius* applied because the "primary purpose" of LA's actions was to reduce the MM directors' ability to influence board decisions. The Court then applied *Blasius* to invalidate LA's board expansion from five to seven.[66]

A NOTE ON HILTON v. ITT CORP.

This Delaware case law was applied by a federal district court in *Hilton Hotels Corp. v. ITT Corp.*, 978 F. Supp 1342 (D. Nev. 1997). In that case, the court was required to determine whether certain defensive actions by the ITT

64. 813 A.2d 1118 (Del. 2003).
65. MM Companies v. Liquid Audio, C.A. No. 19869 (Del. Ch. Oct. 21, 2002).
66. MM Companies v. Liquid Audio, Inc., 813 A.2d 1118, 1132 (Del. 2003).

board in response to a Hilton takeover attempt constituted a violation of fiduciary duty. Hilton had initiated a $55 per share cash offer for all shares and a proxy contest to replace the ITT board. ITT, in reaction, delayed calling its annual meeting (which the court determined it was authorized to do under Nevada law) and then, during this period, structured a reorganization. The restructured firm would be broken up into three separate components. The main part of the company's business would be transferred to a new subsidiary, ITT Destinations, which would hold the company's hotel and gaming assets. Those assets constituted 93 percent of current assets and 87 percent of current revenues. Following creation of ITT Destinations as a subsidiary, its stock would then be spun off in a dividend distribution to ITT shareholders. Significantly, ITT Destinations would be formed with a full stable of antitakeover mechanisms, including, most important, both a poison pill and a staggered board of directors. The existing ITT Corp. did not have a staggered board. In addition, a share vote of 80 percent of the outstanding stock would be necessary in order to authorize the removal of ITT Destinations' directors without cause, to amend the staggered board structure, or to amend the supermajority vote provisions. Apparently, the reorganization did not require a shareholder vote. The spin-off would in no event do so. The transfer to a wholly owned subsidiary of substantially all of the corporation's assets is a little less clear. Presumably, it was thought that that transfer did not require a shareholder vote because the transferee was indirectly held by the same shareholders in the same proportion as was ownership in the transferor.

Hilton sought an injunction against effectuation of the reorganization without shareholder approval. It contended that the action was motivated to protect the incumbency of the board and constituted a breach of fiduciary duty. While ITT was a Nevada corporation, the court looked to relevant Delaware precedents — *Unocal, Blasius,* and *Unitrin* — to shape its answer. By the time the matter reached court, Hilton had raised its bid to $70 per share. The court first determined that the ITT board could reasonably conclude (as it did) that the $70 offer was inadequate. The question became whether the defensive action was preclusive or coercive. The *Hilton* court concluded first that "the installation of a classified board for ITT Destinations, a company that encompass 93% of ITT's assets and 87% of its revenues, is clearly preclusive and coercive under *Unitrin.* The classified board provision for ITT Destinations will preclude current ITT shareholders from exercising a right they currently possess — to determine the membership of the board of ITT." *Id.* at 1348.

QUESTIONS ON HILTON v. ITT CORP.

1. What arguments can be advanced that this action was not "preclusive"?
2. The *Hilton* court invoked the *Blasius* precedent, holding that the defensive action was directed toward affecting the outcome of the pending proxy contest for control of ITT and holding that no sufficiently compelling justification had been put forward. Was this conclusion justified?

3. Under Delaware law, would you argue that the ITT action constituted a "breakup" of the company that invoked a *Revlon* duty to get the highest current value for the shareholders? If the answer is yes, how would the court proceed?

13.9 THE TAKEOVER ARMS RACE CONTINUES

13.9.1 "Dead Hand" Pills

The economic forces that create profit opportunities from hostile takeovers are constantly at work. The state of the law provides one set of constraints that those seeking to seize such an opportunity may have to overcome. When, in the mid-to late 1980s, legislatures and courts reinforced the powers of incumbent managers by validating the poison pill and enacting antitakeover statutes, the hybrid proxy contest/tender offer became a rational reactive strategy for those seeking to exploit takeover opportunities, and this, in turn, led to new efforts by the status quo to counter hybrid takeovers. Thus, the next step was the evolution of the "dead hand" pill.

While in practice a dead hand pill might take a variety of forms, the core idea is simple. A pill cannot be redeemed by the "hostile" board that is elected in a proxy fight for a stated period of time (but variations are possible). Early attempts provided that the company's pill could be redeemed only by the company's "continuing directors," a term defined to mean directors in office at the time of adoption of the pill or nominated to office thereafter by "continuing directors."

Dead hand pills might strike one as a radical proposition. They permit a board to limit the ability of shareholders to designate those with board power, or stated differently, they would recognize a power in current boards to restrict the authority of future boards. An early version of a dead hand pill was struck down by the New York Supreme Court in *Bank of New York Co. v. Irving Bank Corp.*, 528 N.Y.S.2d 482 (1988) (a mild version, which defined "continuing director" to be any person elected by 2/3 of the outstanding shares). A federal district court sitting in Georgia, however, upheld a continuing director dead hand pill under Georgia law. See *Invacare Corp. v. Healthdyne Technologies, Inc.*, 968 F. Supp. 1578 (N.D. Ga. 1997). The Delaware courts were more traditional in their approach to the question.

The Delaware courts first addressed dead hand pills in *Carmody v. Toll Brothers, Inc.*, 723 A.2d 1180 (Del. Ch. 1998). In this case, Vice Chancellor Jacobs held that such a device was invalid because, first, it created two classes of directors (continuing directors and new directors) without the necessary authorization in the company's charter, and second, it unduly conditioned the rights of shareholders to elect new directors. In *Mentor Graphics Corp. v. Quickturn Design Systems, Inc.,*[67] Vice

---

67. 728 A.2d 25 (Del. Ch. 1998).

Chancellor Jacobs addressed a different version of a dead hand pill. In this version, there was no discrimination between old and new directors. Rather, the pill itself provided that, while generally the board had a redemption power, it had no such power for the six months following the election of a new board (or a majority of new directors). The court termed this a "delayed redemption provision." Once more, the Chancery Court struck down the pill, this time explicitly by a *Unitrin/Unocal* analysis. Implicitly, the court said that no abstract threat to the corporation made reasonable the imposition on the shareholders' right to have fully functioning directors in place. The Delaware Supreme Court affirmed *Quickturn* but did not invoke the *Unocal/Unitrin* principle. Instead, its opinion was based on a statutory interpretation of directors' power. It asserted that the present board did not have the authority to restrict the power of future boards, through the adoption of stock rights plans, to exercise their managerial judgment.

The Delaware Supreme Court's rationale for striking down this version of a dead hand pill raises interesting questions. Standard contracts may limit the powers of the corporation and its board in the future but are certainly not invalid because of that fact. As a practical matter, boards continually authorize contracts that — while they do not purport to legally restrict the power of future boards — nevertheless establish conditions (such as liability potential) that constrain the actions of future boards. Plainly, *Quickturn* was not intended to restrict the ability of a corporate board to authorize contracts that establish such constraints on board actions in the future. If that is so, could not today's board legally constrain the power of tomorrow's board to redeem the pill by making such a redemption a trigger for punishing corporate liability? Put differently, today's board would allow a future board to retain its authority but ensure that this authority would be exceedingly difficult to exercise. Thus, for example, redemption could be made by an event of default under a bond indenture with a liquidated damages provision requiring a high payment to bond holders. The point, as ever with pills, would be to achieve an *in terrorem* effect. In any such case, however, the validity of such an attempt to affect future boards would clearly run afoul of the spirit, if not the rationale, of *Quickturn*.

QUESTION

In June 2003, responding to a hostile takeover bid from its Silicon Valley rival Oracle Corp., PeopleSoft initiated a "Customer Assurance Program," (CAP) under which PeopleSoft customers would receive back between two and five their purchase price if Oracle were to acquire PeopleSoft and then reduced the technical support for PeopleSoft's software products, in the form of bug fixes and software upgrades, for up to four years after the customer contract date. By August 2004, the total potential liability under the CAP was approximately $2.0 billion, or more than one-third of PeopleSoft's pre-bid market capitalization. Oracle challenged the CAP in Delaware

Chancery Court, alleging that it was an invalid takeover defense under a *Unocal/Unitrin* analysis, or more generally violated the board's fiduciary duties under the principles set forth by the Delaware Supreme Court in its *Quickturn* decision. PeopleSoft responded that the CAP was not a takeover defense, and in any case was a proportionate response to the threat that Oracle posed to PeopleSoft's customers. In December 2004, the parties reached a negotiated deal at $26.50 cash per share before the court would have ruled on the validity of the CAP under Delaware corporate law. How should the court have come out?

13.9.2 Mandatory Pill Redemption Bylaws

While agents of corporate management were designing the dead hand pill as a countermeasure to the successful technique of linking a proxy contest with a tender offer, protakeover interests (representatives of certain investment funds or institutional investors) were busy cooking up a countermeasure to the poison pill.[68] In particular, some opponents of the pill have sought a technique to gain control of the decision of whether or not to implement a poison pill. The technique developed involves a shareholder bylaw that requires the board of directors to redeem an existing pill and to refrain from adopting a pill without submitting it to shareholder approval.

Shareholder mandatory pill redemption bylaws present two controversial issues. The first is basic: Is a bylaw that mandates the board to exercise its judgment in a particular way a valid bylaw? We ordinarily think of bylaws as defining governance rules — size of board, number of officers, and scope of authority, for example. Can shareholders use the power to enact bylaws to require the board to make particular choices in particular ways? Certainly the articles of incorporation can limit the power of the board, but can shareholders do so through bylaws? The second issue that mandatory bylaws raise is whether managers must include in the company's proxy solicitation, materials respecting any such proposal. These questions are related because *if* it is clear that a bylaw of this type would be invalid under state law, then it is not likely that the SEC will require management to include the proposal. Indeed, SEC Rule 14a(1)(i) specifically states that a board may exclude a proposal that would be illegal or invalid under state law.

Most of the leading Delaware firms have opined that a mandatory bylaw would constitute an invalid intrusion by the shareholders into the realm protected by §141(a) of the DGCL.[69] The idea is that boards have rights and duties to make independent judgments respecting the management of the firm. Under *Moran*, the decision to install a stock rights plan falls within this authority. With respect to exercising powers that fall to the

---

68. As we note below, this arms race has played out against the background fact that, notwithstanding many attempts, it is extremely difficult to establish definitively just what the effects of the pill have been on shareholder welfare.

69. See, e.g., Charles F. Richards & Robert J. Stern, *Shareholder By-Laws Requiring Boards of Directors to Dismantle Rights Plans Are Unlikely to Survive Under Delaware Law*, 54 Bus. Law. 607 (1999).

board under §141 of the DGCL, shareholders — who may in all events elect a different board if they are displeased with the current one — are not given the power to co-manage the firm. Any such reallocation of governance power must be set forth in the corporation's charter.

After an initial back-and-forth in Oklahoma on these issues,[70] these important questions are gradually reaching Delaware. In March 2006, Professor Lucian Bebchuk of the Harvard Law School submitted a 14a-8 proposal to Computer Associates (CA), a Delaware corporation, to amend its bylaws so that the CA board could only adopt a poison pill through a unanimous board vote, and any pill so adopted would automatically expire one year after it was adopted, unless ratified by the CA shareholders. CA submitted a no-action request to the SEC, seeking to exclude the proposal from its proxy materials on the grounds that such a bylaw would violate the board's right to manage the company under DGCL 141(a). The SEC refused to issue a no-action letter, and Professor Bebchuk brought suit in Delaware Chancery Court seeking a declaratory judgment that the proposed bylaw would not violate Delaware law if enacted. In June 2006, the Delaware Chancery Court refused to rule on the question, citing ripeness problems. "Deciding the question posed in this case now," wrote Vice Chancellor Lamb, "would prematurely resolve a highly contentious and important matter before the court knows what pertinent facts might develop in the future."[71] At CA's annual meeting held in September 2006, the proposal recieved a respectable but less-than-majority 41 percent of the shareholder vote, thereby leaving this intriguing legal issue for another day.

The policy question is whether the law should recognize shareholder power to amend the bylaws to eliminate or alter pills. This question raises what we have earlier referred to as an "optimal delegation problem": When are the efficiencies that we gain from delegating authority to centralized managers outweighed by the expected agency costs associated with that delegation? Plainly, in the case of everyday business decisions, the gains are great and the costs modest in comparison (otherwise, we would not observe so many large organizations, which necessarily involve this level of delegation). But equally plainly, the legal infrastructure of corporations reflects the belief that agency costs would be too high if, for example, we denied shareholders the power to appoint directors or approve fundamental transactions. Where then do we suppose that the poison pill fits in the continuum of efficient delegation? While the concept of optimal delegation can give us a framework for making a policy judgment, it cannot provide a scientific answer. An answer requires judgment. How costly is it to evaluate a stock rights plan? (Here we must consider not only the costs of holding

70. In 1999, the Oklahoma Supreme Court held that shareholders may propose and adopt bylaws that restrict the board's power to implement rights plans, absent a restriction in the corporation's charter. *Intl. Brotherhood of Teamsters General Fund v. Fleming Companies, Inc.*, 975 P.2d 907 (Okla. 1999). In response to the Court's holding in *Fleming*, the Oklahoma state legislature passed a statute removing the inherent power of shareholders to amend bylaws, forcing such power to be affirmatively created by the charter. See 18 Okla. Stat. §1013.

71. *Bebchuk v. CA, Inc.*, C.A. No. 2145-N, at 14 (June 22, 2006)

meetings and providing and digesting information but also the implicit costs associated with making decisions that arguably may not be as well informed and deliberated). How likely is it that a pill will deter wanted offers? How likely is it that management will misuse the pill? (If there were no threat that it would be misused, it would be difficult to justify shareholder resistance to its adoption.)

QUESTIONS ON AMENDING CORPORATE BYLAWS

1. Should corporate law permit or prohibit shareholder mandatory pill redemption bylaws? Why?

2. If it were efficient to permit shareholders to proscribe stock rights plans, would you expect to see in, say, post-1990 IPO charter provisions an express grant of power to shareholders to monitor the board in this way? Why or why not?

3. How might you distinguish Professor Bebchuk's proposal at Computer Associates from the standard shareholder pill redemption bylaw? What is the connection between Professor Bebchuk's proposal and the effectiveness of staggered boards as a takeover defense? (recall the "Unfireable CEO" problem in Section 7.2) What do you make of the fact that Computer Associates does not have a staggered board?

4. Assume that Professor Bebchuk's proposal is valid under Delaware corporate law, and that it has been implemented at a public company which you advise. The board, which is staggered, wishes to maintain as much structural defense as possible against unsolicited bidders. Advise them.

In October 2004, as part of a reincorporation from Australia to Delaware, News Corp. agreed with certain of its institutional shareholders to a "board policy" that any poison pill adopted by the News board would expire after one year, unless shareholders approved an extension. One month later, Liberty Media appeared as a potential hostile acquiror for News. The News board promptly installed a poison pill, and announced that, going forward, it might or might not hold to its board policy on pills. Sure enough, in November 2005, the News board extended the pill in contravention of its earlier stated board policy. Shareholders filed suit alleging breach of contract, among other claims. The Delaware Chancery Court (Chandler, C.) refused to dismiss the contract claim for failure to state a claim. In the excerpt below, the Court addresses the defendants' arguments that the agreement between the board and its shareholders was unenforceable as a matter of law.

UNISUPER v. NEWS CORP.

C.A. No. 1699-N (Del. Ch. Dec. 20, 2005)

... Defendants assert that, even if plaintiffs are right about the existence, substance and interpretation of the alleged contract [between the News board and its shareholders], the contract is unenforceable as a matter of law. Defendants offer two arguments in support of this proposition.

A. SECTION 141(A)

Defendants first argue the alleged agreement is inconsistent with the general grant of managerial authority to the board in Section 141(a) of the Delaware General Corporation Law. According to defendants, Section 141(a) vests power to manage the corporation in the board of directors and requires that any limitation on this power be in the certificate of incorporation. Defendants contend that an agreement to hold a shareholder vote on poison pills (or any other issue affecting the business and affairs of the corporation) is unenforceable unless memorialized in the certificate of incorporation.

By definition, any contract a board could enter into binds the board and thereby limits its power. Section 141(a) does not say the board cannot enter into contracts. It simply describes who will manage the affairs of the corporation and it precludes a board of directors from ceding that power to outside groups or individuals.

The fact that the alleged contract in this case gives power to the shareholders saves it from invalidation under Section 141(a). The alleged contract with ACSI [a non-profit organization that advises Australian pension funds on corporate governance] did not cede power over poison pills to an outside group; rather, it ceded that power to shareholders. In effect, defendants' argument is that the board impermissibly ceded power to the shareholders. Defendants' argument is that the contract impermissibly restricted the board's power by granting shareholders an irrevocable veto right over a question of corporate control.

Delaware's corporation law vests managerial power in the board of directors because it is not feasible for shareholders, the owners of the corporation, to exercise day-to-day power over the company's business and affairs. Nonetheless, when shareholders exercise their right to vote in order to assert control over the business and affairs of the corporation the board must give way. This is because the board's power — which is that of an agent's with regard to its principal — derives from the shareholders, who are the ultimate holders of power under Delaware law.[49]

---

49. The alleged agreement in this case enables a vote by all shareholders. Private agreements between the board and a few large shareholders might be troubling where the agreements restrict the board's power in favor of a particular shareholder, rather than in favor of shareholders at large.

B. PARAMOUNT, QVC, AND OMNICARE

Defendants cite three Supreme Court of Delaware cases[50] in support of their second argument that the agreement in this case should be unenforceable as a matter of law. Generally speaking, these cases stand for the proposition that a contract is unenforceable if it would require the board to refrain from acting when the board's fiduciary duties require action.

Stripped of its verbiage, defendants' argument is that the News Corp. board impermissibly disabled its fiduciary duty to shareholders by putting into shareholders' hands the decision whether to keep a poison pill. The three cases cited by defendants do not operate to invalidate contracts of this sort. Each of the three cases cited by defendants invalidated contracts the board used in order to take power out of shareholders' hands. . . .

The contracts in *Paramount* and *Quickturn* were defensive measures that took power out of the hands of shareholders. The contracts raised the "omnipresent specter" that the board was using the contract provisions to entrench itself, i.e., to prevent shareholders from entering into a value-enhancing transaction with a competing acquiror. In this case, the challenged contract put the power to block or permit a transaction directly into the hands of shareholders. Unlike in *Paramount* and *Quickturn*, there is no risk of entrenchment in this case because shareholders will make the decision for themselves whether to adopt a defensive measure or leave the corporation susceptible to takeover. . . .

Omnicare [also] does not invalidate the contract in this case. Unlike the board in *Omnicare*, the News Corp. board entered into a contract that empowered shareholders; it gave shareholders a voice in a particular corporate governance matter, viz., the poison pill. It makes no sense to argue that the News Corp. board somehow disabled its fiduciary duties to shareholders by agreeing to let the shareholders vote on whether to keep a poison pill in place. This argument is an attempt to use fiduciary duties in a way that misconceives the purpose of fiduciary duties. Fiduciary duties exist in order to fill the gaps in the contractual relationship between the shareholders and directors of the corporation. Fiduciary duties cannot be used to silence shareholders and prevent them from specifying what the corporate contract is to say. Shareholders should be permitted to fill a particular gap in the corporate contract if they wish to fill it. This point can be made by reference to principles of agency law: Agents frequently have to act in situations where they do not know exactly how their principal would like them to act. In such situations, the law says the agent must act in the best interests of the principal. Where the principal wishes to make known to the agent exactly which actions the principal wishes to be taken, the agent cannot refuse to listen on the grounds that this is not in the best interests of the principal.

---

50. Defendants cite Paramount Commc'ns Inc. v. QVC Network Inc., 637 A.2d 34, 41-42 (Del.1994); Quickturn Design Sys., Inc. v. Shapiro, 721 A.2d 1281, 1292 (Del.1998); and Omnicare, Inc. v. NCS Healthcare, Inc., 818 A.2d 914, 938 (Del.2003).

To the extent defendants argue that the board's fiduciary duties would be disabled after a hypothetical shareholder vote, this argument also misconceives the nature and purpose of fiduciary duties. Once the corporate contract is made explicit on a particular issue, the directors must act in accordance with the amended corporate contract. There is no more need for the gap-filling role performed by fiduciary duty analysis.[69] Again, the same point can be made by reference to principles of agency law: Where the principal makes known to the agent exactly which actions the principal wishes to be taken, the agent must act in accordance with those instructions. . . .

QUESTION

Several commentators have focused on the Chancellor's language that the board's power "is that of an agent's with regard to its principal." Is this a correct statement of Delaware's approach to corporation law? Recall *Automatic Self-Cleaning Filter*, in Section 4.5. To the extent it represents a departure, what other potential consequences might it suggest?

---

69. See Easterbrook & Fischel, [The Economic Structure of Corporate Law] at 92-93 ("Because the fiduciary principle is a rule for completing incomplete bargains in a contractual structure, it makes little sense to say that "fiduciary duties" trump actual contracts") (emphasis in original).

TRADING IN THE CORPORATION'S SECURITIES

We turn now to a large topic: the obligations of directors, officers, and issuing corporations when dealing in the corporation's own securities. For publicly financed corporations, this is primarily an area of federal law. In the public distributions of securities, the Securities Act of 1933 is the principal statute. Thereafter, for shares that continue to trade in the public "secondary" markets (such as the New York Stock Exchange or NASDAQ), the Securities Exchange Act of 1934 is the primary source of regulatory law. The Securities and Exchange Commission has promulgated extensive regulations under both of these statutes, which dominate the legal regulation of disclosure. While state law is not entirely supplanted in this area, the fiduciary doctrines that play such a large role elsewhere in corporate law are decidedly of secondary significance in this field. Even though the law of mandatory disclosure is principally federal, it is helpful to begin with a review of the fraud remedy and the common law of insider trading. In large part, it was the perceived shortcomings of this area of state law that motivated the Depression-era federal securities statutes.

14.1 COMMON LAW OF DIRECTORS' DUTIES WHEN TRADING IN THE CORPORATION'S STOCK

The nineteenth century was an age of *caveat emptor*—let the buyer beware. Then, as now, fraud was actionable. But prosecuting a claim of common law fraud was not easy, since it required proof of five elements: (1) a *false statement* of (2) *material* fact (3) made with the *intention to deceive* (4) upon which one *reasonably relied* and which (5) *caused injury*. Given these elements, the fraud remedy was generally not available when the buyer or seller simply failed to disclose a material fact without overt deception. Equally important, common law fraud was unavailable to redress the losses of persons trading over impersonal markets (such as stock exchanges), since these investors could not be said to have traded in reliance on statements made by unknown counterparties. Moreover, even where parties transacted face-to-face, nondisclosure of a material fact was not usually considered to be a fraud at common law. A buyer who wanted information generally had to bargain for it by demanding a representation or warranty from his seller. There was, however, one area in which the common law imposed a duty of full and fair disclosure on the seller: in contracts between trustees and their beneficiaries. By the late nineteenth century, such contracts were upheld only if there was proof of full disclosure and substantive fairness. (Sound familiar? Look back to Chapters 2 and 9.)

The tough common law requirements of full disclosure and fairness in contracts between trustees and trust beneficiaries pointed to an obvious question for emergent corporate law at the end of the nineteenth century: Was the purchase or sale of stock by a director or officer of the issuer similar enough to trustee self-dealing to merit analysis under the disclosure and fairness rule? Jurisdictions differed on this question.[1] The majority rule was that a director's only duty was to his corporation and, *a fortiori,* he did not owe a duty of disclosure to those with whom he traded shares. Only a handful of jurisdictions adopted the contrary rule that a director had a duty to disclose material information when he traded opposite shareholders in his company's stock.[2] The United States Supreme Court applied an intermediate rule in *Strong v. Repide,*[3] a case in which a shareholder offered to sell his stock to a company director who knew, but did not reveal, that the company was about to conclude negotiations on a highly favorable contract. The director bought the stock, without disclosing this information or counseling delay, at what soon appeared to be a bargain price. The former shareholder sued to rescind the contract for breach of the duty of loyalty. The Supreme Court affirmed judgment for the former shareholder on the grounds that, where *special facts* exist, a director has an obligation to disclose these material facts or refrain from buying corporate stock in a face-to-face transaction.

Cases involving transactions on the public markets were more difficult for a shareholder plaintiff to prosecute successfully. *Goodwin v. Agassiz* discussed the duty of a director or officer who possesses material nonpublic information and buys stock on a public market as this duty stood on the verge of the enactment of the federal securities laws.

GOODWIN v. AGASSIZ
186 N.E. 659 (Mass. 1933)

RUGG, C.J.:

A stockholder in a corporation seeks in this suit relief for losses suffered by him in selling shares of stock in Cliff Mining Company by way of accounting, rescission of sales, or redelivery of shares. . . .

---

1. See, e.g., Michael Conant, *Duties of Disclosure of Corporate Insiders Who Purchase Shares,* 46 Cornell L.Q. 53 (1960).

2. See, e.g., *Oliver v. Oliver,* 45 S.E. 232 (Ga. 1903).

3. 213 U.S. 419 (1909).

Déjà vu: A 1920s Insider Trade was Ruled by Court
to be Merely a Perk
Wall Street Journal (July 3, 2002)

He possessed all the trappings of a highflying chief executive: a mansion on Boston's Beacon Street, considerable clout within the Republican Party, status as a top international polo player — and a piece of inside information that prompted him to start buying up shares of the corporation he headed, Cliff Mining Co.

It was 1926, and the site owned by Cliff Mining was long past its late-nineteenth century heyday as one of the leading copper producers of Michigan's Upper Peninsula. "The company didn't have a whole lot going for it anymore," says Erik Nordberg, an archivist at Michigan Technological University, which maintains a collection of area mining records.

How tantalizing it must have been when an experienced geologist told Cliff Mining's president, Rodolphe Agassiz, that he believed the company could be sitting on a huge lode. Excited over the prospects, Mr. Agassiz (pronounced Ag-a-see) acquired a sizable amount of company stock, traded on the Boston exchange. Meantime, the lode theory was never disclosed. . . .

Mr. Agassiz hailed from a prominent line. His father's father, Louis, was an eminent natural scientist and teacher who once famously said: "I can't afford to waste my time making money." His father, Alexander, was an esteemed marine zoologist who became fabulously wealthy as part of Michigan's post-Civil War copper-mining boom. He ran Calumet & Hecla Mining Co., which at one point supplied half the nation's copper.

The geologist's hunch failed to pan out. But after Mr. Agassiz snapped up shares of Cliff Mining, a man named Homer Goodwin sued him, arguing he never would have sold his stake had he known of the geologist's report. Mr. Goodwin's shares wound up in Mr. Agassiz's hands. The case worked its way to the Supreme Judicial Court of Massachusetts, which in 1933 issued its ruling. . . .

. . . The facts . . . are these: The defendants, in May 1926, purchased . . . on the Boston stock exchange seven hundred shares . . . of the Cliff Mining Company [belonging to the plaintiff.] Agassiz was president and director and MacNaughton a director and general manager of the company. They had certain knowledge, material as to the value of the stock, which the plaintiff did not have. The plaintiff contends that such purchase in all the circumstances without disclosure to him of the knowledge was a wrong against him. That knowledge was that an experienced geologist had formulated in writing in March 1926, a theory as to the possible existence of copper deposits under conditions prevailing in the region where the property of the company was located. That region was known as the mineral belt in Northern Michigan, where are located mines of several copper mining companies. Another such company, of which the defendants were officers, had made extensive geological surveys of its lands. In consequence of recommendations resulting from that survey, exploration was started on property of the Cliff Mining Company in 1925. That exploration was ended in May 1926, because completed unsuccessfully, and the equipment was removed. The defendants discussed the geologist's theory shortly after it was formulated. Both felt that the theory had value and should be tested, but they agreed . . . that if the geologist's theory were known to the owners of such other land there might be difficulty in securing options [on adjacent properties], and that that theory should not be communicated to any one unless it became absolutely necessary. . . . The defendants both thought, also that, if there was any merit in the geologist's theory, the price of Cliff Mining Company stock in the market would go up. Its stock was quoted and bought and sold on the Boston Stock Exchange. Pursuant to agreement, they bought many shares of that stock through agents on joint account. The plaintiff first learned of the closing of exploratory operations on property of the Cliff Mining Company from an article in a paper on May 14, 1926, and immediately sold his shares of stock through brokers. It does not appear that the defendants were in any way responsible for the publication of that article. The plaintiff did not know that the purchase was made for the defendants and they did not know that his stock was being bought for them. There was no communication between them touching the subject. The plaintiff would not have sold his stock if he had known of the geologist's theory. The finding is express that the defendants were not guilty of fraud, that they committed no breach of duty owed by them to the Cliff Mining Company, and that that company was not harmed by the nondisclosure of the geologist's theory, or by their purchases of its stock, or by shutting down the exploratory operations.

The contention of the plaintiff is that the purchase of his stock in the company by the defendants without disclosing to him as a stockholder their knowledge of the geologist's theory, their belief that the theory had value, . . . and their plan ultimately to test the value of the theory, constitute actionable wrong for which he as stockholder can recover. . . .

The directors of a commercial corporation stand in a relation of trust to the corporation and are bound to exercise the strictest good faith in respect to its property and business. . . . The contention that directors also occupy the position of trustee toward individual stockholders in the corporation is plainly contrary to repeated decisions of this court and cannot be supported. . . .

. . . A rule holding that directors are trustees for individual stockholders with respect to their stock prevails in comparatively few states; but in view of our own adjudications it is not necessary to review decisions to that effect. . . .

. . . The knowledge naturally in the possession of a director as to the condition of a corporation places upon him a peculiar obligation to observe every requirement of fair dealing when directly buying or selling its stock. Mere silence does not usually amount to a breach of duty, but parties may stand in such relation to each other that an equitable responsibility arises to communicate facts. . . . [Nevertheless, p]urchases and sales of stock dealt in on the stock exchange are commonly impersonal affairs. An honest director would be in a difficult situation if he could neither buy nor sell on the stock exchange shares of stock in his corporation without first seeking out the other actual ultimate party to the transaction and disclosing to him everything which a court or jury might later find that he then knew affecting the real or speculative value of such shares. . . . On the other hand, directors cannot rightly be allowed to indulge with impunity in practices which do violence to prevailing standards of upright business men. Therefore, where a director personally seeks a stockholder for the purpose of buying his shares without making disclosure of material facts . . . , the transaction will be closely scrutinized and relief may be granted in appropriate instances. *Strong v. Repide*, 213 U.S. 419. . . .

The precise question to be decided . . . is whether . . . the defendants as directors had a right to buy stock of the plaintiff, a stockholder. . . . The only knowledge possessed by the defendants not open to the plaintiff was the existence of a theory . . . as to the possible existence of copper deposits where certain geological conditions existed. . . . Whether that theory was sound or fallacious, no one knew, and so far as appears has never been demonstrated. The defendants made no representations to anybody about the theory. No facts found placed upon them any obligation to disclose the theory. A few days after the thesis expounding the theory was brought to the attention of the defendants, the annual report by the directors of the Cliff Mining Company for the calendar year 1925, signed by Agassiz for the directors, was issued. It did not cover the time when the theory was formulated. The report described the status of the operations under the exploration which had been begun in 1925. At the annual meeting of the stockholders of the company held early in April 1926, no reference was made to the theory. It was then at most a hope, possibly an expectation. It had not passed the nebulous stage. No disclosure was made of it. The Cliff Mining Company was not harmed by the nondisclosure. There would have been no advantage to it, so far as appears, from a disclosure. The disclosure would have been detrimental to the interests of another mining corporation in which the defendants were directors. In the circumstances there was no duty on the part of the defendants to set forth to the stockholders at the annual meeting their faith, aspirations and plans for the future. . . . Disclosing of the theory, if it ultimately was proved to be erroneous . . . , might involve the defendants in litigation with those who might act on the hypothesis that it was correct. The stock of the Cliff Mining Company was bought and sold on the stock exchange. The identity of buyers and seller of the stock in question in fact was not known to the parties. . . . The defendants caused the shares to be bought through brokers on the stock exchange. They said nothing to anybody as to the reasons actuating them. The plaintiff was no novice. He was a member of the Boston stock exchange and had kept a record of sales of Cliff Mining Company stock. He acted upon his own judgment in selling his stock. He made no inquiries of the defendants or of other officers of the company. The result is that the plaintiff cannot prevail. . . .

QUESTIONS AND NOTES ON GOODWIN v. AGASSIZ

1. Do you disagree with the result? If so, why? How do you suppose public investors today would react to the actions sanctioned by *Goodwin*?

2. Suppose the directors had deliberately tried to create a misleading impression by closing down exploratory operations on the company's property. Would the court have reached a different result?

3. Notice that *Goodwin* was the majority approach among the states when Congress enacted the 1934 Securities Exchange Act. Yet Congress made no attempt to deal with this issue when it drafted the 1934 Act, although this was the same situation — a director buying company stock — that caused the SEC to establish Rule 10b-5 some years later. See § 14.4.2, below.

14.2   The Corporate Law of Fiduciary Disclosure Today

After the enactment of the federal scheme of securities regulation in 1933 and 1934, fiduciary disclosure law atrophied. The "special facts" duty articulated in *Strong* was not a shareholder-friendly doctrine. But pressure to change this doctrine dissipated as the SEC and federal courts aggressively expanded the federal law of disclosure between 1940 and 1975. There were several reasons shareholders opted for federal court relief rather than pressing in state court for change in fiduciary law. First, the 1934 Act provided for the national service of process for federal courts, while it often proved difficult to obtain jurisdiction over all necessary parties in state courts. Second, the amendment of Rule 23 of the Federal Rules of Civil Procedure in 1966 made federal courts an attractive place for class-based litigation. Third, and most important, federal courts created remedies for shareholders and investors through the process of implication.

The federal courts aggressively expanded federal investor remedies by implying private rights of action under the federal securities laws, from *Kardon v. National Gypsum Co.*[4] in 1946, which first implied such a right under Rule 10b-5, through *Cort v. Ash*[5] in 1975, in which the Rehnquist Court began to curtail implied private rights of action under federal law. As a result, almost all litigation of officer and director liability for trading in a company's securities — from the late 1940s to today — has been in the federal courts.

Almost all, but not *entirely* all. State fiduciary duty law continues to play an important role in two situations. First, a corporation can bring a claim against an officer, director, or employee for trading profits made by using information learned in connection with his corporate duties (see § 14.2.1, below). Second, shareholders can invoke state fiduciary duty to challenge the quality of the disclosure that their corporation makes to them (see § 14.2.2, below).

---

4. 69 F. Supp. 512 (E.D. Pa. 1946) (Kirkpatrick, J.). Rule 10b-5 was promulgated by the SEC under § 10(b) of the 1934 Act.
5. 422 U.S. 66 (1975).

14.2.1 Corporate Recovery of Profit from "Insider" Trading

Who is injured by insider trading? One answer might be that inside information is a corporate asset and that the corporation is therefore entitled to any profits made by its agents by trading on it. As you might recall from Chapter 2, this theory is black-letter agency law; an agent may not use her principal's information for personal profit.[6] It does not matter that the principal (or the corporation) is not "injured" in any respect by the agent's trading; equity places a constructive trust on the profits from insider trading in order to discourage fiduciaries from violating their duties.[7]

This "fiduciary" theory could be applied to many insider-trading cases. Assume, as in the *Texas Gulf Sulphur* case, below, that a company's directors buy stock knowing that their corporation will shortly announce an important mineral discovery and later sell their stock to realize a profit after the price of stock rises. Under the fiduciary — or agency — theory, the corporation or its shareholders as a collectivity should be able to sue the insiders derivatively to capture their profit on behalf of the corporation.

Nineteenth-century corporate law, however, simply did not evolve to the point of permitting such suits, and it has been only relatively recently that a few state courts have permitted suits of this sort (as discussed in the *Decio* opinion, below).[8] Two aspects of this fiduciary duty theory are particularly notable. First, since the corporation is seen as "owning" its nonpublic information, it *could* allow its agents to trade on it if there were no other legal considerations. Thus, absent a federal prohibition, a corporation could permit its officers to trade inside information as long as there was no actual deception. (Some academics have defended insider trading on related grounds, which we address in § 14.4.4 below.) Second, the fiduciary duty theory does not attempt to compensate the uninformed stockholder with whom the insider trades. Whether one sees these two aspects as problematic depends on one's view of the "fairness" or "efficiency" implications of permitting those with inside information to trade on it. Put differently, one's view of the utility of this common law theory depends on what one thinks is wrong with insider trading. In any case, the fiduciary duty theory has

---

6. Restatement (Third) Agency § 8.02.

7. Of course, it is difficult to imagine that the corporation is not "injured" in the typical case of insider trading. Either the corporation is also trading, in which case an agent's trading poses an opportunity cost, or the corporation does not — or cannot legally — trade, in which case abstaining from trading presumably benefits the corporation and its shareholders either by the corporation's own lights or in the eyes of the law. But see *Freeman v. Decio*, below, for a different view

8. In *Brophy v. Cities Service Co.*, 70 A.2d 5 (Del. Ch. 1949), a corporate employee traded on inside information, and the corporation sued for breach of fiduciary duty and won. Similarly, in *Diamond v. Oreamuno*, 248 N.E.2d 910 (N.Y. 1969), insiders sold their stock before bad news became public, and a later management sued on behalf of the corporation to recover the "profit" or loss avoided. The court rejected a defense based on the fact that there was no corporate loss, and the plaintiff won. See also *Schein v. Chasen*, 313 So. 2d 739 (Fla. 1975), in which the court rejected a claim based on breach of fiduciary duty under Florida law.

not been widely accepted, at least in its logical common law formulation, although it remains doctrinally sound in our view.

Freeman v. Decio, below, is a federal court of appeals case that declines to adopt a fiduciary duty theory as the law of Indiana.

FREEMAN v. DECIO
584 F.2d 186 (7th Cir. 1978)

Wood, Jr., Cir. J.:

The principal question presented by this case is whether under Indiana law the plaintiff may sustain a derivative action against certain officers and directors of the Skyline Corporation for allegedly trading in the stock of the corporation on the basis of material inside information. . . .

Plaintiff-appellant Marcia Freeman is a stockholder of the Skyline Corporation, a major producer of mobile homes and recreational vehicles. Skyline is a publicly owned corporation whose stock is traded on the New York Stock Exchange (NYSE). Defendant Arthur J. Decio is the largest shareholder of Skyline, the chairman of its board of directors, and until September 25, 1972, was also the president of the company. . . .

Throughout the 1960's and into 1972 Skyline experienced continual growth in sales and earnings. At the end of fiscal 1971 the company was able to report to its shareholders that over the previous five years sales had increased at a 40% average compound rate and that net income had grown at a 64% Rate. . . . Then, on December 22, 1972, Skyline reported that earnings for the quarter ending November 30, 1972, declined from $4,569,007 to $3,713,545 compared to the comparable period of the preceding year. . . . The NYSE immediately suspended trading in the stock. Trading was resumed on December 26 at $34.00 per share, down $13.50 from the preannouncement price. This represented a drop in value of almost 30%.

Plaintiff alleges that the defendants sold Skyline stock on the basis of material inside information during two distinct periods. Firstly, it is alleged that the financial results reported by Skyline for the quarters ending May 31 and August 31, 1972, significantly understated material costs and overstated earnings. It is further alleged that Decio, Kaufman and Mandell made various sales of Skyline stock totaling nearly $10 million during the quarters in question, knowing that earnings were overstated. Secondly, plaintiff asserts that during the quarter ending November 30 and up to December 22, 1972, Decio and Mandell made gifts and sales of Skyline stock totaling nearly $4 million while knowing that reported earnings for the November 30 quarter would decline. . . .

Both parties agree that there is no Indiana precedent directly dealing with the question of whether a corporation may recover the profits of corporate officials who trade in the corporation's securities on the basis of inside information. However, the plaintiff suggests that were the question to be presented to the Indiana courts, they would adopt the holding of the New York Court of Appeals in *Diamond v. Oreamuno,* 248 N.E.2d 910

(1969). There, . . . the court held that the officers and directors of a corporation breached their fiduciary duties owed to the corporation by trading in its stock on the basis of material non-public information acquired by virtue of their official positions. . . . Since *Diamond* was decided, few courts have had an opportunity to consider the problem there presented. In fact, only one case has been brought to our attention which raised the question of whether *Diamond* would be followed in another jurisdiction. In *Schein v. Chasen*, 478 F.2d 817 (2d Cir. 1973) . . . [a majority of a Second Circuit panel], sitting in diversity, . . . not only tacitly concluded that Florida would adopt *Diamond*, but [also] that the *Diamond* cause of action should be extended so as to permit recovery of the profits of non-insiders who traded in the corporation's stock on the basis of inside information received as tips from insiders. . . .

[F]rom a policy point of view it is widely accepted that insider trading should be deterred because it is unfair to other investors who do not enjoy the benefits of access to inside information. The goal is not one of equality of possession of information since some traders will always be better "informed" than others by dint of greater expenditures of time and resources, greater experience, or greater analytical abilities but rather equality of access to information. . . .

Yet, a growing body of commentary suggests that pursuit of this goal of "market egalitarianism" may be costly. In addition to the costs associated with enforcement of the laws prohibiting insider trading, there may be a loss in the efficiency of the securities markets in their capital allocation function. The basic insight of economic analysis here is that securities prices act as signals helping to route capital to its most productive uses and that insider trading helps assure that those prices will reflect the best information available (i.e., inside information) as to where the best opportunities lie. However, even when confronted with the possibility of a trade-off between fairness and economic efficiency, most authorities appear to find that the balance tips in favor of discouraging insider trading. . . .

Absent fraud, the traditional common law approach has been to permit officers and directors of corporations to trade in their corporation's securities free from liability to other traders for failing to disclose inside information. . . .

Yet, the New York Court of Appeals in *Diamond* . . . held that corporate officials who deal in their corporation's securities on the basis of non-public information . . . commit a breach of their fiduciary duties to the corporation. . . .

The *Diamond* court relied heavily on the Delaware case of *Brophy v. Cities Service Co.*, 31 Del. Ch. 241, 70 A.2d 5 (1949), the most significant departure from the traditional common law approach prior to Diamond itself. There, the confidential secretary to a director of a corporation purchased a number of shares of the company's stock after finding out that the corporation was about to enter the market to make purchases of its stock itself, and then sold at a profit after the corporation began its purchases. The Delaware Court of Chancery upheld the complaint in a derivative action on behalf of the corporation to recover those profits. The court stated that the employee occupied a position of trust and confidence toward his employer and that public policy would not permit him to abuse that relation for his own profit, regardless of whether or not the employer suffered a loss. 70 A.2d at 8. The *Diamond* court also relied on Section 388 of the Restatement (Second) of Agency. . . .

[However t]here are a number of difficulties with the *Diamond* court's ruling. Perhaps the thorniest problem . . . is that there is no injury to the corporation which can serve as a basis for recognizing a right of recovery in favor of the latter. . . .

Some might see the *Diamond* court's decision as resting on a broad, strict-trust notion [that] no director is to receive any profit, beyond what he receives from the corporation, solely because of his position. Although . . . this basis for the *Diamond* rule would obviate the need for finding a potential for injury to the corporation, it is not at all clear that current corporation law contemplates such an extensive notion of fiduciary duty. It is customary to view the *Diamond* result as resting on a characterization of inside information as a corporate asset. The lack of necessity for looking for an injury to the corporation is then justified by the traditional "no inquiry" rule with respect to profits made by trustees from assets belonging to the trust Res. However, to start from the premise that all inside information . . . [is] a corporate asset may presuppose an answer to the inquiry at hand. It might be better to ask whether there is any potential loss to the corporation from the use of such information in insider trading before deciding to characterize . . . [it] as an asset. . . . This approach would be in keeping with the modern view of another area of application of the duty of loyalty[,] the corporate opportunity doctrine. Thus, while courts will require a director or officer to automatically account to the corporation for diversion of a corporate opportunity to personal use, they will first inquire to see whether there was a possibility of a loss to the corpora-tion[,] i.e., whether the corporation was in a position to potentially avail itself of the opportunity before deciding that a corporate opportunity in fact existed. . . .

Most information involved in insider trading is not [a corporate asset], e.g., knowledge of an impending merger, a decline in earnings, etc. If the corporation were to attempt to exploit such non-public information by dealing in its own securities, it would open itself up to potential liability under federal and state securities laws. . . . This is not to say that the corporation does not have any interests with regard to such information. . . . However, insider trading does not entail the disclosure of inside information, but rather its use in a manner in which the corporation itself is prohibited from exploiting it. . . .

The injury [to the corporation] hypothesized by the *Diamond* court seems little different from the harm to the corporation that might be inferred whenever a responsible corporate official commits an illegal or unethical act using a corporate asset. Absent is the element of loss of opportunity or potential susceptibility to outside influence that generally is present when a corporate fiduciary is required to account to the corporation. . . .

Since the *Diamond* court's action was motivated in large part by its perception of the inadequacy of existing remedies for insider trading, it is noteworthy that over the decade since *Diamond* was decided, the 10b-5 class action has made substantial advances toward becoming the kind of effective remedy for insider trading that the court of appeals hoped that it might become. Most importantly, recovery of damages from insiders has been allowed by, or on the behalf of, market investors even when the insiders dealt only through impersonal stock exchanges. . . . [I]t is clear that the remedies for insider trading under the federal securities laws now constitute a more effective deterrent than they did when *Diamond* was decided.

QUESTIONS AND NOTES ON FREEMAN v. DECIO

1. Given that the private remedy under Rule 10b-5 is an implied right of action, does it seem curious that the Seventh Circuit here criticized the New York Court of Appeals' *Diamond* case for "judicial regulation"?

2. Is it correct to concede that only investors who trade — and not the corporation — bear the cost of insider trading in a corporation's securities? If shareholders claim the residual value of the corporation, what exactly does it mean to say that "the corporation" is not injured by insider trading? Is this the same as saying that the shareholders are not injured? If not, why not?

3. Note that *Decio*'s analysis has not settled the issue. The Restatement (Third) Agency attests to the continuing soundness of *Brophy* and *Diamond*. Moreover, the absence of venerable nineteenth-century precedent enforcing the corporation's right to recover profits made by its fiduciary by trading on inside information is not dispositive, since all of the nineteenth-century cases were brought by investors, not corporations. When the theory was presented for the first time to the Delaware courts in *Brophy*, there was very little struggle for the answer. See the more recent cases of *ORFA Securities Litigation*, 654 F. Supp. 1449 (D.N.J. 1987); and *Davidge v. White*, 377 F. Supp. 1084 (S.D.N.Y. 1974).

14.2.2 Board Disclosure Obligations Under State Law

Although federal law is the principal arbiter of disclosure obligations, there is an important common law duty of disclosure arising out of recent Delaware cases. The Delaware Supreme Court has gradually articulated a board's duty to provide candid and complete disclosure to shareholders in a series of opinions spanning the past 20 years.[9] Unlike a duty to disgorge profits from insider trading, considered above, this new disclosure obligation is distinctly modern; no nineteenth-century court would have upheld a

---

9. The first case in this line is believed to be *Lynch v. Vickers Energy Corp.*, 429 A.2d 497 (Del. 1981). Other notable cases include *Rosenblatt v. Getty Oil Co.*, 493 A.2d 929 (Del. 1985) and *Zirn v. VLI Corp.*, 681 A.2d 1050 (Del. 1996). See generally Lawrence A. Hamermesh, *Calling Off the Lynch Mob*, 49 Vand L. Rev. 1087 (1996).

duty of loyalty extending from the corporate board to the company's shareholders directly. By contrast, however, this state law duty of full disclosure closely parallels the federal disclosure duty, addressed above, under Rule 10b-5. Indeed, it is unclear which of these duties is broader.[10] Initially, Delaware's Court of Chancery attempted to reconcile parallel federal and state disclosure duties by stating that a duty arose only when the board communicated with shareholders by recommending how to vote or react to a tender offer. Thus, the Chancery Court indicated that state law retained its traditional focus on corporate governance rather than on the effects of corporate disclosures on the investment decisions of individual shareholders. The Delaware Supreme Court rejected this self-imposed limitation and clearly expanded the scope of state disclosure duties to the protection of shareholders in *Malone v. Brincat.*[11]

The director's duty of candor under state law requires them to exercise honest judgment to assure the disclosure of all material facts to shareholders. Failure to disclose a material fact, however, is unlikely to give rise to liability unless this failure represented intent to mislead. Otherwise the common charter waiver of liability for damages, independent of a loyalty violation under statutes such as DGCL § 102(b)(7), will protect directors from good faith (when negligent) failure to adequately disclose. An injunction, however, remains available if a plaintiff can show a failure to disclose a material fact, regardless of the mental state of the directors.

14.3   EXCHANGE ACT § 16(b) AND RULE 16

In contrast to today's attitudes toward insider trading, the Depression-era securities statutes treated it as a secondary matter worthy of only one narrow provision, § 16 of the Securities Exchange Act. Section 16(a) requires designated persons (directors, officers, and 10 percent shareholders of any issuer covered by the Act) to file public reports of any transactions in the corporation's securities. Today, under the regulations implementing Section 403 of the Sarbanes-Oxley Act of 2002, insiders have only two days in which to file these reports (electronically).

In contrast to § 16(a), § 16(b) is a strict liability rule intended to deter statutory insiders from profiting on inside information. Section 16(b) requires statutory insiders to disgorge to the corporation any profits made on short-term turnovers in the issuer's shares (purchases and sales within six-month periods). Although § 16(b) is often said to be a bright-line rule, since it creates liability that does not turn on subjective intent, its coverage can nevertheless require interpretation in light of the presumed intent of the legislature, as we discuss below. Like many bright-line

---

10. For example, whether state law may give rise to a claim by one who merely holds in reliance on an allegedly false statement is unclear. Under Rule 10b-5, however, shareholders have a cause of action only if they buy or sell securities in connection with a misleading statement or material omission.

11. 722 A.2d 5 (Del. 1998).

rules, moreover, § 16(b) is both under- and overinclusive; it is underinclusive because insider trading can occur over a period longer than six months, and overinclusive because short-swing transactions need not involve insider information. But such a rule does economize in administrative costs when compared to a rule that would attempt to be more discriminating.

Section 16(b) raises several administrative problems. One is how to calculate profits on short-swing transactions. In *Gratz v. Claughton*,[12] Learned Hand established the accepted rule that, in matching sales with purchases (or purchases with sales) for § 16(b) purposes, a court must take into account all purchases and sales of the same class of securities occurring within six months of the reportable event (both six months in the past and six months into the future). The technique is as follows: In calculating the profit realized from a sale (or purchase), a covered person must first look back six months and match the number of shares sold (or purchased) with the same number of shares purchased (or sold). The same process is repeated looking forward six months. One then deducts the lower total purchase price from the amount realized on the reportable sale to determine the profit, if any, that is payable to the corporation.[13]

A second administrative problem arising under § 16(b) is delimiting the class of statutory insiders or "covered persons." The statute explicitly covers 10 percent shareholders, officers, and directors. But who is an "officer"? Since the purposes of the statute could easily be defeated through creative use of labels, courts have long held that titles alone are not dispositive of such questions. Thus, a "vice-president" who was in reality a salesman with no managerial duties or access to significant non-public information was not covered by § 16.[14] By contrast, a "production manager" with more senior responsibilities who was not technically an officer under corporate law was covered by the section's prohibition.[15] In both cases, the courts stated that the relevant inquiry concerned whether the putative officer had recurring access to nonpublic information in the course of his duties.[16]

Finally, the most difficult administrative issue arising under § 16(b) lies in formulating the exact criteria for a "purchase or sale." The core meaning of "purchase" or "sale" of securities is easy to understand. But transactions might have the effects of a purchase or sale without having their forms. For

12. 187 F.2d 46 (2d Cir. 1951).

13. In other words, "if one is seeking an equation of purchase and sale, one may take any sale as the minuend and look back for six months for a purchase at less price to match against it. On the other hand, if one is looking for an equation of sale and purchase, one may take the same sale and look forward for six months for any purchase at a lower price." *Id.* at 52.

14. *Merrill Lynch, Pierce, Fenner & Smith, Inc. v. Livingston,* 566 F.2d 1119 (9th Cir. 1978).

15. *Colby v. Klune,* 178 F.2d 872 (2d Cir. 1949).

16. See also *Reliance Electric Co. v. Emerson Electric Co.,* 404 U.S. 418 (1972), where the Court found that plaintiffs could not recover profits made in the second of two successive sales of company stock, even though the sale had been split in order to avoid application of § 16(b), because at the time of the second sale, the defendant was no longer a covered person under the statute (he owned less than 10 percent of the company's stock).

example, suppose an officer borrows money, delivering his holdings of company stock as security, and subsequently defaults on his loan, forcing the bank to sell his stock? Was the original extension of cash a "sale"? If not, why not? Or, more sophisticated still, suppose that a corporate officer uses derivative contracts such as options or futures to place herself in a position to assume the risks and the rewards of stock ownership without dealing in the security itself, or uses swap transactions to cash out the economic interest of her stock while retaining only legal title? To counter this possibility, recent SEC rules bring all derivative combinations that track the financial characteristics of an issuer's securities under § 16(b). See 17 C.F.R. § 240.16b-6 (1998).

Finally, what about the treatment of mergers? One would be hard-pressed to say that target shareholders who receive cash consideration have not "sold" their shares. But what if target shareholders receive stock in the surviving company?[17]

The landmark case of *Kern County Land Co. v. Occidental Petroleum Corp.*, 411 U.S. 582 (1973), resulted from a contest between Occidental and Tenneco to acquire Kern County Land Co. Within a six-month period: (1) Occidental acquired more than 20 percent of Kern; (2) Occidental agreed to bow out and let the Kern-Tenneco merger proceed; (3) the Kern-Tenneco merger closed and Occidental's Kern shares were converted by operation of law into Tenneco shares; and (4) Occidental sold to Tenneco an option to repurchase its (now) Tenneco shares for $9 million cash, with this option price to be applied against the Tenneco purchase price if and when Tenneco exercised its option. More than six months after Occidental's initial acquisition of Kern shares, Tenneco exercised the option, giving Occidental a $19 million profit on its initial investment in Kern.

So far so good. But then, surprisingly, Kern (which continued to exist but now as a wholly owned subsidiary of Tenneco) sued Occidental, claiming that it had violated Section 16(b). Its main theory was that the conversion of the Kern shares into Tenneco shares in the merger constituted a sale giving rise to Section 16 duties on the part of Occidental as a 20 percent shareholder. The second theory was that granting the option for $9 million was itself a 16(b) transaction, either because the acquisition of the Tenneco shares in the merger was a recent purchase or because it was a sale within six months of the Kern shares that had been converted into Tenneco shares.

With respect to the option claim, the U.S. Supreme Court concluded that the option grant was not a sale of the stock; the option merely set up the possibility of a future sale, but one that might never happen or if it did, might happen more than six months from the date of the purchase. Under this reasoning, could a derivative or swap transaction be created that effectively sold (monetized) practically all of the insiders' financial interest in the stock and thus get around the purpose of Rule 16(b)? As we noted above, nowadays, the SEC treats all contracts or instruments that derive

---

17. See 17 C.F.R. § 240.16b-7 (1998) (stating that mergers and reclassifications of 85-percent-owned subsidiaries are exempt from § 16).

current value from the value of a covered security (such as the Tenneco option did) as a security for Section 16 purposes.[18]

With respect to the theory that the merger constituted a sale of Kern shares, the District Court agreed, but, on appeal, the Supreme Court reversed. The Court concluded that this was an "unorthodox" transaction and was not properly treated in the mechanical and technical way that conventional short-term sales are treated. Instead, the Court considered whether this defendant was in a position to profit from inside information. Of course, Kern management had always been hostile to Occidental. Occidental could not access Kern's inside information. In addition, the transaction that was claimed as a sale was a corporate transaction authorized by others, not Occidental alone. Thus, the Court concluded that the merger did not give rise to the risks that Section 16's remedy was designed to protect against and was not covered by Section 16.

While this seems like a fair enough result on the facts, it potentially makes the application of 16(b) more burdensome if courts will look at the particulars of each case.

PROBLEM ON SECTION 16

On September 15, 2001, Raj pays $5.00 per share for 10,000 shares of common stock in XYZ Corp., which constitutes less than 1 percent of all issued and outstanding XYZ common stock. On October 1, he is appointed treasurer of XYZ Corp. On October 30, Raj buys another 5,000 shares of common stock for $5.50 a share. On December 15, he buys another 3,000 shares of common stock for $5.30 a share. On December 25, Raj sells 2,000 shares of common stock for $5.10 a share. On March 1, 2002, Raj resigns as treasurer of XYZ Corp. On March 20, Raj sells his remaining 16,000 shares of common stock for $5.70 a share.

1. What statements must Raj file under § 16(a)?
2. Is Raj liable for any damages under § 16(b)? If so, for how much?

14.4   EXCHANGE ACT § 10(b) AND RULE 10b-5

While the relatively modest § 16 was the Securities Exchange Act's only attempt to deal with insider trading, the 1934 Act left open an indirect route for revisiting insider trading. It broadly empowered the SEC to promulgate rules regulating the trading of securities on national exchanges or through the means of interstate commerce. Section 10 of the Exchange Act is the most important such grant of rulemaking power. It provides in pertinent part:

---

18. See Exch. Act Rel. No. 34-28869 [1990-1991 Transfer Binder] Fed Sec. Reg Rptr. 84,709 (1991).

Section 10. [It shall be unlawful]

(b) To use or employ, in connection with the purchase or sale of any security registered on a national securities exchange or any security not so registered, any manipulative or deceptive device or contrivance in contravention of such rules and regulations as the Commission may proscribe as necessary or appropriate in the public interest or for the protection of investors.

14.4.1 Evolution of Private Right of Action Under §10

The most important rule promulgated by the SEC under § 10(b) — or indeed under any other section of the securities laws — is Rule 10b-5. But Rule 10b-5 had a humble birth. No hearings attended its creation, and no deep deliberation led to its choice of language. The facts prompting the adoption of the rule were rather like those of the *Agassiz* case. The SEC had learned that the president of a company in Boston was "going around buying up the stock of the company . . . at $4 a share and he was telling [the shareholders] that the company was doing very badly, whereas in fact the earnings . . . will be $2 a share for this coming year." (If the facts were as reported, the president was engaging in common law fraud.) To enable the SEC's Enforcement Division to seek an injunction against this activity in U.S. district court, Milton Freeman, a young lawyer working for the Commission, rapidly drafted Rule 10b-5 for the members of the Commission to review. The rest is history.

The rule provides in pertinent part that it shall be unlawful:

(a) To employ any device, scheme or artifice to defraud,

(b) To make any untrue statement of a material fact or omit to state a material fact necessary in order to make the statements made, in the light of the circumstances in which they were made, not misleading, or

(c) To engage in any act, practice, or course of business which operates or would operate as a fraud or deceit upon any person, in connection with the purchase or sale of any security.

In drafting a rule to implement § 10(b) of the 1934 Act, Mr. Freeman had sought only to empower the SEC's Enforcement Division to seek a federal court injunction of fraudulent or misleading conduct. Neither he nor the Commission apparently envisioned creating an implied private right of action under Rule 10b-5. Congress had created private rights of action in the securities laws but had done so sparingly. The legislative framework did not seem to invite additional private rights. Law, however, changes, and in this case, the agent of change was Miles Kirkpatrick, a brilliant federal district judge from Philadelphia,[19] who first recognized an implied private remedy for violation of Rule 10b-5. The case was *Kardon v. National Gypsum Co.,*[20] and the claim was that defendants had conspired to mislead shareholders into selling their stock at depressed prices. Judge Kirkpatrick concluded that, if true, the allegations would support a federal remedy under Rule 10b-5, even though that rule did not state that a private remedy for damages was intended:

> It is not, and cannot be, questioned that the complaint sets forth conduct on the part of the Slavins directly in violation of the provisions of Sec. 10(b) of the Act and of Rule X-10B-5 which implements it. It is also true that there is no provision in Sec. 10 or elsewhere expressly allowing civil suits by persons injured as a result of violation of Sec. 10 or of the Rule. However, "The violation of a legislative enactment by doing a prohibited act, or by failing to do a required act, makes the actor liable for an invasion of an interest of another if: (a) the intent of the enactment is exclusively or in part to protect an interest of the other as an individual; and (b) the interest invaded is one which the enactment is intended to protect. . . . " Restatement, Torts, Vol. 2, §286. This rule is more than merely a canon of statutory interpretation. The disregard of the command of a statute is a wrongful act and a tort.[21]

14.4.2   Elements of a 10b-5 Claim

Whatever theory one adopts to justify a right of private action under Rule 10b-5, such a right must be grounded in the language of both the statute and the rule. The statute empowers the SEC to make rules that protect against "manipulative and deceptive" activity "in connection with the purchase or sale of [covered] securities" or the making of untrue statements of material fact or the omission to state material fact in connection with the purchase or sale of a covered security. Thus, the elements of a Rule 10b-5 implied cause of action must resemble those of common law fraud, but they must also reflect the realities of the market-based transactions at which the rule is chiefly directed.

Recall the elements of common law fraud: a (1) false or misleading statement (2) of material fact that is (3) made with intent to deceive another (4) upon which that person (5) reasonably relies, (6) and that reliance causes harm. In addition to these elements, the language of Rule 10b-5 would seem to mandate that the requisite reliance must be by a buyer or seller of stock, the harm must be to a trader in stock, and the misleading

---

19. In addition to his opinion in *Kardon*, corporate law scholars know Judge Kirkpatrick's opinion in *Insurance Shares Corp. v. Northern Fiscal Corp.,* 35 F. Supp. 22 (E.D. Pa. 1940). (describing when a controller may be liable to fellow shareholders who are looted by the controller's transferee). Judge Kirkpatrick may be thought of as one of the unsung heroes of American corporate and securities law, whose many opinions, although largely forgotten today, continue to have their effects felt indirectly through case law.

20. 69 F. Supp. 512 (E.D. Pa. 1946).

21. *Id.* at 513.

statement must be made in connection with a purchase or sale of stock. Ask yourself whether these conditions are met as you consider the Rule 10b-5 action against insider trading, considered below.

While our discussion of liability under Rule 10b-5 touches upon all of the elements required for recovery we give greatest attention to its two most controversial elements. The first is the *duty* issue in omission cases. Certainly making false statements in connection with a sale of securities falls within the Rule (if other elements are satisfied). But the language of the rule also addresses "omissions." If this language reaches everyone possessing material nonpublic information (for example, someone who acquires such information through diligent research), there is a concern that it goes further than authorized by the language of Section 10(b). After all, the 1934 Act seems concerned about bad conduct: fraud and manipulation. Thus who is obligated to make full disclosure before buying or selling shares? In its 1961 *Cady, Roberts* decision,[22] the SEC essentially side-stepped the duty issue by asserting that the possession of "inside" information itself gives rise to a duty not to trade on it. The Supreme Court, however, focused squarely on the duty issue in its 1980 *Chiarella* case, as we discuss in § 14.4.2.3.

The second element of the 10b-5 cause of action that we explore with some depth is *reasonable reliance*. Again, this issue is framed by the pressure to reshape the fraud remedy into a weapon against misrepresentation in connection with trades on impersonal markets. The doctrinal vehicle for a more aggressive open-market fraud doctrine is the so-called fraud on the market doctrine, which we address below. More briefly, we also treat other elements of a claim: materiality, scienter, loss causation, and measure of recovery.

14.4.2.1　Elements of a 10b-5 Claim: False or Misleading Statement or Omission

A false statement (made with intent to deceive) is the most basic element of common law deceit, and it is likewise a foundation for 10b-5 liability. This is the essence of fraud. By contrast, omissions of material facts are more problematic. At common law, as we noted above, equity imposed an affirmative duty to disclose only when a fiduciary (trustee) was a party to the transaction. In order to stretch 10b-5 liability beyond active misstatements, therefore, the federal courts required a theory on which to predicate a duty to disclose. Three different approaches to this problem have evolved. As the case immediately following this note suggests, the SEC and the Second Circuit Court of Appeals initially took the aggressive position that any possession of relevant, material, nonpublic information gives rise to a duty to disclose or abstain from trading. The U.S. Supreme Court, on the other hand, took a more traditionalist approach in *Chiarella*, finding it

---

22. 40 S.E.C. 907 (1961).

necessary that the insider breach a fiduciary duty in trading on inside information in order to find 10b-5 liability. Last, and more recently, the Supreme Court has adopted the intermediate stance of augmenting the fiduciary duty theory with the more far-reaching misappropriation theory.[23]

SEC v. TEXAS GULF SULPHUR CO.

401 F.2d 833 (2d Cir. 1968)

WATERMAN, Cir. J. (en banc).

This action was commenced in the United States District Court by the [SEC] . . . against Texas Gulf Sulphur Company ("TGS") and several of its officers, directors and employees, to enjoin certain conduct by TGS and the individual defendants said to violate Section 10(b) of the Act, and to compel the rescission by the individual defendants of securities transactions assertedly conducted contrary to law. . . .

This action derives from the exploratory activities of TGS begun in 1957 on the Canadian Shield in eastern Canada. In March of 1959, aerial geophysical surveys were conducted over more than 15,000 square miles of this area by a group led by defendant Mollison, a mining engineer and a Vice President of TGS. The group included defendant Holyk, TGS's chief geologist, defendant Clayton, an electrical engineer and geophysicist, and defendant Darke, a geologist. . . .

On October 29 and 30, 1963, Clayton conducted a ground geophysical survey on the northeast portion of the Kidd 55 segment which confirmed the presence of an anomaly and indicated the necessity of diamond core drilling for further evaluation. Drilling of the initial hole, K-55-1, at the strongest part of the anomaly was commenced on November 8. . . . Visual estimates by Holyk of the core of K-55-1 indicated an average copper content of 1.15% and an average zinc content of 8.64% over a length of 599 feet. This visual estimate convinced TGS that it was desirable to acquire the remainder of the Kidd 55 segment, and in order to facilitate this acquisition TGS President Stephens instructed the exploration group to keep the results of K-55-1 confidential and undisclosed even as to other officers, directors, and employees of TGS. The hole was concealed and a barren core was intentionally drilled off the anomaly. Meanwhile, the core of K-55-1 had been shipped to Utah for chemical assay which, when received in early December, revealed an average mineral content of 1.18% copper, 8.26% zinc, and 3.94% ounces of silver per ton over a length of 602 feet. These results were so remarkable that neither Clayton, an experienced geophysicist, nor four other TGS expert witnesses, had ever seen or heard of a comparable initial exploratory drill hole in a base metal deposit. . . .

---

23. See *United States v. O'Hagan*, below, 521 U.S. 642, *cert. denied*, 519 U.S. 1087 (1997).

During the period, from November 12, 1963 when K-55-1 was completed, to March 31, 1964 when drilling was resumed, certain of the individual defendants . . . purchased TGS stock or calls thereon.[24] . . .

On February 20, 1964, also during this period, TGS issued stock options to 26 of its officers and employees whose salaries exceeded a specified amount, five of whom were the individual defendants Stephens, Fogarty, Mollison, Holyk, and Kline. Of these, only Kline was unaware of the detailed results of K-55-1, but he, too, knew that a hole containing favorable bodies of copper and zinc ore had been drilled in Timmins. At this time, neither the TGS Stock Option Committee nor its Board of Directors had been informed of the results of K-55-1, presumably because of the pending land acquisition program which required confidentiality. All of the foregoing defendants accepted the options granted them.

[D]rilling was resumed on March 31. . . .

On April 8 TGS began with a second drill rig to drill another hole, K-55-6, 300 feet easterly of K-55-1. . . . On April 10, a third drill rig commenced drilling yet another hole. . . . By the evening of April 10 in this hole, too, substantial copper mineralization had been encountered over the last 42 feet of its 97-foot length.

Meanwhile, rumors that a major ore strike was in the making had been circulating throughout Canada. On the morning of Saturday, April 11, Stephens at his home in Greenwich, Conn. read in the *New York Herald Tribune* and in the *New York Times* unauthorized reports of the TGS drilling which seemed to infer a rich strike from the fact that the drill cores had been flown to the United States for chemical assay. Stephens immediately contacted Fogarty at his home in Rye, N.Y., who in turn telephoned and later that day visited Mollison at Mollison's home in Greenwich to obtain a current report and evaluation of the drilling progress. The following morning, Sunday, Fogarty again telephoned Mollison, inquiring whether Mollison had any further information and told him to return to Timmins with Holyk, the TGS Chief Geologist, as soon as possible "to move things along." With the aid of one Carroll, a public relations consultant, Fogarty drafted a press release designed to quell the rumors, which release, after having been channeled through Stephens and Huntington, a TGS attorney, was issued at 3:00 P.M. on Sunday, April 12, and which appeared in the morning newspapers of general circulation on Monday, April 13. It read in pertinent part as follows: . . .

> During the past few days, the exploration activities of Texas Gulf Sulphur in the area of Timmins, Ontario, have been widely reported in the press, coupled with rumors of a substantial copper discovery there. These reports exaggerate the scale of operations, and mention plans and statistics of size and grade of ore that are without factual basis. . . .
>
> The facts are as follows. TGS has been exploring in the Timmins area for six years as part of its overall search in Canada and elsewhere for various minerals — lead, copper, zinc, etc. During the course of this work, in Timmins as

---

24. A "call" is a negotiable option contract by which the bearer has the right to buy from the writer of the contract a certain number of shares of a particular stock at a fixed price on or before a certain agreed-upon date. — Eds.

well as in Eastern Canada, TGS has conducted exploration entirely on its own, without the participation by others. Numerous prospects have been investigated by geophysical means and a large number of selected ones have been core-drilled. These cores are sent to the United States for assay and detailed examination as a matter of routine and on advice of expert Canadian legal counsel. No inferences as to grade can be drawn from this procedure.

Most of the areas drilled in Eastern Canada have revealed either barren pyrite or graphite without value; a few have resulted in discoveries of small or marginal sulphide ore bodies.

Recent drilling on one property near Timmins has led to preliminary indications that more drilling would be required for proper evaluation of this prospect. The drilling done to date has not been conclusive, but the statements made by many outside quarters are unreliable and include information and figures that are not available to TGS.

The work done to date has not been sufficient to reach definite conclusions and any statement as to size and grade of ore would be premature and possibly misleading. When we have progressed to the point where reasonable and logical conclusions can be made, TGS will issue a definite statement to its stockholders and to the public in order to clarify the Timmins project. . . .

The release purported to give the Timmins drilling results as of the release date, April 12. From Mollison Fogarty had been told of the developments through 7:00 P.M. on April 10, and of the remarkable discoveries made up to that time, detailed supra, which discoveries, according to the calculations of the experts who testified for the SEC at the hearing, demonstrated that TGS had already discovered 6.2 to 8.3 million tons of proven ore having gross assay values from $26 to $29 per ton. TGS experts, on the other hand, denied at the hearing that proven or probable ore could have been calculated on April 11 or 12 because there was then no assurance of continuity in the mineralized zone.

The evidence as to the effect of this release on the investing public was equivocal and less than abundant. On April 13 the *New York Herald Tribune* in an article head-noted "Copper Rumor Deflated" quoted from the TGS release of April 12 and backtracked from its original April 11 report of a major strike but nevertheless inferred from the TGS release that "recent mineral exploratory activity near Timmins, Ontario, has provided preliminary favorable results, sufficient at least to require a step-up in drilling operations." . . . The trial court stated only that "While, in retrospect, the press release may appear gloomy or incomplete, this does not make it misleading or deceptive on the basis of the facts then known." *Id.* at 296. . . .

While drilling activity ensued to completion, TGS officials were taking steps toward ultimate disclosure of the discovery. On April 13, a previously invited reporter for *The Northern Miner*, a Canadian mining industry journal, visited the drillsite, interviewed Mollison, Holyk and Darke, and prepared an article which confirmed a 10 million ton ore strike. This report, after having been submitted to Mollison and returned to the reporter unamended on April 15, was published in the April 16 issue. A statement relative to the extent of the discovery, in substantial part drafted by Mollison, was given to the Ontario Minister of Mines for release to the Canadian media. Mollison and Holyk expected it to be released over the airways at 11 P.M. on April 15th, but, for undisclosed reasons, it was not released until 9:40 A.M. on the 16th. An official detailed statement, announcing a strike of at least 25 million tons of ore, based on the drilling data set forth above, was read to representatives of American financial media from 10:00 A.M. to 10:10 or 10:15 A.M. on April 16, and appeared over Merrill Lynch's private wire at 10:29 A.M. and, somewhat later than expected, over the Dow Jones ticker tape at 10:54 A.M.

Between the time the first press release was issued on April 12 and the dissemination of the TGS official announcement on the morning of April 16, the only defendants before us on appeal who engaged in market activity were Clayton and Crawford and TGS director Coates. Clayton ordered 200 shares of TGS stock through his Canadian broker on April 15. . . . Crawford ordered 300 shares at midnight on the 15th and another 300 shares at 8:30 A.M. the next day, and these orders were executed over the Midwest Exchange in Chicago at its opening on April 16. Coates left the TGS press conference and called his broker son-in-law Haemisegger shortly before 10:20 A.M. on the 16th and ordered 2,000 shares of TGS for family trust accounts of which Coates was a trustee but not a beneficiary; Haemisegger executed this order over the New York and Midwest Exchanges, and he and his customers purchased 1,500 additional shares.

During the period of drilling in Timmins, the market price of TGS stock fluctuated but steadily gained overall. On Friday, November 8, when the drilling began, the stock closed at 17 ⅜. . . . On April 13, the day on which the April 12 release was disseminated, TGS opened at 30 ⅛, rose immediately to a high of 32 and gradually tapered off to close at 30 ⅞. It closed at 30 ¼ the next day, and at 29 ⅜ on April 15. On April 16, the day of the official announcement of the Timmins discovery, the price climbed to a high of 37 and closed at 36 ⅜. By May 15, TGS stock was selling at 58 ¼. . . .

[Rule 10b-5] is based in policy on the justifiable expectation of the securities marketplace that all investors trading on impersonal exchanges have relatively equal access to material information. The essence of the Rule is that anyone who, trading for his own account in the securities of a corporation has "access, directly or indirectly, to information intended to be available only for a corporate purpose and not for the personal benefit of anyone" may not take "advantage of such information knowing it is unavailable to those with whom he is dealing," i.e., the investing public. *Matter of Cady, Roberts & Co.*, 40 SEC 907, 912 (1961). Insiders, as directors or management officers are, of course, by this Rule, precluded from so unfairly dealing. Thus, anyone in possession of material inside information must either disclose it to the investing public, or, if he is disabled from disclosing it in order to protect a corporate confidence, or he chooses not to do so, must abstain from trading in or recommending the securities concerned while such inside information remains undisclosed. So, it is here no justification for insider activity that disclosure was forbidden by the legitimate corporate objective of acquiring options to purchase the land surrounding the exploration site; if the information was, as the SEC contends, material, its possessors should have kept out of the market until disclosure was accomplished. *Cady, Roberts*, supra at 911. . . .

An insider is not, of course, always foreclosed from investing in his own company merely because he may be more familiar with company operations than are outside investors. . . . Nor is an insider obligated to confer upon outside investors the benefit of his superior financial or other expert analysis by disclosing his educated guesses or predictions. The only regulatory objective is that access to material information be enjoyed equally, but this objective requires nothing more than the disclosure of basic facts so that outsiders may draw upon their own evaluative expertise. . . .

[W]hether facts are material within Rule 10b-5 when the facts relate to a particular event . . . will depend at any given time upon a balancing of both the indicated probability that the event will occur and the anticipated magnitude of the event in light of the totality of the company activity. Here, knowledge of the possibility, which surely was more than marginal, of the existence of a mine of the vast magnitude indicated by the remarkably rich drill core located rather close to the surface (suggesting mineability by the less expensive openpit method) within the confines of a large anomaly (suggesting an extensive region of mineralization) might well have affected the price of TGS stock and would certainly have been an important fact to a reasonable, if speculative, investor in deciding whether he should buy, sell, or hold. . . .

Finally, a major factor in determining whether the K-55-1 mine discovery was a material fact is the importance attached to the drilling results by those who knew about it. In view of other unrelated recent developments favorably affecting TGS, participation by an informed person in a regular stock-purchase program, or even sporadic trading by an informed person, might lend only nominal support to the inference of the materiality of the K-55-1 discovery; nevertheless, the timing by those who knew of it of their stock purchases and their purchases of short-term calls — purchases in some cases by individuals who had never before purchased calls or even TGS stock — virtually compels the inference that the insiders were influenced by the drilling results. . . .

Our decision to expand the limited protection afforded outside investors by the trial court's narrow definition of materiality is not at all shaken by fears that the elimination of insider trading benefits will deplete the ranks of capable corporate managers by taking away an incentive to accept such employment. Such benefits, in essence, are forms of secret corporate compensation . . . derived at the expense of the uninformed investing public and not at the expense of the corporation which receives the sole benefit from insider incentives. Moreover, adequate incentives for corporate officers may be provided by properly administered stock options and employee purchase plans of which there are many in existence.

The core of Rule 10b-5 is the implementation of the Congressional purpose that all investors should have equal access to the rewards of participation in securities transactions. It was the intent of Congress that all members of the investing public should be subject to identical market risks, — which market risks include, of course the risk that one's evaluative capacity or one's capital available to put at risk may exceed another's capacity or capital. The insiders here were not trading on an equal footing with the outside investors. They alone were in a position to evaluate the probability and magnitude of what seemed from the outset to be a major ore strike; they alone could invest safely, secure in the expectation that the price of TGS stock would rise substantially in the event such a major strike should materialize, but would decline little, if at all, in the event of failure, for the public, ignorant at the outset of the favorable probabilities would likewise be unaware of the unproductive exploration, and the additional exploration costs would not significantly affect TGS market prices. Such inequities based upon unequal access to knowledge should not be shrugged off as inevitable in our way of life, or, in view of the congressional concern in the area, remain uncorrected.

We hold, therefore, that all transactions in TGS stock or calls by individuals apprised of the drilling results of K-55-1 were made in violation of Rule 10b-5. . . .

QUESTIONS ON TEXAS GULF SULPHUR

1. The short-term calls at issue in *TGS* are call options, which give holders the right to purchase stock at a fixed price for a fixed period. Why might wayward insiders prefer to buy calls rather than shares? In contrast, a put option is the right to sell stock in the future at a fixed price. How might a wayward insider profit by trading on puts?

2. Who is harmed by insider trading? The shareholders who trade on the opposite side of the insiders? The shareholders who trade on the same side as the insiders? Does it matter whether inside information is good news or bad?

3. Can a public shareholder who would have bought or sold regardless of insider trading activity be harmed by such activity? If so, is the measure of harm the difference between the price the public shareholder received and the price she would have received had the insider refrained from trading? What else could the measure of harm be? Try to illustrate your views on the appropriate measure of harm from the *Texas Gulf Sulphur* case

4. Are those who know little and seldom trade harmed by insider trading in the few stocks that they do hold? Are savvy (outside) speculators who continuously trade in the same stocks harmed just as much? Might the Wall Street speculators be harmed more than the infrequent traders?

5. Is anyone at all harmed by insider trading if the market correctly anticipates overall levels of insider trading and discounts share prices accordingly? Could we make the same argument about stealing from the corporate treasury—that is, if share prices discount fairly for stealing ex ante, shareholders are not harmed by thieving corporate managers—at least from an ex ante perspective.

NOTE ON THE SUPREME COURT'S EFFORT TO CONSTRAIN RULE 10B-5 LIABILITY IN THE PERIOD FROM 1975 TO 1980

After the influential *Texas Gulf Sulphur* case (and the 1966 liberalization of Federal Rule of Civil Procedure 23, the class action rule), there was an eruption of private litigation under Rule 10b-5 in the lower federal courts. By 1975, the U.S. Supreme Court could be seen as attempting to stem this growth in a series of cases. See, e.g., *Blue Chip Stamps v. Manor Drug Stores,* 421 U.S. 723 (1975) (claimants must be buyers or sellers of stock; holding stock in reliance on misstatement is not enough); *Ernst & Ernst v. Hochfelder,* 425 U.S. 185 (1976) (scienter required to bring a 10b-5 claim). Notable among these cases was *Santa Fe v. Green,* which attempted to preserve state law regulation of internal corporate affairs, including the fiduciary duties that directors and officers owe to the corporation (or as U.S. courts had been saying for most of the twentieth century, the duty owed to the corporation and its shareholders).

SANTA FE INDUSTRIES INC. v. GREEN
430 U.S. 462 (1977)

WHITE, J.:

The issue in this case involves the reach and coverage of § 10(b) of the [1934 Act] and Rule 10b-5 . . . in the context of a Delaware short-form merger transaction used by the majority stockholder of a corporation to eliminate the minority interest. . . .

In 1936, petitioner Santa Fe Industries, Inc. (Santa Fe), acquired control of 60% of the stock of Kirby Lumber Corp. (Kirby), a Delaware corporation. Through a series of purchases over the succeeding years, Santa Fe increased its control of Kirby's stock to 95%; the purchase prices during the period 1968-1973 ranged from $65 to $92.50 per share. In 1974, wishing to acquire 100% ownership of Kirby, Santa Fe availed itself of § 253 of the Delaware Corporation Law, known as the "short-form merger" statute. . . . The statute does not require the consent of, or advance notice to, the minority stockholders. However, notice of the merger must be given within 10 days after its effective date, and any stockholder who is dissatisfied with the terms of the merger may petition the Delaware Court of Chancery for a decree ordering the surviving corporation to pay him the fair value of his shares, as determined by a court-appointed appraiser subject to review by the court. . . .

Santa Fe obtained independent appraisals of the physical assets of Kirby—land, timber, buildings, and machinery—and of Kirby's oil, gas, and mineral interests. These appraisals, together with other financial information, were submitted to Morgan Stanley & Co. (Morgan Stanley), an investment banking firm retained to appraise the fair market value of Kirby stock. Kirby's physical assets were appraised at $320 million (amounting to $640 for each of the 500,000 shares); Kirby's stock was valued by Morgan Stanley at $125 per share. Under the terms of the merger, minority stockholders were offered $150 per share.

The provisions of the short-form merger statute were fully complied with. The minority stockholders of Kirby were notified the day after the merger became effective and were advised of their right to obtain an appraisal in Delaware court if dissatisfied with the offer of $150 per share. They also received an information statement containing, in addition to the relevant financial data about Kirby, the appraisals of the value of Kirby's assets and the Morgan Stanley appraisal concluding that the fair market value of the stock was $125 per share.

Respondents, minority stockholders of Kirby, objected to the terms of the merger, but did not pursue their appraisal remedy in the Delaware Court of Chancery. Instead, they brought this action in federal court on behalf of the corporation and other minority stockholders, seeking to set aside the merger or to recover what they claimed to be the fair value of their shares. The amended complaint asserted that, based on the fair market value of Kirby's physical assets as revealed by the appraisal included in the information statement sent to minority shareholders, Kirby's stock was worth at least $772 per share. The complaint alleged further that the merger took place without prior notice to minority stockholders; that the purpose of the merger was to appropriate the difference between the "conceded pro rata value of the physical assets," App. 103a, and the offer of $150 per share — to "freez[e] out the minority stockholders at a wholly inadequate price," *id.*, at 100a; and that Santa Fe, knowing the appraised value of the physical assets, obtained a "fraudulent appraisal" of the stock from Morgan Stanley and offered $25 above that appraisal "in order to lull the minority stockholders into erroneously believing that [Santa Fe was] generous." *Id.*, at 103a. This course of conduct was alleged to be "a violation of Rule 10b-5 because defendants employed a 'device, scheme, or artifice to defraud' and engaged in an 'act, practice or course of business which operates or would operate as a fraud or deceit upon any person, in connection with the purchase or sale of any security.'" *Ibid.* Morgan Stanley assertedly participated in the fraud as an accessory by submitting its appraisal of $125 per share although knowing the appraised value of the physical assets.

The District Court dismissed the complaint for failure to state a claim upon which relief could be granted. . . . A divided Court of Appeals for the Second Circuit reversed. . . . To the extent that the Court of Appeals would rely on the use of the term "fraud" in Rule 10b-5 to bring within the ambit of the Rule all breaches of fiduciary duty in connection with a securities transaction, its interpretation would, like the interpretation rejected by the Court in *Ernst & Ernst*, "add a gloss to the operative language of the statute quite different from its commonly accepted meaning." *Id.*, at 199. But, as the Court there held, the language of the statute must control the interpretation of the Rule. . . .

The language of § 10(b) gives no indication that Congress meant to prohibit any conduct not involving manipulation or deception. Nor have we been cited to any evidence in the legislative history that would support a departure from the language of the statute. . . .

It is our judgment that the transaction, if carried out as alleged in the complaint, was neither deceptive nor manipulative and therefore did not violate either § 10(b) of the Act or Rule 10b-5.

. . . The finding of the District Court, undisturbed by the Court of Appeals, was that there was no "omission" or "misstatement" in the information statement accompanying the notice of merger. On the basis of the information provided, minority shareholders could either accept the price offered or reject it and seek an appraisal in the Delaware Court of Chancery. Their choice was fairly presented, and they were furnished with all relevant information on which to base their decision. . . .

It is also readily apparent that the conduct alleged in the complaint was not "manipulative" within the meaning of the statute. "Manipulation" is "virtually a term of art when used in connection with securities markets." *Ernst & Ernst*, 425 U.S., at 199. The term refers generally to practices, such as wash sales, matched orders, or rigged prices, that are intended to mislead investors by artificially affecting market activity. . . . Section 10 (b)'s general prohibition of practices deemed by the SEC to be "manipulative" — in this technical sense of artificially affecting market activity in order to mislead investors — is fully consistent with the fundamental purpose of the 1934 Act "'to substitute a philosophy of full disclosure for the philosophy of *caveat emptor*. . . .'" *Affiliated Ute Citizens v. United States*, 406 U.S. 128, 151 (1972). . . . Indeed, nondisclosure is usually essential to the success of a manipulative scheme. . . . No doubt Congress meant to prohibit the full range of ingenious devices that might be used to manipulate securities prices. But we do not think it would have chosen this "term of art" if it had meant to bring within the scope of §10(b) instances of corporate mismanagement such as this, in which the essence of the complaint is that shareholders were treated unfairly by a fiduciary. . . .

The language of the statute is, we think, "sufficiently clear in its context" to be dispositive here, . . . but even if it were not, there are additional considerations that weigh heavily against permitting a cause of action under Rule 10b-5 for the breach of corporate fiduciary duty alleged in this complaint. Congress did not expressly provide a private cause of action for violations of §10(b). . . . [A] private cause of action under the antifraud provisions of the Securities Exchange Act should not be implied where it is "unnecessary to ensure the fulfillment of Congress' purposes" in adopting the Act. *Piper v. Chris-Craft Industries.* . . .

A second factor in determining whether Congress intended to create a federal cause of action in these circumstances is "whether 'the cause of action [is] one traditionally relegated to state law.'" *Piper v. Chris-Craft Industries, Inc.* . . . The Delaware Legislature has supplied minority shareholders with a cause of action in the Delaware Court of Chancery to recover the fair value of shares allegedly undervalued in a short-form merger. . . .

The reasoning behind a holding that the complaint in this case alleged fraud under Rule 10b-5 could not be easily contained. It is difficult to imagine how a court could distinguish, for purposes of Rule 10b-5 fraud, between a majority stockholder's use of a short-form merger to eliminate the minority at an unfair price and the use of some other device, such as a long-form merger, tender offer, or liquidation, to achieve the same result; or indeed how a court could distinguish the alleged abuses in these going private transactions from other types of fiduciary self-dealing involving transactions in securities. The result would be to bring within the Rule a wide variety of corporate conduct traditionally left to state regulation. In addition to posing a "danger of vexatious litigation which could result from a widely expanded class of plaintiffs under Rule 10b-5," *Blue Chip Stamps v. Manor Drug Stores*, 421 U.S., at 740, this extension of the federal securities laws would overlap and quite possibly interfere with state corporate law. Federal courts applying a "federal fiduciary principle" under Rule 10b-5 could be expected to depart from state fiduciary standards at least to the extent necessary to ensure uniformity within the federal system.[16] Absent a clear indication of congressional intent, we are reluctant to federalize the substantial portion of the law of corporations that deals with transactions in securities, particularly where established state policies of corporate regulation would be overridden.

... There may well be a need for uniform federal fiduciary standards to govern mergers such as that challenged in this complaint. But those standards should not be supplied by judicial extension of § 10(b) and Rule 10b-5 to "cover the corporate universe."

NOTE ON SANTA FE *AND FAIRNESS IN GOING-PRIVATE MERGERS*

Santa Fe deals with a short-form, freeze-out transaction under DGCL § 253, which permits a parent that holds 90 percent of the shares in a subsidiary to value the minority interest, merge with the subsidiary, and subsequently pay off the minority shareholders, all without the formality of a shareholder vote. At the time *Santa Fe* was decided, Delaware law offered minority shareholders little protection in a cash-out merger beyond the appraisal remedy. In fact then, as now, few minority shareholders chose to accept the delay and legal cost associated with appraisal litigation. Many commentators regarded with horror the practice, prevalent in the 1970s, of "cashing out" minority shareholders at close to market prices at a time when the stock market seemed depressed. But with *Santa Fe*, the Supreme Court seemed to place the ball clearly back in the court of state law. The Delaware Supreme Court apparently responded to *Santa Fe*'s implied invitation when it issued *Singer v. Magnavox*,[25] which announced more elaborate fiduciary duty protection in self-interested transactions. As we have reviewed in Chapter 12, still later the Delaware Supreme Court decided *Weinberger v. UOP, Inc.*, where it reaffirmed the obligation to pay a "fair price" in such a transaction and also modernized the appraisal remedy.

QUESTIONS ON SANTA FE v. GREEN

1. How do you suppose Morgan Stanley could have valued Kirby's assets at $640/share and its minority stock at $125/share? Could both

---

16. For example, some States apparently require a "valid corporate purpose" for the elimination of the minority interest through a short-form merger, whereas other States do not. ... Thus to the extent that Rule 10b-5 is interpreted to require a valid corporate purpose for elimination of minority shareholders as well as a fair price for their shares, it would impose a stricter standard of fiduciary duty than that required by the law of some States.

25. 380 A.2d 969 (Del. 1977).

numbers have referred to real economic values, given the existing legal framework? Recall that the market price of Kirby stock ranged between $65 and $92.50.

2. What precisely is the distinction between "deception and manipulation," on the one hand, and an allegation of a breach of fiduciary duty, on the other? Might the Court have decided differently if Santa Fe had given Morgan Stanley inaccurate or insufficient valuation data?

NOTE ON DISCLOSURE OF UNFAIRNESS: GOLDBERG v. MERIDOR

1. Although the majority opinion in *Santa Fe* indicates a reluctance to extend Rule 10b-5 into the province of state law regarding corporate mismanagement, lower federal courts did not abandon entirely an effort to transmute a breach of fiduciary duty case into a 10b-5 violation. It seems clear that if D, a director of Corporation C, persuades C's board, by fraud, to sell him stock, C can sue D under Rule 10b-5 even though it can also sue D for breach of fiduciary duty. Similarly, if C's board does not sue D, a shareholder could sue D under Rule 10b-5 in a derivative action (if she can demonstrate that the board's judgment not to sue D is not deserving of business judgment deference). What happens then if a controlling shareholder causes a corporation to issue stock to him at an unfair price, not by making false statements but by dominating corporate directors? Is this actionable manipulation in connection with the purchase or sale of a security under Rule 10b-5?

In *Schoenbaum v. Firstbrook*, 405 F.2d 215 (2d Cir. 1968) (en banc), *cert. denied*, 395 U.S. 906 (1969), decided before *Santa Fe*, Aquitaine was a majority shareholder of Banff Oil Ltd. and had appointed three of its eight directors. It was alleged that Aquitaine used its controlling influence to cause Banff to sell Banff shares to Aquitaine for wholly inadequate consideration. The Second Circuit held that a minority shareholder in Banff could bring a derivative action on Banff's behalf under Rule 10b-5:

> [I]t is alleged that Aquitaine exercised a controlling influence over the issuance to it of treasury stock of Banff for a wholly inadequate consideration. If it is established that the transaction took place as alleged, it constituted a violation of Rule 10b-5, subdivision (3), because Aquitaine engaged in an "act, practice or course of business which operates or would operate as a fraud or deceit upon any person, in connection with the purchase or sale of any security." Moreover, Aquitaine and the directors of Banff were guilty of deceiving the stockholders of Banff (other than Aquitaine).

Reasonable minds apparently might differ because Judge Medina wrote in dissent that the majority opinion was "nothing short of a standing invitation to blackmail and extortion." One might think that *Santa Fe* would require a different answer after it was decided. But what if a plaintiff inserts into allegations about unfair dealings an allegation of failure to disclose the unfairness? Might this self-levitation work to allow the federal courts to hear the case under 10b-5, *Santa Fe* notwithstanding?

In *Goldberg v. Meridor*, 567 F.2d 209 (2d Cir. 1977), *cert. denied*, 434 U.S. 1069 (1978), decided shortly after *Santa Fe*, UGO Corporation was controlled by Maritimecor, which, in turn, was controlled by Maritime Fruit. A UGO shareholder alleged that Maritimecor, Maritime Fruit, and the directors of the various companies had caused UGO to acquire Maritimecor's assets in exchange for UGO stock and that the agreement "was fraudulent and unfair in that the assets of Maritimecor were overpriced." *Id.* at 211. Press releases that described the agreement failed to disclose certain material facts concerning the value of Maritimecor's assets. The Second Circuit, in an opinion by Judge Henry J. Friendly, held that *Schoenbaum* had survived *Santa Fe*. A derivative action could be brought under Rule 10b-5 on the basis that the transaction between a corporation and a fiduciary or a controlling shareholder was unfair if the transaction involved stock and material facts concerning the transaction had not been disclosed to all shareholders:

> *Schoenbaum* . . . can rest solidly on the now widely recognized ground that there is deception of the corporation (in effect, of its minority shareholders) when the corporation is influenced by its controlling shareholder to engage in a transaction adverse to the corporation's interests (in effect, the minority shareholders' interests) and there is nondisclosure or misleading disclosures as to the material facts of the transaction. . . . The Supreme Court noted in [*Green v. Santa Fe Industries, Inc.,*] that the court of appeals "did not disturb the District Court's conclusion that the complaint did not allege a material misrepresentation or nondisclosure with respect to the value of the stock" of Kirby; the Court's quarrel was with this court's holding that "neither misrepresentation nor nondisclosure was a necessary element of a Rule 10b-5 action," . . . and that a breach of fiduciary duty would alone suffice. . . . It was because "the complaint failed to allege a material misrepresentation or material failure to disclose" that the Court found "inapposite the cases [including *Schoenbaum*] relied upon by respondents and the court below, in which the breaches of fiduciary duty held violative of Rule 10b-5 included some element of deception". . . .
> Here the complaint alleged "deceit . . . upon UGO's minority shareholders". . . . The nub of the matter is that the conduct attacked in *Green* did not violate the "'fundamental purpose' of the Act as implementing a 'philosophy of full disclosure.'" . . . [T]he conduct here attacked does. . . .

Goldberg v. Meridor has been interpreted as requiring more than mere nondisclosure of impure motive or culpability. See 7 Louis Loss & Joel Seligman, Securities Regulation 3542 (1991).

2. Courts that adopt the Goldberg approach agree that, in order to succeed under the principle of *Goldberg v. Meridor*, the plaintiff must show (i) a misrepresentation or nondisclosure that (ii) caused a loss to the shareholders. A shareholder vote is an obvious way to satisfy that requirement, but many of the cases in which this theory is deployed do not require a shareholder vote. Thus, a popular technique to show that the failure to disclose caused loss is to allege that a remedy was forgone as a result of this lack of full disclosure. Most commonly, the plaintiff attempts to meet this requirement by arguing that if full disclosure had been made,

the shareholders could have sought injunctive relief against the proposed transaction under state law (i.e., with truthful disclosure, they would have known that the transaction was a violation of fiduciary duty). Courts are in disagreement about the nature of the showing that the plaintiff must make concerning the likelihood that the foregone remedy would have been successful. In *Kidwell ex rel. Penfold v. Meikle*, 597 F.2d 1273 (9th Cir. 1979), the Ninth Circuit held that the plaintiff must show that the shareholders would actually have succeeded if they had brought the forgone suit. In *Healy v. Catalyst Recovery*, 616 F.2d 641 (3d Cir. 1980), the Third Circuit rejected the *Kidwell* test and instead held that the plaintiff must show "there was a reasonable probability of ultimate success." *Id.* at 647.

3. The Seventh Circuit in a series of cases has rejected *Goldberg* and the idea that a 10b-5 action could be predicated upon false disclosure that allegedly led to the plaintiff not availing himself of a state remedy, see e.g., *Harris Trust & Savings Bank v. Ellis*, 810 F.2d 700, 704 (7th Cir. 1987); *Ray v. Karris*, 780 F.2d 636-641-43 (7th Cir. 1985); or the idea that an alleged failure to disclose a breach of fiduciary duty can constitute an actionable omission or manipulation under 10b-5. See *Painter v. Marshall Field & Co.*, 646 F 2d 1092 (7th Cir. 1981).

4. Does *Goldberg v. Meridor* imply anything about the relationship between the level of substantive protection available under state law and the level of protection available to shareholders under Rule 10b-5? What might plaintiffs have argued on *Santa Fe*'s facts in the Second Circuit after the *Goldberg* opinion?

NOTE ON THEORIES OF DUTY TO SUPPORT OMISSIONS CASES

We return now to the development of the law of Rule 10b-5, legal duty, and omissions cases in the wake of *Texas Gulf Sulphur*. As we have noted, cases in which the defendant makes false statements present no problem for theory; false statements are the essence of fraud. But what theory tells us which silent persons who know nonpublic information have an affirmative duty to disclose or abstain from trading? From the time of its *Cady Roberts* decision forward, the SEC has taken the view that the simple possession of inside nonpublic information — no matter the circumstance that lead to that knowledge — gives rise to a duty to "disclose or abstain." But most courts — at least outside of the Second Circuit — have tended to emphasize the need for an act of fraud or manipulation (most recently in *Dura Pharmaceuticals*, 544 U.S. 336 (2005), discussed in our examination of "loss causation" below) and thus have been reluctant to accept the SEC's theory. For such traditionalists it is important to find a doctrinal foundation for a duty to disclose — like the fiduciary duty of the trustee that allowed nineteenth-century courts to impose obligations of disclosure and fairness on trustees dealing with trust beneficiaries. Given the Supreme Court's *Strong v. Repide* case, with its emphasis on "special facts" that give rise to a fiduciary duty to disclose, it was easy for courts and commentators to see the issuer's officers and directors as under a duty that constrained their ability to trade on nonpublic information. But what about those who are not officers or directors but who know nonpublic information? They may fall into several categories: those who are tipped by insiders (tippees) usually as part of scheme to make profits for both; those who get nonpublic information in connection with performing some service for the corporation (service providers, such as lawyers or bankers); and those who invest in information acquisition through legitimate means and in the process learn something material before the public generally appreciates it.

Case law has produced three main legal theories trying to deal with the question of when omissions to disclose may be a predicate for 10b-5 liability, which are sometimes termed the "equal access," "fiduciary duty," and "misappropriation" theories. The problematic nature of these theories arises from the tension between those whose thinking is dominated by an intuitive understanding that the prohibition of insider trading is essential for efficient capital markets operation, and those whose thinking is dominated by the fact that Section 10(b) of the 1934 Act is concerned with fraud and manipulation, which implies culpable behavior in the particular case.

14.4.2.2 Elements of 10b-5 Liability: The Equal Access Theory

In its simplest form, the equal access theory holds that all traders owe a duty to the market to disclose or refrain from trading on nonpublic corporate information. Efficiency considerations aside, the basis for this duty is said to be the "inherent unfairness" of exploiting an unerodable informational advantage — that is, confidential information from which other traders are legally excluded.[26] The equal access theory originates in the expansive setting of the best known (and most ambiguous) sentence in the corpus of insider trading case law: that is, the rationale for invoking Rule 10b-5 offered in *Cady, Roberts & Co.*,[27] the first SEC decision to address insider trading on the open market. In the Commission's words, the application of Rule 10b-5 rested on "two principal elements":

> [F]irst, the existence of a relationship giving access, directly or indirectly, to information intended to be available only for a corporate purpose, and not for the personal benefit of anyone, and second, the inherent unfairness involved where a party takes advantage of such information knowing it is unavailable to those with whom he is dealing.[28]

But taking advantage of this unfairness is unfair to whom, given what sort of relationship? If the unfairness is to other traders based on a duty to disclose and the triggering characteristic is any channel for obtaining confidential information about the corporate issuer, we have arrived at the equal access norm. And it was precisely this path, allowing for detours

---

26. See Victor Brudney, *Insiders, Outsiders, and Informational Advantages Under the Federal Securities Laws*, 93 Harv. L. Rev. 322, 346 (1979).
27. 40 S.E.C. 907 (1961).
28. *Id.* at 911.

and caveats, that the influential Second Circuit seemed to follow during the decade that began with the landmark *Texas Gulf Sulphur* case and ended with (or was impeded by) the Supreme Court case of *Chiarella v. United States,* below.

The doctrinal advantages of the equal access theory are obvious. In its unqualified form, it reaches all conduct that might be popularly understood as insider trading: tippees and financial printers, no less than top corporate officers, may be equally culpable for insider trading, and they may be culpable even if their information originates outside the company, since the essence of "wrongdoing" under this view lies in exploiting an informational advantage over other traders. For this reason, too, the victims of insider trading are easily identified: They are all uninformed traders to whom the insider should have disclosed.[29]

By the same token, however, the conceptual weak points of the equal access theory are also apparent. Even apart from policy concerns, such as the risk of chilling socially useful trading, it is not obvious why the "unfairness" arising from trading on access to superior information defrauds other traders in the absence of misrepresentation or a preexisting disclosure duty. These traders come for their own reasons to the public market seeking to sell (or buy) at the market price. In what sense is information asymmetry alone unfair? Investors continuously exploit differential access to information; indeed, the effort to profit from such disparities is precisely what keeps securities prices informed.[30] Why then should the law seek broadly to impede all trading on nonpublic information? Perhaps a more discriminating theory is necessary even from a public policy (market efficiency) perspective?

14.4.2.3 Elements of 10b-5 Liability: The Fiduciary Duty Theory

The fiduciary duty theory is a natural outgrowth of traditional fiduciary theory that we averted to above. It was adopted in two U.S. Supreme Court decisions of the early 1980s, which remain the authoritative underpinnings of insider trading law under Rule 10b-5. In the first of these cases, the *Chiarella* decision, the Court rejected the equal access theory by overturning the criminal conviction of a financial printer who had traded on confidential foreknowledge of pending takeover bids that he had gained in his employment. More precisely, the Court ruled that the printer did not breach a disclosure duty *to other traders* by trading on nonpublic information. Since the printer had gleaned information from the

---

29. Under Rule 10b-5 jurisprudence, however, only injured purchasers or sellers of securities are allowed a private right of action. See *Blue Chip Stamps v. Manor Drug Stores,* 421 U.S. 723 (1975). The Second Circuit has interpreted Rule 10b-5 to permit a private suit by contemporaneous traders against an insider, with recovery limited to the insider's profit. See *Elkind v. Liggett & Myers, Inc.,* 635 F.2d 156 (2d Cir. 1980).

30. See generally Ronald J. Gilson & Reinier H. Kraakman, *The Mechanisms of Market Efficiency,* 70 Va. L. Rev. 549 (1984).

documents of takeover *bidders,* he lacked a relationship-based duty to shareholders of the *target* companies in whose securities he traded *Chiarella* is excerpted below.

The Supreme Court's second insider trading case, *Dirks v. SEC,* clarified the limits of the fiduciary duty theory by addressing the liability of tippees. Consistent with *Chiarella*'s stress on a fiduciary relationship, *Dirks* portrayed trading by a tippee as a derivative violation of Rule 10b-5. A tipper, who originally may be thought to owe a duty to other traders in his own company's stock, must first violate that duty by tipping improperly; the tippee, who originally owes no duty, then assumes the tipper's duty by trading. Whether tipping is improper in the first instance — and thus whether the tipper violates his duty — is said to turn on whether the insider tips to secure a personal benefit from the tippee. If so, he in effect, trades indirectly on his own tip. In *Dirks,* a former employee exposed a company's ongoing fraud to a securities analyst, who then informed his own clients of the fraud without successfully alerting the public. The Court reasoned that, since the employee had not benefited, there was no tipper violation of Rule 10b-5, and hence, there could be no violation by a tippee. Apart from the doctrinal merits, *Dirks* reflected a strong interest in limiting the liability of security analysts, whose investigatory efforts it depicted as an important contributor to the efficiency of securities prices.[31]

Stepping back then, it is clear that the fiduciary duty theory has at least two important attractions. Its more obvious attraction is that, by isolating a preexisting relationship between insiders and other traders, it supports an analogy to common law fraud that eases the assimilation of insider trading into the statutory prohibition against securities fraud. The less-obvious attraction of the theory is that it allows case-by-case review of the relationship between putative insiders and other traders, and thus permits courts to selectively target insider trading. Such targeting was evident in *Dirks,* where the Court was able to insulate what it perceived to be a socially useful exchange of information between corporate issuers and securities analysts.

However, these doctrinal advantages do not come cheaply. The convenient discovery of a legal relationship linking traditional insiders, such as corporate officers and directors, and traders in the public market is weak support for equating insider trading with conventional fraud. Put another way, the fiduciary duty theory is too clearly a liability filter that fails to answer the question originally raised by the equal access theory: How does trading on one of many kinds of informational disparities defraud uninformed traders? As a liability filter, moreover, the fiduciary duty theory is dramatically underinclusive, since it cannot reach such seemingly clear-cut wrongdoing as the printer's trading in *Chiarella.*

---

31. Dirks also introduced a device for expanding the scope of primary insider trading violations by suggesting that market professionals such as an "underwriter, accountant, lawyer, or consultant" may become constructive insiders for purposes of Rule 10b-5 by virtue of entering a fiduciary relationship with the insider.

CHIARELLA v. UNITED STATES

445 U.S. 222 (1980)

POWELL, J.:

The question in this case is whether a person who learns from the confidential documents of one corporation that it is planning an attempt to secure control of a second corporation violates § 10(b) of the Securities Exchange Act of 1934 if he fails to disclose the impending takeover before trading in the target company's securities. . . .

Petitioner is a printer by trade. In 1975 and 1976, he worked as a "markup man" in the New York composing room of Pandick Press, a financial printer. Among documents that petitioner handled were five announcements of corporate takeover bids. When these documents were delivered to the printer, the identities of the acquiring and target corporations were concealed by blank spaces or false names. The true names were sent to the printer on the night of the final printing.

The petitioner, however, was able to deduce the names of the target companies before the final printing from other information contained in the documents. Without disclosing his knowledge, petitioner purchased stock in the target companies and sold the shares immediately after the takeover attempts were made public. By this method, petitioner realized a gain of slightly more than $30,000 in the course of 14 months. Subsequently, the [SEC] began an investigation of his trading activities. In May 1977, petitioner entered into a consent decree with the Commission in which he agreed to return his profits to the sellers of the shares. On the same day, he was discharged by Pandick Press.

In January 1978, petitioner was indicted on 17 counts of violating § 10(b) of the Securities Exchange Act of 1934 (1934 Act) and SEC Rule 10b-5. After petitioner unsuccessfully moved to dismiss the indictment, he was brought to trial and convicted on all counts.

The Court of Appeals for the Second Circuit affirmed petitioner's conviction. 588 F.2d 1358 (1978). We granted certiorari, 441 U.S. 942 (1979), and we now reverse. . . . This case concerns the legal effect of the petitioner's silence. . . .

[The statute] does not state whether silence may constitute a manipulative or deceptive device. Section 10(b) was designed as a catchall clause to prevent fraudulent practices. . . . But neither the legislative history nor the statute itself affords specific guidance for the resolution of this case. When Rule 10b-5 was promulgated in 1942, the SEC did not discuss the possibility that failure to provide information might run afoul of § 10(b).

. . . In *Cady, Roberts & Co.*, 40 S.E.C. 907 (1961), the Commission decided that a corporate insider must abstain from trading in the shares of his corporation unless he has first disclosed all material inside information known to him. The obligation to disclose or abstain derives from

[an] affirmative duty to disclose material information[, which] has been traditionally imposed on corporate "insiders," particularly officers, directors, or controlling stockholders. We and the courts have consistently held that insiders must disclose material facts which are known to them by virtue of

their position but which are not known to persons with whom they deal and which, if known, would affect their investment judgment. *Id.*, at 911.

The Commission emphasized that the duty arose from (i) the existence of a relationship affording access to inside information intended to be available only for a corporate purpose, and (ii) the unfairness of allowing a corporate insider to take advantage of that information by trading without disclosure. . . .

That the relationship between a corporate insider and the stockholders of his corporation gives rise to a disclosure obligation is not a novel twist of the law. At common law, . . . one who fails to disclose material information prior to the consummation of a transaction commits fraud only when he is under a duty to do so. And the duty to disclose arises when one party has information "that the other [party] is entitled to know because of a fiduciary or other similar relation of trust and confidence between them." In its *Cady, Roberts* decision, the Commission recognized a relationship of trust and confidence between the shareholders of a corporation and those insiders who have obtained confidential information by reason of their position with that corporation. This relationship gives rise to a duty to disclose because of the "necessity of preventing a corporate insider from [taking] unfair advantage of the uninformed minority stockholders." [Citation omitted.]

Thus, administrative and judicial interpretations have established that silence in connection with the purchase or sale of securities may operate as a fraud actionable under § 10(b) despite the absence of statutory language or legislative history specifically addressing the legality of nondisclosure. But such liability is premised upon a duty to disclose arising from a relationship of trust and confidence between parties to a transaction. Application of a duty to disclose prior to trading guarantees that corporate insiders, who have an obligation to place the shareholder's welfare before their own, will not benefit personally through fraudulent use of material, nonpublic information.[12] . . .

In this case, the petitioner was convicted of violating § 10(b) although he was not a corporate insider and he received no confidential information from the target company. . . . [T]he "market information" upon which he relied . . . only [concerned] the plans of the acquiring company. Petitioner's use of that information was not a fraud under § 10(b) unless he was subject to an affirmative duty to disclose it before trading. . . .

The Court of Appeals affirmed the conviction by holding that "[*anyone* —]corporate insider or not — who regularly receives material nonpublic information may not use that information to trade in securities without incurring an affirmative duty to disclose." . . . The Court of Appeals . . . failed to identify a relationship between petitioner and the sellers that could give rise to a duty. Its decision thus rested solely upon its belief

---

12. "Tippees" of corporate insiders have been held liable under § 10(b) because they have a duty not to profit from the use of inside information that they know is confidential . . . The tippee's obligation has [thus] been viewed as arising from his role as a participant after the fact in the insider's breach of a fiduciary duty . . .

that the federal securities laws have "created a system providing equal access to information necessary for reasoned and intelligent investment decisions." ... The use by anyone of material information not generally available is fraudulent, this theory suggests, because such information gives certain buyers or sellers an unfair advantage over less informed buyers and sellers.

This reasoning suffers from two defects. First, not every instance of financial unfairness constitutes fraudulent activity under §10(b). See *Santa Fe Industries, Inc. v. Green* ... . Second, the element required to make silence fraudulent—a duty to disclose—is absent in this case. No duty could arise from petitioner's relationship with the sellers of the target company's securities, for petitioner had no prior dealings with them. He was not their agent, he was not a fiduciary, he was not a person in whom the sellers had placed their trust and confidence. He was, in fact, a complete stranger who dealt with the sellers only through impersonal market transactions.

We cannot affirm petitioner's conviction without recognizing a general duty between all participants in market transactions to forgo actions based on material, nonpublic information. Formulation of such a broad duty, which departs radically from the established doctrine that duty arises from a specific relationship between two parties ... should not be undertaken absent some explicit evidence of congressional intent.

As we have seen, no such evidence emerges from the language or legislative history of §10(b). Moreover, neither the Congress nor the Commission ever has adopted a parity-of-information rule. Instead the problems caused by misuse of market information have been addressed by detailed and sophisticated regulation that recognizes when use of market information may not harm operation of the securities markets. ...

Indeed, the theory upon which the petitioner was convicted is at odds with the Commission's view of §10(b) as applied to activity that has the same effect on sellers as the petitioner's purchases. "Warehousing" takes place when a corporation gives advance notice of its intention to launch a tender offer to institutional investors who then are able to purchase stock in the target company before the tender offer is made public and the price of shares rises. In this case, as in warehousing, a buyer of securities purchases stock in a target corporation on the basis of market information which is unknown to the seller. In both of these situations, the seller's behavior presumably would be altered if he had the nonpublic information. Significantly, however, the Commission has acted to bar warehousing under its authority to regulate tender offers [not under §10(b)].

... Section 10(b) is aptly described as a catchall provision, but what it catches must be fraud. When an allegation of fraud is based upon nondisclosure, there can be no fraud absent a duty to speak. We hold that a duty to disclose under §10(b) does not arise from the mere possession of nonpublic market information. The contrary result is without support in the legislative history of §10(b) and would be inconsistent with the careful plan that Congress has enacted for regulation of the securities markets. ...

In its brief to this Court, the United States [also] offers an alternative theory to support petitioner's conviction. It argues that petitioner breached a duty to the acquiring corporation when he acted upon information that he obtained by virtue of his position as an employee of a printer employed by the corporation. The breach of this duty is said to support a conviction under § 10(b) for fraud perpetrated upon both the acquiring corporation and the sellers. . . .

The jury instructions demonstrate that petitioner was convicted merely because of his failure to disclose material, non-public information to sellers from whom he bought the stock of target corporations. The jury was not instructed on . . . a duty owed by petitioner to anyone other than the sellers. Because we cannot affirm a criminal conviction on the basis of a theory not presented to the jury, . . . we will not speculate upon whether such a duty exists, whether it has been breached, or whether such a breach constitutes a violation of § 10(b).

The judgment of the Court of Appeals is reversed. . . .

BURGER, C.J., dissenting.

I believe that the jury instructions in this case properly charged a violation of § 10(b) and Rule 10b-5, and I would affirm the conviction. . . . I would read § 10(b) and Rule 10b-5 . . . to mean that a person who has misappropriated nonpublic information has an absolute duty to disclose that information or to refrain from trading.

The language of § 10(b) and of Rule 10b-5 plainly supports such a reading. By their terms, these provisions reach *any* person engaged in *any* fraudulent scheme. This broad language negates the suggestion that congressional concern was limited to trading by "corporate insiders" or to deceptive practices related to "corporate information." . . .

. . . The antifraud provisions were designed in large measure "to assure that dealing in securities is fair and without undue preferences or advantages among investors." H.R. Conf. Rep. No. 94-229, p. 91 (1975). These provisions prohibit "those manipulative and deceptive practices which have been demonstrated to fulfill no useful function." S. Rep. No. 792, 73d Cong., 2d Sess., 6 (1934). An investor who purchases securities on the basis of misappropriated nonpublic information possesses just such an "undue" trading advantage; his conduct quite clearly serves no useful function except his own enrichment at the expense of others. . . .

Finally, it bears emphasis that this reading of § 10b and Rule 10b-5 would not threaten legitimate business practices. [It] would not impose a duty on a tender offeror to disclose its acquisition plans during the period in which it "tests the water" prior to purchasing a full 5% of the target company's stock. Nor would it proscribe "warehousing." . . . In each of these instances . . . the information has not been unlawfully converted for personal gain. . . .

The Court's opinion, as I read it, leaves open the question whether § 10(b) and Rule 10b-5 prohibit trading on misappropriated nonpublic information. . . .

QUESTIONS AND A NOTE ON CHIARELLA v. UNITED STATES

1. From where, exactly, does the "relationship of trust and confidence" (the RETAC) between corporate insiders and shareholders come? Not from the common law, certainly, since most states did not make corporate officers and directors trustee-like fiduciaries for the interests of shareholders, as we discussed above. With whom, exactly, are shareholders in a RETAC after *Chiarella*? An issuer's janitor who discovers material information while cleaning at corporate headquarters? The issuer's investment banker who discovers information in the course of confidential negotiations? The taxi driver who overhears a discussion of merger plans on the way to the airport?

2. Can the corporation itself violate a RETAC by purchasing or selling its shares? What if the insider information is bad news and existing shareholders would profit from the sale of treasury shares?

3. Why did the Supreme Court feel compelled to discover a RETAC between corporate insiders and shareholders as opposed to relying on the established fiduciary relationship between corporate insiders and the corporation itself as a basis for Rule 10b-5 liability?

4. Note that Chief Justice Burger's dissenting discussion of the SEC's misappropriation theory marks the debut of that theory as an independent basis of Rule 10b-5 liability.

DIRKS v. SEC
463 U.S. 646 (1983)

POWELL, J.:

Petitioner Raymond Dirks received material nonpublic information from "insiders" of a corporation with which he had no connection. He disclosed this information to investors who relied on it in trading in the shares of the corporation. The question is whether Dirks violated the antifraud provisions of the federal securities laws by this disclosure. . . .

In 1973, Dirks was an officer of a New York broker-dealer firm who specialized in providing investment analysis of insurance company securities to institutional investors. On March 6, Dirks received information from Ronald Secrist, a former officer of Equity Funding of America. Secrist alleged that the assets of Equity Funding, a diversified corporation primarily engaged in selling life insurance and mutual funds, were vastly overstated as the result of fraudulent corporate practices. Secrist also stated that various regulatory agencies had failed to act on similar charges made by Equity Funding employees. He urged Dirks to verify the fraud and disclose it publicly.

Dirks decided to investigate the allegations. He visited Equity Funding's headquarters in Los Angeles and interviewed several officers and employees of the corporation. The senior management denied any wrongdoing, but certain corporation employees corroborated the charges of

---

EQUITY FUNDING

When the Equity Funding scandal became public in 1973, it was the largest corporate fraud that Wall Street had experienced. Equity Funding, a life insurance company, sold the life insurance policies that it generated to other insurance companies, known as "reinsurers." When profits began to lag, however, Equity Funding executives came up with the idea of selling fictitious insurance policies to the reinsurers. The company developed a software program to generate information about the fake policies, which was then sent to the reinsurers to support the sales. In a windowless building miles from the main office, a department known as the "Maple Drive Gang" created fake medical records and application forms to satisfy auditor inquiries. Equity Funding's fraud resulted in over $100 million of false profits.

The story came to light when former employee Ron Secrist informed Raymond Dirks, a stock analyst focused on the insurance industry, of the fraudulent behavior that he had witnessed. Dirks, unsure of Secrist's reliability, investigated the firm for himself by interviewing employees and combing through company records. While performing his investigation, he spoke with colleagues, clients, writers at the *Wall Street Journal*, insurance regulators, and Equity Funding's auditors about the allegations.[32] Most of his contacts were incredulous, and the auditors simply turned his notes over to Equity Funding's management for review. His clients acted immediately, however, by selling large portions of Equity Funding stock. Their actions caused the price to fall so precipitously that the New York Stock Exchange halted trading on Equity Funding shares. The *Wall Street Journal* finally published the story and the ensuing criminal investigation resulted in prison sentences for the perpetrators. The Department of Justice stated in a brief supporting Dirks, "largely thanks to [Raymond Dirks], one of the most infamous frauds in recent memory was uncovered and exposed."[33]

---

fraud. Neither Dirks nor his firm owned or traded any Equity Funding stock, but throughout his investigation he openly discussed the information he had obtained with a number of clients and investors. Some of these persons sold their holdings of Equity Funding securities, including five investment advisers who liquidated holdings of more than $16 million.

While Dirks was in Los Angeles, he was in touch regularly with William Blundell, the *Wall Street Journal*'s Los Angeles bureau chief. Dirks urged Blundell to write a story on the fraud allegations. Blundell did not believe, however, that such a massive fraud could go undetected and declined to write the story. He feared that publishing such damaging hearsay might be libelous.

During the 2-week period in which Dirks pursued his investigation and spread word of Secrist's charges, the price of Equity Funding stock fell

---

32. Ronald L. Soble and Robert E. Dallos, The Impossible Dream: The Equity Funding Story (1975).

33. Department of Justice, *Brief for the United States as Amicus Curiae in Support of Reversal,* 1982 (www.usdoj.gov/osg/briefs/1982/sg820094.txt).

from $26 per share to less than $15 per share. This led the New York Stock Exchange to halt trading on March 27. Shortly thereafter California insurance authorities impounded Equity Funding's records and uncovered evidence of the fraud. Only then did the Securities and Exchange Commission (SEC) file a complaint against Equity Funding and only then, on April 2, did the *Wall Street Journal* publish a front-page story based largely on information assembled by Dirks. Equity Funding immediately went into receivership.

The SEC began an investigation into Dirks' role in the exposure of the fraud. After a hearing by an Administrative Law Judge, the SEC found that Dirks had aided and abetted violations of §17(a) of the Securities Act of 1933, . . . §10(b) of the Securities Exchange act of 1934 . . . , and SEC Rule 10b-5 . . . , by repeating the allegations of fraud to members of the investment community who later sold their Equity Funding stock. . . . Recognizing, however, that Dirks "played an important role in bringing [Equity Funding's] massive fraud to light," . . . the SEC only censured him. . . .

In view of the importance to the SEC and to the securities industry of the question presented by this case, we granted a writ of certiorari. . . . We now reverse.

In *Chiarella*, we accepted the two elements set out in *Cady, Roberts* for establishing a Rule 10b-5 violation: "(i) the existence of a relationship affording access to inside information intended to be available only for a corporate purpose, and (ii) the unfairness of allowing a corporate insider to take advantage of that information by trading without disclosure." 445 U.S., at 227. In examining whether Chiarella had an obligation to disclose or abstain, the Court found that there is no general duty to disclose before trading on material nonpublic information, and held that "a duty to disclose under §10(b) does not arise from the mere possession of nonpublic market information." *Id.*, at 235. Such a duty arises rather from the existence of a fiduciary relationship. . . .

We were explicit in *Chiarella* in saying that there can be no duty to disclose where the person who has traded on inside information "was not [the corporation's] agent, was not a fiduciary, [or] was not a person in whom the sellers [of the securities] had placed their trust and confidence." 445 U.S., at 232. . . . This requirement of a specific relationship between the shareholders and the individual trading on inside information has created analytical difficulties for the SEC and courts in policing tippees who trade on inside information. Unlike insiders who have independent fiduciary duties to both the corporation and its shareholders, the typical tippee has no such relationships.[14] In view of this absence, it has been unclear how a

---

14. Under certain circumstances, such as where corporate information is revealed legitimately to an underwriter, accountant, lawyer, or consultant working for the corporation, these outsiders may become fiduciaries of the shareholders. The basis for recognizing this fiduciary duty is not simply that such persons acquired nonpublic corporate information, but rather that they have entered into a special confidential relationship in the conduct of the business of the enterprise and are given access to information solely for corporate purposes. . . . For such a duty to be imposed, however, the corporation must expect the outsider to keep the disclosed nonpublic information confidential, and the relationship at least must imply such a duty.

tippee acquires the *Cady, Roberts* duty to refrain from trading on inside information.

The SEC's position, as stated in its opinion in this case, is that a tippee "inherits" the *Cady, Roberts* obligation to shareholders whenever he receives inside information from an insider. . . .

In effect, the SEC's theory of tippee liability . . . appears rooted in the idea that the antifraud provisions require equal information among all traders. This conflicts with the principle set forth in *Chiarella* that only some persons, under some circumstances, will be barred from trading while in possession of material nonpublic information. . . .

Imposing a duty to disclose or abstain solely because a person knowingly receives material nonpublic information from an insider and trades on it could have an inhibiting influence on the role of market analysts, which the SEC itself recognizes is necessary to the preservation of a healthy market. It is commonplace for analysts to "ferret out and analyze information," 21 S.E.C. Docket, at 1406, and this often is done by meeting with and questioning corporate officers and others who are insiders. And information that the analysts obtain normally may be the basis for judgments as to the market worth of a corporation's securities. The analyst's judgment in this respect is made available in market letters or otherwise to clients of the firm. It is the nature of this type of information, and indeed of the markets themselves, that such information cannot be made simultaneously available to all of the corporation's stockholders or the public generally.

The conclusion that recipients of inside information do not invariably acquire a duty to disclose or abstain does not mean that such tippees always are free to trade on the information. The need for a ban on some tippee trading is clear. Not only are insiders forbidden by their fiduciary relationship from personally using undisclosed corporate information to their advantage, but they also may not give such information to an outsider for the same improper purpose of exploiting the information for their personal gain. . . .

Thus, some tippees must assume an insider's duty to the shareholders not because they receive inside information, but rather because it has been made available to them *improperly.* And for Rule 10b-5 purposes, the insider's disclosure is improper only where it would violate his *Cady, Roberts* duty. Thus, a tippee assumes a fiduciary duty to the shareholders of a corporation not to trade on material nonpublic information only when the insider has breached his fiduciary duty to the shareholders by disclosing the information to the tippee and the tippee knows or should know that there has been a breach. . . . Tipping thus properly is viewed only as a means of indirectly violating the *Cady, Roberts* disclose-or-abstain rule.

In determining whether a tippee is under an obligation to disclose or abstain, it thus is necessary to determine whether the insider's "tip" constituted a breach of the insider's fiduciary duty. All disclosures of confidential corporate information are not inconsistent with the duty insiders owe to shareholders. In contrast to the extraordinary facts of this case, the more typical situation in which there will be a question whether disclosure violates the insider's *Cady, Roberts* duty is when insiders disclose information to analysts. In some situations, the insider will act consistently with his fiduciary duty to shareholders, and yet release of the information may affect the market. For example, it may not be clear—either to the corporate insider or to the recipient analyst—whether the information will be viewed as material nonpublic information. Corporate officials may mistakenly think the information already has been disclosed or that it is not material enough to affect the market. Whether disclosure is a breach of duty therefore depends in large part on the purpose of the disclosure. . . . Thus, the test is whether the insider personally will benefit, directly or indirectly, from his disclosure. Absent some personal gain, there has been no breach of duty to stockholders. And absent a breach by the insider, there is no derivative breach. . . .

. . . In determining whether the insider's purpose in making a particular disclosure is fraudulent, the SEC and the courts are not required to read the parties' minds. Scienter in some cases is relevant in determining whether the tipper has violated his *Cady, Roberts* duty. But to determine whether the disclosure itself "[deceives], [manipulates], or [defrauds]" shareholders, . . . the initial inquiry is whether there has been a breach of duty by the insider. This requires courts to focus on objective criteria, i.e., whether the insider receives a direct or indirect personal benefit from the disclosure, such as a pecuniary gain or a reputational benefit that will translate into future earnings. . . . There are objective facts and circumstances that often justify such an inference. For example, there may be a relationship between the insider and the recipient that suggests a *quid pro quo* from the latter, or an intention to benefit the particular recipient. The elements of fiduciary duty and exploitation of nonpublic information also exist when an insider makes a gift of confidential information to a trading relative or friend. The tip and trade resemble trading by the insider himself followed by a gift of the profits to the recipient.

Determining whether an insider personally benefits from a particular disclosure . . . will not always be easy for courts. But it is essential, we think, to have a guiding principle for those whose daily activities must be limited and instructed by the SEC's inside-trading rules, and we believe that there must be a breach of the insider's fiduciary duty before the tippee inherits the duty to disclose or abstain. . . .

Under the inside-trading and tipping rules set forth above, we find that there was no actionable violation by Dirks. It is undisputed that Dirks himself was a stranger to Equity Funding, with no pre-existing fiduciary duty to its shareholders. He took no action, directly or indirectly, that induced the shareholders or officers of Equity Funding to repose trust or confidence in him. There was no expectation by Dirks' sources that he would keep their information in confidence. Nor did Dirks misappropriate or illegally obtain the information about Equity Funding. Unless the insiders breached their *Cady, Roberts* duty to shareholders in disclosing the nonpublic information to Dirks, he breached no duty when he passed it on to investors as well as to the *Wall Street Journal.*

It is clear that neither Secrist nor the other Equity Funding employees violated their *Cady, Roberts* duty to the corporation's shareholders by providing information to Dirks. The tippers received no monetary or personal benefit for revealing Equity Funding's secrets, nor was their purpose to make a gift of valuable information to Dirks. As the facts of this case clearly indicate, the tippers were motivated by a desire to expose the fraud. . . . In the absence of a breach of duty to shareholders by the insiders, there was no derivative breach by Dirks. . . .

Reversed.

BLACKMUN, J., dissenting. . . .

No one questions that Secrist himself could not trade on his inside information to the disadvantage of uninformed shareholders and purchasers of Equity Funding securities. . . .

The Court also acknowledges that Secrist could not do by proxy what he was prohibited from doing personally. . . . But this is precisely what Secrist did. Secrist used Dirks to disseminate information to Dirks' clients, who in turn dumped stock on unknowing purchasers. Secrist thus intended Dirks to injure the purchasers of Equity Funding securities to whom Secrist had a duty to disclose. Accepting the Court's view of tippee liability, it appears that Dirks' knowledge of this breach makes him liable as a participant in the breach after the fact. . . .

It makes no difference to the shareholder whether the corporate insider gained or intended to gain personally from the transaction; the shareholder still has lost because of the insider's misuse of nonpublic information. The duty is addressed not to the insider's motives, but to his actions and their consequences on the shareholder. Personal gain is not an element of the breach of this duty. . . .

NOTES AND QUESTIONS ON DIRKS v. SEC

1. *Dirks* was intended in part to create a safe harbor for security analysts. Does *Dirks* allow a corporate manager to release material inside information to a prominent securities analyst as a means of assuring "accurate" reporting on the company? Suppose that the corporate manager gave away inside information only when she honestly believed that the market misvalued her company's stock — and that therefore a favorable analyst's report would raise her company's stock prices to reflect its "real" value?

2. In general, the SEC appears to have no problem in finding a "benefit" to meet the *Dirks* requirement in most tipper tippee cases. When Paul J. Thayer, a former CEO of LTV, was charged with passing information to a group of eight friends, including a young woman who was a former LTV employee, the SEC charged that Mr. Thayer received a personal benefit because of his "close personal relationship" with the woman. Similarly, in *United States v. Reed*, 601 F. Supp. 686 (S.D.N.Y. 1985), the court refused to dismiss an indictment of a tippee who was the son of the tipper even though there was no evidence that the father intended to benefit his son by the disclosure. But see *SEC v. Switzer*, 590 F. Supp. 756 (W.D. Okla. 1984). Barry Switzer, the coach of the University of Oklahoma football team, "accidentally" overheard an acquaintance talking with his wife about problems facing his business while attending a high school track meet. Switzer

was absolved of liability under the *Dirks* standard for trading on this information, since the tipper did not benefit, "directly or indirectly, monetarily or otherwise," from the disclosure (or so the court found).

3. Returning to *Dirks*, why exactly did Secrist *not* breach his duty by telling Dirks about his suspicions of fraud?

4. Consistent with *Dirks*, could a company permit its accountants or lawyers to trade based on nonpublic information in exchange for lower fees? Could a company permit its CEO to trade based on nonpublic information in exchange for a lower salary?

5. On December 27, 2001, Merrill Lynch stockbroker Peter Bacanovic, while on vacation, instructed his assistant Douglas Faneuil to inform their client Martha Stewart that Sam Waksal, CEO of ImClone, and other members of the Waksal family were selling their shares of ImClone stock. That afternoon, Stewart sold 3,928 shares of ImClone at $58 per share. The next day, ImClone announced that the FDA had rejected its application for the cancer drug Erbitux. By Monday December 31st, the ImClone stock price had fallen to approximately $46.50. Under what theory might Martha Stewart, a former stockbroker herself, be liable for insider trading on these facts? Contrary to popular belief, Stewart went to prison in conjunction with these events for conspiracy, obstruction of justice, and lying to investigators, not for insider trading.

NOTES ON RULE 14E-3 AND REGULATION FD

The Supreme Court's narrowing of Rule 10b-5 in *Chiarella* and *Dirks* elicited multiple responses from the SEC, Congress, and lower federal courts. Soon after *Chiarella*, the SEC moved to reassert its equal access conception. It did so with respect to trading on tender offer information by invoking its independent power to regulate tender offenses under § 14(e). Thus, SEC Rule 14e-3 imposes a duty on any person who obtains inside information about a tender offer that originates with either the offeror or the target to disclose or abstain from trading. In effect, this rule reintroduces the equal access norm by regulatory fiat in the limited but important domain of corporate takeovers.

In 2000, the SEC returned to the problem of selective disclosure to security analysts by passing Regulation "Fair Disclosure" (FD). Regulation FD was directed to the practice of issuers sometimes publicly disseminating material business information through a process in which certain (favored) analysts, brokers, or journalists were called to a press conference in which a material piece of information would be released to the public. This release of information was for a corporate purpose and did not constitute a wrong of any sort, and those getting the information could use it. Yet the favored few could clearly derive a trading benefit from early access. "So what?" one might ask. But this practice not only offended a sense of fairness in some but also threatened to corrupt the integrity of the analysts (who, after the disclosures surrounding the collapse of Enron, WorldCom, and much of the U.S. telecom industry, appear to need no additional temptations). In all events, Regulation FD imposes a new regime on the release of material nonpublic information.

§243.100   General rule regarding selective disclosure

(a) Whenever an issuer, or any person acting on its behalf, discloses any material nonpublic information regarding that issuer or its securities to any person described in paragraph (b)(1) of this section, the issuer shall make public disclosure of that information as provided in § 243.101(e):

(1)Simultaneously, in the case of an intentional disclosure; and

(2) Promptly, in the case of a non-intentional disclosure.

[Paragraph (a) covers brokers, dealers, investment advisors, investment analysts and managers, and shareholders who are likely to sell. It does not cover persons who owe a duty of trust and confidence to the issuer, such as attorneys, investment bankers, and accountants.] . . .

§243.101   Definitions.

(a) Intentional. A selective disclosure of material nonpublic information is "intentional" when the person making the disclosure either knows, or is reckless in not knowing, that the information he or she is communicating is both material and nonpublic. . . .

§243.102   No Effect on Antifraud Liability.

No failure to make a public disclosure required solely by § 243.100 shall be deemed to be a violation of Rule 10b-5 (17 CFR 240.10b-5) under the Securities Exchange Act.

QUESTIONS ON REGULATION FD

1. Would Regulation FD have mattered to the outcome of the *Dirks* case?

2. Consider the following excerpt from the *Wall Street Journal*, published on the day that Reg FD went into effect:

> Matthew Berler, an analyst at Morgan Stanley Dean Witter & Co., is pouring over spreadsheets covering 887 financial factors affecting his earning expectations for Georgia-Pacific Corp. In the past, he would call executives at the Atlanta forest-products company to quiz them about the more pertinent variables factored into his model. Such one-on-one guidance, he says, was part of a "continuous check on my modeling." . . . Now, something known on Wall Street as Reg FD has entered the picture, and it means Mr. Berler no longer will have access to all the information he uses in his spreadsheets. The result: He is less certain his earnings estimates will match the profit that Georgia-Pacific reports. . . .[34]

---

34. Jeff D. Opdyke, The Big Chill: Street Feels Effect of the New 'Fair Disclosure' Rule, Wall St. J. (Oct. 23, 2000).

Empirical studies confirm that analyst estimates are less accurate after Reg FD.[35] Is there a social welfare cost arising from less accurate analyst forecasts? And if so, what are the countervailing benefits that Reg FD might provide?

NOTE: THE RESPONSE OF CONGRESS AND THE COURT TO DIRKS

Congress's response to *Chiarella* and *Dirks* was less productive. Repeated efforts to frame a statutory definition of insider trading failed, partly as a result of concern that any fixed definition would be underinclusive. Thus, the definition of insider trading remained in the hands of the courts.

Finally, the lower federal courts — or, more accurately, the Second Circuit — responded to *Chiarella* and *Dirks* by extending the misappropriation theory to reach outsiders who trade illicitly on confidential information. This theory holds that the deceitful misappropriation of market-sensitive information is itself a fraud that may violate Rule 10b-5 when it occurs "in connection with" a securities transaction. This theory leads to an anomaly that might embarrass more scrupulous believers in the constraining power of legal doctrine. Under it, the court finds a duty — the duty that a fiduciary owes to her corporate employer or corporate client (i.e., the source of the inside information) — and predicates an action by the SEC or the Justice Department on the breach of that duty, possibly to protect persons trading in the company's stock. Congressional legislation, considered below, even extends a private action to market trades on the basis of a fiduciary breach to an employer. Thus, the misappropriation theory rearranges the key elements of *Cady, Roberts* once again. Now, the relationship that triggers Rule 10b-5 and the resulting unfairness both refer to the insider's *source* of information. The printer who trades on confidential information defrauds his employer, regardless of his relationship to other traders.

Until the Supreme Court finally adopted the misappropriation theory in *United States v. O'Hagan,* below, it was extremely controversial. Several appeals courts had rejected the theory, largely based on the argument that §10(b) is intended to protect traders in the securities market and not fiduciary relationships more generally.[36]

Nevertheless, the attractions of the misappropriation theory are considerable. Like the equal access theory, it can reach almost all forms of insider trading that are commonly condemned, regardless of whether they involve traditional insiders. Equally important, the misappropriation theory locates a real duty and a "fraud" by focusing on the putative insider's illicit conversion of valuable information rather than on a fictional relationship between the "insider" and uninformed traders. At last, the doctrine seems to reflect the intuitive basis for proscribing insider trading: It is wrong not because informational disparities in the market are suspect

---

35. See, e.g., Anup Agrawal et al.,*Who Is Afraid of Reg FD? The Behavior and Performance of Sell-Side Analysts Following the SEC's Fair Disclosure Rules,* J. Bus. (Nov. 2006).
36. See, e.g., *United States v. Bryan,* 58 F.3d 933 (4th Cir. 1995).

but because it involves the private appropriation of information rights that belong to someone else. But sad to say, it doesn't offer any doctrinal basis for civil recovery by someone other than the entity who owns the information rights — such as uninformed traders in the stock.

UNITED STATES v. CHESTMAN
947 F.2d 551 (2d Cir. 1991) (en banc)

MESKILL, J.:

In this rehearing in banc, we consider for the first time the validity of Rule 14e-3(a), . . . under section 14(e) of the 1934 Act . . . ; we then reexamine two familiar landmarks of the securities fraud landscape, section 10 (b) of the [1934 Act], and the mail fraud statute, 18 U.S.C. § 1341. . . .

[W]e conclude that the Rule 14e-3(a) convictions should be affirmed and that the Rule 10b-5 and mail fraud convictions should be reversed. . . .

Robert Chestman is a stockbroker. Keith Loeb first sought Chestman's services in 1982, when Loeb decided to consolidate his and his wife's holdings in Waldbaum, Inc. (Waldbaum), a publicly traded company that owned a large supermarket chain. During their initial meeting, Loeb told Chestman that his wife was a granddaughter of Julia Waldbaum, a member of the board of directors of Waldbaum and the wife of its founder. Julia Waldbaum also was the mother of Ira Waldbaum, the president and controlling shareholder of Waldbaum. . . .

On November 21, 1986, Ira Waldbaum agreed to sell Waldbaum to the Great Atlantic and Pacific Tea Company (A&P). The resulting stock purchase agreement required Ira to tender a controlling block of Waldbaum shares to A&P at a price of $50 per share. Ira told three of his children, all employees of Waldbaum, about the pending sale two days later, admonishing them to keep the news quiet until a public announcement. He also told his sister, Shirley Witkin, and nephew, Robert Karin, about the sale, and offered to tender their shares along with his controlling block of shares to enable them to avoid the administrative difficulty of tendering after the public announcement. He cautioned them "that [the sale was] not to be discussed," that it was to remain confidential.

In spite of Ira's counsel, Shirley told her daughter, Susan Loeb, on November 24 that Ira was selling the company. Shirley warned Susan not to tell anyone except her husband, Keith Loeb, because disclosure could ruin the sale. The next day, Susan told her husband about the pending tender offer and cautioned him not to tell anyone because "it could possibly ruin the sale."

The following day, November 26, Keith Loeb telephoned Robert Chestman at 8:59 A.M. Unable to reach Chestman, Loeb left a message asking Chestman to call him "ASAP." According to Loeb, he later spoke with Chestman between 9:00 A.M. and 10:30 A.M. that morning and told Chestman that he had "some definite, some accurate information" that Waldbaum was about to be sold at a "substantially higher" price than its market value. Loeb asked Chestman several times what he thought Loeb should do. Chestman responded that he could not advise Loeb what to do "in a situation like this" and that Loeb would have to make up his own mind.

That morning Chestman executed several purchases of Waldbaum stock. At 9:49 A.M., he bought 3,000 shares for his own account at $24.65 per share. Between 11:31 A.M. and 12:35 P.M., he purchased an additional 8,000 shares for his clients' discretionary accounts at prices ranging from $25.75 to $26.00 per share. One of the discretionary accounts was the Loeb account, for which Chestman bought 1,000 shares.

Before the market closed at 4:00 P.M., Loeb claims that he telephoned Chestman a second time. During their conversation Loeb again pressed Chestman for advice. Chestman repeated that he could not advise Loeb "in a situation like this," but then said that, based on his research, Waldbaum was a "buy." Loeb subsequently ordered 1,000 shares of Waldbaum stock.

Chestman presented a different version of the day's events. Before the SEC and at trial, he claimed that he had purchased Waldbaum stock based on his own research. He stated that his purchases were consistent with previous purchases of Waldbaum stock and other retail food stocks and were supported by reports in trade publications as well as the unusually high trading volume of the stock on November 25. He denied having spoken to Loeb about Waldbaum stock on the day of the trades.

At the close of trading on November 26, the tender offer was publicly announced. Waldbaum stock rose to $49 per share the next business day. In December 1986 Loeb learned that the National Association of Securities Dealers had started an investigation concerning transactions in Waldbaum stock. Loeb contacted Chestman who, according to Loeb, "reassured" him that Chestman had bought the stock for Loeb's account based on his research. Loeb called Chestman again in April 1987 after learning of an SEC investigation into the trading of Waldbaum stock. Chestman again stated that he bought the stock based on research. Similar conversations ensued. After one of these conversations, Chestman asked Loeb what his "position" was, Loeb replied, "I guess it's the same thing." Loeb subsequently agreed, however, to cooperate with the government. The terms of his cooperation agreement required that he disgorge the $25,000 profit from his purchase and sale of Waldbaum stock and pay a $25,000 fine.

A grand jury returned an indictment on July 20, 1988, charging Chestman with the following counts . . . : ten counts of fraudulent trading in connection with a tender offer in violation of Rule 14e-3(a), ten counts of securities fraud in violation of Rule 10b-5, ten counts of mail fraud, and one count of perjury. . . . After a jury trial, Chestman was found guilty on all counts.

Chestman appealed. He claimed that Rule 14e-3(a) was invalid because the SEC had exceeded its statutory authority in promulgating a rule that dispensed with one of the common law elements of fraud. He also argued that there was insufficient evidence to sustain his Rule 10b-5, mail fraud and perjury convictions.

A panel of this Court reversed Chestman's conviction on all counts. . . .

A majority of the active judges of the Court voted to rehear *in banc* the panel's decision with respect to the Rule 14e-3(a), Rule 10b-5, and mail fraud convictions. . . .

Chestman challenges his Rule 14e-3(a) convictions on three grounds. He first contends that the SEC exceeded its rulemaking authority when it promulgated Rule 14e-3(a). He then argues that the government presented insufficient evidence to support these convictions. Finally, he contends that his convictions should be overturned on due process notice grounds. . . .

. . . Rule 14e-3(a), the subsection under which Chestman was convicted, provides: . . . One violates Rule 14e-3(a) if he trades on the basis of material nonpublic information concerning a pending tender offer that he knows or has reason to know has been acquired "directly or indirectly" from an insider of the offeror or issuer, or someone working on their behalf. Rule 14e-3(a) is a disclosure provision. It creates a duty in those traders who fall within its ambit to abstain or disclose, without regard to whether the trader owes a pre-existing fiduciary duty to respect the confidentiality of the information. Chestman claims that the SEC exceeded its authority in drafting Rule 14e-3(a) — more specifically, in drafting a rule that dispenses with one of the common law elements of fraud, breach of a fiduciary duty. . . .

In promulgating Rule 14e-3(a), the SEC acted well within the letter and spirit of section 14(e). Recognizing the highly sensitive nature of tender offer information, its susceptibility to misuse, and the often difficult task of ferreting out and proving fraud, Congress sensibly delegated to the SEC broad authority to delineate a penumbra around the fuzzy subject of tender offer fraud. . . . To be certain, the SEC's rulemaking power under this broad grant of authority is not unlimited. The rule must still be "reasonably related to the purposes of the enabling legislation." . . . The SEC, however, in adopting Rule 14e-3(a), acted consistently with this authority. While dispensing with the subtle problems of proof associated with demonstrating fiduciary breach in the problematic area of tender offer insider trading, the Rule retains a close nexus between the prohibited conduct and the statutory aims. . . .

The question presented here differs markedly from that presented in *Chiarella*. It is not whether section 14(e), standing alone, prohibits insider trading in the absence of a fiduciary breach. It is not whether section 14(e)'s broad rulemaking provision, together with SEC action under that authority in the form of Rule 14e-3(a), represent a valid exercise of administrative rulemaking. . . . Our task is easier. Rule 14e-3(a) creates a narrower duty than that once proposed for Rule 10b-5 — a parity of information rule — and, as the language and legislative history of section 14(e) make clear, the rule has Congress' blessing. [The court then found that there was sufficient evidence to support the Rule 14e-3(a) convictions and that the convictions did not violate Chestman's due process rights. Thus, the court affirmed the 14e-3(a) convictions.]

Chestman's Rule 10b-5 convictions were based on the misappropriation theory, which provides that "one who misappropriates nonpublic information in breach of a fiduciary duty and trades on that information to his own advantage violates Section 10(b) and Rule 10b-5." *SEC v. Materia,* 745 F.2d 197, 203. . . . With respect to the shares Chestman purchased on behalf of Keith Loeb, Chestman was convicted of aiding and abetting Loeb's misappropriation of nonpublic information in breach of a duty Loeb owed to the Waldbaum family and to his wife Susan. As to the shares Chestman purchased for himself and his other clients, Chestman was convicted as a "tippee" of that same misappropriated information. Thus, while Chestman is the defendant in this case, the alleged misappropriator was Keith Loeb. The government agrees that Chestman's convictions cannot be sustained unless there was sufficient evidence to show that (1) Keith Loeb breached a duty owed to the Waldbaum family or Susan Loeb based on a fiduciary or similar relationship of trust and confidence, and (2) Chestman knew that Loeb had done so. . . .

The alleged misappropriator in this case was Keith Loeb. According to the government's theory of prosecution, Loeb breached a fiduciary duty to his wife Susan and the Waldbaum family when he disclosed to Robert Chestman information concerning a pending tender offer for Waldbaum stock. Chestman was convicted as an aider and abettor of the misappropriation and as a tippee of the misappropriated information. Conviction under both theories, the government concedes, required the government to establish two critical elements — Loeb breached a fiduciary duty to Susan Loeb or to the Waldbaum family and Chestman knew that Loeb had done so. . . .

We have little trouble finding the evidence insufficient to establish a fiduciary relationship or its functional equivalent between Keith Loeb and the Waldbaum family. The government presented only two pieces of evidence on this point. The first was that Keith was an extended member of the Waldbaum family, specifically the family patriarch's (Ira Waldbaum's) "nephew-in-law." The second piece of evidence concerned Ira's discussions of the business with family members. "My children," Ira Waldbaum testified, "have always been involved with me and my family and they know we never speak about business outside of the family." His earlier testimony indicates that the "family" to which he referred were his "three children who were involved in the business."

Lending this evidence the reasonable inferences to which it is entitled, . . . it falls short of establishing the relationship necessary for fiduciary obligations. Kinship alone does not create the necessary relationship. The government proffered nothing more to establish a fiduciary-like association. It did not show that Keith Loeb had been brought into the family's inner circle, whose members, it appears, discussed confidential business information either because they were kin or because they worked together with Ira Waldbaum. Keith was not an employee of Waldbaum and there was no showing that he participated in confidential communications regarding the business. The critical information was gratuitously communicated to him. . . .

The government's theory that Keith breached a fiduciary duty of confidentiality to Susan suffers from similar defects. The evidence showed: Keith and Susan were married; Susan admonished Keith not to disclose that Waldbaum was the target of a tender offer; and the two had shared and maintained confidences in the past.

Keith's status as Susan's husband could not itself establish fiduciary status. Nor, absent a pre-existing fiduciary relation or an express agreement of confidentiality, could the coda — "Don't tell." That leaves the unremarkable testimony that Keith and Susan had shared and maintained generic confidences before. The jury was not told the nature of these past disclosures and therefore it could not reasonably find a relationship that inspired fiduciary, rather than normal marital, obligations.

In the absence of evidence of an explicit acceptance by Keith of a duty of confidentiality, the context of the disclosure takes on special import. While acceptance may be implied, it must be implied from a pre-existing fiduciary-like relationship between the parties. Here the government presented the jury with insufficient evidence from which to draw a rational inference of implied acceptance. Susan's disclosure of the information to Keith served no purpose, business or otherwise. The disclosure also was unprompted. Keith did not induce her to convey the information through misrepresentation or subterfuge. . . .

In sum, because Keith owed neither Susan nor the Waldbaum family a fiduciary duty . . . , he did not defraud them by disclosing news of the pending tend offer to Chestman. Absent a predicate act of fraud by Keith Loeb, the alleged misappropriator, Chestman could not be derivatively liable as Loeb's tippee or as an aider and abettor. Therefore, Chestman's Rule 10b-5 convictions must be reversed.

NOTES AND QUESTIONS FOLLOWING UNITED STATES v. CHESTMAN

1. In late 2000, the SEC adopted Rule 10b5-2, which clarified when the misappropriation of material nonpublic information by family members or other nonbusiness relations gives rise to liability. Rule 10b5-2 purports to provide a nonexclusive definition of circumstances in which a person has a duty of trust or confidence for purposes of the misappropriation theory. The enumerated "duties of trust or confidence" arise (1) "whenever a person agrees to maintain information in confidence"; (2) whenever two persons "have a history, pattern, or practice of sharing confidences, such that the recipient of the information . . . reasonably should know that the [speaker] expects that the recipient will maintain its confidentiality"; or (3) "whenever a person receives or obtains material nonpublic information from his or her spouse, parent, child, or sibling," provided that the recipient may defend by demonstrating "that no duty of trust or confidence existed," that is, by establishing that he or she neither knew nor reasonably should have known that the speaker expected confidentiality based on agreement or the parties' history.

Query: Could Ira Waldbaum have traded stock of the company under Rules 10b-5 and 10b5-2? Could Shirley Witkin have traded? Could Susan Loeb have traded?

2. A lawyer works for a high-powered law firm and frequently brings work-related documents home. One day the lawyer's (non-spousal) "significant other" (S.O.) sees the documents and notes that they relate to an

impending merger announcement for ABC, Inc., at $30 per share. Yesterday's closing price of ABC was $19.50. May the S.O. buy shares? May he buy options on ABC stock?

3. Assume the S.O. in the above question consults you for advice and you advise him that he may buy ABC stock legally. Your bill for legal services is $10,000. May you suggest to the S.O. that you will waive your legal fees if he permits you to capitalize on his private information by purchasing ABC stock for your own account?

UNITED STATES v. O'HAGAN
521 U.S. 642 (1997)

GINSBURG, J.:

This case concerns the interpretation and enforcement of [SEC] Rule 10b-5 and Rule 14e-3(a). . . . In particular, we address and resolve these issues: (1) Is a person who trades in securities for personal profit, using confidential information misappropriated in breach of a fiduciary duty to the source of the information, guilty of violating §10(b) and Rule 10b-5? (2) Did the Commission exceed its rulemaking authority by adopting Rule 14e-3(a), which proscribes trading on undisclosed information in the tender offer setting, even in the absence of a duty to disclose? . . .

Respondent James Herman O'Hagan was a partner in the law firm of Dorsey & Whitney in Minneapolis, Minnesota. In July 1988, Grand Metropolitan PLC (Grand Met) . . . retained Dorsey & Whitney as local counsel [in] a potential tender offer for the common stock of the Pillsbury Company. . . . Both Grand Met and Dorsey & Whitney took precautions to protect the confidentiality of Grand Met's tender offer plans. O'Hagan did no work on the Grand Met representation. Dorsey & Whitney withdrew from representing Grand Met on September 9, 1988. Less than a month later, on October 4, 1988, Grand Met publicly announced its tender offer for Pillsbury stock.

On August 18, 1988, while Dorsey & Whitney was still representing Grand Met, O'Hagan began purchasing call options for Pillsbury stock. . . . Later . . . O'Hagan made additional purchases of Pillsbury call options. By the end of September, he owned 2,500 unexpired Pillsbury options [each giving the right to purchase 100 shares], apparently more than any other individual investor. . . . O'Hagan also purchased, in September 1988, some 5,000 shares of Pillsbury common stock, at a price just under $39 per share. When Grand Met announced its tender offer in October, the price of Pillsbury stock rose to nearly $60 per share. O'Hagan then sold his Pillsbury call options and common stock, making a profit of more than $4.3 million.

The Securities and Exchange Commission (SEC or Commission) initiated an investigation into O'Hagan's transactions, culminating in a 57-count indictment. The indictment alleged that O'Hagan defrauded his law firm and its client, Grand Met, by using for his own trading purposes material, nonpublic information regarding Grand Met's planned tender offer. . . .

A divided panel of the Court of Appeals for the Eighth Circuit reversed all of O'Hagan's convictions. . . .

. . . We hold, in accord with several other Courts of Appeals, that criminal liability under § 10(b) may be predicated on the misappropriation theory. . . .

The "misappropriation theory" holds that a person commits fraud "in connection with" a securities transaction, and thereby violates § 10(b) and Rule 10b-5, when he misappropriates confidential information for securities trading purposes, in breach of a duty owed to the source of the information. . . . In lieu of [the classical theory of] premising liability on a fiduciary relationship between company insider and purchaser or seller of the company's stock, the misappropriation theory premises liability on a fiduciary-turned-trader's deception of those who entrusted him with access to confidential information.

The two theories are complementary. . . . The classical theory targets a corporate insider's breach of duty to shareholders with whom the insider transacts; the misappropriation theory outlaws trading on the basis of nonpublic information by a corporate "outsider" in breach of a duty owed not to a trading party, but to the source of the information. . . .

In this case, the indictment alleged that O'Hagan, in breach of a duty of trust and confidence he owed to his law firm, Dorsey & Whitney, and to its client, Grand Met, traded on the basis of nonpublic information regarding Grand Met's planned tender offer for Pillsbury common stock. . . .[5]

We agree with the Government that misappropriation . . . satisfies § 10 (b)'s requirement that chargeable conduct involve a "deceptive device or contrivance" used "in connection with" the purchase or sale of securities. We observe, first, that misappropriators, as the Government describes them, deal in deception. A fiduciary who "[pretends] loyalty to the principal while secretly converting the principal's information for personal gain," Brief for United States 17, "dupes" or defrauds the principal. . . .

The misappropriation theory advanced by the Government [also] is consistent with *Santa Fe Industries, Inc. v. Green,* 430 U.S. 462. . . . [I]n *Santa Fe Industries,* all pertinent facts were disclosed by the persons charged with violating § 10(b) and Rule 10b-5 . . . ; therefore, there was no deception through nondisclosure to which liability under those provisions could attach. . . . Similarly, full disclosure forecloses liability under the misappropriation theory: Because the deception essential to the misappropriation theory involves feigning fidelity to the source of information, if the fiduciary discloses to the source that he plans to trade on the nonpublic information, there is no "deceptive device" and thus no

---

5. The Government could not have prosecuted O'Hagan under the classical theory, for O'Hagan was not an "insider" of Pillsbury, the corporation in whose stock he traded. Although an "outsider" with respect to Pillsbury, O'Hagan had an intimate association with, and was found to have traded on confidential information from, Dorsey & Whitney, counsel to tender offeror Grand Met. Under the misappropriation theory, O'Hagan's securities trading does not escape Exchange Act sanction, as it would under the dissent's reasoning, simply because he was associated with, and gained nonpublic information from, the bidder, rather than the target.

§10(b) violation—although the fiduciary-turned-trader may remain liable under state law for breach of a duty of loyalty.[7]

We turn next to the §10(b) requirement that the misappropriator's deceptive use of information be "in connection with the purchase or sale of [a] security." This element is satisfied because the fiduciary's fraud is consummated, not when the fiduciary gains the confidential information, but when, without disclosure to his principal, he uses the information to purchase or sell securities. The securities transaction and the breach of duty thus coincide. This is so even though the person or entity defrauded is not the other party to the trade, but is, instead, the source of the nonpublic information. . . . A misappropriator who trades on the basis of material, nonpublic information, in short, gains his advantageous market position through deception; he deceives the source of the information and simultaneously harms members of the investing public. . . .

The misappropriation theory comports with §10(b)'s language, which requires deception "in connection with the purchase or sale of any security," not deception of an identifiable purchaser or seller. . . . Although informational disparity is inevitable in the securities markets, investors likely would hesitate to venture their capital in a market where trading based on misappropriated nonpublic information is unchecked by law. An investor's informational disadvantage vis-à-vis a misappropriator with material, nonpublic information stems from contrivance, not luck; it is a disadvantage that cannot be overcome with research or skill. See Brudney, *Insiders, Outsiders, and Informational Advantages Under the Federal Securities Laws*, 93 Harv. L. Rev. 322, 356 (1979). . . .

In sum, . . . it makes scant sense to hold a lawyer like O'Hagan a §10(b)violator if he works for a law firm representing the target of a tender offer, but not if he works for a law firm representing the bidder. The text of the statute requires no such result. The misappropriation at issue here was properly made the subject of a §10(b) charge because it meets the statutory requirement that there be "deceptive" conduct "in connection with" securities transactions. . . .

The Eighth Circuit erred in holding that the misappropriation theory is inconsistent with §10(b). . . .

We consider next the ground on which the Court of Appeals reversed O'Hagan's convictions for fraudulent trading in connection with a tender offer, in violation of §14(e) of the Exchange Act and SEC Rule 14e-3(a). . . . [Contrary to the Court of Appeals, w]e hold that the Commission, . . . to the extent relevant to this case, did not exceed its authority. . . .

We need not resolve in this case whether the Commission's authority under §14(e) to "define . . . such acts and practices as are fraudulent" is broader than the Commission's fraud-defining authority under §10(b), for . . . Rule 14e-3(a), as applied to cases of this genre, qualifies under §14(e) as a "means reasonably designed to prevent" fraudulent trading

---

7. Where, however, a person trading on the basis of material, nonpublic information owes a duty of loyalty and confidentiality to two entities or persons—for example, a law firm and its client—but makes disclosure to only one, the trader may still be liable under the misappropriation theory.

on material, nonpublic information in the tender offer context. A prophylactic measure, because its mission is to prevent, typically encompasses more than the core activity prohibited. As we noted in *Schreiber*, § 14(e)'s rulemaking authorization gives the Commission "latitude," even in the context of a term of art like "manipulative," "to regulate nondeceptive activities as a 'reasonably designed' means of preventing manipulative acts, without suggesting any change in the meaning of the term 'manipulative' itself." 472 U.S., at 11, n.11. . . . We hold, accordingly, that under § 14(e), the Commission may prohibit acts, not themselves fraudulent under the common law or § 10(b), if the prohibition is "reasonably designed to prevent . . . acts and practices [that] are fraudulent." 15 U.S.C. § 78n(e).

Because Congress has authorized the Commission, in § 14(e), to prescribe legislative rules, . . . in determining whether Rule 14e-3(a)'s "disclose or abstain from trading" requirement is reasonably designed to prevent fraudulent acts, we must accord the Commission's assessment "controlling weight unless [it is] arbitrary, capricious, or manifestly contrary to the statute." *Chevron U.S.A. Inc. v. Natural Resources Defense Council, Inc . . . .* In this case, we conclude, the Commission's assessment is none of these.

QUESTION ON UNITED STATES v. O'HAGAN

You work for a broker-dealer in Omaha, Nebraska. One day you happen to glance at your neighbor's desk in the open office and notice buy orders from the legendary investor billionaire Warren Buffett for small stakes (0.1 percent of outstanding stock) in five large public companies. Knowing that the market accords considerable deference to Mr. Buffett's views, you buy six-month calls on shares in all five companies. The stock price for one of these companies declines, the stock prices for the remaining four companies rise, and on net, you make $500,000. Have you violated Rule 10b-5 if Mr. Buffett's purchases were never made public? What if they were announced, as you knew they would be, and their announcement triggered the increases in share prices, just as you expected?

NOTE AND QUESTIONS ON THE INSIDER TRADING AND SECURITIES FRAUD ENFORCEMENT ACT OF 1988

You have been secretly and illegally tipped about some very material inside information. You are weak and filled with needs. Why should you be plagued with money problems while others (in fairness, lesser persons really!) have been blessed with abundance. You scratch together what money you can borrow and buy 10,000 shares at $30. The next day your secret information becomes public, and the price of your stock jumps to $45 before you sell. Ahhh! In what amounts are you liable and to whom?

In 1988, Congress passed the Insider Trading and Securities Fraud Enforcement Act (ITSFEA) in response to "serious episodes of abusive and illegal practices on Wall Street."[37] In doing so, Congress intended to increase deterrence of insider trading, in part through increased enforcement and penalties. ITSFEA amended the Securities Exchange Act of 1934 by adding a new §20A, which was incorporated into Title 15 of the United States Code as a new section, §78t-1.

§78t-1. LIABILITY TO CONTEMPORANEOUS TRADERS FOR INSIDER TRADING

(a) Private rights of action based on contemporaneous trading

Any person who violates any provision of this chapter or the rules or regulations thereunder by purchasing or selling a security while in possession of material, nonpublic information shall be liable in an action in any court of competent jurisdiction to any person who, contemporaneously with the purchase or sale of securities that is the subject of such violation, has purchased (where such violation is based on a sale of securities) or sold (where such violation is based on a purchase of securities) securities of the same class.

(b) Limitations on liability

(1) Contemporaneous trading actions limited to profit gained or loss avoided

The total amount of damages imposed under subsection (a) of this section shall not exceed the profit gained or loss avoided in the transaction or transactions that are the subject of the violation.

(2) Offsetting disgorgements against liability

The total amount of damages imposed against any person under subsection (a) of this section shall be diminished by the amounts, if any, that such person may be required to disgorge, pursuant to a court order obtained at the instance of the Commission, in a proceeding brought under section 78u(d) of this title relating to the same transaction or transactions.

(3) Controlling person liability

No person shall be liable under this section solely by reason of employing another person who is liable under this section, but the liability of a controlling person under this section shall be subject to section 78t(a) of this title. . . .

(c) Joint and several liability for communicating

Any person who violates any provision of this chapter or the rules or regulations thereunder by communicating material, nonpublic information shall be jointly and severally liable under subsection (a) of this section with, and to the same extent as, any person or persons liable under subsection (a) of this section to whom the communication was directed.

(d) Authority not to restrict other express or implied rights of action

---

37. H.R. Rep. No. 100-910 (1988).

Nothing in this section shall be construed to limit or condition the right of any person to bring an action to enforce a requirement of this chapter or the availability of any cause of action implied from a provision of this chapter.

Section 20A (78t-1) defines neither what constitutes insider trading nor what constitutes "contemporaneously" buying or selling, which gives a person standing to sue. Instead, it assumes that the courts will continue to employ the standards of the existing case law. Read literally, the first sentence of § 20A would cover a prospective bidder who, knowing that it was about to launch a tender offer or propose a merger, bought shares of the target on the open market. Such a person would not be liable under *Dirks* (because there is no breach of a fiduciary duty), but the person in this example does possess "material, nonpublic information." Despite this hazy drafting, the legislative history makes clear that only those who "misappropriate" the material, nonpublic information should be held liable. Still, even this endorsement of misappropriation theory expands potential liability because under § 20A it appears possible for a shareholder of the target to sue a person who misappropriates information from the bidder. Such a suit could not be brought under Rule 10b-5.[38] Therefore, § 20A provides an alternative to Rule 10b-5. The issue of causation of loss in the context of Rule 10b-5 is left unaddressed, but the legislation adopts a damages rule from *Elkind v. Liggett & Myers, Inc.*, below, that largely trivializes this issue.

14.4.2.4   Elements of 10b-5 Liability: Materiality

BASIC INC. v. LEVINSON
485 U.S. 224 (1988)

BLACKMUN J.:

This case requires us to apply the materiality requirement [o]f § 10(b) of the [1934 Act] and Rule 10b-5 . . . in the context of preliminary corporate merger discussions. We must also determine whether a person who traded a corporation's shares on a securities exchange after the issuance of a materially misleading statement by the corporation may invoke a rebuttable presumption that, in trading, he relied on the integrity of the price set by the market.

[For two years prior to the merger of Combustion Engineering, Inc., and Basic, Inc., in December 1978, the two companies had engaged in private merger negotiations. During this period, Basic made three public statements denying that any merger negotiations were taking place or that it knew of any corporate developments that would account for the heavy trading in its stock. Plaintiffs, former shareholders in Basic who sold their

---

38. See Moss v. Morgan Stanley, Inc., 719 F.2d 5 (2d Cir. 1983).

stock between Basic's first public denial of the merger negotiations and a date just prior to the public announcement of the merger, filed suit on the theory that these statements violated Rule 10b-5. The district court granted summary judgment for the defendants on the theory that preliminary merger negotiations were immaterial as a matter of law because the negotiations between the two companies were not "destined, with reasonable certainty, to result in a merger agreement in principle." The court of appeals reversed, holding that even merger discussions that might not have been otherwise material became so as a result of a statement denying their existence.] . . .

[This] Court . . . explicitly has defined a standard of materiality under the securities laws, see *TSC Industries, Inc. v. Northway, Inc.*, 426 U.S. 438 (1976), concluding in the proxy-solicitation context that "an omitted fact is material if there is a substantial likelihood that a reasonable shareholder would consider it important in deciding how to vote." *Id.*, at 449. Acknowledging that certain information concerning corporate developments could well be of "dubious significance," *id.*, at 448, the Court was careful not to set too low a standard of materiality; it was concerned that a minimal standard might bring an overabundance of information within its reach, and lead management "simply to bury the shareholders in an avalanche of trivial information — a result that is hardly conducive to informed decision making." *Id.*, at 448-449. It further explained that to fulfill the materiality requirement "there must be a substantial likelihood that the disclosure of the omitted fact would have been viewed by the reasonable investor as having significantly altered the 'total mix' of information made available." *Id.*, at 449. We now expressly adopt the *TSC Industries* standard of materiality for the §10(b) and Rule 10b-5 context. . . .

The application of this materiality standard to preliminary merger discussions is not self-evident. Where the impact of the corporate development on the target's fortune is certain and clear, the *TSC Industries* materiality definition admits straightforward application. Where, on the other hand, the event is contingent or speculative in nature, it is difficult to ascertain whether the "reasonable investor" would have considered the omitted information significant at the time. . . .

Petitioners urge upon us a Third Circuit test for resolving this difficulty. Under this approach, preliminary merger discussions do not become material until [there is an] "agreement-in-principle" as to the price and structure of the transaction. . . . By definition, then, information concerning any negotiations not yet at the agreement-in-principle stage could be withheld or even misrepresented without a violation of Rule 10b-5.

Three rationales have been offered in support of the "agreement-in-principle" test. The first derives from the concern expressed in *TSC Industries* that an investor not be overwhelmed by excessively detailed and trivial information. . . . The other two justifications . . . are based on management concerns: because the requirement of "agreement-in-principle" limits the scope of disclosure obligations, it helps preserve the confidentiality of merger discussions where earlier disclosure might prejudice the negotiations; and the test also provides a usable, bright-line rule for determining when disclosure must be made. . . .

None of these policy-based rationales, however, purports to explain why drawing the line at agreement-in-principle reflects the significance of the information upon the investor's decision. The first rationale, and the only one connected to the concerns expressed in *TSC Industries,* stands soundly rejected, even by a Court of Appeals that otherwise has accepted the wisdom of the agreement-in-principle test. "It assumes that investors are nitwits, unable to appreciate — even when told — that mergers are risky propositions up until the closing." *Flamm v. Eberstadt,* 814 F.2d, at 1175. Disclosure, and not paternalistic withholding of accurate information, is the policy chosen and expressed by Congress. . . .

The second rationale, the importance of secrecy during the early stages of merger discussions, also seems irrelevant to an assessment whether their existence is significant to the trading decision of a reasonable investor. To avoid a "bidding war" over its target, an acquiring firm often will insist that negotiations remain confidential. . . .

We need not ascertain, however, whether secrecy necessarily maximizes shareholder wealth — although we note that the proposition is at least disputed as a matter of theory and empirical research — for this case does not concern the *timing* of a disclosure; it concerns only its accuracy and completeness. We face here the narrow question whether information concerning the existence and status of preliminary merger discussions is significant to the reasonable investor's trading decision. Arguments based on the premise that some disclosure would be "premature" in a sense are more properly considered under the rubric of an issuer's duty to disclose. . . .

The final justification offered in support of the agreement-in-principle test seems to be directed solely at the comfort of corporate managers. A bright-line rule indeed is easier to follow than a standard that requires the exercise of judgment in the light of all the circumstances. But ease of application alone is not an excuse for ignoring the purposes of the securities acts and Congress' policy decisions. . . .

We therefore find no valid justification for artificially excluding from the definition of materiality information concerning merger discussions, which would otherwise be considered significant to the trading decision of a reasonable investor, merely because agreement-in-principle as to price and structure has not yet been reached by the parties or their representatives. . . .

Even before this Court's decision in *TSC Industries,* the Second Circuit had explained the role of the materiality requirement of Rule 10b-5, with respect to contingent or speculative information or events, in a manner that gave that term meaning that is independent of the other provisions of the Rule. Under such circumstances, materiality "will depend at any given time upon a balancing of both the indicated probability that the event will occur and the anticipated magnitude of the event in light of the totality of the company activity." *SEC v. Texas Gulf Sulphur Co.,* 401 F.2d, at 849. . . .

In a subsequent decision, the late Judge Friendly, writing for a Second Circuit panel, applied the *Texas Gulf Sulphur* probability/magnitude approach in the specific context of preliminary merger negotiations. After acknowledging that materiality is something to be determined on the basis of the particular facts of each case, he stated:

> Since a merger in which it is bought out is the most important event that can occur in a small corporation's life, to wit, its death, we think that inside information, as regards a merger of this sort, can become material at an earlier stage than would be the case as regards lesser transactions—and this even though the mortality rate of mergers in such formative stages is doubtless high. *SEC v. Geon Industries, Inc.*, 531 F.2d 39, 47-48 (CA2 1976).

We agree with that analysis.

Whether merger discussions in any particular case are material therefore depends on the facts. Generally, in order to assess the probability that the event will occur, a fact finder will need to look to indicia of interest in the transaction at the highest corporate levels. Without attempting to catalog all such possible factors, we note by way of example that board resolutions, instructions to investment bankers, and actual negotiations between principals or their intermediaries may serve as indicia of interest. To assess the magnitude of the transaction to the issuer of the securities allegedly manipulated, a fact finder will need to consider such facts as the size of the two corporate entities and of the potential premiums over market value. No particular event or factor short of closing the transaction need be either necessary or sufficient by itself to render merger discussions material.[17]

As we clarify today, materiality depends on the significance the reasonable investor would place on the withheld or misrepresented information. The fact-specific inquiry we endorse here is consistent with the approach a number of courts have taken in assessing the materiality of merger negotiations. Because the standard of materiality we have adopted differs from that used by both courts below, we remand the case for reconsideration of the question whether a grant of summary judgment is appropriate on this record. . . .

NOTE AND QUESTIONS ON BASIC, INC. v. LEVINSON *AND THE MATERIALITY STANDARD*

1. If materiality is understood in its ordinary sense, how could live and plausible merger negotiations ever be understood as anything *but* material?

2. In framing the "agreement-in-principle" test, the Third and Seventh Circuits appear to have been chiefly concerned with the risk that premature disclosure would scuttle merger negotiations to the detriment of its shareholders. As a matter of policy, should officers and directors be permitted to lie about certain matters, such as merger negotiations, subject to a "fairness" review by a federal judge ex post, to ensure the lies were made to benefit shareholders rather than harm them. Why not? Compare

---

17. To be actionable, of course, a statement must also be misleading. Silence, absent a duty to disclose, is not misleading under Rule 10b-5. "No comment" statements are generally the functional equivalent of silence. See *In re Carnation Co.*, supra. . . .

Jonathan R. Macey & Geoffrey P. Miller, *Good Finance, Bad Economics: An Analysis of Fraud-on-the-Market Theory*, 42 Stan. L. Rev. 1059 (1990) with Ian Ayres, *Back to Basics: Regulating How Corporations Speak to the Market*, 77 Va. L. Rev. 945 (1991).

14.4.2.5 Elements of 10b-5 Liability: Scienter

Common law fraud requires *scienter* or intention to deceive. In 1976, the Supreme Court confirmed that liability under Rule 10b-5 requires specific intent to deceive, manipulate, or defraud. *Ernst & Ernst v. Hochfelder*, 425 U.S. 185 (1976). That authoritative determination of the necessity of scienter has not, however, resolved all of the important issues respecting this mental state requirement. Two issues have been particularly important. The first issue regards *proof*: whether actual intent to deceive must be shown in order to establish liability or whether scienter may be inferred from conduct that is simply willfully or recklessly negligent. You might suppose that intention to deceive is a conscious state, but you would be incorrect in the view of some courts, which have held that the appropriate mental state may be inferred from reckless or grossly negligent behavior.[39]

The second issue is one of *pleading*. This is especially important, since, as we discussed in Chapter 10, shareholder suits that are not dismissed almost invariably settle. Thus, the critical issue for a Rule 10b-5 complaint is whether it can survive a motion to dismiss, which typically occurs at the outset of the litigation. The motion to dismiss tests the legal sufficiency of the complaint and assumes the truth of all allegations. If a complaint can survive a motion to dismiss, the costs and risks of litigation will generally give it a settlement value, regardless of its merits. What then must the plaintiff state in her complaint in order to satisfy her burden to allege scienter at the pleading stage? The practical importance of the holding in *Ernst & Ernst* could be vastly reduced if, for example, that burden could be met by simply alleging that defendants were recklessly unaware of the materiality of an omitted statement.

The courts of appeals have differed on this pleading standard. The Court of Appeals for the Ninth Circuit, for example, adopted the most permissive standard by holding that the plaintiff needed to state in her pleading only that the defendant had acted with scienter.[40] The Second Circuit, on the other hand, applied what appears to be the strictest pleading test. It required the plaintiff to plead "facts that give rise to a strong inference of fraudulent intent."[41] This pleading burden however could be satisfied by alleging facts that specified a motive to defraud and an

---

39. See, e.g., SEC v. Steadman, 967 F.2d 636 (D.C. Cir. 1992) (extreme recklessness); Dennis v. General Imaging, Inc., 918 F.2d 496 (5th Cir. 1990) (severe recklessness); Sundstrand Corp. v. Sun Chemical Corp., 553 F.2d 1033 (7th Cir. 1977) (common law recklessness).

40. Decker v Glenfed Inc., 42 F.3d 1541, 1545 (9th Cir. 1994).

41. Shields v. Cititrust Bancorp Inc., 25 F.3d 1124, 1128 (2d Cir. 1994).

opportunity to do so, if the circumstances pleaded together constituted the required strong inference.

In 1995, Congress adopted the Private Securities Litigation Reform Act (PSLRA) in response to the perception that private securities litigation, principally Rule 10b-5 litigation, had grown too aggressive. The PSLRA enacted a number of provisions designed to stem the tide of such litigation. Of relevance here, for example, it provided that:

> [T]he complaint shall, with respect to each act or omission alleged to violate this chapter, state with particularity facts giving rise to a strong inference that the Defendant acted with the required state of mind."[42]

The legislative history of this Act is complex and in certain places contradictory. Not surprisingly, the courts of appeals are divided as to the meaning of this language. Some circuits take the demanding view that the statutory language itself, in addition to the legislative history, indicates that Congress wanted to strengthen the Second Circuit pleading standing, not simply adopt it. They therefore hold that a plaintiff must minimally plead deliberate recklessness or conscious recklessness as an element of her claim under Rule 10b-5.[43] Other courts have concluded that Congress merely intended to adopt the Second Circuit pleading standard.[44]

The debate is much more textured and subtle than this short report can capture.[45] In any event, two facts are notable. First, in the context of securities class actions, the technical question of how one pleads a mental state may be more important for the suit than the mental state itself that is an element of the cause of action! Second, only the Supreme Court of the United States can resolve this issue, and predictions on how it might do so would be risky.

In all events if the intent of the PSLRA was to constrain the growth in 10b-5 litigation, it has not been successful. Filings of securities class suits continued to grow following the enactment of the act, reaching a high point in 2001 with the numerous corporate frauds that made history that year. From 2001 there has been a decline with filings in 2005 and 2006 appearing to fall back to 1997 levels.[46]

NOTE ON RULE 10b5-1

The SEC promulgated Rule 10b5-1 in mid-2000 to clarify whether it is "use" or "knowing possession" of nonpublic material information at the time of a trade that gives rise to liability under Rule 10b-5. Rule 10b5-1 defines illicit

---

42. 15 U.S.C. §78u-4(b)(2) (1998).

43. See Janas v. McCracken (In re Silicon Graphics Securities Litigation), 183 F.3d 970 (9th Cir. 1999); Makor Issues & Rights, Ltd. V. Tellabs, Inc., 437 F 3rd 603 (7th Cir 2006) (summarizing circuit splits).

44. See, e.g., In re Advanta Corp. Securities Litigation, 180 F.3d 525 (3d Cir. 1999).

45. See, e.g., Symposium, 22 Bank & Corp. Governance L. Rep. 1242 (Aug. 1999).

46. See Stanford Security Class Action Clearinghouse at http://securities.stanford.edu/companies.html.

trading as trading "on the basis of" insider information "if the person making the purchase or sale was aware of non-public material information when the person made the purchase or the sale." This definition, however, was qualified by several affirmative defenses, including (1) proof that a person had given instructions, or adopted a written plan to purchase, before acquiring information; and (2) proof that, in the case of an investing entity, the natural person making the investment on behalf of the entity was unaware of the inside information and the entity itself had implemented reasonable measures to protect against illicit insider trading.

In adopting Rule 10b5-1, the SEC adopted a standard that is closer to the "knowing possession" criterion than to a criterion of "use" based on "awareness" of the insider information.[47] However, the SEC was aware that this standard might prevent companies from structuring securities trading plans and compensation packages with sufficient flexibility. Therefore, the SEC specified an affirmative defense in paragraph (c)(1)(i), whereby defendants may avoid liability by demonstrating that they had entered into an agreement to trade securities on specified terms before becoming aware of the material nonpublic information and that the actual trading of securities was in compliance with the terms of that agreement.

14.4.2.6   Elements of 10b-5 Liability: Standing, in Connection with the Purchase or Sale of Securities

The language of Rule 10b-5 expressly includes the limitation "in connection with the purchase or sale of a security." In *Birnbaum v. Newport Steel Corp.*,[48] it was held, and subsequently followed, that a plaintiff must have been a buyer or seller of stock in order to have standing to bring a complaint about an alleged violation of Rule 10b-5. The SEC sought to have this rule overturned, but courts generally followed *Birnbaum's* lead on this issue.[49]

The Supreme Court addressed this question in *Blue Chip Stamps et al. v. Manor Drugs.*[50] *Blue Chip* arose from an interesting context. The Department of Justice had sued Blue Chip on antitrust grounds, and the suit had been settled by Blue Chip's agreeing to offer its shares for sale to a class of certain persons at a set price. Plaintiff declined the offer to invest but later claimed that the offering document had been materially false. If it had been truthful, the plaintiff alleged, it would have invested. Thus, the plaintiff claimed that it had made a financial decision, relying on a materially false statement, to its detriment. In an opinion that reflected a sensitivity to

---

47. One of the rationales for adopting this standard was the belief that traders will inevitably use information that they possess.

48. 193 F.2d 461 (2d Cir. 1952).

49. Professors Louis Loss and Joel Seligman report that the SEC did so at 8 Securities Regulation 3693 (3d ed. 1991).

50. 421 U.S. 723 (1975).

the risk that 10b-5 liability might become too expansive, the court denied the claim.

Does the same purchaser or seller requirement apply to actions seeking injunctions? Some circuits have thought so. *Cowin v. Bresler,* 741 F.2d 410 (D.C. Cir. 1984) (Blue Chip requires that plaintiff in injunction action also be purchaser or seller). Most courts appear to provide more relaxed standing requirements in this setting, however. See, e.g., *Advanced Res. Int'l, Inc. v. Tri-Star Petro. Co.* 4 F3rd 486(3rd Cir 1998); *Mutual Shares Corp. v. Genesco,* 384 F.2d 540 (2d Cir. 1967) (holding that deceitfully inducing minority shareholders to sell gives minority shareholder who did not sell standing to seek an injunction; a dubious precedent following *Santa Fe v. Green*).

Is a pledge of securities a sale? Again, courts have split on the issue. Compare *Mallis v. Federal Deposit Insurance Corporation,* 568 F.2d 824 (2d Cir. 1977) with *Lincoln National Bank v. Herber,* 604 F.2d 1038 (7th Cir. 1979).

Of course a pledge is just a primitive form of "monetizing" an economic interest. What about more complex forms of non-sale monetizing transactions by officers in company stock? Should they be somehow subject to insider trading regulation? For an interesting window on how much of this there may be, see Carr Bettis, John Bizjak, & Michael Lemmon, *Managerial Ownership, Incentive Contracting, and the Use of Zero Cost Collars and Equity Swaps by Corporate Insiders,* 36 J. Fin. Quantitative Anaylsis 345 (2001).

14.4.2.7 Elements of 10b-5 Liability: Reliance

Reasonable reliance is an element of common law fraud. Reliance as an element of a Rule 10b-5 claim is more complex, since most transactions in shares of public corporations occur in faceless market transactions. Thus, the question bound to arise is, What if a false statement is made by an insider that affects the market price of the stock, but a shareholder never hears the false statement? On the assumption that markets are affected by all public information, we might conclude that the price that such a person gets or pays in transacting in the stock is affected by the false statement. Should this qualify as sufficient reliance to satisfy the element of the rule?

Here we continue with the *Basic, Inc. v. Levinson* opinion excerpted above for its discussion of materiality.

BASIC INC. v. LEVINSON
485 U.S. 224 (1988)

We turn to the question of reliance and the fraud-on-the-market theory. Succinctly put:

"The fraud on the market theory is based on the hypothesis that, in an open and developed securities market, the price of a company's stock is determined by the available material information regarding the company and its business. Misleading statements will therefore defraud purchasers of stock even if the purchasers do not directly rely on the misstatements. The causal connection between the defendants' fraud and the plaintiffs' purchase of stock in such a case is no less significant than in a case of direct reliance on misrepresentations." *Peil v. Speiser*, 806 F.2d 1154, 1160-1161 (CA3 1986).

Our task, of course, is not to assess the general validity of the theory, but to consider whether it was proper for the courts below to apply a rebuttable presumption of reliance, supported in part by the fraud-on-the-market theory.

This case required resolution of several common questions of law and fact. . . .

We agree that reliance is an element of a Rule 10b-5 cause of action. . . . Reliance provides the requisite causal connection between a defendant's misrepresentation and a plaintiff's injury. . . . There is, however, more than one way to demonstrate the causal connection. Indeed, we previously have dispensed with a requirement of positive proof of reliance, where a duty to disclose material information had been breached, concluding that the necessary nexus between the plaintiffs' injury and the defendant's wrongful conduct had been established. See *Affiliated Ute Citizens v. United States*, 406 U.S. 128 at 153-154. Similarly, we did not require proof that material omissions or misstatements in a proxy statement decisively affected voting, because the proxy solicitation itself, rather than the defect in the solicitation materials, served as an essential link in the transaction. See *Mills v. Electric Auto-Lite Co.*, 396 U.S. 375, 384-385 (1970).

The modern securities markets, literally involving millions of shares changing hands daily, differ from the face-to-face transactions contemplated by early fraud cases, and our understanding of Rule 10b-5's reliance requirement must encompass these differences. . . .

Presumptions typically serve to assist courts in managing circumstances in which direct proof, for one reason or another, is rendered difficult. . . . The courts below accepted a presumption, created by the fraud-on-the-market theory and subject to rebuttal by petitioners, that persons who had traded Basic shares had done so in reliance on the integrity of the price set by the market, but because of petitioners' material misrepresentations that price had been fraudulently depressed. Requiring a plaintiff to show a speculative state of facts, i.e., how he would have acted if omitted material information had been disclosed, . . . or if the misrepresentation had not been made, . . . would place an unnecessarily unrealistic evidentiary burden on the Rule 10b-5 plaintiff who has traded on an impersonal market. . . .

Arising out of considerations of fairness, public policy, and probability, as well as judicial economy, presumptions are also useful devices for allocating the burdens of proof between parties. . . . [A] presumption of reliance . . . in this case is consistent with, and, by facilitating Rule 10b-5 litigation, supports, the congressional policy embodied in the 1934 Act. . . .

The presumption [of reliance] is also supported by common sense and probability. Recent empirical studies have tended to confirm Congress' premise that the market price of shares traded on well-developed markets reflects all publicly available information, and, hence, any material misrepresentations. It has been noted that "it is hard to imagine that there ever is a buyer or seller who does not rely on market integrity. Who would knowingly roll the dice in a crooked crap game?" *Schlanger v. Four-Phase Systems Inc.*, 555 F. Supp. 535, 538 (S.D.N.Y. 1982). Indeed, nearly every court that has considered the proposition has concluded that where materially misleading statements have been disseminated into an impersonal, well-developed market for securities, the reliance of individual plaintiffs on the integrity of the market price may be presumed. Commentators generally have applauded the adoption of one variation or another of the fraud-on-the-market theory. An investor who buys or sells stock at the price set by the market does so in reliance on the integrity of that price. Because most publicly available information is reflected in market price, an investor's reliance on any public material misrepresentations, therefore, may be presumed for purposes of a Rule 10b-5 action.

The Court of Appeals found that petitioners "made public material misrepresentations and [respondents] sold Basic stock in an impersonal, efficient market. Thus the class, as defined by the district court, has established the threshold facts for proving their loss." 786 F.2d, at 751. The court acknowledged that petitioners may rebut proof of the elements giving rise to the presumption, or show that the misrepresentation in fact did not lead to a distortion of price or that an individual plaintiff traded or would have traded despite his knowing the statement was false. . . .

Any showing that severs the link between the alleged misrepresentation and either the price received (or paid) by the plaintiff, or his decision to trade at a fair market price, will be sufficient to rebut the presumption of reliance. For example, if petitioners could show that the "market makers" were privy to the truth about the merger discussions here with Combustion, and thus that the market price would not have been affected by their misrepresentations, the causal connection could be broken: the basis for finding that the fraud had been transmitted through market price would be gone. Similarly, if, despite petitioners' allegedly fraudulent attempt to manipulate market price, news of the merger discussions credibly entered the market and dissipated the effects of the misstatements, those who traded Basic shares after the corrective statements would have no direct or indirect connection with the fraud. Petitioners also could rebut the presumption of reliance as to plaintiffs who would have divested themselves of their Basic shares without relying on the integrity of the market. For example, a plaintiff who believed that Basic's statements were false and that Basic was indeed engaged in merger discussions, and who consequently believed that Basic stock was artificially underpriced, but sold his shares nevertheless because of other unrelated concerns, e.g., potential antitrust problems, or political pressures to divest from shares of certain businesses, could not be said to have relied on the integrity of a price he knew had been manipulated. . . .

Justice WHITE, with whom Justice O'CONNOR joins, concurring in part and dissenting in part. . . .

At the outset, I note that there are portions of the Court's fraud-on-the-market holding with which I am in agreement. Most importantly, the Court rejects the version of that theory, heretofore adopted by some courts, which equates "causation" with "reliance," and permits recovery by a plaintiff who claims merely to have been *harmed* by a material misrepresentation which altered a market price, notwithstanding proof that the plaintiff did not in any way *rely* on that price. . . . I agree with the Court that if Rule 10b-5's reliance requirement is to be left with any content at all, the fraud-on-the-market presumption must be capable of being rebutted by a showing that a plaintiff did not "rely" on the market price. . . .

But even as the Court attempts to limit the fraud-on-the-market theory it endorses today, the pitfalls in its approach are revealed by previous uses by the lower courts of the broader versions of the theory. . . .

In general, the case law developed in this Court with respect to § 10(b) and Rule 10b-5 has been based on doctrines with which we, as judges, are familiar: common-law doctrines of fraud and deceit. . . . But with no staff economists, no experts schooled in the "efficient-capital-market hypothesis," no ability to test the validity of empirical market studies, we are not well equipped to embrace novel constructions of a statute based on contemporary microeconomic theory.[4] . . .

Finally, the particular facts of this case make it an exceedingly poor candidate for the Court's fraud-on-the-market theory, and illustrate the illogic achieved by that theory's application in many cases.

Respondents here are a class of sellers who sold Basic stock between October, 1977 and December 1978, a fourteen-month period. At the time the class period began, Basic's stock was trading at $20 a share (at the time, an all-time high); the last members of the class to sell their Basic stock got a price of just over $30 a share. App. 363, 423. It is indisputable that virtually every member of the class made money from his or her sale of Basic stock.

The oddities of applying the fraud-on-the-market theory in this case are manifest. First, there are the facts that the plaintiffs are sellers and the class period is so lengthy — both are virtually without precedent in prior fraud-on-the-market cases. . . .

[T]here is no evidence that petitioner's officials made the troublesome misstatements for the purpose of manipulating stock prices. . . . Indeed, during the class period, petitioners do not appear to have purchased or sold *any* Basic stock whatsoever. . . .

---

4. This view was put well by two commentators who wrote a few years ago:

"Of all recent developments in financial economics, the efficient capital market hypothesis ("ECMH") has achieved the widest acceptance by the legal culture . . .

"Yet the legal culture's remarkably rapid and broad acceptance of an economic concept that did not exist twenty years ago is not matched by an equivalent degree of understanding." Gilson & Kraakman, *The Mechanisms of Market Efficiency*, 70 Va. L. Rev. 549, 549-550 (1984) (footnotes omitted; emphasis added).

Third, there are the peculiarities of what kinds of investors will be able to recover in this case. . . . Thus, it is possible that a person who heard the first corporate misstatement and *disbelieved* it—i.e., someone who purchased Basic stock thinking that petitioners' statement was false—may still be included in the plaintiff-class on remand. How a person who undertook such a speculative stock-investing strategy—and made $10 a share doing so (if he bought on October 22, 1977, and sold on December 15, 1978)—can say that he was "defrauded" by virtue of his reliance on the "integrity" of the market price is beyond me. And such speculators may not be uncommon, at least in this case. . . .

While the fraud-on-the-market theory has gained even broader acceptance since 1984, I doubt that it has achieved any greater understanding.

Indeed, the facts of this case lead a casual observer to the almost inescapable conclusion that many of those who bought or sold Basic stock during the period in question flatly disbelieved the statements which are alleged to have been "materially misleading." Despite three statements denying that merger negotiations were underway, Basic stock hit record-high after record-high during the 14 month class period. It seems quite possible that, like Casca's knowing disbelief of Caesar's "thrice refusal" of the Crown,[11] clever investors were skeptical of petitioners' three denials that merger talks were going on. Yet such investors, the savviest of the savvy, will be able to recover under the Court's opinion, as long as they now claim that they believed in the "integrity of the market price" when they sold their stock (between September and December, 1978). Thus, persons who bought after hearing and relying on the falsity of petitioner's statements may be able to prevail and recover money damages on demand.

And who will pay the judgments won in such actions? I suspect that all too often the majority's rule will "lead to large judgments, payable in the last analysis by the innocent investors, for the benefit of speculators and their lawyers." Cf. *SEC v. Texas Gulf Sulphur Co.*, 401 F.2d 833, 867 (CA2 1968) (en banc) (Friendly, J., concurring). . . .

NOTES AND QUESTIONS ON *BASIC, RELIANCE, AND THE FRAUD-ON-THE-MARKET THEORY*

1. The ECMH is influential in securities litigation and bears on many of our remaining materials. It postulates that (1) prices of stock on the market reflect the material information that is available to the public and (2) information is quickly assimilated into the stock prices. The closely related theory of fraud on the market formed the basis for the Court's determination of the Rule 10b-5 reliance requirement in *Basic*.

A plurality of the *Basic* Court (4-2) determined that defendants' misrepresentations to the public could establish a presumption that plaintiffs had relied on that information, based on the resulting effect on market price, regardless of whether plaintiffs had directly relied upon the false

---

11. See W. Shakespeare, Julius Caesar, Act I, Scene II.

information.[51] Thus, the plurality opinion found that reliance on market price was sufficient to meet the reliance requirement for Rule 10b-5 liability. The effect of this outcome does not act as a binding precedent on the Supreme Court, since a majority of justices did not join on the point. However, the reliance requirement determination of *Basic* has been followed by lower courts.

2. The presumption that a market rapidly responds to all available information may not be valid for all markets in which securities are traded. While empirical evidence strongly suggests that organized U.S. stock exchanges are efficient markets, it is less certain that the "new issue" markets, some "over-the-counter" dealer markets, and the market for municipal bonds are similarly efficient.

3. After *Basic*, investors are presumed to rely on market prices that, if the market is efficient, will fully reflect the issuer's statements. How might an issuer attempt to rebut this presumption?

4. Justice White's dissent is concerned with the issue of damages in a fraud-on-the-market case, especially where plaintiffs are sellers who trade over a comparatively lengthy period prior to the public disclosure of accurate information. Why is the damages issue troublesome?

5. Do you think that the ECMH may be used defensively? If all public information is rapidly absorbed by markets and reflected in prices, can we assume that, if a deliberate misstatement is made, no injury can be caused by that statement once any significant part of the market knows the truth? See, e.g., *In re Apple Securities Litigation*, 886 F.2d 1109, 1116 (9th Cir. 1989).

6. Justice White notes in dissent that the Court is "not well equipped to embrace novel constructions of a statute based on contemporary microeconomic theory." At the time of the Court's decision in *Basic*, the ECMH was widely accepted among legal academics and economists. In 1978, for example, Professor Michael Jensen wrote: "There is no other proposition in economics which has more empirical evidence supporting it than the efficient markets hypothesis."[52] But soon after *Basic* academics began challenging its empirical and theoretical validity. In 1992, Professors Robert Daines and Jon Hanson wrote: "Legal scholars familiar with current financial economics agree that there is now reason to doubt the efficiency of [securities] markets."[53] In 2002, Professor Donald Langevoort summarized the literature as such: "What is impressive in the case against market efficiency is not the strength of any individual claim, but their aggregate weight. . . . If far from dead, market efficiency is at least more contestable than ever."[54] How, if at all, does this trend in academic opinion influence

---

51. Note that the Court did not assess the validity of the fraud-on-the-market theory but instead determined only that the theory could be used to support a rebuttable presumption of reliance. See *Basic*, 485 U.S. at 242.

52. Michael C. Jensen, *Some Anomolous Evidence Regarding Market Efficiency*, 6 J. Fin. Econ. 95, 95 (1978).

53. Robert M. Daines & Jon D. Hanson, *The Corporate Law Paradox: The Case for Restructuring Corporate Law*, 103 Yale L. J. 577, 614 (1992).

54. Donald Langevoort, *Taming the Animal Spirits of the Stock Markets: A Behavioral Approach to Securities Regulation*, 97 NW. U. L. Rev. 135 (2002).

your view of the fraud-on-the-market theory? See also Ronald H. Gilson and Reinier Kraakman, *The Mechanisms of Market Twenty Years Later: The Hindsight Bias*, 28 J. Corp. L. 215 (2003).

14.4.2.8   Elements of 10b-5 Recovery: Causation

In common law fraud, the misrepresentation must be relied on, and that reliance must cause a loss. For example, assume that seller S falsely asserts that asset X has character Y and that buyer B, believing that character Y is important, buys asset X. Should X lose much of its value because market prices for assets of type X decline (both with and without character Y), a court is unlikely to sustain an action by B for rescission, since his loss was a direct result of the risk of the market value for assets X (which he intended to assume). It would be said that the loss was not *caused* by the fraud.

Private actions under Rule 10b-5 also require proof of causation. As the example above suggests, causation may be of two types: transaction causation and loss causation. For liability to attach, a misstatement or omission must both "cause" the plaintiff to enter the transaction and "cause" the plaintiff's loss. But how can an omission *cause* either of these events? If the plaintiff can satisfy the trier of the fact that she would not have entered into the transaction, had the material matter been disclosed, the omission will be said to cause the transaction (transaction loss). Determining loss causation in this context closely resembles proof of damages. Losses that are associated with the transaction (that might have been avoided) and caused by that transaction unless they are shown to result from some factor other than the falseness of the statement that the plaintiff relies upon — general economic factors, for example — ought arguably not be recoverable as damages.

The U.S. Supreme Court's recent decision in *Dura Pharmaceuticals Inc. v. Broudo*[55] illustrates and clarifies the concept of loss causation. Between April 15, 1997 and February 24, 1998, Dura Pharmaceuticals made allegedly false public statements concerning Dura's drug profits and the likelihood of FDA approval of a new asthmatic spray device. On February 24, 1998, Dura announced that it expected lower profits than previously forecast, primarily from slow drug sales. Dura's share price dropped the next day from roughly $39 to roughly $21 per share. In November 1998, Dura announced that the FDA would not be approving the asthmatic spray device; the next day Dura's share price temporarily fell but almost fully recovered within a week. The plaintiff class, consisting of all purchasers of Dura shares between April 15, 1997 and February 24, 1998, brought a 10b-5 claim against Dura for its public statements between April 1997 and February 1998, under a fraud-on-the-market theory.

The District Court dismissed the complaint.[56] On the drug profitability claim, the held found that the plaintiffs failed to adequately allege an

---

55. 544 U.S. 336 (2005).

56. *In re Dura Pharmaceutical, Inc. Secs. Litig.*, 2000 U.S. Dist. LEXIS 15258 (S.D. Cal. July 11, 2000).

appropriate state of mind (i.e., scienter); on the plaintiffs' spray device claim, the court found that plaintiffs did not adequately allege loss causation, because the allegedly false statements with respect to the likelihood of FDA approval did not cause a drop in Dura's stock price. The Ninth Circuit reversed on the spray device claim, requiring only a "pleading that the price at the time of purchase was overstated."[57] The U.S. Supreme Court granted *certiorari*, and unanimously reversed the Ninth Circuit. The Court (Breyer, J.) rejected the Ninth Circuit's "inflated purchase price" approach to causation and loss. The Court reasoned that the fact that a price was inflated by false statement at the time of purchase was logically insufficient, without more, to establish that a loss on sale after truthful disclosure was caused by the misdisclosure. More facts are necessary to show that the loss resulted from the disclosure.

QUESTION ON DURA

What else might plaintiffs show to establish a sufficient claim that the loss was caused by the misdisclosure?

14.4.3   Remedies for 10b-5 Violations

ELKIND v. LIGGETT & MYERS, INC.
635 F.2d 156 (2d Cir. 1980)

MANSFIELD, J.:

[Shareholders brought a class action against Liggett & Myers, Inc. ("Liggett"), for wrongful tipping of inside information about an earnings decline to certain persons who then sold Liggett's shares on the open market.]

This case presents a question of measurement of damages [in a private Rule 10b-5 insider trading class action]. . . .

The district court looked to the measure of damages used in cases where a buyer was induced to purchase a company's stock by materially misleading statements or omissions. In such cases of fraud by a fiduciary intended to induce others to buy or sell stock the accepted measure of damages is the "out-of-pocket" measure. This consists of the difference between the price paid and the "value" of the stock when brought (or when the buyer committed himself to buy, if earlier). Except in rare face-to-face transactions, however, uninformed traders on an open, impersonal market are not induced by representations on the part of the tipper or tippee to buy or sell. Usually they are wholly unacquainted with and uninfluenced by the tippee's misconduct. They trade independently and

---

57. 339 F.3d at 938 (9th Cir. 2003).

voluntarily but without the benefit of information known to the trading tippee.

[Moreover,] it must be remembered that investors who trade in a stock on the open market have no absolute right to know inside information. They are, however, entitled to an honest market in which those with whom they trade have no confidential corporate information. . . .

Recognizing the foregoing, we [suggested in an earlier case] that the district court must be accorded flexibility in assessing damages. . . . [S]everal measures are possible. First, there is the traditional out-of-pocket measure used by the district court in this case. For several reasons this measure appears to be inappropriate. In the first place, . . . it is directed toward compensating a person for losses directly traceable to the defendant's fraud upon him. No such fraud or inducement may be attributed to a tipper or tippee trading on an impersonal market. Aside from this the measure poses serious proof problems that may often be insurmountable in a tippee-trading case. The "value" of the stock traded during the period of nondisclosure of the tipped information (i.e., the price at which the market would have valued the stock if there had been a disclosure) is hypothetical. . . .

Whatever may be the reasonableness of the *nunc pro tunc* "value" method of calculating damages in other contexts, it has serious vulnerabilities here. It rests on the fundamental assumptions (1) that the tipped information is substantially the same as that later disclosed publicly, and (2) that one can determine how the market would have reacted to the public release of the tipped information at an earlier time by its reaction to that information at a later, proximate time. This theory depends on the parity of the "tip" and the "disclosure." When they differ, the basis of the damage calculation evaporates. . . .

An equally compelling reason for rejecting the theory is its potential for imposition of Draconian, exorbitant damages, out of all proportion to the wrong committed, lining the pockets of all interim investors and their counsel at the expense of innocent corporate stockholders. Logic would compel application of the theory to a case where a tippee sells only 10 shares of a heavily traded stock (e.g., IBM), which then drops substantially when the tipped information is publicly disclosed. To hold the tipper and tippee liable for the losses suffered by every open market buyer of the stock as a result of the later decline in value of the stock after the news became public would be grossly unfair. . . .

[A second] measure would be to permit recovery of damages caused by erosion of the market price of the security that is traceable to the tippee's wrongful trading, i.e., to compensate the uninformed investor for the loss in market value that he suffered as a direct result of the tippee's conduct. Under this measure an innocent trader who bought Liggett shares at or after a tippee sold on the basis of inside information would recover any decline in value of his shares caused by the tippee's trading. Assuming the impact of the tippee's trading on the market is measurable, this approach has the advantage of limiting the plaintiffs to the amount of damage actually caused in fact by the defendant's wrongdoing and avoiding windfall recoveries by investors at the expense of stockholders other than the tippee trader. . . .

[However, t]his causation-in-fact approach has some disadvantages. It allows no recovery for the tippee's violation of his duty to disclose the inside information before trading. . . . Another disadvantage . . . lies in the difficult [i]f not impossible burden it would impose on the uninformed trader of proving the time when and extent to which the integrity of the market was affected by the tippee's conduct. . . . [I]n a case where there was only a modest amount of tippee trading in a heavy-volume market in the stock, accompanied by other unrelated factors affecting the market price, it would be impossible as a practical matter to isolate such rise or decline in market price, if any, as was caused by the tippee's wrongful conduct. Moreover, even assuming market erosion caused by this trading to be provable and that the uninformed investor could show that it continued after his purchase, there remains the question of whether the plaintiff would not be precluded from recovery on the ground that any post-purchase decline in market price attributable to the tippee's trading would not be injury to him as a purchaser. . . .

A third alternative is (1) to allow any uninformed investor, where a reasonable investor would either have delayed his purchase or not purchased at all if he had had the benefit of the tipped information, to recover any post-purchase decline in market value of his shares up to a reasonable time after he learns of the tipped information or after there is a public disclosure of it but (2) limit his recovery to the amount gained by the tippee as a result of his selling at the earlier date rather than delaying his sale until the parties could trade on an equal informational basis. Under this measure if the tippee sold 5,000 shares at $50 per share on the basis of inside information and the stock thereafter declined to $40 per share within a reasonable time after public disclosure, an uninformed purchaser, buying shares during the interim (e.g., at $45 per share) would recover the difference between his purchase price and the amount at which he could have sold the shares on an equal informational basis (i.e., the market price within a reasonable time after public disclosure of the tip), subject to a limit of $50,000, which is the amount gained by the tippee as a result of his trading on the inside information rather than on an equal basis. Should the intervening buyers, because of the volume and price of their purchases, claim more than the tippee's gain, their recovery (limited to that gain) would be shared pro rata.

This third alternative, which may be described as the disgorgement measure, . . . offers several advantages. To the extent that it makes the tipper and tippees liable up to the amount gained by their misconduct, it should deter tipping of inside information and tippee-trading. On the other hand, by limiting the total recovery to the tippee's gain, the measure bars windfall recoveries of exorbitant amounts bearing no relation to the seriousness of the misconduct. It also avoids the extraordinary difficulties faced in trying to prove traditional out-of-pocket damages based on the true "value" of the shares purchased or damages claimed by reason of market erosion attributable to tippee trading. A plaintiff would simply be required to prove (1) the time, amount, and price per share of his purchase, (2) that a reasonable investor would not have paid as high a price or made the purchase at all if he had had the information in the tippee's possession, and (3) the price to which the security had declined by the time he learned the tipped information or at a reasonable time after it became public, whichever event first occurred. He would then have a claim and, up to the limits of the tippee's gain, could recover the decline in market value of his shares before the information became public or known to him. . . .

We recognize that there cannot be any perfect measure of damages caused by tippee-trading. The disgorgement measure, like others we have described, does have some disadvantages. It modifies the principle that ordinarily gain to the wrongdoer should not be a prerequisite to liability for violation of Rule 10b-5. . . . In some instances the total claims could exceed the wrongdoer's gain, limiting each claimant to a pro rata share of the gain. In other situations, after deducting the cost of recovery, including attorneys' fees, the remainder might be inadequate to make a class action worthwhile. However, as between the various alternatives we are persuaded . . . that the disgorgement measure . . . offers the most equitable resolution of the difficult problems created by conflicting interests.

In the present case the sole Rule 10b-5 violation was the tippee-trading of 1,800 Liggett shares on the afternoon of July 17, 1972. Since the actual preliminary Liggett earnings were released publicly at 2:15 P.M. on July 18 and were effectively disseminated in a *Wall Street Journal* article published on the morning of July 19, the only outside purchasers who might conceivably have been damaged by the insider-trading were those who bought Liggett shares between the afternoon of July 17 and the opening of the market on July 19. . . .

The market price of Liggett stock opened on July 17, 1972, at $55 ⅝, and remained at substantially the same price on that date, closing at $55 ¼. By the close of the market on July 18 the price declined to $52½ per share. Applying the disgorgement measure, any member of the plaintiff class who bought Liggett shares during the period from the afternoon of July 17 to the close of the market on July 18 and met the reasonable investor requirement would be entitled to claim a pro rata portion of the tippee's gain, based on the difference between their purchase price and the price to which the market price declined within a reasonable time after the morning of July 19. By the close of the market on July 19 the market price had declined to $46 ⅜ per share. The total recovery thus would be limited to the gain realized by the tippee from the inside information, i.e., 1,800 shares multiplied by approximately $9.35 per share.

NOTE AND QUESTIONS ON ELKIND v. LIGGETT & MYERS, INC.

1. The *Elkind* disgorgement measure of damages quickly became the standard measure of damages in private Rule 10b-5 insider trading cases. Does this suggest a reason why there have been relatively few of these cases?

2. Is there a reason why damages in a Rule 10b-5 fraud-on-the-market class action should be measured differently from damages in a Rule 10b-5

insider trading action? As a conceptual matter, shouldn't there be parity between misrepresentations and omissions?

NOTE ON THE SEC'S ENFORCEMENT POWERS

The SEC has a number of different enforcement techniques at its disposal. In federal district courts, it may seek, inter alia, injunctions, monetary penalties (often severe), disgorgement of profits, and accountings or audits. Federal courts also have the power to bar violators of the securities laws from acting as officers or directors of corporations. In addition, the SEC can recommend criminal prosecution, which results in substantial criminal penalties upon conviction.[58] Indeed, with the enactment of the Sarbanes-Oxley Act of 2002, these criminal sanctions were broadened and enhanced. That Act added a new section to the U.S. Criminal Code: § 1348 of Title 18, which makes it a crime, subject to up to 25 years of imprisonment to defraud any person in connection with the security of any issuer covered by the provisions of the 1934 Act. The 2002 Act also increases the maximum fine any individual may be assessed from $1 million to $5 million and, for corporations, from $5 million to $25 million. Maximum incarceration for criminal violation of the 1933 or 1934 Act was raised from 10 years to 20 years.

14.4.4   The Academic Debate[59]

If the doctrinal debate over insider trading has oscillated between a broad fairness norm and a narrower legal concept of securities fraud, the academic debate has ventured even farther afield from popular sentiment by focusing on whether insider trading ought to be regulated at all. Thus, while the case law has explored the borders of impermissible trading, much commentary has toyed with the question of whether even "core" insider trading is necessarily harmful. The most prominent pioneer of this line of inquiry is Professor Henry Manne, whose provocative defense of insider trading has influenced numerous later commentators.[60] This critical tradition is instructive for both the clarity it brings to the policy issues at stake and the potential weaknesses it reveals in a simple contractualist approach to insider trading.

The greatest contribution of the deregulatory tradition has been its clear description of what insider trading is and what banning it accomplishes in terms of the allocation of property rights in the firm. Insider trading is an appropriation of information rights that permits informed

58. See *The Investor's Advocate: How the SEC Protects Investors and Maintains Market Integrity,* at http://www.sec.gov/asec/wwwsec.htm.

59. Portions of this section are drawn from Reinier H. Kraakman, *The Legal Theory of Insider Trading Regulation in the United States,* in European Insider Dealing 39-55 (Klaus Hopt & Eddy Wymeersch eds., 1991).

60. See Henry G. Manne, *Insider Trading and the Stock Market* (1966).

insiders to earn systematically higher trading returns than can uninformed outsiders. However, not all informational advantages that insiders gain from their fiduciary roles are regulated by law. Legal restrictions on insider trading affect only a portion of insiders' higher returns, since existing law merely bars trading on "material" information — that is, obviously market-sensitive facts — and cannot reach insiders' informed decisions to refrain from trading. Thus, as the empirical literature suggests, insiders' trading returns would exceed those of outsiders even if existing laws were perfectly enforced. Moreover, the redistribution of returns from outsiders to insiders that is implied by insider trading is extremely difficult to ascertain. It is unlikely that uninformed traders who trade opposite insiders are the chief losers from insider trading. Perhaps the only observations that can be made with confidence are that outsiders lose in proportion to the frequency of their trades and that comparatively well-informed outsiders lose more than poorly informed outsiders *do* if, as we suppose, the well-informed outsiders trade more frequently and/or invest greater resources and human capital in acquiring information than their less-informed colleagues.[61]

The academic critics of insider trading regulation also correctly point out that the mere fact that insider trading redistributes returns on securities in favor of insiders has little bearing on its fairness in the ordinary sense of the word. All disparities in information among traders have similar effects. Further, if uninformed traders anticipate market-wide levels of insider trading, even this redistributive effect may seem to dissolve from an ex ante perspective: Outsiders will simply pay less for securities, while continuing to earn normal returns on their portfolios. Indeed, if securities prices are efficient and well informed about insider trading — a big "if" but not an implausible one — then outsiders enjoy the automatic protection of prices that already reflect an informed estimate of future insider trading levels.[62] Thus, we need not fear that insider trading will necessarily undermine investor confidence in ways likely to lead to a wholesale exodus of uninformed traders from the market. The critical questions are these: (1) What does insider trading accomplish, good or bad, for the disclosure of trading information and thus the allocational efficiency of the capital markets, and (2) how does, or might, insider trading interact with explicit contractual arrangements between insiders and the corporation?

14.4.4.1 Insider Trading and Informed Prices

Critics of insider trading regulation traditionally argue that, far from undermining the market, insider trading leads to more informed prices that may actually increase investor confidence as well as the allocational

---

61. See David D. Haddock & Jonathan R. Macey, *A Coasian Model of Insider Trading*, 80 J.L. & Econ. 1449 (1986).

62. See, e.g., Kenneth E. Scott, *Insider Trading, Rule 10b-5, Disclosure and Corporate Privacy*, 9 J. Legal Stud. 801 (1980); Easterbrook, *Insider Trading, Secret Agents, Evidentiary Privileges, and the Production of Information*, 1981 Sup. Ct. L. Rev. 309, 324-326 (1981); Haddock & Macey, supra note 61, at 1455-1456.

efficiency of the market.[63] The argument here turns primarily on the value of insider trading as a mechanism for signaling the trading value of information that the firm cannot or will not disclose directly: for example, preliminary merger negotiations or a new product that might be copied by competitors.[64] Such information may find its way into prices only through insider trading. Thus, the claim is that insider trading ought to be tolerated in the interest of informationally efficient prices that ultimately lead to a more efficient allocation of capital.

There is no question that insider trading can convey information into market prices. There are difficulties, however, in drawing policy conclusions from this observation. Consider first the *relative* efficiency with which insider trading is likely to inform prices. Insiders would prefer to trade anonymously, even if their activities were legal, in order to safeguard their informational monopolies. Thus, insider trading is a slow mechanism for releasing information to the market that can fail entirely to move prices if the level of background "noise trading" is sufficiently high.[65] In addition, illegal trading usually concerns "bombshell" information that companies are forced to disclose publicly in the near term in any case.[66] Thus, the deregulation of insider trading may only partially adjust securities prices to reflect information that will be publicly disclosed in a matter of days, weeks, or months. The total contribution of deregulation to informational efficiency thus is unlikely to be large.

Beyond this, it is doubtful that deregulation is the best way to increase the informational efficiency of share prices or that it makes more than a marginal contribution to the allocational efficiency of the market. The proponents of insider trading have been singularly unimaginative in exploring alternatives to deregulation that might have a still greater effect on the informational efficiency of share prices: for example, a requirement that insiders disclose, at some period before trading, the identity and size of their intended trades.[67] The point is not to advocate such a system of disclosed trading but merely to suggest that enthusiasm for the unregulated market has curiously narrowed the policy analyses of commentators in the Manne tradition.

An even more important aspect of the signaling critique of insider trading regulation, which is only now beginning to receive serious attention, is the link between allocational efficiency and informational

---

63. See, e.g., Dennis W. Carlton & Daniel R. Fischel, *The Regulation of Insider Trading*, 35 Stan. L. Rev. 857 (1983).

64. Secondarily, the argument turns on the likely effects of insider trading on insiders' incentives to disclose. If insiders are permitted to trade, are they likely to delay disclosure to exploit the full value of their information, or will they assure more complete disclosure to reap the full profits of their information? Under existing law, are they likely to distort disclosure to enhance price volatility, and hence increase their own profits? The academic debate about these questions is hopelessly speculative.

65. See Gilson & Kraakman, supra note 30, at 629-634; William J. Carney, *Signalling and Causation in Insider Trading*, 36 Cath. U. L. Rev. 863 (1987).

66. The signaling function of insider trading might be considerably stronger without a well-developed mandatory disclosure regime administered by the SEC.

67. See Gilson & Kraakman, supra note 30, at 632.

efficiency. Evaluating the multiple connections between informational efficiency in the secondary markets and allocational efficiency — for example, the importance of informational efficiency for the operation of the primary market, the acquisitions market, and management compensation packages that are linked to share prices — is a complex task that leaves open many questions.[68] The prospects for significant incremental contributions to allocational efficiency from adoption of a regime of open insider trading seem marginal at best. They are particularly suspect, moreover, where the information at issue can be credibly disclosed to the market and is likely to become public in the short term anyway.

14.4.4.2 Insider Trading as a Compensation Device

If concern for the information content of securities prices is an arguable but unpersuasive basis for deregulating insider trading, the parallel claim that insider trading is, or might be, an efficient device for compensating insiders is even less plausible, in our view. The chief weakness of this claim is unrelated to the elaborate (but formally undeveloped) literature suggesting how insider trading *might* interact with other compensation tools in an efficient market for managerial services. Rather, the basic flaw in the compensation-based case for deregulation is the assumption that insiders are likely to contract for efficient compensation in a competitive market and therefore that the right to trade on inside information might realistically serve as just another component of a manager's total compensation package.

The assumption that insider trading need shift only the form rather than the amount of insider compensation is the initial step in the analysis of insider trading as a compensation device. If this assumption is granted, and decision makers charged with the company's success are the chief beneficiaries of insider trading, then the field is open for the difficult task of exploring the incentive properties and other contracting characteristics of insider trading.

The proponents of deregulation have favored insider trading as a compensation device on a number of grounds. Most simply, the expected gain from insider trading is said to have option-like properties that can motivate successful projects by allowing managers to benefit from prior knowledge of increases in share prices. The fact that profits from insider trading increase with the volatility of share prices may crudely offset the natural risk aversion of managers who have invested their entire human capital in a single firm. Moreover, the fact that managers can initiate insider trades and increase their gains without renegotiating their wage contracts is (curiously, in our view) also said to be an advantage: It reduces contracting costs and automatically adjusts the manager's trading bonus to his

---

68. See, e.g., Lynn A. Stout, *The Unimportance of Being Efficient: An Economic Analysis of Stock Market Pricing and Securities Regulation*, 87 Mich. L. Rev. 613 (1988); Marcel Kahan, Normative Aspects of Stock Market Efficiency (Harvard Law School Program in Law and Economics, Working Paper No. 52, Mar. 1989).

proximity to large, value-increasing projects within the firm.[69] Finally, it is argued that firms can recruit managers with the right risk preferences and dispositions by expressly tying compensation to the right to profit from insider trading.

By contrast, typical incentive-based arguments against insider trading review many of these same effects through a dark glass. The option-like character of expected returns from insider trading rewards the selection of projects with volatile payouts, regardless of whether they have a positive or negative expected net payout. The fact that managers can increase their compensation through insider trading without negotiating with the firm merely permits them to "unbundle" the incentive features of their negotiated contracts and deprives the firm of control over total levels of individual compensation. In addition, because trading profits depend on control over information, there is no guarantee that the originators of successful projects will reap the rewards. Indeed, insider trading might be expected to induce a variety of perverse behaviors by managers who would compete to acquire and hoard valuable information rights within the firm. For the economically minded legal scholar, how these arguments balance out is an interesting theoretical question. We have, thus far, very few formal attempts to model the incentive effects of insider trading, even in a simple world in which the market for managerial services is fully competitive, managers deal with firms at arm's length, and firms can perfectly monitor trading by managers.

For purposes of setting legal policy, however, these concerns are largely irrelevant. There is simply no reason to believe that managers' negotiated contracts would correctly anticipate levels of insider trading or that other market controls would operate to check excessive insider trading. Studies of the extent to which existing compensation contracts set rational incentives in other respects are less than comforting. The evidence that top managers, in particular, retain enormous discretion over their own job tenure and compensation in American corporations is overwhelming. The likelihood that this discretion would be exercised benignly if managers were permitted the opportunity to profit from low-visibility insider trading seems extremely small. Put another way, deregulating insider trading would invite managers and similar insiders to extract large rents at shareholder expense without any real check by the corporation or the market.[70] Shareholders might not suffer from an ex ante perspective if securities prices correctly anticipated marketwide levels of insider trading, but then neither would shareholders suffer from outright theft by managers on the same assumption. Moreover, the disparate incidence of the costs of insider trading, which fall most heavily on frequent traders and market makers, may itself interfere with market liquidity and the efficient pricing of securities.[71]

69. See Carlton & Fischel, supra note 63, at 869-872.

70. See Stephen A. Ross, *Disclosure Regulation in Financial Markets: The Implications of Modern Finance Theory and Signaling Theory, in Issues in Financial Regulation* 177 (P. Edwards ed., 1979).

71. The fact that voluntary agreements to prohibit insider trading were uncommon prior to legal regulation is hardly persuasive evidence that insider trading is an efficient

The conclusion that insider trading invites an uncompensated redistribution of returns from uninformed traders to insiders is, if anything, even stronger in the case of outsiders such as investment bankers or financial printers who enter into short-term contracts with the firm. For the most part, no one has seriously proposed that such outsiders ought to be compensated with trading rights in information. There is, however, one troubling exception: arbitrageurs and other intermediaries in the acquisitions market who have frequently benefited in the past from tips about impending takeover bids. Such informational leakages have been tolerated, and sometimes encouraged, by bidders who wish to assure the success of their bids without revealing their identities or overtly violating statutory provisions governing the tender offer process. In these cases, leaked information has indeed served as efficient — albeit now illegal — payment to arbitrageurs for aggregating the stock of target companies, and it does not necessarily redistribute returns from the pockets of bidders, who expect to pay the full price of their tender offers in any event.

SOME FINAL QUESTIONS

1. Examining 6,000 stock trades by U.S. senators between 1993 and 1998, Professor Alan Ziobrowski and colleagues find that senators beat the market, on average, by an astounding 12 percent annually.[72] Does this evidence indicate that U.S. senators are using inside information to trade? What other explanations are possible?

2. The following excerpt shows the complex ways in which insider trading can manifest itself, and the challenges inherent in enforcement today:

ARE DEAL MAKERS ON WALL STREET LEAKING SECRETS?
Wall Street Journal (July 28, 2006)

Suspicious trading patterns — including increased activity and well-timed bets — have cropped up in several companies' securities in advance of news of their involvement in big transactions, suggesting Wall Street's deal-making machine may be leaking confidential information. . . . In advance of the HCA deal, there was a notable uptick in trading in financial contracts tied to HCA's bonds — derivatives known as credit-default swaps. Credit-default swaps are private contracts intended to be insurance policies

---

mode of compensation. Private bans against insider trading would have been uneconomic to enforce in the absence of a centralized public enforcement agency. Moreover, it is difficult to see why managers, as the chief beneficiaries of insider trading, would have been motivated to bar such trading, given a realistic assessment of the scope of managerial discretion permitted by the markets.

72. Alan J. Ziobrowski, Ping Cheng, James W. Boyd, & Brigitte J. Ziobrowski, *Abnormal Returns from the Common Stock Investments of the United States Senate*, 39 J. Fin. & Quant. Anal. 661(2004).

against a company going bankrupt, but they also allow investors to bet on the likelihood of a bond default and are especially popular with fast-trading hedge funds that cater to wealthy clients and institutional investors. The more likely a company is to default, the more expensive its credit-default swaps become. When a company is bought in a leveraged buyout, as is happening with HCA, it assumes dramatically more debt, increasing the likelihood of a default.

In the five days before news of a potential HCA deal was disclosed in The Wall Street Journal on July 19, the price of HCA's credit-default swaps rose 11%, according to data from Markit Group. The market was effectively betting that the likelihood of an HCA default was rising at a time when prices more broadly in that market were rising just 4%, as measured by a Dow Jones index for these instruments. . . . After HCA reached a deal with its private-equity sponsors, prices of its credit-default swaps rose more than 60% and its bonds dived in value. . . . SEC officials say insider-trading enforcement actions have stayed relatively consistent in recent years. Since Oct. 1, 2005, the agency has brought 40 such cases; it had 42 such cases in fiscal 2004 and 52 in fiscal 2002. But that could change as the takeover boom grows. A March study by England's equivalent of the SEC, the Financial Services Authority, found suspicious stock-price movements prior to 29% of the merger announcements it studied between 2000 and 2004. The study recommended more "visible enforcement action.". . .

The merger market is changing in ways that have increased the possibility of leaks and the opportunities for players involved to profit from them before they are public. Deals are taking longer to play out and involve more deal makers. . . . As the deals grow larger, more money, and thus more bankers and lawyers, are coming in "under the tent," in Wall Street parlance. In HCA's $21 billion transaction, announced Monday, six financial firms — Bank of America Corp., Citigroup Inc., Credit Suisse Group, J.P. Morgan Chase & Co., Merrill Lynch & Co. and Morgan Stanley — and at least seven law firms were involved.

Banks and law firms typically are required to submit to market regulators the names of people who worked on a given transaction. The HCA list is 40 pages long, a person familiar with the matter says. . . .

TABLE OF CASES

711

INDEX